'Without question, Brian Boyd deserves lavish praise for his dense door-stopper of a biography, which deftly pirouettes between high scholarship and the need to keep a mere mortal amused for 630 pages. Whether elucidating the emotional terrain Nabokov traversed while writing *Pnin* and *Lolita*, or detailing one of his mammoth cross-country drives into the great wide-open of the American West, Boyd demonstrates that his is a biographer who fully understands his territory. More importantly, he makes us understand that the key to Nabokov's art can be found in his fierce pursuit of rootlessness throughout his life. The restless invention of his fiction paralleled his restless need to avoid the complacency of standing still. Nabokov's American life-and-times have been brilliantly served by an academic who also does not believe in standing still when telling a story... and who even knows how to write'

New Statesman

Brian Boyd

VLADIMIR NABOKOV

The American Years

VINTAGE

VINTAGE

20 Vauxhall Bridge Road, London SW1V 2SA

London Melbourne Sydney Auckland Johannesburg
and agencies throughout the world

First published by Chatto & Windus Ltd 1992
Vintage edition 1993

1 3 5 7 9 10 8 6 4 2

The following sections of this book have appeared elsewhere in slightly different form: chapter 5 (*Shenandoah*) and chapter 24 (*Russian Literature Triquarterly*).

Printed and bound in Great Britain by
Cox & Wyman Ltd, Reading

ISBN 0 09 996230 6

TO BRONWEN

Life is a great
surprise. I do not see why
death should not be an even greater one.

—*Pale Fire*

It cannot be helped. I must know where I stand,
where you and my son stand. When that slow-motion,
silent explosion of love takes place in me, . . . overwhelming
me with the sense of something much vaster, much more
enduring and powerful than the accumulation of matter or
energy in any imaginable cosmos, then my mind cannot but
pinch itself to see if it is really awake. I have to make a rapid
inventory of the universe. . . . I have to have all space and all
time participate in my emotion, in my mortal love, so that
the edge of its mortality is taken off, thus helping
me to fight the utter degradation, ridicule,
and horror of having developed an
infinity of sensation and thought
within a finite existence.

—*Speak, Memory*

CONTENTS

THE AMERICAN YEARS, 1940–1977

PART II: EUROPE

• *VN* •

ILLUSTRATIONS

Nabokov with Dorothy Leuthold, Grand Canyon, 1941

Nabokov at Wellesley College, 1942

Nabokov with Dmitri, Karpovich farm, West Wardsboro, Vermont, 1942

Edmund Wilson and Mary McCarthy, early 1940s

Nabokov with President Frank Reade of Georgia State College for Women, Valdosta, 1942

Vladimir, Dmitri, and Véra Nabokov, Salt Lake City, 1943

8 Craigie Circle, Cambridge, Massachusetts

Nabokov with Dmitri, 8 Craigie Circle, 1942

Nabokov with Véra in park at end of Craigie Circle, 1942

Nabokov with Russian-language class, Wellesley, 1944

Nabokov at the Museum of Comparative Zoology, 1947

Three of Nabokov's detailed diagrams of the pattern of a butterfly wing

A plate from Nabokov's lepidopterological magnum opus, which restructures the classification of the genus Lycaeides

Nabokov teaching Russian literature at Wellesley, 1948

Morris Bishop

Manuscript of the first page of Speak, Memory

Nabokov and Véra, 802 East Seneca Street, Ithaca

Nabokov's index-card notes used in preparing Lolita

Nabokov composing Lolita on index cards in car—a reconstruction for Life magazine, 1958

Nabokov's instructions in his diary about the manuscript of Lolita

Nabokov, holding Pnin, late 1957

Véra and Vladimir at the home of Lauriston and Ruth Sharp, Cayuga Heights, 1957

Nabokov in Professor Sharp's study, 1957

Advertisement for Lolita

Nabokov's last lecture at Cornell

Véra, London, 1959

VLADIMIR
NABOKOV

INTRODUCTION

The new blurb [for the autobiography] seems very satisfactory. I only

think that the fact that I am an American citizen and an

American writer should have been stressed.

—Nabokov to Harper & Bros., 1950

PNIN WOULD sail across the Atlantic on a voyage of cruel humiliation. Kinbote, ejected by fantastic history, arrived in America by parachute. Humbert Humbert showed his immigration papers, smiled stiffly, and smuggled in his secret self. All three owed their existence to the fact that at the end of May 1940, three weeks before German tanks rolled into Paris, Vladimir Nabokov and his family were at last able to flee France and sail for New York.

For years Nabokov had tried to find a job in an English-speaking country, and had landed only the promise of one session of summer-school teaching at Stanford. For months he had attempted to secure a French *visa de sortie* and then an American visa. For weeks he had struggled against his protractedly intensifying impoverishment in order to raise or borrow the money for his family's fare. For hour after hour on their last day in Paris and on the train rattling them through the night to the port of St. Nazaire, he and his wife had fretted that their six-year-old son's sudden high fever would prevent them from boarding their ship. But the next morning Dmitri had recovered, and his parents walked with him through a park down toward the waterfront, waiting for him to discern through a broken row of houses the ship that would take them to America: "We did not immediately point out to our child, so as to enjoy in full the blissful shock, the enchantment and glee he would experience on discovering. . . . a splendid ship's funnel, showing from behind the clothesline as something in a scrambled picture—Find What the Sailor Has Hidden—that the finder cannot unsee once it has been seen."[1]

Nabokov ends his autobiography right there. Why did he choose to end his account of his life thus far at that particular moment, in that particular way?

He completed *Speak, Memory* a decade after arriving in the United

States, five years after taking American citizenship but ten years after finding himself instantly at home in a new country, on a new continent. Through two decades of Western European emigration, he had suffered from a sense of agonizing distance from the Russia he had loved so dearly as a child. Curtained from Cambridge by his nostalgia, isolated from Berlin by language and by choice, irked by his penniless and unsettled existence in Paris, he had found in America the fulfillment of his young dreams.

As a boy, young Vladimir liked to recall a story his mother had read him about another little boy who stepped out of his bed and into the "painted path between silent trees" in a picture on his wall.[2] He often shivered with delight when he looked up at the framed aquarelle on his own bedroom wall, saw the painted path leading through beechwoods, and imagined himself stepping like that fairytale child into a painted forest. Because he sensed from the first the enchantment of America, Nabokov ends his autobiography with himself and his family walking along another path and as if about to step into a picture, as if about to make some magical transition into an unknown dimension or a new world. While still no more than nine or ten, Nabokov had also dreamed ardently of discovering new species of butterfly, as he waded with his net through the sphagnum bog some distance from his parents' manor—a bog to which they had given the name "America" because of its mystery and remoteness. Now in his forties he roamed America's West summer after summer, and his discovery of new species of butterfly and moth made these the most thrilling years of his adult life.

That path at the end of *Speak, Memory* down which three Nabokovs step forward as if into a picture also echoes the opening chapter of the book. There, the four-year-old Vladimir walks hand in hand between his parents along a garden path, and realizes with a shock their age and his, and the fact of his distinctness from each of them. It was his earliest conscious memory, and his first sense of time and self. At the end of the autobiography, Nabokov and his wife walk along another path, each holding Dmitri by one hand and anticipating the shock he will experience when he spies the funnel camouflaged by the surroundings through which it looms. Nabokov felt with a stab of pleasure that that moment of surprised discovery would stay with his son forever—as it did. He always considered that to recognize a future recollection at the moment it happened, to know with certainty that *this* particular moment would later be recalled, was somehow to cheat the tyranny of time, and that to glimpse *someone else's* future recollection was even rarer, a brief escape from the prison of the self.[3]

At the end of the first chapter of *Speak, Memory*, Nabokov describes his father being tossed up in the air by the local villagers, in a Russian gesture of thanks for some kindness he had shown. On the third toss, he would seem to soar in the air "like one of those paradisiac personages . . . on the vaulted ceiling of a church."[4] At the end of the autobiography Nabokov deliberately recalls that moment of live movement freezing into a picture when he and Véra lead their son forward as if into a picture puzzle. In the early chapter, Nabokov uses the image of his father floating aloft to re-create the tranquillity of his childhood, his untrammeled admiration for his father, and at the same time, by a special twist of style, to prefigure his father's senseless assassination decades later. But by a still greater miracle of style he turns his foreshadowing of that ghastly event into an affirmation of his confidence in the ultimate beneficence and harmony of things, despite all the grotesqueries and horrors of history.* In the final chapter of the autobiography, Nabokov chooses to end on a moment of triumph after years of tribulation, a surge of rapture and release despite the encroaching menace of Hitler. And by the force of his art—as we will see when we consider *Speak, Memory* in detail— he designs this real moment in such a way as to represent his sense of an unseen design behind the apparent chaos of life, an unimaginable freedom beyond even the keenest thrills consciousness allows.

Nabokov chose to end *Speak, Memory* by singling out a moment that looked ahead to a radiant America over the horizon. In fact the years between his arrival in the United States and his composing his autobiography had agonies of their own he simply chose to ignore. For Nabokov as a writer, there were fiercer torments ahead of him in 1940 than there had been even in 1919, when he had had to leave Russia forever. *Then* he had worried that he might not be able to develop his Russian as he wanted in the inhospitable climate of exile. Against the odds, he had succeeded, but *now*, after decades of turning his language into a tool more flexible and responsive in his hand than in those of any of his contemporaries, he had to abandon it altogether and write in English.

As a Russian writer, Nabokov had long been hailed by the small but highly literary émigré audience as the most exciting new talent to emerge since the Revolution. Now on his arrival in America he would have to abandon entirely this hard-earned fame and to win respect over again from scratch, at midcareer, in a new language, at

* See *Vladimir Nabokov: The Russian Years*, pp. 7–12.

a time when to be a Russian émigré seemed deeply suspect to much of the American literary intelligentsia.

In Europe he had devoted almost all his time to writing, first by design and then, after Dmitri's birth, by necessity, when other sources of income would have been welcome but proved impossible to obtain, not only in the trap of Hitler's Germany but even in unwelcoming France. Over the ten years prior to his crossing the Atlantic, he had written six and a half novels, two full-length plays, and over thirty stories. In America, where he had to divide his time and energy among the roles of teacher, scientist, translator, critic, and creative writer, it would take him six years to complete his first novel. In his forties, with a family to support, he could land no secure job until almost the end of the decade.

When he began to write his autobiography he still had no security, and yet despite all the uncertainties of his American existence he had planned from the first the book's buoyant conclusion. Unknown to him at the time, that ending in a sense contained within it the solution to the residual frustrations of his new life in America. *Speak, Memory*'s first scene and its last show a young boy walking hand in hand between his parents. A loving family had provided Nabokov with an unexampled serenity of mind that allowed him, despite the most jarring intrusions of history—a revolution, his father's assassination at the hands of rabid Russian monarchists, the death of his brother and close friends in German concentration camps—to affirm his confidence in the underlying generosity of life. Despite the advancing shadow of Hitler at the end of *Speak, Memory*, Nabokov focuses on two parents tenderly watching over the growth of their child's mind.

The sentiments so evident in this conclusion—his regard for the harmony of family love and his conviction that it somehow reflected the essential kindliness of life—had led Nabokov, as so often before, to test his ideas against their apparent inversion or negation. In 1939 he had imagined the tale of a man who marries a woman only to become the stepfather to the young daughter he really craves. Although he did set the story down in Russian, it remained unpublished and he came to deem it unsatisfactory. But the idea was still part of his mental baggage as he stepped down toward the Atlantic with his son.

By the time he began to write his autobiography, the idea of this Russian novella had expanded into the outline for an English—or rather an American—novel about a man who makes his young stepdaughter the prisoner of his lust. Humbert might wish to introduce Lolita to Baudelaire or Shakespeare, but his false relationship to her, his breach of her mother's trust, and his crushing of her freedom mean he can only stunt her growth: he is the inverse of those parents who at the end of *Speak, Memory* welcome, in unspoken harmony, another "blissful shock" of discovery awaiting their child. Unlike them, he takes no thought for the memories with which he will burden the child in his care. And yet despite all that he inflicts on her, Humbert cannot quite crush Lolita's spirit.

Nabokov hoped his autobiography would win him wider recognition and some financial security. It did not. He expected little but his own artistic satisfaction from the novel he was ruminating at the same time: unlike his autobiography, *Lolita* could never be published chapter by chapter in the *New Yorker*, and might not be publishable at all. Nabokov did not foresee that by accepting the imaginative and intellectual challenge of inventing values that so thoroughly inverted his own, he would shock the public into taking notice. He had no inkling that Humbert's story would not only regain for him the literary reputation he had had to leave behind when he emigrated, but would also bring him for the first time the kind of wealth and fame that would allow him to devote himself solely to writing, to cross the Atlantic again in triumph, to regain Europe, to retain America, to carry his words around the world.

One last comment, for the moment, about the final scene of Nabokov's autobiography. As he walked toward the shore with Dmitri, Nabokov recognized the funnel ahead and said nothing, to let his son experience for himself the shock of "discovering ahead the ungenuinely gigantic, the unrealistically real prototype of the various toy vessels he had doddled about in his bath." He ends *Speak, Memory* on this note partly because it sums up his whole artistic credo: his desire to prepare for his readers the sublime surprise of discovery, a surprise that he knows he would ruin were he to point it out himself. Throughout his work he wants to make us gasp with wonder when we see how real things can be behind all that we take for granted; to impart a sense of the artful, deceptive munificence of life, concealing miracles of generosity behind the everyday; to suggest that the world before our eyes is a puzzle, but that its solution lies before us, and that we may somehow be headed toward the "blissful shock" of discovering life's great surprise.

PART I
AMERICA

• *PROFESSOR NABOKOV* •

In America I'm happier than in any
other country. . . . I feel intellectually at
home in America. It is a second
home in the true sense
of the word.

—*Strong Opinions*

CHAPTER 1

Refuge: New York and Stanford, 1940–1941

Today, in a new and beloved world, where I have learned to feel at

home as easily as I have ceased barring my sevens . . .

—*Speak, Memory*

I

NABOKOV had left Russia in 1919 on a crowded little cargo ship,
playing chess with his father on its deck as Bolshevik machine
guns strafed the waters of Sebastopol harbor. Now at the end of
May 1940, despite having been desperately poor for years, he managed to flee France in style. In gratitude for his father's resolute attacks almost four decades before on Russia's officially sanctioned
anti-Semitism, the Jewish refugee charity organization that had char-
tered the *Champlain* assigned Nabokov and his family a huge first-
class cabin, as if to offer them a foretaste of their eventual fortunes in
America.

The crossing was rough on the stomach but calm on the nerves (a
private bath every morning!)—or as calm as the war would permit.
At St. Nazaire the French *sureté* had caught two German spies aboard
the vessel. Out in the Atlantic, a strange jet of vapor pluming above
the gray seas prompted two jumpy young seamen to fire the ship's
new antisubmarine guns—but it was only a whale. Yet the alarm was
real enough: on its next trip to the U.S., the ship was sunk by a German U-boat.[1]

On May 28, 1940, the *Champlain* glided through a lilac morning
mist past the Statue of Liberty and docked at the French Line pier.
After twenty years as stateless Europeans subject to officious bureaucracy at every border, the Nabokovs savored their arrival in America
as an awakening from a nightmare to a glorious new dawn. At the
customs hall, unable to find the key to their trunk (it turned up later
in Véra Nabokov's jacket pocket), they had to wait, while Nabokov
"stood bantering," as he later recalled, "with a diminutive Negro
porter and two large Customs men until a locksmith arrived and

opened the padlock with one blow of his iron bar. The merry little porter was so fascinated by that simple solution that he kept handling the padlock until it snapped shut again." On top of the things in the opened trunk lay the two pairs of boxing gloves Nabokov used for coaching sessions with Dmitri. The two customs officers immediately put them on and began to spar, dancing around Nabokov, while a third customs man studied the small portion of the butterfly collection Nabokov had been able to bring and suggested a name for one species. As Nabokov retold the story decades later, still enchanted by America's easygoing, good-natured atmosphere, he repeated with delight: "Where would that happen? Where would that happen?"²

Standing beside their checked and chalk-marked trunk, Nabokov asked Véra where she thought he could get a newspaper. "Oh, I'll get one for you," said one of the customs men, and came back in a minute with a *New York Times*. Nathalie Nabokoff, the ex-wife of Vladimir's cousin Nicolas, was to have met them with Nabokov's old Cambridge friend Robert de Calry, but the times had been confused and there was no one waiting. They had to take a taxi—to Nabokov it looked like a very shiny, very gaudy bright yellow scarab—to Nathalie Nabokoff's apartment at 32 East 61st Street. Towering new and strange around them, Manhattan somehow looked more vividly hued than Europe, like one of those new colored photographs, and the novelty of the whole scene made the short ride seem to take an age. At their destination they glanced at the meter and registered not the actual 90 cents but "nine, o, oh God, ninety, ninety dollars." The only money they had—what was left over after Paris friends and well-wishers had chipped in for their tickets—amounted to little more than a hundred dollars. Still, what could Véra do but fish out their hundred dollar bill and hand it over? "Lady," said the cabbie, "if I had that money, I wouldn't be sitting here driving a car." And of course, Nabokov added as he retold this story too, "the simplest way for him would have been to give us $10 change and call it a day."³

The newcomers stayed a few days in Nathalie Nabokoff's apartment, then moved across the corridor into the rooms of an actress who was setting off on tour. By June 10 they had found a cheap summer sublet at 1326 Madison Avenue in the apartment of a couple named Lehovich. Oddly enough, Mrs. Lehovich was a niece of the Countess Panin, who had given the Nabokov family a refuge on her estate in the Crimea in 1917, when they were fleeing not Hitler but Lenin.⁴

II

By the time Paris fell to the Germans on June 14, the Nabokovs' former apartment on rue Boileau was already a heap of rubble and the first Russian emigration was in much the same state. New York would become a publishing capital for Russian émigrés—as it is to this day—but the first emigration Nabokov had been part of was over. He had taken his "First Papers" immediately upon arrival in America,[5] and he would soon become an American citizen, an American writer, whose friends were almost all American rather than Russian.

But the momentum of twenty years was not dispersed at once. "Vladimir Sirin's" arrival in New York was noted by the city's daily Russian newspaper, *Novoe russkoe slovo* (*New Russian Word*). He was indeed still Sirin:* he planned to finish at least one more Russian novel, *Solus Rex*, and during his first month in America he set down in Russian his impressions of Paris at war and composed a lofty epitaph for the entire emigration.[6] At the end of the month *Novoe russkoe slovo* interviewed him about his impressions of his new niche. He felt himself splendidly at home, he answered.

> Still, you have to learn to live here. I went up to a self-serve machine, to drink a cup of cold chocolate, put in a nickel, turned the handle, and watched the chocolate pour straight onto the floor. With my absent-mindedness, I had forgotten to put a glass under the tap. . . .
>
> One day I went into a barber's shop. After a few words with me the barber said: "You can see at once that you are an Englishman, you have just arrived in America, and you work in the papers." "How did you figure that out?" I asked, surprised by his penetration. "Because your pronunciation is English, because you haven't had time to wear out your European shoes, and because you have the high forehead and the sort of head typical of newspaper workers." "You're Sherlock Holmes himself," I flattered the barber. "Who's Sherlock Holmes?"[7]

Nabokov's first contacts were naturally within the Russian community. He called on Sergey Rachmaninov, who had twice sent him small amounts of money in his days of direst European poverty,

> and I was eager now to thank him in person. During our first meeting at his flat on West End Avenue, I mentioned I had been invited to teach summer school at Stanford. On the following day I got from him a carton with several items of obsolete clothing, among which was a cutaway (presumably tailored in the period of the Prelude), which he hoped—as

---

* His nom de plume as a Russian writer since 1921.

he said in a little note—I would wear for my first lecture. I sent back his well-meant gift.[8]*

Mikhail Karpovich, the Harvard history professor he had first met and liked in Prague in 1932, invited the Nabokovs to join them at their summer home in Vermont. Meanwhile Nabokov spent the early summer searching for some sort of literary, academic, publishing, or library job, writing to people like George Vernadsky, the Yale historian, Philip Mosely, a Russian historian at Cornell and a keen Sirin fan, and Mikhail Chekhov, the writer's nephew and now a theatrical director. But for the moment Nabokov's financial prospects were no better than in Europe. Once again he was reduced to accepting a small handout—this time, a grant from the Literary Fund, a Russian organization that helped writers and scholars in America—and after the summer vacation he would be compelled to return to language tutoring once more.[9]

Nabokov met Altagracia de Jannelli, the New Yorker who for five years had been acting as his "literary (or rather, anti-literary) agent—a short, fearsome, bandy-legged woman, her hair dyed an indecent red." She demanded from him a genteel book with attractive heroes and moral landscapes, and forbade him to write in Russian. His talks with New York's commercial publishers convinced him that he would have to write something salable like a mystery novel, if only he could manage without clipping his muse's wings.[10]

Although he had no prospects, America kept him buoyant in spirits. Only one thought oppressed him: his close Jewish friends left behind in France, like George and Iosif Hessen, *Sovremennye zapiski* editor Ilya Fondaminsky, and his more recent friends, the harpists Elizaveta, Marussya, and Ina Marinel. Above all his thoughts were with Véra's cousin Anna Feigin, with whom he and his family had lived for years in Berlin. She had not intended to leave at the time the Nabokovs sailed from France, but as Paris fell to Germany she managed to escape to Nice and began to try to reach the United States. Nabokov would spend much energy over the next year obtaining a visa for her—his friend Karpovich would stand surety for her, as he had for Nabokov himself—and for the Marinel sisters.[11]

III

On July 15 the Nabokovs left the mugginess of New York for the Karpovich summer home, the farmhouse on an old maple farm in

* Rachmaninov also gave Nabokov an ultramarine suit that he *did* wear at Stanford.

West Wardsboro, Vermont. This building, with its clapboards badly in need of repainting and starting to sag and spring, was far more modest than the brick-and-timber mansion that in chapter 5 of *Pnin* houses a small summer gathering of Russian émigré intellectuals, but the setting and the atmosphere were the same: a sea of greenery, maple, beech, tacamahac, and pine that Nabokov told an interviewer "looks like some parts of Siberia"—where he had never been—and a decidedly un-Russian fauna: hummingbirds, great sulky porcupines, eerie, elegant skunks.[12]

When still a young man, Mikhail Karpovich had come to America as a minor diplomat, and stayed on after the Revolution. Now at Harvard, he had become the virtual doyen of Russian studies in the United States, for although he wrote little, his students included most of the distinguished American historians of Russia. A magnetic man with a wide personal influence, he had a dynamic concern for herding up living Russians, and did more for Nabokov than any other Russian in America. In 1942, with Mark Aldanov, he would set up *Novyy zhurnal* (*New Review*), a "thick journal" that filled some of the gap left by the Paris *Sovremennye zapiski* and that is now approaching its fiftieth year.

Harvard sociologist Nikolay Timashev and his family were among the guests that summer. Timashev felt that being at the Karpoviches' was like living back in the Russian countryside: "How many fascinating conversations, so typical of the Russian intelligentsia! I recall especially the summer of 1940, when V. V. Nabokov-Sirin was a guest there. We set up a manuscript journal, 'Days of Our life,' with Nabokov, my late wife, Karpovich and others contributing: local news, humor, verse, and comic polemics mostly about the meaning of various Russian words."[13] Two zany literary parodies by Nabokov, recently rediscovered in 1940 issues of *Novoe russkoe slovo*, seem likely to have been written for this journal: nothing else would seem to account for their romping holiday spirit.[14]

Turning this Vermont setting into fiction, Nabokov gives Pnin a near heart attack after a game of croquet so vigorous it surprises the rather cerebral scholars that make up his company at Cook's Castle. Photographs of the Nabokovs' two summers at West Wardsboro, 1940 and 1942, record a much less staid and rarefied world and a much younger one: playhuts and hammocks; a tanned Nabokov, stripped to the waist, so lean and wiry that his ribs show, lolling on a blanket or pushing Dmitri on a mail-order race wagon.

None of the photographs records what made Nabokov's vacation unforgettably thrilling: the chance to fulfill his lifelong dream of catching butterflies on another continent. Before leaving for Ver-

mont, he had written to Andrey Avinoff, the celebrated Russian lepidopterist at the Carnegie Museum in Pittsburgh, to report his recent
discoveries in France and to ask about American lepidoptera. Little
did Nabokov know that by the time he left America he would himself
be the most famous lepidopterist in the world.

While he enjoyed Vermont, his cousin Nicolas was spending the
summer at Wellfleet on Cape Cod, just across the street from Edmund Wilson. Aware of Wilson's keen interest in Russian literature,
Nicolas Nabokov, by then a well-known composer, asked his neighbor to assist with the libretto of an opera to be made from Pushkin's
"Negro of Peter the Great." He also recalled that cousin Vladimir
needed help, and wrote to him in Vermont. At Nicolas's prompting,
Vladimir then wrote to Wilson, who suggested they meet in New
York.[15]

IV

Artists and thinkers of all nationalities and kinds had fled Hitler's
Europe for America: Einstein, Mann, Brecht, Huxley, Auden, Stravinsky, Bartok, Chagall. Unlike these well-publicized immigrants,
Nabokov slipped into the United States without any fanfare. In his
lectures later in the year he could not help a note of regret that while
the Germans who had fled Hitler were at once recognized as the true
heirs of *their* culture, the Russian émigrés of twenty years earlier,
more numerous and more varied, had been overlooked as the active
inheritors of Russian culture.[16] Such a strong prejudice against Russian émigrés persisted in the United States, in fact, that Russian émigré literature would be neglected there, even among Russian specialists, until well into the 1960s.[17]

After reaching the United States with virtually no money and
spending almost four months without landing a job, Nabokov
needed an income desperately. Despite his eminence in Russian émigré letters, he had become an utter unknown. The first sign of hope
was a cable he received in Vermont from the Tolstoy Foundation, an
organization set up by the novelist's daughter Alexandra to help resettle Russian immigrants in America: a job with a New York publisher was being held for him if he came at once. He rushed back to
the city. The Tolstoy Foundation secretary "told him to present himself at the main desk of Scribner's Bookshop, which is located below
their editorial offices on Fifth Avenue. 'And stand up straight,' she
added, 'you'll make a better impression.' At Scribner's he was received by a man named Wreden, whom he had known in Europe,

and who was somewhat nonplussed to see who had been sent over, since the job opening was for a delivery boy on a bicycle."[18] From 9:00 A.M. to 6:00 P.M. every day he was expected to pack books and convey them to the post office, for sixty-eight dollars a month. He declined: he could not even wrap a parcel, let alone support a family on pay like that.[19]

After a week back at 1326 Madison Avenue, the Nabokovs moved in mid-September into a brownstone at 35 West 87th Street, "a dreadful little flat," small and uncomfortable but cheap and close to Central Park.[20]

As a young father, Nabokov had always tried to open Dmitri's eyes to trees, flowers, animals. He would quiz his son on the names of things, reacting with mock fury when the boy confused terms. But he and Véra had given Dmitri no preparation in speaking English before sending him off to his first American school: with Russia itself off-limits, they knew he would learn to speak Russian properly only if he heard it at home. Throughout the family's years in Germany, France, America, and Switzerland, Russian—liberally sprinkled with English or French—would always remain their language of everyday communication.* Shortly after the family came back from Vermont, six-year-old Dmitri returned from his first day at school and proudly announced that he had learned English.[21]

Nabokov had himself been an English tutor for many years in Europe. Now circumstances drove him once more to the stopgap of language teaching, this time in Russian. It could not have been a worse time to look for pupils. Since Stalin's pact with Hitler had allowed the Germans to overrun France and leave Britain isolated and in peril, Russia and its language were anything but popular. Nevertheless, Elena Mogilat, a teacher of Russian at Columbia, managed to introduce Nabokov to some bright, enthusiastic women, including Hilda Ward, who would later help him translate his memoir "Mademoiselle O" from the French. He taught his class of three for four and a half hours and a princely nine dollars a week.[22]

Through other Russians, Nabokov looked for something better. He tried Vernadsky again. He approached Avrahm Yarmolinsky, head of the Slavonic Division of the New York Public Library. He sought the help of Peter Pertzoff at Cornell, who had translated one of his Russian short stories two years before. But nothing turned up, and the Stanford summer-school job for 1941 was still not settled, and

---

* In the few notes he kept in his diary, though, Nabokov would normally write in English, whether he lived in America or francophone Switzerland.

neither the story Pertzoff had translated nor the novel nor the reminiscences Nabokov had written directly in English had attracted a publisher. When the Society of Friends of Russian Culture staged an evening of Sirin readings on October 12, Nabokov delighted a packed hall, but New York's émigré audience could never support him. He *had* to find a job, or someone who would buy his work in English.[23]

On October 8, 1940, he called on Edmund Wilson. Wilson was already the foremost American critic of his time, and had temporarily returned to the *New Republic*, standing in for three months as literary editor in Malcolm Cowley's place. He offered Nabokov books to review, at first on more or less Russian topics (a biography of Diaghilev, a translation of a medieval Georgian epic). Wilson soon wrote of Nabokov to his old mentor at Princeton, Christian Gauss: "I'm amazed at the excellence of the book reviews he's been doing for me. He is a brilliant fellow." A friend of Karpovich also introduced Nabokov to the *New York Sun* and the *New York Times*, and for the next few months, especially in October and November 1940, he reviewed all sorts of work—biography, history, fiction, verse, essays, philosophy—whether with a Russian flavor or not. A review of a John Masefield novel shows some of the bold, free-roaming thought, the dazzling imagery, the verbal grace, and the range that Wilson admired:

> What is history? Dreams and dust. How many ways are there for a novelist of dealing with history? Only three. He can court the elusive Muse of verisimilitude by doing his best to unearth and combine all pertinent facts and details; he can frankly indulge in farce or satire by treating the past as a parody of the present; and he can transcend all aspects of time by entrusting a mummy selected at random to the sole care of his genius—provided he has genius. As neither of the first two methods seems to have been adopted by Mr. John Masefield in his new book [*Basilissa, a Tale of the Empress Theodora*], it may be assumed that he relied upon inspiration to transform a certain remote epoch into the everlasting reality of human passions. Unfortunately, his art is not up to the task; and this being so, a problem of appreciation is set: when the magician alone is deceived into seeing his charms working, must the onlookers stare at the stick which has *not* burst into blossom?
>
> They must.[24]

By dint of tough bargaining with publishers, Wilson had learned to survive in America as a freelance critic and writer without the least intellectual compromise. A champion since the early twenties of unfashionable American writers like Henry James and new figures like Fitzgerald and Hemingway, Wilson had then in *Axel's Castle* become the interpreter of modern European literature—Yeats, Joyce, Eliot,

Valéry, Proust—to a generation of Americans. Convinced, like so many members of the American intelligentsia in the early 1930s, that the depression proved the unworkability of capitalism, he turned toward Marxism and the writing of *To the Finland Station*. There he attempted to show the force of a social explanation of history, which reached a new plateau of power as Lenin turned Marxist historical theory into practice, into the *reshaping* of history. Wilson's intellectual restlessness, his independence of mind, and his honesty led him to see how much was wrong in the Soviet Union when he visited the country in 1935, and well before finishing *To the Finland Station* or meeting Nabokov he had become impatient with any unquestioning allegiance to Marx, let alone to Stalin. His Soviet sojourn had changed him in another way: he discovered Pushkin. Learning the Russian language for Pushkin's sake, he became the first to introduce to a wide American audience the greatest poet since Shakespeare. Now he was eager to probe deeper into Russian literature.

Even before he had read any of Nabokov's Russian fiction—not easy to obtain, and certainly not easy to understand for someone with an uneasy grasp of Russian—Wilson put his hard-won knowledge of the literary marketplace at Nabokov's disposal. He seems to have relied on the excellence of Nabokov's English and the judgment of friends who could vouch for the importance of his Russian oeuvre: Nicolas Nabokov; Harry Levin's wife, Elena, a Sirin fan since as a child she learned by heart the opening of his Russian version of *Alice in Wonderland*; and Roman Grynberg, Nabokov's English-language student in Paris, whose mother and sister had been very kind to Wilson during his time in Moscow.[25]

If Wilson could help Nabokov into the American publishing world, Nabokov more than anyone else could help Wilson to understand Russian literature and promote its cause. Since Wilson had a tendency to seek out friends because they could further his current enthusiasms, it was fortunate for Nabokov that Wilson's affair with Russian happened to be just at its most ardent. Had they met when the older man's attentions had shifted, as they would between the late 1940s and the 1960s, to Haitian literature, Hebrew, Hungarian, and much else besides, their friendship might never have developed. As it was, at one of their first meetings in New York in the fall of 1940, Wilson urged Nabokov to translate one of Pushkin's masterly miniature verse-dramas. "Your suggestion regarding 'Mozart and Salieri' has worked havoc with me," Nabokov wrote Wilson. "I thought I would toy with the idea—and then suddenly found myself in the very deep waters of English blank verse." After Wilson sent him an advance from the *New Republic* for the translation, Nabokov wrote back gratefully: "It is really wonderful to be living at last in a country where there is a market for such things."[26]

At the dinner at Roman Grynberg's where Wilson appears to have suggested translating "Mozart and Salieri," Nabokov was also reintroduced (they had met in Paris) to the writer and translator Max Eastman. In the strongly leftist intellectual climate of America in the 1930s, there were few members of the intelligentsia who had as clear a picture of the horrors of Soviet life—though still short of the bloody truth—as Eastman and Wilson. By presenting himself as the sole foe of fascism, Stalin had successfully manipulated international opinion so that millions of Americans in the 1930s were ready to rally behind the Soviet Union, whatever its flaws. The show trials of 1937–1938 and the Stalin-Hitler pact of 1939 had lost him popular American support, but much of the intelligentsia still accepted everything Stalin did and vilified critics of the Soviet Union.[27] For Nabokov, who had recently been asked "You're a Trotskyite, then?" by an American writer whom he had told he was neither for the Soviets nor for any tsar, it came as a relief to talk to Americans who knew something of Soviet realities.[28]

At the dinner at the Grynbergs' there must have been some discussion of Lenin, for a few days later Wilson sent Nabokov a copy of his new book, To the Finland Station, inscribed "to Vladimir Nabokov in the hope that this may make him think better of Lenin." Though disenchanted with Marxism as a creed, and bitterly anti-Stalinist, Wilson still believed in the moral beauty of Lenin as someone who had a vision of a better future for mankind and the courage to bring it about. Wilson seemed to think that Nabokov need only be exposed to Lenin to understand. Nabokov wrote back at length, praising the book as a whole but offering detailed criticism of the portrait of Lenin.* In fact, as he repeatedly tried to point out to Wilson—and to America at large—Russia, for all the brutal stupidities of tsarist rule, had been moving for six decades, albeit in fits and starts, toward increasing political and cultural freedom, until Lenin seized power and turned what had by February 1917 become a democratic republic into a dictatorship that ruthlessly suppressed all opposition. Stalin's secret police were not a betrayal of Lenin's principles but the natural heirs of his apparatus for total state control.[29]

Though Nabokov was perfectly correct in the lucid criticisms he set before Wilson then and later, Wilson still believed well into the 1950s

---

* To his friend Karpovich, he also noted that he thought both Hegelians and Marxists were rather more complex than Wilson made them. In the same letter he classified Wilson accurately, if paradoxically, as "a narrow eclectic" (Nabokov to Karpovich, December 10, 1940, Bakhmeteff Archive, Columbia).

that "except for Lenin's democratic reign, Russia had remained unchanged from the Middle Ages to Stalin."[30] Because of his Marxist sympathies, he felt confident, he knew Russian history better than Nabokov did. Unaware that in *The Gift* Nabokov had thoroughly researched the origins of Russian radical utilitarianism and in 1933 had even proposed to teach the evolution of Russian Marxism, Wilson simply assumed that Nabokov was uninterested in, and incapable of understanding, social or political issues. Had he ever read the Chernyshevsky biography in *The Gift*, Wilson would have found how much his own analysis of the composition of *Das Kapital* had in common with Nabokov's study of the genesis of Chernyshevsky's *What Is to Be Done?*

Although Nabokov and Wilson shared a passion for Flaubert, Proust, and Joyce, their chief points of contact and friction from first to last would be Pushkin and Russian literature, Lenin and Russian history. But for the moment, their encounters generated intellectual light and personal warmth, not the flame and smoke of battle. For these two opinionated, combative, fiercely independent minds, the brilliance of their frank disagreements was at first just another part of the excitement.

V

Some time in 1940, Mikhail Karpovich introduced Nabokov to Harry Levin. At this point Levin, recently married to a young émigrée, Elena Zarudnaya, was still an untenured young instructor at Harvard and not yet the Harvard Department of Comparative Literature's prize and pride. It was not until the Nabokovs settled in Cambridge, Massachusetts, that they would become close friends with the Levins, but introductions to people like Edmund Wilson and his wife, Mary McCarthy, and the Levins made nonsense of the warning Alexandra Tolstoy had issued to Nabokov: "All Americans are completely uncultured, credulous fools." In 1941, when his friend George Hessen was about to come to the United States, Nabokov's advice was the exact converse: "This is a cultured and exceedingly diverse country. The only thing you must do is deal with genuine Americans and don't get involved with the local Russian emigration." Nabokov was introduced from the start to the best that American intellectual life could offer, and he would make many more American friends in his first years in the United States than he had among non-Russians in twenty years of European exile.[31]

Some of his encounters with the local Russian population justified his warning to Hessen. An émigré teacher of Russian at Columbia complimented him, as soon as he was introduced, on his magnificent aristocratic pronunciation: "All one hears here are Yids." At an émigré party where Nabokov was the guest of honor, he heard the host himself use the word "Yid." Normally extremely correct in his speech—there is not a single obscenity in his published work—Nabokov responded by swearing deliberately and forcefully. When his host reacted with astonishment, Nabokov replied, "I thought this was the language you used in this house," and promptly left.[32]

In America, Nabokov certainly did not ignore old Russian friends from Europe—Nathalie Nabokoff, the businessman and publisher Roman Grynberg, Alexander Kerensky, the painter Mstislav Dobuzhinsky, the writer Mark Aldanov, the former Socialist Revolutionary Vladimir Zenzinov, and the close friends whom he exhorted and helped get into the United States, George Hessen, Anna Feigin, the Marinel sisters. But he made few new friends among Russians. One of those few, the pioneer aviatrix Lucia Davidova, who was a close friend of Stravinsky and Balanchine, pointed out that Nabokov showed no interest in meeting such people. "America is my home now," he later said. "It is my country. The intellectual life suits me better than any other country in the world. I have more friends there, more kindred souls than anywhere."[33]

VI

At the end of November 1940, after a long delay caused by financial complications and more than a year after Mark Aldanov had suggested Nabokov take up the offer he himself could not accept, Stanford University at last wired Nabokov to offer him formally a teaching post for the following summer for a salary of $750. In accepting, Nabokov named four possible courses. Professor Henry Lanz of the Slavic department chose two: Modern Russian Literature, and The Art of Writing, the second to be given in conjunction with the Department of Speech and Drama. Lanz also advised Nabokov that it would be wise to stress "practical playwriting": "In all my advertising notes and pamphlets I strongly emphasize your qualifications as a Russian playwright, for—as you have probably discovered yourself—playwriting in America is the most popular and practical form of literature, and if you will have any number of students in that course they will be from the playwriting class."[34]

In his apartment on West 87th Street and in the New York Public Library, Nabokov spent the fall, winter, and spring preparing a full set of lectures not just for Stanford but for "this or that Eastern col-

lege blurrily looming ahead" where he might teach Russian literature. He later estimated that he prepared perhaps a hundred lectures, at about twenty pages per hour, or about two thousand pages
in all. Never, he wrote to friends, had he had to work so hard.[35]

Nabokov followed Lanz's advice and thought carefully about dramatic composition. He read a handful of playwriting guides, if only
for the satiric treat they offered. A good analogy, he wrote, could be
made between "the vulgarian's (Basil Hogarth's) *How to Write Plays*—
'the art of poking fun,' 'smart lines,' 'feeling the public's pulse,' 'love
scenes'—and a supposed *How to Become a Doctor* consisting of such
chapters as 'decorating the reception room,' 'how to welcome the
prospective patient,' 'a few easy symptoms,' 'fun with a stetho-
scope.' " He read and pulled apart a score of recent American plays,
including Lillian Hellman's *Children's Hour*, Maxwell Anderson's
Winterset, Steinbeck's *Of Mice and Men*, and especially O'Neill's
Mourning Becomes Electra. He also reread a dozen plays by Ibsen,
whom he liked, but concentrated on *Pillars of Society*, which he found
he abhorred. As his ideas on drama bubbled up, he became excited
enough to contemplate writing a book on the subject, to be called,
perhaps, *In Aleppo Once*, and at the same time he jotted down in a
wistful aside: "Oh to write my play about 'Falter'!"[36]

Lanz's letter urging Nabokov to spotlight playwriting had come at
an oddly opportune moment. Just before hearing from Stanford that
he had a firm offer for the 1941 summer course, Nabokov had written
to Mikhail Chekhov, a former actor in the celebrated Moscow Art
Theater and, since his recent arrival in America, director of his own
Chekhov Theater Studio in Connecticut. Nabokov proposed an adaptation of *Don Quixote* for the stage, to be carried out in a manner
akin to that of his own plays, *The Event* and *The Waltz Invention*. He
envisaged an atmosphere tense and alarmed, "like the chaotic condition in which people live"; characters strangely reminiscent of
other characters, and characters who seem to appear before Quixote
again and again, though they are actually different each time; a person who recurs intermittently as if directing the action; a rhythm that
recalls the way we can tell, simply by the intonation of someone talking in the next room, the person being spoken to at the other end of
the line. Nabokov's ideas excited Chekhov, and he asked him to
draw up a sketch for the play, which Nabokov sent him in January.[37]

VII

Meanwhile he had been following another old interest. In Berlin,
Prague, and London, Nabokov had gone to the entomological

branches of those cities' great museums, but only for more or less isolated visits of inspection. Soon after arriving in New York, he made his way to the American Museum of Natural History and plunged with zest into lepidopterological research, working all fall and winter, unpaid, in the entomological section on the fifth floor, sometimes for whole days at a time. He became friends with William Comstock, who put at Nabokov's disposal all the material he needed to compare with his unidentified catch above Moulinet, and analyzed the butterflies' genitalia, a technique Nabokov himself had not yet learned. Nabokov wrote up the findings on his Moulinet rarity, but hesitated to call it a new species, and also published another article on two species he studied at the museum: his first lepidopterological articles that were more than the travel notes of a gifted collector. In gratitude for the help he received there, Nabokov would later donate some three hundred rare butterflies to the museum.[38]

At the end of December, Edmund Wilson left the *New Republic*, but arranged for Nabokov to write a survey article on contemporary Soviet literature, which would fit in with his preparations for Stanford. Early in the new year, Nabokov read the Soviet monthly magazines for 1940, "a ghastly and very amusing task." No longer having the same warm feeling toward the *New Republic* now that Wilson had gone, Nabokov sent his devastating critique to Klaus Mann's ambitious new periodical *Decision*, with which Wilson had also put him in touch. Even straight quotation was damning enough—curiously similar comments by Lenin and the Nazi ideologist Alfred Rosenberg on the "freedom" the artist could have by following the party line, or this precept from a Soviet reviewer to Soviet writers: "A novelist ought not to indulge in the description of misty or cloudy landscape; the Soviet countryside must be shown to be gay and sunny."[39]

As a boy, Nabokov had stopped in Berlin for three months to have his teeth attended to by an American dentist. Now in January 1941, his teeth still a problem, Nabokov once again took advantage of America's dental technology: "Although operation after operation passes painlessly—except for the needle sinking into the tight, gleaming gum—and it is even pleasant to look at the monster that has been extracted, sometimes with an abscess hanging at the root at big as a red candy cherry, the sensations that follow are awful. . . . Most of the extractions have been made, and I think I'll be able to smile for the first time next week." In fact it would be another four months before all eight teeth were out and new dentures were in place. To pay for such things as dentistry and a Manhattan apartment, Véra Nabokov managed to find an excellent secretarial job at *France Forever*, but she was there only a short while before becoming seriously ill. There was even concern that the family might not be able after all to travel to Stanford.[40]

VIII

Early in February, Nabokov delivered his first American college lecture, a guest lecture—a great success—at Wells College, near Cornell, where his cousin Nicolas was teaching music. In New York he had established himself, with the help of Mikhail Karpovich, on the lecture-tour roster of the Institute of International Education. Through the Institute and Prof. Agnes Perkins of the Department of English Literature at Wellesley College, Nabokov was offered two weeks of lectures at Wellesley, beginning on March 15, for $250. The college had been attracted, Nabokov recalled, by the fact that he had translated *Alice in Wonderland* into Russian.[41]

After New York, Nabokov found the oaky calm of New England soothing, and the campus of Wellesley, a private women's college just outside Boston, reminded him in patches and whiffs of Trinity College, Cambridge. During his stay at Claflin Hall, Nabokov was hosted by Agnes Perkins, and by Amy Kelly of the Department of English Composition, later to become known as the author of a best-selling biography of Eleanor of Aquitaine.[42]

Since Wellesley had no Russian department, Nabokov lectured to English classes—although anyone could attend—on Russian literature: "The Technique of the Russian Novel," "The Short Stories of Gorky and Chekhov," "The Proletarian Novel," "The Soviet Drama," "The Soviet Short Story." He thundered against Gorky and Hemingway. He spoke up for the novelists of the neglected Russian emigration, Bunin, Aldanov—and Sirin. Though Soviet literature, he declared, was a provincial courtyard—and he cited liberally to prove his point—émigré literature had continued the public highway of Russian culture. And he again emphasized as he had in his *Decision* article the fundamental similarity of Hitler's Germany and Stalin's Russia, now sharing the spoils of Eastern Europe.[43]

Nabokov's lectures were such a "purring success" that he was paid a bonus, and he was made much of at soirees, banquets, and meetings. By the time he left, moves were already afoot to have him at Wellesley for much longer. He welcomed the prospect: before quitting the campus he wrote to Aldanov that he doubted whether Europe had more attractive universities.[44]

While in Boston, Nabokov had lunch with another contact he owed to Edmund Wilson, Edward Weeks, editor of the *Atlantic Monthly*.

Weeks recalls the strong impression Nabokov's physical appearance made on him then and over the next year or so when they would meet at the downstairs café at the Ritz: "He would come in in a shabby tweed coat, trousers bulging at the knee, but be quite the most distinguished man in the room, with his perfectly beautiful hazel eyes, his fine brown hair, the *élan*, the spark. . . . He just had to walk into the room and the girls looked around—the clothes didn't make any difference. He had a way of carrying himself, a *joie* in his eyes, a zest." After three years of rejections from English-language publishers, Nabokov was surprised at the way Weeks exulted over the translation of "Cloud, Castle, Lake": "We are enchanted, . . . this is genius, . . . this is what we have been looking for, . . . we want to print it at once—give us more." Over the next few years the *Atlantic* would be the outlet for nearly a dozen Nabokov stories and poems.[45]

On the way back to New York at the end of March, Nabokov stopped in Ridgefield, Connecticut, to see Mikhail Chekhov. Their ideas for adapting *Don Quixote* no longer coincided (Chekhov wanted a Christian or rather an anthroposophical apotheosis at the end), and the project was called off.[46] From Ridgefield, Nabokov traveled on a little further to Stamford to spend a night with Edmund Wilson and Wilson's third wife, Mary McCarthy.

Wilson and Nabokov had seen each other several times over the past few months, but it was in Stamford that their keen interest in each other turned into warm friendship. The lean, intense Nabokov, with his full-voweled Russian version of a Cambridge accent, and short, plump, puffy-faced Wilson, with his loud, curiously high-pitched voice, went line by line through the proofs of Nabokov's translation of "Mozart and Salieri." In the glow of their collaboration, Nabokov for once was amenable to emendations, even grateful for them. The two men could not agree on the subject of Russian prosody, a difference that would gradually become tiresome and vexing to them both when repeated on and off for the next twenty-five years, but for the moment they overwhelmed and exhilarated each other with their energy.[47]

Mary McCarthy, then a twenty-eight-year-old former *Partisan Review* editor just starting to write her first fiction, watched them with delight. In her words, "they had an absolute ball together. Edmund was always in a state of *joy* when Vladimir appeared; he *loved* him." As Clarence Brown would remark in a review of *The Nabokov-Wilson Letters*, "both of them well past the midpoint of life, formed the sort of friendship that is normally possible only in youth." Wilson's young son Reuel heard the name "Volodya," but could say it only as "Gardenia." Nabokov thought the name enchanting; Wilson declared with mock grandeur, "you're the gardenia in the buttonhole of Russian literature." Out on a long stroll together, Wilson asked Nabokov whether or not he believed in God. "Do you?" countered Nabokov. "What a strange question!" muttered Wilson, and fell silent.[48]

IX

Though Nabokov had failed to convince Mikhail Chekhov that his *Don Quixote* adaptation was stageworthy, his similarly frenetic *The Event* had its American premiere on April 4, 1941, at the Heckscher Theater in New York. G. S. Ermolov directed and played Troshcheikin; the sets were by Nabokov's friend Mstislav Dobuzhinsky, who had designed sets for Meyerhold, Diaghilev, and Stanislavsky (he was Stanislavsky's favorite designer), and in New York would do the same for the Metropolitan Opera. Nabokov, who had been in Menton when the play premiered in Paris, beamed with pleasure to see it onstage. For decades to come one of the few decorations the Nabokovs would have on their wall—as a rule they entirely neglected their domestic landscape—was a blue-and-white Delftware plate, complete with crack, that Dobuzhinsky had painted on cardboard as a prop for the play.[49]

During April, Nabokov began to translate Russian poetry for his Stanford course. At this stage he translated rhyme for rhyme, preserving an unusual degree of accuracy, although with the inevitable slight equivocation from time to time for the sake of rhyme. The absolutist fidelity and ungainliness of his *Eugene Onegin*, upon which Wilson was to pour such scorn, were still more than a decade away, and for the moment Wilson rated one of the first two short Pushkin lyrics Nabokov sent him as "the best Pushkin translation and one of the best translations of poetry of any kind I ever saw."[50] Over the next months Nabokov translated more Pushkin and Lermontov and Tyutchev.

In the middle of May, Nabokov heard from Wellesley College that it had formally decided to offer him a one-year appointment for the coming year. Though he was to give a few public lectures on comparative literature, to see classes from time to time, and perhaps to read from some of his stories and novels, Agnes Perkins emphasized that almost all his time was to be kept for writing, since the position was intended to be virtually a writer-in-residence post.[51] When Nabokov finished at Stanford, there would be something congenial waiting for him back East.

X

Stanford University would not pay Nabokov any traveling expenses. When one of his Russian-language pupils, Dorothy Leuthold, heard this, she offered to drive the family out West: she had a new car and wanted to test her driving, she would have some exposure to Russian en route, and besides, it would be fun. On May 26 they set out from New York, Nabokov equipped with his four-volume Dahl dictionary, his manuscripts, and his butterfly net.[52]

Nabokov had always cherished exploration as one of his most passionate dreams (see The Pole, "Terra Incognita," The Gift), and he would have relished Elizabeth Hardwick's comment on Lolita after his death: "It is rather in the mood of Marco Polo in China that he meets the (to us) exhausted artifacts of the American scene." His 1941 trip westward was his first venture into the territory of Lolita's motel America: Hotel General Shelby, Maple Shade Cottage, Wonderland Motor Courts, El Rey Courts, Bright Angel Lodge, Mission Court. Nabokov looked around him with an artist's and a scientist's eye, writing with rapture to Dobuzhinsky, his old drawing master, of the changing hues and forms of the landscape, and capturing whatever lepidoptera he could.[53]

They traveled slowly through the Appalachians. As the others sat over their thermos and sandwiches at roadside tables, Nabokov would stalk off, net in hand. They drove through Tennessee and Arkansas, and as he crossed the Mississippi, Nabokov recalled not Mark Twain but Chateaubriand's verdant America. He caught moths at a gas station between Dallas and Fort Worth. Amid the sagebrush of Arizona and New Mexico deserts, he pursued butterflies he had known only in guidebooks or museum trays. In Arizona he was followed for five miles by a horse, "a total stranger." Once he found himself surrounded by coyotes, "unusually likeable, a mother and her pups." And in New Mexico he was nearly arrested for painting a farmer's trees with sugar to attract a certain kind of moth.[54]

On the night of June 7, the travelers stopped on the south rim of the Grand Canyon in the painted log cabins of Bright Angel Lodge. As an "accredited representative of the American Museum of Natural History," Nabokov was issued a permit to collect specimens in Grand Canyon National Park. On June 9, a bright cold morning after snow and rain, he walked down the slushy mule track of Bright Angel Trail with Dorothy Leuthold. A few minutes down the trail, her foot kicked up a midsized brown butterfly, fluttering weakly in the cold. Nabokov saw at once that it seemed to belong to a still undescribed species of Neonympha. He netted it, and then another, and returned proudly to the rim—where Véra and Dmitri had sheltered in the car for warmth—only to find that right beside the car Véra had herself caught two specimens, sluggish with the cold, with nothing but her fingers. [55]

In 1942, Nabokov published a paper on the butterfly and related species.[56] He named his find, the first new species he had discovered, the fulfillment of his most passionate childhood dream, *Neonympha dorothea*, in honor of the woman who had not only kicked up the butterfly but had made it possible for his first crossing of the United States to be an adventure of discovery rather than four days rocking in a train.

XI

When the group reached Palo Alto on June 14, Dorothy Leuthold headed back eastward. The Nabokovs rented a neat little house, a trim Riviera villa, at 230 Sequoia Avenue, just across El Camino Real from the Stanford campus: a sequoia in their own front garden, but no phone and no car.[57]

In the cool blue Palo Alto mornings Nabokov would walk through Stanford's dusty eucalyptus groves to his office and classroom in the Quadrangle, all tan sandstone and rounded arches beneath roofs of Mediterranean tiles. His two courses began on June 24: Modern Russian Literature (Tuesday, Wednesday, Thursday, Friday at 9:00, with only two students enrolled, according to the Stanford register) and The Art of Writing (Tuesday, Wednesday, Thursday at 11:00, four students).[58]

Lean, muscled, tanned, standing before his students in Karpovich's cut-down suit, Nabokov seemed "a man with more energy than he could contain" and read his lectures with such sustained intensity that he was oblivious to the froth and spittle forming on his lips.[59] The surviving text of these Stanford lectures—not to be confused with the published Cornell lectures—explains not only the intensity of Nabokov's manner but the principles of all his criticism.

Always a hard worker, he had prepared thoroughly for class. For the playwriting on which he seems to have concentrated with his creative writing students, he read plays and playwriting guides not widely but energetically and with complete independence of mind. Knowing what he was looking for, he reacted quickly to what he read, writing with such speed that he misspelled words and overlooked grammar but could still express his strong opinions forcefully even in this headlong prose.

Lanz could not have made the suggestion that Nabokov focus on *practical* playwriting to anyone less likely to accept it. Nabokov stressed to his students that "the prime object of a playwright ought to be not to write a successful play but an immortal one." He analyzed the plays he had read not for suggestions to follow but only to show what to avoid: the automatic conventions incompatible with dramatic truth, the tight shackles of determinism that hobble tragedy, the lines of least resistance in exposition and resolution, the fatal desire to pander to the audience.

Nabokov's dismissals of highly regarded writers are notorious. That they are not a writer's envy but the expression of his passion for the possibilities of his art becomes clear in these lectures:

> I must apologize. . . . I so deeply love good literature and hate so bitterly bad literature that my expressions may be stronger than they ought to be.

> I feel much too deeply about permanent values not to apply to modern plays those lofty and imperishable standards which playwrights of genius have observed.

He explained again and again that he was not out to attack authors but to defend and extend literary art:

> What merely interests me is to find the best illustrations of this or that aspect of the technique of writing and just as in science it is not making fun of a creature to note the whims or blunders or the conventional repetitions of Nature in the evolutionary process, so my choice of this or that author is not necessarily the fiercest indictment of him which the list of his fallacies may seem.

What other teacher would tell a group of aspiring writers that for all his reverence for Shakespeare and Chekhov, even these great masters had not done quite enough? In a note to himself, Nabokov summed up his strategy:

> My fundamental standpoint: 1a) drama exists, all the ingredients of a perfect play exist, but this perfect play (though there exist perfect novels, short stories, poems, essays) has not been produced yet neither by Shakespeare nor by Chekhov. It can be imagined and one day it will be written—either by an Anglo-Saxon or a Russian. 1b) exploding the myth of the average audience. 2) the examination of the conventions and ideas

which hamper the possibility of such a play being written—and staged.*
3) rally of positive forces already known, suggestions of method and
new lines based on them.

Nabokov thought that nothing could be worse than the contention
that the audience was everything in a play, that the ideal dramatist
was the one endowed with an intuition for "what the public wants."
He detested the "abject grovelling at the feet of an imaginary audience of nincompoops." "The Theatre is *not* a 'function of the crowd'
for the simple reason that a crowd is composed of individuals." "I
maintain that the public's judgement is much more intelligent than
the management thinks."

A low opinion of the audience necessitated certain standard modes
of exposition, certain necessary signals of future developments, a
false commitment to rising action and the absolute finality of the last
curtain—all of which destroyed the splendid fluidity and surprise of
life and the fact that situations often simply fizzle out. What Nabokov
hoped for instead from drama was "the selective and harmonious
intensification of the loose patterns of chance and destiny, character
and action, thought and emotion, existing in the reality of human
life," "a certain unique pattern of life in which the sorrows and passions of a particular man will follow the rules of his own individuality, not the rules of the theatre as we know them."[60]

Nabokov lectured also on poetry, the short story, the novel, and
the need for an individual style. The published lecture "The Art of
Literature and Commonsense," one of the few pieces that survive
from his creative writing course, ends with the same message as his
playwriting lectures: the need to follow the special rules of the self
while the crowd around "is being driven by some common impulse
to some common goal." Just when an author sits down to write, "the
monster of grim commonsense" will lumber up the steps "to whine
that the book is not for the general public, that the book will never
never—And right then, just before it blurts out the word *s, e, double-
l*, false commonsense must be shot dead."[61] In its dazzling, turbulent
imagery, the lecture is an exhilarating performance, a *demonstration*
of a marvelous writer at work, and at the furthest remove possible

* Nabokov notes in his Russian lectures that Chekhov, "though he almost managed
to create a new and better kind of drama, was cunningly caught in his own snares. I
have the definite impression that he would not have been caught by these conventions—by the very conventions he thought he had broken—if he had known a little
more of the numerous forms they take. . . . he had not studied the art of drama completely enough, had not studied a sufficient number of plays, was not critical enough
about certain technical aspects of his medium"—a judgment that speaks volumes
about Nabokov's own study of the art of fiction (*Lectures on Russian Literature*, 291).

from a collection of helpful hints or a do-it-yourselfer's guide. Nabokov would also from time to time read from his fiction—as if the lectures did not already bear his own special stamp.[62]

One student summed up the Art of Writing course:

> I don't recall taking any notes in that class. It would have been rather like scribbling notes when Michelangelo talked about how he had designed and painted the ceiling of the Sistine Chapel. In any event, I don't recall that he lectured in any conventional sense of the term. He shared with us his creative activity and experience. Never was there richer fare in any course taught on a college campus, but it was as impossible to reduce to notes as to convert a Rolls-Royce into tin cans with a tack hammer.[63]

Nabokov's methods seem to have worked.

However absolute Nabokov may have been in his demands on great writers, he did not expect to find the savior of modern drama right there in his class. He might ask for nothing less than diamonds, but he was ready to concede that coal was carbon too. He was "a most undemanding teacher at Stanford and would be highly appreciative of anything even vaguely resembling acceptable prose. Only barbarous writing would occasionally provoke him to mild ridicule, though he would frequently ask the class for help when he could not understand what someone was trying to do in an assignment."[64]

According to the Stanford bulletin, Nabokov's Modern Russian Literature course covered the "history of Russian literature from 1905 to our times, with survey of the revolutionary movement in earlier Russian literature." In fact, Nabokov seems to have ignored this rubric, for although over the spring he had prepared material on Soviet literature, he evidently taught much from the nineteenth century: he mentions to Wilson having to bestir himself from his sunny deck chair to "talk about Russian versification or the way Gogol used the word 'dazhe' in 'Shinel' ' ('The Overcoat')." Since he found the existing translations of Russian classics not, as Pushkin called them, the post-horses of civilization but "the wild asses of wild ignorance," he had to translate Pushkin and Gogol as he went along—"A Feast During the Plague," "The Overcoat"—until his hand ached.[65]

One constant theme whenever Nabokov lectured on Russian literature was the censorship from the right under the tsars and the censorship from the left under the radicals of the 1840s and 1860s and their despotic descendants in the Soviet Union. As in the creative writing course, where he exhorted his students to defy the American tyranny of the marketplace, Nabokov made his lectures a plea for the right of artists to accept no dictates but their own artistic consciences.

In a climate he compared to Pushkin's prose, cloudless but not hot, Nabokov read and worked in the sun, sitting in his swim shorts on the billiard-table lawn at the back of the house. On free days he would head to the yellow hills of Los Altos for butterflies, and there met his first rattlesnake.[66]

Evenings were often taken up with a busy round of parties, all very formal and "genteel"—Véra Nabokov remembers Stanford as much more formal than Wellesley. (At one party, though, Nabokov introduced a different note when he had to be given a remedy for poison ivy after the day's chase.) Among those the Nabokovs liked to meet socially were Yvor Winters and Henry Lanz and their wives. Lanz, the head of Nabokov's department at Stanford, was a Russianized Finn with whom Nabokov often played chess and whom he found delicate, cultured, and talented. He also discovered another side to him: Lanz was a nympholept, and would drive off on the weekends, neat and dapper in his blazer, to orgiastic parties with nymphets.[67]

Back in January, Edmund Wilson and Harry Levin had both passed Nabokov's name to James Laughlin, the wealthy young scion of a steel family who had just set up the publishing firm of New Directions to launch works of high literary and low commercial value. Nabokov had sent Laughlin the manuscript of *The Real Life of Sebastian Knight*, which was read and recommended by Delmore Schwartz.* In July, Laughlin accepted the book, much to its author's surprise. After three years of rejections, Nabokov had no choice but to accept the low advance of $150. A few days later Laughlin came up to see him from a visit to Los Angeles and sought an option on his next three books.[68]

With term, exams, and marking over by the first week of September, the Nabokovs' friends Bertrand and Lisbet Thompson, now living in San Francisco, came to pick them up and drive them for ten days around Yosemite National Park. This time too, of course, Nabokov was armed with a permit to catch butterflies for the American Museum of Natural History. Once he was so intent on the chase that he stepped on a slumbering bear.[69]

XII

Before Nabokov had left for California, Edmund Wilson, who had just finished a study of Californian writers, had warned his friend against succumbing to Hollywood commercialism and the temptation

---

* For an account of the composition of *The Real Life of Sebastian Knight*, Nabokov's first major work in English, written in 1938, before he abandoned Russian, and for a description and analysis of the novel, see *Vladimir Nabokov: The Russian Years*, pp. 494–502.

to bask idly in the Californian sun. Nabokov knew he had nothing to fear from either, and just before heading east again, he lectured in the Slavic department at Berkeley—at that time headed by Alexander Kaun, the Sirin fan he had met in Paris in 1932—in the hope that his performance would be remembered should a vacancy arise.[70]

On September 11 the Nabokovs left Palo Alto and traveled by train direct to New York and Wellesley.[71] By the time he returned across America, Nabokov was no longer Sirin, a writer confined to the isolation ward of an émigré subculture, but a European intellectual who had found refuge in American universities—and what could be more American than that? From the smiling scenes of his first morning in Manhattan, his first year here had set the pattern for his future as an American. He would settle in the East, but travel through the West summer after summer. He would revel in the intellectual excitement of America. He would study and chase butterflies more zealously than he had ever done, and his teaching and translating and lepidoptera would leave him very little time for his muse. After some difficulties, his English works and even his Russian stories would find a publisher, but there would be no chance for any more of his Russian novels—the vast bulk of his creative output to date—to be published in English until *Lolita* brought him a second fame and allowed him to leave the refuge of academic America.

CHAPTER 2

Visiting Lecturer: Wellesley and Cambridge, 1941–1942

The déménagement from my palatial Russian to the narrow quarters of

my English was like moving from one darkened house

to another on a starless night during a strike

of candlemakers and torchbearers.

—Unpublished note, Nabokov archives

I

NABOKOV'S Wellesley College colleague, the writer Sylvia Berkman, maintains that although she has befriended writers as well known as Robert Frost, she has never met anyone else who seemed to constitute, as Nabokov did, a special kind of his own, an autonomous genus to which not a single other person belonged.[1] His first appointment at Wellesley for 1941–1942 acknowledged his uniqueness by devising a position especially for him: Resident Lecturer in Comparative Literature.

Apart from its being only a one-year appointment, this post suited Nabokov far better than any university position he later held. Since Wellesley had neither a Russian nor a comparative literature department, he was quite on his own. He had been invited to Wellesley, on the strength of his brilliant guest lectures in March, simply to be an inspiration to the college in his role as writer, and he was to be left nearly all his time to do just that: to write. His only obligations were to deliver six public lectures, "possibly on such a theme as 'The Great Russian Writers and Their Importance and Influence on European Culture,' " and a small number of lectures to classes in modern literature departments.[2] The "Resident" in his title was seriously meant: he had to live in Wellesley and was expected to participate in the college's extracurricular life, dining once a week or so at one or another of the various college houses. For all this, he would be well paid: $3,000, an associate professor's salary.

On their return from California the Nabokovs found a place to rent a few minutes' walk from campus on a quiet street in the quiet village of Wellesley: a small but comfortable apartment tucked under the gambrel roof of a large clapboard house at 19 Appleby Road. By 1944, when he formally became part of the teaching staff, Nabokov would have an apartment in Cambridge and would commute from there to Wellesley only on the afternoons of his classes, so that he had little contact with anyone except his students. Things were quite different in this first year, when he was highly visible in and around Wellesley. Colleagues who would soon become friends lived nearby: Agnes Perkins and Amy Kelly, both near retirement age, who had hosted him in March; a youngish couple, Wilma and Charles Kerby-Miller, also both of the English department; and Andrée Bruel of French.

Nabokov liked Wellesley from the start, not least for its appreciation of him. He would later praise the purity of its scholarship, less marred by academic jockeying for prestige and position than neighboring Harvard. He considered the college's interest in the welfare of its students as typical of American kindliness as the open-stack system of its library was of American openness. At first, after his recent "Western orgies," he found it "pathetically dull to watch the good old eastern combination of butterflies on the college lawns," but he also felt more at home in New England than he had "in fair but somehow unreal California, among those blond hills," and he came to enjoy the winding walks through Wellesley's wooded campus, the ivy-twined trees, the innumerable flowers, and gray Lake Waban.[3]

Early in the fall semester, each Wednesday for the first three weeks of October, Nabokov delivered a public lecture in Pendleton Hall to a large audience of staff and students. His opening lecture, "Pushkin as a West European Writer," introduced Pushkin as an exile in his own country, not only subject to the censorship of the tsar but condemned to "a condition of permanent exile which is familiar to all writers of genius but with great Russian writers has always been an almost natural state." His second lecture, "Lermontov as a West European Writer," focused especially on the short lyric "The Dream." The third, "Gogol as a West European Writer," celebrated the irrational magic of "The Overcoat" and Gogol's visual sense that transcended "the hackneyed combinations of blind noun and dog-like adjective that Europe had inherited from the ancients."[4]

Nabokov also gave guest lectures in the Department of English Composition and in the modern literature departments, English, French, Spanish, and Italian. To Spanish students, for instance, he spoke of the use Russian writers had made of Spain: *The Stone Guest*, Pushkin's brilliant version of the Don Juan story; and the Russian intelligentsia's identification with Don Quixote as its members tilted at the windmills of tsarism.[5]

Nabokov and his wife often dined with the Wellesley students in college dormitories or in clubs.[6] His bold opinions and his wide-ranging interests fascinated his young listeners, and he basked in their admiration. The young women—plaid skirts, bobby socks, buttoned sweaters with sleeves pushed up—thought him charming, handsome, and by the standards of well-to-do Wellesley, romantically poor.

II

On his arrival in Wellesley, Nabokov began to write a major article on natural mimicry, with "furious refutations of 'natural selection' and 'the struggle for life.' " It was a theme that had inspired him since childhood. While accepting the fact of evolution, Nabokov thought the Darwinian account of its mechanisms in error:* he could not accept that the undirected randomness of natural selection would ever explain the elaborateness of nature's designs, especially in the most complex cases of mimicry where the design appears to exceed any predator's powers of apprehension. Nabokov sensed something artistic and deceptive in nature, as if its ornate patterns had been deliberately hidden to be rediscovered by the eyes of human intelligence. Although he had completed the paper by the following spring, it was never published and nothing survives except a fragment embedded in *Speak, Memory*.[7]

Nabokov's ideas on mimicry, so fundamental to his whole sense of life, shade rapidly from naturalists' lore into metaphysical speculation. In other respects, his lepidoptery gave off the unmistakable naphthalene scent of the laboratory.

Shortly after settling in Wellesley, he traveled the sixteen miles to Harvard's Museum of Comparative Zoology to check his Grand Canyon catches against the M.C.Z.'s holdings. He discovered right away that most of the butterflies of the Old World in the Weeks collection were badly arranged and poorly housed in glassless trays that offered no protection from dust and museum mites. He called on Nathaniel

---

* At that time, his position was not so unusual as it may seem now. Among professional biologists it was only in the decade 1937–1947 that what Julian Huxley called "the evolutionary synthesis" itself evolved, and settled the differences between naturalists and geneticists that had impeded widespread acceptance, not of evolution per se, but of Darwin's own explanations of the phenomena. See Ernst Mayr, *The Growth of Biological Thought* (Cambridge: Harvard University Press, 1982), 566–68.

Banks, Harvard's head of entomology, and volunteered to set the collection in order. Banks, who had heard from his friend William Comstock at the American Museum of Natural History that Nabokov would call, had open before him on his desk Nabokov's 1920 article "A Few Notes on Crimean Lepidoptera"—a propitious beginning.[8]

Thomas Barbour, the director of the M.C.Z., located some empty glass trays for Nabokov and ordered more, and told him that they would be delighted if he wished to come and arrange the collection in his spare time. It was a very casual offer, and of course he would work without pay, but Nabokov was thrilled to have access to the collection. From October 1941 he would take the tedious subway-and-train or bus-and-streetcar journey at least once a week to the M.C.Z. There, in room 402, with its great cabinets of sliding trays housing rows of neatly pinned and labeled butterflies, moths, and skippers, he was installed at a long bench at the east-facing windows. Within a year that bench would become almost his permanent daytime home.[9]

Nabokov remembered Barbour, the museum's director but not an entomologist, as a genial fellow who liked his *Atlantic* stories, and he always felt grateful for Barbour's sympathy and generosity in allowing him to indulge in research. At the other end of the M.C.Z. hierarchy was a young student volunteer named Kenneth Christiansen, who recalled Nabokov as the most brilliant conversationalist among the many fascinating talkers at the museum, the one people went to if they felt like talk and he was not too busy. Hearing of the boy's interest in dragonflies, Nabokov told him all about them and explained to him the complexities of taxonomy and classification.[10]

Nabokov was not a specialist in the Satyrids, the family to which his Grand Canyon butterfly belonged, but he sat down in the laboratory and worked out how to reclassify his catch. Assembling from the M.C.Z. and other museums around the country a hundred specimens all labeled as the one species, *henshawi* Edwards, he established that some in fact belonged to a second species, his new *dorothea*, and others to a third, *pyracmon*, not previously thought to occur in North America. His Grand Canyon specimens were quite distinct and woke people up: collectors began to amass long series of the butterflies, and confirmed the differences he had discerned.[11]

III

As Nabokov adjusted to the M.C.Z., his first English novel, *The Real Life of Sebastian Knight*, approached publication. Still apprehensive that his English might betray him, Nabokov asked Agnes Perkins to help him read the galleys. Edmund Wilson also saw the proofs and found the novel "absolutely enchanting. It's amazing that you should write such fine English prose and not sound like any other English writer. . . . It is all on a high *poetic* level, and you have succeeded in being a first-rate poet in English. It has delighted and stimulated me more than any new book I have read since I don't know what."[12] Nevertheless, Wilson's competitive edge made him feel obliged to cavil, as he invariably would, at minor verbal quirks, and Nabokov replied, as *he* invariably would, in a letter that pointedly redeployed the supposedly defective constructions.

Already, in late October 1941, Nabokov had dreamed up a new English novel. But as he told Aldanov this, he added that he was longing for Russian and Russia. He was still very much a Russian writer and to relinquish his language was agony. In almost all his literary work over the next few years he would either translate from or write about other Russian writers, or write about Russian subjects. He sent Aldanov "Ultima Thule"—the last chapter of his uncompleted novel *Solus Rex*, the last fiction he would ever write in Russian, and penned in any case before he left Europe—for the first issue of *Novyy zhurnal*. He sent his Lermontov lecture to the English-language *Russian Review*, which had sprung up in the sudden shower of sympathy for Russia after Hitler's invasion in June 1941 had driven the Soviet Union into the allied camp. His first new work after arriving at Wellesley was to translate three poems by Vladislav Khodasevich, a writer like himself who deserved a fame denied him as an émigré. Half a century later these brilliant translations are still the best evidence an English-language reader can have of Khodasevich's genius.[13] Nabokov also wrote his own first English poem since his youth, a lament for the loss of his "Softest of Tongues":

> To all these things I've said the fatal word [*proshchai*, farewell]
> using a tongue I had so tuned and tamed
> that—like some ancient sonneteer—I heard
> its echoes by posterity acclaimed.
> But now thou too must go; just here we part,
> softest of tongues, my true one, all my own. . . .
> And I am left to grope for heart and art
> and start anew with clumsy tools of stone.[14]

Nabokov traveled alone to Wellfleet to spend Thanksgiving with the Wilsons. A much better poem resulted from his encounter there with the latest American appliances: "The Refrigerator Awakes" turns a humdrum machine humming in the darkness into a doorway to the wonders of night and the romance of polar exploration.[15] The *New Yorker*, the best-paying of American magazines, at once accepted the piece, the first of several Nabokov poems it would publish over the next few years.

Wilson, who a couple of months later would tell a publishing acquaintance that Nabokov was the most brilliant man he had ever met and that he would someday write one of the great contemporary novels, wrote a superb blurb for *The Real Life of Sebastian Knight*.[16] Almost three years after Nabokov completed it, the novel was at last published on December 18, 1941. Reviews fell into three categories—rapturous, confused, or hostile, with the first two predominating. Some were quite perceptive: the *Baltimore Sun* identified the book's real theme as "the depths and mysteries of the individuality of the spirit"; the *New York Herald Tribune* considered it an attempt not merely to define "the total unknowableness of any individual but, still more, to intimate the bewitched loneliness of each single human being . . . a little masterpiece of cerebration and execution."[17] But because the novel appeared less than two weeks after Pearl Harbor, it was an immediate flop with the public. Wilson's blurb helped catch the attention of bright young readers—Howard Nemerov, John Wain, Flannery O'Connor, Herbert Gold—for whom during the course of the 1940s the book became a prized private classic. For Nabokov that was far too little, far too late.

IV

Even before Pearl Harbor, the war had been changing Wellesley. Heat-conservation measures and marathon knitting sessions on behalf of servicemen and refugees were now complemented by air-raid drills and war courses in first aid, home nursing, and canteen cookery. In the wider world, a wave of pro-Soviet enthusiasm was rising toward a crest of hysteria as Germany penetrated deep into Russia.

Nabokov appears to have been prompted to write his next novel, eventually to be called *Bend Sinister*, as his private contribution to the war effort: an attempt to show that Nazi Germany and Soviet Russia represented fundamentally the same brutish vulgarity inimical to everything most vulnerable and most valuable in human life. He was deeply engrossed in writing the first chapters of the novel—he had not yet abandoned the practice of writing in sequence, chapter by chapter—in December and January, and optimistically wrote to James Laughlin: "It will be ready for you in three or four months."[18]

Early in February he spoke at Wellesley in a panel discussion organized by the college's Emergency Service Committee. A year before at Wellesley, when Hitler and Stalin had been devouring Eastern Europe together, Nabokov had publicly equated Nazi Germany and the Soviet Union. Now, unable to praise Stalin's Russia but also unable to condemn a country bearing the brunt of a German attack, he stressed the kinship between American and English democracy and the short-lived democracy of old Russia:

> A Russian democrat of the old days, and an American or an English one, despite the differences in forms of government in their respective countries, could meet with perfect ease on a common and natural basis. . . .
>
> Democracy is humanity at its best, not because we happen to think that a republic is better than a king and a king is better than nothing and nothing is better than a dictator, but because it is the natural condition of every man ever since the human mind became conscious not only of the world but of itself. Morally, democracy is invincible. Physically, that side will win which has the better guns. Of faith and pride, both sides have plenty. That *our* faith and *our* pride are of a totally different order cannot concern an enemy who believes in shedding blood and is proud of its own.[19]

V

At the beginning of the second semester, Nabokov gave his second trio of public lectures: on Turgenev's aquarelle style and Tolstoy's unique knack for making the time of imagined events coincide somehow with the reader's time; on the poetry of Tyutchev; and on Chekhov's pathos and his magical interweaving of details seemingly picked at random. He also lectured to Italian students on Leonardo, to English students on the tragedy of tragedy, to zoology students on the theory and practice of mimicry. His name cropped up often in the *Wellesley College News*. One student interviewed him about his aesthetic philosophy. "There is no such thing as art," he told her: "there are artists, but they are individuals with different forms of expression." After listening to his gloomy aspersions on the conventionality of "war art," the reporter asked if he thought art might die out altogether. He laughed in astonishment: "Art is in its infancy!"[20]

In late March he composed perhaps his finest piece of Russian verse, the long poem "Slava" ("Fame").[21] In this haunting, troubling poem, a vague figure who seems all the more eerie and sinister for remaining unspecifiable tries to load the poet with a sense of remorse for having broken with his native land and therefore—now that the emigration is over—with readers everywhere. So far the poem is a bleak reversal of the *exegi monumentum* tradition: you have tried to raise a poetic monument, but no one will ever see it; unlike Pushkin, you are not part of Russia, or famous, and never will be; can your life be anything but a joke? But at last the poet laughs despair away and declares that it is neither fame nor readers that matter, but a special vision that he carries within and that *some* reader might intuit with a shiver:

> That main secret tra-tá-ta tra-tá-ta tra-tá—
>   and I must not be overexplicit;
> this is why I find laughable the empty dream
>   about readers, and body, and glory.
> . . . .
> . . . one day while disrupting the strata of sense
>   and descending deep down to my wellspring
> I saw mirrored, besides my own self and the world,
>   something else, something else, something else.

In later years Nabokov often lamented the anguish of having to abandon his native language in the early 1940s when his Russian muse was so evidently glowing with health: "My private tragedy, which cannot, indeed should not, be anybody's concern, is that I had to abandon my natural idiom, my untrammeled, rich, and infinitely docile Russian tongue for a second-rate brand of English." For a long time he would feel his new language of composition "a stiffish, artificial thing, which may be all right for describing a sunset or an insect, but which cannot conceal poverty of syntax and paucity of domestic diction when I need the shortest road between warehouse and shop. An old Rolls-Royce is not always preferable to a plain Jeep." The one compensation he found for restricting his prose to English was the handful of long Russian poems he wrote in the early 1940s, which, he rightly thought, "improve rather oddly in urgency and concentration" upon all his previous Russian verse.[22]

The day after Nabokov's final public lecture at Wellesley, the departments of Italian, French, Spanish, and German wrote to Ella Keats Whiting, Dean of Instruction, to urge his reappointment: "Through his originality, his creative ability, his keenly critical mind, his stimulating presence and his brilliant use of the English language he has made a definite place for himself at Wellesley College."[23] A powerful alumna sent one hundred dollars to the President's Fund, hoping that it might help toward retaining Nabokov:

I heard a good deal about him from . . . Students and Faculty last year. . . . they all found him stimulating. Then last month I met him at the dinner Miss Perkins gave for Mr. Morgan . . . and again the next day when he and his wife were special guests at a Faculty tea, before his brilliant Tchekhov lecture. . . . the morning after the Tchekhov lecture we discussed it and him at breakfast—French, Italian, Spanish, American professors plus Miss McCrum, and I was astonished that he is actually so great a source of intellectual ferment to Faculty members of all sorts and conditions.[24]

In April, Amy Kelly—who used Nabokov's *Atlantic* pieces in her composition classes—organized with Agnes Perkins a petition to have him retained. Despite all this pressure, nothing moved. He had been hired at Wellesley not simply because of the brilliance of his lectures, but also because his outspoken comparisons of the mediocrity and barbarity of Nazi and Soviet rule had been just what people wanted to hear at the time that the Hitler-Stalin pact was leading to the subjugation of Europe. Now, as Soviet battalions and Soviet citizens desperately tried to resist the German invaders, and as America's entry into the war made the U.S. and the USSR official allies, Nabokov's forthrightness was likely to make him an embarrassment to Wellesley president Mildred McAfee, about to be summoned to Washington as head of the Women's Naval Reserve (WAVES, Women Accepted for Volunteer Emergency Service). Although Nabokov had the sense not to broadcast his anti-Soviet opinions at a time when the Soviet Union was losing so much ground and so many lives to Hitler, President McAfee turned down his permanent appointment on the ground that the special fund from which his initial post had been financed was all but exhausted.[25]

Dejected by the uncertainty of the coming year, Nabokov signed up with the Institute of International Education in April for a lecture tour in the fall. He offered a wide choice of lectures: "The Art of Writing"; "The Novel"; "The Short Story"; "The Tragedy of Tragedy"; "The Artist and Commonsense"; "Hard Facts about Readers"; "A Century of Exile"; "The Strange Fate of Russian Literature"; and a lecture apiece on Pushkin, Lermontov, Gogol, and Tolstoy. The broadsheet advertising Nabokov's availability ended with this ringing praise from Philip Mosely of Cornell: "I should like to add that in my own opinion, and in that of many far better experts than myself, Mr. Nabokov (under his pen-name of 'Sirin') is already the greatest Russian novelist writing today, and contains infinite promise of ever greater achievement. . . . I use these superlatives about his writing deliberately, for I have been reading his work in Russian since 1932."[26]

Nabokov knew that such backing had so far counted for very little. After registering for the army, he almost hoped he might be drafted.

He cheerfully saw himself perhaps leading a platoon by the fall, but he waited in vain to be called.[27]

VI

By May the Wellesley students had end-of-year deadlines to meet and no need for extracurricular excitement à la Nabokov. The first weekend in May, Nabokov visited the Wilsons at Cape Cod for twenty-four hours, taking Pushkin, a butterfly net, and his mimicry article. He met Randall Jarrell, who found him "just wonderful, an extremely charming person." He read Mary McCarthy's first book, *The Company She Keeps*, and was very agreeably surprised, "quite flabbergasted" in fact.[28]

Later in the month he visited Yale, where he was offered a position. It turned out to be no more than that of assistant Russian-language instructor for the summer course, "but as I would have to teach the main professor Russian too, I refused." In fact, Nabokov thought that Professor Trager, who spoke Russian with a thick Odessa accent acquired from his parents in Brooklyn, was not interested in his academic competence "so much as in finding someone who spoke Russian somewhat as he did."* Nabokov told Dean De Vane "the post doesn't suit me, I'm long used to painting them (posts) with my own pigment," although he hoped that they might still invite him as a lecturer on Russian literature. The fortunes of war had made Russia very fashionable, and still Nabokov could find nothing. He confided his exasperation to Wilson: "Funny—to know Russian better than any living person—in America at least—and more English than any Russian in America,—and to experience such difficulty in getting a university job. I am getting rather jittery about next year."[29]

Russia's current popularity did bring one benefit. James Laughlin visited Nabokov in mid-May and commissioned from him a volume of verse translations of Pushkin and Tyutchev and a two-hundred-page critical work on Gogol, for a small advance. Nabokov immersed himself at once in the Gogol book, hoping to send off the finished manuscript by mid-July. For light relief, he wrote at Edmund Wilson's suggestion a poem called "The Man of Tomorrow's Lament": on Superman's wedding night, the Man of Steel's vigor causes his honeymoon suite to explode. Alas, poor Lois! The prim *New Yorker* turned it down, and no manuscript survives.[30]

---

* Nabokov did not exaggerate: another Russian who worked under Trager had difficulty understanding him.

By now Nabokov had finished his first major lepidopterological article, "Some New or Little-Known Nearctic *Neonympha*," and was working two days a week at the M.C.Z., ruling over the lepidoptera room on his own now that his preparator had gone off to war. In June, he learned that he had been appointed a Research Fellow in Entomology at the M.C.Z. for the 1942–1943 academic year. The salary was only $1,000, but it was a part-time post, and until then he had been working for nothing. Besides, it was all the future seemed to hold.[31]

Since Dmitri had been ill all winter and had just had his adenoids removed, his parents badly wanted him to spend a summer in the country but could not have afforded a vacation had the Karpoviches not invited them back to their Vermont farmhouse for the summer. After a few days there in early June, the family returned to Vermont again for July and August. Nabokov converted part of the attic into a comfortable studio and devoted eight to ten hours a day to his Gogol book, slowed greatly by the need to translate so much: "I have lost a week already translating passages I need in the 'Inspector General' as I can do nothing with Constance Garnett's dry shit." He wrote to James Laughlin that he was eager to have *The Gift* published and translated, and explained that he needed as a translator "a man who knows English better than Russian—and a man, not a woman. I am frankly homosexual on the subject of translators." Laughlin suggested Yarmolinsky of the New York Public Library's Slavonic Division, but Nabokov dismissed the idea:

> I have seen Yarmolinsky's and his wife's translation of Pushkin:* their work is conscientious, reasonably exact and careful but they lack my main desiderata: style and a rich vocabulary. Without a good deal of linguistic and poetical imagination it is useless tackling my stuff. . . . I know it is difficult to find a man who has enough Russian to understand my writings and at the same time can turn his English inside out and slice, chop, twist, volley, smash, kill, drive, half-volley, lob and place perfectly every word; Yarmolinsky will gently pat the ball into the net— or send it sailing into the neighbor's garden.[32]

VII

On September 1, 1942, the Nabokovs moved to Cambridge, fifteen minutes' walk from the Harvard campus and the M.C.Z., at 8 Craigie Circle, apartment 35, a dingy little third-floor flat in a four-story brick

* Yarmolinsky would supply literal translations from the Russian to be turned into English rhymes by his wife, the poet Babette Deutsch.

apartment house at the end of a cul-de-sac. They would live here for almost another six years, the one exception to the otherwise nomadic pattern of their American existence. In this two-bedroom apartment, Véra and Dmitri shared one bedroom while Nabokov had the other, where he would write late into the night, walking about, pencil in hand, "under an old lady with feet of stone and above a young woman with hypersensitive hearing," before settling down to sleep for four or five hours.[33]

One hundred dollars' worth of secondhand furniture was all the Nabokovs needed to deck out the apartment. Their friend Wilma Kerby-Miller declared—and everyone close to them at this time says much the same—"I never knew any family who cared less about possessions, food, anything. Their only luxury was Dmitri"—who had expensive toys and went to some of the most prestigious private schools in New England.[34]

Sometimes part of the school fees would be paid off by Véra's giving lessons or working as a secretary at Harvard, but as a rule she had quite enough work as housekeeper and mother and in typing up the pages her husband had left on the floor after the previous night's composition. Wilma Kerby-Miller called her "a one-man woman, she worked with him, helped him, it was her great interest in life. She married a genius, and saw that he had every opportunity."[35] Harry and Elena Levin too were struck by Véra's certainty that her husband was the greatest living writer, and the support she afforded him with her business sense, her secretarial skills, her meticulous compilation of reviews, her sheer conviction and dedication.

Living in Cambridge, the Nabokovs began to see the Levins frequently. Nabokov always regarded himself as a poor talker. Harry Levin, himself no sluggard of the spoken word, thought Nabokov a brilliant conversationalist with an instant sense of the genuine in people and a distaste for the least pretension, which he could deflate in half a sentence. What impressed Levin most of all was Nabokov's inventiveness as a *mystificateur*. Once Ralph Barton Perry, a distinguished Harvard philosophy professor, was a guest at the Levins' house. At that time he was involved as a Concerned Citizen in U.S. relations with its allies, and in the middle of 1943's pro-Soviet fervor he published in the *New Republic* an article entitled "American-Soviet Friendship: An Invitation to an Agreement." Sensing Perry's political sympathies, Nabokov began to weave a spell around him. He claimed to Perry that although Stalin might be present at the Tehran conference, the real Soviet leader was Pavlovsky, the man always standing beside him in the newspaper photographs and posing as no more than an interpreter. It was Pavlovsky who pulled the strings,

Pavlovsky whom the United States would have to learn to understand. Perry took this ad lib apocrypha for gospel.[36]

According to one informant, Harry Levin himself once fell victim to a similar hoax. Early in their relationship Nabokov noticed Levin's air of having read every literary work imaginable. One evening he invented a nineteenth-century novelist and proceeded to fill out details of his life and works, while Levin gave no sign all evening that he had not heard of, let alone had not read, the writer who owed his niche in literary history only to Nabokov's impromptu inspiration.[37]

VIII

Now that they were established in Cambridge the Nabokovs saw more of Edmund Wilson and Mary McCarthy. McCarthy was shocked at the Nabokovs' plain fare and their indifference to their surroundings, to things like the hideous lampshades and the brass ashtrays in their sitting room. On the other hand, when Nabokov visited the Wilsons he made friendly fun of McCarthy's fussing over culinary delicacies by concocting for her fancy treats his own even fancier names. He also disclosed as a grim family secret that at home they might have a carp served up with boiled potatoes and carrots and live off the dish for a week. McCarthy believed him.[38]

Often in Cambridge the Nabokovs would meet the Wilsons in the Levins' much more spacious home. Elena Levin saw the two friends as "such opposite kinds of human: Volodya subtle, reclusive, familial; Edmund blunt, commonsensical, and after three drinks he 'collapsed like a bag of potatoes,' in Volodya's words." Even early on, Harry Levin noticed, the two men, for all the richness of their relationship and their admiration for each other, also grated against each other—and this in the peak years of their friendship. Wilson disliked Nabokov's unrufflable self-confidence and frank self-delight and his dismissiveness of other writers. Nabokov admired Wilson's range of interests but also found it rather amusingly forced. Once Wilson asked him to invite entomologists to a party he was giving at Craigie Circle. None turned up, but, not realizing this, Wilson cornered the two or three guests—actually Nabokov's literature colleagues from Wellesley—assuming they were M.C.Z. scientists, and tried to talk shop. As Nabokov recalled with a smile, his guests "were indeed taken aback by the famous Edmund Wilson's sudden interest in insect lore."[39]

Judging art at its highest and most impersonal, Nabokov had implacable standards, and as a critic he hugely enjoyed hurling writers he deemed interlopers down the slopes of Olympus. At a personal level, on the other hand, he would look for what he could find to like in other people's work. He respected the vulnerability of others and was as sensitive to his friends as he was undemanding of his students. Wilson, on the other hand, had a compulsive competitiveness that meant he had to counterbalance praise with reproach, either providing a list of corrections, no matter how captious, or implying that at the midpoint of a story he had seen a rather better way to finish it than its author had chosen. Wilson seemed to expect the recipient to be charmed by his behavior, by the special Wilsonian tartness of judgment and independence of imagination. Even at an early stage in their relationship, Nabokov detected this irrationality in his friend. Nevertheless he was deeply fond of Wilson, and almost from the start wrote to him with a warmth that Wilson seldom matched. To their common friend Roman Grynberg, Nabokov confided that with Wilson the "lyrical plaint" that adorns Russian friendship seemed to be lacking—as it generally was, he felt, among Anglo-Saxons: "I love a violin in personal relationships, but in this case there is no way one can let out a heartfelt sigh or casually unburden a soft fresh bit of oneself. Still, there's a good deal else to make up for it."[40]

IX

Newly installed in Craigie Circle, Nabokov had no position at Wellesley for 1942–1943 and just a thousand dollars for the coming year's research at the M.C.Z. He desperately needed other income, even if it meant delaying his Gogol book, which had kept him busy from May to September. He applied for a Guggenheim Fellowship for the following year to give him time to work on a novel. Meanwhile he had no choice but to undertake a two-month lecture tour the Institute of International Education had been able to arrange for him.

When in his last decade of life Nabokov planned a second volume of his autobiography, a *Speak On, Memory* or a *Speak, America*, he expected to devote one chapter to his friendship with Edmund Wilson, another to his American adventures in lepidoptera, and a third to this lecture tour.[41] He mentally allotted this thin slice of his American experience a whole chapter partly for the simple practical reason that he had preserved such a complete record of the trip in his long letters to his wife, but also because these travels exposed him to so much of the variety of America. Although his adventures sometimes had a Pninian cast, his observations always reveal an alertness to America that poor abstracted Pnin could never approach.

On September 30 he set off by overnight train for his first lectures, at Coker College in Hartsville, South Carolina. He could not sleep all night, but the next day's landscapes made up for it, their oil-paint hues with a shimmer of green seeming just as he had pictured a valley in the Caucasus might look. When his train pulled in an hour late to Florence, the nearest stop to Hartsville, the connecting bus had long since disappeared. He phoned Coker College; they promised to call back about a car. Feeling tired, bristly, grimy, and irritated, he waited an hour and a half by a restaurant telephone. At last the phone rang and a rich-voiced professor announced he was coming to Florence on business and would take him back at six o'clock in time for his eight o'clock lecture. When Nabokov pointed out that this meant he would have to wait there another three hours, the voice said he would come right away and take him to a hotel.

Not sure he had heard correctly, Nabokov sat in the railway waiting room. After a time he thought he heard a taxi driver calling what sounded like his name. No, it turned out, the name was Yellowwater. The garrulous taxi driver also told him that another cabbie had been ordered to collect someone from the station and to take the person to a hotel, but after running into a truck had asked *him* to pick the customer up. Nabokov thought the hotel was the one he was headed for, and asked again if the taxi had not come for him. Indeed, the person to be picked up was to go to Hartsville, but the taxi driver had not been given his name or the name of the person who had ordered the taxi, and there was no way of finding them out. Nabokov wondered whether he should take the taxi himself straight to Coker College—but then the owner of the rich voice might look for him forever. Deciding that the taxi must have come for him after all, he had himself driven to the Selman Hotel.

There, nobody knew anything, and he had foolishly let the taxi go, and he sensed in a flush of panic that it was all a mistake, that he had been brought here instead of someone else, that the Voice would be looking for him hopelessly at the station. He resolved to call Coker College, so that he could at least find out the Voice's name. Going to the information desk, he heard a person in the crowd telling someone else he could not understand why a taxi he had sent to fetch someone from the station had failed to return. Nabokov butted in and rather desperately asked if it were not *him* he was after? "Oh, no, I am waiting for a Russian professor." "But I *am* the Russian professor." "Well, you don't look like one," he laughed. No photograph had been sent: no wonder, Nabokov wrote to his wife, that the college expected someone with Dostoevsky's beard, Stalin's mustache, and Chekhov's pince-nez, in a Tolstoyan blouse.

Nabokov arrived at Coker College, sprinted through a bath, found his cuffs too starched for cuff links to fit, then in his hurry lost one on the floor. He had to roll up his shirtsleeves under his tuxedo, but as soon as he went down to dinner he disentangled himself from this series of Pninian mishaps by confessing his plight. That relaxed his tension and everybody else's, some cuff links were produced, and from that point on Nabokov's three days at Coker passed without a hitch.

Lodged in comfort in the Coker family mansion, he was introduced to Southern society through the family and its connections. But Nabokov was at least as interested in the region's insect population as its human one. After his lecture that first night, he caught moths in a tumbler on the brightly lit columns of the mansion's colonnade. During the daytime he chased butterflies on his own in the garden of the estate, and with a biology teacher and another lepidopterist out in the countryside. He played tennis with the best player in the college, he went canoeing in a labyrinthine creek winding through cypresses and cedars, he donned dinner jackets three nights in a row, and he received a hundred dollars for his time.[42]

When war conditions caused one engagement to fall through he was diverted to Spelman College, a black women's college in Atlanta, where he arrived on October 7. Depressed by the Uncle Tomism he had already witnessed in the South, he was delighted to spend five days in this "black Wellesley." In his lecture on Pushkin he stressed the poet's Abyssinian grandfather, his immense pride in his African ancestry, his laughing white teeth between negroid lips. "Incidentally," he added, "Pushkin provides a most striking example of mankind at its very best when human races are able to freely mix." The lecture was received with wild enthusiasm.

Apart from his Pushkin lecture, Nabokov also read his own poems and lectured on literature and lepidoptera. He chased insects one afternoon with another biology teacher and a very intense group of young black women. He mingled easily with the students, and hit it off particularly well with the college president, Florence Read, a vibrant, astute older woman who surrounded him with every attention and would become a long-term friend of the Nabokov family. He breakfasted with her every day, discussing everything from the Negro problem to telepathy. She told him he would have to go to chapel at 9:00 A.M., but he protested he was a heretic and hated music and singing. "You'll *love* ours," she insisted, and led him off. Every evening she invited black leaders for her guest to meet over dinner.[43]

His next stop, on October 13, was at Georgia State College for Women at Valdosta, almost on the Florida border. Here he lectured on "Art and Common Sense," on war novels, and on mimicry, and read "Mademoiselle O" and some of his translations of Russian verse. At a very funny and very vulgar women's group—perhaps a forerunner of Charlotte Haze's clubs—he recited his verse only to have the chairwoman tell him afterward with a lyrical leer: "What I loved best was the broken English." He played tennis with Valdosta's president, Frank Reade, and found him as charming and brilliant as Spelman's Florence Read, as irrational as Wilson, as egocentric as himself.* A biology teacher took him for four hours on the chase—and his best day's butterfly catch—in palmetto wilds and pine forests in the Okefenokee swamp. He tried to write a little of his Gogol book and his novel, but everywhere he went people tried to please him from morning until night. His "having a good time," he knew, meant wasting his time.[44]

On the way back from Valdosta he had to stop overnight again in Atlanta. When he called on Florence Read, she presented him with a huge reproduction of a detail of some butterflies in an Egyptian fresco. Nabokov realized at once that since butterfly speciation is singularly rapid and diverse and since butterflies are so well represented in art, millennia-old paintings might have recorded evolution in action. The next day he wrote to Véra that he would write something about it.[45] More than twenty years later, he would indeed begin research for a book on butterflies in art.

X

Though delighted by all the attention he had received, Nabokov was tired, and after one more lecture stop, at the University of the South in Sewanee, Tennessee, he headed back to Boston at the end of October. In Cambridge for ten days, he had time to fall ill, recover, and put in some hard work at the M.C.Z., where—since he had become de facto curator of lepidoptera—Véra in his absence had filled in for him, repinning butterflies from tray to tray. On November 5 he set off reluctantly for the second stage of his tour, knowing that at this time of year the Midwest would offer no butterflies to compensate for the dislocations of travel. Still, he had a superb first day at the Field Museum in Chicago, where he found his *Neonymphas* and showed the staff how to reclassify them and arrange them in their tray.[46]

At Macalester College in St. Paul, Nabokov found that he did not

* Years later he would place Reade undisguised in *Pnin*.

have with him the text of the lecture he was to give on the novel. He decided to speak without notes and found it came out well: he set the students

> a little quiz—ten definitions of a reader, and from these ten the students had to choose four definitions that would combine to make a good reader. I have mislaid the list, but as far as I remember the definitions went something like this. Select four answers to the question what should a reader be to be a good reader:
>
> 1. The reader should belong to a book club.
> 2. The reader should identify himself or herself with the hero or heroine.
> 3. The reader should concentrate on the social-economic angle.
> 4. The reader should prefer a story with action and dialogue to one with none.
> 5. The reader should have seen the book in a movie.
> 6. The reader should be a budding author.
> 7. The reader should have imagination.
> 8. The reader should have memory.
> 9. The reader should have a dictionary.
> 10. The reader should have some artistic sense.

In future years, whenever he taught literature courses at Wellesley or Cornell, Nabokov would tell the story of this quiz. "You know me a little, they did not, those young ladies in Minnesota," he would point out before reporting that the Macalester students had "leaned heavily on emotional identification, action, and the social-economic or historic angle. Of course, as you have guessed, the good reader is one who has imagination, memory, a dictionary and some artistic sense."[47]

The cold and the traveling were beginning to weigh on his spirits. One night, bored, he went to a movie and returned on foot, walking for an hour through the icy wind. He reported to Véra afterward:

> On the way a lightning bolt of undefined inspiration ran right through me, a terrible desire to write, and write in Russian—but it's impossible. I don't think anyone who hasn't experienced these feelings can properly appreciate them, the torment, the tragedy. English in this case is an illusion, ersatz. In my usual condition—busy with butterflies, translations or academic writing—I myself don't fully register all the grief and bitterness of my situation. . . . I have felt with absolute clarity that if it were not for the two of you I would go as a soldier to Morocco, where there are marvelous Lycaenids in the mountains. . . . But how much more than this I would like to write a book in Russian.[48]

A month later he would tell his close friend George Hessen, just arrived in New York, that he felt the Sirin in him beginning to stir again, and that although he had created a person who had in turn created *The Real Life of Sebastian Knight* and his *New Yorker* poems, it all seemed somehow a game he was playing.[49]

The next stop was Knox College, in Galesburg, Illinois. By now he was thoroughly exhausted and depressed. His accommodations had been paid for at Coker College and Spelman, but since all his other travel expenses had come out of his own pocket, the tour was proving a financial failure. Although headed back East, he was expected to travel on to Virginia and to keep on traveling well into December. Instead he had to cancel the next stage of the tour and return to Cambridge on November 18 with a bad attack of flu.[50]

He set off again at the beginning of December, staying for two days in New York to catch up on friends. Visiting the American Museum of Natural History, he gasped with delight when he saw the red type label on his Grand Canyon butterfly.* En route to Washington he wrote a new poem, "On Discovering a Butterfly,"[51] which reads in part:

> I found it and I named it, being versed
> in taxonomic Latin; thus became
> godfather to an insect and its first
> describer—and I want no other fame.
>
> Wide open on its pin (though fast asleep),
> and safe from creeping relatives and rust,
> in the secluded stronghold where we keep
> type specimens it will transcend its dust.
>
> Dark pictures, thrones, the stones that pilgrims kiss,
> poems that take a thousand years to die
> but ape the immortality of this
> red label on a little butterfly.

This, Nabokov's best English poem to date, summed up the great consolation America offered for his having to relinquish the language he had learned as a child: the chance to enact his childhood dream of exploration and lepidopteral discovery. But the fair copy of the poem, typed on M.C.Z. letterhead paper, showed all too painfully the occasional thinness of his English. The ninth line now reads: "My

---

* Normally, specimens in museum collections are identified by small white labels. In the published "original description" ("o.d.") of a new species, however, a particular specimen is designated the type specimen, a sort of Standard Yard for the species, and in the museum where it is housed it is identified by a red label.

needles have teased out its sculptured sex." In the fair copy he sent off to the *New Yorker*, the line ended: "its horny sex."* When the *New Yorker* editors explained why the phrase was impossible, he thanked them "for saving that line from an ignorance-is-bliss disaster. And that nightmare pun. . . . This has somewhat subdued me—I was getting rather pleased with my English."[52] The man who would write *Lolita* still had much to discover in America and in English.

He stopped in Washington—only to visit the Smithsonian Institution and sort out its *Neonymphas*—en route to Longwood College in Farmville, Virginia. On his return to Cambridge he found Véra ill with pneumonia and in the hospital.[53]

In the last weeks of December he managed at last to complete his Gogol book, originally to have been called *Gogol through the Looking Glass* but published as plain *Nikolay Gogol*. He had looked forward to savaging a new translation of *Dead Souls* by Bernard Gilbert Guerney, announced in 1942 under the title *Chichikov's Journeys, or Home Life in Old Russia:* "I am eager—viciously eager—to see 'Home Life.' It is like calling a version of 'Fleurs du Mal'—'The Daisy Chain.' " In fact, the translation proved to be very good, far better than any previous versions in English, and Nabokov not only said so in his book, but even approached Guerney to translate his own Russian novels. Nothing came of their negotiations when Guerney insisted on almost half the royalties.[54]

XI
Nikolay Gogol

Commissioned as a popularizing work, Nabokov's *Nikolay Gogol* has succeeded brilliantly: it has done more for Gogol in the English-speaking world than any other book. Yet from start to finish Nabokov reveals a horror of the obvious summary and the patient exposition of the popularizer. Instead, he chooses the surprising (the book begins with Gogol's death and ends with his birth), the outrageous, the impatient dismissal. As a study of Gogol, it is deliberately incomplete: it picks only the best of Gogol—or rather, only what Nabokov values within the best—and waves away the rest. But what he does touch on is magical.

He warns off those who might turn to Gogol as a realist, a social satirist, a moralist: "If you expect to find out something about Russia,

* The male genitalia of butterflies, essential clues in distinguishing one species from another superficially related one, are complex ("sculptured"), rigid ("horny") armatures.

. . . keep away. He has nothing to tell you. Keep off the tracks. High tension. Closed for the duration. Avoid, refrain, don't. I would like to have here a full list of all possible interdictions, vetoes and threats." Nabokov does smooth and oversimplify when he sets Gogol the magnificent artist of the great works of 1836–1842, *The Government Inspector*, *Dead Souls*, and "The Overcoat," against Gogol the would-be preacher, in his last ten misguided and sterile years of life. Gogol did not simply burn bright and then in his last years turn to ash: even at his best he seemed like a wet log on a fire, smoking, spitting, flaming, sparking, erupting gas from unexpected fissures, all in the most unpredictable sequence and always burning *uneasily*. Nabokov reduces the unease in Gogol. Readers have supposed that he devoted a book to Gogol because he had a greater affinity for him than for other Russian writers. In fact, as his lectures reveal, he cared more for Pushkin, Tolstoy, and Chekhov: his affinity is not so much for the mottled conglomerate of the actual Gogol as for the polished proto-Nabokov he can extract from this recalcitrant ore.

What Nabokov does select from Gogol he invests with superb excitement, often turning things that may be overlooked or seem bland or even inartistic into imaginative triumphs that defy what had seemed acceptable art: the thunderclap suddenness of *The Government Inspector*, and its swarm of secondary characters who can leap into life in the space of an aside; the splendid poetry of the irrelevant in *Dead Souls*, the crazy vitality of its similes, the unrestrained vividness of its visual world; the disturbing vibrations of "The Overcoat."

Although he denies that Gogol may be seen as a realist or a satirist, Nabokov does not proclaim an aesthetic of art for art's sake. He hails Gogol as a critic not of particular social conditions but of the universal vice of deadened sensibility, *poshlost'*, self-satisfied vulgarity. His magnificent definition of *poshlost'* here has fixed the concept in the minds of the cultivated English-speaking world.

Nabokov's commentary rises to a superb crescendo in his final chapter, on "The Overcoat," a brilliant introduction not so much to Gogol as to Nabokov's own aesthetics:

> Gogol was a strange creature, but genius is always strange; it is only your healthy second-rater who seems to the grateful reader to be a wise old friend, nicely developing the reader's own notions of life. . . . Gogol's *The Overcoat* is a grotesque and grim nightmare making black holes in the dim pattern of life. The superficial reader of that story will merely see in it the heavy frolics of an extravagant buffoon; the solemn reader will take for granted that Gogol's prime intention was to denounce the

horrors of Russian bureaucracy. . . . Give me the creative reader; this is a tale for him.

Steady Pushkin, matter-of-fact Tolstoy, restrained Chekhov have all had their moments of irrational insight which simultaneously blurred the sentence and disclosed a secret meaning worth the sudden focal shift. But with Gogol this shifting is the very basis of his art.

Earlier in the book, Nabokov has sometimes merely dismissed any social side to Gogol. Now he explains this not as a rejection of extra-literary values, but in terms of art's refusal to confine itself to a particular time and place.

Russian progressive critics sensed in him the image of the underdog and the whole story impressed them as a social protest. But it is something much more than that. The gaps and black holes in the texture of Gogol's style imply flaws in the texture of life itself. Something is very wrong and all men are mild lunatics engaged in petty pursuits that seem to them very important while an absurdly logical force keeps them at their futile jobs—this is the real "message" of the story.

Soon after *Nikolay Gogol* was published, Nabokov replied to one of his readers, who thought he had expelled all ethics from the world of aesthetics:

I never meant to deny the moral impact of art which is certainly inherent in every genuine work of art. What I do deny and am prepared to fight to the last drop of my ink is the deliberate moralizing which to me kills every vestige of art in a work however skillfully written. There is a deep morality in *The Overcoat* which I have tried to convey in my book, but this morality has certainly nothing whatever to do with the cheap political propaganda which some overzealous admirers in nineteenth century Russia have tried to squeeze out of, or rather into it, and which, in my opinion does violence to the story and to the very notion of art.

By the same token, although you may be right that Gogol did not object to serfdom, the interior moral standards of the book bristle against it. And the reader is more impressed by the bodily serfdom of the peasants and the inevitably following spiritual serfdom of the owners than by the petty roguery of Chichikov.[55]

As his chapter on "The Overcoat" rises to a climax, Nabokov comes closer and closer to outlining aspects of his own aesthetics:

the diver, the seeker for black pearls, the man who prefers the monsters of the deep to the sunshades on the beach, will find in *The Overcoat* shadows linking our state of existence to those other states and modes we dimly apprehend in our rare moments of irrational perception. . . .

. . . At this superhigh level of art, literature is of course not concerned with pitying the underdog or cursing the upperdog. It appeals to that secret depth of the human soul where the shadows of other worlds pass like the shadows of nameless and soundless ships.

One of the chief arguments of *Nikolay Gogol* is that Gogol achieves his weird tiltings and sudden focal shifts by subtle effects of language, and that the only way to experience his magic is to learn the Russian language. Nabokov rightly deplored all prior English translations of Gogol for smoothing over or eliminating precisely those bizarre moves that make him so spellbinding. Only when Nabokov's manuscript was almost completed did Guerney's translation of *Dead Souls* appear. Nabokov referred the reader to Guerney's version as "an extraordinarily fine piece of work." Privately he was harsher and more exact: Guerney's translation "lacks the poetic and musical (and nightmarish!) qualities of the original, but it is fairly exact and is the work of an honest mind."[56]

Nabokov's own extracts from Gogol are vastly superior to Guerney's and are still the only versions that can convey to the anglophone reader why Russians regard Gogol so highly. After Pushkin, Gogol is the most untranslatable of major Russian writers. In his first four years in America, Nabokov had already translated some of Pushkin's finest verse. Unfortunately he did not have time to translate even a single complete work by Gogol. But the long passage from the end of "The Diary of a Madman" that he chooses for the epigraph to *Nikolay Gogol* makes us feel at once in immediate contact with a writer of dazzling, disturbing genius. There could be no better advertisement for Gogol than that one paragraph. What a loss that Nabokov simply had too much of his own work to do to be able to offer English-speaking readers the essential Gogol undiluted.

CHAPTER 3

Scientist, Writer, Teacher: Cambridge and Wellesley, 1943–1944

HUMBERT: Is that a rare specimen?

NABOKOV: A specimen cannot be common or rare, it can only be

poor or perfect.

HUMBERT: Could you direct me—

NABOKOV: You meant "rare species." This is a good specimen

of a rather scarce subspecies.

—*Lolita: A Screenplay*

I

IN 1943 THE STRANGE triple life Nabokov would lead for the next five years began in earnest: lepidopterist, writer, teacher. After returning to Cambridge from his lecture tours, he worked, engrossed, at the M.C.Z. By now he was specializing in his laboratory work not simply on the Lycaenids, one of the eleven North American families of butterfly, but on one of its four subfamilies, *Plebejinae*, the so-called blues.

Identification and classification within this abundant group of small butterflies—many predominantly brown or whitish rather than blue—can often be extremely difficult, and requires examination under the microscope of the structure of the male genitalia. At any other manual work Nabokov felt himself all thumbs, but when he began to dismantle a butterfly he found he suddenly developed very delicate hands and fine fingers and could do anything. He would prize apart under the microscope one hooked lobe of the somewhat triangular genitalia, remove the genitalia from the butterfly, coat them in glycerine, and place them in a mixture of alcohol and water in a separate labeled vial for each specimen. This, he had found, enabled him to turn the organs around under the microscope to obtain a three-dimensional view impossible on a conventional microscope slide. He would later write: "Since I devoted up to six hours daily to this kind of research my eyesight was impaired for ever; but on the other hand, the years at the Harvard Museum remain the most delightful and thrilling in all my adult life."[1]

All through the winter and spring of 1943, Nabokov examined 350 male specimens of the genus *Lycaeides*. The resulting paper, "The Nearctic Forms of *Lycaeides* Hüb[ner]," established the first of his two major principles of broad application in lepidoptery, his analysis of the extremely complex genitalia of the blues. He named the parts of their structure (some of these names have now become the standard terms) and showed that the varying ratios of certain parts could clearly differentiate species. He was also able to deduce an ancestral form of the *Lycaeides* male armature.[2]

At the same time he had new fiction to write. In January 1943 he composed his first English short story, "The Assistant Producer."[3] For once he tells a story that really happened, but by presenting everything as if on a movie screen he makes the facts appear an impossibly trite romantic fiction. In Berlin he had known the celebrated Russian popular singer Nadezhda Plevitskaya, and admired her natural vocal gifts while recoiling from her vulgarity of taste. In 1938 she was sentenced to twenty years' imprisonment for her part in helping her husband—who meanwhile had vanished—to abduct and presumably kill General Miller, head of the émigré All-Russian Military Union in Paris. General Kutepov, Miller's predecessor, had been murdered years earlier.

In "The Assistant Producer," the famous Russian popular singer "La Slavska" marries a White Army general, Golubkov. (In real life his name was Skoblin.) Obsessed with becoming head of the White Warriors' Union, Golubkov becomes a triple agent, serving not only this remnant of the White Army but also the Germans and the Soviets in order to dispose of two, perhaps three of the generals previously heading the union (Wrangel, Kutepov, and Miller). Nabokov tells the story with astonishing speed, color, and precision, rushing from set to set—a Civil War battlefield, Chaliapin's dressing room, soirees at La Slavska's—even as he piles theme upon theme: the singer, the dashing general, the émigré background, the Hollywood studio where a movie might be made from the story, the cinema where one might watch the movie. The story brilliantly inverts life and art: events appear to be purloined from movieland, but in fact come straight from life—which itself seems to have imitated bad art. Having defined *poshlost'* in *Nikolay Gogol*, Nabokov now shows it in action in "The Assistant Producer": the vulgarity of soul of Hollywood art, La Slavska's craft, Golubkov's obsessive dream, and the rank politics of the Russian monarchists, Germans, and Soviets whom this strange pair serve.

II

While his wife had been ill with pneumonia Nabokov had given his son lessons in basic Russian grammar. As Dmitri recalls, "he was as precise, charming and inspiring in this basic discipline as in others."[4] Nabokov had counted on his lecture tour to supplement his meager M.C.Z. fellowship, but travel expenses had left him very little net profit. He had still heard nothing from the Guggenheim Foundation. Meanwhile Wellesley College students, eager to take extra courses that could be seen as "war service" or of value "for service in the period of reconstruction," were buoyed up by the enthusiasm for the Soviet Union that swept America after the decisive defeat of the Germans at the siege of Stalingrad, the turning point of the war on the eastern front.

With Wellesley students anxious to learn and Nabokov needing extra money from teaching, an unofficial, noncredit course in elementary Russian was set up for the spring term of 1943. Nabokov taught one hundred young women, each paying ten dollars for the term, apparently in four classes of about twenty-five each. Two days a week he traveled out to Wellesley after lunch, not returning until after midnight.[5]

The classes were informal and largely unprepared: Nabokov worked through George Birkett's *Modern Russian Course* (he would turn this one grammar over in his hands in front of the class, as if appalled by its lack of bulk), but would digress enthusiastically as fancy prompted. "Please take out your mirrors, girls, and see what happens inside your mouths": "In pronouncing the vowels «а, э, ы, о, у» . . . your tongue keeps back—independent and aloof—whereas in «я, е, и, ё, ю»—the squashed vowels—it rushes and crushes itself against your lower teeth—a prisoner dashing himself at the bars of his cell." He could couple the sober prose of the grammatical rule with the poetry of example, the mnemonics of wit:

Genitive case requires *a* on the end:
    stol poeta   [the poet's desk]
    stul poeta   [the poet's chair]
    stil' poeta   [the poet's style]

He set homework, and marked it gently and politely: "Take care of your 'y'!" "Will you *please* do this one again." And the students who thought they might become Communists he disabused of their illusions about the Soviet Union.[6]

The pro-Soviet euphoria that had swelled Nabokov's class numbers was becoming absurd. *Life* magazine devoted an issue of ill-informed gush to Russia. Hollywood made a film of Ambassador Joseph Davies's fatuously pro-Stalin best-seller *Mission to Moscow*. Bennett Cerf of Random House suggested a formal ban on books critical of the Soviet Union, though it was hardly needed: a de facto ban was already in place.[7]

In a strange fit of optimism or ignorance, the pro-Soviet New York journal *Novosel'e* wrote to Nabokov soliciting new work. Now that the war had turned and it was apparent that Hitler would be defeated, Nabokov, like America's minute anti-Stalinist intelligentsia, felt it was time to protest the glorification of Russia's own mass murderer—even if to a public that did not want to hear. Early in April he sent *Novosel'e* eight fierce lines of Russian verse:

> No matter how the Soviet tinsel glitters
> upon the canvas of a battle piece;
> no matter how the soul dissolves in pity,
> I will not bend, I will not cease
>
> loathing the filth, brutality, and boredom
> of silent servitude. No, no, I shout,
> my spirit is still quick, still exile-hungry,
> I'm still a poet, count me out!

In copied and recopied manuscripts the poem began to circulate among New York's émigré Russian socialists like forbidden literature under the tsars. On seeing the poem, Kerensky burst into tears.[8]

At the end of March, Nabokov heard he had won a Guggenheim Fellowship for "Creative Writing in the field of the novel": $2,500, tax-free, for the year June 1943–June 1944. Nabokov, the first person for whom the Guggenheim's under-forty rule was broken, had Edmund Wilson's strong recommendation to thank (Wilson had himself won a Guggenheim in 1935 in the midst of his Marxist phase to study at the Marx-Engels-Lenin Institute in Moscow). Nabokov was also awarded another year as Research Fellow in Entomology at the M.C.Z. for $1,200, and his position there would be renewed annually until he left for Cornell in 1948. Between lepidoptery and teaching he began to work on the last translations of Pushkin, Lermontov, and Tyutchev for the volume *Three Russian Poets* that Laughlin had commissioned for New Directions.[9]

In mid-April Nabokov traveled to Sweet Briar College, near Amherst, Virginia, which he had been scheduled to visit when he caught the flu at the end of November. On his way to Sweet Briar he stopped in New York, where in addition to Edmund Wilson and colleagues from the American Museum of Natural History he had many close friends from the emigration to see. George Hessen and his father Io-sif, Nabokov's friend and editor at *Rul'*, had arrived safely in December 1942, and it was a serious loss to Nabokov that Hessen *père* died before he could catch up with him again in America. Véra Nabokov's sister Sonia Slonim, her cousin Anna Feigin, and Nabokov's ex-pupil Maria Marinel and her sisters Elizaveta and Ina had all reached New York over the last two years by more or less circuitous and harrowing routes. Now in New York, Nabokov could pay a taxi with a little more aplomb than on his first day off the boat. Meeting the Marinel sisters and Nathalie Nabokoff on the steps of the American Museum of Natural History, he boarded a taxi with them. At their destination he jumped out of the cab first and threw the fare onto the seat: "You know in all those romantic novels the hero throws money down on the seat. I wanted to see how it feels and how it looks."[10]

In Cambridge in May he wrote the story "That in Aleppo Once . . . ," which depicts the kind of hellish wait in the south of France for a passage to America that he had heard about from his New York friends. An émigré writer who has just reached New York from Marseilles and Nice writes to "Dear V.," another émigré writer already settled for several years in America, and recounts his brief and abysmal marriage, more or less synchronous with his attempt to extricate himself and his young wife from Europe. The horrendous shufflings of papers and shuntings of people in the rush for exit visas become mixed up with his wife's disappearances and reappearances and her versions and revisions of what she and the men she has been with have been up to. He would like to believe the recent past has all been a protracted nightmare, but its rhythms are the inexorable rhythms of reality. The letter ends with the pathetic cry the betrayed husband makes to V., asking him to retell his story——as if an artistic shape will allay the private horror of jealousy, the public horror of the refugee. But recalling that Othello had asked, just before stabbing himself, for *his* story to be told, the letter-writer recoils: "Somewhere, somehow, I have made some fatal mistake. . . . It may all end in *Aleppo* if I am not careful. Spare me, V.: you would load your dice with an unbearable implication if you took that for a title."[11]

III

During the spring Nabokov had continued to dictate the Gogol book to his wife. At the end of May he sent the typescript to James Laughlin:

I have just mailed you my "Gogol through the Looking-Glass."

This little book has cost me more trouble than any other I have composed. The reason is clear: I had first to create Gogol (translate him) and then discuss him (translate my Russian ideas about him). The recurrent jerk of switching from one rhythm of work to the other has quite exhausted me. The book has taken me exactly one year to write. I never would have accepted your suggestion to do it had I known how many gallons of brain-blood it would absorb; nor would you have made the suggestion had you known how long you would have to wait. . . .

There are probably some slight slips of the pen here and there. I would like to see the Englishman who could write a book on Shakespeare in Russian. I am very weak, smiling a weak smile, as I lie in my private maternity ward, and expect roses.[12]

Unable to face another summer of goldenrod in Vermont, and anxious to hunt butterflies out West, Nabokov had asked Laughlin if he and his family could stay in Laughlin's hotel, Alta Lodge, Utah. Expecting that the hotel would be empty because of the war, Laughlin was glad to rent out a room, even at a cheap rate. On June 22 the Nabokovs set off by train for Chicago and Salt Lake City. Alta was a ski lodge an hour's drive from Salt Lake City up into the Wasatch Mountains, where it nestled at 8,600 feet on the site of a former mining camp. Nabokov loved the area's landscape, its remoteness, its pioneer past: "the tapering lines of firs on the slopes amid a greyish green haze of aspens"; the thought that twenty years earlier "this place was a Roaring Gulch with golddiggers plugging each other in saloons" just as in Mayne Reid.[13]

For Nabokov, Utah was a fortunate choice: one of the few states in which little butterfly collecting had been done, and with mountain ranges isolated by deserts and therefore likely to have evolved new species. Despite a severe climate with icy winds and noisy thunderstorms, he would walk along the valleys and mountain slopes, whenever the sun came out, from twelve to eighteen miles a day, clad only in shorts and tennis shoes, offering a generous target for gadflies. He wanted to rediscover the haunts of *melissa annetta*, a long-lost subspecies of the *Lycaeides* genus that he had been working on the previous winter, and with the help of nine-year-old Dmitri, he found it on lupine among firs on both sides of the Little Cottonwood River, not far from Alta. Once he invited Laughlin on a collecting hike that lasted four and a half hours. The day was hot even at eleven thousand feet. When Nabokov reached the timberline, he decided to investigate some promising meadows at the base of the final peak. He had no interest in ascending higher, where his butterfly net would hinder him as he climbed on barren rock, but Laughlin headed up to the top of the peak and there put Nabokov's name in the book, much to the latter's annoyance.[14]

At the American Museum of Natural History, Nabokov had become good friends with J. H. McDunnough, the then doyen of American lepidopterists and author of the 1938 *Check List of the Lepidoptera of Canada and the United States*. McDunnough had a particular interest in a family of moths known as the pugs. At night on the brilliantly illuminated plate-glass windows of the Alta Lodge lounge, Nabokov collected for his friend all the unfamiliar pugs he could find. He sent McDunnough his catches, which yielded two species so rare that his captures were designated as type specimens, and two entirely new species, one of which McDunnough gratefully named in his honor *Eupithecia nabokovi*.[15]

Nabokov had rarely felt so good, and as would happen so often in summers to come, the physical well-being and the excitement of chase and capture greatly stimulated his writing. His new novel—eventually to be called *Bend Sinister*—began to take firmer shape. He also discussed with Laughlin the manuscript of his Gogol book. In fact he later misremembered having written the book there, where his only references were a fat, disintegrating, antediluvian volume of Gogol's works, a particularly Gogolesque mayor of the neighboring mining town, and a hash of facts gathered "the Lord knows where" in the days of his omnivorous youth.[16]

His relationship with Laughlin had already become strained: as he wrote to Wilson, "the landlord and the poet are fiercely competing in Laughlin—with the first winning by a neck."[17] Laughlin explained that he thought the book needed more basic information: plot outlines, a straightforward summary of Gogol's life, a list of recommended reading. Nabokov would eventually oblige in an offhanded way, but only after adding to the book a marvelous final chapter so stylized and absurd many readers have mistaken it for fiction:

—"Well," said my publisher . . .

A delicate sunset was framed in a golden gap between gaunt mountains. The remote rims of the gap were eyelashed with firs and still further, deep in the gap itself, one could distinguish the silhouettes of other, lesser and quite ethereal, mountains. We were in Utah, sitting in the lounge of an Alpine hotel. The slender aspens on the near slopes and the pale pyramids of ancient mine dumps took advantage of the plateglass window to participate silently in our talk. . . .

—"Well," said my publisher,—"I like it—but I do think the student ought to be told what it is all about."

I said . . .

—"No,"—he said,—"I don't mean that. I mean the student ought to be told more about Gogol's books. I mean the *plots*. He would want to know what those books are *about*."

I said . . .

—"No you have not,"—he said.—"I have gone through it carefully and so has my wife, and we have not found the plots."[18]

IV

Back in Cambridge in early September, after a return train trip complicated by wartime conditions, Nabokov once again began to teach an informal, extracurricular Russian-language course at Wellesley. This time the one class of twenty-five or so contained a good many staff members and faculty wives. Nabokov was an entertainer and a showman who still managed to impart the necessary information—and some of his enthusiasms. He spent a whole hour talking about Russian sounds and synesthesia, and by the end of the discussion had people agreeing that the letter *x* was the color of shiny tin. Before introducing something new, a long silence would fall as he stood, head bowed, fiddling with the chalk. "I have now something very sad to tell you," he would murmur, raising his eyes. "We have, in Russian, what we call the instrumental case, and it has different endings that one must memorize. But after you have learned these, you will know practically all there is to know about Russian."

One student recorded at the time his playful, coaxing manner:

"Do you know the Russian word for 'nice'? No? Surely we learned it last time." Whatever the word is, no matter how obscure, he is always sure we learned it last time. "Then I shall tell you. It's m-ee-la. Lovely word, meela. Beautiful word." . . . He repeats the Russian several times, musing over it to himself, writes it on the board, then suddenly wheeling around, asks worriedly, "Do you like it? It's really a lovely word. Do you like it?" . . .

He proceeds to correcting the exercises. . . . "Here we go!" and crashes into the first sentence. The students gasp, unable to find any resemblance at all between this torrent of guttural and rolling sound and the letters printed neatly on their papers. He looks up, startled by the dismay on the faces, and shouts, "What is wrong? Don't you all have that?" Striding fiercely to the nearest student, he peers at her notebook. "I-yi-yi-yi-yi, no-no!" He stares unbelievingly at another book. "But what vile 'ch's'!" He pounces on a piece of chalk and writes the character in a slow, careful hand, then gazes at it, impressed by the beauty of the letter.

The lesson proceeds. After reading the simple, English sentences in dramatic, dashing tone, he follows them with remarks in an undertone, such as, "How am I supposed to know 'Where is the book?' " Later he announces, "And now we come to the saddest story ever told, 'She is here. He is there.' " . . . He wonders why the author has persisted in referring to "the brother who plays the organ" and tells us of an exciting sentence in the grammar which asserts that "Those uncles are crossing these rivers."

. . . He asks us to read aloud in Russian—"Aloud" proves to be three brave souls muttering under their breath in a confused jumble. After the sentence has fallen, mutilated, he sighs rapturously, "So good to hear Russian spoken again! I am practically back in Moscow"

—a city where he had never been, and whose accent he deplored.[19]

During the fall Nabokov added to his *Nikolay Gogol* the publisher-author dialogue and a colorful chronology of Gogol's life, and also sent Laughlin the completed manuscript of his translations of the Russian poets. Relations between them remained fraught, however, and when Edmund Wilson suggested to Nabokov they coauthor a book on Russian literature for Doubleday for an advance ten times as large as Laughlin's—Wilson would provide the introductory essays, Nabokov the translations— Nabokov naturally jumped at the chance. Late in November he had his upper teeth removed and a "tip-top plap-plopping plate" fitted, and before visiting the Wilsons in Well-fleet for a weekend at the beginning of December jokingly warned them they might not identify him: "I hope you will recognize me—I shall carry your telegram in my hand." Largely because Wilson moved on to new interests over the next few years, nothing ever came of their projected collaboration.[20]

From the fall of 1943 to the spring of 1944, Nabokov spent most of his time on lepidoptera. After publishing his first major paper on the genus *Lycaeides*, he was elected to the Cambridge Entomological Society. Some members regarded Nabokov as "not professional" as an entomologist. In certain senses of course this was true. He never earned a living solely as an entomologist, and he had neither a Ph.D. in biology, with all the grounding that would have provided in genetics, biochemistry, evolutionary biology, and population biology, nor the detailed understanding of other insect groups—bees, ants, flies, beetles, and so on—that professional entomologists were expected to have, although they might specialize in only one group. On the other hand, because he focused his attention on one order, lepidoptera, or rather on one division within the order (rhopalocera, butterflies but not moths), he knew as much as anyone about the butterfly species of the world, their ecology, distribution, taxonomy, and morphology. He attended meetings of the Entomological Society faithfully, and his wide knowledge of his one field made it possible for him to contribute in others. When for instance someone presented a paper on Southern Hemisphere coleoptera (beetles), Nabokov could suggest interesting parallels between Australasian or South American coleoptera and what he knew of the lepidoptera of these regions. He himself presented a paper on the species concept, insisting, against Ernst Mayr's *Systematics and the Origin of Species* (1943), on the primacy of morphology rather than "population" in any definition of species.[21]

He had a keen amateur interest in birds, trees, shrubs, and flowers. In *The Gift* he had made Count Godunov-Cherdyntsev, though a single-minded lepidopterist, bring back from Central Asia for other naturalist friends a snake, an extraordinary bat, even a whole carpet of alpine vegetation, but above his own bench at the M.C.Z. he had pinned a *Punch* cartoon of a man with a butterfly net in the Gobi desert, and in the distance a tyrannosaurus attacking another dinosaur: "This is all very interesting, but I must remember I'm a specialist in butterflies."[22] Since he had a limited amount of time to indulge in an almost unpaid profession, he gauged his time and capacities carefully. To arrive swiftly at the exhilarations of innovative research he had to specialize narrowly, focusing not merely on the blues but now on one genus, *Lycaeides*, within that subfamily.

After sorting out the *Lycaeides* genitalia and in the process building up at the M.C.Z. the most representative series of American *Lycaeides* in the world, he now turned to their wing markings. With his customary love of detail, he would not settle at the level of precision Schwanwitsch and others had already reached in lepidopterological description, but discovered that the minute scales on each wing were organized in rows radiating out from the base of the wing. This became his second major principle of broad application: by counting the scale rows—something that had never been done before—he could provide a system for specifying with the utmost exactitude the position of any marking on a butterfly wing. Though the technique has not been widely applied since Nabokov's time, one leading lepidopterist well acquainted with Nabokov's work, Charles Remington of Yale, is certain that it will become much more common in the future. It allowed Nabokov to reach new conclusions about the evolution of butterfly wing markings—that the apparent stripes on *Lycaeides* wings evolved not as stripes but by the fusion of initially discrete dots—and hence about the relationship of closely allied species. In the excitement of discovery, Nabokov looked forward to writing a monograph of 250 pages on the *Lycaeides* group.[23]

V

At the end of 1943 he composed a second long Russian poem, "Parizhskaya poema" ("The Paris Poem"). Its thoroughly unsettling opening reflects, as Nabokov explained, "the chaotic, inarticulate agitation when only the rhythm of the future work, but not its direct sense, glimmers in the poet's consciousness." Lines stagger into lilting life, with a shimmer of sense running through a couplet or two, only for meaning to fade, and let the scene behind start to show through: a Russian poet in his room or wandering through Paris at night, his consciousness dispersed, his self scattered. The poem rises on a note of exaltation and collapses again, and only at the end does the poet's lyric voice find command of its material, spurning the desolate fragmentation of all that has gone before and proclaiming a unity and power in life, a mastery and transcendence of the self.[24]

Early in January 1944, Nabokov wrote to Wilson: "Véra has had a serious conversation with me in regard to my novel. Having sulkily pulled it out from under my butterfly manuscripts I discovered two things, first that it was good, and second that the beginning some twenty pages at least could be typed and submitted. This will be done speedily." It would not be the last time Véra Nabokov would nudge her husband back from good work—lepidoptery, translation—to better. Nabokov finished the first four chapters of the novel in an exhausting burst and sent them off to Doubleday.[25]

For the next few months, literary and lepidopterological work followed each other in spasms. Later in life Nabokov would claim at one time that "the pleasure and rewards of literary inspiration are nothing beside the rapture of discovering a new organ under the microscope or an undescribed species on a mountainside," and at another, that "the miniature hooks of a male butterfly are nothing in comparison to the eagle claws of literature which tear at me day and night." Both passions were too intense for him to resist for long. At the end of January he returned "with relief" to his *Lycaeides*, and even thought briefly of revising Holland's *Butterfly Book*, the only book that attempted to represent all the butterflies of North America. He realized the cost of his craving for the excitement of research: "The appalling condition of my purse . . . is my own fault, i.e. I am devoting too much time to entomology (up to 14 hours per day) and although

I am doing in this line something of far-reaching scientific importance I sometimes feel like a drunkard who in his moments of lucidity realizes that he is missing all sorts of wonderful opportunities."[26]

He was still teaching his after-hours Russian-language course at Wellesley, although since fewer students had been able to spare time for another noncredit course in the second semester, staff members—professors of French and Latin and English, and one research librarian—now predominated in the class. Hannah French, the research librarian, remembers Nabokov staying out in the hall smoking until the last possible moment before class. Once, she recalls, "he came in from his train ride from Boston to Wellesley telling of a conversation he had had with a fellow passenger in fairly rapid Russian, challenging us to interpret it." Or he would tell stories in Russian, with many pantomimed gestures, which the class desperately needed, since they recognized only a word or two.[27]

A single guest lecture at Yale in March—on Russian literature rather than elementary Russian language—brought Nabokov as much money as a term of these extracurricular Wellesley classes. But they were not altogether a waste of effort. Already it had become obvious that the Soviet Union would be one of the two leading powers in the postwar world, and in March, Wellesley College decided to offer a course in elementary Russian for credit in the 1944–1945 school year, with Mr. Nabokov as sole instructor.[28]

In the absence of Mildred McAfee, the college president, now in Washington as head of the WAVES, the most powerful figure at Wellesley was the Dean of Instruction, Ella Keats Whiting. She suggested to Nabokov that in designing the course he consult other universities, such as Harvard, to see what methods were in use there.[29] The suggestion was an unfortunate one. Months earlier Nabokov had written to his friend Roman Grynberg complaining about the teaching of Russian in the universities in the area, and added that he would like to write something on the subject. Leading the flock of his bêtes noires was the head of Russian at Harvard, Samuel Hazzard Cross, "who knows only the middle of Russian words and completely ignores prefixes and endings." Nabokov may not have written anything about Cross, but he certainly retold often the story about his friend Karpovich catching Cross, as Nabokov put it, "white-handed": "Karpovich happened to enter a class in which Cross had just finished the lesson; upon seeing Karpovich, he lunged toward the blackboard but did not succeed in completely erasing with the palm of an apprehensive hand the example of grammar which Karpovich managed to see: *on ego udaril s palkoi*, he hit him in the company of a stick, instead of simply [*on ego udaril*] *palkoi* [*with a*

stick]." Enraged at what he considered inept and uncalled-for interference that cast doubt on his own competence, Nabokov fumed:
"Cross me no Crosses."[30]

In May 1944, Nabokov finished the story "A Forgotten Poet," on
which he had been working sporadically all year.[31] A meditation on
the caprices of literary fame and its subjection to extraliterary considerations, it is the wry tale of a Russian poet, supposed drowned at
twenty-four in 1849, who turns up as a seventy-four-year-old at a
memorial gathering in 1899 on the fiftieth anniversary of his death,
and demands the money that has been raised for a monument in his
name—if indeed he really is the poet. Since his disappearance,
Perov—a poet of talent, judging by the samples Nabokov provides of
his verse—has become a hero of the members of the liberal intelligentsia who stage the commemoration. When the organizers eject
the uncomfortable real old man from their meeting, the uncultured
reactionaries take up Perov's cause solely to embarrass their opponents, while the tenderhearted liberals squirm both with guilt for
their heartless dismissal of Perov and with distaste for his quietistic
new views.

Like every one of Nabokov's English works since his arrival in
America, except for short poems and reviews, "A Forgotten Poet"
was decidedly Russian in subject and milieu. Nabokov still did not
feel ready to tackle America or to abandon Russia: even this year,
1944, he would not rule out the possibility that he might write more
Russian fiction for Aldanov's new review. In fact, "A Forgotten Poet"
sums up themes from Nabokov's writing and his situation over the
previous few years. In his recent work on Pushkin and Lermontov,
he had contrasted Pushkin's early death with the "incredible and unnecessary" longevity of the man who shot him, and in 1941, the centenary of Lermontov's death, he had imagined a hypothetical 127-
year-old peasant still wandering a Russian country road, exactly the
age Lermontov would have been had he too not perished in a duel,
at the absurd age of twenty-seven.[32] Nabokov also had in mind in "A
Forgotten Poet" the furor he had himself caused in the émigré intelligentsia when in The Gift he showed the writer Nikolay Chernyshevsky as a bumbler, not the saint that progressive thought had
made him. And surely he was brooding on the capriciousness of his
own fame—his inability to get The Gift published complete in Russian, his having to leave his formidable reputation behind in an émigré Europe that no longer existed—and his hope that one day, perhaps as an old man, he too might receive due acclaim for his first two
decades of work.

VI

Yet "A Forgotten Poet" contains no hint of the personal. A thoroughly *im*personal, superbly understated re-creation of an apparently historical event in a wonderfully evoked Russia of 1899, the story is sober enough to hoodwink readers into accepting Perov as a real poet, just as Khodasevich in 1936 convinced his audience that the Vasily Travnikov from whom he was quoting had really lived in Pushkin's time.[33] Or rather, in "A Forgotten Poet" Nabokov puts us as readers in a position analogous to that of the organizers of the meeting where a man claiming to be Perov comes forward: *they* want to refuse to accept that this could be Perov, yet they know he is utterly plausible in ways difficult to feign; *we* take these pages to be simply a story, but its historical precision and restraint make us wonder whether we know enough Russian literary history to be sure that a poet called Perov did not really exist after all.

The bamboozling sobriety of "A Forgotten Poet" could not possibly be more unlike the bamboozling ebullience of "The Assistant Producer," where Nabokov's technique predominates at every moment to delude us into supposing that a historically accurate record is the wildest film fantasy. Reading "The Assistant Producer" to a composition class at Wellesley in May 1943, Nabokov had explained that he liked "to lure the reader this way and that and then tickle him behind the ear just to see him whirl around."[34] In "A Forgotten Poet" he does the same thing again, but in the reverse direction.

At this point it may be worth commenting on Nabokov's penchant for literary deception. As he explained in his mimicry article and elsewhere, he detected in nature a playful deceptiveness and found nothing more exhilarating than the surprise of seeing through the deception to a new level of truth. He liked to offer the same surprises in literature, feigning falsehood when he was telling the truth or vice versa, for the sake of the reader's pleasure in penetrating the illusion.

He behaved the same way in person. As Elena Levin recalled, "when he tells you the truth he winks at you to confuse you."[35] He would often concoct highly plausible impromptu inventions and pay his listeners the compliment of assuming that they could see through the trompe l'oeil. Those not so well attuned to him often missed the point.

Edmund Wilson was such a person. He became convinced that Nabokov was a malicious practical joker and decided, especially as their relationship deteriorated, that schadenfreude was a key to Nabokov's personality.[36] The worst recorded instance of a hoax Nabokov played on Wilson is no more than this: once "in a convertible, with

Mary McCarthy at the wheel and her husband beside her, Nabokov, who was sitting with his wife in the back, leaned forward and nimbly removed Wilson's awful brown hat—impersonating, as it were, a roguish breeze." Wilson ignored Nabokov and turned to Véra: "Your husband has a rather strange sense of humor."[37]

With his prickly competitiveness, Wilson attempted to ensure he would never be caught out by Nabokov, and as a result imagined hoaxes that had never existed. He telephoned Nabokov shortly after reading *The Real Life of Sebastian Knight* to tell him he had discovered that the whole novel was built as a chess game. Nabokov told him, quite truthfully, that this was not the case. Wilson wrote back to say: "I don't believe a word you say about your book and am furious at having been hoaxed by it (though my opinion of it has rather gone up than otherwise)." A year later, after reading a book of new verse Wilson had sent him, Nabokov complimented him that the opening lines of one of his poems, "After reading, / writing late" were "in tone, rhythm and atmosphere . . . most beautifully like Pushkin's mumble: *mne ne spitsya,* / *net ognya*" ("I can't sleep, there is no light"). A month later Wilson wrote back:

> You know that you played on me unintentionally a more successful hoax than any that you premeditated. I was sure that you had invented the Pushkin poem about lying awake at night which sounded so much like mine. I told Mary and other people so and cited it as an example of the lengths to which you would go in the concoction of literary frauds, and swore that I would not for anything in the world give you the satisfaction of looking it up and of not being able to find it. Then I did look it up one night and found that it did actually exist. I was furious.[38]

Wilson seemed fated to misinterpret Nabokov, but that did not yet impair their friendship or Wilson's generosity. Generosity was something Nabokov needed. He felt terribly short of money. The Russian Literary Fund offered him a subsidy of one hundred dollars; he asked for two hundred dollars and received it. He also visited Cornell for a reading of "A Forgotten Poet" at the Book and Bowl Club, on the invitation of Peter Pertzoff, who had helped him translate two Russian stories for the *Atlantic*. On the way back from Cornell, another Pninian adventure befell him: he disembarked from the train half-awake at Newark instead of New York, and then "in a kind of dull nightmare" had to make his way home by local trains. He hoped to finance publication of *The Gift* in Russian by subscription and use a Russian reading in New York to raise a little more money and as an occasion to launch the book, but the subscription venture was doomed and an unforeseen holiday weekend scotched the reading.[39]

The one thing that did help Nabokov was a new relationship with the *New Yorker*. Over the last two years the *New Yorker* had accepted a handful of his poems, but he had continued to publish his stories in the *Atlantic* for much less than the *New Yorker* could pay. Katharine White, one of the creators of the *New Yorker*, came back from Maine at the beginning of 1944 to work there again. As Wilson told Nabokov, "one of the ideas she came back with was to get you to do stories for them. She had torn out all your things in the *Atlantic*." Wilson encouraged her in her design, and it would be her and the *New Yorker*'s interest in his work that would lead to Nabokov's most satisfying relationship with any American publisher until *Lolita*'s success turned every publisher into an eager suitor. Wilson, knowing of his friend's financial troubles, and for once having money to spare, offered Nabokov a loan that he would not accept. On Wilson's prompting, Katharine White in June 1944 offered Nabokov an advance of five hundred dollars against future contributions to the *New Yorker*, in return for giving the magazine the rights to a first consideration of his new work. He would maintain a first-reading contract with the *New Yorker*, generously increased as his English reputation grew, for another three decades.[40]

VII

On D-Day, June 6, 1944, Nabokov had his own newsworthy story to report. Two days later he wrote to Edmund Wilson:

On the day of the invasion certain "bacilli" mistook my innards for a beachhead. I had lunched on some Virginia ham in a little *Wursthaus* near Harvard Square and was happily examining the genitalia of a specimen from Havilah, Kern Co., Calif. at the Museum, when suddenly I felt a strange wave of nausea. Mind you, I had been most extravagantly well up to that point and had actually brought my tennis racket in order to play with my friend Clark (echinoderms—if you know what I mean) in the late afternoon. Suddenly, as I say, my stomach rose with an awful whoop. I managed somehow to reach the outside steps of the Museum, but before attaining the grassplot which was my pathetic goal, I threw up, or rather down, i.e. right on the steps, such sundry items as: pieces of ham, some spinach, a little mashed potatoes, a squirt of beer—in all 80 cents worth of food. Excruciating cramps racked me and I had just the strength to reach the toilet where a flow of brown blood rushed out of me from the opposite part of my miserable body. Since I have in me a heroic strain, I forced myself to climb the stairs, lock my lab. and leave a note in Clark's office cancelling the tennis game. Then, vomiting every three steps, I proceeded to stagger home, much to the amusement of passers-by who thought I had been overcelebrating the invasion.

Now, you should note, dear Bunny and Mary, that the day before, Véra and Dmitri had gone to New York for [Dmitri's] appendicitis operation . . . so that when I finally crawled into my flat I was quite alone and helpless. I have a hazy recollection: of undressing, in between monstrous distal and proximal discharges; of lying on the floor of my room and issuing a torrent of ham and blood into my waste paper basket; of progressing by spasmodic stages to the telephone which seemed unattainable, standing as it did on the incredibly lofty piano. I managed to sweep the instrument down upon the floor and bracing myself for this last achievement, dialled Karpovich's number. . . .

When [Mrs. Karpovich] heard me gasping into the telephone and pleading for help she said: please do not play the fool (*ne valyayte duraka*)—this is the usual thing that happens to humorists,—and I had quite a time persuading her that I was dying. Incidentally I vomited into the telephone which I think has never been done before. Realizing at last that something was wrong, she jumped into her car and some ten minutes later found me in a state of collapse in a corner of the room. Never in my whole life have I experienced such impossible and humiliating pains. She called an ambulance and in a twinkle two policemen appeared. They wanted to know 1) who the lady was and 2) what poison I had taken. This romantic touch was too much for me, and I swore at them roundly. Then they proceeded to carry me down. The stretcher was not made to negotiate our type of staircase (American efficiency), so I was carried downstairs, squirming and whooping, by the two men and Mrs. Karpovich. A few minutes later I was sitting on a hard chair, in a horrible room, with a Negro baby howling on a table—this was the Cambridge City Hospital—of all places. A young medical student (i.e. had been studying medicine for 3 months only) attempted the ridiculous and medieval procedure of pumping my stomach by means of a rubber hose which he inserted into my nose. It so happens that my left nostril is so narrowed inside that nothing can pass, while my right one is S-shaped. . . . Thus it is hardly surprising that the hose could not pass—and all the while of course I was suffering most hellish pains. When the utter ineptitude of the unfortunate youth dawned upon me, I firmly asked Mrs. Karpovich to take me away—anywhere, and actually signed a document to the effect that I had refused assistance. After this I had my greatest attack of vomiting and *le reste*—the funny thing being that you cannot do the two things at the one time in the W.C. so I kept rolling off and squirting by turns from either end.

Mrs Karpovich remembered that at 6 p.m. (it was about that time now) a doctor was to visit her sick husband. I was carried by a reluctant and meager staff to a taxi and after incredible sufferings found myself shivering under five blankets on the drawing-room couch at the K.'s. By then I was in a state of *complete* collapse and when the doctor (a nice fellow) turned up he could find neither my pulse nor my blood pressure. He started telephoning and I heard him saying "extremely grave" and "not a minute to be lost." Five minutes later (with poor Mr Karpovich quite forgotten . . .) he had arranged the matter and—lo!—I was at the Mt. Aubrey hospital . . . in a semi-private ward—the "semi" being represented by an old man dying from acute cardiac trouble (I could not sleep all night, owing to his groans and *ahannement*—he died towards dawn after telling some unknown "Henry" such things as "My little boy, you can't do that to me. Use me right" etc.—all very interesting and useful to me). At the hospital two or three quarts of some saline stuff were injected into my veins—and I lay with that needle in my forearm all night and most of yesterday. The doctor said it was a case of food-poisoning and called it "hemor. collitis." . . . In the meantime I had been transferred (in spite of my protests) to the general ward, where the radio kept emitting hot music, cigarette ads (in a juicy voice from the heart) and gags without interruption until (at 10 p.m.) I bellowed to the nurse to have the bloody thing stopped (much to the annoyance and surprise of the staff and of the patients). This is a curious detail of American life—they do not actually listen to the radio, in fact everybody was talking, retching, guffawing, wisecracking, flirting with the (very charming) nurses—all the time—but apparently the impossible sounds coming from the apparatus (it is really the first time that I have heard the radio, except for very brief spasms in other people's houses and in the saloon cars during my travels) somehow acted as a "life-background" for the occupants of the ward, for as soon as it was stopped complete quiet ensued and I soon fell asleep). This morning (Thursday 8th) I feel perfectly well,—had a good breakfast (egg was hardboiled, of course) and attempted to take a bath, but was caught in the corridor and bundled back into bed. At present I have been wheeled on to the porch where I can smoke and enjoy my *voskresenie iz myortvikh* (resurrection from the dead). I hope to go home by tomorrow.[41]

When he was wheeled back into the ward things were not so pleasant: the radio, the chatter, a sixteen-year-old boy following the staff around and aping the groans of older patients. To cut down the noise, Nabokov drew the curtain around his bed in the hope of either resting or studying a medical dictionary he had managed to snatch from a bookcase as he was wheeled down the hallway. The staff forbade the curtains, since they implied a patient's sudden death, and confiscated the book as too technical. Nabokov could not stand it all (twenty years later he would remark in an interview, "In hospitals there is still something of the eighteenth-century madhouse"), and when Mrs. Karpovich arrived during visiting hours he outlined in conspiratorial Russian a plan of escape. She returned to the car, he strolled casually to an open side door, and, clad in his dressing gown, ran to the getaway vehicle with two staff members in frantic and unsuccessful pursuit.⁴²* That was the last time anyone made the mistake of trying to put Nabokov in a communal cage.

* In *Ada*, Van Veen will escape from the hospital in similar fashion in Cordula de Prey's car.

CHAPTER 4

Permanent Impermanence: Cambridge and Wellesley, 1944–1946

I

SINCE late 1936, Nabokov had pursued a position teaching Russian literature at an American university. After nearly a decade of searching, the best he could find was a one-year appointment for 1944–1945 at Wellesley as a one-man Russian department teaching no more than elementary Russian language. He felt so dissatisfied at the prospect that shortly before his duties commenced he wrote to a Hollywood agent that he would be ready to come to California as a screenwriter.[1]

Far from writing at high rates for American cinema audiences, Nabokov had not yet composed a single work of fiction with an American setting, and any kind of writing had to compete with his enjoyment of his ill-paid lepidopterological work. Late in June 1944 he briefly visited the Wilsons at Wellfleet. Stimulated by their company, and kept away from the M.C.Z. by a cold that he caught as he rode home by train, he found himself "blessed with a flow of inspiration and . . . composed another tremendous chapter of my novel." By now he had one hundred pages ready, and felt almost sure that the book would be called not *The Person from Porlock* but *Game to Gunm.*[2]*

At the end of July, with Dmitri off at camp in Vermont, the Nabokovs joined the Wilsons at Wellfleet for a couple of weeks, staying at a hotel Wilson had booked for them. Among the guests at the Wilsons' many parties was their neighbor and friend Nina Chavchavadze, who recalled with great feeling the times when as Nina Romanov she had been punted down the Cam by the white-flanneled Volodya Nabokov. He remembered their romance much more dryly.[3]

Despite or perhaps because of their round of festivities, Edmund Wilson and Mary McCarthy were off-balance with each other. Things

---

* Apparently named after the contents designation on the spine of volume 10 of the *Encyclopaedia Britannica*, fourteenth edition (1937–1959), whose entries run from "Game" to "Gunmetal." D. Barton Johnson, the first to identify the source of Nabokov's provisional title, tries to explain why it might have been chosen (*Worlds in Regression* [Ann Arbor: Ardis, 1985], pp. 203–6).

tipped precariously when McCarthy, cleaning up after a party, asked her husband if he would take out the garbage. "Empty it yourself," he said, repeating the phrase with an ironical bow as she struggled through the screen door with two large garbage cans. She slapped him and stamped upstairs. He called her down: "You think you're unhappy with me. Well I'll give you something to be unhappy about," and proceeded to beat her. She fled to New York. Next day Wilson went to the Nabokovs, asking them to move into the house with him, as his live-in cook threatened to leave for fear she might be cited as corespondent in a divorce case. To extricate him from his predicament, they did move in with him for a week.[4]

Back at 8 Craigie Circle in mid-August, Nabokov wrote "another glorious chapter" of his novel. On August 15, *Nikolay Gogol* was published. A *New Yorker* review by Wilson praised the book highly but also criticized rather bitingly what Wilson saw as Nabokov's "poses, perversities, and vanities which sound as if he had brought them away from the St. Petersburg of the early nineteen-hundreds . . . and piously preserved them in exile. . . . His puns are particularly awful." Though Wilson often promised to write a major study of his friend's fiction, this was in fact the only review of Nabokov's work undertaken by the most respected reviewer in America until his celebrated 1965 onslaught on Nabokov's translation of *Eugene Onegin*.[5]

At the end of August, when Dmitri returned brown and tough from camp, the Nabokovs moved out for two weeks to Wellesley, where they boarded with a couple named Fleming (she was a cook, he a carpenter), swam, played tennis, and loafed in the Flemings' lush, leafy garden. Since Edmund Wilson and Mary McCarthy were now back together again—they would separate for good over the coming winter—Nabokov wrote tactfully to his friend, "following Mary's example, I retired . . . to another town (Wellesley, in my case) in order to write a story."[6]

The story was "Time and Ebb," a little masterpiece that blends the immediate and the remote, the mundane and the eerily beautiful.[7] A ninety-year-old Jewish scientist reflects from his hospital bed in the year 2024 not on the world around him—a commonplace after all to his putative audience—but on the strangeness of the world of his childhood, America in the early 1940s. For the first time but not the last, Nabokov brilliantly inverts science fiction. Far from inviting wonder at new gimmicks and gadgets, he postulates a world where flying has been banned, and the airplanes of old—of the present, of 1944—seem magically poetic. Instead of having us gasp at super circuitry, he produces a shiver at the strangeness of the life we take for granted. Back in the narrator's childhood "they played with electricity in various ways without having the slightest notion of what it really was—and no wonder the chance revelation of its true nature came as a most hideous surprise (I was a man by that time and can well remember old Professor Andrews sobbing his heart out on the campus in the midst of a dumbfounded crowd)."

For the first time Nabokov sets one of his stories in America, a setting that at this stage he seems to feel ready to depict for native Americans only when filtered through a prism of futuristic fancy. He records the world around him with wonderful precision and evocative charm: a soda fountain, Central Park, movies, neighborhood stores, trains, planes, taxicabs. In "A Guide to Berlin" he had written that the purpose of literary creation is "to portray ordinary objects as they will be reflected in the kindly mirrors of future times; to find in the objects around us the fragrant tenderness that only posterity will discern and appreciate in the far-off times when every trifle of our plain everyday life will become exquisite and festive in its own right."[8] In "Time and Ebb" he remains true to the same aesthetic—

> old-fashioned "skyscrapers" . . . a misnomer, since their association with the sky, especially at the ethereal close of a greenhouse day, far from suggesting any grating contact, was indescribably delicate and serene: to my childish eyes looking across the vast expanse of park land that used to grace the center of the city, they appeared remote and lilac-colored, and strangely aquatic, mingling as they did their first cautious lights with the colors of the sunset and revealing, with a kind of dreamy candor, the pulsating inside of their semitransparent structure

—but he has become still more inventive and far more capable of evoking a sense of awe at the strangeness of our existing at all.

Time, which we so often let decay into mere habit, is for Nabokov a succession of wonders. By suddenly jerking us outside our own time he confronts us with all we quaintly take for granted. The people of the 1940s

> clung to tradition as a vine still clings to a dead tree. They had their meals at large tables around which they grouped themselves in a stiff sitting position on hard wooden chairs. Clothes consisted of a number of parts, each of which, moreover, contained the reduced and useless remnants of this or that older fashion (a townsman dressing of a morning had to squeeze something like thirty buttons into as many buttonholes besides tying three knots and checking the contents of fifteen pockets).

Nabokov makes us see that by sheer routine acceptance we wear out the beauty and magic of a world whose very existence ought to seem a perpetual, inexhaustible surprise.

II

At Wellesley College Nabokov had the rank of lecturer, a member of the faculty at the professorial level but not on the permanent staff. In this first year he taught Russian 100, elementary Russian language, to eighteen students in three two-hour classes per week, and received a mere $800, even less than the $1,200 he earned at the M.C.Z.[9]

He began with pronunciation: "A Russian vowel is an orange, an English vowel is a lemon. When you speak Russian your mouth ought to distend laterally at the corners. . . . You can, and should, speak Russian with a permanent broad smile." He believed in introducing grammar before all but the barest vocabulary: "Anatomy must precede systematics, and the importance of studying the behavior of a word is greater than that of learning to say in Russian 'goodbye' or 'good morning.' " In theory he advocated that there was no choice but to memorize all the rules: "I must admit to feeling a great deal of disgust for any levelling or oversimplification. . . . The loaves of knowledge do not come nicely sliced."[10]

But in practice his classes were anything but sheer grind. He sat at the head of a seminar table in a small room in Founder's Hall, with his books, papers, cigarettes, matches, and ashtray before him—he now smoked up to four packs of cigarettes a day, lighting a new one from the stub of the old, and crushing the butt out emphatically in the crowded ashtray—while the students were ranged down either side of the table, with one at the opposite end, and were required to take the same place for every class. With his eye for individual differences, Nabokov knew each student well, her personality, her aptitudes, her regular friends. Though he taught with Birkett's *Modern Russian Course* as the class textbook, he would deviate from it at will to deliver poetic sermons on the colors of sounds or the genius of Pushkin or the delights of his latest butterfly hunt.[11]

Early in the fall his regular classes and his guest lectures coalesced in his mind into the longest and perhaps the best of his English poems before "Pale Fire": "An Evening of Russian Poetry."[12] The subject sounds unpromising: a stylized verse account of a lecture that a visiting speaker delivers at a women's college. What makes the poem so successful that it is hard to refrain from simply quoting its 150 lines in full? Perhaps, the contrast between the constraints of the situation—the young college students with their naive questions—and the range of imagination that allows the poet to project onto the minds of his audience the whole landscape of Russia, its remotest history, its natural world, its art. Or the tension between, on the one hand, discipline and economy, and, on the other, the bright colors of fancy, the subterranean throb of passion. The speaker's personal past and his sense of incommunicable loss are both muffled and at the same time expressed in the most romantic terms, as a monarch's flight into exile, and his haunted fear of pursuit:

> Beyond the seas where I have lost a scepter,
> I hear the neighing of my dappled nouns,
> soft participles coming down the steps,
> treading on leaves, trailing their rustling gowns,
> and liquid verbs in *ahla* and in *ili*,
> Aonian grottoes, nights in the Altai,
> black pools of sound with "l"s for water lilies.
> The empty glass I touched is tinkling still,
> but now 'tis covered by a hand and dies.
>
> *"Trees? Animals? Your favorite precious stone?"*
>
> The birch tree, Cynthia, the fir tree, Joan.
> Like a small caterpillar on its thread,
> my heart keeps dangling from a leaf long dead
> but hanging still, and still I see the slender
> white birch that stands on tiptoe in the wind,
> and firs beginning where the garden ends,
> the evening ember glowing through their cinders.

That note of exaltation was not Nabokov's experience in the Wellesley classroom. To Wilson he wrote: "I work a lot. Have financial troubles. Am looking for a good solid professorship somewhere." When he was warned that most of the work in the Slavic department at Berkeley, where an opening had arisen, was "frankly of high school grade," he wrote back that he would still be keen to teach there: it was what he was used to at Wellesley, and at Wellesley his position was not even permanent.[13]

III

Like his father, Dmitri had begun new classes: at Dexter School, where John F. Kennedy had studied fifteen years before. Entering the school poorly adjusted both physically and socially, Dmitri would emerge three years later, at thirteen, already over six feet tall, a top student, an athlete, and a youth of considerable personal poise. Noting his son's progress, Nabokov developed a warm affection for the school and its headmaster, Francis A. Caswell. He would often go along to watch soccer matches, and at halftime would relive his own favorite memories of school by dribbling the ball around with far more flair than the American boys who looked on in admiration. Outside school hours, he would also patiently catch a baseball—an object that meant nothing to him—as Dmitri, trying to become one of those American boys, threw him pitch after pitch.[14]

Although Nabokov taught at Wellesley two or three afternoons a week, almost all the rest of his time was spent at the M.C.Z. In his role as unofficial curator of lepidoptera, he now had an assistant, Phyllis Smith, a high-school volunteer who would carry out routine work after school: spreading butterflies, once he had shown her how; labeling; filing. She remembered his playfulness, his jokes, his word games and puzzles, his uproarious delight at oddities, his loud hearty laugh, the explosions of hilarity that would fill his eyes with tears. But even more she recalls his curiosity: "He asked questions, questions, questions. How-to questions, why questions. He was always collecting facts and opinions. He was learning U.S. customs and attitudes." He took a very probing interest in her parents' recent divorce and apparently nurtured an indulgent hope that they might remarry, even sealing in an envelope he gave her a prediction to that effect. (He was wrong.) She always found him considerate, gentlemanly, almost deferential, although she was so young and her job "the lowest of the low."[15]

By October 1944, Nabokov had completed his "Notes on the Morphology of the Genus *Lycaeides*" and was ready to tackle something new. He had set himself as a long-term project to work out the genitalia of the entire family of the blues (*Plebejinae*), and turned now from his exhaustive analysis of the North American *Lycaeides* to a wider focus: a reclassification of all the neotropical (Central and South American) blues. Some taxonomists ("lumpers") stress resemblances and therefore favor grouping similar kinds together; others ("splitters") focus on differences and prefer to separate kind from kind. As someone who always valued the individuating detail and dismissed generalizations and groups, Nabokov was temperamentally a splitter, but by no means a doctrinaire or extreme one. Like other serious lepidopterists, he deplored the enthusiastic amateur collector's penchant for elevating to the rank of a new species or subspecies what was nothing more than an aberration or a seasonal or geographical form. In his work on neotropical *Plebejinae*, Nabokov introduced seven new genera and revised the remaining two.[16] To older taxonomists, this degree of generic splitting seemed close to vandalism; nowadays, however, generic splitting has become much more widely accepted, and no one has ever found reason to challenge Nabokov's groupings. Even people much more lumpish in inclination than he ever was have accepted his phylogenetic calculation of relationships.[17]

IV

On afternoons when he had to teach, Nabokov would leave his bench at the M.C.Z. just before midday and head for Wellesley by streetcar and bus or subway and train. Returning to Cambridge in the evening, he would ride in one of the car pools set up to cope with the wartime gas shortage. Decades later, Nabokov expected that when he at last sat down to write *Speak, America* he would devote an entire chapter to his days in the car pool.

Occasionally he would ride home with Joan Bishop, Wellesley's placement director, or Sally Collie Smith, the college's publicity officer, but most evenings his chauffeur on the long, slow crawl home would be Isabel Stephens, who taught in the English department at Wellesley and in Cambridge lived just across from the Nabokovs on the corner of Craigie Street. She found him the life of the party, the rouser of tired spirits at the end of a hard day, talking on in "a series of gay witticisms, sometimes ribald, always so amusing that I, as driver, was afraid of laughing too hard—and more than once had to pull over to wipe tears of mirth from my eyes."[18]

He sat in the back of the car, often with Sylvia Berkman or Aileen Ward, the future biographer of Keats. Sylvia Berkman enjoyed his "eerie" playfulness, but on days when teaching had exhausted her, she would ride back in a later car pool rather than feel she had to rise to Nabokov's vitality. Aileen Ward recalls how they used to make up impromptu parodies of poems by Hardy or Housman or whomever. She once asked him how he found time to write. He replied: "In the morning I peer at the genitalia of butterflies; in the afternoon, I teach Russian grammar to students at Wellesley; in the evening I get into bed with a mug of hot milk and write."[19]

In February 1945, Nabokov gave guest lectures at St. Timothy's College in Baltimore and Smith College in Northampton, Massachusetts. Returning from the Baltimore lecture he stopped in New York with George and Sonia Hessen. He had a pleasant evening at the Grynbergs' with Edmund Wilson, who was about to depart as a reporter for the *New Yorker* to war-ravaged Europe. On Nabokov's trip back from New York, a dose of influenza led to a severe attack of intercostal neuralgia, and after reaching Cambridge he spent a week in bed. Warmed by his conversation with Wilson and anxious for his friend's safety in Europe, he concluded a letter to him, "I like you very much." Wilson replied in kind: "Our conversations have been among the few consolations of my literary life through these last years—when my old friends have been dying, petering out or getting more and more neurotic."[20]

Throughout Nabokov's life only one political issue ever excited him: the attitude those outside the country should take toward the Soviet Union. In the closing phases of the war, Soviet conduct in "liberating" Eastern Europe—especially Stalin's refusal to aid the revolt of the Warsaw underground—began to cause a drop in American confidence in Russia and the first revival of the anti-Communist sentiment that would lead to the cold war.[21] In 1944, while the Soviet Union was still seen as a heroic, irreproachable ally, Nabokov's friend, the old Socialist Revolutionary Vladimir Zenzinov, had published—privately, and in Russian, of course—a book called *Meeting with Russia: Life in the Soviet Union: Letters to the Red Army, 1939–1941*, a collection of "letters from home" he had obtained from prisoners taken in the Russo-Finnish War. Nabokov thanked his friend for the book:

> I read it from cover to cover and appreciated the enormous labor and the enormous love you put into it. Gloomy and poor and intolerably happy is the Russia reflected in these pathetic scrawlings, and as you quite rightly remark, nothing, nothing has changed—the same soldiers going mad from the same hunger and grief as five hundred years ago, and the same oppression and the same bare-bellied children in the mud, in the dark. For their sake alone all these vile "leaders of the people" . . . should be destroyed forever. I consider this the most valuable book about Russia of all those that have appeared during these twenty-five despicable years.[22]

Weeks later Nabokov read a newspaper report that Maklakov, the official representative of the Russian émigrés in France, had attended a luncheon reception at the Soviet embassy in Paris and had drunk a toast "to the motherland, to the Red Army, to Stalin." Furious, Nabokov wrote to Zenzinov to relieve his anger:

> I can understand denying one's principles in *one* exceptional case: if they told me that those closest to me would be tortured or spared according to my reply, I would immediately consent to anything, ideological treachery or foul deeds and would even apply myself lovingly to the parting on Stalin's backside. Was Maklakov placed in such a situation? Evidently not. . . .

All that remains is to outline a classification of the emigration. I distinguish five main divisions:

1. The philistine majority, who dislike the Bolsheviks for taking from them their little bit of land or money, or twelve Ilf-and-Petrov chairs.

2. Those who dream of pogroms and a Rumanian tsar, and now fraternize with the Soviets because they sense in the Soviet Union the Soviet Union of the Russian People.

3. Fools.

4. Those who ended up across the border by inertia, vulgarians and careerists who pursue their own advantage and lightheartedly serve any leader at all.

5. Decent freedom-loving people, the old guard of the Russian intelligentsia, who unshakably despise violence against language, against thought, against truth.[23]

Nabokov's indignation at what seemed to be Maklakov's betrayal of democratic principles[24] and his need to state his own position within the emigration combined in his mind with an incident that had occurred during his stopover in New York in February. At dinner with his friends the Grynbergs, Nabokov had met Marc Slonim, an émigré critic with whom he had been friendly in Paris. Sonia Grynberg expected him "to fall into his arms." Instead, Nabokov thoroughly snubbed Slonim, later explaining to Wilson his reason: "He gets 250 dollars from the Stalinists per month, which is not much, but he is not worth even that."[25]* Slonim was remotely related to the family of Véra's father, Evsey Slonim, and this coincidence and Nabokov's judgment of Slonim's politics may together have provided the germ for the story "Double Talk," written in late March and early April 1945.[26]

Nabokov switched the political signposts of the actual event. The story's narrator, a liberal Russian émigré writer, has repeatedly found himself confused during the course of his years of European exile with a reactionary anti-Semitic namesake. Now in Boston, he gets an invitation to a party—and finds when he enters that the invitation must have been for the other man, for he had landed in a conclave of conservative Germanophiles. This unusually topical story—so topical that in book form it would be renamed "Conversation Piece, 1945"—allows Nabokov to explain his own ideological position: his even greater distance from the "very White émigré, of the automatically reactionary type" than from a leftist artist friend "who had for

---

* Nabokov was quite mistaken: Slonim was in fact firmly against Stalin and the Soviet system.

some reason always resented my contempt for the Party line and for the Communist and his Master's Voice." Nabokov mimics superbly the fluent nonsense of ideas he detests: the willful blindness of a Germanophile explaining away the extermination camps; the glib convolutions that make of Nazism a plot inflicted by wicked foreigners on the gentle, cultured German people; the Russian reactionary who opts for Stalin as a new outlet for long-frustrated patriotism.

Before completing "Double Talk," Nabokov wrote a Russian poem, "O pravitelyakh" ("On Rulers"), perhaps the most successful political piece he ever wrote. A superb parody of the intonations and off-rhymes of Vladimir Mayakovsky, the Soviet poet laureate—whom Nabokov regarded as a poet "endowed with a certain brilliance and bite, but fatally corrupted by the regime he faithfully served"—the poem seethes with contempt for those with an awed respect for Stalin or for any of the other great leaders who have inflicted so much suffering on the world.[27]

V

Any new intimacy requires an awkward period of adjustment, and Nabokov's relationship with the New Yorker was no exception. He had signed his first formal first-reading agreement with the magazine; he had met Katharine White at a New Yorker party at the Ritz and spent an evening with her and E. B. White in Boston and liked them both.* For "Double Talk," the first of his stories taken by the New Yorker, he received $812.50, far more than he had ever been paid for a short story. But he was upset about the magazine's compulsion to edit all its contributions. Because of the story's atypical topicality, he accepted some changes, but rejected most: "I am afraid I cannot change or add any of the other sentences mentioned. The 'average reader' does not read the New Yorker. I am very sorry but I really think I have gone as far as my conscience permits in accepting alternatives. I do not want those exasperating little bridges and am quite sure that the good reader will flit across the gaps with perfect ease."[28] He had his way.

---

* He had first read E. B. White in 1940, as he sailed to America on the Champlain. Picking up a magazine in the ship's library, he came across White's definition of a miracle, "blue snow on a red barn"—which to him was a stab of Russia. Whenever he met a writer whose work he liked, he would show his appreciation by recalling a phrase he had cherished for years. Decades later, he recollected that it must have been this little phrase that he paid back with interest to E. B. White (Nabokov letter to Clarence Brown, November 11, 1974, courtesy Clarence Brown).

During the spring, Nabokov had begun to wear glasses for reading, a consequence of his work at the microscope and the first of two transformations from his lean youthful self to the cozily rotund and bespectacled figure of his last thirty years. Early in June, worried by heart palpitations—a recurrent double systole—he visited a doctor. He was advised that the palpitations, although unsettling, were not dangerous, but if he wished to be rid of them he would have to quit smoking. He had tried in vain to give up the habit two or three times before, but this time he stopped overnight and never smoked again. He felt miserable without nicotine and had to keep his cravings at bay by compulsively devouring molasses candy. He rapidly gained weight.[29]

On July 12, he and Véra took their citizenship test with Amy Kelly and Mikhail Karpovich as their two sponsors. Karpovich warned his friend: "Now look here, I want to ask you something—don't joke, please don't joke with them—this is quite serious, you know, don't joke." Nabokov agreed, but then the examiner tested his command of English by giving him a phrase to read aloud: "The child is bold." Silly phrase, thought Nabokov, looking through his new lenses, and, picturing the child as a baby with very little hair, he read out "The child is bald." "No, it is not bald, it is bold." "Yes, but you know, babies don't have much hair." The examiner—"of Italian origin apparently, judging by his slight accent"—had seen at once that Nabokov's English was fine, but was obliged to ask him a question about American history. Nabokov did not even understand the question. The next moment they were kidding each other, roaring with laughter, while Karpovich looked with alarm at these two madmen. "You passed, you passed," the examiner said, as soon as he caught his breath. Nabokov recalled the occasion with as much pleasure as his encounter with the sportive customs men on his first day in America; "I had a wonderful time becoming an American citizen. That was an absolutely wonderful day. . . . That's very characteristic, you know. This rather prim Russian who wants to be very serious and this easygoing American way of settling things. . . . It was very satisfactory, very soothing."[30]

After Dmitri's return from camp the Nabokovs again moved out of their city apartment to the quiet green spaces of Wellesley. This time they boarded at 9 Abbott Street with the Monaghan family, whose jolly Irish heartiness they greatly enjoyed. The Monaghans would later remember Nabokov in terms of his zest for life, his inquisitiveness about everything, and his bags of molasses kisses.[31]

Next door to the Monaghans that summer lived Jorge Guillén and his family. Guillén, six years older than Nabokov and the head of the

Spanish department at Wellesley, was one of the greatest Spanish poets of the most brilliant generation since the Spanish Golden Age. He and Nabokov had known each other since the Nabokovs' year in Wellesley in 1941–1942. Guillén was the only other major writer at Wellesley, and a fellow exile—perhaps even the model in part for the poet at the center of Nabokov's poem "Exile." Though Guillén's English was poor, he and Nabokov could converse easily in French. Often during the summer of 1945, Nabokov would leave off writing his novel to play tennis with Guillén, a man of quick, light movements in a rather French manner and an originality of mind that never ran dry. Nabokov liked him and his work and in *Ada* many years later paid tribute to Guillén's *Cantico*. Guillén in return was a faithful admirer of Nabokov, "poète en deux langues, en prose et en vers, toujours poète." They first met when the onset of war had just expunged Russian émigré culture and Nabokov's reputation within it: no wonder Guillén later commented to his son that he had never known a writer with such a sense that fame was his due.[32]

VI

In the fall of 1945, Nabokov began teaching an intermediate course in Russian in addition to his elementary course. He arranged the timetable so that he could still dispose of the classes on three afternoons each week, by teaching for four straight hours from 12:40 to 4:30. Intermediate students who had had their last elementary class with a gaunt Mr. Nabokov in May were bewildered to encounter a far plumper Mr. Nabokov in September, but the mystery resolved itself when instead of his cigarettes Nabokov "shamelessly inhaled" molasses candy cubes in front of his class, five or six in the course of the hour.[33]

One night at the start of the academic year Nabokov dreamed of his brother Sergey. Although in waking life he supposed Sergey to be safe in the Austrian castle of his lover Hermann, in the dream he saw him in agony on a bunk in a concentration camp. The next day he received a letter from his other brother, Kirill, who had traced Vladimir through his *New Yorker* story. Sergey, Kirill told him, had died of a stomach ailment brought on by malnutrition in a concentration camp near Hamburg. He had been arrested in Berlin in 1943 because of his homosexuality, but five months later his cousin Onya's efforts had secured his release. Hating Berlin, he had managed to find a job in a half-Russian office in Prague. There he openly voiced his contempt for Hitler and Germany and was promptly informed upon and arrested as a British spy.[34] Vexed that Sergey loved not only a man but a German-speaking one, Nabokov had spoken rather harshly of his brother in recent years. Now he was appalled at Sergey's death, filled with admiration at his courageous outspokenness, and mortified that it was too late to make amends.

He also heard from Prague, from his sister Elena, still living there with her young son, and from his mother's faithful friend Evgenia Hofeld, who continued to look after Rostislav, the son of Nabokov's other sister, Olga. Once contact was reestablished with Europe, Nabokov began to send parcels and money to Prague and attempted to bring to the U.S. not only the papers he had had to leave in Paris and the money owing him from the European sales of his books, but also his favorite sister and her family and his nephew Rostislav.[35]

Financially he should have been in a much better position this year. He had a salary of $2,000 at Wellesley, another $1,200 from the M.C.Z., more from the *New Yorker*, and almost $2,500 from the sale of the film rights to *Laughter in the Dark*. Somehow even this much healthier income would soon prove insufficient.

Butterflies still took up most of his time. To Edmund Wilson he lamented, "the urge to write is something terrific but as I cannot do it in Russian I do not do it at all." A month later, nevertheless, at the end of October, he reported that he had written quite a chunk of his novel. By early December he was more than half-finished and still working furiously at it. Exhausted by the week's teaching and research, he would often spend all day Sunday in bed and do nothing but write.[36]

VII

In his application for the position in the Slavic department at Berkeley, Nabokov was backed by Professor George R. Noyes. Oleg Maslennikov, the head of the department, instead chose Nabokov's old friend Gleb Struve, who had many years' experience teaching Russian literature at the university level and had published a standard account of Soviet literature.[37] Stuck at Wellesley, Nabokov was bored simply teaching rudimentary grammar, but reluctant to introduce a course in Russian literature and take all the trouble of preparing it unless he had a permanent position there. By promising to write the lectures herself, Véra persuaded him to seek approval for the course.[38]

At the beginning of 1946 it was still official American policy to regard the Soviet Union very much as an ally. Though Nabokov had a coterie of enthusiastic supporters not only among his students but also in the staff of Wellesley's literature departments, some of the college's key administrators were keen to have Soviet fiction and drama taught. Books like Konstantin Simonov's novel about the siege of Stalingrad, although negligible as literature, were being loudly hailed. Would the anti-Soviet Nabokov be prepared to teach such works? Would he at least be prepared not to disparage our great ally?

Fresh from Washington and her position as head of the WAVES, Mildred McAfee Horton (she had recently married) certainly thought these were the kinds of questions it was her role as president of Wellesley College to put before Nabokov when he asked if he could teach a course in Russian literature. Two years earlier, when the New York Browning Society had invited him to address its members on the relationship between Russian culture and Russian courage in the war, Nabokov had looked over a pamphlet the society had sent him and replied caustically:

> I have read with interest the account of your German studies—I liked the bit about Goethe*—but the end has puzzled me greatly. I have lived in Germany for 17 years and am quite sure Gretchen has been thoroughly consoled by the secondhand, somewhat bloodstained, but still quite wearable frocks that her soldier friend sent her from the Polish ghettos. . . . It is useless looking at a hyena and hoping that one day domestication or a benevolent gene will turn the creature into a soft purring tortoiseshell cat. Gelding and Mendelism, alas, have their limits. Let us chloroform it—and forget. I am sorry of course for music and gemütlichkeit—but not very much, not more in fact than I am for the lacquered what-nots and cherry-trees in bloom (trashy perhaps but sweet) which gemütlich little Japan has contributed.
>
> When I lecture on Russian literature I do so from a writer's point of view, but upon reaching modern times cannot avoid stressing the fact that Communism and its totalitarian rule have prevented the development of authentic literature in Russia during these last twenty-five years.[39]

With the war safely over and his future at stake, Nabokov naturally did not reply in such forthright fashion when Mildred Horton questioned him at the end of January 1946, but she was not happy with his answers. Nor was he, and he wrote to her to make his position clearer:

> What I wish to stress now is that in teaching modern Russian literature it is quite possible to keep out politics. This I have done when teaching

---

* "In Goethe, it is true, were found what seemed to be fundamental flaws in character, flaws which seem also to be inherent in the type of German now in power."

the language (although pretexts for airing one's views on the Soviet regime were by no means lacking), and I see no reason why a similar policy could not be followed when teaching literature. . . .

At present both American and Russian literatures are in a very poor way, but I really do not see why a critical attitude towards obvious shortcomings should be considered biassed politically. Nor am I prejudiced if I say that Simonov's war stories are trashy. On the other hand, Zoshchenko, Olesha, Pasternak and two or three others, all of them living in Russia, have been producing some fine work.

I feel sure that you will understand my point of view. Governments come and go but the imprint of genius remains and it is this imperishable pattern that I should like my students (if any) to discern and admire. . . .

Believe me, I quite appreciate your position of not wanting anything in the way of anti-solidarity propaganda etc., and am convinced that there will be no difficulty in keeping the course within the limits I have traced.[40]

Mildred Horton was not quite so convinced. She approved the literature course for the coming year, but stressed that Nabokov's position was still a one-year appointment and that Wellesley would really prefer a course not in Nabokovian literary criticism but in "literature as a reflection of the culture of its time."[41]

Just before hearing that the course had been approved and he could teach the following year, Nabokov traveled to New York to participate with Ernest Simmons of Cornell in a CBS broadcast on Gogol's *Inspector General.** He stayed with Edmund Wilson, who introduced him to W. H. Auden. Nabokov, who often muffed names, began to compliment Auden on his verse, while actually referring to lines by Conrad Aiken. "I understand now," he wrote back to Wilson, "the wild look that passed in his eyes. Stupid, but has happened to me before."[42]

Once he knew he would be teaching Russian literature in the fall, Nabokov realized he had to rush to complete his novel—its working title had by now changed to *Solus Rex*—before preparing for the new course in the summer. Later he would write that he composed the greater part of the novel "in the winter and spring of 1945–1946, at a particularly cloudless and vigorous period of my life." This was not

---

* Perhaps this was the occasion on which he first heard himself on the radio and was shocked to discover how markedly his English pronunciation was affected by his *grasseyement*, the French rolling uvular *r*, that had also been current in the Russian spoken in educated St. Petersburg before the Revolution. To overcome the quirk, he resolved to disguise the dangerous letter by a little neutral vibration, so that "I am Russian" would not sound as if he came from Roussillon but would emerge as a slightly lisping "I am Wussian" (Bernard Pivot interview with Nabokov, May 1975).

so much autobiographical fact as an attempt to deter any simplistic equations between the oppressive world of the novel and his own mood or circumstances as he wrote. Actually, it *was* a depressing time. Since Wellesley and the M.C.Z. still took up most of his daylight hours, he had to write in the late evenings after two jobs that by themselves would have been a difficult load for most. He had been standing before Wellesley classes in one capacity or another for six years now, and was committed to preparing a demanding new course that he might be able to teach for only one year. "I am in very low spirits," he wrote Wilson, "because there does not seem to be any prospect of a permanent appointment in Wellesley and I am sick of being a badly underpaid instructor. . . . My chief anxiety is the complete lack of security." By May he was also feeling unhappy that despite his first-reading agreement with the *New Yorker* he had had nothing to offer them for over a year, although he was already planning in his mind an autobiography that he had wanted to write for a long time and that he might be able to sell to the *New Yorker* chapter by chapter.[43]

On a warm rainy night in the third week of May, Nabokov completed his novel. By the middle of June, morally exhausted, as flat as an empty balloon, he had revised the book, still entitled *Solus Rex*.[44] By the time it was printed, he would have altered the title to *Bend Sinister*.

CHAPTER 5

Bend Sinister

I

IN THE YEARS between Hitler's rise to power and his defeat, Nabokov wrote more works with a political cast than at any other time of his life, partly in reaction to Hitler, partly in reaction to the communism that so many saw as the only bulwark against fascism. *Bend Sinister* is the most political of all.[1] Set in a Central European country whose inhabitants speak German at one moment, Russian the next, and a moment later an invented blend of the two, the novel subjects its hero to the newly installed dictatorship of Paduk, leader of the Party of the Average Man, whose utterances and acts draw, as Nabokov notes, on "bits of Lenin's speeches, and a chunk of the Soviet constitution, and gobs of Nazist pseudo-efficiency."[2]

By his early forties, philosopher Adam Krug has already become world-famous, the only international celebrity his small country has produced. *Bend Sinister* opens just as Krug's wife dies after an operation. Paduk—who happens to have been Krug's classmate at school—wants Krug to endorse his regime and thereby confer on it international respectability. Even though it may mean the closing of the capital's ancient university, Krug refuses. Confident that his renown will protect him from harm, he rejects advice to emigrate. As his friends are seized one after another, he remains oblivious that their arrests are an attempt to frighten *him*. Still dazed by grief for his wife, he feels he can no longer write or think—and indeed only his mental disarray can explain his failure to perceive his real vulnerability. For when his eight-year-old son, David, is carted off by two of Paduk's pimply young thugs, Krug agrees at once that the moment his son has been safely returned he will do whatever the government wishes.

Even before Krug declares himself ready to cooperate, alas, a series of bureaucratic bungles leads to David's murder. Paduk executes those responsible and offers Krug a trade-off: a score of his liberal friends will be freed if only he will submit. Instead, Krug goes mad and charges at Paduk as if they were back in their schoolyard thirty years before. Two bullets from Paduk's henchmen put an end to Krug's charge and his life.

The plot is as straightforward as it is poignant. The intensity of Krug's love for Olga blinds him to the risks gathering around his son and at the same time prepares us for his capitulation and his final anguish. Krug's world of individual thought and feeling is denied by Paduk and his party, for whom only the group matters, not the individual. But their actions belie their misplaced faith: desperate to obtain the endorsement of their country's outstanding individual, they apply pressure on him through his affection for other individuals progressively closer and closer to his heart. But just when Paduk and his followers have victory in their grasp, their inattention to individuality ruins their strategy: they preserve Arvid Krug, son of Prof. Martin Krug, whose unrelatedness to philosopher Prof. Adam Krug they never quite understand, and destroy Adam Krug's son David, the one lever that could ever have moved him.

An outline of the novel's plot suggests that Nabokov directs *Bend Sinister* by the shortest route to its resounding affirmation of the priority of the individual over the group. Nothing could be further from the truth. Like a porcupine with quills at the ready, the novel sits bristling with devices that make its story difficult to approach. The forces that oppress Krug do not loom over him, implacable and inescapable, but seem lightweight shams, tinsel scarecrows, papier-mâché parrots, almost closer to farce than nightmare ("a little along the lines of *Invitation to a Beheading*," as Nabokov wrote to his sister, "but for bass voice, as it were").[3] And the novel ends not simply with Krug imprisoned and breaking apart with grief for his wife and his son, but with tragedy dispelled when Nabokov intrudes and renders Krug insane by allowing him to see that he is merely Nabokov's fictional character. At the moment of Krug's death, the prison yard dissolves to disclose Nabokov at his desk writing the novel's last words.

Nabokov has always been known as a master of self-conscious fiction, but elsewhere the self-consciousness of his books reflects the mind of a Hermann or a Fyodor, a Humbert or a Van Veen. In *Bend Sinister*, per contra, he stocks the novel with a madly crowded and multifarious arsenal of devices that seem calculated to explode in the reader's face: firecrackers, bat bombs, slings and flaming arrows, petards, dumdums. A scene introduces itself: " 'We met yesterday,' said the room. 'I am the spare bedroom in the Maximovs' *dacha* [country house, cottage]. These are windmills on the wallpaper.' 'That's right,' replied Krug." Narrative clichés, highlighted by italics, bestrew the story. A French professor slips into a parody of gallicized English—"eez eet zee verity"—slips out of it "when the author gets bored by the process—or forgets" and resumes "when the author remembers again." A person's movements are set down as instructions to the actor playing the part. Characters speak in German, Russian, the language of the book's invented country, in bursts of mock-Elizabethan, mock-pidgin, mock-erudition, mock-footnotese. The story's self-promptings blend with a character's: "Describe the bedroom. Allude to Ember's bright brown eyes. . . . Say something. Ask about David." A minor official seems aware he is only a character in a Russian novel when he plaintively rejects a charge Krug levels at him: "I did not delegate anybody. You are in the presence of an underpaid *chinovnik*. As a matter of fact, I deplore everything that has happened in Russian literature."

A few at a time, the self-conscious devices of *Bend Sinister* look colorful and inventive, but the barrage continues until it leaves us shellshocked. And there is more. The novel dips again and again into scholarly arcana: a pastiche of obscure speculations from the scholia of the variorum *Hamlet*; an elevator ride through geological strata; a busily bubbling potpourri of Aurignacian Age art, Victorian telepathy, spiral nebulae, Raphael's icthyological errors in rendering Galilean fish, the Blandinian MSS of Horace; jokes in taxonomic Latin or relineated Melville. Why does Nabokov so often interrupt the political urgency of his straightforward story?

II

To answer that we must remember the circumstances in which he conceived the novel. In 1940, as German tanks neared Paris, he had felt panic-stricken at what might befall Véra and Dmitri, and it was this concern that provided the first impetus for *Bend Sinister*'s plot. Installed in America, Nabokov looked back across the Atlantic at Hitler and Stalin happily straddling the Europe they had agreed to divide between them, and early in 1941 pointed out with contempt to Wellesley audiences the fundamental similarity of these two tyrants allowing no belief but the worship of party and state. By mid-1941, Hitler's invasion of his eastern neighbor had shunted the Soviet Union into the Allied camp, and Nabokov realized with distaste that the new homeland whose freedom he reveled in would soon be called on to pledge its support for the despotic regime that still ruled over Russia.

In the last months of 1941, Nabokov witnessed the mounting enthusiasm for war—which among Wellesley's well-to-do students reminded him of the war fever so easily caught by fashionable Petrograd ladies in 1914. He noted too the swelling admiration for the Soviet Union as a redoubtable ally. His ideas for a new novel began to take shape. He detested the mass mobilization of minds that war required, the air of crisis everyone was supposed to breathe. No, he instinctively responded, it is in the very nature of dictatorship, as it deprives its citizens of their freedom of choice, to inculcate in them a sense of crisis and unite them against some designated opponents: the Jews, the bourgeoisie, the Communists, the kulaks, the Fascists. I will simultaneously attack dictatorship *and* the notion that all good citizens should rally around to attack it—which itself would be just another form of social dictate.

Nabokov's American experiences had shaped his thinking in another way. As a reviewer and a lecturer at Stanford and Wellesley, he had exposed himself during 1941 not only to the Soviet literature of social command but also to the American best-sellers designed to satisfy the decrees of the mass market. In terms of literary quality, he recognized, there was little to choose between the two.[4] But if America seemed borne along more than any other country by the currents of mass culture, she also allowed her citizens to cast off on their own and row wherever they chose if the prevailing drift did not suit. At Wellesley and Stanford and in his research at the American Museum of Natural History and the M.C.Z., Nabokov had discovered this other America: libraries with open access, minds with independent outlooks, and opportunities for research following no directive but one's own curiosity. *Bend Sinister* defends the freedom of the individual mind not only against dictatorships abroad but against the coercion of mass culture or mass mobilization at home or anywhere else. As he had Véra write to an army officer who was thinking of having the novel translated into German in 1948, "one of the main subjects of *Bend Sinister* is a rather vehement incrimination of a dictatorship—any dictatorship, and though the dictatorship actually represented in the book is imaginary, it deliberately displays features peculiar a) to nazism b) to communism c) to any dictatorial trends in an otherwise non-dictatorial order."[5]

Writing at a time of all-out war, Nabokov seems by his indictment of tyranny to have joined the war effort. And in a sense he has. But although politics looks as inescapable in Padukgrad after the revolution as in America at war, *Bend Sinister* takes as its hero a philosopher who refuses to be interested in his country's upheaval. When Nabokov himself hastens to denounce the pernicious stupidity of all totalitarian systems, does his action not imply a reproach of his hero's refusal to act?

No. Nabokov may appear to have written a political novel, but in fact he admits politics into *Bend Sinister* only to argue that politics should be kept out of people's lives. Even in the midst of war he deliberately resists the urgency around him. Immediate considerations required America to ally itself with the Soviet Union and overlook its polity. Instead, Nabokov links Stalin's tyranny with Hitler's: in a work of art that looks beyond the present moment, he will not compromise permanent political values for even the most pressing of immediate needs.

But *Bend Sinister* is not really a political novel at all; it is a philosophical one that aims to set out a certain philosophy of consciousness—which, to be sure, has political consequences. Nabokov starts from the position that individual consciousness matters more than anything else: as he writes in the novel, it is "the only real thing in the world and the greatest mystery of all." Since each of us is enclosed forever in a consciousness to which no one else can ever have access, democracy is "the natural condition of every man ever since the human mind became conscious not only of the world but of itself."[6] Accordingly, Nabokov proclaims allegiance to democracy as a way of life that defends the individual from the pressure of politics. The critical or curious or dreamlike mind can and should wander where it will. As his style bears witness, Nabokov insists throughout *Bend Sinister* on the capacity of consciousness to dart about, to question any convention or assumption, to see things from some other side. And that has its own political value: as one character in the novel declares, "curiosity . . . is insubordination in its purest form." Other than that, Nabokov is not concerned with "politics, or party-regulation, or things like that," with how or why a regime should establish or safeguard individual freedoms, or with the "more or less transient problems of mankind," but only with the fundamental faith that arises from his notion of consciousness.[7]

III

For Nabokov the claim of the primacy of the crowd or the general good over the individual is absurd: the crowd after all is composed of individuals who may have as many different notions of their interest as there are members of the crowd. He makes the meager ideology of Paduk's party a parodic reductio ad absurdum of the notion that individual differences should be limited for the sake of an abstract collective good. A thinker named Skotoma has laid the philosophical foundations of the Party of the Average Man in his theory of Ekwilism, which states that the cause of all our woes is the unequal distribution of the fixed amount of human consciousness the world contains: "Human beings, he said, were so many vessels containing unequal portions of this essentially uniform consciousness. It was, however, quite possible, he maintained, to regulate the capacity of the human vessels. . . . either by grading the contents or by eliminating the fancy vessels and adopting a standard size."

A second source of Paduk's ideas is the padograph that Paduk Senior invents while his son is still a teenager: a sort of typewriter that by means of complicated levers can reproduce an illusion of any given person's handwriting. Though the invention enjoys no more than a passing vogue, Paduk remains loyal to it "as an Ekwilist symbol, as a proof of the fact that a mechanical device can reproduce personality." The fact that it is a cumbersome gimmick producing a superficial imitation of the real with no motive except to impress the easily impressed makes it also a perfect image of Paduk's world.

The third and final source of Paduk's ideas is a comic strip

depicting the home life of Mr. and Mrs. Etermon (Everyman). With conventional humour and sympathy bordering upon the obscene, Mr. Etermon and the little woman were followed from parlour to kitchen and from garden to garret through all the mentionable stages of their existence, which, despite the presence of cozy armchairs and all sorts of electric thingumbobs and one thing-in-itself (a car), did not differ essentially from the life of a Neanderthal couple.

This couple becomes the ideal of the Party of the Average Man. But though it is only fitting that Paduk should find his ideal in a syndicated comic strip, Nabokov points out that the "average" simply does not exist. Even Paduk himself cannot quite hide the fact that although he worships Mr. and Mrs. Etermon, he is himself homosexual and therefore hardly representative of the norm.

Nabokov presents Paduk's notion that we should trim our minds and thoughts to the minds of others as the grossest travesty of humanity. Every value Paduk and his party profess can only ape genuine values, everything they create smacks of the padograph: pure *poshlost'*, a mechanical imitation of thought and feeling that turns into farce, grotesquerie, a gimcrack illusion of impressive efficiency. A lady in a tailor-made suit and a gentleman with a glossy red tulip in the buttonhole of his cutaway come to arrest Krug's friend, the poet and translator Ember:

"Oh, I know what you are going to say"—purred Hustav; "this element of gracious living strikes you as queer, does it not? One is accustomed to consider such things in terms of sordid brutality and gloom, rifle butts, rough soldiers, muddy boots—*und so weiter*. But headquarters knew that Mr. Ember was an artist, a poet, a sensitive soul, and it was thought that something a little dainty and uncommon in the way of arrests, an atmosphere of high life, flowers, the perfume of feminine beauty, might sweeten the ordeal."

Where someone like Orwell, who sees the world in purely political terms, would try to herd us through horror to hysteria, Nabokov refuses to take Paduk and his underlings seriously. Denying the irreplaceable uniqueness of individual consciousness, "the only real thing in the world," Paduk and his party are advocates of the unreal. Nabokov treats them as such, reducing them to preposterous mechanisms around which he arrays all the self-conscious devices he can find.

IV

For Nabokov, consciousness is something we each develop to the degree we feel and think for ourselves. Insofar as we merely accept the emotional and intellectual commonplaces of others, we remain dead. In *Bend Sinister* he sets up a fundamental opposition between Paduk and his followers, champions of an illusory "average" mentality, and Krug, the embodiment of mind at its best.

In 1940, in his first month in America, Nabokov contrasted two notions of human greatness: "Take from da Vinci his freedom, his Italy, his sight, and he will still remain great; take from Hitler his cannon, and he will be nothing more than the author of a rabid brochure, a mere nonentity."[8] Like Hitler, Paduk in power seems superficially impressive. As we first approach the Ruler, we pass through a room drowned by the amplified sound of the heartbeat his doctors monitor. But despite the grotesque amplification, Paduk proves to be heartless, insignificant, easily dismissed: "It is not the first time that an obscure and unlovable but marvellously obstinate man has gnawed his way into the bowels of a country."

Everyone who serves Paduk proves as strangely lifeless as he, though each at the same time refutes Ekwilism by being dead in his or her own way. The three sisters, Mariette, Linda Bachofen, and Doktor Amalia von Wytwyl, embody three different versions of love—one pseudoseductive, another pseudogenteel, the third pseudocompassionate—but their feelings are formulaic, shallow, and ultimately vicious. Krug's love for Olga and for David, by contrast, fills him with wonder at the magnitude of his feeling, which seems not snug and comforting but unprecedented, shocking, unimaginably vast. The main theme of *Bend Sinister*, Nabokov declares, is "the beating of Krug's loving heart, the torture an intense tenderness is subjected to."[9]

In thought, too, consciousness lives up to its name only when it does more than passively accept what is already there. In construing consciousness as something to be averaged out, Paduk merely jumbles together a comic strip, a shoddy invention, and a crackpot theory. Against him Nabokov sets Krug, the foremost philosopher of his day, whose kaleidoscopic mind and passion to extend the limits of truth he lets us see from the inside. Against the Etermons, Mr. and Mrs. Average, he sets the weightiest argument civilization has yet produced for the irreplaceable value of human individuality: William Shakespeare. And against the padograph's claim to replicate anyone's signature by means of a few levers, Nabokov sets Ember's translation of *Hamlet*—a play he has called "probably the greatest miracle in all literature"[10]—a meticulous and arduous attempt to reproduce every nuance of the text and to treat the individuality of another as an inviolable mystery to be respected down to the last quirk.

Nothing could be less like Ember's scrupulous effort than the version of *Hamlet* that Paduk's government allows to be staged. In this travesty, as Ember laments, the blooming young knight Fortinbras, a "fine Nordic youth," "beautiful and sound to the core," becomes the ideological center of the play, displacing the unwholesomely contemplative Hamlet:

> As with all decadent democracies, everybody in the Denmark of the play suffers from a plethora of words. If the state is to be saved, if the nation desires to be worthy of a new robust government, then everything must be changed; popular commonsense must spit out the caviar of moonshine and poetry, and the simple words, *verbum sine ornatu*, intelligible to man and beast alike, and accompanied by fit action, must be restored to power.

Far from accepting that everything ought to be directed toward a common purpose, Nabokov champions the right of minds to follow their own curiosity wherever it may lead. The passage above, closely adapted from the real critical opinions of a German critic, Franz Horn, writing on *Hamlet* in 1823, and sounding not unlike Soviet expropriations of the play in the 1920s and 1930s, forms part of Krug and Ember's frequently obscure discussion of the play. The scholarly minutiae that abound in the novel swarm denser than ever here, as Nabokov lets Krug and Ember parody the whole history of perverse misinterpretations of the play.

Instead of concurring that at a time of crisis everything ought to be reduced to its simplest and made explicable "to man and beast alike," Nabokov makes *Bend Sinister* more difficult, less accessible to the common reader, than any of his other books. As he was composing the novel, he wrote in a Wellesley magazine that the best-seller was "perhaps the worst form of propaganda, the propaganda of current ideas, easily digested brain food, fashionable worries."[11] He objected to any form of leveling or simplification: "Brains must work the hard way or lose their calling and rank."[12] There are no shortcuts to knowledge, there is always more to be known about any subject at all, as he reminds us by confronting us with lumps of arcane information, weirdly looping sentences, snatches of a foreign tongue. The alternative advanced by the Party of the Average Man requires that things should be kept simple for Mr. and Mrs. Etermon, brought down to the lowest common denominator—a policy that would denude the world of its splendid particulars and deny the mind the adventure of apprehending them all.

Skotoma and his intellectual heirs accept consciousness as something to be measured out in small doses. Krug, on the other hand, considers consciousness a marvel, a mystery, a challenge. Incessantly curious about his world, determined not to take the ideas of others for granted, he finds himself dazed by the limitlessness of his grief for Olga, by the paradox of infinite feelings within a finite life. Dim intimations of something beyond lead him to contemplate a "preliminary report on infinite consciousness," but on the very night he conceives of his new project, he and his son are arrested.

V

Paduk's travesty of the genuine values of consciousness reaches its foul climax in David's murder. Taken by mistake to an Institute for Abnormal Children, David is assumed by its director to be

one of the so-called "Orphans," now and then used to serve as a "release-instrument" for the benefit of the most interesting inmates with a so-called "criminal" record (rape, murder, wanton destruction of State property, etc.). The theory . . . was that if once a week the really difficult patients could enjoy the possibility of venting in full their repressed yearnings (the exaggerated urge to hurt, destroy, etc.) upon some little human creature of no value to the community, then, by degrees, the evil in them would be, so to say, "effundated," and eventually they would become good citizens. . . . [David] was left alone and allowed to roam all over the enclosure. . . . After a while the patients or "inmates" (eight all told) were let into the enclosure. At first, they kept a distance, eyeing the "little person." It was interesting to observe how the "gang" spirit gradually asserted itself. They had been rough lawless unorganized individuals, but now something was binding them, the community spirit (positive) was conquering the individual whims (negative).

David is killed in the process of this grotesque therapy, and the proceedings are filmed for the purposes of both research and entertainment. The movie's would-be-jocular captions reveal an insane confusion of values, a horrendous appeal to the lowest level of any conceivable audience. Krug must sit and watch, powerless to assist, before being shown the patched-up body of his murdered child. Nabokov manages to have the death scene overturn all he rates highest in the human spirit: curiosity, in this obscene "experiment" that is no more than a witless travesty of science; imagination, in a film that embodies the inverse of art in a sniggering appeal to everything trite and mean; and tenderness, in this vile assertion of an abstract communal good over the fate of a helpless child.

On the plane of Krug's life, David's death seems a meaningless bungle, the half-cocked consequence of a dictator's decree. But rather than have Krug survive to face the senseless agony of his son's death, Nabokov offers him the refuge of insanity. He permits Krug to realize in a dream that he and all his world are no more than the imaginings of someone on another plane of existence whom he can just detect through a rent in his world. Just before he dies, Krug understands that beyond his whole world looms a different kind of dictator who makes no mistake—"if you like," as Nabokov explained to a publisher, "a kind of symbol of the Divine power"[13]—and who as we can see from our special vantage point subjects Krug to all his misfortunes precisely to affirm Krug's individuality, his tenderness, the poignant vulnerability of mortal life.

At various points throughout the novel there have been intimations in Krug's world of "someone in the know," a "secret spectator," an "anthropomorphic deity." At the moment of Krug's death, Nabokov withdraws from his invented world to disclose himself as its inventor, sitting among a chaos of written and rewritten pages, looking out through the night at a special spatulate puddle on the ground outside, "the one Krug had somehow perceived through the layer of his own life." At the beginning of the novel a person still unnamed—in one sense Nabokov, in another Krug—looks out at this kidney-shaped puddle from the hospital where Olga has died of a kidney operation. Throughout the book, liquid in this shape—a lake, an ink stain—recurs again and again, especially in association with blots and spillages on writing paper. A blot in the shape of "a fancy footprint or the spatulate outline of a puddle" on the statement Dr. Alexander signs, and "a kidney-shaped white puddle" on the desk when Paduk knocks over a tumbler of milk as he takes back the text of a prepared speech Krug refuses to deliver, mark the disastrous uses to which Paduk and his cronies put the written word, and contrast with Nabokov's own puddle in the asphalt and the unknown contours—"unknown, except for a vague, shoe-shaped outline"—of the book Krug wants to write on infinite consciousness, the book that testifies to his intuition that he is somehow linked with an "unfathomable mode of being" beyond.

VI

In all his more political fiction, Nabokov stresses not only the freedom of consciousness of characters subjected to pressures to conform, but also the free play of a directing consciousness over an entire politicized world. In "The Leonardo," his first story written in reaction to the rise of nazism, Nabokov lets an apartment block dwindle to the size of a dollhouse or conjures up trees and clouds from nothing. In *Bend Sinister*, his last "political" work, he shows himself dreaming the novel's whole world. Even when he focuses on an oppressive society's attempt to crush the individual, he cannot allow the implication that social forces are what matter most. No, his manner implies: consciousness calls up and controls these worlds, as some form of consciousness seems to have called life itself into being.

Bend Sinister argues for a political system that will allow individuals to get on with their own lives uninterrupted by the state. Of course politics does not always oblige. Hitler's ambitions shifted the course of twentieth-century history—and shifted Nabokov himself from Europe and Russian to America and English. But whether or not politics interferes in our lives, we mortals will sooner or later find ourselves subjected to the inevitable interruption of death.

At one stage *Bend Sinister* was to have been called *The Person from Porlock*, in honor of the visitor who interrupted Coleridge in the midst of his dream of "Kubla Khan" ("the most famous of unfinished poems," as Nabokov called it).[14] A motif of interruptions defines the contrast Krug begins to apprehend between his state and some uninterrupted mode of being beyond. As Nabokov notes in his 1964 introduction to *Bend Sinister*, Krug is haunted by another famous literary interruption: in Stéphane Mallarmé's "L'Après-midi d'un faune" "the faun accuses the nymph of disengaging herself from his embrace *sans pitié du sanglot dont j'étais encore ivre* ('spurning the spasm with which I was still drunk')." The line recurs—itself in fractured, interrupted form—throughout the novel until the climax of the interruption theme on the night Krug and David are arrested.

Krug falls asleep after an early supper, and dreams an eerie dream that recalls the first night of the novel. Awakening, he feels that for the first time since Olga's death he can write again. Determined that nothing, not even the son he dotes on, will waylay his inspiration, he gives David a perfunctory goodnight that itself interrupts the bedtime story Krug has been spinning out for the boy over the past few nights. Soon after he sits down to write, the pretty young nursemaid, Mariette, begins to make audaciously direct sexual advances. Krug tries to resume his work, but the urge to write has suddenly drained away. When Mariette returns, she manages to entice Krug to a first overt response to her invitation, only to yawn and break off: "I guess I'll go back now." After this insult, she appears almost about to let Krug possess her when a deafening din breaks out at the door: even this pathetically inadequate solace for his solitude is not allowed to run its course, for Mac and Linda have come to arrest Krug, while two young goons seize David. Just as Krug brims with sap like Mallarmé's faun, the fatal interruption comes.

Bend Sinister begins with Olga's death, the first grim interruption in Krug's life, which also blocks his career by rendering him unable to think or write. Paduk's forces too try to interrupt him, but Krug will not let them affect him. But just when he recovers his philosophical gift and can begin his "report on infinite consciousness," he is interrupted by David's clamor for nighttime attention, by Mariette and the evanescent impulses of physical desire, and then by the final, inescapable interruption of the state—which will lead directly to one last "ruthless interruption," David's death.

The implicit contrast between the interruptions of mortal life and the possibility of an infinite consciousness of uninterrupted time somehow beyond human life is central to the novel. Krug's name in Russian means "circle." All his life he has tried to break free of the closed circle of human reasoning. Through the unfathomable magnitude of his feeling for Olga and David, through his passionate attempt to probe his world, to stretch his mind, to accept on trust none of mankind's ready-made answers, Krug comes far closer than most to the limits of the mortal mind, but still remains within the "circular dungeon" of thought. Olga's death adds a new urgency to his quest to understand infinite consciousness. The key image associated with her death and with Nabokov's watching from beyond, the image of the puddle stretching in the middle like a circular cell dividing in two, seems to mark the progress from Krug's circle, $\bigcirc$, through the kidney shape, $\bigcirc\!\bigcirc$, to the lemniscate symbol of infinity, ∞. After David dies, Nabokov allows Krug the relief of insanity, the impossible, maddening insight that he and his whole world have been created by a consciousness on a level of existence beyond his own.

Although Nabokov can pose as the anthropomorphic deity behind Krug's world, even he cannot specify what such an infinite consciousness may be. On his own level, after all, he is a mere mortal himself—as he notes with a bathetic bump in the last line of the novel when a moth flies against the wire netting of his window to interrupt him, too, at his work: "Twang. A good night for mothing." And to know too much about something beyond ourselves might drive us insane as it does Krug. But he allows his role as the author of Krug's being—his tender solicitude for his character, his kinship with a spirit pressing so relentlessly at the limits of consciousness—to prefigure in the only way he can our own possible relationship to a creating consciousness behind *our* world.

Even in his most political novel, conceived in the heat of war, Nabokov turns from the problems of the moment to the might and mystery of consciousness: the power of Krug's mind and heart and soul as he resists the political pressure brought to bear on him; the novel's own resistance, in the name of consciousness, against the group thought that levels individual human minds; and Nabokov's conviction that something beyond consciousness may somehow offer a way out of a world where the self cannot escape the most brutal interruptions.

VII

Bend Sinister is an ambitious work, sensitive to the demands of the moment and at the same time determined to defy them and remain true to its timeless themes. But the novel seems to some readers, myself included, less successful than much of Nabokov's other mature fiction. The plot has its poignancy, but it remains too meager in proportion to the self-consciousness and scholarly obscurity that surround it. Krug's intense concentration of feeling on his wife and son may strike us as less wholly endearing and more cloying and unhealthily exclusive than Nabokov appears to have intended. And the boyhood relationship between Paduk and Krug seems both gratuitous and unconvincing. The schoolboy Krug who could sit on Paduk's face not just once but a thousand times is not merely a bully and a boor but a bore with no conceivable relationship to the Krug of later years.

Announcing to Edmund Wilson that he had just completed the novel, Nabokov remarked, "I do not know whether the thing is likeable but at any rate it is honest, i.e., it comes as close as humanly possible to the image I had of it all along."[15] His doubts were justified. While we can enumerate reasons for the novel's jarring self-consciousness, while we may enjoy the inventiveness and challenge of particular passages, *Bend Sinister* still does not reward us enough as we read to justify all its difficulties and disruptions. In other works Nabokov chooses self-conscious effects that define and arise out of characters and situations, and he conceals most difficulties beneath the obvious charms of his story so that we will discover them only after he has succeeded in luring us back for a closer look at his invented world. But in writing *Bend Sinister* he seems to have recoiled so strongly from the appeals to the crowd made by Hitler or Stalin or even America in pursuit of victory or profit that he seems ready to welcome the risk of a novel that will appeal to very few. The novel's discords seem not so much a "crazy-mirror of terror and art"[16] as a programmatic refusal to satisfy the ordinary interests of readers, lest the book resemble in any way the rhetoric or the rasp of some Paduk or padograph salesman booming through the radios of a million homes.

CHAPTER 6

Teaching Literature at Last: Cambridge and Wellesley, 1946–1948

I

THE FORCED MARCH to complete *Bend Sinister* had brought Nabokov to the brink of a nervous breakdown: "With the feeling I had 1. some serious heart trouble, 2. ulcers, 3. cancer in the gullet and 4. stones everywhere, I had myself thoroughly examined at a good hospital. The doctor (a Prof. Siegfried Tannhäuser) found that I was constitutionally in fine shape but was suffering from acute nervous exhaustion due to the entomology-Wellesley-novel combination, and suggested my taking a two months' vacation."[1] Knowing the advice was sound, Nabokov set off with his family on June 27 on the five-hour train and bus journey to Don-Gerry Lodge on Newfound Lake in central New Hampshire. He chose the place because the New Hampshire stretch of the Merrimack River valley was recorded as one of the breeding grounds of the sole eastern United States representative of the *Lycaeides* genus, the widespread but rare and very isolated *Lycaeides melissa samuelis* Nabokov, which in a 1944 article he had distinguished and named on the basis of museum specimens without ever catching the insect in the wild.[2] He had no luck lepping in New Hampshire: thirty-nine commonplace species but not the one he had come for.[3]

In fact, he had no luck at all in New Hampshire. Everything about the holiday was disappointing:* a highway right beside the lodge; bungalows all cramped in one part of the grounds, and full of townies "out on the country"; shopkeepers; signs stipulating only "gentile clientèle." In a restaurant where Nabokov noticed that phrase on the menu he called the waitress over and asked her if she would serve a couple who tethered their donkey outside and came in with their baby boy. "What are you talking about?" she asked. "I'm talking about Christ!" he replied, and led his family out.[4]

---

* Except for sighting but not catching the extremely rare white W hairstreak butterfly, which most collectors in the Northeast would be lucky to see even in a lifetime's collecting.

Since they had paid in advance, they had no choice but to remain until August 18, when once again they spent the final weeks of the summer vacation in Wellesley. This time they boarded for a month with a prim schoolteacher at 6 Cross Street as Nabokov began to prepare for his lectures. He reread Tolstoy and Dostoevsky, and announced to Wilson: "The latter is a third rate writer and his fame is incomprehensible."[5]

He had sent the manuscript of his novel off to Allen Tate, who had recently become an editor for the firm of Henry Holt. Tate thought the book magnificent, "the only first rate piece of literature that I have had the privilege of reading as an editor." Several months later, when Nabokov objected to the blurb Holt's publicists had drafted for the novel, Tate wrote another blurb himself. Nabokov thought it the best he had ever had:

> Bend Sinister is a dramatic fantasy of modern man menaced by the rising tyrant State which, under the familiar slogans of Equality and Community, extinguishes the free intelligence and all normal human relations. From the opening scene in a hospital, where the hero Adam Krug's wife is dying, to the last scene where the author, like Prospero at the end of The Tempest, takes command of the creatures of his imagination, there is a drama of mounting, of almost intolerable intensity. The "color" of this novel has the weird brilliance of a dream seen under Klieg lights. . . .
>
> The mastery of English prose exhibited here has not been surpassed by any writer of our generation who was born to English.[6]

II

When classes resumed at Wellesley in late September, Nabokov had only five students for elementary Russian and eight for intermediate Russian, but fifty-six for his new Russian Literature in Translation course, although this option was restricted to juniors and seniors. He still taught his classes in three compact blocks, Monday, Wednesday, and Friday from 12:40 until 5:30 without a break. For this year he received $3,250, slightly more than an assistant professor's salary.[7]

Nabokov was not used to teaching in the large lecture rooms in Pendleton Hall. The first time the class met, the students waited eagerly for ten minutes for Mr. Nabokov. Almost despairing, they noticed his face peering through the window, frantically beseeching: "Where does one get in this place?" Both the size of his new class and the nature of his material made him adopt a teaching style much more formal than in his language classes. He read the entire lecture from a prepared text, evolving a subtle up and down movement of the eyes from lectern to listeners. One student who had also taken both his language courses reports that "his presentation—facial expression, gestures, asides, chortles, and vocal acrobatics—and his delightful material combined to convince me that he was speaking ad lib from a beautifully organized memory and a few lecture notes." When he came down with influenza during the term, Véra Nabokov replaced him at the podium for classes on Pushkin's "Queen of Spades." The student realized her mistake: "The words were clearly his, but the melody was quite different; Mrs. N. read beautifully, her delivery was excellent, and her voice and accent were charming, but she *read* what he had written, while he *said* it; and his writing was like his talking."[8]

The lectures were written on a "prepare-as-you-go" basis. Nabokov dictated some to Véra from lecture notes he had prepared in 1940–1941. On other topics Véra not only did drudge work—chasing down references, preparing an outline of dates and other background material—but even composed lectures for him to use. Perfectly attuned to his manner of thought and expression, she provided him an ideal base. Her typescript of a draft lecture on romanticism begins "Volodia, would it be too involved to say . . . that, while during the Middle Ages every facet of human nature was dulled and all the contents of it kept frozen like a Bird's Eye peach, it took roughly speaking four centuries to defreeze it." Always certain that her own talents simply did not count beside her husband's, this remarkable woman characteristically recalled with delight thirty years later that Nabokov kept altering and altering her text until not one word of her original lectures remained.[9]

Nabokov believed that the notion of a crowd of students trying to take down in longhand a lecturer's monologue, which he had written in longhand himself, was idiotic and medieval. Not that he thought the students should not commit what he said to paper: he exhorted them from the start to "take notes, notes and notes." He simply wondered why he had to be there to read the material out to them. Why not, he would later joke, have his voice taped and broadcast over the college radio or recorded so students could replay it at will?[10]

From the first he tried to rouse his Wellesley literature students to a delight in discovery. His introductory exhortations, inspired by his work at the M.C.Z., revealed much more of the man—and of the author of *Bend Sinister*—than his audience could have realized:

> Whichever subject you have chosen, you must realize that knowledge in
> it is limitless. Every subject brims with mysteries and thrills, and no two

students of the same subject discover a like amount of delight, accumulate exactly the same amount of knowledge. . . . Suppose a schoolchild picks up the study of butterflies for a hobby. He will learn a few things about the general structure. He will be able to tell you that a butterfly has always six feet and never eight or twenty. That there are innumerable patterns of butterfly wings and that according to those patterns they are divided into generic and specific groups. This is a fair amount of knowledge for a schoolchild. But of course he has not even come near the fascinating and incredible intricacies invented by nature in the fashioning of this group of insects alone. He will not even suspect the fascinating variety of inner organs, the varying shapes of which allow the scientist not only unerringly to classify them, often giving the lie to the seeming resemblance of wing patterns, but also to trace the origin and development and relationship of the genera and species, the history of the migration of their ancestors, the varying influence of the environments on the developments of the species and forms, etc. etc. etc.; and he will not [have] even touched upon other mysterious fields, limitless in themselves, of for instance mimicry, or symbiosis. This example applies to every field of knowledge, and it is very apt in the case of literature.

When he asked his students at the beginning of the course to consider the value of a university education, Nabokov disclosed his passion for exploring the world's endless detail, a passion that would always be central to his practice as a writer:

The more things we know the better equipped we are to understand any one thing and it is a burning pity that our lives are not long enough and not sufficiently free of annoying obstacles, to study all things with the same care and depth as the one we now devote to some favorite subject or period. And yet there is a semblance of consolation within this dismal state of affairs: in the same way as the whole universe may be completely reciprocated in the structure of an atom, . . . an intelligent and assiduous student [may] find a small replica of all knowledge in a subject he has chosen for his special research. . . . and if, upon choosing your subject, you try diligently to find out about it, if you *allow* yourself to be lured into the shaded lanes that lead from the main road you have chosen to the lovely and little known nooks of special knowledge, if you lovingly finger the links of the many chains that connect your subject to the past and the future and if by luck you hit upon some scrap of knowledge referring to your subject that has not yet become common knowledge, then will you know the true felicity of the great adventure of learning, and your years in this college will become a valuable start on a road of inestimable happiness.

Those lines provide one of the best possible insights into the generosity of Nabokov's art and its power to inspire. His novels are designed to invite their readers into adventures of personal discovery and acts of individual attention and imagination that disclose what an inexhaustible surprise the world can be.

Nabokov emphasized to his students that a nation's literary heritage should not be mined chiefly to understand its national past or its national soul: novelists should not be regarded as "historians, or land-surveyors or guides." He made clear that throughout his lectures he would stress the appreciation of art *as* art.

> Art has been too often turned into a tool to convey ideas—whether political or moral—to influence, to teach, to improve and enlighten and what not. I am not telling you that art does not improve and enlighten the reader. But it does this in its own special way and it does it only then when its own single purpose remains to be good, excellent art, art as perfect as its creator can make. The moment this *only* real and valuable purpose of art is forgotten, the moment it is replaced by a utilitarian aim, however commendable in itself, art [ceases] to be art, and through this loss of its ego, loses not only its sense and its beauty but also the very object to which it has been sacrificed: bad art neither teaches nor improves nor enlightens, it is bad art and therefore has no reasonable room in the order of things.

Nabokov was not interested in conventional academic analysis-for-the-sake-of-analysis, in mapping a specific work and its specific world onto an axis of abstract ideas. He stressed the particularity and sensitivity of the imagination: if you see and smell and taste the world with your own eyes, nose, tongue, if you palpate it with your own imagination, you can extract the happiness lurking in life.

Though he considered a few outstanding authors rather than the overall development of Russian literature, he did not entirely neglect historical and artistic contexts: "No course given on a writer without a preliminary study of past events and tendencies which finally resulted in the advent of that writer has any value for the student. . . . This is why I am going to start this course with some data on what happened in the vast expanse now called Russia, before the most intricate, the most perfect literary art was evolved there, seemingly out of nothing, in the nineteenth century."[11] But he was much more interested in individual authors than in literary movements, in genius as an exception to rather than as a product of its time.

In fact, after a rapid glance over Russian history and eighteenth-century Russian verse, he soon settled on Pushkin. Hannah Green has recorded him in action:

He told us he pronounced *Eugene Onegin* "You-gin One-Gin" in English. He went painstakingly through the translation of "You-gin One-Gin" in the anthology we had, and he corrected certain lines for us. We rewrote these lines in our books in pencil. He told us to. He said that of all the Russian writers Pushkin loses the most in translation. He spoke of the "zooming music" of his poetry, and of the wonderful rhythm, of how "the oldest epithets are rejuvenated in Pushkin's verse," which "bubbles and gleams in the darkness."

He spoke of the structure of *Eugene Onegin* and read aloud the duel. Then, leaving literature aside for the drama of Pushkin's life, he drew on the blackboard a scale diagram of Pushkin's own fatal duel, so that his students could picture the duelling ground. He set the scene in time and place, he reenacted the event, he evoked all its tension and tragedy.[12]

After Pushkin, the remainder of the first semester was devoted to Russia's other great nineteenth-century poets: Lermontov, "iridescent flame," but hardly Nabokov's favorite; Tyutchev, "the cool brilliancy of many waters"; Fet, "the spirit of the air, a wispy cloud, a butterfly fanning its wings."[13] Nabokov would sometimes read the poems in Russian in his tense baritone voice, caressing and rolling and pumping the sounds, then read his own translations in the restrained voice of his second tongue. "Real verse music," he told his students, "is not the melody of the verse. Authentic verse music is that mystery which brims over the rational texture of the line."[14]

III

With his novel at last behind him, Nabokov could now move on to new writing projects as time allowed. He outlined for Doubleday his plans for "a new kind of autobiography, or rather a new hybrid between that and a novel . . . a sequence of short essay-like bits, which suddenly gathering momentum will form something very weird and dynamic: innocent looking ingredients of a quite unexpected brew." He met Allen Tate at the Plaza in New York on October 19 to discuss his future books, and was delighted at Tate's enthusiasm for his work. After receiving an advance of two thousand dollars from Henry Holt for his novel, thanks largely to Tate's zeal, he asked Tate if it might be possible for Holt to give him a sufficient yearly advance to leave teaching, at least for a couple of years, while he wrote another novel and assembled a book of short stories.[15]

No such luck. But he was also appreciated as a writer back at

Wellesley. Selected as one of four poets invited for the annual "Poet's Reading" series—the others were Archibald MacLeish, Robert Frost, and T. S. Eliot—he was introduced to the audience on the night of October 21 as "our department of Slavic Languages," and capped the reading, inevitably, with "An Evening of Russian Poetry."[16]

Nabokov knew appreciation was no substitute for security, and he had not stopped looking for a long-term position. With a resounding letter of reference from Edmund Wilson in his support, he came close to being appointed head of the Russian section of the new Voice of America. But the opening closed when Nicolas Nabokov, whom he had also approached for a reference, secured the job for himself instead. Nabokov was also considered as the potential head of the Russian department at Vassar, but was turned down on the ground that he was a prima donna. When Samuel Hazzard Cross died, Harvard seemed about to appoint Nabokov a professor of Slavic literature. Renato Poggioli, an Italian comparativist and a Russian scholar, paid Nabokov a courtesy call one evening. They had a delightful time discussing literature "and all sorts of other things except the fact that Poggioli had, as Nabokov learned the next day, just been given the post" that he had expected.[17]

One day in November the Nabokovs had their friends Isabel and Rockwell Stephens over for a meal. The phone rang from New York: his publishers were about to send his novel to the printers. Could he *please* decide on a title? He offered his guests three choices: *Solus Rex*, *Vortex*, or *Bend Sinister*. Isabel Stephens voted for *Bend Sinister*, and he agreed.[18]

IV

Wellesley's increased demands on his time and trips to New York to confer with Allen Tate could not keep Nabokov away from his bright bench at the M.C.Z. He was now at work on his definitive monograph on the North American members of the genus *Lycaeides*. Examining two thousand specimens under the microscope, a task that would keep him busy until the spring of 1947, Nabokov gradually established that the North American *Lycaeides* fell into two polytypic species, one with ten distinct subspecies, the other with five. In the early 1950s, Alexander Klots would write in his *Field Guide to the Butterflies of North America*, "the recent work of Nabokov has entirely rearranged the classification of this genus." Nabokov's regrouping of this complex genus has remained valid to the present day, with the exception of one new subspecies first described only in 1972 and named in his honor.[19]

But perhaps it is as well to state that the importance of lepidoptera in Nabokov's life should not be measured by his scientific achievements, even by the unusual combination of literary genius and scientific attainment. At about the time that Nabokov was most deeply engaged in lepidopterological research, Alexander Solzhenitsyn was carrying out experiments in acoustics at the Marfino prison research camp described in *The First Circle*.[20] Solzhenitsyn undertook the work with passion, drawing on his training in mathematics and physics, but for him this kind of research was an accident, and tangential to the obsession that would shape his whole career: his concern for the historical importance of the First World War and the revolution that it brought into being. For Nabokov, on the other hand, lepidoptera were at once a field of research and a passion that had shaped his whole imagination from childhood, and so shaped all his art: his love of the infinite variety, abundance, and generosity of nature, down to its minutest details, his fascinated interest in the marvels and intricacies of pattern, the excitement of discovery, the mysteries of metamorphosis, the appearance of playful deception, and the possibility of conscious design behind nature.

Charles Remington, later to become head of entomology at Yale, began studying for his Ph.D. at Harvard in 1946. While still a graduate student, he founded the Lepidopterists' Society, the only worldwide association of lepidopterists. In his two years at the M.C.Z. and subsequently as editor of the *Lepidopterists' News*, Remington could see better than anyone else the place of Nabokov's work in lepidopterology. He thought Nabokov's contribution to the subject "extraordinary" in a mere six years as a research scientist—six years also shared between teaching Russian and the writing of four books (*Nikolay Gogol*, *Three Russian Poets*, *Bend Sinister*, and half each of *Nine Stories* and his autobiography). Nabokov's reclassifications, his analysis of the diagnostic significance of the genitalia of the blues, and the unprecedented detail of his work on wing markings are all a matter of record in his published articles, but what particularly impressed Remington was the way Nabokov's quick intelligence and his wide knowledge of European butterflies allowed him to spot phenomena in North American lepidoptera that were new to American scholars. Nowadays, for instance, it is taken for granted that many butterflies found in the Rockies do not form colonies but are migratory species that filter up from the warmer climates of the south in favorable summers. Though they may produce one generation during the course of the summer, their larvae—unlike those of the hardier, truly indigenous species—will not survive the winter. As Remington notes, it was Nabokov, recollecting the Vanessas he had seen in his youth flying up from the south through the Crimea in April and reaching St. Petersburg in June, who was the first to point out that a parallel phenomenon occurred in North America.[21]

Nabokov liked to have a running joke on call. Just as he always playfully mispronounced "Eugene Onegin" in his literature classes, Remington remembers, so he would always say "alpha-alpha" rather than alfalfa for the food plant of many of the blues, as if to compensate for the syllable he denied "One-gin." Sometimes after a meeting of the Cambridge Entomological Society he would bring Charles and Jeanne Remington, who occasionally baby-sat for him, home to Craigie Circle. There they would be sat down with their hosts and given a spoon each and a jar of Gerber's assorted fruit jellies. The Nabokovs adored these luminous yellow, green, or red little jars: apricot, quince, beech plum, grape—a fact that should be treasured by all admirers of the story "Signs and Symbols."[22]

V

In February 1947, Nabokov wrote the poem "To Prince S. M. Kachurin," the last of his longish Russian poems but not the first or last of his imagined clandestine trips back to Russia under this or that alias: Martin Edelweiss, Vadim Vadimych, or, here, the Reverend Blank. The poem takes the form of a letter from Leningrad. On the advice of his friend Prince Kachurin, the poet has rashly traveled to Russia in the guise of an American clergyman. But how will he arrange to reach the out-of-bounds country estate of his childhood, the real goal of his trip? He is scared, he wants to go home, *home* to the wild America he dreamed of as a boy, and its brave adventures, far from this stifling vapor of fear.[23]

In the second semester of the college year Nabokov taught nineteenth-century prose. He came into class and told his students he had graded the Russian writers, and they must write down the grades and learn them by heart: Tolstoy, A plus; Pushkin and Chekhov, A;* Turgenev, A minus; Gogol, B minus; Dostoevsky, C minus, or was he D plus?[24] The relative rating of Gogol and Turgenev would probably have come out differently on another occasion; Nabokov loved Gogol as the prose-poet of irrational mysteries, and felt luke-

---

* Pushkin as poet, of course, rated an A plus.

warm about Turgenev's pretty and rather self-satisfied prose. He attacked Dostoevsky, but knew his work well and could find revealing comments to make about his humor and dramatic sense even as he deplored his hysteria, his sentimentality, his artistic muddle. He revered Tolstoy for the flawless vividness of his imagination and his determination to find his own truth. But perhaps most of all he loved Chekhov, who for all his indifference to verbal polish could impart to slight, unexpected details a subtlety and suggestiveness, a delicacy of mood, and an ample pathos that raised the standards of storytelling and disclosed a respect for the individuality and openness of things that Nabokov recognized as akin to his own.

By this point Nabokov intended to give up his research at the M.C.Z. in the fall, when he finished his paper on Nearctic *Lycaeides*. The work was too poorly paid, for one thing, and with Dmitri to put through Harvard in a few years, Nabokov felt alarmed at his financial state. In a bid to improve it, he even asked Wilson if there was room at the *New Yorker* for him to write regular reviews there. The answer was no.[25]

For a little extra cash, he spoke at women's clubs. He served up some verse, his own and translated, at a Boston club supper in December. For an afternoon session of the Ladies' Branch of the Providence Art Club in March 1947, he read his lecture "The Triumphs and Tribulations of Russian Literature." That was a mistake. He had offered the club two topics, "Art and Commonsense" or "Triumphs and Tribulations." On the assumption that "Art and Commonsense" was about painting, the club naturally picked that topic. Nabokov, ill at the time he received their answer, had failed to note it down. On the day of the talk, to the horror of the clubwomen, he began to speak of Russian literature. His audience sat out the talk, but protested afterward. No wonder the figure of Pnin began to take shape in Nabokov's mind.[26]

The women's clubs may have prodded his imagination in another way. In "The Enchanter" in 1939, Nabokov had attempted with only partial success to portray the consuming passion of an older man for young girls, but had decided not to publish the story. One of its most unsavory and unsatisfying parts was the mother of the young girl, who barely existed apart from her diseased and moribund condition. Her successor, on the other hand, is among the undoubted triumphs of *Lolita*: Charlotte Haze, "one of those women whose polished words may reflect a book club or bridge club, or any other deadly conventionality, but never her soul." Nabokov had sensed that he needed "a certain exhilarating milieu" if he was to revive his old idea, and the book clubs he visited may have suggested a new mother for his old story's little girl.[27]

The idea of turning the story into a novel had been forming for months. Early in April Nabokov reported to Wilson, "I am writing two things now 1. a short novel about a man who liked little girls—and it's going to be called *The Kingdom by the Sea*—and 2. a new type of autobiography—a scientific attempt to unravel and trace back all the tangled threads of one's personality—and the provisional title is *The Person in Question*." Here was a second reason for relinquishing his post at the M.C.Z.: as he had discovered in writing *Bend Sinister*, it interfered too much with his literary work, and now he had *two* major books to write. He thought that he had finished his monograph on the Nearctic *Lycaeides* and told Wilson that he would more or less shelve butterflies for a year or so. With fifty-six essays on Dostoevsky waiting for him to mark, there was no danger of his feeling at a loose end.[28]

In May, with his entomological paper drafted and the school year almost over, he could at last sit down to writing a story he had had very clearly in mind for years. In 1943 he had announced in *Nikolay Gogol*: "I shall have occasion to speak in quite a different book of a lunatic who constantly felt that all the parts of a landscape and movements of inanimate objects were a complex code of allusion to his own being, so that the whole universe seemed to be conversing about him by means of signs." Over the next two years he decided the idea should become a short story. On New Year's Day 1946, he had replied to a request from Katharine White for material for the *New Yorker*: "I do have a story for you—but it is still in my head; quite complete however; ready to emerge; the pattern showing through the wingcases of the pupa. I shall write it as soon as I get rid of my novel." A year later, he wrote to her again: "Though my story is all done within me, I have not yet been able to settle down to the business of writing it out."[29]

When he did set on paper what had been so fully formed in his head for years, he produced one of the greatest short stories ever written, "Signs and Symbols," a triumph of economy and force, minute realism and shimmering mystery.[30] An elderly Russian-Jewish couple in New York try to visit their only child, an incurably deranged twenty-one-year-old son, to leave this suicidal boy the most harmless birthday present they can think of: a basket of ten fruit jellies in ten little jars. At the sanitorium they are not permitted to see him: he has once again attempted to take his life. Despondent, they head back the way they came, and things continue to go wrong all the way home. When the husband goes to bed that evening his wife stays up, poring over a photograph album and reliving her son's un-happy life. After midnight, her husband wakes up with a sudden resolution to bring the boy home: "We must get him out of there quick. Otherwise we will be responsible. Responsible!" At this un-accustomed hour, the telephone rings and he gapes apprehensively at his wife. She picks up the receiver, but it is not the sanitorium, only a young girl with the wrong number. They continue to plan for their son's homecoming. The telephone rings again. This time the old woman tells the girl how she has managed to misdial the number. She sits down with her husband to their unexpected festive midnight tea. As she pours, he examines with pleasure the little jelly jars and spells out their labels: "apricot, grape, beech plum, quince. He had got to crab apple, when the telephone rang again." There the story ends. Is it the sanitorium this time, calling to say their son has suc-ceeded in killing himself?

Throughout their lives the old man and woman have quietly borne a steady succession of miseries: the Revolution, European emigra-tion, the death of many of their friends in the gas chambers, their poverty and dependence in America, their son's madness. The mother muses:

> This, and much more, she accepted—for after all living did mean ac-cepting the loss of one joy after another, not even joys in her case—mere possibilities of improvement. She thought of the endless waves of pain that for some reason or other she and her husband had to endure; of the invisible giants hurting her boy in some unimaginable fashion; of the incalculable amount of tenderness contained in the world; of the fate of this tenderness, which is either crushed, or wasted, or transformed into madness.

Against the accumulated horror of their lives Nabokov balances their gentle courage, their love for each other and their son, their resigned humor. When they return from their fruitless visit, the woman hands her husband the jellies and tells him to go straight home: she will buy some fish for supper. But when he reaches the third-floor land-ing he remembers he had given her his keys. "In silence he sat down on the steps and in silence rose when some ten minutes later she came, heavily trudging upstairs, wanly smiling, shaking her head in deprecation of her silliness."

"Signs and Symbols" works brilliantly as poignant realism, but what makes the story such a masterpiece is the Nabokovian twist that turns the real world inside out and into an irresolvable enigma. The boy's illness has been diagnosed as "referential mania." He imagines that everything happening around him is a veiled reference to his personality and existence. He excludes real people from the conspiracy—because he considers himself to be so much more intelligent than other men. Phenomenal nature shadows him wherever he goes. Clouds in the staring sky transmit to one another, by means of slow signs, incredibly detailed information regarding him. His inmost thoughts are discussed at nightfall, in manual alphabet, by darkly gesticulating trees. . . . Everything is a cipher and of everything he is the theme. . . . He must be always on his guard and devote every minute and module of life to the decoding of the undulation of things. The very air he exhales is indexed and filed away.

Detail after detail in the story seems impregnated with doom: "That Friday everything went wrong. The underground train lost its life current between two stations." It is raining hard. They cannot see their son. As they return to the bus shelter they pass by a swaying and dripping tree under which "a tiny half-dead unfledged bird was helplessly twitching in a puddle." On board the bus, the old man's hands twitch, as if in response. A girl sits weeping a few seats away. When they reach home, the husband finds himself without his key. His new dentures are hopelessly uncomfortable. He has just got to bitter crab apple when the telephone rings for the fatal third time.

If we take all these details as signs and symbols, that telephone call will announce that the boy has at last managed to kill himself. But if we accept that that is the case, we have accepted what from within the story's world has to be defined as madness: that everything around the boy forms a message about his fate. If we accept that he has killed himself, then we have to acknowledge every agonizing detail as part of a pattern designed to point toward his tragic fate, to evoke our compassion for him and his parents. From within the parents' world, their son's death seems simply more jagged glass on the pile of miseries that makes up their life. But from outside their vantage point, we can see that *if* the boy has died, then the story bears the mark of a tender concern that shapes every minute detail of a world that from within seems unrelieved, meaningless tragedy. The final blow of death, in one light so gratuitous, in another seems the very proof of the painstaking design behind every moment of their lives. Will the fact of our deaths too perhaps disclose suddenly a pattern of tender meaning running through our lives? Or will we never know, just as we can never know whether that telephone announces a death or simply another irritatingly repeated wrong number, another unneeded vexation?

VI

Bend Sinister was published on June 12, 1947. Unfortunately for Nabokov, Allen Tate, the only person at Henry Holt who really appreciated the book, had already left the firm, and as a result the novel was poorly promoted. Despite glowing notices in *Time* and the *New York Times*, most reviews were mixed ("at once impressive, powerful and oddly exasperating," wrote the *New Republic*), and sales were dismal.[31] But before the book's publication, Nabokov's growing reputation in the *New Yorker*'s catchment area had prompted *Vogue* and *Time* to photograph him working at his desk in the M.C.Z.

Nabokov may have felt he was devoting too much time during his winters to lepidopterological research, but he was not going to forfeit the thrill of the summer chase. With enough money from the advance for *Bend Sinister* to allow him to travel in the summer of 1947, he scouted around for somewhere "fairly wild" in the West. In mid-June the family set off by train for Columbine Lodge, perched at 9,500 feet, just above Estes Park, Colorado. They had a comfortable cabin and a wonderful time, and stayed until early September.[32]

Nabokov thought the flora magnificent. "Some part of me must have been born in Colorado," he wrote Wilson, "for I am constantly recognizing things with a delicious pang." In the last week of June, the species *Boloria freija* was practically over, but Nabokov caught five rather faded specimens near Longs Peak Inn, not in the very wet sphagnum bogs where another species lurked but on marshy meadows in the aspen zone. No wonder that in *Speak, Memory* he would depict himself chasing a *freija*—a circumpolar species of both the Old and New Worlds—through the bog across the river from Vyra and emerging at the end of the marsh onto rising ground with Longs Peak in the distance.[33]

At that altitude the fauna and flora may have resembled the biota at Vyra, but the butterfly collecting was much more strenuous. Nabokov lost twenty pounds pursuing his prey and climbing with Dmitri. Dmitri had tramped in the Rockies before, but this was the first of the real mountain climbing that would become his passion and his parents' nagging fear over the next decade.[34]

Without a car, Nabokov was more tied down than most American collectors. But friends he had met or corresponded with in the lepidopterological world arrived to take him further afield. Charles Remington led him to the Tolland Bog, where seven different *Boloria* species occur together, more than anywhere else in the world. Nabokov was delighted to catch five of the seven species in their one day of collecting.[35]

Don Stallings, a lawyer by profession but also one of America's great collectors, had caught hundreds of blues in the early 1940s. Delighted that someone was taking the time to sit down and solve the classification riddles the group posed, he had turned them over to Nabokov at the M.C.Z. At the end of July 1947 he accompanied the Nabokovs for two days in the Longs Peak area, while thirteen-year-old Dmitri scaled the 14,255-foot summit. Nabokov, fit from so much climbing, bounded up the mountainside, as if—so it seemed to Stallings—in the puckish hope that he and his wife would be exhausted halfway up. They were, and managed to catch only two or three of the *magdalenas* they were after. Next day Stallings announced, "Today we're going to collect *my* way." They scoured the slide and trickle areas around the lower slopes, and caught fifteen *magdalenas*.[36]

Until now Nabokov had killed his catches by putting them in tumblers with carbona-soaked cotton wool. American collectors taught him the much simpler method of pinching a butterfly between one's finger and thumb by the thorax. This killed the creature instantly, so that it could be popped straight into a lightweight little envelope and spread later at one's leisure, even years afterward.

Nabokov's first rush of excitement at Estes Park, recapturing the *freijas* and the sensations and memories of his childhood, came at an opportune moment. On July 2 he sent the *New Yorker* the first completed chapter* of his autobiography, "Portrait of My Uncle."[37] A guided tour of a gallery of colorful ancestors, it gradually narrows its focus to "Ruka"—as Nabokov here calls his uncle Vasily Rukavishnikov—and then to one timeless moment of the remembered past. The editors in the *New Yorker* fiction department were all against the sketch, but Katharine White decided to show it to Harold Ross, the magazine's publisher. Ross was most enthusiastic, and wanted more of the same. His eagerness meant the Nabokovs could afford to stay in the Rockies until the beginning of September. By then, however, Nabokov had become alarmed at the *New Yorker*'s voracious editing of the story, which upset him so much, he told Wilson, that he had almost decided to stop trying to earn his living that way.[38]

VII

At the beginning of September the family returned east by train, stopping in New York, where Nabokov saw for the last time his

---

* Except for "Mademoiselle O," written in French in 1936 before the autobiography was conceived.

friend Gleb Struve, en route from England to his new post at Berkeley.[39]

Back in Massachusetts, Dmitri was sent to St. Mark's School, a prestigious prep school in Southborough, where a scholarship paid just over half of his fees. After his happy years at Dexter School, Dmitri now found himself unready for and at odds with St. Mark's. His father too disliked the place, but found it fired his imagination. In 1951, after finishing his autobiography, still entitled *Conclusive Evidence*, he would remember his shock at the poor standards, snobbishness, and preferential treatment at St. Mark's and would draw up a memo to write a continuation, *More Evidence*, that would devote a chapter to the school and divulge "full details."[40] He changed his mind, and instead assigned portions of the school to *Lolita* (the antiquated game of fives, played at an English day school in the south of France that young Humbert attends) and to *Pnin*, where he sends Victor Wind, Pnin's ex-wife's son, to "St. Bartholomew's," modeled at least in part on St. Mark's.

This year Nabokov taught the same three courses as the year before. A student in his elementary class recalls that on the first day of the term, Nabokov happened to find on his desk a yellow vase with blue flowers. He went to the blackboard, wrote "yellow blue vase," and asked the students what it said. "Yellow blue vase," of course. "That is almost 'I love you' in Russian," he explained, and repeated the phrase, *ya lyublyu vas*, adding: "That is probably the most important phrase that I will teach you."

Students in both classes remember them as informal and Nabokov as fascinating, opinionated, kind, thoughtful, gentle, a man who combined a powerful ego with a very courtly manner. "We were madly in love with him. He was a marvelous man," recalled one. "The classes went by very quickly," said another. "We laughed a lot and talked a lot." The literature class, now with sixty-six students, remained much more formal.[41]

After his recent exposure in *Time*, *Vogue*, and *Mademoiselle*, Nabokov had briefly become a campus celebrity. The *Wellesley College News* ran a profile on him: "Pushkin, Shakespeare and himself constitute his three favorite writers. Mann, Faulkner, and André Gide receive the doubtful honor of being the three writers he most detests."[42] Many of those who find Nabokov's literary opinions too strong have supposed envy must be the spur for his dismissal of other writers. As his unguarded—or deliberately provocative—pronouncement at Wellesley makes clear, he would never have dreamed of stooping to envy a Dostoevsky or a Gorky, a Balzac or a Sartre, a James or a Lawrence. To Russians, Pushkin is their most treasured writer; to the

English, Shakespeare. Nabokov, with both heritages at his disposal, calmly placed himself in their company.*

Just as classes were beginning at Wellesley, Nabokov received a letter signed by a man named Morris Bishop. A professor of Romance languages at Cornell, Bishop had been appointed chairman of a committee to find a replacement for Ernest Simmons, professor of Russian literature. A writer himself—his light verse appeared often in the *New Yorker*—Bishop had admired Nabokov's work since his first stories appeared in the *Atlantic Monthly*. "Some of the sentences," he would later remark, "still return to comfort me in the clairvoyance of a midnight waking." By the late 1940s, he had come to consider Nabokov "one of the best writers of our time." From Sally Collie Smith, the Wellesley publicity officer, he found out that Nabokov taught at Wellesley. In her enthusiasm for Nabokov, she had written to Bishop complaining that Cornell was mentioned often in the *New Yorker* because of both E. B. White and himself, whereas Nabokov, a much more important writer, was at Wellesley: didn't Wellesley, therefore, rate a mention? "Oho, so they've got Nabokov," thought Bishop, and wrote asking him if he would be interested in a professorship at Cornell: "As an old admirer of your work, I think first of you." Should he be offered the post, his duties would presumably include two courses in Russian literature and a course in the general Division of Literature, and no courses in language, which was taught by a separate Division of Modern Languages. It was what Nabokov had been wanting for years.[43]

Visiting Cornell on October 25 to meet Bishop and other senior professors, he made a good impression on everyone. The appointments committee had been apprehensive about choosing a man who had no higher degrees and no stack of scholarly publications, and whose only critical work was his brilliant but eccentric study of Gogol. But they were charmed by Nabokov in person, and impressed by the range of his knowledge and the acuteness of his judgments. Morris and Alison Bishop put him up overnight, and hosts and guest took an immediate instinctive liking to each other. Alison Bishop recalls the vivid impression his playfulness made from the first. He pretended to have lost his return ticket, and made an act of searching for it, until a charming, radiant, enchanted look came over his face when he "found" the ticket again.[44]

Cornell was ready to offer him the position at a salary of $5,000.

---

* In other moods he could be much more modest: "Oh, yes, let people compare me to Joyce by all means, but my English is patball to Joyce's champion game" (*Strong Opinions*, 56).

Despite his predictions, Nabokov was still working a good deal at the M.C.Z., although at a reduced level of financial support. Reluctant to leave Cambridge and the museum if he did not have to, he informed Mildred Horton of the Cornell offer and asked if a permanent position might now be possible for him at Wellesley. She said no, claiming that Wellesley would be delighted to have him continue on a year-by-year basis, but that since the position of Russian as a subject was not secure, the college could not commit itself to a permanent appointment. In fact, the following year Nabokov would be replaced as a Russian teacher by a Pole, Waclaw Jedrzejewicz, who in his second year at Wellesley was made an associate professor. His methods must have appealed to President Horton more than Nabokov's: he introduced Russian songs to his language teaching students and took them along to International Group Singing, and he exposed his literature students to Chaikovsky's Violin Concerto in D so that they could appreciate—in his words—the influence of the steppe on the Russian soul.[45]

Once he knew Wellesley had refused him a permanent place, Nabokov accepted the Cornell post without any qualms.[46] During October, before Cornell's offer had yet been formalized, he had written the next chapter of his autobiography, "My English Education": the Anglophilia of his home, the English governesses of his infancy, the English tutor and drawing master of his boyhood.[47] After sending the piece off to the New Yorker he discovered that they wanted to edit both this and "Signs and Symbols." Only his respect for Katharine White can account for the moderation of his tone in objecting to the very principle of the magazine's editing his work according to its own conception of stylistic elegance:

> I shall be very grateful to you if you help me to weed out bad grammar but I do not think I would like my longish sentences clipped too close, or those drawbridges lowered which I have taken such pains to lift. In other words, I would like to discriminate between awkward construction (which is bad) and a certain special—how shall I put it—sinuosity, which is my own and which only at first glance may seem awkward or obscure. Why not have the reader re-read a sentence now and then? It won't hurt him.

Edmund Wilson staunchly supported him: "I have read the Nabokov stories, and I think they are both perfect. Not a word should be changed." Nabokov meanwhile had been offering all year to help Wilson in the obscenity trial brought against his Memoirs of Hecate County. In fact there was nothing he or anyone else could do; the book was declared obscene.* The Nabokovs spent Thanksgiving with Wilson and his new wife, his fourth, Elena, whom they both liked very much.[48]

VIII

Once Nabokov had accepted the Cornell post, the details of what he was to teach still had to be sorted out in a cross fire of misapprehensions that took six months and twenty letters to fizzle into resolution.

Nabokov was to be the Department of Russian Literature, within which he would teach two courses of his own making, but with the expectation that he would also teach one course in the Division of Literature—preferably one section of the Introduction to Literature, "a sort of Great Books and Stimulating Blather course," as Bishop defined it for him, "the Bible to T. S. Eliot." Nabokov misunderstood: not realizing that there was a set syllabus, including Thucydides, Sophocles, Cervantes, Molière, and Voltaire, hardly staples of his picky literary diet, he eagerly devised his own very Nabokovian introduction to literature. To Thomas Bergin, the chairman of the Division of Literature, he wrote: "What you say about the Literature course seems to me very attractive. I have been turning it over in my mind and I think I would prepare a course consisting of two parts echoing each other: Writers (Teachers, Storytellers, Enchanters) and Readers (Seekers of Knowledge, Entertainment, Magic). Of course, this is only a rough outline of the plan. I would include writers of various countries and categories."[49]

When his mistake was explained, Nabokov accepted the fixity of the Introduction to Literature program, although he did not look forward to teaching a course that seemed too elementary and not enough his own. He also proposed the two courses to be given in Russian: a survey course and a course called The Renaissance of Russian Poetry, 1890–1925, from Blok to Pasternak and Khodasevich. But when some of those involved in teaching things Russian (history, language, politics) suggested that Nabokov perhaps offer a course in English to replace one of his courses to be given in Russian, Nabokov counterproposed that such a course on Russian in English could be given instead of his having to take part in the Introduction to Literature course. "I will tell you quite frankly," he wrote—in Russian—to Professor Marc Szeftel of the history department, "I would much pre-

---

* Since it had at first sold very briskly, Wilson lost a great deal of potential profit when the book was banned. By the time it could be released again in 1959, after the American publication of Lolita, Hecate County had outlived its shock value.

fer this course to replace not one of the proposed Russian courses but the 'Introduction to Literature' itself. Russian literature is my specialty, and I teach it with great pleasure, whereas an incidental course on world literature and at such an elementary level too I must admit attracts me very little." He proposed therefore three courses in Russian literature: a survey in Russian, a survey in English (the overlap was for him of course an excellent economy), and the course from Blok to Khodasevich. What he offered was accepted—and there was still no sign of the Masterpieces of European Fiction course for which Nabokov's teaching at Cornell is now chiefly remembered.[50]

IX

As 1947 turned to 1948 the advancing chill of the cold war began to cause shivers of fear. After its enthusiasm for the Soviet Union during the war, America felt betrayed by Soviet actions and broken promises in Eastern Europe, and many predicted a quick and deadly war in Europe. Early in 1947, Nabokov had written a letter of recommendation to Trygve Lie to help his sister Elena get from Prague to a job as a UN librarian in the West. No opening was immediately available, but by the end of the year she had obtained a UN library post in Geneva. Nabokov was still sending money regularly to Evgenia Hofeld, and had written an affidavit to help extricate her charge, his nephew Rostislav Petkevich, from Czechoslovakia. He was too late: the Communist coup there took place in February 1948. Although Nabokov did not abandon his attempts to have his nephew brought to the U.S., Rostislav would die in Prague in 1960, still in his twenties, of the alcoholism that had been his refuge from a bitter and frustrated life.[51]

The first collection of Nabokov's short stories available in English— three translated from the Russian, one revised from the French ("Mademoiselle O"), and his first five written directly in English— had been published in December 1947 as *Nine Stories*, the last of his books to appear with New Directions. The *New Yorker*'s treatment of his next story, "Signs and Symbols," was once again causing him exasperation. On the proofs the editors had tried to remove, among other things, many of the signs and symbols that serve as the axis of the story's fifth dimension. Nabokov wrote Katharine White, "Frankly, I would prefer you not to publish the story at all if it is to be so carefully mutilated. In fact I am completely against the whole idea of my stories being edited. Among the alterations inflicted on this story there is not a single really necessary one and many are murderous."[52] Fortunately his rights as author prevailed.

Meanwhile he was composing his next autobiographical chapter, "Colette," the story of his first love, Claude Deprès, the girl he met on a beach in Biarritz in 1909. The romance of train travel sets the scene, but for Nabokov romance needed more than a soft-focus lens. He wanted to know the exact word for the black connecting bellows that covered the walkway between sleeping cars. When he could not find it in his dictionaries, he sent Véra to the Widener Library for books on railway lore. He called friends at night asking their help. Once in a poem he had called them black gills. Now he sought prosaic precision to offset the romance, but he had to settle for "intervestibular connecting curtains"—before adding "as black as bat wings."[53]

During the spring of 1948, Nabokov suffered from a long and alarming series of lung troubles that were never satisfactorily diagnosed. One night in late March he began coughing up vast amounts of blood. What seemed like at best a bad case of bronchitis sent him to bed for some weeks, except for visits to the hospital to have a whole picture gallery of X rays taken of his lungs. Someone else's spittle tube was mistaken for his and he was wrongly diagnosed as having tuberculosis. Endless sputum analyses were required before that was definitively ruled out. Meanwhile Véra took over his courses at Wellesley, while he worried about the enormous amount of work still to be finished at the M.C.Z. before his departure for Cornell in June.[54] He also completed "Colette" while lying in bed, and sent the manuscript off to the New Yorker with a plea to Katharine White: "If you accept the story, please let us not have any unnecessary changes. Everything is crystal-clear in the story and my syntax is becoming a grammarian's delight."[55]

In mid-April he had to undergo a bronchoscopy, an exploratory operation under local anesthesia. He watched as the doctors inserted a vulcanized rubber tube down his windpipe. One doctor asked him how he felt. "Controlled panic," he answered. Later he found that they had expected to find cancer, not simply one blood vessel broken for no discernible reason. Nabokov's own retrospective explanation was that it had been his body ridding itself of the damage caused by thirty years of heavy smoking.[56]

After a spell of improvement, Nabokov became seriously ill again in early May and was told he would have to remain in bed for a considerable time.[57] While there, he worked on his next chapter, "My Russian Education," which described his years at Tenishev School mainly as a backdrop for one immortal scene: the agonizing day that he found out from his classmates that his father had called a news-paper editor out to a duel, and might for all he knew already be lying dead. Nabokov told Sylvia Berkman he had to *force* himself to write about his father.[58]

He sent the chapter off to the *New Yorker* in the last week of May.[59] By now he was beginning to recover—although Véra was still teaching his classes—but his doctors insisted he rest through the summer and gave him only a fifty-fifty chance of recuperating by autumn. He feared he might have to back out of the Cornell job at the last minute, but said nothing to Bishop about the seriousness of his condition.[60] His health problems had also caused him great financial anxiety, relieved only when Edmund Wilson prompted the *New Yorker* to advance him money. No wonder he later called this "a time of great mental and physical stress."[61]

During June, while Véra conducted the Wellesley examinations, Nabokov "rested comfortably" by hurriedly preparing for print his long monograph "The Nearctic Members of the Genus *Lycaeides Hübner*," which would appear as a complete issue of the *Bulletin of the Museum of Comparative Zoology*.[62] Nabokov's mode of presentation was ahead of his time. Instead of showing a photograph of a single specimen of a butterfly species or a diagram of the genitalia of a single specimen, he presented when necessary a range of specimens of certain subspecies in nine pages of crowded plates.[63] At the same time—rest, indeed!—he wrote another chapter of his autobiography, "Curtain Raiser," about his friendship with his cousin Yuri and the way their boyish Wild West games gave way to manlier feelings and adolescent adorations: a young American woman at a Berlin skating rink, a coachman's daughter at Vyra.[64]

On June 30, 1948, the Nabokovs left for Cornell. That morning, Véra rang up Sylvia Berkman and asked if Vladimir could come over at 10:00: "I will never get this place cleaned out if he stays here." Nabokov had a carton of butterflies he wanted to store in Cambridge. He asked Harry Levin if he could leave them with him, but Levin made it clear he was interested in books but not butterflies. Nabokov came to Sylvia Berkman quite upset, and she agreed to look after the box. When he had calmed down, he called Véra. He called her fifteen minutes later to see how she was getting on. He called her after another fifteen minutes to see if he could help, and she asked for him to be kept away from the phone. All day long he sat on the sofa, talking to Sylvia Berkman: "I divide literature into two categories, the books I wish I had written and the books I have written." After Véra and Dmitri joined them for dinner, the Nabokovs set off westward, bound for Ithaca, New York.[65]

CHAPTER 7

Russian Professor: Cornell, 1948–1950

I

THEY REACHED Ithaca on July 1, 1948, the day Nabokov's appointment officially commenced. When Morris Bishop had volunteered months earlier to find them a house, Nabokov had accepted with enthusiasm and relief, but warned Bishop "that neither of us being at all familiar with any heating systems (except the central kind), we would hardly be able to cope with any but the simplest arrangement. My hands are limp fools." After more mundane considerations, he added, "I am sorry to give you all these sordid details, but you asked for them." In the house Bishop found for him, Nabokov would eventually finish *Lolita*, and in the afterword to that book he casually turns central heating into poetry as he muses: "Every serious writer, I dare say, is aware of this or that published book of his as of a constant comforting presence. Its pilot light is steadily burning somewhere in the basement and a mere touch applied to one's private thermostat instantly results in a quiet little explosion of familiar warmth." Nabokov may have been anything but a bourgeois homeowner, but the succession of rented homes in his Ithaca years would turn him into a remarkable recorder of suburban America.[1]

He had requested, after his hard winter, a quiet summer in green surroundings. Bishop was able to fill the prescription exactly with 957 East State Street, the home of an electrical engineering professor and the first of the ten professorial homes the Nabokovs occupied in Ithaca: an acre of lawn sloping down under a giant Norway spruce to a screen of trees and a stream, with a study at ground level at the rear of the house overlooking this receding series of greens. At the start of the summer, Nabokov was not fit enough for butterfly expeditions or tennis, but at least he could watch tiger swallowtails flying across the garden as he reclined in the speckled shade. "We are absolutely enchanted with Cornell," he wrote soon after arriving, "and very grateful to the kind fate that has guided us here."[2]

New York State's Finger Lakes are long, narrow glacial lakes cradled within steep stone troughs. At one end of wooded Cayuga Lake sits downtown Ithaca, on a flat basin scoured out by millennia of advancing ice and rock. On one lip of the trough perches Cornell's campus; as the local joke has it, everything at Cornell is on a hill, and to get there you must climb uphill—both ways. Still convalescing, Nabokov had to take the slopes gently at first. He reported to Dean Cottrell, claimed his office, 278 Goldwin Smith Hall, conscientiously acquainted himself with the library, and at once checked out the entomological facilities of Comstock Hall.[3]

The Bishops were away from Ithaca for the summer, but Morris Bishop had seen to it that Nabokov would be met at the university. Since nothing can be more oppressively peaceful than a college town in summer, Bishop had even taken care to ensure Dmitri would not be too bored. He asked two other professors with fourteen-year-old sons to call: William Sale, Jr. of English and Arthur Sutherland of law. (The latter was to become a good friend of the Nabokovs.) In anticipation of the fact that Dmitri would attend a school in New Hampshire, and because they now had a stable income, the Nabokovs prepared to buy their first car. Véra quickly learned to drive: her instructor thought her an outstanding pupil, and as a racing-car driver himself in later years, Dmitri would always be proud of the style and speed with which his mother handled a car. Although the eight-year-old Plymouth four-door sedan they bought was almost falling apart and would be replaced the next year, it was a first step toward those fabled lepping trips to the West the Nabokovs would make almost every summer for the next ten years. All the summer of 1948 offered of real interest was a rare migrant, the snout butterfly, which flew by in its swift and ragged course before Nabokov could reach for his net.[4]

Late in August, Nabokov sent off to the *New Yorker* another chapter of his autobiography, "First Poem," the stylized account of the poem he began to compose at fourteen as he looked out, through the prisms of the pavilion in Vyra's old park, at the remnants of a summer storm.[5] Apart from composing this chapter, he "rested" by preparing his courses. Assuming more of a difference between Wellesley and Cornell students than was to prove the case, he calculated that his new classes could be expected to read three to four hundred pages per week, ten thousand pages in the course of the year. When he had ascertained what was available in the library, he drew up awesome required reading lists and himself reread the Russian classics he would teach. After a little work on Pushkin, he began to think at once of translating *Eugene Onegin*. Ironically, it was to Edmund Wilson that he lightly proposed, "Why don't we write together a scholarly prose translation of *Evgenii Onegin* with copious notes?"

Just such a task—but undertaken very much as a solo effort—would usurp almost all his energy in his last five years at Cornell.[6]

His health improved more rapidly than anyone had expected. His two hundred pounds were soon negotiating the hills with ease, and by August he could even enjoy playing tennis at the Cascadilla courts with Dmitri, who under the Cornell tennis coach had developed an excellent tennis form.[7]

II

One irritant grading into a worry—and a vexation often to be repeated in Ithaca—was that they had to find a new home to rent by September, when Professor Hansteen and his family returned to State Street. Right into August nothing had been found. At last something turned up: "a dismal grayish-white frame house," Nabokov would write in retrospect, "subjectively related to the more famous one at 342 Lawn Street, Ramsdale, New England." Although 802 East Seneca Street was much bigger than they had wanted—two living rooms on the first floor, four bedrooms on the second—it seemed at first a welcome relief to them after their "wrinkled-dwarf Cambridge flatlet."[8]

Though other Cornell professors sent their children to local public schools, Nabokov had enrolled Dmitri at Holderness School in Plymouth, New Hampshire. The school fees consumed one-third of his salary, but he thought the cost well worth it to have his son exposed to foreign languages and shielded from what he saw as the hooligan argot of public-school playgrounds. With Dmitri gone, the house's vastness became even more absurd, and the Nabokovs repeatedly issued invitations to their New York friends—the Wilsons, George Hessen, Roman Grynberg, Vladimir Zenzinov—to come visit. Soon they took in a lodger to recoup some of the house's cost.[9]

As the year drew on, other disadvantages became apparent. In *Pale Fire*, Kinbote's Appalachian home proves impossible to keep warm, perhaps "because the house had been built in mid-summer by a naive settler who could not imagine the kind of winter New Wye had in store for him." The Nabokovs too found they lived in a dreadfully drafty dacha: when they relinquished the house in 1950, the landlady's one complaint would be that they had removed all the keys to the internal doors and stuffed the keyholes with cotton wool.[10]

Always sensitive to noise, Nabokov had complaints of his own to make to the couple in the separate third-floor apartment at the top of the house:

I want further to remind you that your living room is situated exactly over our bedrooms and that practically every word and every step is heard.

Saturday night you had apparently a party and we were kept awake until 1:30 a.m. We think that 11 p.m. is a liberal enough limit, and we would raise no objections if once in a while, at some special occasion, a party you had would go on till 11:30. But I am afraid I must insist that at 11 p.m.—or at 11:30 at the latest—all loud talking, moving of furniture etc. should cease.

Another time two years later Nabokov sent a less peremptory note upstairs, ending with the hope that "if you want me to write those stories you are kind enough to appreciate, you will not shatter the peace of mind within which they are engendered."[11]

III

Unsurprisingly, the only person Nabokov had known well on the Cornell faculty before joining it himself was another lepidopterist, William Forbes, who had been a visiting professor at the M.C.Z. in 1944–1945. Although the presence of a good entomological collection at Cornell was one of the things that reconciled Nabokov to leaving Cambridge and the M.C.Z., he would never become more than an intermittent visitor at Comstock Hall. In his first year at Cornell he researched one brief paper[12] describing a new neotropical blue that he had been sent, but the only lepidopterological papers he wrote after that were a few brief notes. His daytime home in Ithaca would be not a bench with a microscope in Comstock Hall but the high-ceilinged, north-facing office he occupied at the northern end of Goldwin Smith Hall.

For the most part Nabokov also taught in the classrooms of Goldwin Smith. On Friday, September 24, he delivered his first Cornell lecture, for his Russian Literature 151–52 course (Monday, Wednesday, Friday, 11 A.M., Room 248, Morrill Hall). Fourteen students took the course for credit; three others audited. As at Wellesley, the first semester of this course—with Guerney's *Treasury of Russian Literature* as its main text—stretched from the beginnings to Pushkin and Lermontov. There was one major addition: Griboedov's brilliant play *Gore ot uma* (*Woe from Wit*), perhaps the most untranslatable literary masterpiece ever written, combining as it does taut rhyme with all the broken rules and broken sentences of colloquial speech. Nabokov used Sir Bernard Pares's translation, in his own heavily revised version.[13]

He began as he meant to go on:

> Although this course is called "a survey" in the catalog, it is not a survey at all. Anybody is able to survey with a skimming eye the entire literature of Russia in one laborious night by consuming a textbook or an encyclopedia article. *That* is much too simple. In this course, ladies and gentlemen, I am not concerned with generalities, with ideas and schools of thought, with groups of mediocrities under a fancy flag. I am concerned with the specific text, the thing itself. We will go to the center, to the hub, to the book and not vague summaries and compilations.[14]

An hour later he launched his new survey course in Russian, Russian Literature 301–2 (MWF 12 noon, 248 Goldwin Smith). For this course he had ten enrolled students and seven auditors. Among the students was Paul Robeson, Jr., who spoke excellent Russian (his father had sent him to the Soviet Union) and was a devout Communist. Nabokov began by conducting the class in Russian, but although students gamely tried to discuss the works in the language in which they were written, he let them revert to English as the year wore on. Texts, however, were still analyzed in the original. Nabokov ended the semester by taking students through *Eugene Onegin* at the rate of a canto a class, with the aid of his prose translation and line-by-line explanations. He had his students buy a pocket edition that really *could* be fitted in the pocket, and made them dwell on favorite stanzas* that he encouraged them to learn by heart: "You have to work at reopening your memory."[15]

Nabokov had recommended his wife as an instructor in the Russian section of the Division of Languages, but there were no vacancies.[16] Instead she became his constant factotum. She no longer merely typed all his letters but actually conducted his correspondence in her own name, except for a few personal letters or crucial business exchanges. She drove him to and from campus. And with no Dmitri to return to, she regularly sat in on every session of class, acting the part of teaching assistant, handing out papers, writing words and phrases on the blackboard. Some students were shocked at the disparity between her regal poise, her radiant, white-haired beauty—many at Cornell reported that they had never seen a more beautiful older woman—and what seemed to them the subservient role she played.

---

* Especially the dancing of Istomina (1.20), the advent of winter (5.1–2), and the faro table of fate (8.36–37).

With his wife to help him, and his own inherent independence, Nabokov could remain quite apart from the university's administrative structures. Morris Bishop had told him he would be chairman of the Department of Russian Literature, and he had stationery printed with this position marked on the letterhead. But there were no other teachers of Russian literature, and in fact—although Nabokov did not find this out until 1950—there was no separately constituted department of Russian literature. He was indifferent to the institutional proprieties of university life. Once when he received a catalogue of current Soviet publications from the library, he sent it back after scrawling on the cover, "There is no Soviet literature." Although he did participate in monthly Russian Area Studies sessions where faculty members—himself included—would deliver papers in their respective fields, Russian literature or history, politics or economics, he never attended a faculty meeting the whole time he was at Cornell.[17]

IV

Nabokov was not aloof from his colleagues, but he had his own special interests and his own special ways. Passing abstractedly down the corridors of Goldwin Smith Hall with Véra, he might not nod to an acquaintance until she jogged his attention. At other times he could have lightning reactions. When a domestic accident forced the English department's Robert Martin Adams to keep his arm in a sling, he soon grew resigned to heavy-footed academic joshing every time he passed his colleagues. It took Nabokov to raise a smile that lingered: catching sight of Adams, he let out an exultant "Ah, a duel!"[18]

By dint of never discussing the teaching of Russian language at Cornell, Nabokov was able to play tennis with Milton Cowan, head of the Division of Languages. With his superb ground strokes, his long, deep drives, varied with the occasional chop or slice, Nabokov could force an opponent to charge across the court shot after shot just to return the ball right to his feet. But Cowan discovered that if he volleyed sharply, Nabokov would not run for the ball himself. "Consequently, when I needed a point I would go in to the net. Our play settled down to long rallies and a deuce set which went on until we were ready to quit. Neither of us ever won a set as I recall. . . . neither of us felt the need to win."[19]

In *Pale Fire*, Nabokov has John Shade describe the days "when all the streets of College Town led to the game": American football, of course. He himself ignored the crowds and turned up instead to watch Cornell's soccer team, despite its poor standard of play, from the deserted sideline where a few others huddled against the wind. Nabokov's other great pastime of course was chess. The philosopher Max Black had heard he was an excellent chess player and gladly accepted an invitation to play. Black, a former chess champion at Cambridge University, had once defeated Arthur Koestler, a former champion at the University of Vienna, in four moves ("a fluke," Black says). Now he made the mistake, as he recalls, of assuming Nabokov was a very strong player and deliberated carefully over his moves. Nabokov himself knew he was not brilliant at the chessboard: the qualities of imagination that allowed him to be such a superb composer of chess problems had no time to function in chess competition. Still, he rarely found someone who could match him at the board. To the surprise of them both, Black beat Nabokov easily in a game that lasted only fifteen minutes. Nabokov asked for an immediate rematch, and lost just as promptly. Though he saw Max Black often over the next decade, he never invited him to play again.[20]

Black was taken aback that someone of such demanding aesthetic standards as Nabokov could offer him locally made port served in a large glass jar. Another Cornellian also thought that the Nabokovs "don't know the rules."[21] That was true enough: they had their own rules and their own few friends.

At Cornell, their only close companions were Morris and Alison Bishop. Six years older than Nabokov, Morris Bishop, chairman of the Department of Romance Literature, author of biographies of Pascal, Petrarch, and La Rochefoucauld, among many other books, was known on campus for his wit and his oratorical panache. Avuncular and professorial in appearance, urbane and humane, a passionate lover of literature and languages (he knew Greek, Latin, Italian, French, Spanish, German, and Swedish) and a skillful composer of light verse, he was in Nabokov's for once indulgent opinion "a rhymer of genius."[22] Occasionally one of the two friends would send the other a playful limerick and receive by return another limerick written in reply. Bishop for his part regarded Nabokov, even before Nabokov's finest Russian work was translated or his finest English work written, as one of the finest of living writers. As Bishop once remarked to his wife about Vladimir and Véra, "These are probably the two most interesting people we have ever known."[23]

Alison Bishop agreed. A talented painter in a style not unlike the wittier side of Benois or Somov, and keenly interested in problems of aesthetics, she was also an excellent hostess. The Nabokovs went to dine frequently at the Bishops' home in Cayuga Heights, the wealthy wooded suburb north of the Cornell campus, where the Nabokovs would themselves spend their last years in Ithaca. The Bishops' daughter, Alison (now Alison Jolly, the authority on lemurs), recalls Nabokov as "a wonderful man, absolutely wonderful, extraordinarily kind, kind instantly, sweet, accessible. You felt he understood everything about everybody. He didn't say much in conversation, but he listened, even when a child was talking. He had a flypaper feeling for words. He looked large, rumpled, awkward, in contrast to Véra, who was then the most beautiful woman I'd ever seen, with a kind of beauty that was sculptural."[24]

V

Without any language classes to teach and with very small numbers in his literature courses, Nabokov found his job at Cornell "vastly more comfortable and less interfering than Wellesley." But during his first year, with new classes to prepare, he had little time to write. In October, to teach Russia's great medieval masterpiece, *Slovo o polku Igoreve* (*The Song of Igor's Campaign*), he had had to translate the poem himself for his classes. After teaching the *Song*, he began to write a review of a new French edition of the poem prepared by Roman Jakobson, now at Harvard, and Marc Szeftel, a Russian specialist in Cornell's history department. At the same time he started to prepare a careful line-by-line translation of the whole text, which in Jakobson's edition had been rendered into stilted English by Samuel Cross. In January and February, deep in *Eugene Onegin* with his 301 class, he planned the following year to devote a whole course to Pushkin and was beginning to contemplate "a little book on *Onegin*: complete translation in prose with notes giving associations and other explanations for every line—the kind of thing I have prepared for my classes. I am quite certain I am not going to do any *rhymed* translations any more—their dictatorship is absurd and impossible to reconcile with exactitude." He could not foresee that this "little book" would swell to four fat volumes.[25]

During late January and early February, in the vacation between semesters, Nabokov completed his review of the Jakobson-Szeftel *Song*. He also wrote another chapter of his autobiography, "Portrait of My Mother," where he depicts the peculiar mental affinities between himself and his mother, beginning with their shared synesthesia.[26] Nabokov was delighted that within two months of the chapter's publication his precise description of his sensations would be cited in a scholarly article on synesthesia. Véra Nabokov wrote on his behalf to one of the coauthors of the paper, however, objecting to the implication in the draft article that the metaphors he had chosen to specify the exact colors he associated with each letter of the alphabet—"In the brown group, there are the rich rubbery tone of soft *g*, paler *j*, and the drab shoelace of *h*"—were "a concession to literature. He says that, being a scientist (entomologist), he considers his prose scientific and would have used the same 'metaphors' in a scientific article."[27]

Once again his new manuscript was defaced with editorial ink as the *New Yorker* demonstrated its compulsion to query phrase after phrase. In the first of nearly forty replies to Katharine White's questions, he wrote:

> I knew the word "fatidic" when I was a child (probably from a book on mythology that an English governess read to me), but I give in, if you prefer "prophetic voices." (I cannot, however, endure the inserted "but" in the first sentence.) Your attitude toward "fatidic accents" which is exactly what I want to express is a great pity. There was nobody called "Joan of Arc." I prefer, however, her real name, Joaneta Darc. It would be rather silly, for instance, if in a *New Yorker* issue of 2500, I were alluded to as "Voldemar of Cornell" or "Nabo of Leningrad." So, on the whole, I would like to retain "fatidic accents" and "Joaneta Darc" if possible, but you may act as you like.[28]

VI

When the spring term began in the second week of February, Nabokov had an additional course besides his two surveys: Russian Poetry, 1870–1925. This he taught as a seminar at his house, 3:30 to 6:00 every Thursday, with two students taking the course for credit and one auditing. He planned to follow three lines—(1) Tyutchev-Fet-Blok; (2) Benediktov-Bely-Pasternak; (3) (Pushkin)-Bunin-Khodasevich—although he also touched on Balmont, Bryusov, Severyanin, Mayakovsky, Esenin, Gumilyov, and Akhmatova. He insisted that his class master the scansion of Russian verse in order to appreciate the fantastic richness of Blok's irregular rhythms. Forty years later one of his students, though never a literature major or a Russian specialist, explained that that is why he still read Blok for pleasure.[29]

This student, Richard Buxbaum, was also enrolled in the survey course in Russian. Most of the students in the course, he recalls, were leftish in sympathy, and were surprised though not at all bothered by Nabokov's considering the texts of the set works but not their social context. To inoculate his students against the supposition that literature has to have a social purpose, Nabokov made them read Belinsky's influential but execrably written arguments for literature as a civic tool. The vaccine worked.[30]

Three literature courses to teach left Nabokov little time for anything else. He complained to his friend Dobuzhinsky that although he loved the teaching, he would like more time to write: "I have always more to do than I can fit into the most elastic time, even with the most careful packing. . . . At the moment I am surrounded by the scaffoldings of several large structures on which I have to work by fits and starts and very slowly."[31]

In March 1949, he wrote a devastatingly dismissive review for the *New York Times Book Review* of Sartre's first novel: "Sartre's name, I understand, is associated with a fashionable brand of café philosophy, and since for every so-called 'existentialist' one finds quite a few 'suctorialists' (if I may coin a polite term), this made-in-England translation of Sartre's first novel, *La Nausée* . . . should enjoy some success." After listing egregious blunders in the translation, Nabokov thrusts deeper:

> Whether, from the viewpoint of literature, *La Nausée* was worth translating at all is another question. It belongs to that tense-looking but really very loose type of writing, which has been popularized by many secondraters—Barbusse, Céline, and so forth. Somewhere behind looms Dostoevski at his worst, and still farther is old Eugène Sue, to whom the melodramatic Russian owed so much. . . .
>
> . . . When an author inflicts his idle and arbitrary philosophic fancy on a helpless person whom he has invented for that purpose, a lot of talent is needed to have the trick work. One has no special quarrel with Roquentin when he decides that the world exists. But the task to make the world exist as a work of art was beyond Sartre's powers.[32]

Nabokov's attack has been supposed an act of revenge for Sartre's dismissal in 1939 of the French translation of *Despair*. In fact, he had no personal axe to grind, and when the *Times* thanked him for his brilliant review and asked him to review Sartre's *What Is Literature?* he declined: "I have read the French original and consider it to be trash. Frankly, I do not think it is worth reviewing." But he declared that he had wanted for a long time "to take a crack at such big fakes as Mr. T. S. Eliot and Mr. Thomas Mann." To David Daiches, now head of Cornell's Division of Literature, he expressed his hearty support for Daiches's recent article attacking Eliot for his anti-Semitism.[33]

He was in a mood to be fiercely critical. Late in April, during a party he held for his students, he railed against Laurence Olivier's film adaptation of *Hamlet*. One student asked, "But how can you say such things? Have you actually seen the film?" "Of course I haven't seen the film," Nabokov replied. "Do you think I would waste my time seeing a film as bad as I have described?"[34] That same day, the Sartre review was published in New York. When the *Times* arrived in Ithaca, Nabokov was outraged to discover that among much other editing of his piece, his fourth and shortest sample of the translator's howlers had been omitted: "4. The *forêt de verges* (forest of phalli) in the hero's nightmare is misunderstood as being some sort of birchwood." He immediately sent off a fierce telegram accusing the editor of having disfigured his article. Two days later, the Nabokovs had guests at Seneca Street. "I regaled them with a copy of that violent wire. One of my colleagues, a tense young scholar, observed with a humorless chuckle: 'yes, of course, that's what you would *want* to have sent, as we all must have wanted in many similar cases.' My retort, I thought, was not unfriendly, but my wife said later I could not have been ruder."[35]

Nabokov had been asked earlier in the year to speak in New York as part of a Pushkin evening arranged by the local émigrés. He declined, since he could not afford the time to write such a talk, and instead persuaded Zenzinov to invite him to read from his own Russian works. On Friday, May 6, on their first long trip by car, Véra drove him "beautifully, through lively soft-bosomed scenery," to New York. The weekend there was busy. On Saturday night Nabokov read his poems at the Academy Hall on West 91st Street, explaining his Russian verse of the last few years in such a way that even the socially minded in the audience responded with enthusiasm. He and Véra called on their Russian friends Anna Feigin, Nathalie Nabokoff, George Hessen, Nicolas Nabokov; Nabokov played chess with Roman Grynberg, Hessen, Boris Nicolaevsky, and Irakly Tseretelli; and he and Véra attended the émigré Pushkin evening on Sunday.[36] The bizarre claim advanced more than once in print that Nabokov severed his connections with other Russians once he was settled in America has no basis in fact.[37]

In May, Nabokov heard from Doussia Ergaz, his French agent, that she had arranged for Gide's secretary, Yvonne Davet, to translate *The Real Life of Sebastian Knight* into French. Nabokov insisted that he did not want his novel translated except by his own preferred translator, Jarl Priel. When Mme Ergaz complained that he seemed not to care when his books would appear in French, he replied, "You are quite right: I don't attach much importance to whether my books are published in France today or tomorrow because in my own heart of hearts I do not doubt that the day will come when they will be acclaimed."[38] As it happened, he found Yvonne Davet's translation acceptable, and the novel was published by Gallimard in 1951.

As the spring semester wound up at the end of May, Nabokov began to write one more chapter of his autobiography: "Tamara," the account of his haunting love for Valentina Shulgin. By June 20, he had sent it off to the *New Yorker* and was ready to head west for the summer.[39]

VII

Since their old Plymouth looked as though it might not make it even to Chicago, the Nabokovs traded it in for a black 1946 Oldsmobile.[40] Never having taken a car so far before, Véra hoped to share the drive out West with a friend. She asked Dorothy Leuthold, Andrée Bruel, Vladimir Zenzinov. Eventually Nabokov's student Richard Buxbaum offered to come.

On June 22 the Nabokovs picked him up at Canandaigua and set off westward, aiming to reach Salt Lake City by July 5 for a writers' conference Nabokov had been invited to at the University of Utah. A few miles out of Canandaigua, Véra entered the middle lane of a three-lane road and narrowly missed an oncoming truck. She pulled over, silent, and turned to her husband's student: "Perhaps you'd better drive."

Delighted at the idea of Americans taking the trouble to learn Russian, the Nabokovs supported Richard Buxbaum to the point of insistence. They spoke Russian in front of him and not only encouraged him to speak Russian back but chided him gently when he lapsed into English. Buxbaum suggested they could save a little by stopping not at motels but at cheap guesthouses on the outskirts of the towns along the way. Nabokov declined: he would not share a bathroom with other guests.

With *Lolita* already taking shape in his mind, he had a notebook on hand as he traveled. His gift for observation and recollection were always at the ready. Occasionally as they drove on below the Great Lakes and across Iowa and Nebraska someone in the car would casually recall an impression from the previous day's journey, and Nabokov would begin to swamp his companions with details they had all forgotten but now could just recollect having registered. Once as they sat in a restaurant and women left a neighboring table, Nabokov remarked, "Wasn't that *sad*." Although he had been engaged in the lively conversation at his own table, he had heard everything his neighbors had said, and now recounted the whole exchange to his own table, not to impress them, Buxbaum felt certain, but simply because he had found the women's story so touching.[41]

On July 3 they reached Salt Lake City. There they stayed at a sorority house, Alpha Delta Phi, the Nabokovs themselves in a room with a private bath, a condition Nabokov had insisted on before agreeing to come.[42] Others at the conference included Wallace Stegner, whom Nabokov had met at Stanford; Ted Geisel ("Dr. Seuss"), "a charming man, one of the most gifted people on this list,"[43] with a ready wit and a fine ear for language; Martha Foley, motherly but tough-minded, who had twice selected Nabokov's first short stories in English for her *Best American Short Stories* annuals; and John Crowe Ransom, poet, critic, and founder and editor of America's best serious literary review at the time, the *Kenyon Review*. Decades later Nabokov would recall Ransom: "I don't remember his name. White-haired, eye-glasses, he wore a conservative suit and looked like a banker, yet wrote some extraordinary verse: 'Bells . . . Bells'—not Poe!—'Bells for John Whiteside's Daughter,' I liked particularly." He hit it off with the courteous, soft-spoken but nuanced and subtle Ransom, and they showed each other great mutual respect.[44]

Nabokov had a busy schedule: three novel workshops, one on the short story, one on nonfiction (biography), a reading with several other poets, and a lecture, "The Government, the Critic, and the Reader," as he sometimes renamed his old standby, "The Triumphs and Tribulations of Russian Literature." With Wallace Stegner Nabokov enjoyed a hearty tussle in the novel workshops. Stegner had talked on redskins and palefaces: why being unsubtle and robust was better than being over-refined and decadent. Nabokov reacted with glee at having this as a point of disagreement, and set upon Stegner's arguments in a spirit of provocative but good-natured opposition. He also opposed him on the tennis court, playing doubles with Dmitri against Stegner and either Richard Buxbaum or Stegner's son Page, who in 1966 would become the first person to write a book on Nabokov.[45]

After the conference ended on July 16, Nabokov headed north to Wyoming to look for butterflies in the Teton Range. When he had put forward his plans in May, Véra had some timorous queries to make: might he have to encounter grizzlies when he was armed with nothing more than a gauze butterfly net? Nabokov wrote to the lepidopterist Alexander Klots and passed on his wife's fears. Klots replied that Grand Teton National Park was "just another damned touristed-out National Park. . . . Again, reassurance for Mrs. Nabokov about fauna. Tourist traps are much more dangerous."[46]

On the way from Salt Lake City to Jackson Hole, the Nabokovs' car had a flat tire. When Richard Buxbaum and Dmitri got out to change the tire, Nabokov announced, "Well, I'm no use to you," and headed off for an hour with his butterfly net. The next day they arrived at Battle Mountain Ranch, Jackson Hole. Nabokov had chosen the area to look for a particular subspecies he had "described, named, fondled—but never actually taken," *Lycaeides argyrognomon longinus*, which he had defined in his major paper on Nearctic *Lycaeides* on the strength of only three specimens, two caught in 1900, one in 1920. Some felt dubious about a subspecies that seemed almost impossible to find, but Nabokov had chosen the right spot, stayed in the area for a month and a half, and caught some fine long series of the insect.[47]

They soon settled just south of the park proper, at Teton Pass Ranch in Wilson, Wyoming, a pleasant lodge in a large meadow at the foot of the majestic Teton Range. Moose were common in the area, and Alexander Klots had warned Nabokov that when collecting in swampy areas he must give them a wide berth: "I would rather meet ten bears with cubs." As he predicted, humans were even more troublesome. The two owners of the lodge also happened to own a World War II machine gun. One morning, alerted by the stench, Nabokov discovered a bullet-riddled horse by the roadside. When he told his landlords, they chuckled and confessed that it was one of their neighbor's horses and that sometimes "their aim was not so good." Returning from his collecting hikes, Nabokov was "more concerned with the ra-ta-ta fanning around from the lodge than with the ugly moose in the willow bogs around it."[48]

One day Dmitri and Richard Buxbaum were deposited at the base of Disappointment Peak, just next to the East Ridge of Grand Teton, whose 13,700-foot peak rises an abrupt seven thousand feet from the level valley floor. They began climbing the regular route, which called for no special mountaineering gear, until Dmitri, a cocky fifteen, led Buxbaum up the much more difficult east face. They found themselves almost stuck, and lacked the equipment and technique to descend from ledges onto which they had hoisted themselves. Darkness was near when they scrambled out at last to two frantic parents.[49]

Buxbaum hitchhiked back east in mid-August. By the end of the month, Nabokov had lost more pounds and found more butterflies. Taking full advantage of having their own car, the family left Wyoming at the end of August and swung north on the return journey, driving through Minnesota and up above the Great Lakes along the rocky roads of northern Ontario, collecting all the way.[50]

VIII

Back in Ithaca by September 4, Nabokov had three courses to teach in the coming year: the English and the Russian survey courses, scheduled for the same hours as the year before, and a course on Pushkin, Russian 311–12 (Thursdays, 4:15–6:15). Although this was a new course, it consisted of seminars with only four students, and preparation left Nabokov just enough time during the academic year to write the last five chapters he had planned of his autobiography.

As soon as he arrived back from his summer travels, he had hurried to complete "Student Days," a chapter on the nostalgia for Russia that saturated his thoughts at Cambridge, and was able to send it off to the *New Yorker* in mid-October. Before Katharine White disclosed her reaction to the chapter, she saw Nabokov in Ithaca. She and E. B. White had a son studying at Cornell, and while visiting him there at the end of October they visited the Bishops, as they had the previous year, and dined there with the Nabokovs.[51]

Early in November, Katharine White wrote to Nabokov from New York, outlining her response to "Student Days." In one section of his chapter, Nabokov had summarized his youthful attempts to counter the incomprehension among his English acquaintances of the true nature of the Russian Revolution. Katharine White felt that here he lacked his usual detachment and that the bitterness of his tone interrupted the nostalgic mood. He had made the perfectly justified claim that during the last sixty years of the tsars, "despite the fundamentally inept and ferocious character of their rule, a freedom-loving Russian had had incomparably more means of expressing himself, and used to run incomparably less risk in doing so, than under Lenin." Katharine White made the mistake of passing on another editor's query: "and freedom-loving serfs?" She also asked if he could make the passage shorter, less detailed, and less violent. Nabokov replied, "I am terribly sorry, but what you suggest is quite impossible. It is really not my fault that Americans know so little about former Russia. Serfdom was abolished in 1861 (two years before Lincoln's Emancipation Proclamation). I am frank but not bitter." He withdrew the piece from the *New Yorker* and eventually offered it, retitled "Lodgings in Trinity Lane," to *Harper's Magazine*.[52]

Despite such frequent differences, Nabokov and his editor remained on excellent terms. Nabokov wrote to tell her at the end of November that E. B. White's little piece about American eagles and Russian bears was "quite admirable" except for "three unnecessary and lame lines" he specified. She wrote back rather hurt, but he explained: "You misunderstood me. My admiration for your husband's work is boundless, and I love every line he writes. What I really meant was the lameness and futility of hoping the Bears might change (if it were physically and psychologically possible, I would suggest invading the Bears' territory at once)."[53] Nabokov's bracketed afterthought may seem bizarre at this distance, but at the time even Bertrand Russell was ready to advocate a preventive war against Russia before Stalin built up a nuclear arsenal and the power to destroy the world.

Katharine White was a very maternal editor, taking an interest not only in whether a story would be published and in the signs and syntax of the galleys, but also in ways of making the lives of writers easier. Several times she had arranged loans for Nabokov. Over dinner in Ithaca in October, he had told her of his desire to write a chapter on his father, which would require research on the public side of V. D. Nabokov's life at the Library of Congress, a trip he could not afford. Katharine White arranged for the *New Yorker* to pay his expenses. Meanwhile Nabokov had been working on another chapter, "Lantern Slides," about his various Russian tutors, and sent it to her at the end of November. He also outlined to her what was left to write of the autobiography. From the first, he had planned to call it *The Person in Question*.[54] There remained three more chapters to write:

> Chapters 14 (Exile), 15 (Second Person) and 16 (Third Person). Of these the first is concerned with émigré life in Western Europe and has a great deal about literary mores. The second is couched, so to speak, in the second person (being addressed to my wife) and is an account of my boy's infancy in the light of my own childhood. The last is, from my own point of view, the most important one of the series (indeed, the whole book was written with this conclusion and summit in view) since therein are carefully gathered and analyzed (by a fictitious reviewer) the various themes running through the book—all the intricate threads that I have been at pains to follow through each piece. Incidentally, this chapter will include some very nice things about my delightful association with the *New Yorker*.[55]

The novelist William Maxwell, Katharine White's successor as Nabokov's editor at the *New Yorker*, considers that no other *New Yorker* contributor, with the possible exception of Rebecca West, was as loyal as Nabokov to the magazine.[56]

At the beginning of 1949, still in his first semester at Cornell and unable to find time to write anything for the *New Yorker* and thus earn extra income, Nabokov had written to David Daiches, as head of the Division of Literature, to ask him if he might have a raise. No, he might not. Now at the end of 1949, Nabokov had even fewer students in his two survey courses (twelve and seven) than a year earlier, and only four in his Pushkin seminar. Not incomprehensibly, other members of the Division of Literature, and especially Daiches, felt Nabokov a luxury. He had been expected to contribute to general teaching in the Division of Literature and was not doing so; he had a total of only twenty-one students in all three courses combined. Just before Christmas, Daiches wrote to Nabokov warning that university teaching was being scrutinized by efficiency experts and suggesting that it would be much appreciated if he took over Literature 311–12, a course in European fiction then being taught by Professor Charles Weir. This, Daiches hinted, might help with a salary increase or promotion. Nabokov would be free to choose whatever authors he liked, as many Russians as he liked, and he could teach how he liked. He did not hesitate. On the back of Daiches's letter, he devised a rubric that now seems to have a stamp of inevitability, and certainly of Nabokov:

> 311–312 European Fiction. Throughout the year. Credit three hours a term. MWF 12 Mr Nabokov
>
> Selected English, Russian, French and German novels and short stories of the last 150 years will be read. Special attention will be paid to individual genius and questions of structure.[57]

IX

Late in 1949, despairing of finding a journal to publish his long review-essay on the Jakobson-Szeftel edition of *The Song of Igor's Campaign*, Nabokov approached Roman Jakobson directly. Jakobson suggested another possibility—also unsuccessful—but he also had another idea: he would like to include an edition of Nabokov's own translation of the *Song*, with a Russian text edited and brief notes supplied by Szeftel and himself, in a series of Russian classics for students, for which he was acting as general editor. Nabokov replied that he would be happy to revise his translation for this projected edition. He also suggested that the prose translation of *Eugene Onegin* on which he was working might fit Jakobson's proposed series.[58] By the time he had completed the translation of *The Song of Igor's Campaign* in 1959, he would have broken off relations with Jakobson, and his *Eugene Onegin* would still be awaiting publication.

At the end of January 1950, in the break between semesters, Nabokov forfeited his research trip to Washington for the $150 he could get for a lecture at the University of Toronto: once again, "Russian

Literature: Its Triumph and Tribulations."[59] Staying at the Park Plaza Hotel, he began to revolve in his head the first lines of a poem he sent off to Katharine White a month later with the title "The Room":

> The room a dying poet took
> at nightfall in a dead hotel
> had both directories—the Book
> of Heaven and the Book of Bell.[60]

Back in Ithaca, and still short of money, Nabokov agreed to a surprising project: a translation of *The Brothers Karamazov*, with his own introduction and notes, for Pascal Covici of Viking Press. During February and March, meanwhile, he continued to work on the next two chapters of his autobiography, "Exile" and "Second Person." For the latter chapter, a reminiscence, addressed to his wife, of Dmitri's early days, Nabokov had asked Véra to set down her recollections. She typed seven pages, of which he selected only her vivid memories of standing with Dmitri in European winters, watching and waiting for trains: "That incredible amount of heat his big baby body generated!" By mid-March he had finished the first draft of both chapters.[61]

One Friday in mid-March the Nabokovs and the Bishops drove down to New York for a party the *New Yorker* was throwing the next day to celebrate its twenty-fifth birthday. The party, held at the Ritz, was an extraordinary event: over a thousand people invited, and by all accounts a succession of minor disasters. Arriving after supper with the Whites, Nabokov at last met Harold Ross, the *New Yorker*'s founder and first editor, after eight years of indirect meetings through Katharine White, in all sorts of verbal jungles, and lamely joked: "Dr. Ross, I presume?" Ross, who had a reputation for missing the point, missed it again: "No, I'm not a doctor." For the first time since 1948, Nabokov saw Edmund Wilson, who was losing his voice—a notorious bark—with the beginnings of a throat ailment. Hearing that the critic Stanley Edgar Hyman was there, Nabokov marched up to him and asked him what he meant by calling his father "a tsarist liberal." Wilson witnessed the scene: "Hyman, who was evidently afraid that Nabokov was going to attack him physically, replied, 'Oh, I think you're a great writer!—I admire your writing very much!' "[62]

For Nabokov the ill effects of the party lingered for a month. He caught a dose of influenza there that at the end of March brought on an excruciating attack of intercostal neuralgia. Early in April his doctors sent him to the hospital "howling and writhing." Though he knew the symptoms and diagnosed his own condition for the doctors, they refused to believe neuralgia could cause such pain and hopefully tested his kidneys and other organs for two weeks before accepting that the patient might after all be right. At night, when the pains became especially intense, Nabokov received up to three injections of morphine, but each injection kept him "in a state of endurable, dulled pain only for an hour or so."[63] Véra, meanwhile, though suffering from bronchitis herself, once again took Nabokov's place in the classroom.

On his return from New York, just before he was admitted to the hospital, Nabokov had managed to put the finishing touches to "Exile" and "Gardens and Parks," as he had renamed the fifteenth chapter. He now thought of writing still another chapter, to follow "Student Days," "a new venture, a kind of essay on women and love."[64] The advancing illness laid that plan to rest, and the time he lost in the hospital also made him abandon the *Brothers Karamazov* translation. Released from the hospital on April 14, he soon had a bad relapse, missed more classes, and very nearly landed back in the hospital. Only at the end of the month was he able to get up and enjoy life again.[65]

Once more the *New Yorker*'s checking department wanted to change minute details in his latest chapter, like the white of the funnel on the boat that brought Nabokov and his family to America. He would not betray his memory:

> As my policy throughout the book has been to remain absolutely true to a vision of a personal past, I cannot change the color of the funnel although at a pinch I might omit any mention of that color.
>
> As you have probably noticed I often make mistakes when recalling names, titles of books, numbers; but I very seldom err when recalling colors. Since I am absolutely sure (and so are my wife and son) the funnel was white I can only surmise that it was painted white by order of military authorities at St. Nazaire, and that they had taken this liberty with the Champlain's funnel without informing the American office of the French Line. Perhaps some competent person at the Line's office might admit to your checker the possibility of such an occurrence. The voyage was a very dangerous one and it is most unlikely that the liner flaunted its usual black and red.
>
> However, as I do not want to puzzle people, I agree either to delete the word "Champlain" (Galley Nineteen) or to delete the word "white" in the new version of line nine, Galley Twenty (which line I have changed for reasons having nothing to do with the Champlain controversy—there was too great an agglomeration of epithets). I would prefer that you dropped the name of the liner on Galley Nineteen.[66]

Recovered but still shaky, and required to swallow tonic after tonic, Nabokov spent late April and early May writing the sixteenth chapter of his autobiography. On May 14 he completed the chapter, a review as if by another hand of his own memoirs and those of a woman writer he invented for the purpose. After he had traced by means of this "review" all the themes of his autobiography—about which the review is sometimes mildly dismissive—Nabokov decided the deception of the reviewer's mask clashed with the integrity of the memoirist, and dropped the chapter altogether.[67] It still remains unpublished. By now, three years after he had begun it, the book he had decided to call *Conclusive Evidence*—and would later rename *Speak, Memory*—was complete.

CHAPTER 8

Conclusive Evidence / Speak, Memory

I

NO ONE has felt more passion than Nabokov for the radiance of a personal past, and no one has recollected the past with more precision. That alone would suffice to place his autobiography among the greatest ever written. But above all, *Speak, Memory* is the most *artistic* of autobiographies.[1] "The meeting point," as Nabokov himself defines it, "of an impersonal art form and a very personal life story,"[2] it records one man's unique and happy life and at the same time attempts to explore the nature, origins, and destiny of all human consciousness. Again and again its lucid and alluring style and its philosophical probings set up strangely importunate vibrations at a pitch we cannot find. When we discover the right frequency, we will find that without the least falsification of the facts Nabokov has managed to impart to his life a design as complex and harmonious as those of his finest novels.

Some autobiographies succeed by their frankness and fullness, as if memory had been left to speak all its secrets onto an endless reel of tape. Nabokov does not operate that way: unlike his egomaniacal narrators, his Hermanns and his Kinbotes, he does not assume that his life, because it is his, ought to be of interest or concern to others. His purpose is not to tell everything about his life, but to compose a work that by the very artistry of its shaping can express his own deepest convictions far more fully than the thickest transcript of anecdotal reminiscence. The title he chose calls on memory as formally as an epic poet's "Sing, muse. . . ." He had even planned to invoke Mnemosyne, goddess of memory, mother of the muses, until his publisher warned him that *Speak, Mnemosyne* would be commercial suicide.

II

Nabokov wrote *Speak, Memory* in the way he did, not to conceal the truth about his life, but to express his own truth to the fullest, to show not the spontaneous accidents of time past but time itself transcended.

He may write "I confess I do not believe in time," but before he can achieve the timelessness he aims for, he knows he must concede that time is the element in which human lives are lived. He presents himself as an individual developing through time and unravels the threads that combine to make him the unique creature he is. On this level, *Speak, Memory* appears perfectly straightforward, with a chronological structure that records its author's life from his birth in 1899 to his departure from Europe for America at forty, in 1940. Within this outer frame are fifteen chapters, each introducing separable subjects in the order in which they first occur in his life: father, mother, English governesses, Uncle Vasily, French governess, butterflies, first childhood love, Russian tutors, school, adolescence, first poem, first adult love, university, exile, parenthood.

At this level, *Speak, Memory* seduces us by the poetry and accuracy of its evocation of the past. In one scene, Nabokov describes the nocturnal routine of his early childhood. After his mother reads to him downstairs, after she calls out "Step, step, step" as he mounts the stairs beside her with his eyes tightly shut, she hands him over to be undressed and given his evening bath. Beyond the bathroom, the toilet offers another chance to postpone bed:

> The toilets were separate from the bathrooms, and the oldest among them was a rather sumptuous but gloomy affair with some fine panelwork and a tasseled rope of red velvet, which, when pulled, produced a beautifully modulated, discreetly muffled gurgle and gulp. From that corner of the house, one could see Hesperus and hear the nightingales, and it was there that, later, I used to compose my youthful verse, dedicated to unembraced beauties, and morosely survey, in a dimly illuminated mirror, the immediate erection of a strange castle in an unknown Spain. As a small child, however, I was assigned a more modest arrangement, rather casually situated in a narrow recess between a wicker hamper and the door leading to the nursery bathroom. This door I liked to keep ajar; through it I drowsily looked at the shimmer of steam above the mahogany bath, at the fantastic flotilla of swans and skiffs, at myself with a harp in one of the boats, at a furry moth pinging against the reflector of the kerosene lamp, at the stained-glass window beyond, at its two halberdiers consisting of colored rectangles. Bending from my warm seat, I liked to press the middle of my brow, its ophryon to be precise, against the smooth comfortable edge of the door and then roll my head a little so that the door would move to and fro while its edge remained all the time in soothing contact with my forehead. A dreamy

rhythm would permeate my being. The recent "Step, step, step," would be taken up by a dripping faucet. And, fruitfully combining rhythmic pattern with rhythmic sound, I would unravel the labyrinthian frets on the linoleum, and find faces where a crack or a shadow afforded a *point de repère* for the eye.

Nabokov's imagination awakened early in childhood, and throughout his life he held on with an exceptional loyalty and force to all that had stimulated his mind and heart then. All children dawdle their way to bed, all have their rituals of delay, but it takes a Nabokov to remember every detail fifty years later and to re-create sensations like rocking the edge of a door back and forth with one's temple that most of us once knew but had forgotten.

III

He permits us to follow him into the toilet, and he even allows a hint of adolescent erotic self-display. But even here he stresses not his frankness but the artistic imagination evident in the dreamy fancifulness of this young child. And although he can hardly undertake an autobiography without sacrificing some of his own privacy, he refuses to infringe on the privacy of others. His favorite sister, still living, receives a single mention by name in the first version of his autobiography; his close friends in school or in émigré days receive none at all; those he must mention, like "Colette" and "Tamara," he hides behind pseudonyms; and only when they are dead, like his parents, his uncle, or his cousin Yuri, will he let real people play a large part under their own names.

Speak, Memory may show Nabokov's development, but it is no newsreel of his times, no dressing room lined with signed celebrity photographs. Only because their privacy has already been compromised by fame, Nabokov allows himself three pages of concise, astute summaries of leading émigré writers—Khodasevich, Bunin, Adamovich. And he rarely presents more than an accurate reflected gleam of historical events: himself at four, running trains over ice in imitation of the Russian army crossing frozen Lake Baikal to fight Japan, or his son in Berlin, seeing the ubiquitous image of Hitler repeated on the black mustache-smudge of a bed of pansies; a burst of Socialist Revolutionary ardor in a fondly recollected village schoolteacher, a burst of rifle fire as Bloody Sunday erupts nearby.

Only on one matter does Nabokov face history squarely. He persistently attempts to correct Western ignorance of prerevolutionary

Russia and the emigration. As the reaction of his *New Yorker* editors showed, even highly educated Americans could still think Lenin overthrew the tsars and freed the serfs—which is rather like having Napoleon lead the storming of the Bastille or Woodrow Wilson emancipate America's slaves. While deploring the legacy of tsarist tyranny and catastrophic economic inequality, Nabokov stresses the vigorous existence of liberal and radical thought, often socialist and revolutionary in inclination, in prerevolutionary Russia, and its brutal suppression by Lenin. He attacked the common excuse others make for the Soviet Union—that it lacks freedom because Western freedom has never been a Russian tradition—by pointing out that in the years leading up to November 1917, St. Petersburg had, for certain spells, and with lamentable lapses, an independent judiciary and perhaps a more cosmopolitan culture than any Western capital of the time. He also maintains adamantly that in grieving as he did for the past, he mourns not lost property but the unreal estate of memory. Even as a child, with his parents still in command of all their wealth, he could feel the bitterness of exile from his brief but already irretrievable past.

IV

His concern in *Speak, Memory* was not with the headlines or the gossip columns of history, but with a different kind of time. The book opens with a meditation on death, time, mortal consciousness, and "the free world of timelessness" from which we remain barred in life. *Speak, Memory* aims not to record spontaneous, unguarded time but to show the mind triumphing over time, as far as it can, and to intimate something beyond human time. Nabokov pictures himself at the toilet not to catch himself with his pants down, but to stress the spacious time of his daily rhythms, and his perfect recapture of even Vyra's humblest rooms; to link the infant lapsing into reverie with the adolescent composing verse in another bathroom; to connect the child unraveling patterns on the linoleum floor with the adult searching out patterns in time like this very proneness to pattern that links adult and child.

Nabokov's attempt to escape the rigid sequentiality of time begins on the first page of *Speak, Memory* and recurs in meditation after meditation throughout the book. It also shapes the structure of the whole work. Although the chapters succeed one another in chronological fashion, from English governesses to French, from Russian tutors to school, from school to university, each chapter displays a certain looseness, a deliberately understated coherence of subject, a refusal to follow a narrow chronological line. Although there is nothing especially English about them, Nabokov devotes all that space to the two toilets in his Russian home as part of a chapter on his English education. The chapter's sequence is determined by the fact that he was raised by English nurses and governesses between 1903 and 1906, and therefore this chapter must precede the one on his French governess, who arrived in 1906. But within the rubric "My English Education" Nabokov also treats of the general Anglophilia of his home; his mother's reading him English fairy tales before he ascended to bed, and reciting English prayers with him before tucking him in; an English tutor and an English drawing-master of about 1907–1908; and, in a final coda from the 1940s, a conversation with his most important drawing-master, not an Englishman at all but a Russian, about another drawing-master, also Russian. Even within the uninterrupted continuum from his mother's stories in the drawing room to pillow-top prayers, Nabokov consciously resists the pressure of time, to re-create a capacious, immobile, invulnerable space around the toilet where he would sit and dream away the moments, while before rendering that scene he slips ahead to another toilet he would frequent ten years later. As he describes the scene he celebrates the retrieval of time, the fact that memory can recollect, in such amplitude and detail, these two settings—or innumerable other scenes he could rescue from the past, if he happened to require them for his theme.

Speak, Memory's highly wrought style constantly emphasizes its author's total command of the past. This is not the jostling street theater of chance recollection, but a highly controlled performance, with Nabokov in the director's chair: "With a sharp and merry blast from the whistle that was part of my first sailor suit, my childhood calls me back into that distant past to have me shake hands again with my delightful teacher. Vasiliy Martïnovich Zhernosekov had a fuzzy brown beard, a balding head, and china-blue eyes." One scene begins thus:

> A large, alabaster-based kerosene lamp is steered into the gloaming. Gently it floats and comes down; the hand of memory, now in a footman's white glove, places it in the center of a round table. The flame is nicely adjusted, and a rosy, silk-flounced lamp shade, with inset glimpses of rococo winter sports, crowns the readjusted (cotton wool in Casimir's ear) light. Revealed: a warm, bright, stylish ("Russian Empire") drawing room in a snow-muffled house.

He can change the scene suddenly, without warning, to reveal himself in America, fifty years later, as snowy Vyra gives way without warning to snowy New England. Or as a boy he chases a butterfly through a bog near Vyra, and emerges at the end of the marsh in Colorado, only to add:

> I confess I do not believe in time. I like to fold my magic carpet, after use, in such a way as to superimpose one part of the pattern upon another. Let visitors trip. And the highest enjoyment of timelessness—in a landscape selected at random—is when I stand among rare butterflies and their food plants. This is ecstasy, and behind the ecstasy is something else, which is hard to explain. It is like a momentary vacuum into which rushes all that I love. A sense of oneness with sun and stone. A thrill of gratitude to whom it may concern—to the contrapuntal genius of human fate or to tender ghosts humoring a lucky mortal.

Why does Nabokov do such things? Why does he highlight his own mastery of the past? How can he say things like "I do not believe in time"? That phrase introduces the last paragraph of a chapter, and chapter after chapter closes on a similar note of strange exaltation, like the sentence at the end of the first chapter where Nabokov's father, tossed in the air by peasants, becomes a frescoed figure on a church vault while his own body lies below for his funeral. Nothing could be more typical of *Speak, Memory*—or of all Nabokov's mature art—than to install us within a scene so alive it devolves right around us, then subject us to some weird displacement. He can place us in a world so crisply alive we almost gasp in its intoxicating air, and then send us plummeting back to grief. The happiness *and* the grief *and* the mastery of the mind that can encompass both and can simultaneously short-circuit time hint here, as throughout *Speak, Memory*, at the possibility that we might one day find ourselves in a different kind of time where nothing will be lost.*

V

The key to *Speak, Memory* lies in what Nabokov called its "themes," for it is their intricate interrelationship that allows him to conflate both his own evolution in time and his effort to transcend time.

Nabokov stressed that neither one's biological birthright nor one's social setting, nor even their conjunction, can account for the stamp of self. He gives both their due, of course: his parents' intelligence,

---

* For an analysis of the sentence where Nabokov's father is tossed in the air, see *Vladimir Nabokov: The Russian Years*, introduction; for the theme of "a different kind of time" in Nabokov's thought, see chapter 13 of that volume.

memory, and sensitivity, his mother's synesthesia, her love of the visual, his father's robust independence, his humor; the world of St. Petersburg and Vyra, Biarritz and Abbazia, governesses and tutors, love and liberty.[3] But near the start of *Speak, Memory*, he declares he would like to explain his "individual mystery" by something more than environment or heredity. He does not explain how, and in the next section of this first chapter he appears to digress, or to offer a solution that will hardly help. He recounts how General Kuropatkin, on the day he was named commander in chief of the Manchurian army, showed the four-year-old Volodya a rather dull match trick. Fifteen years later, as V. D. Nabokov was fleeing from Bolshevik-held Petrograd to the Crimea, he was accosted on a bridge by a peasant in a sheepskin coat asking for a light. "The next moment each recognized the other. I hope old Kuropatkin, in his rustic disguise, managed to evade Soviet imprisonment, but that is not the point. What pleases me is the evolution of the match theme. . . . The following of such thematic designs through one's life should be, I think, the true purpose of autobiography." This may sound unpromising, a flippant throwaway or, if serious, the misguided manifesto of an affected aesthete. In fact, it is exactly what Fyodor discovers in his own past in *The Gift* ("one of those repetitions, one of those thematic 'voices' with which, according to all the rules of harmony, destiny enriches the life of observant men"),[4] and central to Nabokov's thought.

What we cannot reduce to environment and heredity is the elusive uniqueness of the individual, or if we translate this into terms of time, freedom (if we are looking forward) or individual fate (looking backward). At each moment time is an infinity of branching possibilities, and the self can unfurl as it chooses. But precisely because time branches out so richly, with such a flowering of detail, the retrospective gaze can find, among all the infinite, opulent growth of the past, patterns so often repeated in a single life they seem the very mark of that person's individual destiny.

VI

Nabokov wrote that he had planned *Speak, Memory* "according to the way his life had been planned by unknown players of games."[5] In *The Gift*, Fyodor presents Nikolay Chernyshevsky in a disconcertingly bold and obvious fashion as the plaything of fate. That excursus serves as Fyodor's "firing practice" before stalking the more subtle patterns of fate in his own life. In similar fashion, Nabokov in his own autobiography impersonates fate's role in his father's death in a deliberately obtrusive manner in order to prepare us for the more discreet patterns he can discern when he turns to his own life.

The first intimation of V. D. Nabokov's death, of course, comes at the end of the first chapter, when the local peasants toss him skyward. At the end of another chapter, Nabokov wonders whether he had not kept missing something vulnerable and poignant in his French governess "that I could appreciate only after the things and beings that I had most loved in the security of my childhood, had been turned to ashes or shot through the heart."[6] The chapter that introduces Nabokov at school closes with his discovery that his father has challenged someone to a duel, his dreadful visions of his father killed with rapier or pistol, and his relief on returning home to discover that the duel will not take place:

> Years were to pass before a certain night in 1922, at a public lecture in Berlin, when my father shielded the lecturer (his old friend Milyukov) from the bullets of two Russian Fascists and, while vigorously knocking down one of the assassins, was fatally shot by the other. But no shadow was cast by that future event upon the bright stairs of our St. Petersburg house; the large, cool hand resting on my head did not quaver, and several lines of play in a difficult chess composition were not blended yet on the board.

In the Crimea, Nabokov reports on the harmless people shot and dumped by Bolshevik sailors from the Yalta pier, then adds, "My father, who was not harmless, had joined us by this time, after some dangerous adventures, and, in that region of lung specialists, had adopted the mimetic disguise of a doctor without changing his name ('simple and elegant,' as a chess annotator would have said of a corresponding move on the board)." At the end of that chapter, as their ship sails out of Sebastopol harbor to wild machine-gun fire from the Bolshevik troops onshore, Nabokov and his father remain on deck playing chess. Nabokov prefigures his father's death as an insidious chess problem designed by fate, and yet "the selective apparatus pertains to art; but the parts selected belong to unadulterated life."[7]

VII

Nabokov of course knew his own life in immeasurably finer detail than his father's, and he searches through his own past for a far more elaborate interweaving of thematic designs. The very search, he feels, the disregarding of time as causality and sequence, prefigures something beyond the prison of human time, some state of consciousness where nothing is lost, where there is endless leisure to perceive the harmonies of time, as in Cincinnatus C.'s *there*, where "time takes shape according to one's pleasure, like a figured rug whose folds can be gathered in such a way that two designs will meet—and the rug is once again smoothed out, and you live on, or else superimpose the next image on the last, endlessly, endlessly." [8]

As Nabokov writes, his method is "to explore the remotest regions of his past life for what may be termed thematic trails or currents."[9] One such trail is the theme of garden paths and forest trails. It begins in the scene, Nabokov's first conscious memory, of his walking between his parents along the avenue of oak saplings at Vyra, when he asked his parents' age and for the first time distinctly realized "that I was I and that my parents were my parents." As a slightly older boy, he kneels on his pillow to pray and looks at the aquarelle above his bed, a dusky path winding through a beech wood. Recalling a fairy tale his mother has read him, he imagines climbing into the picture and plunging into that enchanted forest. At the end of the book, he discusses his son's earliest conscious life, and shows the boy walking between his parents not through a family estate but through one public park after another leading from Berlin and Prague to Paris and St. Nazaire, stepping down to the Atlantic shore and their boat for America.

Nabokov's themes interlace like the paths of an elaborate park. As a lepidopterist, he first followed the paths of Vyra's parks. Soon his ambition expanded. Beyond Vyra proper lay a bog the family called "America" because it seemed so far from home. Nabokov describes himself venturing into it in pursuit of butterflies and emerging on the other side to find himself near Longs Peak, in the American Rockies. America itself has become a new theme. As a boy, Nabokov had dreamed of discovering new species of butterfly; as a man, he saw the dream come true in the American West. America's Wild West figures in games young Vladimir plays with his cousin Yuri, inspired by their reading of Mayne Reid's *Headless Horseman*, and as narrator Nabokov suddenly leaps from Captain Reid's "log-walled Texan hotel, in the year of our Lord . . . 1850," and its bright saloon lamps, to note, in a jarring disruption of his childhood world, "in another year of our Lord—namely 1941—I caught some very good moths at the neon lights of a gasoline station between Dallas and Fort Worth."

A lover of young trains (trains are another theme) young Vladimir asks his drawing teacher Mr. Cummings to draw an express for him: "I watched his pencil ably evolve the cowcatcher and elaborate headlights of a locomotive that looked as if it had been acquired secondhand for the Trans-Siberian line after it had done duty at Promontory

Point, Utah, in the sixties." At the end of this chapter, a paragraph later, the adult Nabokov asks his later drawing master Dobuzhinsky about a third teacher, whom he had not liked:

> "And what about Yaremich?" I asked M. V. Dobuzhinski, one summer afternoon in the nineteen forties, as we strolled through a beech forest in Vermont. "Is he remembered?"
>
> "Indeed, he is," replied Mstislav Valerianovich. "He was exceptionally gifted. I don't know what kind of teacher he was, but I do know that *you* were the most hopeless pupil I ever had."

Amusing in its own right, the scene shows the end result of Nabokov's English education and of all the early intimations of America: Nabokov himself, safely installed in the United States, living as an English writer. Moreover, just a few pages after describing the painted beech wood into which he had once dreamed of climbing, he now portrays himself strolling through a beech forest with a famous painter. Like Martin Edelweiss, he lives out the realization of his dream.

Nabokov sometimes highlights his themes by devices like the stark shift to Dallas–Fort Worth or the stealthy glide from the Russian bog to Longs Peak. At other times he slips themes in almost unnoticed (America in the cowcatchered locomotive from Promontory Point, Utah) or overlaps theme on theme until we can barely disentangle one from another (America, forest paths, and the passing-into-the-painting theme as Dobuzhinsky dismisses his pupil's skill). As readers we are left to detect a theme camouflaged against its backdrop or to untie the riddle of numerous interlacing themes—and in fact natural mimicry and its camouflages form a theme of their own, as do riddles and games of every kind. The game and riddle theme has a special justification: commenting on the very subject of *Speak, Memory*'s themes, Nabokov observed that "the unravelling of a riddle is the purest and most basic act of the human mind."[10] *Speak, Memory*'s themes in fact are nothing less than the riddles of time.

VIII

Three other thematic patterns deserve special attention. First, the theme of exile. Even in early childhood, on vacation in the Adriatic, Nabokov mooned in his cot for Vyra and tried to conjure it up in its minutest details. Even then he discovered that "time, so boundless at first blush, was a prison," even then he felt the first pangs of exile, even then his pining for a time where he would not be shut out of his past foreshadowed his adult self. When Nabokov came to write his autobiography, that early sense of exile satisfied his wish to show how thoroughly his childhood already "contained, on a much reduced scale, the main components of his creative maturity."[11]

After his childhood sense of exile from his past came the real fact of exile, his Pushkinian nostalgia in a Pushkinian Crimea, his "Oh, to be in Russia" sighs at Cambridge, his Sirin phase in Berlin and France. Nabokov describes his life in terms of his helical version of Hegel's triad, as "a colored spiral in a small ball of glass": his first twenty years in Russia form the thesis, the next twenty-one of emigration the antithesis, his years in America the synthesis (and, as he would later add in the revised *Speak, Memory*, a new thesis). At the end of the chapter where he introduces this spiral, he describes in detail—this is the climax of the game-and-puzzle theme—the famous chess problem that he designed on the thesis-antithesis-synthesis model, and the bribe that at last secured him his *visa de sortie*, and the Contrôle des Informations stamp—wartime authorization to take written material out of France—on the sheet of paper where he had drawn the chess problem. Why end with that stamp? Because the bureaucratic French stamp on his *visa de sortie* also solved another problem, the real-life problem of exile. After the "pleasurable torments" of the "roundabout route," America—both remote from Russia and a new homeland—provided as neat a synthetic solution to the problem of exile as bishop to c2 in Nabokov's best chess problem.

Another, quite different, theme has shown through for a moment in that "colored spiral in a small ball of glass": the theme of rainbows, spectra, colored glass, jewels. More prevalent than any other theme, it begins with the jewelry Nabokov's mother would produce for her son's bedtime amusement, and the alphabetic building blocks whose array of colors the synesthetic child told his mother were all wrong. It recurs in the "stained glass window" of the toilet where he dreamed as a child, with "its two halberdiers consisting of colored rectangles." It shines in all its glory in the scene of his first poem. After taking shelter from a thunderstorm in a pavilion at Vyra, Nabokov sees the sun return and cast luminous colored rhomboids on the floor from the colored-glass lozenges of the pavilion windows, while outside a rainbow slips into view, and at that moment his first poem begins. Nabokov orchestrates this theme in order to contrast the tangible gems his mother could lend him (and later sell off in exile) with the iridescence of a rainbow, or with the intangible riches of consciousness—the colored sensations of the past and his ability to re-create them in language—that were his real wealth in exile.

The third theme is very different again: the theme of love. Girls and women quickened his heart from an early age: his pretty cousin Onya at three, his governess, Miss Norcott, at four, then—to mention only those he assigns names—Zina, Colette, Louise, Polenka, and at sixteen his real first love, Tamara. From the beginning, Nabokov's romantic feelings and his creative imagination advance hand in hand. This pattern too reaches a climax at that pavilion: there his first poem begins, there he first talks to Tamara. Then the pattern takes a touching new twist. Toward the end of the book, at first intermittently but again and again throughout the last chapter, Nabokov turns to address directly the implicit summation of the whole series, his wife and muse: "The years are passing, my dear, and presently nobody will know what you and I know."

The next sentence continues: "Our child is growing." Love between parent and child encircles the whole book: the toddler at the beginning, walking along a path at Vyra between the parents he revered, the forty-year-old at the end strolling with his wife and the son they adored through a garden in St. Nazaire. Nabokov stresses the essential creativity of parental as of romantic love: his parents' eager desire to awaken his imagination, his and Vera's feeding on demand their son's avid thirst for life.

For Nabokov, the love of parent and child and man and woman are such extraordinary forces they make more urgent than anything else his question: what are the limits of my being?

> It cannot be helped; I must know where I stand, where you and my son stand. When that slow-motion, silent explosion of love takes place in me, unfolding its melting fringes and overwhelming me with the sense of something much vaster, much more enduring and powerful than the accumulation of matter or energy in any imaginable cosmos, then my mind cannot but pinch itself to see if it is really awake. I have to make a rapid inventory of the universe. . . . I have to have all space and all time participate in my emotion, in my mortal love, so that the edge of its mortality is taken off, thus helping me to fight the utter degradation, ridicule, and horror of having developed an infinity of sensation and thought within a finite existence.

In *Speak, Memory*, Nabokov presents parental and sexual love as different currents of life's creative mystery, both stirring us to the depth, both liable to flood the banks of the self. No wonder he attacks Freud more often here than anywhere else. Not only did he have a fierce sense of his own independence and a corresponding disinclination to wear someone else's ill-fitting mythic masks, not only did he have both an extraordinarily precise memory of his early childhood that he had good reason to trust better than Freud's, and an abnormally sharp eye for the unique patterns of his own life, but he detested the way Freud befouled something he held as precious as family love.

IX

At the close of *Speak, Memory*, all its themes come together, like the final dance of the characters around the circus ring at the end of Fellini's *8½*: orderly and slow, irrationally exhilarating, inexplicably ecstatic.

Nabokov begins *Speak, Memory* with a meditation on the origins and ends of individual consciousness, a stylized account of his own lifelong attempt "to distinguish the faintest of personal glimmers in the impersonal darkness on both sides of my life," and a report on the first awakening of his reflexive mind that he deliberately compares with the phylogenetic birth of consciousness in human evolution. He dates his first awakening of self-consciousness to the stroll between his parents in the avenue of oak saplings at Vyra. When he closes the book with a chapter on his son's emerging consciousness, he once again links it with "the riddle of the initial blossoming of man's mind" and with other gardens and parks.

Watching over his infant son, Nabokov broods on the birth of the human brain and of this particular little mind:

> that swimming, sloping, elusive something about the dark-bluish tint of the iris which seemed still to retain the shadows it had absorbed of ancient, fabulous forests where there were more birds than tigers and more fruit than thorns, and where, in some dappled depth, man's mind had been born; and above all, an infant's journey into the next dimension, the newly established nexus between eye and reachable object, which the career boys in biometrics or in the rat-maze racket think they can explain. It occurs to me that the closest reproduction of the mind's birth obtainable is the stab of wonder that accompanies the precise moment when, gazing at a tangle of twigs and leaves, one suddenly realizes that what had seemed a natural component of that tangle is a marvelously disguised insect or bird.

As Dmitri learns to walk and his parents prepare to leave Europe, the gardens and parks through which they take their son lead down toward the sea. By the shore, the boy searches for colored glass and chips of majolica that might be reassembled, in some improbable jigsaw, into a complete bowl—and the gardens-and-parks theme, the spectrum theme and the puzzle theme are all beginning to converge.

At St. Nazaire, as they are about to board the *Champlain* for New York, the Nabokovs stroll through one last garden with Dmitri between them. Nabokov can remember no more of the garden than its geometrical design, which he could no doubt "easily fill in with the colors of plausible flowers, if I were careless enough to break the hush of pure memory."

> What I really remember about this neutrally blooming design, is its clever thematic connection with transatlantic gardens and parks; for suddenly, as we came to the end of its path, you and I saw something that we did not immediately point out to our child, so as to enjoy in full the blissful shock, the enchantment and glee he would experience on discovering ahead the ungenuinely gigantic, the unrealistically real prototype of the various toy vessels he had doddled about in his bath. There in front of us, where a broken row of houses stood between us and the harbor, and where the eye encountered all sorts of stratagems, such as pale-blue and pink underwear cakewalking on a clothesline, or a lady's bicycle and a striped cat oddly sharing a rudimentary balcony of cast iron, it was most satisfying to make out among the jumbled angles of roofs and walls, a splendid ship's funnel, showing from behind the clothesline as something in a scrambled picture—Find What the Sailor Has Hidden—that the finder cannot unsee once it has been seen.

Here the themes spin together and fuse like the colors on a rainbow-striped top, as if motionless, as if in defiance of gravity: gardens and parks, of course, but also puzzles (Find What the Sailor Has Hidden) and America—America, the destination of the ship, the third twist of the spiral, the ultimate synthesis, the solution of the problem of exile: a new home ahead. And still more looms in wait.

Nabokov ends his book with Dmitri about to see through the puzzle's camouflage the "ungenuinely gigantic, the unrealistically real prototype" of his own toy ships. That image recalls an earlier one, Nabokov's one spell of clairvoyance. Lying in bed with a waning fever, young Vladimir vividly visualized his mother taking a sleigh all the way to Treumann's shop, and emerging after having bought a pencil—which for some reason she had given to her footman to carry. Real life caught up with his pellucid vision as his mother entered his room, carrying a monstrous pencil:

> It had been, in my vision, greatly reduced in size—perhaps, because I subliminally corrected what logic warned me might still be the dreaded remnants of delirium's dilating world. Now the object proved to be a giant polygonal Faber pencil, four feet long and correspondingly thick. It had been hanging as a showpiece in the shop's window, and she pre-

sumed I had coveted it, as I coveted all things that were not quite purchasable.

Nabokov knows that thought tapers off as we approach the boundaries of consciousness, but also that if we are to understand the position of consciousness—and for him, that is an "immemorial urge" of humankind—then those boundaries are precisely what we must explore. The return of consciousness after a childhood illness such as he describes here replays in a sense the initial dawn of consciousness, but with an observer now in place. Then in *Speak, Memory*'s final chapter, Nabokov prepares for its ending by suggesting that another echo of the shock of the mind's birth is the shock of seeing through an instance of natural mimicry—a phenomenon he sees as the supreme instance of the splendidly deceptive artfulness of life. With that preparation, he now makes the last scene of the book an image of the mind's birth. As he and his wife take Dmitri down toward their ship, life appears to have staged another playful deception, and mother and father join in, waiting with excitement for the explosive shock their son is about to experience, the sudden jolt to his mind that they know he will never forget.

Nabokov has still not finished. At the end of chapter 1, his father gets tossed up into the sky, and seems to freeze into a celestial fresco on a church ceiling, to soar up from life into the eternity of art. As a boy, Nabokov himself dreams of walking into a painting's forest trail. Now at the close of the book he takes his son along a garden path and notices ahead that they are stepping into a picture-puzzle, toward the ship that will take them to America. That step toward the picture at the end of the last chapter of his life story pointedly matches the end of his first chapter. Then, the vision of his father soaring up into a picture prefigures his father's death. Now he is himself a father, and he depicts himself stepping into a picture and out of the story of his life, as if to imply a step beyond life and into the timeless world of death: a synthetic solution, an exile from life, but also a return home to greater freedom, to the place where all the paths of one's past timelessly meet.

Nabokov wants to suggest that the art behind life prepares for us, as we step into mortality's final picture, as we step from the thesis of life through the antithesis of death into the synthesis of timelessness, another explosion of consciousness as shocking as the mind's original explosion, where with a new clairvoyance we will see the unrealistically real prototypes of our past, where we will find the solution that we cannot unsee once it has been seen.

X

Nabokov lets us look at his world twice over: once within time, once as if beyond. His intuition of the absurdity of receding time makes him treasure his world and try with all his strength of mind to preserve all the precious trifles that otherwise might never be retrieved. Most readers of *Speak, Memory* treasure the book, quite rightly, for its priceless, precise detail.

But Nabokov also invites us to look another way at our world. If we detach ourselves from the everyday coherence of things, if we imagine time not as a rigid sequence of cause and effect but as an accumulation of bright particulars, all accessible within some field of timeless vision, everything might suddenly change. For the very reason that he has stored up so much, Nabokov can detect or construct an astonishingly complex pattern in his past that remains quite invisible at first. He treats his life here just as he has treated the lives of characters like Luzhin, Martin, and Fyodor. He has to: if he believes in the artfulness of life, in a designer behind the apparently undesigned, he ought to be able to detect elaborate design in his own life. Amazingly, he does just that.

And not only that. He discerns design amidst the most unpromising material life could offer: the absurd and bungled assassination attempt that led to his father's senseless murder, the apocalyptic helter-skelter of his own life as a refugee. Nabokov shapes the pattern of fate that points to his father's death as if it were a series of chess moves played by unknown forces. The last move of all before checkmate is the unruly exodus before the Bolshevik advance through the Crimea. Days after the previous evacuee ships have left, the Nabokovs sail out of Sebastopol harbor as machine guns strafe its waters, while Nabokov and his father sit on deck, coolly playing a game of chess with a patched-up set.

The patterns accessible to Nabokov in his father's life prefigure in simple form the ampler design he can make out in his own. Twice history had jolted his own destiny sideways with a sickening lurch: first in that enforced escape from Lenin's Russia and then in his flight from Hitler's Europe. Although nothing could seem more haphazard than the plight of the refugee, Nabokov selects this acme of impersonal chaos as the focus for the design in his own life. His descent with his son toward the waterfront at St. Nazaire, with a special chess problem in his baggage and a picture-puzzle ahead, deliberately recalls his flight with his father from Russia. Even in such apprehensive, ugly, anarchic moments he can detect pattern and point.

He makes his patterns converge on the last line of his life story as if to suggest that, could we only detach ourselves from the world of human time, something surprising might emerge into view: an artfulness and harmony hiding in things, even in things at their worst, watching over life with parental tenderness and leading us to the point where all the patterns meet, to the great transition of death, to the shock of the mind's new birth, to something unrealistically real, larger than the toys we can play with in life, to our passage at last into "the free world of timelessness."

CHAPTER 9

Teaching European Fiction: Cornell, 1950–1951

I

AS A BOY in an Anglophile Russian household, Nabokov used to sit down with his brother and sisters to hear his father read *Great Expectations*. Not wanting to break the spell of those rainy-day readings, he had not broached Dickens on his own, devouring instead Stevenson, Kipling, Wells, Conan Doyle, and Chesterton. As an aspiring poet in his teens and early twenties, he had avidly read English verse, and Shakespeare, Keats, and Browning always remained favorites. Later, he kept up with twentieth-century English fiction, as he did with French and Russian, but he had no extensive knowledge of earlier English novelists. In April 1950, in a brief respite before the final onslaught of his intercostal neuralgia, he had sought Edmund Wilson's advice: "Next year I am teaching a course called 'European Fiction' (XIX and XXc.) What English writers (novels or short stories) would you suggest? I must have at least two. Am going to lean heavily on the Russians, at least five broad-shouldered Russians, and shall probably choose Kafka, Flaubert and Proust to illustrate West European fiction." Wilson recommended Austen and Dickens as incomparably the greatest English novelists, along with the Irishman Joyce. Nabokov reacted with a Russian disdain for lady novelists: "I dislike Jane, and am prejudiced, in fact, against all women writers. They are in another class. Could never see anything in *Pride and Prejudice*." He thought he would choose *Dr. Jekyll and Mr. Hyde* instead. By mid-May he was halfway through *Bleak House* ("great stuff"), taking copious notes, and had decided, after all, to follow Wilson's advice and teach *Mansfield Park*.[1]

Though Nabokov had security of tenure at Cornell as he never had at Wellesley, his salary of $5,000 was not at all high. Since he had begun to publish his autobiography chapter by chapter in the *New Yorker* in 1947, he had received a second income almost equal to his university salary. In the coming year, with a new course to prepare for a large class, a course that would require him to teach books he still barely knew, he would have little time to earn money by writing for the *New Yorker*. His current writing project in any case would hardly be suitable for serial publication, especially in a magazine so prim underneath its sophistication. For what he had in mind—had long had in mind—was *The Kingdom by the Sea*, a novel about an older man's obsessive love for a little girl, a book that even in finished form might remain unpublishable during his lifetime.

With no prospect of a piecemeal additional income while he set to the task of composing the novel, Nabokov urgently hoped for a commercial success from *Conclusive Evidence*. Readers' reactions to the chapters of the book as they appeared in the *New Yorker* had been ecstatic. Playwright S. N. Behrman, for instance, whose *New Yorker* sketches of the legendary art dealer Joseph Duveen Nabokov had been enjoying and would later draw upon for Demon Veen in *Ada*, had written to Katharine White: "The Nabokov pieces are simply marvelous; I deeply cherish them. When are they coming out as a book; that is a book I will want to own and send and send." So far Nabokov's American books had all been dismal commercial flops. With his autobiography he hoped that the intensity of his local reputation might at last translate into book sales across the country. In April he learned that Harper and Brothers would publish *Conclusive Evidence* not in September, in ample time for sales to build toward Christmas, but in ice-bound January.[2]

At Cornell a different kind of disappointment lay in store. He had asked Dean Cottrell why he was not officially listed as the chairman of the Department of Russian Literature. Cottrell's answer was straightforward: there was no such department at Cornell, and Nabokov was simply an associate professor of Russian Literature within the Division of Literature chaired by David Daiches. Citing to Cottrell a 1947 letter from Morris Bishop that specified he would become chairman of the Department of Russian Literature, Nabokov declared himself thoroughly disappointed "to find out, after two years, that the notion I had of my position was based on a misunderstanding."[3] The boxes of stationery he had printed with his supposed departmental title were now so much scrap paper.

Correctly inferring that Russian literature had too few students at Cornell to warrant departmental status, Nabokov wrote two days later to Roman Jakobson at Harvard asking if he knew of any vacancies in the Russian departments of the larger universities, because he was dissatisfied with his present position. One reason was "the very small student enrollment of the Russian Literature Department, the result of the poor preparation they receive at the very mediocre Russian Language Department. Moreover, this poor preparation does not allow me to organize my courses on the level one would normally expect to exist at a first class university."⁴ Perhaps too at this moment Nabokov was hoping, despite his initial acquiescence, to avoid the necessity of preparing new lectures on French, German, and English books even if some of them were works he revered. In the 1930s he had contemplated teaching French literature as a second string to Russian, since at Cambridge he had taken both subjects. But he had never formally studied English literature and had read very little German. No wonder he would have preferred a better-paid job in an autonomous Russian department with students who were capable of handling literary Russian and where he would not be obliged to prepare new material in areas in which he was no specialist.

No escape routes opened up, however, and there was nothing for it but to settle down to the European fiction course, known as "Dirty Lit" on campus in honor of the professor whose course Nabokov was inheriting, Charles Weir, "a sad, gentle, hard-drinking fellow who was more interested in the sex life of authors than in their books." Early in May, Nabokov consulted Weir; by midmonth he was happily ensconced in *Bleak House* and preparing the course that he would teach every year he remained at Cornell.⁵

II

At the end of May, on the day after the last exams in his Russian literature courses, Nabokov traveled to Boston to have his last six lower teeth removed. While there, Véra was stopped for speeding: failing to stop when a police car signaled to her, she was pursued for ten minutes and then crowded into the curb at seventy miles an hour. For that, she lost the Massachusetts part of her license.⁶

On his way back to Ithaca, Nabokov had to investigate a patch of pine-scrub waste by the railroad tracks near Karner, once a whistle-stop on the New York Central Railroad between Albany and Schenectady. In that location *Lycaeides samuelis*, a butterfly he had been the first to classify correctly, had been recorded ninety years ago. He had still not caught the thing himself, despite holidaying in New Hampshire four years before for that very purpose. Now at Karner, near patches of lupine in bloom, he took his first live specimens of the species. A faithful pilgrim, he would make the same stop at the same season every year for several years to come as he traveled to or from Boston.⁷

Back in Ithaca, he cooled his gums with ice creams as he marked exam papers before returning to Boston on June 6 to have dentures put in. A few months later he broke a tooth in his new dentures and wrote in his diary: "What a wonderful experience—to go to a dentist for repairing false teeth, after so many years of torture at their hands." No wonder he felt like firing a parting shot at dentistry in *Lolita*. When Humbert visits Ivor Quilty after finding out that Lolita's abductor is the Ramsdale dentist's nephew, he asks Dr. Quilty how much it would cost to have all his teeth out and a complete set of dentures fitted. As Dr. Quilty lovingly details the complex and costly business, Humbert cuts him short: "On second thoughts, I shall have it all done by Dr. Molnar. His price is higher, but he is of course a much better dentist than you."[8]

Early in June, Nabokov hoped to write a story that could pay for a summer vacation in the Rockies. As he realized how much work lay ahead, his plans shrank: first he postponed the departure, then contemplated a holiday in New Hampshire or perhaps Cape Cod, then had to abandon travel plans altogether.[9]

Once he had completed his revision of the book version of his autobiography in June and sent the revised sixteenth chapter off in July, he could return to *The Kingdom by the Sea*.[10] He had first had the idea of an older man marrying a woman for access to her young daughter in the mid-1930s, in a paragraph of *The Gift*; he had turned the paragraph into a novella, "The Enchanter," in 1939; in 1946 his mind had begun to transform the novella into a novel. By now he had named his heroine Juanita Dark, Joan of Arc—or Joaneta Darc, as he insisted her name should be spelled—with a Spanish lilt.* He had written the fair draft of the first twelve chapters of part 1 of the novel and several passages from part 2.[11]

He had also begun to evolve a new mode of composition. Since he always pictured a whole novel complete in his mind before beginning to set any of it down in words, he could write in any order as he shifted his mental spotlight from one point of the picture to another. For that reason, and because he had grown used to index cards for his lepidopterological research notes, he now began to compose directly on index cards rather than paper, writing out any section he liked—still using a pen, however—and then placing the new cards, in the sequence he had foreseen, among the stack already written.

New methods notwithstanding, Nabokov felt "beset with technical difficulties and doubts" about his new novel.[12] The idea had been too long gestating with too little result, and he had little prospect of finding time to write much at all before having to set the book aside for

* He would abandon the name, of course, but in *Ada* he would use Joan of Arc as a recurrent parallel for Lucette Veen, another martyr to a sexual ardor that perversely parodies family love.

still another year. Even then financial considerations would surely compel him to write something else that he could sell to the *New Yorker*. Perhaps the time had come to abandon the whole thing. Despondent, he carried his pile of index cards out to the garden incinerator leaning in the grass at the back of 802 East Seneca Street. At that point, fortunately for Nabokov and for literature, his wife stopped him and urged him to think it over again. He realized she was right: "the ghost of the destroyed book would haunt my files for the rest of my life."[13]

Late in July, while Dmitri was away at Northwestern University at a high-school debating course, Nabokov wrote to Katharine White:

> I am engrossed in the preparation of a new course. Have finished annotating "Bleak House" and "Mansfield Park" and now shall have to translate—at least in parts—"Madame Bovary," what there is in this line is a mess. In connection with "Mansfield Park" I have been reading Walter Scott, Cowper, Shak.'s "Henry VIII" and Inchbald-Kotzebue's "Lovers' Vows." Am anticipating my students' surprise when I tell them that they will have to read all that too in order to appreciate Jane. My plan is to teach my 150 students to *read* books, not just to get away with a "general" idea and a vague hash of "influences," "background," "human interest" and so forth. But this means work.[14]

But while he could anticipate teaching with excitement, the time he needed to prepare his course was also time he needed to write. As he mentioned to Katharine White just a week later, he was revolving a new story in his mind, "but various matters prevent me from starting to compose it. Feel most anxious to write a novel that is beautifully clear in my mind, but I would need a year untroubled by academic duties to set it in motion. I am in lowish spirits."[15]

Dmitri returned from Evanston taller than ever, 6 foot 5 inches, a lean sixteen. His father played tennis with him every morning before sitting down to correct proofs of *Conclusive Evidence*, the translation into French of his *Real Life of Sebastian Knight*, and the translation into English of *Madame Bovary*. Two weeks into September he had virtually finished preliminary preparation for his new course. He had once admired *Ulysses*, but now he found "bothersome failings among patches of genius": the stream of consciousness seemed a mere convention, the sexual and digestive details too unremitting, Bloom's Jewishness too full of clichés.[16]

Nabokov once defined the sole advantage of a writer's affiliation with a university as access to splendid libraries. After poking around in the Cornell stacks for nineteenth-century studies of Siamese twins, he announced at the dinner table one night, Alison Bishop recalls, "I think I'll write a novel about the life of a pair of Siamese twins." "You will not," answered Véra. By mid-September, in the last few days before the term commenced, he had begun, if not quite the novel he had envisaged, at least "a three-part tragic tale": in the first part a pair of Siamese twins spend their childhood in Turkey before being abducted to America; in the second they marry two normal girls, sisters; in the third "they are separated by surgery, and only the narrator survives, but he too dies after finishing his story."[17] Teaching pressures dictated that only the first part would ever be written.

III

Classes for the 1950–1951 year began on September 22. Nabokov had three students in his survey of Russian literature (Monday, Wednesday, Friday, 11:00–12:00), four in his new seminar course, the Modernist Movement in Russian Literature (Thursday, 3:30–6:00, in his Seneca Street home), which examined Tolstoy's *Death of Ivan Ilich* and *Hadji Murat*, Chekhov's "In the Ravine," "House with a Mezzanine," and *The Seagull*, Tyutchev, Fet, and Blok.[18] Henceforth Nabokov would alternate this modernism course year by year with his Pushkin seminar.

Nineteen-fifty was the year Nabokov first taught outside his field of Russian literature: Literature 311–12 (MWF 12:00–1:00, Goldwin Smith C), almost one hundred and fifty students. As he told Wilson, he planned in this transitional year to rely heavily on Russians: Pushkin, Gogol, Turgenev, Tolstoy, Dostoevsky, and Chekhov. At first he had also considered teaching Washington Irving's "Stout Gentleman," Benjamin Constant's *Adolphe*, and, rather surprisingly, Maupassant's "Diamond Necklace," which he would shatter with such glee in *Ada*.[19] None of the three remained long in contention, and as the teaching year evolved Nabokov also discovered he could dispense with Turgenev and Dostoevsky altogether, so that in the fall term he taught *Mansfield Park*, Pushkin's "Queen of Spades," *Bleak House*, Gogol (*Dead Souls*, *The Inspector General*, and "The Overcoat"), and *Madame Bovary*; in the spring, *Anna Karenin*, *The Death of Ivan Ilich*, *Dr. Jekyll and Mr. Hyde*, Kafka's *Metamorphosis*, Thomas Mann's "The Railway Accident," Chekhov ("In the Ravine," "The Lady with the Little Dog," and *Three Sisters*), *Swann's Way*, and *Ulysses*. In future years he would drop both *The Inspector General* and *The Death of Ivan Ilich* and omit Pushkin, Chekhov, and Mann altogether. The rest easily expanded to fill the gaps.

This course would make Nabokov's name at Cornell. By his last years at Cornell it had become the most popular academic option on campus and was eclipsed in student numbers only by Pete Seeger's folk-song class. In many ways, despite his initial reluctance to undertake it, the European Fiction course was more peculiarly Nabokovian than his Russian classes. Vividly conscious of "the quantity of unreadable books and the quality of the very few readable ones," he wished to concentrate on a few supreme masterpieces.[20] Like his survey courses, the European Fiction course evolved to focus on fewer books studied in increasing detail. *Anna Karenin*, to which he first devoted six classes in his survey course, ended with ten classes there and fifteen in European Fiction; *Ulysses* began with four and filled out to fourteen. Nabokov believed in the internationalism of literature, in individual genius that transcends its circumstances, and in the evolution of literature toward ampler perfection, subtlety, precision; his attention therefore fixed naturally on a few great books of the nineteenth and twentieth centuries.

Nabokov was rated "a great teacher," "a flamboyant, funny lecturer" whose course could attract all kinds of students. His Cornell colleague M. H. Abrams, himself one of the most influential of American teachers of literature, rated him an irresistible lecturer: "Everybody who heard him thought so." One student spoke for many: "He taught me how to read."[21]

IV

What were his secrets as a teacher? To judge by Nabokov's own account he was cold, aloof, and unspontaneous in class: "I had not much contact with the students, and that was something I liked." On another occasion: "I'm a stumbling and faltering speaker. I'd feel much better if there existed a magic eraser to delete said words in retrospect and a magic pencil to form new ones in the air. When I lectured in colleges I'd prepare even topical jokes weeks ahead and nobody laughed."[22] He would tell his colleagues—he would even tell his class—that he thought it would make much more sense to have his lectures on tape, radio, television, or duplicated typescript for students to consult as often as they needed.

His notes were in fact a good deal less polished than he remembered. Most were in his own hand rather than typewritten, and with erasures and insertions, revisions, alternatives, supplementary sheets, looping arrows and sweeping crosses, a plethora of possibilities from which he had to select as he lectured. Already in class in the 1950s he announced plans to publish his lectures, and by the middle of the decade the project seemed under way. As late as the early 1970s he was still expecting to publish the material. Then, after sitting down to read his files over in April 1972, he left a note declaring his lectures "chaotic and sloppy." They "must *never* be published. None of them!" Despite that injunction, three volumes of his lectures have been published since his death, to an enthusiastic reception.[23] In their fragmented, unresolved, and unrevised state, these lectures were not nearly ready for publication, but as scripts for Nabokov's classroom performances they were a resounding success.*

Nabokov did read his lectures, but he had a masterly command of his relationship to his audience, a confident presence, a superb sense of timing, and he knew how to control the rhythm of his speech and his gaze to disguise the fact that he was reading. He seemed to enjoy the act of presentation: although he worked closely from a prepared text he used the notes before him as if he were a conductor giving life to an orchestral score. He would rise to the balls of his feet or rush back and forth from lectern to blackboard in a way that created the impression of enormous physical energy.[24] He was "an exceptional actor, who could give the impression he was divulging a secret, the very essence of things: we thought he was going to reveal all."[25] He had a passion for his subject, a unique way of looking at things, a knack for the provocative and outrageous, a gift for animating the imagination, a genius for the prepared surprise.

He would enter the lecture room with great élan, Véra behind him. In the winter, overcoated to the ears, he would stomp snow from his galoshed feet and remove his coat, which his wife—"my assistant," as he would refer to her in class—would drape over a chair before taking off her own. Then he would draw his notes out of his briefcase. As one student recalls, "I don't think Mr. Nabokov realized how much suspense was involved in this; like watching a handicapped magician, we were never sure whether a fist full of silks would appear instead of the expected rabbit, or a custard pie instead of the promised hard-boiled egg. It was always an adventure."[26]

V

Every semester would begin with mock-imperious abruptness: "You will buy Austen today and start reading at once. *Read every word.*

---

* Véra and Dmitri Nabokov did not see Nabokov's 1972 note, which was later found with his notes for work in progress rather than with the manuscript of the lectures. The lectures as edited for publication contain many puzzling omissions, misreadings, spurious improvements, and even sheer editorial inventions.

Suppress the radio and tell your room-mate to shut up." The surprise
continued when he announced, "great novels are great fairy tales."
Summing up his teaching in later years, Nabokov recalls how his approach

> irritated or puzzled such students of literature (and their professors)
> as were accustomed to "serious" courses replete with "trends," and
> "schools," and "myths," and "symbols," and "social comment," and
> something unspeakably spooky called "climate of thought." Actually
> these "serious" courses were quite easy ones, with the students re-
> quired to know not the books but about the books. In my classes, read-
> ers had to discuss specific details, not general ideas.[27]

The conscious provocateur, Nabokov also roundly dismissed "human interest," "ideas," "realism," until students wondered what
was left.

His answer? The enchantment of the novel itself. As early as 1947,
if not earlier, he had devised his triple formula: "There are three
points of view from which a writer can be considered: he may be
considered as a storyteller, as a teacher, as an enchanter. A major
writer combines these three—storyteller, teacher, enchanter—but it
is the enchanter in him that predominates and makes him a major
writer."[28] "Enchantment" for him meant a writer's power to make
any detail of an invented world spring to life, whether or not it con-
forms to the "real" world outside. He selected from Dickens a quite
incidental messenger who when paid for his errand "receives his
twopence with anything but transport, tosses the money into the air,
catches it over-handed, and retires." "This gesture," Nabokov commented, "this one gesture, with its epithet 'over-handed'—a trifle—
but the man is alive forever in a good reader's mind."[29]

"In reading," Nabokov insisted right at the beginning of his
course, "one should notice and fondle details. There is nothing
wrong about the moonshine of generalization when it comes *after* the
sunny trifles of the book have been lovingly collected."[30] Grand generalizations may seem more impressive, but by relegating them to
second place and bringing detail to the fore Nabokov meant to suggest a principle his students could extend throughout their lives: *no-*
tice the details of your book or your world and it will enrich your
whole life. It was an article of faith for him that only the unobservant
could be pessimists in a world of such variety.

Paradoxically, although he insisted that novels are fairy tales, not
social manifestos or faithful records of their time, he also insisted not
only that their invented worlds should be dwelled on *as if* real, but

also that readers should avail themselves of every scrap of knowledge of the real world that might illuminate the texts.

> In my academic days I endeavored to provide students of literature with exact information about details, about such combinations of details as yield the sensual spark without which a book is dead. In that respect, general ideas are of no importance. Any ass can assimilate the main points of Tolstoy's attitude toward adultery but in order to enjoy Tolstoy's art the good reader must wish to visualize, for instance, the arrangement of a railway carriage on the Moscow-Petersburg night train as it was a hundred years ago. Here diagrams are most helpful.[31]

Teaching *Mansfield Park*, he would stride to the board with a flourish and draw a map of England, a plan of the grounds at Sotherton, another of the interior of Mansfield Park. He would sketch a barouchelandau and provide a chronology of the events of the book. He asked his students questions like: "Edmund tells Fanny that the letter she is going to write to her brother William will cost William nothing because Sir Thomas will frank it. Why can he do it?" (Because he is a Member of Parliament.) When Sir Thomas sets off for Antigua, Nabokov explains exactly where Antigua is, tells how long the journey would have taken, and points out in passing, "the plantations would have been worked by cheap slave labor, the source of the Bertram money."[32] From various details here and there, Nabokov calculates that the income Mr. Norris received from his parish would have been about £700 per year. He treats novels, in other words, as little worlds about which we can and should find out more and more.

Nabokov has often been supposed a devotee of art for art's sake, someone who denies "reality" in order to escape into the refuge of art. That is hardly compatible with his relentless urge to discover more and more about the real world of lepidoptera or more and more factual information that can illuminate the worlds of the novels on his course. He never addressed this paradox explicitly, but I suggest that his remarkable curiosity for information within the novels he taught, and for information in the outside world that could explain the worlds within, reflects his whole metaphysics. Just as the world of a novel has an internal reality that can in no way be applied to the world outside it, but can be made more real, more alive in the imagination, by the application of knowledge from the outside world, so our "outside" world may contain nothing in it to explain a still richer state of reality beyond—while such a state, if we could only reach it, might explain so much more of this world and its reality.

Novels for Nabokov were above all specific worlds that his students should endeavor to know *as* little worlds. The more he could awaken their imaginations and their curiosity to these miniature worlds, the more he might alert his students to the world around them. Once when he asked his class to name the tree visible beyond the classroom window, he was appalled to find that apart from a few vague guesses ("a shade tree?") only a couple of students dared hazard obvious names like "oak," and no one could recognize an American elm.[33]

To explain *Ulysses*, he had consulted a street map of Dublin and set out in detail on the blackboard a map of Stephen's and Bloom's intersecting itineraries, which he required his students to master. For Kafka's *Metamorphosis*, he sketched on the board a diagram of the insect Gregor Samsa turns into, *not* a cockroach, he announced, but a beetle. Teaching *Anna Karenin*, he drew a picture of the attire Kitty would have worn when skating. He clocked and charted the novels partly for the sheer surprise of the exercise, partly to fix the books in his students' minds, partly to exercise their imaginations in the same way music teachers set scales for their pupils' fingers. He encouraged his students not merely to picture the things that he made them see in class but to animate every scene of each of the books with the same imagination and the same vivid curiosity. No one else has ever taught this aspect of reading so well, or made students so able to turn printed words into concrete worlds.

VI

If Nabokov had a gift for inspiring his students to see the *what* of a book, he also had a knack for the *how*. Analyzing Proust's opulent imagery, he would invent his own examples to explain the most rudimentary figures of speech ("simile: the mist was like a veil; metaphor: there was a veil of mist"), then rapidly move toward a hybrid form ("the veil of mist was like the sleep of silence") and apply it to Proust's "wealth of metaphorical imagery, layer upon layer of comparisons. It is through this prism that we view the beauty of Proust's work." He analyzed in detail one complex Proustian image-within-image of a moonlit scene, then contrasted it with the way Gogol might have developed one of his rambling comparisons:

He might have compared the moonlit effect to linen fallen from a wash line, as he does somewhere in *Dead Souls*; but then he might ramble away and say the moonlight on the ground was like sheets and shirts that the wind had scattered while the washerwoman had peacefully slept, dreaming of suds and starch and the pretty new frock her sister-in-law had bought. In Proust's case the peculiar point is that he drifts from the idea of pale light to that of remote music—the sense of vision grades into the sense of hearing.

Lucid explanations of terms, the poetry of example, subtle analysis, brilliant comparison—and then an image of his own summing up the whole effect of Proust: "A garden in a concert hall and a picture gallery in the garden—this is one of my definitions of Proust's art."[34]

No one, not even Flaubert or James, has had a greater sensitivity to narrative methods and conventions than Nabokov. He analyzed Flaubert's mastery of transition and compared it to Tolstoy's. He examined Flaubertian counterpoint (the agricultural fair) and contrasted it with its Joycean counterpart (the viceregal procession). He savored Tolstoy's near-approach to the interior monologue in *Anna Karenin* before criticizing the conventionality of Joyce's stream of consciousness. He made clear his dislike for easy narrative solutions (letters as a means of imparting rapid narrative information in eighteenth-century fiction or Jane Austen, eavesdropping in Proust), and praises in their stead Flaubert's relentless determination to seek out only what the situation will permit. He devised his own terms for describing narrative point of view, the "sifting agent" through or by whom the other characters are seen, or the author's go-between or errand boy, whom Henry James ponderously scrutinizes as the "ficelle" but Nabokov playfully christens the "perry"—and then dismisses with disgust:

> the so-called *perry*, possibly derived from *periscope*, despite the double *r*, or perhaps from *parry* in vague connection with foil as in fencing. But this does not matter much since anyway I invented the term myself many years ago. It denotes the lowest kind of author's minion: the character or characters who, throughout the book, or at least in certain parts of the book, are so to speak on duty; whose only purpose, whose only reason for being, is that they visit the places which the author wishes the reader to visit and meet the characters whom the author wishes the reader to meet. In such chapters the perry has hardly an identity of his own. He has no will, no soul, no heart, nothing—he is a mere peregrinating perry although of course he can regain his identity in some other part of the book. The perry visits some household only because the author wants to describe the characters in that household. He is very helpful, the perry. Without the perry a story is sometimes difficult to direct and propel; but better kill the story than have a perry drag its thread about like a lame insect dragging a dusty bit of cobweb.[35]

Nothing in literature thrilled Nabokov more than writers breaking free of conventions and finding new ways of seeing and telling. He valued new subjects, the agonies of childbirth in *Anna Karenin* or the miseries of childhood in *Bleak House*; new ways of dealing with time, in Proust or Tolstoy; a new force to implication in Flaubert; new ways of perceiving personality, in Proust or Joyce; new depths of the mind's complexity, in Tolstoy or Proust or Joyce; a new precision of the senses in Gogol or Dickens.

"When the sun shone through the clouds, making silvery pools in the dark sea. . . ." Let us pause: can we visualize that? Of course we can, and we do so with a greater thrill of recognition because in comparison to the conventional blue sea of literary tradition these silvery pools in the dark sea offer something that Dickens noted for the very first time with the innocent and sensuous eye of the true artist, saw and immediately put into words.[36]

Literary technique may often have been described with more patience, but rarely with more excitement.

VII

For all the strengths of Nabokov's teaching, his methods also had their considerable limitations. It was no great loss for his students that he never explained the genesis of works of genius in terms of social conditions that others experienced without being able to produce works of genius themselves. It was a genuine gain that he encouraged his students to see literature as a creature of the imagination and not a pretext for pharisaic pronouncements on morality and society. But Nabokov was often reluctant to pass beyond the *what* and the *how* of a book to ask *why* the author makes one particular choice rather than others. Only rarely did he leave description for explanation, as if he did not know that the searchlight of explanation could illuminate and intensify description itself, or that probing the why of what we read ranks as one of the great pleasures of literature. Why does Shakespeare decide to let us all believe Hermione dead? Why does Hamlet but not Gertrude see the ghost the second time the dead king appears? Why does Joyce change his style from chapter to chapter in *Ulysses*, and why does he assign a particular chapter its particular style?

The curious fact is that no writer has made this sort of question more central to his own art than Nabokov has. No other writer has gone so far as to declare that the true drama of a story takes place not among the characters, but between author and readers, just as the true drama of a chess problem takes place not among the pieces but between problemist and solver. Nabokov's work has always posed questions for the reader (why does he introduce Luzhin's wife so abruptly and so pointedly out of sequence, and never name her?), and posed more and more as his art developed, so that by the time of *Ada* the very first sentence, delightfully absurd in itself, can provoke a whole series of questions: why does Nabokov evoke the opening of *Anna Karenin*? Why does he invert it? How does it apply to this novel, or to all the novel's other allusions to *Anna Karenin*?

In his teaching Nabokov rarely pursued such questions, and when he did he often provided hasty or arbitrary answers. He declared that

> *Ulysses*, of course, is a divine work of art and will live on despite the academic nonentities who turn it into a collection of symbols or Greek myths. I once gave a student a C-minus, or perhaps a D-plus, just for applying to its chapters the titles borrowed from Homer while not even noticing the comings and goings of the man in the brown mackintosh. He didn't even know who the man in the brown mackintosh was.[37]

In his lectures Nabokov explained M'Intosh, that enigma wrapped in a raincoat, as Joyce himself inspecting his novel, but he failed to offer a shred of evidence. He dismissed Joyce's use of Homer, despite the title of the novel, despite Joyce's schema for the book, despite a thousand specific details that make the novel funnier and richer and have nothing whatever to do with turning it into a Greek myth. He offered a wonderful analogy for Joyce's altering his style from chapter to chapter:

> If you have ever tried to stand and bend your head so as to look back between your knees, with your face upside down, you will see the world in a totally different light. Try it on the beach: it is very funny to see people walking when you look at them upside down. They seem to be, with each step, disengaging their feet from the glue of gravitation, without losing their dignity. Well, this trick of changing the vista, of changing the prism and the viewpoint, can be compared to Joyce's new literary technique, to the kind of new twist through which you see a greener grass, a fresher world.[38]

But he flatly declares that "there is no special reason" for the style of each chapter—a statement he could not have made had he not dismissed Homer out of hand.

VIII

All too often, university literary studies invite students to operate as literary critics before they have become sensitive readers. At its best, academic criticism involves close reading and protracted analysis of particular texts that can lead to deeper and deeper explanations. When required of students, however, it can allow them to deal with literary works at the level of easy, remote abstractions. Nabokov thought that an absurd betrayal of the particularity of the imagination. As a critic himself, he was simply impatient with the kind of painstaking, step-by-step analysis he had such relish for in his lepidopterological studies. He was ready to devote that kind of exhaustive scrutiny to nature's handiwork, but not to another writer's—not when he could create something just as fine himself. The very impatience of his imagination made him a brilliant teacher and his students not apprentice critics but excellent readers.

He disliked the step-by-step because he found so much more delight in the sidestep, the feint, the sudden leap of surprise, the knight move of the mind. Ross Wetzsteon recalls:

"I want you to copy this exactly as I draw it," Vladimir Nabokov instructed us, after explaining that he was going to diagram the themes of *Bleak House*. He turned to the blackboard, picked up a piece of chalk, and scrawled "the theme of inheritances" in a weird arching loop. "The theme of generations" dipped and rose and dipped in an undulating line. "The theme of social consciousness" wiggled crazily toward the other lines, then veered sharply away.

Nabokov turned from the blackboard and peered over the rims of his glasses, parodying a professorial twinkle. "I want you to be sure to copy this exactly as I draw it."

After consulting a sheet of paper on the lectern, he turned back to the blackboard and scrawled "the theme of economic conditions" in a nearly vertical line. "The theme of poverty," "the theme of political (the chalk snapped under the pressure, he picked up another piece and continued) protest," "the theme of social environment"—all leaping and dipping wildly across the blackboard. Some people simply can't draw a straight line.

Again he peered at us, over his shoulder and over his glasses, in silent reminder to copy this "exactly."

And finally he scrawled the last "theme" in a neat dipping curve, a half-moon on its side, "the theme of art," and we suddenly realized he had drawn a cat's face, the last line its wry smile, and for the rest of the term that cat smiled out of our notebooks in mockery of the didactic approach to literature.[39]

Nabokov's sense of humor was a key to the charm of his lectures. He had running gags: the dusty blackboards were "grayboards," his lectures "monologues." He could give the plainest instruction a comic twist: "And simultaneously, that is in the first days of October, you will dive before I push you, into the Dickens novel." Toward the end of a lecture he might start reading again from the beginning, and watch how some students' heads took a minute or two to rise from their notes while others had already caught on and waited in an expectant hush. Occasionally he would find something so uproarious in Gogol or Dickens or Flaubert that his laughter would infiltrate his lecturing until his wife would have to signal to him from her front-row seat that no one could understand what he was saying.[40]

Provocative, stinging dismissals of major writers and thinkers made Nabokov's students sit up—and on two occasions a student walked out of the class in protest, once when the target was Dostoevsky, once when it was Freud. Beside Kafka, the greatest German writer of our time, Nabokov proclaimed, Rilke or Mann were dwarfs or plaster saints, and one student who took Nabokov's course the same year as Victor Lange's course in German literature recalls making his way from one classroom to another "like a slightly damp fuse between two ammunition dumps." Nevertheless he told Nabokov years later that he "received more intellectual stimulation, sitting in your classroom, even if sometimes seething with indignation, than in all the others put together." And as Ross Wetzsteon recalls, "remarks that seem devastatingly snide in cold print seemed almost affectionate in his warm lectures. He particularly enjoyed reading bad literature aloud—'I can't stop quoting!' he would chortle in glee."[41]

That same caressing of the phrase, naturally, was even more manifest when Nabokov read from the texts he had chosen for his course. He read out great swathes of the novels, with now and again just a brief aside to pinpoint the flash of inspiration: "Mark the candle heavily burning with 'a great cabbage head and a long winding sheet.' No use reading Dickens if one cannot visualize that."[42]

Nabokov homed in on the details that take the imagination unawares, and in class his chief tool was his own gift for the verbal surprise. Three or four times a term he might

> refer to "the passion of the scientist and the precision of the artist," pause for a moment as if he hadn't heard himself quite right, then ask in a mock-baffled tone: "Have I made a mistake? Don't I mean 'the passion of the artist and the precision of the scientist'?" Another pause, peering gleefully over the rims of his glasses, as if awaiting our answer— then "No! The passion of the scientist and the precision of the artist!"[43]

He did not make explicit the fact that he was a writer himself, but let his alert students deduce it. Composing *Madame Bovary*, Flaubert wrote "eighty to ninety pages in one year—that is a fellow after my heart." Stevenson's style, he remarked one day, "is even more florid than mine." *In Search of Lost Time* is not autobiography but "pure fantasy on Proust's part, just as *Anna Karenin* is a fantasy, just as Kafka's 'The Metamorphosis' is fantasy—just as Cornell University will be a fantasy if I ever happen to write about it some day in retrospect."[44]

He expected little of his students in the way of cultural range or intellectual tenacity, but he would not compromise on his imagery: as he once wrote when invited to speak at another college, "I cannot talk 'down' to an audience."[45] He took every opportunity to stir the imaginations of his students, by his language, his opinions, even by sheer performance. Every year he would relive Gogol's death agonies:

> how the hack doctors alternately bled him and purged him and plunged him into icy baths . . . ; Gogol so frail that his spine could be felt through his stomach, the six fat white bloodletting leeches clinging to his nose . . . ; Gogol begging to have them removed—"Please lift them, lift them, keep them away!" Sinking behind the lectern, now a tub . . . Nabokov for several moments *was* Gogol, shuddering and shivering, his hands held down by a husky attendant, his head thrown back in pain and terror, nostril distended, eyes shut, his beseechments filling the large and hushed lecture hall. . . . Then, after a pause, Nabokov would say, dispassionately, . . . "Although the scene is unpleasant and has a human appeal which I deplore, it is necessary to dwell upon it a little longer in order to bring out the curiously physical side of Gogol's genius."[46]

IX

Nabokov stressed to his classes that art appeals to the imagination, and unless it does so it is simply bad art. But precisely for that reason, he also insisted on attacking one moral defect with a forthrightness most university teachers would not dare to accept. Early in the year he would casually refer to *poshlost'*, "look up, mimicking surprise that we didn't know the word, then explain that it was a peculiarly Russian word (as untranslatable as 'corny,' with as many specific instances and as little specific meaning as 'camp'), a kind of subtle vulgarity."[47] Once a year, he would devote a whole lecture to denouncing *poshlost'* or philistinism, a celebrated annual fixture that drew crowds of casual auditors to the lecture hall.*

---

* One year when he gave this lecture, his former student Daniel R. Hunter recalls, he noticed on the blackboard as he entered a roughly drawn circle spattered with chalk dots. He proclaimed to the class, "A true genius takes the work of others and bends it

He took the subject seriously. He valued above all the liberating force of the imagination, the "tingle" that we may experience "in any department of thought or emotion. We are liable to miss the best of life if we do not know how to tingle, if we do not learn to hoist ourselves just a little higher than we generally are in order to sample the rarest and ripest fruit of art which human thought has to offer." Philistinism he saw as the exact reverse, a closing of the imagination, a habit of taking things for granted or at second hand, a desire to conform, a desire to impress oneself and others with sham, unexamined values. He referred to the philistinism of Skimpole in *Bleak House*, Chichikov in *Dead Souls*, Homais in *Madame Bovary*, but he also stressed philistinism as something still thriving in the world around them all, the world of advertising, the world of smug modernity: "Today, of course, a philistine might dream of glass and steel, videos or radios disguised as book shelves."[48]

On other occasions, too, when he incorporated extraliterary values in his lectures, what he had to say was all the more forceful because he refused to accept an appeal to moral uplift as part of the pious decorum of literary study. He introduced Kafka's *Metamorphosis*:

> We can take the story apart, we can find out how the bits fit, how one part of the pattern responds to the other; but you have to have in you some cell, some gene, some germ that will vibrate in answer to sensations that you can neither define, nor dismiss. *Beauty plus pity*—that is the closest we can get to a definition of art. Where there is beauty there is pity for the simple reason that beauty must die: beauty always dies, the manner dies with the matter, the world dies with the individual. If Kafka's "The Metamorphosis" strikes anyone as something more than an entomological fantasy, then I congratulate him on having joined the ranks of good and great readers.[49]

But above all Nabokov stressed throughout his course the value of art in awakening the imagination to delight in the creativity of other minds and the creativity of the world. He would end his courses declaring that what he had tried to impart to his students, the ability to *read* great novels, to become major readers of major writers, would not give them anything they could apply to any obvious real-life problems. "But it may help you, if you have followed my instructions, to feel the pure satisfaction which an inspired and precise work of art gives; and this sense of satisfaction in its turn goes to build up

to his own use," and added two eyes, a nose, and ears to the primitive outline. The image remained there as he delivered his customary lecture on philistinism, where he attacked the banality of advertising and singled out for special scorn the cliché of freckle-faced cuteness in advertisers' drawings of children.

a sense of more genuine mental comfort, the kind of comfort one feels when one realizes that for all its blunders and boners the inner texture of life is also a matter of inspiration and precision."[50]

X

In late September 1950, Nabokov launched his new course with *Mansfield Park.* He had his students read the works mentioned by the characters in the novel: Scott's "Lay of the Last Minstrel," Cowper's "Task," some of Johnson's *Idler* essays, Sterne's *Sentimental Journey*, and of course the play that the young folk rehearse at Mansfield Park, *Lovers' Vows.* He also injected as much historical information as he could into the text. All this literary and historical background seems to have been a way of avoiding Austen herself as much as he could, while instilling in his students the need to read with the utmost precision. For although he tried to disguise it in class, Nabokov could never quite warm to the first writer in his course.

In the first month of his new course, feeling financially pressed, he traveled to Smith College in Massachusetts and to the University of Toronto to deliver guest lectures.[51] On a sheet of paper from Toronto's Royal York Hotel, he wrote to Katharine and E. B. White, "I have no illusions about hotels in this hemisphere; they are for conventions, not for the individual; for a thousand tight salesmen and not for the weary poet (or the weary poet's wife, says Véra). Slamming doors, shunting trains, the violent waterfalls of one's neighbour's toilet. Terrible."[52] Nabokov had been planning the book that had become *Lolita* for years, but in 1950, Juanita Dark and *The Kingdom by the Sea* still had some distance to evolve into the novel we know. The Royal York Hotel seems to have acted as a catalyst for the transformation. At the Enchanted Hunters Hotel, Humbert finally has Lolita in his clutches. The hotel is crowded out by a convention—or rather, a couple of conventions. As he lies with the lightly—too lightly—sleeping Lolita beside him, Humbert squirms at the noise in the corridors as guests say their goodnights. Then the "waterfalls" take over: "someone in a southern direction was extravagantly sick, almost coughing out his life with his liquor, and his toilet descended like a veritable Niagara, immediately beyond our bathroom. And when finally all the waterfalls had stopped. . . ."[53] While Nabokov traveled a great deal most summers in pursuit of butterflies, he and Véra would stay at motels, not hotels, and there is no other description in his letters of a hotel environment like the one he reports from

Toronto. The Royal York appears to have helped Nabokov lay a first foundation for the Enchanted Hunters.

During October, Nabokov also finished the first part of his tripartite story about the Siamese twins, "Scenes from the Life of a Double Monster."[54] Urgently in need of money, he sent it off, incomplete though it was, to the *New Yorker*.

Floyd, the right-hand member of a pair of Siamese twins, recounts the first twelve years of life he and his brother shared in a village on the Black Sea coast: their slow recognition of their abnormality, the curiosity of neighboring villagers, their abortive attempt to escape becoming exhibits in a traveling show. Though vividly written, "Scenes from the Life of a Double Monster" appears to be plainly missing something, as if a skillful juggler were to throw only *one* cup and saucer from hand to hand. For that reason, Katharine White rejected the story, and it remained unpublished until 1958.[55]

At the beginning of November, Nabokov moved on with relief to Dickens:

> We are now ready to tackle Dickens. We are now ready to embrace Dickens. We are now ready to bask in Dickens. In our dealings with Jane Austen we had to make a certain effort in order to join the ladies in the drawing room. In the case of Dickens we remain at table with our tawny port. We had to find an approach to Jane Austen and her *Mansfield Park*. I think we did find it. . . . But the fun was forced. We had to slip into a certain mood; we had to focus our eyes in a certain way.

His condescension was prompted not so much by Austen's gender, as it might seem, as by her adherence to eighteenth-century convention, for he continued:

> In our dealings with Pushkin we were faced by much the same problem because "The Queen of Spades" quite obviously belongs to the dry, brittle, green-tinged world wherein Austen thrived. In order to reveal to you what Pushkin really was behind his rather self-conscious prose, I have had to give you samples of his poetry. An appreciation of the freedom of his verse helped us to enjoy the deliberate austerity and primness of his prose.*
>
> With Dickens we expand. It seems to me that Jane Austen's fiction had been a charming rearrangement of old-fashioned values. In the case of Dickens the values are new. Modern authors still get drunk on his vintage. Here there is no problem of approach as with Jane Austen, no courtship, no dillydallying. We just surrender ourselves to Dickens's

---

* In 1950, exceptionally, Nabokov followed his *Mansfield Park* lectures with two on "The Queen of Spades" and one on Pushkin's verse.

voice—that is all. If it were possible I would like to devote the fifty minutes of every class meeting to mute meditation, concentration, and admiration of Dickens.[56]

Browsing one day in the library, Nabokov chanced on a recent Soviet journal, and in mid-November wrote excitedly to Katharine White, "I have found some extraordinary things, plays and articles, in the Soviet periodical 'Zvezda' for 1949 that cast a brilliant and terrible light on Soviet-American relations. Would you like me to write a piece of 4000–5000 words on the subject? It would contain samples of the Soviet notion of the American way of life culled from some plays and a remarkable warning—in August 1949!—of their Korean policy."[57] This was the year Sen. Joseph McCarthy had begun to bluff his way to prominence. Though they disapproved of McCarthy's random accusations and unscrupulous cross-examinations of alleged Communists, the Nabokovs believed many of his charges were correct, that there was serious Communist infiltration in high places in American officialdom. But Nabokov's own contribution to the cold war never progressed beyond the stage of taking notes for this one article.

At the beginning of December he held a test on *Bleak House*. After the first test in his fiction class a month earlier, he had been appalled at the evident cheating that occurred. This time he announced: "Incidentally, I suggest that for this test, members of teams who work together in study hall sit in a special pattern so as to afford a better chance for mental waves to show what such waves can do in surmounting obstacles. I deplore this preparation in common—the pooling of knowledge and the polling of ignorance—but I suppose it is a tradition."[58]

Nabokov was exasperated at cheating at Cornell throughout his time there. "There was no way for those people not to cheat. It was absolutely impossible to stop them. They would sit with their fraternity brothers or sorority sisters and trade answers." He would modify his instructions before each test, asking friends for instance to leave a space between their seats, lovers to sit in different rows, and fraternity brothers to place themselves at "diagonally opposite ends of the room."[59] Part of the problem, Nabokov felt—and it was a major reason for his wishing his lectures could be made available in recorded form—was the poor note taking he witnessed. Sometimes after class he would ask to see a student's notes. He reported once looking at a page a student showed him:

It read:
metaphores (underlined twice)
after that (;) semi colon, then: parenthesis open, (

parenthesis closed) , nothing inside

Below this: Mary—and a dash—apparently a character in the book.

Below that a date, (1808)

carefully encircled, apparently very important.

Finally, the cryptic phrase: did you get those tickets?[60]

Nabokov was used to writing works he hoped would endure for centuries; now he could see his meticulously chosen words disintegrate the moment they were airborne. Exhorting his class to attend lectures and take notes, he once declared that "there is something confoundedly pathetic about ignoring what a mild old party has so carefully devised."[61]

He finished the term with Gogol and Flaubert, dropping *Fathers and Sons* at the last moment to allow himself more room for *Madame Bovary*. His method with books he taught in translation—unless as with Guerney's versions of Gogol he found them satisfactory, a rare occurrence—was to begin by correcting the worst howlers in class, page after page. Precision of meaning was essential to precision of imagination:

> Various items of Emma's sensuous grace are shown through Bovary's eyes: her blue dress with three flounces, her elegant fingernails, and her hairdo. This hairdo has been so dreadfully translated in all versions that the correct description must be given else one cannot visualize her correctly: "Her hair in two black bandeaux, or folds, which seemed each of a single piece, so sleek were they, her hair was parted in the middle by a delicate line that dipped slightly as it followed the incurvation of her skull (*this is a young doctor looking*); and the bandeaux just revealing the lobes of her ears (*lobes, not upper "tips" as all translators have it: the upper part of the ears was of course covered by those sleek black folds*), her hair knotted behind in a thick chignon. Her cheekbones were rosy."

Nabokov's examinations might include such questions as "All translations of *Madame Bovary* are full of blunders; you have corrected some of them. Describe Emma's eyes, hands, sunshade, hairdo, dress, shoes." In class, still within the scene of Charles Bovary's first glimpse of Emma, he would read on: " 'On the table flies were walking up the glasses that had been used, and buzzing as they drowned themselves in the dregs of the cider. . . .' Note . . . the flies walking up the glasses (not 'crawling' as translators have it: flies do not crawl, they walk, they rub their hands), walking up the glasses. . . ." Great novels are great fairy tales for Nabokov not because they ignore the world, but because they see it so well they re-create it as if by magic: *that* is enchantment.[62]

XI

Every year from at least 1947, Nabokov kept a slim pocket diary for appointments, lecture schedules, publishers' deadlines. Only on rare occasions would he jot down in a hurried hand an epigram, an observation, a record of last night's dream. But for New Year's Day, 1951, Véra Nabokov gave her husband a page-a-day yearbook that he filled daily for over two months until the impulse wore off. It is an extraordinary record of the fertility of his imagination, the range of his curiosity, and the pressures weighing him down.

On January 5 he noted:

Quite an accumulation of work I shall have to complete during January:
   1. finish arranging my notes on Mme Bovary
   2. same in relation to Proust
   3. ponder various phases of my spring course
   4. write the 6000 word article (on Soviet ideas about America, in their plays and stories) that have discussed with Ross. Continuous series of obstacles, with nails sticking out and mutual mimicry of sharp angles of boards and pointed shadows, separating me from the book I would like to write.[63]

The next day:

Also, sur le chantier, and in various stages of completion:
The Kingdom by the Sea
The Double Monster
Book on structure of "Mme Bovary"
Translation in prose of "E. O."
Same of "Slovo" for Jakobson   etc.

In the diary he invented a fictionalized boarder, based on someone he knew in Ithaca, and day after day he tried out this character in various invented poses and imagined dialogues with himself. He forced himself to read more of T. S. Eliot, and recoiled: "What pretentious vulgarity, what tedious nonsense!" He recorded heartrending dreams and queer coincidences, and made a note to himself to write something on dreams, "with especial stress on the[ir] sloppy production—any old backdrop will do." More than a decade later, he carried out the plan in *Ada*. He noted down a repellent advertisement and concluded: "*Must* write something about advertisements." The next day he leafed through *Life* at the Cornell library and recorded in his yearbook, in the form of a conversation between his invented boarder and himself, two wonderfully preposterous advertisements, one for Hanes Fig Leaf Briefs and the other for the zipper with the "grasping and painful" name of Talon Trouser Fastener. Nabokov went on to attack advertisements in his lecture on philistinism, but these priceless samples he would save for *Pale Fire*.*

One entry in the yearbook ruminates briefly on "the future of the immortal soul." Another records from a newspaper item "Leading Figures Dead in Disaster (Railway)": "senior partner of a law firm; general insurance agent; vice president and director of an insurance corporation" and so on. Nabokov saved for an air disaster in *Ada* this ghoulish list of ranks meant to sound so much more impressive than the rankless dead. Items like this he would soon gather in his index cards like "bits of straw and fluff" that he assembled by instinct for new nests he could not yet envisage.[64]

On a day when freezing rain coated the streets of Ithaca with ice, Nabokov looked out the window and recorded a charming scene:

> Small boy—very small (3? 4?)—sliding all the way down our street on the ice-covered sidewalk, ecstatically, on $\wedge$ feet, probably the first time in his life, and falling now and then but getting up with the padded simplicity of a shortlegged dwarf, without helping himself with his hands. He will never forget it.
>
> How often have I taken pleasure in catching a snooping glimpse of another's future recollection.

Six weeks later, he added at the foot of the page: "He *was* a dwarf!"
One day he noted down the scenario for a promising new story:

Three Tenses

A rebellious short-story theme but one that has been breeding in me since November. Young man (Y) invited to dinner by friend, now married to Y's former mistress (but does not know about her relations with Y in the past). Other guests—a young couple (he has never met Y, she has quite recently become Y's mistress). A girl the host has invited to make a sixth does not turn up—they wait, then sit down to a dinner—candle-light affair, summer night after rain, French window open on tiny cast iron balcony (in Paris). Curious exhilarating feeling of superiority and mystery and a tangle of memories and the furious hope that his young mistress's husband will be called to replace a celebrated but very old singer's usual accompanist who is said to be ill. At one point Y and the woman of his past go out onto the balcony—where they lean

---

* Homosexual Kinbote describes the Talon advertisement: "Shows a young gent radiating virility among several ecstatic lady-friends, and the inscription reads: *You'll be amazed that the fly of your trousers could be so dramatically improved*" (*Pale Fire*, 114–15). For reproductions of both advertisements, see Alfred Appel, *Nabokov's Dark Cinema* (New York: Oxford University Press, 1974), 33.

their elbows on the wet railing—glistening dark street below, streetlamp shining through emerald leaves of a lime—she has guessed the situation. Telephone from the South—accompanist ill—husband of present love must go right now, wife remains. All sit together have coffee etc. The wonderful tingle of knowing that presently he will take her to his room across the street (light burns in window, has not put it out). Girl who was to be sixth calls on host for a minute (brother in law died), does not enter, Y. hears her voice. She will be his next and greatest love.

While Nabokov's mind was swarming with all these ideas for future works, he still had other people's books to teach in class—a fact that kept "Three Tenses" forever in the conditional.* In the last week of January he set the first final exams for his European fiction students: "Remember I welcome *originality*, details that have not been mentioned in class but that correspond to details discussed in class."[65] As he sat in front of the exam room, he penned in his yearbook a deft sketch of his hundred and thirty students writing away from 8 A.M. to 10:30 A.M., January 26. Three days later, as he marked the papers, he grumbled to his yearbook: "A chaotic hell of handwritings, in pale pencil, in blue, green, purple ink. My formulas and ideas and images coming back to me in grotesque disguise or crippled and patched up—hideous remnants of my parades and pageants."

With the examination experience fresh in his mind, Nabokov's imagination responded at once to a chance news item:

Axel Abrahamson, a moody B+ student, yesterday committed suicide by taking a fatal dose of potassium cyanide in an Evanston, Ill. apartment (which he shared with his mother), after taking a French exam. at Northwestern. In answering the last question on the exam he wrote in French "I am going to God. Life does not offer me much."

Adopt him. I see the story so clearly. Combine him with notes of Jan. 26. . . . Make him make some pathetic mistake in that last sentence. Change it, of course. . . . Probe, brood.[66]

A story had begun to break free in his mind, and apparently unconnected impressions joined what would soon be an avalanche of inspiration. February 3:

Much warmer after a spell of frost. Brilliant sun. Rows of sharp icicles hanging from eaves casting sharp shadows on the white front of house, and dripping. Watched one set for several minutes to detect the *shadows of drops* falling from the shadows of icicles but observed only one or two though they dripped all the time.

---

* Until it features fleetingly as a novella-within-the-novella in *Transparent Things*.

February 6:

Morning
   Bright vibration of water descending the muddy street. Festooned water flowing down Eddy Street and turning into Buffalo Street. What makes those rows of festoons?

Evening
   On damp-sugar snow dull-red shadow of parking meter due to bright red glow of restaurant sign behind and above.

The next day, Nabokov returned to the suicide note in the examination script:

Turn it into a girl's last note—the P.S. to an exam paper.
French course at W.

>   Tout est fini, école est finie,
>   *cette* examen et *celle* de ma vie.
>   Adieu, jeunes filles.
>   Death begins with a D.

Then, draw attention to . . . the wrong gender in second line (no English speaking person can master genders), to the pathetic and absurd "jeunes filles" for "girls" (because they are told that "fille" means "whore").
   Professor correct papers on train. Poor exam, hardly above "D." First thought the P.S. was the usual addendum—"Had a bad headache, enjoyed your course etc."

On February 8:

Suddenly while in my bath, *new story* came into being *complete*. Somewhere at the back of my mind was Stein, who died recently—his ghost putting a jinx on things. And then all kinds of items I had been storing up came into place *fitted*. Use Jan 29, etc.

"The Vane Sisters" was about to hurtle into being.
   Unfortunately for Nabokov, the rapture of inspiration had descended on him three days after the start of a new term consisting mostly of works he had never taught before and a class larger than he had ever taught. He began with gusto: "The seats are numbered. I would like you to choose your seats and stick to them. This is because I would like to link up your faces with your names. All satisfied with seats? No talking, no smoking, no knitting, no newspaper reading, no sleeping—and for God's sake take notes."[67]
   With his head crammed with projects and a new story importuning him to be written at once, Nabokov, in distress, asked Véra to write to Katharine White:

He has finally settled down to write a story and has delegated all other private matters to me. He has never had so little time for writing. In this respect it is probably the worst year of his life and though he derives much pleasure from his big course and from the students' reaction, the necessity to neglect his writing often makes him feel miserable. Things he had almost completed crumble away one by one because he has not the leisure to put them on paper at the right moment.[68]

On February 14, *Conclusive Evidence* was published to an excited reception from the critics and neglect from the public. Morris Bishop bestowed on Nabokov a "robust compliment" he never forgot: "Some of your phrases are so good they almost give me an erection—and at my age it is not easy, you know."[69] The one thing that did not please readers was the book's title. Edmund Wilson thought it chilly. Nabokov replied: "I tried to find the most impersonal title imaginable, and as such it is a success. But I agree with you that it does not render the spirit of the book. I had toyed with, at first, *Speak, Mnemosyne* or *Rainbow Edge* but nobody knew who Mnemosyne was (or how to pronounce her), nor did *R. E.* suggest the glass edge—'The Prismatic Bezel' (of *Sebastian Knight* fame)."[70] Apart from its unsalability, *Speak, Mnemosyne* was from Nabokov's point of view much the best title: Mnemosyne, as the goddess of memory and the mother of the muses, allowed him to combine the formal epic injunction, an impersonal tribute to memory as the source of imagination, a tribute to his mother as the one who prompted him from the first to hoard and treasure his memories, and even a tribute to his passion for butterflies (in the revised edition of his autobiography Nabokov would feature on the endpapers a sketch of *Parnassius mnemosyne*, one of the butterflies that flits through the pages of the book). Shortly after *Conclusive Evidence*'s American publication, Victor Gollancz asked for the British rights, but, disliking the American title and worried that readers in circulating libraries would be so afraid to mispronounce "Mnemosyne" they would not dare to request a book with that title, he suggested changing the name to *Speak, Memory*. Nabokov agreed.[71]

XII
"The Vane Sisters"

On March 5 he finished his new story, "The Vane Sisters," and started to dictate it to Véra. Five days later, he was still revising. On March 11 he worked all day on the story: "Completely finished, typed, retyped, three copies corrected by 12 p.m."[72]

A teacher at a college in a small New York town one day in late winter follows the bright drops of melting icicles from eave to eave and street to street in an attempt to detect the shadows of the falling drops. As the day wanes, his quest leads him all the way to the edge of town. At his usual eating time, far from his usual eating place, he dines in the only restaurant at hand. As he leaves he loiters a moment to observe the ruddy shadow of a parking meter, tinged by the neon sign above. Just then, a car pulls up and out comes an acquaintance, D., who tells him he has just heard of Cynthia Vane's death.

The narrator reviews his memories of Cynthia and her sister Sybil, a former student in his French course. Cynthia had once come to him begging him to have D. dismissed as a college instructor unless he would either break off his affair with Sybil or divorce his wife. Unbeknownst to Sybil, the narrator speaks to D., who had planned to end the affair in any case. The next day, Sybil in her French exam, after penning some atrocious French, appends a suicide note: "Please, *Monsieur le Professeur*, contact *ma soeur* and tell her that Death was not better than D minus, but definitely better than Life minus D." By the time the narrator marks the script, he is too late to help: she has already taken her life. In New York, months later, the narrator begins to see a good deal of Cynthia, a talented painter, and discovers her obsession with spiritualism and her theory of "intervenient auras. . . . She was sure that her existence was influenced by all sorts of dead friends, each of whom took turns in directing her fate. . . . For a few hours, or for several days in a row . . . anything that happened to Cynthia, after a given person had died, would be, she said, in the manner and mood of that person."

Returning to his home the night D. informs him of Cynthia's death, the narrator, although he has elegantly dismissed all Cynthia's fascination for the hereafter, cannot get to sleep for fear of some sign from Cynthia. Only at dawn does he drift off into a dream somehow full of her but hopelessly vague—yet she had been a painter of extraordinarily precise glass-bright minutiae:

I lay in bed, thinking my dream over and listening to the sparrows outside: Who knows, if recorded and then run backward, those bird sounds might not become human speech, voiced words, just as the latter become a twitter when reversed? I set myself to reread my dream—backward, diagonally, up, down—trying hard to unravel something Cynthia-like in it, something strange and suggestive that must be there.

I could isolate, consciously, little. Everything seemed blurred, yellow-clouded, yielding nothing tangible. Her inept acrostics, maudlin evasions, theopathies—every recollection formed ripples of mysterious meaning. Everything seemed yellowly blurred, illusive, lost.

The story is one of Nabokov's finest. No work of fiction has looked with sharper vision than this, as it records all the surprises of a sunny day in a snowy landscape. Behind the narrator's sharp eyes lurks a character serenely satisfied with himself and condescendingly critical of others. From the refuge of his detachment he coolly notes the imbroglios of other lives: capricious, unstable Sybil and her relationship with D., quietly enchanting Cynthia and her Greenwich Village milieu. Then this tale that has begun with such an intense scrutiny of the visible world leads into a series of fascinating speculations on the invisible world of the hereafter and on the elusiveness of any special signs of its existence, no matter how hard we might peer.

That theme fills the story even on a first reading. But like "Signs and Symbols," "The Vane Sisters" invites us to look out for a secret signal as the narrator strives in vain at the end to detect some precise token of Cynthia. A clue earlier in the story should prompt alert readers to construe the first letter of each word in the story's last paragraph as part of an acrostic message: "ICICLES BY CYNTHIA, METER FROM ME SYBIL." In other words the dripping of the icicles that led the narrator off his usual course toward the restaurant where he meets D. and learns of Cynthia's death have enticed him there under Cynthia's direction. Knowing of his pride in his visual sense, Cynthia attracts his unwitting attention with the icicles she uses to redirect his route: she subjects him to the "intervenient aura" he has so easily laughed away. Sybil, too, adds her little touch, the shadow of the parking meter on the sidewalk, just enough to detain him until D. will emerge from his car, meet the narrator, and inform him of Cynthia's death. The Vane sisters have designed a day in the narrator's life and stamped their mark on it in the very words where he records his frustration at failing to detect any meaningful sign of dead Cynthia. The very terms we employ to express our inability to detect the hereafter, Nabokov suggests, may themselves be the proof of the beyond, a proof we cannot read until we get outside the stories of our lives.

"The Vane Sisters" sums up a great deal of Nabokov's art: meticulous attention to the outer world of shine and sludge, an exact eye for the inner world of desire, despair, detachment, and yet an urgent compulsion to discover something that might lie beyond; a brilliant command of the normal virtues of fiction, but at the same time a shimmering promise behind the words: a problem set before us (why does that last paragraph sound so strange?), indirect hints that our imaginations can turn toward a solution, and a chance for us to experience the surprise of a discovery that utterly transforms the story and its world.

Nabokov sent "The Vane Sisters" to Katharine White, hoping for an immediate advance if she liked it, for he was in "awful financial difficulty."[73] A week later, she turned it down. He immediately sent it elsewhere, but quietly, patiently explained the story in detail to her and voiced his despair at her having failed to understand his best story. His letter shows how acutely, how critically, how humanely he could assess his characters, even those who seem almost drawn in his image. He dismisses the French professor—whose very Nabokovian fondness for the visual might make him seem singled out as one of the elect—as "a somewhat obtuse scholar and a rather callous observer of the superficial planes of life" who sees Cynthia merely "in terms of skin, hair, manners, etc. The only nice thing he deigns to see about her is his condescending reference to a favorite picture of his that she painted—frost, sun, glass—and from this stems the icicle-bright aura through which he rather ridiculously passes in the beginning of the story when a sunny ghost leads him, as it were, to the place where he meets D. and learns of Cynthia's death." Cynthia, on the other hand, Nabokov sees in terms of "her forgiving, gentle, doe-soul that had made him this gift of an iridescent day (giving him something akin to the picture he had liked, to the only small thing he had liked about her)." Nabokov then turns to look Katharine White in the eyes:

> You may argue that reading downwards, or upwards, or diagonally is not what an editor can be expected to do; but by means of various allusions to trick-reading I have arranged matters so that the reader almost automatically slips into this discovery, especially because of the abrupt change in *style*.
>
> Most of the stories I am contemplating (and some I have written in the past—you actually published one with such an "inside"—the one about the old Jewish couple and their sick boy) will be composed on these lines, according to this system wherein a second (main) story is woven into, or placed behind, the superficial semitransparent one. I am really very disappointed that you, such a subtle and loving reader, should not have seen the inner scheme of my story.[74]

XIII

When Nabokov had seen Mikhail Karpovich in Boston in June 1950, his friend had suggested that when he took sabbatical leave for the

1951–1952 academic year, Nabokov might replace him for his Russian literature courses at Harvard in the spring semester of 1952. With Dmitri to be a freshman at Harvard that year, Nabokov was eager to follow up Karpovich's offer, and by the end of March 1951 arrangements were settled: he would be a visiting lecturer in Slavic languages and literatures, teaching a survey course in Russian nineteenth-century literature and another course on Pushkin.[75]

By late March Nabokov was lecturing on *Dr. Jekyll and Mr. Hyde* and Kafka's *Metamorphosis*, which he examined along with Gogol's "Overcoat" as part of a triad of transformations. Once again he had to ˌcorrect the set text in class, and he knew just enough German to ascertain, with Véra's help, where the English diverged from Kafka. He also disposed of the edition's critical introduction: "This drivel should be disregarded," says a note on his copy.[76] It seems extraordinary that Nabokov, already a master of English prose rhythm and the orchestration of verbal sound—later in the year he would write Humbert's lilting invocation to Lolita—often felt it necessary to mark the pronunciation of words in his lecture notes, the vowel length of the "i" in "drivel," the syllable stress in "despicable." Even the torrent of his tirades had to be carefully channeled in advance.

Nabokov had intended to teach Dostoevsky's *Notes from Underground* (which he irreverently rechristened *Memoirs from a Mousehole*), but abandoned the idea. Feeling obliged in this first year to follow Weir's format and include two German authors, he devoted one lecture to Thomas Mann's story "The Railway Accident," which he subjected to a ruthless paragraph-by-paragraph attack.[77] Nabokov never repeated the lecture, and was glad to pass on to the much more congenial world of Proust.

At the end of April, the New York chapter of the American Association of Teachers of Slavic and East European Languages held its annual meeting at Cornell. Nabokov was to be the luncheon speaker, talking on "The Translator as Teacher" and his experience of translating *Eugene Onegin*. The Nabokovs arrived half an hour late, explaining to an audience by now quite frantic that there had been trouble with the car. As Cornell's only teacher of Russian literature, Nabokov had been assigned a seat next to Associate Professor Gordon Fairbanks, the head of Russian-language teaching at Cornell. When Nabokov saw this, he emitted a quite audible "No!" and took himself off to another table where he sat down with an acquaintance, Albert Parry, a professor at Colgate University and a longtime Sirin fan, and greeted him in pointedly effusive fashion to reinforce the snub.[78]

Ever since arriving at Cornell, Nabokov had been frustrated by the way the Russian language was taught on campus. The Division of Modern Languages was controlled by linguistics experts who did not necessarily know the languages they were to impart. That was certainly the case for Russian. Fairbanks frankly admitted to his students that he was learning Russian as he went along and that he could teach the language on the basis of linguistic theory. As early as 1948, Nabokov had noted in his diary in outraged amazement, "F. teaches all his groups *theory*, not the language."[79]

In the Division of Modern Languages, set up in the 1940s to meet war conditions, the major goal was mastery of the spoken language, taught by native speakers, with a linguistics specialist to teach the formal rules. Not only did Fairbanks have to keep just ahead of his students in the text, he did not know enough Russian to assess the competence of the three supposed native speakers who assisted him. One of the three came from the Caucasus region and could barely write Russian. After nearly ten years at Cornell, this assistant applied for a job teaching Russian at Columbia and cited his years of experience at Cornell. Those who interviewed him at Columbia later told Avgusta Jaryc, one of the genuine native speakers in the Cornell Russian language program, what an imposter they had encountered: someone who knew almost no Russian at all and claimed he had taught nearly ten years at Cornell![80]

Unable to teach his Russian literature courses to ill-prepared students, Nabokov had a relationship with the Division of Modern Languages not unlike a miniature cold war—he even wrote of the "iron curtain . . . between Goldwin Smith . . . and Morrill Hall"—that threatened to erupt into a miniature Korea. In February 1951, he had noted down in his yearbook the idea for a story, "The Assistant Professor Who Was Never Found Out," which would conflate Fairbanks and Harvard's Samuel Cross. Instead he saved his contempt until *Pnin*, where Professor Blorenge stands in for Fairbanks, and French serves as a thin disguise for Russian.[81]

As spring advanced, Nabokov began classes on *Ulysses*. This year, though not in subsequent years when he came to know the book better, he contrasted *Ulysses* unfavorably with Proust's masterpiece. He objected to the novel's continuous preoccupation with sex, to its needless obscurity, to the misrepresentation of human thought in its stream-of-consciousness passages ("no one walks around from morning to night remembering their past life—except authors").[82] But he had some superb insights to offer: the double dream of Stephen and Bloom, or the hallucinatory nighttown chapter as not Bloom's dream or Stephen's but the whole book dreaming itself.

Late in May Nabokov traveled to New York to be presented with an award from the National Institute of Arts and Letters. He sorely needed the $1,000 he received. After the ceremony, during which Elizabeth Bishop, Brendan Gill, and Randall Jarrell had also received awards and read from their work, he was rather taken aback, sitting on a bus with Jarrell, to find that the young poet did not want to talk about poetry, only about the reputations of other poets.[83]

On June 2, Nabokov conducted the final examination for his European fiction course. Once again he breathed life into dead time by jotting down carefully "all the little movements, curl twining, pimple-teasing, roving eyes, etc. peculiar to exams. Will come handy some day."[84] No other professors monitored exams at Cornell, normally a chore left to graduate students. No other professors insisted as Nabokov now began to do that students must write in ink. No others, certainly, asked their students questions like Nabokov's—but then no one *taught* like Nabokov either. And although all teachers sighed with relief when their teaching was over and they could turn single-mindedly to their own research and writing, no one else at Cornell had a project anything like Nabokov's *Lolita*.

CHAPTER 10

Finding Time for *Lolita*: Cornell and Harvard, 1951–1953

I

BY JUNE 1951, Nabokov could look back on the first year of his European fiction course as murderous. He was eager to escape to the West, where he could chase butterflies, revive his spirits, and carry on with *Lolita*. Never, he complained, had he been so anxious to write.[1]

Before leaving Ithaca he had things to attend to. Early in June he had an animated conversation with Milton Cowan, head of Cornell's modern languages division, over Gordon Fairbanks's ignorance of Russian. After the encounter he drew up a memorandum to himself. At a time when McCarthyism was forcing hundreds of American university teachers from their positions, he hinted at the gravity of exposing students to "the incredible errors (historical boners and the presentation of Soviet propaganda statements as *facts*)" in Fairbanks's *Russian Area Reader*. But, he added, the errors were due not to misplaced political sympathies and not to mere naïveté but to the fact that Professor Fairbanks simply "does not know Russian."[2] His complaint to Cowan had no effect.

With no time all year to write for the *New Yorker*, Nabokov was short of money, especially since his son had not obtained a scholarship for Harvard in the fall. He had to borrow from his friend Roman Grynberg, explaining: "I can't write stories for money, a pathological cold seizes my joints—and something else has me, a novel. . . . If you could advance me a thousand, the phantoms would take themselves off and the productive part of my soul could clear up." He had undertaken *Lolita* in the supposition that his Cornell post and good sales for his memoirs would support him while he wrote a book that might prove unmarketable. He wrote to Edmund Wilson that he was sick of having his books "muffled up in silence like gems in cotton wool. The letters from private individuals I get are, in their wild enthusiasm, ridiculously incommensurable with the lack of interest my inane and inept publishers take in my books. . . . I am completely in the *dèche*, am in miserable financial difficulties, see no way out of academic drudgery (ill-paid to boot)."[3]

Teaching at Harvard at least was not ill-paid. Every fall John Finley taught Harvard's Humanities 1 (Epic: *Iliad*, *Odyssey*, *Aeneid*, *Divine Comedy*, and *Paradise Lost*), which led in the spring to Harry Levin's Humanities 2 (Novel: *Don Quixote*, *Sorrows of Werther*, *Bleak House*, *Moby Dick*, *War and Peace*). For the spring of 1952, Levin had other commitments. Would Nabokov care to take over the course, substituting his own choice of novels? Yes, he would. He would be at Harvard then in any case to replace his friend Karpovich for two small Russian literature courses and to monitor Dmitri's progress, and needed the extra income a large new course would bring. He was much less keen to accept Levin's arguments that he would have to teach at least one new novel. After Humanities 1 swept through more than two millennia from Homer to Milton, Levin pointed out, it would be absurd if Humanities 2 immured itself entirely within the nineteenth century. Could he not reach back in time to *Don Quixote*? Nabokov remained reluctant to undertake another major book, especially as he knew no Spanish, but eventually had to concede.[4]

Before leaving the East and university cares behind, the Nabokovs had one last chore. The large house they had rented since September 1948 at 802 East Seneca Street was ruining them financially: they would have to move. Selling off their few items of furniture, even their piano, they piled their remaining belongings high up behind the frosted doors of Nabokov's offices in Goldwin Smith Hall and left the rest in storage with Dean of Ithaca.[5] From now on they would become nomads, renting cheap accommodations in the West every summer and moving, during the months they had to be at Cornell, from one home of a professorial family absent on sabbatical to another.

II

In the last week of June, their aging Oldsmobile set off westward. In a paper he had finished early in 1948, Nabokov had named and described *Lycaeides argyrognomon sublivens* on the strength of nine male specimens in the M.C.Z. Keen to capture the first female *sublivens* and simply to study the insect in the field, he had Véra head for Telluride, Colorado, where the M.C.Z. specimens had been caught half a century earlier. For afternoons and rainy days he took with him his copious notes for *Lolita*, "a novel I would be able to finish in a year if I could completely concentrate upon it." Dmitri meanwhile had traveled ahead to Los Angeles for a national high-school debating tournament.[6]

All along the route, Véra had to brave rains, thunderstorms, and floods. With no chance to collect butterflies, Nabokov instead gathered impressions for *Lolita*. In a special diary he execrated smelly motels and extolled delicate skies. June 28: "Yesternight highbrow trucks like dreadful huge Christmas trees in the darkness." June 29: "the first mesas, the first yuccas." June 30: "Night. St. Francis. Old farmer with a mummy's neck, furrowed and tanned. A grim El Greco horizon. Alternating stripes of water and green corn—of brightness and darkness opening like a fan as we drive by—somewhere in Kansas."[7]

As his wife drove on, Nabokov sometimes jotted down her casual phrases: "The little headlights are lighting up like one candle from another"; "My Oldsmobile gulps down the miles like a magician swallowing fire. Oh, look at that tree sitting on its haunches!"[8] John Synge improbably pictures Elizabethan dramatists reaching for their inkhorns and inserting into their plays phrases they have just heard at dinner from their mothers or their children, and adds that "in Ireland, those of us who know the people have the same privilege." Nabokov never drew directly on his wife's phrases—and she was speaking in Russian, not English—but the entries in his diary hint at the imaginative atmosphere around him every day.

After checking into a thin-walled motel room that might let through the sound of the honeymooners next door, Nabokov would often retire again to the car. Sitting in the back seat, in his private mobile studio—the only place in America with no noise and no drafts, he later told reporters—he would carry on with *Lolita*, writing in pen or pencil on a batch of index cards firm enough to serve as their own miniature writing desk. And in bed at night—if he wanted to do more than drift into insomnia—he needed earplugs to keep out the zip and whine of cars passing on the highway outside.[9]

At the beginning of July the Nabokovs stopped at the Skyline Ranch, just south of Telluride, a damp, unfrequented, defunct mining town 9,000 feet up in a breathtaking cul-de-sac at the end of two atrocious roads, one from Placerville, the other from Dolores. Two days later, when Dmitri joined them, they moved to Telluride's one motel, the "optimistic and excellent Valley View Court." Every evening a prodigious rainbow would straddle the town, and often the Nabokovs could watch what in *Pale Fire* would be dubbed

> that rare phenomenon
> The iridule—when, beautiful and strange,

> In a bright sky above a mountain range
> One opal cloudlet in an oval form
> Reflects the rainbow of a thunderstorm
> Which in a distant valley has been staged.

As he admitted, Nabokov bungled his family's vacation—all this mist and rain—but he got what *he* wanted.[10]

With legs still a footballer's but with breasts bouncing on his heavy frame, he would climb up every day to at least 12,000 feet along various more or less steep trails in search of *sublivens*:

> Every morning the sky would be of an impeccable blue at 6 a.m. when I set out. The first innocent cloudlet would scud across at 7:30 a.m. Bigger fellows with dark bellies would start tampering with the sun around 9 a.m., just as I emerged from the shadow of the cliffs and trees onto good hunting grounds. At around 10 a.m. there would come the daily electric storm, in several installments, accompanied by the most irritatingly close lightning I have ever encountered anywhere in the Rockies, not excepting Longs Peak, which is saying a good deal, and followed by cloudy and rainy weather through the rest of the day.

On July 15 he hiked up Tomboy Road. After three hours of walking and collecting en route he passed through Social Tunnel, an archway in the solid granite, at about 10,500 feet. A little further on, he came to a steep, almost overhanging slope on his left, "quite an enchanted slope, in fact, with hummingbirds and humming moths visiting the tall green gentians that grew among the clumps of a blue lupine, *Lupinus parviflorus*, which proved to be the food plant of my butterfly." For on that slope he found a few males of *sublivens* emerging. Three days later on the same slope he discovered the spectacular female. During the whole month of July he caught some sixty specimens of the butterfly on this slope, but despite climbing to 14,000 feet and exploring in every other direction he found no other trace of the species.[11]

To Nabokov's readers, Telluride and nearby Dolores and this enchanted slope above the town with its hummingbirds and humming moths and its prize female have an extra, unforgettable enchantment. At the end of *Lolita*, Humbert Humbert looks from an old mountain road down at a small mining town in a valley and hears wafting up the valley the vapory peal of children at play: "I stood listening to that musical vibration from my lofty slope, to those flashes of separate cries with a kind of demure murmur for background, and then I knew that the hopelessly poignant thing was not Lolita's absence from my side, but the absence of her voice from that concord." The scene Humbert evokes is exactly the scene Nabokov records in a letter to Edmund Wilson: "An old-fashioned, absolutely touristless mining town full of most helpful, charming people—and when you hike from there, which is 9000', to 10000', with the town and its tin roofs and self-conscious poplars lying toylike at the flat bottom of a *cul-de-sac* valley running into giant granite mountains, all you hear are the voices of children playing in the streets—delightful!" By the time he had worked that scene into *Lolita*, Nabokov had turned the private spell the scene cast over him into a seamless part of Humbert Humbert's own enchanted but much more sordid and sorrowful world. That world was rapidly becoming more real as the wet and the wind kept him indoors day after day.[12]

At the beginning of August, the family headed northwest through the Rockies, with Dmitri at the wheel terrifying his parents as he spun the car elegantly around tight corners above waiting abysses. Dmitri stopped at Jenny Lake in the Tetons, where he would spend the first two weeks at the Petzoldt-Exum mountaineering school, climbing the mountains along their most difficult and dangerous sides while his parents tried not to picture him with too much nightmarish vividness. Nabokov felt constantly alarmed, but could only approve of this "extraordinary overwhelming passion" that meant as much to his son as his lepidoptera did to him. He felt full of admiration for the alpinists who taught Dmitri, and he approved with a nod of recognition the way the physical exertion of mountaineering was somehow transmuted into a spiritual experience.[13]

He thought it a blissful relief to return to Véra's even tempo as she drove him a hundred miles further to West Yellowstone, Montana. Up in the hills there, they rented Duck Ranch—or rather, its two habitable rooms—for a ridiculously small sum, and had the place absolutely to themselves. "Aspens, pines, more warm-blooded animals than I have ever seen in one place"—including a herd of cattle that called once to mill around their cabin—"not a human for miles around, a distant gate we had to unlock when we drove through on a road with more flowers than sand—and all this for a couple of dollars per day."[14] Though Nabokov spent every possible moment on butterflies, *Lolita* made her claims too, in this unlikely spot, whenever the weather closed in.

III

By the end of August, the Nabokovs had picked Dmitri up and driven back to Ithaca. Their new address was 623 Highland Road, the home of an engineering professor. Cayuga Heights, to the north of the Cornell campus, stretches through the hills above Cayuga Lake, along heavily wooded, winding streets where the lawns come right to the roadway, unlined by any sidewalks. A suburb thickly dotted with Cornell professors, it would become the Nabokovs' preferred choice for their annual migration. Smaller than their big box house on Seneca Street, their Highland Road home was far quieter, more comfortable, and more picturesque, nestled among leaves already showing hints of autumn orange.[15]

Despite the season, Nabokov came down with sunstroke and spent two weeks in bed. "Silly situation: after two months of climbing, shirtless, in the Rockies, to be smitten by the insipid N.Y. sun on a dapper lawn. High temperature, pain in the temples, insomnia and an incessant, brilliant but sterile turmoil of thoughts and fancies."[16]

Among his new neighbors were Arthur and Rosemary Mizener. Arthur Mizener had just joined the Cornell faculty after the publication of his biography of Fitzgerald. Shaking hands with him for the first time, Nabokov at once pronounced judgment: "*Tender is the Night*, magnificent; *The Great Gatsby*, terrible." Mizener later summed up his friend:

I have never known anyone more learned in the literal sense of the term than Vladimir; the quantity, the precision, the depth of his knowledge was an astonishment and a delight. . . .

The innocence that went along with this remarkable mind was most obvious in his vanity, which was considerable and entirely inoffensive. I once introduced him to a student who said he had gone to all Vladimir's lectures on the European novel, though he was not taking the course; Vladimir immediately led the student across the room and introduced him to Véra Nabokov with a full account of the student's delight in his lectures.[17]

Over the previous few months the Ford Foundation had begun to set up in New York a new Russian-language publisher, the Chekhov Publishing House, in affiliation with its East European Fund. Its aim was to publish work by Russian émigré authors like Bunin, Aldanov, and Nabokov-Sirin, or by Soviet authors like Bulgakov or Akhmatova, who had become "internal émigrés." Thanks to the Ford Foundation's support, the Chekhov Publishing House could afford to pay advances that were larger and to sell copies at prices that were lower than émigré books could otherwise expect in America. In mid-September Nabokov sent to the Chekhov Publishing House—not yet formally in existence—the manuscript of *Dar* (*The Gift*).[18]

In the 1930s, when his Russian novels were published first in serial form in *Sovremennye zapiski*, the *Sovremennye zapiski* editors had refused to publish chapter 4 of *The Gift*, the almost novel-length satirical biography of the socialist hero Nikolay Chernyshevsky. Nabokov had been unable to secure its publication in toto and in book form in the émigré press, and his attempts to have it published in Russian after his arrival in the United States had met with no more success. Now, nearly twenty years after he had begun writing it, he had the satisfaction of knowing that what many would come to regard as the greatest Russian novel of the century would be published.

In mid-September the Nabokovs took Dmitri to register at Harvard, then drove back to Cornell for a term before returning to Harvard themselves in the spring. At Cornell, Nabokov had now been moved from the general Division of Literature, under David Daiches, to the more congenial Department of Romance Literature, under the friendly aegis of Morris Bishop. His salary increased, for the first time since his arrival, from $5,000 to $5,500, although he still felt underpaid "in a ridiculous and insulting manner." Instruction resumed on September 21: the fiction course, from Austen to Tolstoy, a Pushkin seminar, and his Russian survey course. For the last of these there were only two regular students. Fairbanks, Nabokov complained, was killing off students' chances of being able to read Russian literature in the original, and in future years he had no choice but to teach the survey course in translation.[19]

He began to prepare his lectures on *Don Quixote* for Harvard. Meanwhile, in his Cornell fiction course, he had begun to sharpen his class tests into pointed pedagogic tools to prod students into minute attention to the worlds of the novels. "I shall give you tests because study without monitoring is like writing on water," he announced. On October 4, his class faced its first test on *Mansfield Park*: "The seats are numbered. . . . Any consultation will be fatal. . . . What did Julia do immediately after her sister's wedding? . . . What did Mr. Price's daily newspaper cost him?" Reports of his exacting particularity must have begun to spread, for most students answered correctly: "Julia accompanied her sister on the latter's honeymoon—a curious custom of the day. . . . Finally the fact that Mr. Price invariably borrowed the paper from a neighbor throws a bright light on his way of life." In the classroom and elsewhere Nabokov thundered against hallowed authors, and he later liked to project an image of the ferocity of his literary standards as a teacher, referring to the Ds or Fs he issued or to his pencil ripping the paper as he crossed out a preposterous answer. In fact he was not a hard marker,* and in Mizener's words,

---

* When he returned test papers, he would read out in class the names of people whom he had given grades of 90 or higher and call them to the front of the class.

"except when his literary judgment was involved, he was extremely soft with his students."[20]

He was not soft, however, on cheating.* Unlike other Cornell professors, Nabokov monitored examinations, in the hope his vigilance would minimize cribbing. One year the toilets were set up by some students as an information center. After Nabokov discovered this he warned students in future years to go to the toilet before the examination commenced, as they would be allowed out later only on condition that he took their scripts as they left, marked immediately all that had been written so far, and devised new and more difficult questions for them to answer on their return.[21]

During October Nabokov applied for another Guggenheim Fellowship to allow him to work on the annotated translation of *Eugene Onegin* that for years he had been hoping to prepare. He also noted among his current projects a critical book "on several European novels (*Madame Bovary*, *Bleak House*, etc.)."[22] But his creative work made more urgent demands.

Throughout the month he put "the equivalent of a dozen distant thunderstorms in nervous energy" into a story largely inspired by the intense admiration and apprehension Dmitri's mountaineering exploits aroused in him. In the midst of composition, Morris Bishop testified, Nabokov "would sometimes appear, shaking, in the office, to confess that he had not slept all night; words and phrases had done demonic dances in his mind till morning. There was no use telling him to slow down, to take it easy; the creative spirit demands suffering of its adepts." Nabokov had to resign himself to a recurrent rhythm of not sleeping at all one night, taking a sleeping pill the next, then trying in vain the third night to sleep without a pill as words continued to whirl through his head.[23]

IV
"Lance"

At the beginning of November, he sent off to the *New Yorker* the result of all this energy, "Lance," the last short story he ever completed and one of his best.[24] At some unspecified time in the future, Mr. and Mrs. Boke see their only son off on the first manned expedition to another planet, and hope against hope for a return they can hardly expect. At the end of the story Lance does return, only to announce

* In a 1960s interview, he would list cheating as one of the three worst things human beings could do (*Strong Opinions*, 152).

that one of his friends has been mysteriously killed in the expedition but that nevertheless he himself will be off again in November.

Nabokov makes the story a giddy exploration of style: a flamboyant, explosive dismissal of the gleaming gadgets and tarnished conventions of science fiction, a roll call of the heroes of medieval chivalric romance (Mr. Boke's scholarly specialty), a cascade of mountaineering terms (Lance climbed assiduously in his teens). Nabokov sets images spinning until we lose our bearings, as Lance must be losing his, wherever he is headed, or as his parents lose theirs in their attempt to imagine the unknown world where their son might be alive or dead. At one moment the narrator confidently commands space and time; at another he appears just a poor mortal, evoking a long-dead great-uncle, recalling a recurrent childhood dream, afraid to screw in a light bulb: like humanity itself, achieving amazing feats of courage and invention but still not sure what the imagination can bring back from the great unknown surrounding the little world we know. Recounting Lance's story as science fiction or as ancient romance, letting him mount the skies as he would scale an icy crag or assail an enemy hilltop, Nabokov jumbles perspectives in sickening fashion to make us feel in the pit of our stomachs two preposterous and ungraspable facts: that space and time stretch off toward infinite remoteness from our immediate here and now, and that death's vast emptiness surrounds our little well-lit stretch of life.

"Lance" is a story about courage: Lance's courage in heading into space and the courage through the centuries of sailors leaving for uncharted seas and unmarked dooms; the courage of his parents as they wait helplessly behind, like a million fishermen's wives or soldiers' brides; or the courage of humankind, knowing that death looms ahead but still carrying on bravely with life, knowing how much colder the cosmos becomes the further we venture from home, but still ready to struggle deeper into the unknown.

Evidently Nabokov's first impulse for the story was Dmitri's passion for mountain climbing, which reminded him of both his own passion for butterflies and his youthful dreams of danger, the feats of daring he shared with his cousin Yuri until Yuri rode to his death in a cavalry charge. Above all the story derived from his and Véra's fears for Dmitri's safety. "Lance" is almost the last of a series of works on the theme of parents' love for their children and their dread of losing them: *Bend Sinister*; "Signs and Symbols"; *Conclusive Evidence*, which ends with Dmitri being led away from danger by his parents; the radical, repulsive inversion of the whole theme in Humbert's love and loss of Lolita, still at the center of Nabokov's mind as he composed "Lance"; and two gentler variations on the theme,

Pnin's poignant love for Victor, his ex-wife's son, and Shade's lament for his dead daughter.

"Lance" was also the result of Nabokov's studies in medieval French literature at Cambridge and a more recent, gleefully derisive, exploration of pulp science fiction. The story's medieval romance and parodic science fiction made its texture the densest and most difficult of all his short fiction, and after the *New Yorker*'s rejection of "The Vane Sisters" in the spring, he felt gloomy about the prospects of their taking the piece. In fact, Katharine White loved "Lance" and persuaded Harold Ross to publish the story, despite Ross's protests that he could not understand it. Nabokov received $1,256 for "Lance," which the *New Yorker* paid for "at an unusually high word rate," Katharine White informed him, "just on the basis of its originality."[25]

Despite their enthusiasm, the *New Yorker* editors still wanted to tinker with the story. Nabokov's replies to their queries reveal his passion for exactitude, his diligence in research, and his good-humored patience at so much fussy interference:

> 3. Asclepias is more exact, since the name milkweed is applied not only to asclepias but to some totally different plants. I shall give in if you really prefer milkweed but my sense of precision will suffer. Suffer intolerably, in fact.
>
> 4. *Selenographers will confirm this, but then their lenses serve them better.* I do not understand your query. I *am* speaking here of selenographers—not of astronomers in general, but of those among them who chart the moon and whose lunar maps confirm what planetary maps suggest (deserts), since selenographers, who are nearer to the object they observe, can rely on their lenses better than those who observe more distant planets. I am afraid I cannot change anything, especially since the moon is alluded to in the beginning of part 3.
>
> Please try to see telescope to telescope with me!
>
> 5. "Spacers" is the word used in "science fiction" magazines, which I have studied with the utmost repulsion. This gem should be kept. . . .
>
> 9. . . . As to Biola and Vala, which must be left untouched, these are names of scientists and names of girls which I have culled from science fiction magazines. They are meant, by the science fiction authors, to represent names of the remote future or connected with remote planets.
>
> 10. I am sending you a picture from Galaxy Science Fiction magazine which illustrates my point. The whole discussion of the science fiction business in my story is supposed to lead up to, and culminate in, this centaur passage.* I had other pictures of these four-legged beauties from

---

* "Inhabitants of foreign planets . . . have one remarkable trait in common: their

other magazines but have lost them. This one will do, I think. He is shown in front view. I doubt very much that the loincloth conceals anything that could not be shown. . . .

27. *Through the driving rain . . . and stops short at the gate, near the dripping liriodendron.* The "liriodendron" is absolutely essential here; in fact the "tulip tree" mentioned earlier was mentioned *only* because its sole duty was to lead up to "liriodendron." You will note the absolutely essential "l," "r" and "dr" (*dr*iving *r*ain, *dr*ipping li*r*iodend*r*on) which are summed up in the name of the tree; for just as the sound of "hystricomorphic," in the same sentence, suggests hysterical haste so the sound of "liriodendron" suggests a lyrical cry of joy and (in the "dr") the skidding of the hooves. Almost thirty centuries ago Homer used these simple tricks and I do not see why I should not.

"Liriodendron" is as important as the whole thing is. So please let it grow undisturbed in this damp corner of my story. . . .

For the benefit of your research people, I would like to mention (so as to avoid any duplication of labor): that the planet is very like Mars; that at least seventeen states have Pinedales; that the end of the top paragraph Galley 3 is an allusion to the famous "canals" (or, more correctly, "channels") of Schiaparelli (and Percival Lowell); that I have thoroughly studied the habits of chinchillas; that Charrete is old French and should have one "t"; that Boke's source on Galley 9 *is* accurate; that "Lancelotik" is not a Celtic diminutive but a Slavic one; that "Betelgeuze" is correctly spelled with a "z", not an "s" as some dictionaries have it; that the "Indigo" Knight is the result of some of my own research; that Sir Grummore, mentioned both in Le Morte Darthur and in Amadis de Gaul, was a Scotsman; that L'Eau Grise is a scholarly pun; and that neither bludgeons nor blandishments will make me give up the word "hobnailnobbing."

As usual, I appreciate very much the delicate care you take in steering my meaning through all my obscurities toward all those reading lamps which, I hope, get more numerous every year.[26]

If the *New Yorker* staffers were nonplussed by "Lance," some of the magazine's readers were positively vexed. To one, who wrote complaining that neither she nor any of her friends had been able to see anything more in the story than a feeble parody of science fiction comics, the *New Yorker* replied:

In "Lance" he is, of course, satirizing "science fiction" but he is also using it as the basis of an underlying serious theme which, as we inter-

---

intimate structure is never depicted. In a supreme concession to biped propriety, not only do centaurs wear loincloths; they wear them about their forelegs."

pret it, is the constancy of human emotions in an ever-changing world.
Extraordinary as an interplanetary expedition seems to us now, the emotions involved in the undertaking are no different from the emotions felt
in medieval days when Lancelot, the knight, went into battle, or the
emotions stirred up today when a son goes off to war. There is the same
tension, the same awkward departure, the same fear of the unknown,
the same anxious waiting on the part of parents, the same courage under
stress, the same sad loss of a friend, the same joyful return, the same
inarticulateness in trying to communicate what one has felt and seen.
No matter what changes the world goes through, our human relationships, our feelings, our reactions remain basically the same, and what
seems extraordinary for us even to imagine now will be reacted to in
quite an ordinary way when it comes to pass.

Genius may be misunderstood in its own time, but it can also be superbly apprehended. Nabokov was touched by the letter, and wrote
Katharine White: "Please tell its author that he or she has summed
up the thing in a perfectly admirable way, saying exactly what I
would have liked to say (but would not have been able to do so lucidly). It gave me great pleasure, great satisfaction."[27]

V

In October and again at Thanksgiving, the Nabokovs had driven to
Harvard to see Dmitri and to make arrangements for their spring
term there. Early in December they journeyed to New York, where
on December 8 the Russian émigré community staged a Nabokov
reading at the Master Institute Theater. Nabokov spent the first half
of the evening talking on Gogol (1952 would mark the centenary of
Gogol's death), and the second half reciting his own Russian poems.
While in New York he also lunched with Pascal Covici of Viking
Press, who was eager to publish whatever he could by Nabokov. Nabokov offered him his new novel and a collection of his lectures, to
be called *The Poetry of Prose*. He could not predict when he could complete the novel since he had to combine it with short-term produc-
tions merely "in order to vegetate."[28]

Back in Ithaca, he continued to prepare for his Harvard course and
to teach his three Cornell courses. *Lolita*, meanwhile, was still growing. Nabokov undertook research of all kinds. He sought out a book
on the recently discovered cave paintings at Lascaux, which gave him
what he needed for the novel's last paragraph, where Humbert
hopes to make Lolita "live in the minds of later generations. I am

thinking of aurochs and angels, the secret of durable pigments." At
the other end of the time scale, he needed to know current schoolgirl
slang. He traveled on buses, noting down in his diary snatches he
overheard: "She's quite a kid," or "Listen, I met ———," or "It's a
sketch," "It's a riot," "It's a panic." He took "one arm of a little girl
who used to come to see Dmitri, one kneecap of another." He visited
a school principal on the pretext of placing his little daughter. He
searched out recent studies of the physical and psychological development of American schoolgirls, recording on his index cards perti-
nent details from such works as "Attitudes and Interests of Premen-
archal and Postmenarchal Girls" and "Sexual Maturation and the
Physical Growth of Girls Age Six to Nineteen." He noted newspaper
reports of accidents, sex crimes, and killings: "a middle-aged morals
offender" who abducted fifteen-year-old Sally Horner from New Jer-
sey and kept her for twenty-one months as his "cross-country slave,"
until she was found in a southern California motel; G. Edward Grammar's ineptly staged murder of his wife in a poorly faked motor accident; a man charged with murder who confessed to wrapping his
extra cartridges in a handkerchief, as Humbert would do. He consulted a history of the Colt revolver, gun catalogues, an article on
barbiturates, a book on Italian comedy. He took song titles from juke-
boxes, and phrases from teen magazines, women's magazines, home
decorating guides, billboards, motel guest notices, Girl Scout manu-
als, and more overheard conversation ("I have *zillions* of them," "She
was loads of fun").[29]

He had been eager for years to find the time to work on *Lolita*. It
seems odd that in his little free time he continued to work on much
less compelling projects, like the foreword to a Chekhov Publishing
House collection of Gogol stories that he wrote over the Christmas
vacation. Perhaps he simply feared that no one would dare to publish *Lolita* and that therefore he needed other writing projects. Late
in January, he wrote to Pascal Covici: "My novel is coming along well
and is rapidly approaching the pen-and-paper stage." He hoped to
have time in Cambridge for a concerted attack on *Lolita*. Meanwhile,
hemmed in by examination papers, he wrote to Edmund Wilson: "I
am sick of teaching, I am sick of teaching, I am sick of teaching."[30]

VI

At the beginning of February, the Nabokovs arrived in Cambridge
and settled in at 9 Maynard Place, near the Charles River and a
twenty-minute walk west from the Harvard campus. They had ob-

tained the house through their friend Sylvia Berkman, a friend of the couple subletting the place, the writer May Sarton—"a charming lesbian lady," Nabokov thought—and Judith Matlack, who was taking sabbatical leave. Nabokov loved the ramshackle quarters, with all their bibelots and a good *bibliothèque*. He laughed at the protracted and rather fussy orgasm that took place every five minutes or so among the steam pipes of the radiator in his comfortable, sunny study at the top of the house.[31] And he doted on May Sarton's tiger cat, Tom Jones—the Nabokovs renamed him Tomski*—later to become famous as the hero of Sarton's book *The Fur Person*. In that work, Tom Jones's owner describes the long trestle table by the study window and the straight chair she kept there:

> Nabokov removed this austere object and replaced it with a huge overstuffed armchair where he could write half lying down. Tom Jones soon learned that he was welcome to install himself at the very heart of genius on Nabokov's chest, there to make starfish paws, purr ecstatically, and sometimes—rather painfully for the object of his pleasure—knead. I like to imagine that *Lolita* was being dreamed that year and that Tom Jones' presence may have had something to do with the creation of that sensuous world. At any rate, for him it was a year of grandiose meals and subtle passions.[32]

When Tom Jones fell ill, the Nabokovs took him to the vet and visited him regularly until he could come home again. Kinbote's disdain for the cat he inherited in Judge Goldworth's house was not his maker's.[33]

At Harvard, Nabokov was officially Visiting Lecturer in Slavic Languages and Literatures for the spring term. He taught two Russian courses, Slavic 150, Modernism (Tyutchev, Nekrasov, Fet, Dostoevsky, Tolstoy, Chekhov, Blok, Khodasevich, and Mayakovsky), and Slavic 152 (Pushkin). But his major teaching task was Humanities 2, The Novel. On Tuesdays and Thursdays from 10:00 to 11:00 A.M. he lectured in the Sanders Theater, Memorial Hall, before "an abyss of five hundred students." In the front row sat Véra, erect, attentive, and white-haired, chalk at the ready to write any difficult terms on the blackboard.[34]

Priming his friend before he took over his course, Harry Levin had warned him that few of the students, though bright and curious, were "interested in literature from an artistic point of view; they

---

* Not simply, as it looks, a case of adding the "-ski" suffix to Russify the name; the Nabokovs compounded May Sarton's play on "tomcat" and *Tom Jones* by superimposing an allusion to the character Tomski in Pushkin's "Queen of Spades."

want these novels, frankly, to open windows for them into the lives of people at other times and places." Nabokov was disappointed to find from his own observations that most of the students had no real interest in the novels and preferred merely to be told about them at second hand. But far from accepting either that fact or Levin's advice, he continued to insist on the artfulness of art and the particularity of the imagination. In reply to Levin, he began the course by disabusing his students:

> We shall do our best to avoid the fatal error of looking for so-called "real life" in novels. Let us not try and reconcile the fiction of facts with the facts of fiction. *Don Quixote* is a fairy tale. . . . With its preposterous inns full of belated characters from Italian storybooks and its preposterous mountains teeming with lovelorn poetasters disguised as Arcadian shepherds, the picture Cervantes paints of the country is about as true and typical of seventeenth-century Spain as Santa Claus is true and typical of the twentieth-century North Pole.[35]

He devoted six lectures to *Don Quixote*. It seems he began his preparation with only remote memories of the novel and a favorable predisposition toward its hero, but as he reread the text minutely, he soon found himself shocked by its crudeness and savagery. Cruel heroes like Humbert Humbert and Van Veen and victims of cruelty like Adam Krug and Timofey Pnin have led some readers— including Edmund Wilson—to suppose Nabokov had a perverse love of inflicting pain. In fact, it should be perfectly apparent that he was outraged by cruelty. Certainly no one could have mistaken his appalled reaction to *Don Quixote*. He detested the belly laughs Cervantes wanted his readers to derive from his hero's discomfiture, and he repeatedly compared the vicious "fun" of the book with Christ's humiliation and crucifixion, with the Spanish Inquisition, with modern bullfighting. Some small boys lift up the tails of Rocinante and Sancho's gray nag and insert bunches of prickly furze: "The animals begin leaping and rearing and toss their riders to the ground. Those will laugh at this who just love bucking horses in commercial rodeos—bucking nags fitted with special corrosive belly straps."[36]

Nabokov enjoyed thundering against *Don Quixote* in front of so many students, and told Harry Levin what he thought of the book. "Harvard thinks otherwise," Levin replied gravely. Uncommon though Nabokov's estimate of *Don Quixote* was, it was certainly not perverse: Morris Bishop shared his friend's opinion and was always unhappy when as a professor of Romance literature he could not avoid teaching Cervantes.[37]

Upsetting received opinions was always one of Nabokov's great pleasures. Don Quixote, the critics wrote, was a perpetual loser. Nabokov checked the book in detail, scene by scene, and found this was not so. He even tallied Don Quixote's victories and defeats as games in a tennis match that proves surprisingly close: "6-3, 3-6, 6-4, 5-7. But the fifth set will never be played; Death cancels the match." And although he was impatient with anyone who thought that the sentimentalized image of Don Quixote, the woebegone righter of wrongs, fairly represented Cervantes' book, he paid eloquent tribute to Don Quixote as an independent cultural symbol: "He has ridden for three hundred and fifty years through the jungles and tundras of human thought—and he has gained in vitality and stature. We do not laugh at him any longer. His blazon is pity, his banner is beauty. He stands for everything that is gentle, forlorn, pure, unselfish, and gallant."[38]

After *Don Quixote*, Nabokov continued with his regular Cornell material on *Bleak House*, *Dead Souls*, *Madame Bovary*, and *Anna Karenin*, adding occasional comments to reinforce the continuity between the Epic and Novel sections of Humanities 1 and 2. He never repeated his *Don Quixote* lectures at Cornell, but he did retain his additions to the lectures on other novels. These interpolations on the evolution of literature provide some of his finest comments on fiction. Lauding the scene of Kitty giving birth in *Anna Karenin*, Nabokov observes that "the whole history of literary fiction as an evolutionary process may be said to be a gradual probing of deeper and deeper layers of life. It is quite impossible to imagine either Homer in the ninth century B.C. or Cervantes in the seventeenth century of our era—it is quite impossible to imagine them describing in such wonderful detail childbirth." Or in describing the pathos of *Bleak House* and approving the rich stream of Dickens's pity for children, he remarks

> how different is this world of Dickens from the world of Homer or from the world of Cervantes. Does a hero of Homer's really feel the divine throb of pity? Horror, yes—and a kind of generalized routine compassion—but the keen sense of specialized pity as we understand it today . . . ? For let us nurse no doubt about it: despite all our hideous reversions to the wild state, modern man is on the whole a better man than Homer's man, *homo homericus*, or than medieval man.[39]

VII

One of Nabokov's chief reasons for coming to Harvard to teach this term was that it would be the end of Dmitri's first year there. To his

sister Elena Sikorski he reported Dmitri's interests as "mountaineering, girls, music, track, tennis and his studies (in that order)." In an
escapade that typified his freshman form, Dmitri and another climbing friend one night scaled the ivy-clad walls and tower of Memorial
Hall. When a campus policeman accosted them, he replied, "It's all
right. My father lectures inside," and the amazed policeman let them
go. Dmitri's first term had begun tempestuously, and his parents
awaited his results with apprehension. As they feared, his marks reflected his lack of effort.[40]

The Nabokovs had many others to see in Cambridge besides their
son. One evening their friends Harry and Elena Levin had them to
dinner with the Jakobsons. Nabokov set the evening off to a bad
start. He and Jakobson had agreed back in 1949 to work together on
an English edition of *The Song of Igor's Campaign*, but now Nabokov
could not recall Jakobson's patronymic: as always, he had difficulty
remembering the names of those he did not care for. The Levins'
daughter had just been given a tape recorder, at that time still very
much a novelty, and guests were asked to choose favorite poems to
recite. Both Nabokov and Jakobson opted for Pushkin, and it became
a competition between St. Petersburg and Moscow accents. Jakobson
also recited some Khlebnikov, whose verse Nabokov could not stand.
Nabokov's muttered comment "Eto uzhasno" ("That's terrible")
came out quite distinctly when the tape was replayed. On another
occasion the Levins invited Mary McCarthy. She found Nabokov
greatly changed from a decade earlier: no longer the gaunt émigré
conditioned by austerity that she had seen in him in the early 1940s,
but a bon vivant, fatter, rubicund, more expansive in every way.[41]

Through Harry Levin, Nabokov met the poet Richard Wilbur,
whose work he came to rate very highly.* Wilbur had read in *Partisan
Review* Nabokov's memoir "First Poem," and commented on the extraordinary minutiae, such as a drip glissading from a wet leaf's tip,
that Nabokov's memory preserved for decades. Alas, every detail
was true, Nabokov replied, because he was a victim of total recall.
On another occasion, at a dinner at Harvard's Society of Fellows, Wilbur noted the equanimity and detachment with which Nabokov listened to a sherry-maddened Junior Fellow holding forth on the ugli-
ness of Russian women.[42]

Through the Levins, the Nabokovs also began to see much of William and Alice James. William, a painter, was the son of the great

---

* Once when Wilbur came to Cornell for a poetry reading, arriving weary and unfed
after a delayed flight, he looked down and saw Nabokov "sitting alone in the very
front row, and passionately wished that I had eaten something, that I felt better, that
my poems were better."

philosopher, a favorite of Nabokov's, and a nephew of the novelist. Nabokov thought William James "a dear soul with an admirable delicacy of string-tone," and treated the older man—aged seventy in 1952—in his most warmly ceremonious fashion.[43]

No pages in the small appointment books Nabokov kept between 1943 and his death are more thumbed and soiled than those relating to the spring of 1952. He and Véra kept up with their Wellesley friends: the Stephenses, the Sweeneys, the Kerby-Millers, Andrée Bruel, and Sylvia Berkman. They saw the Jakobsons, Renato Poggioli, the poet John Ciardi (Dmitri's best grades had been in English under Ciardi), May Sarton, Arthur Schlesinger, Isaiah Berlin, Mark Schorer, Richard Ellmann, the young Adrienne Rich. At William James's, Nabokov met Robert Lowell and talked about Lowell's old school, St. Mark's, astounding the poet with his detailed knowledge of the place—soon to find its way into *Pnin*.[44]

In February, a routine X ray revealed Nabokov had a " 'Shadow behind the Heart'—something that has been haunting me for more than ten years and that no doctor has been able to explain—but what a wonderful title for an old-fashioned novel!"* In his anything but old-fashioned *The Real Life of Sebastian Knight*, Sebastian Knight himself dies young of a heart ailment. In February 1952, hero and book were resurrected in a French translation, *La vraie vie de Sebastian Knight*, which the French press hailed as "un chef d'oeuvre," "un des plus beaux, des plus riches, des plus neufs, des plus passionnants romans que nous ayons lus depuis longtemps."[45]

Late in March, Nabokov read in the Morris Gray poetry series at Harvard's Sever Hall, in a season that had begun with William Carlos Williams and would end with Wallace Stevens. With less than two weeks to go before the reading, he panicked at finding he had none of his English poems with him. To fill the gap, he composed the poem "Restoration" and then, with only three days to go, wrote another poem, "Pity the elderly grey translator," which he could use to lead into his own translations of Pushkin, Tyutchev, and Nekrasov, which he had on hand for his modernism course. He read from *Conclusive Evidence* at Wellesley, and was to have lectured on Chekhov at Toronto, but called it off, despite a loyal following there, rather than face the Boston-Toronto-Boston train journey over a weekend between classes. He spoke on Gogol at Dartmouth College before an audience of eight—the organizer had not remembered to advertise—

---

* This too finds its way into *Pnin*, where Chateau remarks on Pnin's having "a shadow behind the heart": "Good title for a bad novel."

but he summoned up his resolve and concentration and gave "a wonderful lecture."[46]

At the end of March he began translating *The Song of Igor's Campaign*, and finished after two weeks' hard work. He mimeographed the result for his class, and took the translation back to Cornell with him for future years, while unauthorized copies continued to circulate at Harvard and Columbia for the rest of the decade until his new translation was published in 1960.

Early in April he heard that he had been awarded his second Guggenheim Fellowship. Although he had applied for it in order to translate *Eugene Onegin*, it was considered to be an extension of his 1943 fellowship, and therefore was awarded for "creative writing." Now he could apply for unpaid leave from Cornell for the spring 1953 term, and he optimistically looked forward to the numerous projects that suddenly seemed feasible. In May he talked over with Pascal Covici his translation of *The Song of Igor's Campaign*, in an edition with notes by Jakobson and Szeftel, his own *Eugene Onegin* translation, his new novel, a new volume of memoirs, and a volume of literary criticism.[47]

His Harvard lectures ended late in May. As exams commenced, he invited Edmund and Elena Wilson to dinner when they came through Boston at the beginning of June. Wilson accepted, adding, "I think that the time is approaching when I am going to read [Volodya's] complete works and write an essay on them that will somewhat annoy him."[48] A curious way of accepting a dinner invitation, but typical of the long autumn of their relationship. The slight chill perceptible in their letters would be instantly dispelled in a rush of warmth when the two friends actually met, but it would soon creep back into their correspondence in their desire to prove their frankness to each other by promising biting criticism to come. Yet the onset of their feud still lay thirteen years ahead.

VIII

Three Nabokovs left Cambridge on June 20, 1952: Dmitri, racing ahead in his newly acquired 1931 Model A Ford, and his parents, following in their Oldsmobile. They stopped overnight in Ithaca to store things for the summer, and headed west for Wyoming, reaching the Lazy U Motel in Laramie at the end of the month.[49]

Nabokov had planned to work intensively on *Lolita*, but he was utterly exhausted by his university year. Seven weeks after leaving Cambridge he wrote to Edmund Wilson: "I have not read a book (save for a collection of Henry James' short stories—miserable stuff, a complete fake, you ought to debunk that pale porpoise and his plush vulgarities some day) nor written a word since I left."[50]

He had come to Wyoming to check on the range of distribution of his blues. Véra drove him just a little past Laramie, through Medicine Bow National Forest, the most beautiful drive they had yet seen in the Rockies. They stopped at Riverside, "(one garage, two bars, three motor courts and few ranches), one mile from the ancient and obsolete little town Encampment (unpaved streets, wooden sidewalks)." While Dmitri worked as a head gardener and pool lifeguard at an inn in nearby Saratoga, his parents had a little log cabin to themselves. Nabokov had chosen to begin his collecting some two hundred miles south of the previous season's, where the Continental Divide extends through the snow of the Sierra Madre range, to see whether he could find geographical intergrades between various species of the genus *Colias* and whether he could account geographically for hybridization in his *longinus* subspecies.[51]

He had one interesting surprise in his first week. *Vanessa cardui*, a butterfly he had observed in Europe migrating up from beyond the Black Sea through the Crimea to the St. Petersburg area, seemed to be migratory here too. In the first week of July he saw the species in colossal numbers above the timberline, and found from an alert ranger that the first spring flock had passed five weeks earlier. He was able to trace the species' progress as he moved northwest during the season himself, and to establish the phenomenon of intrazonal migration in North America, butterflies "moving early in the season from subtropical homes to summer breeding places in the Nearctic region but not hibernating there in any stage."[52]

On July 4, tiny Riverside treated itself to a rambunctious celebration: one of the town's two bars, crowded with drunks, boomed music out for a half-mile radius until the local policeman took the barman into custody.[53] That seems to have found its echo in *Lolita*: there, Lolita's own Independence Day, the day she escapes at last from Humbert in a town just west of the Continental Divide, coincides with some rowdy "great national celebration"—July 4—that Humbert is too ill to recognize.

Many of *Lolita*'s first readers confused Nabokov with Humbert. Few could have imagined the real author's activities at the time he was writing the book. Shortly after Independence Day, acting on a hunch, he visited "a remarkably repulsive-looking willowbog, full of cowmerds and barbed wire," and found the species *Boloria toddi* more abundant than anywhere else in the West, but "very difficult to capture, their idea of sport being to sail to and fro over the fairly tall sallows that encompassed the many small circular areas . . . into which the bog was divided by the shrubs."[54]

In mid-July the Nabokovs, with Dmitri, moved northwest to Dubois, nearer their old haunts of 1949 (the Grand Tetons, to which Dmitri now returned to climb) and 1951 (Yellowstone). A letter from Edmund Wilson's daughter Rosalind, forwarded from place to place, at last caught up with them at Dubois's Rock Butte Court. Now working for Houghton Mifflin, Rosalind Wilson recalled Nabokov's frequent comments on mimicry and invited him to write a book on the subject. Véra replied on his behalf, full of enthusiasm: "The question of mimicry is one that has passionately interested him all his life and one of his pet projects has always been the compilation of a work that would comprise *all* known examples of mimicry in the animal kingdom. This would make a voluminous work and the research alone would take two or three years." Eagerness on such a colossal scale only ensured that Houghton Mifflin was scared off the proposal.[55]

The Nabokovs continued to roam about in Wyoming, settling at the beginning of August into Corral Log Cabins in the little town of Afton, which they found altogether enchanting and blessed with a wonderful climate. After reaching Afton, Nabokov's nerves began to calm down. By the second week in August he could report to his friend Roman Grynberg that he still had not quite come to after his terrible winter and spring efforts, but that his nervous system had righted itself and stopped walking along a slack rope of tangled barbed wire. He put some finishing touches to his translation of *The Song of Igor's Campaign*. Since in applying for his Guggenheim Fellowship, which commenced on August 1, he had stipulated that he wished to translate *Eugene Onegin*, he conscientiously began the translation and fondly hoped to have it finished by the autumn of 1953.[56]

IX

The family had set out west in two vehicles, but as Dmitri had already worn out his first car and sold it in Jackson Hole, they had to return in one. By September 1 they were back in Ithaca, this time at 106 Hampton Road, the home of a professor of chemical engineering, and once again in Cayuga Heights: a little house on the top of a hill, with an enormous picture window overlooking most of Cayuga Lake and the hills beyond. By now Véra had acquired a well-earned reputation in Ithaca as an immaculate housekeeper. She and her husband were ideal tenants, much sought after. And they never complained about having to shift once or twice a year after a summer on the move. Rather, Morris Bishop recollected, "they delighted in the frequent change of scene. They took pleasure in constructing the character of their absent hosts from the artifacts of their homes—the objects of art, the books, the mechanical robotry, the minglings of pretension and makeshift."[57] Nabokov's amused curiosity could turn even the walls and floors around and beneath him into a laboratory for *Lolita*, *Pnin*, and *Pale Fire*.*

After driving Dmitri back to Harvard in mid-September, his parents returned to Cornell for another term. Nabokov now had two hundred students in his European fiction course, six for his course in Russian modernism, and thirty for his survey of Russian literature.[58] This time for the first year he taught the survey using only English translations (Guerney's *Treasury of Russian Literature*, his own *Three Russian Poets*, his mimeographed *Song of Igor's Campaign*, and his embryonic *Eugene Onegin*). From 1952 to 1957 the same pattern persisted: the European fiction course, the English-language survey of Russian literature, and in alternate years an advanced seminar on either Pushkin or what Nabokov conservatively called "Modernism" in Russian literature (Tyutchev, Fet, and Blok in verse; Tolstoy and Chekhov in prose) with texts in Russian but classes in English.

Teaching came far easier this year. By now his courses had become familiar routines, requiring no new preparation; he was well rested after the effort of the previous year; and he had the relief of knowing that with the spring term of 1953 on leave his time would be his own from the coming January until late September. Once the administrative torments of the beginning of the academic year were over, he could begin to work in sustained fashion on *Lolita*.

In mid-October he wrote to Pascal Covici that he was on the point of completing his new novel—"on the point of completing" from the position of someone in training for years and now entering the stadium for his crucial run. He explained that for reasons of his own he wished to publish the novel under an assumed name, and asked Viking Press to make a legally binding promise of secrecy in all dealings

* Before the Nabokovs had left Ithaca for Cambridge at the beginning of the year, Meyer and Ruth Abrams had wanted them to take their house for the 1952–1953 academic year. Although the Abramses showed them eagerly through their large Cayuga Heights home, with its fine view over the lake, the Nabokovs seemed uninterested. Only when they entered the nursery, and Nabokov saw all sorts of things left over from their child's infancy, did his eyes light up: "How charming, Véra, we'll take it." But since the Abramses wanted tenants all year, the arrangement fell through when Nabokov was granted leave for the spring term of 1953.

about the book. To ensure his signature could still be made out on the finished canvas, however, he included among the book's characters a woman named Vivian Darkbloom. Early in November he reported to Covici that he hoped to have at least part of the manuscript ready within a few weeks.[59]

The Chekhov Publishing House, meanwhile, after publishing the full Russian text of *The Gift* in the spring, had requested other Nabokov works. He had hoped they would republish in Russian his other major early novels, *The Defense* and *Invitation to a Beheading*, but he was asked instead to translate one of his English novels. He counteroffered a translation of *Conclusive Evidence*, and on being promised the normal advance of $1,500, accepted with delight. His friend Roman Grynberg had translated a chapter at the beginning of the year, but Nabokov had thought it all impossibly brutal in Russian.[60] If it were to be translated, it would have to be in his own version.

For now, he spent almost all his time writing *Lolita*, until his "plump freckled hand" was worn out, but he still maintained a lively presence in the classroom. "Brothers sit apart. Sisters sit apart. All use ink," he announced with playful curtness before a November examination in his European fiction class. Once he came into his modernism class, sat down at the desk, staring before him, and started shaking his head with a puzzled, half-shocked, half-amused smile. "You will never believe this! Do you know what happened to me today? In the middle of the European literature class, a girl suddenly got up and walked out! I was talking about that Viennese quack, . . . and she just got up and walked out on me!" He seemed not so much offended or hurt as amused and even impressed by the student's courage in registering her protest on Freud's behalf.[61]

Over the Christmas break, Dmitri and his friends set off in a converted hearse on an expedition to climb Mexico's tallest mountain, the 18,855-foot Orizaba. His father traveled no further than New York for another public reading before the émigré community on December 21: a talk on Blok in the first half, his own prose and verse in the second.[62]

Three weeks of the fall term remained after classes resumed. In his European fiction class his last lectures were on *Anna Karenin*. One cloudless January day he found both himself and his students losing concentration. Among the students was his future critic and friend Alfred Appel, Jr., who recalls that Nabokov

> stopped lecturing, abruptly, and, without a word, strode to the right-hand side of the stage and snapped off the three overhead light fixtures. Then he walked down the five or six steps to the floor of the lecture hall,

clumped up the aisle to the back, two hundred dismayed heads turning together . . . to watch him as he silently pulled down the shades of three or four windows (the other window shades were already drawn, thanks to an Art History slide show in the previous class). Nabokov retreated down the aisle, up the stairs, and returned to stage right and the control switch. "In the firmament of Russian literature," he proclaimed, "this is Pushkin!" The ceiling light on the far left of the planetarium went on. "This is Gogol!" The middle light went on. "This is Chekhov!" The light on the right went on. Then Nabokov descended the stage once again, marched to the rear and the central window, and released the window shade, which sprang back on its roller (bang!), a solid white beam of sunlight streaming into the room, like some emanation. "And that is Tolstoy!" boomed Nabokov.[63]

With that crack and flash from on high, every waverer in the class was converted at once.

X

After examinations finished on January 30, Nabokov had eight months of leave. Happy to have an occasion to be near Dmitri, who was still paying little attention to his studies, he planned to spend the last months of the winter in Harvard's Widener and Houghton libraries, carrying out the research for his annotations to *Eugene Onegin*, before leaving as soon as the season would permit for the first place where butterflies would emerge in the American montane zone, in southernmost Arizona on the Mexican border.

On February 1 the Nabokovs arrived at 35 Brewster Street, Cambridge, which they had taken until April. The house, obtained once again through their friend Sylvia Berkman, belonged to her friend the poet Robert Frost, absent for his customary winter sojourn in Florida. Stone-cold inside, the place was at once rechristened the Jack Frost House by its new tenants. Frost had locked up his study, and the Nabokovs felt disconcerted and made unwelcome by that barricaded den in the middle of the house. They did not stay long.[64]

By mid-February they had moved to a hotel apartment right on campus, the Ambassador Hotel (now Coolidge Hall), 1737 Cambridge Street, Suite 617. The new quarters suited them ideally for two months of intensive work: only five minutes' walk to the Widener Library, and no housekeeping duties, so that Véra remained free to act as research assistant and transcriber of all the materials her husband tracked down.[65]

Nabokov spent from 9:00 A.M. every day until 2:00 the next morning working on his commentary to *Eugene Onegin*. He began in the Widener stacks by reading the sourcebooks *Pushkin i ego sovremenniki* (*Pushkin and His Contemporaries*) and Khodasevich's work on Pushkin. He studied ten translations of *Eugene Onegin*, four English, four German, two French. He read "*all* the books Pushkin refers to in 'E. O.' Even Burke. Even Gibbon. Of course, Richardson and Madame Cottin," and he read them all in French, as Pushkin would have done. He reread La Fontaine and Voltaire and waded through a whole swamp of seventeenth- and eighteenth-century French authors who might have influenced Pushkin in thought, phrasing, or versification. He even found the dream guide that Tatiana consults to try to interpret her prophetic dream. By the time he left Cambridge his commentaries had swollen to three hundred pages and he expected the whole book now to be six hundred pages long. Little did he know that he had glimpsed only a third of the beast.[66]

Social calls provided the only break in the daily grind. Of course the Nabokovs saw Dmitri often, and worried about his progress. With the Levins away, they called most frequently on William and Alice James, and through them met novelist Elizabeth Bowen. Nabokov saw his friend Allen Tate, "tight as a drum," at a reading at Radcliffe. He met the critic and poet I. A. Richards.[67] And he invited Tom Jones for a reunion and tea at their Ambassador Hotel suite. May Sarton has described the scene:

> Naturally attendants were required. Judy and I took him in a taxi. I had misgivings, for although Tom Jones was a gentleman cat, he was still a cat, . . . and cats are subject to violent anxiety at any uprooting, so we were all three rather nervous as we went up in the elevator, Tom Jones in my arms.
>
> The welcome was warm indeed, not only tea for the attendants, but a dish of raw liver cut into small delicate pieces was laid on the floor for the hero of the occasion. What happened was distressing. Tom Jones, subject to a fearful attack of agoraphobia, vanished under a velvet sofa and refused to come out during the painful hour of our stay. We had finally to move the sofa and extricate him brutally when it came time to go. The reunion, as Nabokov had fondly imagined it, . . . was not a reunion. It was a disaster.[68]

XI

Early in April the Nabokovs packed their trunk, filled up with gas, and headed for Arizona via Birmingham, Alabama. "Joggy and jittery and buzzy with insomnia" and once more on the verge of a breakdown after another spell of overwork, Nabokov decided to set Pushkin aside for a few months and start fixing and copying out the final text of *Lolita*.[69]

Eight days after leaving Cambridge, the Nabokovs' tired Oldsmobile panted into Portal, Arizona, in the southeast corner of the state, almost on the border of Old and New Mexico. There they had arranged in advance to rent a cottage on a ranch designed by its owner as a kind of wildlife preserve. Spectacular birds in great numbers visited the cactus-and-yucca waste outside the windows. From the cactus desert it was an hour's drive every morning up to the aspens of the Chiricahua Mountains where, if the weather permitted, Nabokov devoted himself to butterflies from 8:00 A.M. to noon or later. Here he hoped to take long series of *maniola*, which another entomologist had demoted—wrongly, Nabokov thought—to a subspecies of *dorothea*, his 1941 Grand Canyon find. Then from 2:00 P.M. until dinner he would work on *Lolita*.[70]

After the first week of fine weather, it became cold and windy. Day after day he rose at 6:00 A.M in the hope that it would prove warm and calm enough for collecting, but day after day he was disappointed. *Lolita* profited, and he made excellent progress as he transcribed the text in longhand. To vary a day of enforced writing, he would sometimes translate parts of *Conclusive Evidence* into Russian.[71]

It seemed unfair to have traveled thousands of miles to escape the chill of a New England spring and then find nothing but cold and gales. The Nabokovs began to think of moving again. When her husband killed a fair-sized rattlesnake—seven rattles—a few feet from their doorstep, Véra was ready to move at once.[72]

At the beginning of June they left for Ashland, Oregon, via several Californian lakes, collecting en route. Their destination was dictated partly by the fact that Dmitri's mountaineering club would be climbing in British Columbia in July. (After the season was over, Nabokov reported to his sister that he and Véra had spent their time in "worrying constantly about him—I doubt if we'll ever get used to it.") There were other reasons. Nabokov had traveled all through the East and South and Midwest on his lecture tours or en route to his hunting grounds throughout the Rockies, but he had never explored the Pacific Northwest, and he wanted to make Humbert Humbert defile with his "sinuous trail of slime" every state in America. Besides, there were—there *had* to be—good entomological reasons for lingering in Oregon. In 1949, in his major scientific monograph, Nabokov had observed: "Darkest Africa seems to be better known lepidopterologically than the coastal stretch of Western North America from Mendocino northwards."⁷³

The Nabokovs rented a tiny house in Ashland, 163 Mead Street, the home of a member of the faculty of the Southern Oregon College of Education who had gone east for the summer. The house, perched on a hill even steeper than their steepest Ithaca address, was surrounded by a garden of roses and irises. Oregon seemed beautifully lush and soothing after arid, windy Portal. Despite his 190 pounds, Nabokov walked eighteen miles a day in the mauve and green hills around Ashland. No rain hindered the chase, and results were excellent. He confessed to his sister that this season his passion for butterflies turned into a genuine mania.⁷⁴

At the same time he found Ashland singularly favorable to literary inspiration. *Lolita* was by now purring along steadily, and had reached the point where he could begin to dictate his finished chapters to Véra at the typewriter. With all but the final touches in place, his imagination was once again open to other creative ideas. In June or early July he composed the poem "Lines Written in Oregon," and the superbly haunting comic poem, "The Ballad of Longwood Glen." The *New Yorker* rejected the second, which Nabokov would rework off and on for another four years.⁷⁵

During June and July he also wrote a story about a Professor Pnin. Sending it to Katharine White at the end of July, he added a curious comment, decidedly out of keeping with his later admiration for Pnin the man: "He is not a very nice person but he is fun." He hoped that it could be the first of a series for the *New Yorker*: since it might be difficult to place *Lolita*, it was important to write something he could sell while publishers considered Humbert's macabre confessions.⁷⁶

Putting pressure on himself to finish *Lolita*, he kept writing steadily. Véra wished she could prevail on him to take a short rest, but he carried on dictating finished copy to her, crumpling each old manuscript sheet once it had served its turn and discarding the pages out the car window or into a hotel fireplace.⁷⁷ Now that *Lolita* was soon to face public scrutiny—and, as its author hoped, in an anonymous edition—its manuscript pages seemed almost too hot to handle, too dangerous to keep.

XII

At the beginning of September the Nabokovs headed home for Ithaca. On their way back they called on Dmitri, in a tent on the banks of Jenny Lake in the Tetons. Earlier in the summer he had manned a bulldozer and overturned a truck on a road construction project in Oregon, climbed the Selkirks in British Columbia, and signed with his parents an agreement that he would forfeit the right to a car and participation in track if his average fell below B for the coming year. His parents journeyed slowly eastward, and saw him installed at Lowell House in Cambridge—sporting a beard, having already worn out his third secondhand car, and eager to buy a first secondhand plane—before they headed back to Ithaca.[78]

Just before classes resumed they moved into 957 East State Street, the house where they had spent their first months in Ithaca in 1948, now the home of another member of the Cornell faculty. Morris Bishop secured Nabokov another salary increase, to $6,000.[79]

In his first full year at Cornell since 1950–1951, Nabokov had 207 students in his European fiction course, 34 in his survey of Russian literature in translation, and one in his Pushkin seminar. That sole student, who met Nabokov one afternoon a week in his State Street study overlooking a sloping lawn and a tree-lined creek, recalled it as "a stimulating year with a gentle man."[80]

Nabokov wrote to Edmund Wilson that his summer had passed in such intense work he now found academic duties positively relaxing. Relaxing? In addition to his teaching he now had five writing projects under way. He had more or less finished his translation of *The Song of Igor's Campaign*, and hoped to complete *Eugene Onegin* over the coming winter. His and Véra's translation of *Conclusive Evidence* into Russian had to be ready in the spring of 1954. By now too he had planned *Pnin* as a novel of ten chapters, had worked out the structure of the book and his own appearance as a character in the last chapter, and hoped to complete it within the year.[81]

Before carrying on with these projects he wanted to finish *Lolita*. Regaining momentum rapidly after his return to Ithaca, he was soon working sixteen hours a day to complete the novel. He had no time even to read the newspapers, and he arranged for Cornell to pay Véra to mark his midterm and end-of-term exams. On December 6, 1953, he wrote in his diary with relief: "Finished *Lolita* which was begun exactly 5 years ago." The 450-page typescript, with no author's name on the title page, was ready to be taken to a discreet publisher in New York.[82]

CHAPTER 11

Lolita

When you do read *Lolita*, please mark that it is a highly moral affair.

—Nabokov to Edmund Wilson, 1956

I am in favor of childhood.

—Interview, 1958

I

*L*OLITA will never cease to shock.[1] Seesawing wildly from emotion to emotion, it jolts us off balance line after line, page after page. A case study in child abuse, it also manages against all the odds to be a passionate and poignant love story. Humbert exalts Lolita with the utmost delicacy and fervor, and he exploits her with the utmost determination. Lionel Trilling's comment thirty years ago still holds true—"in recent fiction no lover has thought of his beloved with so much tenderness, no woman has been so charmingly evoked, in such grace and delicacy, as Lolita"[2]—except that Lolita is no woman but a twelve-year-old girl, prisoner of her stepfather's lust. With one hand Humbert caresses her gently, with the other he twists out of her grasp the bribe he has given her for the "fancy embrace" of fellatio.

Because Nabokov leaves the story to Humbert, every page of the novel crackles with tension: between Humbert's free self-consciousness and his unrelenting obsession, between his sense of guilt and his confidence that his special case renders other people's codes of conduct irrelevant. He seems to represent the human mind at its freest and best, lucid and unimpeachably self-aware, and then discloses the mind's awesome capacity to blind itself and other minds as it rationalizes away the pain it has caused. He confesses frankly to unequivocally vile behavior, even castigates himself as a monster, yet somehow almost inveigles us into acquiescing in his deeds.

Even more than other Nabokov characters, Humbert epitomizes the insatiable hunger of the human imagination, but—and this special twist *makes* the whole novel—his attractive urge to transcend the self decays at once into nothing more than its own foul parody, into the mere promotion of self. In writing *Lolita* Humbert expresses so splendidly his yearning for something more than life allows that he seems at moments to speak for us all—until we recoil from such complicity. We see him attempt to escape the trap of time, and hope for a moment he may have found a way out for everyone; then we shudder, look again at the bars on his cage, and sigh with relief.

In other ways too the novel swings from extreme to extreme. From his first words ("Lolita, light of my life") to his last ("my Lolita"), Humbert fixes his gaze intently on his dream-child. En passant, however, he guides us through all of America's forty-eight contiguous states, casting his outsider's ironic eye over glad ads and *Screen Spleen*, teenage America, housewives' America, the tidy turf of suburban lawns and the loud signs of a thousand quiet Main Streets. Nabokov permits an unrelenting focus on Humbert's passion, but he also wrote just before beginning the novel that he was "always ready to sacrifice purity of form to the exigencies of fantastic content, causing form to bulge and burst like a sponge-bag containing a small furious devil."[3] Life suddenly flashes off to one side—"My very photogenic mother died in a freak accident (picnic, lightning) when I was three"—or peers up odd alleys (Humbert's ex-wife and new husband on all fours eating bananas in a year-long ethnological experiment) or veers crazily off course: to arctic Canada, where Humbert spends nearly two years on an expedition supplied with "*Reader's Digest*, an ice cream mixer, chemical toilets, paper caps for Christmas," or to Grainball City, where he wakes up one morning beside Rita ("Who?" many a reader will ask) to see snoring on the other side of the bed a complete stranger, sweating in thick, dirty underwear, with old army boots on. Not even Rita or Humbert or the youth himself—he turns out to be totally amnesiac—knows who or where he is, or why he wakes up in this book.

II

No other novel begins so memorably: "Lolita, light of my life, fire of my loins. My sin, my soul. Lo-lee-ta: the tip of the tongue taking a trip of three steps down the palate to tap, at three, on the teeth. Lo. Lee. Ta." Humbert invokes Lolita with a passion more appropriate to a lyric poem than to a novel—and sustains that intensity throughout.

Some readers worry about language that sounds so good: has Nabokov not sold off sense to the bawds of euphony? Christopher Ricks points out after all that in an English "t" the tongue taps the alveolar ridge, not the teeth.[4] But that is precisely Nabokov's point, and Humbert's: Lolita's name is not to be pronounced in the American manner, with a thick "d" sound ("Low-leed-uh"), but Spanish style. Lolita was conceived on her parents' honeymoon in Vera Cruz: Dolores and her nickname are mementoes of two weeks in Mexico. A native francophone, a scholar of Romance languages, a pedant and a self-conscious idolater, Humbert wants his readers to relish the name as he did, with the special Latin thrill he reserves for his Lolita, his Carmencita. *Lolita*'s language may sound extravagant, but its words are exact: the elements of a coherent fictional world, the chemistry of Humbert's very special mind.

That mind jumps from mode to mode and mood to mood: "She was Lo, plain Lo, in the morning, standing four feet ten in one sock. She was Lola in slacks. She was Dolly at school. She was Dolores on the dotted line. But in my arms she was always Lolita." Humbert sees her as sharply and in as many lights as he sees America, but the name he calls her by is not the name she, her mother, her friends, or her teachers ever use. He appropriates her on his own terms, just as he will appropriate all of America to make a paradise for himself and a prison for his little girl.

A few lines later Humbert slips into archness, then suddenly jars us: "You can always count on a murderer for a fancy prose style." *Lolita* will not let us settle and sink roots: it preserves a consistent pitch of high passion, but it also skips from mood to mood in more manic fashion than almost any other novel. Humbert's style can be at once or by turns extravagant and precise, hysterical and self-conscious, ecstatic and venomous, frank and deceptive, vain and self-reproachful. He ruins one person's life and ends another's, and yet he makes us laugh: he is tragic hero, tragic villain, and court jester all in one. His mobile mind can gyrate freely and still remain narrowly obsessed by his passion. And this is one of the glories of the novel: that Nabokov creates a style to fit every furrow in Humbert's brain and at the same time startles us from line to line with both the freedom of the human mind and its perverse capacity to entrap itself and others.

III

No one could defend Humbert's behavior. After all, he even admits to murder at the outset. No one, that is, but Humbert: "Ladies and gentlemen of the jury," he addresses us, "exhibit number one." *Lolita* begins as his statement for his trial, and though it soon becomes a memorial to Lolita, the whole book also remains a brilliant case for the defense.

Humbert's strategy of course is to seem as if he is not defending himself at all. Once he realizes that he cannot parade his past with live Lolita before the courtroom, that he will have to keep the manuscript of his confession unseen until Lolita herself has died, he addresses the jury parodically, facetiously, as if to mock the idea that he might really want to exonerate himself before his readers. He confesses everything. He reviles himself insistently throughout the book, calling himself a monster and a pervert. But he lays charges against himself in order to disarm us with this display of moral scrupulousness—of course he wouldn't dream of defending himself for what he has done to his beloved Lolita—and to encourage us to accept the way he really sees himself. Even some very good readers have seen him just as he wants them to.

Despite his self-castigation, Humbert actually presents himself as a poor, sensitive soul, tormented by a love that may seem sordid to an uncomprehending world but in his own case is something uniquely poetic, at the highest pitch of romantic intensity. Lolita by contrast seems an essentially vulgar and soulless young girl who is lucky, he almost implies, to be ennobled by such love, to be lifted up to a region far above her prosaic teenage world of cynicism and sodas, and who takes advantage of his besotted love to milk him for his money.

Some readers have accepted even this picture. In his review of *Lolita*, Robertson Davies declared that the book's theme "is not the corruption of an innocent child by a cunning adult, but the exploitation of a weak adult by a corrupt child."[5] His reaction is a common one. But how can that be possible, when Humbert quite freely confesses what he did to Lolita and to the man he murdered?

Humbert begins his manuscript in custody after murdering Quilty and publicly proclaiming what he has done. He envisages the full story of his love for Lolita as a convincing defense against the murder charge, while at the same time he acts as his own prosecutor on a charge not laid against him, his treatment of Lolita. "Had I come before myself," he writes at the end of the book, "I would have given Humbert at least thirty-five years for rape, and dismissed the rest of the charges."

But we know that he did not rape Lolita in any ordinary sense. At twelve she had lost her virginity at summer camp, and when she and Humbert meet again after her mother's death it is she who suggests that they try out the naughty trick she has just learned at camp. Handing down to himself that sentence for rape, Humbert seems far more self-accusatory than the case warrants. His stance works so well that a reader as subtle as Lionel Trilling can assign the murder eight words out of the eight thousand he writes about *Lolita*—a not atypical response.

So much for Humbert's overall strategy. What of his particular tactics? Nabokov grants Humbert every argument that the child-abuser could want, and more: psychological trauma in childhood (the Annabel Leigh story); the arbitrariness of any prohibition against sex with the young when other times, other cultures have allowed it; his efforts at restraint, before Lolita (marrying Valeria and finding himself tied to "a large, puffy, short-legged, big-breasted and practically brainless *baba*") and until Lolita seduces him; her having already lost her virginity; the transcendent poetry of nymphet love ("there is no other bliss on earth comparable to that of fondling a nymphet. It is *hors concours*, that bliss, it belongs to another class, another plane of sensitivity"), the artistry ("you have to be an artist and a madman"), the metaphysical thrill of a journey to that "intangible island of entranced time where Lolita plays with her likes."

Above all, Humbert dwells on the radiance of his passion for Lolita. After several grim years in America, he suddenly receives a gift from fate: sunbathing Lolita, peering at him over dark glasses, like a reincarnation of his Annabel on that Riviera beach so many years ago, and a miraculous triumph over time. His appetite grows as he feasts on her every feature, his ardor swells, his prose soars, and she does not notice a thing (or so he claims) as she sprawls across him on the sofa and he brings himself to orgasm, "a glowing tingle which *now* had reached that state of absolute security, confidence and reliance not found elsewhere in conscious life."

Still, he stresses, he took care to avoid upsetting Lolita's innocence until she—fresh from camp and eager to show him a special sort of teenage fun—suggests they make love. Once they become technically lovers Humbert calls himself a brute and a monster, but at the same time appeals to our sympathy by pointing to the poignant gap between his ecstatic devotion to Lolita and her complete failure to experience passion on his plane. There she would be, as he sat her on his lap in an armchair, "a typical kid picking her nose while engrossed in the lighter sections of a newspaper, as indifferent to my ecstasy as if it were something she had sat upon, a shoe, a doll, the handle of a tennis racket."

Then Clare Quilty skulks onto the scene and whisks Lolita away. Humbert stresses Quilty's sordid villainy: a pervert, a degenerate, a drug-taker, a pornographer whose passing fancy for Lolita stands in complete contrast to his own rarefied love. Humbert's killing of Quilty is no more than the proof of the purity of his passion.

Though Lolita has left him, Humbert's love remains. When he finds her again, seventeen, married, hugely pregnant, he treasures her still, though she is long past her nymphancy: "I looked and looked at her, and knew as clearly as I know I am to die, that I loved her more than anything I had ever seen or imagined on earth, or hoped for anywhere else." He asks her to come away with him, and even when she turns him down he gives her all the money he has. And he ends the book with an epiphany: above a mountain valley, just after she has left him, he hears the sounds of children at play wafting up through the stillness, "and then I knew that the hopelessly poignant thing was not Lolita's absence from my side, but the absence of her voice from that concord."

Such is Humbert's case. It seems extraordinarily persuasive, and some ladies and gentlemen of the jury are certainly convinced. After summarizing *Lolita*'s plot, Trilling writes: "We have come virtually to condone the violation. . . . I was plainly not able to muster up the note of moral outrage. . . . Humbert is perfectly willing to say that he is a monster; we find ourselves less and less eager to agree with him."[6] Like so many readers, Trilling has accepted only Humbert's version of himself; he has reacted to Humbert's eloquence, not Nabokov's evidence. By making it possible to see Humbert's story so much from Humbert's point of view, Nabokov warns us to recognize the power of the mind to rationalize away the harm it can cause: the more powerful the mind, the stronger our guard needs to be.

IV

Outside the novel, Nabokov's own judgment of Humbert was blunt: "a vain and cruel wretch who manages to appear 'touching.' "[7] *Lolita* bears him out.

Humbert is puffed up with vanity. He boasts of his looks, his libido, his discriminating sensitivity, his intelligence, his love. Extolling his own high standards, he injects the venom of his considerable contempt into Valeria and Maximovich, Charlotte, Quilty, America, even Lolita herself. He is brutally indifferent to other lives. He marries Valeria simply as a safety valve for his sexual tension. He bullies her, and even though he detests her, the cobra hood of his pride swells up when she decides to leave him for another man: "I now wondered if Valechka (as the colonel called her) was really worth shooting, or strangling, or drowning. She had very vulnerable legs, and I decided I would limit myself to hurting her very horribly as soon as we were alone." Marrying Charlotte only for access to Lolita, Humbert is calculatingly dishonest from the start. He even contemplates getting Charlotte pregnant merely in order that "a prolonged confinement, with a nice Caesarean operation and other complications in a safe maternity ward sometime next spring, would give me a chance to be alone with my Lolita for weeks, perhaps—and gorge the limp nymphet with sleeping pills."

Humbert *is* a moral monster, as the novel shows in such detail. One of the marvels of the book is that while it presents such damning facts it also allows Humbert full scope to lure inattentive readers into acquiescence—until Nabokov confronts them with their facile complicity.

Though Humbert feigns concern for Lolita's purity, he paws her as much as he can without putting himself at risk. At the Enchanted Hunters he lures her into taking a sleeping pill to put her at his complete disposal for the night. Legally, technically, morally, this would have been rape, had the pill's failure to work not kept him at bay. The next morning, Lolita proposes a naughty routine she has learned at camp, and Humbert can only seize the opportunity, never mind the consequences, never mind that *he* knows that *she* does not know the implications of what she has proposed.

Over the next two years Humbert manipulates Lolita as he had Valeria and Charlotte. He exploits her naïveté, her fear of reform school, her physical weakness, her material dependence on him. He keeps her just happy enough for her to remain at his disposal. He is unfair in the most rudimentary sense, promising her something before they make love only to withdraw the promise immediately afterward. He is revoltingly persistent in his sexual demands, he has numbed her into submission through fear of exposure and physical force, he habitually ignores her state of mind "while comforting my own base self." He is foully jealous. He is a consummate hypocrite: he denies Lolita freedom for fear she will meet boys her own age but attempts to insist she bring her classmates home as "a bevy of page girls, consolation prize nymphets, around my Lolita." Humbert claimed in his defense the arbitrariness of any legally stipulated age of innocence, but there is nothing arbitrary about cheating and cruelty and imprisonment. His awareness of her pain and grief, which he allows to be read in his favor, does not modify his behavior a whit: he hears "her sobs in the night—every night, every night—the moment I feigned sleep."

Like Iago, Humbert catches our imagination by the sheer zeal of his vice, though even Iago cannot match the convolutions of Humbert's selfishness. When it is time for the school bus, Humbert parks the car "to watch the children leave school—always a pretty sight.

This sort of thing soon began to bore my so easily bored Lolita, and, having a childish lack of sympathy for other people's whims, she would insult me and my desire to have her caress me while blue-eyed little brunettes in blue shorts . . . passed by in the sun."

Nabokov makes this hypocrite, swindler, bully, jailer, rapist, murderer a perfect study in the psychology of crime. So much of Humbert's character predisposes him toward his crimes: his exaggerated sense of his own importance, his fierce frustration at the thwarting of his desires, his knack of seeing himself as someone wronged, his long years of manipulating and deceiving people this side of the law. We watch his stealthy advance, from mesmerized temptation through wary opportunity to the sudden leap at an irresistible prize; and once the forbidden fruit has been plucked, we discover his savage determination to protect his right to feast from that sumptuous tree.

V

Humbert is a triumph of the imagination. For all the distance between his character and himself, Nabokov grants us immediate access to Humbert's mind. For all Humbert's vices, Nabokov refuses to make him a subhuman ogre and even selects him to express his own positives: the inordinate riches of consciousness, the intensity of passion, the tenderness of the senses, the mind's many-branched awareness within the moment.

> The implied sun pulsated in the supplied poplars; we were fantastically and divinely alone; I watched her, rosy, gold-dusted, beyond the veil of my controlled delight, unaware of it, alien to it, and the sun was on her lips, and her lips were apparently still forming the words of the Carmen-barmen ditty that no longer reached my consciousness. Everything was now ready. The nerves of pleasure had been laid bare. The corpuscles of Krause were entering the phase of frenzy. The least pressure would suffice to set all paradise loose. I had ceased to be Humbert the Hound, the sad-eyed degenerate cur clasping the boot that would presently kick him away. I was above the tribulations of ridicule, beyond the possibilities of retribution. In my self-made seraglio, I was a radiant and robust Turk, deliberately, in the full consciousness of his freedom, postponing the moment of actually enjoying the youngest and frailest of his slaves.

"In the full consciousness of his freedom": nothing could demonstrate better than such a passage the freedom, the manifold awareness, that for Nabokov is the great prize of consciousness. But in the last lines—the radiant and robust Turk, the frail young slave—he touches on the converse, consciousness as imprisonment: Humbert's imprisonment within his own obsession, Lolita's entrapment in his designs. It is no accident that Nabokov releases Lolita from Humbert's grasp on July 4, Independence Day: Humbert may aver that his bliss transports him to a plane beyond life, but for Nabokov such a claim only travesties the liberation *he* hopes consciousness may attain.

VI

What of Lolita? Humbert remarks at one point: "And neither is she the fragile child of a feminine novel." No, she certainly is not.

No novelist knows the art of preparation better than Nabokov, who begins to characterize Lolita even before we see her. In part 1, chapter 10, Humbert inspects the Haze house, though in fact he has no intention of renting a room there, and all the disarray only confirms his fastidious disgust: an old gray tennis ball, a brown apple core, bedraggled magazines, a white sock on the floor, a still glistening plum-stone. But an alert reader can guess that these things that offend Humbert constitute Lolita's spoor, fresher the closer he gets. And then, around the corner of the page, Humbert's heart leaps with delight: Lolita on the piazza, his Riviera love revived!

Lolita is a real child who leaves things around the house, like any preteen American girl; a recapture, for Humbert, of his Annabel Leigh; and very much herself. Nabokov's command of detail has never been so good. Humbert watches Lolita pick pebbles up with her toes and flick them (*ping*) at a can; her toenails show flaked remnants of cherry-red polish, and across her toe she has a bit of adhesive tape—so much less likely and therefore so much more vivid in the mind's eye than an ordinary Band-Aid would have been. Nabokov has caught perfectly Lolita's mixture of "dreamy childishness and a kind of eerie vulgarity": her slangy speech, her magazines, her clothes and fudge and sodas. She wavers between child and would-be grown-up. She develops a crush on Humbert, she senses his excitement and copies movie mannerisms as she plays up to it, but whereas with Humbert their encounters create a steamy, hothouse feeling, whose atmosphere he certainly does not want to lighten by allowing in a fresh breeze from outside, Lolita perfectly naturally enjoys the game of flirtation with a handsome man of movie-star age, and then rushes off to hear about the dead something the maid has found in the basement.

Humbert thinks Lolita irredeemably vulgar and trite, endowed with nymphet magic and grace thanks to his discerning eye but otherwise without special interest. Charlotte Haze seems to confirm the assessment. Intolerant of her daughter's youth, she chafes at all that makes Lolita adolescent. Humbert notes the same things, at first with both the fascination of an anthropologist reporting an alien life and the force of a lover ready to exalt what he knows another might see as Lo's limitations. The situation changes after the Enchanted Hunters, when Humbert takes over the role of parent as well as lover. Suddenly he finds her as exasperating, moody, and cunning as her mother had thought her. He decrees her to be mentally "a disgustingly conventional little girl." He deigns to find charming her showing another child "some of her few accomplishments."

Amazingly, many readers of the book accept Humbert's judgment at face value; Lolita is "a charming brat lifted from an ordinary existence only by the special brand of love"[8] bestowed on her. Such readers misconstrue Lolita only because they are accustomed to books that oversimplify life. Nabokov refuses: he creates a Lolita far more rounded and rich than that flat image—and allows even Humbert himself in the last third of the book to recognize that that portrait does her no justice.

For Nabokov, Lolita's ways are the passing fads of youth and no indication of her adult potential. In the years he wrote *Lolita* he would tell his Cornell students:

A philistine is a full-grown person whose interests are of a material and commonplace nature, and whose mentality is formed of the stock ideas and conventional ideals of his or her group and time. I have said 'full-grown person' because the child or the adolescent who may look like a small philistine is only a small parrot mimicking the ways of confirmed vulgarians, and it is easier to be a parrot than a white heron.[9]

We encounter Lolita chiefly as the subject of Humbert's rhapsodies or the object of his lust. For all the lyrical description of her lashes, the bloom on her arm, the lilt of her laugh, Humbert makes few attempts to sound her mind—and as he concedes, the very falsehood of their relationship makes it impossible for him to discuss with her "an abstract idea, a painting, stippled Hopkins or shorn Baudelaire, God or Shakespeare, anything of a genuine kind." But the little we hear from Lolita indicates she has a sharp and witty mind. At the Enchanted Hunters Hotel, still dreaming of possessing her while preserving her innocence under cover of darkness and drugs, Humbert pontificates: "Two people sharing one room, inevitably enter into a kind—how shall I say—a kind—" only for Lolita to jump in with mischievous glee: "The word is incest." She mocks his speech ("You talk like a book, *Dad*"); she mimics him ("Was the corroboration satisfactory?"). She casts an eye over her mother's aging car, and finds it "sort of purplish about the gills."

At fourteen Lolita already displays talent as an actress and as a tennis player. Humbert marvels that on the tennis court Lolita, "so cruel and crafty in everyday life, revealed an innocence, a frankness, a kindness of ball-placing. . . ." In fact, this child Humbert thinks difficult shows remarkable patience under his tyranny and confinement, and reveals real animation on the few occasions when there is cause. Even Humbert can see that he has broken something in her: her innate grace as a tennis player is no match now for her complete loss of the will to win.

That little glimpse of her tennis game shows something of what has been broken in her spirit. But some of 1958's more sensitive reviewers felt appalled that Nabokov had not shown Lolita ultimately wrecked by Humbert, a prostitute, psychically crippled.[10] Nabokov knew the odds for someone debauched at twelve, subjected to Humbert's apprenticeship in sex for pay, sodomized by Clare Quilty, but he also wanted to show Lolita as an extraordinary young girl who triumphs over her fate in the only way left to her.[11]*

When he shows us Lolita three years after she has run away from Humbert, Nabokov gives us neither slick sentimental comfort nor the grim pathos of "inevitable" tragedy, but only a girl with shrunken expectations battling with courage and calm moral poise. Three years before, she had declined any part in Clare Quilty's group-sex pornography; now she even refuses to tell Humbert just *what* things she declined: " 'Oh, things . . . Oh, I—really, I'—she uttered the 'I' as a subdued cry while she listened to the source of the ache, and for lack of words spread the five fingers of her angular up-and-down-moving hand. No, she gave it up, she refused to go into particulars with that baby inside her." Married to uneducated, poor, deaf, shy Dick Schiller, she knows she will never thrill to his wit as she once did to Quilty's, but he is still "a lamb," and she is proudly pregnant, and determined to make a life for her child, and smilingly assured as she turns down Humbert's last request that she come to live with him. Three months later she is dead in childbirth.

VII

Writing of Pushkin, Nabokov once observed quite accurately that his subject was the threefold formula of human life: the irretrievability of

---

* Of all the thousands of characters in his work, Nabokov once said, Lolita came second in his list of those he admired most as people. Top of the list came Pnin, another courageous victim.

the past, the insatiability of the present, and the unforeseeability of the future.[12] This might be the only formula one could apply to such an unformulaic novel as *Lolita*.

First, the irretrievability of the past. Humbert introduces his life in terms of his love for Annabel Leigh in the enchanted Riviera of his childhood princedom by the sea: "But that mimosa grove—the haze of stars, the tingle, the flame, the honeydew, and the ache remained with me, and that little girl with her seaside limbs and ardent tongue haunted me ever since—until at last, twenty-four years later, I broke her spell by incarnating her in another." But although part of Humbert's sense of the splendor of his love for Lolita is that she reincarnates Annabel, he also knows Lolita cannot really fill the place of his first love. With Annabel, he could share his passion and his thoughts; with Lolita, he can only secure access to her body.

Humbert's love for Lolita herself also reflects the theme of the irretrievable past. He enjoys his first year with Lolita, touring the motels of every state, but he knows it cannot last forever. He settles down at Beardsley, but Lolita's desire for freedom to be with other teenagers rather than with throbbing Humbert makes the tension rise day by day in their Thayer Street home. When Lolita suggests they simply pack up and head west again, Humbert is overjoyed: he looks forward to reliving what to him anyway was the paradise of that first year of fervent nymphet love. What he does not know, of course, what he finds out too late, is that on this second trip, this supposed reprise of the past, everything has changed: Lolita has arranged the whole thing with Clare Quilty, and Quilty's car trails them all the way out west, like a shimmer of unease, a mirage of retribution, a shadow of guilt. The attempt to repeat the past only shows how impossible it is to relive.

"The insatiability of the present" sums up Humbert's sexual cravings: his aching desire for Annabel, back in his thirteenth summer, when her parents always intervened between the youngsters and their fulfillment; the hopeless yearning of his lonely years in Paris; the new and agonizing intensity of his longing for Lolita. In Humbert's diary, in the early stages of his life at the Haze house, he details the unexpected raptures of his daily proximity to Lolita, but all these chance contacts of flesh against flesh only make more tantalizing the lure of still richer rewards.

Of course Humbert gets Lolita at last, but the theme of insatiability simply progresses to another stage, the insatiability of his sexual demands: "thrusting my fatherly fingers deep into Lo's hair from behind, and then gently but firmly clasping them around the nape of her neck, I would lead my reluctant pet to our small home for a quick connection before dinner." Even the bliss of possession does not suffice: "My only grudge against nature was that I could not turn my Lolita inside out and apply voracious lips to her young matrix, her unknown heart, her nacreous liver, the sea-grapes of her lungs, her comely twin kidneys."

And when Lolita disappears, a new desire seizes hold of Humbert: he must at all costs identify, track down, and dispose of the man who took Lolita from him and taunted him in the process. But when he does kill Quilty, his victim's frivolous manner of facing death, his refusal to see it as the solemn discharge of a rival's passion, robs the very moment Humbert has so longed for of all its satisfaction.

VIII

Lost love and unappeasable desire may make *Lolita* a tragic tale, but the book is also a fabulously witty construction. No small measure of its wit derives from the third of the three ironies of time: the unforeseeability of the future.

Fate seems to have toyed with Humbert ever since he decided to spend a summer in Ramsdale in the home of a family with "two little daughters, one a baby, the other a girl of twelve, and a beautiful garden, not far from a beautiful lake." On the day he arrives, the McCoo house has just been burned down, and although his reason for lingering in Ramsdale has vanished (actually, as it turns out, Ginny McCoo was anything but a nymphet) he cannot wriggle out of inspecting the Haze home. Everything he sees there makes him squirm with disgust—and then he sees Lolita and swoons with delight.

From that point on disappointed plans seem to alternate with magical rewards. Shortly after Humbert enters the Haze household, both Charlotte and Lolita, eagerly looking forward to a day at the lake with their handsome new lodger, buy themselves new bathing suits. First promising sign. But it rains. First setback. It rains the next day. Second setback. The day after, Lolita makes Humbert's heart race when she asks him in a voluptuous whisper: "Make Mother take you and me to Our Glass Lake tomorrow." Second excited anticipation. By now both Charlotte and Lolita are keener rivals than ever for Humbert, and when Charlotte packs Lolita off to bed to have Humbert to herself, the child erupts ("I think you stink"), forcing her mother to retaliate by canceling the excursion. Third setback. Naturally Humbert has to conceal where his affections lie, and Charlotte worries that her daughter's attentions might irk the retiring scholar. Two days later she asks hesitantly: "Would it bore you very much

. . . to come with us tomorrow for a swim in Our Glass Lake if Lo apologizes for her manners?" Third positive sign. Lolita refuses to apologize, and again the lake is out. Fourth setback. Another rainy day, and Humbert too buys himself new swimming trunks. Fourth anticipation.

Again clouds overshadow the lake, and Humbert wonders "Is it Fate scheming?" Fifth setback. More hail and gale, but the weather bureau promises a fine weekend, and Humbert dreams of the lake, in the fifth bright anticipation. That evening he had recalled his last day with Annabel—their "final attempt to thwart fate" on the deserted sands of a Riviera beach with somebody's lost pair of sunglasses as the only witness—and in his sleep that night he visits Hourglass Lake, tells Charlotte he has left his wristwatch or his sunglasses "in that glade yonder," and plunges with his nymphet into the wood: "The Quest for the Glasses turned into a quiet little orgy with a singularly knowing, cheerful, corrupt and compliant Lolita behaving as reason knew she could not possibly behave." This is the most rapturously complete foretaste of all. In Humbert's dream, the next day's future looms as a retrieval of his time with Annabel on the shores of the Riviera: he is standing the hourglass on its head, making time run backward. His diary breaks off, and he notes that the reader will have marked "the curious Mirage of the Lake. It would have been logical on the part of Aubrey McFate (as I would like to dub that devil of mine) to arrange a small treat for me on the promised beach, in the presumed forest." Actually Charlotte has now invited one of Lolita's classmates along for the excursion to occupy her daughter and leave Humbert to herself (sixth setback), but Mary Rose has a temperature and the picnic must be postponed once more. Seventh setback, but on this occasion, Humbert's disappointment is amply recouped by the fervent pleasures of the davenport scene: sixth big plus.

By now nothing will stop Charlotte's plans to have time alone with Humbert. She dispatches Lo to summer camp (eighth disastrous setback); she invites Humbert to propose, and he, envisaging fatherly caresses on Lolita's return, quickly accepts: seventh forward step. By the time they reach Hourglass Lake they are, against all expectation, a married couple—and by the side of the lake Charlotte breaks the news that as soon as Lo returns from camp she will be shipped away to boarding school. Ninth setback, this time positively ruinous. Shocked by the announcement, Humbert has to have time to think, and tells Charlotte he has forgotten his glasses in the car. So much for his dream of bliss by Hourglass Lake.

Humbert realizes he is trapped. His lighthearted vision of controlling Charlotte through her passion for him will not work: the moment he protests and attempts to keep Lolita near, he will give himself away. There seems to be only one solution; to kill Charlotte. As they swim out into the lake together, Humbert realizes that kind fate has arranged the scene for the perfect murder. No one else is around except two men building a wharf on the other side of the lake, much too far off to see him holding Charlotte under the water, just close enough to hear his feigned cries for help once her lungs are safely waterlogged.

But Humbert cannot do it: as she swims trustfully and clumsily at his side, he realizes he will never be able to make himself put her to death. They return to the beach. Charlotte undoes her bra to catch the sun on her back; she hears a rustle behind her and snarls: "Those disgusting prying kids." In fact it is their friend Jean Farlow, an amateur painter, who came to the lake early in quest of rare light effects and now after the morning's session brings her easel down for her husband, John, to collect her in his car. The Hourglass Lake chapter ends:

> "I almost put both of you into my lake," she said. "I even noticed something you overlooked. You [addressing Humbert] had your wrist watch on in, yes, sir, you had."
>
> "Waterproof," said Charlotte softly, making a fish mouth.
>
> Jean took my wrist upon her knee and examined Charlotte's gift, then put back Humbert's hand on the sand, palm up.
>
> "You could see anything that way," remarked Charlotte coquettishly.
>
> Jean sighed. "I once saw," she said, "two children, male and female, at sunset, right here, making love. Their shadows were giants. And I told you about Mr. Tomson at daybreak. Next time I expect to see fat old Ivor in the ivory. He is really a freak, that man. Last time he told me a completely indecent story about his nephew. It appears—"
>
> "Hullo there," said John's voice.

Longsighted Jean would have spotted the "perfect murder" and had Humbert clapped straight into prison. Whew, Humbert can think: tenth catastrophic setback narrowly averted: he could have been locked away from Lolita until she had long passed her nymphancy.

Let us linger for a moment over this last glimpse of Hourglass Lake: a perfectly straightforward dialogue, apparently, with none of the fancy phrasing of "Lolita, light of my life." In fact, these lines are far more complex than the novel's opening passage—where Nabokov hands the pen over to indulgent Humbert the Hummer—and provide the perfect answer to those who think he writes for display or for local sparkle at the expense of structure. As so often, Nabokov offers us something immediately—the irony of the "perfect" murder—while he hides much more. For behind that irony, time has other reasons to smile.

Humbert had savored the Hourglass Lake project as a chance to relive his summer on the sand with Annabel, but now he witnesses a mocking replay of the past. Then he was about to possess Annabel when two onlookers emerging from the sea spoiled the brimming passion of the present; now Jean Farlow recalls two children here at sunset making love—and as an onlooker herself she would have spoiled the murder Humbert contemplated after he found that Hourglass Lake and life in the Haze household would not live up to their promise of the Riviera revived.

Other pleasures lie half-concealed. Earlier in the chapter, Charlotte had told Humbert that Jean had been at the lake early one morning and had seen the Negro servant from the house opposite

> taking a dip "in the ebony" (as John had quipped) at five o'clock in the morning last Sunday.
> "The water," I said, "must have been quite cold."
> "That is not the point," said the logical doomed dear. "He is subnormal, you see."

Charlotte's genteel racism is matched by her friend John Farlow's. In an earlier scene, as Humbert discusses Ramsdale with the Farlows, John remarks: "Of course, too many of the tradespeople here are Italians, but on the other hand we are still spared—" Sharp-eyed Jean, suspecting dark-featured Humbert may be a Jew, cuts off her husband's smug anti-Semitism: " 'I wish,' interrupted Jean with a laugh, 'Dolly and Rosaline were spending the summer together.' " Now, at Hourglass Lake, Jean refers to Leslie Tomson's dawn swim without Charlotte's gratuitous assumption that it suggests he is somehow subnormal, and inverts her husband's "in the ebony" quip (the cue to Charlotte's slur: Nabokov has watched how racism spreads) by picturing Ramsdale's fat old dentist Ivor Quilty swimming "in the ivory." Right then, her husband's arrival cuts off her and her liberalism, as she had cut off his racism: a perfect structural reprise.

IX

Back now to the ironies of time. After each setback in Humbert's life, it seems as if fate has been stringing him along; after each miraculous gift, as if fate has acted in accordance with his wildest dreams. As though in compensation for all Humbert's trials at Hourglass Lake, fate has Charlotte run over by a car: the perfect murder, the only perfect murder: you wish her dead, and dead she is. Eagerly accepting McFate's offering, Humbert prepares to pick Lolita up from camp. He arms himself with soporifics for his prey, but this new scheme turns to dust: Lolita remains quite unaffected by the drugs, his plans prove all to no avail. Then comes the greatest irony of all: after Humbert's agonizingly slow stalking of Lolita, it is she who "seduces" him. He hears her wake next to him and suggest they make love: while he and Charlotte were lying quietly on the sands of Hourglass Lake, Lolita at camp was losing her virginity beside another lake.

All the ironies of time in part 1 of the novel lead toward this surprise in the Enchanted Hunters Hotel. All the ironies of time in part 2 arise from the fact that Humbert does not realize until almost the end of the book that the person who took Lolita from him was Clare Quilty, the man who wrote the play, *The Enchanted Hunters*, that is staged at Lolita's school. In part 1 we know from the first—from "light of my life, fire of my loins. My sin, my soul"—that Humbert and Lolita must have become lovers, and even though we do not know *how* this will happen, we measure each inch of Humbert's hesitant progress toward her against our knowledge of the fact that he eventually enjoys her as a lover. Even before the start of part 2, we know that Humbert is a murderer, but we do not know *whom* he has murdered.

The whole of *Lolita* inverts the detective story pattern: we begin with a murderer, identified on the first page of the novel, and have to guess at the victim: we face not a whodunit but a "whocoppedit." False "suspects" are paraded and dismissed. Flaring with anger at Valeria and her lover Maximovich, Humbert thinks of killing both. Trapped by Charlotte into marriage without Lo, he pictures in vivid detail holding her down to drown, then decides he lacks the nerve.

Lolita herself lingers longer as likely victim. Conscious of her "Hispanic" origin, Humbert calls her his Carmen; he plays with a popular song she fancies ("O my Carmen, my little Carmen! . . . And, O my charmin', our dreadful fights . . . And the gun I killed you with, O my Carmen, The gun I am holding now") and comments, in crimestory lingo: "Drew his .32 automatic, I guess, and put a bullet through his moll's eye." For a long time Carmen images are relegated to the wings; then they suddenly sweep across the stage in the Elphinstone chapter, just before Lolita's escape, and once more three years later, when Humbert catches up with her at last. With his .32 in his pocket, he implores her to come with him ("Carmen, voulez-vous venir avec moi?"). She refuses, and the theme sounds one last time: "Then I pulled out my automatic—I mean this is the kind of fool thing a reader might suppose I did. It never even occurred to me to do it."

In fact of course Humbert has been hoping to track and kill not her but her abductor, though he cannot identify his target. He lies in wait for a male teacher at Beardsley. Wrong man. He loads his pistol for Lolita's husband. Wrong again. He asks Lolita the name of the man who took her from him:

> Softly, confidentially, arching her thin eyebrows and puckering her parched lips, she emitted, a little mockingly, somewhat fastidiously, not untenderly, in a kind of muted whistle, the name that the astute reader has guessed long ago.
>
> Waterproof. Why did a flash from Hourglass Lake cross my consciousness? I, too, had known it, without knowing it, all along. There was no shock, no surprise. Quietly the fusion took place, and everything fell into order, into the pattern of branches that I have woven throughout this memoir with the express purpose of having the ripe fruit fall at the right moment; yes, with the express and perverse purpose of rendering—she was talking but I sat melting in my golden peace—of rendering that golden and monstrous peace through the satisfaction of logical recognition, which my most inimical reader should experience now.

" 'Peace,' indeed!" snorts Alfred Appel in his *Annotated Lolita*.[13] Few if any first-time readers will guess the name Lo whispers or experience anything like that golden peace. As if taunting us, Humbert withholds the name for another twenty pages. Even if we flick back two hundred pages to Charlotte saying "Waterproof," we will not find the abductor's name.

Shrugging, we resume the final thirty-odd pages of the story. At last, as Humbert sets off in search of his prey, he imparts the name: "In the methodical manner on which I have always prided myself, I had been keeping Clare Quilty's face masked in my dark dungeon where he was waiting for me to come with barber and priest." From this point to the end of the novel Quilty, clowning his way through his own murder, struts across center stage. As Quilty's image looms larger, as he becomes more and more dominant in Humbert's mind, we feel more troubled than ever that Humbert could assume we should have known the name without his prompting.[14]

Once again Nabokov has inverted the detective-story formula. He at last identifies the victim, but instead of summing up all the clues at the point where he divulges Quilty's name, he informs us they have already been provided. We must therefore return to the beginning ourselves to track the man down. As we reread—and in order to encourage us to reread, Nabokov packs the whole book with the kind of time-lapse surprises, delayed discoveries, concealed jokes, and hidden enrichments of his fictive world that he strews around Hourglass Lake—we discover in amazement and amid all the excitement of the chase just how much we missed: more than a score of references to Quilty before Lolita discloses his identity.

Now, for instance, with the image of the murdered Quilty clearly in view, we can see why the word "waterproof" flashed through Humbert's mind as Lolita divulged the name. At Hourglass Lake Jean Farlow had been about to mention Quilty (nephew of the Ivor she imagines in the ivory) and even to disclose the fact that his fondness for little girls had nearly landed him in jail, when her husband's arrival interrupts her, and Humbert breaks off the chapter. Then Fate had almost warned Humbert, but thought better of it; now, Humbert himself almost holds up a hint for his first-time readers, but quickly palms it again.

Quilty, we learn, is a successful playwright, a pretentious hack with a taste for drink, drugs, and underage dollies. He had been a guest speaker at Charlotte's club two years before Humbert reached Ramsdale and had even perched little Dolly Haze on his knee. He had been a guest at the Enchanted Hunters Hotel when Humbert registered, and knowing Lolita was not Humbert's daughter, had enviously divined the intentions of his fellow pervert. He writes a play inspired by the hotel's name, and when Lolita's school decides to stage it he visits to watch rehearsals. He recognizes the pretty teenager in the lead role, and finds out she knows of his penchant for pretty pubescence. They become lovers. They plan her escape from Humbert. Humbert drives Lolita to Elphinstone, with Quilty pursuing him in cat-and-mouse fashion, at first in his own car, then in a succession of rented vehicles, while Humbert wonders whether that unshakable image in his rearview mirror is a detective, a rival, or the product of his own paranoia.

Just before the drive from Beardsley to Elphinstone, when Quilty first starts to shadow him, Humbert warns the reader "not to mock me and my mental daze. It is easy for him and me to decipher *now* a past destiny; but a destiny in the making is, believe me, not one of those honest mystery stories where all you have to do is keep an eye on the clues. I once read a French detective tale where the clues were actually in italics; but that is not McFate's way." Humbert records Quilty's mysterious manifestations but keeps his identity hidden. To understand his story, Humbert feels, we too must sense how utterly helpless he had been to fathom Quilty's intent, no matter how plain it may all seem now. When the future remains still unknown, we have no idea what signs to watch for; once it has happened, we look back at the past and everything seems to signal the approach of the impending event.

Smarting still, three years later, Humbert ascertains Quilty's address and hunts him down. He does not hesitate a moment: his undeviating romantic intensity demands Quilty's death. And here comes the final irony of the unforeseeable future: Humbert has planned this murder, he has composed a poem that he wants Quilty to read out before he dies, to make sure Quilty knows *why* he is dying; but the way Quilty behaves and the way the whole scene evolves turn the murder into a farce that seems to have been scripted by Quilty: "the ingenious play staged for me by Quilty," as Humbert dejectedly calls it.

Humbert had tried to corner Lolita in a room in the Enchanted Hunters, but it was she who turned to him and invited him to take his prey. Now at Pavor Manor he has tried to stage a final curtain call for the author of *The Enchanted Hunters*, but once again it is his victim who rewrites the future he had drafted with such care.

X

Lolita may not be written in the flat manner of conventional realism, but it takes place in a very accurately observed America. Yet as we search through the novel for Quilty's trail, something eerie, enchanted, and rather disconcerting seems to emanate from *The Enchanted Hunters*.

It is no more than a mild coincidence that the distinguished playwright who visits Charlotte Haze's book club and seats Lolita on his lap should have an uncle, the dentist Ivor Quilty, who lives right behind the Haze home. It becomes rather more surprising that he should happen to be a guest at the Enchanted Hunters Hotel, in a small town several hours' drive away, on the night Humbert and Lolita become lovers; that he should suspect Humbert's intentions; that he should enviously taunt him in the dark; that he should even occupy the next room.

At the hotel, of course, Humbert himself proves to be the most enchanted of hunters. After stealthily stalking Lolita for months, he runs her to ground at the hotel, only to find himself bagged by his prey—to his unutterable delight.

But it becomes thoroughly bizarre that Quilty then writes a play called *The Enchanted Hunters* as Humbert and Lolita tour America's motels, and that this play culminates in a scene that seems to echo what happened at the hotel. In Quilty's play the farmer's daughter—the role Lolita takes on when her school stages the show—confronts the Poet who insists that she and everyone else in the play are his invention. She leads him to her farm to prove that "she was not a poet's fantasy, but a rustic, down-to-brown-earth lass"—just as Lolita at the hotel becomes unexpectedly real when she leads Humbert to her innermost lair. Humbert himself is a poet, and more than once he has put his Lolita into verse, and he writes of the davenport scene: "What I had madly possessed was not she, but my own creation, another, fanciful Lolita—perhaps, more real than Lolita; . . . having no will, no consciousness—indeed no life of her own." At the Enchanted Hunters Hotel he wants to possess her in her sleep, to keep her part of his enchanted dream. But she proves unforeseeably real and independent of his imaginings, as she turns to him with the whispered suggestion that they make love. Despite his picturesque fancy, she proves herself a down-to-brown-earth lass.

Quilty could not possibly have known until he himself becomes Lolita's lover two years later—in other words, until *after* his play was written—what happened between Humbert and Lolita that night at the Enchanted Hunters. His play turns out to be almost an enchanted snare for Lolita: certainly, she takes the lead role, he visits her school as the play's author, and she takes *him* off to prove that she is not just the part he invented. But when he wrote that play there was no way Quilty could have foreseen that Humbert and Lolita would settle in the provincial town of Beardsley, or that Lolita's school there would stage this very play, only recently premiered in New York, or that Lolita would win the lead, or that he would have time to travel hundreds of miles for the rehearsals of this high-school production. The play seems almost to suggest some strange control over the future on Quilty's part, yet logic screams out that that is impossible.

Within days Lolita and Quilty become lovers. They arrange to have Humbert drive Lolita west to Elphinstone. Throughout the journey, Humbert finds himself under the spell of an enchanted hunter who seems to know his every move in advance and constantly reminds him he is being stalked. When Lolita absconds from Elphinstone, Humbert's only lead is the trail of riddling aliases that Quilty has left in hotel registers on the way, extravagant, allusive concoctions tuned by the unknown fiend to Humbert's mind and manner. Now when Humbert has become the hunter himself, in search of vengeance, he discovers his quest for clues to be another spell cast by his prey: he finds himself compelled to follow the route that mocking Quilty has carefully scripted in advance.

Something disconcerting and sinister is afoot: it seems almost as if

Quilty has Humbert completely in control, as if Humbert were no more than a character in one of Quilty's plays, a figment of his imagination. To anyone such an idea is repellent; to Humbert, doubly so. He prides himself in transforming and molding Lolita according to the dictates of his imagination: now he finds someone else has usurped the role and made *him* a plaything of his fancy. He seethes at the very thought.

As soon as Lolita divulges Quilty's identity, Humbert heads off to stage a murder in which Quilty will play the role *he* wants. He arrives at Pavor Manor "lucidly insane, crazily calm, an enchanted and very tight hunter." When the half-drugged Quilty hazards a wrong guess as to the intruder's identity, Humbert taunts him in anticipation of the puppet show he has prepared: "Guess again, Punch." At gunpoint Humbert compels him to read a poem that will serve as his death sentence:

> Because you took advantage of a sinner
> . . . .
> because you stole her
> . . . .
> took a dull doll to pieces
> and threw its head away
> because of all you did
> because of all I did not
> you have to die.

"The term 'poetical justice,'" Humbert smugly notes, "is one that may be most happily used in this respect." Quilty reads the poem as instructed, but then adds facetious critical comments before folding the sheet up and handing it back: "Well, sir, this is certainly a fine poem. Your best as far as I am concerned." He refuses to take either Humbert or Lolita with the grand seriousness Humbert requires, and his extravagant behavior sets the tone for the whole grim farce, even as Humbert begins to shoot. The scene becomes more and more phantasmagoric, right up to the moment of Quilty's death, and Humbert leaves in the most dejected spirits: "This, I said to myself, was the end of the ingenious play staged for me by Quilty. With a heavy heart I left the house." Even in murdering Quilty, Humbert cannot wrest control from him. Even as he dies, Quilty scripts the show.

Quilty has managed to ruin Humbert's satisfaction, but in any case Humbert sees the murder as only preparation for writing *Lolita*. He ends the book: "And do not pity C. Q. One had to choose between him and H. H., and one wanted H. H. to exist at least a couple of months longer, so as to have him make you live in the minds of later generations. I am thinking of aurochs and angels, the secret of durable pigments, prophetic sonnets, the refuge of art. And this is the only immortality you and I may share, my Lolita."

Humbert writes *Lolita* with two aims: to immortalize Lolita as *his* Lolita, and to put the dead Quilty at his command as he never could in life. With Quilty dead, Humbert exacts a revenge more soothing than the murder itself, as he turns his rival into a puppet who now dances to *his* control of time as he pointedly shapes the pattern of Quilty's appearance and disappearance within the past.

Quilty's *Enchanted Hunters* had seemed to cast a spell over Humbert's future: now as he retells the story Humbert controls Quilty's time at will. Quilty may have sabotaged Humbert's murder script, but Humbert's mastery of his rival's exits and entrances makes *Lolita* itself the perfect revenge, the perfect crime.

XI

By the same stroke Humbert also makes *Lolita* the perfect defense of the crime it caps. Just at the point where Quilty's image begins to come into clear focus, as Humbert listens to "Mrs. Richard F. Schiller," Humbert's self-defense reaches a new pitch. He gazes at Lolita as she talks, at "her ruined looks and her adult, rope-veined narrow hands . . . hopelessly worn at seventeen. . . . You may jeer at me, and threaten to clear the court, but until I am gagged and half-throttled, I will shout my poor truth. I insist the world know how much I loved my Lolita, *this* Lolita, pale and polluted, and big with another's child." She is no longer a nymphet, no longer a projection of his fancy, but a real person whom he loves just as she is. As the love theme soars, so does the theme of guilt. On his way to Ramsdale in search of Quilty's address, Humbert reviews his case: "Alas, I was unable to transcend the simple human fact that whatever spiritual solace I might find, whatever lithophanic eternities might be provided for me, nothing could make my Lolita forget the foul lust I had inflicted upon her . . . a North American girl-child named Dolores Haze had been deprived of her childhood by a maniac." Humbert now records the most damning images of Lolita's maimed childhood and the clearest evidence of his own iniquity. Then as he waits for the police to reach him after he has killed Quilty he recalls his great epiphany, the remote sounds of children at play, the hopeless poignancy of Lolita's absence from that concord.

When Humbert comes to murder Quilty, his victim displays no interest in Dolores Haze, then or now, and refuses any responsibility for her fate. Humbert by contrast carefully positions his noblest declarations of love and his most poignant admissions of guilt on each side of the scene in which he kills Quilty. For love of Lolita, for the pain of her loss, he has to eradicate this degenerate who refuses to take her seriously.

XII

But although Humbert can shape his story and turn *Lolita* itself into the ideal revenge and the ideal defense, he cannot control the patterns of time. He closes his book hoping Lolita will live well into the twenty-first century, but only five weeks after his own imminent death she dies in childbirth, at seventeen. His book may possibly immortalize Lolita, but his conduct has quite certainly hastened her death. The girl he pretended he might have killed as his Carmen he has indeed killed young by thrusting her so early into the adult world.

As if in revenge for Quilty's toying with his own fate—although he has himself done the same to Lolita—Humbert seeks out Quilty, tries to script *their* final scene together, fails, and then tries to reassert final control over Quilty in the way he directs the story of *Lolita*. But a fate beyond him has again woven into the patterns of time another design that redounds not at all to his credit.

All his adult life Humbert has prepared plans in which others play a passive role he assigns them—only to find that they are as real as he is, and have plans of their own. In Europe he decides to marry solely to keep himself from raping nymphets. He chooses Valeria because at first he finds her imitation of a young girl not without charm, if no substitute for the thing itself. Disenchantment sets in at once, and he bullies her, he abuses her, he reduces her to a "stock character" with no right to a life of her own, and certainly no right to tell him, as they leave that bureau,

"There is another man in my life."

Now, these are ugly words for a husband to hear. They dazed me, I confess. To beat her up in the street, there and then, as an honest vulgarian might have done, was not feasible. Years of secret sufferings had taught me superhuman self-control. So I ushered her into a taxi which had been invitingly creeping along the curb for some time, and in this comparative privacy I quietly suggested she comment her wild talk. A mounting fury was suffocating me—not because I had any particular fondness for that figure of fun, *Mme Humbert*, but because matters of legal and illegal conjunction were for me alone to decide, and here she was, Valeria, the comedy wife, brazenly preparing to dispose in her own way of my comfort and fate. I demanded her lover's name. I repeated my question . . . *"Mais qui est-ce?"* I shouted at last, striking her on the knee with my fist; and she, without even wincing, stared at me as if the answer were too simple for words, then gave a quick shrug and pointed at the thick neck of the taxi driver. He pulled up at a small café and introduced himself.

Quivering with rage, Humbert wonders whether to kill Valeria or her lover or both and decides he will limit himself to hurting Valeria very horribly as soon as they are alone. Fortunately, they never are.

Humbert does not notice the silent link between Valeria and her lover and Lolita and Quilty. Valeria and Maximovich have prearranged that as she emerges with Humbert from the *préfecture* and tells him there is someone else in her life, Maximovich will follow just behind them in his taxi. That plan evolved behind his back annoys Humbert in some obscure way: he has been drafted into a scene others have stage-managed. Ten years later, Quilty pursues Humbert in another car in another prearranged plan and taunts him with the fear that his destiny is under someone else's control. Humbert retaliates by killing Quilty and trying to make his corpse jerk at the twitch of his pen. Humbert presents his murder of Quilty as the romantic deed of a betrayed lover, but he was ready to kill Maximovich and Valeria—or at least to beat Valeria brutally—not because he had ever loved her but simply because his control had been usurped, his pride affronted.

Humbert marries Charlotte Haze too without love, and only for access to Lolita. Charlotte, however, has her own plans. Envious of her daughter's youth, wanting to be alone with her handsome new lodger, anxious that scholar Humbert should not be chased off by what she supposes are Lo's bothersome attentions, she sends her daughter to camp. At Hourglass Lake she announces to her new husband that she will send Lo straight from camp to St. Algebra. Again, Humbert finds that because somebody else has plans of her own, the situation he has slyly set up for his own advantage has suddenly turned into a trap. His first reaction is to murder her; fortunately for them both, he does not. Once again Nabokov arranges Humbert's instinctively murderous reaction at this forfeiture of control to match his later reaction to Quilty. The camp to which Charlotte has taken Lolita is called, of all possible names, Camp Q (Lolita tells Humbert that everyone calls Quilty "Cue," and he thinks: "Her camp five years ago. Curious coincidence"). It is run by a Shirley Holmes, almost Sherlock Holmes, as if to prefigure the detective whom Humbert at first supposes his pursuer to be ("Detective Trapp," he dubs him, and Quilty returns the favor one night by appearing before Humbert in a Dick Tracy mask). And Humbert learns to shoot Chum, the automatic with which he kills Quilty, in the woods around Hourglass Lake.

The pattern occurs once more, in an ironic variation, before its final manifestation. Humbert tries to capture Lolita with his sleeping pills at the Enchanted Hunters, but instead she has her own ideas, and prepares to spring her trap on him: she invites him to make love. Delighted, Humbert walks right in—and once they are lovers, makes that fact in its turn a trap for the defenseless child.

When Quilty's play *The Enchanted Hunters* becomes a lure for Lolita, Humbert finds once again that he has ceded control, that his girl has plans of her own, that his nympholepsy has landed him in another trap. This time he merely pretends he wants to murder his Lolita, his Carmen, but from the first he also proves deadly serious about taking the life of the person who dared usurp his control.

Four times Humbert, in pursuit of his fantasies, devises plans in which others play a preset role he assigns them. Four times he finds that they have wills of their own, and his plans run awry. Each time except for the pleasant surprise at the Enchanted Hunters, he whirls around in bitter fury, looking for someone to destroy. And each time a McFate beyond Humbert's world inscribes this pattern into Humbert's life.

XIII

At the end of *Lolita*, Humbert heaps reproaches on himself for all he has done to Lolita since that fatal day at the Enchanted Hunters. He contrasts his grief and remorse with Quilty's inhuman indifference to losing Lolita and to *her* losing her future. For that callousness, Humbert implies, Quilty deserves to die.

Nabokov disagrees: unattractive as Quilty may be, his murder remains a crime that reflects harshly on the criminal. To indicate his judgment and yet elude Humbert's alertness in his own defense, Nabokov has deliberately paired the two major scenes that end the two parts of the novel—the fateful mornings of the "seduction" at the Enchanted Hunters and the murder at Pavor Manor—in order to stress that on both occasions Humbert displays the same passionate, deliberate, calculating self-centeredness, the same disregard for the live reality of another person.

As he stalks Quilty at his manor, Humbert calls himself "an enchanted and very tight hunter." What he fails to realize here is that fate or Nabokov has constructed a whole system of parallels between the Enchanted Hunters episode and the episode of the murder. In both cases, Humbert spends the previous night in Parkington—though no other scenes occur there in the novel, and there is no geographical need for hotel and Quilty's home to be at all near each other in a story that encircles the United States more than once between these two scenes. Both nights Humbert spends there he cannot sleep. Before the first night, he telephones long-distance from Parkington to Camp Q; before the second, he calls long-distance to "Cue's" manor. Before both encounters, Humbert prepares pills or ammunition explicitly compared to each other and both comically ineffective: his amethyst capsules to make Lolita sleep, a "boxfull of magic ammunition," and the bullets that seem only to intensify Quilty's manic state: "in distress, in dismay, I understood that far from killing him I was injecting spurts of energy into the poor fellow, as if the bullets had been capsules wherein a heady elixir danced." Prior to pouncing on his prey Humbert in both cases pockets the keys, as perhaps might be expected from the logic of the situation. Quite unexpectedly, however, both scenes contain hints of anti-Semitism. The Enchanted Hunters advertises its location "Near Churches," a discreet code in midcentury America that only Gentiles were welcome. On Humbert's arrival the hotel receptionist at first informs him there are no rooms free: in the telegram he had sent, his name had come out as "Humberg." And Quilty at Pavor Manor tries to dismiss guntoting Humbert: "This is a Gentile's house, you know. Maybe, you'd better run along."

What are we to make of this pointed pairing of apparently unrelated scenes?

Humbert carefully places after the murder that haunting and famous scene on the mountain trail overlooking the valley filled with the sound of schoolchildren at play. "I stood listening to that musical vibration from my lofty slope, to those flashes of separate cries with a kind of demure murmur for background, and then I knew that the hopelessly poignant thing was not Lolita's absence from my side, but the absence of her voice from that concord." In the position Humbert has given it, this becomes the last distinct scene of the novel. Even a fine reader like Alfred Appel can treat this moment of epiphany for Humbert as his "moral apotheosis,"[15] a final clarity of moral vision that almost redeems him. Certainly, Humbert does indeed feel profound and sincere regret here, albeit too late, but that is only one part of a complex whole. He places this image of himself to stand in contrast to Quilty, whom he has just murdered, though the vision itself occurred not then but three years earlier, when Quilty took Lolita from him. What difference does the timing make? Think about it. For two years Humbert had been quite lucidly aware that he was keeping Lolita a prisoner and destroying her childhood and her spirit, but he continued to hold her in his power. So long as he could extract sexual delight from her, he could remain deaf to his moral sense. Only after her disappearance, when she was no longer available as the thrice-daily outlet for his lust, did he allow his moral awareness to overwhelm him as he looked down into that valley.

But that was a very selective insight. Humbert places that scene at the end to show he can be selfless, and his rhetorical strategy persuades a good many readers. Nabokov assesses things differently, and although he gives Humbert complete control over his pen, he finds a way to inscribe his own judgment within what Humbert writes. By the covert parallels he constructs between the climaxes of the novel's two parts, he indicates that in both scenes there is the same romantic sense of the imperious dictates of desire, the same overriding quest for self-satisfaction even at the expense of another life.

Overlooking that serene valley, Humbert feels already a lust for revenge as importunate as his old craving for Lolita. Before, during, and after his "moral apotheosis" on the mountainside, he remains for three years absolutely committed to savoring the "intolerable bliss" of killing the person who has robbed him of Lolita. With the pressure of another sweet satisfaction looming ahead, he is just as obsessive, just as willfully blind as before. When he pursues Lolita all the way to the Enchanted Hunters, he is as oblivious to her as someone who has her own existence outside his "needs" as he is to Quilty when he pursues him so single-mindedly to Pavor Manor. Humbert demonstrates how easy it is to let moral awareness turn into sincere regret after the fact, but how much more difficult to curb the self before it tramples others underfoot. The emphasis throughout Lolita on the contrast between a forward and rear view of time is ultimately a moral one.

CHAPTER 12

Lolita into Print, *Pnin* onto Paper:
Cornell, 1953–1955

I

IN THE SECOND week of December 1953, Nabokov took to New York a corrected typescript of the book he had called a time bomb. He had no idea its timer was set so far ahead: *Lolita* would take nearly two years to be published, and another three to explode across America.

After recording a talk on the art of translation for the BBC, Nabokov dined with Pascal Covici of Viking Press and handed over his manuscript. A month later, back in Ithaca, he received the verdict: the book was brilliant, but a publisher who took it on would risk a fine or jail. He sent it straight on to Simon and Schuster.[1]

His contract with the *New Yorker* paid him generously for allowing the magazine first consideration of everything he wrote for publication. To fulfill the terms of his agreement, he would have to show the *New Yorker* the manuscript of *Lolita*, although he knew there was no chance of the magazine publishing even an excerpt. But before he would let Katharine White see the novel, he sought reassurance that she could decide on the manuscript without anybody else but her husband, E. B. White, setting eyes on it. Or if someone else had to read it, could its authorship be kept concealed from him or her? Nabokov did not even want to entrust his text to the mails: if Katharine White felt she must read it, he would have to bring it to New York himself. After sending her Covici's report on the risks of publishing the book, he asked if she would still want to see it. He also asked if she thought it likely he could preserve his anonymity once the book was published. No, she replied: from her experience, an author's identity sooner or later leaked out.[2]

Curiously, at the very time Nabokov was trying to do all he could to ensure that *Lolita* could not be connected with Cornell, he was himself involved in a censorship row on campus. Deane Malott, the Cornell president, wanted to expel the young Ronald Sukenick, later to become well known as an avant-garde novelist, for having published his story, "Indian Love Call," in a new campus literary magazine, *The Cornell Writer*, of which Sukenick was fiction editor. The story's subject, as Sukenick later recalled, was the "suppression of teenage lust in the deenergized fifties," and its most offending phrase no more than the word "birdshit." Nabokov himself coyly avoided all "obscene" terms in his own work, even in *Lolita*, but he had been asked by the *New Yorker* to remove "bright dog dirt" from one story and in 1954 would have to dematerialize the brilliant final line of his poem "On Translating *Eugene Onegin*" by turning "Dove-droppings on your monument" into the bland "The shadow of your monument." He disliked censorship far more than he disapproved of the kinds of expression his upbringing had taught him to consider improper, and he played an active role in the Division of Literature's campaign to ensure the obscenity charges brought against Sukenick and his coeditor were dropped.³*

In January 1954, Nabokov wrote the second chapter of *Pnin* (Pnin moves in with the Clementses and receives a visit from his ex-wife, Liza Wind). He sent it off to the *New Yorker* on February 1 only to have it turned down as too "unpleasant."⁴ The nastiness of Liza and Eric Wind in exploiting Pnin and in inflicting their psychoanalysis on others seemed too much for a magazine that had hoped for more of Pnin's mild misadventures.

At the same time as he mailed off "Pnin Had Not Always Been Single," Nabokov sent Viking chapters 1 and 2 and an outline of the novel that differs in several important respects from the finished book. It would consist of ten chapters.

> In the next eight chapters, the insecurity of Pnin's job becomes evident while simultaneously it transpires that owing to some juggling, which Dr. Eric Wind blames on his first wife, Eric's marriage to Liza is invalid, and in the midst of her intrigue with "George" she returns for a while to Pnin. Owing to a further impact of circumstances, Pnin finds himself solely responsible for the welfare of Liza's boy. There are some surprises and alarums. Then, at the end of the novel, I, V. N., arrive in person to Waindell College to lecture on Russian literature, while poor Pnin dies, with everything unsettled and uncompleted, including the book Pnin had been writing all his life.

Pascal Covici argued that Pnin's death would be wrong. Nabokov thought highly of Covici, and whether for Covici's reasons or his

---

* Several issues later, Sukenick heard that Nabokov liked his stories, and decided to call on him. In response to Sukenick's anxious questions about his own writing and his modernist literary heroes, Nabokov talked only about cricket, about which Sukenick knew and cared nothing. Nevertheless, Sukenick felt, Nabokov was being "very friendly in some monumentally oblique way" he could not understand (*Down and In: Life in the Underground* [New York: Beech Tree Books, 1987], pp. 80–81).

own he eventually refused to let the heart trouble in the book's open-ing chapters kill Pnin off at the end. Ejected from Waindell on the last page of the novel, Pnin would in fact turn up in *Pale Fire*, ten-ured, promoted, and thriving as head of the Russian department at Wordsmith University.[5]

At the beginning of the spring term, the Nabokovs moved into an-other faculty home, at 101 Irving Place, not far from their State Street address. Alfred Appel, Nabokov's student this year, recalls sitting behind his professor, the author of *Laughter in the Dark*, at an Ithaca cinema screening *Beat the Devil*,

> the bizarrely humorous Truman Capote–John Huston shaggy-dog thriller. Nabokov was so amused that his loud laughter became conspic-uous immediately. Véra Nabokov murmured *"Volodya!"* a few times, but then gave up, as it became clear that two comic fields of force had been established in the theater: those who were laughing at the movie, and those who were laughing at (nameless) Nabokov laughing at the movie. At one juncture of the film, actor Peter Lorre approaches an artist who is painting a portrait of a man. Lorre studies the picture, a profile view, and then complains, in his famous nasal whine, "That doesn't look like him. It has only one ear!"* Nabokov exploded—that is the only verb—with laughter. It seemed to lift him from his seat.[6]

Occasions like this when Nabokov had time away from his writing desk were few. Early in January he had sought an extension from the Chekhov Publishing House for his Russian translation of *Conclusive Evidence*, due at the end of February. Grudgingly he was allowed un-til the end of March, and he had to race to meet that date.

In the original autobiography Nabokov had been able to assume little interest on the part of his American audience in things Russian or in Vladimir Nabokov. Now in preparing his book for an émigré audience to whom V. D. Nabokov and Vladimir Sirin were major fig-ures and every memory of Russia a treasure, there was much to in-sert, much he could not omit. Since in its Russian form, the book could afford to be even more nostalgic than in English, its Russian title, *Drugie berega* (*Other Shores*), lifts a phrase from a famous Pushkin lyric in which the poet revisits a scene from his past.[7] And now that Nabokov himself was revisiting his past in the language in which it was lived, his memory seemed to recall more, and more exactly, than when he wrote in English.[8] The new material he added blurred the outlines of certain chapters—a blurring that would remain when he retranslated *Drugie berega* for the revised *Speak, Memory* in the mid-1960s. Chapter 3 of *Conclusive Evidence*, "Portrait of My Uncle," had

---

* Actually, the line was "Only has one eye."

been a lighthearted romp through Nabokov's ancestors before settling on what were to him much more important: his own ineradicable memories of one near twig on the family tree, his Uncle Vasily. In the Russian version, Nabokov not only incorporated more about Vasily but skewed the chapter by dwelling at considerable length on the idyllic, quintessentially Russian landscape around the Oredezh.*

Nabokov found the recomposition and translation into Russian of Russian memories he had first expressed in English a harrowing experience. To Katharine White he wrote that after the agony of his atrocious metamorphosis from a Russian to an English writer in the early forties, he had sworn he "would never go back from my wizened Hyde form to my ample Jekyll one—but there I was, after fifteen years of absence, wallowing again in the bitter luxury of my Russian verbal might." On April 1, after a winter of relentless pressure, he completed *Drugie berega*.[9]

II

Two days later he was in New York to make another recording for the BBC (his poem "An Evening of Russian Poetry" and some Pushkin translations). He lunched with Wallace Brockway of Simon and Schuster and agreed to edit *Anna Karenin*, revising Constance Garnett's translation and supplying an introduction and notes.[10]

Owing to two spring terms spent at Harvard, Nabokov had not taught Kafka, Proust, and Joyce since 1951, the first year of his Masterpieces of European Fiction course, and was conscious his lectures on these authors needed much revision, especially if, as he hoped, he was to publish them one day.[11] In the second week of April he began to lecture on Kafka's "Metamorphosis." Alfred Appel recalls him making two huge blackboard drawings, four feet by two, of Gregor Samsa and his six feet, as seen from the side and from above.

> Since there is no sustained description of Gregor in the narrative, Nabokov proceeded to enumerate some fourteen entomological characteristics and mannerisms of Gregor, that, distributed through the text, served to define him as a scarab or dung beetle—"a bug among humbug," Nabokov would say, referring to Gregor's dreaded family. Next, Nabokov would explain the transformation in starkly fundamental human terms, asking us to imagine Gregor's spectral existence as a salesman, the unreality of all those hotel rooms in strange towns: "Where am

---

* As Gennadi Barabtarlo points out, Nabokov also added a passage poignantly evoking the prose style of Ivan Bunin, in a memorial tribute to the émigré Nobel laureate, who had died since the publication of *Conclusive Evidence*.

I? [Gregor, awakened by a nightmare, sitting up in an unfamiliar bed.]
Who am I? *What* am I?"

In his next lecture Nabokov announced that a new translation of the
book had arrived in the morning mail. He shuddered and grimaced
as he held up the expensive new illustrated edition "whose translator
had substituted 'cockroach' for 'gigantic insect' in the famous opening sentence. '*Cockroach!*' Nabokov repeated. . . . 'Even the Samsa
maid knows enough to call Gregor a dung beetle!' "

On another occasion, Nabokov had no choice but to ad lib, but
after landing himself in a Pninian situation, extricated himself with
the kind of Nabokovian style he thought he had only in his finished
work. Rushing along a few minutes late to join the thirty or so others
in Nabokov's Russian literature in translation class, Alfred Appel noticed with relief that his professor, also late, was walking ahead of
him along the dark hall. When Nabokov hurried into a classroom,
Appel realized it was one door too soon:

> I entered the class to find Professor Nabokov several sentences into his
> lecture; not wanting to waste another minute, he was stooped over his
> notes, intently reading them to thirty stunned students, a shell-shocked
> platoon belonging to an even tardier don. Trying to be as transparent as
> possible, I approached the lectern and touched Nabokov on the sleeve.
> He turned, and peered down at me over his eyeglasses, amazed. "Mr
> Nabokov," I said very quietly, "you are in the wrong classroom." He
> readjusted his glasses on his nose, focused his gaze on the motionless
> . . . figures seated before him, and calmly announced, "You have just
> seen the 'Coming Attraction' for Literature 325. If you are interested,
> you may register next fall."

Folding up his notes, he left, entered the right classroom, and,
chuckling to himself, announced to his real students, "A most extraordinary thing has just happened, most extraordinary." Without
explaining further, he began to lecture.[12]

On April 17, Nabokov headed west by train for three days as a
guest lecturer at the University of Kansas, Lawrence, for the sizable
sum of $400. He found Lawrence a charming place full of bright peo-
ple, and greatly enjoyed his time there. His busy schedule reflected
the range of his interests. On day one, he lectured on Tolstoy in the
morning to a class studying masterpieces of world literature, spoke
on the art of writing in the afternoon, and in the early evening had a
tea followed by a discussion with Russian literature students. The
next day he talked with entomology students after lunch and in the
evening spoke on "Gogol, the Man and the Mask" for the fifth of the
University of Kansas Humanities Lectures, a major annual fixture.

On day three he lectured on contemporary French literature in the afternoon, and in the evening on Proust.[13]

Back in Ithaca, Nabokov exhorted his students to overcome the approaching summer heat and tackle *Ulysses* head-on. On rereading *Ulysses* himself for his course in 1950, Nabokov had found his earlier enthusiasm for the novel needed to be qualified by considerable reservations, and he had no doubts that Joyce ranked far below Proust. Now in 1954 he devoted six lectures to Proust and for the first time nine lectures to Joyce—to expand in future years to thirteen. He would later declare that his efforts to prepare *Ulysses* for the lecture room were the best part of the education he received at Cornell. "You will enjoy," he told his students, "the wonderfully artistic pages, one of the greatest passages in all literature, when Bloom brings Molly her breakfast. How beautifully the man writes!"[14]

Nabokov liked to claim that every word he uttered in class was prepared in writing beforehand. One incident late that May vividly belies his claim. In the drowsy heat of the classroom, Appel recalls, Nabokov gave a start:

> "Did you hear that? A cicada is singing, perhaps in this room." Suddenly Professor Nabokov has our attention, the sort paid to any harmless fellow when he is about to formulate his madness. "Yes, a cicada. I think it is on that window sill," he says, pointing to the right. "Please check it for us," he asks a young man slumped by the window. . . . "It's *two* grasshoppers," the student reports. . . . The class laughs, a breeze stirs. . . .
>
> "Do you know *how* the cicada makes its music and *why*?" asks Professor Nabokov. . . . He draws the insect on the blackboard; then he explains, and his voice rises in excitement and he stammers as he extends the digression, adding lore about the cicada and information about its appearance in art—the mosaics of Pompeii!—and literature.

On the final day of class Nabokov read out in tones of steadily mounting rhapsody the last three pages of Molly Bloom's soliloquy, and after the final "yes and his heart was going like mad and yes I said yes I will Yes" he stopped, announced "Yes: Bloom next morning will get his breakfast in bed." He said no more, collected his text, and left. On that abrupt note, the course was over.[15]

III

Before heading off for the summer, Nabokov spent the first two weeks of June hard at work in the Cornell library, annotating *Anna*

Karenin and planning the introduction he would write for the novel during the vacation. In preparation for the journey, he looked for a healthier car. Wary of any kind of machine and averse to all kinds of purchase, he would consult friends at wearisome length before committing himself. This time he settled at last on a frog-green Buick. As a final preparation for departure, he shut up his two copies of *Lolita*, one a corrected typescript in two black spring binders, one an uncorrected typescript in a box. He locked them both within the desk in his office, placed the key inside another box concealed in the middle drawer of his filing cabinet, then locked the office itself.¹⁶ *Lolita* would not escape.

In the middle of June, three Nabokovs set off in one car on a direct line through Cleveland and Wichita to Taos, New Mexico. There they had rented for the summer—for only $250—a very attractive-sounding house ten miles out of town. When they arrived they found, instead of three acres of orchard and garden, an adobe construction perched by the road with a narrow and almost impassable strip of kitchen-garden in the back. There was nowhere to walk or even sit outside in privacy. The promised rushing mountain river was an irrigation ditch. They did not care for the "painful quaintness" of the house. Dust and sand drifted down constantly from the ceiling. Mice droppings littered shelves and drawers. Flies buzzed in through the doors and faulty screens. In a south wind the smell of the sewer pervaded the house. At first they wanted to flee immediately, but then decided to see if they could stick it out.¹⁷

Taos itself was if anything even less attractive: "a dismal hole full of third-rate painters and faded pansies," Nabokov snorted, "an ugly and dreary town with *soi-disant* 'picturesque' Indian paupers placed at strategic points by the Chamber of Commerce to lure tourists from Oklahoma and Texas who deem the place 'arty.' " Only one feature made the location bearable: some admirable canyons, not far afield, which despite difficult hunting conditions yielded interesting butterflies. Dmitri drove his father there in a World War II jeep that came with the house.¹⁸

Throughout June and the first half of July Nabokov worked on *Anna Karenin*, completing the notes and a foreword for the first of the novel's eight parts and correcting blunders in Constance Garnett's text. When NBC asked him to translate another Russian classic of sorts, the libretto Chaikovsky co-wrote for the opera *Eugene Onegin*—a notoriously hideous travesty of Pushkin—Nabokov refused to have anything to do with its "criminal inanities."* In a third reaction to

---

* He would parody them fifteen years later in the second chapter of *Ada*.

Russian classics, he offered Dmitri occasional hints for his Harvard thesis, on a topic he had suggested himself: Shakespeare's influence on Pushkin.[19]

Nabokov learned in mid-July that Simon and Schuster's editors had at last turned down Lolita as "sheer pornography." After Viking Press had rejected the book in January, he had observed to Katharine White that he "had to write that book, for artistic reasons, and I really don't care much what happens to it next." By now his attitude had changed. In the book's early stages he had been uncertain that he could make it work, but now that it was done and his confidence in its worth had not declined a jot, he could no longer rest until it was published. He was ready to offer an agent a huge commission of 25 percent to place the book. Early in August he wrote to Doussia Ergaz of the Bureau Littéraire Clairouin in Paris, who had arranged the publication of French versions of some of his Russian and English books, and asked her to find somebody in Europe who would publish Lolita in English. She thought she could arrange it.[20]

By now the Nabokovs had lasted eight weeks in their rented adobe house. Their reward for perseverance was an unpleasant surprise. Two animals had entered the poorly covered water tank and drowned, and as their bodies decomposed all three Nabokovs became ill, Véra severely so. On Tuesday, August 10, she was driven to a doctor in Albuquerque. His diagnosis of her liver condition was so alarming that on Thursday morning she was put on a train to New York, to be met there by her cousin Anna Feigin. The men followed by car. After thoroughly examining her, doctors in New York pronounced Véra well. Fortunately, there would be no worse consequence of this "hectic hash of a summer" than an increase in the family debt.[21]

IV

After an uncomfortable squeeze into Anna Feigin's apartment on West 104th Street, the Nabokovs were able to move back to Ithaca on September 1, two weeks ahead of schedule, into number 30, Belleayre Apartments ("sic!" notes Nabokov), at 700 Stewart Avenue, right on the edge of the campus. Nabokov now asked Doussia Ergaz to hold off her search for a European publisher for Lolita, as James Laughlin of New Directions had asked to see the novel. Laughlin had published The Real Life of Sebastian Knight when no one else would take on something so strange, and although Nabokov had been disappointed by the meager financial rewards of publishing with New

Directions, it seemed worth a try. Always ready to launch the original and the challenging, Laughlin nevertheless found *Lolita* too great a risk: it would be unthinkable, he wrote, to publish the book without destroying Nabokov's reputation and his own. [22]*

As soon as he reached Ithaca, Nabokov resumed work on his masses of notes and drafts for *Eugene Onegin*, fearing that if he did not bring the project to a reasonable stage of completion he might tire of it all. He returned to New York for an English Institute conference at Columbia University, where on September 14 he presented a paper called "Problems of Translation: *Onegin* in English," a brilliant, impassioned attack on rhymed translations, a convincing demonstration of the impossibility of conveying the explicit sense and the implicit assocations behind Pushkin's lines to an English reader by any means except absolute literal fidelity. The conference organizer, Reuben Brower, reported to Nabokov that his paper had a succès fou. [23]

Lectures at Cornell resumed in the last week of September. By now Nabokov was much happier than he had been in his first years at Cornell. His salary had risen to $6,500, [24] his largest course was extremely popular, he was engaged in scholarly projects of note (*Eugene Onegin*, *The Song of Igor's Campaign*, the *Anna Karenin* edition, and the planned book on masterpieces of European fiction), he had already managed to write two creative masterpieces since arriving in Ithaca (*Conclusive Evidence* and *Lolita*), and now that he had no new material to prepare for class he had much more time free during the college year for his own work as a Russian scholar or an English writer.

He spent the fall term working feverishly to finish *Eugene Onegin*, only to realize it would still take him many more months. Meanwhile Edmund Wilson had suggested that Nabokov show *Lolita* to his current publisher, Farrar, Straus. Roger Straus turned the book down and counseled Nabokov against publishing it pseudonymously, for although that might at first safeguard Cornell, it would weaken the book's chances in court. There, the only possible defense would be that it was a first-rate work of art by a reputable man of letters who had handled a repellent subject with perfect literary tact. [25]

Edmund Wilson himself was next to receive the manuscript. He recoiled at once. One night in a typically Wilsonian gesture he called Nabokov up at 11:00 P.M., asked him to identify a moth he had caught, and did not say a word about the novel, although his friend

---

* He also wrote that Nabokov's style "is so individual that it seems to me absolutely certain that the real authorship would quickly be recognized even if a pseudonym were used" (Nabokov, *Selected Letters*, 153n).

had been eagerly awaiting his response.[26] Despite his immediate personal dislike of the book, Wilson nevertheless remained determined to help it find a publisher. When Jason Epstein of Doubleday visited him at Wellfleet, he took the two black binders down from a shelf: "Here's a manuscript by my friend Volodya Nabokov. It's repulsive, but you should read it." Elena Wilson and Mary McCarthy, however, were still ahead of Epstein in the queue. According to the version Nabokov learned some time later, Wilson read only half of the manuscript: in order to have it seen by as many as might be able to help with publication, he had reserved one of the binders for himself and passed the other on to Mary McCarthy. Only at the end of November did Nabokov receive Wilson's report of Elena Wilson's judgment (very positive), McCarthy's (negative and perplexed), and Wilson's own: "I like it less than anything else of yours I have read."[27]

Nabokov took some months to reply: "Belatedly but with perfectly preserved warmth," he began, "I now want to thank you for your letters." His reply *was* a warm one, but over the next year, after hearing how cursorily Wilson had scanned the book, he could not conceal a different kind of warmth as he tried to prod his friend into reading *Lolita* properly: "I would like you to read it some day"; "When you do read *Lolita*, please mark that it is a highly moral affair."[28]

After her hasty reading, Mary McCarthy handed the manuscript on to Philip Rahv, editor of *Partisan Review*. Rahv thought *Lolita* charming, and was prepared to consider publishing an extract, provided his colleagues were game. But Nabokov asked for anonymity, and Rahv too counseled that that would only arouse suspicion, imply something shoddy, and rob the book of its best defense.[29]

In December came Jason Epstein's turn. He wanted to publish, but Doubleday's president heard what the novel was about and vetoed the idea at once.[30] Viking, Simon and Schuster, New Directions, Farrar Straus, and now Doubleday all thought it impossible to publish the book and avoid prosecution. It was high time to look abroad.

V

In the last week of January, Nabokov presided over the fall term exams: "Clear hand. One blue book. Ink. Think. Abbreviate obvious names (e.g. MB). Do not pad ignorance with eloquence. Unless medical advice is produced, nobody will be permitted to retire to the WC." His examination questions still continued to surprise. Although he did ask his students to describe Chichikov's physical appearance, he also made them identify passages a mere two lines long from the novels on the course, and complicated the task by incorporating a plausible dummy culled from a newspaper. Far from ignoring history, he checked that students kept an eye—an eye for detail, not for generalization—on the markers of time: "Places and people in *Dead Souls*, *Bleak House* and *Madame Bovary* are products of their authors' creative fancy but they are also fitted, more or less loosely, into certain historical frames. Discuss: 1) Time of described events and time of writing; 2) Elements (besides "horses") that identify the times in each novel; and 3) What you consider to be their international and everlasting features."[31]

As the term drew to a close, Nabokov finished the next chapter of *Pnin*—chapter 3, "Pnin's Day," a quiet Tuesday of mishaps and rewards at the Waindell College Library—and on February 1 sent it off to the *New Yorker*.[32] On the same day he mailed the manuscript for another book. The Chekhov Publishing House had asked him to translate his English novels into Russian, but he thought it much more important that *The Defense* and *Invitation to a Beheading*, his best books in Russian after the recently republished *The Gift*, should once again be made available. When the Chekhov press made it plain they would prefer something that had never appeared before in book form in Russian, he offered them *Vesna v Fial'te* (*Spring in Fialta*), a collection of short stories that was to have been published in France in 1939 but was abandoned as war drew close. They accepted his suggestion.[33]

In mid-February, as soon as Doubleday returned *Lolita*, Nabokov sent the manuscript on to Doussia Ergaz in Paris. He suggested she show it to Sylvia Beach, proprietor of the famous Left Bank English-language bookstore, Shakespeare and Company, who had dared to publish *Ulysses* in Paris after every English press seemed certain to refuse it. Nabokov had met and liked her in Paris in 1937, and no doubt would have welcomed the chance to have *Lolita* line up with *Ulysses*. But Sylvia Beach's publishing days were over, and Ergaz instead showed the manuscript to Mme Duhamel of La Table Ronde, publishers of the English-language *Paris Review*.[34]

By late February Nabokov was halfway through chapter 4 of *Pnin*. In April he was still "up to his chin in *Pnin*" and determined to finish the novel over the summer. In May he switched to his *Eugene Onegin* translation. By the beginning of June the translation seemed quite complete, and he hoped to have the commentaries in order by Christmas.[35]

After shipping *Lolita* to France, he had joked to Edmund Wilson: "I suppose it will be finally published by some shady firm with a Viennese-Dream name—e.g. 'Silo.' " His jest proved truer than he would have wished. In April, Doussia Ergaz met Maurice Girodias, founder and owner of Olympia Press.[36]

Girodias was the son of Jack Kahane, who in the 1930s had published Henry Miller's *Tropic of Cancer* and *Tropic of Capricorn* and much outright pornography. In 1953, finding himself penniless, Girodias decided to follow in his father's steps, to make some quick money by publishing in English, in Paris, every book rejected by Anglo-American censorship that came his way. He had a real taste for literature, but although by the end of the decade his Olympia Press list would include Samuel Beckett, Henry Miller, Lawrence Durrell, J. P. Donleavy, William Burroughs, and the English translations of Jean Genet, he deliberately chose, as he explained to *Playboy*, "to be indiscriminate, to bring out good books as well as bad ones: the only standard was the ostracism to which they would have been subjected." Three-quarters of his list was pornographic trash, but he accepted the title of pornographer "with joy and pride."[37]

Doussia Ergaz, knowing little about the new press, judged Girodias by the art-book subsidiary, Editions du Chêne, which he had recently sold to a major French publisher, and by the fact that he was currently publishing the English version of *L'histoire d'O*, much lauded that season. Unlike every other publisher to whom *Lolita* had been offered, Girodias naturally was not daunted but positively enticed by warnings of the novel's perverse sexual intensity. In mid-May Ergaz reported to Nabokov that Girodias was enraptured by the book and offered concrete terms for immediate publication. Nabokov cabled acceptance immediately, and in the letter that followed expressed his delight at all Ergaz had to report of Girodias's record ("several years as director of the Editions du Chêne, a financial flop but the publisher of artistically admirable books issued with a care and perfection not often seen").[38] Nabokov later explained:

> I had not been in Europe since 1940, was not interested in pornographic books, and thus knew nothing about the obscene novelettes which Mr. Girodias was hiring hacks to confect with his assistance, as he relates elsewhere. I have pondered the painful question whether I would have agreed so cheerfully to his publishing *Lolita* had I been aware in May, 1955, of what formed the supple backbone of his production. Alas, I probably would, though less cheerfully.[39]

He was too relieved that he could at last publish his best novel to notice the strange odor of other comments Girodias made on the book and Ergaz passed on: "He finds the book not only admirable from the literary point of view, but he thinks that it might lead to a change in social attitudes toward the kind of love described in *Lolita*, provided of course that it has this authenticity, this burning and ir-repressible ardor."⁴⁰ Girodias appeared to assume that Nabokov *was* Humbert, and felt perfectly content to deal with such a man and to promote such a cause.

Even before reading *Lolita*, Girodias had strongly urged Nabokov to put his name on the novel. Nabokov asked Ergaz not to permit this unless Girodias made it an absolute condition.⁴¹ Until this late date he had kept the book and its subject concealed even from Morris Bishop, his closest friend at Cornell, but now he sought Bishop's advice about anonymity. Bishop proved not to be the person to ask: he thought the story of a man who loves little girls absolutely taboo in America, and rightly so. He imagined furious letters raining down on Cornell—"Is this the deranged creature you picked to teach my daughter? I am going to withdraw her from the university, along with the endowment I proposed"—and feared that the authorities might dismiss the very man he himself was most anxious to keep at Cornell. He found he could not read the novel through: Humbert seemed just too slimy. Offended, Nabokov replied: "It is the best thing I ever wrote." The disparity of judgment put a strain on their friendship for months. Thirty years later Alison Bishop wondered how her husband would feel if he could know that their granddaughter, at fifteen, had just read *Lolita* as an assignment for her high-school English class.⁴²

Nabokov's family advised him to wait rather than commit himself to the low royalty scale Girodias offered, but he felt he simply had to have the thing off his shoulders. The uncertainty interfered with his other work, and he wanted to have the contract signed before leaving for the summer. Above all, he wanted *Lolita* published as soon as possible, and Girodias promised an extremely rapid production schedule. On June 6, Nabokov signed a contract for the novel with Olympia Press.⁴³

VI

Ten days later, when he and Véra visited Harvard for Dmitri's commencement, they found his cum laude a pleasant surprise. In the spring, Dmitri had been accepted at Harvard Law School, and Nabokov hoped that his son, winner of the New England high-school debating championship in his last year at Holderness, might distinguish himself along the same legal and oratorical path as V. D. Nabokov. After years of voice training and singing in choirs, Dmitri was far more interested in projecting his fine bass voice from a concert or an operatic stage than a soapbox or a courtroom floor. On being accepted at law school, he had told his parents: "I've showed you I can do it, but now I would like to study singing." Nabokov was alarmed. He knew that although he himself had two incomes, as writer and teacher, he had no money to spare, and he feared Dmitri might never be able to support himself at such an unlikely profession as operatic singing. He sought advice from his friends. Wilma Kerby-Miller counseled: "Give him two years. He could always go to law school then. But don't decide through fear." Nabokov liked the advice. Dmitri auditioned and was accepted at the Longy School of Music in Cambridge.[44]

As summer drew on the Nabokovs decided that this year they would not travel west. Nabokov had no desire to relive the terrors of Taos, he had very little money, and above all he was desperate to finish *Pnin*. Just before setting off for Dmitri's commencement, he had sent the *New Yorker* the fourth chapter, "Victor Meets Pnin"; out of the final total of seven, three more remained. On their way back from Cambridge, he and Véra looked for somewhere they could spend the summer in a Riviera setting. After a cold wind sweeping across a wide expanse of wet sand in New Hampshire failed to conjure up images of Menton, they decided they would find nothing in the East much superior to Ithaca and its lakes and glades.[45]

In the spring, with Dmitri's graduation looming, Nabokov had asked Jason Epstein if Doubleday could use someone to translate Russian literature for them. Late in June, Epstein followed up the inquiry, visiting the Nabokovs in Ithaca. They all took to one another warmly,* and came to the decision that Dmitri should translate Lermontov's novel *A Hero of Our Time* with his father, while Nabokov would translate *Anna Karenin* on his own. Translating would be good discipline for Dmitri, Nabokov thought—he remembered his own father applying pressure on him to complete his translation of Rolland's *Colas Breugnon* when he was Dmitri's age—as well as a supplementary skill perhaps more marketable than operatic training. Besides, it might encourage Dmitri to spend more of his summer in Ithaca. Dmitri spent two weeks there working on the translation before heading for the Canadian Rockies. Less fit after his final year's studies than in previous years, he twice peeled off the rocks. Deciding that without more commitment he ought to abandon climbing before he killed himself, he returned to Ithaca to spend another two weeks among the red rocks of Lermontov's Caucasus.[46]

* Véra Nabokov surprised Epstein by producing the new pistol she had bought with the first half of the *Lolita* advance her husband had just received.

Nabokov himself was working furiously to complete *Pnin*. Inspiration flowed steadily.[47] Because of all his other commitments, he had so far taken a long time to transfer *Pnin* from mind to paper, but after a slow start he would race through the summer of 1955 to complete the book.

A lap ahead, *Lolita* had also been slow to get from typescript to print, but like *Pnin* it rushed toward the finish line through the summer of 1955. By July 12, Nabokov had received the first proofs and was delighted with the speed. Girodias was hurrying to have *Lolita* published by August, since Olympia Press's only active period was the summer, when English and American tourists thronged Paris, eager to buy the hot novelettes unobtainable at home. Uneasy that the book would appear in such company, especially now that he had agreed to publish under his own name, Nabokov asked for review copies for the *Partisan Review*, the *New Yorker*, the *New York Times*, the *Saturday Review*, and the *New York Herald Tribune*. "You and I know," he wrote Girodias, "that *Lolita* is a serious book with a serious purpose. I hope the public will accept it as such. A *succès de scandale* would distress me." He had already asked Girodias to ensure that copyright would be in the author's name. By ignoring that request, Girodias would endanger Nabokov's rights in America and initiate ten years of friction between them.[48]

VII

In mid-July the Nabokovs left their small Stewart Street apartment for 808 Hanshaw Road, yet another cozy little professorial house in Cayuga Heights. Remaining in Ithaca was proving to be a mistake. The heat was intense, the humidity oppressive. Ithaca old-timers rated it the worst summer they had even known.[49]

On July 20, Nabokov delivered a guest lecture at the Russian summer school in Middlebury College, Vermont. On the return journey he and Véra called on the Wilsons for a few hours at Wilson's ancestral upstate New York home, Talcottville. It was their first visit to the famous "Old Stone House." Wilson, slumped in a chair as he drank on the white-pillared porch, warned Nabokov that he must secure copyright for *Lolita*, since two or three American firms made it their business to pirate foreign editions, and *Lolita* would be just the kind of book for them.[50]

The day after his return, Nabokov mailed the *New Yorker* chapter 5 of *Pnin* ("Pnin under the Pines"), his hero's visit to the Russian émigré colony at "Al Cook's" summer home. The magazine rejected the chapter because Nabokov refused to remove references—all historically accurate—to the regime of Lenin and Stalin: "medieval tortures in a Soviet jail," "Bolshevik dictatorship," "hopeless injustice." The next day, he sent off the final galleys of *Lolita*. Suddenly searing pains shot through his back: an acute attack of lumbago, brought on perhaps by the combination of overwork and high humidity. Two days later, when a room became available at the Tompkins County Memorial Hospital, he was rushed there by ambulance. After eight days he was discharged, but despite massage and diathermy treatments the pain lingered for another two weeks.[51]

While confined to bed, as he drifted in and out of a hospital library copy of Hemingway's *Old Man and the Sea*, Nabokov thought out in detail an additional chapter he could insert between chapters 4 and 5 of *Pnin*: "Pnin recovering in the hospital from a sprained back teaches himself to drive a car in bed by studying a 1935 manual of automobilism found in the hospital library and by manipulating the levers of his cot. . . . The chapter ended with Pnin's taking his driver's examination and pedantically arguing with the instructor who has to admit Pnin is right." But he had already written most of the final two chapters, and although "Pnin at the Hospital" remained clear in his mind down to the last curve, the impulse to write it faded over the course of the year.[52]

In the middle of August, before Nabokov's sprained back had fully recovered, Edmund Wilson visited for two days. Apart from Nabokov's anxiety that he might risk dismissal from Cornell for moral turpitude, Wilson had never seen his friend so cheerful. Nabokov showed him his *Eugene Onegin* translation and the already voluminous commentary. Everyone enjoyed the visit, with the help of Wilson's gift of a magnum of Piper-Heidsieck, which they "merrily consumed" on the porch. But Wilson's tone in reporting the trip to a friend two days later shows a strange chilliness toward Nabokov: less friendship than amazed fascination at the opinions of an eccentric he tolerates solely for the stimulus of his shock value.[53]

On August 23, Nabokov sent the *New Yorker* chapter 6 ("Pnin Gives a Party"), and three days later completed the last chapter, "I Knew Pnin."[54] At the end of the month he shipped the book off to Viking with the provisional title *My Poor Pnin*. He had hoped to spend a little time at the seaside—he certainly needed a rest after writing half a novel over the summer—but his lumbago returned. By late September, at Katharine White's suggestion, he had added a final polish to Victor's bowl for "Pnin Gives a Party." Two days after Professor Nabokov's new term had begun, Professor Pnin's story was done.[55]

CHAPTER 13

Pnin

I

O F ALL Nabokov's novels, *Pnin* seems the most amusing, the most poignant, the most straightforward: a portrait of a Russian émigré whose difficulties with English and with America make him a comic legend throughout the campus, somewhere in New York State, where he teaches Russian.[1] But the novel soon poses awkward questions. How can we laugh at another person's misfortunes? How can consciousness and conscience exist in a world rife with pain?

None of Nabokov's works was written as a money-spinner, least of all *Lolita*, the novel that would earn him most. But because he anticipated that *Lolita* might be difficult to publish, he had begun *Pnin* in 1953 in the hope that a series of detachable, story-length chapters might earn him an immediate income as he sold each one to the *New Yorker*. The individual chapters of his autobiography had been enthusiastically received by *New Yorker* readers, and *Pnin* rapidly proved even more popular.

At first a figure of fun, drolly exotic for all his desire to blend in with American ways, Pnin soon becomes an object of pathos as an exile, an ex-husband, a man alone, mocked and misunderstood. Chapter 1, the first of seven, shows Pnin en route from Waindell to Cremona to deliver a guest lecture. From the start of the chapter, as he rocks happily along in the wrong train, blithely unaware of his mistake, we are invited to view him as a comic butt: absurd in appearance (ideally bald, potato nose, massive torso atop spindly legs); constantly at war with objects (alarm clocks, eyeglasses, zippers); grotesquely foiled by the English language; so warily determined to avoid mistakes that he ensures they always occur; vastly amused himself at the minor calamities he brings down on his own head. Everything in the chapter appears to prompt us to laugh at the setback Pnin is about to discover ahead, only to plunge into even more comically proliferating complications once he quits the train.

But only a year before writing this chapter, only a few months before conceiving *Pnin*, Nabokov had reread *Don Quixote* and lectured on Cervantes at Harvard. He had reacted with outrage to *Don Qui-*

xote's cruelty, to the book's implicit invitation to its readers to enjoy Don Quixote's pain and humiliation. *Pnin* is Nabokov's reply to Cervantes. It is no accident that the book's risible name, that "preposterous little explosion," almost spells "pain."

Pnin has become as much a source of mirth on the Waindell campus as the Knight of the Mournful Countenance once was in old Castile. But if the opening of *Pnin* appears to ask us to hoot at the novel's hero, Nabokov suddenly turns the story about. Lurching off the bus, Pnin collapses on a park bench. In a seizure that may just be a heart attack, his mind travels back to a spell of childhood illness in St. Petersburg. Pnin with his seizure and his sudden vision of his childhood, Pnin the object of his mother's love, a half-delirious schoolboy looking anxiously out from his sickbed and trying to discern the pattern of his wallpaper, becomes much too immediate and vivid a person, too real and durable to be reduced to a series of comic pratfalls. He has a complex inner existence Don Quixote is never allowed, and his pain suddenly matters. Mistake-prone Pnin comes to sum up all human mishaps and misfortunes, the strange blend of comedy and tragedy in all human life.

II

Chapter 1 eventually turns out happily for Pnin, but in chapter 2 a still more poignant note sounds. His ex-wife, psychotherapist and émigré poet Liza Wind, comes to visit. Repeatedly unfaithful, she had finally left him in France in 1938 for another psychotherapist, Eric Wind. In April 1940, just as Pnin prepared to escape to America, Liza returned to him, seven months pregnant, declaring she had come back to him for good. Only on the ship across the Atlantic does Pnin discover that Eric Wind is also on board, that Wind has not yet been able to obtain a divorce from his first wife, and that Liza has rejoined Pnin only for the sake of quick entry into America. Now in 1952, with no illusions about Liza's character but unable to alter his staunchly devoted love, Pnin thrills with joy at the prospect of her visit. But she comes to inform him only that since her second marriage is also headed for the rocks, she wants his financial help in putting her son through boarding school.

Of course he will oblige. He sees her off, and walks back through the park, filled with longing "to hold her, to keep her—just as she was—with her cruelty, with her vulgarity, with her blinding blue eyes." Although his mind knows Liza to be selfish, cruel, intellectually and spiritually false, his heart has never been able to resist her.

Nabokov has refined almost beyond recognition the coarse joke of Don Quixote's devoted love for the slatternly peasant he sees as his Dulcinea. But the dignity of Pnin's devotion and the tragedy of his solitude remain inseparable from his apparent absurdity: "I haf nofing," he wails at the end of the chapter, "I haf nofing left, nofing, nofing!"

As he colors in Pnin's past, Nabokov also outlines his present. *Pnin* offers us as accurate and memorable a picture of academic America as *Lolita*'s Lawn Street and its whirlwind of motels provide of America at home and on the move: "The 1954 Fall Term had begun. Again the marble neck of a homely Venus in the vestibule of Humanities Hall received the vermilion imprint, in applied lipstick, of a mimicked kiss. Again the *Waindell Recorder* discussed the Parking Problem. Again in the margins of library books earnest freshmen inscribed such helpful glosses as 'Description of nature,' or 'Irony.' " Nabokov had little contact with his students, and Pnin, the sole appointment in Russian within a precarious adjunct to the German department, has almost no one to teach. But Nabokov etches every other aspect of American academic life with the same mixture of affection and acid he employed in *Lolita*: the rhythm of the school year; the layout of the campus; the guest lecture; the faculty lunch; the rivalries and intrigue and gossip; the farce, as he saw it, of linguistics, psychology, and the social sciences; academic social life as a blend of essential isolation and repetitious conviviality.

Chapter 4 focuses on Liza and Eric Wind's son, Victor, fourteen years old and an artistic genius from very early childhood. Nabokov not only convinces us of Victor's painterly gift—and makes us wish there had been just such an artist—he also makes Victor's happy divergence from every norm a pretext for continuing the attack he has already launched on the Winds' psychoanalysis: "To the Winds, Victor was a problem child insofar as he refused to be one."

Pnin invites Victor to visit. Because Victor is the son of the woman Pnin loves, because he is the son Pnin never had—as he set off across the Atlantic with eight-months-pregnant Liza, Pnin had been filled with excitement at the prospect of the baby's first cry—and simply because he is so unselfish by nature, Pnin is eager to meet the little boy. He buys him a soccer ball and a Jack London novel. But Victor turns out to be nearly six feet tall and surprisingly mature, and Pnin's nervous dinnertime chatter about sports—boxing in Lermontov, tennis in Tolstoy, croquet and *gorodki* in his own Russian childhood—comes to a dismayed halt when Victor declares he has no interest whatever in games. Returning to his lodgings, Pnin rushes upstairs ahead of Victor to throw out into the wet night the ball he has bought for the boy. The last section of the chapter opens on a plangent note as the ball rolls down the lawn and is swept into a rain-swollen brook. Another fervent hope dashed, another humiliating defeat for Pnin.

Except that the chapter then grades into a triumph for Pnin that only we readers can see. Chapter 4 opened with Victor's dream of the king, his father, about to flee his revolution-torn land, pacing a beach as he waits for a motorboat to whisk him away. Victor's dream-father has nothing to do with Eric Wind, "a cranky refugee doctor" he had never much liked. On the other hand, since everything his mother alludes to "invariably took on a veneer of mystery and glamour, the figure of the great Timofey Pnin, scholar and gentleman, teaching a practically dead language at the famous Waindell College . . . acquired in Victor's hospitable mind a curious charm, a family resemblance to those Bulgarian kings or Mediterranean princes who used to be world-famous experts in butterflies or sea shells." At the end of the chapter Pnin's meeting with Victor seems an abject failure, an awkward encounter of two complete strangers with no chance of rapport. They retire to bed. Pnin—to whom Victor has of course told nothing of his recurrent dream—begins to dream of himself "fantastically cloaked, fleeing through great pools of ink under a cloud-barred moon from a chimerical palace, and then pacing a desolate strand . . . as [he] waited for some mysterious deliverance to arrive in a throbbing boat from beyond the hopeless sea."* Somehow, the twinned dreams seem to cast Pnin in the role of Victor's spiritual father.** Unobservant and inflexible, Pnin is anything but an artist himself, but as a later chapter shows, Victor intuits behind Pnin's awkwardness of manner a precious nobility of spirit.

Nabokov wrote *Pnin* not only after rereading *Don Quixote*, but after writing *Lolita*. From the first he designed Pnin as a contrast to Humbert. Humbert, a foreigner easily accepted in America, thanks to his good looks and his suave English, conceals a rotten heart beneath his reputation as a scholar and a gentleman. Pnin's noble, generous heart, on the other hand, beats within the body of a clown whose

* Nabokov commented in an interview that "the boy at St. Mark's [a slip for St. Bartholomew's, and further confirmation that the fictional school is closely based on Dmitri's St. Mark's] and Pnin both dream of a passage from my drafts of *Pale Fire*— . . . that is telepathy for you!" (*Strong Opinions*, 84). Nabokov did not think up *Pale Fire* until two years after writing this chapter of *Pnin*, and did not begin writing the novel for another three years after that.

** Like the *Don Quixote* themes, the twinned dreams arose from Nabokov's class on the novel, where he invariably stressed the twinned dreams of Anna and Vronsky and of Stephen and Bloom.

Nabokov on the rim of the Grand Canyon with Dorothy Leuthold, June 1941. To improve her Russian and try out her first car, Dorothy Leuthold offered to drive Nabokov and his family out to Stanford. En route, in the Grand Canyon, Nabokov discovered his first new species of American butterfly, which he named *Neonympha dorothea* in her honor.

Nabokov at Wellesley college, February 1942. He would continue to smoke heavily for another three years. (*Wellesley College Archives; photo by Sally Collie-Smith.*)

Nabokov with eight-year-old Dmitri, at the Karpovich farm, West Wardsboro, Vermont, summer 1942. He and his family had also spent the summer of 1940, their first in America, with the Karpoviches.

Right: Nabokov on his lecture tour, October 1942, showing a tray of mounted butterflies to President Frank Reade of Georgia State College for Women, Valdosta. Reade rates a mention by name in *Pnin*.

Below: Edmund Wilson and Mary McCarthy, 1941–1942. *(Sylvia Salmi.)*

Vladimir, Dmitri, and Véra Nabokov, Salt Lake City, summer 1943. They spent the summer at New Directions publisher James Laughlin's Alta Lodge, Sandy, Utah.

8 Craigie Circle, Cambridge, Massachussetts, where the Nabokovs lived from 1942 to 1948. Nabokov uses the view from the third-floor windows (the central row in this picture) at the beginning of *Bend Sinister*.

Nabokov with Dmitri outside 8 Craigie Circle, late 1942.

Nabokov with Véra in the park at the end of Craigie Circle, 1942.

Nabokov with Russian language class at Wellesley, 1944.

Nabokov at his regular perch in Harvard's Museum of Comparative Zoology, 1947. Since stopping smoking in the summer of 1945, he had put on weight. *(Robert Kelly,* Life Magazine © *Time Warner Inc.)*

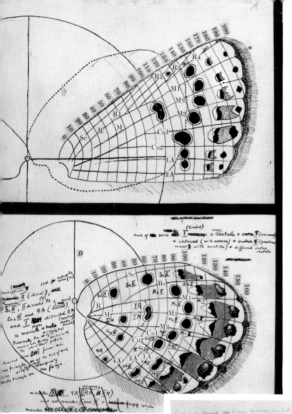

Right: A plate from Nabokov's lepidopterological magnum opus, researched and written between 1944 and 1948 and published in 1949. In this paper restructured the classification of the complex North American genus *Lycaeides*. The photograph resembles the layout of the museum trays Nabokov sorted for the Museum of Comparative Zoology in the early 1940s, and anticipates the design he wanted for his uncompleted *Butterflies of Europe* in the early 1960s.

Three of Nabokov's detailed diagrams of the pattern of a butterfly wing. His study of the evolution of wing markings in the Lycaenidae was one of a series of major papers on that family that he worked on between 1944 and 1948.

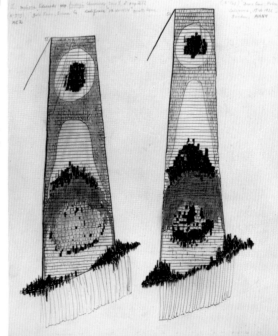

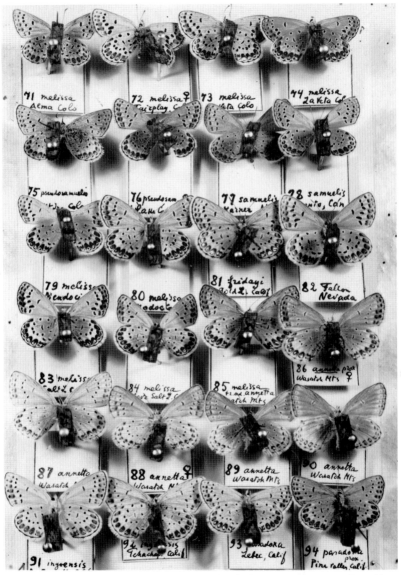

(continued from previous page) Numbers 75 and 76 belong to a subspecies, *Lycaeides melissa pseudosamuelis*, newly defined by Nabokov in this article. Numbers 77 and 78 represent a subspecies, *Lytcaeides melissa samuelis*, that he had defined in 1944, had tried to capture in New Hampshire in 1946, but did not catch until 1950 near Karner, New York (this is the butterfly that flits into *Pnin*). Numbers 85–90 are specimens Nabokov himself caught near Alta, Utah, in 1943, of two different species (*melisssa* and *annetta*) whose intergrading he could show by these closely matched series.

Nabokov teaching at Wellesley in his Russian literature in translation course, early 1948. (*Wellesley College Archives; photo by MacLaurin.*)

Morris Bishop, who invited Nabokov to Cornell and became his best friend there. (*Alison Jolly.*)

Manuscript of the first page of *Conclusive Evidence*, later renamed *Speak, Memory*. From the 1960s, *Speak, Memory* has often been mened by anthologists for examples of English prose at its best. The manuscript of the book's opening shows how difficult such prose can be to compose. It took at least five tries to find the first few words of the opening sentence: "The cradle rocks above an abyss, and commonsense tells us that out existence is but a brief crack of light between two eternities of darkness." *(Library of Congress collection; photo by Christopher Sykes.)*

Nabokov and Véra outside 802 East Seneca Street, Ithaca, where much of *Lolita* was written.

Above and next page: Nabokov's index-card notes used in preparing *Lolita*: statistics on the height, weight, and age of young girls; details culled from a gun catalogue for Humbert's murder weapon, Chum; and some juke-box tunes. Nabokov composed *Lolita* in pencil and on index cards, a method he would later adopt for all his later novels. However, he destroyed the manuscript of *Lolita* itself, preserving only a hundred of the cards containing his preparatory jottings. *(Library of Congress collection; photos by Christopher Sykes.)*

I went over to ...
to ...
you ...

A History of the Colt Revolver
by Charles T. Haven
and Frank A. Belden
1940   N.Y.   (Turn)

Colt catalogue for 1940

    Colt automatic pistol   pocket model
Calibers .32 - for the .32 automatic cartridge
    Capacity of magazine. Cal. 32. 8 cartridges
    Length of arm all 6 ¾ inches   Stocks: checked
Walnut.   Finish : Full Blued
                              [indicating graphically
                               in these drawings]
with the
Slide Lock in safety position
    ⟶ (drawing of pointing hand) ⟶
The automatic may be carried left cocked with [

Wall-o-matic   (5¢)   Left

    You SammyKaye
    Maybe, Como + Fisher   ↖ The gorgeous
    Wishin' Russ Morgan
    Walkin' to Missouri S. Kaye
    God's Little candles Red Fo
    Botch a Me   Rosemary Clooney
    Pretty Boy Jo Stafford
    Forgive me Peggy Lee
    A Full Time Job Eddy Arnold
    Here in my Heart Tony Benne

    You may be the Sweetheart
                          Ink Spots
    Sleepin Tony Bennett [Two
                              (Turn)

---

ready for instant ...
that danger of accidental cocking.   ...

    A light weight arm, compact in design, smooth
and flat, powerful and accurate
    This model is particularly well adapted for use
in the home and car, as well as on the
person [!]   A significant point
in its construction is the solid breech.

    (diagrams)
Rear sight   front sight   smokeless
                                          powder

    magazine spring   magazine
                           with cartridge
                    8 cart. / home   push the magazine well
                                     into the butt
                                     press home

In writing *Lolita*, Nabokov not only composed on index cards but often did so while seated in the family car during his summer butterfly trips. He staged this reconstruction for *Life* magazine in September 1958, as *Lolita* headed to the top of the American best-seller list. *(Carl Mydans,* Life Magazine © *1959 Time Warner Inc.)*

Nabokov's diary for September 16–19, 1954. Note under September 18, the date he had planned to return from his summer, his memo about the whereabouts of the manuscript of *Lolita*. At this stage he still planned to publish the book pseudonymously and was apprehensive that someone might find it.

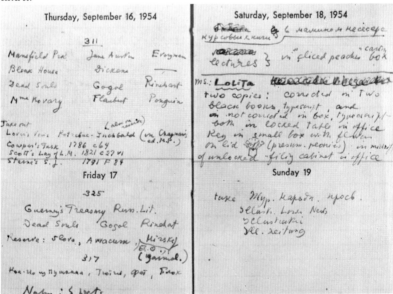

Nabokov, late 1957. This and the next two photographs were taken just after Nabokov's nomination for a National Book Award for *Pnin*, the book he is holding in his lap. *(The Department of Manuscripts and University Archives, Cornell University Library.)*

Véra and Vladimir at 880 Highland Road, Cayuga Heights, the home of Lauriston and Ruth Sharp, 1957. Waxwings often flew into the plate-glass window behind the Nabokovs in this, their favorite Ithaca home. The house and the surrounding garden supplied many other images for *Pale Fire*, an early version of which was taking shape in Nabokov's mind this year, but Bandit, the cat lying to his right in this photograph, fared better at Nabokov's hands than Judge Goldsworth's poor pet at Kinbote's. *(The Department of Manuscripts and University Archives, Cornell University Library.)*

Right: Nabokov at work on his monumental translation of and commentary on Pushkin's *Eugene Onegin*, in Professor Sharp's study, 1957. In the foreground lie three of the eleven fat folders of Nabokov's typescript. (*The Department of Manuscripts and University Archives, Cornell University Library.*)

Left: Advertisement for *Lolita*, *New York Times Book Review*, August 24, 1958.

Right: Nabokov's last lecture at Cornell, January 1959. *Lolita* had by now earned enough to enable him to retire. (Veckojournalen.)

Véra, in London for the launch of the British *Lolita*, 1959. *(Colin Sherborne.)*

The Nabokovs smile for the paparazzi in Milan, November 1959. *(News Blitz, Milan.)*

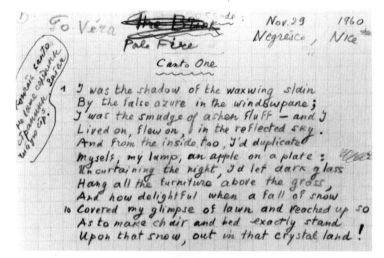

An index card from the manuscript of *Pale Fire* showing the beginning of John Shade's poem "Pale Fire". According to Shade's neighbour Kinbote, Shade composed his poem on index cards, and dated each one. In the real world, Nabokov too – uncharacteristically dated all the index cards for *Pale Fire*, poem and commentary. Note the first title, crossed out; the marginalia in Russian at top left, typing instructions for Véra; and the tidiness that indicates this card is a fair copy. Other cards swarm with erasures, deletions and insertions. *(Library of Congress collection; photo by Christopher Sykes)*

Nabokov with his brother Kirill and his sister Elena on the Promenade des Anglais, Nice, December 1960.

every phrase in English is an unwitting joke. Humbert marries Charlotte Haze for his own sordid ends. Pnin marries Liza only to become the pawn in her callous games. And where Humbert abuses his role as Lolita's stepfather, Pnin's relation to a son not his own will be the purest and most touching triumph in his story. The gifts Humbert buys Lolita are mere bait for his trap. The gifts Pnin buys Victor seem emblems of the hopelessness of his desire to win the boy's heart, but the magnificent bowl Victor later sends Pnin—can one imagine Lolita ever wanting to offer Humbert a gift?—seems nothing less than Victor's tribute to a man he could have been proud to call his father.

By the beginning of chapter 5, Pnin has just learned to drive. We watch him utterly lost on his way to the summer home of an émigré friend who every second year assembles around him a colony of Russian intellectuals. Behind the wheel Pnin once again seems almost an idiot, but when he finally reaches his Russian friends, everything changes. Among those who share his background, his precise knowledge of Russian culture—Nabokov passed on to Pnin his own recent, still unpublished discoveries about *Anna Karenin*—suddenly seems of the highest value. His language becomes graceful, dignified, and witty, and the pedantry he shares here with his peers no longer seems misplaced fussiness but rather the index of a well-stocked mind with a passion for accuracy. Even as a sportsman he unexpectedly excels on the croquet lawn familiar to him from youth. And in his heartrending recollection of an old sweetheart, Mira Belochkin, incinerated at Buchenwald, he throbs with all the agony of the purest compassion.

Pnin in a sense represents the best of the Russian emigration. From time to time throughout the book Nabokov pays tribute to the writers and scholars and the courageous liberal and socialist-revolutionary democrats who formed the emigration's core, the sum of its cultural significance, and he eloquently distinguishes them from the cheap popular picture, jewels and generals, balalaikas and borsch, just as he insists on Pnin's essential dignity and nobility despite the easy travesties of his alien ways.

Pnin's American exile has meant a series of rented rooms in other people's homes. In chapter 6, an exile still, he swells with pride when he rents his first whole house, and decides to throw a "house-heating" party. But he lacks security of tenure, and he does not yet know what we have just learned: that his position is about to vanish when his protector Dr. Hagen leaves Waindell for a better post elsewhere. All the time Pnin basks in his pride as host, we remain aware that disaster looms. At the end of the cozy evening, when he overhears that Pnin hopes to see someone about buying the house, Hagen decides he must break the sad news: Pnin will have to leave Waindell and face a future more homeless than ever.

At the party, Pnin has served up punch in a resplendent glass bowl Victor had sent him. Though deeply touched by Victor's kind gesture, unworldly Pnin does not guess until his guests exclaim over it with delight that the bowl is a precious rarity that must have cost Victor over a hundred dollars of his holiday earnings. After Hagen's news, Pnin washes the dishes from the party. As the great bowl soaks in the foaming suds, Pnin's clumsy hands drop a nutcracker, and he hears the muffled tinkle of shattered glass. Overcome with despair, he hurls the dish towel into a corner and stares out at the blackness beyond his open back door. His eyes film over with tears. Bracing himself, he returns to the sink, dips his hand into the foam, and cuts himself on a jagger of glass. "Gently he removed a broken goblet. The beautiful bowl was intact." Victor's tribute will be the one victory that nothing can destroy.

III

Chapter 7 closes the novel and suddenly opens it up. Only now does the story's hitherto virtually faceless narrator come to life as a distinct individual, someone who turns out to have first met Pnin when they were both boys in Russia. To judge by every detail he divulges—his family had lived on the Morskaya, he became a lepidopterist in his youth, his first names are Vladimir Vladimirovich, he is now a prominent Anglo-Russian novelist and an American academic—he is none other than Vladimir Nabokov.

This Vladimir Nabokov had an affair with Liza Bogolepov just before she married Pnin. In fact, after he simultaneously wooed her and told her that the Akhmatovesque poetry she wrote was utter rubbish, she reacted by attempting suicide.* Pnin meanwhile had written her a marriage proposal, and friends fearing for her stability advised her to accept it. She showed the letter to Nabokov: "This is an offer of marriage that I have received. I shall wait till midnight. If I don't hear from you, I shall accept it." And it is none other than Vladimir Nabokov who has now been invited to take up a new post in Waindell's English Department at the very time Pnin must leave Waindell. He offers Pnin the chance to remain in a Russian division he will set up, but Pnin cannot accept.

* When Akhmatova read *Pnin* she was deeply offended by Nabokov's clever parodies of her early style (Lydia Chukovsky, *Zapiski ob Anne Akhmatovoy* [Paris: 1980], 2:383).

In *Bend Sinister*, his previous third-person novel, Nabokov had played the part of an anthropomorphic deity: Vladimir Nabokov, eager to catch a moth he hears pinging against his window screen as he sits in his study one warm, wet night writing the novel's last lines, is the god controlling Krug's whole world. In *Pnin*, Nabokov enlists his own image again to opposite effect: the Vladimir Nabokov who has actually invented Pnin and his surroundings now seems merely a character on Pnin's level, recording the life of someone whose path happens to have crossed his own again and again.

Krug lives within an invented country, a nightmare reflection of the real world. Pnin's world, on the other hand, seems comfortingly familiar, and Nabokov first invites us to join the coziness by laughing at Pnin's expense. Within the familiar world of Russian émigrés in academic America, Nabokov himself was a recognizable landmark, yet when he introduces himself as Pnin's friend, everything in the story starts to subside and tilt, as a house built on permafrost turns its foundation to a bog by its own inner heat.

Aristocratic, poised, successful in love and work, narrator Nabokov could not be less like poor awkward Pnin. Where Pnin bungles elementary English, Nabokov proves a marvelous stylist in his adopted language. But he lacks Pnin's moral fineness. Defensive of his own privacy, he passes quickly over his embarrassing role in Liza's attempted suicide, but then publishes in toto Pnin's letter to Liza, violating Pnin's own wistful principle ("Why not leave their private sorrows to people? Is sorrow not, one asks, the only thing in the world people really possess?"), even though the proposal Pnin sets before Liza reveals the poor man at his most vulnerable, a tortoise without his shell of privacy. Aware of his awkwardness and unattractiveness, Pnin confronts these shortcomings squarely in his letter, rising nobly above them to promise Liza "everything I have, to the last blood corpuscle, to the last tear, everything. And believe me, this is more than any genius can offer you because a genius needs to keep so much in store, and thus cannot offer you the whole of himself as I do. I may not achieve happiness, but I know I shall do everything to make you happy."

At the end of the chapter Nabokov arrives at Waindell on the day Pnin is supposed to leave. Although not actually replacing Pnin, although he even offers him a post, Nabokov seems almost to be squeezing him out, and his academic rise contrasts with poor Pnin's decline. Nabokov spends the night at the home of Jack Cockerell, head of the English department and the most indefatigable Pnin mimic on campus. Earlier in the novel Pnin had even overheard

Cockerell's impersonations and almost caught a glimpse of him in midact. Now Cockerell treats Nabokov to an anthology of Pniniana:

> I was tired and not overanxious to be entertained throughout the supper with a floor show, but I must admit that Jack Cockerell impersonated Pnin to perfection. He went on for at least two hours, showing me everything—Pnin teaching, Pnin eating, Pnin ogling a coed, Pnin narrating the epic of the electric fan which he had imprudently set going on a glass shelf right above the bathtub into which its own vibration had almost caused it to fall.

By midnight, the intoxicated Cockerell declares that he is sure Pnin has not yet left town, and suggests they call him up. No one answers, but the phone has not been disconnected. Nabokov feels "foolishly eager to say something friendly to my good Timofey Pahlich, and so after a little while I attempted to reach him too." Pnin answers, trying in vain to disguise his voice before hanging up. Cockerell proposes driving over to Pnin's house and serenading him. But his wife intervenes, "and after an evening that somehow left me with the mental counterpart of a bad taste in the mouth, we all went to bed." The chapter ends with Cockerell announcing at breakfast later that morning: "And now . . . I am going to tell you the story of Pnin rising to address the Cremona Women's Club and discovering he had brought the wrong lecture."

This distasteful sequence confronts us with *our* complicity in treating Pnin as an object of amusement. On the last page of the novel, Pnin leaves Waindell in his absurd little car, with a mangy mongrel he has befriended. He appears admirable in his proud independence, while the suave Nabokov seems a sheepish accomplice in Cockerell's obsessive, mean-spirited mockery. But we in turn are the accomplices of this narrator who from the moment he promised us the story of Pnin's discomfiture en route to Cremona at the beginning of the novel has done nothing but describe Pnin's misadventures.

Nabokov—the author, not the narrator—suggests how far the easy images we make of one another fall short of the truth and become less than human. Unwilling to see beyond Pnin's looks, his clumsiness, his cracked English, most at Waindell College fail to recognize Pnin's high standards and refuse to see that his bizarre idioms may be an index less of innate grotesquerie than of the pain and dislocation of exile. People like Cockerell, or Vladimir Nabokov (the narrator) as he listens to Cockerell, or us as we are made to share in narrator Nabokov's eagerness for Pnin's next comic mishap, become like the cruel duke and duchess ghoulishly feasting on Don Quixote's misfortunes.

To see others as simply figures of fun, as objects of mockery, is for Nabokov a failure of the imagination that can have disastrous consequences. At Pnin's party Dr. Hagen passes on the latest story about the wife of Professor Idelson, not at all unlike the gleefully dismissive anecdotes passed around about the grotesque foreigner Professor Pnin. Laurence Clements refuses to listen to this mildly anti-Semitic story; Pnin waves his hand in disgust at Hagen and says: "I have heard quite the same anecdote thirty-five years ago in Odessa, and even then I could not understand what is comical in it."* At this level the comic stereotyping of another human being and the refusal to consider the vulnerable individual behind the stereotype may seem—to the thoughtless—harmless enough. But at the moral center of the novel stands Mira Belochkin, put to death in Buchenwald simply because she was Jewish and therefore less than human to those who accepted a millennium of derisive dismissals. She comes to represent humanity at its best and most vulnerable when Pnin muses on the confused reports of her last days: "The only certain thing was that being too weak to work (though still smiling, still able to help other Jewish women), she was selected to die and was cremated only a few days after her arrival."

On one level *Pnin* seems a simple character study of an unhappy man whose every move seems to make others laugh. But by the bold surprises of the final chapter Nabokov disrupts the novel to make us conscious of our own reactions to Pnin's plight: our images of others, our laughter at others, our pity for others' pain. *Pnin* concerns itself throughout with the problem of pain. Pnin confides to Hagen his plans to teach a course on the pain in human history: "On Tyranny. On the Boot. On Nicholas the First. On all the precursors of modern atrocity. Hagen, when we speak of injustice, we forget Armenian massacres, tortures which Tibet invented, colonists in Africa. . . . The history of man is the history of pain!"

IV

On one occasion, when the Vladimir Nabokov of the last chapter visits Paris in the 1930s and sits around with others in an émigré apartment, Pnin warns a friend not to believe a word Nabokov says. "He makes up everything. He once invented that we were schoolmates in Russia and cribbed at examinations. He is a dreadful inventor." Cu-

---

* Nabokov noted to Katharine White: "Hagen's story had a faint antisemitic flavor which Pnin, a good Russian liberal, discovered. And the Idelsons had not come because they discovered the Hagens had been invited too."

riously, Pnin here seems to garble the very precise memories Nabokov had once recounted of young Pnin, but Pnin's charge puts the
testimony of both in question. Then, on arriving at Waindell twenty
years later, Nabokov does not meet Pnin at all. Out walking early the
next morning, he sees Pnin driving away from Waindell, heading off
for a new day, a new journey, a new life, as if in escape from someone who has always harassed him by knowing or pretending to
know too much.

Yet Nabokov has seen nothing of Pnin at Waindell. How does he
know of all Pnin's adventures there? Presumably through the testimony of people like Cockerell. But when Nabokov returns to his
host's, Cockerell is about to regale him with the story of Pnin rising
to address the Cremona Women's Club and discovering he had
brought the wrong lecture. That is not the Cremona story we read at
the beginning of the novel. There, Pnin crams all three papers (two
lectures and one student essay) in his pocket to guarantee he will
have the one he wants. The first chapter stops short before Pnin rises
to speak at Cremona, but the narrator makes it plain he would have
preferred to end on a note of doom had it been at all possible. Cockerell's story then must be wrong, but how does the narrator know
what really happened at Cremona?

Much of the Cremona story could perhaps be constructed from
versions of Pnin's amused reports of his own mishaps. But one part
of the story certainly could not be: Pnin's detailed thoughts during
his seizure.

The report of the onset of Pnin's seizure begins:

> I do not know if it has ever been noted before that one of the main char
> acteristics of life is discreteness. Unless a film of flesh envelops us, we
> die. Man exists only insofar as he is separated from his surroundings.
> The cranium is a space-traveler's helmet. Stay inside or you perish.
> Death is divestment, death is communion. It may be wonderful to mix
> with the landscape, but to do so is the end of the tender ego.

Discreteness *is* a basic characteristic of life, and the discreteness of
person from person and mind from world forms a major theme in
Pnin. As Nabokov wrote in another context, there is an "unbridgeable division between ego and non-ego."[2] The world to be known remains outside the mind. No wonder then that Pnin or any of us
makes mistakes. Set in an institution dedicated to the pursuit of
truth, the whole novel is about mistakes: the comic mistakes Pnin
repeatedly makes (with a word, a library card, a washing machine, a
train schedule) or the more serious mistakes we make about other
people (the mistakes almost everyone at Waindell makes about Pnin).

Precisely because minds are discrete, Pnin's friend "Vladimir Nabokov" obviously cannot know the detailed vision of Pnin's childhood illness that follows chapter 1's meditation on discreteness. Either we suppose that the narrator simply concocts a few plausible lies about his friend's inner life—but then in this case the true, poignant Pnin, the Pnin who still cares for Liza and recollects Mira and dreams Victor's dream is simply an unwarranted fabrication, and the book ceases to be of interest—or we admit to ourselves that Vladimir Nabokov the narrator and friend of Pnin and lover of Liza is an invention of the real Vladimir Nabokov, who as author has the power to create people from inside and out.

In other words, the *real* Pnin, the poignant inner Pnin, can exist only if we accept the fictionality of the whole story. The novel begins with a thoroughly "real" world and seems to encroach still further on the real when Vladimir Nabokov turns out to be Pnin's friend, but we end up forced to admit that Pnin can exist as a creature whose inner self we can know and value only so long as we recognize that he is invented.

V

In *The Tempest*, Shakespeare hands Prospero his own powers over the world of the play, thereby making his hero thoroughly unreal but at the same time allowing him to embody multiple meanings: erring man, betrayed brother, ousted prince, arch-colonizer, playwright, the personification and pinnacle of human culture, even God Almighty. In *Pnin*, Nabokov works the opposite way, introducing himself as a mere character into a world brimming with familiar reality. Strangely, this too generates level upon level of meaning.

On the first level, Nabokov suggests that in life nothing can overcome our ignorance of another's innermost self. By confronting us with the contrast between the Nabokov on Pnin's own plane and the Nabokov outside this plane who can see every particle of Pnin, he stresses that only if we could step onto another plane of being, only if we could pass beyond that discreteness that defines our mortal condition, could we ever know the rich measure of other lives. But he does not leave it at that.

Chapter 1 invites us to laugh at Pnin's mounting mishaps on his jinxed journey to Cremona: the perfect material for a Cockerell anecdote. Then suddenly we peer into the recesses of Pnin's soul in a way Cockerell or narrator Nabokov could never know, and for the first time we must face the reality of Pnin's pain. In the midst of his seizure, Pnin recalls a childhood illness, the chill in his ribs, the stinging of his eyelids, and his feverish mind trying desperately to unravel two riddles. What is the object that that squirrel on the screen in his bedroom holds in its front paws? A nut? A pinecone?

> He set himself to solve this dreary riddle, but the fever that hummed in his head drowned every effort in pain and panic. Still more oppressive was his tussle with the [pattern on the] wallpaper. . . . It stood to reason that if the evil designer—the destroyer of minds, the friend of fever—had concealed the pattern with such monstrous care, that key must be as precious as life itself and, when found, would regain for Timofey Pnin his everyday health, his everyday world.

Pnin feels he must unravel the pattern. So should we, for as many readers have noted, a pattern of squirrels runs throughout the novel.[3]

As his seizure took him back to his past, Pnin recalled Dr. Yakov Belochkin, the pediatrician who treated him for his childhood fever. Belochkin is the father of Mira Belochkin, the sweetheart of Pnin's youth and the woman whose death in Buchenwald poses more urgently than anything else in the book the question whether ours is a world of pointless pain. It can be no accident that the name "Belochkin" derives from the Russian *belochka*, a diminutive of *belka*, a squirrel.

The squirrel pattern that recurs in every chapter of *Pnin* seems to intimate a number of possible metaphysical answers to the problem of human pain: a patterner of human lives, a designer of fate, who apportions pain with the utmost compassion and concern; a reprieve from present anguish as death allows one to step from the prison of time into the free world of timelessness; or a tender interest in particular mortal lives on the part of those who once cared for them when they too were mortal.

In his fever, Pnin could not discover what that squirrel held in its paws. But now, as the pain of his seizure slackens its grip, he finds himself on a park bench in Whitchurch: "A gray squirrel sitting in comfortable haunches on the ground before him was sampling a peach stone." Suddenly it seems as if his riddle has been answered, and over the course of the next few lines, Pnin recovers, heads back through the town to the railroad station, retrieves his bag, and finds at once a way to reach Cremona and his lecture on time after all.

In this first chapter, life has piled misfortune after misfortune on Pnin as if there *were* some evil designer of the sort Pnin sensed in his childhood delirium. Then, as if by magic, the apparently insurmountable obstacles separating him from Cremona are suddenly withdrawn. Nabokov the narrator grumbles, "Harm is the norm. Doom should not jam." Behind him, however, some other force seems to arrange a kindlier disposition of fate, and incorporates the squirrel and its peach stone in refutation of the idea of an evil designer or a pointless pain.

Now that the panic and the pain are over, in fact, it appears as if Nabokov has designed Pnin's seizure to revive in Pnin that rich recollection of his past, that generous measure of his having lived through so much, and to awaken our sense of the poignant reality of Pnin's inner self. Pnin's pain here is not part of some wantonly malevolent design but a means of extracting the treasures of the character's private past and our present pity. Perhaps there may be some force beyond mortal lives with an ultimately kindly purpose behind what can seem the willfully imposed vexations of an individual life or even the long history of human suffering, a force that aims to impose the shadow of unhappiness only to light up pity and tenderness at some other level of existence.

In chapter 4, still supposing that Victor will be at the age where he would enjoy an animal picture postcard series, Pnin sends him a card depicting a gray squirrel. Two chapters later we discover that Victor, in return for Pnin's kindnesses, has sent him the celebrated glass bowl. A guest at Pnin's party comments that "when she was a child, she imagined Cinderella's glass shoes to be of exactly that greenish blue tint." In reply to his guest, pedantic Pnin points out that in the first versions of the story Cinderella's shoes were not originally made of glass "but of Russian squirrel fur—*vair*, in French," later corrupted to *verre*. Not for nothing does Nabokov point out that below his topheavy torso Pnin dwindles down to curiously feminine feet: he turns out to be a Cinderella of sorts, apparently spurned by fortune but eventually reaping that deserved token of Victor's allegiance, a glass bowl of Cinderella tints* in place of the fairy-tale slippers. Through Pnin's scholarly gloss, the squirrel pattern returns in its most unexpected and most triumphant guise.

During the childhood illness recalled in chapter 1, Pnin had been in the grip of pain. Now the distance of time has banished the pain but preserved intact the intensity and even the charm of those hours in the sickbed. Setback after setback lies in wait for Pnin on the way

* Among the many exhilarating things Victor learns from his admired art teacher, Lake, is "that the order of the solar spectrum is not a closed circle but a spiral of tints from cadmium red and oranges through a strontian yellow and a pale paradisal green to cobalt blues and violets, at which point the sequence does not grade into red again but passes into another spiral, which starts with a kind of lavender gray and goes on to Cinderella shades transcending human perception."

to Cremona, until an attack that seems to threaten his very life revives those earlier memories. Once the danger passes, once time has anesthetized these moments, the afternoon's strange twists and turns will soon form another of Pnin's own comic anecdotes that he can barely retell for laughter: the passage of time, the ability to stand outside one's past, can turn even pain into pleasure. Perhaps after death the whole of life can be resavored in a similar way, as Pnin's anguish can now turn into tenderness and delight.

In chapter 3, Pnin passes a statue some pranksters have defaced. "Huliganï" (hooligans), he fumes. A moment later a skimpy squirrel dashes over the snow "where a tree trunk's shadow, olive-green on the turf, became grayish blue for a stretch, while the tree itself, with a brisk, scrabbly sound, ascended, naked, into the sky. . . . The squirrel, invisible now in a crotch, chattered, scolding the delinquents who would put him out of his tree." All day Pnin's thoughts have echoed Pushkin's fears of death. Will death come to him "*V boyu li, v stranstvii, v volnah*? In fight, in travel, or in waves? Or on the Waindell campus?" That squirrel seems some sort of answer. Three pages later, Pnin almost becomes a squirrel himself: it is a treat in the library to see him "pull out a catalogue drawer from the comprehensive bosom of a card cabinet and take it, like a big nut, to a secluded corner and there make a quiet mental meal of it, now moving his lips in soundless comment." And on the same page as the squirrel, Pnin fumes at "huliganï," in pointed parallel to the squirrel "scolding delinquents." Why the connection? Surely because Nabokov sends the squirrel up a tree that itself bewilderingly "ascended, naked into the sky." When Katharine White queried that expression, Nabokov refused to rephrase it.[4] Pnin need not fear the death that has been on his mind all day, the squirrel in that tree seems to imply: for him death will involve some kind of ascent.*

In chapter 2, Pnin agrees to Liza's unexpected request that he contribute to Victor's schooling. Walking back from the bus station, he wishes he could keep her, with her cruelty, her vulgarity, "with her impure, dry, sordid, infantile soul. All of a sudden he thought: If people are reunited in Heaven (I don't believe it, but suppose), then how shall I stop it from creeping upon me, over me, that shriveled, helpless, lame thing, her soul?" Just at this moment a squirrel encounters Pnin on the path, climbs up to the brink of a drinking fountain, and thrusts its face toward him, cheeks puffed out. Pnin under-

---

* In his poem "The Ballad of Longwood Glen," written in the month he began *Pnin*, Nabokov has his hero Art Longwood climb a tree, never to be sighted again by mortal eyes, which cannot make out "the delirious celestial crowds" that "greet the hero from earth in the snow of the clouds."

stands, and after some fumbling presses the lever the right way. Eyeing him with contempt, the squirrel drinks deeply and departs without the least sign of thanks. In its greed and ingratitude it seems an image of Liza herself and a reply to Pnin's meditation. No, he need not fear Liza's soul will ever linger and cling: when it has what it wants, the squirrel leaves him, just as Liza's soul will. She could not encumber him in heaven. As spiritless and selfish as the squirrel, she has no more chance of reaching there than that little animal.

But perhaps, that uncannily prompt squirrel implies, Pnin's supposition that people may be reunited in heaven has more to it than he thinks: *something* seems to be watching over the private ruminations of his soul.

Chapter 5 opens in a strange fashion. Pnin, lost on his way to his Russian friend's summer house, is observed as if from high above, from a tower on Mount Ettrick, by "the adventurous summer tourist (Miranda or Mary, Tom or Jim, whose penciled names were almost obliterated on the balustrade)," or again by "Mary or Almira, or, for that matter, Wolfgang von Goethe, whose name had been carved in the balustrade by some old-fashioned wag." There is actually no one on the tower, but Nabokov continues to imagine a "sympathetic soul," a "compassionate eye" observing Pnin lost below. The only living thing on the tower in fact is an ant on the balustrade, lost, bothered, and baffled "much in the same way as that preposterous toy car progressing below." A squirrel is suddenly shot at in the trees but escapes unharmed. "Another minute passed, and then everything happened at once: the ant found an upright beam leading to the roof of the tower and started to ascend it with renewed zest; the sun appeared; and Pnin at the height of hopelessness, found himself on a paved road with a rusty but still glistening sign directing wayfarers 'To The Pines.' " When Pnin reaches the Pines, he meets a friend of Mira Belochkin's and in the midst of another seizure sinks into his agonizing reverie about Mira and her death. As he emerges from his reverie, he walks "under the solemn pines. The sky was dying. He did not believe in an autocratic God. He did believe, dimly, in a democracy of ghosts. The souls of the dead, perhaps, formed committees, and these, in continuous session, attended to the destinies of the quick."

The pointedly disguised repetition of "mira" ("Miranda or Mary . . . Mary or Almira")⁵ in the names of the imagined observers looking down on lost Pnin, and the squirrel (*belka*) whose escape from death seems to trigger Pnin's long-delayed discovery of the right route—an echo of the squirrel that marked Pnin's finding a way to reach Cremona after all—now take on an eerie suggestiveness. Pnin's moment of despair that "no conscience, and hence no consciousness, could be expected to subsist in a world where such things as Mira's death were possible" seems to have been answered. Someone seems to watch over Pnin and his pain—someone, perhaps, it might not be wrong to think is Mira Belochkin herself.

Our first glimpse into Pnin's inner recesses occurred during his seizure, when he recollected Dr. Belochkin's visit to his feverish young self and his attempt to make out what the squirrel on the screen concealed in its paws. Now in chapter 7, Vladimir Nabokov's first glimpse of Pnin ends the series of squirrels. Once again, pain initiates the pattern: young Vladimir suffers agony in one eyeball when a speck lodges inextricably under one eyelid; he visits Dr. Pavel Pnin, Timofey's father; he glimpses Timofey himself and notices, among other objects in the Pnin children's schoolroom, a stuffed squirrel.

Later in the chapter, Nabokov's scorn and dismissal drive Liza to attempt suicide. To anchor her drifting future she decides to marry Pnin, but in a last attempt to arouse Nabokov's jealousy she gives him Pnin's proposal and then, after her marriage, tells Pnin what she has done. Pnin knows that Nabokov in reading that letter has glimpsed far deeper into his heart than he would ever have wished another man to see. When he meets his rival later, he angrily denies his own misconstrued version of Nabokov's recollections of him as a child, as if to discredit anything else Nabokov may say about him. Again and again throughout the novel's last chapter, Nabokov the narrator's glimpses of Pnin—in childhood, in Pnin's letter to Liza, in the course of his inebriated evening with Cockerell—seem to cause Pnin pain. He shows Pnin no deliberate malice, but his own recurrent good fortune seems a pointed, almost deliberate contrast that makes Pnin's unhappiness all the more bitter. At the same time Pnin fears that Nabokov will take unscrupulous advantage—as indeed he does—of the brief glimpse Pnin's proposal to Liza allowed of his inner self. Nabokov knows just enough of Pnin to be able to pad out the story with more: not enough to record the truth of Pnin's life, but enough to make of him a stuffed squirrel, a lifeless substitute that as raconteur he can set out on display.

So after suggestions of Mira Belochkin's kindly eye watching from beyond death, or the kindly designer of the squirrel pattern in Pnin's fate, we return once again to the disconcerting conclusion of the final chapter. On this more human level Nabokov sets all of Pnin's life available to him as author against the little that Nabokov the narrator can see, to stress that *in this life* none of us can know directly another's pain. But if we cannot *know* the pain our actions cause others, we can and should try to imagine it. Only through the imagination can we mortals act with sufficient thought for another's pain, and on this level of our real lives even a novelist's or a novel-reader's imagination—this novelist, Vladimir Nabokov, this reader, you or I—will often fall short.

CHAPTER 14

Lolita Sparks: Cornell, 1955–1957

My poor Lolita is having a rough time. The pity is that if I had made

her a boy, or a cow, or a bicycle, Philistines might never have

flinched.

—Nabokov to Graham Greene, 1956

I

A LAUGHINGSTOCK to his colleagues, Pnin leaves Waindell as the suave and successful Nabokov arrives to take up a post. By the early 1950s the real-life Nabokov was indeed a local success as a *New Yorker* writer and a lecturer. But although he had the completed manuscript of *Lolita* beside him as he wrote *Pnin*, he could not foresee that as the decade wore on his fame would spread not only on campus but across the country and around the world, until by 1959, within a few months of publishing *Lolita* in America, he could leave Cornell on his own terms.

Much of Pnin's character we see in terms of the reactions of his colleagues. How was Pnin's creator seen by *his* colleagues when he was simply a respected writer and not yet a celebrity? Was he in any sense a Pnin? Or was there someone else on campus who filled the role better?

Many have identified Marc Szeftel, a Russian émigré and a Cornell professor of Russian history, as Nabokov's model for Pnin. Some even reproach Nabokov for cruelly mocking Szeftel in the person of Pnin. Since Nabokov considered Pnin "an attractive and admirable person," far superior intellectually and morally to those who mock him, the reproach seems strangely misplaced.[1] But did he draw a portrait of his colleague?

Nabokov admired Szeftel's work with Roman Jakobson in their edition of *La geste d'Igor*, and for that reason had agreed in 1950 to work with them on an English edition of Russia's greatest medieval poem.[2] In Ithaca, Nabokov saw Szeftel both professionally, at staff seminars for those involved in Russian area studies (history, economics, politics, literature, and so on), and socially. But he always denied that Szeftel was his model.

As a lecturer Szeftel was chaotic, and his thick accent made him difficult to understand. Twenty years after the event Alfred Appel told Nabokov how he and other students called one another just before their Russian history exam in an attempt to decipher their notes. Everyone had the phrase "the bloody purchases," but no one could make sense of it, until in the exam a question asked about the Blood Purges. As he so often did, Nabokov laughed at the story until tears streamed down his face—a Pninian trait in himself—but then he mused with warm appreciation: "What an innocent man." Nabokov remembered one Pninian moment: Szeftel standing with him in an elevator at Cornell and saying casually, with a sigh, as if he had forgotten that Nabokov was the author of the book: "We are all Pnins!"[3]

Nabokov had had his own mishaps on lecture tours, and frequent nightmares about teaching: losing his lecture notes, having a heart attack in class.[4] As an émigré, a teacher of Russian, a professor at Stanford, Wellesley, Cornell, and Harvard, and a widely traveled guest lecturer, he knew scores of Russians in academic America. He had caught a long series of specimens in the fine net of his observation before publishing his original description of the species, Russian émigré professor, and naming Pnin as type specimen. He had no need of a single model, but he was delighted to find in a remark like Szeftel's that he had defined the species correctly. He once asked fellow émigré Albert Parry, who taught at nearby Colgate: "Aren't you cross with me for Pnin?" "Me? Why?" "Oh, every Russian in America who teaches anything Russian recognizes himself in Pnin and gets very angry with me." When Parry answered that he saw nothing of himself in Pnin, he thought Nabokov looked quite disappointed.[5]

Unlike Pnin, Nabokov himself inspired neither derision nor commiseration. Where Pnin could often be humorless, Nabokov feasted on the absurdity of the world, and consciously deployed his comic gift as a way both to breach and to maintain his distance from others. In the process, he earned a reputation as a wit and an entertainer.[6] As singular as Pnin, he was rarely alone: with Véra at his side, in the car, in the corridor, in the classroom, he could not have resembled less his poor solitary Pnin. One professor recalled seeing the Nabokovs out shopping, like two lovebirds. Nabokov caught sight of him and became ebulliently jocular about the new possibilities of colored toilet paper: one could do all sorts of things with it, festoons, party hats. . . .[7]

Nabokov disconcerted some by his difference and his evident love of that difference. He was more amused than discomfited to learn there was talk "in the lower depth of the faculty at Cornell of my stressing too much 'structure' and too little 'Ideas.' I shall not change my approach."[8] But although he delighted in upsetting the decorums of academic analysis, although he remained aloof from faculty meetings and the students seated in tiers before him, he struck both colleagues and students as remarkably kind and even deferential on an individual basis. One female student remembers the contrast between Nabokov's thundering in the first class of the year against radios and dormitories and group study—instead of which, he suggested, they should all be locked in individual soundproofed study cells—and the graciousness of the Nabokov welcome when she had to withdraw from his class because of a schedule conflict. Véra invited her into the office, Nabokov asked to take her coat, they made her at home, and then as she left Véra accompanied her down several flights of stairs. "I'd never been treated like that. I was completely nonplussed."[9]

Some days Nabokov would be so abstracted walking along the corridor that Véra would have to draw his attention to people he should greet. On other days he could be alert and buoyant. M. H. Abrams once saw him heading home for the weekend with a stack of books up to his chin: 1820s volumes of the *Edinburgh Review*. "Some wonderful articles there," remarked Abrams. "Articles? I never read the articles! It's the advertisements I look for!" Nabokov replied, eager to glean a few more of the fashions and fads of Pushkin's time.[10]

Ephim Fogel, then a young teacher in Cornell's English department, remembers Nabokov warmly as decent and kind, "the hearty man who would spend time talking to a very junior instructor." Knowing that Nabokov was translating *A Hero of Our Time*, Fogel named his favorite among the novel's detachable stories. Nabokov replied that he thought that story weak, but then deliberately softened the criticism by adding that it had been Chekhov's favorite too. One year Fogel taught Shakespeare in Goldwin Smith B the hour before Nabokov's European novel course. Between two classes, Nabokov observed: "I see you have given them a quiz on *King Lear*. . . . Did you ask them the names of Lear's dogs?" Fogel took a deep breath, then quoted the passage to show that he knew it: "The little dogs and all—Tray, Blanche and Sweetheart—see, they bark at me." Drawing on one of his favorite instances of the follies of translators, Nabokov asked: "You know, in the most frequently read nineteenth-century Russian version of that speech, do you know what it says?" No, Fogel replied. "The hounds are barking at my heels!" Fogel admits that although he thought he knew *King Lear* back to front, he had never considered those three dogs. When he taught Shakespeare in later years he would begin with Nabokov's question, and the irreducible particular choices that make the greatest of all writers so elusive and inexhaustible.[11]

Peter Kahn, a Cornell professor of fine arts, also remembers Nabokov's command of specific detail. Another Cornell professor, from a prominent local family, commissioned a stained glass window in St. John's Episcopal Church in downtown Ithaca. Nabokov approached Kahn, a painter, to design the window. He agreed, but *which* St. John was it? Though profoundly indifferent to Christianity, Nabokov was unfazed, Kahn reports, and

> recited fifty-five sainted Johns, in that sort of order in which he loved to categorize. He told about the main saints, and the minor saints, and the banished saints, and the Popes that were saints, and so on and so on. Actually we had two windows in that little chapel, and there are two major St. Johns. One of them was apparently St. John the Baptist, and the other was St. John the Evangelist. And Nabokov knew all the attributes, and the symbols that are associated with the two saints. I designed the windows, and to my astonishment found that he knew about the technique of stained glass windows.[12]

For most of his time at Cornell, after he was shifted from the Division of Literature to the Department of Romance Languages, Nabokov's closest contacts were with teachers of French literature like Morris Bishop and Jean-Jacques Demorest. Demorest recalls Nabokov coming into his office and proceeding in mock-seriousness to synchronize watches with him. Demorest adds:

> He always managed to pop a question before I opened my mouth. If we were alone, he spoke French. Habitually, the question was loaded and unexpected. . . . He would begin with: "Bonjour, Jean-Jacques. To your knowledge, did Stendhal ever pen a decent sentence?" "Does anyone worth reading in France still believe that fellow Dostoevski could write?" "Do you think your country will ever again beget authors as perfect as Bossuet and Chateaubriand? No? You agree?"[13]

With Victor Lange of the German department—who taught a course in the European novel much less successful than his own—Nabokov's teasing had much more of an edge to it. Nabokov the mystificator enjoyed playing up to his more stolid colleague's bewilderment at him. He would explain, for instance, that he graded his students' first papers of the year very carefully and then collected but never bothered to read any of their later work: the first mark simply became the final grade for the course. "Nobody ever improves. . . . What you are, you remain; what you know, perhaps you retain; but what I tell them now is not likely to increase their qualitative ranking. . . . Nobody has ever challenged me." Decades later, interviewed about his famous colleague, Lange still mistook Nabokov's hoaxes for fact.[14]

II

Nabokov had applied early in 1955 for a full year's sabbatical but was granted leave only for the spring term of 1956. In September 1955 he therefore resumed his courses, but with only a single term of teaching ahead: his masterpieces course as far as Flaubert, his Russian survey course to Gogol, and his Pushkin seminar. By the time he had begun the term and sent off the manuscript of *Pnin*, he had become extremely worried about *Lolita*. He had not received the promised page proofs and had no replies from Girodias to his queries about copyright and about when or even whether the book had been published. At last in October he received the two pale olive-green paperback volumes of *Lolita* in the Olympia Traveller's Companion series. They were attractive and elegant, Nabokov noticed, but swarming with typographical errors and with copyright assigned in Olympia Press's name as well as his own.[15]

By now his *Eugene Onegin* commentaries were beginning to take final form. He still thought the commentary would fill no more than four hundred pages, and hoped to send the completed manuscript to a publisher early in 1956, after two months more research in Harvard's libraries. In October he sent Katharine White his essay on Pushkin's Abyssinian great-grandfather, Abram Gannibal, and a piece on Tatiana's and Onegin's libraries, and continued to work on the commentaries all term with "fantastic concentration." Véra also noted that he was at work on another story, perhaps the first flicker of *Pale Fire*.[16]

In mid-November he spent two days in New York. Although he called on Edmund Wilson and his closest Russian friends, he had taken the midweek trip to see publishers and editors. Pascal Covici of Viking, long an enthusiastic admirer of his work, had to turn down *Pnin* as too short and too much a collection of sketches to succeed as a novel. Nabokov next sent the book to Harper and Brothers. To guard against the misconception that it was a series of mocking vignettes, he stressed its moral point with unusual directness:

> In Pnin, I have created an entirely new character, the like of which has never appeared in any other book. A man of great moral courage, a pure man, a scholar and a staunch friend, serenely wise, faithful to a single

love, he never descends from a high plane of life characterized by authenticity and integrity. But handicapped and hemmed in by his incapability to learn a language, he seems a figure of fun to many an average intellectual, and it takes a Clements or a Joan Clements to break through Pnin's fantastic husk and get at his tender and lovable core.[17]

Harper and Brothers was still unconvinced.

Nabokov was not having much luck with his New York contacts. Philip Rahv had hoped to print excerpts from *Lolita* in the *Partisan Review*, but abandoned the plan on the advice of his lawyer. Now Katharine White informed Nabokov that for reasons of health she would have to move from the *New Yorker*'s editorial staff to general magazine policy. He told her: "Your decision has distressed me. I look back at our cloudless association. . . . Your kindness, your gentleness and understanding." He had often been exasperated at greater editorial interference in his work than he was ever to encounter elsewhere, but he was also more prepared to consider her judgments and suggestions than those of any other editor. As E. B. White observed, Nabokov "did recognize in Katharine a special intelligence that was congenial to his own, and that he respected and was willing to gain from."[18] In future years Nabokov would enjoy the warm and witty tributes to his work that he received from Katharine White's editorial successor at the *New Yorker*, the talented novelist William Maxwell, but after writing the final *Pnin* chapters he would never again write fiction designed even in part for the *New Yorker*. Although his relationship with the magazine remained cordial and lucrative, it would no longer be intimate.

Early in the new year came the first sign of a change of fortune for *Lolita*. Because of its Olympia Press origins, the book had been neither reviewed nor advertised, but in mid-January 1956, Nabokov discovered that Graham Greene had selected *Lolita* as one of the three best books of 1955 in the Christmas issue of the London *Sunday Times*.*

At the end of January, Nabokov had to sit down to his last batch of marking before the end of the year. Some months earlier he had had in mind another couple of *Pnin* stories that would show his hero after leaving Waindell. Now he thought up another story for Pnin's last day: Pnin burns a student paper, decides it has a flash of genius, and retrieves it.[19] Like the other late Pnin ideas, this never materialized.

---

* The others were *Boswell on the Grand Tour* and the Swiss writer Herbert Luthy's *State of France*.

III

At the beginning of February the Nabokovs set off on icy roads for one final stint of research on *Eugene Onegin* at Harvard. There they installed themselves in number 10, Continental Hotel Apartments, 16 Chauncy Street.[20]

Once again they had many friends to see: Harry and Elena Levin, Billy and Alice James, Mikhail and Tatiana Karpovich, Arthur and Marion Schlesinger, Wilma and Charles Kerby-Miller, Jorge Guillén, Sylvia Berkman. At the Levins' Kirkland Place home they met John Dos Passos in a merry and mellow mood.[21]

They also made a dinner date there with Edmund and Elena Wilson, now living in their upstate New York home. One of Wilson's pet projects was to have the better poets among his friends—W. H. Auden and Edwin Muir, for instance—help him compile a unique anthology at his Talcottville house by inscribing a few lines of their verse on his windowpanes with a diamond pencil. Nabokov agreed to contribute. Wilson arranged to meet him early at the Levins, before their host had returned from a class. He brought with him a plate of glass and his diamond pencil, and since he wanted no mistakes as the lines were inscribed, he took Nabokov to Levin's study. When Levin returned and found his study door closed—he always kept it ajar—he naturally opened it. Wilson turned around, made it clear he should not enter, and ordered him to close the door. Turning white, Levin replied that he wasn't used to being shut out of his own study, and stormed off upstairs. Nabokov pointed out to Wilson ("who was a little thickskinned, as I am perhaps thinskinned," commented Levin) that he should not be so rude to his host and must apologize. He did.[22]

The Nabokovs also saw a good deal of Dmitri, now studying voice, piano, German, and musicianship at the Longy School of Music, just around the corner from their apartment. He was still supposed to be translating *A Hero of Our Time* for a publisher's deadline only a few months off, but he had become more interested in the possibility of using his aged MG as a racing vehicle than in establishing credentials as a translator. Covered in snow or buckling and curling still more under the rain, his copy of the Russian text of Lermontov's novel, front cover missing, lay spread open day after day in his permanently topless MG. As he passed the car, his father would check and record in his diary Dmitri's slow progress, or, more often, note with despair that the book was still open at the same page.[23] That meant his summer work load was piling up.

He had of course come to Cambridge for work of his own. When he had first been awarded a half-year sabbatical, he had hoped to interleave the final research for *Eugene Onegin* and the compiling of a book from his European fiction lectures. But *Eugene Onegin* continued to expand. Even devoting himself exclusively to the one project, he was kept furiously busy in the Widener and in his apartment, copying, taking notes, writing.[24]

One Sunday at the end of February, casually flipping through the *New York Times Book Review*, Nabokov read in Harvey Breit's "In and Out of Books" column about a literary squabble developing in Britain over a book entitled *Lolita*. At the end of January, John Gordon, editor of the sensationalist *Sunday Express*, had used his weekly column to vent his outrage at Greene's recommending the novel: "Without doubt it is the filthiest book I have ever read. Sheer unrestrained pornography. . . . Anyone who published it or sold it here would certainly go to prison. I am sure the *Sunday Times* would approve, even though it abhors censorship as much as I do." Greene had responded with the ironic suggestion that a John Gordon Society should be formed, a body of censors "to examine and if necessary to condemn all offensive books, plays, paintings, sculptures and ceramics." With no inkling of *Lolita*'s future, Nabokov was vexed that his book had been labeled pornographic and that a scandal appeared about to break. But there was nothing he could do.[25]

There was nothing he needed to do. Greene held a first meeting of the John Gordon Society on March 6. Attended by people like Christopher Isherwood, Angus Wilson, and A. J. Ayer, it earned excellent publicity for modest proposals like keeping Scrabble words clean and inviting publishers to print a book band: "Banned by the John Gordon Society." Already the story had caught the eye of Gallimard, France's most prestigious publishing house, who quickly arranged to publish *Lolita* in French. Since Gallimard's director was known to have become extremely prudish, this was an enormous advance in the novel's public respectability. And the *Nouvelle revue française*, France's most distinguished literary magazine, planned to print a large advance extract.[26]

In his March 11 column, Harvey Breit reported a flurry of mail in response to his initial story. Now he felt he could name the author— he had interviewed Nabokov for the *Times* in 1951—and stress his literary credentials. He cited letters emphasizing the book's high quality: "The novel is much less detailed in its descriptions, and far more decorous in its vocabulary, than many novels on recent bestseller lists." "It shocks because it is great art, because it tells a terrible story in a wholly original way. It is wildly funny, coarse, subtle and tragic, all at once." Other readers compared it to the work of Dostoevsky, James, Proust, Fitzgerald, and Nathanael West. Within four days Nabokov had been contacted by four American publishers: Reynal, Knopf, Harper's, and even Indiana University Press. *Lolita* was on the move—and in New York, Olympia Press copies were selling for up to twenty dollars.[27]

Staff at the BBC studios in New York were keen admirers of Nabokov's work and had already recorded him reading his poetry. Now they wished to have him read some of *Eugene Onegin*. Early in March he traveled to New York to record chapter 1 of Pushkin's poem, along with some of his own commentaries. Later in the month, back in Cambridge, he and Véra proudly watched Dmitri singing in a concert. During April, they drove out to visit the Wilsons at their Cape Cod home, and returned to Cambridge "invigorated and refreshed by the mental sea breeze."[28]

IV

At the beginning of May, they left for Ithaca, stopping en route at Karner to catch another generation of blue *samuelis* butterflies among the blue lupines. They had at first planned to collect in California, but then decided to return to the Rockies.[29]

By May 15 they were settled in a ranchito they had rented outside the village of Mt. Carmel in southern Utah. They enjoyed their "heavenly" and rather wild setting amid sage and cedar, and a superb summer's collecting among the eroded pillars of Bryce Canyon National Park, an hour's drive away, or the red and pink cliffs of Zion National Park, even closer, or the vast vistas of the north rim of the Grand Canyon, just a little further from home base.

Even in Utah and Arizona, where rain almost never interfered with the chase, one could not collect butterflies all day long. Back in their log-and-stone cottage, the Nabokovs had to sacrifice rest time for work. Dmitri was off in Maine, rehearsing for the summer opera in Kennebunkport, but his unfinished translation of *A Hero of Our Time* was with his parents. They had to slog hard through May and June to complete and rework the translation for Doubleday's deadline.[30]

Nabokov was now ready to enter an agreement with Doubleday for an annotated edition of *Anna Karenin*. Much more exciting was Jason Epstein's suggestion that Doubleday should publish something on his butterfly work. Nabokov jumped at the opportunity: "It would contain my adventures with leps in various countries, especially in the Rocky Mountains states, the discovery of new species, and the description of some fantastic cases of adaptation. I think I could achieve a fantastic blend of science, art and entertainment."[31] Like all Nabokov's butterfly books, it was not to be.

By the first week in July, the Lermontov translation was complete and Nabokov began to write an introduction. As the heat intensified and the rattlesnakes multiplied, Véra declared it was time to move on. On July 12 they started to meander home, stopping in leisurely fashion along the way to catch butterflies. First they headed into Wyoming, revisiting Afton and then driving further north to the high altitudes of Beartooth Pass (10,940 feet). There, based in Silver Gate and Cooke City, Montana, they had a wonderful time late in July, then drove north again to Minnesota before turning back southward for some "very special" butterflies in southern Michigan. In the first week of August they were back in Ithaca, thoroughly content with a remarkable summer.[32]

V

They had planned to travel on to Kennebunkport, but Dmitri's opera season was almost over. For the next half year they settled in another professorial home in Cayuga Heights, at 425 Hanshaw Road, comfortable but too large for them and their few belongings.[33]

Unlike young Dmitri, his father was punctilious about deadlines. Reuben Brower, organizer of the 1954 English Institute session on translation at Columbia, had asked for essays from the participants by September 1956. Other academics and translators thought the deadline so elastic that the essay collection would not be published until 1959, but Nabokov, although he had already published his own paper from the conference in *Partisan Review*, now sat down to write something new. He had his own motives. It was now some years since he had made his first discoveries in preparing the *Eugene Onegin* commentaries, and publication still seemed another two years away. Anxious to establish the priority of his findings, he made the essay a summary of his principal lines of inquiry.[34]

Dmitri returned from Maine run down and fifteeen pounds lighter after poor food and too little sleep. Nabokov reworked the Lermontov translation with him one final time, and began to draft the superb comparative study of English and Russian prosody that would later become an appendix to *Eugene Onegin* and be published as a book in its own right.[35]

Amidst all this work, he was not happy that classes had to resume on September 19. He felt extremely frustrated. He had hoped to complete *Eugene Onegin* in April or May but could now see he might still spend another year on the project. He was not tired of the Pushkin—in fact, he was delighted to keep on making new discoveries—but was irritated that teaching duties continued to defer its completion. Besides, until *Eugene Onegin* was out of the way he could not embark on the new novel beginning to take shape in his mind.[36]

Meanwhile his latest novel remained unpublished. *Pnin* had been turned down by Viking and Harper and Brothers because of its brevity. Although Doubleday had similar reservations, it decided in August 1956 to take the novel, and rapidly moved into production. At the beginning of October, Nabokov howled in pain at the projected cover illustration for the book, and sent all the instructions and photographs he could to ensure that the person on the cover would be *his* Pnin:

> I have just received the sketches. They are executed with talent, the picture as art goes is first-rate, but in regard to my Pnin it is wrong: The sketch looks like the portrait of an underpaid instructor in the English department or like a Republican's notion of a defeated Adlai, when actually he should look like a Russian muzhik clean-shaven. I am sending you some photographs of Pnin-like Russians, with and without hair, for a visual appreciation of the items I am going to discuss.
>
> 1. The head should look quite bald, without any dark margin, and must be ampler, rounder, smoother, more dome-like. Note Zhavoronkov and Yegorov for the type of head, which however should be bigger in Pnin's case, not egg-shaped. Maslov would be perfect, minus hair.
>
> 2. The glasses should be definitely tortoise-shell ones, with heavier, somewhat squarish frames.
>
> 3. The nose is very important. It should be the Russian potato nose, fat and broad, with prominent nostril curves. See Zhukovski for nostrils, and Obraztsov for a replica of Pnin's fat glossy organ; but Pavlov and Maslov are also good.
>
> 4. The terribly important space between nose and upperlip. This must be simian, large, long, with a central hollow and lateral furrows. See Zhavoronkov, Baykov, Yegorov, Zhukovski. The latter's lips are very Pninian. Pnin's bad teeth should not show.
>
> 5. The cheeks and jowls. Jowls and jaw should be large, broad, massive. See Baykov, Zhavoronkov, Yegorov.
>
> 6. The shoulders should be very broad, square, padded. Pnin wears a ready-made American suit of four years ago.
>
> 7. The tie should be a flamboyant one.
>
> Now, instead of all this, the sketches show a puny Professor Milksop, with an egg-shaped face, flat nose, short upper lip, non-descript chin, sloping shoulders and the necktie of a comedy bookkeeper. I have noticed long ago that for some reason illustrators do not read the books

they illustrate. In my book, all the details listed above are mentioned in the first chapter, and repeated further on. . . .

Splendid idea to have Pnin hold a book. The title on the book he holds should read

ПНИН

В. НАБОКОВ[37]

Nothing could reveal better the precision with which Nabokov always imagined his fictive worlds, or the care he took in this particular case to make Pnin's features quintessentially Russian. With the same scrupulous care for national characteristics, Nabokov had made Pnin explain to his friend Laurence Clements the language of Russian gesture. Pnin's interest in gesture, Nabokov later acknowledged, was really his own, and the book on gesture that he makes Clements write was one he had considered undertaking himself.[38] Nabokov knew less of architecture than Hardy, less cityscape than Dickens or Joyce, less about twills and tweeds and buttons than Arnold Bennett, but no other novelist has taken such care to master the timeless particulars of the novelist's craft: color, light, shade, weather; birds, flowers, trees; the eloquent details of eyes, lips, faces, necks, limbs, hands.

VI

Lolita would have to wait a little longer than *Pnin* for its first American dust jacket. In France, Gallimard's high priests were enchanted by the book and planned a great effort for its launch. Particularly enthusiastic was novelist Raymond Queneau, whose 1959 novel *Zazie dans le Métro* would translate *Lolita*'s puckishness into the streets of Paris and a lighter mood.[39]

In mid-October, Nabokov traveled to New York to consult with Jason Epstein. Epstein was determined that Doubleday should be Nabokov's publisher—they already had *Pnin* and *A Hero of Our Time*—and should publish *Lolita*. A decade earlier, Doubleday's president, Douglas Black, had been taken to court over Edmund Wilson's *Memoirs of Hecate County*. After fighting a $60,000 court case, he had lost, and the book had been banned. He had resolved then and there to have another fight if he could find the right book. Aware of this, Epstein hoped that *Lolita* might be the book, but he also knew that despite Black's pride in his record on behalf of freedom of speech, he was terrified of *Lolita*.[40]

To publish *Lolita* without losing a court battle, defenses had to be dug deep. In September, Epstein had proposed to Nabokov that the next number of *Anchor Review*, an irregular literary review issued by Doubleday's paperback division, should contain a longish and carefully chosen series of excerpts from *Lolita*. Nabokov agreed with delight, and came to New York for a council with Epstein, Melvin Lasky, the editor of *Anchor Review*, and Fred Dupee of Columbia, a literary scholar and former editor of *Partisan Review*, who was eager to write a long introductory essay. Together the four men selected the passages from the novel to appear in *Anchor Review*: ninety pages, almost a third of the text.[41]

Nabokov returned to Ithaca and wrote his elegant afterword, "On a Book Entitled *Lolita*," completing it after two weeks of intense work.[42] Witty and profound, this nimble, elusive, deceptive essay on the genesis of *Lolita* and the nature of its art defends the novel from any charge of pornography by its sheer certainty that a novel on *this* artistic level need not descend to self-defense.

Lolita's fortunes would not stand still. In June the United States Customs had seized, then passed on, an Olympia Press copy of the novel. Although not an official ruling, it was an encouraging sign. By November another copy had been confiscated and then released, and this now seemed tantamount to official sanction. Unaware that customs had let the book go, Howard Nemerov wrote to the *New York Times*: "By the mere corruption of taste, and by the ample provision of substitutes for literature, our society is already so well protected against good writing that Mr. Nabokov's book might be allowed to enter the United States without occasioning the fear of any general deterioration of morals or improvement of minds." He also compared *Lolita* to *Ulysses*, as others would inevitably do. Nabokov thanked him for his friendly gesture.[43]

Publicity grew. Olympia Press copies of *Lolita* were seized in London libraries at about the same time as America's most serious intellectual magazine, *Partisan Review*, published *Lolita*'s first review ("just about the funniest book I remember having read"). Swedish, Danish, and German publishers had asked to buy rights for their countries.[44]

Doubleday too was ready to sign for the novel, proposing that Nabokov receive 75 percent of the royalties of the American edition and Olympia Press 25 percent, the normal proportion of royalties awarded an English-language publisher licensing the first English edition in another country's market. Since overall royalties normally begin at 10 percent of the retail price and rise to perhaps 15 percent as more copies are sold, Girodias could have expected a 2.5 percent royalty for himself, rising to 3.75 percent. Instead, he insisted he should have a royalty of 10 percent, leaving the author a mere 5 percent. He also misled Nabokov's Paris agent about the contents of his contract. Disturbed by both developments, Nabokov consulted a lawyer and on his advice declared the contract with Girodias null and void on the basis of a technicality: Olympia had failed to deliver statements as the contract stipulated. Girodias ignored Nabokov's declaration, but exacerbated their relations further by proposing, now that the U.S. Customs had cleared the book, that he advertise the Olympia Press edition openly in the United States. Nabokov had warned Girodias repeatedly that if more than 1,500 copies of a book printed outside the United States were brought into the country before publication of an American edition, copyright would be lost and anybody could legally publish the book without paying a cent to the author or his first publisher. Girodias once again took little heed.[45]

Then came something he could not ignore: the French Ministry of the Interior's sudden ban at the end of December on the sale in France of *Lolita* and twenty-four other Olympia Press titles. It soon became known that the request had come from the British Home Office, anxious, in the wake of the publicity generated by the John Gordon affair, that British tourists were bringing back across the Channel too many copies of *Lolita* and other Olympia books. In the thick of the Suez crisis, the French ministry was ready to obey the request of its ally.

In acceding to the request, the French government unwittingly loosed a host of preposterous ironies. Henry Miller and Frank Harris, banned on the Olympia Press list, were already available in France in French editions. J. P. Donleavy's *Ginger Man*, also banned, was freely published in England. *Lolita*, now banned in its English edition, was in the process of being translated quite legally into French for France's most venerable publishing house. And since *Lolita* could be legally brought into the United States once it was smuggled out of France, France was proving itself more pudibund than the Anglo-Saxon countries. Most absurd of all from a legal point of view was that the ministerial decree against Olympia's books could only invoke a law restricting subversive *political* publications.

Maurice Girodias promptly sued the French government to have the ban lifted. The French press eagerly supported his case and his indignant defense against governmental encroachment on traditional freedoms. By the end of 1956, the French press had singled out *Lolita* from all the other books on the banned list, and by January 1957 the whole matter had become known in France as "l'affaire *Lolita*."[46]

VII

January's thick snowfalls turn Cayuga Heights into a picturesque dream and driveways into a nightmare for those who have to shovel snow—a task Nabokov never had to perform. He had no time. According to his answer to a faculty survey this year, he spent ninety-one hours per week on intellectual work: six delivering lectures and another two in his seminar, eighteen in preparation and marking, thirty in research, and another thirty-five in writing. Rising at 7:30, he would eat two oranges, shave, take a bath (never a shower), dress, and write or prepare lectures. At 10:00 and 11:00 he had classes three days a week, and one day his two-hour seminar at home. After 12:30 he worked steadily until dinner at 7:00. Then he might visit or entertain, play chess, or dictate his day's work to Véra, who would type it for further revision. About 10:00 he would retire to bed and read until 1:00 A.M.[47]

By the end of the fall term, in the whitest depths of winter, he was finishing his "Notes on Prosody." As he wrote to a friend, his Pushkin opus was still growing, "but what things I'm finding, what discoveries I'm making!" He drew up an outline for a comparative literature course in English, French, Russian, and German poetry, one hundred poems to be mimeographed in the original and translated in class, and discussed in terms of forms and meters and themes such as Arcadia and the evolution of landscape.[48]

For an academic deep in the worst drudgery of teaching and excited by research there can be little more soothing than planning a new course: its purity of outline, its logic of structure, its distance from the draining business of preparation and presentation. But the ideal new course does not make the current courses disappear. In class, he asked his European fiction students what a "bodkin" was. Although some remembered the term from Hamlet's soliloquy, no one broached the silence. Nabokov promptly assigned Hamlet to read, and announced he would set a question on the play in the final exam, a few days away. The Dickens question was bizarre enough: "Discuss his style, such as character impersonation, eloquence, word-play, etc. Do his lips move when Esther takes over?" The Hamlet question, which could be tried for additional points, would stump most who think they know the play: "What gentleman of Normandy teaches what Dansker to scrime in Hamlet?" A few days later, wading through his pile of blue books, Nabokov came across the inevitable: "In Dickens there are many illiterations."[49]

Unbeknownst to Nabokov, another escape from his Cornell routine was in the offing: not simply a new course but a new university. McGeorge Bundy, dean of arts at Harvard, had written to all departmental chairmen to put forward names of people they might want on the staff whose talents were too wide in scope to fit into conventional departmental structures and who might for that reason be overlooked. At that time Harry Levin was chairman of the Department of Modern Languages, including Slavic. Mikhail Karpovich of Slavic had some doubts about Nabokov's telling naive students that Dostoevsky was a detective-story writer, but on balance still agreed with Levin to put Nabokov's name forward. Mark Schorer in English also wanted Nabokov. Bundy approved the recommendation, but it had to return to the department. There Roman Jakobson, the star performer in Harvard's Slavic troupe, staunchly opposed someone else who might take top billing and attacked Nabokov for his quirky ideas on Dostoevsky and other great Russian novelists. Nabokov's advocates asked if he were not a very distinguished novelist in his own right. Jakobson replied: "Gentlemen, even if one allows that he is an important writer, are we next to invite an elephant to be Professor of Zoology?" No one managed to parry that thrust.[50]

VIII

At the beginning of February the Nabokovs moved to another Cayuga Heights address, 880 Highland Road, the home of Professor Lauriston Sharp. They would not take on the Sharps' dog, but agreed to look after Bandit, a Siamese cat with a milky stare who proved more difficult than Tom Jones. A cedarwood ranch-style house designed by a local artist, 880 Highland Road was the Nabokovs' favorite Ithaca home and the one that resonates most in his work, in the echo chambers of *Pale Fire*. A large picture window looked down through the snows of a bare beech wood. At night, uncurtained, the window made all the furniture appear to stand out in that crystal land.[51]

Across the Atlantic, "l'affaire *Lolita*" showed no signs of dying down. Girodias tried to press Nabokov to bring his own action against the French government, but Nabokov had no money for the case and no desire to ruin *Lolita*'s chances for serious American publication by stressing its proximity on Olympia's banned list with works like *Until She Screams* and *How to Do It*.[52] He hoped that those of his books already translated into French might be republished to take advantage of the current publicity stirred up by the appeal against the ban. He still had no inkling that *Lolita* would permanently change his life and his fortunes.

Working relentlessly since 1955 to complete *Eugene Onegin*, he had had no time to write the *New Yorker* stories that had provided him with such a valuable second income over the past decade. Feeling the financial pinch, he once again sent the magazine his "Ballad of Longwood Glen." He had kept reworking the piece ever since the *New Yorker* had rejected it in 1953, and now warned Katharine White to consider it very carefully:

> With my usual modesty I maintain it is the best poem I have composed—far superior, for instance, to the *Evening of Russian Poetry*.
>
> At first blush this ballad may look to you like a weird hybrid between Shagall and Grandmother Moses. But please stick to it as long as you can bear, and by degrees all kinds of interesting shades and underwater patterns will be revealed to the persevering eye. If you still hate it, please feel no qualms—just send it back.[53]

Nabokov is right: this apparently childish little curiosity is one of his best poems. Art Longwood, a small-town American, takes his family for a picnic. Showing his crippled son how to pitch, he throws a ball into a tree. Though he never climbed trees in his timid prime, he overcomes his fears and climbs and climbs.

> Up and up Art Longwood swarmed and shinned,
> And the leaves said *yes* to the questioning wind.
>
> What tiaras of gardens! What torrents of light!
> How accessible ether! How easy flight!
>
> His family circled the tree all day,
> Pauline concluded: "Dad climbed away."
>
> None saw the delirious celestial crowds
> Greet the hero from earth in the snow of the clouds.
>
> Mrs. Longwood was getting a little concerned.
> He never came down. He never returned.

Sightseers, tree surgeons, detectives, and firemen rush to the scene, and even a lyncher keen "to see justice done." The tree is cut down, and still nothing found. "They varnished the stump, put up railings and signs. Restrooms nestled in roses and vines." Art's wife remarries,

> And now the Deforests, with *four* old men,
> Like regular tourists visit the glen;
>
> Munch their lunches, look up and down,
> Wash their hands and drive back to town.

Nabokov mentioned Chagall and Grandma Moses, but other painters also spring to mind. The poem seems pure Norman Rockwell—until it begins to revolve around a mystery that transforms it in the direction of one of Turner's luminous lightscapes.

Art's name is perfect: down-home American, it also implies an "art" that belongs to a very different milieu. The whole poem's point is the gap between Art's fate and the uncomprehending lunch-munchers. What is death doing in the midst of snug life? And what is it in Art that removes him from life into a special and somehow triumphant kind of death? His courage? His longing? His dreaminess ("Silent Art, who could stare at a thing all day, Watched a bug climb a stalk and fly away")? This time, the *New Yorker* accepted the poem.

IX

Early in March, Ivan Obolensky came to visit Nabokov in Ithaca to bid for *Lolita*. Unlike Doubleday, the new firm of McDowell Obolensky was ready to publish this spring, and willing to stake everything on its success. Two years later in Britain *Lolita* would make the fortunes of another young company, Weidenfeld and Nicolson, but McDowell Obolensky was just a fraction too early.

With little in his coffers, Nabokov inclined toward McDowell Obolensky's terms until Jason Epstein telephoned and warned that *Lolita* really needed the resources and reputation of a larger firm. If court action were begun against the novel, the *New York Times* would refuse to accept advertisements for it, and other newspapers would follow suit. The post office would not allow announcements through the mail, and bookstores would hardly risk stocking the book. If it were published in the usual way, *Lolita* would be bound to lose in any American court. The only possible solution, Epstein suggested, was to continue to surround the book "with academic praise and high critical authority, letting her peep out of the pages of the *Anchor Review* until eventually, little by little, the country gets used to her."[54]

To steer Nabokov out of his financial straits, Epstein offered him a contract for his *next* novel. He eagerly accepted. As he had written Epstein a year earlier, in another outburst of gratitude and admiration: "I have never had a publisher like you!"[55]

Nabokov appears to have been brooding on a new novel since at least late 1956, and perhaps a year earlier. In Victor's and Pnin's dreams of a king's escape by sea from a chimerical European country riven by revolution, Nabokov had touched on the "Ultima Thule" theme that had so stirred his imagination in the past. In the early 1940s, after abandoning Russian and *Solus Rex*, he had reworked the theme of revolution and the invented land into *Bend Sinister*, but without the romantic shimmer of *Solus Rex*'s Ultima Thule. Now on

March 6, 1957, he took a fresh index card and wrote: "The story starts in Ultima Thule."⁵⁶

In an interview just after the publication of *Pale Fire*, Nabokov described the strange process of accumulating scraps of information for a novel he cannot yet see but senses he will shortly glimpse in a flash of inspiration: "All I know is that at a very early stage of the novel's development I get this urge to garner bits of straw and fluff, and eat pebbles. Nobody will ever discover how clearly a bird visualizes, or if it visualizes at all, the future nest and the eggs in it." For the first three months of 1957, he had been garnering straw and fluff for the unseen nest of *Pale Fire*. When at the end of January he noted that the snowflakes were a "dull dark white against the light white,"⁵⁷ a line of the "Pale Fire" poem he would write for John Shade four years later was already almost fully formed.

In this receptive state of mind the Highland Road home he had moved into in early February and found so congenial contributed much more to what he would eventually insert in *Pale Fire*. But the synopsis of a new novel called *Pale Fire* that he sent to Jason Epstein at the end of March 1957 bears the oddest relationship to the *Pale Fire* he would eventually begin to write at the end of 1960. Here there is still no Shade, no homosexual king, no poem, commentary, and index. Only the ex-king's flight to America, a hint of Gradus, and Shade's relentless probing of the inadmissible abyss of death seem already in place.

> My main creature, an ex-king, is engaged throughout *Pale Fire* in a certain quest. This quest, or research (which at one point, alas, involves some very sophisticated spiritualism), is completely divorced from so-called faith or religion, gods, God, Heaven, Folklore, etc. At first I thought of entitling my novel *The Happy Atheist*, but the book is much too poetical and romantic for that (its thrill and poetry I cannot reveal to you in a short and matter-of-fact summary). My creature's quest is centered in the problem of heretofore and hereafter, and it is I may say beautifully solved.
>
> The story starts in Ultima Thule, an insular kingdom where a palace intrigue and some assistance from Nova Zembla clear the way for a dull and savage revolution. My main creature, the King of Thule, is dethroned. After some wonderful adventures he escapes to America. Certain political complications lead President Kennedy to answer evasively when questioned about the displaced personage.
>
> He lives more or less incognito, with the lady he loves, somewhere on the border of Upstate New York and Montario: the border is a little blurry and unstable, but there is a bus to Goldenrod, another to Calen-

dar Barn, and on Sundays the Hudson flows to Colorado. Despite these—on the whole quite innocent—little defocalizations, the locus and life-color are what a real-estate mind would call "realistic," and from the picture window of my creature's house one can see the bright mud of a private road and a leafless tree all at once abloom with a dozen waxwings.

The book is regularly interrupted, without any logical or stylistic transition, right in the middle of a sentence (to be blandly continued a few lines further) by glimpses of an agent, a Mr. Copinsay, from Thule, whose job is to find and destroy an ex-king. Mr. Copinsay, who is of Orkney descent, has some dreadful troubles of his own, and his long journey (through all the drains of the book) is full of nightmare difficulties (he gets entangled in a West-Indian cruise at one point). However, he does reach Goldenrod in the final chapter—where a surprise awaits the reader and him.

I am writing this in a hurry, have to correct exams.[58]

A month later Nabokov wrote to Katharine White that he was bubbling over with inspiration and chafing at the academic routine that consumed so many of the hours he could otherwise devote to writing.[59] By the time he could work uninterrupted on his next novel, he would have broached a different project altogether: not the ur-*Pale Fire* he had begun, but one wing of *Ada*.

X

Pnin was published on March 7, 1957. For the first time since his arrival in the United States, Nabokov saw one of his books hailed from coast to coast. Timofey Pnin is of course the most immediately appealing of heroes, and his story the most straightforward in all Nabokov's mature novels. But there was more to the book's success than that. *Pnin*'s maker was also becoming known as the author of the still-unreviewable *Lolita*—as "one of the subtlest, funniest and most moving writers in the United States today"[60]—and all the major dailies and weeklies at once had their eyes on his new novel. Two weeks after publication, *Pnin* went into its second printing.[61] Nothing like this had ever happened to Nabokov.

Pnin loses his university job. Nabokov himself in March 1957 was very aware of the risk he ran of losing his own position at Cornell on the ground that Olympia's court action against the French government aligned *Lolita* with so much pure pornography. In class, however, there was no trace of Pnin in his maker. One student recalls

Nabokov thundering against Freud early in the spring term of 1957: "about halfway through the heating pipes began clanking and reached a literally deafening pitch, over which Mr. Nabokov shouted 'The Viennese fraud is *railing* at me from his grave.' "[62]

Like Tolstoy and Joyce, Chekhov and Bunin, Nabokov thought little of Dostoevsky, and, as he insisted, he was not enough of an academic to teach books he did not like. Once an English graduate student who had learned Russian in the army came to see him about a thesis on Dostoevsky. "Dostoevsky? Dostoevsky is a very poor writer." "Well," said the student, "isn't he an influential writer?" "Dostoevsky is not an influential writer," Nabokov replied. "He has had no influence." The student persisted: "Hasn't he influenced Leonov?" Nabokov threw up his hands and said: "Poor Leonov! Poor Leonov!" The interview was over.[63]

In mid-March, Nabokov was lecturing in his survey of Russian literature when a student rose to his feet and requested that he be allowed to talk about Dostoevsky for a class period if Nabokov would not. Afterwards Nabokov stormed to the English department office, quite apoplectic with rage, and demanded the student be expelled. He was not. Instead the student began to boycott most of Nabokov's classes in protest against his treatment of committed writers. Often reluctant to credit the intelligence of those who disagreed with him, Nabokov for the remainder of the term noted in his diary whether the "idiot" was present or not in class: only six times out of twenty. The young man, a star student, one of the brasher young fiction writers in Cornell's creative writing program, received an F on the exam. He went to Arthur Mizener and M. H. Abrams to complain. Convinced that Nabokov was overreacting, they asked him to reconsider the grade. He would not. As Nabokov warned his students, he required a certain kind of answer. Perhaps the student chose not to play by the rules of the game, and made it inevitable he would not score. Or perhaps Nabokov simply decided to rule him offside.[64]

In April, before returning midterm papers on *Anna Karenin*, Nabokov explained to his students just why he set them such specific questions. An essay question on some general idea would be likely to produce misleading results. "Let us assume that I had said: L[adies] and G[entlemen]. You have one hour and I want each of you to write a paper on the theme: *Tolstoy's attitude to family life*. This is, indeed, a standard question, and it would seem, theoretically, that in answering it the brilliant students would glitter, the good students would shimmer and the average students would shed a subdued light." But he imagines two sample students, X and Y, both "good, kind, lovable, young people—and neither gives a hoot for literature," and he reproduces comically accurate, hopelessly waffly mock-answers by "the debonair fraud X and poor humble Y who can't even crib intelligently."

> If each gets a 50 (which is generous) then each comes to the instructor and says: Look—I've written about family life, and I've written about marriage and I've said that Tolstoy stood for family life—and I've said. . . . They are right. They have. They have been given a general idea to discuss and they have discussed it in a general way. And this is why I prefer the specific question—demanding a specific answer.
>
> Let us now turn to the specific questions in this midterm test.
>
> Question one was: how does Anna find out that Steve and Dolly are reconciled?
>
> The point was did the *image* remain in your minds. The beautiful little theme of *hesitation* on Anna's part—has this been noticed? Steve and Dolly had talked things over, and Steve had gone to his study. Presently Dolly appears. She says to Anna she wants to move her downstairs where it is warmer. Anna looks intently at Dolly—*are they reconciled*? Now Steve strolls in. Asks what they are discussing. *"Reconciled" thinks Anna.* Dolly answers Steve—and her tone seems to Anna cold and neutral. *Not reconciled* thinks Anna. Steve says to Dolly: Oh nonsense. You always make difficulties. *Reconciled* thinks Anna. Dolly answers her husband: All *you* do is to tell the servant what to do and then you leave him to make a mess of it—and Dolly's lips wrinkle at the corners with her habitual mocking little smile. *Full, full reconciliation*—thinks Anna with joy.
>
> You see the image? A reader who only remembers that Dolly had a mocking smile and so Anna then knew they were reconciled, has missed a whole piece of Tolstoy's incomparable art, this wonderful interplay, the *sequence* of emotions which makes the image. I did not hope that anybody would remember the passage word for word, but I did hope that somebody would notice the ups and downs of Anna's emotions as she watched the couple and the way Tolstoy manages to depict Anna and the couple.[65]

An explanation like this indicates perhaps better than anything else the strengths of Nabokov's approach: not to have his students play at being critics, which so few of them would ever become, but to turn them into first-rate readers, "major readers of major authors."

XI

After Nabokov had hurried to meet the deadline for his essay on translating Pushkin for Reuben Brower early the previous fall, Brower at last replied in late March that he would prefer the article already published in *Partisan Review*. By now Nabokov was more anxious than ever to lay claim to the priority of his findings on *Eugene Onegin*: Pushkin's knowledge of foreign languages; the gallicisms in his Russian diction; the role of French translations as a filter through which Western European writers reached Russian readers; the sources for Pushkin's *Eugene Onegin* rhyme scheme; and a few specific echoes and allusions. He took the material from the essay Brower rejected, translated it into Russian, and sent half to his friend Roman Grynberg's journal *Opyty* (*Experiments*) and half to Karpovich's *Novyy zhurnal*.[66]

But *Lolita* was even more of a worry to Nabokov the writer than *Eugene Onegin* to Nabokov the scholar. He was now ready to choose an American publisher, but accepted that the moment for publication itself had not yet arrived. He would have liked Doubleday to sign for the novel, but Girodias's demands continued to make it difficult for any publisher in the United States to consider an agreement.

In Paris early in April Girodias published *L'affaire Lolita*, a book consisting of excerpts from the novel, Dupee's article for the *Anchor Review*, Nabokov's "On a Book Entitled *Lolita*," all translated into French, and an article by Girodias on the ban. Girodias now added the publication of *L'affaire Lolita* to the court action he had brought against the French government, as instances of his major contribution to *Lolita*'s fortunes and as justification of his demand to be richly rewarded for any American edition.[67] In fact, he fought the court case and published *L'affaire Lolita* to remove the ban on twenty-four other books on his list as well as *Lolita*, and he seemed to forget that he had already claimed an absurdly high royalty *before* the French Ministry of the Interior issued the ban in the first place. Graham Greene, John Gordon, and Jason Epstein had done as much as Girodias to advance *Lolita*'s name, and, as Nabokov pointed out, he as author had also made a certain contribution.

In March, Nabokov tried to ascertain from Girodias on what basis he would agree to American and British editions of the novel. Before receiving a clear answer, he and Véra drove to New York to meet with publishers. Chief among them was Epstein, who asked Nabokov if Doubleday could publish a volume of his short stories. The more visible evidence of his literary respectability, the better for *Lolita*.[68]

Epstein had also mentioned the *Eugene Onegin* project to the Bollingen Press. Nabokov talked with John Barrett and Vaun Gillmor of Bollingen and came away with "a fairy-tale impression" of the meeting: it seemed there would be no problem in having them publish even this multivolume monster or in having it published with all the care he could ask for. Late in March he had written to Edmund Wilson that he was completely engrossed in *Onegin* and simply had to finish it this year: "This is the fifth or sixth version [of the translation] that I have made. I am now . . . welcoming the awkward turn, the fish bone of meager truth."[69]

He had had a contract for years with the Bollingen Press for an annotated English edition of *The Song of Igor's Campaign* to be prepared with Marc Szeftel and Roman Jakobson. All three contributors had been paid an advance. Although in no position to repay his share, Nabokov wanted to withdraw from the joint edition rather than work with Jakobson. To his delight, Bollingen agreed not to demand he return his part of the advance. He promptly wrote to Jakobson, explaining that he wanted to withdraw from their joint project on account of "your little trips to totalitarian countries." He had heard that the year before, in Moscow for a conference, Jakobson had wept at his return to the city, and had promised to come back soon. Nabokov was in fact convinced that Jakobson was a Communist agent. At a time when university faculties were hostile to the search for Communists on their campuses, Nabokov befriended the FBI agent assigned to Cornell and declared he would be proud to have his son join the FBI in that role. No wonder it was impossible for him to work alongside Jakobson.[70]

Nabokov could be suspicious in other ways too. During his year at the Sharp home he and Véra invited friends for a cocktail party. Arthur Mizener began to talk to a group of guests

> about another party, this one given by the poet Delmore Schwartz during the summer of 1950, in Gambier, Ohio, while the annual Kenyon School of Letters was convening. Schwartz's guests were discussing the continuing controversy surrounding the awarding of the Bollingen Prize to Pound, an Axis collaborator. Schwartz, who had consumed a fair share of his own liquor, began to argue with Robert Lowell, who had been one of the Bollingen judges. Angrily, Schwartz accused Lowell of being an anti-Semite, too; and Mizener, retailing all this for the Nabokovs' guests, said that he had to sympathize with Lowell because Cal was an honorable man, and so forth. Host Nabokov, who had been listening at some remove, suddenly paled and tugged at the sleeve of another guest, Professor M. H. Abrams, pulling him around the corner and out of the room. "What am I going to do, Mike?" asked the stricken Nabokov. "Arthur is a friend of mine but I am going to have to throw him out of my house." "Why?" asked Abrams, quite amazed. "For telling that anti-Semitic story!" replied Nabokov.

Abrams managed to calm his friend down, but Nabokov was still on edge, and later consulted Philip Rahv, the editor of *Partisan Review*, to find if there was any trace of anti-Semitism in Mizener's past.

There was not, but Nabokov, shocked by the casual anti-Semitism he found among his academic colleagues, remained hypersensitive to any hint of a slur.[71]

XII

Late in May, Edmund Wilson came to visit the Nabokovs for the weekend. Once again the two men revived their dispute about English and Russian versification, a conflict that had already simmered for a decade and a half and that in 1965 would erupt into the literary explosion of the year.

Summing up for his guest the notes on prosody he had recently added to his *Eugene Onegin*, Nabokov indicated that he still followed the assumption he had once set before Wilson: "I am quite, quite sure that Russian versification can be explained better to an English poet by the vague similarities between it and English versification than by the blatant differences between the two languages." Wilson noted in his diary: "Volodya's insistent idea that Russian and English verse are basically the same is, actually, I have become convinced, a part of his inheritance from his father, a leader of the Kadets in the Duma and a champion of constitutional monarchy for Russia after the British model, a belief that these two so dissimilar countries are, or ought to be, closely associated." Wilson's reaction here seems typical of his behavior toward Nabokov in this phase of their friendship. Rather than listen to Nabokov, he constructed an absurd biographical explanation of what he supposed his friend to be saying. In fact, Nabokov was fully aware of the "blatant differences" between the two prosodic systems, and a few months earlier had written that even if by some miracle an English version of *Eugene Onegin* could render Pushkin's exact sense *and* the whole constellation of his rhymes, the miracle would be pointless, since the English conception of rhyme does not correspond at all to the Russian.[72]

When Nabokov announced that Pushkin's knowledge of English and other languages was rudimentary, Wilson once again dismissed Nabokov's discovery and resorted to jaundiced psychology: "These false ideas, of course," he declared in his diary, "are prompted by his compulsion to think of himself as the only writer in history who has been equally proficient in Russian, English and French." But Nabokov had at first assumed like many others that Pushkin knew English, German, Greek, and Italian, and only on examining the detailed evidence did he find Pushkin continually starting and restarting to learn these languages and never reaching the point where he could easily read foreign poets other than the French in the original.[73]

Wilson kept his most critical thoughts to himself, and even in the matters where they constantly disagreed he and Nabokov could still enjoy each other's company. Nabokov challenged his guest to read *Eugene Onegin* aloud. Wilson started to perform with disastrous gusto, putting the wrong syllabic stress on the first word that had more than one syllable: "Moy dyaDYA," which means, and matches, "My uncLE." He garbled every second word, Nabokov reported, "turning Pushkin's iambic line into a kind of spastic anapest with a lot of jaw-twisting haws and rather endearing little barks that utterly jumbled the rhythm and soon had us both in stitches."[74]

The author of *Memoirs of Hecate County* and the author of *Lolita* shared an amused taste for sexual spice in their literary dishes. As Wilson later reported, he brought his friend "*Histoire d'O*, that highly sophisticated and amusing pornographic work, and in return he sent me in my quarters a collection of French and Italian poems of a more or less licentious character, which I think he had been consulting in connection with his translation of Pushkin." The morning Wilson left, Nabokov came out to see him off. Wilson, sitting propped up in the back of the car with his gouty foot on the seat, congratulated Nabokov on looking fresh after his bath. Nabokov leaned into the car and murmured, in parodic homage to *Histoire d'O*, "Je mettais du rouge sur les lèvres de mon ventre."[75]

XIII

Pushkin kept Nabokov at his desk in Ithaca throughout the summer of 1957. Late in June he was able to send the Bollingen Press the first third of the book: the introduction, the translation and commentary for chapter 1, and the notes on prosody. Dmitri, about to spend the last six months of the year in national military service, had begun to work on the detailed index his father wanted to provide for the book.[76]

Although extremely busy, with no time for anything but *Onegin*, Nabokov was enjoying the beautiful grove he had to work in. Ever since the spring, he had kept a close eye on the rich bird life around the house: flickers, bluejays, waxwings. He had repositioned his bed so that he could see the shagbark tree in the garden with its attached child's swing, an old car tire. He did not mow the lawn, but would sit out happily at work in the two-foot-high grass. In the evening light, he and Véra would throw horseshoes at a pin-oak tree, and neighbors could hear the sound of their laughter ringing through the air. Cat-minding, window, waxwings, shagbark, swing, horseshoes—everything about the place was kindling for *Pale Fire*. One July day, Nabokov wrote a poem ("The setting sun has lit the tips / Of TV's giant paperclips") that he would revise four years later for John Shade. But all the enchantment of the setting could not relieve him of the pressure to complete *Eugene Onegin*. Early in August he was still hoping to finish the commentaries in the course of the month, and reported himself "sometimes utterly exhausted and dejected."[77]

Not long ago he had dreaded that *Lolita* might jeopardize his position at Cornell. By now that danger had passed. In late spring the Dean of Arts at Berkeley had even called him up after reading *Lolita* to invite him to the University of California as a visiting lecturer. In June the *Anchor Review* appeared with almost a third of the novel, Nabokov's afterword, and Fred Dupee's weightily academic appraisal of the novel. Not the slightest outcry was raised. Bookshops all over America were rapidly selling under-the-counter copies of the Olympia *Lolita* at a high markup. Internationally, *Lolita* was suddenly establishing Nabokov as a leading author: in the three major Continental book markets, three major publishers—Rowohlt in Germany, Gallimard in France, and Mondadori in Italy—had signed for *Lolita* and would continue to publish as much Nabokov as they could. It was high time to arrange that his book be published in his own country.[78]

Nabokov had to warn Girodias against making a false move. With copies of *Lolita* being sold briskly even in a local Ithaca bookstore, he was alarmed that the United States might rule more than 1,500 copies had been imported and copyright forfeited. He also warned that two recent adverse court decisions on other books had made the defense of *Lolita* no easier, although it would probably be acquittable by the time it reached the Supreme Court. Doubleday was ready to make a definite offer for *Lolita*, although not to publish immediately. Girodias, however, insisted on a royalty for himself of 7.5 percent for the first 10,000 copies and 10 percent after that. Epstein wrote to Girodias, "The terms of your proposal are so vastly excessive that we cannot even discuss them." To Nabokov he added that Girodias's claims were not only unthinkable but also naive: by asking for so much, he would only ensure that no American edition could be published.[79]

XIV

In September 1957, now on a university salary of $8,500, Nabokov for the first time had to abandon his small seminar course altogether:

there were simply no prospective students adequately trained in Russian.[80] On his arrival at Cornell in 1948, he had commenced duties as a professor of Russian literature, teaching three courses in his subject, two in the original Russian, and had resisted teaching non-Russian literature at all. Now, although he had devoted all his time and energy for years to scholarly work in Russian literature, he had ended up, through circumstances not of his own making, teaching only one course in Russian literature, and even then in English, to about thirty-five or forty students, and one course in European fiction to classes that had become ten times that size. By now he was known on the Cornell campus as the author of *Pnin* and *Lolita* and as a lecturer who should not be missed.

In his study, meanwhile, he continued to polish his glosses. Sitting at his desk throughout the fall, he would from time to time feel a thud shake the whole house. Just in front of the Sharps' large picture window stood some rosebushes. At this time of year cedar waxwings often became quite drunk on the swelling rose hips, and flew into the window. Normally they would simply stun themselves, although occasionally they might break their necks. Early in October, Nabokov noted down the waxwings' kamikaze customs. It would be another three years before he would write for John Shade: "I was the shadow of the waxwing slain / By the false azure in the windowpane." But the everlasting notes on *Eugene Onegin*, which were preventing him from settling down to write *Pale Fire*, were also silently transforming the new novel, implanting in some recess of his mind the idea of a novel in the form of poem and commentary and index. All the assiduous reading in eighteenth-century French and English poetry that he had undertaken to explain Pushkin's gallic diction and to render Pushkin's lines in an equivalent English lexicon had also begun to make it possible for him to add to his story of a refugee king the story of an American poet and eighteenth-century scholar living amidst waxwings and shagbarks and echoes of Pope. As he scanned the stacks of Cornell's library for the sake of *Eugene Onegin*, he kept an alert eye out for arcana. Three days before he recorded his observations of the waxwings, he noted down a reference to the Old Norse *Kongs-skuggsio*, a title which translates as "The Royal Mirror." That image, the "bodkin" in *Hamlet* that provided the first hint for suicidal Kinbote's name, the waxwing, the story of an exiled king, Nabokov's own commentary to Pushkin's long poem: in retrospect, it looks as if everything for *Pale Fire* was at hand. In fact it would be another three years before the conception of the novel we know suddenly rushed into Nabokov's mind.[81]

At the end of October 1957, Nabokov traveled to Poughkeepsie to talk on Pushkin and European literature at Vassar, then drove on to

New York to see Jason Epstein. Two months earlier Doubleday had been frightened off *Lolita* by Girodias's greed. Aware of his demands, MacDowell Obolensky was ready to offer an enormous royalty of 20 percent, a figure more experienced publishers would not dream of. Girodias reacted to this by declaring he should have 12.5 percent and Nabokov only 7.5 percent. Faced by such outrageous demands and the risk of *Lolita*'s losing all copyright protection through Girodias's continuing to stock the American black market, Nabokov once more declared his contract with Olympia void, again by resorting to the technicality of Olympia's failure to submit statements on time.[82]

MacDowell Obolensky now withdrew its offer. Meanwhile first Walter Minton of Putnam's and then Simon and Schuster had asked if they could negotiate with Girodias. Nabokov was happy to let anybody else try to come to terms with the man.[83] By now he simply wanted nothing more to do with him.

There were other *Lolita* worries. Girodias's brother, Eric Kahane, was translating the novel for Gallimard. He had translated the excerpts and afterword for *L'affaire Lolita* in a rush and at the expense of accuracy, and Nabokov was extremely concerned that he had still heard nothing from Kahane and seen nothing of the translation itself, whose French he wanted to check. Swedish he knew nothing of, but he was disturbed to hear that the Swedish translation of *Lolita* highlighted the passages of erotic tension and omitted as much as possible of the rest of the novel. He demanded the edition be immediately withdrawn and a faithful version of the novel prepared.[84]

Fame was beginning, frustrations and all. *Lolita* was already hotly circulated on the Cornell campus. One student came up to Nabokov after a lecture, Olympia *Lolita* in hand, and simply bowed to him. *Pnin* was nominated for a National Book Award, and students, his own and others, kept bringing copies to be autographed. A Nabokov cult developed among Cornell's ambitious young writers: the future novelist Thomas Pynchon, science fiction writer Joanna Russ, novelist Richard Fariña (*Been Down So Long It Looks Like Up to Me*), critic Roger Sale, editor Michael Curtis. At Cornell's literary club, the Book and Bowl, Marc Szeftel and Richard Fariña read from *Lolita*, which Szeftel then placed in the context of Nabokov's Russian oeuvre. One undergraduate, the future experimental novelist Steve Katz, even showed Nabokov the typescript of his novel, *The Steps of the Sun*. "It occurs to me I don't know anything about the world of this novel, its boundaries, its presuppositions, its values," Nabokov wrote on the manuscript, but he could give some basic literary advice: "Nothing ages faster than 'stark realism.' . . . You have to *saturate* yourself with English poetry in order to compose English prose. You must know your tool. You do not. You cannot begin all over again with the *Canterbury Tales*, in comic-strip English. . . . *Suggestion*: Read: Milton, Coleridge, Keats, Wordsworth."[85]

Out in the wider world, *Lolita* continued to emit contradictory signals. While black-market sales persisted across the country, a magazine popular that year carried "A Review of a Novel You Can't Buy." But if *Lolita*'s fate remained uncertain, that of *Eugene Onegin* was at last resolved. By the beginning of December, Nabokov had put the final touches to the eleven fat folders—introduction, translation, commentaries, and appendices—of the largest literary project he had ever undertaken.[86]

CHAPTER 15

Eugene Onegin

My method may be wrong but it is a method.

—"Reply to My Critics"

. . . the gaunt, graceless literalist groping around in despair for the

obscure word that would satisfy impassioned fidelity and

accumulating in the process a wealth of information which

only makes the advocates of pretty camouflage tremble or sneer.

—"Reply to My Critics"

I

I SHALL be remembered by *Lolita*," Nabokov predicted in 1966, "and my work on *Eugene Onegin*."[1] In size and in effort expended, his controversial translation of Pushkin's masterpiece and the twelve hundred pages of accompanying commentary dwarf all his other works. He devoted as much time to making Pushkin available to English-speaking readers as he would need to compose all three of his own English masterpieces, *Lolita*, *Pale Fire*, and *Ada*. Was it worth all that effort? How close do the four volumes of his *Eugene Onegin* get us to Pushkin—and to Nabokov? How could a writer supposedly concerned above all with style rather than content produce a translation that deliberately eschews every stylistic grace in order to render with ruthless fidelity the exact verbal meaning of Pushkin's lines, at the cost of all their magic? And how could someone who consistently tried to detach fiction from "real life" provide more information than any other critic on the minutest details—time and place, flora and fauna, food and drink, dress and gesture—of Pushkin's and Onegin's worlds?

Pushkin *was* worth the trouble. He may well be—Nabokov certainly thought he was—the greatest of all poets after Shakespeare.[2] His *Eugene Onegin* is not only the greatest poem in Russian, but has been rated arguably Russia's greatest novel. Without question it is the most important single work in Russian literary history and in Russian literary hearts. "Russians," Nabokov has written, "know the conceptions of 'homeland' and 'Pushkin' are inseparable, and that to be Russian means to love Pushkin."[3]

No other writer of Nabokov's stature has ever been so deeply committed to his country's literature and contributed so much to it before being compelled to switch to another. In *The Gift*, his richest Russian novel, his hero's growth as a writer is also a development toward Pushkin: Fyodor even ends the novel by farewelling his book in a paragraph that, although printed as prose, has the meter and rhyme scheme of a *Eugene Onegin* stanza. In his English fiction, in Sebastian Knight's Paris, Pnin's Waindell, Kinbote's Zembla, and Van Veen's dream-bright, Russified America, he continually let the shadow of the Russian past play over the present. And as someone with a combined command of Russian and English that has never been matched, he was in a unique position to bring Russian literature to the English-speaking world.

In the early 1940s he had responded to that mission, writing a book on Gogol and publishing some splendid verse translations of nineteenth- and twentieth-century Russian lyrics by Pushkin, Lermontov, Tyutchev, Fet, and Khodasevich. In 1945 he published a verse translation of three stanzas from *Eugene Onegin*. The next year he began to teach a survey course in Russian literature in English translation at Wellesley College, and appears to have translated a few other portions of *Eugene Onegin* into verse for his classes.[4]

When he moved to Cornell in 1948, Nabokov expected scholastic standards to be considerably higher than at Wellesley, and prepared to teach not only his English-language survey course but another that examined Russian literature in the original. A detailed study of *Eugene Onegin* naturally constituted a large part of the first semester's work. When he vented his disgust at the "rhymed paraphrases" of *Eugene Onegin*, every line of which he had to revise for his students, his wife casually remarked, "Why don't you translate it yourself?" Just before the semester began, he suggested to Edmund Wilson that they write together a scholarly, copiously annotated prose translation of *Eugene Onegin*. At the end of his first Cornell year, in May 1949, he thought of offering a publisher a little (little!) book on *Eugene Onegin*: "complete translation in prose with notes giving associations and other explanations for every line—the kind of thing I have prepared for my classes." The next year, capitalizing on his thorough preparation, he introduced an advanced seminar on Pushkin, and in January 1950, before the first semester was over, he reported to Roman Jakobson that he was working on a prose translation of the poem.[5]

He still had *Conclusive Evidence* to complete, a new course to prepare on European fiction from Austen to Kafka, and *Lolita* to transfer
from image to index cards. Not until 1952–1953, during the tenure of
a second Guggenheim Fellowship, did he begin concerted work in
the libraries of Harvard and Cornell. When he broached the project
in earnest in August 1952, he predicted he could complete it by the
fall of 1953.[6] As it turned out, he would toil over the commentaries
until the end of 1957.

Had he known how much time it would eventually consume, Nabokov might never have begun. But once in motion, the challenge
became irresistible: "the more difficult it was, the more exciting it
seemed." He surprised himself by evolving a new theory of translation that became progressively more rigorous and, he could foresee,
progressively more certain to shock. He went through five or six
complete versions during the 1950s until announcing in 1957: "I have
at last discovered the right way to translate *Onegin*. . . . I am now
breaking it up, banishing everything that honesty might deem verbal
velvet." Another last-minute and still stricter revision followed in
January 1963.[7]

Meanwhile throughout the 1950s his research for the commentary,
at Cornell and in Harvard's Widener and Houghton libraries, had
become as compulsive as his work at the microscope on his bench at
Harvard's Museum of Comparative Zoology in the 1940s. Though he
had no more than a Cambridge B.A., Nabokov was temperamentally
a scholar as well as an artist, and had been so ever since his first
childhood butterfly researches in the 1900s and his youthful private
investigation of Russian verse meters in the 1910s. He was delighted by all he was discovering and still had to discover, and by all
that other commentators had taken for granted and that he could
prove wrong.

As he prowled quiet stacks on the dusty trail of Pushkin and whatever Pushkin had read, Nabokov did not know that *Lolita* was about
to bring him worldwide fame. But he did hope that *Eugene Onegin*
would attract attention by its violation of the decorums of translation,
and he deliberately planted at least one booby-trap for future reviewers.[8] During the six-year gap—a saga in itself—between his completing the book and the day in 1964 when the Bollingen Press's four
handsome cream-colored volumes went on sale, Nabokov had become the hottest property on the literary market. *Lolita* had not only
brought him its own *succès de scandale et d'estime*, but had also led to
the publication of his collected English stories and his English poems,
and the first translations of his Russian fiction, *Invitation to a Beheading*
(1959), *The Gift* (1963), and *The Defense* (1964), with the promise of

more to come. His new novel, *Pale Fire*, had been hailed as one of the great works of art of the century.

But there was another side to the chasm between the composition and the publication of his Pushkin. As early as 1956 he had become anxious about establishing priority for his findings, and had published some of his more important discoveries in Russian and English.[9] As delay after delay widened the gap between Bollingen's acceptance of the manuscript in 1958 and publication in 1964, Nabokov worried more and more that someone might preempt him. His fears were borne out. In 1963, Walter Arndt published a verse translation of *Eugene Onegin* that adhered strictly to the complex stanza form of the original, and Arndt received for his efforts—irony of ironies—the Bollingen Prize for the translation of poetry. Nabokov responded with a devastating critique in the young *New York Review of Books*.[10]

The vehement indignation of this review and the conscious provocativeness of the absolutist standards in his own translation created a volatile atmosphere for the publication of his *Onegin* a few months later. Reactions were explosively contradictory. John Bayley, a novelist and Pushkinist himself, hailed the work: "A better commentary on a poem has never been written, and probably not a better translation of one. . . . So sensitive is Nabokov's version that it becomes poetry in its own right." Others found Nabokov's rhymeless literalism no more than a nail scratched across the record of Pushkin's verbal music. Loudest of all who decried the translation was Edmund Wilson. Not only had Nabokov produced "a bald and awkward language which has nothing in common with Pushkin," but he had demonstrated "the perversity of his tricks to startle or stick pins in the reader . . . to torture both the reader and himself by flattening Pushkin." Nabokov replied angrily, Wilson counter-replied, Nabokov counter-counter-replied, and others like Anthony Burgess and Robert Lowell joined the fray to create the fiercest transatlantic literary feud of the mid-1960s.[11]

In one way, Nabokov the provocateur had succeeded beyond his dreams: not only his own fame but the challenge of his extremist views had brought Pushkin more attention in the English-speaking world than he had ever had. In another way, the ferocity of the skirmish was something of a personal tragedy. Few realized that for Nabokov it marked the end of the most intense literary friendship he had ever known. For despite all their differences of outlook, Wilson and Nabokov during the 1940s and 1950s had exhilarated and exasperated each other with their common love of literature and their uncommon love of Pushkin.

While battle raged through 1965, Nabokov found as he turned to defend particular lines in his translation that his practice had not been quite as severe as his theory—which itself, far from yielding in the face of opposition, was becoming still more uncompromising. Early in 1966, *Ada* began to come to him in a rush, but as soon as inspiration paused he returned to his translation and during the last three months of 1966 revised it to make it still more fiercely literal, "ideally interlinear and unreadable."[12] As with the first version, a complicated series of publishing mishaps again caused an inordinate delay in publication, this time until 1975.

II

Why, after his own highly acclaimed verse translations during the 1940s, did Nabokov come to reject all rhymed translations and to insist on such absolute literalism? Are verse translations really so impossible to combine with literal accuracy? Are their divagations from literal sense not more than compensated for by the echo of the original's verbal music?

To answer these questions I compared Pushkin's text with Nabokov's two translations and the three most widely available English rhymed versions. Babette Deutsch's, first published in 1936, is the freest and most poetically fluent of the three.[13] Walter Arndt's 1963 version, the jauntiest, has often been preferred to Nabokov's by Russian scholars reviewing Nabokov's work. Sir Charles Johnston's 1977 translation, the most ponderous as verse, has also received much acclaim.[14]

As I reread Pushkin, I decided before looking at any of the translations to settle on a sample stanza and see how the different translators coped. Five: XXXII seemed ideal. It begins with Tatiana Larin's confusion as Onegin is seated before her at the banquet for her name-day party. She has seen Onegin twice before. On the day her sister Olga's fiancé, the young poet Lenski, brought Onegin to visit, romantic Tatiana had at once fallen in love with the moody stranger, and in a trance of passion spent the night penning him an ardent declaration of love. The evening of the day after she sent the letter, Onegin had called and coolly turned down her offered love. Since this visit he has avoided the Larin home and retreated into the solitude of his own estate. Six months after his lecturing to Tatiana against youthful indiscretion, Onegin finds from Lenski that he has been invited to Tatiana's name-day party. In his current reclusive mood he feels unenticed: "But there will be a mass of people and all kinds of such scum." No, Lenski assures him, only the family. Under pressure, Onegin consents to come.

He and his young friend arrive as dinner is served, and are placed opposite Tatiana. Onegin notices her deep embarrassment at having to face the man to whom she had bared her soul, only to receive such a chilly rebuff. Exasperated at Lenski's having exposed him to Tatiana's discomfort and to a vast crowd of tiresome country neighbors, Onegin in Five: XXXI vows to avenge himself on his friend. Later that evening he will flirt with Olga to the point where Lenski storms away from the party and next day challenges him to a duel—which will end in Lenski's death.

When Onegin sits down before the flustered Tatiana, it is therefore a key moment in the novel, but what particularly attracted me to this stanza was its typically Pushkinian mobility. In the midst of this emotionally charged situation, the poet suddenly dispels the charge in a jocular parenthetical comment on an oversalted pie, lingers in lively description of the banquet fare, then glides away again into a passionate personal recollection. Everything is terse and direct. Pushkin moves from one subject to another with no fuss, no nonsense—even as he shows his playfulness—and no waste, no mistakes. One of the great charms of Pushkin—something no other poet can match—is the sense that he comes at whatever he finds in life without hesitation, savors it to the full, masters it, and passes on. This surely is the secret of what Edmund Wilson calls Pushkin's "infinite sympathy and his equally universal detachment":[15] one moment he can be *in* Tatiana's and Onegin's predicament, the next he can suddenly cut off to bring the scene of the feast to vivid life, and then soar away in playful recollection to a passionate moment in his own life, before once more returning in the next stanza to the pop and fizz of the party.

Now let us turn to Five: XXXII. Pushkin's original is interlineated on the left with Nabokov's revised version; Arndt on the right. I selected Arndt for closest scrutiny because he was the target of Nabokov's celebrated review, because reviewers of Nabokov had most often chosen him as a basis for comparison, and because his translation of this stanza happens to be the worst of those examined. The kinds of flaws Arndt reveals here are present in all the verse translations, differing in proportion from stanza to stanza, but never absent for more than a moment.

1   *Konéchno, ne odín Evgéniy*
    Of course, not only Eugene   Tatyana's plight, of course,
                                                  was noted

2   *Smyatén'e Táni vídet' mog;*
    Tanya's confusion might have seen;   Not by Eugene alone, but
                                           now

3   *No tsél'yu vzórov i suzhdéniy*
    but the target of looks and comment   Their scrutiny was all
                                           devoted

4   *V to vrémya zhírnyy bĭl piróg*
    Was at the time a rich pie   To a plump pie that made its
                                           bow

5   *(ĭ. neschást'iyu, peresolyónnïy);*
    (unfortunately, oversalted);   (But proved too salt, alas!)
                                           Already

6   *Da vot v butĭlke zasmolyónnoy,*
    and here, in bottle sealed with pitch, In pitch-sealed flasks arrives
                                           the heady

7   *Mézhdu zharkím i blan-manzhé,*
    between meat course and blancmangér,   Champagne 'twixt meat-
                                           course and blancmange

8   *Tsimlyánskoe nesút uzhé;*
    Tsimlyanski wine is brought already,   And in its wake, in serried
                                           range,

9   *Za nim stroy ryúmok úzkih, dlínnïh,*
    followed by an array of glasses,   The glass that slimly, trimly
        narrow, long,   tapers

10 *Podóbno tálii tvoéy,*
    similar to your waist,   So like your slender waist,
                                           Zizi,

11 *Zizí, kristáll dushí moéy,*
    Zizi, the crystal of my soul   Heart's crystal, you that
                                           used to be

12 *Predmét stihóv moíh nevínnïh,*
    the subject of my innocent verse,   Game for my first poetic
                                           capers,

13 *Lyubví primánchivïy fiyál,*
    enluring vial of love,   Allurement's phial that I
                                           adored.

14 *Tĭ, ot kogó ya p'yan bĭvál!*
    you, of whom drunk I used to be!   Drunk with the wine of love
                                           you poured!

Notice first that Arndt's opening lines destroy the dramatic situation. Throughout *Eugene Onegin* no one except Tatiana and Onegin knows or guesses that she has any feelings for Onegin, let alone that she has written him a passionate declaration and been spurned. The whole point of Pushkin's first quatrain is that despite Tatiana's embarrassment being too visible to hide, no one but Onegin notices. It is a secret bond between the two, almost a moment of sympathy for Tatiana on Onegin's part. But in Arndt's translation, as in Deutsch's (but not in Johnston's, which often benefits from Nabokov's), that slight switch from "not only Eugene *might* have seen Tanya's confusion" to "*noted* Not by Eugene alone," that simple failure to render the contextual sense of the modal verb, alters Pushkin's drama. It also makes nonsense of the story to come. In Six: xviii, Pushkin muses over Lenski on the eve of the fatal duel: "If he had known what a wound burned the heart of my Tatiana!" If, in other words, Lenski had known of her love for Onegin, he might never have issued the challenge at all. Later, in Seven: xlvii: "and her heart's secret . . . she mutely guards meantime and shares with none." Had that one moment of confusion at the name-day party publicly given her away, she would not be the Tatiana we know now, able to nurse her ardent secret in such icily poised, unbreachable reserve.

Line 3. "*Their* scrutiny": in the context of Arndt's lines, the natural antecedent seems to be Tatiana and Eugene. For a moment it seems (in Arndt) that while others also note Tatiana's confusion, Tatiana and Eugene have passed on to scrutinizing the pie. This makes little sense, and readers are forced to decide for themselves what must have happened.

Line 4. "A plump pie that made its bow." Pushkin has simply *bil pirog* (lexically, "was [a] pie"). A "chancrous metaphor," as Nabokov complains of another Arndt image,[16] a shameless filler that travesties Pushkin's spareness, rightness, precision. Pushkin would *never* use an image so execrable, even when he parodies Lenski's trite elegies.

Lines 6–8 Charles Johnston renders: "now they're bringing bottles to which some pitch is clinging"—which almost conjures up a scene of the servants having a pitch-fight down in the cellar. The hideous continuous present for the sake of a feminine rhyme ("they're bringing" / "is clinging") is a fault common to all the verse translators.* Rhyme, which of course was responsible for Arndt's pie "now" making its "bow" (and later to nourish a rhyme Arndt will have some

---

* Johnston elsewhere manages to turn Pushkin's "I only observe, in parenthesis" into "But, inside brackets, I'm contending" (Four: xix), as if Pushkin were a Lilliputian in a Brobdingnagian printing shop.

"sentimental" folk "fed on lentil"), is one of the great charms of Pushkin: so subtle, so exact, seemingly so subordinate to direct plain sense. And Pushkin never uses off-rhymes. How exactly is Arndt's "blancmange" to rhyme with "range"? No wonder John Bayley compares the artificial efforts of the verse translators to a dog dancing on its hind legs.[17]

Arndt tritely calls his champagne "heady" in line 6, while omitting "Tsimlyanski" in line 7, a cheap Russian sparkling wine which like the blancmangér serves to define the Larins' rather modest circumstances. In the next line Arndt sins in minor but persistent fashion against Pushkin's purity and economy. He introduces a dead metaphor, "in its wake," instead of Pushkin's plain *za nim* ("after it"), which makes the proclaimed orderliness of the "serried range" of glasses bob up and down rather precariously. Need it be said that Pushkin takes care not to mix images? In line 9, a *single* "glass" is somehow "in serried range." In line 10, Zizi's waist, already compared to a glass that "slimly, trimly" tapers, need not be defined by Arndt a third time as "slender." Unlike Conrad, Pushkin shows no fondness for buttering buttered butter: *his* glasses are simply "narrow" and "long," and after that he knows enough not to tell us again that Zizi's waist is slender.

Now we arrive at the phrase "you that used to be Game for my poetic capers." "Game for" suggests "ready to brave something risky," but the sense does not fit. "Game" and "capers," in this banqueting scene, could be venison and its condiment. No? What does the line mean, then? Why should we be satisfied that it rhymes with "tapers," and not care that it refuses to yield sense until we refer to Pushkin or Nabokov?

Only two lines to go. Instead of Pushkin drunk with love for Zizi we have in Arndt the image of leering Zizi pouring out more wine to make Pushkin tipsy—except that since Zizi is the phial, she is in Arndt's image somehow pouring out herself.

Out of fourteen lines, only one in Arndt's translation does not betray Pushkin. How does Nabokov compare? In line 3, *suzhdeniy* would normally be translated "judgments" or "opinions," not "comments" (*zamechaniy*): Nabokov wants to make clear here that the judgments are the guests' vocal exclamations. In line 13, he selects the bizarre "enluring" because Pushkin, instead of the usual *zamanchivïy*, "alluring," draws on an archaic equivalent with a different prefix, and Nabokov revives the archaic English "enlure" to match. The final line seems ungainly in Nabokov's version, but although in English one can be drunk *on* love, drunk *with* love, or made drunk *by* love for a woman, each of these prepositions has connotations he takes care to rule out: drunk on her (Pushkin snoring prostrate on Zizi), drunk with her (a tipsy glint in her eye and his), made drunk by her (Arndt's smirking wine-pourer returns). "Of" avoids even the faintest unwanted association.

Of course that last line, so carefully considered, would be an abomination as an independent line of English verse: "you, of whom drunk I used to be." Unquestionably Nabokov's lines are not only unrhymed but often flat and gracelessly awkward, unlike Pushkin's, and it was this that many reviewers found a cruel betrayal of Pushkin and sufficient reason to prefer Arndt's nonsense jingles. But placed under Pushkin's line, approximating Pushkin's order and rigorously faithful to his sense, Nabokov's last line here is simply and typically illuminating. Nabokov pays Pushkin the compliment that his exact meaning matters—and how can we take literature seriously if we do not believe this?—and that his music cannot be matched.

III

Readers of verse have long known that a poem can be truly appreciated only in the language in which it was conceived. As Samuel Johnson remarked: "Poetry, indeed, cannot be translated; and, therefore, it is the poets that preserve languages; for we would not be at the trouble to learn a language, if we could have all that is written in it just as well in translation. But as the beauties of poetry cannot be preserved in any language except that in which it was originally written, we learn the language."[18] For Johnson, that meant learning Greek, Latin, French, German, Spanish, and Italian. Even he might have balked at adding Russian to his list. Nabokov's translation is designed for those who may not have the time to master Pushkin's language but know that a great poet cannot be read at second hand.

As Anthony Burgess puts it:

And so most of us read Mallarmé and Leopardi in the original, with a crib on the opposite page. We read Dante that way also, and *El Cid* and Lorca—Romance poetry being what our schools have best equipped us to read. We also read Goethe and Hölderlin, even though we had no formal lessons in German. After all, the Teutonic languages are more cognate with English than the Romance. It is when we start to move East that the trouble begins.

The trouble begins because of strange alphabets (they take only an hour to learn, but this is too long for many) and because of the apparent lack of familiar linguistic elements (few people are any good at piercing disguises). Here, it seems, arty translations are in order.

But as he points out with a few concrete examples, even a translation as successful as Edward Fitzgerald's completely betrays its original. He concluded: "If we want to read Omar, then, we must learn a little Persian and ask for a good, very literal, crib. And if we want to read Pushkin we must learn some Russian and thank God for Nabokov."[19]

Although many read poetry in its language of origin, with a supporting crib, Nabokov has been far more vehement than anyone else in execrating the arty translation that passes itself off as a more or less adequate simulacrum of the original poem. But in the context of his other work, his vehemence makes perfect and very serious sense. In *Invitation to a Beheading* and again in *Bend Sinister* he insisted that unless one makes the effort to understand and appreciate the uniqueness of things—a tree, a person, a poem—one lives in an unreal world of cheap imitations, a nightmare waxworks of interchangeable because dimly perceived parts.

This, in fact, is a key to Nabokov's work: not that nothing is real, as many readers idly suppose he says, but that it is only as the mind tries to peer past the generalization or the commonplace that things actually start to *become* real, individual, detailed, differentiated from one another. It is our taking things for granted, our supposing that they are easily accessible to the mind because no more complex than our handy labels, that turns things and thinkers into inhabitants of a two-dimensional, depthless world like the one surrounding Cincinnatus C. In this sort of world—but not in Nabokov's—a poem is just a jingle, and one poem that jingles in a way similar to another will be an adequate surrogate, and never mind too much what it means.

IV

If readers from Dr. Johnson to Anthony Burgess have preferred to eschew easy rhymed dummies and to confront instead the intricacies of the original, why did Nabokov's translation provoke so much criticism? There is one overwhelming reason: the translation was *not* printed, as it should have been, in interlinear fashion, beneath Pushkin's transliterated lines. The verse versions of other translators of course were never meant to appear this way: interleaved with Pushkin, they would confuse anyone with little or no Russian and reveal to anyone who knows more of the language their stuffing and stucco. But Nabokov *designed* his translation to be read closely with the Russian text, then let the translation appear without the original printed on the same page. No wonder his phrasing seemed grotesque.

In the mid-1950s, when Jason Epstein at Doubleday was keen to publish all the Nabokov he could, Nabokov told him he would like to have his *Eugene Onegin* set out threefold: the Russian original, a transliteration, and his translation. Epstein laughed and said if he could print the thing on *three* facing pages, he would.[20] Nabokov soon decided the Cyrillic script was unnecessary, and even expressed in the commentary his fervent wish that Cyrillic and all other non-Roman scripts would soon be replaced by Roman.* Although in April 1955, when he thought he had completed the translation, he still expected to print it with the Russian *en regard*,[21] he seems to have decided against that plan by the time he prepared the fair copy of his commentary in 1957. Why?

He had spent four years more on *Eugene Onegin* than he had anticipated, and by late 1957 he simply wanted to finish and move on to his new novel. Throughout the 1950s, moreover, he had had continual difficulties in publishing his work. Despite his close relationship with the *New Yorker*, the magazine had turned down two of his last three stories and his best English poem. No press in America had dared to touch *Lolita*, and he had been obliged to have it published by a Paris pornographer. Even poor, harmless, popular *Pnin* was rejected by Viking and Harper and Brothers. Already Nabokov had eleven hefty folders of translation and scholarly notes. Would he find a publisher at all, if he swelled his manuscript still more by addding a transliteration? And he could not afford to wait: what if his findings seeped out, or other researchers stumbled on his discoveries while he waited for a publisher?

Individual lines or stanzas on which Nabokov wishes to comment in detail are sometimes presented within the commentaries as Five: xxxii was printed above: transliterated Russian interlineated with the translation, and with the accented syllables of all Russian words of more than one syllable marked. For anyone learning Russian, accents are a dark wood full of threatening noises. All Russian words, no matter how long, have only one accented syllable. Learning precisely where the accent falls for each word—especially in a word whose accent shifts from stem to ending and back as different inflectional endings are added—is far from easy. It seems curious that Nabokov, who went to such inordinate lengths in his commentary to explain

---

* *Eugene Onegin*, 3:399n. This makes all the stranger Nabokov's decision to include, and only in a separate volume, a photographic facsimile of the 1837 edition of *Eugene Onegin*, in minuscule Cyrillic print.

the principles of Russian prosody and to provide every other scrap of information relevant to the poem, chose not to provide a stressed interlinear transliteration of the whole poem, for without accents marked, even advanced Russian students might have difficulty in pronouncing correctly and ascertaining the metrical flow of almost every line.

In revising his text in 1966, Nabokov followed Pushkin's lineation exactly, even at the cost of a wrenched and unnatural word order in English. To Gleb Struve he wrote that his text had now become "ideally interlinear," yet even this revised version fails to provide an interlinear, transliterated, accented Russian text. When someday Nabokov's translation is published in this fashion, I expect every reviewer who knows Pushkin in the original and who has preferred verse translations over Nabokov's uncompromising literalism will recant.

V

Not that there are no problems in his translation. In theory he sternly opposed a translation as a surrogate for a great poem, but even he could not quite relinquish the idea altogether. He preserved an iambic meter in his lineated prose, claiming that retaining this one vestige of verse form "assisted rather than hindered fidelity."[22] Actually he kept the regular rhythm not to further fidelity but simply because he disliked free verse and believed no great poetry had ever been written outside the discipline of formal meter. To preserve the meter, One: VIII's plain *tseliy den'* ("the whole day") becomes the jarringly jejune "the livelong day." When Nabokov has Onegin tell Tatiana in Four: XIII he would have chosen her "If life by the domestic circle I'd want to limit," he introduces unnecessary obscurity into Pushkin's clarity rather than opt for the less scannable but more natural and lucid "If . . . I *had* wanted to limit." For the sake of this routine rhythm Nabokov repeatedly sacrifices a plain English that would reflect Pushkin's plain Russian sense—even though, as he shows in his commentary, Russian and English iambic meters are not in any case equivalent.[23]

One of the great strengths of Nabokov's commentary is his alertness to pre-Pushkinian intonations in French and English poetry of the seventeenth to nineteenth centuries. But he sometimes incorporates into the text of his translation an association that would have been better confined to the commentary. In Six: XXI he renders a Pushkin line "Whither, ah! whither are ye fled" rather than adhere to the literal "receded," and explains that he prefers "to echo the cry so often heard in English seventeenth- and eighteenth-century poetry." His examples from 1656 to 1818, from John Collop, Thomas Fletcher, Pope, James Beattie, Anne Laetitia Barbauld, Barry Cornwall, and Keats, are impressive in their range. But Pushkin could have written the Russian for "Whither are ye fled," and chose not to. Nabokov should have respected his choice. Of course "*livelong* day" and "Whither are ye *fled*" are not at all of the order of Arndt's "pie that made its bow," but it seems absurd that after having argued so persuasively and so absolutely for rigorous literal fidelity Nabokov should occasionally betray his principles for such dubious gains.

A more serious problem arises not from his falling short of literalism but from his desire to push it too far. *Absolute* fidelity presupposes that a perfect one-to-one correspondence can be found between the words of the Russian original and the available lexicon of English, when no such match is often possible. Sometimes Nabokov hits on coinages or revivals that precisely because they do render the Russian with impeccable word-for-word accuracy create a crisp and novel poetry in English: "With frostdust silvers / his beaver collar" (One: xvi); "The mannered tomcat sitting on the stove, / purring, might wash his muzzlet with his paw" (Five: v). More often the search for the perfect equivalent runs up against the impossibility of the enterprise. As Nabokov tries to tune more and more finely, he gets a sudden blast from another station, since what corresponds more closely to the Russian in one direction differs from it harshly in another. In One: xxiv, he describes Onegin's scissors as "curvate." He later explained that he felt the more natural choices would "not quite do justice to Onegin's regularly bent manicure scissors."[24] But nor does the rare "curvate" do justice to the naturalness of Pushkin's *krivïe*, the common word for "curved" or "crooked."

Often Nabokov endeavors to specify the values of a Pushkin word so precisely that he selects an English word which not only conveys the direct sense but serves as a complex gloss. In the first version of One: xlvii, he writes: "rememorating intrigues of past years, / rememorating a past love." When challenged about his choice, he explained: "In order to indicate the archaic note in *vospomnya* (used by Pushkin . . . instead of *vspomnya*, or *vspomniv*, or *vspominaya*) as well as to suggest the deep sonorous diction of both lines (*vospomnya prezhnih let romany, vospomnya* etc.), I had to find something more reverberating and evocative than 'recalling intrigues of past years.' "[25] His reply suggests what a brilliant find the archaic *rememorate* was for Pushkin's archaism, but without this explanation—not present in

Nabokov's commentary—the word *rememorate* itself in the translation fails to convey the information Nabokov intended it to contain.

Again and again Nabokov squeezes a valuable gloss into one word of the translation, one rare word tracked down in long hours of searching through Webster's Second International Dictionary. But for the appropriateness of the English word to be valued, for the nuances of Pushkin's word to be savored, a separate prose gloss is still essential. Another example: "he scrabs the poor thing up" for *bednyazhku tsaptsarap* (One: XIV). Once again, on being challenged, Nabokov explained his choice of verb, marked as a dialect word in Webster's: "This *tsaptsarap*—a 'verbal interjection' presupposing (as Pushkin notes when employing it in another poem) the existence of the artificial verb *tsaptsarapat'*, jocular and onomatopoeic—combines *tsapat'* ('to snatch') with *tsarapat'* ('to scratch'). I rendered Pushkin's uncommon word by the uncommon 'scrab up,' which combines 'grab' and 'scratch.' "[26] Once more we need the gloss that his published commentary did not provide before we can appreciate Nabokov's mot juste, and Pushkin's.

One cannot compress into a single English word as much information as Nabokov often has at his disposal about a particular word in Pushkin, and then expect the English-speaking reader to infer correctly, say, that "scrab" has been chosen not because its Russian counterpart is a dialect word for "grab" but because the original term fuses Russian verbs for "snatch" and "scratch." Nabokov's diligence in searching so widely for words so exactly right would be exemplary *provided* he explained in every case in a separate prose gloss just why he had to forage so far.

Nabokov aimed to render Pushkin with such accuracy that he could incorporate the full harmonics of meaning, overtone as well as base note. In advocating such absolute precision he occasionally played the deliberate provocateur. At one point he translates Pushkin's *obez'yana* not as the literal "monkey" but as "sapajou" (a spider monkey). Edmund Wilson leaped at the word. Nabokov replied, with a confident smile:

He wonders why I render *dostoyno staryh obez'yan* as "worthy of old sapajous" and not as "worthy of old monkeys." True, *obez'yana* means any kind of monkey but it so happens that neither "monkey" nor "ape" is good enough in the context.

"Sapajou" (which technically is applied to two genera of neotropical monkeys) has in French a colloquial sense of "ruffian," "lecher," "ridiculous chap." Now, in lines 1–2 and 9–11 of Four: VII ("the less we love a woman, the easier 'tis to be liked by her . . . but that grand game is

worthy of old sapajous of our forefathers' vaunted times") Pushkin echoes a moralistic passage in his own letter written in French from Kishi-
nev to his young brother in Moscow in the autumn of 1822, that is seven
months before beginning *Eugene Onegin* and two years before reaching
Canto Four. The passage, well known to readers of Pushkin, goes:
*"Moins on aime une femme et plus on est sûr de l'avoir . . . mais cette jouissance
est digne d'un vieux sapajou du dix-huitième siècle."* Not only could I not
resist the temptation of retranslating the *obez'yan* of the canto into the
Anglo-French "sapajous" of the letter, but I was also looking forward to
somebody's pouncing on that word and allowing me to retaliate with
that wonderfully satisfying reference.[27]

Nabokov would have been far better to have left *obez'yan* as "monkeys" and to introduce the "sapajou" subtext in a gloss (in the revised edition, he did add this gloss to his commentary, but kept the
translation intact). "Sapajous" may have been what Pushkin had in
mind, but *obez'yan* was what he wrote, and what readers of Pushkin's
time (who after all had not yet read Pushkin's collected letters) would
hear, before, if at all, they heard the overtone of "sapajou." For Nabokov to be more precise than Pushkin is for him to become less than
literal.

Elsewhere Nabokov's desire to record within the translation Gallic
overtones as well as the primary Russian tone can distort his literalism by turning a plain Russian word into an English freak. He repeatedly translates *nega* ("pure comfort" grading into "sweet bliss"),
a favorite among Russian Romantic poets, short and easily rhymed,
into the archaic "mollitude." For *nega*, Nabokov does provide sensitive descriptions of its range of meanings, and he also notes that in
using the word, "Pushkin and his constellation were trying to render
the French poetical formulas *paresse voluptueuse, mollesse, molles dé-
lices*, etc., which the English Arcadians had already turned into 'soft
delights.' "[28] A worthwhile observation, but since Russians of Pushkin's time encountering *nega* would have thought the word quite self-
explanatory in context, and since Pushkin was not seeking to *remind*
his readers of the French *mollesse*, why should Nabokov render this
natural Russian word by the archaic, extremely obscure "mollitude"?
Once again he tries to incorporate his gloss within a single word of
the translation. Once again, as with "sapajou," the choice seems to
reflect his combative spirit: he wants to jar readers accustomed to
daintily smooth translations, and he wants to insist that his own
translation is *not* meant to stand on its own, to work as English, to
remain independent of its original, but that it is simply a series of

signals designed to point at Pushkin and turn us back to the effort of understanding every nuance of *Eugene Onegin*.

VI

Even more jarring than a lexical curio like "mollitude" are the much more frequent wrenchings of English word order. In the revised translation there occur horrors like these, from Eight: xxviii:

> Of a constricting rank
> the ways how fast she has adopted!
>
> . . . .
>
> And he her heart had agitated!
> About him in the gloom of night,
> as long as Morpheus had not flown down,
> time was, she virginally brooded.

When a great stylist produces such ungainly English, he has evidently decided on awkwardness for awkwardness' sake. As Nabokov wrote to Edmund Wilson in 1957, he welcomed "the awkward turn, the fish bone of the meager truth."[29] He deliberately translated Pushkin *out of* Russian rather than *into* English. He had his reasons.

He had undertaken his translation in the first place because he simply could not teach *Eugene Onegin* with the rhymed paraphrases available. Throughout his long years of labor, as his project expanded out of all recognition, he remained faithful to his original motivation. In his foreword to the published translation, he wrote: "Pushkin has likened translators to horses changed at the posthouses of civilization. The greatest reward I can think of is that students may use my work as a pony."[30] They do. In university libraries throughout the English-speaking world, volume 1 of the four-volume set, the translation itself, has not only long since lost its dust jacket, but its spine has given way and been rebound, the cloth covering is frayed around the edges, the stiff boards have turned soggily limp through constant use. In a draft blurb Nabokov wrote for his book in 1962, he noted that "Although the ordinary reader (if such a being exists) is welcome to glance through this work, its hoped-for user is the college instructor."[31] One such instructor, Elena Levin, declares categorically: "You can't teach *Eugene Onegin* without it."

But perhaps I should quote her in full: "It's unreadable—but you can't teach *Eugene Onegin* without it."[32] Why is it so unreadable?

Most people who aim to persuade others to a contrary point of view will try to discover something in common, some way of seeing what can be agreed on, as a basis for step-by-step discussion. Nabokov's methods are different. Although he often holds opinions he knows to be at odds with those of the majority of his audience, he prefers not to argue point by point but to shock, to startle, to take the imagination by surprise in order to disrupt and dislodge a settled conviction. One of his reasons for keeping his translation unreadable is certainly to upset those who have preferred their translations fluent and effortless.

A more serious reason is his insistence on challenging his readers to consult and confront Pushkin. By refusing to offer smooth, self-sufficient English, he can issue a constant, line-by-line reminder to students—or to the general readers who he hoped might be "moved to learn Pushkin's language"[33]—that they must keep returning to the Russian.

Above all he wanted to represent every turn of Pushkin's thought with the utmost exactitude. He rightly deplored the verse translations whose rough approximations never permit that precision and in fact can be hailed as "readable" "only because the drudge or the rhymster has substituted easy platitudes for the breathtaking intricacies of the text." Pushkin has often been praised, Nabokov notes in an unpublished Russian lecture, for qualities like "harmony, clarity, proportion, fullness of sound, fullness of being." These aspects of Pushkin are real enough, but they still fail to sum up his elusive spirit. They are generalizations, labels, and as such are insufficient, leaving "the person who sees in Pushkin only Olympian radiance . . . puzzled by this or that obscure or bitter line." One Russian reviewer of Nabokov's translation admitted that despite having known *Eugene Onegin* in the original for fifty years, it is "only now, thanks to Nabokov's help, that I have become aware of certain ambiguities in Pushkin's text and of the possibilities of varying interpretations."[34]

Often the awkwardness of Nabokov's translation merely reflects accurately Pushkin's peculiar compressions, where other translators reduce unprecedented locutions to easy banalities. But at other times one looks at his translation and thinks there can be no excuse, no reason in Pushkin, for this or that particularly repellent sequence of nominally English phrases. I had planned to analyze samples like those quoted at the beginning of this section to show Nabokov's revised translation at its most grotesque and to reprove him for willful perversions of natural English. But when I turned to the verse translations of the same lines, I found their English no more acceptable than Nabokov's—though for different reasons—and infinitely less faithful to Pushkin.

If we compared such atrocities of Nabspeak as the example quoted above from Eight: xxviii (Tatiana's rise in station) with the verse translators' versions we would merely repeat the conclusions we drew from comparing Nabokov's Five: XXXII (Tatiana's confusion) with those of Arndt, Deutsch, and Johnston. Line after line, stanza after stanza, the verse translators exhibit the same defects. Each may have his or her own special stamp—Deutsch's glibness, Arndt's skewed English, Johnston's cumbersome and defocalizing abstractions—but they are all forced again and again by the exigencies of rhyme into facile, mixed, and muddled images, fillers, tautologies, repetitions, obscurities, confusions, and self-contradictions that sully Pushkin's purity of thought. Not only do they substitute jingles for Pushkin's full-throated music, not only do they fail to render his meaning, but their sacrificing reason for rhyme destroys what is so irresistible in Pushkin: the harmony between sure thought, sure words, and his sure mastery of his world.

Nabokov, on the other hand, distorts English deliberately and transparently. Deliberately, to remind us that this English has no independent life of its own, and has value only when placed alongside Pushkin's Russian. And transparently, because when his words take up their natural place under their Russian counterparts—as we saw in the case of the grotesque "you, of whom drunk I used to be"— they suddenly allow us to see through to Pushkin. Like the lenses of a microscope, they seem at first merely to assault the eye that tries to peer through them, until we slip the specimen under, and the glass instantly loses its disconcerting opacity. Through the perfect translucence of the polished, minutely calibrated lenses, the intricate veins of the new find leap into focus.

Nabokov chose as an epigraph for the introduction to his translation a sentence from Pushkin, his favorite Russian writer of the early nineteenth century, on Chateaubriand, his favorite French writer of the time, and his *Le paradis perdu:* "Nowadays—an unheard-of case!—the first of French writers is translating Milton word for word and proclaiming that an interlinear translation would be the summit of his art, had such been possible." That seems like Nabokov's oblique statement of intent for his own translation of *Eugene Onegin.* When his translation is printed as it should have been, with a transliterated and accented Russian text between its lines, not only will it no longer seem unreadable, but the English-speaking world will find Pushkin himself within reach.

VII
Commentary

Nabokov's translation occupies only a part of one of the four volumes of his *Eugene Onegin.* The remaining twelve hundred pages of notes, which took up the vast bulk of the time he spent on the project, form the most detailed commentary ever made on *Eugene Onegin*. Although some reviewers found aspects of Nabokov's annotations intensely exasperating, overall judgments ranged only from John Bayley's "a better commentary on a poem has never been written" to the repeated observation that as a commentary on *Onegin* it was "the best in any language."[35]

The commentary is the result of a prodigious amount of research from 1948 to 1958, a decade during which Nabokov also wrote an autobiography (first in English, then in Russian), two novels, and a number of stories; set up and taught four new courses at Cornell and Harvard that have already produced three books and could give rise to a fourth; translated and annotated *The Song of Igor's Campaign*, and cotranslated Lermontov's *A Hero of Our Time*. He had known *Eugene Onegin* from the age of nine or ten, he had written a brilliant imitation of the poem in 1926, he had lectured on it and written about it in the 1930s, and he had begun to teach it at Wellesley in 1946. With his intimate prior knowledge of the poem, his superb powers of recall, and his acute sensitivity to verbal intonation, he could scour through masses of seventeenth-, eighteenth-, and nineteenth-century Russian, French, and English literature in the libraries of Cornell, Harvard, and New York City, ready to seize on the smallest phrase that might recall or elucidate Pushkin.

The variety, depth, and exactitude of his information are extraordinary. Pushkin ends his poem noting that "many, many days" have rushed by since he first envisaged Tatiana and Onegin, and Nabokov notes laconically: "Three thousand seventy-one days (May 9, 1823–Oct. 5, 1831)." Annotating a typical stanza, Three: XXXII, where Tatiana stays up all night to write her letter, Nabokov describes Pushkin's drawings in the margins of his draft (his father in profile, Tatiana in a flimsy shift); explains the sound and sense of the "untranslatable Russian exclamation *oh* of weariness and distress"; tells us how one sealed letters before envelopes were invented; indicates the nuances of a Russian diminutive; describes the evening ablutions and night attire of a young Russian lady in the provinces in 1820; sums up Pushkin's travels at the time he wrote this section of the poem; and translates in full a rejected stanza.

Reluctant to omit any information readers might conceivably need, Nabokov registers all the available bibliographical details about Pushkin's poem. Though barred from the manuscripts, difficult of access even for Soviet Pushkinists, he was nevertheless able to reconstruct a new sequence for the surviving fragments of "chapter 10," a reconstruction now accepted by Soviet scholars.[36] Working after a century of investigations into the life of Russia's national poet, he could add little new biographical information, but he retells aspects of Pushkin's life with verve and an eye for the entangled themes of dueling and destiny.

But his major contribution to Pushkin studies was in terms of purely literary rather than biographical or bibliographical scholarship. His wide reading and his alertness to literature as convention, device, and effect allowed him to show far more thoroughly than ever before the extent of Pushkin's reliance on French literature, and on English via French. With typical wit and grace and one of his invariably pointed evaluations, he notes a French echo in Tatiana's letter to Onegin: "Tatiana may have seen (among the contributions to her sister's album, perhaps) an elegy of 1819 by Marceline Desbordes-Valmore (1786–1859), a kind of female Musset minus the color and the wit,"[37] and then quotes the appropriate lines.

Much of the life of the commentary comes from what one critic calls Nabokov's spirited précis that spare us the tedium of consulting a source or an allusion ourselves.[38] From his summary of Rousseau's *Julie, ou la nouvelle Heloïse*:

> Smallpox, which later was to afflict for purpose of plot or emotional interest so many handsome characters . . . is caught by Saint-Preux from sick Julie, whose hand he kisses before starting on his *voyage autour du monde*; he comes back from it badly pock-marked, *crottu* (pt. IV, Letter VIII), but her face is spared except for some fugitive *rougeur*; he wonders if they will recognize each other; they do; and presently Saint-Preux is gorging himself on curds and whey at Julie de Wolmar's house, in a Rousseauesque world of eggs, *laitages*, vegetables, trout, and generously watered wine.
>
> Artistically, as fiction, the novel is total trash, but it contains digressions of some historical interest, and the glimpses it affords of its author's morbid, intricate, and at the same time rather naïve mind are far from negligible.[39]

Nabokov provides all he can to bring an English-speaking reader closer to Pushkin's verse music. An appendix to the commentary contains an innovative and much-acclaimed comparative study of English and Russian prosody, adducing examples from English poets from Gower and Chaucer, by way of Surrey and Shakespeare, Charles Crotton and Matthew Prior, to William Morris and T. S. Eliot. Nabokov tracks down in the fables of La Fontaine two sequences of lines that prefigure by chance the complicated rhyme scheme of the fourteen-line stanza Pushkin invented for *Eugene Onegin*; he sums up the effect of the rhyme: "This opening pattern (a clear-cut sonorous elegiac quatrain) and the terminal one (a couplet resembling the code of an octave or that of a Shakespearean sonnet) can be compared to patterns on a painted ball or top that are visible at the beginning and at the end of the spin";[40] and he presents two brilliant stanzas of his own in the *Eugene Onegin* pattern to show English-speaking readers just what the stanza can do.

He treats us to a superb fifty-page summary of the novel's structure; to a running commentary, thoroughly independent and happily irreverent, on its narrative and psychological flow; and to analyses and evaluations of the magic or the failed spells of individual lines and stanzas. And to enable us to picture the little world of the poem, he provides all kinds of information, more precise than had ever been assembled before, about the time and place of its events and about its social and its natural spheres: modes of dress and gesture, species of berry and tree.

VIII

If Nabokov's commentary has become indispensable to all serious students of Pushkin's masterpiece, what does it reveal about Nabokov himself? Some reviewers complained about the aimless heterogeneity of its information; others suspected it—especially since it appeared after *Pale Fire*—of harboring a secret "artistic" aim, perhaps as a send-up of scholarship. In fact, the commentary is neither aimless pedantry nor covert art. It is a serious, impassioned work of scholarship that while fully committed to serving Pushkin—and precisely because of that commitment—reveals as much about Nabokov as many of his novels.

Through all four volumes Nabokov advances the claims of the particular over the general, the detail over the generalization, the unique and irreplaceable individual over the group or the generic surrogate. Each of us, he feels, must discover the world's particularity for ourselves. To relinquish our curiosity and to accept blandly the convenience of ready-made generalities is to turn a live world into unreality, into a superstore of prepackaged goods, stick-on labels, artificial lighting, into the nightmare existence of *Invitation to a Beheading*. "To be sure," he declares, "there is an average reality, perceived by all of us, but that is not true reality; it is only the reality of general ideas, conventional forms of humdrummery."

"Average reality," he adds, "begins to rot and stink as soon as the act of individual creation ceases to animate a subjectively perceived texture." Everyday "reality," if it is only this pile of dead commonplaces, has no existence worth the name. Genuine reality, on the other hand, in a world of infinite differentiation, "is a very subjective affair"—which does not mean that it is mere solipsistic fancy: "I can only define it as a kind of gradual accumulation of information; and as specialization."[41] Only by this "accumulation of information," by vigilant determination to push beyond the easy generalization, can the mind approach the endless particularity of things, reanimate its world, and make the most of life or art.

In an unpublished dust-jacket blurb he drafted for *Eugene Onegin*, Nabokov wrote: "A display of general ideas in the notes to a poem is akin to a paraphrase in the translation of its text. Both generalities are absent from the present work."[42] Attempting in his translation to render word by word every rough and rare particularity of Pushkin's sense and to resist the currently accepted mode of translation, he undertook his commentary in a similar defense of Pushkin's particulars and an equally determined opposition to the dominant mode of literary criticism: "In art as in science there is no delight without the detail, and it is on details that I have tried to fix the reader's attention. Let me repeat that unless these are thoroughly understood and remembered, all 'general ideas' (so easily acquired, so profitably resold) must necessarily remain but worn passports allowing their bearers short cuts from one area of ignorance to another."[43]

IX

Nabokov rejects the philosophical, social, and historical generalizations so customary in literary criticism, and stresses instead the uniqueness of Pushkin's invented world. He guides us through its various parts, encouraging us to imagine Onegin's surroundings as precisely as Pushkin allows. Assembling disparate indicia, he pinpoints the likely latitude and longitude of the Larin-Lenski-Onegin estates, and describes their vegetation and their spatial and imaginative distance from Pushkin's own Boldino or from immemorial Arcadias. He tells us what Onegin might have worn and how he would have had his hair cut in 1819. He makes us *see* a gesture:

> The Russian gesture of relinquishment that *mahnul rukoy* (or *rukoyu*) conveys is a one-handed downward flip of hasty dismissal and renouncement. If analyzed in slow motion by the performer, he will see that his right hand, with fingers held rather loose, sketches a half turn from left to right, while at the same time his head makes a slight half turn from right to left. In other words, the gesture really consists of two simultaneous little movements: the hand abandons what it held, or hoped to

hold, and the head turns away from the scene of defeat or condemnation.[44]

Nabokov the naturalist refuses to accept that Pushkin's English readers should be blind to Russian nature. To translate the name of a Russian tree, he insisted it was necessary to question the accepted dictionary equivalent, a catch-all term that really caught nothing. The word he wanted had to do more than simply fill out a line, it had to fire the imagination as the Russian equivalent fires a Russian mind:

Dictionaries usually translate *cheryomuha* as "bird cherry," which is so vague as to be practically meaningless. Specifically, *cheryomuha* is the "racemose old-world bird cherry," Fr. *putier racémeux*, *Padus racemosa* Schneider. The Russian word, with its fluffy and dreamy syllables, admirably suits this beautiful tree, distinguished by its long racemes of flowers, giving the whole of it, when in bloom, a gentle pendulous appearance. A common and popular woodland plant in Russia, it is equally at home among the riverside alders and on the pine barren; its creamy-white, musky, Maytime bloom is associated in Russian hearts with the poetical emotions of youth. This racemose bird cherry lacks such a specific English designation (it has a few generic ones, all of them either uncouth or homonymous, or both) as would be neither as pedantic nor as irresponsible as the nonsense names that harmful drudges carefully transport from one Russian-English dictionary to another. At one time I followed the usually reliable Dahl's *Dictionary* in calling the tree "mahaleb," which proves to be, however, another plant altogether. Later I coined the term "musk cherry," which renders rather well the sound of *cheryomuha* and the fragrance of its bloom, but unfortunately evokes a taste that is not characteristic of its small, grainy, black fruit. I now formally introduce the simple and euphonious "racemosa" used as a noun and rhyming with "mimosa."[45]

Contrast with this the attitude of Babette Deutsch, who in rendering Tatiana's pre-auroral vigils on the balcony, replaces Pushkin's "and, morning's herald, the wind whiffs, and the day rises by degrees" with her own: "day would soon be on the march, And wake the birds in beech and larch" (Two: XXVIII). Nabokov asks what those birds and trees are doing here: "Why this and not, for instance: 'And take in words to bleach and starch' or any other kind of nonsense? The charming point is that beeches and larches, not being endemic in west central Russia, are the very last trees that Pushkin would imagine growing in the Larins' park."

Nabokov's love of the quiddity of things, and his refusal to accept substitutes like Deutsch's "beech and larch," lead to some delightful asides. On Pushkin's word "truffles," he begins a note that will introduce references to truffles he has uprooted in early nineteenth-century English and French literature: "These delicious fungi were appreciated to a degree that we, in a palateless age of artificial flavors, might hardly credit."[46] On Pushkin's "beefsteaks," he observes: "The European beefsteak used to be a small, thick, dark, ruddy, juicy, soft, special cut of tenderloin steak, with a generous edge of amber fat on the knife-side. It has little, if anything, in common with our American 'steaks'—the tasteless meat of restless cattle. The nearest approach to it is a *filet mignon*."[47]

X

Nabokov insists, more than any other commentator, on details of food, fashion, flora, as if Pushkin's characters inhabited a real world. Yet on the other hand he denies that they have any historical significance as representatives of Russian society. How can he affirm vividly one reality and deny the other? Is he not perversely inconsistent?

No. In the first place, he accepts readily the specific details thrown up by Pushkin's imagination, and yet he cannot see what these have to do with a generalized notion of Russia either common in Pushkin's time (and the more common it was, the less likely it was to have satisfied Pushkin's highly individual imagination) or advanced since then by this or that historical generalizer. And in the second place, he knew how much Pushkin's art draws on the art of other places and other times.

The romantic young poet Lenski might seem to typify the Romantic era, but Nabokov cautions: "It would be a mistake to regard Lenski, the lyrical lover, as a 'typical product of his time,' " and goes on to cite among others a passage from Shakespeare's collaborator Fletcher that sounds like pure Lenski. He writes of Tatiana, as "a 'type' (that pet of Russian critics)":

Ninety-nine per cent of the amorphous mass of comments produced with monstrous fluency by the *ideynaya kritika* (ideological critique) that has been worrying Pushkin's novel for more than a hundred years is devoted to passionately patriotic eulogies of Tatiana's virtue. This, cry the enthusiastic journalists of the Belinski-Dostoevski-Sidorov* type, is your pure, frank, responsible, altruistic, heroic Russian woman. Actu-

---

* Nabokov echoes here the equivalent of "every Tom, Dick and Harry," "Ivanov-Petrov-Sidorov."

ally, the French, English and German women of Tatiana's favorite novels were quite as fervid and virtuous as she.[48]

In the notes to the final chapter of the poem Nabokov cites enough
close parallels from Rousseau, Constant, Mme de Krüdener, Goethe,
Richardson, and the like to prove his case.

Onegin himself has been repeatedly dissected by social anatomists.
Nabokov locates the literary antecedents of young Onegin's morose-
ness of spirit in English spleen and French ennui and demonstrates
that by 1820 they were "a seasoned cliché of characterization that
Pushkin could play with at leisure, on the flowered brink of parody,
by transforming West-European formulas into virgin Russian." But
Russian critics have wanted to turn Onegin into something more. To
the quest for explanations of Onegin's condition, Nabokov observes,

> Russian critics applied themselves with tremendous zeal, accumulating
> in the course of a dozen decades one of the most boring masses of com-
> ments known to civilized man. Even a special term for Onegin's dis-
> temper has been invented (*Oneginstvo*, "Oneginism"); and thousands of
> pages have been devoted to him as a "type" of something or other (e.g.,
> of a "superfluous man" or a metaphysical "dandy," etc.). Brodski (1950),
> standing on the soapbox that had been provided a hundred years ago
> by Belinski, Herzen, and many others, diagnosed Onegin's "sickness"
> as the result of "tsarist despotism."
>
> Thus a character borrowed from books but brilliantly recomposed by
> a great poet to whom life and library were one, placed by that poet
> within a brilliantly reconstructed environment, and played with by that
> poet in a succession of compositional patterns—lyrical impersonations,
> tomfooleries of genius, literary parodies, and so on—is treated by Rus-
> sian pedants as a sociological and historical phenomenon typical of Al-
> exander I's regime (alas, this tendency to generalize and vulgarize the
> unique fancy of an individual genius has also its advocates in the United
> States.)[49]

One of the best of such American critics was Edmund Wilson. In
his review of Nabokov's *Eugene Onegin*, Wilson criticized as Nabokov's "most serious failure" his not understanding the central situation that leads to Lenski's death in his duel with Onegin. Wilson offers a supposedly deep-level explanation of the sort that Nabokov in
reply exposes as reductive, insensitive to the particulars of the characters Pushkin presents, and all too easy:

> Pushkin stresses the fact that Onegin "sincerely loves the youth" but
> that *amour propre* is sometimes stronger than friendship. That is all. One
> should stick to that and not try to think up "deep" variations which are

not even new; for what Mr. Wilson inflicts upon me, in teaching me how to understand Onegin, is the old solemn nonsense of Onegin's hating and envying Lenski for being capable of idealism, devoted love, ecstatic German romanticism and the like "when he himself is so sterile and empty." Actually, it is just as easy, and just as irrelevant (yet more fashionable—Mr. Wilson is behind the times), to argue that Onegin, not Lenski, is the true idealist, that he loathes Lenski because he perceives in him the future fat swinish squire Lenski is doomed to become—and so he raises slowly his pistol and . . . but Lenski in malignant cold blood is also raising his pistol, and God knows who would have killed whom had not the author followed wisely the old rule of sparing one's more interesting character while the novel is still developing. If anybody takes "a mean advantage," as Mr. Wilson absurdly puts it (none of the principals can derive any special "advantage" in a *duel à volonté*), it is not Onegin, but Pushkin.[50]

Where Wilson falsely exalts Pushkin by accounting for Onegin's strange behavior with a grandiose generalization that ignores prickly details, Nabokov scrutinizes the minute play of circumstances that leads up to the duel, takes pains to establish the accepted practices and the precise rituals of the dueling code, and with a detached spirit and an acute eye lists the discrepancies in Onegin's conduct that reveal Pushkin's authorial sleight-of-hand in constructing his character. By not rushing to Wilson's sweeping statements (Onegin seeks "revenge on Lensky for being capable of idealism"), Nabokov performs a double service. He makes Pushkin spring to life as a writer, deciding on this or that delicate adjustment and sacrificing Onegin's consistency in order to convince us of the duel and its outcome. And he also makes Onegin come alive in the way that Pushkin makes him live: not, as he points out by way of contrast, like Benjamin Constant's Adolphe, physically featureless but emotionally consistent and vital, but the very reverse. Onegin, although psychologically suspect as a character as Pushkin moves him from one emotional situation to another, remains "superbly stereoscopic, a man with a wardrobe, a man with a set of recognizable gestures, a man existing forever in a local world colored and crowded with Pushkin's people, Pushkin's emotions, memories, melodies and fancies. In this sense, Pushkin transcends French neoclassicism; Constant does not."[51]

XI

When Nabokov shifts from Pushkin's invented world to Pushkin's place in the world of literature, he shows the same preference for the unique over the typical, the original over the conventional. "A group is always impressive to historians of literature," he snorts, but for him all great literature is "the product of individuals, not groups":

> There are teachers and students with square minds who are by nature meant to undergo the fascination of categories. For them, "schools" and "movements" are everything; by painting a group symbol on the bow of mediocrity, they condone their own incomprehension of true genius.
>
> I cannot think of any masterpiece the appreciation of which would be enhanced in any degree or manner by the knowledge that it belonged to this or that school; and, conversely, I could name any number of third-rate works that are kept artificially alive for centuries through their being assigned by the schoolman to this or that "movement" in the past.
>
> These concepts are harmful chiefly because they distract the student from direct contact with, and direct delight in, the quiddity of individual artistic achievement (which, after all, alone matters and alone survives); but, moreover, each of them is subject to such a variety of interpretation as to become meaningless in its own field, that of the classification of knowledge.[52]

Parody for Nabokov's Sebastian Knight is a means of exposing an idea as moribund, or perhaps of investing it with miraculous new life. He can even use it as "a kind of springboard for leaping into the highest region of serious emotion." In *Eugene Onegin*, in the same way, parody allows Nabokov to redeploy or reanimate decrepit literary ideas or to leap to the breeziest heights of literary history. He declares that the origins of what he classifies as the first, generalized form of romanticism

> can be traced back to the contrived Arcadia of Italian and Spanish romance. From its lowland meadows distraught lovers—wretched knights and young scholars—would repair to its montane zone and run amuck there in amorous madness. Clouds masked the moon and brooks murmured in pastoral poesy as allegorically as rack and rill were to do above and below Lenski's tomb some three centuries later. In the eighteenth century, Swiss and Scottish guides pointed out to the panting poet the waterfall and its lugubrious conifers. From there it was an easy mule's ride to the desolate Byronic scene.[53]

Nabokov loathes the literary fashions and formulas that can lure even original minds into mere imitation, and he repeatedly and unsparingly assesses Pushkin in terms of his individuality or his derivativeness in this or that stanza. One stanza's allusions to gondoliers singing Tasso belong "to the tritest commonplaces of Romanticism, and it is a pity Pushkin used so much talent, verbal ingenuity, and lyrical intensity to render in Russian a theme that had been sung to death in England and France. The fact that it leads to the perfectly original and adorable nostalgic digression in One: L spites its beauty but does not condone it."⁵⁴

If Nabokov disliked Pushkin's variations on romantic themes, he positively deplored Pushkin's allegiance to the aesthetics of the eighteenth century, that "pedestrian age," "that most inartistic of centuries." He saw eighteenth-century neoclassicism as a glorification of the derivative, an affront to originality, and he lamented that "for years, Pushkin, not to speak of the minor poets of his day, could not get rid of these Wounds, Charms and Ardors, of these clusters of cupids coming from their porcelain beehives in the eighteenth-century West."⁵⁵

Even worse was the eighteenth century's "pathological dislike . . . for the specific 'unpoetical' detail and . . . its passion for the generic term." A keen observer of landscapes, Nabokov despised the poetic Arcadianism that he saw as the source of the early, generalized, phase of romanticism:

> "Arcadian" poetry, pastorals and the like, presupposing a bucolic space time within which refined shepherds and shepherdesses tend immaculate flocks amid indestructible meadow flowers and made sterile love in shady bosquets near murmuring rills. That sheep look like toads and can devastate a continent did not concern poets. The overrated Virgil was a popular exponent of the theme on the burnished threshold of an ormolu era.

He found Pushkin too often content to continue within the convention: "As a poet, Pushkin does not show any genuine knowledge of the Russian countryside (as Turgenev and Tolstoy were to show fifteen years after our poet's death). Stylistically, he remains true to the eighteenth-century concepts of generalized 'nature.' "⁵⁶

Aware that the novelty of a writer's contribution is impossible to evaluate without a thorough knowledge of his literary antecedents and context, Nabokov can show Pushkin's uniqueness all the more convincingly because he never exaggerates it in the wrong place. He remains keenly and at times even contemptuously aware of all that Pushkin adopts from imitations of imitations, and still reveres his innate originality, singling out for praise any marked novelty of intonation or description. Alert to Pushkin's gift for the specific detail, especially in rendering city life, he regrets that "in the depiction of nature [Pushkin's] leanings were always on the side of the eighteenth century" and welcomes the few occasions where he shows the influence of "the second, specific, phase of romanticism, its interest in 'ordinary' details and in 'realistic' trivialities."[57]

XII

The esteem for individuality that at times leads Nabokov to reprove Pushkin for following the crowd affects even his textual scholarship. Within volume 1, he translated only the complete text as it has come down to us from the second edition (1837), the last Pushkin super- vised in his lifetime. In volumes 2 and 3, he also translates and an- notates stanzas Pushkin deleted, variants, drafts, and every scrap of any textual interest, but he refuses to allow any alteration of the es- tablished text: "there would be scarcely one masterpiece left untam- pered with and unchanged from beginning to end if we started to republish a dead author's works in the form we *think* he might have wished them to appear and endure." He has too much respect for the mystery of another's self to tinker with anything in the final ver- sion Pushkin oversaw, even if "an omitted line, the place of which seems still warm and throbbing in the established text, explains or amplifies something of great artistic value," and even if in a few in- stances "we feel dreadfully certain that only the grotesque require- ments of a despotic regime forced our poet to delete passages, to alter lines of development, to abolish whole sets of marvelous stanzas."[58]

Which leads us from textual minutiae to the very different dimen- sions of politics, and one last aspect of Pushkin's individuality that Nabokov celebrates in his commentary: Pushkin's natural indepen- dence of spirit and his innate love of freedom. In his unpublished Cornell lectures Nabokov refers to Pushkin's "craving for perfect spiritual liberty," and in support of that impulse, he translates and annotates in full in his commentary Pushkin's "Liberty: An Ode." He shows Pushkin's sympathies for the Decembrists, his distance from their conspiracy, the natural "artistic immunity" that he expressed along with his commiseration for the exiled rebels, and the absurdity of the Soviet critic Brodski's attempts to prove that Pushkin was "a solemn admirer of revolution" when in fact he "hated equally the despotism of the Tsar and the despotism of public opinion . . . the rabble in the palace and the rabble in the street." In his lectures Na- bokov also stressed the individual conscience as one of Pushkin's vi- tal themes, especially the unencroachable artistic conscience, "that idea of the inner mission of the Poet, of his carrying within him the criterion of truth, right and beauty." Pushkin's "uncompromising artistic resistance to any interference," Nabokov suggests, was one of the factors that contributed to "his inevitable doom."[59]

XIII

If he sees Pushkin as an intuitive champion of the individual, Nabokov in his commentary projects an image of himself as the very deliberate champion of the particular and the individual. One aspect of the image is the implicit opposition he establishes between his own lone effort, his tracking down every original source he can find, and the scholarly habit of relying on the accumulated information—and the accumulated error—of other scholars.

His long appendix on Abram Gannibal, Pushkin's African great-grandfather, serves as a comic demonstration of the elusiveness of particulars and the degradation of "facts" as they are repeated from mouth to mouth and book to book. By retracing Abram Gannibal's version of his childhood and testing it against what can be discovered of Gannibal's possible homeland at the time—a few maps, the first travelers' reports, the few available scraps of local history—Nabokov shows that despite the assertions of earlier investigators like "Anuchin, blindly followed by Vegner and other ovine compilers,"[60] almost nothing of Pushkin's ancestor's early life can be ascertained.

Within the commentary itself, Nabokov repeatedly rejects received opinions and familiar facts. He reproves the scholiast who in his anxiety to impress with the sheer number of his references, "neither bothers to verify the items he copies out (or has others copy out for him) nor cares if his source, or his science, errs." Again and again he attacks Professor Dmitri Chizhevski of Harvard, author of a 1953 commentary on *Eugene Onegin*, for errors in transcribing titles of works—some simply nonexistent, and even shown to have been so decades earlier—that Chizhevski plainly had never consulted himself.[61] Nabokov, by contrast, emphasized that his scholarship was his own, that he had read for himself every work he mentions, that he is ready to present his own highly individual summary and judgment of every book he needs to describe. Though he acknowledges the discoveries of other Pushkinists, especially Lerner, Shchyogolev, Gofman, and Tomashevski, he presents his commentary as an exemplum of what can be accomplished by direct individual effort rather than reliance on secondhand knowledge.

Just as he chooses Chizhevski to represent the degeneration of original inquiry into unquestioned academic tradition, so Nabokov selects the Soviet scholar N. L. Brodski, author of a 1950 commentary on *Eugene Onegin*, as the negation of the individual scholarly conscience. A Soviet toady who refers to the "army of the tsar" when the Russians are beaten by Napoleon and the "army of the people" when Napoleon is beaten by the Russians, Brodski tries to demonstrate Onegin's "unconscious bolshevism." What offended Nabokov above all was Brodski's "servile eagerness" to make his scholarship serve the current dictates of the state, to an extent that prompted Tomashevski, the finest of Soviet Pushkinists, to dare, even under Stalin, to make "some crushing remarks on Brodski's maneuvers."[62]

Nabokov delights in denouncing Soviet interference in free scholarship: "Prevented as I am by a barbarous regime from traveling to Leningrad to examine old playbills in its libraries, I cannot say for sure what 'Cleopatra' Pushkin had in view." But he goes much further. He will not bow even to the gentler pressure of Western scholarly decorum: "I refuse to be guided and controlled by a communion of established views and academic traditions." His only duty, he felt, was to his own conscience. Although in the course of his commentary he praised scores of writers, from Shakespeare and Chateaubriand to Shevïryov and Shelley, he never hesitated to criticize those, however enshrined in literary history, who fell short of his artistic standards. After exposing Dostoevsky's careless reading of Pushkin and summing him up as "a much overrated, sentimental and Gothic novelist of the time," he adds, "Dostoevski the publicist is one of those megaphones of elephantine platitudes (still heard today), the roar of which so ridiculously demotes Shakespeare and Pushkin to the vague level of all the plaster idols of academic tradition, from Cervantes to George Eliot (not to speak of the crumbling Manns and Faulkners of our times)."[63]

If Nabokov asserted his right to topple those he considered Pushkin's false rivals, he was even more indignant in denouncing Pushkin's false interpreters. He regularly places other translators in the stocks—and, it must be said, could have placed each of them there on a hundred other occasions for equally serious crimes. Along with them he sets a trio of Russian adaptors of Pushkin: Chaikovsky, whose opera *Eugene Onegin* all literate Russians recognize as a banal travesty; Ilya Repin, the painter, in whose "most famous and most execrable picture of the Lenski-Onegin duel, in which everything, including the attitudes and positions of the combatants, is ludicrously wrong"; and the "miserably bad" engraver Alexander Notbek (Nabokov does not exaggerate) whose 1829 illustrations of *Eugene Onegin* inspired Pushkin to two acid epigrams. Asked by Bollingen Press to delete references to a more recent artist's "hideous and absurd illustrations," Nabokov responded that his criticism was "so dear to me that I would prefer giving up the publication of my entire work rather than surrendering that passage." An overstatement, no doubt, but the decay of the unique contribution of genius as it becomes corrupted by "average reality" was too central a theme of his whole enterprise for him to withdraw the attack.[64]

Against the arty translators and the arty adaptors, Nabokov places his own fidelity to Pushkin and his own fidelity to particulars. When Pushkin sends Onegin speeding to a St. Petersburg ball, "the twin lamps of coupés . . . project rainbows on the snow." Unlike an Arndt, who would sacrifice this clear image for the sake of a rhyme with "shutters" and turn it into the empty "brush the snow with rainbow flutters," Nabokov simultaneously encourages us to imagine Pushkin's scene and promotes the still more specific: "My own fifty-year-old remembrance is not so much of prismatic colors cast upon snowdrifts by the two lateral lanterns of a brougham as of iridescent spicules around blurry street lights coming through its frost-foliated windows and breaking along the rim of the glass."[65]

While encouraging the reader to see Pushkin in as much detail as possible, Nabokov indicates at the same time that he himself aims to pursue detail much further than eighteenth-century aesthetics would allow Pushkin, and much further than twentieth-century criticism, with its ideational bent, expects an explicator to venture. Although he stresses Pushkin's innate independence of mind, he makes plain that Pushkin was often willing to accept this or that ready-made formula or phrase, and presents himself by contrast as unswervingly committed to individuality and originality, determined to resist any pressure to conform to common standards or to betray his absolute defense of the particular.

Throughout, his *Eugene Onegin* is a defense of the free twists and particular turns of Pushkin's mind and art and a wholesale defense of the independence of the individual and the passion for the particular that to Nabokov are the essence of all art.

XIV

Two curious defects in Nabokov's commentary must be noted.

When he first began to work on Pushkin, Nabokov wrote, he had supposed Pushkin had a perfect command not only of Russian and French but also of English, German, and Italian.[66] In his finished commentary, on the other hand, he would insist that Pushkin knew no languages well except Russian and French, and especially that his English was so flimsy that he could read English works only in

French translation: the Byron Pushkin knew was Byron filtered through Amédée Pichot's prose translation.

What evidence does Nabokov have for insisting so often on "Pushkin's inability to master the rudiments of the English language"? He notes six mistakes in Pushkin's attempts to translate Byron in 1821 or 1822, Wordsworth in 1833, and Byron again in 1836. This evidence seems to suggest in fact that while Pushkin's English was decidedly shaky (though an error in rendering Byron's "guileless beyond . . . imagining" is *not* proof that Pushkin "does not know the simplest forms of English"), he repeatedly tried to grapple with English poets in the original.[67]

Nabokov regularly notes of this or that English poet that Pushkin read him "of course" in so-and-so's French. But when, as Nabokov himself notes,[68] Pushkin wrote a Coleridge epigram in a friend's album, are we to suppose he had read it in French but when calling on his friend brought with him the unread English text so he could set down the lines in their original phrasing? Advancing his untenable thesis, Nabokov resorts to uncharacteristic bluster. When he mentions Pushkin's *Feast at the Time of the Plague* (1830), a translation of a scene from John Wilson's *City of the Plague*, he calls it "a blank verse translation (made from a French prose version). . . . Pushkin must have got hold of a fairly accurate version, perhaps with the English original *en regard*."[69] But this French version is purely hypothetical, and neither the British Library nor the Bibliothèque nationale lists a single translation of John Wilson's play into French. A study of Pushkin's text shows five outright blunders in translating over a hundred and fifty lines of Wilson's play: mistakes that are clearly Pushkin's, and more evidence that most of the time he not only could but often did follow English verse without French intermediaries.[70] Still more evidence: among Pushkin's recorded conversations are observations on *Othello* that derive directly from Coleridge's *Table Talk*—which has never been translated into French.[71]

After Nabokov's work, most Pushkinists now accept that Pushkin knew rather less English than had once been assumed, and that he probably read English literature, especially English fiction, more often in French versions than in the original. But scholars also rightly refuse to accept Nabokov's dogmatic assertions that Pushkin knew too little English to read Wordsworth or Byron or Coleridge in anything but French versions. Nabokov hoped to settle the argument, and land one last decisive blow on Edmund Wilson, when he wrote to the *New Statesman* in 1968 conceding "that Pushkin had almost as much English in the 1830s as Mr. Edmund Wilson has Russian today."[72] Wilson's Russian wobbled much more in the 1960s than it had in the 1940s, but Nabokov's comparison still backfires. He had once planned to write a volume on Russian poets with Wilson, and he had even suggested to Wilson in 1948 that they undertake together a scholarly translation of *Eugene Onegin*. He knew the flaws in Wilson's Russian, but he also knew that despite them his former friend had read thousands of pages of Russian literature in the original, and with a literary sensitivity he had once seen fit to praise. Why could not Pushkin have read even a fraction as much English?

Nabokov's irrationally unconditional denial that Pushkin could encounter English verse in the original seems explicable in only one way. Just as he implicitly contrasts his own hunger for specific detail with Pushkin's acceptance of the eighteenth-century taste for generalized nature, or his own insistence on originality with Pushkin's readiness to appropriate the images or incidents of other writers, so he seems to wish at all costs to oppose his own determination to encounter great literature in the original and Pushkin's readiness to accept it at second hand.

XV

Lesser flaws mar Nabokov's "Notes on Prosody," his second appendix to the commentary. This ninety-page monograph has been highly praised: a Russian scholar can note there is no better work on the subject of Pushkin's prosody; an English critic, that it breaks important new ground in its treatment of English prosody.[73] But despite many brilliant observations, "Notes on Prosody" 's central comparison of English and Russian verse meters seems much less illuminating than it could be.

When Nabokov analyzes samples of English iambic tetrameters and compares them to Pushkin's iambs, he misleads. He marks a regular foot as o, and a foot without an accent on the expected stress as what he terms a "scud," x.[74] Pushkin's pattern of xs appears much more varied than those of any of the English poets. So it is, but only for the strange reason that Nabokov's diagrams ignore the metric variations that distinguish English poetry from Russian.

All Russian words have only *one* syllabic accent, even if they stretch, as they often do, to six or more syllables. Since in any extended passage of Russian a high proportion of words will be polysyllabic, the modulation most natural in Russian verse is the "scud," the foot where the meter leads one to expect a stress but none comes. Pushkin is a master of such modulation. But in an equivalent passage of English there will be proportionately far more accented syllables, because there will be fewer polysyllabic words—which moreover often carry secondary accents in English—and far more stressed monosyllables, verbs, nouns, and adjectives. In English the "scud," an absence of accent on the metrical stress, is one frequent modulation, but the introduction of syllabic accents where no stress is expected (a "tilt" or a "false spondee") is equally natural and often much more dramatic.[75] In his tabulation Nabokov ignores these modulations by omitting spondees altogether and grouping "tilts" as "scuds."[76]

The result of this is that most of the more interesting modulations of an English iamb are overlooked. Because the italicized syllables in the following examples are unaccented, Nabokov declares Tennyson's "*In expectation of* a guest" and Marvell's "*To a* green Thought *in a* green Shade" to be examples of lines with first and third foot scuds, a common Pushkinian pattern.[77] But one of the things that makes Marvell's line so deservedly famous is that each time the word "green" occurs it is also strongly accented (although not quite as heavily as the noun it accompanies), so that the second and fourth feet are false spondees. If we were to mark false spondees by a z, the pattern of Marvell's line would be not Tennyson's Pushkinian xoxo but the highly un-Pushkinian xzxz.

What renders Nabokov's diagrams still more treacherous is that even within the misleading symbols he has adopted he frequently errs in recording the meter. Donne's line "Interinanimates two soules" he marks xxoo, which means he reads the first four syllables as unaccented and the sixth ("-mates") and eighth ("soules") as accented.[78] In fact, of course, the fourth syllable receives the main accent of "interinANimates," and the seventh syllable also seems accented. The line could be marked xooz or, according to Nabokov's own system, xooo, but certainly not xxoo.

Apart from frequent misscannings such as this—presumably the result of haste—what seems striking about "Notes on Prosody" is that Nabokov fails to make as clear as his usual lucidity permits the real contrasts between English and Russian meter. Russian iambs are modulated by a much richer pattern of unaccented stresses (scuds) than English, English by a more diverse pattern of irregular feet (scuds, tilts, and false spondees, in Nabokov's terminology) than Russian. Nabokov's diagrams are slight modifications of the metrical schemas he learned in 1918 from Andrey Bely's *Symbolism* (1910) and applied at once to classical Russian poetry and his own prolific youthful verse. His adherence in "Notes on Prosody" to these diagrams and their emphasis on scuds rather than other modulations seems to have two sources. First, his unusual reliance on the forces that shaped him in youth. When writing "Notes on Prosody" he did not reconsult Bely's work, which he had not read for nearly forty years, nor did he rethink thoroughly enough how applicable Bely's system would be to English poetry. Second, his reliance on these diagrams appears to reflect a desire to suggest that the language whose verse filled him with such rapture through his teens and twenties, as reader and writer, is somehow richer in its musicality than English. Nabokov's detailed comments on English poets reveal a fine appreciation of the subtleties of English prosody, but his examples and diagrams seem designed to show the metrical laurels fit not on the heads of the English poets he selects but on Pushkin's brow alone.

XVI

Nabokov's *Eugene Onegin*, unique in his career, can have few parallels anywhere else in literary history. In the twentieth century creative writers by the hundreds have been attached to universities, but none has performed at Nabokov's literary level, let alone produced such a monumental work of scholarship. Almost a century ago A. E. Housman held his melancholy at bay in the long gaps between unexpected creative bursts by devoting his whole scholarly career to editing Manilius, a writer barely read even by Latin scholars. Nabokov, on the other hand, consecrated more than four years of intense effort, at a time when he was at the height of his inventive powers—in the years he wrote *Lolita* and *Pnin* and was itching to start *Pale Fire*—to the greatest of Russian poets.

Perhaps we would have to turn to an earlier century, to the Age of Criticism, to Nabokov's detested eighteenth century, to find similar examples of major authors at work on other major authors: Dryden translating Virgil, Pope translating Homer, Johnson editing Shakespeare. But the translations are utterly incomparable. Dryden and Pope did not so much translate Virgil and Homer as rewrite them, as the Roman poet and the Greek might have written had they been English gentlemen, devotees of decorum, of powder and polish and rhyme. Nabokov was far too conscious of the inviolable differences between one person and another to countenance such a procedure. Rather than presume to know how Pushkin might have expressed himself in English, he abjured all style in his own English in order to refer the reader back to Pushkin's Russian.

Johnson as the editor of Shakespeare in some ways comes closer to Nabokov. In their literary principles, they could not be further apart. Johnson opts for common sense, for reason, for the amplest generalizations he can make about "general"—that is, human—"nature."

Nabokov extols the surprise of personal perception, the play of individual fancy, the irreducible detail that the general view can overlook but never explain. But both have a proud independence of mind and an unquenchable vigor of expression. Both refuse to be daunted by the genius of their subjects, and demand the best of them, according to their own high standards: Johnson chastises Shakespeare for a Nabokovian pun, Nabokov reproves Pushkin for a Johnsonian dictum. As an edition of Shakespeare, Johnson's had rivals in its own day. As a commentary on *Eugene Onegin*, Nabokov's has none. But both will be read long after more subdued and balanced works are deep in dust.

What makes Johnson's Shakespeare so immediately memorable, ironically, is the exceptional penetration of mind he brings to discussing the common operations of the mind—and to a specific Shakespeare phrase. Nabokov's Pushkin, on the other hand, may at first appear thoroughly disconcerting because he begins at a level of minute precision that can seem pointless and disjointed and that allows him so much less opportunity than usual for his own talent for the sweeping phrase, the provocative reflection, the many-sided observation. But gradually we can discover how staunchly the scrupulous, even jarring fidelity of the translation and the meticulous detail of the commentary serve what is unique and irreplaceable in Pushkin—and by the same token form such a powerfully consistent summation of Nabokov's own philosophical position and his character. Through all four volumes of his *Eugene Onegin* runs a plea for the specific and the individual, and for the effort needed to perceive them both. Loyal to the irreducible particulars of Pushkin's genius, to Pushkin's natural, effortless individuality, Nabokov also inevitably demonstrates his own innate singularity, so much of which lies in his more conscious, more thoroughgoing, more dogmatic, pursuit of the particular.

CHAPTER 16

Lolita Explodes: Cornell and After, 1957–1959

Lolita is having an unbelievable success—but all this ought to have

happened thirty years ago.

—Nabokov to Elena Sikorski, 1958

I

ALTHOUGH Nabokov completed *Eugene Onegin* at the end of 1957, the explosions it would cause in the literary world had to wait until its publication in 1964. But as he added the final corrections to his Pushkin typescript, the advance tremors of a much larger eruption had begun to shift the ground under his feet: *Lolita* was about to be published in America.

Two problems still stood in the way of publication: the risk that the book might be banned, and the demands of Maurice Girodias. Of the publishers who had been ready to proceed despite the threat of prosecution, both Jason Epstein of Doubleday and Ivan Obolensky of McDowell, Obolensky had withdrawn in the face of Girodias's intransigent demands for at least half of Nabokov's royalties. Only one late entrant remained: Walter Minton of G. P. Putnam's Sons.

Lolita's fate seems destined to have been colorful at every turn. Despite all the publicity surrounding the novel since 1955—Graham Greene's praise, John Gordon's denunciation, the French ban, the black-market sales, the *Anchor Review* campaign—Walter Minton had his attention belatedly drawn to the novel only in the summer of 1957. According to a 1958 story in *Time*, written by a woman Minton had become involved with, it was another lover, "onetime Latin Quarter showgirl" Rosemary Ridgwell, who suggested the book to him and received a handsome finder's fee for her efforts.[1]

When Minton had approached him at the end of August 1957, Nabokov had been glad to let him begin negotiating directly with Girodias. By late fall, recognizing Minton's determination, he asked him if he would be prepared to defend *Lolita* all the way to the Supreme Court if necessary. Minton replied that no publisher could make that blanket guarantee, but promised that Putnam's would present the book in such a way as to minimize its chances of prosecution.² Nabokov accepted his arguments.

Then there was Girodias. Deeming him utterly untrustworthy, Nabokov could not bear the thought that he and his descendants might remain in Girodias's clutches for decades, until the copyright on *Lolita* expired. Because of Girodias's failure to pay him on time and to adhere to conditions he had agreed to, Nabokov had declared his contract with Olympia Press null and void.³ Girodias ignored the declaration, and French courts seemed likely to side with him. For the moment there was no way to publish in America except on terms Girodias would agree to. Instead of accepting the usual publisher's licensing fee of 20 or 25 percent of the author's royalties, Girodias persisted in demanding nothing less than 50 percent. Minton was ready to offer a high royalty of 15 percent (7.5 percent each, therefore, for Nabokov and Olympia), and counseled Nabokov strongly through January and February 1958 that in view of the current interest in *Lolita* he would have more to lose by the delay a lawsuit would guarantee than to gain by the favorable ruling it just might make possible. Reluctantly, Nabokov accepted, and on March 1 mailed back to Minton his signed contract. More than four years after completing the novel, he had at last found an American publisher ready to gamble that the courts would not prevent *Lolita* from reaching an American audience.

In France, meanwhile, the book had not fared so well. Olympia's English edition had been banned in December 1956. Only in January 1958 was Girodias able to win his case in court against the French government and have the ban rescinded. Despite this ban, Gallimard had been pushing ahead with its plans to publish a French edition, and in January 1958, Nabokov was relieved to discover that the first installment of the French translation, by Girodias's brother Eric Kahane, was much less careless and inexact than he had dreaded.⁴

II

Dmitri Nabokov had ended his military service just before Christmas 1957 and returned home with his throat in poor repair after a persistent virus he had picked up in the army. For three months he remained at home in snowbound Ithaca under the care of his parents' doctor, until he had recovered sufficiently to resume his vocal studies in New York. He began to work under his father's supervision on the vast index needed for *Eugene Onegin*. There was no need to hurry. Unable to guarantee that they could publish the book within a year, as Nabokov had wanted, Bollingen Press returned *Eugene Onegin* to him at the end of January. He sent it on to Knopf.[5]

Early in February, in a driving blizzard, the family moved from the Sharps' house to another professorial home in Cayuga Heights, 404 Highland Road, their final Ithaca address, a large red-brick house that proved much colder than the compact ranch-style home they had just vacated. This would be only the second full winter they had to spend in Cayuga Heights, one and a half winding miles through snowdrifts to the Cornell campus, and they felt its force. Other blizzards followed, and by mid-March, when snow had made driving impossible and walking difficult, Dmitri had to play the Saint Bernard, donning skis and knapsack to bring back supplies from the nearest shop, a mile away.[6]

The so-called spring term began on February 10 with Nabokov announcing to a chorus of groans: "By Monday February 24 you should have finished reading *Anna Karenin*, after which you will have almost a month to reread it twice before the midterm exam." When the exam came on March 19, he asked the students a question they would never forget, even if they could not recall the answer: "Describe the wallpaper in the Karenins' bedroom."[7] Answer: part 4, chapter 17: Anna, expected to die of puerperal fever, watches with relief as Karenin magnanimously shakes hands with Vronsky, but just before delirium sets in once again, she points at the wallpaper and exclaims, "How tastelessly these flowers are done, not at all like violets."

During March, Nabokov met C. P. Snow at a cocktail party at the Mizeners' ("horrible," he notes in his diary) and Lionel Trilling at a party at the Abrams'. M. H. Abrams recalls that Nabokov stood at one end of their long living room with a group of people around him and Trilling at the other end with the rest.

> Neither looked at the other. Finally it was time for the party to break up, and so they began simultaneously to drift to the door, each with his own entourage. I had introduced them before, but they had done no more than acknowledge the introduction. But now I took care to ensure that they would have to say something to each other. Nabokov remarked [with a smile as broad as the sun, another memoirist recalls], "I understand, Mr. Trilling, you don't like my little *Lolita*." And Trilling replied, "No, that isn't true. What I've said is that I'm putting off the rereading of it until this summer, when I have the time *really* to come to grips with it."[8]

That summer Trilling's provocative long essay on *Lolita* would appear in the month the novel was published. At one of these two parties, or another about the same time, Nabokov encountered a very pretty woman leaving just as he arrived. She mentioned she had just read his "Scenes from the Life of a Double Monster," the story about Siamese twins written in 1950 but published only now. "Did you like it?" he asked. "I loathed it," she replied, and swept by him to the door. Nabokov recounted the incident with gales of laughter.[9]

In Highland Road one of the Nabokovs' neighbors was the philosopher Max Black. Noticing Nabokov's radiant smile one morning, Black asked him why he was feeling so happy. He had been revising the French translation of *Lolita*, Nabokov explained, and had just hit upon a beautiful equivalent for "cheerleader."[*] Another day, when Black's car was stuck in the snow, Nabokov helped push it free, an incident that now prefigures in Black's mind the scene from *Pale Fire* where Kinbote slips on his neighbors' icy driveway and by his fall dislodges the Shade car from its snowy rut. Black feels convinced that the scenery around the Shade and Goldsworth homes in *Pale Fire* was based on what the Nabokovs could see from their Highland Road home.[10]

Certainly *Pale Fire* seemed to be still alive. At the end of March, Nabokov wrote to Jason Epstein that it was "crackling and spreading," although in fact the fire seems not to have caught, for no more of it is heard until a new flash of inspiration in November 1960 made the novel blaze out in a new direction. In the meantime Nabokov's creative fancy had begun to attune itself to ideas and sensations that would later slowly coalesce into *Ada*. But in the short term, there were publishers to deal with: when Knopf declined *Eugene Onegin*, Nabokov sent it on to Cornell University Press; in England, Weidenfeld and Nicolson expressed an interest in publishing *Lolita* if it could also publish all Nabokov's other available works; and in France, Gallimard also wanted all the Nabokov it could have.[11]

III

On campus too he was in demand. Jean-Jacques Demorest, head of the Department of Romance Literatures, was able to obtain a substantial raise, from $9,000 to $11,000, for the department's most popular and most celebrated teacher.[12] A public lecture Nabokov gave opened the twelfth Cornell Festival of the Contemporary Arts on April 10. He was to deliver "Readers, Writers and Censors in Russia," his standby lecture for public occasions since 1941, but now

* *Allumeuse*: literally, "a woman who ignites," but with the colloquial overtone of "flirt."

given new relevance by *Lolita*'s predicament. *Lolita* drew the crowds. In fact, the Nabokovs could find nowhere to park their car, and cruised around and around in the hope that somebody would leave, "until we realised," as Nabokov explains,

> that all available space near the lecture-hall would remain occupied until the performance, my performance, was over. Finally we had to seek out a rather remote spot, and started at a brisk walk, almost a run, for the lighted building.
>
> People were waiting there—everyone had come, except a last runner; for on the way we were suddenly overtaken by a lone Japanese who sprinted past us at a pace far surpassing anything we could attain. There was something uncanny about his solitary velocity and streamlined shape as he made for the porch and dashed up the steps and plunged into a crowded place which existed for him at the moment only insofar as it included the lecturer. But the lecturer was still outside, almost paralysed by the weird feeling that a ghost must feel when debarred from the events of his relivable past.[13]

It can be no accident that this passage, one of the few Nabokov actually set down of his long-projected *Speak on, Memory*, contains this kind of metaphysical shiver: *that* was precisely what he was searching for in order to construct a second volume of his autobiography.

It mattered less to Nabokov that the evening was a triumph. But it certainly was—once he at last entered Olin Hall, dressed for the occasion in an academic gown in Cambridge blue. The text of his speech now opens his *Lectures on Russian Literature*, but at the time he provided the Festival Committee with a pithy résumé: "Mr. Nabokov's lecture will deal with the tribulations and triumphs of authors of genius who happen to be Russian. It will cover the nineteenth century and the first half of the twentieth. He will describe the various forces which fight for the possession of a writer's soul. He will examine what the tsar and the dictator, the moral policeman and the political moralist, the phantom of a consumer and the reality of a conscience demand of an artist." The highlight of the talk was a dramatized reading ostensibly from Fyodor Gladkov's novel *Energiya*, "Socialist Realism's ideal love-scene—boy and girl with pneumatic drill." Behind the lectern, Nabokov would imitate first the young man clutching the drill and saying "I lo-lo-lo-lo-lo-love you," and then change tones and rhythms to speak for the girl replying in kind as her truck throbbed by. Everyone in the audience, including Cornell president Deane Malott, was helpless with laughter. Nabokov peered over the top of his glasses, which had slipped down to the tip of his nose, and confessed with delight: "I can't stop quoting." One regular student of his thought that that moment encapsulated Nabokov's teaching methods, "that wonderfully gleeful way he had of making fun of something and revealing his enjoyment of it at the same time." Nabokov concluded the scene with his own interpolation: "Then, as he dreams of becoming a good Communist, of mastering Marx, the trembling of the drill rocks him with a joyful paroxysm."[14]

Publishing and publicity were taking up a good deal of his time. After having decided that the distance, the cost, and the uncertainty of arbitration made it not worthwhile trying to sue the Swedish firm of Wahlström and Witrand for their adulterated and abridged translation of *Lolita*, he found out that their *Pnin* was almost as bad. By late April he was busy checking the proofs of the Putnam *Lolita*, of Doubleday's collection of his stories, *Nabokov's Dozen*, and of Gallimard's *Lolita* and *Pnin*.[15]

Sensing that events would soon come too thick and fast to recall, the Nabokovs began a short-lived diary on which Nabokov would later pencil the heading "Hurricane Lolita."[16] The entries for the first day (May 20), before the hurricane started to blow, capture some of the unpredictable heterogeneity of a typical Nabokov day: family, friends, neighbors; writing, reading, teaching, and lepidoptery. A call from New York: Jason Epstein asks Nabokov to translate Tolstoy's short novels (he will think it over—and decline). Sad letters from Geneva (his sister Elena, whose husband is dying) and Prague (his sister Olga, raving about the charm of her four-year-old grandson, but saying nothing about her alcoholic son). A vignette of compassion and comic incomprehension à la Nabokov, although it could be a scene straight from *Pnin*:

> Tiny white bitch, tiny bell tinkling, inspected lawn, dandelions, violets, dark garage, steps down to garden, porch, door, entered with me, refused milk sop, sniffed all the carpets—Telephone! "Is my dog there?" "Yes, she is. In fact she is sniffing and trotting all over the house, I tried to give her some bread and milk—" "*Bread* and *milk*?" "Yes . . . well . . ." "Look: Miss Dodd is supposed to come to take care of a patient . . ." ("Dodd" not "dog").

He spreads a batch of butterflies caught in Wyoming in 1952, the first chance he has had for several hectic years to sort out his old catches. He prepares an analysis of *Ulysses*'s Ormond Hotel chapter for the next day's classes. He reads *Notes and Queries* for 1870, in search of the kinds of bizarre arcana he will later stuff into odd pockets of *Pale Fire* and *Ada*. Dinner with Morris and Alison Bishop at their daughter's sorority, then another call from New York to round off the day:

Dmitri, hopeful of a place in an opera group for which he has just auditioned and of a job with the *Current Digest of the Soviet Press*.

IV

After two years of uninterrupted work in his relentless drive to complete *Eugene Onegin*, Nabokov had been looking forward for months to returning with his wife to "our native West."[17] On June 10, their black 1957 Buick started off for the Rockies. This time they planned to explore further to the north than ever before. During their last summer in the West, in 1956, they had settled in southern Utah before moving north out of rattlesnake country into northern Wyoming and the southern edge of Montana, which they had thoroughly enjoyed. Now they returned another three hundred miles further north to the Glacier Parks region, on Montana's border with Alberta. There was another reason for choosing such a location. Nabokov optimistically expected to be back in Ithaca in August to supervise the printing of *Eugene Onegin*.[18] In a more northerly climate, where the butterfly breeding season was shorter, he could sample more of the year's lepidopteral life than in the southern Rockies, where the season could stretch from April to September.

Acclimatizing themselves, the Nabokovs traveled up through the Great Lakes area, from Niagara Falls through central Michigan and along the southern rim of Lake Superior, collecting en route. On June 19 they installed themselves in Lake View Cabins, between Babb and St. Mary, at the eastern edge of Glacier National Park, in a primitive one-room cabin with dim electricity and a hot shower that ran cold. But it was worth it: marvelous flowery meadows, frequented by butterflies that Nabokov wanted, reached almost to the doorstep, while nearby glistened a secluded fairy-tale lakelet surrounded and hidden by aspens.[19]

After a week of good weather, a storm that dropped hailstones the size of hazelnuts announced a brusque change. A raging gale set in, and while the foul weather continued the Nabokovs decided to reread *War and Peace*. The wind howled so fiercely against the cabin walls that Nabokov could scarcely hear his wife read. Before long they decided in any case—or at least so Nabokov teased an interviewer—that the book was childish and dated, a mere historical novel, not worth continuing.[20]

Early in July they crossed the Canadian border to spend ten days in Alberta's Waterton Lake National Park among the white-crowned sparrows and the red-faced, red-bellied whistling marmots. They had planned to travel further north still, to Banff and even Jasper, but the wind and the cold forced them to cancel their plans, and they retreated southward again. By mid-July they had reached Helena, Montana, then set off southeast to the Bighorn Mountains in northern Wyoming. One afternoon, quite exhausted, Nabokov asked Véra if they could stop in the next settlement. There they found a dirty little hut with two lockless doors at opposite ends, but no door inside for the toilet. "Where are you folks from?" asked the landlord. "Upstate New York." "Good enough so long as you are not from the Big City. All sorts of folks come from there trying to jew you." "What is wrong with the Jews?" asked Véra. "Oh, they always try to knife you, get the better of you." "Well, I am Jewish," she replied, "and I have no intention of swindling you." His smiles and apologies were too late, the local cafés too grimy, and the Nabokovs drove on to Sheridan, forfeiting the night's rent to their righteous host.[21] Strange to think that only a year later they would be traveling first-class and would soon be able to settle for decades in one of Europe's best hotels.

By July 18 they had reached Devil's Tower, Wyoming, then headed across to South Dakota for two days' collecting in the Black Hills. Homeward bound, they took the northern route again (Minnesota, Wisconsin, and Michigan), reaching Ithaca at the end of July after covering eight thousand miles in seven weeks. Thanks to the weather, their collecting had yielded little in quantity, but Nabokov was delighted with the excellent quality of his finds.[22]

Even in the West they had not been isolated from *Lolita*. In Babb, Nabokov had received an advance copy of the Putnam edition, and was pleased with the book's discreet cover—lettering only, no picture of a little girl—and Putnam's discreet publicity. A long article on Nabokov in the *New Republic* by Conrad Brenner, a talented young stylist working in the Eighth Street Bookshop, caught their attention. Véra noted in her diary that the critique finally granted V. "a long overdue recognition of true greatness. There hardly ever was an author as indifferent to praise or invective as V.—'I have too high an opinion of myself to mind'—but, I think, he rather enjoyed the Brenner article."[23]

On his return to Ithaca, Nabokov found a letter from Harris-Kubrick Pictures asking if the film rights to *Lolita* were free—a bold request at a time when films were far more tightly policed than fiction and *Lolita* still had to be tested in American bookstores. The next day the Nabokovs headed for New York, where they discovered that a book club, the Readers' Subscription, planned to make *Lolita* its August selection. On August 4, Minton held a cocktail party for representatives of the leading periodicals and papers in the President's Room of the Harvard Club. The Nabokovs were delighted to find that Minton, who had seemed slow-moving, owlish, and unsparking when he visited them in Ithaca, now appeared intelligent, knowledgeable, and very tactful. Nabokov enjoyed himself, Véra noted in the diary, "and therefore was amusing, brilliant and—thank God—did not say what he thinks of some famous contemporaries."[24]

V

Back in Ithaca, August became humid and unpleasant. Nabokov continued where he had left off in May, spreading his old summer catches at a rate of fifty or more a day.[25] He seemed to know he would soon be moving on.

The book that was about to allow him to make that move reminded him once again it was no ordinary novel. Lolita had been banned in France at the end of 1956, only for the ban to be ruled illegal in January 1958. Now news came that in July the French government had imposed another ban under another law, this time barring it from any bookshop display or from sale to those under eighteen. If France behaved this way, what would puritan America do?

American publication was scheduled for Monday, August 18. The day before, a dozen Sunday newspapers reviewed the book. As with later reviews, two-thirds were enthusiastic, a third puzzled, taxed, peeved, irked, or outraged. Elizabeth Janeway's sensitive analysis in the New York Times Book Review decided in Lolita's favor:

> The first time I read Lolita I thought it was one of the funniest books I'd ever come on. . . . The second time I read it, uncut, I thought it was one of the saddest. . . . Humbert is every man who is driven by desire, wanting his Lolita so badly that it never occurs to him to consider her as a human being, or as anything but a dream-figment made flesh. . . . As for its pornographic content, I can think of few volumes more likely to quench the flames of lust than this exact and immediate description of its consequences.

The next day, in the daily New York Times, Orville Prescott took the opposite view. Summarizing the furor, he proclaimed: "Lolita, then, is undeniably news in the world of books. Unfortunately, it is bad news. There are two equally serious reasons why it isn't worth any adult reader's attention. The first is that it is dull, dull, dull in a pretentious, florid and archly fatuous fashion. The second is that it is repulsive. . . . highbrow pornography."

A few hours after Prescott's review hit the newsstands, Minton wired Nabokov: "EVERYBODY TALKING OF LOLITA ON PUBLICATION DAY YESTERDAYS REVIEW MAGNIFICENT AND NYTIMES BLAST THIS MORNING PROVIDED NECESSARY FUEL TO FLAME 300 REORDERS THIS MORNING AND BOOK STORES REPORT EXCELLENT DEMAND CONGRATULATIONS" He wrote that afternoon: "I telegraphed you this AM there were over 300 reorders on publication day. It is now 3:00 PM and there are over 1000!" The "1000" was crossed out and "1400" written underneath, and "—another order just arrived." Another note came in the same mail: "Over 2600 reorders today—mostly all from New York but they are beginning to arrive from out of town by wire, phone, etc."[26]

On August 21, Putnam's advertised *Lolita* in the *New York Times*: "4 days old and already in its 3rd Large Printing. 62,500 copies in print." Three days later, a full-page ad in the *New York Times Book Review* cited rave reactions from Dorothy Parker ("a fine book, a distinguished book—all right, then—a great book"), Graham Greene, William Styron, Harry Levin, Lionel Trilling, and others. At a time when Joyce's *Ulysses* seemed perhaps even more clearly the benchmark for modern fiction than many think it today, writers inevitably compared these two shocking books and their troubled histories. George P. Eliot was cited in the *New York Times Book Review* advertisement: "Like *Ulysses* before it, *Lolita* by high art transmutes persons, motives and actions which in ordinary life are considered indecent into objects of delight, compassion and contemplation."

Irving ("Swifty") Lazar, who had by now become Nabokov's Hollywood agent, announced in the *New York Times* on September 13 that *Lolita* was the first book since *Gone with the Wind* to sell 100,000 copies in its first three weeks. Véra Nabokov meanwhile had noted in her diary in the week of the book's publication: "V. serenely indifferent—occupied with a new story [the unfinished 'The Admirable Anglewing'], and with the spreading of some 2000 butterflies." Three weeks after publication he could report to his sister Elena on *Lolita*'s "unbelievable success—but all this ought to have happened thirty years ago." The financial coup was a surprise and a comforting assurance for the future, but he thought the critical acclaim merely his belated and inevitable due. Three years later, after the *Times Literary Supplement* had hailed her husband as unexcelled and perhaps unequalled for sheer literary talent among all English writers of his time, Véra Nabokov wrote to a friend that "without *Lolita* this would have taken another fifty years to happen."[27] But there had never been any shadow of doubt in her mind or his that this was the sort of recognition he deserved. The scale of *Lolita*'s success seemed not nec-

essary confirmation but a pleasantly unexpected reward for their un-
flinching confidence.

VI

Success made the press and the public stare. Early in September,
with *Lolita* about to jump from tenth to fourth place on the best-seller
list, *Life* sent its best writer to Ithaca. As Nabokov reported to Minton: "I spent two delightful days with Paul O'Neill, who pumped me
very delicately with great skill and acumen." A week later photographer Carl Mydans and his caption writer came for another two-day
session. Mydans snapped Nabokov in front of a mantelpiece on
which fifty of his books were ranged; with the eleven folders of the
Pushkin manuscript; working out on the punching ball in the basement; playing chess with Véra; poring over his butterflies; talking;
writing at his desk, on his bed, in the yard, in the car; catching a
butterfly in Six-Mile Creek, killing it, boxing it; and standing in front
of an innocent motel. Curiously, *Life*, pudibund family magazine that
it was, hesitated about running the story. Only in April 1959 would
it appear, and then not in the domestic but only in the international
edition, presumably, as Véra Nabokov wryly noted, to protect American farmers and their daughters from evil influence.[28]

While the Nabokovs and the *Life* reporters were seated at lunch,
Morris Bishop called up to offer his congratulations. What for? Did
they not read the *New York Times*, Bishop asked. Not always, but Volodya has been buying it almost every day this week, because he is
fascinated by the Nimer murder case (an eight-year-old boy suspected of murdering his parents). But no, they had not yet looked at
today's. Bishop then read out the announcement that movie rights
had been sold to Harris-Kubrick Pictures for $150,000 plus 15 percent
of the producers' profits. Nabokov had known an agreement was
looming, but had thought nothing was yet final.[29]

When the contract arrived, his reaction was bizarre—and uniquely
Nabokovian. He recalled a curious dream he had had the year his
uncle Vasily Rukavishnikov died in 1916. Uncle Vasya had said to
him: "I shall come back to you as Harry and Kuvyrkin." Within the
dream, the two names had signified a duo of (otherwise nonexistent)
circus clowns. Forty years later, Nabokov still recalled the dream and
now saw the dream-duo as a foreshadowing of Harris and Kubrick,
in another theatrical setting. In 1916 he had become a wealthy young
man when he inherited Uncle Vasya's fortune, only to lose it the next
year in the revolution. Now Harris and Kubrick had returned him at
one stroke to the ranks of the wealthy. That kind of combinational

replay is the stuff of his fiction. No wonder he would make Van Veen engage in a serious study of the "precognitive flavor" of dreams "in the hope . . . of 'catching sight of the lining of time.' "[30]

Other reactions were considerably more mundane. The secretary of the Women's Club of the Ithaca Presbyterian Church telephoned to ask if Nabokov would address the club. As Véra noted in the diary: "This is not *Lolita*'s literary merits. It's merely the 150 'grand' mentioned by the *Times*. To think that 3 yrs ago people like Covici, Laughlin, and also the Bishops, strongly advised V. *never* to publish *Lolita*, because, among other things, 'all the churches, the women's clubs' and so forth would 'crack down on you.' "[31]

The warnings had not been entirely without foundation. Over the past three years the chances of sexually frank fiction being published unopposed had improved, and *Lolita* herself had benefited from the concerted efforts of serious publishers and critics. Now in the United States itself there were few flickers of outrage. On September 17 the Cincinnati Public Library banned *Lolita*—and the next week the novel reached the top of the best-seller list. Another book club made the novel its selection of the month, and *Nabokov's Dozen* came out on September 21 to very favorable reviews.

Minton was now trying to secure a publisher for *Lolita* in England, where obscenity laws were far tougher. Late in September a British magistrate declared the novel obscene and imposed a £200 fine on a bookseller who tried to sell the Olympia edition to a plainclothes policeman. Publishers and printers faced much stiffer penalties, and genuinely feared being sent to jail for publishing the book.[32]

Nabokov was proud that, despite all the fears, his adopted homeland had not even come close to banning *Lolita*: "America is the most mature country in the world now in this respect." On the other hand, although he had become the subject of interviews in periodicals ranging from the *Cornell Sun* and the *Ithaca Journal* to *Life* and *Newsweek*, he was no fan of American openness if it began to intrude on his privacy. The Library of Congress had recently persuaded him to donate his papers gradually to their archives in return for tax concessions. Nabokov asked for a fifty-year restriction on whatever material he sent. The library would have preferred access to the papers to be free, and tried to persuade him to lift the restriction, but he remained adamant.[33]

VII

Nor was he happy when reporters showed up on the first day of the new school year, and he made them sit high in the back rows of the

Goldwin Smith B auditorium, where the light was too poor for photographs. Richard Fariña and other young Cornell literati wanted to interview Nabokov for a campus magazine, the *Trojan Horse*, but James McConkey and Baxter Hathaway of Cornell's English department, neither enamored of Nabokov, opposed the idea. Stephen Jan Parker, an undergraduate student of Nabokov's that year, distinctly recalls "the considerable jealousy on the part of other faculty members over Nabokov's notoriety. After all, from their point of view, here was a colleague who had been aloof and antisocial, strong in his convictions and not academically bent, who now was becoming rich and famous. It just wasn't fair."[34]

Nabokov had his own gripes. When the Soviets launched their Sputniks in 1957–1958, Americans suddenly felt a need to know more about the cold war opponent they had regarded as backward. At the beginning of the 1958–1959 school year, the *Cornell Sun* reported that campus enrollments in elementary Russian had doubled. The newspaper's informant, Richard Leed of the Division of Modern Languages, also stated that there was a slight increase in the number of students taking "advanced courses in Russian language and literature." Nabokov was stung into action. He wrote immediately to the *Sun* that he was the only instructor in Russian literature at Cornell and that Russian Literature 315–16 and 317–18 were the only advanced courses offered: "They presuppose some knowledge of the Russian language. This is the second year in succession that neither of these courses could be given for lack of qualified applicants."[35]

Since there were no other teachers of Russian literature, Nabokov's Russian courses were placed under the aegis of the Department of Romance Literatures. On the day he wrote to the *Sun*, he also wrote a formal protest to Professor Jean-Jacques Demorest, the current head of the department:

As you know, the prerequisite for enrolment in my course 315–316 is "qualification in Russian." By "qualification" I understand the ability to read and write, a knowledge of grammar, and as much of a vocabulary as, say, is needed for the understanding, with my assistance, of Pushkin's text. This fall three students, all of them bright talented boys whom it would have been a pleasure to teach, wished to enrol in Russian Literature 315. All three had taken Russian 101–102 in the University's Modern Languages Department. That course, I am told, is designed to give "proficiency" in Russian. I examined the three students asking them to 1. translate a simple Russian poem of 12 lines into English; 2. to perform a few simple exercises in declension and conjugation; and 3. to replace the blanks in a few sentences as given in the seventeenth lesson of a "Beginner's Manual" ("Conversational Russian"). After a brief spell of stunned contemplation, all three students declared that the task was utterly hopeless, that they did not understand the words and that they were utterly unprepared for that type of work.

I should have found this situation inexplicable had I not been aware of the farce taking place year after year in the Russian Dept. at Morrill Hall. At the root of the evil there is one simple fact: the head of the Russian Language Dept., Prof. G. Fairbanks, does not have any Russian. He cannot speak it, he cannot write it. I believe he can teach the linguistics of any language, including Armenian, Korean, Hungarian and what not—but that is all he can do. So that our students are taught not the Russian language itself but the method of teaching others to teach that method.

On the other hand, since Dr. Fairbanks knows no Russian, he has no means to ascertain whether or not the instructors he appoints have sufficient Russian for the task assigned to them. The result is that the young instructors (mostly graduate students appointed by him) are likewise incapable of reading and writing Russian.

When I joined the Cornell faculty in 1948, three Russian ladies with excellent knowledge of the language and teaching were in charge of the Russian language courses. Two of them have long left, to be replaced by ludicrously incompetent young instructors whose major field frequently lies outside the Russian Language Dept. The only courses in Russian language that still have value are those given by Mrs Jaryc. It is plain that one excellent instructor cannot outbalance the disastrous nonsense going on in the other classes.

The situation of the Russian Language Dept. has been steadily deteriorating over a number of years and now it has really reached a point at which continued silence on my part would be disloyal to the University.[36]

Nothing came of his protest.

Meanwhile, he continued teaching literature in his own way. The day after his letter to Demorest, he began *Mansfield Park* by warning his class to "OMIT IDIOTIC INTRODUCTION!!!!!"[37] Preparing for his course in Russian literature in translation, he began, as soon as the term started, to correct his version of the masterpiece of medieval Russian literature, *Slovo o polku Igoreve* (*The Song of Igor's Campaign*), both for use in class and in order to leave a copy on reserve in the library for his thirty-odd students. Though he did not yet know it, this fall would be the last term he would ever have to teach—and just when his and Dmitri's *Hero of Our Time* translation could be prescribed for the first time (it had been published in March), just when his version of the *Slovo* was taking final shape, just when his finally corrected manuscript of *Eugene Onegin* could also be placed on reserve.[38]

If he was in some ways better prepared than ever, he was also more distracted than ever as New York placed urgent demands on his time. On the third weekend of term, in mid-October, the Nabokovs drove to New York to watch Dmitri perform the role of Fernando in *Il Trovatore* for the Broadway Grand Opera Association, a little group with a big name. Since finding an apartment on West End Avenue in the spring, Dmitri had combined his training as a singer with work as a translator and editor for the *Current Digest of the Soviet Press*. After the success of *Lolita*, he had agreed early in September, despite a shortage of time, to translate his father's *Invitation to a Beheading* from the Russian, the first Nabokov novel to be translated into English since the family's arrival in America.

There were other business matters to attend to. Now that he had money and a name that could mint more, Nabokov wanted to consult a New York lawyer about investing his income and securing it against inflation and about safeguarding the copyright on his old Russian books. To meet the lawyer, he had to cancel his Monday classes. A week later he did the same again, taking a train to New York for a *Herald Tribune* Books and Authors luncheon at the Waldorf-Astoria. This time the Nabokovs stayed at the Windermere Hotel, just down the street from Dmitri's apartment—it would become their regular New York perch over the next six months—and fitted in eight meetings with publishers on the Monday and Tuesday before returning by the night train for Wednesday morning's classes.[39] Obviously this could not continue, and Nabokov applied for a year of unpaid leave from Cornell.

VIII

In mid-September, with *Lolita* at number four on the best-seller list, the English translation of *Doctor Zhivago* was published. By the end of September, *Lolita* was number one. After seven weeks in that position Nabokov's novel would be bumped down to number two by Pasternak's. Chance had contrived it that the two most successful representatives of the two streams of modern Russian literature, the Soviet and the émigré, should fight it out in the American marketplace.

After *Novy mir*, the leading Soviet literary periodical, rejected *Doctor Zhivago* in 1956, Pasternak had given the manuscript of the novel to an agent of the Italian publisher Feltrinelli to publish abroad. Aware of the risk he ran, he farewelled Feltrinelli's agent: "You are as of now invited to my execution"—an eerie echo of Nabokov's *Invitation to a Beheading* (literally *Invitation to an Execution*). Pasternak also gave another copy of the manuscript to Georgy Katkov, asking him to have it translated and published in England. In the course of discussing the difficulty of translating the book, especially the verses at the end, Katkov named an ideal translator: "a poet, who is completely bilingual: Vladimir Nabokov."

Pasternak replied: "That won't work; he's too jealous of my wretched position in this country to do it properly." A curious remark, for ever since socialist realism had been proclaimed the official Soviet aesthetic in 1934, Pasternak had had to survive by diverting his creative energies to translation. Though more courageous than any other Soviet writer except perhaps Mandelstam, he could keep alive while others died in Stalin's purges only by remaining virtually silent. Now even after the mild and brief post-Stalin thaw he was unable to publish his work in his own country and risked his life by publishing it elsewhere. What was there for Nabokov to envy? Not Pasternak's gifts as a lyric poet, which he happily acknowledged—he called Pasternak "a kind of masculine Emily Dickinson," no mean compliment—but had criticized him as much as thirty years previously for the jarring infelicities he thought intrinsic to Pasternak's poetic style. And certainly not Pasternak's limited talent as a novelist. As Georgy Adamovich, Nabokov's staunchest critical foe in the emigration, would later say: "I do not care for Nabokov, but, of course, he is an amazing craftsman and storyteller. There is no comparison between his novels and *Doctor Zhivago*, a feeble production, though an important one."[40]

Reading an advance copy of *Doctor Zhivago* in August, Nabokov wrote to Jason Epstein that it was "dreary conventional stuff." In the year following the book's American publication, the press and others repeatedly sought Nabokov's opinion of it, even asking him for a review. He answered Dwight MacDonald early in October: "Had not *Zhivago* and I been on the same ladder . . . I would have been glad to demolish that trashy, melodramatic, false and inept book." Later he explained that he was also wary—before American acclaim was intensified in reaction to Soviet vilification—that an early and outspoken negative critique might have influenced other reviewers, harmed the book's reception, and left Pasternak "more vulnerable than ever." After the Soviets had denounced the book themselves, Nabokov still refused "to go out of my way to demolish it in public" but did not mind being frank, when asked for an opinion, about his rejection of the novel on artistic grounds. Artistically, he would tell reporters, "*Doctor Zhivago* is a sorry thing, clumsy, trite and melodramatic, with stock situations, voluptuous lawyers, unbelievable girls, romantic robbers and trite coincidences."[41]

As it climbed up the best-seller list in October, two or three rungs below *Lolita*, Nabokov joked, echoing Cato's call for the destruction of Carthage: "*Delenda est Zhivago!*"[42] Then on October 23, Pasternak was awarded the Nobel Prize. He accepted, and the Soviet press immediately denounced *Doctor Zhivago* as "artistically squalid" and a "malicious lampoon" on the Soviet Union. *Pravda* claimed that if there were "a spark of Soviet dignity left in him," Pasternak would have rejected the prize. On October 27 the Soviet Writers' Union voted to expel him. He was called a pig "who befouls the place where he eats and befouls those by whose labor he lives and breathes." On October 29, Pasternak declined the prize.[43] *Lolita* had caused a sensation, but it had never been scandalous front-page international news, and *Doctor Zhivago* quickly vaulted to the top of the best-seller list.

Even before the campaign of orchestrated abuse, the Nabokovs had been convinced (quite unwarrantedly) that the whole history of *Zhivago* was a Soviet plot. Since Feltrinelli was a Communist—albeit an Italian one—they assumed that he was under Moscow's control, that the story of the manuscript's having been smuggled out of the Soviet Union was a fabrication, and that Soviet opposition to the book's publication was only a ruse to boost its foreign sales and earn much-sought-after foreign currency, "which they would eventually pocket and spend on propaganda abroad."[44]

In the West, *Doctor Zhivago* was hailed for its courageous criticism of the Soviet system. How could Nabokov suppose the Soviets themselves had engineered its success? Although publicly he professed to judge the novel only from an artistic point of view, privately he in fact objected equally strongly to its politics. Recognizing *Doctor Zhivago*'s anti-Stalinist stance, he found it also fundamentally antiliberal in its glorifying Lenin's overthrow of Russian democracy.[45] Since Pasternak never challenged Lenin's elevation of the Communist party over the will of the people, Nabokov saw *Doctor Zhivago* as merely a justification of an antidemocratic system, a subtler kind of Bolshevik propaganda.

Edmund Wilson's reaction could not have been more different. In the 1930s he had boldly risked the contempt of his own comrades on the left by criticizing Stalin. Now he saw in Pasternak an idealized reflection of the most difficult change in his own career, a magnified version of the way he might have acted had he been a Russian and endowed with Pasternak's talent. As America's most authoritative critic, Wilson had never reviewed any of Nabokov's novels, while repeatedly promising to write an overview of his friend's entire oeuvre. But now he devoted the most excited review of his career to Pasternak, concluding: "*Doctor Zhivago* will, I believe, come to stand as one of the great events in man's literary and moral history. Nobody could have written it in a totalitarian state and turned it loose on the world who did not have the courage of genius."[46]

IX

Western governments promoted *Lolita* almost as much as the Soviets had inadvertently assisted *Doctor Zhivago*. The French government had rebanned the English *Lolita* in July, and now in November, Maurice Girodias sought 32,500,000 francs in damages from the Ministère de l'Intérieur. In Britain a new obscenity bill was introduced into the House of Commons in September, allowing for a book to be judged as a whole rather than by passages divorced from context and permitting the defense to summon expert witnesses to testify to literary merit. Most publishers now preferred to wait for the bill to be passed into law before offering to commit themselves to *Lolita*—which would crop up frequently in the coming parliamentary debates.[47]

Nabokov hoped the English rights would be taken by Bodley Head, largely because Graham Greene, now one of the firm's directors, had already done so much for the book and declared himself ready to go to jail for it: "there couldn't be a better cause!" Minton, however, sensed that Greene's public ridiculing of John Gordon in 1956 was still strongly resented in influential quarters, and virtually insisted on Weidenfeld and Nicolson. This promising young firm, now nine years old, was ready to offer a bigger advance than Bodley Head's and to commit itself in writing to defend the book. Nabokov let Minton have his way. Late in November, when Weidenfeld signed up *Lolita*, one British publishing pundit muttered to the press: "Sixty per cent chance of gaol."[48]

In America, *Lolita* was becoming a household word and a regular subject of jokes by television hosts like Steve Allen, Dean Martin, and Milton Berle. The process of vulgarization would ultimately lead to such horrors as the life-size Lolita doll with "French and Greek apertures" advertised in the mid-1970s. In 1958, standards were very different—and Nabokov's own stricter than most. He was quite shocked when a little girl of eight or nine came to his door for candy on Halloween, dressed up by her parents as Lolita, with a tennis racquet and a ponytail, and a sign reading L-O-L-I-T-A. Before the novel's publication, he had insisted to Minton that there be no little girl on the book's cover, and now as a *Lolita* movie looked more and more possible, he warned Minton that he "would veto the use of a real child. Let them find a dwarfess."[49]

In mid-November, on the day Nabokov signed the movie contract, he was also awarded a year's leave of absence from Cornell. Whether or not leave could commence in February depended on his being able to find someone to take his place at the lectern for the coming spring term. He wrote immediately to a number of friends asking if they could suggest a replacement. Before he could receive a reply, he found he had still less need of a university post: the paperback rights to *Lolita* would be bought by Fawcett Crest for $100,000.[50]

At the end of the month the Nabokovs again took the train to New York. This time the main reason was a television trialogue—Nabokov, Lionel Trilling, and the interviewer—for the Canadian Broadcasting Commission. He had been offered $500, but held out for twice the amount. Unlike all Nabokov's later television interviews, this show was unscripted and live: an interview in Toronto with General Montgomery from 10:00 to 10:15, before a link-up with New York. There, the Radio City studio was colorfully made up as a plausible simulacrum of Nabokov's sitting room: books, chrysanthemums, candles, teapot, and teacups. Since the stores were closed and there was nowhere to buy tea—which he never drank anyway—Nabokov offered a passable surrogate to fill the teapot: a small bottle of brandy he had bought for the return train trip.

In later interviews Nabokov would characterize his writing methods by saying that he wore out erasers faster than pencil lead. He was an assiduous, meticulous reviser, and for that reason began to insist in his interviews of the 1960s that questions be submitted in advance so that he could write and revise his answers in advance. He knew that he was no orator, and one of the notable characteristics of his speech was a habit of verbal erasure, repetition, and readjustment, the result of his trying out the best possible words and the best possible order as he continued to speak. In his novel *The Real Life of Sebastian Knight* he describes Sebastian's manner of not striking out trial phrases which he had replaced by others, so that one of his manuscripts begins thus: "As he a heavy A heavy sleeper, Roger Rogerson, old Rogerson bought old Rogers bought, so afraid Being a heavy sleeper, old Rogers was so afraid of missing to-morrows. He was a heavy sleeper. He was mortally afraid of missing tomorrow's event glory early train. . . ." Live speech provides one with no eraser, no retrospective "delete," and the tape of Nabokov's CBC interview records incantatory repetitions that almost rival Sebastian Knight's: "My baboon Humbert Humbert, for after all Humbert Humbert is a baboon, a baboon of genius but a baboon." At other times the repetition has more purpose: "I have invented in America my America and just as fantastic as any inventor's America." Still, there are flashes of Nabokov at his best. After he dismissed those who recoiled from *Lolita* as "just common scolds and old philistines," he was asked to define what he meant by "philistines," and replied: "Ready-made souls in plastic bags." Véra and Dmitri, sitting with two technicians in the empty auditorium, watched with delight. When the interview ended, Véra and her husband had to dash from the studio, and even so just caught the night train back to Ithaca.[51]

X

Lolita's strange tale had still more twists to make. In France, the Conseil d'état ruled that the Ministère de l'Intérieur after all had the right to act as it did: *Lolita* in her Olympia guise would once again be banned. In Britain, the Home Secretary R. A. ("Rab") Butler, Nabokov's acquaintance from Trinity College days, introduced a new Obscene Publications Bill, and when *Lolita* cropped up in the debate, Nigel Nicolson, the second half of Weidenfeld and Nicolson and the Conservative M.P. for ultraconservative Bournemouth, defended his firm's decision to publish the book on the grounds that "*Lolita* has a built-in condemnation of what it describes."[52] Five days before Christmas, Nabokov's European agents sent Japanese, Norwegian, and Israeli contracts for the book, to add to the Danish, Swedish, and Dutch editions already published, and the French, German, Italian, and Finnish versions in the process of translation.

Back in Ithaca, reporters from across the United States and Europe called Nabokov on the phone or knocked at his door. He received invitations to lecture at six universities and the Library of Congress. Students lined up outside his office waiting for him to sign copies of *Lolita* as Christmas gifts for their parents: so much for the complaints his advisers at Cornell had dreaded a few years before. Not that America had *no* complaints to make. The Texas town of Lolita debated changing its name to Jackson. A city official in Los Angeles blew the whistle when he found the public library circulating the book—and Putnam's promptly received another large order from California. Nabokov found in his fan mail a pot holder embroidered with the word "Lolita" and felt sure it had come from Edmund Wilson as a derisive tribute to a potboiler. "Take me to your Lolita," said one cartoon among many, and Groucho Marx announced: "I've put off reading *Lolita* for six years, till she's 18."[53]

As December deepened, so did the snow, but by now the Nabokovs had relief in sight: a willing replacement had been found. When Herbert Gold, a young novelist recommended by Nabokov's former Wellesley colleague, Aileen Ward, arrived to be looked over by Cornell, the Nabokovs coached him carefully, anxious that nothing should go wrong. They advised him on how much to drink in order to be a good fellow, but suggested he be not *too* good a fellow, told him to be polite and to brush his teeth. Although he was far too charged up to sleep, they insisted he would need a nap before the ritual martinis. Addressing each other in English rather than their habitual Russian—a sure sign of a stage whisper in that household—they "woke" their unsleeping guest by asking outside his door: "Do you think he'd like sherry when he wakes up?"

A fine conversationalist, Gold passed the ordeal of the official inspection, and as he settled into Ithaca found Nabokov generous with him, not condescending, not avid of adulation: "He didn't demand worship. You got on well with him if you teased him. He demanded friendly competition." Nabokov liked to simultaneously flatter and tease Gold by smuggling into this or that unlikely corner of the conversation a line from Gold's *The Man Who Was Not with It*. When Gold failed to recognize the phrase in its new context, Nabokov would laugh: "You do not know your own work."[54]

XI

On January 19, Nabokov delivered his last two lectures at Cornell. This time he was all smiles for the reporter from the Swedish periodical *Veckojournalen*, who kept snapping pictures of the professor professorially peering over his glasses, a delighted grin on his face, at his students grinning, laughing, and applauding his latest phrase.[55]

He needed the reprieve from teaching to catch up with all his literary affairs. He was completing his revision of the French translation of *Lolita*, which Gallimard was anxious to publish immediately to challenge the French government's ban on the Olympia edition. He had reached a pitch of frustration with Girodias, who continued to imply that he was responsible for *Lolita*'s success. "*I* wrote *Lolita*," Nabokov had to remind him. Unable to trust Girodias, he had also become highly suspicious of his own European agents, Doussia Ergaz and Marie Schébéko of the Bureau Littéraire Clairouin. Surmising that they had acted on Girodias's behalf, he fired a number of wounding comments their way over the course of the coming months, until his meeting with them in Paris in October cleared away misunderstandings and restored their former friendship.[56]

When he came home for Christmas, Dmitri had brought with him the first installment of his translation of *Invitation to a Beheading*. His father deemed it excellent, and urged Dmitri to drop his job and work full-time on the translation of his father's books.[57] This marked the beginning of the long, still unfinished series of Dmitri's translations from the Russian: first in conjunction with his father, until all the novels and the collected stories were published, the last a year before Nabokov's death; and then, on his own, the poems and the uncollected stories, plays, and essays. At various points in the 1960s, Dmitri's operatic career would allow him too little time to keep up with his father's and publishers' schedules, and other translators would be brought in for this or that book. As if to compensate, the Italian that Dmitri learned while studying opera in Milan would enable him to translate some of his father's work into Italian in the 1970s and 1980s. After his father's death, as his mother entered her eighties, Dmitri would then take on from her the role of supervising the publication of his father's literary leftovers: his Cornell and Harvard lectures, his selected letters, his uncollected stories.

Nabokov naturally preferred his son to any other translator. Dmitri accepted his father's principle of literality and knew that an undulating or knobbly Russian phrase should not be flattened into plain English. Where other translators often felt Nabokov's exacting corrections and innumerable rephrasings a threat to their professional competence, Dmitri could simply welcome the improvements.

Even without needing to be translated, *Lolita* required meticulous preparation to be published in England. George Weidenfeld mapped out a strategy and drew on the talents of literary figures who supported the book's right to an audience.[58] Bernard Levin published a brilliant defense of the novel ("Massive, unflagging, moral, exquisitely shaped, enormously vital, enormously funny") in the *Spectator*. Twenty-one writers, including Compton McKenzie, Iris Murdoch, V. S. Pritchett, Stephen Spender, and Angus Wilson, wrote a joint letter to the *Times*: "We are disturbed by the suggestion that it may yet prove impossible to have an English edition of Vladimir Nabokov's *Lolita*. . . . Prosecutions of genuine works of literature bring governments into disrepute and do nothing to encourage public morality. When today we read the proceedings against *Madame Bovary* or *Ulysses*—works genuinely found shocking by many of their contemporaries—it is Flaubert and Joyce whom we admire, not the Public Prosecutors of the time."[59] Levin's comments and the *Times* letter would be published in an appendix to the English *Lolita* that listed reactions from nine countries and from writers like Graham Greene, Alberto Moravia, Dorothy Parker, V. S. Pritchett, and Lionel Trilling: more necessary insurance against prosecution.

George Weidenfeld was committed to *Lolita* and eager to republish all Nabokov's works, for their own sake and in support of their author's seriousness. Nabokov welcomed this but issued one caution. In promoting his work, they must avoid anything of the "Mr. Nabokov is a second Pasternak" sort. "Pasternak is the best Soviet poet, and . . . Nabokov is the best Russian prose writer but there the parallel ends; so just to prevent any well-meaning publicity from taking the wrong turn, I would like to voice my objection to *Doctor Zhivago* which may brim with human interest but is wretched art and platitudinous thought."[60]

As Weidenfeld wrote to Nabokov, the battle for *Lolita* had been raging furiously in the lobbies, debating rooms, and ministerial cubbyholes of the House of Commons, in the press, and on television, making it the most talked-about book in Britain months before publication. In February, Nigel Nicolson's problems with his Bournemouth constituency kept *Lolita* very much in the news. He had already been in trouble with his local party organization for opposing government policy on Suez, but now, as another M.P. admitted, "*Lolita* is the main issue. Suez has been replaced."* Nicolson soon lost his seat.[61]

In the week of his last Cornell classes, Nabokov withdrew his *Eugene Onegin* from Cornell University Press. "They started to groom it for print," he wrote to Edmund Wilson, "and had actually taken care of the square brackets when an impossible clause in their contract forced me to take back my poor monster": after requiring him to forfeit his royalties in their academic edition, they had insisted in a share in the royalties of any future trade editions. Jason Epstein mentioned the book's plight to Bollingen Press. Since Bollingen had recently been told that letting *Eugene Onegin* go was the greatest mistake it had ever made, it was delighted to find the book available once more. At the end of January, Bollingen's Vaun Gillmor phoned Nabokov to say that Bollingen wanted the manuscript, and the decision to publish was final. Nabokov was as pleased as his new publisher.[62]

In their last month in Ithaca the Nabokovs had no rest. Nabokov was busy revising his translations of *The Song of Igor's Campaign* for

---

* Strangely, Nicolson's parents, Sir Harold Nicolson and Lady Vita Sackville-West, were also fiercely opposed to the publication of *Lolita*, despite the sexual unconventionality of both of their lives (see the *Diaries of Sir Harold Nicolson* and Nigel Nicolson's *Portrait of a Marriage*).

publication. He had also collected a considerable number of shorter Russian poems he had translated into English—by Lomonosov, Zhukovsky, Batyushkov, Pushkin (lyrics and short dramas), Tyutchev, Fet, Blok—and hoped to publish them as a volume. It never appeared, and many of the translations now appear untraceable. Sorting through papers to send off to the Library of Congress, he also discovered the manuscript of "Volshebnik" ("The Enchanter"), the unpublished 1939 story that marked his first attempt at the *Lolita* theme, and suggested translating and publishing it while interest in *Lolita* ran high. But the story would have to wait until Dmitri translated it in 1986.[63]

While Véra handled his correspondence, now ten to fifteen letters a day, Nabokov was collecting material for the story "The Admirable Anglewing."[64] He had begun to brood on it while sorting and pinning his catches the previous summer. From the notes that survive, it appears that the story would have told of an entomologist who lends a fantastic butterfly rarity, perhaps a genetic aberration, perhaps a new species, to a colleague, only for someone in the latter's family to lose or destroy the specimen and attempt to substitute a black-and-white Admirable whose wings have been cut out to match the alar contours of the missing prize—a ploy hideously unconvincing to a lepidopterist's eye. The story would have used more technical detail about lepidoptera than any of Nabokov's other published fiction. He continued to work on it in June 1959 and perhaps later still, and his reasons for abandoning it can only be guessed at. Perhaps he felt the story's moral (that there *are* no substitutes for the unique individual) was too plain; perhaps he could not reconcile his own wish for uncompromising scientific exactitude and his sense of the lay reader's resistance to technical minutiae.

Or perhaps it was simply that other ideas intervened. Nabokov had been actively planning *Pale Fire* between 1956 and early 1958, but his blueprints had apparently faded into limbo. In their place a new project emerged, to turn up after many transformations as the key to *Ada*. In mid-February 1959, he noted down:

Space, time, the two prime mysteries. The transformation of nothing into something cannot be conceived by the human mind.

The torrent of time—a mere poetical tradition: time does not flow. Time is perfectly still. We feel it as moving only because it is the medium where growth and change take place or where things stop, like stations.[65]

With these lines, Nabokov had begun a Bergsonian meditation on time that would preoccupy and thwart him for years, until late in 1965, he suddenly conceived of *Ada* and realized that there was a space in that baroque edifice already prepared for "The Texture of Time." As he jotted down these first reflections, he had no inkling of the finished *Ada*, but in some curious way his mind seems to have been ripe for the novel, for between abandoning *Pale Fire* in the spring of 1958 and the flash of inspiration that reanimated it in November 1960, he was to store up a host of apparently unconnected impressions that would find their place years later in *Ada*.

XII

When Herbert Gold entered the office he took over from Nabokov, he found on the desk a copy of *Doctor Zhivago* heavy with marginal annotations ("*poshlost'*!" "idiocy!" "repetitious!") and the note "Dear Mr. Gold, I leave you my copy of *Dr. Van Cliburn*."⁶⁶* The rest of their possessions the Nabokovs placed in storage at Dean of Ithaca, and drove off for the last time on February 24. A bad skid on icy roads left them with one final memory of upstate New York.⁶⁷

Reaching Manhattan the next day, they moved into a pleasant apartment in the Windermere Hotel. Over the next six weeks they saw a good deal of Dmitri, Véra's sister Sonia Slonim, and her cousin Anna Feigin, but they had come to New York on business. In the first four days there Nabokov was interviewed by *Time*, *Life*, the *New York Times Book Review*, and the London *Daily Mail* and *Daily Express*, and turned down interviews on three television programs. A month later, *People* magazine could comment: "Never in the history of publishing has a book caused such a rumpus."⁶⁸

Nabokov heard a rumor that Maurice Girodias planned to name the new Paris nightclub he was opening—with the money he had gained from *Lolita*—after the novel itself.⁶⁹ Although the venture never materialized, Nabokov's brushes with the caprices of fame made their way into *Ada*, where a film made from Van Veen's long-neglected first book, *Letters from Terra*, becomes a *Star Wars* kind of success,** and Eric Veen's Villa Venus brothels enjoy a brief but colorful and elegant vogue. *Lolita* becomes a book by Osberg—Borges, as we know him, with whom Nabokov would be so often compared

---

* In 1958, after Van Cliburn's victory at the Chaikovsky Competition in Moscow, his recording of Chaikovsky's Piano Concerto No. 1 had hovered for months at or near the top of the LP charts, along with Johnny Mathis and *South Pacific*.

** "L.F.T. tiny dolls, L.F.T. breloques of coral and ivory, appeared in souvenir shops, from Agony, Patagonia, to Wrinkleballs, Le Bras d'Or. . . . From the tremendous correspondence that piled up on Van's desk during a few years of world fame. . . ."

in the 1960s—and romantically inclined handmaids are all agog over *Docteur Mertvago*.*

On March 1, Nabokov met his future English publisher for the first time. With the example of Girodias in mind, he at first cast a suspicious eye over George Weidenfeld, but was won over by his determination to publish during the next three years not only *Lolita* but also *Bend Sinister, Invitation to a Beheading, The Real Life of Sebastian Knight*, either *The Gift* or *The Defense*, and then *Nikolay Gogol, Speak, Memory*, and *Laughter in the Dark*.[70] Not all the program would be adhered to as planned that day, but Weidenfeld's fledgling firm would soon soar on the strength of *Lolita*. Over the next three decades he would continue to publish almost every Nabokov work he could, whether freshly written or newly revived. During the 1960s and 1970s, Nabokov's most loyal publisher and Weidenfeld's best author would become firm friends.

Nabokov sent off the last batch of proofs for the French *Lolita*. He talked over with the Bollingen staff the possibility of presenting the *Eugene Onegin* translation and Russian text *en regard*.[71] He spent six weeks completely revamping his translation of *The Song of Igor's Campaign* and compiling a set of annotations that "has inherited a Eugene gene and is threatening to grow into another mammoth," as he wrote to Edmund Wilson; "Russia will never be able to repay all her debts to me."[72] That was plain fact, not empty boast. After beginning his American academic career by providing the most influential introduction in English to Russia's most difficult nineteenth-century prose writer, Gogol, he had now rounded it off by translating and annotating the greatest poems first of modern and now of ancient Russia.

XIII

After the experience of the previous year's rough weather, stark accommodation, and short season, the Nabokovs headed south in search of a longer and more soothing summer. Nabokov needed a good rest, and they took the trip slowly, by a circuitous southern route, collecting all along the way. Setting off on April 18, they stopped for four days among the flowering dogwood and the alluring lepidoptera of Gatlinburg, Tennessee. As the British House of Commons prepared for the third reading of the Obscenity Bill, as Australian federal police and then New South Wales state police burst into the offices of the Sydney *Nation*, looking in vain for the copy of *Lolita*

---

* *Zhivago* derives from the Russian for "alive," *Mertvago* from "dead."

from which the paper had typeset Quilty's death scene, as *Lolita* was published in France to dazzling acclaim, the Nabokovs drove on through Birmingham, Alabama, and San Antonio, Texas, while all around them, in front and behind, tornadoes raged, rivers overflowed, thunderstorms roared, and all they saw of it was a cloudburst or two.[73]

At Uvalde in southern Texas a thunderstorm turned the dry riverbed beside their motel into a lush floral meadow—which Nabokov would transform in *Ada* into "the daze of desert flowers that the rain had brought out." They stopped for four more days at Big Bend National Park, "a magnificent semitropical place, the newest (and wildest) of our national parks," where they were warned that collecting could be complicated by overplayful mountain lions and ubiquitous rattlesnakes. A young Canadian they met borrowed the butterfly net and brought back a rattler. Nabokov for his part was proud to have caught "a rather wonderful, apparently undescribed, green hairstreak close to *M. siva.*"[74]

In mid-May they reached Flagstaff, Arizona, and the next day drove into Oak Creek Canyon, a picturesque spot fifteen miles to the south. The narrow canyon drops steeply down from the seven-thousand-foot-high plateau and its ponderosa and piñon pines, through the maples, oaks, ash, and poplar flanking the slender creek. Further down, the rocks become red, rounded, and broken knolls, like fat knobbly fingers—Max Ernst country—and junipers begin to oust other trees. A little lower still, prickly pear and sagebrush mark the beginning of desert country. Enticed by the prospect of a mixture of arctic and subtropical fauna to match the flora, Nabokov decided to stay. He called Dmitri from a glass booth in the wilderness and asked him to send the rest of the *Invitation to a Beheading* translation at once.[75] That too would form part of the "daze of desert flowers" scene in *Ada* ("I rang you up at your hotel from a roadside booth of pure crystal still tear-stained after a tremendous thunderstorm"). Nabokov's appreciation of the fantastic quality of his recent fortunes and his America seem very much part of the strange world of Antiterra.

On a hunch, the Nabokovs stopped and took a cabin in a string of cottages called Forest Houses. Their landlord, Bob Kittredge, turned up the next day with a glossy pamphlet in his hand: the spring list of Weidenfeld and Nicolson, with a full-page advertisement for *Lolita* and another smaller advertisement for his own novel. Kittredge and his wife, both sculptors, had built their six or seven wooden cabins in delightful taste, isolated from each other and the highway but right by the creek. The nights were cool, the days sunny, and the Nabokovs came to love the place in the two months they remained.[76]

XIV

In May, after nine months on the American best-seller lists, *Lolita* moved up again from fourth place to third. At the end of the month Mondadori's version of the novel was published in Italy. And in the first two days in June, a reporter from *Sports Illustrated*, Robert Boyle, came to catch Nabokov wielding his net. By luring Boyle to Oak Creek Canyon, *Lolita* brings us Nabokov the lepidopterist in action—a blend of sport and science, information and play—and perhaps our finest moment-by-moment image of Nabokov the man.[77]

On the first morning, swathed in dungarees, sport shirt, and sweater, Nabokov emerged from his cabin at 8:30 to test the air and the morning sun. "It is now 9 o'clock," he announced: as one of his running jokes, he would keep advancing every watch and clock he could find, in the hope that this might make Véra move faster and allow him to reach his butterflies all the sooner. As he admitted, though, the butterflies would not be up for another hour, until the sun rose over the canyon rim and had time to dry the dewy grass.

Taking Boyle inside, he opened a volume of *Colorado Butterflies* to a page showing Nabokov's wood nymph, the *dorothea* he had discovered in the Grand Canyon in 1941. "I know it occurs here, but it is difficult to find. It flies in the speckled shade early in June, though there's another brood at the end of the summer, so you came at the right time."

At 9:35, Nabokov standard time, he reached for his net and cloth cap and led Boyle down a foot trail beside Oak Creek. He pointed with the handle of his net to a butterfly clinging to the underside of a leaf. "Disruptive coloration," he explained, indicating white spots on the wings. "A bird comes and wonders for a second. Is it two bugs? Where is the head? Which side is which? In that split second the butterfly is gone. That second saves that individual and that species." Briefly buoyed up by catching a beautifully fresh *Melitaea anicia*, pinching its thorax, storing it in a glassine envelope in a small Band-Aid box in his pocket, he pressed on for another hour and a quarter before exclaiming with delight: "Ah. Oh, that's an interesting thing! Oh, gosh, there it goes. A white skipper mimicking a cabbage butterfly belonging to a different family. Things are picking up. Still, they're not quite right. Where's my wood nymph? It is heartbreaking work. Wretched work."

Véra, her day's letters done, greeted them as they returned to the cabin. "Let us hurry, darling," Nabokov cajoled her. Smiling indulgently, she followed him out to the car, which would not start. "The car is nervous," he proffered in explanation. At last it started, and Véra drove them off. At a spot several miles north, Nabokov caught several interesting specimens, but still no wood nymph, as he noted sadly.

Once he swished the net triumphantly and trapped two butterflies. . . . "Lygdamus blue—female," he said. "This other, by freakish chance, is a male blue of another species that was flying with it. That's adultery. Or a step towards adultery." He let the offending male fly free unpunished.

Another time Nabokov swung and netted three butterflies, one an angle wing. "It has a curiously formed letter C. It mimics a chink of light through a dead leaf. Isn't that wonderful? Isn't that humorous?"

After lunch in Sedona they tried a grove further south, found nothing, and drove back to Sedona to shop. Nabokov followed Véra into the supermarket. As she hesitated over the cold cuts, he confided to Boyle: "When I was younger I ate some butterflies in Vermont to see if they were poisonous. I didn't see any difference between a monarch butterfly and a viceroy. The taste of both was vile, but I had no ill effects. They tasted like almonds and perhaps a green cheese combination. I ate them raw. I held one in one hot little hand and one in the other. Will you eat some with me tomorrow for breakfast?"

The next day Nabokov planned to explore in the vicinity of the ghost mining town of Jerome, an hour's drive away. Early the next morning he was "as chipper and as restless as ever. 'Come on, darling,' he called to Mrs. Nabokov during breakfast. 'The sun is wasting away! It's a quarter to 10.' Mrs. Nabokov took her time. 'He doesn't know that everyone is wise to him,' she said. At 10:10, Nabokov at last succeeded in luring her behind the wheel. 'We are going to Jerome,' he said happily. 'The wood nymph should be out, I hope, on Mingus Mountain.' " Stopping at Jerome, elevation 7,023 feet, the Nabokovs each took a net from the back and walked up a dirt road bordered by pines.

A yellow butterfly danced crazily by. Nabokov swung and missed. "Common," he said. "I'm just getting warmed up." Unfortunately, a 15-minute search of the terrain revealed nothing. Nabokov turned toward an iris-covered meadow. "I can't believe there won't be butterflies here," he said. He was mistaken. "I'm very much disappointed," Nabokov said, after searching the meadow. "*Rien, rien.*"

Nabokov returned to the car. "It was very sad. 'And then I saw that strong man put his head on his forearms and sob like a woman.' "

They tried another luckless location and drove back toward Jerome.

"Sad," said Nabokov. " 'His face was now a tear-stained mask.' " Five minutes later, he had Mrs. Nabokov stop at Mescal Canyon. "We may be in for a surprise here," he said. Alas there was none. He walked up the dirt road alone. Mrs. Nabokov lent her net to their visitor. With a whoop of joy, the visitor snared a white-winged beauty. Cupping it in his hands, he showed it to Nabokov who dismissed it airily. "A winged cliché." . . . As the car swung out for the journey home, Nabokov spread his arms and said sadly, "What can I say? What is there to say? I am ashamed for the butterflies. I apologize for the butterflies."

A few days later, Nabokov wrote to Boyle: "I have seen my *dorothea* twice and twice missed it." But over the next six weeks he and Véra managed to catch some remarkable butterflies and to unwind completely from the stresses of the last few arduous years.[78]

XV

Not that it was all landscape and lepidoptera. At the beginning of June, Nabokov began revising Dmitri's *Invitation to a Beheading* translation,[79] and by the end of the month he had added his own high-spirited foreword to the novel and sent it off to Putnam's. The afterword he had written for *Lolita*, part of the strategy of making the novel more "respectable," presumably suggested the model he was to follow for all the forthcoming translations of his Russian novels, which might not offend readers but could well perplex those who knew nothing of the émigré circumstances in which they were written.

The introductions he wrote over the next sixteen years contain some of his breeziest autobiographical and autocritical writing. Nabokov never liked to reveal the hidden springs of his fiction, for he wanted readers to exercise their own eyes and minds. But at the same time he liked to disclose some of the secrets of the work in question—and then feign by his patter that he had not done so at all. He placed the clue before the reader's eyes, but left it still concealed: Find What the Author Has Hidden.

At Oak Creek Canyon he also wrote a little more of "The Admirable Anglewing," the last story he ever attempted to write: in the future, he decided, he would conserve his energy for ampler tasks. He sent indignant letters to his agents in France. He received a haunting description (clear day, mild wind, lake, gasoline-scented air) of the burning of six thousand copies of the unsatisfactory Swedish translations of his books on a garbage dump near Stockholm: two thousand copies apiece of the first and second editions of *Lolita* and the sole edition of *Pnin*. And he made sure his publishers would not couple Edmund Wilson's name with his.[80]

New Directions was about to capitalize on Nabokov's new success by reissuing *The Real Life of Sebastian Knight* for the first time in eighteen years. In 1941 it had sold poorly but gradually earned a high reputation among a few discerning readers drawn to it by Wilson's enthusiastic dust-jacket comments. Nabokov now wrote to Laughlin to ensure that the blurb was not reprinted. One reason was his objection to the practice of pestering writer A to gush in response to the latest work of writers B, C, and D. Another was his distaste for Wilson's conduct and standards in writing so ecstatically about *Doctor Zhivago* while dismissing *Lolita* before reading it to the end—as Wilson had freely confessed. Nabokov also wrote to Walter Minton to make sure Putnam's did not tap Wilson for comments on any of his books: "Personally, I am against all endorsements—especially the ones that come from old friends. In this case, however, I am prompted to say what I say by my utter disgust with Edmund's symbolico-social criticism and phoney erudition in regard to *Doctor Zhivago*."[81]*

XVI

In the second week of July, Nabokov received a call from James Harris and Stanley Kubrick inviting him to Hollywood to write the screenplay for *Lolita*. They offered a considerable sum, but Nabokov felt only revulsion at the idea of tampering with his novel. After a lull in the local lepidoptera, however, he and Véra decided they might as well drive on to California. On July 20 they left Oak Creek Canyon for Los Angeles, staying until the end of the month at the Beverly Hills Hotel. As negotiations with Harris and Kubrick dragged on, Nabokov came to feel he could write nothing along the lines they suggested: to appease the watchdogs and moral shepherds of American

---

* In Wilson's review of *Doctor Zhivago* (*New Yorker*, November 15, 1958), he strongly censured the translation, and in the process misconstrued a simple but crucial phrase that in the words of one critic could be "clearly understood by a first-year Russian student" (Blake, in Hayward, *Writers in Russia*, lv).

cinema Harris and Kubrick wanted him to end the film with Lolita and Humbert married, and with an adult relative's blessing![82]

After crisp, dry Oak Creek Canyon, Los Angeles felt hot and humid. If Nabokov's imagination were to be triggered at all into finding a solution that would satisfy his own artistic sense and his producers' caution, he would need a few days of quiet thought in mountain air. He and Véra set off at the end of July for Mammoth Lakes in the Sierra Nevadas, hoping to be soothed by the pines and the solitude. Instead they thought the place awful, shabby, and dusty, and thick with a shabby and dusty crowd.[83]

They moved on to the Brockway Hotel, on the banks of sapphire and emerald Lake Tahoe, where Dmitri joined them. Nabokov found the new location delightful to look at but no more conducive to inspiration—perhaps because "a calamitous growth of manzanita precluded the presence of good butterflies." After two weeks of sterile meditation, he was ready to leave by mid-August. He and Véra headed east, following the northernmost route they could devise and collecting along their way through in the northern U.S. and Canada.[84]

They reached New York at the beginning of September, and stopped at Manhattan's Park Crescent Hotel, at 87th Street and Riverside Drive.[85] Nabokov had just over three weeks to settle his affairs with publishers and lawyers before sailing off for three months in Europe with Véra.

Although *Lolita* would sell fourteen million copies around the world by the mid-1980s, Nabokov naturally assumed in September 1959 that after more than a year on the best-seller lists (236,700 copies sold over bookstore counters, another 50,000 through book clubs),[86] the book's sales would soon drop. Accordingly, he set up with his lawyers a trust fund to ease his tax burden by spreading forward over the coming years the high income of the last twelve months, especially from paperback and screen rights. He sent another batch of his papers off to the Library of Congress. He also met with Wallace Brockway and his editor William McGuire of the Bollingen Press. While working on *Eugene Onegin*, Nabokov had found poring over *Webster's Second International Dictionary* in the libraries of Cornell and Harvard one of the most pleasant and fruitful parts of his research. Assuming that he would soon be checking the proofs of his translation, he persuaded McGuire to buy him a copy of the dictionary to take with him to Europe.[87]

The Nabokovs had planned to remain there no longer than three months.[88] For the past three or four years, since his Cornell salary had risen sharply and the expense of Dmitri's Harvard education had been left behind, Nabokov had been hoping to travel to Europe. He had kept in touch with his sister Elena ever since the war, but had not seen her since 1937. Widowed in 1958, she was now a librarian in Geneva. Recently he had also resumed contact with his brother Kirill, once something of a poet, now a travel agent in Brussels. Nabokov had never been close to his other sister, Olga, though he had always been concerned about Rostislav, the son she neglected, and regularly sent money for the young man's support. But Olga and Rostislav and his young family lived in Prague, and for Nabokov even to draw back an edge of the iron curtain was unthinkable.

A major reason for the Nabokovs' planning no more than a few months in Europe was their wish not to be too long away from America while Dmitri continued his musical studies in New York. Of course if Nabokov was to teach at Cornell next spring he would also need to be back at the end of January. Véra had long thought her husband's joint teaching and writing too much of a burden for him, and now that they were about to head off to Europe and to welcomes from Lolita's French and English and Italian publishers, they realized they could hardly be back for the spring semester. Besides, the thought of returning to the physical demands of an Ithaca winter and to regular classes when there was no longer any need seemed too tiresome to contemplate. In September, Nabokov wrote to Cornell's president, Deane Malott, tendering his formal resignation.[89]

Yet six days later, when the Nabokovs boarded the Liberté bound for Le Havre, they had still no idea how much of a change Lolita had wrought in their lives. The following February, for a reason they could not yet see, they would indeed return to the United States for a few months, and they would always remain proudly American, but after this first departure, they would never settle in America again.

In 1940, Nabokov had sailed into New York penniless and unknown, to a country he had long tried to reach and now gratefully accepted as a refuge and hoped to make into a home. Leaving behind him a Europe where he had always felt himself an émigré detached from the society around him, he had entered into American life, mastered its ways, traveled and described its highways. Eking out what was often a meager and unsteady existence, he had still found America the land of opportunity, a place where he could become a scientist, teacher, and scholar—and even, suddenly, a writer of world renown. He had refused to settle anywhere, preferring to move from one house or apartment or motel unit or cabin to the next. At the same time, while he maintained as always his inviolable spiritual independence, he had had to join institutions like Stanford, Wellesley, Harvard, and Cornell because he simply could not afford not to.

Now he could afford to do just as he pleased: to devote himself wholly to his art, to maintain his distance from the world around him, and to settle down without the cares and responsibilities of property or without putting down roots he might have to pull up again. Europe, he would discover, would be the place where a Nabokov of unconstrained means could satisfy this uniquely Nabokovian set of needs, by paying for permanent transience on his own terms, in his own suite in an *hôtel de luxe*.

PART II
EUROPE

• *V N* •

My life thus far has surpassed splendidly
the ambitions of boyhood and
youth. . . . At fifteen I visualized myself
as a world-famous author of seventy
with a mane of wavy white hair.
Today I am practically
bald.

—*Strong Opinions*

CHAPTER 17

Chased by Fame: Europe, America, Europe, 1959–1961

I

"STATUE of Liberty thumbing a ride to Europe," noted Nabokov in his diary the day his ship sailed out of New York Harbor, September 29, 1959. He had come to America from Europe an unknown. Now, after almost two decades, he was headed back toward a Europe eager to acclaim him, on a boat whose library housed in his honor an elaborate display of his books, *Lolita* and *Pnin* and the just-published *Invitation to a Beheading* and *Poems*. He was still sensitive to impressions for *Ada*, still amused at the flightiness of fame, and would recollect the *Liberté* years later as he set the scene for Lucette's mid-Atlantic suicide: a display window on her liner contains "half a dozen glossy-jacketed copies of *Salzman* . . . impressively heaped between a picture of the handsome, thoughtful, now totally-forgotten, author and a Mingo-Bingo vase of immortelles."[1]

Over cocktails, the ship's captain—who, Véra thought, knew his Freud but not his *Lolita*—insistently probed *why* her husband had chosen to write about such a subject. The head of Bobbs-Merrill, the firm that had published his first novel in America, *Laughter in the Dark*, tried to lure Nabokov away from Putnam's. The whole boat swarmed with his readers and admirers, especially, Véra noted, the female variety.[2]

After a pleasant crossing—Nabokov always found the leisurely pace and the uncrowded space of transatlantic liners much more soothing than he imagined air travel must be—the *Liberté* docked at Le Havre on October 5. The Nabokovs took the train to Paris. When they had left in May 1940, German tanks were about to occupy the city. Now Americans and cars were staging a second occupation. Visitors to the Salon d'Auto could find no hotel vacancies left, and roomless American tourists were standing about on street corners discussing their predicament.[3] Not knowing yet that automobiles and tourists had changed the Europe they remembered, the Nabokovs abandoned Paris and traveled straight on to Geneva.

There they stayed for ten days at the Hotel Beau-Rivage and saw

Lolita in at least three languages staring at them from every bookstore window. Seven years older than his sister Elena, now a librarian in Geneva, and twelve years older than his brother Kirill, a travel agent in Brussels, Nabokov had shared with them little of his Russian past and even less of his émigré life, seeing almost nothing of them throughout the 1930s. Elena still remained more sentimental than Vladimir, Kirill more prankish, but by now the age gap between them mattered much less than in the past, and their European reunions were relaxed and warm. Strolling along lakeshore or seashore, reclining in the grass, parleying in hotel rooms, Vladimir and Elena and Kirill would sift through the family past, the two younger siblings occasionally calling their brother's autobiography to account, challenging minor details, dismissing this or that event as family legend or rumor or anachronism. Their comments would help him fine-tune the second edition of his autobiography that his new fame soon demanded.[4]

II

By now the Nabokovs expected to spend eight or nine months in Europe, settling in the warmth of southern Italy or Sicily for the winter, then moving north to the Riviera or northern Italy for the spring and to Switzerland for the summer.[5] But first they had to run a gauntlet of flashbulbs and microphones.

Two weeks after passing through Paris, they returned, this time to a room reserved in advance at the Hotel Continental. Because of the government's ban on the book, *Lolita* had been continuously in the news in France for three years, and had sold phenomenally well since its publication in April. The Parisian press gave Nabokov no rest.[6]

Not that his French publishers had rest in mind—although when Gallimard staged a mammoth reception for Nabokov in its dignified salons on October 23, it could not know there would be repercussions in print years and even decades later. There were two thousand present: book people coming from the Frankfurt Book Fair, journalists from the world's press, critics and writers from the Paris literary world. Publisher Ivan Nabokoff, son of Nabokov's cousin Nicolas, recalls the guest of honor as helpless, ill at ease with the hubbub and crush, and asking him "Please stay with me."[7] Perhaps Nabokov's disorientation explains the evening's strange events.

Maurice Girodias was not to have been invited by Gallimard, but the person handling the invitations thought it might be rather fun if she sent Girodias one too. Girodias concurred, anticipating that if a scandalous scene took place between himself and Nabokov the publicity might sell another fifty thousand copies. According to Girodias, cameras did flash as Doussia Ergaz introduced him to Nabokov, but after exchanging a few sentences (as Girodias recalled) or no more than a polite grin at someone he had no idea was Girodias (as Nabokov and others remembered), Nabokov turned and made his way to Véra's side. Girodias was nonplussed at such a mild anticlimax to their fierce transatlantic feud.[8]*

The encounter was even less memorable than Girodias thought. That evening, as they drove away from the party, Doussia Ergaz asked Nabokov how he found Girodias. He replied, with a surprised look and to Ergaz's judgment in perfect good faith, that he had not seen the man. Ergaz realized that in the midst of the noise and the crowd of people eager to meet him, Nabokov had taken Girodias for someone unconnected to him. Ergaz told Girodias of Nabokov's reaction; two years later Girodias would publish in *Playboy* a memoir that included a stretched and stylized version of their meeting and of Nabokov's denial that it had taken place; Nabokov in turn would publish a reply explaining how he had indeed not known it was Girodias whom Ergaz had brought before him. Meanwhile, the Nabokovs' response to Ergaz's question was to pool their reactions to the man both now knew to be Girodias and decide they "did not like him a bit." The whole incident seems symptomatic of the long, tangled relationship between Nabokov and Girodias: they did not quite meet, they could not agree on how they did not meet, they would dispute in public over their failure to do more than shake hands.[9]

III

Another handshake at the Gallimard party occasioned a still more delayed reaction in print. Zinaida Shakhovskoy, the sister of Nathalie Nabokoff, cousin Nicolas's first wife, had helped Nabokov arrange public readings of his works in Brussels in the early 1930s and had become a warm friend during the course of the decade. Now settled in Paris, she came up to Nabokov at the party, ready to embrace him. "Bonjour, madame," he said coldly, as if to a stranger.

---

* Véra Nabokov has her own clear recollection of the scene: "Somebody had brought Girodias and his brother, the translator [of *Lolita* into French, Eric] Kahane, to introduce them to me. Nabokov either was not in the vicinity, or walked away as they approached. I exchanged two or three words with Kahane (not with Girodias), and then left them. Girodias was *not* introduced to Nabokov."

This time, at least, three witnesses—Véra Nabokov, Irina Komarov, and Zinaida Shakhovskoy herself—agree that Nabokov made that pointed snub, but no one knows why. Some time afterward, Nathalie Nabokoff came to ask why her sister had been rebuffed. Véra began to explain that she didn't know, and that she was surprised too. In fact, in 1939, Véra had reproached Zinaida for anti-Semitism, a charge that the latter was not ready to forget. Now, in a recent letter to Nabokov, Zinaida had not sent greetings to Véra or even referred to her at all, as if she did not exist. Always touchily protective of his wife, Nabokov—but not Véra herself—was greatly annoyed. After referring only to this last fact, Véra was interrupted by Nathalie Nabokoff, although she had been intending to add that she thought the main reason for her husband's snub must have been Zinaida's supercilious tone in an article she had just written about his work.[10]

Nabokov had good reason to find the article offensive, as he certainly did. Under the pen name Jacques Croisé, Shakhovskoy declared that the emotional desert of Nabokov's years of Continental exile had been so complete that in his memoirs "he would even forget the friends of his darkest days." Shakhovskoy seems to have resented the fact that *Conclusive Evidence* did not name her, although the émigré pages of Nabokov's memoirs quite deliberately avoided his private life, limiting themselves to a few comments on those who contributed to Russian émigré literature, in tones far from cold (Fondaminsky, "a saintly and heroic soul who did more for émigré literature than any other man"; Khodasevich, "wrought of irony and metallic-like genius, whose poetry was as complex a marvel as that of Tyutchev or Blok"; "wise, prim, charming Aldanov").[11]

Citing the opinions of Hermann in *Despair* as if they were Nabokov's own and not those of a madman and a murderer he despised, Shakhovskoy declared that in Nabokov's world "goodness does not exist, all is nightmare and deceit. Those seeking intellectual comfort would be better swallowing poison than reading Nabokov." Speaking in his own voice, on the other hand, Nabokov had declared his belief in the "goodness of man" as "a solid and iridescent truth . . . a central and tangible part of one's world." Shakhovskoy suggests that the deceptions in Nabokov's "black writings" afford him the same kind of pleasure as his cruellest villain, Horn (Axel Rex), derives from watching a blind man sit down on a newly painted bench. Shakhovskoy did not understand that for Nabokov tenderness and kindness were the essence of art, and that he presented characters like Horn in a spirit of outrage at their travesty of his dearest values. As a final demonstration of her perspicacity, Shakhovskoy identified *Lolita* as "a penetrating and cruel satire on American life." She ignores Humbert's lament that his and Lolita's "long journey had only defiled with a sinuous trail of slime the lovely, trustful, dreamy, enormous country" they had traversed, or Nabokov's own cry in his afterword that the charge that *Lolita* is anti-American "pains me considerably more than the idiotic accusation of immorality."[12]

After hearing from Nathalie Nabokoff only the first half of Véra's explanation for the snub at the Gallimard reception, Zinaida Shakhovskoy held Véra Nabokov to blame. In 1973 she published a story about a writer living in surroundings recognizably Nabokov's, who after his wife's death puts away her photograph and at once feels a surge of release and freedom. Ten years after Nabokov's death, Shakhovskoy published *V poiskakh Nabokova* (*In Search of Nabokov*), a memoir-critique whose theme, none too covert, is that Nabokov's talent as a writer withered under an alien (Jewish) influence—Shakhovskoy herself was Russian Orthodox, and her brother an Orthodox archbishop—until he lost all the benefit of his Russian culture and the spiritual values of the Orthodox faith and became a rootless, alienated, spiritless decadent. Shakhovskoy told me: "I wrote that book against Véra. And if you say so, I will deny it."[13]

One of the charges Shakhovskoy made in her book was that after leaving Europe in 1940, Nabokov began to drift away from any interest in Russia or allegiance to Russian friends. In fact, of course, he consecrated years of work to making Pushkin, Gogol, and *The Song of Igor's Campaign* available to English-speaking readers, his autobiography and *Pale Fire* and *Ada* are steeped in nostalgia for Russia, and he had kept in close touch with a score of Russian relatives and old and new friends. Shakhovskoy was also quite wrong to suppose that after returning to Europe Nabokov ignored former Russian friends. After his cold "Bonjour" to her, Shakhovskoy managed to say: "J'espère que vous vous souvenez d'Irène quand-même." "Bien sûr," replied Nabokov, turning to Irina Komarov, the sister of his friend Savely Kyandzhunstev, who had given Nabokov valuable financial support in the late 1930s. He took her telephone number, and a few days later invited her to dinner. During the course of an evening of warm reminiscences he asked if he could repay the money Savely had lent him in his grimmest years in Paris. He also called on Raisa Tatarinov (now Tarr), the woman who had organized a literary circle around him in the 1920s and 1930s; on his cousin Nicolas; and on Evgenia Cannac, a member of the Tatarinov circle in the 1920s who in the 1960s would translate one of Nabokov's Russian novels into French.[14]

He visited France's Musée d'Histoire Naturelle. He saw his English publisher, George Weidenfeld, and met for the first time Claude Gallimard and the man who would later become the closest of his new European friends, his German publisher, Heinrich Maria Ledig-Rowohlt. Above all in that one week in Paris he met the press: representatives of *Jours de France*, *Nouvelles littéraires*, *France-Soir*, *L'Exprès*, *France-Observateur*, *Lettres nouvelles*, *La nouvelle revue française*, *Il giorno*, and the Canadian Broadcasting Corporation.[15]

Arts, a French literary weekly, asked Nabokov whom he would like most to meet among French writers. Françoise Sagan, perhaps? No, Nabokov replied, he was interested only in Raymond Queneau and Alain Robbe-Grillet, whom he thought by far the most talented French writers. Though *Arts* had established itself as a foe of Robbe-Grillet and had declared the *nouveau roman* dead, it gamely went along with Nabokov's preferences. Queneau was out of town, but *Arts* had Robbe-Grillet interview Nabokov, who found him as original in person as on paper. They met again twice over the next few days. The Nabokovs were amused at Robbe-Grillet's wife, a diminutive actress, who came dressed as Lolita and played the part of the nymphet. To everyone's delight, the waiter, after taking orders from the "adults" for aperitifs, turned to her and asked: "Et un Coca-Cola pour mademoiselle?"[16]

IV

After crossing the Channel on October 28, the Nabokovs were whisked by car, courtesy of Weidenfeld and Nicolson, to London. There he was interviewed for the best literary program on British television, *The Bookman*, and before this second screen appearance asked for the questions to be submitted in advance so that he could compose and revise his answers ahead of time. Tired out from Paris, he turned down several other television interviews, and accepted only one of six radio interviews requested. John Wain interviewed him for the *Observer* and others for the *Evening Standard* and the *Spectator*. He had dinner with Graham Greene and discovered during the course of the conversation that Greene had thought from a passage in *Lolita** that Nabokov too was a Catholic convert, but gradually realized his mistake. Nabokov nevertheless found him entertaining

---

* Part 2, chapter 31: "A couple of years before, under the guidance of an intelligent French-speaking confessor, to whom, in a moment of metaphysical curiosity, I had turned over a Protestant's drab atheism for an old-fashioned popish cure, I had hoped to deduce from my sense of sin the existence of a Supreme Being. On those frosty mornings in rime-laced Quebec the good priest worked on me with the finest tenderness and understanding."

company. The next day he had lunch with the writers V. S. Pritchett and Philip Toynbee, both of whom would often review his work, Roy Jenkins, the first proponent of a revised obscenity bill, Nigel Nicolson, and others.[17]

Since it still seemed frighteningly possible that Weidenfeld and Nicolson and Nabokov himself might be prosecuted when *Lolita* was published in Britain on Friday, November 6, the campaign to emphasize Nabokov's respectability was still not over. On November 4 he traveled to Cambridge to deliver his "Russian Classics, Censors, and Readers" lecture at King's College. It was a glittering success, as was the splendid banquet Noel Annan, then provost at King's, set up for Nabokov. Despite the acclaim, Nabokov found Cambridge "in some respects curiously provincial in comparison with its American counterparts."[18]

The next day, the eve of publication, Nabokov was back in London. With the book's legal fate still in the balance, *Lolita*'s grand launching at the Ritz began nervously, but the enlightened British newspapers and M.P.s turned up en masse in support. During the evening Nigel Nicolson received a call from an anonymous clerk in the office of the Director of Public Prosecutions within the Home Office: the government had decided not to prosecute *Lolita*. Nicolson climbed up on a table and made the announcement to a cheering crowd—and *Lolita* caused still another furor when newspapers protested at the government tip-off.[19]

After almost four years of public controversy in England, *Lolita* sold out on publication day. Although the Weidenfeld and Nicolson edition would be banned for some time in Australia, New Zealand, and South Africa—and other editions would be banned in Belgium and Burma—there was no more trouble in British courts.

V

The day after *Lolita*'s English publication, the Nabokovs set off from London for Rome. Looking out from their balcony in the Grand Hotel, strolling along the Pincio, standing amidst the dust of centuries in the Colosseum, shopping along the Via Veneto, watching black-garbed Italian matrons feeding fish-heads to sleek stray cats, gazing at the endless flow of taillights through the glistening black night, they found the city wonderful. They had expected to be less the focus of attention here than in Paris and London, but paparazzi followed them so often that they decided they would have to return incognito in the spring to savor Rome on their own. Knowing no Italian and almost nothing of modern Italian literature, they had little reason to meet with local literati, and when they did dine with Alberto Moravia they found him boring. The weather turned cold, and it began to rain steadily. Exhausted after a solid month of interviews, meetings, and dinners with strangers, Nabokov was ready to retreat somewhere to write.[20]

He had been nursing a new novel in his mind for several weeks. In mid-November he headed for Sicily with Véra, in search of sunshine and warmth. They stopped at the Hotel Excelsior in Taormina, but hoped to find a furnished house for the winter and establish the quiet Nabokov needed.[21]

Like the mainland, Sicily throbbed with cars and even enormous buses squeezing with barely any clearance through the narrow corridors between rows of ancient houses. Instead of the tranquillity and warmth they sought, the Nabokovs encountered thunderstorms, hail, and unrelenting rain. They disliked Taormina—dismissed in *Ada* as "Minotaor, the famous artificial island." Sicilian reporters and photographers chased Nabokov, the local newspaper shop displayed in a frame of blue pencil lines his photograph and interviews clipped from local papers, and the numerous German tourists and a German film crew shooting in their hotel whispered and stared.[22]

Unhappy with his surroundings and unable to contemplate settling there, agitated because he still could not find space to write, Nabokov was crossing the gardens of Taormina one green rainy night when his mind suddenly reverted to the possibility of adapting *Lolita* to the screen. In "a small nocturnal illumination, of diabolical origin, perhaps, but unusually compelling in sheer bright force," he saw the Enchanted Hunters sequence of the novel as if on color film, and as he listened to the soundtrack discovered the aesthetically satisfying solution he had searched for and failed to find in Beverly Hills and on the shores of Lake Tahoe.[23]

VI

Still, his ideas were incompatible with Harris and Kubrick's requirements, and in search of a more congenial climate he and Véra traveled north to Genoa on November 27 in what seemed to them second-class carriages now labeled first, but no substitute for the luxurious first class of prewar Europe. They hoped to stay only two or three days at the Colombia Excelsior Hotel until they could discover a place outside the city to rent. Rain or no rain, they thought Genoa and the colors of its painted house-fronts enchanting. They searched in vain for a little villa they could rent in Genoa, in Nervi, in Rapallo, but no one wanted to rent just for the winter, and Nabokov began to wonder how Anna Karenin and Vronsky managed to find *their* Italian villa.[24]

At least in Genoa the press lost sight of Nabokov and he could have peace at last. On November 30, still without a separate room in which to write, he noted down in his diary: "Began L. to T." Elsewhere in the diary he had set out other titles for the new novel—*Dear Terra, Terra Incognita, Letters from Luna*—but evidently he had decided for the moment on *Letters to Terra*, a prefiguration of a major motif in *Ada*, Van Veen's first book, *Letters from Terra*. Van's novel-within-the-novel tells the story of Theresa, a roving reporter from an American magazine on Terra, who sends messages to a scientist on Antiterra (the world of Van and his readers), falls in love with him, and flies to him through space only to discover that she seems microscopic in size to the huge humid eye of her lover. Her messages had exaggerated the bliss of Terra, "had been, in fact, the instrument of 'cosmic propaganda'—a brave thing to admit, as agents of Terra might have yanked her back or destroyed her in flight."[25]

Enchanted by the romance of space travel, Nabokov toyed between 1959 and 1966 with several plots combining that romance with an interplanetary love story and at the same time an oppressive sense of superpower secrecy. Late in 1964 he would respond to a request from Alfred Hitchcock with this synopsis:

> A girl, a rising star of not quite the first magnitude, is courted by a budding astronaut. She is slightly condescending to him; has an affair with him but may have other lovers, or lover, at the same time. One day he is sent on the first expedition to a distant star; goes there and makes a successful return. Their positions have now changed. He is the most famous man in the country while her star rise has come to a stop at a moderate level. She is only too glad to have him now, but soon she realizes that he is not the same as he was before his flight. She cannot make out what the change is. Time goes on, and she becomes concerned, then frightened, then panicky. I have more than one interesting dénouement for this plot.[26]

An undated note in Nabokov's files records this brief plot for another star romance: "Act I. He is about to travel to a planet. She does not love him. He does her. Act II. Away. News? No news? Act III. Back. We never discover has he been really 'changed' or is it starmadness." There was also a note for dialogue at the end of act 3; "My little [car make] is not running as well as it should. I shall probably sell it." "Now that's funny—you said this once before—exactly like that." "Did I?" "Wait a moment. You sold it long ago!" "So I did, so I did. I must be running out of speeches." The astronaut tries another speech but it also turns out to have been said in the first act, and he dies soon after this scene.[27]

A year after the letter to Hitchcock, in September 1965, Nabokov told interviewer Robert Hughes of his plan to write a little book called *Letters to Terra*, about a zoologist heading for an unknown planet who writes letters back to earth to his actress lover, very dear to him but not very faithful.

> There's not a single word about reaching the planet. It's all in the wings, behind the scenes. We must feel that something absolutely awful is happening to him, when he hasn't the right to talk about his experience. This is, after all, a governmental secret while . . . the flight is in progress. So he writes about all kinds of matters. He develops a tremendous love for the [earth]. The farther he gets, the dearer earth is to him, not the other way around, you see. And now and then he uses a kind of obscure circumlocution to explain something about his colleagues whom he doesn't like—they are very matter-of-fact people—or about his new experience. And finally he arrives. There are going to be twenty letters and the twentieth letter is a rather hopeless letter. He knows it is the last letter, but he doesn't dare say it is the last letter. They are doomed, those people, for reasons which we can't understand.[28]

Several months after this interview the idea for *Ada* came to Nabokov, and the interplanetary theme found a new twist in the relations between Antiterra and Terra, between Ada's unanswered letters to Van and Van's *Letters from Terra*, and between Lucette's entanglement in various kinds of letters and her apparent messages from the next world.

By then the initial mixture of the romantic and the sinister had been altered beyond recognition. But in November 1959 it seems that Nabokov's inspiration was his sense of the sheer romance of living in an age when men might first venture into space, and his disgruntlement at the prospect that it might be the Soviets who had a head start. In 1961, Yuri Gagarin would circle the ionosphere; a year later John Glenn followed suit, and Nabokov would still maintain that there was no *proof* there had been a man in space, that they may have simply discovered a way to fool the radar, that it was all probably no more than "cosmic propaganda."[29]

Back on terra firma—in Rome, to be precise—Nabokov had been filmed for a newsreel the day before he left the city. Now in Genoa the Nabokovs heard that the newsreel had been screened. Trying out their rudimentary Frenchified Italian, they asked about the movie "*actualités*," and in reply received elaborate instructions for the way to the "*tualetta*."[30]

Early in November they had asked publisher Arnoldo Mondadori to help find a singing teacher for Dmitri in Milan. At the beginning of December, as Dmitri set out for Europe on the *United States*, his parents traveled north from Genoa to Lugano, on the Swiss side of the Italian lake district. In the Grand Hotel they took for the first time two adjacent rooms, their standard practice from then on to allow Nabokov the space to write uninterrupted. But the day after arriving in Lugano something happened to prevent him from writing *Letters to Terra*. Stanley Kubrick cabled that he had rejected Calder Willingham's screenplay for *Lolita*: "Convinced you were correct disliking marriage Stop Book a masterpiece and should be followed even if Legion and Code disapprove Stop Still believe you are only one for Screenplay Stop If financial details can be agreed would you be available." Nabokov cabled back that he might consider it, and added by letter that he felt much more in the mood to do it than he had in the summer.[31]

VII

On December 13 the Nabokovs took a taxi to Milan, to the Hotel Principe e Savoia. This time it was the turn of their Italian publishers, Arnoldo Mondadori and his son Alberto, to give them the royal treatment and another grand reception. They had also come to Milan to meet Maestro Campogalliani, the singing teacher recommended by the director of La Scala, to arrange for an audition for Dmitri.[32]

With still more journalists lining up for photographs and quotable phrases, Nabokov now asked if interviews could be held in groups of three or four, as he was no longer young and these things wore him out. He still felt unable to settle on anything: not ready to commit himself to a *Lolita* script while protracted and possibly fruitless negotiations dragged on in Hollywood between Lazar and Kubrick, he still could not focus on *Letters to Terra*.[33]

On Christmas Day the Nabokovs drove to San Remo, where first Dmitri, in his new Triumph, and then Elena Sikorski and her son Vladimir, joined them at the Hotel Excelsior-Bellevue. Dmitri began to work busily on translating *The Gift*, and the rest of the family seemed to want in on the act. When Kirill had volunteered to translate *Lolita* into Russian, his brother asked him to send a sample. Kirill, it was resolved, would try part 1 of the novel, Elena part 2. By the following March, Elena's son too would be translating the story "Krug" ("The Circle") into French.[34]

Two days after reaching San Remo, Nabokov wrote a Russian poem, "Kakoe sdelal ya durnoe delo" ("What is the evil deed I have committed"), a parody of the poem Pasternak had written earlier in the year on being forced to decline the Nobel Prize. Nabokov was aware that many émigré Russians regarded Pasternak as a saint for *Doctor Zhivago* and himself as a sinner for *Lolita*, but his poem ended with the oblique suggestion that despite his remoteness from the Soviet era, Russia would one day erect a monument to him:

> Amusing, though, that at the last indention,
> despite proofreaders and my age's ban,
> a Russian branch's shadow shall be playing
> upon the marble of my hand.[35]

Early in January 1960, the Nabokovs crossed the French border to install themselves somewhere for the winter at last, in the Hotel Astoria, Menton. Despite the name, the building was not so much a hotel as a block of furnished apartments. Theirs, number 5, had plenty of space, complete privacy, and a large balcony overlooking the azure sea. Only the recurrent roar of motorcycles racing along the avenue Carnot spoiled the prospect.[36]

Just when they had found a secure lair, and just when Dmitri had been taken on by Maestro Campogalliani, the Nabokovs received a telegram from Lazar with terms for the screenplay: $40,000 plus another $35,000 if Nabokov received sole credit for the screenplay, plus transportation to Los Angeles and back and expenses there for six months or more. Nabokov cabled back his acceptance the same day.[37]

Laurence Olivier, David Niven, and Marlon Brando were all interested in the part of Humbert. In fact, everyone wanted to be in on *Lolita*. A French film, *Les Nymphettes*, was announced; an Italian film, *Le Ninfette*, even claimed—falsely—to be a free adaptation of *Lolita*. Over the next year the Nabokovs heard of Greek, Turkish, Latin American (Mexican, Venezuelan, and Uruguayan), Indian (Orya, Bengali, Assamese, Malayalam, and Gujarati), and five Arabian editions of the novel under way, almost all pirated. Some Continental newspapers proposed that since Uncle Sam had become a subject of caricature rather than a respected emblem of the United States, Lolita could serve in his place.[38]

Despite *Lolita*'s triumphs, Nabokov wrote to Morris Bishop that "Europe is not a hit with me. I feel bored and dejected. . . . Time has tampered with the places I knew, and those I visited now for the first time did not promise any memories worth storing." Part of his dissatisfaction no doubt was that for four months he had not been able to settle down to write, and that he had not yet had a taste of chasing after European butterflies. He booked a passage to New York for Feb-

ruary 19, but since he and Véra were leaving their "big but very inexperienced son" alone in Europe, they planned to return at the end
of the year.[39]

Early in February, Nabokov received a notice that he had been
elected a member of the American National Institute of Arts and Letters. He replied:

> This is a difficult letter to write. I have to choose between bad manners
> and the betrayal of principle. Sadly, but without hesitation, I choose the
> first. Believe me, I am deeply touched and feel greatly honored by the
> distinction you propose to confer on me, and the little rosette is perfectly
> charming but, alas, I must return it.
>
> I could not imagine belonging to an organization without being active
> in it—yet, in my case, any organizational activity is utterly out of the
> question. Socially, I am a cripple. Therefore, all my thinking life I have
> declined to "belong." I have never joined any union or club (not even a
> faculty club), have never served on any committees, taken part in faculty
> meetings, or been a member of any organization whatsoever. I have
> gratefully accepted grants from organizations I respected—but would
> never accept an honorary degree from a university no matter how much
> I respected it. What should I do, what could I do, as a member of your
> Department of Literature? Even making a speech at a public ceremony
> is as impossible for me as saying grace is for a good atheist. In conse-
> quence, my name on your distinguished list would be meaningless.[40]

Nabokov would consistently turn down all the honorary doctorates
and memberships offered him over the course of this and the following decade. The only organization he agreed to belong to—he paid
an annual subscription but asked to be left off any membership list—
was the Lepidopterists' Society.

VIII

Since Nabokov did not care to fly, the trip from Menton to Beverly
Hills took twelve days by train and boat and train again. On February
18 he and Véra clambered into their Paris-bound sleeping car "amid
the mimosas and cypresses in the aquarelle elegance of a Riviera evening." At Le Havre the next day they boarded the liner the *United
States*. Instead of the upper-deck cabin they had booked, they found
that the management had transferred their famous passenger to a
suite, at no extra cost and with a bonus of fruit and whiskey. As
always, Nabokov found the crossing supremely restful.[41]

He had asked Walter Minton to reserve him a room in New York
with "two beds and a bath, and no communicating doors to adjacent

rooms, full of coughing people with radios." During four busy days of discussions in the city, he was pleased to hear that his Bollingen editors expected *Eugene Onegin* to be published in the spring of 1961. At the end of February he and Véra left New York by train for Chicago. Snow fell all the way from Chicago to California, and it was a relief for them at last to descend the Pacific slope of the San Bernardino Mountains and find the eternal Californian spring, palms and mimosas and flowers and sun.⁴²

As soon as he arrived, Nabokov met Kubrick at his Universal City Studios and "debated in an amiable battle of suggestion and counter-suggestion how to cinemize the novel. He accepted all my vital points, I accepted some of his less significant ones." Nabokov decided he could undertake the screenplay, and the next morning, "sitting on a bench under a lovely bright yellow-green *Pyrospodia* tree in a public park not far from the Beverly Hills Hotel (one of whose cottages Mr. Lazar had taken for us) I was already attending with all my wits to the speech and pantomime in my head." A week later Kubrick had the Nabokovs meet Tuesday Weld, "a graceful ingénue," the scenarist thought, "but not my idea of Lolita."⁴³

By March 10, the Nabokovs had moved into a pleasant rented villa at 2088 Mandeville Canyon Road, off Sunset Boulevard in Brentwood Heights, an area thick with movie-star homes, floodlit tennis courts for parents, stables for their daughters' horses. The Nabokovs' house, not large but comfortable, sat amidst a garden of avocado and tangerine trees, hibiscuses and palms frequented by a host of melodious songbirds. Nabokov found inspiration in the lawn chair under the jacaranda and in the green-and-blue hills of the canyon. On one side, the house bordered on a well-settled road. On the other began a walk that stretched for miles through wild country where he could stalk butterflies for hours without meeting a soul. He and Véra would have been ready to settle permanently in "charming semitropical" California if their son had not been singing in Milan. As it was, they could only be transients, and they rented a Chevrolet Impala for six months to take them to the supermarkets and along the superhighways of Los Angeles.⁴⁴

Once Nabokov was installed in Mandeville Canyon, Kubrick sent him a rough outline of the scenes they had agreed on, all of part 1 of *Lolita*. By then Kubrick's attitude had convinced Nabokov "that he was willing to heed my whims more closely than those of the censor." Nabokov wrote with great enthusiasm, hurrying to finish ahead of time, although financially it would have been to his advantage to run the full term. "All qualms dissolved in the pleasure of the task," he later wrote, and in his foreword to the published screenplay he recalled:

I worked with zest, composing mentally every morning from eight to noon while butterfly hunting in the hot hills, which, except for some remarkably skittish individuals of a little-known Wood Nymph, produced nothing noteworthy, but *per contra* teemed with rattlers whose hysterical performance in the undergrowth or in the middle of the trail was more comical than alarming. After a leisurely lunch, prepared by the German cook who came with the house, I would spend another four-hour span in a lawn chair, among the roses and mockingbirds, using lined index cards and a Blackwing pencil, for copying and recopying, rubbing out and writing anew, the scenes I had imagined in the morning.

Elsewhere Nabokov noted that new scenes and new conversations "were now produced as naturally as if the core of the novel was evolving a new life of its own." With a week of March still to go, he submitted the first of three acts to Kubrick. Meanwhile he was also reading proofs of *Eugene Onegin* and *The Song of Igor's Campaign*. Dmitri's translation of the first chapter of *The Gift*, too, would have to be checked. Nabokov liked its quality but its meagre quantity threatened to skew publishing schedules, and he recommended to Walter Minton that a second translator should be brought in.[45]

Late in April, Nabokov sent Kubrick the second act. Only the buzz of legal worries distracted him a little from his contented composing under the Californian sun. With agent Irving Lazar he would fight all year for his right to publish his screenplay, while Kubrick's lawyer persistently stalled: Kubrick wanted to avoid any chance of invidious comparisons between Nabokov's designs and his own finished film. James Harris brought a suit against the French movie *Les Nymphettes*, until it proved only a flop, not a rival. Unauthorized Lolita dolls in Italy vexed them briefly but were soon forgotten. And once again Nabokov searched—for the moment in vain—for ways to break with Girodias.[46]

Life around Beverly Hills had its more relaxed side. Irving Lazar found the Nabokovs tennis courts. He and his wife, Mary, would become good friends with the Nabokovs, and would later call on them in Switzerland almost every year. Lazar also introduced Nabokov to people like John Huston and Ira and Lee Gershwin, and to the whole Hollywood social scene. At his first cocktail party, at producer David Selznick's, Nabokov met a rangy, craggy-looking man sporting a deep suntan. "And what do you do?" he asked. "I'm in pictures," John Wayne modestly replied. At another party Nabokov met an attractive brunette to whom he spoke French, and told her she had a wonderful Paris accent. "Parisian, hell," replied Gina Lollobrigida. "It's Roman French." He did not always put his foot in it—at one party, Marilyn Monroe took quite a liking to him—but conscious of being out of step, he soon dropped out of the cocktail party circuit.[47]

Early in June he sent Kubrick four new scenes for acts 1 and 2 and began working on the prologue. He and Kubrick had at first met every fortnight or so, but "outlines ceased altogether, criticism and advice got briefer and briefer, and by mid-summer I did not feel quite sure whether Kubrick was serenely accepting whatever I did or silently rejecting everything." On June 17, he sent the prologue: a flash-forward to Quilty's murder, then back to Annabel Leigh and Valeria. He then broached act 3, but with this last section mapped out and four months' intense writing beginning to take its toll, he left with Véra late in the month for a ten-day rest in the High Sierras, stopping in Big Pine, Inyo County: cold, rugged, but exhilarating, especially when he caught butterflies like the Inyo Blue.[48]

Back in Mandeville Canyon on July 9, Nabokov sent the third act of the screenplay, which included several scenes of Quilty with Lolita, "since otherwise he would have remained a ghostly, uncharacterized and implausible figure." Nabokov had not expected to enjoy his work in Hollywood so much, and was pleased with what he had accomplished: "The screenplay became poetry, which was my original purpose." Kubrick was less happy, and told Nabokov the screenplay was "much too unwieldy, contained too many unnecessary episodes, and would take about seven hours to run." He had a whole barrage of suggestions to make for alternative scenes within act 3, and it took Nabokov until August 11 to send the last new sequences. He then set about cutting the whole screenplay down to size, an operation he later claimed "was the toughest, but also the most exhilarating part of the six-month task." On September 8, when he sent Kubrick the corrected screenplay, a practically new version of the play, his feelings were in fact considerably more mixed: "I still feel painful twinges in my torn ligaments (the elimination of the marvelously moodful motel dialogue in Act Two hurt most) but I do think that the play has gained in unity and neatness." James Harris and Stanley Kubrick declared it the best screenplay ever written in Hollywood.[49]

IX
Lolita: A Screenplay

Collaboration and compromise, so necessary in the production of any film, were always anathema to Nabokov. Had he been a director, he declared, he would have advocated and applied a system of total tyranny, directing the play or the picture myself, choosing settings and costumes, terrorizing the actors, mingling with them in the bit part of guest, or ghost, prompting them, and, in a word, pervading the entire show with the will and art of one individual—for there is nothing in the world that I loathe more than group activity, that communal bath where the hairy and the slippery mix in a multiplication of mediocrity.

For that reason it was important to him from the first that however much producers, directors, actors, cinematographers, and editors might alter what he had written, he be allowed to publish his screenplay so that he could preserve and present his vision intact. When he was at last permitted to publish his screenplay in the 1970s, he would politely point out that he did so "not in pettish refutation of a munificent film but purely as a vivacious variant of an old novel."[50]

His claim that the most exhilarating part of his task was excising at Kubrick's request half of what he had spent months composing might also seem mere politeness. But the shorter screenplay—the version he published—is in fact much superior to the still unpublished first version. The early version is diffuse and often strangely pedestrian. Nabokov not only tried to transfer too much of the novel onto the screen, but he also tried to explain far too ponderously what he had been able to suggest so swiftly and lightly in the novel.

For all that, even the first version of the screenplay offers much to astound anyone who knows *Lolita* well. Tentative and structurally unresolved, this first version offers for many parts of the story alternative sequences whose sheer color often reveals how far Nabokov's imagination could jump in trying out diverse solutions to particular artistic problems. At the beginning of the published screenplay, Humbert kills Quilty in a brisk and wordless version of the protracted and voluble death scene at the end of the novel. The first version of the screenplay also begins with the death scene, but here not only is almost all of the novel's eccentric dialogue retained, but Quilty even wears a mask Humbert gives him ("Put it on. I want a few words with you before you die, and I can't hold my fire if I see your real face").[51] Apparently Nabokov sought an equivalent for the novel's keeping Quilty's identity concealed for so long.

In the novel, Humbert arrives with apparently ailing Lolita in Elphinstone, where playwright Quilty plans to steal her from him. At this point the draft screenplay starts to stray from the novel into a Nabokovian funhouse of comic visual images. The mountain burg of Elphinstone is preparing for a Gabriel Goff gala. "Goff, a black-bearded railway robber, held up his last train in 1888, not to rob it but to kidnap a theatrical company for his and his gang's entertainment. The stores in Elphinstone are full of Goff faces, bearded pink masks, and all the men have grown more or less luxuriant whiskers." A motel manager suggests Doctor Fogg as the best physician to attend to Lolita's illness. While Humbert is momentarily absent, Quilty arrives wearing a Goff mask but impersonating Dr. Fogg. Under Humbert's very eyes, he subjects Lolita to a physical examination:

Quilty

. . . Muh. (Examines Lolita who is now sitting up bending forward) Muh.

This sound with which he punctuates his manipulation resembles a purr of degustation, a comfortable grunt, a moan of glee. He is making the most of the situation and the artistic delight he takes in the farce almost surpasses his impatience to abduct the nymphet.

Humbert

Is it some kind of virus?

Quilty

Muh. Ahum. Hot spine, cold tummy. (Lolita squirms hiding her uncontrollable mirth.) Yes. Alas, yes. (Gloating over Lo) Don't be bashful, my lass. I have to inspect your uvula. (To Humbert) Bring me a glass of water, captain.[52]

With its doubles, its masks, its transparent and multiple theatricality, its involutions and inversions, this scene appears almost a parody of the puppet-show side of Nabokov. Perhaps the scene was simply too long, or perhaps it conflicted with the relative solidity of Humbert's and Lolita's world too starkly to remain in the revised version of the screenplay. But the exuberant imagination evident here, not content merely to copy the novel onto the screenplay but ready to reinvent it, also dominates the published screenplay. There, although plot and characters remain inviolate, almost every scene is new in manner or content.

Some scenes are dramatic equivalents of effects that cannot be translated directly from page to screen. Immediately after Humbert's first glimpse of Lolita in the novel and his decision to stay in the Haze home, he switches from retrospective narrative to his diary, where he tabulates the ways in which Lolita's proximity causes his sexual tension to mount over the next few weeks. In the screenplay Nabokov instead prolongs that first scene with Lolita sunbathing on the veranda. As Charlotte attends to his luggage, Humbert sits down with Lolita. Rigid with desire, unable to relate to her in a natural way but unable to leave her, he grills her about her life with an ominous, awkward, duplicitous intentness. We can see, as Lolita cannot, the shadow waiting to fall on her life, but at the same time Nabokov makes the scene glint with comedy, the comedy of the discrepancy between pursuer and pursued (Lolita: This a quiz? Humbert: I only want to know more about you. I know that you like to solarize your solar plexus. But what else do you like?), the comedy of the unstated (when Charlotte returns, Humbert heads off to change: "I never thought it would be so warm in Ramsdale").

That scene has no counterpart in *Lolita*, but it quietly dramatizes what seems a natural part of the novel's world. Much of the screenplay, on the other hand, can astonish the reader familiar with *Lolita*. On the second page of the novel, Humbert tells us, "My very photogenic mother died in a freak accident (picnic, lightning) when I was three"—the best parenthesis in literature, in Tom Stoppard's judgment. The only other reference Humbert makes to his mother comes almost three hundred pages later: "When my mother, in a livid wet dress, under the tumbling mist (so I vividly imagined her) had run panting ecstatically up that ridge above Moulinet to be felled there by a thunderbolt, I was but an infant." But in the screenplay Nabokov zanily rounds off that scene:

Humbert's Voice
. . . she was killed by a bolt of lightning during a picnic on my fourth birthday, high in the Maritime Alps.

CUT TO:
A Mountain Meadow—A thunderhead advancing above sharp cliffs
Several people scramble for shelter, and the first big drops of rain strike the zinc of a lunchbox. As the poor lady in white runs toward the pavilion of a lookout, a blast of livid light fells her. Her graceful specter floats up above the black cliffs holding a parasol and blowing kisses to her husband and child who stand below, looking up, hand in hand.

Nabokov was determined to incorporate into the screenplay the flutter of fantasy easily lost by the matter-of-fact eye of the camera. His irrepressible technical inventiveness disrupts and delights. Dr. John Ray, Humbert's psychiatrist and the man who brings Humbert's manuscript confession to light, bizarrely intrudes in the voice-over during the scene where Valeria tells Humbert, as they drive around in a Paris taxi, that she is leaving him forever—with the taxi driver, as it turns out. Dr. Ray comments:

She had never been so voluble.

Humbert

You've never been so voluble. All right. Let's get this straight—

Dr. Ray's Voice

My patient is flabbergasted. As Professor Gast used to say: "Woe to him who gets stuck in his own guilt complex like an angry fly." Mr. Humbert cannot react rationally, he splutters. That's the famous *Place de l'Etoile*, Place of the Star. Need good brakes. Oops. See what I mean?

The taxi driver is strangely erratic.

Valeria

It's all finished now. I'm going to be free. There's another man in my life and I'm leaving you.

Humbert

What man? What are you talking about? How dare you?

Dr. Ray's Voice

Dare indeed. A very curious situation. Humbert is accustomed to making the decisions. Now the fate of his marriage is no longer in his hands. I think the cab driver ought to have turned left here. Oh, well, he can take the next cross street.

One of the fascinations of the *Lolita* screenplay is that despite the different incidents and the different medium, character and plot remain so stable. Nabokov's changes, curiously, only confirm the stability. In the novel we see through Humbert's eyes. Self-reproachful though he may be, Humbert depicts himself as the suavest of monsters. Lolita, on the other hand, he presents as someone whose mind barely matters in comparison with his own mighty romantic imagination that incarnates in her his lost Annabel Leigh. A sensitive reader can deduce, however, that Humbert is a good deal more boorish and Lolita a good deal subtler and kinder than Humbert expects we will notice. Unlike the novel, the screenplay presents a more objective record. It repeatedly registers Lolita's intelligence, her tenderness (to a dog, a rabbit, a poor squashed squirrel), and Humbert's rigidity and rudeness.

But if the screenplay revitalizes the book, it also diminishes it. *Lolita* was conceived as a novel, and much of its fire comes from three interrelated facts in its fiction. Unlike all the characters in the novel, even Lolita herself, we as readers can see right into the mesmeric intensity of Humbert's mind. On the other hand, because we see through Humbert's eyes, we do not discover the identity of Humbert's pursuer and tormentor and Lolita's abductor until Humbert himself does, so that Quilty remains shadowy, ominous, but larger than life in his unseen control over Humbert's destiny. And yet again, because by the time he tells his own story Humbert is aware of its latest events, he can toy with our ignorance of the ironies of unfolding time.

Nabokov does what he can to make Humbert retain his perverse intensity even though he must now be seen from the outside. At one early point he inflicts a nervous breakdown on Humbert just as he addresses a women's club. While the faces before him ripple and twist, Humbert diverges from Poe's poetry, the subject of his lecture, and begins to set before the horrified audience his own secret definition of nymphet. As a shape on the screen, nevertheless, Humbert can never have the force his mind has on the page. Projected flatly before us, Quilty too loses his spectral shimmer. In the novel he seems ubiquitously elusive; in the screenplay he becomes blatantly intrusive. Nor does the placing of the murder at the beginning do much to solve the problem of the lost ironies of time. In the novel we know from the start that Humbert has murdered someone, but we do not know whom. The succession of false candidates—Valeria, Charlotte, Lolita herself—and our last-minute discovery of Quilty's identity remind us as we read how utterly unpredictable is time, that force that Humbert tries to cast a spell on by imprisoning Lolita on his "island of entranced time." Of all the eerie power of Humbert, Quilty, and McFate, only faint traces remain in the screenplay.

Nabokov confesses in his introduction to the published screenplay: "By nature I am no dramatist." He is right: he is a novelist, a poet, a master of the hidden resonances and the delayed inferences that the printed page can accommodate but stage or screen cannot. Nabokov's gifts as a novelist depend on his ability to observe the world of fact in consummate detail at the same time as he allows full scope to the play of the imagination. But his respect for fact means that in drama he adheres to the limitations of real conversation: he will not permit characters to speak with the eloquence he can achieve with pencil and eraser and time. One of the most poignant aspects of the novel is the gap between the poetry of Humbert's passion and the little he can *say* to Lolita, or the even littler she will allow him to say. In the screenplay, that little is almost all we get.

In works designed as plays, Nabokov devises plots that can show how powerfully an imagination like Morn's, Waltz's, or Troshchei-kin's can color its world. In *Lolita* the novel, Humbert's confessional imagination provides that lurid filter, but in the screenplay, despite a few moments of vivid fantasy, the colors seem plain. Often the best things in the screenplay seem to be the unfilmable stage directions where Nabokov's own imagination tints the details he selects. On the first page the camera that shows us Pavor Manor and Quilty asleep "also locates the drug addict's implementa on a bedside chair, and with a shudder withdraws." When Charlotte invites Humbert to learn the latest dance steps, he rises from his chair "not because he wants to be taught but because the ripe lady might roll into his lap if he remains seated." Into an elevator at the Enchanted Hunters step Humbert and Lolita and "three rose-growing ladies each looking like a rock garden." Humbert at the supermarket "broods among the fruit, a rotting Priap, listening to a melon, questioning a peach, pushing his wire cart toward the lacquered strawberries." At one point someone approaches Charlotte at the driver's window of her car: her old and rather gaga neighbor Mr. Jung, "who is a little deaf and seems to listen with his mouth." With brilliant acting and direction, the gaping mouth that supplements the straining ear might succeed on screen, but they could never be as pointed as the last six words of that surprising but unerringly accurate phrase.

X

By the beginning of September 1960, as Véra typed the final version of the screenplay, she and her husband had decided to stay in Mandeville Canyon until October: he had begun a new novel, and moving would disrupt his work. Whatever the new book was—*Letters from Terra*? *The Texture of Time*?—Nabokov expected to carry out research for it at the local library. Shooting for *Lolita* was scheduled to begin in November, perhaps in Rome, and Nabokov anticipated being present on location, as Harris and Kubrick had requested in the summer. There was more film work in the offing: a Hollywood producer had approached him to write the screenplay for *A la Recherche du temps perdu*, and he was eager to try.[53]

After seven months without seeing Dmitri, the Nabokovs were anxious about their son, his fast cars and fast-changing women: "It is very unhealthy for us to worry like this (we are 120 years old)," Nabokov wrote Dmitri, "and we simply cannot understand why you don't understand this." Then they heard the good news: in an international opera competition in Reggio Emilia, Dmitri had earned, as first-prize winner among the basses, the right to a debut at Reggio next spring. On a private court in Hollywood meanwhile, his parents were playing tennis three times a week with a "magnificent" professional, and Nabokov felt he was hitting better than ever. To his friend

George Hessen, a keen sportsman, he wrote: "If they asked me what were the best things *Lolita* had brought me, I would answer, the melody in Milan and the sound of our rackets here."[54]

By late September, Harris and Kubrick had signed James Mason for the part of Humbert, chosen Peter Sellers for Quilty, and had decided to shoot the film at Elstree Studios near London. At his Beverly Hills home Kubrick showed Nabokov photographs of a few of the eight hundred potential Lolitas. Pointing to Sue Lyon, Nabokov said: "No doubt about it: she is the one." Luckily Kubrick agreed: he had already selected her after a conclusive screen test. Later, however, Nabokov would observe that the ideal Lolita would have been Catherine Demongeot, who played the title role in Louis Malle's 1960 film of Raymond Queneau's *Lolita*-inspired *Zazie dans le Métro*.[55]

Twenty-six-year-old Dmitri, buoyed by his success in Reggio, had let a self-styled publicity agent persuade him to stage a fake casting contest for the part of Lolita with "national newsreel coverage, a jury of Scala singers and other acquaintances, and a predetermined winner." For two days his Milan apartment was invaded by "decidedly postpubescent aspiring nymphets, some with provincial mothers in tow." When his father saw a magazine photograph of the "finalists" surrounding Dmitri on his oversized, satin-covered bed, he cabled his son at once to stop the "*Lolita* publicity" immediately. By letter he warned that this puerile stunt would only harm Dmitri in the eyes of those who took music seriously.[56]

On October 12, Dmitri's parents headed east from Los Angeles by train, en route to Europe. Harris and Kubrick had already left for England after locking themselves in an office and, over thirty grueling days, completely reworking the script they had praised to Nabokov's face.[57] Nabokov would put just a trickle of himself into Mlle Larivière, the children's governess in *Ada*, who, after blossoming forth into fame, remains for too long blithely unaware of the way her novel *Les enfants maudits* has become more and more travestied the further its film version advances.

In New York, Nabokov met Shelley Winters, recently picked to play the part of Charlotte Haze. He consulted his lawyers about his relations with Kubrick, with Girodias, and with the Internal Revenue Service. He checked up on the details of *Eugene Onegin*. To Walter Minton he suggested that Putnam's should publish the Belgian writer Franz Hellens, whom he had met and admired in the 1930s. When nothing came of his prompting, Hellens gratefully thanked Nabokov anyway and declared it was his own fault for wanting to reach a public that lived on the moon.[58]

Nabokov had planned to travel on from New York to the Riviera and to settle down, after all the latest proofs and translations had been checked, to his new novel. Whatever that novel was—*The Texture of Time* or *Letters from Terra*—it would be set aside for an older project suddenly revived in a new form. On reaching New York on October 15, the Nabokovs had taken room 503 in the Hampshire House, with "a wonderful view over Central Park: the Gobelin clumps of trees, and, along its edges, mysterious skyscrapers shaded with a lilac wash under a Poussin sky." In the same letter to his sister, Nabokov writes that he has "thought up something big." Six days later, in his Hampshire House bathroom, the plan came to him with such clarity he set it down in his diary: "*The Theme* a novel, a life, a love—which is only the elaborate commentary to a gradually evolved short poem." Sparked anew by the structure of his *Eugene Onegin*, *Pale Fire* was about to blaze.[59]

XI

At the beginning of November the Nabokovs left New York on the *Queen Elizabeth*. As Ivan Nabokoff had recommended, they ate in the grill rather than the main restaurant. In *Ada* Lucette dines with Van on the night she dies, in the grill of the *Admiral Tobakoff*, where they feast on grugru shrimps (the yellow larvae of a palm weevil) and roast bearlet. Nabokov could afford the A-deck of the *Queen Elizabeth*, but his own tastes were much plainer: he detested underdone meat, all inner organs—kidneys, brains, liver, tongue, sweetbread—and any seafood other than fish. For the voyage he also added Bonamine to his diet to fend off seasickness. Lucette's travel pills would have the more allusive and more ominous trade name of Quietus.[60]

Arriving at Cherbourg on November 7, the Nabokovs spent a day with their Paris publishers and agents before taking the train to Milan, where they stopped again at the Principe e Savoia. Dmitri of course was their main reason for being there, but the Mondadoris also held a party in their honor, and once more reporters crowded around.[61]

But this time Nabokov would not let publicity impinge. He had come to Europe to find congenial surroundings where he could write, and on November 26, he and Véra headed straight for the Riviera. While they looked for an apartment in Nice, they stopped at the Hotel Negresco on the promenade des Anglais. Entering the large circular lobby, under the hotel's distinctive pink-scaled dome, Nabokov vividly recalled running around it as a child—only to find that in fact the hotel had not been built at the time. As the cameras began to turn for *Lolita*, Nabokov had a beginning of his own to make: on November 29, he took up an index card and wrote the twelve brilliant opening lines of the poem "Pale Fire." He would later rate the poem—entitled "The Brink" on his first index card, until he deleted it and inscribed in its place "Pale Fire"—"the hardest stuff I ever had to compose." As with *The Gift*, where he started with Fyodor's life of Chernyshevsky, he wanted to tackle the most difficult part first.[62]

Early in December the Nabokovs moved into apartment 3 at 57 promenade des Anglais, a few doors down from the Negresco. With Americans crowding the city for its cloudless weather, and with most of the promenade rebuilt in small modern apartments, the Nabokovs had had a hard time finding what they wanted. The old building they found, shabbily grand, "a hideous yellow birthday cake Victorian villa," gave them all the space they required, and although its high ceilings and large windows made for a cold winter, the view over the palms of the promenade to the sea more than made up for the drafts and the chill.[63]

As soon as their bags were brought in, Nabokov carried on with the poem. Despite Sunday afternoon traffic jams and the inescapable Vespas whining along below, he found the place highly conducive to his work. He remained completely immersed in his task, and saw no one. An indefatigable writer all his life, he had not been ensconced in a novel since completing *Pnin* in 1955. *Eugene Onegin* had required all his time until early 1958, and, left untended, the first flickers of *Pale Fire* in 1956 and 1957 had died out. When *Lolita*'s success made it clear he could leave Cornell, he hurried to round off his last scholarly work on *The Song of Igor's Campaign*, to answer reporters, negotiate with publishers, check translations, and adapt *Lolita* for the screen. He had enjoyed working on the screenplay, but *Pale Fire* was completely new, unprecedented, bizarre, and beautiful, and he composed with zeal, "imbibing [inspiration] while it lasted for hours on end."[64]

There were few diversions: visits from Dmitri, a shorter visit from Elena and her son, three half-hour games of tennis a week with a fine old coach. Nabokov found that even when he did try to relax the muse would fight to get started again. He composed a good deal of the poem in his head as he strolled along the promenade to unwind. Even that fed into the poem, as he passed the experience on to Shade:

> too weary to delete I drop my pen
> I ambulate—and by some mute command
> the right word comes and perches on my hand.

Nabokov has written of Pope's genius for placing the best possible words in the best possible order, a genius that as Pope's manuscripts reveal materialized during the process of revision. As Nabokov revised these lines of Shade's neo-Popean poem, he deleted the word "comes," replaced it with "streaks," crossed it out again and inserted the word that had flitted into his mind by some felicitous fluke: "the right word flutes and perches on my hand."[65]

In this phase of unrelenting creative concentration, the occasional radio or newspaper interview—even the sudden flurry in the second week of January, as Gallimard launched the French version of Nabokov's autobiography, and the French, Swiss, German, Israeli, Irish, and British press all pounced on him—seemed a welcome break from his labors.[66]

Rather less welcome was the most disconcerting and tragic of all the attentions inflicted on him by fame. A young Swedish woman, an enthusiastic fan, had sent the Nabokovs clippings about him culled from the Swedish press in the late 1950s. Out of gratitude, Véra Nabokov had casually suggested that if she happened to be in the Riviera she could call to see them while they were there. Unexpectedly she flew to Nice for a fortnight expressly to meet the Nabokovs, who therefore felt obliged to entertain her. They soon realized she had an extraordinary literary talent, even in English, and a remarkably quick and well-stocked mind. They also discovered she was a lesbian and had a Dostoevskian temperament, alternating between exhilaration and despair, adulation of the Nabokovs and abuse.

Complaining of her difficult life in Sweden, she soon convinced herself that she needed to move to the United States. Over the next year the Nabokovs would help her with information about Harvard and even a letter of recommendation. Only after her arrival in Cambridge did the Nabokovs begin to discover through their friends there that she was schizophrenic. Later in the 1960s she would translate *The Gift* superbly into Swedish, but when she turned to tackle *Pale Fire* she began to insert inventions of her own, and the translation was never published. As the decade wore on, she sent the Nabokovs such a torrent of letters and erotic and abusive autobiographical fantasies about her involvement with them that after years of begging her to stop they would have to resort to the threat of handing the matter over to their lawyers.[67]

Despite the young Swede's visit, Nabokov continued to write assiduously and contentedly throughout January 1961. Early in the month he had completed canto 2, with its poignant story of Shade's daughter taking her life after another sharp reminder of her unattractiveness to men. Two weeks later Nabokov wrote to his son warning

him of the consequences of his attractiveness to women—and rhyme
rolled on:

> I have interrupted my literary labors to compose this instructive little
> jingle:
>
>> In Italy, for his own good,
>> A wolf must wear a Riding Hood.
>
> Please, bear this in mind.
>
>> Love, Father.

By February 11, Nabokov had finished the whole poem: nine hundred and ninety-nine superbly shaped lines in ten weeks.[68]

A week later he wrote to Walter Minton that he was in the middle
of the novel and hoped to finish it in a few months: "It is a fantastically beautiful thing." For his commentary, he began to mine the de-
posit of stray facts that for years he had been building up on index
cards, especially zoological, geographical, and cultural details that he
had sensed hung together and now helped form Kinbote's Zembla.[69]

After a poor return from the funds they had invested in the stock
market, the Nabokovs began to contemplate buying some land in
Switzerland. But they were still not committed to Europe, and rather
than buy a car they simply rented a humble Peugeot. At the end of
March, Véra drove her husband to Geneva to spend Easter with his
sister and to check out some background scenery for *Pale Fire* (Gradus
passes through Geneva as well as Nice on his way to America). At
the beginning of the month Nabokov had attended a meeting of the
entomological section of Nice's naturalists' society, then had headed
off for butterflies around Grasse and Vence. Now in Geneva he visited the Institut d'Entomologie in the Musée d'Histoire naturelle.
Véra fell in a Geneva street and tore a ligament in her foot, and it was
not until April 5 that they had a chauffeur take them back in their
rented car to Nice. On his return, Nabokov began correcting his son's
English translation of *The Gift*. Over the next two weeks he also traveled four times to a hill near Villeneuve-Loubet and in twelve hours
of searching among the strawberry trees on its ridge managed to
catch three specimens of the rare Chapman's Hairstreak. Reporters
for the *Nice-Matin* who interviewed him after one day's chase found
him aglow with excitement and pride at his catch.[70]

XII

As the tourist season approached, an increasingly noisy and con-
gested Nice threatened to throttle the inspiration it had fostered. The
Nabokovs planned to leave and find somewhere to settle down for

the summer in Italy or Switzerland before returning to the United States to winter in New York. By April 26, Nabokov had brought *Pale Fire* to a point at which he could set it aside, and Véra drove him off to Reggio Emilia for Dmitri's operatic debut in *La Bohème*. Journalists turned up to report on the famous writer's son, but that proved a lucky break not so much for Dmitri as for another singer who had also won the right to a debut here in the same competition: a young tenor named Luciano Pavarotti, whose career the occasion launched. The Nabokovs spent eleven days in Reggio, watching Dmitri three times in *La Bohème* and twice in *Lucia di Lammermoor*.[71]

On May 8 they drove on to Stresa, intending to spend three or four weeks moving around the Italian lakes before staying for two months in Switzerland, at Champex-Lac. But as soon as he arrived anywhere that summer Nabokov plunged into *Pale Fire*, and it seemed pointless to disturb him. In Stresa the weather was wet and so windy that narrow Lago Maggiore looked like a raging ocean, but the Nabokovs found the area's green-and-blue vistas so beautiful and its tiled roofs stepping down to the shore so full of old-time glamour that they were happy to stay.[72]

The tumultuous skies kept Nabokov away from his butterflies and at his desk. He resumed checking Dmitri's translation of the first chapter of *The Gift*, and completed it on May 23: three hours a day for thirty-five days, or an hour and a half for every page, much of the time spent on rendering into rhymed English the samples of Fyodor's early Russian verse, which he had asked Dmitri to leave untranslated. After *The Gift*, Nabokov then turned to check Bart Winer's editing of his *Eugene Onegin* commentary, which had been arriving sporadically since September 1960.[73]

Few families can have ever worked together as the Nabokovs did. While Nabokov himself had been polishing Dmitri's English translation of *The Gift*, Véra had mastered the rudiments of Italian grammar in order to check the Mondadori translation of his English and Russian poems word by word against the dictionary.[74]

Dmitri's success in Reggio had led to a concert engagement in Milan. Early in June his parents traveled to the city to hear him sing two arias and a duet from Anton Rubinstein's opera *The Demon*. A week later they drove back to Martigny, in the upper Rhone valley, and the next day wound ten perilous miles up a mountain road to the tiny village of Champex, pretty below (lake, green hills), spectacular above (white peaks thick with snow, even at this point in the summer). There they rented rooms in the Grand Hôtel Alpes et Lac until August 15, hoping *Pale Fire* might be completed by then. Véra also hoped there would be more sun than in Stresa so that her husband would rest from writing each day for at least the duration of the butterfly chase. He did hunt at various spots along the Valais, at Verbier, Crans, and Saas-Fee. Although he would be delighted by any rarity, blues always remained his special interest. He had come to Champex in the hope of catching a particular blue, and twice had had Véra drive him all the way to the Simplon Pass to find it. After five weeks he had caught only three specimens of the species he wanted.[75]

But most of the time it rained. For his first month at Champex, Nabokov had to check the copyedited typescript of his *Eugene Onegin* commentary while spending the bulk of the writing day on Kinbote's commentary to *Pale Fire*. By July 13 he was writing Kinbote's foreword, and four days later noted in his diary "finished at least half of *Pale Fire*." High summer brought visitors: Dmitri, who came to stay for ten days; Elena; cousin Nicolas and his friend the composer Igor Markevitch; George Hessen. Dmitri, fresh from another concert success in Italy, climbed Le Grand Combin in a formidable two-day excursion, and Nabokov confided to his sister that *ruka tyanetsya krestit'sya* ("my hand feels drawn to make the sign of the cross") when Dmitri returned from one of his dangerous feats.[76]

At the end of July the Nabokovs drove east up the Valais to the Hotel Bellevue at Simplon Kulm. Nabokov was ready to stay two weeks to catch the butterfly he especially wanted, though he had several other rarities in mind. Véra hoped he would catch them all quickly so they could leave a place that seemed both forlorn and godforsaken, yet swarmed with tourists.[77]

XIII

Nabokov must have fared well in four fine days on the trail, for they left the Simplon Pass on August 7 and drove to Montreux. With the town busy for the summer, they had to take a room in the Hotel Belmont, some distance up from the lake. Perhaps, they thought, they might divide their time between the United States and Switzerland, but at any rate they had decided to rent a place in Montreux, Lausanne, or Geneva—or perhaps even buy one, although prices had just jumped and new restrictions on foreign ownership had been introduced—and to make a trip to Italy before settling down somewhere on Lake Geneva.[78] There were two main reasons for choosing Switzerland: Dmitri was not far away in Milan, and the local lepidoptera offered both change and continuity. In the American West, Nabokov had specialized in the alpine butterflies that had much in common with those familiar to him from his boyhood around St. Petersburg. Now if he based himself in Switzerland he could master a third fauna adapted to severe winters and short summers.

There was another more immediate reason for the Lake Geneva location: for Gradus's journey in *Pale Fire* he needed a little of Switzerland as well as the France he had assimilated sufficiently in Nice, and he needed to create Zembla "out of the rejects of other countries" in Europe. One index card from Nabokov's manuscript, dated September 1, shows how the evening light over Montreux seeped into *Pale Fire*:

> How much happier the wide-awake indolents, the monarchs among men, the rich monstrous brain that can derive intense enjoyment and exquisite heartbreak from the balustrade of a terrace at nightfall, from the lights and the lake below, from the distant mountain shape melting into the dark apricot of the afterglow, from the black conifers outlined against the pale-ink of the zenith, and from the ruby and emerald flounces of the water along the silent, sad, forbidden shoreline. Oh my sweet Boscobel![79]

Nabokov found Montreux as fruitful for his work as Champex had been: an enchanting place, and beautifully sunny through late summer. In mid-August he dined at the Markevitches' in nearby Villars-sur-Ollon, and met Peter Ustinov. Ustinov recommended the Montreux Palace Hotel, where he and his family lived, and by the end of August the Nabokovs had signed up for an apartment there from October 1, hoping that *Pale Fire* could be finished before they left Montreux in the spring.[80]

Deep in his novel, Nabokov nevertheless wanted to see Dmitri play the part of Don Basilio in *Il Barbiere di Siviglia*, and he and Véra drove down to Milan on September 20. Dmitri had made himself up to imitate Chaliapin's version of the role, and the audience and critics loved his part. But doting father though he was, Nabokov could not stay for a second performance, and he hurried back to Montreux and *Pale Fire*. Already he and Véra had become attached enough to Switzerland to consider that they might delay their return to America until the fall of 1962.[81]

For a famous expatriate writer one source of contact with America was to be found in the books optimistic publishers sent him to read. After he had received *Catch-22*, Véra wrote back on his behalf that he made it a rule not to give his opinion "since he is a harsh judge. But he agrees to make an exception in this case. . . . : 'This book is a torrent of trash, dialogical diarrhea, the automatic produce of a prolix typewriter.' Please do not repeat this either to the author or to his publisher."[82]

At the beginning of October the Nabokovs moved into the Montreux Palace. During the quiet season its old wing, Le Cygne, was turned into furnished apartments, and as long-term occupants the Nabokovs were allowed two adjacent sets of rooms, 35–38, for the price of one. The suite would prove much more draft-resistant than their apartment in Nice, and although outdoors it was less balmy, Montreux, warmed by the sun reflecting off the lake and protected from the north wind by the mountains rising steeply behind the town, was much the warmest place on the Swiss Riviera. The Nabokovs could play tennis until the end of October, despite thick snow on the surrounding peaks. In any light they found the play of colors on the lake a delight to look at from balcony or promenade, and now, as the tourists moved off, Nabokov, with his naturalist's eye, feasted on the rich variety of waterfowl—coots, crested and black-coated grebes, black-hooded gulls, tufted ducks—that came to join the swans for winter on the lake. In a small town filled with newsstands displaying papers from a dozen countries and in a dozen languages, Nabokov was delighted to have discovered somewhere that seemed both central—not cut off from the world—and quiet, after the traffic noise of Nice.[83]

One noise he was conscious of was the tread of Ustinov's feet on the floor overhead. Nabokov was by now anxious that he had not yet seen the *Lolita* movie, although Kubrick had been promising for months to arrange a private showing as soon as he could. Ustinov, who had been filming at Elstree in a studio adjacent to the *Lolita* set, had caught occasional glimpses of the film and reassured Nabokov that he had heard everyone concerned with it declare it marvelous.[84]

During his first four months in Montreux, Nabokov completed *Pale Fire* in half the time he calculated it would have taken to write it elsewhere. By early November he had engaged Jaqueline Callier, who had a part-time job typing the Montreux Palace Hotel's English correspondence, to type up the *Pale Fire* commentary from the fair-copy pencil version on his index cards.[85]

Just after finishing his most luminous tale, turning the story of a northern king's overthrow by a gray revolution into pure color and magic, Nabokov read Abram Tertz's* "On Socialist Realism." He thought Tertz's case was stated with intelligence and brilliancy, but also commented that it was what he had been saying to his students for twenty years.[86]

Late in November he was still incorporating final revisions into the

---

* Pseudonym of Andrey Sinyavsky.

typescript. On December 4 he noted in his diary: "Finished *Pale Fire*, begun a year ago, 29 November (in its present form)." Two days later he sent two copies to Walter Minton at Putnam's: "I trust you will plunge into the book as into a blue ice hole, gasp, re-plunge, and then (around p. 126) emerge and sleigh home, metaphorically, feeling the tingling and delightful warmth reach you on the way from my strategically placed bonfires."[87]

CHAPTER 18

Pale Fire

I

IN SHEER beauty of form, *Pale Fire* may well be the most perfect novel ever written.[1] Each scene stands out with crystalline clarity and at the same time flips from right to left, from meaning to madness, in the crazy mirror of Kinbote's mind; each crisp but comically unstable moment challenges us to discover its place in what feigns to be chaos but turns out to be consummate order. *Pale Fire* also allows Nabokov the most perfect expression of his themes he could ever find. Kinbote and Zembla set up a shimmer of strange significance around everything in Shade's poem, as if another reality lurked behind his self-contained world: madness, or the key to the riddle he has spent his life trying to unlock?

More than any other novel, *Pale Fire* is committed to the excitement of discovery. The foreword opens as Kinbote's scholarly summary of John Shade's "Pale Fire," but the facade soon begins to crack: outbursts of spontaneous petulance ("There is a very loud amusement park right in front of my present lodgings"); academic intrigue swirling around the manuscript left by a dead poet; imputations against the competence of its present editor and annotator.

Two pages into the foreword, Kinbote tells us that his poor friend Shade proclaimed to him on the last day of his life that he had reached the end of his labors. Kinbote adds: "See my note to line 991." At this point we can either continue with the foreword, and catch the note when we come to it, or trust the author enough to suppose there is some reason for that suggestion and turn to the note. If we take the second course, we can witness at once Kinbote's curious attachment to Shade. As he returns home, Kinbote sees Sybil Shade driving toward town and immediately calls to see what his "dear neighbor was doing. . . . I grant you I very much resembled a lean wary lover taking advantage of a young husband's being alone in the house!" He finds Shade on "the arborlike porch or veranda I have mentioned in my note to lines 47-48." Do we continue the note to line 991—which has already begun to make the relationship between poet and commentator quite bizarre—or do we divert to the earlier note? If we do, we are referred forward almost at once to the note to line 691, and though we are running out of fingers to insert as bookmarks, and though we wonder whether we will ever reach the foreword again, we may agree to one last try. In the note to line 691, we find that a disguised king in exile has parachuted to America and that he is none other than our commentator, Dr. Kinbote. The trail of cross-references loses its mazy look and returns us, on our way back to the foreword, to the note to line 991. There we discover this passage:

> "And if you agree to show me your 'finished product,' there will be another treat: I promise to divulge to you *why* I gave you, or rather *who* gave you, your theme."
>
> "What theme?" said Shade absently, as he leaned on my arm and gradually recovered the use of his numb limb.
>
> "Our blue inenubilable Zembla, and the red-capped Steinmann, and the motorboat in the sea cave, and—"
>
> "Ah," said Shade, "I think I guessed your secret quite some time ago."

To readers ready to follow this chain of cross-references, Nabokov signals that their curiosity will be well repaid: we are only two and a half pages into the foreword, but already we know that Kinbote has a secret, and we know what that secret is, and we know much more besides—Kinbote's rampant homosexuality, his mad egocentricity, his preposterous unreliability—that we should not yet realize. Nabokov has granted us a glimpse of forbidden knowledge and a foretaste of the delights of discovery.

This little excursus can serve as a paradigm for reading all of Nabokov. He has a reputation for teasing his readers for the sake of teasing, or for taunting them with the implication of his own superiority. Far from it: he teases us to test us, because he has so much confidence in the enterprise of good readers—he has written that a writer's audience "is the most gifted and varied in the world"[2]—and because to attentive and imaginative readers he is the most generous of writers. He knows that there is no substitute for the excitement of a discovery we make ourselves, and he encourages us to exercise our curiosity and imagination in a world that may often resist the mind but that can afford endless rewards to those who approach it in a spirit of inquiry and confidence that it has worthwhile secrets to yield. Nabokov never succumbs to the false notion that truth is easy: there will be many frustrations—like the apparent labyrinth of cross-references here—and we will have to make a bracing effort of attention and imagination. But for those who are prepared to look at their world that way—or at one of Nabokov's books—Nabokov assures us that the effort will be exhilaratingly worthwhile.

II

Not every reader will follow that first trail of cross-references right to the end—although those who do find their own way through without prompting are likely to be addicted to Nabokov for life. But throughout *Pale Fire*, Nabokov makes it difficult for any reader not to sense that there are surprises to be discovered every step of the way. And as we stumble upon the treasure he has planted, *Pale Fire* offers us not only two bright worlds for the price of one, but also the mad comedy of their conjunction.

Into the 999 lines of "Pale Fire," John Shade compresses the whole of his settled life in the college town of New Wye in Appalachia, easily recognizable as Ithaca:*

> Flew back to our small town.
> Found that my bunch of essays *The Untamed
> Seahorse* was "universally acclaimed"
> (It sold three hundred copies in one year).
> Again school started, and on hillsides, where
> Wound distant roads, one saw the steady stream
> Of carlights all returning to the dream
> Of college education.

At sixty-one, Shade looks over his life in the face of death: his own, his daughter's, anyone's. The poem rises at its center to a poignant climax as Shade recounts his daughter's suicide—a scene I have watched evoke tears on a bus near Novgorod, in a kitchen in Toronto, in a classroom in Auckland. I wonder how many other modern poems could produce an effect like that.

Shade's whole existence has been a war waged against "the foul, the inadmissible abyss" of death, and though life has mocked all his attempts to discern what lies beyond, he concludes with a wry but

---

* New Wye of course suggests "New Y." and New York State. The Wordsmith campus and the Goldsworth house evoke for those familiar with Cornell the university's renowned Wordsworth collection and Goldwin Smith Hall, where Nabokov had his office. The three local lakes, Ozero, Omega, and Zero, add a Slavic, a Greek, and a Romance touch to the Finger Lakes, especially Owasco, Cayuga, and Seneca, the three closest to Ithaca.

serene confidence that the harmony of his art augurs well for the future:

> And if my private universe scans right,
> So does the verse of galaxies divine
> Which I suspect is an iambic line.
> I'm reasonably sure that we survive
> And that my darling somewhere is alive,
> As I am reasonably sure that I
> Shall wake at six tomorrow, on July
> The twenty-second, nineteen fifty-nine,
> And that the day will probably be fine.

In fact, as we learn at the end of the commentary, Kinbote calls on Shade just minutes after he has completed the poem and invites him over for a celebratory wine; as they walk across the lane, a gunman shoots at them, killing Shade. Life savagely negates all Shade's confidence in a harmony behind and beyond it.

Kinbote then takes the manuscript of Shade's poem and arranges its publication with his notes, explaining that "without my notes Shade's text simply has no human reality at all since the human reality of a poem such as his (being too skittish and reticent for an autobiographical work), with the omission of many pithy lines carelessly rejected by him, has to depend entirely on the reality of its author and his surroundings, attachments and so forth, a reality that only my notes can provide."

From the first of Kinbote's notes to the last entry in the index, we find ourselves again and again zooming off "to Zembla, my dear country." Shade's poem only has to mention "my bedroom" for Kinbote to turn to the crown prince's bedroom in Zembla in the weeks between his mother's death and his coronation. One of the Queen's ladies-in-waiting orders her daughter Fleur de Fyler to lay siege to Charles Xavier in his bedroom, though she knows that in amatory matters Zembla inverts the rest of the world. Here, male homosexuality seems almost the norm, and "manlier" than love between men and women—and in this respect the new king will be eminently fit to head his people.

The style of this sublimely preposterous scene, as of the rest of the commentary, is much leaner and more direct than that of *Lolita* or *Ada*—a plainness of texture necessary in a book whose structure resembles an Escher castle—but at the same time magical because of the bright invention behind every verbal formulation. The topsy-turvy mores of Zembla impart a weird instability to the first sentence in Kinbote's note: "Our Prince"—at this stage Charles Kinbote still refs to Charles Xavier in the third person, as he had to, for security reasons, when regaling Shade with the king's adventures—"Our Prince was fond of Fleur as of a sister but with no soft shadow of incest or secondary homosexual complications." Unaroused by Fleur's physical charms, Kinbote need only describe her via an outrageously comic and typically Zemblan reworking of the Cinderella story that Nabokov has concocted for him: "It was rumored that after going about with a porcelain cup and Cinderella's slipper for months, the society sculptor and poet Arnor had found in her what he sought and had used her breasts and feet for his *Lilith Calling Back Adam*; but I am certainly no expert in these tender matters." Countess de Fyler bribes the prince's groom of the chamber and his bodyguard, and plants Fleur in his room while she herself keeps guard in a small antechamber. But Fleur has no hope of seducing him, and barely tries: "She wore on the second day of their ridiculous cohabitation nothing except a kind of buttonless and sleeveless pajama top. The sight of her four bare limbs and three mousepits (Zemblan anatomy) irritated him, and while pacing about and pondering his coronation speech, he would toss towards her, without looking, her shorts or a terrycloth robe." The prince does not defile or deflower Fleur de Fyler, despite her name, and their "chaste romance" ends when the Prime Councilor and three Representatives of the People burst in to protest: "Amusingly, it was the Representatives of the People whom the idea of having for queen the granddaughter of a fiddler infuriated the most."

To the magic strangeness of Zembla, Nabokov adds the Ruritanian romance of revolution, the King's escape, his stumbling flight through the mountains. Kinbote retells this story in sequence through the first half of the commentary, interspersing it with his New Wye present: his installation in Judge Goldworth's house, next door to Shade, their growing friendship, his exhorting Shade to compose an epic on Charles the Beloved's flight, his frantic efforts to catch sight of the poet, at work on a long poem that Kinbote feels confident must be his own Zemblan saga. The second half of the commentary continues the story of Kinbote and Shade through the weeks of "Pale Fire" 's composition, but counterpoints these Appalachian scenes with the steady approach through space and time of Jakob Gradus, a thuggish killer for the Zemblan Extremist group the Shadows. For the man who kills Shade just after he had put the last touches to his poem was not aiming at Shade but at Kinbote, the disguised king, and was certainly not, as he claimed to the police, plain "Jack Grey."

Kinbote's mind may be too obsessed to follow Shade's poem for long, but Nabokov takes pains to allow the three stories of Charles II's flight, Kinbote's friendship with Shade, and Gradus's stalking of the disguised king to develop sequentially through the commentary for the sake of readers unprepared to venture beyond page-by-page order. But he also invites even the most conservative reader to discover the comedy of the disparity between the poem and the commentary, to flip back and forth from text to madly tangential gloss. Nothing could be more remote from Shade's "my bedroom" (the bedroom he had as a child, in the house where he still dwells)—and the unruffled, homely life in small-town America that his phrase implies—than the surreal sharpness of Fleur de Fyler's siege and all the rest of Kinbote's fragile past.

III

Kinbote's commentary on Shade's "Pale Fire" is a riotous scholarly nightmare. True, he does offer revealing glimpses of Shade's life, details of the poem's composition, parallel passages from other Shade works, some fine rejected variants, and helpful glosses on difficult words, images, and allusions. But he also expounds irrelevant Zemblan customs in enchanting detail, while knowing too little about obvious Americana to understand the joke in "Red Sox Beat Yanks 5–4 On Chapman's Homer." He has no Shakespeare in his mountain cabin except a Zemblan translation of *Timon of Athens*, and so cannot even trace the source for the very title of the poem he is annotating.*

Nabokov has devised Kinbote's obsession and the fictional situation that surrounds him so that Kinbote acts out in comically literal form all the perennial perversions of the critical mind: the critic's desire to appropriate the text, to insinuate himself into it, to make it say what he would like it to say, to thrust himself between text and reader; his delusion that he is somehow responsible for all that is best in the work, or that it could have been better still if only his own prescription had been followed; his desire to spy on the artist at the moment of creation and to pry into his private life, as if that would explain the work; his sense that he is the one person in close harmony with the mind of genius; his desperate desire to achieve immortality by attaching himself to an immortal work.

Unable to express himself in verse, Kinbote presses the story of Charles the Beloved on Shade "with a hypnotist's patience and a lover's urge." Supposing that Shade's long poem is indeed his own

* See below, pp. 436–37.

Zemblan adventure, he peers compulsively through uncurtained windows to catch Shade in the act of composition. He "appropriates" the manuscript in the worst possible fashion, stealing the thing from the poet who lies bleeding on the path, and then wears the index cards of the manuscript distributed about his person. He discovers as he reads it that there is no trace of Charles the Beloved, and attributes that to the envious censorship of Sybil Shade. Nevertheless he publishes the poem himself, with notes that forcibly reroute us from Shade's world to his own. He fabricates variants in an attempt to prove that the Zembla story has been Shade's real inspiration, and arranges his notes "to sort out these echoes and wavelets of fire, and pale phosphorescent hints, and all the many subliminal debts to me." Despite his closeness to Shade as Shade writes the poem, despite his repeated encroachments on Shade's privacy, Kinbote's monstrous ego obtrudes so that he can see almost nothing of Shade's poem or his life. The fantastic index records the measure of his obsession: Sybil Shade, the woman Shade addresses throughout his poem, is dismissed in one line ("*Shade, Sybil*, S's wife, *passim*"), while Shade himself receives a page of detailed references and Kinbote and Charles II almost three.

IV

Kinbote can hardly wait for us to detect the real story of *Pale Fire*: first, that he has inspired the poem Shade would really have preferred to write, and that New Wye subjects him to its calumny only because it envies his brief but glorious friendship with Shade; and second, that he is himself the disguised king of Zembla, pursued all the way from his homeland by relentless assassins, of whom Gradus is only the first.

Nabokov expects that with just a little more time we will discover the real real story beneath Kinbote's version of his world.[3] Kinbote's very attempts to refute the aspersions against him comically confirm them:

> It is so easy for a cruel person to make the victim of his ingenuity believe that he has persecution mania, or is really being stalked by a killer, or is suffering from hallucinations. Hallucinations! Well did I know that among certain youthful instructors whose advances I had rejected there was at least one evil practical joker; I knew it ever since the time I came home from a very enjoyable and successful meeting of students and teachers (at which I had exuberantly thrown off my coat and shown sev-

eral willing pupils a few of the amusing holds employed by Zemblan wrestlers) and found in my coat pocket a brutal anonymous note saying: "You have hal.....s real bad, chum," meaning evidently "hallucinations," although a malevolent critic might infer from the insufficient number of dashes that little Mr. Anon, despite teaching Freshman English, could hardly spell.

We can deduce from the number of dots and from the context of the wrestling display that Kinbote should have deciphered the missing word simply as "halitosis": his hysterical misreading only verifies his persecution mania and his obliviousness to the fact that he is not nice to be near.

Again and again Kinbote's attempts at self-defense raise doubts about the reality of what he records. "A certain ferocious lady" in New Wye tells him in the middle of a grocery store:

> "You are a remarkably disagreeable person. I fail to see how John and Sybil can stand you," and, exasperated by my polite smile, she added: "What's more, you are insane."
>
> But let me not pursue the tabulation of nonsense. Whatever was thought, whatever was said, I had my full reward in John's friendship. This friendship was the more precious for its tenderness being intentionally concealed, especially when we were not alone, by that gruffness which stems from what can be termed the dignity of the heart.

Is the friendship as Kinbote sees it, or is Shade's gruffness proof that he wishes to keep his distance from his neighbor? When Kinbote refers to Shade's anecdotes about Judge Goldsworth, his eager defense of his own reality undermines it still further:

> He did not bring up, my sweet old friend never did, ridiculous stories about the terrifying shadows that Judge Goldsworth's gown threw across the underworld, or about this or that beast lying in prison and positively dying of *raghdirst* (thirst for revenge)—crass banalities circulated by the scurrilous and the heartless—by all those for whom romance, remoteness, sealskin-lined scarlet skies, the darkening dunes of a fabulous kingdom, simply do not exist.

When we first encounter this, before we learn how Shade was killed, we do not know what to make of it all, but Nabokov invites us to file this and similar passages away in memory and to test Kinbote's world against them as it revolves more fully into view.

By reading between Kinbote's lines, by seeing through his denials and by piecing together scattered shards of information, we can soon make out behind the obvious disjunction between Shade's poem and

Kinbote's Zembla the subtler disparities between the real New Wye and Kinbote's. Kinbote sees himself as Shade's intimate friend and his male muse, the envy of New Wye. In fact, although Shade shows more tolerance than others toward a disconcerting eccentric, although his essential humaneness makes him unwilling to hurt a tiresome neighbor, although he even derives pleasure from the wild colors of Kinbote's fancy, he also sees quite clearly Kinbote's repellent self-obsession and offensive insensitivity to others. Much of the comedy, the irony, and the moral force of *Pale Fire* derives from the contrast between Kinbote's outrageous behavior—his importunate demands, his orgy of spying on Shade—and Shade's gentle forbearance that Kinbote construes as a mark of special favor.

A more shocking discovery creeps up on us by the end of the novel. Although Kinbote has introduced Gradus in his first note, although he has sketched Gradus's life as glassmaker and blundering revolutionary, although he has recorded in detail Gradus's pursuit of Charles the Beloved's trail in Paris, Geneva, Nice, and New York, Gradus the regicide exists only in Kinbote's imagination. The man who shot Shade is just who he says he is, Jack Grey, escapee from an Institute for the Criminal Insane to which he was sentenced by Kinbote's landlord, Judge Goldsworth, who is absent on sabbatical. Mistaking Shade for Goldsworth—the two men look alike—Grey aimed for the poet, not the disguised king. Suddenly the bottom drops out of scene after scene that Kinbote claims to have reconstructed from "an interview, perhaps even two interviews," with the jailed killer.

V

Beyond this discovery lies another, more unsettling still: Kinbote and his whole Zemblan past appear to be nothing but the demented fantasy of Vseslav Botkin, a refugee scholar in the Russian department at Wordsmith.[4] His anguish in exile has led him to construct the compensatory refuge of Zembla, a homophile homeland where *he* is king—at least until the evil Shadows plot revolution.

Kinbote lives within a complex and intricate network of delusions typical of the classical paranoiac. Not only do his delusions have the fixity and logical coherence of all paranoia, but he even manifests in rotation the symptoms of all three main kinds: the grandiose, the persecutory, and the erotic. Delusions of grandeur are the rarest and usually the most severe form of paranoia, and in contrast to the grandiose delusions in mania and schizophrenia they tend to be well-organized, relatively stable, and persistent.[5] Nothing could fit the bill more exactly than the Zembla that intrudes into Kinbote's commentary and ousts everything of New Wye but Shade and Kinbote from the index. Kinbote has built up his Zembla to cope with an overwhelming sense of loss—and that it is the loss of Russia emerges irresistibly. *Zemlya* is Russian for "land," and Nova Zembla or Novaya Zemlya part of Russia's far north. Shade's poem conjures up a dying exile who "suffocates and conjures in two tongues / The nebulae dilating in his lungs." Kinbote glosses hysterically:

> *Line 615*: two tongues
>   English and Zemblan, English and Russian, English and Lettish, English and Estonian, English and Lithuanian, English and Russian, English and Ukrainian, English and Polish, English and Czech, English and Russian, English and Hungarian, English and Rumanian, English and Albanian, English and Bulgarian, English and Serbo-Croatian, English and Russian, American and European.

While no other pair is repeated, English and Russian recur four times, and every other second language belongs to a country within the former Soviet sphere.

Erotic paranoia involves the fixed belief that one is loved sexually by another person, usually famous, who indicates affection through innumerable little signs. Kinbote has an unwarranted conviction of special favor in the eyes of Wordsmith College's most celebrated figure, John Shade, a favor that passes beyond "glorious friendship" and into the erotic. Seeing Sybil drive away, Kinbote stalks Shade down like "a lean wary lover taking advantage of a young husband's being alone." "Would he ever come for me?" Kinbote tells us he used to wonder, "waiting and waiting in certain amber-and-rose crepuscules, for a ping-pong friend, or for old John Shade."

Avid for a glimpse of Shade at work, Kinbote lurks in the shadows around his friend's home. But when he returns to the Goldsworth house, the shadows of fear begin to stir all around him. Every night he dreads assassination. He naturally believes that he was the real target of the man who shot John Shade. In his imagination, Jack Grey at once becomes the regicide Jakob Gradus, who thus confirms that Kinbote's nightly panics were no more than justified wariness. Beneath the insane exaggerations of persecution mania we can see the real cause for his fears: at Wordsmith his mental imbalance, his colossal self-conceit and self-obsession, and his undisguised homosexuality all make him the butt of constant scorn. But his fears seem to have a still deeper cause: they seem to be a transmutation of his own relentless urge to commit suicide, an urge he knows he will be unable to resist once his commentary is complete, his book published, his Zembla safely immortalized.[6]

In Kinbote's paranoia, Nabokov deliberately upends Freud. The philosopher Karl Popper points out that the distinguishing characteristic of a scientific attitude to knowledge is a readiness to accept criticism, especially evidence that conflicts with one's own theory. The opposite attitude is to look only for verifications of one's ideas—the method that allows people to believe in astrology, rain dances, soothsaying, and a great deal else. Once this second attitude is adopted, Popper writes, "every conceivable case will become a verifying instance," and it is this attitude that allows Freudians to explain any form of human behavior with absurd and worthless ease in terms of Freudian theory. Popper suggests only one exception: "Freud's explanation of paranoia in terms of repressed homosexuality would seem to preclude the possibility of active homosexuality in a paranoid individual."[7] Nabokov knew his Freud well, and he chose the one Freudian theory that even Popper had to concede was precise enough to be refutable, then neatly refuted it by making Kinbote so credible as both paranoid *and* actively, rampantly homosexual, and also by providing his own reasons, so much saner than Freud's, for Kinbote's madness.

But Kinbote is not so much a case study or even a critique of Freud as a zanily unforgettable character composite—critic, neighbor, lunatic, king—whose madness allows Nabokov to set him in the sharpest opposition to John Shade. Shade's poem, with its highly formal verse pattern and the Parthenon-like elegance of its architecture, subjects powerful emotions to deliberate control. Kinbote's commentary yields to the lurch of his obsessions, and ranges from comic self-satisfaction ("I trust the reader has enjoyed this note") to helpless panic ("Dear Jesus, do something"). Nabokov contrasts Shade's self-control and Kinbote's emotional riot, Shade's love for Sybil and Kinbote's desperate loneliness, Shade's luminous fulfillment and Kinbote's consuming despair, Shade's kindness and sensitivity and Kinbote's crazy selfishness. Shade embodies the imagination at its best, able to break free of the narrow confines of self; Kinbote's deranged mind represents the imagination not as escapee but as jailer, herding everything he sees into the dungeon of his own crazy ego.

VI

The rift between poem and commentary begins as bright parody, comedy, romance, but ends in a streak of tragedy and a stark opposition of love and loneliness, hope and despair, lucidity and madness. But as we read *Pale Fire* what seems most important of all is the shock of discovery, the unstable relationship of part to part that invites us to detect level after level of meaning: neighbor and annotator Kinbote as Charles II of Zembla, Gradus as no more than Jack Grey, Kinbote as the paranoid and suicidal Botkin. And yet as our knowledge of Kinbote grows and we probe the chasm between his world and Shade's, we also begin to sense an eerie congruity between poem and commentary that invites us to look deeper still. Not for nothing did Nabokov say, in an interview at the time of *Pale Fire*'s publication, "You can get nearer and nearer, so to speak, to reality; but you never get near enough because reality is an infinite succession of steps, levels of perception, false bottoms, and hence unquenchable, unattainable."[8]

One of Nabokov's invitations to discovery is the title of Shade's poem. Shade writes, after deploring his own habit of choosing allusive titles:

> But *this* transparent thingum does require
> Some moondrop title. Help me, Will! *Pale Fire*.

Kinbote's gloss begins well: "Paraphrased, this evidently means: Let me look in Shakespeare for something I might use for a title. And the find is 'pale fire.' " But then he adds: "But in which of the Bard's works did our poet cull it? My readers must make their own research. All I have with me is a tiny vest pocket edition of *Timon of Athens*—in Zemblan! It certainly contains nothing that could be regarded as an equivalent of 'pale fire' (if it had, my luck would have been a statistical monster)." The good rereader will notice Kinbote's comment on a variant version of two lines early in the poem:

> One cannot help recalling a passage in *Timon of Athens* (Act IV, Scene 3) where the misanthrope talks to the three marauders. Having no library in the desolate log cabin where I live like Timon in his cave, I am compelled for the purpose of quick citation to retranslate this passage into English prose from a Zemblan poetical version of *Timon* which, I hope, sufficiently approximates the text, or is at least faithful to its spirit:

> > The sun is a thief: she lures the sea
> > and robs it. The moon is a thief:
> > he steals his silvery light from the sun.
> > The sea is a thief: it dissolves the moon.

Readers with their suspicions aroused—and this ought to be everybody—should check the original:

> The sun's a thief, and with his great attraction
> Robs the vast sea; the moon's an arrant thief,
> And her pale fire she snatches from the sun;
> The sea's a thief, whose liquid surge resolves
> The moon into salt tears.

Those who make the effort* are rewarded not only with the source of Shade's title, but with a hilariously plausible parody of mistranslation (note that sun and moon change sex, which seems just right for a translation into Zemblan) and a flash of Shadean wit: Shade complains of the widespread practice of purloining titles from other works, then himself filches from Timon's diatribe against universal thievery.⁹

Kinbote dares publish a commentary of "Pale Fire" without even checking in Shakespeare the source of the poem's title. But curiously, although he remains ignorant of the source, he echoes it twice—just when he discusses the relationship between poem and commentary: "I have reread, not without pleasure, my comments to his lines, and in many cases have caught myself borrowing a kind of opalescent light from my poet's fiery orb, and unconsciously aping the prose style of his own critical essays." After he reads "Pale Fire," Kinbote finds to his chagrin that it does not commemorate his escape from Zembla, but as he rereads he thinks he detects "echoes and spangles of my mind, a long ripplewake of my glory. . . . My commentary to this poem, now in the hands of my readers, represents an attempt to sort out those echoes and wavelets of fire, and pale phosphorescent hints, and all the many subliminal debts to me."

Timon of Athens and its "pale fire" play a curious role in the king's escape from his Zemblan palace. As he removes the cupboard shelves that conceal a secret tunnel, the king picks up a tiny copy of *Timon Afinsken*, the Zemblan translation of *Timon of Athens*, which he takes with him all the way through the tunnel, across the mountains, over the Atlantic to New Wye, and on to the desolate log cabin where he lives "like Timon in his cave." He finds his way through the tunnel by the dim light—or the pale fire—of a flashlight and emerges in a theater after passing under Coriolanus Lane and Timon Alley. And these strange streets find their own eccentric echo in Shade's New Wye, on the Wordsmith campus, where Kinbote encounters a celebrated avenue planted with all the trees mentioned in Shakespeare.

There are other curious coincidences. Gradus and Kinbote share

---

* In fact, the good reader can follow the cross-reference from Kinbote's early "the sun is a thief" note to his gloss on the title, and chase down the clue at once: a double bonus for curiosity.

the same birthday; Shade too was born on the same day, but seventeen years earlier. In his poem Shade notes that an artist called Lang has painted Sybil Shade's portrait. Kinbote comments, "a modern Fra Pandolf no doubt." The allusion of course is to Browning's "My Last Duchess"—and Kinbote himself has been married, to Disa, duchess of Payn and Mone. In the poem, Shade addresses his wife as a Vanessa butterfly ("come and be caressed, My dark Vanessa, crimson-barred, my blest"); Kinbote notes that a recognizable Vanessa appears on the escutcheon of the dukes of Payn. Kinbote comments, on the lines where Shade describes his wife, that his own Disa

> bore a singular resemblance not, of course, to Mrs. Shade as she was when I met her, but to the idealized and stylized picture painted by the poet in those lines of *Pale Fire*. Actually it was idealized and stylized only in regard to the older woman; in regard to Queen Disa, as she was that afternoon on that blue terrace, it represented a plain unretouched likeness. I trust the reader appreciates the strangeness of this, because if he does not, there is no sense in writing poems, or notes to poems, or anything at all.

Nowhere else does Kinbote adopt such an urgent tone: and why does he write "there is no sense in writing *poems*, or notes to poems, or anything at all"?

Perhaps strangest of all is the coincidence that links Kinbote's Zembla with the opening lines of Shade's poem:

> I was the shadow of the waxwing slain
> By the false azure in the windowpane;
> I was the smudge of ashen fluff—and I
> Lived on, flew on, in the reflected sky.
> And from the inside, too, I'd duplicate
> Myself, my lamp, an apple on a plate:
> Uncurtaining the night, I'd let dark glass
> Hang all the furniture above the grass,
> And how delightful when a fall of snow
> Covered my glimpse of lawn and reached up so
> As to make chair and bed exactly stand
> Upon that snow, out in that crystal land!

These images—the azure sky reflected on the outside of Shade's window by day, his room reflected from inside at night as if it were standing out in "that crystal land" of snow—not only haunt the whole poem but seem strangely mirrored in the commentary. There we find Kinbote telling someone, before he knows of the poem, that "the name Zembla is a corruption not of the Russian *zemlya*, but of Semblerland, a land of reflections, of 'resemblers.' " One Zemblan translator enthusiastically calls his and Kinbote's language "the tongue of the mirror." When the king escapes through the mountains, he is disturbed by an uncanny false reflection of himself in the "limpid tintarron" of a mountain lake—tintarron being a precious glass stained an azure blue and made by Sudarg of Bokay, "a mirror-maker of genius" whose name if reversed as if in a mirror yields Jakob Gradus, himself a glassmaker and a Shadow.

What are we to make of these reflections between poem and commentary? Are the coincidences there because of Nabokov's sheer pleasure in design? Or should we heed what he would write in his next novel: "Some law of logic should fix the number of coincidences in a given domain, after which they cease to be coincidences, and form, instead, the living organism of a new truth"?[10]

VII

To answer this we need to return to Shade's poem.

As a poem, "Pale Fire" is a brilliant achievement in its own right. Like a genial host, Shade invites us right into his home, his spacious life, his ample past, but at the same time concentrates intently on a single theme. His has been a quiet life, but he has still been jarred by the fact of death—his parents, Aunt Maud, his daughter, his own fits and seizures—and by the idea of death. He has dedicated his art and his life to exploring and fighting death's abyss, and he relates his resolute but frustrated forays into the abyss with passion and wry detachment.

Tender, brave, wise, and witty, the poem builds its lucid lines into the shapeliest of structures with all the assurance of a masterpiece. If we add to line 999 a repetition of the first line, and so count the last line as line 1,000—and Shade and Kinbote both indicate we are to read this way—the poem's four cantos fall into two equal groups of 500 lines each, each of the central cantos being exactly twice the size of the two outer ones, or one third of the whole, so that the poem divides in different ways into the ratios 1:2, 1:3, 1:4, 1:6. The clarity of the poem's structure, the surprise of its prosody—it is written in heroic couplets—and the name and number of its parts, seem to make it a deliberate challenge to both Pound's *Cantos* and Eliot's *Four Quartets*, the latter of which Shade explicitly dismisses. Nabokov revitalizes rhyme, revels in the pleasure of a verbal compression achieved without sacrifice of sentence structure or sense, and piles up a vault full of visual and aural *trouvailles*. A man stands at his window with the light on, and as a dark snowy day sinks, the neutral light outside turns blue—indigo in the east, still a more luminous blue in the west—and the man gazing through his window begins to see himself reflected on the inside pane. Nabokov has Shade put it thus:

> A dull dark white against the day's pale white
> And abstract larches in the neutral light.
> And then the gradual and dual blue
> As night unites the viewer and the view.

English poetry has few things better to offer than "Pale Fire."

The poem works superbly on its own, but because it also forms part of a larger work it asks to be read in a second way. In the opening lines Shade imagines himself as the shadow—a literal shadow, but also the ghost—of a waxwing that flies into his window, whose reflected azure suggests a continued sky. In imagination, Shade becomes both the smudge of ashen fluff, the bird's corpse on the ground, and its spirit soaring on into the blue reflected world. "And from the inside, too," from his study, he projects himself onto the windowpane, or as if onto the snowy landscape outside. These images dissolve into pictures of Shade's house and his reminiscences of the calm childhood he spent here—calm, that is, until at the end of canto 1, as he plays on the floor with "a clockwork toy / —A tin wheelbarrow pushed by a tin boy," he has the first of a series of fits: a sudden sunburst in his head, a sense of being tugged at by playful death:

> And then black night. That blackness was sublime.
> I felt distributed through space and time.

Canto 2 opens with Shade's adolescent qualms about survival after death and his dedication to fighting death's mysteries, and closes with the heartrending scene of his daughter's suicide. Canto 3 begins with an amusedly dismissive account of

> I. P. H., a lay
> Institute (I) of Preparation (P)
> For the Hereafter (H), or If, as we
> Called it

where Shade has been invited to lecture on death for a term. That tasteless venture, he explains, teaches him "what to ignore in my survey of death's abyss." During a talk before a poetry club twenty years later, Shade has a heart attack. In a state of clinical death, he has a spellbindingly limpid vision of a white fountain that seems somehow charged with unspeakable significance—and he wakes. Months later he comes on a magazine account of a woman who in her own near-death experience has also seen a tall white fountain. He drives three hundred miles to talk with her, and discovers there was a fatal misprint: it should have been "*Mountain*, not *fountain*."

> Life Everlasting—based on a misprint!
> I mused as I drove homeward: take the hint,
> And stop investigating my abyss?
> But all at once it dawned on me that *this*
> Was the real point, the contrapuntal theme;
> Just this: not text, but texture; not the dream
> But topsy-turvical coincidence,
> Not flimsy nonsense, but a web of sense.
> Yes! It sufficed that I in life could find
> Some kind of link-and-bobolink, some kind
> Of correlated pattern in the game,
> Plexed artistry, and something of the same
> Pleasure in it as they who played it found.
>
> It did not matter who they were. No sound,
> No furtive light came from their involute
> Abode, but there they were, aloof and mute,
> Playing a game of worlds, promoting pawns
> To ivory unicorns and ebon fauns;
> Kindling a long life here, extinguishing
> A short one there; killing a Balkan king.

But when he reaches home, even this new insight fails: even to Sybil he cannot express this vision of "the real point, the contrapuntal theme."

Canto 4 appears to leave death alone, as Shade broods instead on the problems of poetic composition. For instance: line after line of verse may rush into his mind while his hands are busy shaving. As he adjusts razor and skin, his imagination roams:

> And now a silent liner docks, and now
> Sunglassers tour Beirut, and now I plough
> Old Zembla's fields where my gray stubble grows,
> And slaves make hay between my mouth and nose.
>
> *Man's life as commentary to abstruse*
> *Unfinished poem.* Note for further use.

The poem ends after a day of composition, "a sustained / Low hum of harmony" that allows him

> A feeling of fantastically planned,
> Richly rhymed life.
>
>   I feel I understand
> Existence, or at least a minute part
> Of my existence, only through my art,
> In terms of combinational delight.
>
> . . . .
>
> I'm reasonably sure that we survive
> And that my darling somewhere is alive,
> As I am reasonably sure that I
> Shall wake at six tomorrow, on July
> The twenty-second, nineteen-fifty-nine,
> And that the day will probably be fine;
> So this alarm clock let me set myself,
> Yawn, and put back Shade's "Poems" on their shelf.

But as he notes, it is not bedtime yet, and he looks out at the tranquil suburb and the lucent evening:

> A dark Vanessa with a crimson band
> Wheels in the low sun, settles on the sand
> And shows its ink-blue wingtips flecked with white.
> And through the flowing shade and ebbing light
> A man, unheedful of the butterfly—
> Some neighbor's gardener, I guess—goes by
> Trundling an empty barrow up the lane.

The poem ends with its last rhyming couplet unfinished—unless we return to the first line, which would round off structure and rhyme with "I was the shadow of the waxwing slain"* and Shade's avowal that he has projected himself into the azure, that he is both corpse and the creature flying on in the reflected sky. Just at this moment, after having declared that he is reasonably sure he will wake tomorrow, he leaves his veranda and walks over with Kinbote to his death, and in a few minutes lies "with open dead eyes directed up at the sunny evening azure." As he composes his last lines he winds his alarm clock to rouse himself the next morning, looks outside at a gardener—Kinbote's black gardener, in fact—trundling an empty

---

* As an additional clue to Shade's intentions, the rhymes "lane" and "slain" would share the *consonne d'appui* (the matching consonant before the rhyme vowel), for which Shade pointedly confesses his special fondness just before the poem ends.

barrow up the lane, and then steps out to that lane and death: a sequence that repeats with miraculous exactitude the end of canto 1, and Shade's first childhood fit, his first taste of death, as he played with a tin wheelbarrow pushed by a tin boy, a clockwork "little Negro of painted tin."[11]

The coincidences crowd the end of the poem and its implicit return to the beginning too profusely for there to be any doubt. Shade has left his poem unfinished, and acted out the suggestion that follows "Old Zembla's fields": *"Man's life as commentary to abstruse / Unfinished poem.* Note for further use."

As John Shade, autobiographical poet, he may assert all he likes his confidence in waking up safely tomorrow, but he knows on the other hand that he is as subject to the unpredictable contingencies of life as anyone else. He can dramatize that discrepancy in the starkest possible way by stepping outside his poem and his self and right there subjecting himself to an accidental killing, like the waxwing stunned against the azure, but then project himself into the Kinbote who flies on in the reflected sky of the commentary. For as his poem itself makes clear, he senses the need somehow to reach beyond his death, and to allow himself a meaning he can express not through the text of his life but only through the texture of interacting poem and commentary, self and nonself, life and whatever follows afterward. He wants to try to enter another soul and to play the role of life-dealer and death-dealer, to suggest as if from beyond the confines of his own existence how his own death may suddenly turn the dead end of his whole life's search into the portal of discovery.

VIII

Nabokov has built Shade up in such a way as to leave no doubt that his poet could have conceived the idea of hiding behind his commentator's mad mask. As a Pope scholar, Shade has before him the example of Pope's *Dunciad*, a poem also in four books and in heroic couplets, with eccentric annotations by an invented critic and a comic index: a parody of egotistic scholarship. As an eighteenth-century specialist, he also knows Swift's *Battle of the Books*, in which "a malignant deity, call'd *Criticism*. . . . dwelt on the top of a snowy mountain in Nova Zembla." The same specialty ensures his familiarity with Boswell, who in his *Life of Johnson* manifests a comically insistent eagerness to introduce Johnson to Scotland, *his* distant northern land, and a self-display that often reads like Kinbote in a more guarded version. And as a writer and an academic, Shade is of course accustomed to polished prose as well as verse—Kinbote even admits to "aping the prose style of [Shade's] own critical essays"—and to the quirks of criticism so absurdly parodied in Kinbote.

It is Shade who points out that Kinbote is "the author of a remarkable book on surnames"—a hint if ever there was one. According to Nabokov's dictionary, Webster's Second, a kinbote is a bote or compensation "given by a homicide to the kin of his victim." Jack Grey, the man who kills Shade, certainly does not give Kinbote to Sybil, nor would she want him. The only way the name makes the sense that Nabokov indicates it ought to have is if Shade, in compensation for the shock of fictively killing himself off, presents Sybil with the maddening but supremely colorful Kinbote, whose attacks on Sybil, if reflected through one more mirror so that we can read them the right way around, are of course a tribute to her staunch loyalty. And "Botkin" is just as apt. Webster's Second records one meaning of bodkin—or as Kinbote insists, "botkin"—as "a person closely wedged between two other persons," like Kinbote trying to thrust himself between John and Sybil Shade. Its main meaning, of course, is a stiletto, and in this sense it evokes Hamlet's "When he himself might his quietus make / With a bare bodkin" and the suicide that will remove the figmentary interloper between the two Shades as soon as he has finished his commentary and index.

Although several critics have proposed Shade as the sole author of poem and commentary,[12] one or two others have instead proposed Kinbote as the person responsible for the swarm of echoes between the two parts.[13] Kinbote has one advantage over Shade: according to the plot, he is not dead at the time the commentary is written. But just as Nabokov takes care to show that Shade could have invented the whole, he takes pains to rule out Kinbote. Kinbote admits to being "a miserable rhymester"—a fact horribly verified by the inept variants he fabricates to make it appear that Shade had been planning a poem on Charles II's escape. The whole point of his commentary lies in the fact that he cannot express himself in verse and so cannot immortalize his Zemblan fantasy. He lacks the control ("and damn that music") even to organize a critical commentary, let alone to construct a flawlessly shaped poem. He is deranged, transfixed by his obsession, and has no interest in other people, least of all in inventing a happy heterosexual who writes a poem that has nothing to do with him. And he is certainly not the sort of person to write a commentary deliberately riddled with ironies at his own expense— like the halitosis/hallucinations blunder, or the fact that he does not even know the source of the poem's title. A Kinbote who is a master of English poetry, who could invent with such sympathy John and

Sybil Shade, and who is capable of extraordinary self-detachment would not only have no need of Zembla as a mental refuge, he would not be Kinbote. Kinbote as author of both poem and commentary seems no more plausible than hazarding that *The Tempest* may be Caliban's dream.

IX

One last piece of evidence proves conclusively that Nabokov had Shade in mind as the author of foreword, poem, commentary, and index. Four years after *Pale Fire*, when he drafted the foreword to the revised *Speak, Memory*, Nabokov concluded with a comment on the new index to his autobiography. He added as an envoi:

As John Shade says somewhere:

> Nobody will heed my index,
>   I suppose,
> But through it a gentle wind *ex*
> *Ponto* blows.[14]

In the final version of his foreword to *Speak, Memory*, Nabokov decided not to divulge *Pale Fire*'s secret, to leave it for readers to discover quite unaided, but this draft leaves no doubt that he saw Shade as the compiler of the index, months after Jack Grey or Jakob Gradus supposedly shoots him through the heart.

What could Shade intend by killing himself off and allowing his "shadow" to impersonate a mad neighbor? Paraphrasing Nabokov's invented philosopher of the hereafter, Pierre Delalande, Fyodor writes in *The Gift*: "The unfortunate image of a 'road' to which the human mind has become accustomed (life as a kind of journey) is a stupid illusion: we are not going anywhere, we are sitting at home. The other world surrounds us always and is not at all at the end of some pilgrimage. In our earthly house, windows are replaced by mirrors; the door, until a given time, is closed; but air comes in through the cracks."[15] Because of Shade's childhood seizures and his heart attack, because he has slipped on the floor of life's house and peeked through the crack under the door before scrambling to his feet again, Shade knows there is something outside those windows that can only reflect life back at him.

As Shade writes in the opening lines of his poem, he projects himself out into the mirror world, and lives on, flies on, in the reflected sky of Zembla as his mirror-image, Kinbote. In a mirror, images are duplicated but with directions reversed, as if from the A of Appalachia to the Z of Zembla. Both Kinbote and Shade are writers, university teachers, and neighbors, but otherwise they inhabit opposite poles. Kinbote is a vegetarian, where Shade "must make a definite effort to partake of a vegetable." Kinbote is bearded, tall, of "erect carriage," and athletic; Shade clean-shaven, short, twisted, clumsy. Kinbote is homosexual, lonely, with constantly changing partners; Shade heterosexual and happily married for almost forty years to his high-school sweetheart. Kinbote is a pietistic but anguished Christian, Shade happily agnostic, Kinbote insane, Shade lucid and at ease with his world. While Kinbote is above all an exile, Shade has lived all his life in the same house. Compulsively drawn to suicide, Kinbote rates the best method as falling to one's death, and he cannot avert his gaze from this "inviting abyss." Shade affirms confidently he will wake the next morning, he devotes his whole life to exploring and fighting the "inadmissible abyss" of death, and he flies straight to his imagined death in the azure mirror of Kinbote's world when he runs into glassmaker and Shadow Jakob Gradus.

How does Shade's creation of Kinbote's mirror-world allow him to express what he cannot express directly in his own voice?

Shade has always been only too aware of the limits to what can be known by each mind, being only one mind—

> I alone
> Knew nothing, and a great conspiracy
> Of books and people hid the truth from me

—and by any mind, being only mortal:

> Space is a swarming in the eyes, and time,
> A singing in the ears. In this hive I'm
> Locked up.

Through the imagination Shade unlocks the possibilities closed to him by the limits of his mind and his experience. To imagine himself for the length of a line as the shadow of a waxwing is not enough: he wants to try to enter another soul, the soul of someone as remote from himself as possible, a foreigner, a madman, a homosexual, a suicide. In *The Real Life of Sebastian Knight*, V. suggests that "the hereafter may be the full ability of consciously living in any chosen soul, in any number of souls, all of them unconscious of their interchangeable burden."[16] Shade wants to try out what it might be like to have such an unheralded freedom from personality.

But as he knows from his time at I.P.H., any direct attempt to chart the hereafter runs up against the absurdity of trying to express the unthinkable in human terms. Perhaps a better way to suggest what might lie beyond would be to define the rigid limits of the human mind and to suggest that in death all these limits are reversed as easily as the images in a mirror. Hence Shade concocts Kinbote, whose very being defines the prison of personality in the starkest terms.

No one could be more obnoxious as a neighbor or colleague than Kinbote. But within the recesses of his mind there is a "streak of magical madness": even in him there is something priceless and irreplaceable. Precisely because we value the differences between people, the independence of the human spirit, we cannot permit others to intrude on the privacy of the soul. Kinbote ignores that basic human decorum. Although he breaks into a sweat of dread every night at the thought that someone may be spying on him, he himself tries compulsively to pry into the secrets of Shade's mind, and the outrage his behavior provokes kindles much of *Pale Fire*'s moral heat.

On the one hand, Shade kills himself off to enter the soul of Kinbote, as if to suggest the liberation of personality that may be possible beyond death. On the other, he creates Kinbote, who more than anyone shows what it is to be sentenced for life to imprisonment within the self and who at the same time tries to force his way into the inner sanctum of someone else's soul.

X

Pale Fire portrays the isolation of the soul as the fundamental condition of mortal life. Besides the necessary moral tax of privacy, our individual isolation exacts another cost: the burden of human solitude. Despite all his "ping-pong boys," Kinbote is abysmally lonely—and this of course places him in absolute contrast to John and Sybil Shade. Paying tender homage to Sybil in his poem, Shade pictures married love as a breach in the solitude of the soul, an advance peep at some ultimate space beyond human loneliness that we might reach in death. In the commentary, Kinbote's envious rancor against Sybil for all she shares with Shade and for her sterling defense of his privacy is Shade's own inverted tribute to their married love.

Kinbote himself is a married man. For reasons of state, Charles the Beloved has taken as his queen Disa, duchess of Payn and Mone. Although she loves him helplessly, he cares nothing for her. Dreams of Disa nevertheless torture his sleep, and his dream-love for her exceeds "in emotional tone, in spiritual passion and depth, anything he had experienced in his surface existence. This love was like an endless wringing of hands, like a blundering of the soul through an infinite maze of hopelessness and remorse." Kinbote points out Disa's striking resemblance to Sybil, and exclaims "there is no sense in writing poems, or notes to poems, or anything at all" if we do not appreciate the strangeness of this. In fact, his dreams of Disa are a gleam showing through from the world of his maker. And at the center of his recurring dream, he knows Disa has

> just come across a telltale object—a riding boot in his bed—establishing beyond any doubt his unfaithfulness. Sweat beaded her pale, naked forehead—but she had to listen to the prattle of a chance visitor or direct the movements of a workman with a ladder who was nodding his head and looking up as he carried it in his arms to the broken window. One might bear—a strong merciless dreamer might bear—the knowledge of her grief and pride but none could bear the sight of her automatic smile as she turned from the agony of the disclosure to the polite trivialities required of her. She would be canceling an illumination, or discussing hospital cots with the head nurse, or merely ordering breakfast for two in the sea cave—and through the everyday plainness of the talk, through the play of the charming gestures with which she always accompanied certain readymade phrases, he, the groaning dreamer, perceived the disarray of her soul and was aware that an odious, undeserved, humiliating disaster had befallen her, and that only obligations of etiquette and her staunch kindness to a guiltless third party gave her the force to smile.

For Nabokov the ability to show "staunch kindness" to others in the midst of one's own private agony is the highest of ethical principles, something that recurs as a moral touchstone in stories, plays, and novels he wrote over a span of forty years. Here it figures in a dream within the fantasies of a madman who has himself been invented by someone who is already a fictional character, but the series of lenses and mirrors through which we see Disa's kindly forbearance only serves as a powerful optical instrument to intensify and resolve the image. In this hopelessly poignant picture of Disa, John Shade and his maker allow a dream within a madman's mirror-world to suggest that human kindness and human love foretoken the transcending of personality perhaps possible in a state of being beyond death where "curiosity, tenderness, kindness, ecstasy"[17] are the norm.

XI

In canto 2 of "Pale Fire," Shade relates the night of Hazel Shade's death in a haunting counterpoint: theme, John and Sybil Shade restlessly watching television; countertheme, their brilliant but fat, ugly, and depressed daughter at twenty-three on her first blind date. Her partner recoils when he sees her, invents a feeble pretext, and escapes; she leaves the two friends who have arranged the date and takes the bus partway home.

> The lake lay in the mist, its ice half drowned.
> A blurry shape stepped off the reedy bank
> Into a crackling, gulping swamp, and sank.

In the commentary, Kinbote organizes a similar counterpoint as he coordinates Shade's composition of "Pale Fire" with Gradus's approach to New Wye—and for him, Gradus's approach is the inexorable approach of his own suicide. Pondering his future in the last lines of his commentary, Kinbote writes: "But whatever happens, wherever the scene is laid, somebody, somewhere, will quietly set out—somebody has already set out, somebody still rather far away is buying a ticket, is boarding a bus, a ship, a plane, has landed, is walking toward a million photographers, and presently he will ring at my door—a bigger, more respectable, more competent Gradus."

Shade chooses to place Kinbote the suicide in further counterpoint to his own poem, in the hope that this study in the solitude of the soul will help him to understand his daughter's death. Shade realizes he cannot know all the mysteries hidden in Hazel's soul, but he does know that she has been provoked to suicide by the prospect that she will have to spend her days without a partner. In creating Kinbote's desperate loneliness, Shade attempts to express the hope that even within the loneliness and despair that drove Hazel to her death there may have been something to match the private, magical radiance that Zembla has within Kinbote's mind.

XII

Although in the poem "Pale Fire" Shade shows himself convinced of something beyond death, every attempt to detect it, from I.P.H. to the mysterious mirage of the fountain, leads to a dead end. But when he leaves the facts of his own life and steps into the looking-glass world of Zembla, he feels free to speculate here as he cannot do in person.

One tactic he adopts is to stage Kinbote's escape from Zembla as a transition from one world to another. As a boy, the future king removes some cupboard shelves and their contents, including a translation of *Timon of Athens*, to follow his coeval and beloved bedmate Oleg, duke of Rahl, down a secret tunnel and under Timon Alley.

"Oleg walked in front: his shapely buttocks encased in tight indigo cotton moved alertly, and his own erect radiance, rather than his flambeau, seemed to illume with leaps of light the low ceiling and crowding walls." A noise at the other end frightens them back. Soon after the discovery of the secret passage, the young prince almost dies of pneumonia. "In his delirium he would strive one moment to follow a luminous disk probing an endless tunnel and try the next moment to clasp the melting haunches of his fair ingle." Oleg's death at fifteen "helped to obliterate the reality of their adventure. A national revolution was needed to make that secret passage real again."

After the revolution Charles the Beloved is incarcerated in the room from which the tunnel leads. On his first night there, "distant spasms of silent lightning" flash through the window. "The bedside light was just strong enough to put a bright gleam on the gilt key in the lock of the closet door. And all at once that spark on that key caused a wonderful conflagration to spread in the prisoner's mind" as he recalls his venture through the tunnel with Oleg. As the king prepares to descend the tunnel again, the theme of electricity crackles and flashes once more: "Distant lightning still throbbed now and then in the window. The King finished his drink in the dark and replaced the empty tumbler on the night table where it knocked with a subdued ring against a steel flashlight prepared by the thoughtful authorities in case electricity failed as it lately did now and then." He removes the cupboard shelves in the dark, and an object falls with a miniature thud. Guessing what it is—*Timon Afinsken*—he takes it as a talisman. Safely down in the tunnel, he switches on his flashlight: "The dim light he discharged at last was now his dearest companion, Oleg's ghost, the phantom of freedom." As the tunnel passes through the foundations of a museum, he notes "a headless statue of Mercury, conductor of souls to the Lower World," and emerges in the national theater beside Timon Alley.

Apart from "Pale Fire" itself, the longest and best of John Shade's poems we see is "The Nature of Electricity":

> The dead, the gentle dead—who knows?—
> In tungsten filaments abide
> And on my bedside table glows
> Another man's departed bride.
>
> And maybe Shakespeare floods a whole
> Town with innumerable lights,
> And Shelley's incandescent soul
> Lures the pale moths of starless nights.
>
> Streetlamps are numbered, and maybe
> Number nine-hundred-ninety-nine

> (So brightly beaming through a tree
> So green) is an old friend of mine.

> And when above the livid plain
> Forked lightning plays, therein may dwell
> The torments of a Tamerlane,
> The roar of tyrants torn in hell.

In recounting the king's fantastic escape, Shade fills the air with electricity, with hints of a phantom presence and a passage to another world, with the pale fire of a flashlight and the *Timon* from which "Pale Fire" takes its name. The king's transition from Zembla to Appalachia seems a transition from one world to another, from life to death. And it satisfies the condition Shade requires for his "faint hope":

> I'm ready to become a floweret
> Or a fat fly, but never, to forget.
> And I'll turn down eternity unless
> The melancholy and the tenderness
> Of mortal life; the passion and the pain
> . . . .
> Are found in Heaven by the newlydead
> Stored in its stronghold through the years.

For as he crosses from Onhava to New Wye, Kinbote takes all his memories with him.

XIII

In creating Kinbote, Shade can also mimic the role of the gods, wielding over an imagined world the sort of control he supposes some higher force may exercise over his own life, "Playing a game of worlds, promoting pawns / To ivory unicorns and ebon fauns."

In the role of storyteller, Kinbote himself tries to exert a much cheaper and nastier form of such control over Gradus, both through the counterpoint of the poem's composition and Gradus's approach and through his comic attempts at narrative revenge. He exults in the power over Gradus that language permits, and describes with relish even the internal turmoil of incipient diarrhea:

> We know already some of his gestures, we know the chimpanzee slouch
> of his broad body and short hindlegs. We have heard enough about his
> creased suit. . . . We see, rather suddenly, his humid flesh. We can even
> make out (as, head-on but quite safely, phantom-like, we pass through

him, through the shimmering propeller of his flying machine, through the delegates waving and grinning at us) his magenta and mulberry insides, and the strange, not so good sea swell undulating in his entrails.

He depicts Gradus meeting a graceful young boy with "nothing on save a leopard-spotted loincloth," whom Kinbote then promptly reclads—he is successively "wreathed about the loins with ivy," and sporting "black bathing trunks," "white tennis shorts," his "Tarzan brief"—in implicit mockery of Gradus for failing to observe and savor such a sweet young thing.

Shade pointedly controls Kinbote, too, but his manner is much less malign. He surrounds Kinbote's escape not only with gleams of ghostly electricity, but with image after image of chess as a game of fate. Imprisoned in his tower before being transferred to the room from which the tunnel leads, the king has "the amusing feeling of his being the only black piece in what a composer of chess problems might term a king-in-the-corner waiter of the *solus rex* type." Later he will suggest "Solus Rex" to Shade as the title for his Zemblan epic. Just before the young prince enters the tunnel with Oleg, his English and French tutors Mr. Campbell and Monsieur Beauchamp sit down for a game of chess; as the boys emerge from the tunnel again, they find the tutors ending their game in a draw. On a stone bench outside the king's cell the night he escapes, two guards sit playing lansquenet, an invented game which, deriving from the German *Landsknecht* (mercenary foot soldier),[18] seems a Zemblan variant of chess. As the king passes through the tunnel, he notes beside the statue of Mercury "a cracked krater with two black figures shown dicing under a black palm." Dressing in the dark for his escape, the king had donned some sports clothes he found in the cupboard, not noticing until too late the tracksuit's bright scarlet hue: he has become the Red King—the red *chess* king, of course—from *Through the Looking Glass*.[19] In his escape over the mountains (note to line 149) he skirts a pool where he sees his scarlet reflection moving when he stands still: an eerie scene in which he seems almost to pass through his own reflection. According to Tweedledum and Tweedledee, they and Alice are all part of the Red King's dream, but although Kinbote dreams up his own version of Shade as his passionate friend, it is Alice in fact who is the dreamer, and Shade who controls every move of *his* red king.

As this red king skirts his reflection in a mountain lake, he shivers with eerie *"alfear* (uncontrollable fear caused by elves)" and begins to recite to himself the lines of Goethe's "Elf-King" in German and Zemblan. John Shade reworks Goethe's lines into his poem, too, just as he and his wife play chess to distract themselves from haunting thoughts of the daughter they have lost in another lake:

> And when we lost our child
> I knew there would be nothing: no self-styled
> Spirit would touch a keyboard of dry wood
> To rap out her pet name; no phantom would
> Rise gracefully to welcome you and me
> In the dark garden, near the shagbark tree.

> "What is that funny creaking—do you hear?"
> "It is the shutter on the stairs, my dear."

> "If you're not sleeping, let's turn on the light.
> I hate that wind! Let's play some chess." "All right."

> "I'm sure it's not the shutter. There—again."
> "It is a tendril fingering the pane."

> "What glided down the roof and made that thud?"
> "It is old winter tumbling in the mud."

> "And now what shall I do? My knight is pinned."

> Who rides so late in the night and the wind?
> It is the writer's grief. It is the wild
> March wind. It is the father with his child.

Shade hears nothing in the wind but his own sense of loss and an echo of a poem that ends with a child dead in its father's arms. But he will himself write a poem—canto 2 of "Pale Fire"—where to comprehend Hazel's death he will assume the part of fate playing its inexorable game with his daughter and her anxious parents, and then he will step further out, through the looking glass, to become both the red-tipped waxwing and its shadow, or both the red king advancing toward suicide and the supernatural chess player who moves him along. Only by playing a game of worlds can he understand his own world.

XIV

Within the poem, Shade knows he will see and hear nothing of Hazel after her death: no phantom, no self-styled spirit. But within the commentary he redesigns a spectral episode from his daughter's past that Kinbote records but whose significance he fails to detect. As a college student, Hazel Shade becomes interested in reports of weird sounds and lights in an old barn. She investigates the barn herself at night, and sees "a roundlet of pale light" flit across the dark walls. She interrogates "the luminous circlet": in the hope that it might have some message, she recites the alphabet again and again, waiting for its small jump of approval at the next letter of the message. Kinbote transcribes the meager result: "pada ata lane pad not ogo old wart alan ther tale feur far rant lant tal told." Observing that "the barn ghost seems to have expressed himself with the empasted difficulty of apoplexy," Kinbote tries to decipher in the message an allusion to Hazel's impending suicide, but he can find nothing. He has looked in the wrong place. As Nabokov has noted privately, the message can be decoded as a garbled warning via Hazel "to her father and hint at the title of his poem to be written many years later. *Padre* should *not go* to the *lane* to be mistaken for *old Goldswart* (worth) after finishing his *tale* (pale) *feur* (fire) [which in Shakespeare is accompanied by] the word 'arrant' (*farant*) [and this] with '*lant*' makes up the Atalanta butterfly in Shade's last scene. It is '*told*' by the spirit in the barn." The message appears to come from Shade's Aunt Maud, who had raised him as a child, had a pronounced penchant for "images of doom,"[20]* had suffered impaired speech after a stroke just before her death, and for a brief period after her death had seemed to be the force behind the poltergeist phenomena surrounding Hazel.

Why does Shade give Kinbote this scene to record, with its pale spectral fire matching the luminous disks in the tunnel through which Kinbote escapes? The point of the pale-fire message is that it can make no sense to anyone at the time: it suddenly becomes pregnant with meaning only at the moment of Shade's "death." And in fact Shade has constructed the whole commentary so that the poem will spring to new life through the device of his fictive death: the image of the waxwing, the story of his lifelong struggle against death, his childhood trances, his adult seizure; his "not text but texture," his "playing a game of worlds," his unfinished poem that invites completion by "I was the shadow of the waxwing slain."

Shade stages his own death in such a way that it will seem as meaningless and undeserved as possible. Just after he has completed his masterpiece, he falls victim to the misdirected revenge of a mad assassin; already almost meaningless, this ridiculous death is then robbed even of this much sense by another madman who appropriates both the murder and the still-warm text of "Pale Fire." Within the restrictions of truth to his own life, Shade can orchestrate the

---

* Like the threefold reference to the Atalanta butterfly that, as Gennadi Barabtarlo points out, flits into Shade's last lines and then accompanies Kinbote and him on his last fatal stroll toward the Goldsworth home: "pada *ata lane* pad *not* ogo old *wart alan* *ther* tale feur far *rant* *lant tal* told" (*Nabokovian* 13 [1984]: 28).

poignant counterpoint around Hazel's death that bravely incorporates her wasted life into a larger pattern. Within the wild freedoms of the commentary, he arranges his own still more gratuitous death to become part of a breathtakingly rich pattern. Perhaps from the other side of life any death, no matter how seemingly pointless, may become the center of a glittering web of meaning.

XV

Of course the more we accept Shade as the author of both poem and commentary, the less we can be sure that someone who has invented Zembla and his own murder has not already transformed the life he presents in the poem in order to make poem and commentary fit. The more autonomy we see in Shade the artist, the less distinct become the outlines of Shade the man. He begins, in other words, to grade into Nabokov.

Like Shade, Nabokov wishes to express in terms of fiction what he cannot express directly in a sober account of his own life: a confidence that through the magic mirror of his art he can somehow resolve the mystery of death that must otherwise remain impenetrable in life. Like Shade, too, he accepts the idea of worlds within worlds. He grants Shade the role of sober verse chronicler of his own life, assigns Kinbote the task of telling how Shade comes to collide fatally with Gradus, and then allots Shade the extra role of unseen creator of Kinbote and Gradus, unseen interpreter of death's design. He suggests that Shade, in acting as he does, in trying to understand death and the unknown forces beyond life by playing their own game, proves his aims close to those of *his* unseen maker, Nabokov, and then, on the last twist before the expanding spiral disappears from sight, Nabokov implies the hope that his own work in its turn may be somehow close to the aims of whatever mysterious forces lurk further beyond.

Kinbote's Zembla is the mad Botkin's attempt to cope with the misery of his isolation and exile. Shade's art is an attempt to cope with the apparent waste of his daughter's life—or of any life—in death. But in the relationship between poem and commentary Shade makes it plain that although his artistic concerns arise out of his own life, he has to transcend his own life to express all he wants. In canto 2, he imposes the discipline of his art on the tragedy of Hazel's death, but to satisfy his own hopes he has to invent Botkin-Kinbote's despair and his own gratuitous death. Beyond his two characters, Nabokov himself has to cope with both kinds of grief: the loss of Russia, and his father's pointless murder. Nabokov's feelings for Russia are plainly—albeit enchantedly—reflected in the looking-glass world of Zembla, but that he has constructed *Pale Fire* in an effort to make sense of a life in which something as tragic and absurd as his father's murder could happen must at first seem far less likely. A few historical facts should set doubts to rest. V. D. Nabokov's birthday was July 21, the day of Shade's murder. In that Berlin hall in 1922, the assassins Taboritsky and Shabelsky-Bork shot V. D. Nabokov through the heart, although they had planned to kill Milyukov,[21] just as Gradus or Grey intends to kill Kinbote or Goldsworth but certainly not the Shade whom he shoots through the heart. And after V. D. Nabokov died, it was one S. D. Botkin—like "Nabokov," "Botkin" is a distinguished Russian name—who succeeded him as the acknowledged head of Russian émigré organizations in Berlin.

Pale Fire is a dazzling technical tour de force, a comic delight, an imaginative treat, a study of life and death, sanity and madness, hope and despair, love and loneliness, privacy and sharing, kindness and selfishness, creativity and parasitism, and above all a thrilling ride of discovery. All the successive fictive levels that spin around Shade's death make *Pale Fire* an exhilarating intellectual feat, but the miracle of it all is that at the center of this book in which every fact seems radiant with multiple meaning lies the most grotesquely tragic moment of Nabokov's life. Out of that foul burst of chaos, he creates resplendent order.

CHAPTER 19

Mask and Man: Montreux, 1961–1964

I

A TRAIN from Zurich or Geneva passing through Montreux en route to the Simplon Pass and Italy climbs up from Lausanne for its first high glimpse of Lac Léman. Below, vineyards drop steeply down to the water. A dove-blue haze seems to thicken on the south, French, side of the lake, against the deep-blue bases of the Savoy Alps, which rise abruptly from the shore they overshadow. On the sunny north side the railroad dips down, below opulent homes positioned for the panorama, to skirt the shore, the gently rippling lake, a black swan, a cluster of coots quietly bobbing on the water. As the train climbs hillward and then dips shoreward again, the snow-capped molars of the Dents du Midi loom into view behind the upper Rhône valley at the end of the lake.

Mountains and lake settle into position for their most enchanting pose. A steamer cuts its silent swath in to shore. The region's old wealth, its vineyards that once descended to the shore, retreats before its new wealth, its mansions and apartments and hotels. "Prochain arrêt, Montreux," announces the conductor.

A minute later you emerge from the railway station onto the gray cobbles of the avenue des Alpes, and, crossing the road, patter down the Escalier de la Gare to reach the Grand-Rue, almost at lake level, where the town's main shopping street beckons to the tourists disgorged by the tour buses lining the other side of the road. Cross the Grand-Rue and then a narrow strip of public garden, and you stand on the quai lapped by Lake Geneva. Either way you turn, toward Rousseau's Clarens on the right or Byron's Chillon on the left, you can walk past trees of every kind and every climate, planted by a gardener of genius. Palms by the parapet thrive even under a short-lived winter coat of snow. Firs, elms, cypresses, ginkgos, paulownias, and cedars vie for attention with the mountains and lake in front or the mountains behind.

A quarter of a mile along to the right, the promenade passes by the gardens of the Montreux Palace Hotel. During the exceptionally mild fall of 1961, Nabokov had often sat on a bench there between hotel and lake, at the foot of a weeping cedar. With pencil poised above the stack of index cards that served as his portable desk, he would hesitate for a moment, scan the mountains across the lake for another phrase to confer on Kinbote, and write on, in "one of the most enchanting and inspiring gardens I know."[1]

The Montreux Palace itself would be Nabokov's home until his death. Its two wings run a whole block along the north side of the Grand-Rue, its kitchens extend back up to the avenue des Alpes. A hotel first arose on the site of the smaller wing in 1837. Rebuilt to its modern dimensions in 1865, this Hôtel du Cygne became part of the Montreux Palace when the main hotel was built in 1906.

For their first year in Montreux, the Nabokovs lived on the third floor of the old wing, in quarters that faced the lake, except for Nabokov's study, which faced north toward the graceful curves of nearby Mont Cubly and the peaks behind. Fanciful derivations of the town's name became one of the Nabokovs' standing jokes. Vladimir would maintain that Montreux was named Mont Roux in honor of Mont Cubly's russet autumnal coat. Not so, demurred Véra: the name must come from "montre," after the jewelers' shops on the Grand-Rue.[2]

At the beginning of their second year in the Palace the Nabokovs would move up to the sixth and topmost floor of the old wing, where their rooms occupied almost the whole lakeside frontage of the Hôtel du Cygne. Further from the street noise and with no footsteps thudding overhead, they liked their new quarters too much to move.

From the reception desk on the hotel's main floor radiate grand foyers and salons with high ceilings, gilt architraves, rows of chandeliers, wan fin de siècle murals. But this imposing decor provides no clue to the way the Nabokovs' rooms would remain until renovation in 1990: surprisingly modest and cramped, and furnished in the hotel's haphazard antiquated-eclectic style. Nabokov once described their suite:

> Our quarters consist of several tiny rooms with two and a half bathrooms, the result of two apartments having been recently fused. The sequence is: kitchen, living-dining room, my wife's room, my room, a former kitchenette now full of my papers, and our son's former room, now converted into a study [or rather, by the time of its conversion in the 1970s, an office for Nabokov's secretary]. The apartment is cluttered with books, folders, and files. What might be termed rather grandly a library is a back room housing my published works, and there are additional shelves in the attic whose skylight is much frequented by pigeons and Alpine choughs.[3]

Nabokov's narrow bedroom, which doubled as his study, overlooked the lake and the sun streaming onto it down the Rhône valley in the morning or reflected red on its surface as it sank beside the Dent d'Oche in the evening. Only that pool of constantly changing light below makes the room seem at all large enough to have satisfied a restless imagination for a decade and a half.

II

Why did the Nabokovs choose Switzerland? Their main reason for coming back to Europe at the end of 1960 had of course been to stay near their son in Milan, a distance of only a few hours' drive. Nabokov's sister, too, lived an hour away, in Geneva. Switzerland offered the alpine butterflies that were Nabokov's particular passion. The country was spectacularly beautiful, peaceful, and untroubled by the demonstrations and strikes and chaos that would have made Italy or France a nightmare for an author always anxious about his American and English publishing deadlines and the safe return of proofs. For pure efficiency, he could not have chosen better. One morning in Montreux he broke his lower dentures, mailed them to Lausanne at eleven o'clock in the morning, and received them back repaired at nine o'clock that evening.[4]

Why Montreux? The town, though small, serves a cosmopolitan world. Its location made it easy enough for publishers, editors, and agents to call, often en route from the Frankfurt Book Fair, while its small size helped minimize the intrusions of idly curious tourists. "I am an old man, very private in all my habits of life," Nabokov observed after more than ten years in Montreux, "who has preferred fruitful isolation in Switzerland to the stimulating but distracting atmosphere of America."[5] He had never quite planned to settle in Montreux, and did not quite realize he had done so until the late 1960s. It was simply that there was always another project requiring his immediate attention and never any pressing reason to move.

Why a hotel? Even in the 1920s, at one of Raisa Tarr's literary parties, Nabokov had answered, when asked where he would like to live, "In a large comfortable hotel." He knew clearly why he had never chosen to own a house, even in America: "The main reason, the background reason, is, I suppose, that nothing short of a replica of my childhood surroundings would have satisfied me. I would never manage to match my memories correctly—so why trouble with hopeless approximations?" And, he added, he did not much care "for furniture, for tables and chairs and lamps and rugs and things—

perhaps because in my opulent childhood I was taught to regard with amused contempt any too-earnest attachment to material wealth." Living in a hotel, he pointed out, "eliminates the nuisance of private ownership." Though he had never wanted to be severed from the things of his childhood, he never wanted to be attached to any other material possessions whatever. Apart from memories, he hoarded nothing, not even good books. A hotel life, he said, "confirms me in my favorite habit—the habit of freedom." It simplified postal matters; it ensured first-class service.[6]

Nabokov was an extremely generous tipper for whom doors always swung open. Not that he simply bought service; from an early age he had been taught never to be rude to servants and to treat people as individuals, not members of a class. Among his idiosyncrasies as an adult were his unusual alertness to the unique person occupying this or that position. He liked humor as an instrument for probing all kinds of people, a way of assessing their powers of observation and flexibility of mind. He played with everybody, hotel staff, publishers, friends, and he liked best those who played back. To some extent his playfulness was a shield for his own privacy as well as a delicate test of other people's character, but he also saw it as exercise for the imagination, balm for the spirit, and lubrication for smooth social contact. Certainly the Montreux Palace staff found him polite, cheerful, generous, open, amused, and interested in them as individuals. They adored him, and were quite surprised to discover that the outside world thought him aloof and remote.[7]

Of course there were reasons for the world's impression: his choice of Switzerland as a retreat, the majestic spectacle of the Montreux Palace Hotel, the preconditions he laid down for interviews: "Nowadays I take every precaution to ensure a dignified beat of the mandarin's fan. The interviewer's questions have to be sent to me in writing, answered by me in writing, and reproduced verbatim. Such are the three absolute conditions." Lifelong preferences drove him to impose these terms: his passion for accuracy; his sense of privacy, which dictated that casual chat should not become public fact; his distrust of his own impromptu powers of expression. But in the 1960s and 1970s, when he was simply "VN" to the literary world, he also chose to create in the Nabokov persona the image of someone immeasurably satisfied with himself and often immeasurably contemptuous of others. That daunting mask served as a protective mechanism—less extreme than J. D. Salinger's or Thomas Pynchon's rigorous reclusiveness—against the casually curious. The hotel staff could form a protective forward phalanx around him: "Mr. Nabokov's cables may be delivered only at *dix heures*, M'sieur."[8]

One aspect of his private life that he did divulge to reporters was a summary of his daily routine: "I awake around seven in winter: my alarm clock is an Alpine chough—big, glossy, black thing with big yellow beak—which visits the balcony and emits a most melodious chuckle. For a while I lie in bed mentally revising and planning things. Around eight: shave, breakfast, enthroned meditation, and bath—in that order." As his seventies approached he tended to sleep even less well than before and to rise even earlier, sometimes putting in five hours of writing in the morning. Before lunch, while the hotel's cleaning crew rampaged through their rooms, vacuum cleaners blaring, he would take time for a short stroll with Véra along the lake. He never had the least interest in the window-shopping the Grand-Rue offered: he might notice pedestrians or sound out the shopkeepers he had to deal with, but he had no curiosity about the goods on display. He preferred to stroll along the quay observing the birds, the trees, the water, the light, and perhaps a lady with her little dog. After the one occasion when he did make the mistake of entering a shop on impulse and buying some pearls, he turned his blunder into another standing joke: "I am going out. Can I bring you back something? Some bread? Milk? Pearls?"[9]

On weekdays a local woman, Mme Fürrer, came to make lunch at one o'clock. Nabokov would be back at his desk by one-thirty and work steadily until six-thirty. Normally he would have started the day in "the vertical position of vertebrate thought," standing "at a lovely old-fashioned lectern I have in my study. Later on, when I feel gravity nibbling at my calves, I settle down in a comfortable armchair alongside an ordinary writing desk; and finally, when gravity begins climbing up my spine, I lie down on a couch in a corner of my small study."[10]

At half past six he would stroll to one of the newspaper kiosks of the avenue des Alpes or another on the Grand-Rue for English papers. In his early twenties, terrified of losing his Russian in exile, he had studied Dahl's dictionary assiduously every day. Now in French-speaking Switzerland he regularly scanned through his Webster's, noting down curios like "kinbote," "versipel," "caruncle," "borborygmus," and "granoblastic." But he also kept up with current idioms as well as literary news through a generous diet of periodicals. His daily fare was the *New York Herald Tribune,* and he also read *Time, Newsweek,* the *Saturday Review,* the *New York Review of Books,* the *Spectator,* the *New Statesman,* the *Listener,* the *Times Literary Supplement,* the London Sunday papers, the *New Yorker, Esquire, Encounter,* and *Playboy.* He made a point of buying from three different newspaper vendors—he knew each of them by name—so that they could all benefit from his custom.[11]

Mme Fürrer returned again to prepare dinner, served punctually at seven. Nabokov would rarely work in the evening. Normally he would sit with Véra to enjoy the sunset, and perhaps play a game of chess. Only occasionally would he find his second wind and stand before his lectern to begin the cycle again. Otherwise, bed at nine, and reading: usually "several books at a time—old books, new books, fiction" (but never mysteries or historical novels), "nonfiction, verse, anything—and when the bedside heap of a dozen volumes or so has dwindled to two or three, which generally happens by the end of the week, I accumulate another pile." He would switch the light out at half past eleven, "and then tussle with insomnia till one a.m. About twice a week I have a good long nightmare with unpleasant characters imported from earlier dreams, appearing in more or less iterative surroundings—kaleidoscopic arrangements of broken impressions, fragments of day thoughts, and irresponsible mechanical images, utterly lacking any possible Freudian implication or explication."[12]

III

Daytime brought other nightmares. When Nabokov moved into the Montreux Palace late in 1961, he was able to concentrate intensely on *Pale Fire* after almost three years of being jostled about by fame. But once *Pale Fire* was completed, his first years in Montreux became a time of frustration. At Cornell at the beginning of the 1950s he had been irked by all he wanted to do and could not in the time left after teaching: finish his autobiography and *Lolita*, translate *Eugene Onegin*, turn new ideas into new stories. Now in the early sixties he had written *Lolita* and *Pale Fire*, *Speak, Memory* and *Eugene Onegin*, and he found himself thwarted in another sense by all he had already accomplished and the fame it had brought. By 1962 the immediate pressures of fame had eased—he no longer had to face interviews by the score—but long-term pressures took their place as publishers sought his old books in new translations, or reissues of his newer works with new forewords or new revisions, or new projects entirely.

As a rule Nabokov was an exceptionally prompt proofreader, but in the rush to finish *Pale Fire* he had delayed checking the last of the edited commentaries to his *Eugene Onegin*. After he had submitted *Eugene Onegin* to Bollingen a second time early in 1959, his book's progress was delayed for a year by inefficient preparation of copy on the part of an inexperienced member of the Bollingen staff. Another year and a half had passed as Bart Winer alternated his painstaking copyediting of Nabokov's four volumes with work on Kathleen Coburn's definitive edition of the complete Coleridge. At first curt with his copyeditor, Nabokov had soon realized Winer's experience and his zeal for detail were well worth the delay. Soon he was accepting more suggestions from Winer on *Eugene Onegin* than from any other editor he had had in the course of his career, and late in 1961 he had asked the Bollingen Press to devise a formula acknowledging his help. When the Bollingen office suggested thanking him for "a meticulous and intelligent job," Nabokov changed it to "meticulous and brilliant." Galleys of the commentary began to arrive by the end of 1961, but very slowly, and by early January 1962, four years after he had completed the book, Nabokov had become anxious at the accumulated delays and felt that his sense of the whole project was slipping away from him.[13]

The first two weeks of 1962 Nabokov spent correcting the French *Pnine*. For the next two months, until mid-March, he revised Michael Scammell's translation of the last four-fifths of *The Gift*, spending up to seven hours a day on the task.[14] At the same time he had *Pale Fire* proofs to attend to, and comments to offer Walter Minton on advertising the book. Minton felt it would help if he clarified and tabulated the Zembla theme. Nabokov was horrified. Véra wrote for him:

Vladimir is very happy about your plans for publicity but he is not at all happy about your suggestion to have "a cast of characters with the land of Zembla included and identified." Here are Vladimir's objections to it:

   1. The image of Zembla must creep up on the reader very gradually, which it starts to do early in the Commentary. Its abrupt revelation would destroy this thematic development.

   2. It would also throw the eerie Index completely out of balance.

   3. Since the entire book is supposed to be the production, without any editorial interference, of the mad commentator, he would hardly be likely to introduce such a cast of characters.

   4. Nobody knows, nobody should know—even Kinbote hardly knows—if Zembla really exists.

   5. Zembla and its characters should remain in a fluid misty condition and not be degraded to the rank of items in a directory.

   6. We do not even know whether Zembla is pure invention or a kind of lyrical simile to Russia. (Zembla: *Zemlya*)

   7. And perhaps *most* disastrous would be the effect of your suggestion on the last line of the book, its crucial line, its melting horizon, with its

suggestion of unfinished interrupted life, "Zembla, a distant northern land"—without any reference to verse or page.[15]

Some weeks later, Véra added: "He does not think you need worry too much about the identification of Zembla. Together with being completely articulate all art should leave a certain margin for the reader's imagination to get some exercise. 'A distant Northern land' has poetry, nostalgia, almost a heartbreaking sob in its sound. If we say 'a non-existent Northern land' it becomes a label on an empty bottle."[16]

Advance reports of Lolita had circulated for years before Putnam's published the American edition in 1958. Now Minton decided to try the reverse approach for Nabokov's new novel: no information would be released, except that the book's subject remained a closely guarded secret and reviewers were sent advance copies only after committing themselves to disclosing nothing before publication day. The strategy worked, and newspapers clamored for information.[17]

On February 20, Irving Lazar telephoned to report on the movie of Lolita. Since Nabokov disliked the telephone, especially long-distance calls, Véra answered. Lazar told her the picture was marvelous, Sue Lyon miraculous, James Mason excellent throughout, and Peter Sellers so good they had to add to his part. Adding to Vladimir's screenplay was exactly what they did not want, Véra replied. In fact, Kubrick had not only reworked Nabokov's script with James Harris but during rehearsals he had encouraged his actors to improvise lines, which he often retained in shooting. As James Mason commented, moreover, Kubrick "was so besotted with the genius of Peter Sellers that he seemed never to have enough of him."[18]

Moves were now afoot to have Roger Vadim direct Laughter in the Dark, in the hope that Brigitte Bardot would star. After Simone de Beauvoir's Brigitte Bardot and the Lolita Syndrome, Playboy asked Nabokov to write an article on Bardot. Nabokov was chary of Playboy, which had published Girodias's memoir "Pornologist on Olympus" the previous year and had not printed his own denial quickly enough for his liking. He also pointed out that although he was flattered by their confidence in his versatility, he had never seen Bardot either on the screen or in life, and the entire project had no interest for him.[19]

In March he saw one of the very few movies he sought out in the nearly twenty years of his final European period: Robbe-Grillet's L'Année dernière à Marienbad, a film that delighted him not so much by its labyrinthine compulsiveness as by its originality and its romanticism.[20]

Between April 9 and 13, the Nabokovs made a short trip to Cannes to look at some land they might have bought but decided against. On their return they learned that *Lolita*'s premiere would take place in New York in June. They had been anxious to see the movie for almost a year, and Nabokov announced he would be present at the first showing even if it took place in the Antarctic. He reserved a cabin on the *Queen Elizabeth* at once.[21]

Early in May, with *Pale Fire* just published at the end of April and the *Lolita* movie imminent, *Newsweek* interviewed him in depth in Montreux for a cover story. *Pale Fire* would occasion a wide range of reactions, from the perplexed to the ecstatic. The most remarkable and influential was Mary McCarthy's "Bolt from the Blue." McCarthy felt and conveyed the excitement of discovery Nabokov can generate, but became overintoxicated in tracking down the novel's literary allusions, and introduced a great many irrelevant ingenuities of her own. (Nabokov noted that "90% of her symbols were not fathered by me.") She ended by proclaiming the book "one of the very great works of art of this century."[22]

Pale Fire's double authorship and the suspicion that Kinbote might be a mask for Shade or Shade for Kinbote combined with the first sentence of Nabokov's *Lolita* postscript* to launch the first of the attribution jokes that became more and more unfunny as the 1960s wore on. Translator Michael Scammell suggested in print that Mary McCarthy was just a front for Nabokov; Herbert Gold that the name Scammell in turn was the master's mask. Over the next few years when A. Alvarez, Alfred Appel, Conrad Brenner, Alan Brien, Andrew Field, Carl Proffer, and Edmund Wilson wrote on Nabokov, they were all declared to be Nabokov pseudonyms. This increasingly depressing ritual was redeemed only by Nabokov fan Martin Gardner, who in his *Ambidextrous Universe* attributed the poem "Pale Fire" solely to John Shade, as if Nabokov had never existed. In *Ada*, Nabokov returned the compliment: " 'Space is a swarming in the eyes, and Time a singing in the ears,' says John Shade, a modern poet, as quoted by an invented philosopher ('Martin Gardner') in *The Ambidextrous Universe*, page 165."[23]

IV

On May 31, the Nabokovs boarded the *Queen Elizabeth* in Cherbourg. Expecting that they might return to America for good early in 1963, they had scheduled only a two-week stop in New York. On the voy-

---

* "After doing my impersonation of suave John Ray, the character in *Lolita* who pens the Foreword, any comments coming straight from me may strike one—may strike me, in fact—as an impersonation of Vladimir Nabokov talking about his own book."

age over Nabokov recorded in his diary details of light and water that would prove useful in *Ada* and continued to correct proofs of *Eugene Onegin*, just as Van would work on proofs during Lucette's last voyage.

Nabokov disembarked on June 5 and stayed at the St. Regis Hotel on Fifth Avenue for two "very busy, very amusing, very tiring" weeks in New York, starting with a solid bank of interviewers the day he landed. He deposited his rare Chapman's Hairstreaks at the American Museum of Natural History. He saw friends, lawyers, and publishers, notably William McGuire of Bollingen Press. He dined with Stanley Kubrick, Sue Lyon, and James Mason.[24]

After an advertising campaign featuring the famous photographs of Sue Lyon in bikini and with lollipop and heart-shaped sunglasses, *Lolita* opened on June 13 at Loew's State on Times Square. Nabokov arrived at the gala premiere in a limousine, "as eager and innocent as the fans who peered into my car hoping to glimpse James Mason but finding only the placid profile of a stand-in for Hitchcock." He had in fact seen the film at a private screening a few days before, where he had discovered "that Kubrick was a great director, that his *Lolita* was a first-rate film with magnificent actors, and that only ragged odds and ends of my script had been used." Before Kubrick he concealed his disappointment, pronouncing it a great film and Sue Lyon marvelous: "There are even some things in it I wish were in the book" (he had in mind especially the ping-pong game between Sellers and Mason at the beginning of the film).[25] Acting and directing were superb, and the scenes of the murder, of Charlotte angling for Humbert, and of Humbert's visit to married Dolly Schiller worked magnificently. But with Sue Lyon looking seventeen and Humbert's passion for nymphets entirely omitted, the film lost all the tension and horror of the novel. Under the eye-catching photos of Sue Lyon and the lollipop had appeared the question: "How did they ever make a movie of *Lolita*?" Critics answered: "They didn't."[26] Audiences recognized as much, and after the first few weeks box-office returns dropped sharply. Years later Kubrick himself confessed: "Had I realized how severe the [censorship] limitations were going to be, I probably wouldn't have made the film." He also named the film his only manifest failure, and explained it by the fact that the book was simply too good to adapt for the screen.[27] Nabokov's own unpublished comments on the film's relation to the novel sum it all up: "a lovely misty view seen through mosquito netting," or, less gently, "a scenic drive as perceived by the horizontal passenger of an ambulance."[28]

V

Sailing from New York on June 20 on board the *Queen Elizabeth*, Nabokov gathered more ideas that would find their way into *Ada*'s shipboard scenes.* Six days later he was back in the Montreux Palace. Summers are noisy and restless in Montreux as tourists arrive by the busload, the trainload, the boatload, and the Nabokovs regularly escaped into the mountains. This year they tried Saas-Fee, but found it so unappealing they moved the next day, July 2, to Zermatt. Charmed by the ban on automobiles and the horses-and-buggies for hire in their stead, they decided to stay at the Hôtel Mont Cervin until August.[29]

Net in hand, Nabokov would set off at a quarter to eight in the morning and choose one of four or five possible trails. Depending on the weather, his hike could last from three to five hours and cover fifteen kilometers. In high summer he would often start off on a cable car or his favorite, a chairlift, precursor of *Ada*'s jikkers (magic carpets): "I find enchanting and dreamy in the best sense of the word to glide in the morning sun from valley to timberline in that magic seat, and watch from above my own shadow—with the ghost of a butterfly net in the ghost of a fist—as it keeps gently ascending in sitting profile along the flowery slope below, among dancing Ringlets and skimming Fritillaries." Sometimes he might spend two or three hours in the same meadow waiting for a particular butterfly, then after the day's chase head back downhill, perhaps stopping at a friendly little inn for a drink.[30]

Early in July, Nabokov heard to his amusement and amazement that *Pale Fire* had reached the bottom of the best-seller list, aided no doubt by his face on the cover of *Newsweek* in every magazine stand in America. In mid-July a BBC television crew came to film him for the program "The Bookman." The crew of six spent two days following him all over Zermatt, mostly in horse-cabs, packing and unpacking and repositioning camera and microphones to capture the Matterhorn in the background as he caught butterflies and talked. Droves of tourists followed the spectacle. What did they make of Nabokov, in baggy shorts and bare chest, smiling as he announced: "I am not

---

* For instance, he noted in his diary: "From Games Deck he trained a telescope on letter being written on Sun Deck." In *Ada*, part 3, chapter 5, Van looks for Lucette: "She was not on the Games Deck from where he looked down at some other redhead, in a canvas chair on the Sun Deck: the girl sat writing a letter at passionate speed and he thought that if ever he switched from ponderous factitude to light fiction he would have a jealous husband use binoculars to decipher from where he stood that outpour of illicit affection."

a Western Union messenger, I do not send any messages, I do not deal in general ideas, I am not a general"?[31]

As usual, Elena Sikorski came to join her brother and sister-in-law for part of the summer. So did Nabokov's old schoolmate Samuil Rosoff, his best friend at St. Petersburg's Tenishev School. Although they had exchanged warm letters in the 1930s, they had not seen each other since 1919. To their delight they found themselves as close as ever, and Nabokov declared the reunion "a complete victory over time." While Rosoff was there, photographer Horst Tappe followed Nabokov over scree and mountain meadow and was rewarded by a famous image: Nabokov grinning from under the raindrops on his parka hood, fit, relaxed, and benign in his happy hunting ground.[32]

Early in August the Nabokovs drove down, via Montreux and Grenoble, to Cannes, stopping en route for a day of excellent butterfly collecting at Gap in the Hautes-Alpes. After the larches of Zermatt, they would spend a month under the shade of the olives at Castellaras above Cannes, where they had rented a house. They had thought of buying some land in a new development there, where the Ustinovs were planning to build a house, but they discovered it to be a sort of kibbutz for millionaires, where the old idlers who sat on park benches discussed the rise and fall of their shares. The Nabokovs had not been in the Riviera in the summer since 1939 and could not believe how crowded and charmless it had become. When they did venture down to the sea, Nabokov reported to Herbert Gold, with a squeamish shudder, "we find the water glazed with the various ointments of innumerable and rather repulsive bodies contaminating the coast." They left with no regrets.[33]

VI

Back in the Montreux Palace on September 15, they moved into the sixth-floor rooms that would become their permanent quarters: much less spacious but also less costly, and with a still more magnificent view over the lake. Although it was not a home where they could be completely *chez eux*, it had too many advantages for them to think of moving, and they decided to remain all through 1963, provided it would not affect their United States citizenship.[34]

In August, Dmitri had come down with a mysterious and alarming affliction, a painful swelling in the joints that would take months to diagnose and a year and a half to recede completely. His father also had another reason to be worried. After almost two years at the printers', *Eugene Onegin*'s galley proofs still remained unfinished. Everything had conspired to impede progress: the printers had settled on a distinguished but rare typeface which they had taken a long time to deliver, they had to cope with recruiting problems, they had had to delay while moving their premises, they had found themselves with a strike on their hands. One typesetter had been at work for so many years on nothing but the *Onegin* project that he had become known on the shop floor simply as "Dr. Onegin." Late in September 1962, Nabokov wrote to William McGuire that "the sense of losing contact with my own EO is excruciating, especially since I am unable to postpone much longer my next work."[35]

By October, Dmitri's illness was in remission and he had found another way to cause his parents anxiety. Always a keen and precipitate driver, he now began to race the Triumph TR 3A he had bought in 1959 and had had modified for competition. Unfortunately for his parents, a fifth and a third place in his first two races confirmed his zeal. His parents had a more timid new venture of their own: they bought the only piece of land they would ever own,* a small plot of a thousand square meters in the village of Les Diablerets in the Bernese Alps, forty minutes' drive from Montreux. Their land adjoined a much larger plot the Ustinovs had bought: since they were unused to such a purchase, Peter Ustinov felt, they had needed someone else to lead the way. Although the Ustinovs built on their land, the Nabokovs never erected the summer chalet they had dimly envisioned on theirs.[36]

Late in October, George Weidenfeld visited Montreux, as he often would after the Frankfurt Book Fair. By now he had a good sense of Nabokov:

> He was subtle, he was oblique, he was self-mocking and testing all the time; but he was a warm friend. . . . He had a marvellous freshness in getting to the point of people, and a marvellous memory. He'd say, do you remember so-and-so who you brought to lunch nine years ago, and he would repeat every detail of a conversation, recalling the colour of a person's dress, the way she tilted her head or pursed her lips or wrote imaginary calligraphic signs in the air.[37]

On this visit Nabokov and Weidenfeld agreed on two projects: a reissue of *Speak, Memory* with a new foreword, and a book on *The Butterflies of Europe*, a complete catalogue of all the butterflies of Europe west of Russia, with color photographs of all species and the main

---

* Apart from the patch of land they purchased near Kolberg in Germany in 1929, which they soon had to forfeit.

subspecies, and notes by Nabokov on classification, habitat, and behavior.[38]

Nabokov's American publisher had a bright thought of his own. Since Michael Scammell's translation of *The Defense* was now complete, and since *The Gift* had not yet been set in type, perhaps the more accessible and the more humanly endearing of the two novels should appear first. No, answered Nabokov, who had recently checked the translation of *The Gift* but had not yet reread *The Defense* and tended to disparage most of his early fiction until he found himself pleasantly surprised on rereading it. *The Gift* was unquestionably his greatest novel in Russian, he declared, and more important by far than *The Defense*, which was written before he had found and completely realized his artistic self.[39]

VII

Montreux had produced another exceptionally warm and sunny fall. After the doctor advised him not to give up exercise during the winter, Nabokov and his wife "trotted" every morning along the promenade, thankful that swans were almost the only onlookers. The new regimen did not last long.[40]

Nabokov's work load that fall was still more exceptional than the weather. For once he had no urgent deadlines, and with time on his hands he decided he would like to undertake the index to *Eugene Onegin*. "An index to a work like this," he wrote to William McGuire, "should reflect its virtues and its shortcomings, its tone and personality (as I have proved in *Pale Fire*). It should be an afterglow and not a yawn."[41] McGuire and Bart Winer, aware of the rich strain of madness and wild humor running through *Pale Fire*'s index, were understandably alarmed, but Nabokov did not wait for their reaction, and worked throughout November on the task. By December 1 he had completed the index, filling with his six-by-four-inch cards three giant sixteen-inch shoe boxes, and had begun to check and correct.

Meanwhile the printers had drawn to William McGuire's attention that Nabokov's latest additions overlapped and cut across previous proof changes. Nabokov sighed that they were "symptoms of a growing dullness of mind on my part in regard to my own work which was finished, as you know, almost five years ago. I cannot sufficiently stress the importance of speeding up publication."[42]

Bollingen flew Bart Winer from London on December 14 to ensure that Nabokov was not marring a serious scholarly work with a frivolous index. They need not have worried: Nabokov's only concern was to ensure the index's scholarly thoroughness and accessibility for English- and Russian-language readers alike. He aimed to provide in the index the full first name and patronymic for all Russians mentioned, although in the text he had preferred to omit patronymics so as to avoid disconcerting English readers; and to record every title or first line of a Russian work three times, once in Russian, once in English, and once in Russian again under the author's name.[43]

In Montreux, Winer directed his astute gaze at more than textual detail. He was amazed at the relationship between the Nabokovs: "When you were in their presence the love flowing from one to another was the most extraordinary thing. I've never seen love like that before." Véra was the only person who could correct her husband, the one whose word he would take over any Russian critics. "*Priyatel'* " he had translated "pal" rather than the more usual "friend," a choice many reviewers would object to. Nabokov turned to Véra for support. "You're wrong," she told him, in a firm, steamroller tone, and he looked suitably flattened—but kept his choice.

Winer discovered Nabokov's dislike for people who saw things in general terms and neglected the particular. As they strolled along the promenade one day, Nabokov pointed out a bird on the water: the crested grebe. "Oh yes," said Winer, without interest, and carried on with the conversation. Nabokov was put out, but turned his annoyance to amusement and instruction by signing his next letters to Winer "the Crested Grebe."[44]

From as early as 1955, Nabokov had worried that his *Eugene Onegin* findings might be preempted by other scholars. Now almost five years after completing the project, he had heard that a graduate student in New York was working on a comparative study of English and Russian prosody. Winer sensed the depth of his concern, and recommended to Bollingen that as compensation for their long delay they immediately produce an offprint from the corrected plates and distribute it privately and for free. Two hundred copies of the separatum were run off in the spring of 1963.[45]

Another kind of "separatum" Nabokov could publish for much better financial returns. He had had a first-reading agreement with the *New Yorker* for decades, but had not published anything there since 1957, and no fiction since 1955. Although the magazine's policy was to publish no translations and nothing that had been published before in any form, Nabokov asked at the end of 1962 if they would like to see his Russian stories. When the *New Yorker* said yes, he sent Dmitri's translation of "Terra Incognita," which was accepted at once.[46] During 1963 and 1964, Nabokov published in the *New Yorker* more Russian stories, excerpts from *The Gift*, and all of *The Defense*, the first time the magazine had ever accepted a complete novel.

VIII

In the late fall of 1962, Dmitri had hoped his father might be able to buy him a new car to race, but his illness returned and this time was diagnosed as Reiter's syndrome. He spent January and February 1963 in a clinic in Zurich. During January his father heavily revised the translation of *Eugene Onegin* that he had thought finished in 1957. He wrote to McGuire in explanation: "That little virgin has been left too long with the shipwrecked sailor on Christmas Island, and in result the beautiful and once intact page proofs of my translation of the poem have undergone a number of changes." In fact, the changes were very heavy, and set back the book's production schedule still further, especially as all the cross-references in the thousand pages of commentary had to be altered to match the new translation. Two weeks into the year, Nabokov complained that he was "swamped, flooded, overrun and ravaged by proofreading my huge *The Gift* . . . and my infinite *Eugene Onegin*."[47]

Searching for relief from these chores, he thought of writing new chapters for *Speak, Memory*, and to Véra's regret became more and more fascinated by the *Butterflies of Europe* project. At the end of January he found another diversion. His brother's and sister's attempts to translate *Lolita* into Russian had appalled him, and he now began to translate the first few chapters of the novel into Russian for his friend Roman Grynberg to include in his literary miscellany *Vozdushnye puti* (*Aerial Ways*). He wrote to Grynberg that when he switched from Russian to English, it was like a champion ice skater's switch from blades to rollers: "Now I am writing something in Russian for you, and the reverse transition, from asphalt to ice, is terrible." He soon found himself liking the new rhythms, however, and became so carried away that he did not cease until he had put in three weeks of intense work. In the second week of February he stopped with sixty pages translated and the intention of completing the task sooner or later. To ward off the day "some oaf within or without Russia will translate and publish the book," he would do the whole thing himself.[48]

Throughout February he also checked Dmitri's translation of *The Eye*. On February 13, after leaving *Lolita*, he picked up his old notes on *The Nature of Time* and began to develop further his story, half romance, half philosophical meditation. To this profusion of his own projects—*Eugene Onegin, The Gift, The Eye,* the Russian *Lolita, The Nature of Time*—more was added when a man named René Micha visited to discuss a Nabokov number for his periodical *L'Arc.* For this special issue Véra began to compile a bibliography of her husband's works. Meanwhile, in Germany, Dieter Zimmer was translating Nabokov's autobiography. His publisher, Ledig Rowohlt, had noticed how much effort Zimmer had put into compiling a Nabokov bibliography for his own use, and suggested it appear as a supplement to *Speak, Memory.* In America, Nabokov was nominated for an Academy Award for the *Lolita* screenplay, for which he had received sole credit, and in mid-March *Playboy* sent Alvin Toffler (of future *Future Shock* fame) over for a long interview that he refined with Nabokov until they had perfected the illusion of spontaneity.[49]

The Nabokovs had been thinking of buying some land in Sardinia. Now a friend of a friend invited them to stay in his large, half-renovated ex-convent at Calenzana on Corsica. They headed off in mid-April by train and steamer, and spent a week on the island to see if they might want to settle there. Nabokov was delighted to discover how many Corsican butterfly races looked like species distinct from their Continental counterparts, and how many Corsican subspecies were the most striking representatives of their species.[50]

Back in Montreux at the end of the month, he found other projects in motion. After reviewing numerous sample translations of *Pale Fire* submitted to him by Gallimard, he at last found one to satisfy him. About to leave Montreux for the summer, he asked William McGuire if the edited *Onegin* index was ready: "This question is prompted not by natural curiosity, but by the anxious and dreadful thought that if not, I shall have to travel from alp to alp with three enormous, stone-heavy cartons of index cards (without which I cannot check the Index) in the boot of my car or in the rucksack-encumbered vestibules of funiculaires."[51]

One project at least had come to fruition. *The Gift* had waited fifteen years between composition and first complete publication in Russian. Now at the end of May it appeared in English, with more translated novels waiting in the wings. Advertised as "the greatest Russian novel to appear in the last fifty years," its appearance confirmed the depth and range of Nabokov's talent. A *New York Herald Tribune* review was not atypical: "As if we all didn't know, there is a giant among us. . . . That one man could write *The Real Life of Sebastian Knight, Lolita,* and *Pale Fire* seems extraordinary, but that the same fellow could also turn out *Pnin, Conclusive Evidence,* and *The Gift* is not only almost incredible but downright annoying. . . . One almost wishes he would go away, or have lived a hundred years ago."[52]

IX

On the day *The Gift* was published in America, May 27, the Nabokovs drove up the Valais to Loèche-les-Bains (Leukerbad), where Dmitri was spending the summer at the Rheumaklinik. His parents stayed at the Hotel Bristol, which like the local weather proved anything but grand. They had hoped to travel around Switzerland in their Peugeot, perhaps to St. Moritz, but the doctors' reports on Dmitri made them reluctant to move anywhere before mid-July, when they had reserved hotel rooms in Les Diablerets. Once again summer proved a time for visitors—Nabokov's sister Elena, George Hessen, Raisa Tatarinov—and some good lepping in the Pfynwald, a small forest near Süsten, which Nabokov would commemorate in *Ada*.[53]

Dmitri joined his parents after they moved to the Grand Hotel in Les Diablerets, and Véra's cousin Anna Feigin and sister Sonia Slonim followed to fill out the family. Nabokov had little luck with the weather, and thus a good deal of time for literary chores. After quickly checking the initial installment of the edited *Onegin* index, he wanted to continue. To William McGuire he emitted a self-mockingly eloquent but nonetheless earnest wail: "It would be a pity if the serenity of my relations with the Bollingen Series should be obscured by pre-auroral cloudlets just as the sun of publication day is about to rise; but I must really urge you to do your utmost to have that sluggish sun rise—to haul it up with pullies, or yank it out with hooks, if need be—but to have it emerge at last." The final part of the index arrived, he checked it, he returned it, and a new worry arose. Bollingen's lawyers wanted him to tone down his outbursts against translators and adaptors who had perverted Pushkin. In a letter signed "Vladimir Adamant Nabokov" he emphatically objected to deleting his epithets: "This is a matter of principle. Omitting them would mean admitting censorship—and censorship is the villain of my book. If a paraphrase is ridiculous and if an illustration is monstrous, I will say so." As he pointed out, three of his recurrent targets were dead, and "the dead cannot take legal action against the quick."[54]

Nabokov returned to Montreux on August 19. He was to have traveled to London at the beginning of September for a television interview with Jacob Bronowski and perhaps a thorough look at the British Museum's collection of European butterflies, but to cap off a not very happy summer Dmitri's illness suddenly took a turn for the worse, and he was readmitted to the Rheumaklinik at the Zurich Cantonal Hospital.[55]

Time-Life had asked Nabokov for an introduction for a new edition of *Bend Sinister*, which he composed in the first week of September. To George Weidenfeld he wrote that he was keener than ever to tackle the butterfly book once his current projects were finished. He expected to feature color photographs of about 2,000 specimens (male, female, and underside). After mailing his last *Eugene Onegin* corrections at the end of September, he sat down to test the arrangement of specimens on the plates. Over the next six weeks he drew 2,000 outline figures on eighty thirteen-by-ten-inch plates. Later he would have to add more than half as much again, and had the project not been called off in 1965 it would no doubt have continued to expand like *Eugene Onegin*, whose proofs he was still checking even now, thirteen years after he had declared that the translation and commentary would take him one year.[56]

At the same time as he began the butterfly-book plates he also started to correct Michael Scammell's translation of *The Defense*, practically rewriting entire paragraphs. Only at the end of November did he finish at last this "oppressive task." While working on butterflies and chess, he perceived in a delightful flash an entire new novel he would in fact never write: "The biography of a practical joker. Some of the tricks are purely psychological and very subtle. But there is also that false member. He stages one day an elaborate illusion of his own death but accidentally dies in the process. And *The Life of a Practical Joker* is only the illusion of a biography." After finishing the butterfly plates in mid-November, Nabokov revised Dmitri's translation of the story "Lik" and, with Véra's help, turned next to revising the German translation of *Speak, Memory*.[57]

X

Politics normally caused Nabokov simply to step aside, but when politics threatened to implicate him, he would make a point of announcing his sidestep. Early in December he sent René Micha a statement to print in the Nabokov special issue of *L'Arc*:

> It is not my custom to display my political credo. Nevertheless a certain sympathy for Castro that I believe I detected in the Cuba issue of *L'Arc* forces me in this issue to make a little clarification of my principles. I do not care a fig for politics as such. I despise all force which strikes at liberty of thought. I am against any dictatorship, right or left, terrestrial or

celestial, white, grey or black, pink, red or purple, Ivan the Terrible or Hitler, Lenin, Stalin or Khrushchyev, Trujillo or Castro. I accept only governments that let the individual say what he likes.[58]

René and Ghislaine Micha were deeply upset. They regarded L'Arc as an apolitical cultural review, and thought his manifesto would make it political. If they had a limited political interest, they wrote Nabokov, they would not be publishing a special issue on him, whose works they had both loved for twenty-five years. Nabokov was charmed and mollified by their reply, but wrote: "You tell me that I put L'Arc in an impossible situation; but the situation in which the Cuban issue has placed me is no laughing matter either. You tell me that my publisher Gallimard has published authors of very diverse political views; agreed, but a publishing house is a grand hotel, Place de la Gare, where one doesn't worry about one's neighbor, whereas a review is a salon where everyone remembers yesterday's guest." He suggested as a compromise that they print his note without the first two sentences, and they agreed.[59]

More familiar to English-speaking readers than this politically sensitive Nabokov was the Nabokov persona of his forewords and interviews. On December 15, he composed the foreword to The Defense, where he wrote that he would

> like to spare the time and effort of hack reviewers—and, generally, persons who move their lips when reading and cannot be expected to tackle a dialogueless novel when so much can be gleaned from its Foreword— by drawing their attention to the first appearance of the frosted-window theme (associated with Luzhin's suicide, or rather sui-mate) as early as Chapter Eleven, or the pathetic way my morose grandmaster remembers his professional journeys not in terms of sunburst luggage labels and magic-lantern shots but in terms of the tiles in different hotel bathrooms and corridor toilets.*

He then proceeded to list several evocative scenes of Luzhin amidst tiles, none of them in fact in the novel: a trap for idle reviewers. While some reviewers indeed fell into the trap, a number of others objected to the contempt behind "persons who move their lips when reading."

Nabokov's forewords are both extremely helpful and as weirdly deceptive as his novels themselves and, as he saw it, the world of nature. He would offer as clues what turned out to be new puzzles, or disclose genuine clues to subtly camouflaged patterns while feign-

---

* In his own tiled bathroom in the Montreux Palace, Nabokov kept a chessboard, with chessmen in place, beside the toilet.

ing irrelevant patter or obstructive pronouncements. His forewords formed part of the irascible and arrogant Nabokov persona, in part a game, a parody, a running joke, in part a means of deterring the curiosity-seekers who might think they could intrude on his time simply because he had become famous.

Nabokov certainly did like his own work and turned that into a jest in itself, as in *The Defense*'s foreword ("this attractive novel") or the covering note he sent Minton: "I am enclosing with this letter one of my racy introductions which, I am sure, you will not fail to enjoy as much as I have writing it." But his protective public persona was not the real Nabokov. His German publisher Ledig Rowohlt, a keen reader and translator of American fiction, once wrote: "I have met many famous American authors as different from one another as Dos Passos, Faulkner, Hemingway, Updike, Wolfe, but never encountered with any of them such warmth and simple friendliness, so much understanding and self-assured lack of ostentation" as with Nabokov. In private life Nabokov was kind, courteous, "the ultimate gentleman." He liked people who were honest, kind, observant, and endowed with a sense of humor, from whatever walk of life they came. He could appreciate "the observant and intelligent people who bring me fruit and wine, or come to repair radiators and radios."[60]

XI

But he also demanded the highest standards of those who did choose to engage in pursuits of the mind. On December 16 he began to write his devastating review of Walter Arndt's rhymed translation of *Eugene Onegin*.[61]

Nabokov would have had reason for anger of a personal and competitive kind at Arndt's translation. He had begun his own translation in 1950 and completed it in 1957, the year that Arndt began his version, and yet Arndt's appeared before his. Arndt had sent him samples in 1957 and 1959, and Nabokov had commented frankly then on the blunders in Arndt's Russian and his knowledge of the literary and historical background, on the betrayals forced by rhyme, on the nonequivalence of the same metrical pattern in Russian and English. But now Arndt's published version mentioned Nabokov's name in the preface and in the blurb in such a way that it could be construed that he endorsed the translation. To make matters worse, Nabokov, who because of the demands he placed on his own translation had waited nearly six years since he first gave the Bollingen Press his version, now learned that Arndt's translation had been awarded, by people unconnected with the Press, the Bollingen Prize in Translation.[62]

Many would think Nabokov's review of Arndt a mercilessly cruel attack by a man who could never brook competition. In fact, Nabokov was far too self-assured to think of Arndt as a competitor in his knowledge of Russian, or English, or Pushkin, or the art of poetry. He saw himself—correctly, I think—as rightly indignant in Pushkin's defense. After all, Arndt did betray Pushkin's sense and style line after line, and to expose the betrayal Nabokov needed do little more than use Arndt's errors against him.

Certainly Nabokov was as unforgiving of scholarly error as he was unsparing of lapses from his standards of artistic truth, but rivalry will not explain his rigor. Although he could completely dismiss writers like Balzac, Dostoevsky, Mann, and Faulkner, he could also praise others like Flaubert, Tolstoy, Kafka, and Joyce, whom he thought far above the challenge of those he dismissed, and he had no doubts about which group he belonged to. Just as he could extol a few fellow novelists, so too he could be generous to a few translators or scholars working in his fields. In the early 1940s, some time after he had begun to write his *Nikolay Gogol* book with the intention of denouncing English translations of Gogol and offering his own instead, Nabokov had discovered the new translations of *Dead Souls*, *The Inspector General*, and "The Overcoat" by Bernard Gilbert Guerney, and called the first "an extraordinarily fine piece of work," and all three "excellently rendered."[63] When he reviewed Higgins and Riley's *Field Guide to the Butterflies of Britain and Europe* in 1970, after having set aside for the moment his own *Butterflies of Europe*, he pointed out flaws in their book but hailed it as "marvelous" and ended on this note: "The feat of assembling all those Spanish and African beauties in one book is not the least glory of Higgins' and Riley's unique and indispensable manual."[64] When Nabokov attacked Arndt, he did so not because Arndt had translated Pushkin as well in his way as Nabokov had done himself, but because still another rhymester had mutilated Pushkin.

At the end of 1963, Nabokov's own *Butterflies of Europe* was becoming more and more ambitious. He planned to have all the species represented by butterflies from the original type locality, so that all the Linnaean species, for instance, would be illustrated by Swedish specimens. When necessary he would also have certain species represented in different seasonal variations. After his first main run through all the species at the end of December 1963, he had decided on 310 species represented on 88 plates. By June 1965 he would have

346 species and about 800 subspecies represented by about 3,000 specimens on 128 plates.[65]

XII

During the first week of January, Nabokov began checking the French *La Défense Loujine*, translated by his friends Evgenia and René Cannac.[66] The easy relations he could have with them were not the norm. He expected from his translators the same unstinting accuracy and complete comprehension that had been his own standard in translating *Eugene Onegin*, and at the same time he reserved the right to make minor adjustments for a new audience, to provide English or French allusions in place of the original Russian or English ones, or to clarify local details about émigré life for an English and American audience or about American life for a French one. Even when he pointed out very courteously the inaccuracies he wanted eliminated, translators—especially in France—often resented the interference as a challenge to their competence. One example of his difficulties with translators will have to stand for many.

He had begun checking the French *Pale Fire* in October 1963 and would not finish until January 1965. Early in January 1964, he received an arrogant, hostile, and imperceptive letter from one of the two translators, Maurice Edgar Coindreau, who spoke also on behalf of his colleague Raymond Girard. Although Nabokov always decided on exactly the phrasing he wanted in English translations of his books, whether the translation was wholly his own or based on Dmitri's or another professional translator's work, he was quite modest in the case of French translations, never insisting on a particular French phrase but only on the English meaning: "I am only giving the sense, not the best French." Coindreau and Girard had to accept Nabokov's corrections when their understanding of the English was evidently faulty. They had rendered the phrase "Stormcoated, I strode in" as "J'entrai à la maison comme un ouragan." Nabokov commented: "No, no: 'stormcoat' is a warm coat, furlined and belted. The sense is: 'j'entrai dans la chambre sans enlever ma pelisse.' " But in other cases they repeatedly refused to believe that they had not rendered the English accurately.[67]

Coindreau told Nabokov he was wrong to object to their translation of his "shagbark" (hickory). Nabokov had written that *noyer* was impossible; Coindreau insisted that their version was correct "because hickory belongs to the walnut (*noyer*) family. See Webster." Nabokov replied: "You tell me that according to Webster *hickory* belongs

to the *walnut family*. Quite right, but you have confused family and
genus. To translate *hickory* by 'noyer' is every bit as strange as translating . . . 'cat' by *tiger* and *jaguar* by 'lynx' because all four are in the
family *Felidae!*" "That tree must stay," he added. "The description
which follows in the text does not fit a noyer!" Of course he is right.
The unusual precision of his description would be nonsensical applied to any other tree:

> I had a favorite young shagbark there
> With ample dark jade leaves and a black, spare,
> Vermiculated trunk. The setting sun
> Bronzed the black bark, around which, like undone
> Garlands, the shadows of the foliage fell.
> It is now stout and rough; it has done well.

Coindreau and Girard adopted the translation "jeune hickory."[68]

Nabokov took care to make things as comprehensible to a French
audience as to his original American one. When his translators had
rendered "Old Faithful" as "Fidèle," he commented: "Old Faithful is
the nickname of a geyzer in Wyoming, a punctual old thing: 'Vieux
geyser fidèle.' " Some of his glosses for translators are invaluable for
readers in any language. Fondly contemplating suicide, Kinbote says
"no wonder one weighs in one's palm with a dreamy smile the compact firearm in its case of suede leather hardly bigger than a castle-
gate key or a boy's seamed purse." Noticing that "a boy" had been
rendered in French into the neutral "un enfant," Nabokov proposed
instead " 'le petit sac couturé d'un bambin' (or better) 'le scrotum
d'un garconnet' (Dr. Kinbote is not a nice person)."[69]

XIII

Edmund and Elena Wilson arrived in Montreux on January 11, 1964,
for a three-day visit with the Nabokovs. It was the first time they had
met since 1957, and the last time they would ever meet. Since *Lolita*'s
publication their correspondence, once so lively, had tapered off to a
mere ten letters in almost six years, but in person there seemed no
sign of any cooling in their relationship. Ledig and Jane Rowohlt,
who were also visiting the Nabokovs at the time, were entranced by
the sparking spectacle the two men provided: "The conversational
fireworks . . . on the virtues of literature, ending in a mock-serious
dispute about the virtues of their respective razors."[70] Not, *this* time,
the cutthroat kind.

On January 15 a phone call came from New York: the *New Yorker* wanted to publish *The Defense*, a full-length novel, complete in two issues, and would pay Nabokov $10,400. Only a month earlier, *Playboy* had taken his novella-length *The Eye* for $8,000.[71]

Maurice Girodias was not finding publishing so profitable. Early in March in Paris he was sentenced, on a number of charges relating to his Olympia Press activities, to a year in prison, a fine, and a prohibition from publishing for twenty years (extended in an October ruling to eighty years). Although Girodias would appeal, Nabokov hoped this might at last enable him to break free of Olympia.[72]

By March, Dmitri's health had improved, he had resumed his singing studies, and he had acquired a car to race for the coming season. As compensation for his illness, his parents had helped him buy an Alfa Romeo TZ, a special racing coupe of which only a few were built, and which had to be custom-tailored to accommodate his height. To Peter Ustinov, a car-racing aficionado, Nabokov played up the role of total incompetent in the practical side of life: "Was I overcharged?" he asked. "What is a sports car? Is it a car with a very particular kind of engine?"[73]

He could not tie up a parcel, Nabokov would maintain, but his hands were dextrous in the extreme at manipulating butterflies under the microscope or catching them on the wing. During the winter he continued to work on his *Butterflies of Europe*. As he drew up its taxonomic principles, he began to contemplate another butterfly project. Oscar de Liso, setting up in New York a new publishing house by the name of Phaedra, had asked him if he would like to write a book on some such subject as "aristocrats of Philadelphia, or the very high class of Ireland" and provide the text for a hundred pictures of his choosing. If the number of pictures could be considerably increased and in high-quality color, Nabokov replied, he would indeed be interested in compiling a book on *Butterflies in Art*, a subject that had interested him for many years. Even in 1949 he had spoken of it as something he had long wanted to write about, perhaps ever since the time he had determined the country of origin of a painting by identifying the local form of butterfly it depicted. Since butterflies evolve into new subspecies and species at a prodigious rate, the problems such a study could resolve, Nabokov mused, might include these: "Were certain species as common in ancient times as they are today? Can the minutiae of evolutionary change be discerned in the pattern of a five-hundred-year-old wing?" He would go back as far as the butterflies of ancient Egypt, painted on the walls of Theban tombs, and as far forward as seventeenth-century Dutch still lifes. Over the next few years the project would take him around many pinacothecas, large and small, throughout Italy, and although the work would never see publication, it would at least help stock the lavish picture-galleries of *Ada*.[74]

XIV

Late in 1963, Nabokov had agreed to come to New York for the launching of *Eugene Onegin*. He and Véra set off from Montreux on March 17, 1964, crossed the Atlantic on the *United States*, and in New York stayed at the Hampshire House. There Nabokov saw friends, entomologists, lawyers, publishers, and agents. With Walter Minton of Putnam's he discussed the possibility of publishing his lectures. Finding Oscar de Liso enthusiastic about the projected *Butterflies in Art*, he carried out some research on still-life painting. Anxious to publish the *Lolita* screenplay, he consulted with the William Morris Agency. After they prompted him to consider putting one of his stage plays up for performance, he had Dmitri translate *The Waltz Invention* over the summer. The agency also proved instrumental in his eventual move from Putnam's. For some time Nabokov had not been happy with the return from his Putnam's books. Now the people at William Morris confirmed that he could obtain much better terms.[75]

At the end of March the Nabokovs headed for Ithaca by train to rummage through the boxes they had placed in storage there in February 1959, when they had expected to be absent from the United States for no more than a few months. Morris and Alison Bishop came to pick them up from the Erie-Lackawanna line at Owego station. After greeting his old friends, Nabokov turned around and clapped his hands in an imperial summons for a porter. There were no porters for miles around. Symptomatic, thought Morris Bishop: his friends seemed to him now very grand-ducal, riding high, and out of scale with the America they were revisiting.[76] But the Nabokovs still planned to return to America for good. In the warehouse of Dean of Ithaca they hunted out only the lepidopterological papers and the lectures Nabokov thought he would need in the near future; the rest of their papers remained in storage rather than being shipped to Montreux.

Nabokov flew back to New York on April 2. Three days later he gave a reading at the Poetry Center of the Y.M.H.A. After an introduction by Susan Sontag, he read "The Ballad of Longwood Glen" and some of Kinbote's commentary, and stirred his audience with the account of Hazel Shade's poignant fate.[77]

On April 9 he traveled to Cambridge, Massachusetts, for another reading. Beforehand he met a young Harvard graduate student in Russian named Andrew Field, who presented him with a copy of V. D. Nabokov's *Sbornik statey po ugolovnomu pravu* (*Essays on Criminal Law*), 1904, which he had bought in the Soviet Union. Nabokov had never read the book and was particularly delighted to receive it now, just as he was about to search out more about his father's career for his revised version of *Speak, Memory*. Field would go on to write several books on Nabokov.[78]

The same day, also at the Commander Hotel, Nabokov met a Harvard undergraduate, Peter Lubin, who would later write a couple of brilliant short pieces on Nabokov, one a hilarious mock-interview that is the most successful Nabokov parody ever written. Lubin recalls sitting in the downstairs bar as workmen took long mirrors off the wall, and shivering with delight at the absurd appropriateness of the moment to Nabokov's love of literary mirrorings and coincidences. Lubin asked Nabokov what he was currently reading. Keith Waterhouse's *Jubb*, he replied, and he liked it. Checking out the book himself, Lubin was charmed that Nabokov had derived such pleasure from a book like this with no grand reputation.[79]

Nabokov's evening at Sanders Hall, sponsored by the *Harvard Advocate*, would be his last public reading ever. Professor Harry Levin, introducing his friend to the audience, looked lean and dapper in his close-fitting suit that emphasized by contrast the ample, almost baggy clothing Nabokov had always preferred. Nabokov prefaced his readings with his customary self-mocking self-delight and his customary sense of timing. "The Ballad of Longwood Glen," he explained, "I composed in Wyoming, one of my favorite states . . . of existence. It is also one of my favorite ballads." He offered a passage from *Pale Fire* "for those who committed the grave mistake of not reading my novel." He read "An Evening of Russian Poetry," turning to Harry Levin at the instruction: "My little helper at the magic lantern, insert that slide. . . . The other way, the other way." Sitting in the enthusiastic audience was the especially enthusiastic John Updike, who thought the reading splendid.[80]

Back in New York, Nabokov learned that his brother Kirill had died of a heart attack in Munich. For some time Kirill had worked for Radio Liberty, which broadcast from West Germany to the Soviet Union, and he was just preparing a program on his brother at the time of his death. In his hotel after he died, his brother's works were found spread out all around his bedroom.[81]

Although last-minute delays would postpone the publication of *Eugene Onegin* until June, the Bollingen Press held its reception for Nabokov on April 21 as planned. After more than six years of waiting, Nabokov was delighted with the appearance of the four-volume boxed and beribboned set (it went on to win awards for typography) and with the party itself. Two days later he and Véra sailed back to Europe on the *United States*.[82]

XV

Véra, who had quietly suffered severe abdominal pains throughout her American trip, spent May in a diagnostic clinic. After weeks of tests she at last had an exploratory operation—and had her appendix removed. In his new car Dmitri began the car-racing season with a prize in every race, until he and his car flew over the embankment at Monza, without permanent damage to either. Nabokov himself meanwhile spent May and early June preparing his tentative list of European butterflies and the localities from which he wanted specimens. With Véra in the clinic, and unable to drive their car himself, he took day excursions by train into the mountains behind Montreux to hunt butterflies in places like Château d'Oex—which would feature in *Ada* as Van's birthplace, Ex.[83]

In satisfying the post-*Lolita* demand for his early Russian work, Nabokov's practice until this point had been to make very few revisions apart from brief explanations of details of émigré life and explicit identifications of Russian literary allusions or the substitution of non-Russian equivalents. He even told Michael Scammell, the translator of *The Defense* and most of *The Gift*, that one reason for commissioning others to prepare the base translation was to help him resist the temptation to revise his early work. Once he had polished the English translation to his satisfaction, he would then arrange for subsequent translations into other languages to be made from the English rather than the Russian text, not only because there were far more translators available from English than from Russian, but also because Nabokov regarded the English-language versions with their minor glosses as textually definitive for non-Russian readers. Early in June 1964, however, *Playboy* sent him the galleys of *The Eye* well ahead of the publication date in the hope that he might make extensive revisions. At first cool toward *Playboy*, he had by now become grateful for their generous remuneration, the complete freedom they allowed him, and their ready consultation with him over publishing conditions. Since they offered a $1,000 bonus as an inducement, he spent the last weeks of June adding "some rainbow patches."[84] A typical example: in Russian, *The Eye* closes with Smurov trying to affirm his happiness: "And what do I care if she marries another? She and I have had heart-rending meetings by night, and her husband shall never find out about these dreams I've had of her." In the English version, that becomes: "And what do I care if she marries another? Every other night I dream of her dresses and things on an endless clothesline of bliss, in a ceaseless wind of possession, and her husband shall never learn what I do to the silks and fleece of the dancing witch."

Between mid-July and mid-August the Nabokovs stopped at the Hotel Beau-Séjour in Crans-sur-Sierre in the Valais, a spa where Véra could recover while her husband pursued more butterflies. He found the place rather dismal ("Three layers of cloud today, and cold shivers in the aspens"), and by August 18 they were back in the Montreux Palace.[85]

During August, Nabokov checked his son's translation of *The Waltz Invention*. He had hoped to travel to London in September, but since the British Museum had not yet checked its collections against his list, he had to postpone his trip.[86]

Late the following month *The Defense* appeared in America. Outstanding among the many reviews was John Updike's *New Republic* appraisal. He named Nabokov "distinctly . . . the best writer of English prose at present holding American citizenship. . . . He writes prose the only way it should be written—that is, ecstatically. In the intensity of its intelligence and reflective irony, his fiction is unique in this decade and scarcely precedented in American literature."[87]

Just at the time the novel was published, Jane Howard arrived with photographer Henry Grossman to interview Nabokov for *Life*. After she sent him her questions a month ahead of time, Nabokov had returned his answers with a postscript.

Dear Miss Howard, allow me to add the following three points:

  1. My answers must be published accurately and completely: verbatim if quoted; in a faithful version, if not.
  2. I must see the proofs of the interview—semifinal and final.
  3. I have the right to correct therein all factual errors and specific slips ("Mr. Nabokov is a small man with long hair," etc.)[88]

Despite the rigid instructions, Jane Howard found Nabokov entertaining and expansive during her two days with him, and would later make the trip to Montreux again simply for pleasure, as other interviewers had also done and would do. After she submitted her draft of the interview, Nabokov insisted she respect his sense of propriety. His tone—gentle, friendly, self-deprecating, considerate of others, almost apologetic at seeming the censor—belies the image of the arrogant ogre of Montreux:

> Thanks for letting me see your jottings. I am returning them with my notes and deletions. I do hope you won't find the latter too discouraging. You have done your job extremely well, but I didn't. Much of what I said was idle talk, mainly and lamely meant to entertain you and Mr. Grossman in between business.
>
> I am a poor *causeur*, and this is why I prepare my answers to interviews in writing; and since this method takes up time, I very seldom grant interviews. Several things that I said, and that you took down, are quite unfit for publication. I cannot discuss my obesity in public. I do not want to embarrass a heroic, and now ailing, cosmonaut by recalling a fishy television program. I find it unseemly to speak of my pedigree or of the butterflies bearing my name. I cannot be made to criticize contemporary writers. I have sufficiently worried poor Zhivago. . . .
>
> Let me repeat that it was a great pleasure to talk to you. We all three enjoyed your and Henry Grossman's visit tremendously. Please, do not resent my fastidious and fussy alterations. I did take a lot of trouble with the written answers I sent you.[89]

CHAPTER 20

Ada Stirs: Montreux, 1964–1966

I

AS EARLY as 1958, Nabokov had started to assemble ideas for a fictive meditation on time. At the beginning of 1963, a year after completing *Pale Fire*, he returned to his notes on "the nature of time." By 1964 he expected his next work of fiction to be *The Texture of Time*, and told reporters how problematic it was proving:

> The difficulty about it is that I have to devise an essay, a scholarly-looking essay on time and then gradually turn it into the story I have in mind. The metaphors start to live. The metaphors gradually turn into the story because it's very difficult to speak about time without using similes or metaphors. And my purpose is to have these metaphors breed to form a story of their own, gradually, and then again to fall apart, and to have it all end in this rather dry though serious and well-meant essay on time. It proves so difficult to compose that I don't know what to do about it.[1]

When Jane Howard came to interview him in September 1964, he told her too of his project. On her return she sent him Gerald Whitrow's *The Natural Philosophy of Time*, another source he would eventually incorporate into *Ada*'s ample flow.[2]

Back in July, Véra had written to Walter Minton that her husband was "finishing" a new book. But the evidence of his diaries and manuscripts suggests that while he often expected a breakthrough must come soon, the project had advanced little over the last year: when he was not checking or revising translations, writing forewords, or answering interviews, he had spent most of his time on *Butterflies of Europe*. But at the end of September 1964, even before he received Jane Howard's gift, he resumed serious work on *The Texture of Time*.[3]

In mid-October he drew up the heading "An Experiment" on one of his index cards and began to note down his dreams in order to test the contention of J. W. Dunne in *An Experiment with Time* that time works backward as well as forward and dreams can often appear precognitive because they allow the reverse direction of time, in which future precedes present, to leak into our minds. The results proved nothing, although they did satisfy Nabokov's taste for coincidence, and the experiment naturally led him to analyze his own dreams. He categorized their types: "1. Professional and vocational (in my case: literature, teaching, and lepidoptera); 2. dim-doom dreams (in my case fatidic-sign nightmares, thalamic calamities, menacing series and riddles); 3. obvious influences of immediate occupations and impressions (Olympic games, etc.); 4. memories of the remote past (childhood, school, parents, émigré life); 5. 'precognitive'; 6. erotic tenderness and heart-rending enchantment." He also noted such special characteristics as "very exact clock-time awareness but hazy passing-of-time feeling," or "fairly sustained, fairly clear, fairly logical (within special limits) cogitation."[4] All this self-analysis would provide the basis for Van Veen's anti-Freudian lectures on dreams in *Ada*.

Nabokov had returned to *The Texture of Time* partly because he was waiting on the British Museum. He needed to know exactly which of the butterfly species that he would incorporate in his book were represented in the museum by specimens from the type localities he stipulated. The museum's delays and silences were keeping him in a constant state of perplexity and irritation, he complained. Throughout November he continued with both the butterfly book and his new novel—"novel or novelette," Véra wrote, "he is still not certain of its eventual length."[5]

Nor, apparently, of its direction, for on December 1 he resumed his Russian translation of *Lolita*, last worked on in February 1963. Two weeks later, *Lolita*'s first publisher was declared bankrupt. Although the judgment would be set aside in April 1965 for lack of interest on the part of Olympia's creditors, the bankruptcy would become, after four more years of legal struggles, Nabokov's basis for terminating his contract with Girodias. Recently he had refused Girodias the right to print anything from *Lolita* in *The Olympia Reader*. Girodias suggested that without an excerpt from his press's most famous book he would have to write the story of his relations with Nabokov and Minton, steering just clear of libel. Nabokov wrote to Minton to tell Grove Press, publishers of *The Olympia Reader*, "that Girodias's letter is that of a blackmailer, and he should be aware of what a blackmailer should expect."[6]

Late in the fall the Nabokovs had sold their Peugeot: Véra was suffering from pains in her wrists and had "stopped enjoying fighting ice and snow" on the roads. On Christmas Day itself, to avoid the crush of Italians returning from Switzerland just before Christmas, they took the train to Padua to stay for two weeks in nearby Abano, at the Hotel Due Torri, where Véra took the "fango" treatment (hot mud-baths) to relieve her pains. There in the rain and snow and cold they continued translating *Lolita* together.[7]

Back in Montreux on January 10, Nabokov as usual found himself pulled in several directions. He carried on translating *Lolita*. He had to reconsider some of the classifications for his *Butterflies of Europe*, and contemplated traveling to Paris to hurry up the Musée nationale and to Spain for the coming butterfly season. In mid-February, he began to revise his own 1935 translation of *Despair*. Although he had anticipated that he would have to make major changes, he found less to do than he expected. An important passage describing Hermann's mental dissociation from his wife while making love had been "stupidly omitted" from both Russian and English editions in the more reticent 1930s, but was now reinstated from his manuscript. He added some fresh images, some vivid local details, some fictional preparations for later events, and the brilliantly comic final paragraph in which Hermann bellows down to the crowd and the police below as if he were the director of a movie in which the crowd is required to hold the police and allow the archcriminal about to emerge to make a clean escape. On March 1, Nabokov devised the first chess problem he had composed for many years. Perhaps the fact that he was once again writing Russian prose—the translation of *Lolita*—had rewound a spring in his imagination. And at the end of the month he finished transposing into the language of his birth the novel that owed most to his adopted country.[8]

II

For the most part, Nabokov's translation of *Lolita* is as literal as any of his other translations.[9] He opts for sense over sound: "Lolita, light of my life, fire of my loins" loses its lilt to become "*Lolita, svet moey zhizni, ogon' moikh chresel*'." In compensation, he finds what Clarence Brown calls "routinely brilliant" Russian equivalents for English wordplay, and equivalents or glosses or parallels for English and French allusions.[10] In the Russian, the allusive nightmare of Quilty's cryptogrammic paper chase combines comedy and camouflage at least as well as the original English. Quilty's collaborator, the anagrammatic enigma Vivian Darkbloom, becomes "Vivian Damor-Blok (Damor, her stage-name; Blok, after one of her first husbands)," as if Quilty's shady coauthor has a past record of intimate theatrical collaborations, or as if the mystery and romance of "Darkbloom" has turned into a new avatar of Blok's romantic, nebulous "Incognita."

The translation will prove a useful sourcebook for the English *Lo-*

lita, for it often makes explicit what is left only strongly implicit in the original: the misplaced anti-Semitism behind the initial refusal of a room to "Humberg" at the Enchanted Hunters, or the precise terms under which Lolita earns her pocket money. "Her weekly allowance, paid to her under condition she fulfil her basic obligations, was twenty-one cents at the start of the Beardsley era," says the English version, but the Russian further stipulates that she had to fulfill those "basic obligations" three times a day.

Nabokov had ended his afterword to the English *Lolita* by referring to his "private tragedy . . . that I had to abandon my natural idiom, my untrammelled, rich, and infinitely docile tongue for a second-rate brand of English."[11] He began his new afterword to the Russian translation by telling his readers that the process of translating had been one of disillusionment: "Alas, that 'marvelous Russian language' that I thought awaited me somewhere, blossoming like a faithful springtime behind a tightly locked gate whose key I had kept safe for so many years, proved to be nonexistent, and beyond the gate are nothing but charred stumps and the hopeless autumnal vista, and the key in my hand is more like a jimmy."[12] Many Russians reportedly agree, finding the translation clumsy and stiff. Others do not. Nina Berberova, perhaps the most important novelist other than Nabokov himself to emerge in the emigration, dismisses his claim that his Russian strings had grown rusty. Gennadi Barabtarlo, who after Nabokov's death would translate *Pnin* into Russian, considers Nabokov's last Russian opus "in many *stylistic* respects his finest," sufficient to place it "on the very top step of the frozen escalator of Russian masterpieces."[13]

Part of the reason for the disparity of judgments is that the Russian language in the Soviet Union has undergone a steady vulgarization. Nabokov consciously resisted that process, and to many a Soviet ear the effect seems stilted. To others, though, it reflects Nabokov's attempt to write for an audience in a future Russian where art and language could once again be free, true, individual. As Clarence Brown notes, Nabokov translated *Lolita* "for the same hypothetical reader that kept his countrymen Baratynsky and Mandelstam going: for the 'friend in posterity,' as they both explicitly put it. But to write for the future implies a faith that there will be a future," and that, he concludes, is patriotism of the highest order. Vladimir Weidle, the émigré critic, prophesies that in the long run Nabokov's translation will be fertile for Russian literature and an even greater phenomenon there than the English *Lolita* in English literature.[14]

In the afterword to his translation, Nabokov compares the expressiveness of Russian and English: both cope equally well with the poetry of landscape, movement, and emotion, but abstractions, the implications of the unsaid, and everything to do with fashion, sports, science, and technology become in Russian wordy and ungainly. To his friend Bertrand Thompson, Nabokov wrote that Russian was "a good 'From' language but a terrible 'Into' one. The main trouble is with technical terms: they are either longwinded and roundabout or facetious. In translating, for example, windshield wipers you can render it by a forty-letter phrase or choose between 'little paws,' 'janitors' and 'twins'—all of them vulgarisms used in the USSR." In this instance, he chose "twins," but his unique command of both English and Russian led him to many precise and felicitous equivalents not listed in any standard English-Russian dictionary—and now assembled in a special *English-Russian Dictionary of Nabokov's "Lolita"* that will become an invaluable lexicographic tool.[15] Rather more marketable, though, would be another offshoot of the Russian *Lolita*: *Ada*, whose ironic vision of technology ("petroloplane," "dorophone") and disconcerting appropriation of American states for its Russian estates owes much to Nabokov's experience of turning *Lolita*'s Americana into Russian.

III

In the spring of 1965, construction works on every side of the Montreux Palace made the place too noisy for a writer with hypersensitive hearing. After buying a new car, a Lancia Flavia, the Nabokovs headed off late in April for Gardone Riviera on Lake Garda. On the way there, Nabokov stopped in Milan, where he searched the Pinacoteca Ambrosiana for his *Butterflies in Art*. There he admired Caravaggio's butterfly-less but beautiful "Basket of Fruit"—and he would soon make an invented Caravaggio one of the most memorable of *Ada*'s many paintings.[16]

At Gardone's Grand Hotel, Nabokov had a room with a balcony directly overlooking Lake Garda. Late every morning, after roaming the surrounding hills in search of real-life butterflies, he would return to work intensely on *The Texture of Time*. He also read and enjoyed Anthony Burgess's Malay trilogy and began to read Saul Bellow's *Herzog*, but found himself too bored to continue. Dmitri visited often. After more successes in car-racing, thirty-one-year-old Dmitri now had more cups than his mantelpiece could hold. To his parents' enormous relief he decided that summer to give up the sport and devote himself to opera. One day, just as he had been about to leave for another race, he found that his friend the tenor Giuseppe Campora and his wife had locked his race car in their front yard and refused to open the gate. He persuaded them to release the car, and duly won a trophy in the next day's competition in Trieste, but was so moved by their faith in him as a singer that he made it his last serious race.[17]

When lovely Gardone became too hot for comfort, the Nabokovs moved back to Switzerland and up to higher ground. On July 7, a week after arriving at Suvretta House, St. Moritz, Nabokov read Edmund Wilson's review of his *Eugene Onegin* and at once cabled Barbara Epstein at the *New York Review of Books*: "Please reserve space in next issue for my thunder."[18]

Reviews of *Eugene Onegin* had been appearing for almost a year. All praised the sheer quantity of information in the commentary, though some reproached Nabokov for capricious selections, digressiveness, or captiousness of tone. All praised the literal accuracy of the translation, but most wished that Nabokov had tried to match both the music and the naturalness of Pushkin's language, to make the poem seem *not* a mere translation. A brief exchange of letters with a previous translator, Babette Deutsch, early in 1965, had served as a preliminary skirmish for the battle that was now about to commence.[19]

Wilson began his review by referring to his friendship with Nabokov, then launched into a fierce personal attack:

> Since Mr. Nabokov is in the habit of introducing any job of this kind which he undertakes by an announcement that he is unique and incomparable and that everybody else who has attempted it is an oaf and an ignoramus, incompetent as a linguist and a scholar, usually with the implication that he is also a low-class person and a ridiculous personality, Nabokov ought not to complain if the reviewer, though trying not to imitate his bad literary manners, does not hesitate to underline his weaknesses.

Of course Nabokov had made no such announcement, and in fact commended and drew on translators like the Ivan Turgenev–Louis Viardot team and André Lirondelle, and commentators like Lerner, Shchyogolev, Khodasevich, Tomashevski, Tynyanov, and others. And as Clarence Brown comments, Wilson seems to have overlooked the modesty of Nabokov's aims: to translate only the exact sense without presuming, as verse translators did, that he could offer a fair approximation of Pushkin's music and grace.[20]

Wilson's principal charge was that the "bald and awkward language" of Nabokov's translation had nothing in common with Pushkin, and he sought to explain it thus:

One knows also the perversity of [Nabokov's] tricks to startle or stick pins in the reader, and one suspects that his perversity here has been exercised in curbing his brilliance; that—with his sado-masochistic Dostoevskian tendencies so acutely noted by Sartre—he seeks to torture both the reader and himself by flattening Pushkin out and denying to his own powers the scope for their full play.

Aside from this desire both to suffer and make suffer—so important an element in his fiction—the only characteristic Nabokov trait that one recognizes is the addiction to rare and unfamiliar words.

Throughout his work Nabokov stresses that a world as rich as ours cannot be easily understood. On the other hand, for that very reason it proves a delight to discover, if one makes the effort. In writing fiction, he constructs his invented worlds to match, so that at first they resist the mind in certain ways in order to offer us more in the long run. But this central aspect of Nabokov's work Wilson had for many years misconstrued as a desire to humiliate and torment the reader. Nabokov's *Onegin* operates on the same principle as his fiction: like the world itself, Pushkin's masterpiece is a complex marvel, and there can be no easy substitute for mastering its priceless particulars. Far from desiring to vex his readers, Nabokov hoped to offer them the full flavor of Pushkin: by choosing, for instance, an unusual word like "rememorating," he could convey both the archaism and the vocalic resonance of Pushkin's choosing *vospomnya* instead of the more usual *vspomnya*. Wilson instead read that generosity of intent as a penchant for willful cruelty.

Wilson criticized some of Nabokov's rare words as nonexistent, only because he had not deigned to look them up in Webster's. He ignored Nabokov's choice of method, his attempt to provide a humble pony, his deliberate decision not to offer smooth English so that he could direct readers to the irreplaceable Russian. To quote Clarence Brown once more, Wilson spent most of his time in the review complaining that the translation

did not read smoothly, contained unusual words, and was even downright wrong. In making the latter point, Wilson committed the almost unbelievable hubris of reading Nabokov several petulant little lessons about Russian grammar and vocabulary, himself blundering all the while. (Where were the Russian friends to whom he constantly alludes?) He also disliked the tone of everything, found the manners of his 'personal friend' to be characteristically unsupportable, dismissed the commentary not so much for any faults he found as for its conveying more than anyone wished to know, and ended with an insulting compliment on the physical appearance of the books.[21]

IV

Why did Wilson aim such a willfully peevish attack at someone who had long been a close friend? Wilson's great talent had always been for turning up stones with the queerest crabs underneath, for discovering literary interest where others had not yet looked—in, say, the Civil War writers he incorporated into *Patriotic Gore*. Nabokov, on the other hand, maintained that literature mattered not at the level of the tolerable but only at that of the supreme masterpiece, where a work of art seems to extend the limits of the humanly possible, and he had long irritated Wilson by his readiness to dismiss writers with reputations as high as those of Balzac, Stendhal, Dostoevsky, or Mann. But in his relations with friends he always tried to signal the strengths of their books, whereas Wilson regarded it as a virtue, a rather endearing trait—proof of his frank and unbiased judgment— to criticize friends harshly to their faces. "Disagreement truly interested him," writes Edith Oliver. " 'Embarrassing!' he said. 'What does that mean? I have never known what that meant.' He felt that anything in print . . . was discussable."[22]

But even that attitude cannot explain the seething animosity of his attack on Nabokov. We must return to the beginnings of their relationship.

Nabokov, who always liked a sparring partner, welcomed the boldly combative spirit in Wilson. At the same time, he never felt Wilson was any competition. When Andrew Field later wrote of their relationship that there was "hardly a moment when the tension of being competitors is dropped," Nabokov asked him to replace it with " 'when the tension between two highly dissimilar minds, attitudes and educations is slackened.' We were never competitors. In what, good gracious?"[23] On their common ground, Russian language and literature and history, Nabokov knew he was incomparably better informed than Wilson. Nor did he have any doubts that as a writer he was in a different class from his friend or for that matter any other contemporary he had read.

Wilson came to resent Nabokov's dismissal of other writers and his unshakable self-assurance, and as early as 1945 he wrote to him of "your insatiable and narcissistic vanity." Nabokov played up to that image, deliberately teasing his friend. When Wilson wrote that he had begun to learn chess, for instance, Nabokov had replied: "I hope you will soon be playing well enough for me to beat you."[24]

Nabokov's confidence that Wilson was no competitor only intensified his friend's drive to prove that he could challenge and even outdo Nabokov. Wilson wrote fiction himself, and in the years when he first knew Nabokov he was composing his favorite among his books, the stories of *Memoirs of Hecate County*. As he read Nabokov's works, he regularly imposed alternative continuations that he implied would be better than Nabokov's own versions. He liked *Laughter in the Dark* "better before it got rather implausible toward the end. I thought that the unfortunate hero was going to develop color audition and detect the whereabouts of the girl by hearing her red dress, or something." He read *Pale Fire* with amusement, "but it seems to me rather silly. . . . I expected that the professor would turn out to be the real King and that the commentator would be the assassin." He subjected *The Real Life of Sebastian Knight*, "Rusalka," and *Bend Sinister* to the same strange treatment.[25]

In these rewritings of Nabokov, Wilson's rivalry operated at an instinctive level. Criticism offered him a more conscious and more potent weapon. He was, after all, often considered the best American critic of his time. As early as 1947 he had proposed an article on Nabokov's works as a whole. In 1952 he proudly announced to Véra Nabokov that he would soon set to reading all her husband's works and would write an essay on them "that will somewhat annoy him." Throughout the next ten years he would repeat the promise and the threat again and again. He had come to the conclusion that he had discovered the secret source of Nabokov's art in schadenfreude, and that he had a psychological explanation for this in line with his thesis in *The Wound and the Bow* that artistic creativity springs from trauma. In Nabokov's works "everybody is always being humiliated" because "he himself, since he left Russia and as a result of the assassination of his father, must have suffered a good deal of humiliation." Nabokov later responded to this: "the 'miseries, horrors and handicaps' that he assumes I was subjected to . . . are mostly figments of his warped fancy. . . . He has not even bothered to read *Speak, Memory*, the records and recollections of a happy expatriation that began practically on the day of my birth."[26]

If the charge of schadenfreude could be leveled at anyone, it would not be at Nabokov, who detested bullfighting and hunting and all cruelty to animals, but at Wilson. As Nabokov noted in his diary in 1967 on reading one of Wilson's *New Yorker* pieces, "Only a scoundrel could write that he could understand 'the sexual satisfaction' of seeing a woman stepping on a milk-glutted kitten and causing it to explode."[27]

The eroticism of Wilson's *Memoirs of Hecate County* had ensured only that the book was banned from sale and forgotten. When *Lolita*, on the other hand, brought Nabokov fortune, fame, and ringing acclaim, it sharply intensified Wilson's irritation that he could not quite compete and that Nabokov knew it. In the year of *Lolita*'s American appearance, Wilson failed to reply to one of Nabokov's letters, and when Nabokov wrote again, suspecting the cause of Wilson's silence, he took care not to mention *Lolita* by name. But he still tried to keep the friendship alive: "You have quite forgotten me," he wrote late in 1960, after Wilson again failed to reply to another letter. After seeing Wilson in 1962, their closest common friend, Roman Grynberg, wrote to Nabokov asking what had made Wilson so angry with him. "Envy? But you are so different!"[28]

V

Pushkin had always been their meeting-ground, and would now become their battlefield. In 1962, William McGuire wrote that Dwight MacDonald and Wilson wanted to see the *Onegin* proofs. Nabokov replied: "Sorry—I definitely do not wish them to be shown to anybody, least of all to Wilson." A year later, however, when the proofs were finalized, he gave McGuire permission to send them to Wilson, "but if he starts questioning things, please don't inform me of his questions."[29]

When the first favorable review of *Eugene Onegin* appeared in the summer of 1964, the Bollingen Press was delighted. Nabokov set little store by the acclaim: "The only good of it is that some of its banal compliments might be useful for . . . a full-page advertisement. . . . Otherwise, I have no illusions about these articles. None of the reviewers is really competent." The Bollingen Foundation kept looking forward to Wilson's article, but Nabokov warned that he did not expect much from it: "As I have mentioned before, his Russian is primitive, and his knowledge of Russian literature gappy and grotesque. He is a very old friend of mine, and I do hope our quarter-of-a-century correspondence . . . will be published someday."[30]

Nabokov had not anticipated he would learn from Wilson's review, but he was shocked to find the degree to which "a dear friend" could be "transformed into an envious ass." After reading the article, Nabokov wrongly supposed that Wilson had already read the *Onegin* proofs and written his article before visiting him in Montreux early in 1964, but meanly said nothing of the impending attack. In fact, although Nabokov had given McGuire permission to send Wilson proofs in September 1963, Wilson had begun to read the translation only in its published version and in the summer of 1964.[31]

In his commentary to *Eugene Onegin*, Nabokov wonders why on one occasion "Pushkin, vindictive Pushkin, with his acute sense of honor and *amour-propre*" did not call out to a duel a famous rake who had challenged him with an insulting epigram. Endowed with a Pushkinian sense of amour propre himself, Nabokov never thought for a moment of not defending himself. Yet his first riposte was a surprisingly gentle letter to the *New York Review of Books*. After alluding to his long friendship with Wilson and his gratitude for Wilson's past kindnesses, he went on to list and explain eight blunders in Wilson's Russian and his English and let these facts speak for themselves. He concluded: "I suggest that Mr. Wilson's didactic purpose is defeated by the presence of such errors (and there are many more to be listed later), as it is also by the strange tone of his article. Its mixture of pompous aplomb and peevish ignorance is certainly not conducive to a sensible discussion of Pushkin's language and mine."[32]

In the same issue appeared Wilson's reply. He had consulted with Max Hayward, whose translation of *Doctor Zhivago* he had harshly criticized in 1958, only to disclose even then how patchy his own Russian was. Since that date the two men had become drinking buddies, and Hayward now formulated a riposte for Wilson. Nabokov had written: "I do not think Mr. Wilson should try to teach me how to pronounce this or any other Russian vowel." Now Hayward prompted Wilson to take issue with Nabokov's description of one Russian consonant and to declare that the sound as Nabokov explained it was "a feature of ByeloRussian. Now, I have heard Mr. Nabokov insist on the superiority of the Petersburg pronunciation to that of Moscow, and I am rather surprised to find him recommending the pronunciation of Minsk."[33]

Anthony Burgess, who earlier in the year had reviewed the *Onegin* translation, would later recall modestly that after reading Wilson's attack and Nabokov's reply, "small reviewers like me scuttled out of the crossfire and left it to the giants."[34] In fact, in the letters columns, review pages, and editorials of the *New York Review of Books*, the *New Republic*, *Poetry*, and elsewhere, others continued to join the fray, and Nabokov was vexed that many who knew no Russian or missed the point of his translating the way he did took Wilson's side and hissed at the hideousness of a translation he had never tried to prettify.

In late October and early November he wrote a long article on the whole furor destined for the *New York Review of Books* but ultimately published in *Encounter*. He began by saying he never responded to criticism of his creative work, but that scholarship "possesses an ethical side, moral and human elements. It reflects the compiler's honesty or dishonesty, skill or sloppiness. If told I am a bad poet, I smile; but if told I am a poor scholar, I reach for my heaviest dictionary." He defended literality, disposed quickly of a few criticisms made in other reviews, then turned to the Wilson article, no longer with restraint in his voice but gloating over "the unusual, unbelievable, and highly entertaining opportunity . . . of refuting practically every item of criticism in his enormous piece. . . . It is a polemicist's dream come true."[35]

Discussing every example of his own seemingly bizarre renderings that Wilson had tried to fault, he showed that "all have pedigrees of agony and rejection and reinstatement, and should be treated as convalescents and ancient orphans, and not hooted at as impostors by a critic who says he admires some of my books." His precision and erudition were devastating, his irony unsparing:

In translating *slushat' shum morskoy* (Eight:IV:11) I chose the archaic and poetic transitive turn "to listen the sound of the sea" because the relevant passage has in Pushkin a stylized archaic tone. Mr. Wilson may not care for this turn—I do not much care for it either—but it is silly of him to assume that I lapsed into a naive Russianism not being really aware that, as he tells me, "in English you have to listen *to* something." First, it is Mr. Wilson who is not aware that there exists an analogous construction in Russian, *prislushivat'sya k zvuku*, "to listen closely to the sound"—which, of course, makes nonsense of the exclusive Russianism imagined by him, and secondly, had he happened to leaf through a certain canto of *Don Juan*, written in the year Pushkin was beginning his poem, or a certain *Ode to Memory*, written when Pushkin's poem was being finished, my learned friend would have concluded that Byron ("Listening debates not very wise or witty") and Tennyson ("Listening the lordly music") must have had quite as much Russian blood as Pushkin and I.[36]

After the publication of "Nabokov's Reply" in Britain, the *Observer* described the affair as the bloodiest literary brawl since F. R. Leavis went for C. P. Snow's jugular vein, and in its honor the Royal Shakespeare Company performed a highly successful reading of Nabokov's translation at the Aldwych. There was something unintentionally apt about comparing the Nabokov-Wilson broil to Snow's and Leavis's arguments for and against uniting the "two cultures" of science and art. Nabokov was a scientist, and in preparing his *Butterflies of Europe* he had told Weidenfeld he would prefer if necessary to feature a slightly damaged specimen from a species' type locality rather than a fresher specimen from elsewhere: "We shall always sacrifice 'beauty' to science with the result that genuine beauty will be achieved." In *Eugene Onegin* he followed the same principles: he sacrificed the facile "beauty" of imitating Pushkin's verse form at the

Above: Nabokov with Elena, Reggio Emilia, Italy, late April 1961. *(Zenith Press.)*

Left: Proud parents with Dmitri dressed for his operatic debut, as Raimondo in *Lucia di Lammermoor*, Reggio, early May 1961.

Top left: The Montreux Palace Hotel. The Nabokovs lived here, mostly on the sixth (top) floor of the nearer (Cygne) wing, from 1961 until Nabokov's death. Véra remained in the apartment until 1990. The one sunshade on the sixth floor shielded their narrow living room, number 64. The next window to the left, partly obscured, was Véra's bedroom; the next, 62, Nabokov's; the next a bathroom and unused kitchen, and the next, room 60, at first Dmitri's bedroom and then an office. On the near side of the sunshade was the Nabokovs' kitchen. The remaining two windows on the front facade of the building, and on the east flank, belong to another apartment. The noisy Grand-Rue runs below. *(R. T. Kahn.)*

Newsweek cover photo, on the occasion of *Pale Fire*'s publication, 1962. (Newsweek, *June 25, 1962.)*

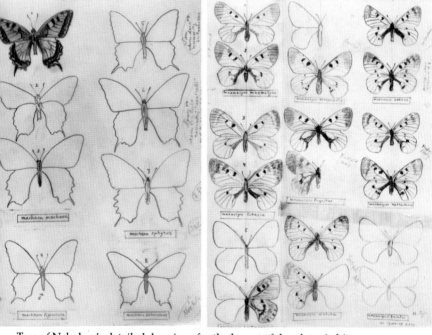

Two of Nabokov's detailed drawings for the layout of the plates in his
Butterflies of Europe, which he worked on in 1962 and 1963 until the cost of the
project deterred publishers. The plates were to begin with Linnaeus's original
butterfly genus, *Papilio*, and the first plate would have featured subspecies of
Papilio machaon, the Old World Swallowtail. The other plate depicts subspecies
of the Parnassian *mnemosyne*, a species that becomes a sort of tutelary deity in
Speak, Memory, which Nabokov would have liked to call *Speak, Mnemosyne*.
Interested readers may compare the second butterfly on the lefthand column,
the female of *mnemosyne mnemosyne*, with Nabokov's 1965 drawing of the same
insect in the revised *Speak, Memory* (1966).

Nabokov, in his living room at the Montreux Palace, May 1964, examines with delight the boxed set of the four volumes of *Eugene Onegin*, just published more than eight years after he completed the manuscript. *(Henry Grossman.)*

Above: Dmitri, Vladimir, Véra. May 1964. *(Henry Grossman.)*

Left: Nabokov on balcony of his living room at the Montreux Palace, June 1964.

Nabokov with Webster's Dictionary. *(Photo by Philippe Halsman 1966, © Yvonne Halsman 1991.)*

Left: Nabokov in his bedroom-cum-study, where he did most of his writing, beginning the day's composition at the lectern the hotel staff had found in the attic, then transferring to the armchair, and then, as gravity tugged harder on his old muscles, stretched out on his bed. *(Horst Tappe.)*

Below: Nabokov on bench in garden of Montreux Palace, with box of index cards serving as miniature desk. *(Henry Grossman.)*

Nabokov not discouraged by the rain that has ended the day's butterfly hunt. *(Horst Tappe.)*

Nabokov correcting proofs—a major task in the 1960s and 1970s, as his canon expanded at both ends, past and present, Russian and English. *(Jean Waldis.)*

Nabokov composing at his lectern, 1966. Note, from rear to right foreground, the open window with view down to and across Lake Geneva, the long index box with the cards from some major project to Nabokov's left, the butterfly he has drawn on the lampshade to his right. (*Photo by Philippe Halsman 1966,* © *Yvonne Halsman 1991.*)

Right: Searching for butterflies, September 1966. *(Photo by Philippe Halsman 1966, © Yvonne Halsman 1991.)*

Below: Searching for the *mot juste.* Montreux Palace, September 1966. *(Photo by Philippe Halsman 1966, © Yvonne Halsman 1991.)*

Véra and Vladimir, October 1968. Visitors often remarked that the two—here aged sixty-six and sixty-nine—looked like young lovers. *(Photo by Philippe Halsman 1966, © Yvonne Halsman 1991.)*

In October 1968, just as he was finishing *Ada*, Nabokov pulled this mischievous face for Philippe Halsman, saying it would be right for the cover of his new novel. *(Photo by Philippe Halsman 1968, © Yvonne Halsman 1991.)*

A more serious shot from the same session, this image was used for the American *Ada*—the English edition opted for the more impish image—and for most of Nabokov's books of the 1970s. *(Photo by Philippe Halsman 1968, © Yvonne Halsman 1991.)*

Time cover illustration, on the occasion of *Ada's* publication, May 1969. *(Copyright 1969 Time Warner Inc. Reprinted by permission.)*

Nabokov; his wife; his sister, Elena; his wife's cousin, Anna Feigin; and Louise Fürrer, Anna Feigin's *dame de compagnie*, in their typical summer milieu. Saanen, near Gstaad, August 1971. *(Dmitri Nabokov.)*

The Nabokovs, August 1971. *(Dmitri Nabokov.)*

Nabokov on La Videmanette, above Gstaad, the day he told Dmitri he felt he had accomplished all he had ever dreamed of as a writer, August 1971. *(Dmitri Nabokov.)*

Nabokov outside the chalet-apartment near Saanen, September 1972. *(Dmitri Nabokov.)*

To Véra

Arlequinus arlequinus ♂

Montreux
August, 1974

Nabokov's butterfly inscriptions on his books for family and friends became more elaborate and more vividly colored in the 1960s and 1970s. The harlequin butterfly on Véra's *Look at the Harlequins!* is a hybrid of the stained glass rhomboids of *Speak, Memory* and the harlequin pattern in the past of Vladimir and Véra Nabokov.

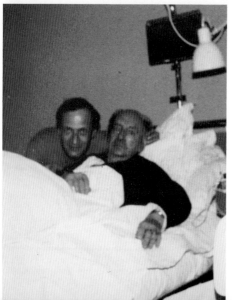

Above: Alfred Appel on a visit to the Nabokovs. Zermatt, 1974. *(Nina Appel.)*

Left: The last photo of Nabokov, with Dmitri, in the hospital in Lausanne, April 1977.

expense of his sense and opted instead for the ruthless fidelity that could achieve a deeper truth and therefore a more genuine beauty.[37]*

There were a number of aftershocks of the controversy: a couple of brief blasts and counterblasts in print from Wilson and Nabokov early in 1966 and again in 1968, and a rather more curious private exchange. Wilson seemed to feel that his criticism had been simply robust frankness rather than vicious hostility, and sent a copy of the article to his and Nabokov's friend Roman Grynberg. Grynberg wrote to Nabokov that, ever since, Wilson had been waiting for his reply: "He doesn't see how pathetic he is." Then Wilson surprised Nabokov by sending him a Christmas card at the end of 1965 that would have been "charming and even witty in other circumstances." The next year he sent another card: "I'm sorry our controversy has come to an end. I have rarely enjoyed anything so much." With stiff politeness Nabokov replied: "Although I did not relish quite as much as you tell me you did our 'controversy,' I would like to thank you for your Christmas greetings." Two years later he noted in his diary: "Odd dream: somebody on the stairs behind me takes me by the elbows. E. W. Jocular reconciliation." It was not to be.[38]

VI

Despite Wilson's review, despite the cold, the clouds, the rain, and even some slight snow, Nabokov enjoyed the month of July 1965 that he spent in St. Moritz. When the clouds cleared, the scenery and the butterflies were spectacular. On the steep slopes of Alp Grum, covered with alpine lilies, he netted a very rare, very local yellow-banded ringlet and emitted cries and whoops of delight.[39]

By August 10 he was back in the Montreux Palace, where he had begun to stake out his sixth-floor suite as Nabokov territory by sketching on the shades of standard lamps nonexistent but plausible butterflies or insinuating grotesque little creatures into the curlicues of the wallpaper design. A month after his return, he announced to George Weidenfeld his decision not to continue with the butterfly book. His plans had been on such a scale—over a hundred large-format six-color plates—that Weidenfeld had been trying to arrange for an international consortium of European publishers to share the costs. Uncertain that the project would proceed, Nabokov had found the continuing suspense at first irritating and then insupportable, es-

---

* "Shorn of its primary verbal existence," he wrote in "Problems of Translation: *Onegin* in English" (1955), "the original text will not be able to soar and sing; but it can be very nicely dissected and mounted, and scientifically studied in all its organic details."

pecially since it drained off creative energy he could channel elsewhere. Reluctant to abandon the project, Weidenfeld immediately offered a $10,000 advance, but Nabokov would not budge.[40]

Lepidoptera's loss was literature's gain, but his *Butterflies of Europe* would have been a fascinating work, both in its two hundred pages of text and in its plates. Nabokov had written a great deal of the text before abandoning the project. Recording the distribution of a particular species, he might drop in a casual personal reference that testified to his extraordinary memorial exactitude: one species extended "along the Atlantic Coast southwards at least to Biarritz (where I remember taking it as a boy, in September 1909, in a pine wood)," another as far as Perpignan, "where I have seen it [in 1929] haunting orchards in March in close proximity to *podalirius podalirius*, the ordinary Pyrenean form." The notes show where his eyes first learned to observe, to distinguish, to recall what he had observed: "The skipping, zigzagging flight of this species and those of the *tynandras* group is quite different from other Erebias. The independent-looking motion and, in fresh specimens, underside bluish-grey flash of the hind wing are especially remarkable."[41]

In taxonomic matters he was moderate, judicious, reasonable in tone, not the extreme splitter some have supposed. He knew better than to value the slightly variant specimen proudly elevated to a distinct subspecies by the amateur collector. Eighteen different "subspecies" of the popular *apollo* had been claimed for the Tyrol alone, "making of that small but touristically very accessible region a perfect paradise for race names." From the approximately two hundred named *apollo* subspecies doomed to be carried forever in complete catalogues, he selected only ten that seemed important, representative, and distinct.

Like the text, the plates showed Nabokov searching for beauty and truth at the point where art and science meet. He wanted his plates in the matte finish of pasty aquarelle paper so that the color photographs might bear some resemblance to paintings. On the other hand, the butterflies would be placed as if in a museum collection "in two or three vertical rows (as 'series' of specimens are pinned in glassed trays) of four to eight specimens in each row." Under every specimen he wanted a typeset label to match the handwritten labels attached to real specimens in three-dimensional collections: his would indicate the species name; the date, location, and altitude of the specimen's capture; and the collection from which it had come. Everything was as firmly in place as the worlds of his novels were before he began to write: the dimensions, in millimeters, of those little labels; the two sizes of type for the labels, one for the species name, another for the rest of the data; the exact number and aspect of specimens he would need of every species; the exact arrangement of which species and subspecies to fit together on which plate.

VII

Although at the time he Russified *Lolita* Nabokov had had no plans for immediate publication, he would have to wait only two years for the translation to be published by Phaedra.[42] Early in 1965, Phaedra had been little more than a letterhead, but having aroused Nabokov's interest by offering to publish his *Butterflies in Art*, its director, Oscar de Liso, was able to secure for his firm a number of Nabokov works that Putnam's considered commercially unviable: the novella *The Eye*; the four stories issued as the slim *Nabokov's Quartet*; the play *The Waltz Invention*; and the Russian *Lolita*.

The promotion campaign for Phaedra's first book, *The Eye*, published early in the fall of 1965, revealed the naked hope of profit but little publishing acumen and less taste: "A James Bond–type book by the author of *Lolita*! . . . a spy story in Ian Fleming and John Le Carré tradition." As soon as he saw the advertisements, Nabokov cabled "For goodness' sake don't compare me in ads to Bond or Le Carré whoever they are." Following the lead of an early review, de Liso altered the terms of the comparison to Turgenev, Fitzgerald, and Conrad. Véra wrote back: "He does not want to be compared to anyone in the advertisements because you should realise that you are publishing the work of a completely individual writer. . . . If you want to compare, please compare the present work to his other publications. . . . recommend his books as just that: his books."[43]

In mid-September, Robert Hughes arrived from the United States to film Nabokov for National Educational Television. Every phase of the interview he conducted proves a revelation about Nabokov's reputation and manner and mind. Hughes had first written to Nabokov with a cautious, almost timorous request, enthusiastic but obviously fearing he might be barked at. Nabokov responded with delight and suggested they meet for dinner.[44] Over the week following the dinner, Hughes and his camera crew filmed Nabokov catching late-season butterflies, playing a comic game of blitz chess with Véra, pottering at the study end of his bedroom, strolling by the lakeshore, and chatting on a bench in Glion on the slopes above Montreux.

The published interview in *Strong Opinions* contains only a fraction of all that the crew recorded.[45] Nabokov was expansive about the past, playful in the present. Alluding to his translation of *Lolita*, he offered to read its opening lines. "Of course, incrrredible as it may seem," he said, with his distinctive St. Petersburg burred "r," as he peered over his glasses, his eyes atwinkle, "perhaps not everybody remembers how *Lolita* starts in English," and for the sake of such unfortunates he read out Humbert Humbert's invocation before turning with relish to declaim Gumbert Gumbert's (Humbert suffers in transliteration the same fate as Shakespeare's Gamlet). He explained about his current and coming projects, *The Texture of Time* and *Letters to Terra*. He showed the kinds of ingredients for future works he listed on index cards: jottings on heraldry, a possible simile awaiting a subject to attach itself to, Freud's grotesque confession that because he failed botany at the university he became, symbolically, a deflowerer.

Nabokov thought he spoke poorly, but others disagreed. His sentences might often grope for direction, he might hesitate and revise what he had said, but the record of this interview shows the quickness of his imagination and memory and observation in spontaneous conversation. When Hughes said he would like to have been able to film as they happened certain scenes from the past, especially scenes with writers in the parts, Nabokov quickly took him up:

> Yes, yes, of course. Shakespeare in the part of the King's ghost. That is said to have been one of his best roles. Stalking along, stalking along. Or take some of the American writers. Herman Melville at breakfast feeding a sardine to his cat. Nice little morning. Poe's wedding. Lewis Carroll's little picnics. Things like that. Or in American history. Russians leaving Alaska, delighted with the deal. We could have, perhaps, at the very end, a seal applauding!

After the filming was over, Hughes wrote from America that it had been one of the pleasantest experiences of his life. But when he sent the typescript, Nabokov was aghast:

> I am greatly distressed and disgusted by my unprepared answers—by the appalling style, slipshod vocabulary, offensive, embarrassing statements, and muddled facts. These answers are dull, flat, repetitive, vulgarly phrased and in every way shockingly different from the style of my written prose, and thus from the "card" part of the interview. I always knew I was an abominably bad speaker, I now deeply regret my rashness, and in fact must apologize for yielding so foolishly to the mellow atmosphere of your Glion terrace. I have kept what I managed to stomach of this spontaneous rot, and shall be grateful to you if you make still heavier cuts in that section. . . . In some cases it seemed a pity because I would have expressed it so well, so concisely, if I had written it

down beforehand. But that does not matter much now—you have
plenty of material without the deleted pages. . . .

I am terribly sorry if my extensive cuts are causing you any disappointment, but I am sure you will understand that after all I am almost
exclusively a writer, and my style is all I have.[46]

When the final text arrived, Nabokov noted he could not find any
trace of Dmitri's bathroom singing, which they had agreed to include. Always eager to promote his son's career, he wrote:

If the choice is between my son's singing and one of the two sequences
you mention (chess problem—novel writing and pleasure of writing) I
would of course prefer to have his sequence instead of mine. Why not
have him for one half of the minute somewhere in the background of
any of the more or less mute happenings and allow only one half of a
minute for him alone? Embarrassing though it is, I want to remind you
(without stressing it) that I gave you all the time you wanted and asked
for no reward except that little bit of singing.

When he saw the finished film in February, Nabokov found all reason
for alarm dispelled, and congratulated Hughes, although Dmitri's
voice remained unheard, on an "artistic, vivacious, clever and wholly
delightful" film.[47]

VIII

By late 1965, protest against America's Vietnam policy had become
vociferous and widespread, especially after Johnson ordered the
bombing of North Vietnam. Unlike most other American intellectuals, Nabokov thought of Vietnam almost entirely in light of the
crushing of freedom that the region would suffer after any extension
of Soviet influence. As pleased with President Johnson's Vietnam
policy as with his civil rights legislation, he sent the president a telegram at the time of his gall-bladder operation wishing him a "speedy
return to the admirable work you are accomplishing."[48]

Late in October, Nabokov began to draw up his reply to Edmund
Wilson, envisioning it as a third appendix to *Eugene Onegin*.[49] Early
the next month he wrote the afterword of his Russian *Lolita*, with its
explanations of the trials of translating from English into Russian.
Curiously this postscript bears the dateline "7 November 1965, Pa-
lermo," but there is no other evidence to suggest Nabokov was anywhere other than in Montreux throughout the fall.

On November 1 he began amplifying and revising *Speak, Memory*,

504

a project he had wanted to tackle for ten years.[50] He had added much to *Conclusive Evidence* in 1954 when he translated it into Russian. Now he was as famous in the English-speaking world as he had been in the émigré one and could assume, as in *Drugie berega*, that his own life and background had an intrinsic interest for his readers. He worked from both his original English and its Russian expansion, adding more detail, more dates, photographs, a foreword, an index, and endpaper maps of the Nabokov estates. As a result the new book makes his life much more tangible than it had seemed when seen solely through the bright veils of his prose. The evidence has become still more conclusive.

Nabokov wanted it that way. When he translated his autobiography into Russian in the early 1950s, the fact of writing in Russian about a Russian past seemed to reactivate and sharpen his memory. Now he probed his past still more painstakingly, and once again he proved himself ready to sacrifice approximate beauty to exact truth. The first chapter of *Conclusive Evidence* had recorded his earliest recollection, a festive walk along the alley of oaklings at Vyra, hand in hand with his parents, and his discovery of their ages. He had assigned the occasion to his father's birthday, which linked up neatly with the prefiguration of his father's death at the end of the chapter. Although no one else could now challenge him on the date of his recollection, his own concentrated retrospection caused him to redate the event to 1903, not 1902, and to reassign it tentatively to his mother's birthday in August rather than his father's in July. The chapter would lose a little of its symmetry, but he did not flinch: his sense of artistry had to make way for his sense of history.

At the beginning of December, Nabokov heavily rewrote some parts of Dmitri's translation of *The Waltz Invention*. Although he incorporated these extensive changes in the margins of the proofs—a most unusual procedure for him—some were far from last-minute flourishes, deriving as they did from ideas that had taken shape in 1939 as he began to prepare the play for a performance that was subsequently cancelled. While he was at work on the play, the Radio Liberty organization for which Kirill had worked approached him with an offer to republish some or all of his Russian novels for clandestine distribution in the Soviet Union. They would be published without an indication of Radio Liberty's involvement, under the imprint of Editions Victor, and would not be for sale despite a price added for show. Although the scheme was not political (other books planned for publication included Camus's *L'etranger* and a book that emerged in Russian as *Dublintsy* by Dzhems Dzhois), and although Nabokov was keen to have his *Lolita* published first, Radio Liberty settled on *Invitation to a Beheading*, to be followed a year later by *The Defense*.[51]

IX

Nabokov had always been impatient and implacable in defending his personal honor. He had been outraged in 1961 when *Playboy* could not print at once his rejoinder to Girodias's "Pornologist on Olympus," but his schedule had now become so tight, with three proof deadlines looming, that he could not even find time for a rejoinder to Girodias's recent "*Lolita*, Nabokov and I" (also entitled "A Sad, Ungraceful History of *Lolita*").[52] Just at this busy moment, after a few days of mounting expectancy, arrived the first flash of *Ada*, which he noted down before the vision had a chance to fade:

> Sea crashing, retreating with shuffle of pebbles, Juan and beloved young whore—is her name, as they say, Adora? is she Italian, Roumanian, Irish?—asleep in his lap, his opera cloak pulled over her, candle messily burning in its tin cup, next to it a paper-wrapped bunch of long roses, his silk hat on the stone floor near a patch of moonlight, all this in a corner of a decrepit, once palatial whorehouse, Villa Venus, on a rocky Mediterranean coast, a door standing ajar gives on what seems to be a moonlit gallery but is really a half-demolished reception room with a broken outer wall, through a great rip in it the naked sea is heard as a panting space separated from time, it dully booms, dully withdraws dragging its platter of wet pebbles.[53]

Reworked, that scene would stand at the center of *Ada*, in a haunting, desolate passage that must rate as one of the finest dreams in all of literature.

Although Nabokov did not yet see the contours of the whole novel, the changes he was making to *Speak, Memory* had prepared his mind for *Ada*. In its context in the novel, the dark romantic dream in that flash of inspiration mingles the ardor of love and the ache of exile, Van's exile from Ada, from Ardis, from the perfect past of his youth. Revising *Speak, Memory*, Nabokov had immersed himself once more in the evocation of a luminous past centered on summers at the family manor. *Ada* would retain that mood of rapturous recall, but replace the warm security of family love with the insatiable heat of adolescent desire and the need to keep the rest of the family at bay.

One immediate impetus for *Ada* was Nabokov's reworking of *Speak, Memory*'s chapter 12, his account of his love for "Tamara," Valentina (Lyussya) Shulgin. With Lyussya he had spent two summers in the Vyra area, as Van spends two summers with Ada at Ardis; with Lyussya, he found the interim between the summers a trial ("She contended afterward, in her rare moments of moodiness, that our love had not withstood the strain of that winter; a flaw had appeared, she said. . . . There it was, the same ominous flaw, the banal hollow note, and glib suggestion that our love was doomed since it could never recapture the miracle of its initial moments"),* as Van's life seems bitter and bleak between the summers of "Ardis the First" and "Ardis the Second." The letters Lyussya Shulgin sent Nabokov in the Crimea, after their affair seemed to be over, made him suddenly feel "all the pangs of exile," just as Van's ultimate exile from Ardis seems all the more jangling on the nerves when he reads Ada's letters. Nabokov could not quite get rid of the oppression until he incorporated Lyussya in his first novel, and Van can cope with his distance from Ada only by writing Letters from Terra.

In Conclusive Evidence, Nabokov reports that, during his trysts with Lyussya on the grounds of his uncle's estate, his tutor spied on them through a telescope. The young Nabokov soon put a stop to this by complaining to his mother. In Drugie berega, he adds that it was his uncle's steward who informed him about the snooping. In Speak, Memory, he recalls still more clearly: his tutor was one day "observed by my uncle's purple-nosed old gardener Apostolski (incidentally, a great tumbler of weeding-girls) who very kindly reported it to my mother." Eavesdropping and spying on Van and Ada's frenzied antics form a central motif in Ada, involving sister Lucette, the maid Blanche, kitchenhand Kim, and one of Blanche's lovers, old Sore, "the ribald night watchman."54 Though partly a parody of Pasternak's naive use of eavesdropping (Blanche's favorite book is Les Amours du docteur Mertvago), this strand of the novel also plainly echoes Nabokov's past. In Speak, Memory, too, Nabokov becomes more explicit about his sexual initiation with Lyussya and mentions "the coarse graffiti linking our first names." In Ada, Van and Ada's amours during their first summer at Ardis become "a sacred secret and creed, throughout the countryside."

"Once, at sunset, near the orange and black river," Nabokov adds to Speak, Memory, "a young dachnik (vacationist) with a riding-crop in his hand bowed to [Lyussya] in passing; whereupon she blushed like a girl in a novel but only said, with a spirited sneer, that he had never ridden a horse in his life." In Ada a riding crop will mark Van's first

---

* In Drugie berega the phrasing seems still closer to the mood of Ada: those first lyrical moments of their love the summer before "already seemed, that homeless winter, an irretrievable paradise, and this winter itself, exile."

pang of fear that Ada may prove unfaithful. "And another time,"
Speak, Memory also adds, "as we emerged onto a turn of the highway,
my two little sisters in their wild curiosity almost fell out of the red
family 'torpedo' swerving toward the bridge." That sentence's comic
tone and its ogling little sisters prepare the way for the comedy of
Lucette's compulsive spying on her insatiable siblings and for the
crucial scenes of Ada and Lucette together on the charabanc.

X

After completing his revisions to the main text of *Speak, Memory* early
in January 1966, Nabokov compiled the index—like *Pale Fire*'s, a thoroughly Nabokovian index, in this case a master key to unlock the
book's themes—and wrote the foreword.[55] It was his fifth foreword
or afterword (along with those for *The Eye, Despair*, the Russian *Lolita*,
and *The Waltz Invention*) within the past twelve months, a fair measure of the hectic pace of his production schedule.

At last he could turn to refuting Girodias's aspersions: basically,
that sheer greed had led him to attempt to dump Girodias after an
American edition of *Lolita* looked likely. His documentation was ir-
refutable, his manner one of controlled exasperation:

> From the very start I was confronted with the peculiar aura surrounding
> his business transactions with me, an aura of negligence, evasiveness,
> procrastination, and falsity. . . . What always made me regret our asso-
> ciation were not "dreams of impending fortune," not my "hating" him
> "for having stolen a portion of Nabokov's property," but the obligation
> to endure the elusiveness, the evasiveness, the procrastination, the
> dodges, the duplicity, and the utter irresponsibility of the man.[56]

Girodias did not reply.

Nabokov appears to have been in a restless state, aware that a major new work loomed, but not yet sure what it would be. While sorting through his files for the Girodias material he began to catalogue
all the multiple editions and translations of his books piled up in his
study and the *chambre de débarras*. At the beginning of February he
translated the poem "Sentimental'nyy marsh" ("A Sentimental
March") by the Soviet writer and singer Bulat Okudzhava. It was the
first time Nabokov had ever translated any work by a Soviet author
in a spirit of homage rather than scorn.* The previous October, he

---

* Except for excerpts from Yuri Olesha's story "The Cherry Stone," translated for his
classes at Cornell.

had read the poems of Osip Mandelstam in the new edition that his friend Gleb Struve had coedited and sent him. "Marvelous and heart-rending," he had written Struve at once. Now, sending the Okudzhava translation to the *New Yorker*, Véra Nabokov explained its motive: "V's blood boils when he sees what purports to be translations from the Russian of, say, poor, defenseless, doubly murdered Mandelstam by some of our modern practitioners." Nabokov had in mind especially the limitations of Robert Lowell's "imitations" of Mandelstam, recently published in the *New York Review of Books*. He was not alone in his judgment. When Andrey Voznesensky heard that Lowell had declined President Johnson's invitation to the White House, he declared he wanted Lowell as his translator. Max Hayward and Patricia Blake counseled Voznesensky against it: if he had written "horse," they warned him, Lowell would turn it into "raspberry." In an exchange with Lowell in *Encounter* in May on the subject of his *Onegin* translation, Nabokov asked Lowell to "stop mutilating defenceless dead poets—Mandelshtam, Rimbaud and others," and later in the year he would write to Struve expressing the hope that somebody would attack Lowell "for his illiterate and cretinic reworkings of poor, marvelous Mandelstam." In *Ada* he would undertake the job himself* and at the same time pay a compliment to Okudzhava's "soldier dit[ty] of singular genius."[57]

But early in February, *Ada* had still to materialize and Nabokov was still restless. "Toy with story 'The Admirable Anglewing,' in between rather boring Girodias stuff," Nabokov instructed himself in his diary, after flicking through his old index cards for ideas. He obeyed, but his old notes of 1958 and 1959 once again failed to come to life.[58]

XI

His fitfulness was about to end. On February 16, he and Véra drove along Lake Geneva's waterfront to Vevey, the next town in the direction of Lausanne, to dine with James Mason and their friend Countess Vivian Crespi at the Countess's chic hotel, the Trois Couronnes.

In *Ada* the crucial scene of Van and Ada's ultimate reunion takes place in the Hotel Trois Cygnes, an obvious fusion of the Trois Couronnes and the old Cygne wing of the Montreux Palace. Their meeting face-to-face proves a disaster, and on a flimsy pretext Ada leaves for the Geneva airport. Van ascends bitterly to his room and carries

---

* Part 1, chapter 2's intermezzo during the travestied stage adaptation of *Eugene Onegin* parodies Lowell's garblings of Mandelstam.

on writing *The Texture of Time* to keep despair at bay. The next morning he steps out onto his hotel balcony, and sees Ada exultantly gesturing up to him from the next-room balcony a floor below. She has returned in the middle of the night; he rushes down to her; they are reunited forever. What the reader will gradually discover is that the phone call the previous evening sets up the elements of a pattern woven through Van and Ada's moments of passionate reunion and poignant parting, through all the unforgettable mornings that have been the turning points of their lives. The unexpected sight of Ada on that balcony, and the eerie way the moment links up with other peaks of their past, proves in Van's own life the two central arguments of his *Texture of Time*: the utter unpredictability of the future, and the past as not a rigid succession but a storehouse of remembered images and concealed patterns that contain the key to the mysterious designs of our lives.

"Only in February 1966," states Nabokov, "did the entire novel leap into the kind of existence that can and must be put into words. Its springboard was Ada's telephone call."[59] At last he had the resolution he had sought for *The Texture of Time*, a way to allow a philosopher's metaphors about time to "breed to form a story of their own, . . . and then again to fall apart" and sink once more into a meditation on time. And now he had a means of integrating this with the Juan-Adora–Villa Venus passage he had jotted down six weeks earlier, and its mood of exile from love, its desolate inversion of *Speak, Memory*'s perfect past. The novel started to flow at once, the day after the dinner at the Trois Couronnes. Four days later, he hit upon the name "Ada." Another five days, and he noted in his diary: "New novel progressing at an alarming rate—at least half a dozen cards daily."

Lolita and *Pale Fire* had both been a long time in the making—*Lolita* from as early as 1935, *Pale Fire* from 1939—and had been repeatedly deferred, absorbing strange energies and heading in new directions before being set down in a rapid final rush. *Ada* followed a similar pattern. It depended of course on Nabokov's childhood memories—refracted through a baroque prism—of Vyra and Lyussya, but it had begun* with *The Texture of Time* in 1958 and *Letters from Terra* in 1959. All sorts of subsequent experiences had fed into the novel: the whirlwind of fame stirred up by *Lolita*;** transatlantic crossings; the *Lolita*

---

* Apart from a notebook sketch and a poem, both from 1918, that anticipated the inverted relationship of Antiterra and Terra.

** Herbert Gold told Nabokov that the meat patties served at a San Francisco drive-in had been called "lolitaburgers." In *Ada*, Van has "a few years of world fame" when his forgotten novel *Letters from Terra* is revived as a hit movie, an ur-*E.T.*: "L.F.T. clubs screenplay, reflected in *Ada*'s stage or screen adaptations of *Eugene Onegin*, *Les enfants maudits*, *Don Juan's Last Fling*, and *Letters from Terra*; the Russianizing of the American *Lolita*; the *Butterflies of Europe* and *Butterflies in Art* projects, which fed into Ada's biologizing and Lucette's art history; *Eugene Onegin* and the resultant controversy about translation; the reworkings of *Speak, Memory*; the surprise in *Ada* of old age as a golden sunset, a conclusion conditioned by the unexpectedly serene view the Nabokovs had over Lake Geneva and the 1960s.

Ada sums up everything that mattered to Nabokov. Russia, America, and exile. Family love, romantic love, first love, and last love. Three languages, three literatures: Russian, English, and French. All his other careers outside writing: lepidoptera, translation, his teaching the masterpieces of European fiction. But he did not indulgently pile up his private concerns and his private dreams. He took his world apart and painstakingly reconstructed it, square by square, to incorporate all the meaning and magic he could assemble.

XII

Before he could complete his new novel, Nabokov would have a new publisher. Walter Minton of Putnam's was irked that Nabokov was publishing so much with Phaedra: *The Eye* was several months old; *The Waltz Invention* had just been published at the end of February; the foreword for *Nabokov's Quartet*, a collection of four stories, had been composed early in March; the Russian *Lolita* had just been accepted. But Phaedra published only books Minton was not prepared to take, and offered larger advances and more advertising than Putnam's allowed for its much more substantial Nabokov works. Nabokov had felt disturbed for years that his poor advances and modest sales from his Putnam's books were the result of poor promotion of all his work since *Lolita*. If the *New Yorker* could snap up *The Defense* and *Playboy* take *The Eye* and *Despair*, why could Putnam's not find him readers?[60]

Among those most grateful for the rush of new Nabokov books, whether from Putnam's or from Phaedra, were university literature departments. Academic America had begun to catch up with Nabokov. By now *Pnin*, *Lolita*, *Pale Fire*, and the unrevised *Speak, Memory* were widely taught in U.S. colleges. The first critical book on Nabo-

---

sprouted. L.F.T. girlies minced with mini-menus out of roadside snackettes shaped like spaceships."

kov's work, by Page Stegner, would come out later in the year.[61] Andrew Field, working on his *Nabokov: His Life in Art*, sent some of his manuscript for Nabokov to check, and received this gentle rebuke:

> I wonder if you would very much mind my saying that I am emphatically opposed to the automatic use of Freudian *idées reçues*. You handle, for instance, the term "castration symbol" as if it were an irrefutable truth whereas actually it is on the same level as our ancestors' notion that the liver of a lynx is a sure cure for leprosy or a hysterical girl's stigmata are a heavenly sign (I apologise if you are a practising Roman Catholic). I think that such an original and independent mind as yours should avoid the clichés of the couch.[62]

Often pestered by graduate students who hoped to turn the object of their research into the main source of their information, Nabokov generally ignored such thoughtless requests,[63] but whenever he was asked he helped those compiling books on him for publication. Over the next decade his compulsion to scrutinize such manuscripts in meticulous detail would add to all the other literary chores his perfectionism imposed, from drafting and revising interview answers to supervising translations into four different languages.*

These chores, of course, were for the sake of his own work. But when the Library of Congress asked him if he would be prepared to translate Lincoln's Gettysburg Address into Russian for a multilingual pamphlet, he responded to the request as to a patriotic duty, and in April interrupted the swift flow of *Ada*'s composition to provide the translation.[64] Perhaps in compensation, "Abraham Milton" found his way into accommodative *Ada*.

XIII

No lover of music, Nabokov always had a very keen interest in painting, but cared little for abstract art. Among contemporaries he valued painters like American landscape artist Peter Hurd, who could record the real with a sense of poetry, or Balthus, who at this late stage in the history of art could still find new poses and moods and implications for the human body and the play of light. But his favorite contemporary artist was not a painter but the cartoonist Saul Steinberg, who could raise unexpected questions about the consequence of a style or even a single line, or could open up a metaphysical riddle

---

* In the case of translations into German, of which his knowledge was rudimentary, he naturally had to rely heavily on Véra.

with as much wit as an Escher or a Magritte and with far more economy. Nabokov invited him to call in on Montreux, and after hosting him to dinner early in March reported "a wonderful time with wonderful Saul Steinberg."⁶⁵

Otherwise Nabokov was anxious this year to have complete isolation. He hoped to find a quiet, secluded spot with nothing but butterflies—on whose trail he could still sift ideas and phrases and fancies—and work. This year Véra gave out summer addresses only in strict confidence: "We are trying to go into hiding." In mid-April they set off for Italy, stopping for a couple of days in Monza, where Dmitri had now moved from nearby Milan. They investigated Bologna's art gallery, and found nothing, then explored Florence for two weeks, tracking their way through more than a dozen galleries. As Nabokov pointed out, the search was not easy. Still lifes, unfashionable to twentieth-century tastes, are "gap-fillers, generally hanging in dark places or high up. A ladder may be necessary, a flashlight, a magnifying glass! . . . Since I don't find many of the pictures in the regular display rooms I try to find the curator because some pictures may turn up in their stacks." Early in May he and Véra spent two days in the old streets of Pompeii "amidst remarkable beauty and no less remarkable tawdriness." Searching for *Ada*'s sake as much as for the *Butterflies in Art* project, they tried to see the erotic frescoes behind the closed doors of the old brothel, the Lupanare. They were told at the office it was impossible because the place was under repair. When they reported this to their guide, he was convulsed with laughter. "That's what they tell everybody. The truth is that the Pope considers the place indecent." The guide could not stop laughing as he repeated "il Papa, il Papa," and pressed his palms together in mock prayer.⁶⁶

On May 7, Véra drove around the snaky coast to Amalfi, where they hoped to remain until July moved them to cooler altitudes. Despite the beauty of the town they did not care for the way their hotel, a thirteenth-century Capucine convent, perched in midair between sea and crags. After only two weeks they moved on, staying for four profitable days in Naples. There in the Museo Nazionale, Nabokov saw the famous Stabian fresco of a girl strewing flowers, and knew he had to place her in *Ada*'s opening chapter.⁶⁷

The last week of May and all of June they spent in Chianciano Terme, a small town set in a charming Tuscan landscape but virtually unknown to non-Italians. They were almost the only foreigners in their hotel, although a German television crew found its way even here to conduct an interview. Good weather and good locations around Chianciano allowed Nabokov to spend day after day chasing

butterflies. Then as the heat advanced he and Véra retreated north-
ward, stopping for a day in Parma—Parmigianino's sketches for the
vaulting of Santa Maria della Steccata feature in *Ada*'s second chapter—before heading up to Ponte di Legno, a tiny ski resort in the
Italian Alps, almost on the border with Switzerland and Austria.
Here, from the end of June until August, they shivered in the Grande
Albergo Excelsior, and Nabokov chased butterflies assiduously every
time the rain eased to let through a few feeble peeps of sunshine that
did little to relieve the unseasonable cold.[68]

In mid-August they returned to Switzerland, staying at the Grand
Hotel and Kurhaus at Bad Tarasp in the Engadin. Penelope Gilliatt
came to interview Nabokov for *Vogue*. She saw him as a tall, loping
man whose gait and peering gaze reminded her somewhat of Jacques
Tati. By recording Nabokov's impromptu remarks and ignoring his
prepared ones, she was able to present a lively picture of his casual
ebullience. In the hotel basement were spa baths whose soothing
treatment Véra still required. The day he met Gilliatt, Nabokov had
been up since six, as usual, and had taken a spa bath himself: "I
discovered the secret of levitation. One puts the flat feet braced
against the end of the bath and rises covered with bubbles like a fur.
I felt like a bear. A memory of a former state." She asked him about
Pasternak, and he talked at great length and in great detail about the
weaknesses of Pasternak's celebrated translations of Shakespeare
and of *Doctor Zhivago*. " 'And the metaphors. Unattached comparisons. Suppose I were to say "as passionately adored and insulted as
a barometer in a mountain hotel," ' he said, looking out at the rain.
'It would be a beautiful metaphor. But who is it about? The image is
top-heavy. There is nothing to attach it to.' " Weeks later, when he
saw the typescript, he admired Gilliatt's story but asked for many of
"a careless babbler's reported remarks" to be deleted. They were not,
and his howl came too late.[69]

XIV

At the beginning of September, the Nabokovs moved back to the
Montreux Palace. Finding more sun and warmth than they had in
Italy, they made the most of the hotel's poolside chairs. Photographer Philippe Halsman arrived with his wife to take pictures for an
article Herbert Gold was to write for the *Saturday Evening Post*. A Lat-
vian by birth, Halsman spoke Russian and had been a Nabokov fan
since the 1930s, and he and his subject established an immediate rapport. Halsman aimed to capture Nabokov as the writer in his habitat:

sitting before his open Webster's, or staring into space for a word, or with Véra resting her head on his shoulder and gazing lovingly at the man who dedicated all his books to her. Halsman had just come from photographing Lyndon Johnson, who as Herbert Gold reports was difficult to photograph

> because he was vain. . . . Johnson kept ripping the film out of his camera. He didn't like certain ears that he had, and certain hairs, and certain warts, and certain sides of his face; it was very hard to get just what he wanted. About Nabokov, however, . . . I asked . . . "Why is it there's not a single bad photograph?" . . . [Halsman replied:] "He doesn't take a bad photograph because he doesn't give a damn." And this is true. He had photographs of him sitting, walking, strolling, chasing butterflies . . . and every photograph was great because Nabokov was enjoying being himself.

Nabokov thought Halsman's pictures the best ever taken of him.[70]

Herbert Gold arrived on September 11 to interview Nabokov formally for the *Paris Review* as well as to garner what he could for the *Saturday Evening Post*. As required, he had sent the questions in advance. When he checked into the Montreux Palace Nabokov came up to the desk with an envelope in his hand: "Here is your interview. You may go home now." Gold had a moment of terror before catching the glint in Nabokov's eye. In fact, Gold stayed for two weeks, stipulating that he liked Montreux, could entertain himself, did not want to interrupt Nabokov's work, and would wait to hear from him. Nabokov telephoned at nine o'clock the next morning: "Mr. Gold, I'm finished with my day's work. What are we going to do now?" They walked, they talked, they swam. Another morning he telephoned at the same hour: "You called for two whiskies, Sir?"[71]

He reproached Gold for telling unfounded anecdotes about him ever since they had first met at Cornell in 1958. One was that Nabokov had said of a mutual friend: "Of course, he is a very nice fellow. Of course, do not lend him any money. Of course, he is completely untalented. Of course, he is a liar and a hypocrite. Of course he is a pederast. Of course, isn't that good you know him, he's a *very nice fellow*."[72] When Gold published this in the *Saturday Evening Post*, Nabokov played the most elaborate hoax he had concocted since the Vasily Shishkov affair. He wrote to the magazine that it was "most unfair" of Gold to have quoted this conversation about a common friend:

> That friend was, and is (for he is still very much alive—and very much upset) no other than Sam Fortuni, the poet. Sam tells me that he has

seen Mr. Gold only once, forty years ago, and would have never dreamed of asking him for a loan. I may add that—in refutation of the statements attributed to me—Sam does have some talent, loves women, always tells the truth, is not a particularly nice fellow, and does not exist.

This is one of the reasons I invariably beg interviewers either to stick to the script which I supply in the form of written answers to their written questions, or else, if they prefer their own impressions to my expressions, to let me check the article for factual slips before publication.

Despite his promise to do so, Mr. Gold has not complied with my request. I could not have dreaded the German TV team's impending visit which was to include my admirable translator Dieter Zimmer whom I was very keen to meet. . . . There are other embarrassing inaccuracies in the article but these will suffice as examples. I hope Mr. Gold, who seems to like anagrams, will take a good look at the name of our poor old furious poet.

Otto Friedrich, managing editor of the *Post*, was puzzled. If this Sam Fortuni existed, or even if there existed a Sam Fortuni somewhere whom Nabokov had never met, the letter's identification of him as the subject of the quoted comments would be libelous. But if it was an anagram, no one could decipher it, "and there is even one student of Nabokoviana who argues that the hint of an anagram means that it isn't an anagram." He asked if he could print Nabokov's letter with all reference to Sam Fortuni omitted. Nabokov wrote back insisting the letter be printed in full, and added:

Since I state in my letter that "Sam Fortuni" is my invention, and his name my riddle, it cannot be true that there is anything libelous in my comments, even if an old poet of that name could dig himself up and stomp, very drunk, into your office. . . .

The very simple combination SAM FORTUNI = 12345678910 = 35178942106 = MOST UNFAIR (a phrase actually used in my letter) might be unscrambled, if you like, in an editorial footnote for the benefit of inexperienced Nabokovians.

Nabokov was delighted that Friedrich printed both letters in full with Friedrich's own letter sandwiched between them.[73]

On his return to Montreux, Nabokov had continued with *Ada*, which was still "going strong." For nine weeks he also checked the French translation of *The Gift*, usually from six to ten in the morning, turning to *Ada* between two and seven in the afternoon. But he had other tasks too. He read a murky thermofax copy of the manuscript of Andrew Field's *Nabokov: His Life in Art*, and thought it superb. Field stressed the breadth of Nabokov's Russian oeuvre and the need to see his newer works in light of the old. His book in fact would be most useful for listing and summarizing Nabokov material still inaccessible at that time to most non-Russian readers. Field was also determined to be original in critical method, and although few reviewers saw any signs that he had succeeded, Nabokov at least welcomed the ambition. Field had run afoul of Russian scholars in America, and Nabokov, who had himself so often been at odds with conventional academe, thought that this antagonism too might be only a reaction to and confirmation of Field's originality. Field in fact had provoked such a reaction largely because his high confidence in his own powers was based on a rather shallow knowledge of Russian and a shaky commitment to accuracy. Nabokov began to send Field the first corrections of the many errors in his manuscript—far more than enough to have earned Nabokov's contempt in any normal scholarly situation—but smiled indulgently at the blunders because of Field's adulatory tone and his excitement about Nabokov's work.[74]

At the same time, in late September, Nabokov also had two other tasks to perform for young American academics: he supplied corrections to the manuscript Carl Proffer had sent of his *Keys to Lolita*, and he prepared interview answers for Alfred Appel for a forthcoming special Nabokov issue of *Wisconsin Studies in Contemporary Literature*.[75] It was a mark of his current standing that the journal's regular hundred pages would swell to three times that size for Nabokov.

Field, Proffer, and Appel were to be key figures in the first phase of Nabokov scholarship. Field's *Nabokov: His Life in Art* would become the best-known critical work on its subject, and Field would go on to compile a Nabokov bibliography and two biographies. Despite the tone of authority he assumed, his work, at first energetic but more proclamatory than penetrating in its critical judgments, soon became disastrously careless and seriously unbalanced, and by the mid-1970s he and the Nabokovs would be communicating only through lawyers. Proffer's academic work, by contrast, was breezy, unpretentious, and avowedly provisional, but in 1969, Proffer would set up Ardis Press, soon to develop into the largest publisher of Russian works outside the Soviet Union. He and his wife, Ellendea, would become the publishers of all Nabokov's works in Russian, Nabokov's lifeline to the growing number of his readers in the Soviet Union, and rare but welcome visitors. Appel's work,[76] by far the best as criticism, offered the deepest insights that had yet been made into Nabokov's fictional techniques, his detail, his humor, and his humanity, and this former Cornell student of Nabokov's would become a close friend.

A fourth major figure in Nabokov scholarship was his frequent

German translator and the compiler in 1963 of his first bibliography: Dieter Zimmer, later to become literary editor of *Die Zeit* and general editor of the twenty-three-volume German annotated edition of Nabokov's works. Two days after Appel left at the end of September, Nabokov turned to answer the questions Zimmer had sent him, and Zimmer himself arrived in Montreux early in October with a television crew who stayed a week. Nabokov had spent almost two decades in Germany before the war. Would he ever return for a visit, Zimmer asked? "No, I shall never go there again, just as I shall never go back to Russia. . . . As long as I am still alive there may be brutes still alive who have tortured and murdered the helpless and the innocent. How can I know the abyss in the past of my coeval—the good-natured stranger whose hand I happen to clasp?"[77]

September and October would always be busy months in Montreux, with the arrival of those who had waited for Nabokov's return from his summer travels, but this particular autumn was "a madhouse of interviews, photographers, publishers . . . and TV." Nevertheless, *Ada* continued to advance steadily, and on October 25, Nabokov could note in his diary that his box of *Ada* index cards was "heavy and alive."[78]

CHAPTER 21

Flying High: Montreux 1966–1968

I

ALTHOUGH in 1958, reviewers, readers, and writers across America had hailed *Lolita*, Nabokov himself was not well known except as the author of *Lolita* itself, *Pnin*, and a few fine *New Yorker* stories. A decade later, his literary reputation was at its height. The publication of his Russian fiction had revealed the depth and breadth of his oeuvre, while *Pale Fire* showed he could produce another surprise as great in scale as *Lolita* yet wholly different in kind. By the second half of the 1960s he was often acclaimed the greatest writer alive, the standard against which other writers should be measured, the one certain choice for a Nobel Prize.

In taking on *Lolita* when no one else had dared, Putnam's had earned the right to become his regular American publisher. But by the time Putnam's acquired the novel, *Lolita* had already built up a huge advance reputation, and so long as the courts did not intervene, its sales prospects had never been in doubt. Since *Lolita*'s runaway success, Nabokov had become more and more disappointed that Putnam's had done so little to promote sales of his subsequent work. Walter Minton, he felt convinced, had resigned himself to Putnam's other Nabokov books earning no more than a succès d'estime, and so had projected limited sales, offered modest advances, and advertised little. Nabokov also had another complaint. Despite the huge amount of effort he expended in reworking all his Russian books into English, he received no extra compensation for delivering them impeccably translated.[1] All this seemed particularly galling in the fall of 1966, when he was about to interrupt *Ada* for several months to revise the translation of *King, Queen, Knave*. A novel as accessible as that "bright brute" should attract a wide audience, and although *Ada* would be a much more difficult read, its eroticism and lyricism, its comedy and color and scale should still result in it too having excellent sales—*if* it were well promoted.

Obliged to show *King, Queen, Knave* to Putnam's, Nabokov wanted to know beforehand whether or not the advance Minton would offer was worth accepting. He had already been approached for the film rights to *King, Queen, Knave*, and in passing the request on to the William Morris Agency, he had had Véra ask what terms they thought he could obtain for the novel itself. At the end of October, Véra flew to New York for a week to discuss her husband's publishing future. There she reiterated to Minton their dissatisfaction with Putnam's advances and advertising. She heard Minton's answer as: "Vladimir is an author who is better served by a few smaller ads than by big ones." (Minton, on the other hand, remembered saying "by *numerous* small ads than by one or two very large ones.") When Véra pointed out that her husband did not agree, Minton replied: "Véra, this amounts to an author telling his publisher how to publish his works." On that note, she telephoned Switzerland. Hearing Minton's response, Nabokov asked her to instruct the William Morris Agency to ascertain—while respecting all Putnam's rights—what fee other publishers would pay to secure a package deal of his next three books.[2]

II

In Montreux, Nabokov had his own work to do. On October 26, the very day after recording that his *Ada* cards were "heavy and alive," he left the novel pulsing healthily in his imagination and turned his attention to revising *Eugene Onegin* for a new edition. Exactly a year earlier he had written in "Nabokov's Reply": "My EO falls short of the ideal crib. It is still not close enough and ugly enough. In future editions I plan to defowlerize it still more drastically. I think I shall turn it entirely into utilitarian prose, with a still bumpier brand of English, rebarbative barricades of square brackets and tattered banners of reprobate words, in order to eliminate the last vestiges of bourgeois poesy and concession to rhythm." He spent all of November 1966 heavily revising his translation, although he attacked it far less savagely than this battle cry promised. Regrettably, he did not rout iambic rhythm. Fortunately, he did redeploy his own phrases to achieve an exact line-by-line fit with Pushkin, often imparting a still stranger order to his English but bringing only a short step away an interlinear presentation of translation and original. He eliminated a few phrases less than absolutely literal, and introduced a correlative lexicon to ensure that where possible a given English word would always signal only one word of Pushkin's Russian, a plan he had adopted in preparing his first edition but then abandoned.[3]

Why did he set *Ada* aside to revise *Eugene Onegin* for an edition he knew would not be published for years? Of course, he had no need to fear that the novel's shape would start to blur: he had long been accustomed to carrying plots intact in his mind for a year or so even before setting anything on paper, and his novels seemed to gain in both complexity and coherence from this mental marinade. While writing *The Gift*, he had broken it off to compose a whole new novel, *Invitation to a Beheading*, a play, *The Event*, thirteen stories—a full Nabokov's dozen—and two translations into English of other full-length novels, *Despair* and *Laughter in the Dark*. In America he had combined *Bend Sinister* with laboratory work at the M.C.Z. and teaching at Wellesley, and *Lolita* and *Pnin* with teaching at Cornell and Harvard. But in the past, money had always restricted his choices. Knowing *The Gift* would be long in the making, he had needed to write and sell shorter pieces in the interim. Now he had no pressing need for money, and certainly could hope for little more from a revised *Eugene Onegin*. The only explanation for his suddenly breaking from *Ada* seems to be that after returning to his translation during the *Eugene Onegin* controversy in late 1965 and early 1966, he had felt compelled to tighten it to meet his most rigorous standards, and had held off only until the first irresistible rush of inspiration for *Ada* had played itself out.

Ada was still beating strongly in his mind, and in his eargerness to return to it, he would rise to begin work at six o'clock every morning. But he had other projects to attend to. At the end of November he had completed the simultaneous revision of the French translations *Le Don* and *Le Regard* (*The Eye*) and had reached the last chapter of *Eugene Onegin* when he began to revise Dmitri's literal translation of *King, Queen, Knave*.[4]

In mid-December he received a cable from the William Morris Agency: Funk and Wagnalls was ready to advance him $150,000 for his next three books. For some time Minton had been disturbed that Nabokov was ready to offer his work to other publishers, although he realized that in view of the amounts Phaedra paid for the commercially unpromising books it had taken, he could hardly complain. Still, he was upset at Nabokov's feeling that Putnam's had not done enough for him and that he deserved bigger advances. Nabokov wrote to soothe Minton, describing their association as always serene but adding: "If the difference between your offer [$7,500 for *King, Queen, Knave* in hardback, perhaps $16,000 with the paperback included] and that of another publisher were a matter of a couple of thousand dollars in the advance, I would not allow myself to be tempted. But . . . it is much more than that."[5]

A few days later his placatory attitude changed. Putnam's had been keeping Nabokov's high earnings from *Lolita* and paying them out to him at a rate of $25,000 per year to help him avoid punitive tax rates. Now Minton hinted he might dump all the money on Nabokov at once. Nabokov regarded that as blackmail, and blackmail—it would become a prominent theme in *Ada*—always made him see red. Instead of cowing him, Minton's threat made him defiant: "I will not act under coercion." No longer feeling he owed allegiance to someone who had sought to manipulate him, he became positively eager to switch publishers.[6]

III

On its launching early in January 1967, *Speak, Memory*—the last new Nabokov book Putnam's would publish*—was received with overwhelming enthusiasm. Symptomatic of Nabokov's critical status at this time was the *New Republic*'s two-part review by Alfred Appel, the magazine's longest literary review since Edmund Wilson's two-part essay on *Finnegans Wake*. Perhaps the most penetrating analysis of Nabokov's art to have appeared up to this time, the article identified the aim of all his work as "the transcendence of solipsism." Véra Nabokov wrote to Appel that his essay was so brilliant and profound she could not resist telling him of the pleasure it gave her husband: "If he ever broke his rule not to thank critics, this would have been the occasion. (This is cheating a little, as you may notice.)"[7]

Throughout January and February, Nabokov continued to revise *King, Queen, Knave*:

> I foresaw having to make a number of revisions affecting the actual text of a forty-year-old novel which I had not reread ever since its proofs had been corrected by an author twice younger than the reviser. Very soon I asserted [ascertained?] that the original sagged considerably more than I had expected. I do not wish to spoil the pleasure of future collators by discussing the little changes I made. Let me only remark that my main purpose in making them was not to beautify a corpse but rather to permit a still breathing body to enjoy certain innate capacities which inexperience and eagerness, the haste of thought and the sloth of word had denied it formerly. Within the texture of the creature, those possibilities were practically crying to be developed or teased out. I accomplished the task not without relish.[8]

Not since he rewrote *Camera Obscura* to produce *Laughter in the Dark* in 1937 had he undertaken such a thorough revision of one of his

---

* Except for *The Enchanter*, which in 1986 Dmitri would give to Putnam's.

novels. The first chapter alone had taken a week's work, and he carried on with the same intensity, operating on the book "in the most intimate parts of its anatomy." Certainly, the revised version of this novel of adultery becomes much franker in sexual matters: Nabokov adds young Frank's masturbation prior to his affair with Martha, Martha's coldness in the face of Dreyer's sexual dominance, and her sexual fervor with dominable Franz. But the sexual frankness also means greater psychological depth, on the one hand, and on the other more stress on the novel's theme of dehumanization, on the playing-card values of king, queen, and knave.[9]

Nabokov altered the novel at every level. In its texture: imagery, psychological shimmer, physical detail, incidental characters. In its structure: preparation for later events; internal reflections (the mannequin motif, the playing-card motif, the new motif of the *King, Queen, Knave* movie); external reflections of "Mr. Vivian Badlook," Nabokov and Véra, and "Blavdak Vinomori." In its characterization: Franz's lone lyrical recollections of his hometown river; Martha's relentlessly conventional soul; Dreyer's rich fantasy. And, finally, in its narrative technique: plot conventions unconsciously adopted by a young novelist and too deeply embedded in the story to discard were now rescued by an explicit twist of self-conscious irony. To those who can read both the Russian and the English versions, the differences between the two constitute an exhilarating lesson in the resourcefulness of an experienced imagination.

For Nabokov did not reconstruct the book at all: the most fleeting change sufficed. In the Russian, "Dreyer briefly cast up his eyes and made no reply" to one of his wife's repeated complaints. In the English, Nabokov need only insert after "cast up his eyes" the phrase "to a makeshift heaven" to make a flat sentence plump out: he now prods us into visualizing Dreyer's expression, he speculates (half-mockingly, but perhaps half-seriously?) on its evolutionary origins, he indicates the irony of that provenance to Dreyer's happily godless spirit.

Later, Nabokov would call his revisions to *King, Queen, Knave* "lighthearted and highhanded." In some ways they were. In the middle of his revision, he read Russian scholar Ronald Hingley's *New York Times* review of both *Speak, Memory* and Page Stegner's rather pallid *Escape into Aesthetics: The Art of Vladimir Nabokov.*[10] Hingley professed to enjoy Nabokov, but took issue with Stegner's description of him as "deeply compassionate": "His works in general secrete about as much milk of human kindness as a cornered black mamba." But worse to Nabokov than Hingley's repeatedly reading his works in the wrong light was the comparison he made of the Russian and English versions of Nabokov's autobiography and his insinuation that details added later were inventions. Hingley writes: "Thus lush incrustation piles on incrustation as Nabokov switches from one language to the other; one now awaits further and even fruitier reworkings in which he shall appear, like some exotic snake, to be growing ever newer and more grotesquely maculated skins." Right, Nabokov evidently thought, if he wants to compare my Russian and English texts, let him try this. In the Russian version of *King, Queen, Knave*, a mannequin in the sporting-goods section of Dreyer's department store has no name. Now Nabokov adds (I have italicized the changes): "*The shopgirls had dubbed him Ronald.* . . . From the way *Ronald* held his racket *it was obvious he could not hit a single ball—even an abstract ball in his world of wood.*" Nabokov chose to satisfy Hingley's expectation that future translations would sport "grotesquely maculated skins" by stressing "Ronald's" unappetizing surface: "The *dead* body was a *brownish green color with darker blotches* and paler discolorations." Hingley described as "delectably caddish" the photographs that Nabokov had chosen of his younger self for *Speak, Memory*. Nabokov spun the adjective back: "Because of the open collar Ronald's *fixed condescending grin* became even more *caddish* and indecent." Have a look at this when you next collate my translations, Nabokov seems to warn. For the moment this is between you and me, but watch whom you call unkind.[11]*

IV

When George Weidenfeld visited Montreux in late January, he found Nabokov excited about *Ada* and quite evidently "in a most active and ebullient phase of his working life." But at the end of the month Nabokov had to take a week off from *King, Queen, Knave*, not to return to *Ada*, but to scour through the galleys of Field's *Nabokov: His Life in Art*. He still regarded the book highly, despite correcting Field on a multitude of "quite astounding" mistranslations, garbled plot summaries, and fatuous critical assertions.[12]

---

* Hingley noticed, and for years enjoyed retelling the story. His recollection had become hazy with repetition by the time he identified "Ronald" in print: "[Nabokov] so resented my own reviews that he interpolated a revenge-fantasy figure, intended to represent me, into a rewritten version of his novel *King, Queen, Knave*. This is the odious character called Ronald who ends up dead in a ditch with his nostrils full of black dust" ("Sting in the tale," *Evening Standard*, November 15, 1990). Hingley has forgotten that Ronald was a mannequin, that he was present, though unnamed in the original, and that since he never leaves the shop floor, he suffers no greater indignity than having his tie removed. Hingley also misses the precision of the protest: as before, the venom and vengeance he thinks he finds in VN seem largely his own invention.

During January, Nabokov had agreed that *The Defense* should be the second of his Russian novels to be republished by Radio Liberty and distributed in the Soviet Union. Over the next two months, he received from Radio Liberty transcripts of the first excited Soviet readers' responses to *Invitation to a Beheading*. What amazed and delighted the Nabokovs most was a lengthy, intelligent, and subtle reaction to *The Gift* and *Invitation to a Beheading* from a twenty-five-year-old: "We really did not know that readers in this age bracket, nurtured on Sholohov and his likes, *could* judge literature from the purely aesthetic point of view." Later in the year Nabokov would hear from an American friend who had visited Leningrad that the office workers occupying his old home at 47 Herzen (formerly Morskaya) Street were quite used to foreigners visiting the building on his account.[13]

At the beginning of March, after three months' work, Nabokov finished revising *King, Queen, Knave*, which he had already begun to dictate to Véra. The same day he received a letter from Peter Kemeny of McGraw-Hill. Ed Booher, the company president, wanted to elevate McGraw-Hill's cultural status by acquiring a novelist who could make up for their having virtually no fiction list. Kemeny wrote: "We regard you as the greatest writer of fiction at work today, the most profound and inventive master of the English language, the novelist whose work one must be most convinced will endure. I and my colleagues ask you to allow the most successful and powerful book publisher in America to place its resources in your service. . . . Our financial agreements would be the most generous possible." How could anyone resist? Two weeks later Kemeny wrote again to make the offer still more tempting. McGraw-Hill would publish *all* of Nabokov's books—novels, stories, plays, critical and scientific works—and eventually a uniform collected edition. Could he come and see them? Naturally, he could.[14]

V

Someone as desirable as Nabokov had become to publishers was also sought after by the world at large. Despite the daunting surroundings of the Montreux Palace, despite having the hotel desk below as a sentry post and a portcullis, the Nabokovs came to feel like Tolstoy at Yasnaya Polyana, harassed by pilgrims trekking to the shrine they still inhabited. Their spring and summer travels were an essential escape. On April 4 they headed off for charming Camogli, on the Italian Riviera between Genoa and Rapallo. In the mornings, Nabokov hiked as many as fifteen kilometers up steep paths in pursuit of butterflies, but with meager results. In the afternoons, he carried on with *Ada*.[15]

Dmitri visited, as usual. As usual, so did Nabokov's sister Elena. She booked for herself a room in a pension at the other end of the village, and warned that she would be very vexed if they altered her reservation. Nabokov thought this a case of the reverse snobbery he sometimes accused her of. He checked out her pension and wrote to her with comic exagerration that he had found it squalid and sordid— an impression confirmed when he was solicited by a young boy. He implored her to let him pay for the difference between her pension and their own luxurious Hotel Cenobio dei Dogi, but she refused. After her arrival Nabokov whisked her away to his own hotel.[16]

In mid-April a French court declared the agreement between Olympia Press and Nabokov canceled as of December 1964, when Girodias had first been declared bankrupt: success at last for Nabokov, after ten years of trying to extricate himself from Olympia. At the end of the month McGraw-Hill's envoy Peter Kemeny, a much more welcome publisher, arrived for two days. He and Nabokov quickly established a warm relationship, and he agreed to McGraw-Hill's taking everything Nabokov wished to make available: stories, plays, and poems; the *Lolita* screenplay; a *Speak on, Memory*; his *Butterflies in Art*; his lectures; and perhaps an annotated *Anna Karenin*.[17]

After ten weeks in Camogli, concentrating intensely on *Ada*, Nabokov on June 13 left the coast and the summer heat for the altitude of the Maritime Alps at Limone Piemonte, a ski resort near the French border. He had chosen the area for a particular butterfly, the rare subspecies *Boloria graeca tendensis*, and climbing at 7,000 feet found "all that he had dreamed of" in the lepidoptera line. Even here, though, he found himself the prey of journalists who had tracked him down to the Cita Grand Hotel.[18]

In America too he was the focus of much attention. Alfred Appel had begun to work on his *Annotated Lolita*, and kept him busy answering his many queries. Field's *Nabokov: His Life in Art* came out to largely positive reviews and an audience that could not have enough of Nabokov. And in a glass tower on the Avenue of the Americas, Ed Booher worked out the basic conditions of Nabokov's agreement with McGraw-Hill: a $250,000 advance for a package of eleven books, a royalty of a munificent 17.5 percent from the first copy sold, and instead of the usual 50 percent of income from paperback editions, an author's split of 65 percent, rising to 80 percent.[19] Meanwhile, *Ada* flowed on.

VI

The Nabokovs had planned to spend late August still higher in the Alps, at Chamonix, but canceled their reservations in protest against de Gaulle's attitude to the United States and Israel after the Six-Day War.[20] Early in the month they returned instead to Montreux to face the annual ritual of moving their possessions back into their apartment from the *chambre de débarras* across the corridor.

During the summer Nabokov composed a number of chess problems, sending some to the *Sunday Times* and the *London Evening News*. Perhaps he had been asked to contribute on the strength of his problem in *Speak, Memory*, newly released in England, or perhaps he was already planning to have McGraw-Hill publish *Poems and Problems*. At any rate, his final ten years would become, like his twenties and thirties, a time of lively interest in chess-problem composition.

He had planned to travel to New York in September or October to discuss publishing arrangements with McGraw-Hill, who indicated it was prepared to help him set up a corporation to relieve his tax burden. But the chance of his finding the time dwindled rapidly as he became inextricably immersed in *Ada*, working from morning to night.[21]

As soon as he had returned to Montreux, however, visitors arrived: Peter Kemeny; his old friend of London and then Paris days, Lucie Léon Noel; William McGuire of Bollingen Press and his wife, Paula, who left surprised at the warmth of their reception. A French television crew came for three days in the first week of September, and a journalist from Geneva for still another interview. As curiosity seekers continued to call, Nabokov began to lament that so many articles in places as prominent as *Life*, *Vogue*, and the *Saturday Evening Post* had featured his photograph before the imposing backdrop of the Montreux Palace Hotel.[22]

He was happy, of course, to see those he knew and liked. One such couple was Phyllis and Kenneth Christiansen. She had been his research assistant at the Museum of Comparative Zoology between 1944 and 1946, and both had baby-sat Dmitri. They had arrived rather alarmed at the prospect of meeting a celebrity, but found Nabokov unchanged and were moved by the heartiness of his welcome. In the M.C.Z., Nabokov had plied his young assistant with query after query. Now, delighted to see her again, he astonished her by remembering everything about her and her family and by having understood her so well. He continued to ask direct, probing questions about her, her parents, her sister. Down in the hotel lounge, over coffee after lunch, he turned recollection into a game: "*Now* Phyllis, we are at the M.C.Z., you and I, and I want you to tell me: what was the name of the janitor who used to be a clown at the circus?" He posed the question in a pseudo-formal manner, with a twinkle of expectation in his eye. "And what was the name of the cleaning woman who had a crush on him?" He cast his mind over the denizens of the M.C.Z. and their divergent destinies, and resavored them all. As the Christiansens left, he kissed Phyllis's hand with a courtly flourish. "This has been really nice," he said, then, catching himself in a banality, retrieved it: "*Huh!*—Well, that is not a cliché. I just coined that phrase: 'r-e-e-e-ally *nice*.' "[23]

VII

In *Ada*, Van Veen talks of professional and vocational dreams: hideously flawed galley proofs, nightmarish lectures. Nabokov had such dreams recurrently, he confided to Alfred Appel: losing his notes, or slumping forward over the lectern, convulsed by a heart attack. One dream he recorded in the middle of September found its way almost straight into *Ada*: "Dream last night: late for my lecture (had to return for my notes). Flock of sheep before me threatening to delay me still more. It occurs to me suddenly that I can simply cross the whole passage out, especially as I had used it before and it was too long. This I do—and arrive in time at the lecture hall."[24]

In waking life, he would cross out passages of *Ada* only to replace them with something ampler. On the day after noting down that dream in his diary, he added another note: "Returned energetically to *Ada*, started copying out old cards (with a thousand revisions and recopyings) of Part One (Ardis) and writing, and rewriting, new cards of same Part One." As he often explained, he would conceive of a novel in such detail that he could write it on his index cards in any order, rather than from first chapter to last. But once all the contours were in place he would then sit down to a long, intense phase of recopying from the beginning and hauling his text into more or less final form. During the brilliant Indian summer of 1967, he started this final run at *Ada* at a frenetic pace. He would begin the day's writing in bed at five-thirty, then rise at eight-thirty for a simple breakfast of cornflakes, while Véra read him the most important mail. He would continue at his lectern until ten-thirty, have a hot bath, take a stroll with Véra while the hotel staff cleaned the rooms, a frugal lunch, and a two-hour nap, then return to writing again from three o'clock until six-thirty or seven.[25]

After dinner he and Véra would play a game of Russian Scrabble on a board Vivian Crespi had given them early in the year. Scrabble coincidences struck Nabokov's imagination: "There is something of the planchette in this game," he observed to his sister. One evening as he was collecting the tiles for the first round, he mentioned Elena's recent dream that Fyodor's dream at the end of *The Gift* had really happened. "*Zabavno* [amusing]," he reflected, and then discovered *zabavno* in his scrabble rack. A few days earlier he had been telling Véra that he had four people (*chetvero*) dining in *Ada*, and *chetvero* (seven letters in Russian) turned up in his rack. No wonder he appropriated Russian Scrabble for the theme of portents and prophecies in *Ada*.[26]

In mid-October, after the Frankfurt Book Fair, Ed Booher visited Montreux, and Frank Taylor, editor-in-chief of McGraw-Hill's trade book division, came to discuss the scheduling of Nabokov's books. As an editor who had long operated at the highest levels, Taylor was familiar with many world literary figures, but he had never felt intimidated at meeting any of his authors until he came to Montreux. His terror was dispelled instantly by Nabokov's friendly welcome. Taylor liked Véra's firmness, too, but it was Nabokov himself he was eager to talk to closely, to share in his "wonderful creative intensity," and to have Nabokov to himself he accompanied him on his daily stroll to buy newspapers.[27]

By November 18, part 1 of *Ada* was "*more or less* copied out in presentable form (but still many little chapters unfinished or missing)." A week into December, the first chapters were ready to type.[28] Earlier in the year Véra had typed out *King, Queen, Knave* and had felt hopelessly weighed down by that extra burden piled on top of the correspondence. Someone else would have to tackle the massive task *Ada* was shaping up to be. Jaqueline Callier, who had typed *Pale Fire* and the English translations prior to *King, Queen, Knave*, agreed to come in again for *Ada*, and would soon become Nabokov's part-time librarian and then part-time secretary.

At the end of November, Véra flew to New York to arrange for her cousin Anna Feigin to come to Montreux. Almost eighty and nearly blind, Anna Feigin, once so altruistic and accommodating, could now be nervous, impatient, and demanding, and still refused to make the move Véra had been urging all year. While in New York, Véra also joined the family lawyer, Joseph Iseman, to negotiate the final McGraw-Hill agreement with Frank Taylor and Ed Booher. At the beginning of December, Nabokov was formally signed up with McGraw-Hill, and would remain with the firm until he died.[29] For the next six or seven years, until economic changes made him seem almost unaffordable and corporate changes eliminated his editors, his relationship with McGraw-Hill would continue on the most harmonious of terms.

While Véra negotiated in New York, Elena Sikorski was brought in from Geneva to keep her brother in running order by brewing his two cups of morning coffee—he simply did not know even how to make the coffee he drank every day—answering the phone, sitting across the Scrabble board from him in the evenings—duties he set out for her in a parodically pedantic schedule, complete with a topographical plan of the apartment, that he drew up as a comic thank-you for her trouble. Véra had not wanted him to be left on his own: she was worried about the intensity of his work on *Ada*, which had lasted now in one sustained streak since August. Even three weeks after her return from New York, she still had not been able to persuade him to take time from his writing to cast an eye over the McGraw-Hill agreement.[30]

VIII

Early in the year the Nabokovs had invited Andrew Field to visit. Since then, McGraw-Hill had decided to mark their acquisition of Nabokov by publishing an updated and expanded version of Zimmer's bibliography of his works, and Field had recently been asked to undertake it. On December 26 he arrived for dinner with his future second wife, Michele, and watched as Nabokov opened an envelope from Edmund Wilson and a Christmas card, shaped like a butterfly and propelled by a wound-up rubber band, shot out and lurched across the room, a vestigial gesture of friendship that could not stay airborne long.[31] When Nabokov and Field broke off *their* relations, not even that much would remain.

In the first week of January 1968, Nabokov's Hollywood agent Irving Lazar and his wife came to visit. Producer Harold Prince (*West Side Story, Fiddler on the Roof*) wanted to stage a musical on the improbable basis of *Lolita*. Lazar also wanted to consider the prospects for an early sale of the movie rights to *Ada*. There were other theatrical prospects. Joseph Papp had asked to produce a stage adaptation of *Invitation to a Beheading* for the New York Shakespeare Festival. Oxford University's Russian Club was in rehearsal for the world premiere of *Izobretenie Val'sa* (*The Waltz Invention*), using a text that included translations into Russian of the new material added to the English text. It was staged on March 8 and 9, 1968, in a pattern reminiscent of the 1938 premiere of *Sobytie* (*The Event*), the first night a disaster, the second a great success.[32]

The story of Nabokov's transfer to McGraw-Hill broke in New York on January 12. When asked by reporters why he had switched publishers, Nabokov replied: "Putnam's position was that Mr. Nabokov was much too good a writer to fuss about such sordid trifles as more money for more books and Mr. Nabokov's position was that no matter how good he was he should get enough to buy pencil sharpeners and support his family." At the end of the month, Ed Booher proposed to Nabokov that to mark his first book with them, *King, Queen, Knave*, McGraw-Hill would simultaneously republish the Russian original, *Korol', dama, valet*.[33] In the twenty years between Nabokov's switching to English in 1938 and the American publication of *Lolita*, he had had to take his first four English novels from publisher to publisher, and to abandon altogether the attempt to have his Russian novels translated, let alone republished in the unprofitable Russian. How different were things now!

As one of its first Nabokov works McGraw-Hill would also publish the *Annotated Lolita*. Its editor, Alfred Appel, arrived in Montreux with his wife, Nina, two days after the Lazars left, to revise his annotations in tandem with Nabokov. Nabokov was enthusiastic about Appel's work, though at times he asked him to prune luxuriant detail and tone down his irrepressible humor, hardly apropos in scholarly annotations that a publisher would want compactly bound into affordable copies of the novel. But Nabokov delighted in someone like Appel, who did not sit reverently waiting for the master's words but could hold his own and even cheerily characterize himself as a "Jew d'esprit."[34]

At dinner one evening Nabokov's eyes lit up when Appel, rubbing one of his shoes against a trouser leg, caused its loose sole to flap right open, as if he were playing the part of Chaplin's tramp. While his sole was being repaired Nabokov loaned him some zippered after-ski boots, two sizes too big. As they strolled along through an unusually cold Montreux winter, Appel had to keep stopping and pulling up his socks. Walking beside him in his camel-hair coat, Nabokov could not stop chuckling at his friend's plight. Then, when a car hurtled past along the narrow Grand-Rue and Appel jumped out of the way, only for one of his shoes to be left on the sidewalk, Nabokov roared with laughter: "He can't fill Nabokov's shoes!" Appel's own shoes were ready the next morning, and at nine-thirty Nabokov collected them and knocked at the Appels' door. "Who is it?" asked Appel. "It's the boy," replied Nabokov. Nina Appel, practically undressed, ran for cover when the door opened, but both she and her husband could see Nabokov observing the room, taking it all in, watching how they performed when they were caught off guard. His novelist's eye was always alert, Appel felt, whether to strangers, visitors, or hotel staff, always ready for the expression or the gesture that revealed the person behind the social mask.[35]

Despite all his visitors and a severe cold that developed into pleurisy, Nabokov continued apace with *Ada*, finishing his fair copy of part 1 on February 5 and passing on to part 2 as soon as he had checked the *King, Queen, Knave* proofs and written the responses for yet another interview.[36]

Partly in reaction to the winter's intense cold, partly to make it easier to care for Anna Feigin, the Nabokovs had thought seriously of taking an apartment in Tuscany for the coming winter. But on March 8, Véra's sister Sonia cabled from New York that Anna Feigin's faculties were rapidly deteriorating and she needed urgent care. Two weeks later Véra flew across the Atlantic and brought her cousin back to Montreux, where she found her an apartment and live-in help. Now, even if the Nabokovs had been thinking seriously of settling elsewhere, Anna Feigin's condition would keep them where they were.[37]

One night in March, Nabokov had a dream that the hotel was in flames, and that he saved "Véra, my glasses, the *Ada* typescript, my dentures, my passport—in that order!" Perhaps that may have sparked off his next novel, *Transparent Things*, and the fire-fed nightmare at its terrible center. Then early in April, Nabokov became restive as he had to set aside his current novel for his previous one. On April 1 his German publisher Ledig Rowohlt arrived with his chief foreign editor and *Pale Fire*'s translator to revise *Fahles Feuer* in conjunction with Nabokov, who had an advanced smattering of German, and Véra, who spoke it well. All day every day for a week, from as early as nine-thirty in the morning to as late as ten at night, the five assembled while the translator read steadily through his text from beginning to end. The Nabokovs thought the translation excellent, but still stopped the reading after almost every sentence to query a rendering, check a nuance, or suggest an improvement.[38]

Splendidly effective though it was, this mode of translation was exhausting for a couple of near-seventy-year-olds. After returning to *Ada* for a few days more on part 2,* Nabokov took his reward for the unrelenting pace and the unprecedented productivity he had managed since August—six hundred typescript pages over the fall and winter—and headed off on April 17 for spring, butterflies, and rest at Cernobbio, on Lake Como. A week later he and Véra were summoned back to Montreux by a sudden but short-lived alarm over Anna Feigin's condition. *Ada* seemed fated to give him no rest.[39]

---

* An incidental note from this time in Nabokov's diary: April 10, 1968: "Begun watering my claret"; April 11, 1968: "Stopped watering my claret."

IX

While assembling for Field pages of additions and corrections to Zimmer's Nabokov bibliography, Véra had mentioned to him there were many otherwise unrecorded poems in some one hundred and fifty letters that Nabokov had written to his mother in the 1920s and 1930s and that had just arrived—courtesy of the new freedoms Dubček had introduced into Czechoslovakia—from his sister Olga in Prague. The news of the letters precipitated Field's decision to ask if he could undertake Nabokov's biography. At the end of May, Véra replied that her husband "warmly welcomes" the project and "could not imagine anyone else whom he would want to accept as his biographer"—the other obvious choice, Appel, knew no Russian—but at the same time made it clear that they would approve few informants and allow only controlled and limited access to their papers.[40] Meanwhile Field had the bibliography to finish.

Others had Nabokov projects of their own. *King, Queen, Knave* was published at the end of April to enthusiastic reviews, and like *Speak, Memory* became a Book-of-the-Month-Club selection. Even before its publication, a $100,000 contract had been negotiated for movie rights. Frank Taylor called from New York about the possibility of sending representatives of major Hollywood studios to Montreux to bid for *Ada* on the strength of the typescript, and announced to the press that the asking price for movie rights would be $1,000,000. Edward Weeks, editor of the *Atlantic*, approached Nabokov for the rights to serialize the whole of *Ada*. Robie Macauley, *Playboy*'s fiction editor, flew to Switzerland in pursuit of the same quarry.[41]

Meanwhile, *Laughter in the Dark*, conceived almost forty years earlier with an eye to the screen, was at last about to be filmed over the summer, with Tony Richardson to produce the movie from a screenplay written by Edward Bond. Richard Burton had been signed to star, but after turning up on the set drunk or late and hung over several days in a row, he was dropped and replaced by Nicol Williamson.[42] Despite all this talent, the film would prove flat and unprofitable.

X

As summer approached, the Nabokovs prepared to flee Montreux again. With Anna Feigin in their party, they could not travel far, and on May 10 they settled for the Hôtel des Salines in Bex-les-Bains, a twenty-minute drive away in the upper Rhône valley. Véra instructed her closest correspondents to keep the address strictly secret, since it was too close to Montreux to deter zealous sightseers. During a rainy and uneventful summer, Nabokov continued to work on *Ada*, while Véra emended and added to the Zimmer bibliography for Field. She also placed advertisements in Europe's Russian weekly, *Russkaya mysl'*, to try to obtain some of Nabokov's rarest early works and make their collection bibliographically complete. In mid-June she and her husband traveled to Italy for a week to hear Dmitri sing in two concerts in Milan and San Remo, and only at the beginning of July did the weather improve enough for butterflies to emerge around Bex and offer a little competition to *Ada*, which was "coming along beautifully."[43]

Early in July, Véra drove her husband to the Parc Hotel in Verbier, a mountain resort across the Rhône valley, and left him to chase butterflies while she returned to look after her cousin. By now he was writing part 3 of the novel, and still the fates conspired in *Ada*'s favor as he faced "the foulest (and most productive!) weather imaginable." When a friend of Anna Feigin's arrived in Bex on July 19 to relieve her for three weeks, Véra drove back to Verbier to rejoin Vladimir at once.[44]

Around the world, 1968 was a year of political turmoil. Nowhere could have been further from it all than a mountain resort in the Valais. The Nabokovs had little sympathy with the student uprisings "except in the few countries with real and grim dictatorships." In Dubček's Czechoslovakia, the country that seemed likeliest to shake off its oppressive yoke, a lively interest had developed in Nabokov's work. Rights were even granted for a Czech edition of the antitotalitarian *Invitation to a Beheading*—and then Soviet tanks rolled in to squash that and millions of other hopes. Across the Atlantic, chaos was expected at the Democratic party's national convention in Chicago, and *Esquire* magazine, suspecting that the affair would turn into theater of the absurd, invited Jean Genet, William Burroughs, and Terry Southern to cover the occasion, and sent out another invitation to Nabokov—Nabokov, of all people to approach to write *anything* on commission, let alone about current politics! Predictably, he declined,* preferring to remain with his head in Antiterra.[45]

Early in August he returned to the Montreux Palace. Six hundred and seventy-one pages of *Ada* had now been typed up, and he was nearing the end of part 3. He asked for the planned visits from Hol-

---

* "I . . . still believe it must have been some sort of joke on the part of *Esquire*—inviting *me* who can't tell a Democrat from a Republican and hates crowds and demonstrations" (*Strong Opinions*, 126).

lywood studio heads to be deferred until October so that he could show them part 3 complete. September as usual brought another television interview, this one led by Nicholas Garnham for the BBC. As usual, too, Nabokov wrote out his answers in advance, but was delighted to find that this time he could read them out from a tele-prompter.[46]

By mid-September he was at work on *Ada's* part 4, *The Texture of Time*. In August he had anticipated this short section of the novel might cause him trouble, as it had four or five years earlier, and he predicted he would not finish it until Christmas. Now, drawing on the notes he had started in 1957, he completed part 4 in only three weeks.[47]

Ada's earliest readers had already begun to arrive. First came Frank Taylor at the end of September, then throughout October a succession of movie moguls. Agent Irving Lazar was delighted at the parade: "I don't know of any author who is so highly regarded and a novel which was so eagerly awaited that the heads of studios will come to Switzerland to read the novel and are told the conditions under which they can read it, and in reading it are not being told simultaneously that they are the *only* ones who are reading it." Robert Evans of Paramount, who arrived at the beginning of October, came with the idea of having Roman Polanski direct. Then at three-day intervals followed representatives from CBS, Twentieth Century-Fox, and Columbia. Last of all was Richard Lester. Each of them had to take the typescript and, before leaving, send the bids up to the Nabokov's floor, like petty princes offering tribute to an emperor.[48]

As Nabokov drafted the fair copy of *Ada's* last few chapters, he could look back in wonder at that young or middle-aged Nabokov completing other major works in circumstances that now seemed impossibly remote. *The Gift* he had finished in poverty on the Riviera, then had to wait fifteen years for a publisher prepared to publish it in toto. He had had to compose *Lolita* while burdened by teaching duties and the uncertainty that the book would ever be published; after a long series of rejections, he could have it accepted only by a Paris pornographer. Now, major publishing houses, major magazines, and major studios were all ready to vie for *Ada* before he could even round the novel off.

Instead of resting after he finished part 4 on October 5, he plunged into part 5 the next day, and finished this last short section and the novel's built-in blurb on October 16, on the last of some twenty-five hundred index cards. "I feel very empty and fragile," he wrote Frank Taylor.[49]

In *Ada*, Van and Ada die in their bed, flattened out as it were *"into* the finished book, . . . into the prose of the book or the poetry of its blurb." In the very week he was putting the final touches to Van's valedictory blurb, Nabokov was posing for his own two-dimensional image to appear on the dust jacket, along with his hero's last lyrical self-advertisement. Two days before he finished *Ada*, he welcomed Philippe and Yvonne Halsman back to Montreux with a bottle of Mouton Rothschild. Afterward, Philippe Halsman would write that he felt more sheer unadulterated intellectual pleasure in Nabokov's company than in the company of anyone else he had ever captured on film, even Einstein. On this assignment his aim was no longer to photograph the writer at work in his habitat but simply to take the "portrait . . . of a genius." For one shot, Nabokov pulled an impishly quizzical expression and declared that it would be just right for *Ada*.[50] That puckish portrait appeared on the cover of the English *Ada*, along with Van's blurb, but the American edition featured another from the same Halsman session, a serious, inscrutable expression that would be repeated on other McGraw-Hill covers and would look somehow mysteriously different on each: now jaded, now chilling, now weary, now poignant, and then simply inscrutable again, as if Nabokov were saying: "Make of me what you will."

CHAPTER 22

Ada

I

ADA, NABOKOV'S longest and most ambitious novel, sets us down in his strangest and most contradictory world, his most colorful and comic, his most lyrical and discordant, his most unsettling and profound.[1] Line by line, page by page, chapter by chapter, he piles one bizarre choice on another. He sets the action on a planet, Antiterra, whose geography appears identical to ours but whose history follows its own strange forks. He bestows on Van and Ada fabulous wealth, high birth, supreme intelligence, athletic vigor, tireless sexual energy, and an ardent love affair that lasts well into their nineties. So enraptured are they by the story of their own love, and so eloquent in evoking its charm, that we cannot help sharing their delight. Yet Nabokov makes them not only brother and sister but almost male and female variants of a single design, so that their passion and their pride begin to reek of self-love and self-advertisement. And after holding up the first two summers of their affair for lingering, rhapsodic inspection, he lets the next eighty years of their lives plummet away, jerking from day to decade with ever-increasing speed and an ever-dwindling sense of control.

But then genius always opts for strange choices. Beethoven makes the last movement of his last symphony swell with song; Monet paints the same facade five times from the same point of view; Shakespeare forces a mad king, a fool, and a bedlamite beggar out into the windswept night—and we would not wish any of those moves unmade. *Ada*'s quirks testify not, as some critics have thought, to idle caprice or a failure of distance and design, but to Nabokov's desire to express more than he ever has before: "My purpose is not to be facetiously flashy or grotesquely obscure but to express what I feel and think with the utmost truthfulness and perception."[2] Never in more perfect command of his material, he fractures his world and reassembles it not simply for the fun of it all—though that is real enough—but in order to reexamine it more thoroughly than ever before.

II

Lecturing to his students at Cornell and Harvard, Nabokov always stressed that great writers are above all great enchanters. In *Ada* he offers enchantment itself in the story of Van and Ada's extraordinary affair, which dominates the novel from start to finish. Against all the odds, their rapturous first love for each other, in their early teens, proves also to be serene last love, as they reflect in old, old age on the summer, so remote, so near, when they first fell in love. Here Nabokov fuses two of his brightest themes—first love and the might of memory—with the theme of faithful married love, which he normally treats only by reticence (Fyodor and Zina, himself and Véra, John and Sybil Shade), by ironic or tragic negation (the Dreyers, the Luzhins, the Kretschmars, the Humberts, the Pnins) or through the pain of loss (Chorb, Sineusov, Krug). As brother and sister, Van and Ada cannot marry, but they spend their last forty-five years happily together. Their good-luck story wards off even the threat of lonely bereavement that might stretch its shadow over their sunset love, for they die together in their nineties, die as if *into* the manuscript record of their past that they continue to revise until the last, as if into the timeless romance of their love.

Ada's special texture adds to its strange allure. A psychologist and a philosopher, Van Veen in 1922 writes *The Texture of Time*, one of his major works, and reprints it in toto as part 4 of *Ada*. *Ada* itself, which he writes and revises between 1957 and 1967, is in a sense an expansion of the ideas of his earlier treatise. Van—with Nabokov behind him—deliberately sets up multiple rhythms of time and multiple relationships to time to turn *Ada* into an extraordinary study of that most elusive of concepts: but time as pure passion, not a cerebral abstraction.

In *The Texture of Time*, Van severs space from time and rejects time as direction even as he is driving headlong across Switzerland toward Ada. In *Ada*, in similar fashion, he appears to concede the idea of time's direction only to turn around and challenge it. Part 1 of the book, more than half its length, covers two summers Van spends at Ardis manor with Ada: their first summer together, in 1884, and a second, four years later, in 1888. "Ardis the First," his 1884 sojourn, begins with the fourteen-year-old Van's initial distaste for his "cousin" rapidly turning to love and to agonies of impossible yearning: after all, Ada is only twelve, she is his cousin, he dare not even show his interest in her for fear that she might recoil in disgust or raise the alarm. Then starts the headlong slide toward the consummation of their love—a swift, undeviating advance that would itself

seem to confirm what Van the philosopher dismisses as "the direction of Time, the ardis of Time, one-way Time."* But what really stirs
our own sense of excited anticipation as we read is that we already
know that their love is a fact. Each early phase in their coming together has become a milestone that we are allowed to see immediately they will fondly recall: "When I kiss you *here*, he said to her
years later, I always remember that blue morning on the balcony."
And what makes the Ardis scenes so enchanting is not the speed of
their love, not the "ardis of Time," but that their time seems so expansive, so timeless, stretching out like any child's unending summer, and with detail after detail still immediate and intact eighty
years later.

Van returns to Ardis in 1888, having seen Ada over the last four
years on only two occasions, for an hour apiece. Dreading that time
will have changed everything, he arrives "unexpected, unbidden,
unneeded; with a diamond necklace coiled loose in his pocket. As he
approached from a side lawn, he saw a scene out of some new life
being rehearsed for an unknown picture, without him, not for him."
He sees Ada in the distance in a new long dress "with no sleeves, no
ornaments, no memories," and watches Percy de Prey kiss her hand
and then hold it while he speaks to her and then kiss it again. Van
walks off in icy fury and tears the necklace he has brought for Ada
"into thirty, forty glittering hailstones, some of which fell at her feet
as she burst into the room" to tell him that he is wrong, that nothing
has changed, that she loves only him. At this point Ardis the Second
becomes a glorious retrieval of the past, a metaphysical triumph over
time, never more magical than in the picnic for Ada's birthday that
seems to replay detail after detail from the picnic on her birthday four
years earlier. Then the miracle crashes to the ground: Van discovers
Ada has been unfaithful not only with robust Percy de Prey but with
the family's plaintive and pathetic music teacher, Philip Rack. In a
rage, he storms from Ardis in pursuit of his foes.

When part 1 introduces young Van and Ada falling in love, we also
see behind them or through them the old Van and Ada collaborating
fondly on the story of their past, still passionately in love decades
later. The sunflecked happiness of the Ardis sections, the gentle drift
of time through those two summer idylls, the bright unity of season
and setting, the magical recapture of time, and the glimpse of the old
Van and Ada still in love establish powerful expectations for the rest
of the book. They are rudely dashed. Part 2, only half as long as part
1, is more than half over before the lovers meet again, four years

---

* "Ardis," as Ada points out, means in Greek "the point of an arrow."

later, when Ada at last overcomes Van's jealous resentment. The intervening chapters have seemed jagged and disturbingly disjunct, and when Van and Ada meet, it is not at Ardis. Ardis, indeed, will never recur.

Part 3 in turn is only half as long as part 2, and we reach the eighth and last chapter of this part before Van and Ada meet once more, twelve years later, for a short series of snatched adulterous trysts. Part 4 is not even half the length of part 3, and now a whole seventeen years later in time. When Van and Ada see each other in fifty-year-old bodies, they are so shocked at each other's appearance and at their awkward unfamiliarity with each other that they abandon their attempt at reunion. Only on the last page of part 4—and the few remaining pages between right thumb and fingers warn that part 5 cannot be much more than half of part 4—do Van and Ada at last stop the catastrophic slide of time, the rapid radioactive decay of their elemental passion.

Just before part 4 closes, Van and Ada seem to have wasted their lives and their love. What can part 5, a meager sixteenth of part 1, retrieve? But part 5 begins triumphantly: "I, Van Veen, salute you, life, Ada Veen, Dr. Lagosse, Stepan Nootkin, Violet Knox, Ronald Oranger. Today is my ninety-seventh birthday." The triumph continues: by the time he writes that, Van has spent forty-two years of cloudless love with Ada, the last ten reworking the story of their enchanted beginnings at Ardis.

Time's arrow had seemed to be hurtling away with greater and greater speed through an ever colder and more ragged sky. But no matter how strong the force of expectation, it cannot determine the shape of the future: against all likelihood, Van and Ada's course changes utterly in 1922, and from that point on they live together in harmony for as long as almost any happily married couple. Ultimately, time for Van and Ada has proved to be not an ineluctable arrow but a rhythm of passionate union and bitter separation and the continual accumulation of a fondly shared past.

Ever since writing *The Tragedy of Mr. Morn* in 1924, Nabokov had been searching for a way to express his sense of a human life evolving in time. Not until *Ada* did he find how to show all he wanted: life not as one-way motion, not as the dramatic action and reaction of forces narrowing relentlessly to some inescapable climax, but as something much freer, with surprising jolts and changes of direction that nevertheless in retrospect fall into a unique pattern that characterize one person's individual fate. And at the same time, *Ada* records rhythms that are common to us all: the seemingly endless expanse of childhood time, the accelerating collapse of the years, the steadily swelling stores of memory.

III

When Nabokov identified a great novel by its power to enchant, he meant by that its appeal to the alert imagination of the reader. If *Ada* as a whole has its fairy-tale spell, its parts often show that Nabokov's gift for individual scenes has never been more magical.

Take one typical scene. Twelve-year-old Ada, as Van explains, has her private philosophy of happiness: "An individual's life consisted of certain classified things: 'real things' which were unfrequent and priceless, simply 'things' which formed the routine stuff of life; and 'ghost things,' also called 'fogs,' such as fever, toothache, dreadful disappointments, and death. Three or more things occurring at the same time formed a 'tower.' . . . 'Real towers' . . . were the joys of life." Shortly after his arrival at Ardis, before he and Ada dare voice their feelings, Van leaves the hammock in which he has slept out in the summer night and joins Ada on the balcony where she is having breakfast in the early-morning blue.

> Her plump, stickily glistening lips smiled.
>
> (When I kiss you *here*, he said to her years later, I always remember that blue morning on the balcony when you were eating a *tartine au miel*; so much better in French.)
>
> The classical beauty of clover honey, smooth, pale, translucent, freely flowing from the spoon and soaking my love's bread and butter in liquid brass. The crumb steeped in nectar.
>
> "Real thing?" he asked.
>
> "Tower," she answered.
>
> And the wasp.
>
> The wasp was investigating her plate. Its body was throbbing.
>
> "We shall try to eat one later," she observed, "but it must be *gorged* to taste good. Of course, it can't sting your tongue. No animal will touch a person's tongue. When a lion has finished a traveler, bones and all, he *always* leaves the man's tongue lying like that in the desert" (making a negligent gesture).
>
> "I doubt it."
>
> "It's a well-known mystery."

Her hair was well brushed that day and sheened darkly in contrast with the lusterless pallor of her neck and arms. She wore the striped tee shirt which in his lone fantasies he especially liked to peel off her twisting torso. The oilcloth was divided into blue and white squares. A smear of honey stained what remained of the butter in its cool crock.

"All right. And the third Real Thing?"

She considered him. A fiery droplet in the wick of her mouth considered him. A three-colored velvet violet, of which she had done an aquarelle on the eve, considered him from its fluted crystal. She said nothing. She licked her spread fingers, still looking at him.

Van, getting no answer, left the balcony. Softly her tower crumbled in the sweet silent sun.

At this stage of the novel, Van has passed beyond the stage of wondering "was she really pretty, at twelve? Did he want—would he ever want to caress her, to really caress her?" He has been initiated into her private "philosophy." He spends his nights haunted by his longing for Ada, and on this particular morning wakes up resolute: "He was fourteen and a half; he was burning and bold; he would have her fiercely some day!" But when he sees her his desire has to remain as mute as it is here.

The scene is shot through with the tension between anticipation of an impossible dream and fond recollection after the dream has come true. Almost before the scene starts, Van recalls passionately recollecting it to Ada years later; within the scene, he silently anticipates ("my love's bread and butter") a happiness he still has no knowledge will ever come to pass. The crumb steeped in nectar, the throbbing wasp, the oilcloth, the honey-smeared butter define in an instant the space within which silent expectation stirs. Around the little that happens we feel the pressure of what does not happen—Ada does not tell Van that his presence makes the moment "priceless," that he is her third "Real Thing"—and what we anticipate *will* happen, that Van will find out that Ada, far from being too young for love, already adores and desires him. Young Van does not know this; young Ada cannot simply tell him; but we and the older Van and Ada all know it—and we all look forward to the moment when young Van and Ada can frankly declare their love and recall to each other this moment and the feelings they dared not voice.

IV

Alongside the enchantment of much of *Ada* there also seems much that some readers find anything but enchanting. Three aspects of the novel particularly rankle: its sheer difficulty, or rather the sense it continually imparts that one may have missed this or that local obscurity, recondite allusion, half-buried joke; its lack of form, its centripetal sallies, its eruptive heterogeneity; and the attitude toward Van and Ada that the book seems to invite. John Updike, one of Nabokov's most enthusiastic readers, begins his review of *Ada* by declaring that "when a book fails to agree with a reader, it is either because the author has failed to realize his intentions or because his intentions are disagreeable," and then proceeds to quote *Ada's* first speech in the first full scene of the novel, at the end of the first chapter.[3] Let us look at that scene.

After a tangled summary of marital relationships that parodies the family forebears paraded across the entrance of many a nineteenth-century novel—Aqua Durmanov has married her cousin Demon Veen; her twin sister Marina has married her, Aqua's, and Demon's cousin Dan Veen—part 1, chapter 1 discloses two naked and unnamed children rummaging in the attic at Ardis Hall. They have come across evidence of their parents' past: a wedding photograph in a newspaper, a reel of a home movie, and a herbarium belonging to Marina. The leaves and flowers labeled in the middle of the herbarium, dated between September 1869 and March 1870, seem to act out "a regular little melodrama." To us, the sample entries are colorful but hardly much of a story:

> Golden [ginkgo] leaf: fallen out of book "The Truth about Terra" which Aqua gave me before going back to her Home. 14.XII.69.
>
> Artificial edelweiss brought by my new nurse with a note from Aqua saying it came from a "*mizernoe* and bizarre" Christmas Tree at the Home. 25.XII.69.
>
> Petal of orchid, one of 99 orchids, if you please, mailed to me yesterday, Special Delivery, *c'est bien le cas de le dire*, from Villa Armina, Alpes Maritimes. Have laid aside ten for Aqua to be taken to her at her Home. Ex en Valais, Switzerland. "Snowing in Fate's crystal ball," as he used to say. (Date erased.)
>
> *Gentiane de Koch*, rare, brought by *lapochka* [darling] Lapiner from his "mute gentiarium" 5.I.1870.
>
> [Blue-ink blot shaped accidentally like a flower, or improved felt-pen deletion] *Compliquaria compliquata* var. *aquamarina*. Ex, 15.I.70.

From this meager evidence the children make a host of fantastically elaborate deductions much more mystifying than the herbarium itself:

> "I deduce," said the boy, "three main facts: that not yet married Marina and her married sister hibernated in my *lieu de naissance*; that Marina had her own Dr. Krolik, *pour ainsi dire*; and that the orchids came from De-

mon who preferred to stay by the sea, his dark-blue great-grand-mother."

"I can add," said the girl, "that the petal belongs to the common Butterfly Orchis; that my mother was even crazier than her sister; and that the paper flower so cavalierly dismissed is a perfectly recognizable reproduction of an early-spring sanicle that I saw in profusion in hills in coastal California last February. Dr. Krolik, our local naturalist, to whom you, Van, have referred, as Jane Austen might have phrased it, for the sake of rapid narrative information (you recall Brown, don't you, Smith?), has determined the example I brought back from Sacramento to Ardis as the Bear-Foot, B,E,A,R, my love, not my foot or yours, or the Stabian flower girl's—an allusion, which your father, who, according to Blanche, is also mine, would understand like this" (American finger-snap). . . .

"Good for you, Pompeianella (whom *you* saw scattering her flowers in one of Uncle Dan's picture books, but whom *I* admired last summer in a Naples museum). Now don't you think we should resume our shorts and shirts and go down, and bury or burn this album at once, girl. Right?"

"Right," answered Ada. "Destroy and forget. But we still have an hour before tea."

All we can deduce from this is that Van and Ada at fourteen and twelve are immeasurably bright, self-conscious, and self-satisfied. From *Ada*'s first sentence, we have been made aware that there may be much that eludes us in the world of this book. Now the young hero and heroine stand before us, glorying in the fact that nothing escapes *them*, and even—for they seem almost aware of us looking over their shoulders—deliberately shutting us out of any chance of understanding their exchange. Has their maker miscalculated?

Nabokov always values the excitement of discovery, but as a scientist, a scholar, and a writer, he also recognizes the effort that discovery requires. He stresses the world's resistance to the mind that tries to apprehend it, as well as the delights ahead for the mind that exercises the curiosity and imagination to overcome as much of that resistance as it can. Never have these two sides of his epistemology played such a role in his fiction as in *Ada*. At one point, as Van and Ada meet for a last passionate tryst at the end of their first summer together, the novel lapses into code and emerges again, leaving us with a momentary twinge of frustration but at the same time tantalizing us. Is this scene simply too hot to print, even more ardent than all the vividly erotic scenes we have already been permitted to witness at Ardis? But the passage continues with Ada handing Van the code for their correspondence during their time apart—their inces-tuous relationship must of course remain a secret—and providing us at least with some reason for that burst of code. Still no key to the code, however, and the scene closes with no explanation of the ci-phered words. Only in the next chapter do we find the code itself, and if we scurry back to "making *klv zdB AoyvBno . . .*" we can now read it as "making *his way through the brush and crossing a brook to reach* Ada in a natural bower of aspens; *they embraced.*" The promised For-bidden Masterpiece proves entirely innocent, and that joke itself is more than reward enough for the tease. Again and again throughout *Ada* Nabokov adopts the same tactics: an obvious obscurity, remind-ing us that we have no instant access to knowledge, and then a ret-rospective clarification, for those prepared to take the new evidence and search back for the hidden reward.

That is the pattern of the three chapters that comprise *Ada*'s pro-logue. The convoluted story of Van and Ada's parents obscurely glimpsed in the attic scene begins to unfold with dizzy speed and dashing romanticism in Demon and Marina's affair in the next chap-ter. Then in part 1, chapter 3, Van summarizes Aqua's uncertainty that she is really his mother:

> At one time Aqua believed that a stillborn male infant half a year old, a surprised little fetus, a fish of rubber that she had produced in her bath, in a *lieu de naissance* plainly marked X in her dreams, after skiing at full pulver into a larch stump, had somehow been saved and brought to her at the Nusshaus, with her sister's compliments, wrapped up in blood-soaked cotton wool, but perfectly alive and healthy, to be registered as her son Ivan Veen. At other moments she felt convinced that the child was her sister's, born out of wedlock, during an exhausting, yet highly romantic blizzard, in a mountain refuge.

When Aqua escapes from her next madhouse and rushes to Demon's house she finds all her things still in place in her bedroom: proof to her poor shattered mind that Demon has been faithful to her all along. In fact, Marina "had conceived, *c'est bien le cas de le dire*, the brilliant idea of having Demon divorce mad Aqua and marry Marina who thought (happily and correctly) she was pregnant again"—but when she smugly divulges her intentions Demon throws her out of the house.

Nabokov intends the paragraph from which these two passages come as the key to his impossibly, parodically impenetrable exposi-tion. No attentive reader should fail to note that the "*lieu de nais-sance,*" the "X," and the "*c'est bien le cas de le dire*" have occurred to-gether before. Why the repetition? With only twenty pages to flick back through, we ought to have curiosity enough to begin the search. Once we track the phrases down to the attic scene, we realize we now have enough information to comprehend what Van and Ada deduce.

Demon and his cousin Marina have conducted an intense but on-again, off-again affair from the beginning of 1868. In March 1869, "in the ecstasy of reconciliation neither remembered to dupe procreation," but before they discover Marina to be pregnant with Van, they have argued and parted again, and by late April Demon—who swoops through life at a breakneck pace—marries Marina's twin sister Aqua "out of spite and pity." She too becomes pregnant, but when Demon abandons her to return to Marina, Aqua has her first breakdown, retreating to a mountain sanitorium at Ex in Switzerland. Under cover of looking after Aqua, Marina conceals her own pregnancy from the world by retreating to Ex. Van is born on January 1, 1870 (the day Demon, with typically extravagant panache, sends those ninety-nine orchids). Two weeks later Aqua, six months pregnant and less than sane, skis into the stump of the larch that provided her Home with its Christmas tree. Her unborn child is killed, but Marina takes advantage of her sister's mental muddle to substitute her two-week-old Van for the bloody fetus. Two years later Marina again becomes pregnant by Demon. When Demon refuses to divorce Aqua and dismisses Marina for even suggesting the idea, Marina belatedly accepts the proposal her dull cousin Dan had made the previous year. Van is therefore raised as Demon and Aqua's child and Ada as Dan and Marina's, but they are full brother and sister.*

V

In the midst of writing *Ada*, Nabokov noted that "in art, as in nature, a glaring disadvantage may turn out to be a subtle protective device."[4] Not only does the swift, zany melodrama of Van and Ada's parentage more than compensate for the stilted stasis of the attic scene, but there is also fierce pleasure to be won from the realization that we can now construe what had seemed the incomprehensible evidence in the herbarium. In showing us that we can solve even something that appeared so opaque, if only we trust him enough to exert the effort, Nabokov invites us not to read on stolidly, page after page, but to look around, to explore, to discover, and he guarantees

* Nabokov's meticulous planning ensures that they are also putative first cousins, second cousins, and third cousins.

in advance that he will make the rewards concealed behind any future difficulties worth the effort.

That in itself is a great part of his point in *Ada*, and in its introduction in particular. For what he has created here is nothing less than a parody of the very idea of narrative exposition, of an author carefully unfolding just what the reader needs to know in order to follow the tale about to commence. Information does not come to us a piece at a time, neatly labeled and sorted. Rather, this teeming world assaults us with more than we can assimilate, and Nabokov therefore violates conventional exposition for the very reason that the convention violates life.

His point is a serious one, arising from a considered and consistent epistemology. But that does not preclude his having fun—for after all part of his very epistemology is his sense that life keeps playful surprises hidden for us to find. Like a good nineteenth-century novel, *Ada* in its attic scene presents us with all the family relationships we must master, only to proffer them in such profusion that the exposition seems to expose nothing—until the ensuing chapters allow us to discover what we need to know. But nothing could be less like a nineteenth-century novel, less like the worlds of meek Fanny Price, Amelia Sedley, or Esther Summerson, than an exposition that exposes little Ada standing there naked in the first scene of the novel, before her naked brother and lover.

Nabokov pushes the parody further as he takes aim at two other stock storytelling devices older than Oedipus: a mysterious birth, and the recognition scene that uncovers this mystery. In tragedy, the hero is likely to have already married his mother or his sister when the grim disclosure comes. In comedy or romance, a humble shepherdess may be prevented from marrying her noble lover until she suddenly proves to be of noble origin. Or a more sophisticated kind of comedy may merely toy with tragedy's horrified reaction to incest, leaving the characters aghast—that Fanny should be the sister of Joseph Andrews, that Mrs. Waters should be the mother of Tom Jones—even as we recognize from the book's overall comic tone that the relationship will somehow prove *not* to be taboo. We are doubly caught, by ironic amusement at the unnecessary lamentations of the stricken characters and by tantalized curiosity: how will a second recognition scene dispel the shadow of incest?

Nabokov can parody the tradition of the mysterious birth and the recognition scene in which incest is discovered much more radically than was possible for Fielding. In the best romantic manner the circumstances of *both* lovers' births have been hidden, and are both discovered together. Since they have already become lovers before finding out that they are brother and sister, Van and Ada ought to be destined for tragedy. Yet far from being a cataclysmic horror, or even the toyed-with shadow of that horror, the disclosure, which would be a dramatic peak in a traditional tale, passes almost unnoticed and is quietly dismissed. To Van and Ada it is no more than welcome additional proof of the specialness of their case and of the naturalness of their mental harmony. They will continue to be the passionate and lucky lovers at the center of the tale: not only is their relationship not shattered, but it will endure for more than eighty years to come. Just where Van and Ada flout the oldest of taboos, Nabokov himself upends all the rules of his craft by piling right on top of his exposition the recognition scene that should come only after long delay and steadily rising suspense, to hurtle us down toward a final denouement. In an exposition that at first glance seems to refuse to tell us anything, Nabokov lets us in on much more of the plot than we had any right to expect. And just where the characters of a traditional tale would be overwhelmed with revulsion, Ada turns to naked Van and tells him there is still time for another round of love-making before tea.

VI

Nabokov's care in controlling the complexities of the attic scene and his mastery of structure as he parodies its expository role should help allay the first two of the common objections to *Ada*. What of the third, the attitude Nabokov expects us to take toward Van and Ada? Does he not have too little distance from his inordinately gifted protagonists?

There is much to enchant in the story of Van and Ada's passion, and in the final passage of the novel, Van's lyrical built-in blurb, he stresses *only* the enchantment. That attitude pervades the attic scene. As the celebrant of his past, Van in his role as narrator seeks to reveal the uniqueness of young Van and Ada: their brilliance, their uncommon and even uncanny affinity, the carefree quality of their incestuous love. The capacity of this fourteen-year-old boy and his twelve-year-old sister to deduce as much as they do from the very spare, very oblique evidence in the herbarium is awesome, and it is amusing and exactly right that two bright young "cousins" who not long ago were strangers and are still eager to command each other's admiration should engage in this contest of mutual one-upmanship.

Yet there is also something decidely distasteful about this arcane exchange. Since Ada is consciously trying to outdo her brother, it is perfectly plausible that her "I can add . . . that . . . ; that . . . ; and that . . ." should echo so exactly Van's "I deduce . . . that . . . ; that . . . ; and that. . . ." To Van the narrator, the similarity of the children's remarks proves the singularity of their mental kinship. But to us the similarity can only seem an unattractive basis for the children's love. Van and Ada feel so attracted to each other precisely because they are so unnaturally alike: each has found a duplicate self to worship. Passionate love for someone else proves unpleasantly close to ardent self-love, as if Narcissus were to find that the adoring Echo and the reflection he yearns for are one.

Not only are Van and Ada eerily alike, but their exceptional giftedness also makes them unlike everybody else. That Van and Ada sense this difference and relish it and augment it is evident in every detail of the conversation. They are proud that they can deduce what others could not, proud of their ability to respond to and take even further each other's cryptic concision. They elaborate their sentences as if for an audience that is deliberately being shown that it cannot comprehend, as if they wish to stress and savor their superiority to any imaginable listener. Their pride blazes like a ring of fire set to mark the charmed circle of their understanding and to keep the rest of the world at bay.

Van and Ada's dialogue jars, and I think it is meant to jar. But why?

Nabokov wrote of his chess problems, but with an eye to his novels, that although he tried to conform "to classical rules, such as economy of force, unity, weeding out of loose ends, I was always ready to sacrifice purity of form to the exigencies of fantastic content, causing form to bulge and burst like a sponge-bag containing a small furious devil."[5] *Ada*, the story of the two children of a man named Demon, is full of these furious little devils. Of course, the novel has its own special harmony of form, in the rhythm of Van and Ada's meetings and partings, the accelerating decline of the years, and the triumphant final reunion that allows them to bask in the radiant, lingering recollection of their first falling in love. As the attic scene suggests, too, *Ada* has other architectural lines of development kept under strict authorial control. But again and again Nabokov disrupts the novel's sense of balance by sudden outbursts of obscurity from the overexcited pen of Van Veen or the overexcited mouths of Van and his sister. In her first speech, twelve-year-old Ada, with her extraordinary vocabulary and syntax, her casual mastery of botanical taxonomy, literature, and Roman art, and her evident immodesty in displaying the range of her knowledge and the speed of her thought, typifies the novel's sudden, strange, bewildering eruptions of multiple allusion, multilingual punning, and multilayered arcana.

At such moments, all three of the major problems in reading the novel fuse: opacity of sense, apparent imbalance of design, unease with character. Has Nabokov succumbed to the temptation simply to dazzle us with his own cleverness, and can he not see how unattractive that impulse would be? On the contrary, I suggest, far from showing off, Nabokov has never kept so much of his own design so well concealed.

Van and Ada submit passages like their exchange in the attic as proof of their own brilliance. Nabokov lets us read them instead as evidence of their self-satisfaction—and their dishonesty. As narrator, Van playfully calls himself and Ada in this scene "Nicky and Pimpernella" or "Pimpernel and Nicolette," in honor of a newspaper comic strip they unearth in the attic, "the now long defunct Goodnight Kids, Nicky and Pimpernella (sweet siblings who shared a narrow bed)." As a character within the scene, young Van responds to Ada's reference to the famous fresco of the flower girl from Stabia, near Pompeii, by calling her "Pompeianella," as if he has overheard the nicknames in old Van's narrative—or as if old Van, pen in hand, has polished and repolished the ostensibly impromptu brilliance of his young self and his sister. Insisting on absolute fidelity to memory, Nabokov himself kept dialogue out of his memoirs, knowing that no one can recall conversations accurately decades after the fact. Van, on the other hand, loads *his* memoirs with masses of extended, intricately elaborate dialogue supposedly recollected eighty years later. Or rather, as we should suspect, he reworks all that direct speech, during the ten years he spends writing the book, in order to exaggerate the flair of the young Veens. As Nabokov commented in an interview, Van Veen could have exerted a good deal more self-control over his memory than he chose to.[6]

Amidst all the enchantment, the romance, the color, and the comedy of *Ada*, the book's lapses into smartness of tone or its sudden squalls of exhibitionistic allusion can set the teeth on edge. But Nabokov knows what he is doing. Just as he shows that for the human mind the delights of discovery are inextricably related to the frustrations of opaque fact, just as he portrays glory and grief as inevitably intermingled even in what seems the fairy-tale world of Ardis and Antiterra, so he suggests that even minds with such effortless command and range as those young Van and Ada seem to disclose in that attic scene can have their own severe limitations and their blindnesses. And while "vain Van Veen" and his no less competitive sister happily indulge in abstruse self-display, Nabokov behind them has prepared and quietly concealed still more surprises for those who care to look.

VII

The attic scene introduces us to Van and Ada as lovers not simply unperturbed by their discovery that they are brother and sister, not cousins, but positively smug at the evidence that their closeness excludes the outside world. But this first scene also marks the exclusion of their half-sister Lucette—and her tragic involvement in Van and Ada's affairs.

Lucette receives one throwaway line in the attic scene. After recording Ada's birth and making it clear she is Demon's child, although her mother is married to Dan, Van notes: "Another daughter, this time Dan's very own, followed on January 3, 1876." Later we learn how this little girl becomes enmeshed in Van and Ada's fate. As the older siblings make love at Ardis, they have to evade Lucette's natural curiosity. In the desperation of desire, they try all sorts of stratagems.

In one scene, perhaps the most fateful of all, Van manipulates Lucette's affections before stealing off with Ada to the attic. Mustering all his charm, he tells Lucette in a conspiratorial whisper that he will present her with his book of "the most beautiful and famous short poems in the English language," "one of my most treasured possessions," if she can go to her room and learn an eight-line poem by heart in an hour.

> "You and I" (whispering) "are going to prove to your nasty arrogant sister that stupid little Lucette can do anything. If" (lightly brushing her bobbed hair with his lips), "if, my sweet, you can recite it and confound Ada by not making one single slip—you must be careful about the 'here-there' and the 'this-that,' and every other detail—*if* you can do it then I shall give you this valuable book for keeps. . . ."
>
> "Oh, Van, how lovely of you," said Lucette, slowly entering her room. . . .
>
> Van hastened to join Ada in the attic.

Van is proud of his stratagem at the time, but he recalls this moment with a grim shiver seventeen years later when Lucette drowns herself out of thwarted love for him.

At the age of eight, Lucette falls in love with her big "cousin" visiting Ardis for the first time. She succumbs to his charm, she imitates her big sister's passion, and she falls victim to Van and Ada's playing upon her devotion. She is also initiated into sex far too early: she cannot help knowing Ada and Van are up to something in this or that corner of manor or park, and like any eight-year-old child she cannot resist stealthily satisfying her curiosity. At twelve, on Van's next visit to Ardis, she finds herself caressed by Van at Ada's instigation—ostensibly to confuse the child and make it impossible for her to complain of Van and Ada's own caresses, but also to distract Van while Ada tries to wind up her affairs with Philip Rack and Percy de Prey. Two years later, with Van still refusing to forgive Ada and with Ada as sexually insatiable as ever, fourteen-year-old Lucette is introduced by her sister to lesbian lovemaking. When Lucette is sixteen, Ada pulls her into bed with herself and Van and leads Van's fingers over with her own to fondle Lucette, stretched out "in a martyr's pudibund swoon"—until Van ejaculates and Lucette can make her escape.

At twenty-five, despite this whole series of too-early initiations, Lucette remains a virgin, emotionally frail, compulsively but helplessly in love with Van. Hearing that he has booked a passage on a transatlantic liner, she joins the ship, determined to seduce Van—who has accepted Demon's edict that he must not see Ada while their parents remain alive—or to commit suicide if she fails. Before leaving Paris, she writes a letter to Van's American address, just in case he fails to turn up on the crossing. In that letter, which Van receives only after her death, she cites the whole poem she had proudly learned at eight—while Van and Ada were in the attic.

Unlike Van and Ada's cryptic exchanges, Nabokov's essential points are not designed to shut others out. They simply require that we observe, remember, and connect. In order to decipher the melodrama in the herbarium for ourselves, we had only to recall and return to the attic scene as soon as we read about Aqua two chapters later. That was an easy clue, an enticement to the kind of active participation that reading *Ada* demands. The next, more unexpected discovery about the attic scene is a little more difficult—the scene of Lucette being cajoled into learning the poem by heart occurs more than a hundred pages after the attic scene, and three hundred pages before her death—but Nabokov leaves it up to us to discover that what matters most about the attic scene is the little girl shut out. Van and Ada in that dusty room may celebrate a passion that excludes the rest of the world, but they have already ensnared someone else's fate with theirs.

VIII

At first it may seem absurd to suggest that Lucette's absence from the attic is almost the very point of the novel's opening scene. But the more one reads *Ada*, the more the little girl whom Van and Ada overlook and shove aside as they blindly pursue their passion comes to stand at the very center of the novel. There is no space here for the detailed evidence; interested readers may consult my *Nabokov's Ada*.[7] Let me simply restate some conclusions.

Van and Ada are brilliant, ardent, and eloquent. They claim that they are special, a law unto themselves, and that their passion exalts them above all normal considerations. But we all seem special to ourselves, and Van and Ada, with all their prodigious good fortune and their concomitant self-esteem, are at one level simply this private sense writ large. They act as if they *are* Antiterra, a world unto themselves.

Nabokov demurs. We cannot be worlds of our own. We would not be human without our contact with others, and the joys Van and Ada celebrate depend on being able to share so much of each other's feelings. With the privilege open to human consciousness of being able to imagine another's feelings comes the responsibility to avert another's pain.

Whether or not we choose to attend to the feelings of others whom our behavior affects is of course up to us. Van and Ada at first treat Lucette as no more than a fetching but ordinary and ultimately irrelevant little sister who makes a nuisance of herself by getting in the way of their extraordinary passion. But she cannot be simply set aside: as innumerable patterns running through *Ada* clearly demonstrate, her fate is inextricably involved with theirs.

That is the real point of the novel's incest theme. Family life and family love reveal us at our most interdependent, our most vulnerable. Never are we more responsible than within the family for the ways our lives touch those immediately around us. *Ada*'s playful allusions to Chateaubriand appear to make light of the whole subject of incest,* but good readers will recall or discover that Chateaubriand's beloved sister Lucile is thought to have committed suicide, and will note that the first Chateaubriand allusion in the novel refers only to Lucette, and that every subsequent allusion also involves Lucette or prefigures her death.[8] Van and Ada may dismiss incest, but Nabokov does not. Though Van and Ada's mental toughness leaves

---

* Which perfumes, of course, Chateaubriand's *Atala* and *René* and his *Mémoires d'outre-tombe*.

them quite unscathed, the bewildering secret of their passion turns the much more normal Lucette into a hysterical, frail, sex-obsessed young woman, headed for disaster.

Nabokov chooses incest as a standard by which to assess all human responsibility. Van and Ada celebrate to the hilt the joys of their love. Behind them Nabokov insists that the price of all the pleasure we can have through our intimate interconnections with others is our responsibility to others, a responsibility that increases the more closely our fates are linked with theirs.

IX

Aboard the *Tobakoff* on the last night of her life, as she sits beside Van while they watch a prerelease movie, Lucette hopes that her looks and her passionate proximity have won Van over at last. From the shockingly unexpected moment when Ada appears on the cinema screen—like her mother, Marina, Ada has become an actress—Lucette senses Van start to slip out of her spell again. Almost immediately, three prim old maids walk out of the cinema in disgust at the role Ada plays, and the Robinson couple—"old bores of the family"—sidle up and plump themselves down next to Lucette. Although she needs desperately to reapply pressure on Van, Lucette turns to the Robinsons "with her last, last, last free gift of staunch courtesy that was stronger than failure and death." Van seizes the opportunity to make his escape. Safe in his room, he masturbates twice to rid himself of the sexual excitement Lucette has aroused all day and to immunize himself against any renewal of the temptation: after all, he does not want to complicate his, Ada's, and Lucette's lives any further. When Lucette at last succeeds in extricating herself from the Robinsons and calls him up from her cabin, he feigns to have another woman there. Admitting defeat in her last-ditch attempt to win Van's love, Lucette stuffs herself with sleeping pills and jumps overboard to her death.

Her simple politeness toward the Robinsons, her refusal to show anything less than kindness even to people she does not care for and in the face of her own overwhelming need, represents for Nabokov human conduct at its most heroic. Contrast that with the way Van and Ada, in the imperious throes of their passion, treat not near-strangers but their susceptible little sister: they manipulate her affections, they play on her fears, they lock her up, they deprive her of her innocence with no regard to the consequences.

By a whole array of oblique, concealed, but precisely calibrated interconnections, Nabokov sets Lucette up as a silent standard by which to judge all of Van and Ada's conduct: Van's fierce jealousy and sexual hypocrisy, his viciousness in dealing with his rivals or foes, his casually exploitative attitude toward women, his casual dismissal of the men he cuckolds; Ada's sexual insatiability, her thoughtlessness, her deliberate and elaborate duplicity. Again and again he associates their shortcomings, from sneering scorn for others to out-and-out savagery, with the passionate self-centeredness that allows them to overlook Lucette until it is too late.[9]

By means of Lucette, Nabokov makes *Ada* a radical exploration of the moral consequences of human consciousness. He lets Van and Ada revel in the infinity of their emotion for each other, and then shows the absurdity of their acting as if the privilege of such feeling could exist without their being interconnected with other lives and without their being responsible for each of those interconnections. Subjecting his hero and heroine to rigorous scrutiny, he sets out an exhaustive criticism of the romantic egotism that in certain lights and at certain moments they can make seem so seductive. And he shows that even the greatest gifts of consciousness offer insufficient protection against the blindness of the ego—unless, like Lucette politely greeting the Robinsons, we remain determined not to let the tumult of our own feelings cause even the slightest injury to innocent others.

But Nabokov does not point out the flaws in Van and Ada's conduct from the beginning. In telling their story, Van and Ada celebrate their love in scenes like that breakfast on the balcony whose charm few can resist. Nabokov lets this charm inveigle us into dismissing Lucette, until it is too late, as no more than an amusing impediment to Van and Ada's resplendent love. He grants them such romantic verve, he makes us so eager for their next radiant reunion, that we can easily overlook the way they behave toward others. When we discover how scrupulously Nabokov has assessed Van and Ada's every action by the standard of Lucette, it can come as a salutary shock to see how inattentive we have been, how easily we have succumbed to the partiality of Van's vision.

Yet *Ada* paints far too complex a picture of life to be a mere denunciation of Van and Ada from end to end. Much of their behavior may be repellent, and the book does not stint at exposing their flaws, but they are not moral monsters like Hermann or Axel Rex or Humbert Humbert. In their last forty-five years together they hurt nobody by their love. For sixty years Van has regretted his treatment of Lucette and now tries to incorporate that regret into *Ada*. He ends his memoir with a euphoric blurb advertising the "pure joyousness and Arcadian

innocence" of his idyll at Ardis. The blurb mocks itself: Van knows
its buoyant blitheness reflects only his own first raptures at Ardis, not
his later discovery that life always mixes radiance and remorse.

X

Now we must return once again to the scene in the attic. While Van
and Ada make love there, Lucette learns by heart a short poem of
Nabokov's invention. The poem depicts a dead person's ghost talking to a mortal, and we find its text only in a letter that Lucette sends
Van before her last fatal voyage and that he reads only after her
death. Lucette and letters—epistolary, alphabetical—form a strange
pattern that extends throughout *Ada* and that reveals that Nabokov
not only centers on Lucette *Ada*'s study of the moral responsibilities
of consciousness, but that he also focuses on her the novel's exploration of metaphysical possibilities beyond human consciousness.

Once again, I refer readers interested in the detailed evidence to
Nabokov's Ada.[10] A few items in the pattern should be mentioned, to
indicate its persistence and point. Estranged from Ada after her infi-
delities during their second summer at Ardis, Van publishes a novel,
Letters from Terra—about communications from a planet many on Antiterra suppose a Next World—over the pseudonym "Voltemand,"
the name of a letter carrier in *Hamlet*. That year he receives a passionate love letter from the fifteen-year-old Lucette, who, distraught by
Ada's inveigling her into lesbian love-play, puns "in an Ophelian
frenzy on the feminine glans." Still full of the bitterness of jealousy,
Van refuses even to receive the letters Ada sends him by special cou-
rier, until Lucette herself brings a letter from Ada to Van at Voltemand Hall, Kingston University. In the scene in which she delivers
the letter—thus herself reenacting Voltemand's role—the agitated
Lucette hysterically recalls the letters for "clitoris" in an unforgettable
game of Russian Scrabble she played with Van and Ada. Or, rather,
she reminded Van of this in her first letter to him, which he now
incorporates into her dialogue in the reconstructed scene, while he
replies to her with the closing words of Hamlet's letter to Ophelia.

Before following Ophelia to a watery grave, Lucette mails to Van's
Voltemand address her last-ever letter, which he reads only after her
death, and which cites that poem about a ghost talking to a mortal.
Four years later, before his first reunion with Ada since Lucette's
death, Van dreams of Ada and Lucette fused as "one of the Vane
sisters"—which psychologist Van can appreciate as an oneiric recom-
bination of the letters of his first and last names, but which only we

can recognize as an allusion to Nabokov's story where two dead sisters attempt to communicate to the unwitting narrator in an acrostic formed by the initial letters of the last paragraph in his story. Then, just before his next and final reunion with Ada, Van thinks of the dead Lucette as a "bird of paradise" and "a mermaid in the groves of Atlantis"—phrases that echo not only the "bird of paradise" and "mermaid" he called her in his last letter to her, many years ago, but also the "micromermaid" he used to describe the heroine from Terra in his *Letters from Terra*.

The pattern reaches its climax at the turning point of the whole novel.

For all their unabated love, Van and Ada appear to have squandered their adult years first in jealousy and bitterness, then in obedience to the edict issued by Demon—the one person other than Ada whom Van unequivocally respects—after he discovers his children cohabiting. To ensure they remain apart, Demon pressures Ada to marry Andrey Vinelander. In 1905, the year Demon dies, Van and Ada meet for a round of gleeful adultery in Mont Roux. Just when they are about to abscond together, Ada finds out that her husband is dying of tuberculosis. She cannot abandon him in such a condition—and then the poor fellow takes another seventeen years to die. After his death, fifty-year-old Ada and fifty-two-year-old Van agree to a reunion in Mont Roux.

Despite the lapse of almost two lonely decades, Van still hopes he can recapture his youthful past with Ada. On reaching the hotel where the reunion is to take place, he calls up from the lobby to Ada's room. Her young voice seems to hold out the promise that they can reconnect with their remote past, but when she descends, they find each other old and fat and almost strangers. A chance remark from a neighboring table momentarily promises to dispel the tension, but the awkwardness returns. The reunion is a failure. Issuing a flimsy promise to see him soon, Ada declares she must dash for the Geneva airport.

Despondent, Van ascends to his room, takes his nightly sleeping pill and—to keep his thoughts of Ada at bay until the pill takes effect—continues writing his *Texture of Time*. The next morning he wakes and thinks suddenly he *must* pursue Ada at once or lose her forever. Or should he simply leap from the balcony and down to his death? As he steps out on the balcony, he sees Ada standing on a balcony below:

> Pensively, youngly, voluptuously, she was scratching her thigh at the rise of the right buttock. . . . Would she look up? All her flowers turned

up to him, beaming, and she made the royal-grant gesture of lifting and offering him the mountains, the mist and the lake with three swans.

He left the balcony and ran down a short spiral staircase to the fourth floor. In the pit of his stomach there sat the suspicion that it might not be room 410, as he conjectured, but 412 or even 414. What would happen if she had not understood, was not on the lookout? She had, she was.

When, "a little later," Van, kneeling and clearing his throat, was kissing her dear cold hands, gratefully, gratefully, in full defiance of death, with bad fate routed and her dreamy afterglow bending over him, she asked:

"Did you really think I had gone?"

"*Obmanshchitsa* (deceiver), *obmanshchitsa*," Van kept repeating with the fervor and gloat of blissful satiety.

"I told him to turn," she said, "somewhere near Morzhey ("morses" or "walruses," a Russian pun on "Morges"—maybe a mermaid's message). And *you* slept, you could sleep!"

"I worked," he replied, "my first draft is done."

After it had seemed that one-way time would hurtle him inexorably, ever more rapidly, toward a desolate death, Van is now back with Ada for life. And he has finished his *Texture of Time*—the events of which have just borne out his argument better than he could ever have hoped. The future is utterly open: when he wrote his final arguments the night before, all his eager hopes for his reunion with Ada had been cruelly shattered; now, the next morning, against all expectation, she is back, and all their remoteness banished. Even better, Van's glimpse of Ada on the balcony below suddenly establishes a pattern running through all the key moments of their lives: that first glorious wasp-and-honey morning on the balcony at Ardis, and their last morning at Ardis in 1884; a single tryst, one morning near Ardis in 1886; their first and last mornings at Ardis in 1888, and the morning of the ensuing duel; the first and last mornings of their Manhattan reunion in 1892–1893; and their first and last mornings at Mont Roux in 1905. Without that 1922 balcony scene to crown the pattern, it would never have been detected—and like so many other patterns in *Ada* it seems invisible even on a rereading, until unexpected and unmistakably exact details* suddenly click together.[11] This present moment on the balcony at the end of *The Texture of Time* proves with a gasp of surprise Van's other point in his treatise—that it is the pat-

---

* Like two "structurally perfect stools" Van has on two of these mornings—another feature of the novel Updike objected to, because he could not discern the concealed structural perfection of which they form a part.

tern of the past that matters more than anything else in time—and that for Van and Ada the triumphant pattern of their lives is the rhythm of their meetings and partings.

But what does it mean when Ada says "I told him to turn . . . somewhere near Morzhey ('morses' or 'walruses,' a Russian pun on 'Morges'—maybe a mermaid's message)"? Morges is a real town more than halfway from Montreux to Geneva; "Morzhey" is Russian for "of walruses," and "morse," besides suggesting a Morse code message, is an English synonym for "walrus." In the notes he appended to the Penguin edition of *Ada*, Nabokov glosses the "mermaid's message" as an "allusion to Lucette." Lucette of course has drowned twenty-one years earlier: Ada, it appears, jokingly suggests that her own change of mind, en route to Geneva airport, has been prompted by the dead Lucette.

To us as readers who can detect all the patterns of Lucette and letters, Lucette and messages from the beyond, which converge on this pivotal point of the novel, that idea seems no mere joke, but a possibility Nabokov has woven throughout the novel.[12] He suggests that Lucette is on some kind of Terra—another world inaccessible from this Antiterra, with a different relation to time—and that Van, for all his lifelong attempts to probe the mysteries of that putative planet, has not been able to recognize even the message that makes all the difference to his and Ada's lives. Kindly Lucette induces Ada to return to Van, and she does so in such a way that their morning glimpse of each other will set the seal on the pattern of the magic mornings running through their lives, a pattern that can be seen only from her timeless point of vantage, or from ours, outside the novel's world and time.

XI

Van's lifelong effort as psychologist and philosopher to probe the mysteries of consciousness and time and Terra arise from his fascination with Aqua, the woman he thought of as his mother until after her suicide in his fourteenth year. The novel traces the theme of Van's career as a minor-key parallel to the major-key theme of his love for Ada. Whenever he and Ada part, he returns to the sorry refuge of his work—a pattern that changes only when his career and his love fuse in the harmony of the novel's close, in *The Texture of Time* and the later works that he and Ada write together, ending with *Ada* itself.

Like the herbarium in the attic, *Ada*'s location on Antiterra and the planet's relation to our own had been a colorful but unexplained mystery in the novel's opening chapter. But like the herbarium, Antiterra and Terra become a good deal more comprehensible in the last of the three chapters that form the novel's prologue, as Van explains Aqua's madness and its relation to the widespread belief in the existence of Terra. The "L disaster" in the mid-nineteenth century, which somehow gave rise to the notion of Terra, is too well known to Van's Antiterran readers for him to retell the whole story. From what he does disclose, however, we can piece together that this global catastrophe somehow discredited electricity, even made it unmentionably obscene, at the same time as it spawned the idea of Terra. Terra—apparently our earth, as dimly envisaged by Antiterrans—matches Antiterra in terms of physical geography, but the history of the two planets has numerous mismatches,

> because a gap of up to a hundred years one way or another existed between the two earths; a gap marked by a bizarre confusion of directional signs at the crossroads of passing time with not *all* the no-longers of one world corresponding to the not-yets of the other. It was owing, among other things, to this "scientifically ungraspable" concourse of divergences that minds *bien rangés* (not apt to unhobble hobgoblins), rejected Terra as a fad or fantom, and deranged minds (ready to plunge into any abyss) accepted it in support and token of their own irrationality.

Aqua, like other sick minds, "identified the notion of a Terra planet with that of another world and this 'Other World' got confused not only with the 'Next World' but with the Real World in us and beyond us." As her madness deepens, she reaches a stage where she imagines she can hear water talking, and feels tickled at the thought that "she, poor Aqua, had accidentally hit upon such a simple method of recording and transmitting speech, while technologists (the so-called Eggheads) all over the world were trying to make publicly utile and commercially rewarding the extremely elaborate and still very expensive, hydrodynamic telephones and other miserable gadgets that were to replace those that had gone . . . to the devil" with the banning of electricity.

In light of the later "mermaid's message" from drowned Lucette, in light of all the images throughout the novel that prefigure or picture her watery death, in light of her subliminal centrality to the whole novel, the terms of Aqua's madness suddenly look rather different. Nor is it any accident that the disaster that makes Antiterra so different from our world and has "the singular effect of both causing and cursing the notion of 'Terra' " is known as "the L disaster," the first letter of Lucette's name,* or that the force that then becomes a surrogate for electricity, by some weird hydraulic principle, is water, the element in which Lucette drowns, the element that holds Anti-terra together.

Before the herbarium scene, *Ada*'s first chapter introduces the four protagonists of the prologue:

> On April 23, 1869, in drizzly and warm, gauzy and green Kaluga, Aqua, aged twenty-five and afflicted with her usual vernal migraine, married Walter D. Veen, a Manhattan banker of ancient Anglo-Irish ancestry who had long conducted, and was soon to resume intermittently, a pas-sionate affair with Marina. The latter, some time in 1871, married her first lover's first cousin, also Walter D. Veen, a quite as opulent, but much duller, chap.

Such blatant patterning—twins Aqua and Marina, and their hus-bands, two "Walters"** and so almost "water," or Aqua and Marina all over again—seem too preposterous to be anything but parody: a parody of all "family background," a parody of all character pairing and contrast.

Some readers are disturbed by patterns so obvious they seem to be there for the pattern's sake alone, as if in mockery of all seriousness of intent. But those who persist can discover the point behind the pattern. Twins Aqua and Marina are tragically, inseparably commin-gled, as sisters Ada and Lucette will be a generation later, and the turbulent fates of the four elder Veens coalesce to sweep Aqua into a state of mind in which she first thinks she sees Terra, then thinks she hears water talking, then takes her own life. Her madness and death prefigure both Lucette's suicide, after *her* fatal entanglement with *her* sister, and the messages Lucette seems to send from her watery grave or from Terra the Fair.[13] Even the absurdly obtrusive quartet of aqueous names that stares us in the face right from the start of the novel, then, cannot be seen at full value until we understand Lu-cette's role as the representative of all those shoved aside by impa-tient passion, and until we understand that her presence has shaped the whole world Van and Ada have seemed to claim for themselves.

In the same way, Nabokov suggests throughout *Ada* that the pat-tern of our life may be right before our eyes but remain utterly mean-ingless so long as we stay trapped in human time. Through the spe-cial conditions of his art he invites us to retrace events until we end up in a new relation to the novel's time, until everything flashes with

---

* Van at one point writes her a letter addressed simply "Poor L."
** The "Ds" stand for Demian (known as Demon) and Daniel (Dan), respectively.

new meaning as we see more clearly than ever both the constraints of mortal life and the freedoms that might lie beyond.

Or are we taking too seriously the absurd Aqua-Walter-Marina-Walter or the dorophones that gurgle and splutter their convulsive course through the novel? Is Nabokov not simply having fun? May he not be saying that art is a game in a world that itself seems a game we cannot understand?

He has remarked, however, that only a single letter separates the comic from the cosmic.[14] In *Ada* he asks us whether there is not something playful behind life—not in the sense of something that reduces life to a meaningless game, but something that makes it all richer than we could ever have dreamed, richer even than this wondrous and well-stocked world.

XII

Ada works throughout by unexpected relationships beneath the apparent ones, just as Van and Ada turn out in that scene in the attic to be full brother and sister and not the cousins they seem. The whole novel is, among much else, a study of the very idea of relationship. Before its first sentence, Nabokov sets out a family tree, as if to picture pure relationship in stark diagrammatic form. In the first paragraph of the novel's first chapter, he toys with the ideas of resemblance and difference, with the relations between part and whole, model and mimic, the individual literary work and its wider tradition, and he provides the first glimpses of that constant play of similarity and dissimilarity, on large scale and small, between Antiterra and Terra. As the chapter draws to a close, up in Ardis's attic, he introduces not only incest—family relationships doubled back on themselves—but also that troubling similarity between Van and Ada.

As a lepidopterist interested in the distinctions and the connections between species, Nabokov had from an early age studied problems of resemblance and difference and relationship. He brooded on them at length in his lepidopterological work in the 1940s: "The idea of 'species' is the idea of difference; the idea of 'genus' is the idea of similarity. What we do when trying to 'erect a genus' . . . is really the paradoxical attempt to demonstrate that certain objects that are dissimilar in one way are similar in another."[15] He returned to the problem again in his notes for the *Butterflies of Europe* project he worked on after he finished *Pale Fire*—where he has John Shade observe that "resemblances are the shadows of differences"[16]—and before he began *Ada*.

Ada re-creates in microcosm the way the mind apprehends its world through discovering more differences, more similarities, more relationships. In the most radical dismantling and recomposition of his world he ever attempted, Nabokov constructs his Antiterra as if from scratch, compounding patterns of sound and word, color and contour, object and character, date and event, into networks whose very profusion mimics that of our own Terra and proves the greatest obstacle to disentangling their sense. But the sense is always there.

CHAPTER 23

Tidying Up: Montreux, 1968–1972

I

IN THE FOUR YEARS after he completed *Ada*, Nabokov's rate of original composition slowed down markedly as he tidied up his files, his life, and his life's work. He felt "dreadfully drained" after the intense effort of *Ada*, and his imagination needed fallow time.[1] His contract with McGraw-Hill required him to produce another nine books in short order. Always prepared to devote himself to the propagation of his own oeuvre, he spent much of the time left after translating and selecting material for McGraw-Hill in helping his French, German, and Italian translators, his American critics and biographers, and interviewers from all over the world.

Ever since *Lolita*, his papers had mounted up relentlessly. Véra filled carton after carton with newspaper clippings she had not had the time to sort and paste in albums. She stuffed correspondence with publishers and fans into punched folders and pouched folders, into envelopes and boxes and drawers. As one of the many favorable conditions of his McGraw-Hill contract, Nabokov had obtained the right to as many as fifty copies of his books instead of the usual six, so that he could immediately supply his work to foreign publishers, translators, and film producers. All these extra packages cascading into the steady flow of hardback, paperback, and innumerable foreign editions from a fifty-year career threatened to engulf the Nabokovs' small rooms in a sea of paper.

At the time he invented Van Veen's secretary and typist, Nabokov had had no secretary of his own except Véra, although during the 1960s Jaqueline Callier had taken the index-card fair copies of his novels to type out at home in triplicate. At the end of October 1968, a week after she completed the 880 pages of the *Ada* typescript, Nabokov engaged her as a secretary for three afternoons a week, and more than twenty years later, now in her seventies, she still works the same hours for Véra Nabokov. Room 60 in the Nabokovs' suite, at first Dmitri's bedroom, had become the storehouse for their chaotic files and now became Mme Callier's office.[2]

Like the staff of the Montreux Palace, Jaqueline Callier was ready to do anything for Nabokov. Kind and solicitous toward her, he would turn a request into a shared jest and never rebuke her for an error but explain gently what he wanted. At first she spent several months simply bringing order to the files and books, and as manuscripts were completed would take them home to type. Gradually she also took over from Véra the typing of business correspondence—always dictated by Véra herself, never by Nabokov.[3]

By now Andrew Field, in the process of compiling Nabokov's bibliography and preparing to work on his biography, had become eager to see the papers that since 1959 the Nabokovs had left in thirty-five boxes with the storage company Dean of Ithaca. During the 1960s the Nabokovs had still expected they would resettle in America and had had no reason to bring their papers to Europe. Nabokov was still averse to taking root too firmly ("I also intend to collect butterflies . . . in Peru or Iran before I pupate," he joked to one interviewer), and even at the end of the 1960s, especially on blue spring days, he and Véra were prone to yearn for a quiet, sunny spot in California. By now, however, he was almost seventy, reports from America made the country sound troubled and turbulent, and he realized he was not likely to move from Montreux. In November 1968 he wrote to Dean of Ithaca and, after balking at the cost of shipment, had the papers sent over in 1969.[4]

While Field looked ahead to Nabokov's biography, Nabokov himself looked back to a second volume of his autobiography, *Speak on, Memory*, or *Speak, America*: a chapter on his years at the M.C.Z., perhaps another on his butterfly hunting, one on his relationship with Edmund Wilson, one on his lecture tours, perhaps one on the car pool to Wellesley, another on Cornell, another on *Lolita*'s misfortunes and fortunes.[5] He wanted to impose artistic order on his life as he imposed physical order on his papers, and to set down his own inner view of his past before Field recorded the outer.

He was also conscious of advancing age. In their late nineties, Van and Ada, for all their happiness, admit that life has become a succession of pains and pills. Although especially in spring and summer Nabokov struck visitors as healthy, robust, and much younger than his years, his own diaries from the late 1960s record his battles with the frustrations of old age. His lifelong insomnia had become worse than ever. A fourth severe attack of neuralgia intercostalis produced aftershocks for month after month. When he bent down for a book or a pencil, he could all too easily sprain his back. His psoriasis returned. Colds, infections, aches, heart palpitations came and went. At one point he notes in his diary: "Stomach flu . . . will not resume idiotic consumption of pills with side effects," but new ailments soon drove him to new medications.[6]

II

Although exhausted by *Ada*, he soon found himself with an idea for a new novel. At the end of November he recorded in his diary:

> "You are a swine, Mr. Tamworth," said a deep voice in the next room.
>
> Idea for a short novel: through a thin wall and slitty door a lodger (say, Atman) hears every sound and word in next room. These occasions increase till gradually the *other* room takes over and the people in it listen to Atman's adjacent life.[7]

Atman and Tamworth would both feature fleetingly in Nabokov's next novel, *Transparent Things*, although not at all in a manner this passage prefigures. But what did breed in Nabokov's mind until his new novel took shape was the idea of witnessing another life, of unnaturally thin or even transparent walls between one consciousness and another.

While that idea gestated, Nabokov turned early in December to translating his best Russian poems for a collection he would entitle *Poems and Problems*: thirty-nine Russian poems, presented in the original and in facing translations; the fourteen English poems he had published in a slim volume in 1959; and eighteen chess problems, all but two composed in or since 1965.* He had planned to travel to Rome with Véra on December 10 to explore the city for his *Butterflies in Art*, but canceled the trip to avoid strikes and riots.[8]

As he remained in Montreux, poring over his old Russian verse and devising new chess problems, his latest English fiction continued to surge ahead. Frank Taylor, as editor-in-chief at McGraw-Hill and an adorer of *Ada*, was determined to find something in the novel he could "edit"—and felt pleased when he managed to locate a single word he could query. By the end of December the first galleys had been sent for Nabokov to check. Just as well, for *Ada* had been chosen as a selection of the Literary Guild book club for May 1969, and with that deadline the production schedule for such a long book would be very tight. *Playboy* also wanted to take a good deal of the novel, but since its excerpts would now have to appear before May, it had to be satisfied with only eight chapters—still a generous serv-

---

* His unpublished problems of the 1940s and 1950s have been lost, he notes in *Poems and Problems*. In view of his hectic schedule in those years, it is likely they were few.

ing—from the "Ardis the First" section of the novel. As if this were not already success enough, Columbia Pictures bought the film rights to the novel for $500,000 plus an escalation clause. Then to cap it all, Henry Grunwald, the editor of *Time*, cabled that he wanted to do a cover story on Nabokov to coincide with the publication of *Ada*. Nabokov was delighted.[9]

He read galleys and page proofs of the novel steadily through January and February 1969. Andrew Field visited for four days late in January, for the first time since it had been agreed he could write Nabokov's biography. It would prove symptomatic of his efforts that in the first chapter of his biography he would misdate this visit, just as he misdated and mislocated his first-ever meeting with Nabokov. During his longest visit for the biography, he would stay a month at the Eurotel, across the Grand-Rue from the Montreux Palace. Despite that, Field would still manage in his biography to call the street on which both hotels stand not the Grand-Rue, which runs down by the lake, but the avenue des Alpes, which runs up by the railway station.[10] For the moment the Nabokovs remained blithely unaware of Field's predilection for imprecision.

In mid-March, *Time* reporters Martha Duffy and Ronald Z. Sheppard sent their interview questions by telex and turned up themselves four days later to find neatly typed answers like the memorable "I have never seen a more lucid, more lonely, better balanced mad mind than mine." After a photographer and the artist preparing the *Time* cover portrait had also been and gone, the Nabokovs traveled for a week by train and taxi to their regular hotel in Lugano, the Splendide Royale. They planned to return to Montreux, and at the end of April to sail from Genoa to New York for the publication of *Ada* and the presentation of the American Academy of Arts and Letters Merit Medal that Nabokov had been awarded. But a severe pain in one of Véra's eyes was diagnosed as a detached retina, and two oculists agreed that she could not travel—nor could she prevail on her husband to travel to America on his own.[11]

III

Even at a distance, they could enjoy the initial reaction to *Ada*. On May 4, the day before publication, Alfred Appel's rapturous appraisal appeared in the *New York Times Book Review*: "A supremely original work of the imagination. . . . further evidence that [Nabokov] is a peer of Kafka, Proust and Joyce. . . . a love story, an erotic masterpiece, a philosophical investigation into the nature of time."

Other reviewers acclaimed *Ada* as Nabokov's ultimate masterpiece, his culminating statement, the greatest of his sixteen novels. Alfred Kazin in the *Saturday Review* declared that "*Ada*, coming after *Lolita* and *Pale Fire*, makes a trilogy with no contemporary peer."[12]

Morris Bishop wrote to Nabokov that *Ada* had won probably the best critical reception since Virgil's *Aeneid*.[13] It had reached the front page of the *New York Times Book Review*, by far the most influential organ of the American book trade; the front cover of *Time*, the most widely read weekly in the world; and the opulent interior of *Playboy*, the most successful monthly of the decade. Nabokov's reputation was at its zenith.

Ada's very success soon provoked a counterreaction. Although it climbed to number four on the *New York Times* best-seller list (behind *The Godfather*, Jacqueline Susann's *The Love Machine*, and *Portnoy's Complaint*) and stayed on the list for twenty weeks, reviewers began to attack it. Philip Toynbee declared it an appalling piece of unremitting exhibitionism. Two years later, Mary McCarthy would suggest that the novel was so bad she would have to reassess Nabokov's earlier work, even *Pale Fire*, which she had praised so highly. To her, *Ada*'s anachronisms were Nabokov's supreme revenge on the modern world: "There he at last reinstates himself in a supranational, supercilious palace of culture, with a queen by his side; the mirror pair of children, like the Ptolemys, are brother and sister."[14] Her denunciation anticipated a widespread disenchantment with Nabokov as the 1970s wore on. Despite the sparkle and glow of *Ada*, so exciting to many readers, others wondered if there were not something horribly indulgent about it all—its language, its structure, its characters, its morality? Was the initial ecstatic reaction to the book not merely a magnified echo of Van Veen's self-adoring blurb, and if so, what was that worth?

Nabokov had anticipated such reactions, and had noted down May 5 in his diary as the publication date of "Nabokov's Folly." Almost two months later, Morris Dickstein responded to the first reviews by calling *Ada* the most overpraised novel of the decade, in a *New Republic* review entitled precisely "Nabokov's Folly." Nabokov remained unmoved by the adverse comments unless they touched on his or Véra's life. As he explained to an interviewer: "I do get annoyed when people I never met impinge on my privacy with false and vulgar assumptions—as for example Mr. Updike, who in an otherwise clever article absurdly suggests that my fictional character, bitchy and lewd Ada, is, I quote, 'in a dimension or two, Nabokov's wife.' " He sent a letter to the *New York Review of Books*, where Matthew Hodgart had reviewed *Ada*. Addressing Hodgart directly, he objected "violently to your seeing in reunited Van and Ada (both rather horrible creatures) a picture of my married life. What the hell, Sir, do you know about my married life? I expect a prompt apology from you."[15]

Over the coming years many would be driven away from Nabokov by their assumption that Van and Ada's self-indulgence was Nabokov's self-indulgence, their self-delight his self-delight. As his responses to Updike and Hodgart make plain, nothing could be further from the truth: "I loathe Van Veen."[16] To appreciate the novel, one has to reject the a priori assumption that Nabokov is blind to Van and Ada's stupendous self-satisfaction.

One also has to reject the assumption that the novel lacks artistic control. Much more complex, crowded, and challenging than his other fiction, *Ada* was often compared by vexed reviewers to *Finnegans Wake*. But Nabokov knew and disliked Joyce's polyglot monolith and took care to pack into *Ada* maximum meaning with minimum loss of readability. Endowed with a narrative gift Joyce lacked, he moves the story along with speed and color, laughter and lyricism. Of course he also reminds us line after line that there is much we are missing, but he provides the clues to the problems he poses. His aim is not to mock incomprehension but to invite detection. If we trust him enough to assume he has a reason for what he does—and all artistic response depends on that trust—we can discover not only the surprise and the inventiveness behind choice after choice, but also Nabokov's rigorous determination to incorporate in this luxuriant fantasy as much psychological, ethical, metaphysical, and epistemological truth as he can.

IV

At the time *Ada*'s publication was eliciting acclaim for Nabokov in the U.S., he was also beginning to rouse attention in the USSR. Carl and Ellendea Proffer reported from Moscow that he was widely read there, his books passing from hand to hand like best-sellers. But while almost no one in literary circles would admit to not having read him, only one person the Proffers had met dared keep Nabokov's books at the front of his bookshelves. Some pages of Nabokov's works had recently been read at an official evening devoted to émigré literature, and one university even planned an essay on *Invitation to a Beheading* for its scholarly journal but balked at the last moment. For the first time the *Concise Literary Encyclopedia* published in Moscow included an article on Nabokov. Although he was described as "extremely contradictory, with traits of artistic snobbery," the encyclopedia's editors were rebuked in the Soviet press for the "dangerously objective" approach to ideological enemies exemplified by the mere inclusion of Nabokov.[17]

In June, Elena Sikorski visited Leningrad for two weeks, the first time any of Nabokov's immediate family had ventured into the Soviet Union. Firmly committed for his own part to avoiding all contact with dictatorships of left or right, Nabokov had always tended to regard anyone who visited the Soviet Union as either a dupe or a knave. In the case of his favorite sister, he was merely apprehensive about her welfare. She returned safely enough, bearing photographs of Vyra and Rozhdestveno and a stone from the foundation of the old manor's main staircase. For the next ten years, as long as her health permitted, she would return to Leningrad every summer.[18]

Véra's health, on the other hand, had kept the Nabokovs in Montreux at the beginning of the summer of 1969. Now in mid-June, her oculist gave her permission to travel, and on June 20 they returned to Lugano's Hotel Splendide Royal. Ledig Rowohlt visited, worried that *Ada*'s obscurities would make the novel hopelessly difficult to translate. At his friend's request Nabokov reluctantly prepared a preliminary series of notes to the novel to assist translators.[19]

Since Anna Feigin's doctors had declared that her heart condition ruled out a retreat to the hills for the summer, the Nabokovs spent July with her in a house they rented in the little village of Cureglia, four kilometers from Lugano. After years of alpine summers, they found the humid lowland heat sapping and unrestful, although Nabokov still managed to walk fifteen kilometers a morning in pursuit of butterflies. While at Cureglia, he received an invitation from Kenneth Tynan to contribute to an anthology of anonymous pornographic pieces to be commissioned from well-known writers, a request perhaps prompted by reviewers who had dismissed *Ada* as pornographic. Nabokov replied curtly: "I have no interest whatever in pornography and cannot imagine myself being titillated by what I write."[20]

But that month he did become a voyeur of sorts. He had set *Ada* on Antiterra partly in response to his sense of the romance of space travel. As a boy he had been exhilarated by voyages of discovery; as a man he had written a play about Captain Scott, a story about exploring the jungles of South America, a novel that follows an explorer into the mountains of Central Asia, and another story that launches its hero toward an unnamed planet. Now he rented a television set to watch every moment of the "marvelous adventure" of the first moon landing. Asked for a comment for the *New York Times*, he cabled his reply: "Treading the soil of the moon, palpating its pebbles, tasting the panic and splendor of the event, feeling in the pit of one's stomach the separation from Terra—these form the most romantic sensation an explorer has ever known."[21]

V

At the end of July, Carl and Ellendea Proffer called on the Nabokovs in Lugano on their way back from the Soviet Union. After testing them out in Russian, the Nabokovs quickly switched to English, but they took at once to these tall, ebullient, energetic young Slavists. They especially liked in Ellendea Proffer her refusal to be awed by anybody, her readiness to say exactly what she was thinking and to ask exactly what she was wondering about. She tried to find out how the Nabokovs first met. Characteristically, Nabokov himself, who could be as expansive in person as he was fiercely reserved about what could be set in print, was ready to answer her. Equally characteristically, Véra, all reserve, stopped the inquiry by asking: "Are you from the KGB?"—but with her own acute interest in people, she later asked Ellendea how she and Carl had met (and of course received an answer).

Like others, Ellendea Proffer noted the centrifugal mobility of Nabokov's conversation: in Isaiah Berlin's terms, he was the fox, not the hedgehog.* When the conversation touched on Solzhenitsyn, one of literature's great hedgehogs, Nabokov made it clear that although he had grave reservations about Solzhenitsyn's artistic gifts he had none about his courage or his political importance, and would never say anything negative about his work in public because in this case his political merits far outweighed his literary defects.

Naturally, Nabokov listened eagerly to the Proffers' reports about his own popularity in the Soviet Union. After asking them about the dissident writers they had met, he and Véra arranged for jeans to be sent in their name to poet Joseph Brodsky, at that stage a keen admirer of Nabokov. As Carl Proffer later commented, the Nabokovs would be very generous to dissidents, in their quiet way, over the years to come.[22]

* In his book on Tolstoy, *The Hedgehog and the Fox* (London, 1953), Berlin recalled the ancient line "the fox knows many things, but the hedgehog knows one big thing" in order to contrast those "who relate everything to a central vision, one system more or less coherent or articulate" and those "who pursue many ends, often unrelated and even contradictory." He brilliantly characterized Tolstoy as someone instinctively a fox but convinced it was better to be a hedgehog.

The first three weeks of August the Nabokovs spent in Adelboden in the mountains of the Bernese Oberland. "Horribly cold, damp, dreadful," Nabokov noted in his diary. "Never again!" On August 22 they returned to Montreux, where Nabokov prepared another interview for the BBC, who came to film him early in September. During the early fall, he wrote out a fuller version of the "Notes to *Ada*" he had begun for Rowohlt, and now signed them "Vivian Darkbloom." They would be published as an appendix to Penguin editions of the novel, but, during his lifetime, nowhere else—as if he wished to avoid making them, like Pushkin's notes to *Eugene Onegin* or Eliot's to *The Waste Land*, an accidentally integral but distracting component of the received text itself.[23]

In mid-September, Simon Karlinsky paid his first visit to the Nabokovs. Brought up in émigré Harbin, Karlinsky had been a Sirin fan before reaching his teens, and had published some of the earliest American academic criticism on Russian émigrés like Nabokov and Tsvetaeva. Meeting Nabokov, he found himself subjected to more than one kind of test. When drinks were ordered, it was a mark in his favor that he could address the waiter in French. Nabokov asked him point-blank: "Do you know French literature?" Karlinsky replied that he had studied Chateaubriand and other French preromantics at Harvard. Nabokov commented that to write "about Pushkin and also about me" one had to know French literature. "Field doesn't. Nor Appel. Nor Proffer," he observed ruefully.

The next day Nabokov told Karlinsky it would disrupt the rhythm of his work if they met for dinner, but they could have a stroll together and then tea. As they set off, Nabokov said, "Well, I've really enjoyed your visit after all our correspondence." Karlinsky was puzzled by his tone. "I want to give you something to remember me by," Nabokov added as they approached a newspaper kiosk. "A leg-pull," thought Karlinsky. Nabokov asked, "Would you like the *New York Times* or the Paris *Herald Tribune*?" Karlinsky evaded gracefully: "Why do you deign to pamper a poor man like me?"—a line from the playwright Ostrovsky that tickled Nabokov's fancy but did not deter him from insisting on a choice. Karlinsky said he would take the *Tribune*, and Nabokov passed the decision on in French to the newspaper vendor, then bestowed his grand purchase on Karlinsky: "Here in memory of this marvelous visit. . . ." "I shall cherish this the rest of my life," Karlinsky wryly promised. They returned to the Palace, where Véra was serving tea. As they sat down, Nabokov asked, "You didn't really think this was the present, did you?" Karlinsky has a dry humorless tone that masks the sense of humor often disclosed by his elfin smile, and Nabokov had raked him over the coals to see how he would react. Now he presented him with a type-script of the still-unpublished "Notes to *Ada*," doubly valuable as advance scholarly information and as a bibliographic rarity (Nabokov manuscripts in private hands are as hard to find as coelacanths). When people would ask Karlinsky later whether Nabokov was cruel and whimsical, he would answer: "No, he's funny and whimsical."[24]

In "Notes to *Ada*," Nabokov had indicated the allusions in *Ada* to "ludicrous blunders" in Robert Lowell's versions of Osip Mandelstam's poems. Now in the last week of September he wrote "On Adaptation," a noble defense of "a great poem" by Mandelstam, a poem whose high heroism and severe Siberian beauty Lowell's adaptation quite destroys. Nabokov asked *why* adaptation rather than faithful translation? "What, then, is there especially adaptive or adaptational in an obvious travesty? This I wish to be told, this I wish to comprehend. 'Adapted' to what? To the needs of an idiot audience? To the demands of good taste? To the level of one's own genius? But one's audience is the most gifted and varied in the world. . . ."[25]

VI

On October 7 he began writing the first draft of his new novel, *Transparent Things*. In his gloomy Adelboden hotel in August he had been disturbed by a woman he could overhear in the next room, whining and clamoring for Toto. "Dog? Cat?" he wondered in his diary. "Ah, qu'il est beau, ah, qu'il est gentil!" he heard her exclaim when someone from a farther room arrived with Toto. Over the next few days, Nabokov had continued to speculate: "If it's a little dog, it never barks. Cat? Bird?" He began to speak very loudly in his room to inform the neighbors he could hear all they said. After two weeks, he identified the couple, a woman in her fifties and her gloomy, gray man, and the next day he solved the mystery: "Papa wanted to get up early and go for a walk, but she said: 'Ah non. D'abord on fait Toto.' He had to perform. Nauseating neighbors!" The theme of listening in on another life with which Nabokov had dallied a year earlier in his diary "idea for short novel" had now intruded all too vividly on real life, confirming the distaste he expresses in *Transparent Things* for the disregard of privacy in modern architecture and modern life. In *Transparent Things* he would also make gloomy, gray Hugh oblige his wife's chillingly unnatural sexual demands—quite different from those of Nabokov's hotel neighbors, but surely not unrelated.[26]

Before he could advance far in the novel, he had to make time for visits from publishers and the press. When Charles Orengo of Fayard arrived and acquired the French rights to *Ada*, Nabokov warned him that none of his previous French translators was up to the challenge the novel posed. To conserve his time, Nabokov had turned down interview requests from New York, London, Holland, and Milan, but since his Italian publishers were rushing to have *Ada* out before Christmas—only seven months after the appearance of the first English-language edition—he agreed to six Italian interviews in Montreux in late October. Mondadori's chief editor also came to confer with him about troublesome passages in the novel—which, although still not without bad blunders in translation, would reach the number one position on the Italian best-seller lists early in the new year.[27]

Traditionally, late October is the time the Nobel Prize for Literature is announced. Since the early 1960s, Nabokov's name had often been mentioned in connection with the prize, and he knew he had been nominated again this year. On *Ada*'s publication, John Leonard of the *New York Times* had written, "If he doesn't win the Nobel Prize, its only because the Nobel Prize doesn't deserve him." Leonard's remark would prove prophetic: Nabokov would join the greatest writers of the twentieth century—Chekhov, Joyce, Proust, Kafka*—who were never awarded the prize. But in 1969 his selection seemed particularly likely. Early in the fall, *Life* magazine had asked Frank Taylor to contact them as soon as there was any Nobel news, and he passed their request on to the Nabokovs. Then in late October the Nabokovs fielded a call from Sweden. "Stockholm calling . . . Stockholm calling," they heard—and the connection broke. After moments of mounting expectation, the call came through again: a woman who wanted help with her thesis.[28]

After the Nobel Prize went to Solzhenitsyn in 1970, Solzhenitsyn wrote to Nabokov that *he* was far more deserving of the award, and acting on that conviction he nominated Nabokov himself. But whatever other writers, reviewers, and readers may have thought, the Swedish Academy never managed to agree on Nabokov.[29]

VII

During November, Nabokov checked his *Eugene Onegin* one last time. Hoping McGraw-Hill could bring out the translation in a paperback edition with minimal notes—ten pages of annotations, eight lines on

---

* Tolstoy, the obvious candidate for the first prize, was passed over in favour of Sully-Prudhomme. When the following year he was awarded the prize, he declined.

Pushkin's life—he mailed his typescript off to Frank Taylor, announcing: "I am now through with that diabolical task forever. I feel that I have done for Pushkin at least as much as he has done for me."[30]

McGraw-Hill, it turned out, could not publish the revised translation until Princeton University Press—who had taken over *Eugene Onegin*'s original publishers, Bollingen—published the second edition of the complete poem and commentary. But by the time the second complete edition appeared, another six years would have elapsed and McGraw-Hill would have all but lost interest in Nabokov. Meanwhile, at the end of 1969, he needed another new book to make up the eleven he had contracted for. With Andrew Field coming for four days in mid-November, Nabokov prepared to set his past in order, unpacking the cases of papers that had arrived from Ithaca and reading his old diaries in preparation for *Speak on, Memory*.[31]

Late in 1969 he also began to assemble the fair copy of *Poems and Problems*. As a final argument in his case against rhymed verse translations, he tried to produce the exception that would prove his rule that a rhymed poem in one language could not fit with perfect fidelity into a poem of the same stanza form in another language. He hoped to compose a poem simultaneously in Russian and English, a poem on the very subject of this strange endeavor ("So start along the tightrope . . . riding two bicycles") that would demonstrate by its absolute equivalence in two languages how far other verse translations inevitably fell short of this ideal. But even he could not keep the two bicycles moving together, and he ditched the project entirely.[32]

Early in December he thought he had finished *Poems and Problems* and mailed it off, only to find over the next six weeks as he checked through his papers of the 1920 and 1930s that there were other poems that demanded inclusion.[33] In his introduction to the volume he disparaged his English poems for their slightness, and discussed the strangeness of translating his own Russian poems with the loyal and reverent fidelity he had shown toward Pushkin: "One has to fight a vague embarrassment. . . . one feels rather like a potentate swearing allegiance to his own self or a conscientious priest blessing his own bathwater. On the other hand, if one contemplates, for one wild moment, the possibility of paraphrasing and improving one's old verse, a horrid sense of falsification makes one scamper back and cling like a baby ape to rugged fidelity."

But he felt no embarrassment about the combination of poems and problems. "Finally, there is the chess. I refuse to apologize for its inclusion. Chess problems demand from the composer the same virtues that characterize all worthwhile art: originality, invention, conciseness, harmony, complexity, and splendid insincerity. . . . Problems are the poetry of chess."[34] During the late 1960s and early 1970s, his most prolific chess years, Nabokov subscribed to *The Problemist*, and would rate the problems in each new issue. "Very poor," "difficult but crude," "pointless," "dull," "childish," "hideous duals," "horrible," he penciled in a single issue. "Cooked and recooked." "Cannot see any beauty here." He was equally hard on his own mistakes. Writing to the editors of *The Problemist*, he could deplore "the wretched dual in my self-mate in 5" or declare it not worth the bother to eliminate a rook in another problem: "I prefer scrapping the wretched thing altogether." But his problems were rated highly. On the strength of his first few contributions to *The Problemist*, he was invited in January 1970 to join the American team as a composer in future international chess-problem tournaments. Boris Spassky would single out one of the problems in *Poems and Problems* for special praise. The fellow fanatics who subscribed to *The Problemist* would characterize his problems of the 1960s and 1970s as not necessarily difficult but witty and remarkable for their originality of composition. Like *The Gift*, *Lolita*, *Pale Fire*, and *Ada*, his problems differ radically from one another in design, but share this much: they depend not on forceful conflict but on the sheer unexpectedness of the central design itself: the surprise of a wandering king, like Kinbote let loose from his Zembla; false solutions as complex as the single true solution; a queen who for all her might proves in the way and must exile herself to a remote corner of the board; a compelled circuitousness on the part of an attacking rook; a flash of unexpected symmetry; a sudden vista of variations; an amusing abundance of discovered checks.[35]

VIII

Poems and Problems was the first book Nabokov had completed since *Ada*, and the third of the eleven he needed for McGraw-Hill. Late in January 1970, he began book four, spending a month revising Michael Glenny's translation of *Mary*.[36] After this, only one of his Russian novels remained to be translated.

Although Nabokov's seventieth birthday had taken place in April 1969, just before the publication of *Ada*, Alfred Appel had organized as a belated present a special Nabokov issue of *Triquarterly*. Nabokov had been eager to check it beforehand for factual accuracy, but Appel would not let the wraps come off his gift until he could offer it intact. Nabokov received the bulky volume at the end of February: tributes from people like Saul Steinberg, Anthony Burgess, Herbert Gold,

John Updike, John Barth; criticism from Karlinsky, Appel, Carl Proffer, Peter Lubin, and others; and reminiscences from Nina Berberova,
Morris Bishop, and others. When Appel hinted that a little essay in
reply would be welcome, Nabokov spent two weeks on the difficult
task of drafting public thank-yous to forty-two separate contributors.
He was grateful; he was tactful. Thanking Ross Wetzsteon for a superb memoir on his Cornell years, he began: "I remember most of
the best students in my Cornell classes. Mr. Wetzsteon was one of
them"—thereby complimenting Wetzsteon and seeming to recollect
him but allowing the careful reader to deduce that he probably could
not. He was unstinting in praise: Robert Alter's critique of *Invitation
to a Beheading* was "practically flawless," "a most brilliant reflection of
that book in a reader's mind." Only George Steiner came in for nothing but criticism. Nabokov had poked covert fun at Steiner's essay
"To Traduce or to Transfigure: On Modern Verse Translations" as
early as the first sentence of *Ada*. Now he dusted him off: "Mr Steiner's article ('Extraterritorial') is built on solid abstractions and
opaque generalizations. A few specific items can be made out and
should be corrected."[37]

Setting off for Rome with Véra on March 19, Nabokov took with
him on the train the index cards for *Transparent Things*, another sample translation of *Ada* in French, his chess problems and chess
pocket-board, two butterfly nets, his *Butterflies in Art* notes, and a
magnifying glass to check the entomological detail on his painted
prey. It was not easy to track down. He tramped through the whole
of the Vatican Museum to find only one butterfly, "a Zebra Swallowtail, in a quite conventional *Madonna and Child* by Gentile, as realistic
as though it were painted yesterday."[38]

At the beginning of April, he took the train and ferry south to Taormina in search of live butterflies, sun, and refuge from the American tourists who considered him their property. Véra returned for
two weeks to Montreux before flying down to rejoin him. This time
the trip to Taormina was a success, and Nabokov found the rare Sicilian butterflies he had come for. In mid-May the Nabokovs returned
to Montreux to be near Anna Feigin while her *dame de compagnie* took
her vacation.[39]

Alan Jay Lerner arrived for two days in late May to discuss the
musical of *Lolita*, a project for which Nabokov had had high hopes
since it had first been mooted more than a year earlier. His play *The
Waltz Invention* had had its English-language premiere in Hartford,
Connecticut, in January 1969, and in March of that year Joseph
Papp's New York Shakespeare Festival had staged Russell McGrath's
ponderously symbolic adaptation of *Invitation to a Beheading*. Neither

had won much critical or popular acclaim, but Nabokov hoped that a *My Fair Lolita* might prove a smash hit. He had another motive: he also hoped that Dmitri, now singing in Medellín and Caracas, could be used to record a background song for the show.[40]

IX

In the last week of June the Nabokovs drove up the Valais to spend a month at the Grand Hotel in Saas Fee. "After many gropings and false starts," Nabokov noted in his diary on June 30, *Transparent Things* "burst into life (8:15 PM, after raclette with white wine)."[41] Off at last, he kept writing steadily for the next two months.

Late in July he returned with Véra to Montreux. Even here he ventured out for butterflies, taking the train up to the Rochers de Naye or the Dent de Jaman and walking and stalking his way down.[42] A descent of a thousand meters was nothing for this seventy-one-year-old, and valuable preparation for *Transparent Things*, where climbing and descending a Swiss mountainside proves one of clumsy, sedentary Hugh Person's worst waking nightmares.

Montreux in the summer left the Nabokovs accessible to tourists. Occasionally, just to see some new faces, they would agree to share an afternoon drink with some persistent and promising strangers, like Charles Givan and his wife, both English graduate students from California, who later wrote an account of the hour they were allotted in the Green Salon. When Nabokov found out that Givan would teach creative writing, he wondered whether creativity could be taught at all, but then added, "The great thing which can, I suppose, be taught, is to avoid the cliché of one's time." He also urged Givan to have his students learn to write down conversations they had overheard and learn to remember and reproduce them accurately. "And they could learn what a dentist does—learn about different professions. That's very old-fashioned. Flaubert's idea. Learn the little secrets of a trade, of the different professions, so that they can write about them."[43]

Nabokov himself had learned from a Montreux stationer many details about the manufacture of the pencils he bought to write with, and he would use the information to extraordinary effect in a strange digression on the history of a pencil in *Transparent Things*. The novel was progressing well in Montreux's beautiful late-summer weather: mornings by the hotel pool, lunch there at its open-air café, afternoons at the lectern.[44]

In the last week of August, he broke off *Transparent Things* to turn to *Glory*, the last of his Russian novels to be turned into English. Dmitri, in an active phase of his singing career, had recently been performing in North and South America—rather defeating the purpose of his parents' residence in Europe—and although he had begun the translation three years before, he had been able to complete less than two-thirds of it. Véra set about translating the rest, and Nabokov continued to revise the family translation on and off until December.[45]

At the end of August, Alfred and Nina Appel arrived for a five-day visit. Strolling with Appel along the lakeside, Nabokov pointed out the filth polluting Lake Geneva: "I saw it coming in the States twenty years ago, and would tell people that," he said, shaking his head, and then went on to inveigh against the faddist aspects of the current outcry against pollution.[46] He was fascinated by all that was happening in the United States, although he had an overcolored sense of the violence and social unrest of the late 1960s. He asked if Appel's classes at Northwestern University had been disrupted by demonstrations. No, Appel replied,

> "My classroom problems are not political." . . . I told him about a nun who sat in the back row of one of my lecture courses, and who one day complained after class that a couple near her were always spooning. "Sister," I had said, "in these troubled times we should be grateful if that's all they were doing." . . . "Ohhh," moaned Nabokov, mourning my lost opportunity, clapping his hand to his head in mock anguish. "You should have said, 'Sister, be grateful that they were not forking.' "[47]

Appel was entranced by Nabokov's conversational manner:

> Nabokov clearly relishes good gab; gossip, anecdotes and jokes pour forth from him, and he is one of those people whose laughter threatens to unseat them. To emphasize a point or underscore a punch line, he will often lower his head, wrinkle his brow, and peer over the top of his eyeglasses, a parody of a professor. His face, even at less animated moments, is very expressive, mobile; photographs reveal its protean qualities. "I've frequently been told that I don't look like me," he says, pausing for a moment to enjoy the paradox. "Recently, a stranger, a tourist, approached me in the [hotel] garden, and said, 'I know you! You're . . . you're . . . *you're General MacArthur's brother!*' " Nabokov shakes with mirth, and dabs his eyes with his handkerchief, and catches his empty coffee cup and saucer as they are about to topple from his lap.

Appel describes well Nabokov's manner of testing and revising what he says: "He has a habit of repeating a phrase that he has just spoken, of spearing a word in midair and toying with the pieces. 'No, tape recorders are out,' he says. 'No speaking off the Nabocuff. When I see one of those machines I start hemming and hawing . . . hemming and hawing. Hemingwaying all over the place.' "[48] Appel, who had come to interview Nabokov for *Novel*, was able to fill two-thirds of the interview with transcripts of Nabokov's impromptu remarks rather than his prepared index-card answers, and noted "there are no differences in manner, style and tone between his oral and written responses. . . . Nabokov's voice is firmly, consistently his."[49]

Appel was as struck by the content as by the contours of Nabokov's conversation. He observed Nabokov's manifest admiration of Véra's mind.* Once as she corrected him and left the room, Nabokov turned to Appel: "Vera's Russian is stupendous." Another time he declared that her memory was better than his own. But Appel noted that Nabokov himself seemed interested in everything and able to recall it all. With his own enthusiasm for popular culture, he was delighted to discover that Nabokov loyally followed in his daily newspapers the comic strips *Buzz Sawyer* and *Rex Morgan, M.D.* A keen film scholar, he asked Nabokov what movies he had seen in Berlin in the 1920s and 1930s. Nabokov fondly recalled Charlie Chaplin and the Marx Brothers and recounted in precise detail scene after scene from Laurel and Hardy movies that he had not seen for thirty or forty years.[50]

A former art history student, Appel also asked Nabokov about his *Butterflies in Art*. Nabokov answered with animation, for he was still eagerly pursuing the project, and in the middle of September he and Véra traveled by train to Venice to spend a week scouring its galleries and churches. They adored the city.[51]

On his return, he switched easily from his *Butterflies in Art* back toward his abandoned *Butterflies of Europe*. The *Times Educational Supplement* had written to him asking if he would care to review Higgins and Riley's *Field Guide to the Butterflies of Britain and Europe*. By now, although certainly not the greatest lepidopterist in the world, he was by far the most famous, and the previous year had been asked to write the foreword to Higgins and Riley's book but had had too little time. Apart from his demolition of Arndt's *Eugene Onegin* in 1964,

---

* Nabokov could be generous toward others too. At the time of Appel's visit he had just been offered an honor from an American literary institution, and told Appel that he was declining it because they promised him no money and were simply trying to attach *his* prestige to *their* name. "Of course if it was a *real* honor, that would be different." Appel asked: "What would you consider a real honor?" "A real honor, Alfred, is when someone like you comes halfway across the world to see me."

Nabokov had not written reviews since the early 1950s, but those last reviews had been of Klot's *Field Guide to the Butterflies of North America* and of Audubon's *Butterflies, Moths, and Other Studies*. Less than two weeks after it sent the book to Nabokov on the off-chance, the *Times Educational Supplement* was delighted to receive back his highly favorable review.[52]

Butterflies were one of his few temptations to diversion. In October he turned to his *Lolita* screenplay, partly to satisfy his McGraw-Hill quota, partly because he wanted the screenplay out before the possible publication of Lerner's libretto for the musical *Lolita*.[53] Another year would in fact elapse before he could obtain a release from Kubrick to publish the screenplay, and by then the musical would have long since folded and faded from memory.

With the screenplay ready to print, Nabokov turned to the proofs of *Poems and Problems* and to revising the French *King, Queen, Knave* and the translation of *Glory*—a novel he found he liked much more than he had expected. Nevertheless, he felt a great sense of relief when he finished with *Glory*. On December 2 he wrote in his diary: "Two pages left! . . . the entire thing corrected by me, an excruciating task that took three months to complete with a few interruptions. Last Russian novel, thank God." Eight days later: "Finished correcting and collating three typescript copies of *Glory*. *Vraiment—ouf!*" By now it was almost four months since he had worked on *Transparent Things*, but after some hesitation he decided to risk interrupting the novel once again to visit America for the musical *Lolita*.[54]

X

On December 31, 1970, Andrew Field and his wife, Michele, arrived to see the New Year in with the Nabokovs. Field remained in Montreux for a month, meeting with Nabokov a dozen times at hours that would not disturb the rhythms of his work.[55] It would be the last time he saw Nabokov except to drop off the manuscript of his biography in two years' time.

Tensions were already starting to show. A vigilant Nabokov was not an easy subject for a biographer. Always highly impatient with inexactitude and indignant at any divergence from the truth as he saw it, he trusted his own memory and denounced as false other people's images that did not accord with his own. Still dabbling with *Speak on, Memory*, he had become worried that it would turn into a mere chronicle, epic or episodic in comparison with the lyrical *Speak, Memory*: "If the distant past is highly organized poetry," he reflected, "the recent past is nothing but rough topical prose." He told Field: "There is an absence of that glow of affection I felt for *Speak, Memory*. It will not be violins but trombones."[56]

He had always liked to command memory to perform for him, but to fish up a recollection for someone else to prepare and serve up for public consumption made him uneasy, self-conscious, defensively playful. Joining Field after a nap, a little groggy on his feet, he played the part of his own biographer: "I remember him shuffling in looking old and wretched, and a moment later he was bubbling with good spirits." Another time he fell behind Véra and urged Field in a stage whisper not to let him forget to tell about his daughter and his previous wife. On a third occasion, feigning that he did not know Field was within earshot, he asked Véra: "Do you think I should tell him about IT?"[57]

He was an expert tease. Once he told an interviewer, quite truthfully, that he didn't need friends who read books, but simply bright people, "people who understand jokes." Then he added with resignation: "Véra doesn't laugh. She is married to one of the great clowns of all time, but she never laughs." The poor interviewer failed to see the joke—Nabokov prized in Véra the best sense of humor he had ever met in a woman—and by recording the lament straight, the interviewer unwittingly revealed he had himself failed Nabokov's test. One day Nabokov mocked Field's solemn harping on the myth that Nabokov's father was an illegitimate son of Tsar Alexander II. He danced a little jig: "Yes, sometimes I feel the blood of Peter the Great in me!" Véra, who had already observed Field's failure to understand her husband's jokes, shouted out that he must not say such things—and Field took that as confirmation that the Nabokovs feared this supposed family secret.[58]

Field's insistence on the rumor that V. D. Nabokov was the son of either Alexander II or his brother, Grand-Duke Konstantin—the very existence of these alternatives should have made him realize the story was pure speculation—was the result of his talking to other members of the Nabokov clan with a romantic reluctance to distinguish fact from fancy. Field's reliance on other informants led to the first serious squaring off between biographer and biographee.

Nabokov expected Field to ask him questions; he would supply the answers. He had in fact been answering Field's biographical queries by mail since 1965. Since Field had become the official biographer, Nabokov had furnished much more information, the last before the current round of live interviews in a long interview by mail in the summer of 1970. After having sorted out his Montreux files, sent for his Ithaca papers, and ordered photostats of material he had donated to the Library of Congress, he assumed that Field would have in Montreux everything he needed for a serious biography.

As early as the fall, however, he had been annoyed to hear that Field had interviewed others, looking for "human interest" that Nabokov thought could only spoil the book.[59] He was still more upset to discover that in December, Field had placed an advertisement in New York's Russian-language daily soliciting contacts with those émigrés who had known Nabokov. This was a normal enough procedure for a modern biographer, but then there was a great deal of modern biographical practice—the invasion of privacy, the inventions of *biographie romancée*, unlicensed psychological speculation—that Nabokov had objected to for decades. He made it plain to Field on January 23 that he thought Field's action, without his knowledge or permission, quite improper.

From his hotel Field wrote an apology, assuring Nabokov of his friendship. Nabokov felt soothed, but asked Véra to tell Field by phone that he wanted a complete list of all the people he had interviewed and planned to interview. Field obliged, and left Montreux a week later almost reconciled.[60]

XI

Nabokov had long supported his family in Prague—first his mother and her friend Evgenia Hofeld, then his nephew Rostislav Petkevich, and now his sister Olga. By now he was also sending money to Elena Yakovlev, the sister of his friend Mikhail Kaminka, and had begun to send money to help dissident writers in the Soviet Union, to the Russian Literary Fund in America, which had supported him in his émigré years, and to the Union of Russian Jews, which had helped him emigrate to America. Some years before, he had sent a check to his school friend Samuil Rosoff for the League for the Abolition of Religious Coercion in Israel, and now he sent more to the Israel Defense Fund.[61]

He took a lively interest in Israel. His father had resolutely opposed Russian anti-Semitism and had close Jewish friends, Avgust Kaminka and Iosif Hessen. Their sons, Mikhail and George, in turn became Nabokov's own best friends. His wife was Jewish. He had lost close friends in German concentration camps. Naturally, therefore, he supported U.S. policy in the Middle East and opposed Soviet aid to Israel's Arab opponents. He had been invited to Israel as an official guest by Israeli ambassador Arie Levavi in December 1970. Nabokov demurred, but by February 1971 the thought of hunting

new butterflies and visiting Samuil Rosoff made him ready to contemplate his first taste of the Middle East since passing through Con-
stantinople in 1919. Although other invitations from Israel followed
over the next few years, somehow age, illness, and work in progress
recurrently deferred the trip.[62]

Had he visited Israel as he planned in the spring of 1971, he would
have had to defer *Transparent Things* yet again. He still hoped to finish the book—only a novella, after all—by January 1972,[63] but evidently he felt it was still not resolved enough in his mind for another
prolonged burst of attention, for he was also eager to travel to New
York in April for the Broadway opening of *Lolita, My Love*. The play's
failure spared him the journey. At its tryout in Philadelphia it was
panned as vacuous and bland ("nice little flop," Nabokov noted
calmly in his diary), and a new tryout in Boston a month later with a
new director, a new Lolita, and some new songs fared no better.

In the spring of 1971, with all his Russian novels translated, Nabokov began the next phase of finalizing his canon: his Russian stories. He revised Dmitri's translation of "Ultima Thule," cotranslated
with him "Solus Rex," and translated "Torpid Smoke" on his own.[64]

Spring-cleaning this year for the Montreux Palace included repainting the hotel's facade. To avoid the distraction of the noise, Nabokov
escaped at the end of March to the south of Portugal, where he could
expect warm weather, a good crop of early butterflies, and the quiet
he needed to work on *Transparent Things*. For the first time in Europe
he took a plane. Flying from Geneva to Lisbon, he enjoyed the heartbreaking loveliness of the scenery at low elevations—a sensation he
would draw on for the conclusion of his new novel. Praia da Rocha
and the whole Algarve coast turned out to be horribly cold, with a
storm-swept, booming sea and a rattling wind. After taking two
weeks to catch only one specimen apiece of two different butterfly
species, Nabokov had had enough, and he and Véra flew back to
Montreux a week early.[65]

During April, Nabokov translated more stories, and happily accepted Simon Karlinsky's offer to translate "A Russian Beauty." (Karlinsky received ten dollars for the completed translation, a sum he
thought so comical he had the check framed for his wall.)[66]* Stephen
Jan Parker came to visit. Parker, who a year after Nabokov's death
would set up the first scholarly journal devoted to Nabokov studies,
had taken Literature 311 in the last year Nabokov taught at Cornell,
and had recently completed one of the first doctoral dissertations on

---

* When the Nabokovs heard of this from Alfred Appel, they sent Karlinsky another
forty dollars. "A Russian Beauty" *was* the shortest of Nabokov's mature stories.

Nabokov. He arrived in Montreux with trepidation, and left three hours later warmed by Nabokov's cordiality. The conversation ranged everywhere from Malamud to Mandelstam, from Cornell to the Russian countryside, from Solzhenitsyn to Stravinsky. Laughing until the tears flowed, Nabokov regaled Parker with a vision of the CIA editions of *The Defense* and *Invitation to a Beheading* parachuting down into the Soviet Union, a parcel of bright orange books being blown in the wrong direction.

He asked Parker's help: did he know the name of the fabric used in blinds on European trains? For a whole month he had been trying to find the right word to use in the scene in *Transparent Things* where Hugh meets Armande. He had made inquiries at the Montreux railway station; he had written to the railways. Parker did not know, and Nabokov would have to settle for "semitransparent black fabric."[67]

The Nabokovs had planned to return to Sicily in May but canceled their reservations to avoid a strike and headed instead for the Midi. As a precaution against disaster they flew down to Nice, as they had to Lisbon, on different days. The rain poured and the mistral tossed the holm oaks almost every day of their three weeks in the tiny resort of Tourtour near Draguignan in the Var, but the poor weather at least kept Nabokov steadily at work on *Transparent Things*.[68]

Back in Switzerland he was driven to Anzère-sur-Sion in the Valais to pursue butterflies on his own. At the Hôtel des Masques—good name—he asked for a room facing south, but because of construction noise (another motif in *Transparent Things*) the manager gave him both a room facing south and another facing north so that he could move from one to the other to escape the din.[69]

Véra had fallen ill at Tourtour, and a bad reaction to antibiotics after her return briefly put her in the hospital. Nabokov returned to Montreux to be close to her, although in the mornings he still roamed the nearby hills for butterflies, cursing the pesticides that had killed off his prey. Véra returned from the hospital, *Transparent Things* started trickling again, and all the butterflies—simply suppressed, it turned out, by bad weather—suddenly emerged. Véra's fortnight of bed rest had left her with circulatory trouble in her feet, and Nabokov spent the evenings with her on their sun-drenched terrace reading her Solzhenitsyn's *August 1914*.[70]

XII

For August 1971, the Nabokovs rented three apartments in a chalet-style apartment house between Gstaad and Saanen: one for themselves and Dmitri; one for Anna Feigin and her *dame de compagnie*; and one for visitors, Nabokov's sister Elena Sikorski, and Véra's sister Sonia Slonim, who also lived now in Geneva. After the morning's chase Nabokov would work on *Transparent Things* while his son translated more of his Russian stories. "Dreary region. Wretched butterfly hunting," noted Nabokov in his diary.

But one fine morning he and Dmitri climbed the 2,200-meter La Videmanette, above Rougemont. Dmitri recollects that his father told him that day, "in one of those rare moments when father and son discuss such matters, that he had accomplished what he wished in life and art, and was a truly happy man. His writing, he went on, was all there, ready inside his mind, like film waiting to be developed. A sensation, he said, akin to Schopenhauer's vision of events as they unfold."[71] They were not to know this would be the last good hike they would ever share.

After that serene moment Nabokov returned to the Residence Wyssmüllerei to find a new critical book on his work, William Woodin Rowe's *Nabokov's Deceptive World*.[72] Rowe and his wife had visited the Nabokovs in Montreux the previous year and caused no offense. His book was a different matter. Nabokov had no objection to its first half, but its second half professed to unearth buried sexual references throughout his work, regardless of context and sense. "Eye" can mean female pudendum, Rowe declares, and therefore so can the letter "i," and therefore same thing can be implied in the "I" that begins Indiana, Illinois, and Iowa. Rowe is not the first to have convinced himself of preposterous conclusions by the simple expedient of automatic self-confirmation, excluding alternative explanations and conflicting evidence, and the hilarious retort Nabokov penned for the *New York Review of Books* at the end of August could serve as a warning to many a mechanical mind:

> One may wonder if it was worth Mr. Rowe's time to exhibit erotic bits picked out of *Lolita* and *Ada*—a process rather like looking for allusions to aquatic mammals in *Moby Dick*. But that is his own choice and concern. What I object to is Mr. Rowe's manipulating my most innocent words so as to introduce sexual "symbols" into them. The notion of symbol itself has always been abhorrent to me. . . . The symbolism racket in schools attracts computerized minds but destroys plain intelligence as well as poetical sense. It bleaches the soul. It numbs all capacity to enjoy the fun and enchantment of art. . . . Pencil-licking is always a reference to you know what. A soccer goal hints at the vulval orifice (which Mr. Rowe evidently sees as square).
>
> . . . The fatal flaw in Mr. Rowe's treatment of recurrent words, such

as "garden" or "water," is his regarding them as abstractions, and not realizing that the sound of a bath being filled, say, in the world of *Laughter in the Dark*, is as different from the limes rustling in the rain of *Speak, Memory* as the Garden of Delights in *Ada* is from the lawns of *Lolita*.[73]

XIII

On his return to Montreux, Nabokov discovered another reason to rush into print. Early in the year he had written his first real letter to Edmund Wilson since their *Eugene Onegin* clash:

Dear Bunny,

A few days ago I had the occasion to reread the whole batch (Russ., *vsyu pachku*) of our correspondence. It was such a pleasure to feel again the warmth of your many kindnesses, the various thrills of our friendship, that constant excitement of art and intellectual discovery.

I was sorry to hear (from Lena Levin) that you had been ill, and happy to learn that you were much better.

Please believe that I have long ceased to bear you a grudge for your incomprehensible incomprehension of Pushkin's and Nabokov's *Onegin*.[74]

Wilson responded to this generous letter with another harsh misreading of Nabokov's motives, reporting to a friend: "Nabokov has suddenly written me a letter telling me that he values my friendship and that all has been forgiven. He has been told that I have been ill, and it always makes him cheerful to think that his friends are in bad shape. He was mourning for Roman Grynberg at least ten years before he died."[75] Nabokov never learned of these remarks, but in September he received a photocopy of a few pages about himself from Wilson's *Upstate: Records and Recollections of Northern New York*, which showed that as early as 1957 Wilson had been harboring similar feelings, although they were at that stage leavened by others more charitable.[76] Nabokov wrote in outrage to the *New York Times Book Review* to refute Wilson's willful incomprehensions: "What surprises me, however, is not so much Wilson's aplomb as the fact that in the diary he kept while he was my guest in Ithaca he pictures himself as nursing feelings and ideas so vindictive and fatuous that if expressed they should have made me demand his immediate departure."[77]

In mid-September he began revising the first pages of the French translation of *Ada*. He planned to set aside two months for the entire translation: apparently he had reached the point where he was ready for the final run at *Transparent Things* and wanted to clear his desk of other commitments before he began. But although he waited in suspense through the month of October, nothing more arrived of *Ada ou l'ardeur*.[78]

He had been asked to participate in major television programs in the United States, France, Switzerland, and elsewhere, but he accepted only one request, a joint BBC–Bavarian TV interview. A much more elaborate affair than he had anticipated, the interview required eight days of filming and discussion, eight days he had hoped to devote to *Transparent Things*.[79]

Before he could return to the novel, he had to spend the first three weeks of November correcting the endless galleys of his revised *Eugene Onegin*. Although he aimed to offer the translation as a paperback for McGraw-Hill after the publication of the revised Bollingen edition of translation and commentary, this second Bollingen edition would prove as jinxed as the first—a strike by electrical employees, a printer's slowdown, a mismatched inking job, and more—and would not appear for more than another four years, at the very end of 1975.[80]

On November 23, after a five-month pause, *Transparent Things* began its final, steady "retrickle." So engrossed did Nabokov become that Véra had difficulty persuading him to discuss even major business decisions she did not feel she could handle alone. Throughout January and February the novel was advancing "at a spanking pace," interrupted only by the time Nabokov took off to compose two chess problems and the three days he needed for a generously paid interview for *Vogue*. In March he was still "deep, deep in his new book." On the last of his fair-copy index cards, he recorded the date and the precise hour—April 1, 6:30 P.M.—that he wrote out the six words of the weirdly disconcerting final sentence of *Transparent Things*.[81]

CHAPTER 24

Transparent Things

I

NABOKOV wanted his new novel to be as unlike his previous one as possible: instead of a vast and opulent romance, a slim novella; instead of a luxuriant never-never land, a few shabby corners of his immediate Swiss surroundings; instead of *Ada*'s sunshot nostalgia, a drab present seen under the grayest and chilliest of lights. *Transparent Things* brings us back from Antiterra to earth with a thump and a wince.[1]

But this posed a problem. Although his natural first audience was an American one, Nabokov was out of touch with American slang and the rapid social changes of the 1960s. Except when he was constructing a fantastic environment, he always limited himself to milieus he could observe as well as or better than any of his readers. In the 1940s and 1950s he watched American college towns closely enough to invent Beardsley and Waindell and Wordsmith, but he knew nothing of the likes of the Berkeley and Cornell and Columbia of the late 1960s. After years of chasing butterflies from state to state, he had accumulated far more evidence than most Americans of the motel America he would record in *Lolita*. Now his passion for lepidoptera had introduced him to another specialty, the hotels and slopes of Swiss mountain resorts, and these became his new story's milieu.

He still needed an American nexus. Over the last decade of his residence in Europe the kinds of Americans he had seen most were bright, youngish editors like Bart Winer, publishers like Frank Taylor, and academics like Alfred Appel. Accordingly, he made Hugh Person an editor and proofreader—a job all too familiar to Nabokov himself in recent years—who visits Switzerland to meet the novelist Mr. R., a naturalized American expatriate of German origin who writes English far better than he speaks it.

There was of course one young American—who often proofread his books—whom Nabokov had seen much more than any other: his son Dmitri. Inverting Dmitri helped him invent Hugh Person. Where Dmitri enjoyed his father's confidences and admired him unstintingly, Hugh remains remote from his father, for whom he feels little but impatience and sullen scorn. Dmitri had long had an active, colorful love life; inept and almost impotent Hugh Person has little experience with women and even less luck. Dmitri was a passionate mountain climber and an accomplished skier; Hugh has Dmitri's height and powerful hands but finds even struggling up to the bottom of a cableway an inferno of pain and frustration.

In *Ada*, Nabokov had assigned Van's birth to the year his father was born. Now he chose a protagonist roughly his son's age, and with a reverse Dmitri in mind could construct Hugh as a counter to Van Veen. Van, in his youth a gravity-defying acrobat and an inexhaustible libertine, has his life enriched by eighty years of love for Ada, and in his nineties writes down with her fond help the story of their rhapsodic love. Hugh Person finds gravity a nightmarish humiliation as he struggles to clamber up an alpine path in the wake of Armande and the sporty young men who bound along with her. Wretchedly unhappy, he marries Armande, loves her helplessly despite her coldness of soul, and accidentally kills her after one short shared winter. Of a literary bent but without the talent to make his time with Armande live on the page, Hugh tries instead to revisit their past. But when he stops at the hotel where they spent their first night together, the hotel burns down and brings his short, unhappy life to an end.

II

Everything frustrates Hugh, even inert matter, and he must find refuge from the inimical outer world in the inner one of his emotions. But family love offers no comfort, and sexual love proves little better. The night his father dies, Hugh procures his first prostitute to keep at bay his consciousness of his father's presence "in every dark corner of solitude," but the girl refuses to stay the night and leaves him alone with his belated remorse. Back in America his romantic life seems restricted to a single, unrepeated evening with the promiscuous Julia Moore.

If Hugh's visible life appears lackluster, he still has his thoughts and dreams. From time to time he makes a vivid entry in his diary; a letter to the London *Times* merits inclusion in an anthology, *To the Editor: Sir*; two lines of a poem he published in a college magazine still seem an auspicious beginning; but as he laments, he is only a proofreader, not a poet. On his second trip to Switzerland, to call on the writer, Mr. R., he encounters a young woman on a train and later records the meeting in his diary:

Wished to know if I like my job. My job! I replied: "Ask me what I *can* do, not what I *do*, lovely girl, lovely wake of the sun through semitransparent black fabric. . . . I can compose patches of poetry as strange and new as you are, or as anything a person may write three hundred years hence, but I have never published one scrap of verse except some juvenile nonsense at college. . . . I can levitate one inch high and keep it up for ten seconds, but cannot climb an apple tree. . . . I have fallen in love with you but shall do nothing about it. In short I am an all-round genius."

Of all the improbable dreams of transcendence Hugh records here, his love for Armande seems the likeliest. But when he arranges to meet her for some summer skiing, she turns up with three athletic young males, one of whom is her current lover, and the promised "stroll" up to the cableway, all steep ups and slippery downs, proves agony as he labors, "hot, wretched Hugh, behind Armande's blond bun, while she lightly followed light Jacques." He fails to make it to the cableway. The next day, despite new boots and alpenstock, he still falls behind and loses his way. Only on the fourth try does he at last reach cableway and ski-slopes, where he can only sit sipping drinks on the café terrace and try to catch sight of lithe Armande.

After an argument with Jacques, she has Hugh take her back down the mountain. As they descend the winding path and Hugh tries to pluck up the nerve to kiss her, she announces casually: "And now one is going to make love." She leads him to a mossy patch in the fir forest that she has evidently tested with others. Disconcerted, Hugh just manages to perform, and afterward blurts out:

> "I hate life. I hate myself. I hate that beastly old bench." She stopped to look the way his fierce finger pointed, and he embraced her. At first she tried to evade his lips but he persisted desperately. All at once she gave in, and the minor miracle happened. A shiver of tenderness rippled her features. . . . Her eyelashes were wet, her shoulders shook in his clasp. That moment of soft agony was never to be repeated . . . yet that brief vibration in which she dissolved with the sun, the cherry trees, the forgiven landscape, set the tone for his new existence with its sense of "all-is-well" despite her worst moods, her silliest caprices, her harshest demands.

That kiss also proves the last moment when his love for Armande appears to offer Hugh the promise of release from the solitude of the self. Miscalculating his prospects, eager for a life of parties in New York, she marries him quickly and returns with him to America. There her chilliness of spirit sets the tone of their relationship. Despite his discomfort, she insists they make love dressed as if for a party and without the least break in their elegant chitchat. Unfaithful to him even on their honeymoon, she enjoys a dozen lovers during the three solo skiing trips of her first and last winter in America.

Love, Hugh had hoped, might create an allowable transparency between his soul and hers within the privacy of marriage. But with Armande he finds the values reversed, just as they are in her mother's strangely transparent house, where everything seems to take place "in full view of the public." Hard, untender Armande shuts Hugh out—and lets others in. But Hugh's feelings do not change: "He loved her in spite of her unloveableness." Lying awake beside her, fretting that "preparing other people's books for publication was a debasing job," he can still reflect "that no manner of permanent drudgery or temporary dissatisfaction mattered in the face of his ever growing, ever more tender, love for his wife."

III

Hugh's only life remains his inner life. But when his imagination manages to escape the outside world, it is not for the freedom of the artist he feels within him, nor for the ecstasy of the lucky lover, but only to sink into the thralldom of sleep. All his life he has found night a grim giant. A somnambulist as a boy, seen by his college roommate to wrestle a bedside table while still in the throes of a dream, Hugh still has nightmares night after night. One March evening in New York, several months after marrying Armande, he dreams that the woman he loves—in the dream a fusion of Giulia Romeo, the whore he picked up the night his father died, and of Julia Moore—wants to leap from their burning building. He knows it would be madness for her to jump that far, and he holds her back. She struggles and slips and even falls, but still he holds her, as he soars through the air like "Superman carrying a young soul in his embrace!" He wakes up to find Armande on the floor, strangled by his own hands.

That fatal dream destroys the one happiness in his life, robs him of his freedom (he spends the next eight years shuttling between prison and madhouse), and reenacts the worst alarm and humiliation of his life. For on the last night of their honeymoon, in their hotel at Stresa, Armande had become agitated by a hotel fire on the television news and insisted they practice descending the ornate facade of their old hotel, which had no fire escape. Inept Hugh panics just below the ledge of their fourth-floor room and scrambles up again, thinking Ar-

mande, scaling the wall beneath him, has fallen. Eventually he locates her in a third-floor room (she had entered through the window), wrapped in a blanket on the bed of a stranger with whom she
has clearly made love.*

Psychiatrists insist that Hugh's dream is the expression of his unconscious desire to kill Armande. Hugh—with Nabokov's backing—
fiercely denies this "odious rot." Although Armande never understood or shared his need for some intimacy of the spirit, he still holds
onto the privacy of his marriage and refuses to discuss what the
prison psychiatrist calls "in his professional jargon 'conjugal sex.' "
Since no one can prove that there was the slightest awareness, the
slightest directive on the part of the waking Hugh when his dream
self killed Armande, the ultimate verdict has to be that he acted in a
trance, and the mystery of the soul remains intact.

On his final discharge, Hugh, haunted by dreams of Armande in
the Swiss setting where he first met her, and unable to cope with his
loss in any other way, makes a pilgrimage to his past, just like Chorb,
in Nabokov's 1925 story "The Return of Chorb," who when his wife
dies during their honeymoon helplessly retraces their steps all the
way to the room where they spent their first night together. For
Hugh, frustration looms again. He can remember the floor but not
the room number of the hotel in Witt where he spent his first night
with Armande. In any case the whole third floor is occupied and he
has to make do with a vile fourth-floor room. Anxious to reclimb the
trail to the cableway and find the setting for that unforgettable kiss,
he soon finds the tight new boots he has bought scrape the skin off
his feet, "resulting in a red eye burning there through every thread-
bare thought." He becomes utterly lost: all he can retrieve of his early
climbs is the anguish and the exasperation.

When he returns to the hotel, his devoted efforts seem about to
reap their reward. Checking along the third-floor corridor, he recollects the room he and Armande had shared—313—and discovers
down at reception that the occupant of the room has suddenly been
called home, and he can move in after dinner. He retires early to bed,
and tries to conjure up the image of Armande entering through the
door.

> Person, *this* person, was on the imagined brink of imagined bliss when
> Armande's footfalls approached—striking out both "imagined" in the

---

* Nabokov drew in part on Dmitri's occasional practice, much frowned on by his
mother, of mysteriously appearing in his parents' living room (Montreux Palace, Room
64) after having made what was for him the short and easy diagonal outside climb
from his own usual bedroom at the Palace, Room 52.

proof's margin (never too wide for corrections and queries!). This is where the orgasm of art courses through the whole spine with incomparably more force than sexual ecstasy or metaphysical panic.

At this moment of her now indelible dawning through the limpid door of his room he felt the elation a tourist feels, when taking off.

The controlled imagination of art seems to overcome gravity and time and the solitude of the self, and Hugh's fancy soars up as if on a plane zooming for the clouds and beyond. As his reverie shades into dream, air-hostess Armande approaches. Abruptly, the dream-plane explodes with a roar and a cough, and Hugh awakes, coughing, to find the hotel on fire. Before he can reach the window, the smoke has choked him to death. In place of imagined fulfillment, he encounters only one last merciless humiliation.

IV

Except that Hugh's life, like *Transparent Things*, ends this way:

Rings of blurred colors circled around him, reminding him briefly of a childhood picture in a frightening book about triumphant vegetables whirling faster and faster around a nightshirted boy trying desperately to awake from the iridescent dizziness of dream life. Its ultimate vision was the incandescence of a book or a box grown completely transparent and hollow. This is, I believe, *it*: not the crude anguish of physical death but the incomparable pangs of the mysterious mental maneuver needed to pass from one state of being to another.

Easy, you know, does it, son.

That bizarre final line is perhaps the strangest in fiction. Who says it?

Presumably whoever is responsible for the first words of the novel, in what is—here we can delete the perhaps—the strangest beginning any story ever had:

Here's the person I want. Hullo, person! Doesn't hear me.

Perhaps if the future existed, concretely and individually, as something that could be discerned by a better brain, the past would not be so seductive: its demands would be balanced by those of the future. Persons might then straddle the middle stretch of the seesaw when considering this or that object. It might be fun.

But the future has no such reality (as the pictured past and the perceived present possess); the future is but a figure of speech, a specter of thought.

Hullo, person! What's the matter, don't pull me. I'm *not* bothering him. Oh, all right. Hullo, person . . . (last time, in a very small voice).

When *we* concentrate on a material object, whatever its situation, the very act of attention may lead to our involuntarily sinking into the history of that object. Novices must learn to skim over matter if they want matter to stay at the exact level of the moment. Transparent things, through which the past shines!

These jarring shifts between voice and voice continue throughout the novel. Even before we discover that in another way Hugh Person's life will be just as jarring, the novel poses the problem: who is saying these lines, and why, and what do they mean? How do they relate to the human scene that begins to unfold in chapter 2, as Hugh emerges from a taxi to reenter the Ascot Hotel where eight years ago he spent his first night with Armande?

If we read carefully we soon deduce—certainly before the novel ends—that the narrators are the ghosts of mortal men and women watching over Hugh. Throughout the novel Nabokov continues to surprise us with the economy and inventiveness and disconcerting comedy of his disruption of conventional narrative technique, as he defines the powers of these transparent things and at the same time defines by contrast the limitations of mortal Hugh. Unlike Hugh, who has such trouble with the spatial world, these spectral presences can flit instantly from place to place. Unlike any mortal, they can also flit from time to time, and even have to be on guard against a sort of temporal gravity inviting them to sink into the history of an object or a space. A pencil in a drawer in Hugh's hotel room becomes an adventure of discovery in its own right as the narrators dip back "a number of seasons (not as far, though, as Shakespeare's birth year when pencil lead was discovered)" to trace its origins. The graphite

is now being cut into the lengths required for these particular pencils (we glimpse the cutter, old Elias Borrowdale, and are about to mouse up his forearm on a side trip of inspection but we stop, stop and recoil, in our haste to identify the individual segment). See it baked, see it boiled in fat (here a shot of the fleecy fat-giver being butchered, a shot of the butcher, a shot of the shepherd, a shot of the shepherd's father, a Mexican) and fitted into the wood.

Hugh's tragedy is that no one can see the vitality within him—and that Armande is not even interested in looking. But the disembodied narrators can enter any mortal mind they choose. The busy main street of Witt "teems with transparent people and processes, into which and through which we might sink with an angel's or author's

delight, but we have to single out for this report only one Person."
They can understand human nature at any depth. Hugh is one of
those who earns his living in a humdrum way that befalls those brilliant young people who lack any special gift or ambition: "What they
do with the other, much greater portion, how and where their real
fancies and feelings are housed, is not exactly a mystery—there are
no mysteries now—but would entail explications and revelations too
sad, too frightful, to face. Only experts, for experts, should probe a
mind's misery."

Although the narrators can peer into any chosen soul, they cannot
take human personality quite seriously: "This Henry Emery Person,
our Person's father, might be described as a well-meaning, earnest,
dear little man, or as a wretched fraud, depending on the angle of
light and the position of the observer." Helped by the peculiar possibilities in Hugh's name, the narrators juggle distance and closeness, sympathy and detachment. With her French accent, Armande
calls Hugh "You," and occasionally the narration itself switches into
the second person: "You swerved toward her, thinking she was
alone." Hugh becomes "our Person" (almost "our body"—rather bizarre, coming from these discarnate beings) or "our dear Person,"
"my good Hugh," and then abruptly "Hugh, a sentimental simple-
ton, and somehow not a very *good* person."

The narrators can play with human personality because they have
passed so far beyond its limits. They speak of themselves with an
impersonal "one" or an "I" or "we," juxtaposing one mode of self-
reference with another. This evidence of grammatical "person" suggests that in the shadowy regions of being from which the narrative
voice descends, identity is much more fluid than on the mortal level:
"The dead are good mixers, that's quite certain, at least."

V

Nevertheless we can single out the dominant voice within the narrative chorus. "Here's the person I want. Hullo person!" begins the
novel. On Hugh's second trip to Switzerland he had met the novelist, R., who boomed out in greeting: "Hullo, Person!" The novel
ends "Easy, you know, does it, son," and in an earlier passage we
discover that R. has a habit when speaking English of trotting out
hackneyed formulas and skewing them: "To make a story quite short
. . . I had not been feeling any too healthy, you know, during the
winter. My liver, you know, was holding something against me." He
is also the only character in the novel to use the familiar "son," as

when he says to Hugh "You shake your head in advance and you're jolly right, son." The speaker of the novel's last line and its first can be no one but R.*

R. dies of his rotten liver a year or so before Hugh's final trip to Switzerland. During his life, he had become fond of Hugh ("Person was one of the nicest persons I knew") and concerned about his plight after Armande's grisly death. As a writer, R. had appreciated as infinitely precious the "favors of death knowledge," and had even written in his fiction of the "umbral companions" that might lurk unseen at the shoulders of mortals.

At the beginning of the novel's present time, dead R. has himself become one of these umbral companions, and tries to catch Hugh's attention in order to warn him about registering at the Ascot Hotel. He appears to have seen that a hot-tempered young waiter has just been dismissed after a farcical fight in the hotel restaurant and has already begun to plan his revenge: he will set the place alight.[2] Since "direct interference in a person's life does not enter our scope of activity," the other specters there at the beginning of the novel's present—perhaps the ghosts of some of the many characters who have already died in the course of this short book—discourage R. from any further intrusion, but at the end of the novel R. can welcome Hugh over the threshold of death and into a state of being where he need no longer be trapped by space and time and self.

After Hugh's arrival at the hotel, after his failure to hear the advice of R.'s ghost, the narrators wait for his fate to unfurl. They mark time by probing Hugh's past and enfolding within their account of his final trip to Switzerland the story of his three previous visits. Aware that Hugh may be headed for doom, they mimic the role of destiny as they explore the past and especially Hugh's father's death during his first trip to Switzerland. Reveling in their knowledge *now* of an outcome unknown at the time, they can investigate the profusion of the past and highlight patterns and parallels as if playing the part of fate.

In recounting Hugh's father's death, the narrators exploit chance synchronicities to create an almost comic profusion of omens and intimations, as if mocking mortal unawareness of the doom ahead, as if affirming their own closeness to destiny's design. For some reason their patterns place particular emphasis on falling. The morning of his death, Henry Person hoists up the venetian blind to look at the weather and lets it redescend in "a rattling avalanche." As his death looms closer, the ominous notes sound more and more frequently. A

* Nabokov confirms the identification in an interview (*Strong Opinions*, 195).

girl in mourning enters the clothes store. "A dingdong bell* and a blinking red light at the grade crossing announced an impending event: inexorably the slow barrier came down."

Although Henry Person simply dies in the changing room of a Swiss clothing store as he tries on new trousers too tight for him, the narrators depict his death as a fall: he "died before reaching the floor, as if falling from some great height." They appear to render his death this way and to prefigure it with other images of falling because they suspect his death will in turn prefigure Hugh's own death if he jumps from the fourth floor to escape the hotel's imminent destruction by fire. Of course they remember Hugh's inability to climb down the facade of the hotel at Stresa and his fatal attempt to stop a fatal jump in his dream. Throughout the novel—from the night his father dies, when Hugh looks out from another fourth-floor hotel room and feels "the pull of gravity inviting him to join the night and his father"—the narrators single out patterns of climbing and falling and accord them even more marked emphasis than the numerous glimpses of fire.

But in fact they do not know the future. "Perhaps if the future existed, concretely and individually," a voice speculates as the novel commences. But the future does not exist except as empty space to be filled in by a few of the infinity of branching possibilities at every moment. As the narrators concede, "some 'future' events may be likelier than others, O.K., but all are chimeric, and every cause-and-effect sequence is always a hit-and-miss affair." While observing the obstreperous waiter who created havoc in the hotel's restaurant, they appear not to have noticed destiny's quiet but decisive move on another corner of the board. The lady in room 313 will be called home urgently, and Hugh will take her place. In a bedroom with a different orientation, he will wake up to the fire and make for the door and fling it open "instead of trying to escape, as he thought he could, through the window which stood ajar and banged wider as soon as a fatal draft carried in the smoke from the corridor." Because of that mistake, he loses vital seconds as he turns toward the real window and starts to succumb to the smoke. Instead of falling, he will choke to death. Thanks to the "accidental" intrusion of another line of causality, the future has not turned out quite as the narrators expected.

---

* Apart from the obvious Romeo-and-Juliet pattern, *Transparent Things* is as bare of allusions as *Ada* is richly decked out in them, but "dingdong bell" recalls Ariel's dirge for Ferdinand's "dead" father: "Full fathom five thy father lies. . . . Sea-nymphs hourly ring his knell. . . . Hark! now I hear them—ding-dong, bell."

VI

On the other hand, that shift of rooms, that death by fire, seems to allow Hugh into a new existence where no room can lock one in or lock one out from other lives. Hugh need no longer feel the torment of a solitary room, as he did the night of his father's death. He need not shut out strangers as he was compelled to do to retain his sanity in prison, where he would behave in a manner that ensured his transfer to the "ineffable paradise" of solitary confinement. He need not wait in vain for love, for someone to open the door of his self, as Armande had never done in the past but as he hoped she would somehow do on the last poor night of his life.

Hugh enters the novel searching for the room he shared with Armande and unable to find it. From his point of view at the time the wrong room means only frustration. Now, from the point of view of the transparent things he has just joined, he will discover that even a humble pencil, a forgotten object in a forgotten drawer in an unloved room, can become a source of endless fascination.

The day his father dies, Hugh searches out a prostitute to avoid spending the night in the solitude of the room he shared with his father the night before. As he makes blundering love to Giulia Romeo in the rooming house she has led him to, the narrators dip a century into the past to view a Russian novelist, a minor Dostoevsky, who once occupied that very room. For the narrators there is no solitude now, for they can search out and participate in the lives of whomever they like.

At college, Hugh shares a room with a student named Jack Moore, who one night prizes him apart from the table he has tried to crush in his sleep. That moment and Jack Moore's very name will take on a strangely prophetic ring. After Giulia Romeo, Hugh's next bed partner appears to be Julia Moore, who, when she returns to Hugh's apartment to have him make clumsy love to her, remembers the much better lover she once had in this same room. Had Hugh known her thoughts at the time, he would have been mortified. Now, from the perspective of the transparent things—even of R., himself once Julia's lover—such an image loses its sting and becomes instead only part of fate's pattern of secretly pre-occupied rooms.

Julia's presence in Hugh's room and his life in turn enriches the pattern. R. has incorporated Julia—renamed June—in his novel *Figures in a Golden Window*, which ends with her death by fire. The very night Julia spends with Hugh begins as they watch a play that has to be stopped when the theater catches fire. On his way to meet R. in Switzerland, Hugh takes a train seat opposite Armande, notices her, as the low sun gilds the carriage windows, reading a book called *Fig-*

ures in a Golden Window—which Armande has just been given by her friend Julia—and starts up a conversation by remarking (funny coincidence) that his firm published the novel.

The next day Hugh meets R. for the first time, and, eager to recount the coincidence, alludes to Julia. Although Hugh knows she and R. were once lovers, he does not mention, of course, the secret of his own brief link with Julia. Later in the week, when Hugh meets Armande for the second time, Julia is also present, and Hugh thinks with fascination that, like R., Armande remains unaware of his one night with Julia. He recalls R.'s famous novella *Three Tenses*:

> A fashionable man in a night-blue tuxedo is supping on a lighted veranda with three bare-shouldered beauties, Alice, Beata and Claire, who have never seen one another before. A. is a former love, B. is his present mistress, C. is his future wife. . . .
>
> The charm of the Past Tense lay in its secrecy. Knowing Julia, he was quite sure she would not have told a chance friend about their affair— one sip among dozens of swallows. Thus, at this precious and brittle instant, Julia and he (*alias* Alice and the narrator) formed a pact of the past, an impalpable pact directed against reality as represented by the voluble street corner, with its swish-passing automobiles, and trees, and strangers. The B. of the trio was Busy Witt, while the main stranger— and this touched off another thrill—was his sweetheart of the morrow, Armande, and Armande was as little aware of the future (which the author, of course, knew in every detail) as she was of the past that Hugh now retasted.

On one occasion, R. and Julia Moore and Armande and Hugh all come together—along with Giulia Romeo, Jack Moore, and Jimmy Major, and the honeymoon night at Stresa's Hotel Borromeo on Lake Maggiore. Late on the last evening he ever spends with Armande, Hugh has been working on the proofs of R.'s new novel, *Tralatitions*. Unlike Hugh, R. has no qualms about broadcasting *his* amatory secrets, and uses his novel to depict Julia's infidelity. After Hugh retires to bed, routine worries drift through his mind and he broods on his wife's betrayals. Reminded of Julia by the proofs he has been reading, he muses that he too betrayed Armande in a sense "by concealing from her the one night spent with another girl, premaritally, in terms of time, but spatially in this very room." As he drifts off to sleep, his memory blends a host of images: Armande's betrayals and the fire drill of Stresa, her descent from the room he did not want her to leave and into the room he was horrified to find she had entered; Julia and the fire on the night she spent in his room; Giulia Romeo and the brief hour he spent in her room before returning to solitude and thoughts of hurling himself to his death. From all this rises the dream in which Hugh as Mr. Romeo restrains his Juliet from jumping from their room—and he wakes up to find Armande strangled.

VII

This dream and the cumulative patterns of rooms and names it draws on foreshadow Hugh's final transfer to another room and his death by suffocation. To the transparent things, that unexpected shift of rooms invalidates their hunch about his death. But at another level his move into the room of the lady with the little dog perfects the pattern and the poignancy of his death. The lady with the little dog recalls Chekhov's famous tale of adultery, while Hugh's descent from the fourth floor to a third-floor room recalls Armande's first infidelity, that night at Stresa, when she clambered from the fourth floor into a stranger's room a floor below. His death mocks his hopes of reviving his past: all he can revive are the humiliations of his life with Armande.

The complexity of the whole pattern of names and rooms, fires and falls, seems inevitably to imply a patterner who has planned the whole design, even the exact mode of Hugh's death, from the very first. Our narrators, our transparent things, have looked around into the evidence of the present and the pattern of the past, and deduced that Hugh will fall from his hotel room to his death. They are mistaken. They do not invent but merely relate: they have not created or designed Hugh's world. On the other hand, they can understand its design and the force behind it better than mere mortals. Concluding their digression of the pencil, they declare:

> Here's the board that will yield the integument of the pencil in the shallow drawer (still not closed). We recognize its presence in the log as we recognized the log in the tree and the tree in the forest and the forest in the world that Jack built. We recognize that presence by something that is perfectly clear to us but nameless, and as impossible to describe as a smile to somebody who has never seen smiling eyes.

Despite being endowed with powers beyond the human, the narrators remain mere narrators, not the authors of their world, not the Jack that built the world that Jack built. Why does Nabokov construct his transparent things in precisely this manner, so that they can highlight the pattern they perceive in the past, but cannot anticipate its outcome?

If human consciousness transcended death, he suggests, it might acquire an infinite capacity to see into anything, matter or mind, present or past: it might acquire all the powers of fictional narrators, especially the power to perceive complex pattern in the past. But any knowledge of the future would still remain utterly beyond even any expanded form of human consciousness. For if "future" events existed, if the future had the same kind of reality that "the pictured past and the perceived present possess," human actions would not be free.

Nevertheless, there might be a force vastly beyond even any possible extension of human consciousness, whose powers might be metaphorically equivalent to those of an author, and whose metaphysical difference from even any extension of human consciousness might be metaphorically, "tralatitiously," suggested by the difference between an invented narrator and a real author beyond the work.

Authors can plan "ahead," as mere narrators cannot, for they exist quite outside the time of their created worlds. Of course, although they can invent their worlds and plan their events, these microcosms become more than clockwork only if they can give their creatures reality and independent life, if they allow whatever design they want to impose on their world, however complex, to be consistent with the preservation of chance (the lady with the dog) and choice (Hugh's free decision to stay on at Witt, despite the narrators' wish to put pressure on him). Each point in space, each instant in time, each impulse of consciousness must be allowed its own independence—a room of its own—along with whatever part it might be made to play in a wider pattern of overlapping rooms.

Within the small compass of *Transparent Things* and the bleak life of Hugh Person, Nabokov ruptures the relationship of reader, character, and author more radically than he has ever done, in order to explore some of his oldest themes: the nature of time; the mystery and privacy of the human soul, and its simultaneous need to breach its solitude, the scope of consciousness beyond death; the possibility of design in the universe.

Ada's ebullience and lyricism and color had made it a best-seller. *Transparent Things*, with its squalid world and its heartless characters, seems almost designed not to appeal. But readers who like high-energy surprise, readers who can stand the invigorating shocks Nabokov prepares in line after line, will recognize that while the story will not be for everyone it is a masterpiece.

Nabokov loved this life, its endless particulars, its infinity of sensation and thought and feeling. If in *Transparent Things* he chooses to make Hugh's world appear arid and anguished, he does it only in order to suggest, as the story's secret spaces open out, how vast an expansion death might be.

CHAPTER 25

Reinventing a Life: Montreux, 1972–1974

At least the plain truth of documents is on my side. That, and only

that, is what I would ask of my biographer—plain facts.

—*Strong Opinions*

such humdrum potterings are beneath true scholarship

—*Pale Fire*

I

AFTER COMPLETING *Transparent Things* at the beginning of April 1972, Nabokov read over his Cornell and Harvard lectures with a view to publishing them at last, as he had promised for years. He was not impressed with what he found. Among his papers he inserted this note: "My university lectures (Tolstoy, Kafka, Flaubert, Cervantes, etc. etc.) are chaotic and sloppy and must *never* be published. None of them!"[1]

Two weeks later he set off with Véra by train for a short rest in Amélie-les-Bains, a small resort in the Pyrénées Orientales, near the site of their first butterfly expedition back in 1929. Intermittent patches of sun during three weeks of gray windy weather allowed him to capture a few remarkable butterflies.[2]

By now Andrew Field had begun to write his biography, *Nabokov: His Life in Part*. Shortly after Nabokov returned from Amélie to Montreux in early May he received a letter from his cousin Sergey Nabokov, a journalist now living in Brussels and a keen amateur of Russian genealogy who a decade earlier had volunteered his celebrated cousin information on the Nabokov family background for the revised *Speak, Memory*. Since early 1971, Field had been insisting Sergey assign top priority to helping him explore the Nabokov family tree. Sergey had willingly obliged but had become concerned at the strange direction of Field's recent letters: his desire to return again and again to the idea that Nabokov's father might be the bastard son of Tsar Alexander II or his brother Grand-Duke Konstantin; his unfounded assumption that he knew a great deal about Russian history; his misconstruction of all the evidence set before him. Field had also written to Sergey of his pique at having often been called an agent or lackey of Vladimir Nabokov and of his plan to prove his independence by special efforts not to seem too much a friend of the family.[3] Nabokov invited his cousin to come stay with him in Switzerland for a few days over the summer to discuss the problems Field was posing.

He had his own reasons to worry about Field. At the beginning of the year, while he was absorbed in the final drafts of *Transparent Things*, *Glory* had been published in the United States. The novel's foreword, written a couple of years earlier, had contained one of Nabokov's customary blasts at Freud: "Nowadays, when Freudism is discredited, the author recalls with a whistle of wonder that not so long ago . . . a child's personality was supposed to split automatically in sympathetic consequence of parental divorce. His parents' separation has no such effect on Martin's mind, and only a desperate saphead in the throes of a nightmare examination may be excused for connecting Martin's plunge into his fatherland with his having been deprived of his father." Martha Duffy, who had interviewed Nabokov for *Time*'s cover story on the occasion of *Ada*'s publication, now reviewed the new novel, asserting at one point that Nabokov had given "particular hell to Critic Andrew Field," who had written in *Nabokov: His Life in Art* that Martin's return to Russia was "a reenactment of his father's lonely death."[4]

Véra wrote at once to Field that Nabokov was terribly embarrassed by Duffy's remark, that he had had Freud, not Field, in mind, and that he had not recalled Field's phrase because when he read *Nabokov: His Life in Art* he "tended to skip your speculations so as not to be tempted to interfere in matters of opinion." Nabokov had hoped Field would react in print to Duffy's "unfortunate joke," but when he did not, Nabokov himself in March 1972 wrote a letter to the editor of *Time* explaining that he had never dreamed of insulting "a dear friend of mine. . . . a learned and talented man." When *Time* did not print the letter, Nabokov decided to incorporate it in *Strong Opinions*, his forthcoming collection of public prose (interviews, essays, letters to the editor). He had also sent the letter at once to Field.[5]

Unappeased, Field replied that he was well aware Nabokov had never been much inclined to be drawn into questions of other people's honor, good name, or memory. When Nabokov protested that that was unfair, and asked him what he meant, Field could only cite Nabokov's reluctance to write an "in memoriam" tribute to Amalia Fondaminsky in 1935. Nabokov's hesitation to pen that piece had been perfectly natural in view of the fact that he barely knew her: he had met her for the first time only three years before her death and had seen her only during the course of a single month, November 1932. Nevertheless in that instance he had agreed to write what turned out to be a vivid and poignant memorial. But Field was in no mood to be fair.[6]

Along with his reproachful letter Field also sent Nabokov an excerpt from the file that *Time* had assembled in preparation for its cover story. Asked about the publication of his Cornell lectures, Nabokov had replied—he had at that stage been planning to publish the lectures soon for McGraw-Hill—that he was keeping his notes to himself, "however much Andrew Field may want them."* *Time*'s reporter continued: "Field at the moment is teaching on the wrong side of Australia but he has a reputation for aggressiveness and arrogance and he appears to have settled on Nabokov for his life's work. Nabokov may know a Quilty when he sees one." Sending Nabokov this passage from the *Time* files, Field now stressed that his main concern was that *Nabokov* understood that he was not Field's life's work, and that Field was not anything but wholly "his own man" in all that he ever wrote or would write.

The comment in *Time*'s files had wounded Field's pride, and after reading it he had in 1970 fired his first salvo against the magazine in print.[7] Now, in the initial draft of his Nabokov biography, he would devote almost twenty pages to attacking the magazine, a statistic that suggests his own ego was as much to the fore in the biography as Nabokov's life. By now Field had determined to prove his independence from Nabokov in the biography by trying to avoid him as a source of information.

A year hence, when Nabokov saw the result, he would no longer call Field learned and talented. The Nabokovs had for years seen evidence of Field's blunders in translation, scholarship, and interpretation, and had corrected them, for little thanks, in the manuscripts of *Nabokov: His Life in Art* and *Nabokov: A Bibliography*. Won over by Field's enthusiasm and energy, by his sense of his own originality and his eagerness to extol Nabokov's, they had pardoned him for errors they would have been outraged at in anybody else. But once Field proved himself no longer the eager admirer, they began to see for themselves the shortcomings that others like Gleb Struve had long deplored and tried to warn them about.

---

* Nabokov had heard that Field had tried to pressure others into handing over to him student lecture notes from Nabokov's Cornell classes.

II

On June 19, the Nabokovs headed for Lenzerheide in the Grisons in eastern Switzerland. Three days later Sergey arrived. Over four days of discussion he and his cousin decided that however strained relations between biographer and subject might become, Sergey should continue to send Field information to minimize the defects caused by his ignorance.[8]

After a miserably rainy month, Nabokov returned to Montreux and wrote to Field asking to see what he had written so far and making it clear that he would not want him to put more time into the biography if it could not be approved after all. He warned specifically that he would not countenance any argument with *Speak, Memory*.[9]

Early in August he carried out a little more work on *Strong Opinions* before heading as he had the previous August for the Residence Wyssmüllerei near Gstaad, where once again room was reserved for Dmitri, for Anna Feigin, and for Elena. Just back from her summer trip to Leningrad, now an annual affair, Elena regaled her brother with tales of the coarseness and the daily falsehoods of Soviet life. Her accounts would soon inspire him for the first time to describe the Soviet Union as if from within, when in *Look at the Harlequins!* he sends apprehensive Vadim Vadimych back to the land of his birth.[10]

On his return to Montreux at the end of August, Nabokov found a letter from Field, who insisted that his manuscript was not ready to be shown and that he had expended far too much effort on three round-the-world trips to stop the project now. Nabokov replied:

> First of all let me make it quite clear that I am not interested in your producing what you call a "flattering portrait." There must be some perilous patches of dimness in your general vision of me as a person if you think I could suggest such a thing. What I do suggest now, even more strongly than before, is that it would be unfair to both of us if I left unchallenged wrong background details and impossible suppositions. You speak of "mutual obligations." My only duty is to spot errors and stop futile investigations. Your only duty is to show me every word of the biography and accept all my corrections of factual mistakes.[11]

Before beginning the biography, Field had assured Nabokov that "the final word as to what would be better deleted will rest in your hands," and it was on that understanding that Nabokov had agreed to show Field his papers, submit to interviews, and authorize his closest friends to cooperate with Field.[12] Now, four years later, Nabokov continued:

I should have warned you, perhaps, before you started upon your project, that despite a semblance of joviality and ready wit, I am really a rather dreary and lonely person in terms of visible life. . . . The number of friends I have had or have is quite abnormally small and amongst them the two or three intimate ones I ever had are now dead. The jolts of my era kept creating gaps in space and gulfs in time between me and the few people dear to me. . . .

In these circumstances V.N.'s biographer can learn very little by getting in touch with V.N.'s sporadic relatives, schoolmates, literary acquaintances or academic colleagues, and the worst he can do is to collect the vulgar gossip that always buzzes around a ripe old author ready to be biographized. . . . I cannot imagine a reliable history of my life if it is to be based on the meager and sometimes grotesque communications gathered from strangers at the cost of the prodigious efforts you mention in your letter of August 16. . . .

To sum up: the only rational and artistic way to write the history of an individual of my dismal kind (whose only human and entertaining side is the gift of inventing clouds, castles, lakes) would be to follow his development as a writer from his first opaque poems to *Transparent Things* (a copy of which will reach you by mid-October). Somehow I suspect that this is precisely what you plan to do despite your losing so much precious time on bizarre attempts to establish whether a tsar, or at least a grand-duke, was my father's real father.

Two weeks after that letter Nabokov noted in his diary the idea for a new novel: " 'He had finished his task.' Start from there—with the flush and the bloom and the mist present throughout the book, but specified only by allusion to *several* forms of art: poetry, music, painting, architecture etc."[13] This cryptic note seems to reflect the glow of achievement that Dmitri witnessed the previous year as he stood with his father on the slopes of La Videmanette. In this first flash of a novel that he still glimpsed only vaguely, Nabokov expected to stress the hero's ultimate accomplishment, though in an oblique manner. In its final form, *Look at the Harlequins!* would indeed conclude with "the flush and the bloom" of fulfillment, but until its close the novel would offer only futility, misdirection, the disquiet of non-arrival—apparently an echo of Nabokov's groans as he contemplated the possibility that an inept biography might drown out with its static the note of achievement in his own life story.

A week later he noted in his diary that to satisfy his McGraw-Hill agreement he had only *Strong Opinions* and the second collection of his Russian stories, *Tyrants Destroyed*, to complete, and he listed the projects ahead that could become the basis for another multibook contract: his new novel; the paperback, one-volume *Eugene Onegin*; a third volume of his Russian stories; his lectures (he had changed his mind again); and an anthology of Russian poets in translation. Later he would add *Speak on, Memory*, especially if McGraw-Hill would agree to pay his expenses in revisiting parts of America he needed to describe. Meanwhile he was irked by the difficulties of assembling all the material for *Strong Opinions*. The chore was not eased by his anxiety to write his new novel. Such a brief gap between initial inspiration and his readiness to commence writing a new novel was without precedent in his long career.[14]

Throughout the first two weeks of October he continued to prepare his interviews and essays for *Strong Opinions*. Since he had to submit the last book to McGraw-Hill by January 1, he could afford no rest after completing *Strong Opinions* and turned immediately to revising Dmitri's translations of the stories for *Tyrants Destroyed*.

III

Late in October, he received a long cable from Edmund White, a senior editor for the new *Saturday Review of the Arts*, which planned to publish a special Nabokov issue for its inaugural number at the beginning of the new year. Would Nabokov care to write them a two-thousand-word essay? William Gass, Joyce Carol Oates, Joseph McElroy, and White himself would be writing on what Nabokov meant to them. Could he in turn single out any American writers he admired?[15]

Normally Nabokov never contributed commissioned articles to magazines, but, softened perhaps by the prospect of a special issue, by White's mention of mutual friends Simon Karlinsky, Peter Kemeny, and William F. Buckley, and by the thought that a little essay like this could nicely round out *Strong Opinions*, he agreed. He spent a good deal of November painfully composing this brief essay, "On Inspiration."[16]

One of his finest prose pieces, it records his own experience of the strange physiology of inspiration, the first glow and flash of a new novel and the caprices and insistent demands inspiration could make during the process of composition. He explained that he always assigned grades to the stories in anthologies that hopeful publishers continually sent him, and awarded the grades solely on the basis of their artistic inspiration. In some of these anthologies—this he did not say—Nabokov descended as far as Z-, but on this occasion the scourge of Mann and Faulkner, Stendhal and Dostoevsky, was in a

mellow mood: "Examples are the stained-glass windows of knowledge. From a small number of A-plus stories I have chosen half-a-
dozen particular favorites of mine." He marshaled extracts from
Cheever, Updike, Salinger, Gold, Barth, and Delmore Schwartz,
pausing each time to explain his choice or the difficulty of choosing
from such riches.

Several months later, Nabokov would read Edmund White's own
first novel, *Forgetting Elena*, and think *it* an example of inspiration.
Asked in a 1975 interview whom he most admired among current
American writers, he answered Edmund White (and Updike, and
Salinger). By that comment alone, this notoriously severe reader—
who until this point had promoted to American audiences only three
unfamiliar writers, two Russian (Andrey Bely and Vladislav Khodasevich) and one Belgian (Franz Hellens)—would do more than anyone else to launch White's career.[17]

In mid-November, Alfred and Nina Appel visited Montreux for
five days. While there they acted as witnesses to Nabokov's will, pro-
bated at the Montreux Palace by a notary in a cheap mortuary suit,
with top hat and wing collar and an unmistakable odor. When he
left, Nabokov leaned over to Appel: "Did you notice that death
smelled?" Death and suits came up once again as Appel told Nabokov that his favorite passage in all of Nabokov was the closing sentence of *Speak, Memory*'s first chapter, the sentence that transforms
the image of Nabokov's father being tossed in the air into a prefiguration of his death or of his immortality. Nabokov turned aside, his
eyes filled with tears: "Yes, he looked so handsome in that white
suit." No wonder he felt so apprehensive that Field seemed to be
preparing an attack on *Speak, Memory*. When the talk once again returned to Field, Véra asked Appel: "Why didn't you warn us?"[18]*

From late November to early January, Nabokov steadily revised
the stories for *Tyrants Destroyed*. On the publication of *Transparent
Things* in America in November, he noted in his diary: "Reviews oscillating between hopeless adoration and helpless hatred. Very amusing." One reviewer, after hailing *Pale Fire* as "the most imaginative
and soundest work of imaginative literature executed during this half
of our century," called *Transparent Things* "an unlovely and unlove-
able book that begins to touch the reader only the second time
around. It is a masterpiece, of course." Even John Updike began his
review with a confession: he did not understand this enigmatic little
tale. Despite the puzzlement it caused, *Transparent Things*, like *Pnin*

---

* Although he had had his own misgivings about Field, Appel had not dared to
voice them earlier, lest it seem he wished to oust Field from a project he would have
dearly loved to undertake himself.

and *Pale Fire* before it, would be nominated for a National Book Award, and like them it would fail to take the prize.[19]

Early in a foggy December, Lord Snowdon arrived to photograph Nabokov—a month after Yousuf Karsh had been on a similar mission—for the special issue of *Saturday Review of the Arts*. Nabokov enjoyed Snowdon's company as he clambered up to the hotel roof or stopped on a mistily soulful hillside, in shops, cafés, and restaurants, and back in his office, to pose for one of the most diverse portfolios of portraits any photographer had assembled of him.[20]

In the first week of January 1973, Nabokov, always punctilious about deadlines, completed *Tyrants Destroyed* to fulfill the terms of his eleven-book, five-year agreement with McGraw-Hill only four days late.* Meanwhile Véra, whose back had been causing her pain for some time, was now plunged into agony by two slipped discs. When eighty-five-year-old Anna Feigin died on January 6, after five years' nursing in Montreux by the Nabokovs, Véra was in too much pain to attend her cousin's funeral. Nabokov too felt death encroaching:

> Woke up at dawn with diurnal part of brain still in dream gear. "That's it!" I thought grimly as I sat up and saw that in the space between bed and window *two* guillotines, facing each other, had already been set ("That's the way they do it, of course—in one's bedroom"). Vertical and horizontal shadows in the barred and broken twilight, that I can never get accustomed to, kept imitating the horrible machines for at least five seconds. I had even time to wonder if V. in the adjacent bedroom was being "prepared" to join me. I should get thick curtains but I don't like to wait for sleep in total darkness.

A week later Véra was taken to a hospital in Geneva. Though she was away for only a few days, Nabokov recorded in his diary: "The feeling of distress, désarroi, utter panic and dreadful presentiment every time V. is away in hospital, is one of the greatest torments of my life."[21]

IV

In mid-January, Andrew Field stopped in Montreux just long enough to drop off the 678-page typescript of his *Nabokov: His Life in Part* and

---

* The books he had given McGraw-Hill were: *King, Queen, Knave* (published 1968), *Ada* (1969), *Mary* (1970), *Poems and Problems* (1971), *Glory* (1971), *Transparent Things* (1972), *A Russian Beauty* (1973), *Strong Opinions* (1973), *Bend Sinister* (1973, a new edition of the 1964 subscription-only *Time* version, with Nabokov's new introduction, of the original 1947 novel), *Lolita: A Screenplay* (1974), and *Tyrants Destroyed* (1975).

lunch with Nabokov. Véra was to have read the book first, but she was in no condition for that now. Late in the month Nabokov read and enjoyed the typescript of Bobbie Ann Rowling's *Nabokov's Garden*, one of the first dissertations on *Ada*, by the woman who as Bobbie Ann Mason would be hailed a decade later for her stories (*Shiloh, In Country*) of people who could not be more different from the cosmopolitan and superendowed Van and Ada. On January 28, Nabokov began reading Field's typescript.[22] He thought he had braced himself for the worst, but what he found outdid his gloomiest apprehensions.[23]

Early in February, Field wrote insisting he needed any comments by the beginning of March. Hurrying to satisfy Field's schedule, Nabokov clocked up a hundred hours of work on the manuscript over the first three weeks of February. Already on February 6 he could note: "Have corrected 285 pages of Field's 680 page work. The number of absurd errors, impossible statements, vulgarities and inventions is appalling." Marking them all in red pencil, he had the offending passages typed out with his notes: one hundred and eighty pages in all, and even then he had overlooked scores of major and minor blunders. There were simply too many errors for him to catch them all.[24]

When he sent Field the whole batch of corrections on March 10, he added a final comment:

> Upon rechecking this collection of quotes and notes I find myself wondering what strange "block" prevented you from simply consulting me in hundreds of instances when my wife or I could have come to your assistance. I am thinking especially of those narrative items—incidents, anecdotes, situations and the like—where you quite obviously had to fill in with plausible-looking little inventions (some of them quite innocent but crude and banal in their innocence) the blanks in your information. A phrase has to be rounded out, articles of clothing, or food, etc., have to be briefly—and harmlessly it would seem—listed, the little feet of the limping anecdote have to be orthopedically shod—and since by no amount of imagination can one conjure up the details one does not know in a setting with which one is not familiar, the description of the event becomes at best a clumsy cliché and at worst an offensive farce. You *must* have been aware of these blanks and pitfalls, and what puzzles me is how you could have been so reckless, so cocksure in your repeated use of quick fillers which *statistically* had so little chance to work. Why could you not have asked me again and again (with samples of your successive tries) about the factual touches you needed to make the event true to the place, to the time, to the person?

What *was* the strange block in Field's mind? During his first contretemps over the biography in January 1971 he had written to Nabokov that he doubted there was much about his personal life he did not know.[25] As his manuscript now showed, he remained uninformed even of basic facts about Nabokov's public life and literary output, let alone his private life (When did Nabokov begin school? When did he leave home? When did he leave Germany? When did he write his books?). How *could* he know so little?

V

Nabokov had not made things easy for his biographer. He had a hypertrophied sense of privacy: "I hate tampering with the precious lives of great writers and I hate Tom-peeping over the fence of those lives—I hate the vulgarity of 'human interest,' I hate the rustle of skirts and giggles in the corridors of time—and no biographer will ever catch a glimpse of my private life."[26] He had placed a fifty-year restriction on the papers he deposited in the Library of Congress. He hid behind literary masks, and then retreated still further from the public gaze to the comparative privacy of Montreux. Ensconced there, he fired off brusque letters to various editors protesting against factual inaccuracies or infringements of his privacy, and agreed to interviews only if the questions were submitted in writing well in advance, so that he could prepare his answers too in writing—and then check the whole thing in proof.

Such attitudes certainly made Field's task difficult, but they could have been no surprise: they were well known to the whole literary world before he offered to write Nabokov's life. When the offer came, Nabokov decided it would be safer to allow a biography while he was still there to minimize errors, just as he had preferred to Russify *Lolita* himself rather than envisage a lame translation being force-marched into Russian when he was no longer there to correct it at every step.

Setting aside his reluctance, Nabokov let Field see much material from the Library of Congress and his own archives. He answered questions punctiliously by mail and expansively in person. But he naively expected Field to consult only himself and a few designated friends, for he distrusted the memories of others, especially of anyone less than favorably disposed toward himself. Even his own incidental anecdotes and unguarded comments failed to satisfy him the moment they were transcribed onto paper. A writer's finished written words should suffice, he thought: his diaries and letters and casual chitchat were not public property. He had fixed the image of his Russian past forever in *Speak, Memory*, and his American years he wanted to reserve for *Speak on, Memory*.

Nevertheless, he was still ready to offer information to Field. Field, however, had reached a point where he thought he no longer needed it and no longer wished to ask it from Nabokov. He had always thought extraordinarily highly of his own powers, and even in *Nabokov: His Life in Art* had announced, in a foreword that made reviewers recoil, his desire to prove himself an artist in his own right.

One bizarre consequence of his ambition was that he confused disdain for mere accuracy with proof of artistry. He wrote to Véra Nabokov that the thing he was proudest of in *Nabokov: His Life in Art* was "500 pages without a footnote."[27] He despised "wombat work" such as translation. He positively boasted of the howlers the Nabokovs pointed out even in *Life in Art*, such as translating *velikan* (from *velikiy*, "big," "great") not as "giant" but as "volcano" (and in a phrase that then emerged as "a volcano in her womb"!).[28]

And yet, Field seemed to think, he was not only an artist but also a champion of truth. Nabokov had always had an acute sense of how difficult the truth could be to ascertain and to express. Field by contrast tended to confuse the truth with whatever *he* had found out or written down, no matter how garbled. He therefore interpreted Nabokov's readiness to challenge *his* findings or emend what *he* had written not as his concern for the truth of his life but as his desire for a falsified life.

Field convinced himself that Nabokov was trying to restrict his artistic independence, his freedom to record the facts in his own special way. On that assumption, nothing could demonstrate his own commitment to truth better than proving his independence from Nabokov. Field now welcomed any piece of evidence, no matter how flimsy or easily invalidated, that came from someone other than Nabokov, especially if Nabokov actually opposed it. Even those who alluded to the story that Nabokov's father may have been the bastard son of Alexander II disbelieved it, and so did Field for that matter: never mind, Nabokov objected to it, so the "information" must somehow be important enough to return to again and again.

Speak, Memory became especially suspect: it was after all the place par excellence where Nabokov was trying to tell *his* version of his past. Although Nabokov had set out in *Speak, Memory* his experiences at Tenishev School, Field preferred to describe Tenishev by means of alternative sources, such as Osip Mandelstam's memoir *The Noise of Time*. Mandelstam recorded that the school uniform was of an English character, so to Field that detail deserved a mention, although by Nabokov's own day, as his autobiography makes clear, uniforms had been phased out—a fact Field simply overlooked. To Mandelstam, the teacher Vladimir Gippius was an inspiration. Field therefore declared Gippius a major influence on Nabokov's life, even though Nabokov had been exposed to literature in three languages long before Tenishev and had already formed his own strong opinions quite at odds with those of Gippius. Nabokov's vehement objections to Field's conjecture ("I knew nothing about Gippius' critical articles. I liked his poetry but could not stand him and his 'committed' enthusiasm for political discussion. . . . The Tenishev school's inflicting Gippius upon me is no reason for your repeating the process") only seemed to confirm to Field that he must be right. By dint of eschewing *Speak, Memory*, Field was even able to have Nabokov enroll at Tenishev at the wrong age and in the wrong class.[29]

Occasionally Field challenged *Speak, Memory* directly. Nabokov describes in his autobiography his father's triumphal return from the prison sentence he served for signing the Vyborg manifesto, the archivolts of fir needles and the crowns of bluebottles that the local villagers had arranged to greet him as he passed through Rozhdestveno. After reading the memoirs of Nabokov's aunt Nadine Wonlar-Larsky, Field drew up his own alternative version, in which Nabokov's grandmother "staged a successful counter-manoeuvre by threatening the peasants with economic reprisals if they demonstrated in support of her son."[30] In fact a letter written the day after the procession by another eyewitness, Nabokov's uncle Konstantin, confirms *Speak, Memory*'s account exactly, and if Field had bothered to read even the Wonlar-Larsky recollections with any care, he would have seen that they too actually confirmed the triumphal homecoming.* But despite Nabokov's detailed rebuttal, Field still thought he knew more than an eyewitness.

To Field's claim that *Speak, Memory* had "avoided facts," Nabokov replied that he could not let these lines stand "unless, in a special note, you list, Andrew, *all* the incorrect facts in *Speak, Memory* with the chapter and page."[31] As it happens, there are at least twenty-one demonstrable errors in *Speak, Memory*, but Field knew too little of the details of Nabokov's life to identify a single one, and let the charge drop.

At the time of their initial decision to permit Field to proceed, the Nabokovs had made it clear that they expected to control what was

---

* Wonlar-Larsky makes clear that only the inhabitants of Maria Nabokov's village, Batovo, but not those of the other local villages, Rozhdestveno, Gryazno, and Vyra, refrained from the celebrations.

made available to him.[32] Later, in an ebullient moment during one of Field's early trips to Montreux, Nabokov had playfully—and unthinkingly—offered him "a field day" with the material.[33] His instinct for privacy soon checked his enthusiasm, and while he gave Field much—manuscripts, letters, information, anecdotes—he soon shrank from the thought of showing him even his recent diaries. To have had access to more, Field would have needed to demonstrate his trustworthiness. Instead, his ignorance of the contexts of Nabokov's life, his gift for mistranscription, misreporting, mistranslation, and misconstruction, and his desire to prove his independence by contradicting Nabokov even when he was the sole available source had ensured Nabokov's reluctance to show him more.

Nevertheless, ever since 1965 the Nabokovs had furnished Field with information. Even now, Nabokov wrote to Field in a firm but friendly tone, saving him from making hundreds of gross errors and forwarding him masses of new information. Although deeply upset by the biography's inaccuracies and insinuations, Véra added to her husband's letter a long missive of her own, which supplied most of the best information Field obtained about her early life and background.[34] He took it over wholesale, without a word of thanks to her. Rather than gratitude for all the errors detected and the new information proffered, Field would show only resentment toward Nabokov's injunctions against his misinformation. Although he had promised to accept Nabokov's complete right of veto, Field now prepared to fight for the right to preserve his errors.

VI

Field's distorted "VN" inspired the real Nabokov to make his next novel a deliberate travesty of his own life and of *Speak, Memory* in particular. As his apprehensions about Field's work had deepened in September 1972, Nabokov had written to his lawyer that his works were a sufficient history of his artistic life and that his private life was nobody's concern. Two weeks later he had had the first flash for a new novel that would be steeped in his own sense of fulfillment but with the fulfillment somehow offstage. Now, three days after beginning to read Field's manuscript, he announced to McGraw-Hill that he would begin a new novel on March 1. But he could not contain himself. On February 6, the day he noted in his diary how appalled he was by Field's "absurd errors, impossible statements, vulgarities and inventions," he began to write *Look at the Harlequins!*[35]

Looking back on his life and inverting it for his new novel, Nabokov at seventy-three could also look ahead and see that death might catch him unawares. With that in mind, he left a note on his manuscript that it should be destroyed unread if the book remained unfinished. He also wrote to Princeton University Press that it was eighteen months since he had first corrected the galleys of the revised *Eugene Onegin*, and now two months had passed since Princeton had written that another batch of proofs was on its way:

> For all I know, the silence you inflict upon me can go on eternally. It is a ridiculous, incomprehensible and intolerable situation.
>
> You know well how much I would want Princeton University Press to bring out EO², but I will be 74 soon, and would like to see my edition printed before confronting an irate Pushkin and a grinning E. Wilson* beyond the cypress curtain.³⁶

He had the revised *Eugene Onegin* in mind for his new McGraw-Hill agreement, the terms of which would not be settled for another year and a half. Meanwhile in April he and Dmitri began to translate the first stories for his next McGraw-Hill book, *Details of a Sunset*, the last of his four volumes of collected stories.

Plagued by insomnia all his life, Nabokov had suffered more and more as old age drew on. Late in April he noted down in his diary in amazement: "For the first time *in years* (since 1955? 1960?) had this night a six-hour stretch of uninterrupted sleep (12–6). My usual extent of sleep (apart from periodical insomnias), even if induced by more or less potent pills (at least thrice daily) is a 3+2+1 or at best 4+2+2 or at frequent worst 2+1+1+2+1-hour affair with intervals (+) of hopelessness and nervous urination."³⁷

In early May, Field sent Nabokov the revised draft of his manuscript, now reduced to 480 pages. In his covering letter Field claimed that he had had conclusive evidence for everything he had written and that even his errors had their sound reasons, such as an incorrect street name taken faithfully from a reportorial transcript. He reproached Nabokov for having given him so little help and suggested they had perhaps reached a stalemate. In reply Nabokov wondered at "the miraculous fact of your not being really responsible for *any* of the blunders in your book." He pointed out that there were two ways out of their situation: "Either we scrap the entire project (which would be a pity) or you keep the promise you made me at the very start of the venture. I quote: '. . . the final word as to what would be better deleted will rest in your hands.' " He also made it clear that he sniffed blackmail in Field's hint that if they were going to quarrel

---

* Wilson had died in 1972.

there were some things not in the biography they ought to discuss first.[38]

Before leaving Montreux for the summer to concentrate on his new novel, he had time only for a brief glance through the revised biography, but as he told his New York lawyer in apprising her of the situation, that glance sufficed to reveal that "most of the rot and nastiness is still there. . . . I cannot tell you how upset I am by the whole matter. It was not worth living a far from negligible life . . . only to have a blundering ass reinvent it."[39]

VII

This year the Nabokovs' annual exodus from Montreux had to be delayed until Véra's back had recovered sufficiently. At last at the beginning of June they fled Montreux, interviews, and endless Penguin proofs, to travel by taxi—Véra could still not drive—all the way down to the Adriatic Coast, to Cervia, just south of Ravenna. Here amidst pine and brine Nabokov happily immersed himself again in his novel, on which he had had almost no chance to work since February. After three weeks at Cervia they moved up to Cortina d'Ampezzo, the oldest of the winter sports resorts in the eastern Italian Alps. Delighted by the Valle d'Ampezzo and its butterflies, Nabokov kept on composing at a brisk pace.[40]

Staying longer at Cortina than they had planned, they returned to Montreux on August 3 to attend to urgent proofs.[41] There Nabokov found Field's reply to his ultimatum. Warning Nabokov to brace himself, Field reproached him for having concealed aspects of his life from him. The two most important, he complained, were " 'the Romanov connection' and your separation from your wife." Field wrote that of course he would not mention the "separation" (more of that in a moment), but that he knew Nabokov thought about and feared the Romanov rumors, so they had to remain whether true or not.[42] Apart from Nabokov's jocular "I feel the blood of Peter the Great in my veins!" Field could cite only one piece of evidence for Nabokov's "thoughts and fears": a diary entry, of which Field had a photostat, in which—or so he claimed—Nabokov records a dream of intercourse with his own grandmother. How that would have proved Nabokov feared his father might be a royal bastard remains evident only to Field, and in fact the diary entry (March 25, 1951) concerned not Nabokov's grandmother but an old woman in Ithaca, where Nabokov was living at the time. Here it is in full:

> Dream: am attempting a cold and joyless copulation with a fat old woman (whom I know slightly and for whom I have as much desire as for a gorilla or a garbage can). The day before somebody in my presence was telling somebody that a third party, a man I knew, was—for goodness' sake—marrying a "fat old woman" whom I did not know, but whose name sounded rather like that of the one I dreamt of the night after.[43]

This was Field's hard evidence that Nabokov dreaded the Romanov connection, and the sort of unwarranted mistake he could make even with a photostat at hand, the sort of use he found for the private materials to which Nabokov granted him access.

Field also reproached Nabokov for implying that he had threatened blackmail, yet even as he disclaimed any threat he reiterated it in another form: if Nabokov did not like Field's third book on him, how much less he would like the fourth if his opposition forced Field to write it. An outraged Nabokov replied:

> Your ignoble letter of July 9, 1973 arrived only now, upon my return to Montreux from Cortina d'Ampezzo, thus taking a month to reach me. I would attribute to the workings of a deranged mind some of its wild rubbish—such as my dreading the blood of the Tsars in my veins, or that filthy lie about a "separation" from my wife, or your comic complaint that I failed to inform you that she is "related to Marc Slonim" (she isn't—and who cares anyway?), or my telling my three-year-old son in Berlin: "spit on those flowers that look like Hitler faces" (in our set, children were forbidden to spit); but mental derangement is one thing, and blackmail another, and blackmail is the word for your threats to publish my informal utterances on two afternoons of tape-recording, the garbled recollections of strangers, and the various rumors that fell into your unfastidious lap, if I continue to insist on your deleting from your book the errors of fact, the blunders of fancy and the vulgar malice, which still mar your "revised" edition.
>
>   Since I cannot conceive what rational considerations can prompt the unfortunate author of a biographical work riddled with mistakes to refuse the help, free of charge, offered him by the only individual in the world who is able to set straight the incidents, situations and other matters recklessly botched by that biographer, I shall persevere and send you my corrections, as promised, in the course of this month, and if you refuse to accept them you will face the consequences.[44]

By the "separation" he had mentioned, Field had had in mind Nabokov's brief 1937 affair with Irina Guadanini, about which he had heard from Nabokov's friend George Hessen. This was the one matter Nabokov really did not want Field to know about. But Field as usual had it wrong. Although Nabokov had moved to France before Véra and Dmitri could leave Germany early in 1937, there had never been any marital separation. Field's inaccuracy gave Nabokov the opportunity to denounce the story of a "separation" in the fiercest terms in order to ensure Field's silence on the matter and to avoid inflation of the incident by gossip.

Nabokov now set about correcting Field's revised typescript. The revisions included many changes Nabokov had demanded, but they also omitted many others. When Nabokov set straight an anecdote whose point Field had missed, Field naturally was happy to adopt Nabokov's version. On the other hand, he often refused to relinquish not only what Nabokov thought might infringe on his own or someone else's right to privacy but even unmitigated errors easily checked against the facts. When he did incorporate corrections, he did so in a resentfully perfunctory spirit. Informed that an event he had assigned to "a wet autumnal day" had in fact taken place "in July," he had simply retyped the phrase as "a wet autumnal day in July." When Nabokov pointed out that Bunin, whom Field had described as "a very little man" was "not of small stature," Field altered to "a very little man (he was of average height)."[45] Such contempt for the tiresome business of getting things right marred phrase after phrase of Field's revised text.

While Nabokov was correcting Field's second draft, Simon Karlinsky arrived in Montreux, on his way back to the U.S. from his first trip to the Soviet Union. Nabokov planned to send the narrator of *Look at the Harlequins!*, his mock-double, émigré Vadim Vadimych, to Leningrad. Now he told Karlinsky, "What I need from you is your very first impression of Petersburg [he did not say Leningrad] the moment you stepped from your bus." Karlinsky hardly needed to hesitate: "Loud women's voices, swearing obscenely." As he walked into his hotel he had heard the elevator woman cursing mightily; when he reached his floor, another barrage issued from the *dezhurnaya* (the woman stationed on every floor in Soviet hotels to keep an eye on guests); the next morning he had heard a third woman's voice down in the courtyard blasting out in the same style. In *Look at the Harlequins!* Nabokov appropriated Karlinsky's impressions while inventing his own dialogue:

A flushed athletic *liftyorsha* wearing several bead necklaces was in the act of being replaced by a much older woman of the pensioned type, at whom she shouted while stomping out of the lift: "*Ya tebe eto popomnyu, sterva!* (I'll get even with you, dirty bitch)"—and proceeded to barge into me and almost knock me down (I am a large, but fluff-light old fellow). "*Shto-ty suyoshsya pod nogi?* (Why do you get underfoot?)"[46]

Before his sister Elena's trip to Leningrad that summer, Nabokov had supplied her with a long list of details she was to check out on her travels, from the smells in street and corridor to the patterns on the blinds of Aeroflot planes. *Look at the Harlequins!* devoted little space to V.V.'s Leningrad expedition, but described it with such an accurate eye and ear and nose that readers who had traveled to the Soviet Union felt sure Nabokov must have returned there incognito.

A few days after Karlinsky's departure, Nabokov sent off to Field his corrections to the revised text of the biography: "The style and tone of your work are beyond redemption, but if you wish to publish it at all you must accept *all the deletions and corrections in the present list.*"[47] Apart from a letter in October requesting Field's acknowledgment that he had received these corrections, Nabokov would never write to him again.

Over the next three years Nabokov's lawyers and Field's editors battled it out. Field incorporated many of the most important changes on Nabokov's reduced list of corrections, but when *Nabokov: His Life in Part* was published in 1977, a few weeks before Nabokov's death, most of the book's flaws remained. One informed comment on the finished product will have to stand for many: "Not only a vast compendium of error but so nauseatingly mannered and self-important as to have a kind of morbid appeal only for those fascinated by literary and scholarly pathology."[48]

VIII

Infuriated that Nabokov's insistence on an accurate account of his life had delayed the biography, Field retaliated by publishing in 1986 *VN: The Life and Art of Vladimir Nabokov.*[49] In part a conflation of *Nabokov: His Life in Art* and *Nabokov: His Life in Part*, Field's fourth Nabokov book would prove the worst of all. The decay of what he had once known about his subject, already so marked in his previous book, had advanced several stages further. Field could no longer remember salient facts about Nabokov's world or his life. The two most significant dates in modern Russian history are 1861, the emancipation of the serfs by Alexander II, and 1917. On the very first page of his new book Field installed Alexander II on the throne in 1868, seven years too late to free the serfs and an unlucky thirteen behind the true date. In the earlier version of the biography, Field had thought the Russian

Revolution began in February 1916 rather than a year later; now he not only repeated his mistake but even brought the October Revolution forward to September.* Nor could he recall even major milestones in Nabokov's life: when he finished Cambridge, when he first met Véra (various indices in Field's text placed their meeting in 1921, 1922, or 1924 but not in the correct 1923), when he left America, when he settled in Switzerland.

As for the plan of revenge, it backfired time after time. In 1973, refuting Nabokov's accusation of blackmail, Field had written back that he could easily wait until Nabokov's death and then write a book entitled, say, *He Called His Mum Lolita*—but of course, he added, he could never write a book of that sort.[50] Now, having outlived Nabokov, he had after all produced a book of exactly "that sort," for in the new biography he claimed that Nabokov did indeed write to his mother as "Lolita." Since *Lolita* begins and ends with Humbert's address to Lolita, and is one long rhapsody to her, Field's claim would of course transform utterly our sense of Nabokov's private life and his most famous work.

Nabokov had shown Field photocopies of his letters to his mother, but out of a combination of firm Old World decorum and his own acute sense of privacy he had deleted the salutation. Field, like the rest of the literary world, knew of Nabokov's imperious insistence on privacy but chose instead to regard whatever Nabokov withheld as almost certainly a compromising secret. As so often, he chose to twist into service the little information he had at hand, whether or not it snapped in the process. Nabokov's mother was called Elena. In Russian, first names form diminutives, and the regular diminutive for Elena is "Lyolya." In the excised salutation, Field counted space for seven letters and deduced—eureka!—that Nabokov must have added a suffix and called his mother "Lolita."

---

* Even when his February 1916 blunder was pointed out, Field maintained in the English paperback edition of his book that the Russian Revolution "did indeed take place in 1916/17." As I commented in *TLS* (June 17–28, 1988): "Only in the strange world of Field's mind. Field simply remains oblivious to the fact that in the real world the February Revolution took place in February 1917, not February 1916 as two of his books have it. By defending his formulation 'February 1916, when the provisional government of Alexander Kerensky overthrew the Czarist regime,' Field proves he does not know that (1) the mood of Russia in February 1916 seemed many years away from revolution; (2) the February Revolution took place in 1917; (3) the first provisional government was formed only after street riots and the Petrograd garrison's desertion had made revolution a fact; (4) *Kerensky's* provisional government was formed not in February 1916 nor even during the February Revolution but five months later still, in July 1917. Field somehow fails to recognize his elementary historical howlers, even when they are pointed out to him. How does one deal with such a man?" And Nabokov had hundreds of such errors to persuade Field to change.

Except that, as the originals prove, the word deleted in the copies was *radost'*, which means simply "joy" or "dearest."[51] Everything was wrong about Field's would-be embarrassing conjecture. There are six letters in "Lolita," not the seven spaces Field counted in the deleted word. The diminutive of "Elena" is "Lyolya," not, as Field records it, "Lolya," and in Russian a Spanish suffix added to a Russian word is simply impossible, so that neither the first nor the second half of "Lolita" could have been formed from the diminutive of Nabokov's mother's name. And in Nabokov's set in any case it was quite unthinkable for a son to address his mother by her first name or a diminutive.*

Even in his first Nabokov book in 1967, Field had made no secret of his ambition to be immortalized by the artistry of his work. In compiling his 1977 and 1986 versions of Nabokov's biography he enacted in real life the roles of Nabokov's two invented inept biographers, *The Real Life of Sebastian Knight*'s Mr. Goodman, happily ignorant because so serenely confident of the power of conjecture, and *Pale Fire*'s Kinbote, who intrudes on the privacy of John Shade but misconstrues everything because his own desire for glory gets in the way. Field may find immortality all right, but more likely in the pit than in the pantheon.

IX

After completing and mailing off his corrections to Field's revised manuscript in September 1973, Nabokov had set aside a week to revise the translation of the German *Ada*. Ledig Rowohlt adopted once again the method that had proved so successful for *Pale Fire*, bringing two translators to Montreux for the Nabokovs to check their superb version of *Ada* line by line. Six days of conferences, seven or eight hours a day, took the team only a third of the way through the novel. They would have to come back for more.[52]

Nabokov had not touched *Look at the Harlequins!* since Cortina. Now, with Field and *Ada* out of the way, he was at last able to return to the novel on September 25. Although he had worked on it only in February and over the summer, he now began in earnest with the final consecutive draft. Throughout the fall he continued at an alarming rate, working "smoothly and merrily" for five hours a day, finishing part 1, almost a third of the book, on November 20.[53]

He still feared that death might strike before he could complete the novel. Earlier in the year he had written on the inner lid of his box of

---

* Field later maintained that although Nabokov had apparently written "*radost'*" rather than "Lolita," that did not invalidate his point. Somehow *his* errors remain truths.

index cards for the novel's manuscript, "To be destroyed *unread* if unfinished." Now in his fair copy he adopted a system of catchwords (each card carries isolated at the top the last word of the preceding card) and for the first time he numbered each card, and now altered his note about destroying the cards to read: "unnumbered cards only." If he died before the novel's completion, in other words, the numbered, fair-copy cards could be preserved and read in the right order, and the rest destroyed.[54]

At the end of November, Nabokov received a call from the U.S.: he had won the $10,000 National Medal for Literature, a prize conferred annually on a single author for his or her total output. Recent recipients included Thornton Wilder, W. H. Auden, Marianne Moore, and Robert Penn Warren. In accepting the award, Nabokov made it clear he could travel to New York in April for the presentation dinner only if he could first complete *Look at the Harlequins!* Throughout December and January he kept composing steadily, stopping only to pore over Véra's Christmas gift, the thirteen fat volumes of the Oxford English Dictionary, and to devote five more days early in February to another revision conference for the German *Ada*.[55]

On February 14 the news broke that Alexander Solzhenitsyn had been deported to Germany. After receiving the Nobel Prize in 1970, Solzhenitsyn had written to Montreux suggesting that Nabokov deserved the prize more than he did himself, and forwarding a copy of his letter to the Swedish Academy nominating Nabokov for the prize. Fearing that it might endanger Solzhenitsyn to receive correspondence from an old émigré, Nabokov had not replied. Now that Solzhenitsyn was out of Soviet clutches, Nabokov wrote that very day, welcoming him to the freedom and safety of the West.[56]

Throughout February and March he remained deeply engrossed in *Look at the Harlequins!* and uncertain when he would finish. In late February his attending the National Medal for Literature ceremony looked unlikely. Early in March his fast pace made it seem as if he might just complete the novel in time, but as he set down what he had expected to be the last third of the novel, it swelled out to become the last half of a book longer than he had anticipated. By mid-March, he had to formally decline the award dinner. As it turned out, he could still have gone. Less than three weeks after drafting a statement for Dmitri to deliver at the ceremony, he rose even earlier than usual on the morning of April 3 and began writing at four-thirty. By nine o'clock that morning he had finished the last novel he would ever complete.[57]

CHAPTER 26

Look at the Harlequins!

I

*L*OOK AT *the Harlequins!* seems to announce its intentions even before its story starts.[1] After the title page follows a list of "other books by the narrator," six Russian and six English, a parodic telescoping of the Nabokov canon. Item number two, for instance: *Pawn Takes Queen*, a comic conflation of *King, Queen, Knave* and *The Defense*. In Nabokov's second novel Franz does take Dreyer's queen, Martha, and he is a pawn—much more a pawn in fact than a knave. Like Nabokov's third novel, *The Defense*, the invented *Pawn Takes Queen* is serialized in a Russian émigré journal, and a woman who has read the latest installment approaches its author at a party: "She had adored that treacherous conversation between the Pawn and the Queen about the husband and would they really defenestrate the poor chess player?"

Vadim Vadimych N——, whose full surname we never learn, is a parody of his maker, Vladimir Vladimirovich Nabokov,* or of popular misconceptions of Nabokov the man and the artist. Since madness is the clichéd shadow of genius, Nabokov makes Vadim as much a neurotic as a novelist, hospitalized again and again as he succumbs to his anxieties and hallucinations. Since another cliché presupposes writers recycle their lives in their works, Vadim's youthful loves yield "quite a number of erotic passages scattered like rotting plums and brown pears throughout an aging novelist's books."

Critics have often thought Nabokov obsessed with self-reference, with doubles, with puppetlike characters whose chief function is to reveal a glimpse of the puppet-master's hand. In *Look at the Harlequins!*, Nabokov offers up a parodic exaggeration of these misguided versions of himself. One of the many fears that drives Vadim mad is his intermittent apprehension that his life was "the non-identical twin, a parody, an inferior variant of another man's life": Nabokov's. Even the book's very title reflects back on itself, for Vadim often com-

* As the novel itself points out, "in rapid Russian speech longish name-and-patronymic combinations undergo familiar slurrings," so that "Vladimir Vladimirovich," for instance, "becomes colloquially similar to 'Vadim Vadimych.' "

presses its name into the acronym *LATH*, and in the commedia dell'arte, one of Harlequin's identifying emblems is invariably his wooden lath.

More than any other Nabokov work, *Lolita* defined the popular image of its author. Even some otherwise sophisticated readers supposed that he could render Humbert so vividly only because he must have had a penchant for little girls himself. Mocking the myth, Nabokov has Vadim tempted by eleven-year-old Dolly von Borg. Vadim resists her charms then, but not when she reenters his life at twenty-four. After learning of his affair with Dolly, his second wife Anna flees with their four-year-old daughter Isabel. Seven years later, after Anna's death, Vadim takes custody of Bel, who at eleven combines the precocious giftedness of Pnin's surrogate son, Victor Wind, with the sexual allure of Lolita Haze. Vadim resorts to a third marriage, not as in *Lolita* to obtain access to a nymphet daughter, but to keep himself from violating her. But Bel, despising her new stepmother for the vulgarity under her elegant veneer and resenting her father for stooping to marry such a woman, closes off her mind against them both. The very move Vadim makes to protect Bel ends up stunting the growth he had tried to ensure.

Vadim reacts to this twist of fate by writing *A Kingdom by the Sea*—the working title of *Lolita*—a wish-fulfillment fantasy in which the hero makes a ten-year-old girl his concubine, only for the relationship to mature into mutual love and eventually, when the girl turns eighteen, marriage and a happy life together that lasts until the two reach a combined age of 170. *A Kingdom by the Sea* makes Vadim's fortune, but his relationships with Bel and her stepmother are already ruined. He is seventy by the time he meets the real heroine of *Look at the Harlequins!*: "You," whose name we never learn. Exactly the same age as Bel—and briefly in her class at school—she shares her birthday not only with Bel but also with Lolita. But by the time her path crosses Vadim's she is a permissible twenty-seven years old. At long last, after a lifetime of frustrated love, Vadim finds fulfillment with a woman in whom his daughter's budding precocity has opened out into brilliant bloom.

II

Many readers—and for a long time I was one—have responded to the novel summed up so far as to a tired self-referential joke. In *Look at the Harlequins!* Nabokov seems simply to have taken common criticisms of his work or common misapprehensions about his life and subjected them to a reductio ad absurdum.

To those who consider him inhumanly cold, he offers a Vadim who never sparks to life and a series of women all without warmth until the entry of You. Even her radiance on the novel's last pages fails to redeem the emptiness of the rest. Vadim himself seems irritating and impossible from the first. Initially that appears full of comic promise: he virtually invites himself to Villa Iris, he refuses to notice his reluctant hosts' polite and not-so-polite attempts to dismiss him, he breaks open the whiskey he had brought for Ivor, he walks around a strange house naked, he helps himself to the wine in the fridge for breakfast. He seems likely to prove as much a concentrate of comic insensitivity as Kinbote, but for many readers his apparent role as only a parody Nabokov makes him dwindle in vitality and independent viability to a point where it becomes hard to take an interest in him or his fate.

To those deterred by the lifelessness of the characters, the style can seem no better. Few can value the spell of Nabokov's verbal art more than Martin Amis, who comments in his review of the novel: "The really unnerving deficiency of *Look at the Harlequins!* is the crudity of its prose. . . . In the book's 250-odd pages I found only four passages that were genuinely haunting and beautiful; in an earlier Nabokov it would be hard to find as many that were not."[2]

In his final novel, Nabokov inverts and parodies himself in language as in everything else. Vadim's casualness, his sheer offhandedness, stands in deliberate contrast to his creator's impassioned precision and control. The first chapter begins with Vadim not bothering to count: "I met the first of my three or four successive wives. . . ." The chapter ends with deliberate limpness and an abrupt change of subject—"The melancholy fact was that his sister—but, perhaps, he had better postpone the explanation of her case till we and the bags were installed more or less"—only for the ensuing chapter to fail to follow this drooping signpost.

Of course this slackness reflects Vadim's mental disarray, and pointedly matches his social shamblings. More often, Nabokov simply deprives Vadim of the romantic vibrato of his own prose. Perhaps this too is deliberate, appropriate certainly for Vadim, who has been initiated into sex long before love, and indeed the novel contains brilliantly funny images of deromanticized sex. Other passages seem to show Nabokov's language hardened into mannerism, a spangle of bright detail stuck on cardboard characters and cardboard backdrops. Perhaps the motley failures of style are *all* deliberate, the patches of Vadim's harlequin self. If so, the missing magic of Nabokov's language can seem too high a price to pay. Joyce could mimic nastiness, shallowness, dreaminess, or verbal tiredness in *Ulysses* and leave us in no doubt about his aims or the triumph of his achievement. Here in *Look at the Harlequins!*, Nabokov's language can seem disconcertingly fussy, disappointingly graceless. Surely even that disappointment is not deliberate self-parody?

Perhaps Nabokov's undertaking such a thorough self-inversion was a mistake from the first. He may have been too disconcerted by Field's assault on *Speak, Memory* to write his own inversion of an inversion of his life with the composure his art required. Perhaps he conceived, wrote, and revised the book too quickly, as the speed of composition suggests and the unusually abundant crop of errors in the first edition possibly confirms. Perhaps he was lured by the sheer difficulty of the design, a sort of literary equivalent of a sui-mate in chess-problem composition, where the very aim is to ensure the defeat of one's own forces, and succeeded only by defeating himself in a way he never intended.

Or perhaps *Look at the Harlequins!* is simply not the self-centered self-parody it at first seems to suggest.

III

"You" serves notice that the novel is more than a parodic jigsaw of Nabokov's life and works: it will also be a specific inversion of *Speak, Memory*, the one Nabokov work that draws directly on his life. For as readers of the autobiography know, *Speak, Memory* quietly introduces someone named only "you" who steps to the fore as the book ends: Nabokov's wife, to whom his whole memoir is addressed.

Speak, Memory concentrates on Nabokov's life up to his last year at Cambridge, 1922, then skims rapidly to stop at 1940 and his passage to America. It focuses on family love and the amours of childhood and youth but touches on the great love of Nabokov's adult life only by implication. *Look at the Harlequins!* on the other hand *begins* with Vadim leaving Cambridge and meeting his first adult love and continues into his old age via a succession of wives and loves.

Speak, Memory's first chapter was published separately as "Perfect Past," and the radiant happiness of the past pervades the book. *Look at the Harlequins!* offers the obverse. After preparing to meet Vadim's first wife, Iris, the novel breaks off to ask: "What kind of childhood did *you* have, McNab?" Vadim answers himself: "Atrocious, intolerable. There should be a natural, internatural, law against such inhuman beginnings." Nabokov remembered Russia, his home, and his family with passionate adoration. Vadim skips over his catastrophic past as quickly as he can: "I saw my parents infrequently," he says in his hit-or-miss fashion (his father actually dies several months before Vadim's birth). "They divorced and remarried and redivorced at such a rapid rate that had the custodians of my future been less alert, I might have been auctioned out finally to a pair of strangers of Swedish or Scottish descent." Nabokov revered his father's liberalism and his dedication to the highest standards of European culture. He has to desecrate his past to transform Vadim's father into "a gambler and a rake. His society nickname was Demon. . . . His politics were of the casual, reactionary sort. He had a dazzling and complicated sensual life, but his culture was patchy and commonplace." And even then this Demon may not be Vadim's real father: Vadim could well be the bastard son of Count Starov, a descendant of German and Russian nobility and even the English royal line.

The very title of *Look at the Harlequins!* turns *Speak, Memory* awry. Nabokov had wanted to call his memoirs *Speak, Mnemosyne*, in honor of the Greek goddess of memory and mother of the muses, and more specifically in honor of his own mother, who would lead her little son through the estate and instruct him, in conspiratorial terms, "*Vot zapomni* [now remember]," as she drew his attention to this or that loved thing in Vyra.[3] She *was* the mother of his imagination: her instructions to him to hoard the present until it turned into the priceless past shaped his very being. She allowed him to daydream, she let him have all the time he wanted to pursue his butterflies—and in proposing the title *Speak, Mnemosyne*, Nabokov had also wanted to commemorate his love for lepidoptera by way of *mnemosyne*, a butterfly species he had chased at Vyra.

Young Vadim, on the other hand, already harboring at seven or eight the secrets of a confirmed madman,[4] is told by a grandaunt to stop daydreaming, stop moping: "Look at the harlequins!" As neither boy nor grandaunt know, "harlequin," like "mnemosyne," is the name of a butterfly.

"What harlequins? Where?"

"Oh, everywhere. All around you. Trees are harlequins, words are harlequins. So are situations and sums. Put two things together—jokes, images—and you get a triple harlequin. Come on! Play! Invent the world! Invent reality!"

I did. By Jove, I did. I invented my grand-aunt in honor of my first daydreams.

While in name and nature *Speak, Memory* records young Vladimir's responsiveness to his mother's injunction to attend to and remember his world, *Look at the Harlequins!* testifies to Vadim's slippery hold on his unsteady world.

As Nabokov probes his past in *Speak, Memory*, his exceptional control over the harmony and design of his life both establishes his identity as an artist whose medium is time and serves to explain how he came to master this unprecedented art. Vadim, on the other hand, is comically slipshod, confused, deluded about his patchy past. His memoir opens with him apparently not able to recall just how many wives he has amassed in the course of his life. Nor can he be sure about his first glimpse of his first wife, Iris. One possible first sighting merges with a drunken recollection of a visit to a psychiatrist, which in turn leads into a scene in a dentist's reception room that gradually metamorphoses into a party—various befuddled impressions identify it as a funeral, a birthday, a wedding—that Vadim has in fact declined to attend. After describing in detail his dinner with Iris and her brother Ivor on the night of his arrival, Vadim even confesses: "Those first days at Villa Iris are so badly distorted in my diary, and so blurred in my mind, that I am not sure if, perhaps, Iris and Ivor were not absent till the middle of the week."

Speak, Memory's apparently effortless control bespeaks a mind with the firmest grasp on its world. Neurotic Vadim, by contrast, breaks down repeatedly, his mental alarm bells set off by almost any switch: drink, darkness, headaches, neuralgia, the turmoils of love, the terrors of space. Before proposing to each of his wives, he feels compelled to explain his inability to *imagine* himself walking along in one direction and turning around so that what was left has now become right and vice versa—something he can do of course without thinking in everyday life. To Vadim this mental quirk, although perfectly harmless in itself, seems a possible harbinger of irreversible insanity. Four times, once to each of his prospective wives, Iris, Anna, Louise, and You, he insists on explaining this bizarre flaw. Obsessed with the thought that his mind is so special, so precarious, he does not notice that everyone else—including his readers—thinks it all inconsequential and even boring.

As You tells him on the last page of the book, he has simply confused space and time. The narrator of his latest novel, she explains,

speaks of space but he means time. His impressions along the HP route (dog overtakes ball, car pulls up at next villa) refer to a series of time events, and not to blocks of painted space that a child can rearrange in any old way. It has taken him time—even if only a few moments—to cover the distance HP in thought. By the time he reaches P he has accumulated direction, he is saddled with it! Why then is it so extraordinary that he cannot imagine himself turning on his heel? Nobody can imagine in physical terms the act of reversing the order of time. Time is not reversible.

Nabokov, on the other hand, as he announces at the beginning of *Speak, Memory*, has been interested all his life in time, in finding out why our minds cannot return to roam within the accumulated reality of the past. In his case it is not a sign of madness or obsessive self-concern, not a supposition that the whole world must revolve when he turns around, not an insignificant and idiosyncratic tic, but a philosophical mystery that affects every human mind: what is the point of storing up in the present an infinite wealth of experience if it all sinks into an irretrievable past?

IV

Many early reviewers were puzzled by Nabokov's first title for his autobiography. In a little-known interview he once explained that he chose *Conclusive Evidence* for the two *v* sounds together at the center of the title, as a secret link looping together Vladimir and Véra.[5] Like its title, the whole autobiography was designed as a tribute to his wife. When she emerges late in the story as the "you" to whom the book has been addressed, it becomes apparent that the love affairs of childhood and youth that Nabokov has described with mounting intensity will find their apotheosis in her. But he will *not* describe their relationship directly. A condition of their opening themselves to each other must be that the secrets they share remain secrets. Nabokov begins the last chapter of his autobiography affirming the privacy of their intimate lives: "The years are passing, my dear, and presently nobody will know what you and I know."[6]

In *Look at the Harlequins!*, by contrast, Vadim discloses the most grotesque details even of his sexual relations with his wives. Virginal Anna's primness during his first attempt at making love with her renders Vadim an impotent wreck, but an open-mouthed kiss restores his vigor: "I hastened to possess her. She exclaimed I was disgustingly hurting her and with a vigorous wriggle expulsed the blooded and thrashing fish. When I tried to close her fingers around it in humble substitution, she snatched her hand away, calling me a dirty *débauché* (*gryaznyy razvratnik*). I had to demonstrate myself the messy act while she looked on in amazement and sorrow." But when You comes on the scene, Vadim changes. Suddenly the romance so characteristic of *Speak, Memory* and so absent until this point from *Look at the Harlequins!* floods into Vadim's life, and he refuses to say any more: "Reality would be only adulterated if I now started to narrate what you know, what I know, what nobody else knows, what shall never, never, be ferreted out by a matter-of-fact, father-of-muck, mucking biograffitist."

Soon after their first meeting in 1923, Vladimir Nabokov and Véra Slonim had discovered that they might have met earlier in their lives, through common friends in St. Petersburg, on a rural road near Vyra, in an office in émigré Berlin. Nabokov construed these near-encounters in the past as fate's first attempts to bring them together, proof of the persistence of its design. He would turn that idea into a minor motif in two of his novels and the major structural principle of a third, The Gift. Fifty years after meeting Véra, he would still muse over other possible forays of fate. Perhaps his nurse and Véra's had talked together when taking their separate charges for a stroll through some St. Petersburg park.[7] Or he would tell visitors that however history had turned out, revolution or no revolution, he and Véra would have still met and married.[8] Look at the Harlequins! begins with Nabokov's slyly inverted tribute to fate's persistence in bringing himself and Véra together: "I met the first of my three or four successive wives in somewhat odd circumstances, the development of which resembled a clumsy conspiracy, with nonsensical details and a main plotter who not only knew nothing of its real object but insisted on making inept moves that seemed to preclude the slightest possibility of success."

Not only the novel's first sentence but its very title and the whole opening sequence constitute an oblique tribute by Nabokov to his first meeting with Véra. When he encountered her for the first time at a charity ball, she was wearing a mask (he wrote a poem about it, "The Encounter," a few weeks later).[9] He had that mask in mind when he introduced Harlequin—who always wears a mask—into the title of Vadim's memoir, for he privately rechristened the book Look at the Masks![10] In real life, during that first meeting in 1923, Véra appears not to have lowered her mask lest her looks interfere with Nabokov's response to her mind and manner. In the novel, when Vadim arrives virtually uninvited at Villa Iris, Ivor conspires with his sister to deter the unwanted guest by adopting a mask that reverses Véra's: Vadim can see Iris's face all right, but she pretends to be deaf and dumb.

V

Central to the design of Speak, Memory are the "themes" that Nabokov weaves through the book, especially the theme of spectra, rainbows, prisms, jewels, and colored glass. Through that theme he contrasts the gemstones that briefly supported him and his family in exile with the much greater, though intangible, riches of consciousness, the colored treasures of memory and imagination that sustained him through a whole lifetime. The theme begins with the colored alphabet blocks he played with as a child. When he remarks to his mother that their colors are all wrong, she quizzes him and finds that, like her, he associates particular letters with particular colors. As he describes all the hues and shades of the spectrum by way of the letters that evoke them, Nabokov links the rise of his unique verbal imagination and his mother's role in fostering the early growth of his mind. From that point on, women and words are repeatedly joined by the rainbow arc of the spectrum theme. While he listens to his Swiss governess reading aloud some work of French literature, for instance, young Vladimir allays his boredom with the lesson by staring entranced through the colored glass lozenges of the veranda at Vyra. As he falls in love time after time, the theme of colored glass develops: thus, his last glimpse of Colette, his first passionate childhood love, brings to mind a "rainbow spiral in a glass marble." The theme reaches its explicit climax as Nabokov fuses the roles of love and art in his life by way of the "wine-red and bottle-green and dark-blue lozenges of stained glass" in the pavilion at Vyra. There he finds the inspiration for his first poem, an elegy dealing "with the loss of a beloved mistress—Delia, Tamara, or Lenore—whom I had never lost, never loved, never met, but was all set to meet, love, lose"; there, a year later, in that same "rainbow-windowed pavilion," he meets for the first time the girl he calls Tamara (Valentina Shulgin), his first true love.[11] Within a year, he has published his first book of passionate love poems dedicated to her. A decade later, he will publish his first novel, a passionate evocation of his lost love for her that even quotes at length from her love letters.

Just as the series of explicit young loves recorded in *Speak, Memory* culminates in the love for Véra that he leaves largely implicit but no less emphatic for that, so the theme of the link between his art and his love for women reaches its tacit crescendo in Véra. As the structure of *Speak, Memory* suggests, her role in inspiring his art has been as much greater than Tamara's as his love for her exceeds his love for Tamara—but that too is something he will not permit us to see.

In *Look at the Harlequins!* Nabokov reworks the patterns of *Speak, Memory*. The distinguishing mark of Harlequin's appearance is of course his costume of multicolored lozenges, evoked by Nabokov in the title of the novel in oblique but deliberate allusion to the colored glass lozenges of the pavilion, the most explicit link between *Speak,*

Memory's themes of love and art. And Vadim's first three wives are all constructed as virtual color negatives of Véra, the implicit center of *Speak, Memory*'s pattern: all three break the nexus between love and art so central to Nabokov's own life.

Iris, the first of the three—her very name, after the Greek goddess of the rainbow, signals the reintroduction of the spectrum theme—is "a sleek little flirt" with a disconcerting sense of humor that bespeaks her indifference to Vadim and leaves him at a perpetual disadvantage. Vadim writes her a metaphysical love poem—it must rate as one of Nabokov's best Russian poems—and explains to Iris its sense in English. Feigning not to realize the poem is for her, she offers just this devastatingly dismissive comment on its somber tones: "Your girl must be having a jolly good time in your company." Although at first anything but interested in him, Iris begins to toy with Vadim simply because he is at hand. She becomes curious about his mind and his literary talent, and agrees to marry him. As Vadim develops as a writer, she takes desultory lessons in Russian but never succeeds in learning the language and ends with "a dull habitual aversion" to it. In compensation for being debarred from his writings, she decides to become a writer herself, although she lacks talent, and her endlessly rewritten detective novel never approaches completion. Véra on the other hand was fascinated by Nabokov's work even before she met him; she had a command of Russian that could leave him in admiration and awe, and a literary talent she preferred to set aside in order to serve her husband's greater gifts.

Besides all the other ways she contrasts with Véra, Iris also happens to be unfaithful, and dies at the hands of an unstable ex-lover. Composing prolifically to ward off his grief over her death, Vadim looks for a Russian typist. Eventually he finds Anna Blagovo. Inept at the keyboard, ignorant of his work, she proves constitutionally incapable of remembering anything he has written. Although she types every word of *The Dare* ("and most of its commas") she retains not even an outline of its plot. A virgin and a prude, she puts herself on guard against what she suspects are Vadim's designs on her. Somehow her very chilliness and the frail charm of her helplessness inflame Vadim's desire. He proposes, she accepts. Like Iris, Anna is a portrait by inversion of Véra Nabokov—a superb and dedicated typist, secretary, and editor who remembered every detail of her husband's work and every line of his poetry. But as if to caution against anyone supposing *that* his reason for marrying Véra, Nabokov has a woman named Lyuba Savich respond to an advertisement Vadim places before he finds Anna. Although Lyuba is imposingly beautiful, an excellent typist, an ardent fan of his writings, and eager for his love, Vadim finds her and her ardor simply not to his taste, and he dismisses her before he discovers Anna.

Easily dominated, Anna finds herself drawn away from Vadim by the next person to take an interest in her: an unattractive, mean-minded woman whose strong Soviet sympathies ought to be the last thing to appeal to an émigrée like Anna. Indomitable Véra, of course, would prove staunchly loyal to Nabokov and would remain if anything even more fiercely opposed than he was to the tyranny both their families had fled.

After Anna's death, Vadim gains custody of Bel and marries the beautiful young socialite Louise Adamson solely to keep himself from succumbing to his love for his daughter. Despite Louise's looks and her poise, Vadim has no illusions about her. A snob and a name-dropper excited by success, she has read none of his books but marries him in the expectation that he will win the world's most prestigious literary prize. She poses as a woman of high taste but manifests a vulgar compulsion to acquire the latest and most expensive electronic gizmos and to follow all the most philistine fads. She too inverts facets of Véra Nabokov. Although dedicated to her husband's work and eager to see it achieve the prominence she had no doubt it deserved, Véra had no interest whatsoever in reflected glory for herself. She would even have preferred to be left entirely out of her husband's biography. Severe in her artistic standards, she made it almost a point of honor to be indifferent to material circumstances and material possessions—except perhaps a few good books.

Of Vadim's fourth wife, You, we see almost nothing. But Vadim's protective reticence about her itself proves her not a contrast but a deliberate parallel to the "you" of *Speak, Memory*. Before the mask of secrecy drops, Vadim lets us see how he met her. As he emerges from his office at Quirn University, the string around a batch of his letters and drafts breaks. Coming from the library along the same campus path, You crouches down to help him collect his papers. "No, you don't," she says to a yellow sheet that threatens to glide away in the wind. After helping Vadim cram everything back into his folder she notices a yellow butterfly settle on a clover head before it wheels away in the same wind. "*Metamorphoza*," she says, in her "lovely elegant Russian."

In this one short scene, she helps a writer assemble his papers; she notices a butterfly; she cannot help disclosing the alertness of her imagination: she *is* Véra, putting two things together—a joke, an image—to make a triple harlequin. And then Vadim terminates the scene to announce that reality would only be adulterated if he started to tell "what you know, what I know, what nobody else knows." All the same, we do find out a little more about You. She has a superb command of Russian and English, an original mind, a deep appreciation of Vadim's art. She seems to know him better than he knows himself. She treats him with sweet firmness, constant solicitude, unswerving loyalty. No wonder Vadim dedicates all his translated books to her—as Nabokov did to Véra.

In *Speak, Memory*, Nabokov builds steadily though the romance of childhood love and the richer romance of adolescence to hint at the still richer romance of his adult love for "you." In *Look at the Harlequins!*, despite Vadim's falling for one wife after another, there is almost none of the tender enchantment of *Speak, Memory*. The helplessness that passes for romance in his feelings for Iris yields to his perverse bemusement at Anna and then to his cool appraisal of Louise's superficial charms. Much of the terrible hollowness of Vadim's life stems from our sense that this writer has no one to write for. Then suddenly, at seventy, romance rushes into his life as You crouches down by his side. And that makes all the difference: she is the muse he has been searching for all his life, the muse Nabokov had all *his* writing life in Véra.

VI

In *Speak, Memory*, Véra as "you" serves to anchor another structural design. After the secure filial love Nabokov feels for his parents comes the agitation of his ardor for Colette, Polenka, and Tamara, which in turn swells at the end of the autobiography into love for Véra as together they watch over their child. In the Hegelian terms Nabokov adopts for *Speak, Memory*, this ending synthesizes familial and romantic love, and provides the thesis for a new cycle of life, a new round of love.

Once again *Look at the Harlequins!* turns the positives of *Speak, Memory* into negatives only to culminate in the surprise positive of You. In Vadim's childhood, family love has no place, and "love" appears only in terms of a few stylized vignettes of juvenile eroticism. In his adult years awkward or misplaced passion precludes real romance. And his love for girls young enough to be his daughters only lands him in trouble—until You redeems it all. Dolly, although of an age to be Iris and Vadim's child, is no daughter but only a sexual temptation who destroys what family Vadim has. A decade later Bel, his true daughter, proves "the sole splendor, the sole breathtaking mountain in the drab plain of [his] emotional life." An adolescent prodigy, she thrives more than ever under his parental care, unaware how close she comes to turning into the victim of his desire. When Vadim resorts to Louise as a sexual safety valve, he causes something to shrink in Bel as she rejects him and his values along with the woman he has married despite *her* values.

Fifteen years later he meets You, who as she bends down to pick up his papers asks about and reminds him of Bel. She has everything his daughter had had—her intelligence, her originality, her effortless command of Russian and English, her literary sensitivity—developed to the stage he had hoped to help Bel herself attain. As Vadim's fourth wife, You fulfills romantic aspirations thwarted for seventy years. As his daughter's coeval, she satisfies his desire to pass on all he can to another generation. And when she stands at his side as he is reborn to consciousness again after the protracted, deathlike seizure that afflicts him when he proposes to her, she acts in loco parentis. Playing the part of parent, partner, child, she fuses three kinds of love in one.

VII

Vadim proposes to You, as he has to his other prospective wives, by confessing his peculiar inability to imagine reversing his direction in space. You manages to resolve this pattern too, and to turn a series of apparently trivial, irksome, repetitive confessions into something much richer.

Vadim's confessions grate for good reason: they are patently the disturbing consequence of his neurotic personality. Compulsively repeated rituals are characteristic of a certain type of neurosis, which can occasionally arise not merely from anxiety—and Vadim has more than enough of that—but precisely from preoccupation with quasiphilosophical enigmas like those that trouble him.

But Vadim's confessions disclose more than his own character. In context, each is also a revelation about the woman to whom he makes his confession. When he asks Iris to imagine the plane-tree avenue between her villa and the post office, her own mental impression of the vista outdoes his in vividness: that last plane tree by the gate in his abstract schema is actually a lamppost in a coat of ivy, the notice whose traces he recalls on another trunk can be identified as Ivor's, and so on. As always, she has him at a disadvantage.

Vadim falls in love with Anna because of the challenge of her physical and mental remoteness, and as product and proof of that distance he addresses her a stiffly formal letter of confession and proposal. Wooly-headed Anna does not bother to read through the difficult "poetic" bits, skips to the end, and, although she tries to follow Vadim's instructions for accepting the proposal, manages to bungle even them.

Since Louise is a social animal, it is no accident that drunken Vadim inflicts his confession and proposal to her on a dinner party where others constantly chip in, and the frankly bored Louise has to be restrained from leaving the table to make a long-distance call to a recent lover. She hears him out, she too accepts, but as a dedicated follower of fashion, she responds to his confession by also offering to take him to an "absolutely divine" analyst.

Vadim makes a fourth and final confession and proposal when he asks You to read a section on the Specter of Space from the just-completed manuscript of his latest novel, *Ardis*. Alone of his wives she can respond to his work. Weeks later, when Vadim recovers from the seizure that coincides with her reaching the end of his text, she tells him she has not liked the fragment at all. "Meaning she would not marry a madman? Meaning she would marry a sane man who could tell the difference between time and space." Vadim values her comment ("I'm grateful, I'm touched, I'm cured!"), although something still remains unresolved: "Your explanation, however, is merely an exquisite quibble—and you know it; but never mind, the notion of trying to twirl time is a *trouvaille*."

VIII

You stresses the impossibility of trying to reverse one's direction in time, of trying to walk not forward to the unfolding future but back into the barricaded past. As if in sympathy, each of the confessions at the beginning of Vadim's marriages secretly predicts the disaster at the marriage's end, and so marks the absolute contrast between a forward and a rearward view of time, between the bright wave of hope as love swells and the frothy scum and rattling pebbles as it retreats. Gearing himself up for his first confession to Iris, Vadim describes the plane-tree vista between the villa gate and the post office. He and Iris head off along this path to the sea. En route, Iris notes a spectacular green butterfly that a passing lepidopterist dismisses as a common Pandora. Down on the beach Vadim as usual stays in the shallows while Iris swims for the horizon. When he sees another young man encircle Iris with his motorboat like a moth around her hot flame, jealous Vadim instinctively swims toward her, finds himself out of his depth, and succumbs to a deadly spasm of total cramp.

A wave returns him to blessed sand, and when Iris emerges he makes his confession and his proposal.

She accepts, they are married, but the happiness he has expected does not eventuate, not only because she cannot learn Russian and therefore cannot read his books, but also because he suffers unallayable cramps of jealousy. When he asks her whom she is writing to she will invariably answer that the letter is to an old schoolmate, to her brother, to a teacher of Russian, but Vadim always knows "that in one way or another the letter would reach the post office at the end of the plane-tree avenue without my seeing the name on the envelope." One night in 1930, he and Iris dine with Ivor at the Paon d'Or—an anagram of "Pandora," and with a glass case of showy but common Morpho butterflies on display—only for Iris to be killed on their return from the restaurant by the lover whose last imploring letter she has spurned. Nabokov has arranged the fatidic Pandora butterfly and the swimmer's cramp just before the confession, and then within the confession itself the plane-tree vista, with its inset post office, in order to foreshadow Iris's fatal infidelity.

In similar fashion, the other confessions and proposals unwittingly anticipate the end of the hopes they embody. Vadim's proposal by letter to Anna Blagovo prefigures the letter that Anna and her mentor Ninel Langley send after discovering his affair with Dolly Borg, and that announces he is never to see his wife or his daughter again. The dinner where Vadim proposes marriage in order to ensure he will be no more than a loving father to his daughter, will be echoed four years later by a dinner that marks the end of his marriage and of all contact with his beloved Bel.

What of Vadim's final confession? What future does *it* foreshadow? It is the strangest of them all. Vadim gives You a section from his latest novel describing his inability to contemplate turning around to walk back in the direction from which he has come. As she reads, he sets off on his evening stroll, but with his recently composed text still fresh in his mind, he can picture every word she reads and keep mental pace with her as her eyes scan each manuscript card. Just as he envisages her at the end of his text, he reaches the end of his walk and prepares to turn and head back to meet her. He cannot. The intensity of his love for her and the vividness of his sense of her have made him so conscious of both ends of the distance separating them that his inability to turn in theory now manifests itself in reality. Rigid, he falls to the ground. Over the next three weeks in the hospital, he remains physically paralyzed, sensorially dead, while his mind hurtles through hallucinatory landscapes. Only very slowly do sensation and self begin to seep back.

Until this last confession and proposal, through all of Vadim's previous marriages, there has been no connection whatever between his love and his art as a writer. Now during this scene, for the first time in his life, these two parts of his existence come together, in almost miraculous fashion. The scene records a kind of ecstasy, a standing outside the self: knowing the depths of her artistic responsiveness, Vadim can follow You's thoughts as she reads his index cards. Art always allows for a kind of transcendence of the self, as one person participates in the visions of another's imagination, but here the force of Vadim's love for You grants him a still more immediate transcendence of the self, a virtual telepathic trance, an entry into her mind as she reads.

At their highest, both art and the mental harmony of married love suggest to Nabokov a kind of foretaste of what death may bring: the release of the self from its prison. But in life even these glimpses of a freedom beyond must remain highly conditional. Just at the moment where Vadim's last confession-cum-proposal seems to blur the boundaries between life and art (You reading from Vadim's novel as he acts out the novel's scenario), between self and other (Vadim virtually *in* her mind, reading his own text even as he heads away from her), and between life and death—just at that moment he has to turn around and face the anxiety that after all he does not know You's thoughts, that she might be repelled by his confession, that she might reject his proposal.

On one level his strange seizure is just what he has feared all along, an extreme form of the phenomenon students of neurosis call conversion reaction, a bodily displacement of a mental stress. On another level, as Vadim explains, it seems a foretaste of death, a trial run beyond life, a total shutdown of the body and the senses while thought and imagination career on.

As sensations gradually return, Vadim still has to grope desperately for his identity. He has other questions: "What was, apart from my own identity, that other person, promised to me, belonging to me?" He does not fully wake to consciousness of his own self until he suddenly apprehends *who* has just paused at his hospital door: "I emitted a bellow of joy, and Reality entered."

IX

Waking to consciousness like this had constituted another key structural pattern in *Speak, Memory*. In the opening chapter of his autobiography Nabokov describes how one day as an infant, walking between his parents down an avenue of oaklings, he had asked about their ages and his. When their answer made him understand with a shock their separate identities and his own, he felt catapulted to full consciousness, plunged into the radiant and mobile medium of time. In the book's final chapter he describes himself and Véra watching over the birth of Dmitri's mind. He ends with the image of them both anticipating with delight the shock Dmitri will receive as he walks between them and suddenly realizes that up ahead looms a ship's funnel, "showing from behind the clothesline as something in a scrambled picture—Find What the Sailor Has Hidden—that the finder cannot unsee once it has been seen."

In Vadim's first confession to Iris, with its vista of plane trees, Nabokov deliberately evokes *Speak, Memory*'s avenue of oaklings. When Vadim follows another pathway during his final confession and steps as it were into the pages of his own book, the sudden shock of his seizure, the resolution of his lifelong puzzle as he wakes to a sense of self, to a sense of Yóu, and to her explanation of his own mind's relation to time, the path recalls both *Speak, Memory*'s first scene and its last, the path Dmitri takes, the illusion of walking as if into a picture, the exhilarating shock his parents have prepared, the sudden explosion of consciousness that in *Speak, Memory* Nabokov offers up as an image of the mind's blissful bursting through death.

Death: that word explains why Vadim cannot quite accept You's explanation that he has simply confused a possible return through space with an impossible return through time. In his kaleidoscopic coma he has as it were hurtled through death. Neither he nor she quite realizes that his dreaded image of not being able to turn in the opposite direction is not a mere muddle of time and space but an unconscious image of escape from mortality's prison of irreversible time, the prison Nabokov defines at the beginning of *Speak, Memory* and declares he has tried to break free from by every means short of suicide. For beyond death, Nabokov suspects, consciousness will be able to head backward through time, just as the mind can move back and forth through the timeless world of a work of art.

Late in 1925, the year Nabokov married Véra, he wrote two works, *Mary* and "The Return of Chorb," structured around a contrast between time and space, between a possible return in space and an impossible return in time. For the first time in his career, Nabokov had begun to find a way to relate his love of the world of human emotion to his quest for something beyond, without resorting to the apostles and angels he had all too casually invited into his early poetry and prose.[12] He would still have much to learn as a writer, but in 1925 he mastered what for his art would be by far the most important lesson of all. Since *Look at the Harlequins!* begins with a tribute to Nabokov's first meeting with Véra, since the novel ends with Vadim's confession and proposal to You and her resolution of its terms, and since the decisive change in Nabokov's art immediately followed his marriage to the woman who would become the "you" of *Speak, Memory*, there seems good reason to suppose that Nabokov ends *Look at the Harlequins!* with an oblique tribute to the role Véra played in 1925 in helping him to redefine his art. Did he confess to her before they married about his sense of the insanity of a world where every present became a past as inaccessible as if it had never been? What did she say? This must surely remain the most tantalizing case in all Nabokov's artistic life of "what you know, what I know, what nobody else knows."

X

Vadim's neurotic fixation on the unimaginable transition from direction AB to direction BA had always been a mark of his obsession with self: he could not conceive of himself turning around because he would have had to revolve the whole world of which he was the center. But as his seizure retreats, his sense of self returns only as he becomes aware of You waiting there tenderly beside him, ready to accept his proposal.

Before his first confession and proposal to Iris, Vadim had written her a philosophical love poem that closed by suggesting that in the mystery of love, "maybe, the hereafter stands slightly ajar in the dark." But the depths of love he had expected to sound with Iris proved to be shallows. Now as he returns to consciousness after his proposal to You and his collapse, he has not quite passed through death, he has not yet escaped the prison of irreversible time, but he *has* found a way beyond the self in the depth of his love for You.

In *Speak, Memory* Nabokov depicts his life as it passes through family love, romantic love, parental love, each stage a metamorphosis and an expansion of his creative consciousness. He also discloses his sense of an art behind life, a conscious design behind the world, ready to rouse human consciousness first to life itself and then perhaps to a still greater freedom beyond life. If the imagined worlds of mortal art allow intimations of immortality and a freedom from the confines of self and time, mortal love, he suggests, allows us a special chance to escape the cell of the self. And as lovers become parents, as they in turn awaken another young mind to consciousness, they share in the delighted generosity of the unknown art that may lie behind nature.

In *Look at the Harlequins!*, by contrast, Vadim's life begins without family love, and his mind grows neurotically, agonizingly askew. Romantic love collapses time after time, and the women in his life, far from playing muses to his creative endeavors, remain deaf and blind to his art. His tangled relations with his daughter end by stunting her growth and her once-subtle appreciation of the creative side of life. But then at seventy, after living out the conventional span of mortal life, he discovers You. He proposes to her in a sequence of events that fuse life and art, life and death, self and other. As he emerges from his seizure, he has You at his bedside watching over a rebirth of his consciousness, allowing him beyond self in the intensity of his love, and fulfilling the hopes he had had for his daughter's growing young mind. All *Speak, Memory*'s three generations of love as generators of consciousness are suddenly concentrated in one.

Just before Vadim rediscovers his identity he gropes about for his name, reaching comically close (Naborcroft? Nabarro?) to Nabokov. A joke, certainly, but more than that: Nabokov suggests that at this point Vadim has approached much nearer to his creator than ever before, just as Nabokov himself at the end of *Speak, Memory*, with *his* "you," remembering the birth of his own consciousness and watching over the growth of his son's, feels as near to the creative principle behind life as he does in the creation of his art.

XI

Nabokov knew he had had exceptional happiness in life. In *Look at the Harlequins!* he restates the truths he drew from his own lucky life in terms of someone whose existence is marred by madness and emotional emptiness. That too may be in part a tribute to Véra. After Nabokov began to reject the all-too-accessible imagery of religious and poetic convention for his own analysis of space and time, he had one other major step to take in his art. His early work had often expressed his confidence in the ultimate harmony of things much too directly, in his lyrics, in a story like "Grace," in the warm glow of *Mary*. Within a year of his marriage, he began not simply to affirm his vision but to test it by subjecting it to the challenge of inversion or the threat of negation. Although he already saw art and married love as foreshadowing some ultimate escape from the self and time, he chose in his next novels to focus instead on those who fall short of or invert the values of art (Dreyer, Luzhin, Horn, Hermann) or of shared love (the Dreyers, the Luzhins, the Kretschmars, Hermann and Lydia). But despite the apparent dominance of these reverse sides of his own values, Nabokov's fiction continued to affirm his confidence in a point and a pattern behind life and death: the only difference was that now he made his affirmations richer and stronger by focusing on and ultimately refuting all that seemed to contradict his trust in the underlying harmony of things.

Véra Nabokov shared her husband's delight in the world and trust in the values of the imagination. But where Nabokov was of a self-confessedly buoyant and optimistic disposition, she admits to often seeing the worst side of things first. Perhaps this second change in Nabokov's art, in the year or two following his marriage—his testing his positives by confronting them with their apparent negation, only to reaffirm them at a more complex level—also owes something to his wife's presence beside him.

Nabokov creates Vadim as an inversion of himself not to score points off a character he has made his own inferior, and not to mock misapprehensions about his own life deduced from the superficially heartless worlds of many of his books, but rather to sum up his own impulse to test his art and his happiness against its apparent converse. He suggests that even someone like Vadim, subjected to a lifetime of solitude and hopeless yearning, may find fulfillment at or beyond the margin of life, may discover a way outside the self even richer than the release of love, a way to make the unimaginable transition from forward-facing time to a time with free entry to the past, and a way to resolve his dread that he is only the shadow of some force beyond him. And it is You who helps retrieve Vadim from the realization of his worst fears, You who restores him to his self and who points beyond it.

In the hitherto loveless world of *Look at the Harlequins!* the only relation between love and art seems to have been the erotic passages modeled on Vadim's life that he has "scattered like rotting plums" through his books. Now You discloses the true, priceless link between love and art: at their depths both offer a way beyond the self. And in a very clear sense this You is also Véra Nabokov, the "you" of *Speak, Memory*. A novel that appears terminally narcissistic turns out to be one sustained love song, and no less passionate for all its play.

CHAPTER 27

Unanswered Questions: Montreux, 1974–1977

I . . . have not yet finished milking my mind.

—Nabokov interview, 1974

"I thought you said he had shot himself. That would have been so

much more romantic. I'll be disappointed in your book if it all

ends in bed."

—*The Real Life of Sebastian Knight*

I

EVEN BEFORE he completed *Look at the Harlequins!* at the beginning of April 1974, Nabokov had been eager to tackle his next book. In March, Véra had written warning the Appels, who had planned to join them over the summer, to come before August, because by then her husband would probably be engrossed in his new novel. At the end of April, Nabokov signed a new agreement with McGraw-Hill that anticipated his delivering them six books over the next four years: *Look at the Harlequins!* immediately, a last volume of translated stories a year hence, his next novel in two years' time, a volume of his Russian plays by the end of 1976, his lectures, and new translations of his choice of Russian nineteenth- and twentieth-century verse, by the end of the summer of 1978. Early in May he wrote to Fred Hills, editor-in-chief at McGraw-Hill, that he had "a new novel mapped out rather clearly for next year" and therefore would like *Look at the Harlequins!* published quickly so that the two novels could reach the market spaced as widely apart as possible.[1]

It had always been a peculiarity of Nabokov's method of composition that he would envisage a novel in his mind complete from start to finish before writing it down. Although he would have his new novel, *The Original of Laura*, in his head for three years, a series of accidents and illnesses would keep him from transferring to his index cards more than a patch or two of his bright mental picture.

A year before Nabokov's first stumble toward death, the pressure of other work kept him from his new novel. Two days after completing the fair copy of *Look at the Harlequins!* he and Véra began the third and final session of revisions for the German *Ada* with Ledig Rowohlt and his translators, eight consecutive days' work. A chilly spring aggravated the recurrent neuralgia of Nabokov's last years, but his creative energies were undiminished.[2] Although his nerves still jangled after the rush to complete *Look at the Harlequins!*, he composed a number of chess problems in the month of his seventy-fifth birthday, and three weeks later noted down the first idea for still another new novel: "Inspiration. Radiant insomnia. The flavour and snows of beloved alpine slopes. A novel *without* an I, without a he, but with the narrator, *the gliding eye*, being implied throughout."[3]

During May, he sorted through his letters from Edmund Wilson to send to Elena Wilson, who was assembling her husband's correspondence for *Letters on Literature and Politics*. He wrote her: "I need not tell you what agony it was rereading the exchanges belonging to the early radiant era of our correspondence," and suggested that they publish as a separate volume the complete Nabokov-Wilson letters of the 1940s and 1950s.[4]

Henri Hell and Bernard de Fallois of the French publishing firm of Fayard arrived on May 21 with the long-awaited typescript of Gilles Chahine's translation of *Ada*, which they hoped to make the literary event of the next spring season. Nabokov immediately set about checking the translation, the first pages of which he had seen and partially revised in 1971, after a long search for a satisfactory translator. Chahine had suffered a breakdown turning such a long and complex novel into French for this most exigent of authors—who now found the result chaotic.[5]

Since he wished to minimize delays in processing the proofs of *Look at the Harlequins!* Nabokov canceled a summer vacation in Italy, choosing to remain in reliable Switzerland, where he reserved accommodations in Zermatt for June and July. To figure out which dictionaries and texts he needed on his "vacation" for various urgent proof-reading and translating tasks seemed a hellish chore: "My complicated packing," he mused in his diary, "strangely corresponds to my torments over the composition of a sentence." On June 5 he took a taxi to Zermatt's Hôtel Mont-Cervin. Véra followed a week later.[6]

Nabokov chased butterflies whenever the fickle weather and his meager spare time allowed it. Two entries in his diary show that he took with him other special attributes of his world. Sketching an outline of the Matterhorn's peak, he accentuated its likeness to the styl-

ized profile of Pushkin—the subject of so many of the celebrated marginal doodles in Pushkin's manuscripts—and wrote a brief verse on
Pushkin and death. But another diary note reveals him responding
to a side of life some readers thought he ignored:

> Heard from my balcony young sad woman (all day trundling hay from
> one hut to another, opposite the S. façade of Mount Cervin Hotel):
>   La vie? (Screaming) Mais quelle vie? Toi tu dors ou tu bois. Moi je
> *travaille*, je travaille. C'est ma vie![7]

Late in June, Fred Hills arrived with the page proofs of *Look at the
Harlequins!* Like other visitors, he found Nabokov

> quite unlike his formidable image in literary debate—utterly charming,
> affable, worldly, ready to discuss any subject with ease and pleasure.
> Part of his charm when you were alone with him was that he made you
> feel more intelligent and articulate than you might think yourself. His
> stance was to accept you for the moment as an equal. . . . Without ever
> losing the sense of the personal and specific that might be the subject of
> the discussion he had the ability to raise it to the level of an idea. To chat
> with him was to waltz in the realm of ideas, never staying with any one
> for long. He was impatient with any impulse to belabor a subject.

Leading Hills up a mountain trail, giving him a snap course on the
butterflies as they began the ascent and a snap quiz as they finished
the descent, Nabokov did not hide his delight that a man more than
three decades his junior could not keep up with the pace of his
climb.[8]
In mid-July, a week after Hills left with the corrected page proofs
of *Look at the Harlequins!*, the Appels arrived. Alfred Appel found Nabokov in great shape and as anxious as ever to be off on the chase. It
had rained the first two days of their visit:

> "Oh, when will it clear, *when* will it clear?" groaned Nabokov, pacing
> the hotel lobby as though the world had been created the previous
> night, and he had to examine at once its resplendent marvels, describe
> and name them. On the third day there was light; and early that morn-
> ing—far too early that morning—we accompanied the seventy-five-year-
> old writer-naturalist on a butterfly hunting trip. . . . Nabokov, squinting
> and scanning the horizon, talked on steadily, mainly about the flora and
> fauna around us. "Tolstoy saw that [dense shrubbery] best . . . and you
> remember how Chekhov described those berries in—*ah!* There's one,
> what I've been looking for [name in Latin]"; and Nabokov was off, up
> and over some boulders, net aloft, an assault squad of one in pursuit of
> a pale-yellow butterfly. After depositing his capture ("Wonderful speci-

men, wonderful!") in the worn old Johnson & Johnson Band-Aid tin that
had served him since the forties, the climb continued ("That hostel has
the sweetest of Alpine butters, I speak as an expert, we can stop on the
way down"), Nabokov's good spirits rising with the altitude, save for
one quiet moment during our ascent when he paused on the path and
gestured towards the hillside."This is the timberline of my youth. See
those trees."[9]

Human nature too caught his gaze. Appel observed that Nabokov
was definitely a *vieillard encore vert*, not a senior citizen, and still had
a keen eye for young beauty.[10]

Most of his working time in Zermatt, four to five hours a day, Nabokov spent revising the French *Ada*, at least half an hour per page.
Because of his translator's breakdown, he considered himself obliged
to revamp the whole text: the translator's life would be ruined, he
felt, if he did not bring it up to standard. Appel told him that was the
publisher's responsibility, not his, and that he had his own creative
work to do. When Véra turned to her husband, urging him to heed
Appel's advice, he replied: "It would be dishonorable not to see it
through." Véra smiled resignedly at Appel, as if to say: "There's no
one like him." For the moment that settled the discussion, but a few
days later Nabokov did ask Fayard to appoint someone to weed out
the mannerisms in Chahine's translation. With Jean-Bernard Blan-
denier's preliminary revisions, Nabokov's pace would soon speed up
to an average of twenty minutes per page.[11]

As a last taste of almost pure vacation, the Nabokovs spent five
days at the end of July at Sarnico on the Lago d'Iseo, between Ber-
gamo and Brescia, in a house Dmitri had been lent by friends. While
Dmitri roared about the lake in his motorboat, Nabokov collected on
the slopes above. Once or twice, Dmitri took his father across the
lake to collect on Mont'Isola, the largest inland island in Europe,
which had evolved its own entrancing fauna.[12]

II

At the beginning of August, Nabokov returned to the Montreux Palace. With the end of summer exercise he regained his winter dimensions despite monitoring his weight: eighty-five kilos, his diary soon
recorded, "gained two kilos since returning to Montreux despite my
drinking only half a litre of Bordeaux daily and no beer." In his last
European years Nabokov regularly drank with gusto, perhaps four
glasses of wine over the course of the day and a glass or two of

grappa when visitors came, but he held his drink well and no one ever knew him drunk or even tipsy.[13]

As usual his return from his summer vacation meant a steady stream of visitors lining up for interviews: an academic for his own research, journalists for the *Daily Telegraph* and *Esquire*, Swiss and German television. And now Soviet writers too were beginning to call.[14]

Between the 1920s and the 1960s there had been a sharp division between émigré and Soviet literature. Now émigré literature was moribund, with Bunin, Khodasevich, and Tsvetaeva long dead and Nabokov writing in English. In the 1960s and especially the 1970s the division within Russian literature between Soviet and émigré began to break down as many Soviet writers escaped censorship at home by publishing in the West and often followed their works abroad. After Sinyavsky, Brodsky, Solzhenitsyn, and Victor Nekrasov, Aksyonov, Sokolov, Voinovich, and Zinoviev would soon follow.

Foremost among the publishers of innovative Soviet writing in the West would be Carl and Ellendea Proffer of Ardis Press, Ann Arbor. In 1968, McGraw-Hill had republished the Russian original of *King, Queen, Knave* at the same time as it launched the translation. Nabokov hoped it would repeat the favor for his next and last novels to be translated from the Russian, *Mary* and *Glory*, but McGraw-Hill had barely sold any copies of *Korol', Dama, Valet* and was reluctant to undertake *Mashen'ka* and *Podvig* without the participation of someone who had better access than it did to the Russian-language market. In 1974, Ardis therefore copublished *Mashen'ka* and *Podvig* with McGraw-Hill. By the fall of that year the Proffers were preparing to republish more Russian Nabokoviana on their own, and by mid-1975 they had decided to reprint his complete Russian works.[15]

The Proffers also kept the Nabokovs in touch with Russian writers and Russian readers. Joseph Brodsky had been a fervent admirer of Nabokov until Carl Proffer passed on a softened version of Nabokov's criticism of one of his poems: from that point on, Brodsky began to disparage the older writer. Nadezhda Mandelstam, on the other hand, had argued fiercely with Brodsky at the end of the 1960s *against* Nabokov, but by the mid-1970s had changed to open admiration. She later confessed that her earlier dismissals had sprung solely from envy.[16*]

Supposing that the Soviet secret police were omnipotent within their own territory, Nabokov had suspected that when Solzhenitsyn

---

* She had not been aware that some of the clothes the Proffers had brought her had come from money supplied by Véra Nabokov. See above, p. 570.

published work in the West while still resident in the Soviet Union, he must have done so with KGB compliance.[17] Only when Solzhenitsyn was expelled at the beginning of 1974 and continued his charges from the West did Nabokov decide that even the Soviets must have responded in some measure to world public opinion in not imprisoning their most influential critic. Spurred by the hope that it might now be worth the effort to stand up for Soviet dissidents, he wrote a public appeal in May 1974 on behalf of Vladimir Bukovsky. It appeared in the *Observer*:

> Bukovsky's heroic speech to the court in defence of freedom, and his five years of martyrdom in a despicable psychiatric jail will be remembered long after the torturers he defied have rotted away. But that is poor consolation for a prisoner with rheumatic carditis who has been transferred now to a Permian camp and will perish there unless a public miracle rescues him. I wish to urge all persons and organisations that have more contact with Russia than I have to do whatever can be done to help that courageous and precious man.[18]

At the end of the year, Nabokov would hear from Carl Proffer about the trial of Vladimir Maramzin and the confiscation and burning of Maramzin's books, among them his copy of the Russian *Lolita*. Nabokov sent a telegram to the Leningrad branch of the Soviet Writers' Union: "Am appalled to learn that yet another writer is martyred just for being a writer. Maramzin's immediate release indispensable to prevent an atrocious new crime."[19]

In mid-September 1974, Victor Nekrasov came to visit Nabokov in Montreux, the first writer Nabokov had met who had grown up entirely within the Soviet system. A month later Vladimir Maximov visited and proved somewhat more to Nabokov's taste.[20] And between these two visitors, Solzhenitsyn and his wife were expected to call.

In August, Nabokov had read *The Gulag Archipelago*. There, Solzhenitsyn had referred to the complete Soviet suppression of all signs of émigré intellectual life—such as for instance the existence of the "unprecedented" writer Nabokov-Sirin. Nabokov's reaction to Solzhenitsyn and *The Gulag Archipelago* was more mixed: "His style is a kind of juicy journalese, formless, wordy and repetitious, but endowed with considerable oratorical force. The lasting virtue of the work is its trenchant historical truth annihilating the smugness of old Leninists."[21]

As soon as he heard of Solzhenitsyn's arrival in the West, Nabokov had written to welcome him and to let Solzhenitsyn know he would be happy to meet him. In the fall of 1974, still stationed in Zurich, Solzhenitsyn planned a tour with his wife that would take them through Montreux. When he wrote suggesting a time, Nabokov penciled it in his diary—"October 6, 11:00 Solzhenitsyn and wife"—but did not realize that confirmation was expected. According to Solzhenitsyn's biographer Michael Scammell:

> By the time of the Solzhenitsyns' departure from Zurich, there had been no reply to their letter, and although they telephoned the house each day, no answer had come by the time they reached Montreux. Uncertain of what this silence meant, they reached the hotel, crawled past the end of the driveway debating whether to go in, and eventually decided to drive off, fearing that Nabokov might be ill or have some other compelling reason for not seeing them that day.

When Maximov visited the Nabokovs two weeks later, he heard from them that they had ordered lunch for four in a private dining room, and sat waiting for their guests over an hour. They were still most puzzled and distressed that the Solzhenitsyns had failed to turn up at all. Maximov visited the Solzhenitsyns shortly afterward, learned their side of the story, and telephoned Nabokov at once to explain how the confusion had arisen. But, Scammell writes, "the two principals did not speak to one another, and in the end did not meet."[22]

III

Early in October, Nabokov began translating for the last volume of his Russian stories, *Details of a Sunset*. Dmitri had prepared draft translations of some stories, while his father tackled others on his own. But the chief task facing him for the winter was the remainder of the harrowing French *Ada*. He knew he had to rid himself of all his translations before settling down to the new novel "that keeps adding nightly a couple of hours to my habitual insomnias." In the last week of November he resumed the French *Ada* in earnest, working from six o'clock to nine o'clock each morning and sometimes two more hours in the late afternoon to meet the January deadline, while also preparing *Details of a Sunset* for the same deadline and correcting the usual number of proofs. Sometimes the search for the right rendition of a single phrase would take longer than the twenty minutes he needed for the average page. He wrote his French publisher: "The Italian translation of the poor girl was *bâclée*, bungled, botched, in less than two months. The German one took years to ripen, the publisher and translator coming here for numerous sessions. But it is to the French *Ada* that I am giving the blood of my brain, and I will not be spurred on by anything short of a private illusion of perfection."[23]

As he noted how much of the translation remained, he stepped up the pace until by late December he was spending almost all day on *Ada*. Outside, the winter was the mildest since the Nabokovs had settled in Montreux, with not a single flake of snow. Inside, it was the most severe. Despite rising to commence work at six o'clock, the seventy-five-year-old Nabokov not only worked all day, switching to *Details of a Sunset* in the afternoon, but also began to train himself to take no more than a quick dinner at six-thirty before returning to his room for another stint at *Ada*. The demanding hours and the pressure of the deadlines—especially nerve-racking since they prevented him from starting "the only thing that is important to him: his new book"—were a major factor, Dmitri Nabokov feels certain, in weakening his father during his last two years of life.[24]

Nabokov finished revising the *Ada* translation in the third week of February 1975. The pressure did not ease even then, as he still had to correct galleys and page proofs steadily through March and April to meet the May publication date. Curiously, despite the punishing strain of the task, he was ready in April to contemplate another still more demanding: translating *Ada* entirely by himself "into Russian—not sovjargon and not soljournalese—but romantic and precise Russian."[25]

Late in 1974, Teddy Kollek, the mayor of Jerusalem, had invited Nabokov to visit as an official guest. Nabokov responded, joking that he eagerly looked forward to pursuing butterflies in the Moab hills, and kept searching for a time when work pressure would leave him free to take up the invitation. In April 1976 he would reserve an apartment at Mishkenat Sha'ananim, an old building restored for visiting artists and scholars, for the month of April 1977, but when that time arrived he would be fit to leave Montreux only by ambulance.[26]

When Kollek's invitation first came, Israel at least offered a dream of escape while business chores piled up over the onerous winter of 1974–1975. Dealing with these chores proved more difficult than ever, for Véra had by now become rather deaf and her secretary had fallen ill.[27]

The literary trust Nabokov had set up fifteen years earlier to ease his tax burden had outlived its usefulness and had to be wound up. Once the paperwork was done Nabokov sent the trustee, his friend William McGuire, a whole case of Chivas Regal in thanks.[28]

Field's biography also had to be dealt with. After threatening that he would be denied permission to quote from all unpublished Nabokov materials, Nabokov's New York lawyers began negotiating early in 1975 with Field's editor at Viking. Over the next fifteen months they would manage to have Field eliminate or revise almost all the passages Nabokov objected to most strongly.[29]

Another serious concern was the long delays in McGraw-Hill's payments, especially for income derived from foreign rights. In part the delays were caused by McGraw-Hill's enormously complex accounting procedures, but Nabokov also feared his publisher was cooling toward him. Sales of *Transparent Things*, *Strong Opinions*, and *Lolita: A Screenplay* had been very poor. Published in the fall of 1974, *Look at the Harlequins!* had had a mixed critical reception, often being deplored by keen Nabokov readers but welcomed by hacks who found it less taxing than *Ada* or *Transparent Things*. Though nominated for a National Book Award, *Look at the Harlequins!* too sold rather poorly. McGraw-Hill was both tightening its belt and losing what slight appetite it had had for fiction. It also had little interest in promoting Nabokov: because of the inflation and currency exchange provisions built into his first agreement with McGraw-Hill, the recent rise in inflation and weakening of the dollar ensured his publisher now made almost no profit on his works.[30]

Vexed at having to deal with so many separate departments within McGraw-Hill, the Nabokovs asked to coordinate their correspondence through Beverly Loo, the subsidiary rights manager and executive editor of the general books division. Although she traveled to Europe twice a year, Loo felt too daunted to see the Nabokovs. After her fall 1974 trip, however, Véra Nabokov suggested it would have been appropriate for her to visit. Loo took that as a command, and in mid-April 1975 stopped in Montreux for the first time. They had arranged to meet in the hotel's main lounge. Only Nabokov was there, pacing up and down. Although he had never met her and had not been told she was an Asian, he came straight over to her and at once put her at her ease. Over the coming years she rapidly found herself accepted as almost a member of the family.[31]

In May 1975 the publication of *Ada ou l'ardeur* occasioned a spate of interviews in the French media. Most important by far was Nabokov's appearance on Bernard Pivot's extremely influential television book program, *Apostrophes*. Pivot's persistence overcame Nabokov's resistance to a live show filmed before a live audience, albeit on Nabokov's own special terms: instead of the usual round table discussion, only Pivot was to ask him questions, all to be sent in advance. Nabokov had to travel to Paris for the broadcast, which took place on May 30 at 9:40 P.M., past his usual bedtime. He read his carefully drafted answers from cards propped against a stack of books piled before him. To many in Pivot's regular audience, accustomed to a lively and often anarchic debate among a number of invited authors,

Nabokov's responses seemed appallingly unspontaneous. Only occasionally did he allow himself an unplanned jest, as when Pivot offered him tea from a teapot that in fact contained only whiskey. To the laughter of the invited guests, all in on the substitution, Nabokov pretended to study the color of the liquid as Pivot poured, and commented that it looked a little strong. When Pivot offered to pour more, Nabokov responded: "It's coffee this time, I think." Pivot himself would later name the broadcast with Nabokov as his proudest memory in the whole history of the show, and he would rescreen the program again and again.[32]*

In France, *Ada* repeated the excellent critical and popular success it had had in Italy and Germany. *L'Exprès* hailed it as "le plus beau livre de souvenirs depuis Proust et Chateaubriand," two book clubs selected it, and it rose to number two on the best-seller list.[33]

IV

The cost of *Ada*'s French triumph had been high, and on June 18, Nabokov left with his wife for a much-needed rest at Davos. The tranquillity and beauty of the mountains and the chance to chase butterflies restored his spirits only to deal a cruel blow to his flesh. Late in July, now seventy-six, he was climbing at 1,900 meters when he fell painfully down a steep, slippery slope. His butterfly net slid still further to become wedged on the branch of a fir. Climbing after his net he suffered a second, even more painful fall and could not get up. He laughed at his predicament—Hugh Person stuff, this—and waited for the cablecar to glide overhead. Seeing him laughing as well as waving, those on board assumed there was nothing wrong. Only when the cablecar operator noticed the tanned old man in shorts still in the same spot as they skimmed past again did he realize he needed help, and at the end of his run sent two men down to carry Nabokov out on a stretcher. He had had to wait two and a half hours between his fall and his rescue.[34]

He had not broken any bones, but had to spend several days in bed. Although by the end of the month he was out chasing butterflies again with another net—the first one was still hanging on that branch "like Ovid's lyre"—some of those close to him thought he never seemed quite the same after his fall.[35]

Certainly after Nabokov returned at the end of July from the crisp

* "C'est un écrivain d'une qualité très rare, un des meilleurs du vingtième siècle. . . . Je suis heureux d'avoir tant insisté. Quel homme c'était! Quel humour! Quelle érudition! Quelle finesse!"

air of Davos to sweltering Montreux he felt increasingly unwell. Early in September he reported to the Montreux Hospital for a urographic test. That and other tests showed he had a tumor on the prostate, quite likely cancerous. On October 15 he entered a small private hospital in Lausanne, the Clinique de Montchoisi, and was operated on the next day. To everyone's relief the growth turned out to be a benign adenoma. Two weeks later Nabokov returned home, still exhausted after his illness. Against his physician's advice he resumed work immediately, and so slowed down an agonizing convalescence.[36]

At the beginning of December he announced he was "returning zestfully to the abyss of my new novel," tentatively entitled *A Passing Fashion*, and on December 10 he began writing steadily, at least three cards per day. Despite a mild infection that set in as a delayed consequence of the operation, he was deep in the new novel by late January and even hoping to complete it by midsummer. Age and nervous energy had made his insomnia worse and worse, quite "hopeless" in fact as each new pill became ineffective after two or three nights. Early in February he compiled a progress report in his diary: "New novel more or less completed and copied 54 cards. In 4 batches from different parts of the novel. Plus notes and drafts. 50 days since Dec. 10, 1975. Not too much." By mid-February he had decided on the book's final title, *The Original of Laura*, and reported to Fred Hills, "I am having a marvelous time with my new novel."[37]

Other projects were afoot. Delighted with Ardis's plans to reset all his Russian stories for a two-volume collected edition, he decided to translate into Russian all the modifications he had made in turning the stories into English. By March he had changed his mind, and asked Ardis to choose instead between either a small volume of his "patriotic" verse—fifteen or twenty poems he had considered too topical for *Poems and Problems*—or a largish edition of his collected Russian verse. The Proffers naturally preferred a volume of his collected poems.[38]

Another plan had been on Nabokov's mind since the spring of 1974, when he had sifted through his correspondence with Edmund Wilson. Now in January 1976 he suggested to McGraw-Hill that it publish the Nabokov-Wilson letters. Impressed by Simon Karlinsky's copious and astute annotations in his edition of Chekhov's letters, he recommended Karlinsky to Elena Wilson, who agreed with his choice.[39] But neither the Russian poems nor the *Nabokov-Wilson Letters* would reach the bookstores until two years after his death.

In his diary Nabokov continued to monitor the progress of *The Original of Laura*, affectionately abbreviated *TOOL*. "Proceeding at the rate of 5 or 6 cards per day," he noted at the beginning of April, "but a lot of rewriting," A few days later: "transcribed in final form 50 cards = 5000 words." He worked energetically throughout the month, and by April 20 reported optimistically to McGraw-Hill that he had passed the hundred printed page mark, about half of the novel. A week later he anticipated completing it before the summer was over. It was not to be.[40]

V

The last book he ever finished and the last of his books to appear in his lifetime, *Details of a Sunset and Other Stories*, was published in the spring of 1976. It was received enthusiastically by those who reviewed it—it consisted mostly of unperplexing early Nabokov stories, with an average date of 1928—but it did not catch the public eye. Its predecessor, *Tyrants Destroyed and Other Stories*, had just been nominated for a National Book Award only to fail—like *Pnin*, *Pale Fire*, *Transparent Things*, and *Look at the Harlequins!*—to win the award itself.

The attention Nabokov received from writers and readers in the mid-1970s in fact was oddly mixed. Right up to his death he could be hailed as "surely the greatest literary artist living today." Writers like Updike and Burgess, Solzhenitsyn and Robbe-Grillet, leading figures of the three literatures he knew well, singled him out as a genius or as the most interesting writer of the last few decades. But as J. D. O'Hara wrote in the year Nabokov died, he occupied "a strange position in the Alps of contemporary literature, at once admired and forgotten."[41]

There were a number of reasons for his singular status. So many new works had appeared over the past fourteen years—*Pale Fire*; *The Gift*; *The Defense*; the four-volume *Eugene Onegin*; *Despair*; *The Eye*; *Nabokov's Quartet*; *Speak, Memory*; *The Waltz Invention*; the Russian *Lolita*; *King, Queen, Knave*; *Ada*; *Mary*; *Poems and Problems*; *Glory*; *Transparent Things*; *A Russian Beauty*; *Strong Opinions*; *Lolita: A Screenplay*; *Look at the Harlequins!*; *Tyrants Destroyed*; the revised *Eugene Onegin*; and now *Details of a Sunset*, twenty-nine volumes in all—that readers and critics were saturated. McGraw-Hill, with its declining interest in fiction and in an author whose works now earned them a minuscule return per volume, did little to promote his new books.

As Nabokov dug deeper in the barrel of his literary past for his new translations, he came up with books like *Details of a Sunset* or *Mary*, which for all their merits could not generate the sort of excitement

The Gift and *The Defense* had aroused when they were translated in the early 1960s. At the other end of his career, his latest three English novels had all provoked discontent. While many thought *Ada*'s exuberance revealed a failure of both moral insight and artistic control, *Transparent Things* disconcerted by its uncompromising spareness, and *Look at the Harlequins!* by its apparent narcissism. Teachers of American literature who had eagerly taught *Lolita*, *Pnin*, *Pale Fire*, and *Speak, Memory* in the mid-1960s had become alarmed at the amount of Russian *Ada* seemed to suggest they needed to know. Andrew Field's *Nabokov: His Life in Art*, which still remained the best-known critical work on its subject, provided no evidence to support his high claims for Nabokov's position in modern literature, and impoverished Nabokov's themes by reducing them to a concern for the role of the artist.[42]

Intellectual fashions too had changed. With the rise of feminism, novelists like Doris Lessing and Margaret Atwood aroused excited attention. Someone so decidedly male as Nabokov, equipped by his upbringing with gentlemanly notions of honor and more comfortable with woman as muse than woman as writer, seemed a relic of the past. After all, it was he who had created Humbert, for whom Lolita barely exists except as a mere object of *his* emotion and *his* imagination. It could be easily overlooked that for Nabokov Lolita was quite a different creature, a person in her own right, and one of the characters he found most admirable in all his works, or that his book seethed with indignation of Humbert's manipulation of *all* the women in his life.

In the 1960s and 1970s, as the world tried to shake off the legacy of colonialism and to recognize the limitations of a Eurocentric view of history, readers turned to Latin American, Caribbean, and African novelists as different as García Márquez, Naipaul, and Achebe. Nabokov, on the other hand, was more decidedly European in emphasis than any other writer of his time, less sympathetic to "boring ethnopsychics"[43] or to any kind of folk or primitive art. On the other hand he also dismissed much of the Western heritage, from medieval Christianity to modern Marxism, from Greek drama to French neoclassicism; he had no illusions about the savagery of colonization; he strongly opposed racism of all kinds. But by the 1970s that seemed not enough to balance his unswerving allegiance to the best of Western culture, the best of Western freedoms.

Nabokov had always been at odds with his times, although he also knew that he needed to localize the timeless in human emotion by mastering the particulars of his own time and place. Asked in 1963 about his literary future, he had imagined opening a newspaper of

2063 and finding on the book page: " 'Nobody reads Nabokov or Ful-
merford today.' Awful question: Who is this unfortunate Fulmer-
ford?"[44] During the 1960s his reputation had been second to none.
Now, one critic could declare that Nabokov had had his years of
glory but had become "an anachronism with little to offer serious
readers"—although another, a few weeks before Nabokov's death,
could still call him "the Western world's foremost writer."[45] By the
beginning of the 1990s, after a posthumous lull, a resurgence of interest in Nabokov was clearly in evidence, in the U.S., France, Germany, Italy, and the USSR, and more are now ready to name him the
foremost writer of the mid-twentieth century, and one of the greatest
of all times.

VI

Nabokov had more immediate worries. On April 24, 1976, the day
after his seventy-seventh birthday, he noted in his diary: "At 1 a.m.
was raised from brief sleep by horrible anguish of the 'this-is-it' sort.
Discreetly screamed, hoping to wake Véra in next room yet failing to
succeed (because I felt quite alright)." A week later he caught his foot
on something in his bathroom floor, tripped, and crashed, jarring the
back of his head. Concussed, he was rushed by ambulance to CHUV,
the Vaud Canton hospital complex in Lausanne, and remained there
for ten days. On his return he found that even on a short stroll his
legs felt like lead. Nights were no lighter as sleeping pills proved less
and less effective. Constantly trying out the new capsules his doctors
prescribed, he noted that one taken on three consecutive nights
caused rich hallucinations. "Never again!" he vowed.[46]
    At the end of May he and Véra planned to leave on June 8 for six
or seven weeks' holiday at Flims in the Engadine. Early in June, an
attack of lumbago made him postpone his departure for a week.
Three days before the new departure date, his temperature began to
rise. He was soon seriously ill with an undiagnosed infection and
had lapsed into semiconsciousness by the time he was admitted on
June 17 to Montchoisi, the private clinic in Lausanne where he had
had his prostate operation the previous October.[47]
    In his clear moments Nabokov read. Shortly before his latest return
to the hospital, he had enjoyed a novel Carl Proffer sent in trepidation from Ardis Press, Sasha Sokolov's *School for Fools*. Nabokov declared it "an enchanting, tragic and touching book," the best example
of recent Soviet fiction he had seen. He had also read with rapture
Howe's *Butterflies of North America*, "the kind of work that we,

American lepists, have been awaiting ever since Holland's wretched and dishonest compilation appeared in the 'revised' edition of 1932." He took this to the hospital with him, along with a third book that elicited a third kind of professional admiration: Charles Singleton's six-volume translation of the *Divine Comedy*. He found both translation and commentary excellent, and wrote to his friend William McGuire at the Bollingen Press, the book's publisher: "What a triumphant joy it is to see the honest light of literality take over again, after ages of meretricious paraphrase!"[48]

But his most poignant reading was of an unfinished book. Day after day, perhaps fifty times during several weeks of delirium, he returned to *The Original of Laura*, so complete in his mind, and kept reading it aloud to "a small dream audience in a walled garden. My audience consisted of peacocks, pigeons, my long-dead parents, two cypresses, several young nurses crouching around, and a family doctor so old as to be almost invisible."[49]

The doctors outside his delirium still could not ascertain its cause. Apparently Nabokov at first had a touch of bronchial pneumonia, but the real reason for his fever was not discovered until Dmitri suggested sodium and potassium tests—which showed levels of both low enough to cause what was by now almost a semicomatose state—and additional tests that focused on the area where his father had been operated on in October. Nabokov was found to have an infection of the urinary tract grave enough to warrant his immediate transfer to the hospital.[50]

Accordingly on July 9 he was moved into the Nestlé Hospital within the CHUV complex. Since it was understaffed, private nurses were hired to attend him. By late July he was beginning to recover but was still very feeble and exhausted by the weeks of high fever. Normally he was at a peak of fitness by late summer—this season was the first to go by without a butterfly expedition since his work on *Eugene Onegin* had kept him at his desk in 1957—but now his prolonged spell with no exercise whatsoever impeded his recovery. Véra too had had a wretched summer, with two short sojourns in the hospital herself after she had damaged her spine trying to support her husband as he fell, and found she could still move her right shoulder and arm only with great difficulty.[51]

A cocky young doctor at CHUV assured Véra that her husband was on the mend, and on September 7 Nabokov was discharged from CHUV. He and Véra at once checked in for two weeks of convalescence and physiotherapy at the Valmont Clinic at Glion, a sanatorium for the rich and famous situated on the slopes above Montreux and with spectacular views over Lake Geneva and the Savoy Alps.[52]

VII

On September 21, after more than three months of hospitalization, Nabokov returned to the Montreux Palace. Beverly Loo visited at the end of the month and found him frail, shuffling along with difficulty, but with his mind and spirit undimmed. She too had been in the hospital recently, and said she enjoyed it. "I don't mind being in hospital either," Nabokov said. "Oh, you complain all the time," laughed Véra. "Only because you're not there. I would never mind a hospital stay if I could take you, wrap you up in my top pocket and take you with me." His comment only confirmed Beverly Loo's observation that Nabokov was "absolutely madly in love with Véra . . . you could see it in every look."[53]

Late in September he was still suffering from pain in his legs and occasional slight temperatures, but on September 30 he recorded with delight that not only was his temperature normal, but "pain in legs suddenly vanished after 3 months. *I can even run!*" Over the rest of the year he began the selection process for his collected Russian verse, marking with a blue or red pencil cross the poems he liked in his own slender manuscript albums of 1917–1923, his mother's thick marbled albums of the 1910s and 1920s, and Véra's albums of clippings she had taken from the émigré press since the early 1920s.[54]

Weakened by his fever, his dearth of exercise, and his continued lack of sleep, Nabokov felt what by his standards seemed "a terrible laziness." He continued to work on *The Original of Laura* in his head, where it was by now practically finished, but the physical effort of writing it all down still posed a problem. Dictating was out of the question. Even deadlines did not help. Although the French publisher Julliard pressed him to assess sample translations of *Tyrants Destroyed*, the sheer physical effort of handling two texts proved too much.[55]

At the end of November he did manage an interview. He still sounded like his old self: "My caloric diet usually consists of bread and butter, transparent honey, wine, roast duck with red whortleberry jam, and similar plain fare. . . . My literary regime is more fancy, but two hours of meditation, between 2 a.m. and 4 a.m. when the effect of a first sleeping pill evaporates and that of a second one has not begun and a spell of writing in the afternoon, are about all my new novel needs."[56] Although even months after his last return from the hospital he still felt groggy, he tried to allow no sign of weakness, no sense that his life might be closing off. He said he still looked forward keenly to butterfly collecting in Israel in May 1977; he was still ready to answer another interviewer—his last—early in February 1977 that he anticipated returning to the United States at the first opportunity. He spoke to friends who came to visit as if his new novel was almost completed. But that last BBC interview belies the vigor he still tried to inject into his words. His skin looks gray and flabby, he breathes hard, he moves very slowly. He seems rigid, his voice lacks spring, he makes verbal lapses even as he tries to read his prepared answers. His insomnia was worse than ever, he felt weak all day long, and he would never recover enough energy to transfer more than a fraction of his new novel from mental image to written text.[57]

VIII

Nevertheless, in February 1977 his condition seemed to be improving, although he still had to walk with a cane and day after day had to forfeit his afternoon spell of writing when another sleepless night left his mind too numb for the rigors of composition. During an unseasonably warm March, Dmitri would walk his father, thin and weak, a few hundred feet up and down the Grand-Rue: "Father always had a cheerful quip for the druggist and news-vendor," Dmitri recollects, "and never once complained of his weakness." Bella Akhmadulina, the leading Soviet woman poet, visited early in March. Unaware how vibrant Nabokov had looked two summers before, she thought him in good health and high spirits. Certainly he still continued to tease and amuse friends and strangers with all the energy he could muster.[58]

In mid-March, Dmitri drove to Geneva to hear a friend sing in *The Marriage of Figaro*. Exulting in the mild spring air, he had taken no coat. When he emerged from the theater a cold wind had blown up. He caught a chill, a day later had a dry cough, and the next day was in bed with that year's particularly virulent influenza. His mother too succumbed. Although Dmitri had begged his father not to come too close, Nabokov padded into his son's room that evening with a trayful of food and a volume of Musset for him to read.[59]

"A couple of days later," reports Dmitri, "his voice grew husky, and he started clearing his throat more often than usual; but for several days he insisted he was fine." Soon he was in bed with a rising temperature. By March 19 he had a very high fever and was taken by ambulance back to the Nestlé Hospital in Lausanne. Looking around a room that was a mirror image of the one he had been assigned the previous summer, Nabokov noted in his diary, "Everything begins anew." Influenza soon led to a touch of bronchial pneumonia that kept him in the hospital for seven weeks.[60]

Montreux was in the throes of a wretched autumnlike spring when he returned on May 7. A few days later Carl and Ellendea Proffer visited. Since their one previous visit they had republished five of Nabokov's Russian books and were gearing up to put all the rest into print. Nabokov was delighted: how different all this was from his plight a quarter of a century before. But the Proffers, who had seen Nabokov at seventy in such radiant health, were shocked now to see him so stooped and shrunken. Moving freely but evidently in pain, he seemed no slower mentally and still tried to amuse them, joking about his Andalusian daughter or pretending to sit on a trayful of tea things on a couch.[61]

He was still cheerful, and still writing The Original of Laura when he was able. But on May 18 he recorded in his diary: "Mild delirium, temp. 37.5°. Is it possible that everything starts anew?" His handwriting had become unsteady, his concentration poor. His sister Elena, no mean Scrabble player, enjoyed losing to her brother at Russian Scrabble. When she visited now and played another game, the greatest verbal magician of his time lost by two hundred points.[62]

In the first days of June his temperature began to rise slightly, oscillating between 37.1 and 37.6 degrees centigrade, but without any change in his general condition. On June 5, with his temperature up to 38 degrees, he was taken back to the Lausanne hospital complex to try to establish why he could not shake off the fever that had been bothering him on and off ever since his prostate operation. Tests of every kind failed to identify the cause.[63]

His condition seemed irritatingly irresolvable, even serious, but hardly life-threatening. He tried to read Field's Nabokov: His Life in Part, just published at last in the U.S., but was bored and put it aside. In mid-June he was still looking forward to a little trip to Cannes with Véra as soon as he was strong enough to travel. A few days later one of his doctors announced that he had identified the trouble as pseudomonas, a common hospital bacillus, but that test too proved negative.[64]

By now Nabokov was very weak and the doctors could only administer antibiotics in rather haphazard fashion. Toward the end of June, Véra retorted to a doctor who told her that her husband was getting better that she thought he was dying. The doctor insisted that if *he* said his patient was better, he was better. But Nabokov continued to weaken, and even the doctors became apprehensive. Dmitri writes: "As Mother and I waited for the professors' pregnant pauses to give birth, the air of condescending reassurance had disappeared, and one had the troubling sensation that the physicians' manner was changing from bedside to graveside." Nabokov's attitude, hopeful so long, had changed to one of resignation.[65]

Parting from his father for the second to last time, Dmitri kissed his forehead as he always did for a goodbye or a goodnight. Nabokov's eyes suddenly welled with tears. When Dmitri asked him why, he replied that a certain butterfly was already on the wing, and his eyes made clear that he expected never to see it again.[66]

As Dmitri recalls, "The end was quick: a chance draft from door and window simultaneously left open by an incautious, sneezing maid." Nabokov's temperature rose to 39 degrees, then 40 degrees. A massive bronchial congestion set in, and great quantities of fluid were drained from his lungs. Antibiotics and physiotherapy did nothing to keep his condition from deteriorating.[67]

On June 30 he was moved into intensive care. As the bronchial congestion worsened, his breathing became labored. Still another medical expert had been called in and was to visit the patient for the first time on July 2. But that bright, sunny day it was obvious Nabokov was slipping away. Véra and Dmitri sat in the room with him, sure he was conscious but simply too weak to react to their presence. At ten minutes to seven that evening he emitted an abrupt threefold groan, his heart stilled, and he was dead.[68]

IX

The immediate cause of death was clear—the fluid buildup in his lungs—but the reason he had succumbed to fever so frequently over the previous eighteen months remained a mystery.[69]

Nabokov's body was cremated at a simple nonreligious funeral service in Vevey on July 7, 1977, with only a dozen family members and friends present, including Véra, Dmitri, Elena, Nabokov's cousins Nicolas and Sergey, his German publisher, Ledig Rowohlt, Beverly Loo, and his Montreux friends Martin and Margaret Newstead. The next day only Véra and Dmitri were present when his ashes were interred, under the shadow of the chateau of Chatelard, in Clarens cemetery. Another Nabokov lies buried there, his great-aunt Praskovia-Alexandria Nabokov, née Tolstoy, 1837–1909, her grave marked by a statue. Nabokov's tomb, by contrast, is simply a broad unornamented slab of marble, a deep bruised blue in color, with the terse inscription: "VLADIMIR NABOKOV ECRIVAIN 1899–1977."

Two weeks after his funeral, an American memorial service was organized by Beverly Loo. On New York's hottest day for forty years—the temperature reached 104 degrees Fahrenheit, the humidity was stifling—there was standing room only as five hundred people packed the McGraw-Hill auditorium to hear Harold McGraw, Alfred Appel, Julian Moynahan, Alfred Kazin, John Updike, and Dmitri Nabokov pay tribute.⁷⁰

But Nabokov's true memorials are elsewhere. In the remarks of two freshmen Alfred Appel overheard after his first class for the year on *Lolita*: "Don't you love every sentence?" "Yes. Which are your favorite passages?"⁷¹ Or on the jacket notes for a 1989 Soviet recording of Nabokov's prose: "You feel compelled to reread every sentence several times, enjoying its rhythm, its metaphors, its similes. Reverently preserving in his own work the best traditions of Russian prose, the prose of Pushkin, Lermontov, Chekhov and Bunin, Nabokov creates his own mode of writing, unique in its system of images and in the fluidity and musicality of its phrasing."⁷²

That note on a Melodia record sleeve marks the most surprising development of all in the decade since Nabokov's death. He was rehabilitated in the Soviet Union in July 1986, at first tentatively and then in a rush: by 1988 even *Invitation to a Beheading* and *The Gift* were available to Soviet readers, albeit at first in texts with some politically sensitive passages suppressed. Nabokov came to be regarded officially as a national treasure. Evenings devoted to his work were staged in the hall of the former Tenishev School, and 47 Hertzen Street, the sites of Vyra and Batovo, and the manor of Rozhdestveno became part of an official Nabokov tour. He became so popular he was jokingly referred to as "*the* writer of perestroika." In the English-speaking world, Dmitri Nabokov supervised the publication of his father's lectures and letters, and translated more stories, poems, and plays, now for the first time without his father's ultimate revision. Véra Nabokov, although slow and frail, translated *Pale Fire* into Russian, supervised the translation of *Pnin*, and even, in her eighties, talked of translating *Ada* too into Russian. Despite her son's entreaties that she visit him in Florida, and perhaps stay on if she liked it, she would not move from the Montreux Palace, or from the double plot of her husband's grave less than half a mile away.⁷³ In 1990 she had to vacate the Montreux Palace when the Cygne wing underwent major renovations, and found an apartment overlooking the hotel and still closer to the cemetery. After her death, on April 7, 1991, her ashes were buried in the same urn as her husband's.

X

Nabokov had begun to speculate about death in his own distinctive fashion even before the best friend of his childhood had his forehead ripped open by a fusillade of bullets or the father he loved so dearly was shot through the heart. In novel after novel he would draw on all the power of his imagination to depict the surprise of death: Luzhin plunging down to the ground as if into a chessboard; Smurov shooting himself yet continuing to recount his story; Martin disappearing into the landscape as if he had stepped into a picture; Cincinnatus standing up, after he is beheaded, to walk toward creatures like himself; Van and Ada dying together into their book; Hugh Person choking amidst dancing flames as he is welcomed over the threshold of death by the dead narrator, and much, much more.

In December 1974, almost three years before his death, Nabokov set down a first tentative title for *The Original of Laura*: *Dying is Fun*.[74] As far as can be seen from this side of the screen, dying for him would be no fun at all, no final bedazzling transition. The great unanswered question of death would be obscured by a series of minor infections that left unanswered the questions his wife and son put to his doctors. Slowly robbed of the strength he needed to set down the story he saw so distinctly, Nabokov in turn would leave us as readers with our curiosity about his last novel forever unanswered.

In an unpublished, unfinished continuation of *The Gift*, he had once written: "The bitterness of an interrupted life is nothing compared to the bitterness of an interrupted work: the probability of a continuation of the first beyond the grave seems infinite by comparison with the hopeless incompleteness of the second. *There* perhaps it will seem nonsense, but *here* all the same it remains unwritten."[75] The best answer to that comes from a work Nabokov did finish and publish:

> "But we still have to decide about the damned last wish. Well, what have you selected?" . . .
>
> "To finish writing something," whispered Cincinnatus half-questioningly but then he frowned, straining his thoughts, and suddenly understood that everything had in fact been written already.[76]

ACKNOWLEDGMENTS

A S I WROTE in *Vladimir Nabokov: The Russian Years*, this has never been an official or authorized biography, but it would never have been undertaken and written had not not Véra Nabokov condoned my researches. She gave me access to her husband's papers in Montreux and the Library of Congress, she submitted to endless interviews, and she trusted to what I would do with my independence. In return I let her see all I wrote and took note of her painstaking comments on matters of style, fact, and interpretation in every part of my text and at several stages of its composition. Our occasionally lively, even fierce, disagreements have never impinged a jot on my freedom to write what I construe the evidence requires.

Dmitri Nabokov has repeatedly tried to square my need for information with his strong desire to defend his parents' instinct for privacy. Although publicly hostile to any negative opinions of his father based on ignorance or impercipience, he has also respected and defended my independence and my right to the sometimes severe judgments I pass on individual Nabokov works.

Nabokov's sister Elena Sikorski, now living in Geneva, has always been eager to guide me through the past she and her brother knew and to pass on all the information she has received from her extensive network of Soviet sources. Nabokov's cousin Sergey Nabokov of Brussels has given me all the information he could about the genealogy of the Nabokov family. Sergey Nabokov, Elena Sikorski, and Dmitri Nabokov have also commented in detail on the parts of my text covering the periods with which they were most familiar: family background, 1910s–1920s, and 1940s onward, respectively.

I would also like to thank the following individuals for sharing their recollections of Nabokov and/or making available correspondence and other documents. Many have been exceptionally generous.

In the United States: Meyer H. and Ruth Abrams, Ithaca, N.Y.; Robert M. Adams, Santa Fe; Vladimir Alexandrov, New Haven; the late Elizaveta Marinel-Allan, New York; Robert Alter, Berkeley; Samuel Anderson, Lawrence, Kans.; Svetlana Andrault de Langeron, St. Petersburg, Fla.; Alfred and Nina Appel, Evanston, Ill.; Marina Astman, New York; Gennady Barabtarlo, Columbia, Mo.; Natalia Barosin, New York; Nina Berberova, Princeton; Sylvia Berkman, Cambridge, Mass.; Alison Bishop, Ithaca, N.Y.; Max Black, Ithaca, N.Y.;

Alexander Brailow, Keuka Park, N.Y.; Clarence Brown, Princeton; F. Martin Brown, Colorado Springs; Matthew J. Bruccoli, Columbia, S.C.; Richard M. Buxbaum, Berkeley; Frank Carpenter, Cambridge, Mass.; Phyllis and Kenneth Christiansen, Grinnell, Iowa; Milton Cowan, Ithaca, N.Y.; Lucia Davidova, New York; Jean-Jacques Demorest, Tucson; Jason Epstein, New York; Ephim Fogel, Ithaca, N.Y.; J. Vail Foy, Moscow, Idaho; John G. Franclemont, Ithaca, N.Y.; Hannah French, Rye, N.H.; Orval and Helen French, Ithaca, N.Y.; Herbert J. Gold, San Francisco; Hannah Green, New York; Albert J. Guerard, Palo Alto; Claudio Guillén, Cambridge, Mass.; John Hagopian, Binghamton, N.Y.; Joel Hedgpeth, Santa Rosa, Calif.; T. C. Heine, Jr., Waverley, Iowa; Frederic W. Hills, New York; Glenn Horowitz, New York; Marjorie Horowitz, Montclair, N.J.; Daniel R. Hunter, McLean, Va.; the late Archbishop Ioann, Santa Barbara; the late George Ivask, Amherst, Mass.; Augusta Jaryc, Ithaca, N.Y.; D. Barton Johnson, Santa Barbara; Alison Jolly, New York; Michael Juliar, Highland Park, N.J.; H. Peter Kahn, Ithaca, N.Y.; Simon Karlinsky, Berkeley; Sergey Karpovich, Washington, D.C.; Edward Kasinec, New York; Wilma Kerby-Miller, Palo Alto; Alexander B. Klots, Putnam, Conn.; James Laughlin, Norfolk, Conn.; Irving Lazar, Beverly Hills; Harry and Elena Levin, Cambridge, Mass.; Beverly Jane Loo, New York; Peter Lubin, Cambridge, Mass.; James McConkey, Ithaca, N.Y.; Robert McGuire, New York; William and Paula McGuire, Princeton; Beatrice McLeod, Ithaca, N.Y.; John Malmstad, Cambridge, Mass.; Sidney Smith Marshall, West Chester, Pa.; William Maxwell, New York; Arthur and Rosemary Mizener, Ithaca, N.Y.; the late Nathalie Nabokoff, New York; Stephen Jan and Marie-Luce Parker, Lawrence, Kans.; Katherine Reese Peebles, Boston; Ellendea and the late Carl R. Proffer, Ann Arbor, Mich.; Mark Raeff, New York; Charles Remington, New Haven; Roger Sale, Seattle; May Sarton, York, Maine; Michael Scammell, Ithaca, N.Y.; Arthur M. Schlesinger, Jr., New York; Robert Scholes, Providence; R. Lauriston and Ruth Sharp, Ithaca, N.Y.; Don Stallings, Caldwell, Kans.; Isabel Stephens, Woodstock, Vt.; Leon Stilman, St. Petersburg, Fla.; Mary and the late Gleb Struve, Berkeley; Ronald Sukenick, Boulder, Colo.; Susan Summer, New York; the late Marc Szeftel, Seattle; Frank Taylor, New York; Elizabeth Trahan, Monterey, Calif.; Aileen Ward, New York; Edward Weeks, Boston; Ross Wetzsteon, New York; the late E. B. White, North Brooklin, Maine; Ella Keats Whiting, Bedford, Mass.; Richard Wilbur, Cummington, Mass.; Ronald S. Wilkinson, Washington, D.C.; Bart Winer, New York.

In France: the late Alexandre Bacherac, Paris; Evgenia and René Cannac, Paris; Vera Kliatchkine, Paris; Irina Komaroff, Paris; E. A.

Lijine, Paris; the late Mary McCarthy, Paris; Tatiana Morozoff, Paris; Ivan and Claude Nabokoff, Paris; Mme Jean Paulhan, Paris; Frederic Raphael, St. Laurent-La-Vallée; Alain Robbe-Grillet, Paris; Louba Schirman, Paris; Zinaida Shakhovskaya, Paris; Maria Vereshchagina, Paris; Edmund White, Paris.

In the Soviet Union: Anatoly Alexeev, Leningrad; Evgeny Belodubrovsky, Leningrad; Natalia Buynyakov, Leningrad; Alexander Dolinin, Leningrad; Valentin Fyodorov, Moscow; Tatiana Gagen, Moscow; Evgeny Shikhovtsev, Kostroma; Natalia Styopin, Moscow; Sergey Task, Moscow; Natalia Teletov, Leningrad; Natalia Tolstoy, Leningrad; Oleg Volkov, Moscow.

In Switzerland: Carlo Barozzi, Montreux; Jacqueline Callier, La Tour-de-Peilz; the late Louise Fürrer, Territet; Pierre Goeldlin de Tiefenau, Lausanne; the late Martin and Margaret Newstead, Fontanivent; Heinrich-Maria and Jane Ledig-Rowohlt, Vaud; Peter Ustinov, Vaud.

In England: Julian Barnes, London; Michele Field, London; Jane Grayson, London; Francis Haskell, Oxford; Jarmila Hickman, Oldham; W. F. Madelung, Oxford; Tamara Talbot-Rice, Fossebridge; George, Lord Weidenfeld, London.

In Canada: Patricia Brückmann, Toronto; John Melby, Guelph; Elizabeth Lonsdale Webster, Toronto.

In Spain: Hélène Jakovlev, Tarragona; in Germany: Dieter E. Zimmer, Hamburg; in Finland: Pekka Tammi, Helsinki; in Ireland: Jack Sweeney, Corofin; in New Zealand, Michael Gifkins.

The collections and staff of the following archives, libraries, and museums have been helpful, often invaluable:

Auckland Public Library; Bayerische Staatsbibliothek, Munich; Bibliothèque de documentation internationale contemporaine, Paris-Nanterre; Bibliothèque d'études orientales et slaves, Paris; Bibliothèque municipale, Antibes; Bibliothèque municipale, Menton; Bibliothèque nationale, Paris; British Library; Bryn Mawr College Library; Cambridge University Library; Central State Archive of Literature and Art, Moscow; Central State Archive of the October Revolution, Leningrad; Central State Historical Archive, Leningrad; Central State Historical Archive of the City of Leningrad; Columbia University Library; Cornell University Library; Deutsche Staatsbibliothek, Berlin; Dom Plekhanova, Leningrad; Harvard University Libraries (Houghton, Lamont, Widener); Helsinki University Library; Hoover Institute; Humanities Research Center, University of Texas at Austin; Institute of Russian Literature and Art (Pushkinskiy Dom), Leningrad; Lenin Library, Moscow; Library of Congress; Musée

Cantonal de Zoologie, Lausanne; Museum of Comparative Zoology, Harvard; Preussischer Kulturbesitzunginstitut, Berlin; Princeton University Library; Rozhdestveno Local History Museum; Saltykov-Shchedrin State Public Library, Leningrad; Stanford University Library; Trinity College Library, Cambridge; Universitni knihovna (Klementinum), Prague; University of Auckland Library; University of California Library, Berkeley; University of Illinois Library, Urbana; University of Lund Library; University of Toronto Library; University of Uppsala Library; Vilis Lācis State Library, Riga; Washington University Library; Wellesley College Library; Yale University Library; Yalta Local History Museum.

In particular I would like to thank Dr. E. S. Leedham-Green of the Cambridge University Archives for suggesting much I would not have known to look for; Eila Tervakko and the staff of the Slavonic Division, Helsinki University Library, for always being there to offer assistance but letting one explore their splendid collection so freely on one's own; the staff of the Columbia University Library Rare Books and Manuscripts section, especially Stephen Corrsin, Susan Summer, and Ellen Scaruffi, who ensured I missed nothing in the constantly expanding Bakhmeteff Archive; Fred Bauman and Charles Kelly of the Manuscript Division at the Library of Congress; Natalia Buynyakova of the Central Historical Archive of Leningrad Province for offering such prompt and precise pointers to the most diverse materials; the harassed but valiant staff at the Bibliothèque de documentation internationale contemporaine; the attentive, prompt, and eager staff at the Humanities Research Center; and the cheerfully cooperative staff at the Hoover Institute Library.

I would like to express my gratitude to the New Zealand University Grants Committee for awarding me a Claude McCarthy Fellowship, without which I could not have begun this project; to the University of Auckland for further research grants and for allowing me the time to complete the task; and especially to the University of Auckland English Department, and particularly Professors Don Smith, Terry Sturm, and Mac Jackson, for their continued support and forbearance.

For comments on matters of fact and style in my manuscript I would like to thank the following: Professor Simon Karlinsky, University of California, Berkeley, and Professor Gennady Barabtarlo, University of Missouri, Columbia, who both read the manuscript closely and made many superb suggestions about matters literary and historical; Professor D. Barton Johnson, University of California, Santa Barbara, and Professor Stephen Jan Parker, University of Kansas, who read and commented astutely on the entire manuscript; Professor Robert Alter, University of California, Berkeley; my editors at Princeton, Robert Brown, Beth Gianfagna, and Jane Lincoln Taylor; and above all, my first reader, Bronwen Nicholson. For generous help with computers, I must thank David Joel; and with typing, Bronwyn Joel and, once again, Bronwen Nicholson.

Unless otherwise indicated, all photographs are from the Vladimir Nabokov Archives, Montreux.

ABBREVIATIONS

ALL BOOKS are by Vladimir Nabokov unless otherwise noted. All unpublished material, except for interviews conducted or letters received by the author, derives from the Vladimir Nabokov Archives unless otherwise indicated. Within critical sections on individual Nabokov works, page numbers for quotations from the work in question will not be cited in the notes except in the case of *Eugene Onegin*.

Ada	*Ada or Ardor: A Family Chronicle*. New York: McGraw-Hill, 1969.
Appel, *AnL*	Alfred Appel, Jr., ed. *The Annotated Lolita*. New York: McGraw-Hill, 1970.
Appel, *NDC*	Alfred Appel, Jr. *Nabokov's Dark Cinema*. New York: Oxford University Press, 1974.
Appel and Newman	Alfred Appel, Jr., and Charles Newman, eds. *Triquarterly* 17 (Winter 1970), Nabokov special issue; repr. as *Nabokov: Criticisms, Reminiscences, Translations, and Tributes*. New York: Simon & Schuster, 1970.
BB	Brian Boyd
BS	*Bend Sinister*. 1947; repr. New York: Time, 1964.
CE	*Conclusive Evidence*. New York: Harper, 1951.
ColB	Bakhmeteff Archive, Columbia University
CornUA	Cornell University Archives
DB	*Drugie berega*. New York: Chekhov Publishing House, 1954.
Defense	*The Defense*, trans. Michael Scammell with VN. New York: Putnam's, 1964.
DN	Dmitri Vladimirovich Nabokov (son)
DN, *CC*	DN, "Close Calls and Fulfilled Dreams: Selected Entries from a Private Journal," *Antaeus* 61 (Autumn 1988): 299–323.
DQ	*Lectures on Don Quixote*, ed. Fredson Bowers. New York: Harcourt Brace Jovanovich/Bruccoli Clark, 1983.
DS	*Details of a Sunset and Other Stories*, trans. DN with VN. New York: McGraw-Hill, 1976.

EIN	Elena Ivanovna Nabokov (mother)
EO	Alexander Pushkin. *Eugene Onegin*, trans. and with commentary by VN. New York: Bollingen, 1964; rev. ed., Princeton: Princeton University Press, 1975.
ES	Elena Sikorski (née Nabokov) (sister)
EW	Edmund Wilson
Field, *Life*	Andrew Field. *Nabokov: His Life in Part*. New York: Viking, 1977.
Field, *VN*	Andrew Field. *VN: The Life and Art of Vladimir Nabokov*. New York: Crown, 1986.
Gibian and Parker	George Gibian and Stephen Jan Parker, eds. *The Achievement of Vladimir Nabokov*. Ithaca: Cornell University Center for International Studies, 1984.
Gift	*The Gift*, trans. Michael Scammell and DN with VN. New York: Putnam's, 1963.
GS	Gleb Struve
Hoover	Hoover Institute, Stanford University
HRC	Harry Ransom Humanities Research Center, University of Texas, Austin
IB	*Invitation to a Beheading*, trans. DN with VN. New York: Putnam's, 1959.
KDN	Konstantin Dmitrievich Nabokov
KQK	*King, Queen, Knave*, trans. DN with VN. New York: McGraw-Hill, 1968.
KW	Katharine White
LATH	*Look at the Harlequins!* New York: McGraw-Hill, 1974.
LC	Library of Congress
LCNA	Nabokov Archives, LC
Lects	*Lectures on Literature*, ed. Fredson Bowers. New York: Harcourt Brace Jovanovich/Bruccoli Clark, 1980.
LectsR	*Lectures on Russian Literature*, ed. Fredson Bowers. New York: Harcourt Brace Jovanovich/ Bruccoli Clark, 1981.
Lolita	1955; New York: Putnam's, 1958.
LS	*Lolita: A Screenplay*. New York: McGraw-Hill, 1974.
Mary	Trans. Michael Glenny with VN. New York: McGraw-Hill, 1970.
MUSSR	*The Man from the USSR and Other Plays*, trans. DN. New York: Harcourt Brace Jovanovich, 1984.

N1	Unpublished VN notes to Andrew Field, February 20, 1973, VNA.
N2	Unpublished VN notes to Andrew Field, August 31, 1973, VNA.
ND	*Nabokov's Dozen*. Garden City, N.Y.: Doubleday, 1957.
NG	*Nikolai Gogol*. Norfolk, Conn.: New Directions, 1944.
NRS	*Novoe russkoe slovo*. Daily. New York.
NWL	*The Nabokov-Wilson Letters*, ed. Simon Karlinsky. New York: Harper & Row, 1979.
NYRB	*New York Review of Books*
NYTBR	*New York Times Book Review*
NZ	*Novyy zhurnal*. Journal. New York.
Perepiska	*Perepiska s sestroy*. Ann Arbor: Ardis, 1985.
PF	*Pale Fire*. New York: Putnam's, 1962.
PP	*Poems and Problems*. New York: McGraw-Hill, 1971.
Quennell	Peter Quennell, ed. *Vladimir Nabokov: A Tribute*. London: Weidenfeld & Nicolson, 1979.
RB	*A Russian Beauty and Other Stories*, trans. DN and Simon Karlinsky with VN. New York: McGraw-Hill, 1972.
Rivers and Nicol	J. E. Rivers and Charles Nicol, eds. *Nabokov's Fifth Arc: Nabokov and Others on His Life's Work*. Austin: University of Texas Press, 1982.
RLSK	*The Real Life of Sebastian Knight*. Norfolk, Conn.: New Directions, 1941.
SL	*Selected Letters, 1940–1977*, ed. DN and Matthew J. Bruccoli. New York: Harcourt Brace Jovanovich/Bruccoli Clark Layman, 1989.
SM	*Speak, Memory: An Autobiography Revisited*. New York: Putnam's, 1966.
SO	*Strong Opinions*. New York: McGraw-Hill, 1973.
Stikhi	Ann Arbor: Ardis, 1979.
SZ	*Sovremennye zapiski*. Journal. Paris.
TD	*Tyrants Destroyed and Other Stories*, trans. DN with VN. New York: McGraw-Hill, 1975.
TLS	*Times Literary Supplement*
TT	*Transparent Things*. New York: McGraw-Hill, 1972.
VDN	Vladimir Dmitrievich Nabokov (father)

NOTES

INTRODUCTION

1. *SM*, 309–10.
2. *SM*, 86.
3. For the theme of future recollection, see *TD*, 131; *Gift*, esp. 16, 106, 354; *Lolita*, 88.
4. *SM*, 31–32.

CHAPTER 1. REFUGE

Epigraph to Part 1: *SO*, 10.
Epigraph: *SM*, 277. VN was ceasing to cross his sevens by January 1943 (VN to Edward Weeks, January 1943, HRC).

1. VéN to A. A. Goldenweiser, July 4, 1957, ColB; *N1*; Field, *Life*, 226; VN to Karpovich, May 29, 1940, ColB; *NRS*, June 23, 1940; DN, *Enchanter*, 103; DN, *CC*, 303; DN to BB, October 14, 1990.
2. *SO*, 54; DN, *CC*, 302; *N1*; *NRS*, June 23, 1940; Field, *Life*, 231.
3. Robert Hughes interview with VN, September 1965, from TS, VNA; *N2*; *NRS*, June 23, 1940; Field, *Life*, 231; VéN to BB, July 10, 1988.
4. *N2*; VéN, Page-a-Day Diary, VNA; BB interview with Nathalie Nabokoff, March 1983; VN to Mstislav Dobuzhinsky, June 10, 1940, ColB; Page-a-Day Diary, VNA; Field, *Life*, 234.
5. VN to C. A. Pearce, [ca. June 1943], VNA.
6. "Opredeleniya," TS, LCNA.
7. *NRS*, June 23, 1940.
8. *SO*, 290.
9. VN to Vernadsky [June 1940], and to Karpovich [ca. September–October 1940], ColB, and to Litfund, December 21, 1961, VNA.
10. *SL*, 33–34; VN to Karpovich [ca. June 10, 1940], ColB.
11. VN to Karpovich [ca. June 10, 1940], and Nabokov-Karpovich correspondence, ColB; *SL*, 33, 35–36.
12. Beth Kulakofsky, *Wellesley College News*, March 21, 1941; Page-a-Day Diary, VNA; *NWL*, 66–67.
13. *NZ*, 59 (1959): 192.
14. "Zud" (signed "Ridebis Semper"), *NRS*, October 17, 1940; "Pokupka Sardinki Nepmanom" (unsigned), *NRS*, October 19, 1940.
15. EW, *Letters on Literature and Politics*, 361–62; *NWL*, 29; VN to EW, October 7, 1940, Yale.
16. Unpublished lecture, VNA.
17. Proffer, *Widows of Russia*, 128.

18. Alfred Appel, Jr., in Rivers and Nicol, 7 (Appel misspelled the name "Wraden"); VéN to BB, July 10, 1988.

19. VN to Karpovich, September 19, 1940, ColB.

20. Page-a-Day Diary, VNA; VéN to Mary Wilson (McCarthy), December 28, 1940, Yale.

21. DN interview with BB, December 1981.

22. Albert Parry, NRS, September 10, 1978; VéN to A. A. Goldenweiser, July 12, 1962, and VN to Karpovich [ca. October 1940], ColB.

23. VN to Yarmolinsky, October 7, 1940, ColB; to Pertzoff, August 30, 1940, LCNA; NRS, October 12 and 15, 1940.

24. VN to EW, October 7, 1940, Yale; EW, Letters on Literature and Politics, 373; VN to Karpovich, November 11, 1940, ColB; "Mr. Masefield and Clio," New Republic, December 9, 1940.

25. BB interview with Elena Levin, March 1983; NWL, 30.

26. VN to EW [ca. December 12, 1940], Yale; NWL, 31.

27. For a fine summary of the American intelligentsia's shifting attitudes to the Soviet Union between 1930 and the 1950s, see William O'Neill, A Better World: The Great Schism: Stalinism and the American Intellectuals (New York: Simon and Schuster, 1982).

28. Glory, xii.

29. See Simon Karlinsky's superb summary of this theme in his introduction to NWL.

30. Karlinsky, NWL, 23. Only in 1971, in his introduction to the 1972 edition of To the Finland Station, did Wilson acknowledge the flaws in his portrait of Lenin.

31. BB interview with Harry Levin, March 1983, and with VéN, December 1986; Field, Life, 235.

32. Field, Life, 235; VéN notes for Field, 1986, VNA.

33. BB interview with Lucia Davidova, April 1983; Douglas Davis interview with VN, National Observer, June 29, 1964.

34. Henry Lanz to VN, November 28 and December 15, 1940, VNA.

35. N1; Hughes interview TS, VNA; SO, 5; SL, 36.

36. Unpublished lecture notes, VNA.

37. Mikhail Chekhov to VN, December 12, 1940, and Eugene Somoff to VN, January 13, and May 13, 1941, VNA.

38. SO, 5; DB, 53; VN to Karpovich [ca. October 1940] and October 7, 1940, ColB; VN, Lysandra Cormion, 267; VN to William Comstock, February 20, 1942, VNA.

39. EW to VN, December 27, 1940, VNA; NWL, 37; proofs of article, "Soviet Literature 1940," VNA. The article never appeared in Decision.

40. VN to Mark Aldanov, January 29, 1941, ColB; NWL, 45; VéN to A. A. Goldenweiser, January 14, 1941, and July 12, 1958, ColB; Field, Life, 236.

41. NWL, 37; VN to Karpovich, October 7, 1940, and January 26, 1941, ColB; Edgar Fisher, Institute of International Education, to VN, January 28, 1941, VNA; SO, 286–87; Perepiska, 25.

42. VN to Aldanov, March 29, 1941, ColB; *NWL*, 40; *Wellesley College News*, March 6, 1941.

43. *Wellesley College News*, March 6, 13, and 21, 1941; VN to Aldanov, March 29, 1941.

44. *NWL*, 41; VN to Aldanov, March 29, 1941.

45. BB interview with Edward Weeks, April 1983; *NWL*, 40; VN to Peter Pertzoff, March 1941, LCNA.

46. VN to Aldanov, March 29, 1941; BB interview with VéN, February 1983.

47. VéN to Mary Wilson (McCarthy), December 28, 1940, and VN to EW, January 5, 1941, Yale; *NWL*, 38, 41, 42; *N1*; VN to Karpovich, April 5, 1941, ColB.

48. BB interview with Mary McCarthy, January 1985; Clarence Brown, *Saturday Review*, June 23, 1979; *N1*.

49. *NRS*, April 6, 1941; BB interview with Nathalie Nabokoff, March 1983.

50. *NWL*, 42.

51. Agnes Perkins to VN, May 17, 1941, VNA.

52. Dorothy Leuthold to VN, n.d., VNA; *NWL*, 45.

53. Hardwick, *NYTBR*, October 19, 1980; unpublished notes, VNA; VN to Mstislav Dobuzhinsky, July 25, 1941, ColB.

54. VN to Aldanov, ca. July 20, 1941, ColB; *SM*, 201; *We* (Wellesley College), December 1943, 32.

55. Unpublished notes, VNA; "Nearctic *Neonympha*," 66; VN to William Comstock, February 20, 1942, VNA; *SL*, 114; BB interview with VéN, January 1980.

56. "Nearctic *Neonympha*."

57. Unpublished notes, VNA; *N1*; Page-a-Day Diary, VNA.

58. Stanford University Bulletin, 1940–1941; VN notes on Stanford correspondence, VNA.

59. VN to Karpovich [Summer 1941], ColB; Field, *VN*, 209.

60. The last quotation comes from *MUSSR*, 341 (text corrected according to MS, VNA), the rest from Stanford lecture notes, VNA.

61. *Lects*, 373.

62. VN to Aldanov, ca. July 20, 1941.

63. Cited in Field, *VN*, 209.

64. Field, *VN*, 210.

65. *NWL*, 46; VN to Mstislav Dobuzhinsky, July 25, 1941, ColB.

66. VN to Aldanov, ca. July 20, 1941.

67. Page-a-Day Diary, VNA; VéN notes re: Field, 1986; BB interview with Albert J. Guerard, May 1983, and with VéN, December 1981; VN to Aldanov, ca. July 20, 1941; Field, *VN*, 210–12.

68. *NWL*, 38, 45; *N1*; BB interview with Harry Levin, March 1983; VN to Karpovich, July 7, 1941, ColB; James Laughlin to VN, July 1, 1941, VN to Laughlin, July 7, 1941, VNA.

69. Page-a-Day Diary, VNA; unpublished notes, VNA.

70. *NWL*, 43; VN to Karpovich, August 12, 1941, ColB; Monroe Deutsch,

University of California, to VN, August 7, 1941, VNA; BB interview with Simon Karlinsky, May 1983.

71. VN to Laughlin, September 10, 1941, VNA.

CHAPTER 2. VISITING LECTURER

Epigraph: unpublished note, VNA.

1. BB interview with Sylvia Berkman, April 1983.

2. Mildred McAfee to VN, June 30, 1941, WCA.

3. Field, *Life*, 263; VN to Edward Weeks, September 19, 1941, HRC; *Perepiska*, 29.

4. *Wellesley College News*, October 2 and 16, 1941; unpublished lectures, VNA; VN, "The Lermontov Mirage," *Russian Review* 1, no. 1 (November 1941); *NG*, 86.

5. *Wellesley College News*, November 20, 1941.

6. *The Last Word*, April 1943, 19.

7. VN to Aldanov, October 20, 1941, ColB; *NWL*, 48. For his ideas on mimicry, see *SM*, 124–25, *DB*, 116–17, *Gift*, 122–23, and unpublished "Vtoroe dobavlenie k *Daru*," LCNA.

8. VN to Joseph Bequaert, July 6, 1950, VNA; *N1*; Field, *VN*, 207.

9. Thomas Barbour to VN, October 17, 1941, VNA; VN to Aldanov, October 20, 1941; BB interview with Frank Carpenter, April 1983.

10. *N1*; *SL*, 102; BB interview with Kenneth Christiansen, April 1983.

11. "Nearctic *Neonympha*," 61–80; BB interview with Charles Remington, February 1987. The distinctions Nabokov made have proved valid, but experts in the Satyrids have subsequently discovered more about the relationship of these butterflies to their generic context. Thus the genus to which they belong has been broken up since Nabokov's time, and the three species he studied are now assigned to *Cyllopsis* rather than *Neonympha*; within that genus, Nabokov's *dorothea*, *maniola*, and *avicula* have been recognized as North American subspecies of a basically neotropical species, *pertepida*; and the North American subspecies of *pyracmon* has been named *nabokovi* in honor of his discovery that the species occurred in the Nearctic as well as in Central America.

12. *NWL*, 49–50; *SO*, 292.

13. VN to Aldanov, October 20, 1941; *SL*, 37–38. For the Khodasevich translations, see *New Directions in Prose and Poetry*, *1941* (Norfolk, Conn.: New Directions, 1941); repr. *Triquarterly* 27 (Spring 1973); and Karlinsky and Appel, *Bitter Air of Exile*.

14. *Atlantic Monthly*, December 1941, 765.

15. Pub. *New Yorker*, June 6, 1942; *PP*, 153–54. Cf. *NWL*, 52.

16. Robert Linscott, reader's report, August 2, 1944, Columbia, Random House Collection; *NWL*, 58.

17. *Baltimore Sun*, January 11, 1942; *New York Herald Tribune*, January 25, 1942.

18. VN to James Laughlin, January 3, 1942, VNA.

19. *Wellesley Magazine*, April 1942, 212.

20. *Wellesley College News*, February 19 and 26, March 5 and 12, April 2, and May 7, 1942.

21. MS, VNA; pub. *NZ* 3 (1942); *PP*, 102–13.

22. *Lolita*, 318–19; *SO*, 106, 54.

23. Dated March 12, 1942, WCA.

24. Gracie Humphrey to Mildred McAfee, April 10, 1942, WCA.

25. Mildred McAfee to Amy Kelly and Agnes Perkins, April 30, 1942, WCA; *NWL*, 62.

26. Institute of International Education information sheet, April 1942, LCNA.

27. VN to Aldanov, May 20, 1942, ColB; VN to Marinel sisters, April 26, 1942, Michael Juliar Collection; VN to Henry Allan Moe, August 1, 1947, VNA.

28. *NWL*, 60–61; *Randall Jarrell's Letters*, ed. Mary Jarrell (Boston: Houghton Mifflin, 1985), 67.

29. *NWL*, 64; Field, *Life*, 247; VN to George Vernadsky, May 28, 1942, ColB; *NWL*, 66.

30. VN to Aldanov, May 20, 1942, ColB, and to James Laughlin, June 7, 1942, VNA; *N1*; *NWL*, 66; Thomas Barbour to VN, June 10, 1942, LCNA.

31. VN to Aldanov, May 20, 1942; *NWL*, 66; Thomas Barbour to VN, June 10, 1942, LCNA.

32. VéN to A. A. Goldenweiser, May 27 and June 11, 1942, ColB; *SL*, 41, 42–43.

33. *NWL*, 79; *BS*, xi; *Perepiska*, 22.

34. BB interview with Sylvia Berkman, April 1983; Wilma Kerby-Miller, cited in Field, *VN*, 241.

35. VéN to A. A. Goldenweiser, July 1, 1958, ColB; BB interview with Wilma Kerby-Miller, May 1983.

36. BB interviews with Harry and Elena Levin, March 1983 and February 1987; Harry Levin to BB, July 23, 1990; Barbara Breasted interview with Elena Levin, WCA.

37. BB interview with Aileen Ward, April 1983.

38. BB interview with Mary McCarthy, January 1985.

39. BB interview with Harry and Elena Levin, March 1983; *N1*.

40. VN to Roman Grynberg, December 16, 1944, ColB; VN to VéN, October 17–18, 1942, VNA.

41. Unpublished notes for work in progress, VNA.

42. VN to VéN, October 2–3 and 5, 1942, VNA.

43. VN to VéN, October 7, 1942, VNA; unpublished lecture notes, VNA; *Spelman Messenger*, November 1942, 9.

44. VN to VéN, October 18, 1942, VNA; *NWL*, 91; *Atlanta Constitution*, October 20, 1942.

45. VN to VéN, October 20, 1942, VNA.

46. VN to VéN, October [ca. 11, 14, and 20], 1942, and November 5, 1942, VNA; *NWL*, 85–86.

47. *Lects* 2–3; unpublished lecture notes, VNA.

48. VN to VéN, November 10, 1942, VNA.

49. Cited in Field, *Life*, 249.

50. *SL*, 43; *NWL*, 87, 89.

51. *NWL*, 89, 91; VN to VéN, December 7, 1942, VNA; poem pub. *New Yorker*, May 15, 1943, and as "A Discovery," *PP*, 155–56.

52. VN to C. A. Pearce [ca. January 1943], VNA.

53. VN to Cyril dos Passos [ca. October 1, 1945], VNA; Austin Clark to VN, December 15, 1942, VNA; *NWL*, 91.

54. *SL*, 43; VN to James Laughlin, June 24 and August 7, 1946, VNA.

55. *SL*, 56–57.

56. *SL*, 44.

CHAPTER 3. SCIENTIST, WRITER, TEACHER

Epigraph: *LS*, 128.

1. Anne Guérin interview with VN, *L'Exprès*, January 26, 1961; *SL*, 102; "Morphology of the Genus *Lycaeides*," 108; *SO*, 109.

2. *Psyche*, September–December 1943, 87–99.

3. MS, LCNA; pub. *Atlantic Monthly*, May 1943; *ND*, 75–93. The *ND* version accidentally omits two long final paragraphs from the correct version in *Nine Stories* (New York: New Directions, 1947), 95.

4. DN to Stephen Jan Parker, October 24, 1984.

5. *NWL*, 96–97.

6. 1943 Diary, VNA; Breasted, "Vladimir Nabokov at Wellesley," 22; *NWL*, 96; class notes of Jean Stadeker, WCA; Barbara Breasted interview with Katherine Reese Peebles, WCA.

7. See O'Neill, *Better World*, 59–60, 77–78.

8. *NWL*, 100–101, 103, 132; VN to Sophia Pregel-Brynner, April 2, 1943, Illinois; pub. *PP*.

9. Henry Allan Moe to VN, March 23, 1943, VNA; Paul, *Edmund Wilson*, 117; VN to James Laughlin, April 4, 1943, VNA.

10. Diary, VNA; BB interview with Elizaveta Marinel Allan, March 1983.

11. *NWL*, 102; pub. *Atlantic Monthly*, November 1943; *ND*, 141–53.

12. *SL*, 45.

13. VéN to BB, July 27, 1988; *NWL*, 106–7.

14. VN to Aldanov, August 6, 1943, ColB; *NWL*, 107; "Nearctic Forms," 97; *N1*.

15. J. McDunnough, "New North American Eupithecias (Lepidoptera, Geometridae)," *Canadian Entomologist*, September 1945, 168–76; BB interview with Charles Remington, February 1987.

16. VN to Aldanov, August 6, 1943, ColB; VN, "Zametki perevodchika— II," *Opyty* 8 (1957): 45–46.

17. *NWL*, 106–7.

18. *NG*, 151–52. Ellipses in original.

19. Katherine Reese, *We* (Wellesley) 1, no. 2 (December 1943): 6–7, 32; BB interview with Katherine Reese Peebles, April 1983.

20. VN to James Laughlin, November 9, 1943, VNA; *NWL*, 111–12, 112–13, 115; VN to EW, November 29, 1943, Yale.

21. BB interviews with Frank Carpenter, April 1983, and Charles Remington, February 1987; lepidoptera MSS, VNA.

22. BB interview with Kenneth Christiansen, April 1983.

23. VN to Louis Griewisch, cited in *Lepidopterists' News* 7, no. 2 (1953): 54; "Nearctic Members," 483; BB interview with Remington, February 1987; *NWL*, 131.

24. VN to Roman Grynberg, December 25, 1943, ColB; pub. *NZ* 7 (1944), repr. *PP*, 114–25. VN's explanation comes from his introductory notes for a 1949 reading in New York, MS, Zenzinov Collection, ColB.

25. *NWL*, 121, 126.

26. *SO*, 100, 190; *NWL*, 126–27, 135.

27. Hannah French to BB, August 14, 1983; Barbara Breasted interview with Hannah French, WCA.

28. *NWL*, 132; *Wellesley College News*, April 1, 1944. VN received $150 at Yale, $120 for the Wellesley classes.

29. Ella Keats Whiting to BB, August 3, 1983.

30. VN to Grynberg, December 25, 1943, ColB; *N1*; BB interview with Sylvia Berkman, April 1983; Field, *Life*, 263; VéN to BB, September 5, 1988.

31. *NWL*, 135; pub. *Atlantic Monthly*, October 1944, repr. *ND*, 39–54.

32. *Three Russian Poets*, 37; "The Lermontov Mirage," 39.

33. See *VNRY*, pp. 424, 509.

34. Jane Harris to VN, May 26, 1943, VNA.

35. BB interview with Elena Levin, March 1983.

36. *NWL*, 234; EW, *Letters on Literature and Politics*, 578, 733; EW, *Upstate*, 161–62; EW, *NYRB*, July 15, 1965; EW, *Window on Russia*, 231, 236.

37. *N1*; Field, *Life*, 259.

38. *NWL*, 52, 90, 92.

39. VN-Zenzinov letters, May 1944, ColB and VNA.

40. *NWL*, 125; KW to VN, June 23, 1944, VNA; VN to EW, June 8, 1944, Yale.

41. VN to EW, June 8, 1944, Yale.

42. *N1*; Penelope Gilliatt interview with VN, *Vogue*, December 1966, 279; Field, *Life*, 253.

CHAPTER 4. PERMANENT IMPERMANENCE

1. VN to Alvin Manuel, August 15, 1944, VNA.

2. *NWL*, 136; VN to Edward Weeks, July 21, 1944, HRC.

3. *NWL*, 138–42; BB interview with Mary McCarthy, January 1985; VéN to Joan Daly, April 6, 1976.

4. Grumbach, *Company She Kept*, 117–18.

5. *NWL*, 139; EW, *New Yorker*, September 9, 1944.

6. *NWL*, 142; BB interview with VéN, November 1982; Scrapbook, VNA.

7. Pub. *Atlantic Monthly*, January 1945; repr. *ND*, 155–64.

8. *DS*, 94.

9. WCA.

10. "On Learning Russian," 191–92.

11. Sidney Smith Marshall to BB, August 20, 1983; Marshall, "Yellow-Blue Vase," 25–26; *NWL*, 142; *BS*, vii.

12. *New Yorker*, March 3, 1945; repr. *PP*, 158–63.

13. *NWL*, 146; George R. Noyes to VN, December 19, 1944, VN to Noyes, August 6, 1945, VNA.

14. BB interview with DN, December 1981; Francis Caswell to VN, January 10, 1960, VNA; Page-a-Day Diary, VNA.

15. BB interview with Phyllis Christiansen, April 1983; Phyllis Christiansen to BB, June 15 and August 17, 1983.

16. "Neotropical *Plebejinae.*"

17. *SO*, 320; BB interview with Charles Remington, February 1987; Alexander Klots to VN, n.d. [1949], VNA. Cf. VN, "Klots' *Field Guide*," 41. One genus, *Hemiargus*, does not at present follow VN's reclassification into three genera, *Hemiargus*, *Cyclargus*, and *Echinargus*, but Charles Remington suspects that the genus may be resplit when it receives more scholarly attention.

18. Isabel Stephens to Barbara Breasted, February 25, 1971, WCA.

19. Barbara Breasted interview with Sylvia Berkman, November 20, 1970, WCA; BB interview with Aileen Ward, April 1983.

20. *NWL*, 148; VN to EW, March 1945, Yale; *NWL*, 149.

21. O'Neill, *Better World*, 98.

22. VN to Zenzinov, ca. February 28, 1945, ColB.

23. VN to Zenzinov, March 17, 1945, ColB.

24. The Maklakov incident had in fact been seriously misreported (see Zenzinov to VN, June 11, 1945, ColB).

25. VN to EW, February 1945, Yale.

26. VN read the story at an evening meeting of a Wellesley English composition class on April 17 (*Wellesley College News*, April 26, 1945). Pub. *New Yorker*, June 23, 1945; repr. *ND*, 125–40.

27. Dated April 14, 1945, MS, VNA; pub. *NZ* 10 (1945): 172–73; repr. *PP*, 128–33.

28. VN to Gus Lobrano, May 25, 1945, and to Katharine White, May 25, 1945, VNA.

29. VN to Marusya and Elizaveta Marinel, April 30, 1945, Juliar Collection; *NWL*, 154; BB interview with VéN, November 1986.

30. Robert Hughes interview with VN, from TS in VNA.

31. Page-a-Day Diary, VNA; BB interview with VéN, November 1982; Marion Monaghan to Mary Lyons, November 24, 1970, and to Barbara Breasted, WCA.

32. BB interviews with VéN, January 1982, and with Claudio Guillén, April 1983; Jorge Guillén inscription to VN on *Cantico*, January 15, 1945, VNA.

33. *Perepiska*, 29; Sidney Smith Marshall to BB, August 20, 1983; DN to BB, October 14, 1990.

34. *NWL*, 156; ES to VN, October 9, 1945, VNA; VN diary, 1969, VNA.

35. VN to Aldanov, December 8, 1945; VN to Tatyana Osorgin [ca. December 20, 1945], VNA; *Perepiska*, 27.

36. *NWL*, 156, 157, 159; VN to Aldanov, December 8, 1945, ColB; *Perepiska*, 29.

37. BB interview with Struve, May 1983; VN to Noyes, August 6, 1945, VNA.

38. John O'Hara to VéN, February 9, 1980, VNA.

39. *SL*, 47–48.

40. VN to Mildred Horton, February 6, 1946, WCA.

41. Mildred Horton to VN, February 14, 1946, WCA.

42. *NWL*, 160, 163.

43. *BS*, xi; *NWL*, 164, 168; *Perepiska*, 39.

44. *BS*, xi–xii; *SL*, 68; VN to Jarl Priel, June 22, 1946, VNA.

CHAPTER 5. BEND SINISTER

1. Written 1941–1946; pub. New York: Henry Holt, 1947; repr. with introduction by VN, New York: Time, Inc., 1964.

2. *BS*, xiii.

3. *SL*, 67.

4. Unpublished lecture notes, VNA.

5. *SL*, 80.

6. "What Faith Means," 212.

7. "What Faith Means"; *SL*, 49.

8. "Opredeleniya," from TS, LCNA.

9. *BS*, xiv.

10. Unpublished lecture notes, VNA.

11. Ibid.

12. "On Learning Russian," 192.

13. *SL*, 50.

14. *Lects*, 180.

15. *NWL*, 168.

16. *BS*, xvi.

CHAPTER 6. TEACHING LITERATURE AT LAST

1. *NWL*, 170.

2. "Nearctic Members," 540.

3. VN to Charles Remington, July 20, 1946, Remington Collection.

4. *NWL*, 170; DN and VéN to BB, August 29, 1988.

5. *NWL*, 170, 172; VN to James Laughlin, August 25, 1946, VNA; BB interview with VéN, December 1982.

6. Allen Tate to VN, October 23, 1946, VN to Tate, March 24 and May 2, 1947, VNA; *Wellesley College News*, October 9, 1947.

7. WCA; *NWL*, 172.

8. *Wellesley College News*, October 17, 1945; *SO*, 5: VN to English Institute, April 6, 1954, VNA; Sidney Smith Marshall to BB, August 20, 1983; unpublished lecture notes, VNA.

9. Unpublished lecture notes, VNA; J. D. O'Hara to VéN, February 9, 1980, VNA.

10. *SO*, 104, 124; unpublished lecture notes, VNA; Alan Nordstrom interview with VN, *Ivy*, February 1959. He restates the idea in *Pnin*, *Ada*, and *LATH*.

11. Unpublished lecture notes, VNA.

12. "Mister Nabokov," in Quennell, 36, 39.

13. Unpublished lecture notes, VNA.

14. Green, "Mister Nabokov," 39–40.

15. *SL*, 69, 70–71; VN to Tate, October 21, 1946; Tate to VN, October 14, 1946, VNA.

16. *Wellesley College News*, October 24, 1946.

17. EW to R. D. Clark, September 26, 1946, Yale; *NWL*, 182; Albert Parry, in *NRS*, July 9, 1978; Field, *Life*, 263–64; *N1*.

18. BB interview with Isabel Stephens, April 1983.

19. Klots, *Field Guide* (Boston: Houghton Mifflin, 1951), 164. The subspecies named after VN was *Lycaeides argyrognomon nabokovi* Masters: see Hodges et al., *Check List of the Lepidoptera of America North of Mexico*, 56.

20. See Scammell, *Solzhenitsyn: A Biography* (New York: Norton, 1984), 255–60.

21. BB interview with Remington, February 1987; VN, "Butterfly Collecting in Wyoming," 51.

22. BB interview with Remington, February 1987.

23. MS sent to EW on February 22, 1947, *NWL*, 187; pub. *NZ* 15 (1947): 81–83; repr. *PP*, 134–41.

24. Green, "Mister Nabokov," 37.

25. *NWL*, 181–82.

26. VN to Miss Jones, November 7, 1946, VNA; Edith Donato to VN, March 15, 1947, and VéN to Edith Donato, March 19, 1947, VNA.

27. *Lolita*, 39, 317.

28. *NWL*, 188; VéN to ES, April 6, 1947, Sikorski Collection.

29. *NG*, 59; *SL*, 65; VN to KW, January 8, 1947, VNA.

30. Pub. *New Yorker*, May 15, 1948; repr. *ND*, 67–74.

31. VéN to New American Library, June 12, 1952; *New Republic*, September 7, 1947.

32. VN to KW, April 17, 1947, VNA; *NWL*, 190.

33. *NWL*, 190; VN to Alexander Klots, April 22, 1948, VNA; *SM*, 138–39.

34. VN to Phyllis Christiansen, August 25, 1947, VNA; BB interview with DN, December 1981.

35. BB interview with Remington, February 1987.

36. BB interview with Don Stallings, February 1987; DN and VéN to BB, August 29, 1988.

37. VN to KW, July 2, 1947, VNA; pub. *New Yorker*, January 3, 1948; *SM*, chap. 3.

38. KW to VN, July 15, 1947, VNA; *NWL*, 192.

39. VN to James Laughlin, August 21, 1947, VNA; Page-a-Day Diary, VNA; Gleb Struve to VN, September 23, 1947, VNA.

40. February 18, entry, Yearbook (for 1951), VNA.

41. Barbara Breasted interview with Jean Handke Proctor, November 1970, WCA; Marjorie Horowitz to BB, July 19, 1983. VN wrote out the test questions, dated October 3, 1947, in his copy of Bondar's *Simplified Russian Method*, 6th ed. (New York: Pitman, n.d.), VNA.

42. *Wellesley College News*, October 9, 1947.

43. Bishop, "Nabokov at Cornell," 234, 235; KW to VN, August 18, 1948, Bryn Mawr; BB interview with Alison Bishop, April 1983; Morris Bishop to VN, September 13, 1947, VNA.

44. BB interview with Alison Bishop, April 1983. Appel (Rivers and Nicol, 9) is incorrect: VN had not been invited to lecture on the occasion of this visit.

45. Mildred Horton to VN, November 10 and December 8, 1947, VNA; *Wellesley Alumnae Magazine*, May 1952, 230.

46. VN to Bishop, November 14, 1947, VNA.

47. Pub. *New Yorker*, March 27, 1948; chap. 4 of *SM*.

48. *SL*, 77; EW, *Letters on Literature and Politics*, 409–11; *NWL*, 216.

49. Bishop to VN, November 17, 1947, VNA; *SL*, 78.

50. VN to Szeftel, March 2, 1948, VNA.

51. VN to Trygve Lie, January 2, 1947, *Perepiska*, 45–46; Kirill Nabokov to VN, November 2, 1947, VNA; George Hessen to VN, October 10, 1947, VNA; VN correspondence about Rostislav Petkevich, VNA.

52. VN to KW, March 13, 1948, VNA.

53. BB interview with Sylvia Berkman, April 1983; Isabel Stephens to Barbara Breasted, February 25, 1971, WCA; unpublished poem "Ekspress proletaet," December 6, 1918, in album, VNA; *SM*, 144.

54. Field, *VN*, 255; *NWL*, 199, 272; *N2*; *SL*, 102–4.

55. VN to KW, April 5, 1948, VNA; pub. *New Yorker*, July 31, 1948; chap. 7 of *SM*.

56. *NWL*, 199; *N1*; Field, *Life*, 254.

57. VéN to Elena Wilson, May 9, 1948, Yale.

58. Pub. September 18, 1948; chap. 9 of *SM*; Field, *VN*, 231.

59. VN to William Maxwell, May 25, 1948, VNA.

60. VN to Morris Bishop, May 27, 1948, VNA, and to KW, May 30, 1948, Bryn Mawr.

61. *NWL*, 200; VN to KW, May 30, 1948; *SM*, 10.

62. *NWL*, 203; *Bulletin of the M.C.Z.* 101, no. 4 (February 1949): 479–541.

63. BB interview with Charles Remington, February 1987.

64. Sent to KW, July 5, 1948; pub. *New Yorker*, January 1, 1949; chap. 10 of *SM*.

65. VN to KW, June 23, 1948, VNA; BB interview with Sylvia Berkman, April 1983.

CHAPTER 7. RUSSIAN PROFESSOR

1. VN to Bishop, November 30, 1947, VNA; *Lolita*, 317.

2. VN to Bishop, May 15 and July 24, 1948; *NWL*, 204; VN to KW, July 5, 1948, VNA.

3. Diary, VNA.

4. Bishop to VN, May 30, 1948, Burton Jacoby to VN and VéN, June 24, 1969, and VN diary, VNA; *NWL*, 205.

5. VN to KW, August 21, 1948, VNA. The story was rejected by the *New Yorker* as too technical in its discussion of Russian prosody; pub. *Partisan Review*, September 1949; chap. 11 of *SM*. Cf. *VNRY*, 107–9.

6. Diary and unpublished lecture notes, VNA; *NWL*, 205.

7. VN to Bishop, July 24, 1948, VNA; *NWL*, 205.

8. *TD*, xi; VN to Roman Grynberg [Fall 1948], ColB.

9. VN to ES [ca. December 1948], private collection, and to Karpovich, September 28, 1948, ColB.

10. *PF*, 19; *SO*, 230; William Orndorff, letter to editor, *Cornell Alumni News*, February 1984.

11. VN to Croghans, November 7, 1948, and July 3, 1950, VNA.

12. "New Species of *Cyclargus* Nabokov," 273–80.

13. Diary; VN to Eric Bentley, July 21 and August 10, 1958, VNA.

14. Unpublished lecture notes, VNA.

15. BB interview with Richard Buxbaum, May 1983.

16. VN to Roman Grynberg, March 31, 1949, ColB.

17. Bishop to VN, April 27, 1948, VNA; Field, "Russia's 'Other' Poets"; VN diary, VNA; Gordon Ackerman interview with VN, *Weekly Tribune*, January 28, 1966.

18. McConkey, "Nabokov and 'The Window,' " 29; BB interview with Ephim Fogel, April 1983; Robert Martin Adams to BB, August 31, 1989.

19. Cowan, in Gibian and Parker, 222–23; for VN's tennis style, cf. also BB interview with Richard Buxbaum, May 1983, and DN to BB, September 22, 1988.

20. BB interview with VéN, December 1982; Mizener, "Professor Nabokov," 56; BB interview with Max Black, April 1983.

21. Black interview; Gilbert Weeks, cited by Alison Bishop, interview with BB, April 1983.

22. Diary, November 22, 1973, VNA.

23. Cited by KW, letter to VN, August 18, 1948, VNA; Alison Bishop in Gibian and Parker, 217.

24. BB interview with Alison Jolly, March 1983.

25. *NWL*, 210, 209, 216, 227.

26. *Song of Igor's Campaign* review and "Portrait of My Mother" chapter

sent to KW, February 10, 1949, VNA; latter pub. *New Yorker*, April 9, 1949, chap. 2 of *SM*.

27. VéN to Gladys Reichard, June 17, 1949, VNA; Reichard, Jakobson, and Werth, "Language and Synesthesia."

28. VN to KW, March 4, 1949, VNA.

29. Diary, VNA; BB interview with Richard Buxbaum, May 1983.

30. Buxbaum interview.

31. VN to Mstislav Dobuzhinsky, February [20], 1949, ColB.

32. *NYTBR*, April 24, 1949; repr. *SO*, 228–30.

33. VN to Herbert Lyons, March 14, 1949, VNA; *SL*, 90–91; VN to David Daiches, April 13, 1949, VNA.

34. Buxbaum interview; VN diary, VNA.

35. *SO*, 229–30.

36. VN to Zenzinov, January 21, 1949, ColB; *NWL*, 228; Roman Grynberg to VN, May 28, 1949, ColB; diary, VNA; *NWL*, 228.

37. See Shakhovskoy, *V poiskakh Nabokova*; Field, *VN*, 289. Field declares that VN spurned Russian contacts "in the 1950s."

38. VN to Doussia Ergaz, May 16, 1949, VNA.

39. VN to KW, June 20, 1949, VNA.

40. Field, *Life*, 272; DN to BB, September 22, 1988.

41. Buxbaum interview.

42. Diary; unpublished Notes for Work in Progress, VNA.

43. VN, cited in Field, *Life*, 272.

44. Cited by Appel, in Rivers and Nicol, 12; Buxbaum interview.

45. Pamphlet, "The Second Writers' Conference at the University of Utah," July 5–16, 1949; Buxbaum interview; BB interview with Wallace Stegner, May 1983.

46. VN to Alexander Klots, May 16, 1949, Klots to VN, July 2, 1949, VNA.

47. Buxbaum interview; diary; *NWL*, 227; BB interview with Charles Remington, February 1987.

48. VN to KW, August 1, 1949, VNA; Buxbaum interview; Klots to VN, July 2, 1949, VNA; Field, *Life*, 272; *N1*.

49. Buxbaum interview; DN, *CC*; DN to BB, September 22, 1988.

50. VN to Donald Eff, May 8, 1949, VNA; BB interview with VéN, January 1980.

51. VN to KW, October 17, 1949, and KW to VN, November 1, 1949, VNA.

52. *SM*, 263–64; VN to KW, November 9, 1949, VNA; pub. *Harper's Magazine*, January 1951; chap. 13 of *SM*.

53. *SL*, 95; VN to KW, December 2, 1949, VNA.

54. BB interview with William Maxwell, April 1983; *SL*, 95; VN to KW, December 2, 1949; *NWL*, 186.

55. *SL*, 95.

56. BB interview with William Maxwell, April 1983.

57. Daiches to VN, December 21, 1949, VNA; cf. Daiches in Donoghue, "VN: The Great Enchanter."

58. Jakobson to VN, January 9, 1950, VN to Jakobson, January 16, 1950, VNA.

59. *SL*, 96; diary.

60. VN to KW, March 4, 1950, VNA; pub. *New Yorker*, May 13, 1950; repr. *PP*.

61. Covici to VN, November 21, 1949; *SL*, 97; VN to KW, February 19 and March 13, 1950, VNA; VéN TS, VNA.

62. *NWL*, 233; EW, *Letters on Literature and Politics*, 482; *SL*, 110–11; Harold Ross to VN, January 11, 1951, VéN to Alfred Appel, October 12, 1977, VNA; diary.

63. *NWL*, 236–37; VN to KW, April 16, 1950, VNA; diary.

64. *SL*, 99. "Exile" pub. *Partisan Review*, January–February 1951, chap. 14 of *SM*; "Gardens and Parks" pub. *New Yorker*, June 17, 1950, chap. 15 of *SM*.

65. VN to Pascal Covici, April 15, 1950, and to KW, April 29, 1950, VNA.

66. Note in *CE* MS (May 5, 1950), VNA.

67. VéN to KW, May 5, 1950, VNA; diary; VN to KW, August 2, 1950, VNA.

CHAPTER 8. CONCLUSIVE EVIDENCE/SPEAK, MEMORY

1. Written 1935–1936 ("Mademoiselle O" and unpublished English reminiscences) and 1947–1950; pub. *Mesures*, April 1936, and *Atlantic Monthly*, January 1943 ("Mademoiselle O," chap. 5 of book), *New Yorker*, January 1948–June 1950 (chaps. 1–4, 6–10, 12, 15), *Partisan Review*, September 1949 and February 1951 (chaps. 11 and 14), *Harper's Magazine*, January 1951 (chap. 13); in book form, as *CE* (New York: Harper, 1951) and as *SM* (London: Gollancz, 1951); in VN's expanded Russian translation as *DB* (New York: Chekhov Publishing House, 1954); rev. and expanded English edition, *Speak, Memory: An Autobiography Revisited* (New York: Putnam's, 1967).

2. Unpublished chapter of *CE*, LCNA.

3. For VN's treatment of these influences, see *VNRY*, esp. chap. 2.

4. *Gift*, 211.

5. Unpublished chapter of *CE*, LCNA.

6. This sentence ended chap. 5 in *CE*; in *SM*, VN placed new material after this, and to compensate included another foreshadowing of VDN's death in the final movement of chap. 2.

7. Unpublished chapter of *CE*, LCNA.

8. *IB*, 94.

9. Unpublished chapter of *CE*, LCNA.

10. Ibid.

11. Ibid.

CHAPTER 9. TEACHING EUROPEAN FICTION

1. *NWL*, 236, 238, 241, 246.

2. S. N. Behrman to KW, April 19, 1950, cited in KW to VN, April 1950, and VN to John Fischer, April 20, and May 20, 1950, VNA; *SL*, 100.

3. Leonard Cottrell to VN, May 2, and VN to Cottrell, May 3, 1950, VNA.

4. VN to Jakobson, May 5, 1950, VNA.

5. *SO*, 128; 1950 diary, VNA.

6. VN to EW, June 3, 1950, Yale.

7. 1950 diary; VN to EW, June 3, 1950; "Klot's *Field Guide*," 41.

8. 1951 Yearbook, February 9, VNA; *Lolita*, 293.

9. *NWL*, 251; 1950 diary.

10. VN to John Fischer, June 5, July 13 and 20, 1950, VNA.

11. VN to Carl Proffer, May 1, 1968, VNA; *Lolita*, 314.

12. *SO*, 105.

13. *Lolita*, 314.

14. *SL*, 106.

15. VN to KW, August 2, 1950, Bryn Mawr.

16. *NWL*, 251; VN to Roman Grynberg, September 11, 1950, ColB.

17. BB interview with Alison Bishop, April 1983; VN to Andrew Field, September 26, 1966, VNA.

18. 1950 diary.

19. Ibid.

20. 1951 diary, May 27, VNA.

21. Ross Wetzsteon, "Nabokov as Teacher," 241; Martha Duffy, cited in *SO*, 128; Abrams, in Donoghue, "VN: The Great Enchanter," from TS in VNA; Ian Alexander interview with Elizabeth Lonsdale Webster, November 7, 1980, Canadian radio.

22. Gerald Clarke interview with VN, September 1974, from TS in VNA; 1969 diary, VNA.

23. Unpublished lecture notes, VNA; *SO*, 294; note, VNA. The lectures were published as *Lectures on Literature* (1980), *Lectures on Russian Literature* (1981), *Lectures on Don Quixote* (1983), all edited by Fredson Bowers, pub. New York: Harcourt Brace Jovanovich/Bruccoli Clark.

24. BB interview with Elizabeth Lonsdale Webster, April 1983.

25. Martha Updike, *Libération*, August 31, 1986.

26. Daryl Turgeon to VéN, February 10, 1966, VNA.

27. Unpublished lecture notes, VNA; *Lects*, 2; *SO*, 128.

28. *Lects*, 5. For date, 1947 diary, August 3 and 28–30, VNA.

29. *Lects*, 124.

30. *Lects*, 1.

31. *SO*, 156–57.

32. Unpublished lecture notes, VNA; *Lects*, 18.

33. "The Servile Path," in Reuben A. Brower, ed., *On Translation* (Cambridge, Mass.: Harvard University Press, 1959), 103.

34. *Lects*, 212–13, 220; unpublished lecture notes, VNA.

35. *Lects*, 56, 98.

36. *Lects*, 164, 116.

37. *SO*, 55–56.

38. *Lects*, 289.

39. Appel and Newman, 240–41.

40. *SO*, 294; unpublished lecture notes, VNA; Field, *Life*, 237–38; Robert Hughes interview with VN, September 1965, from TS in VNA.

41. VN to Joan Daly, April 6, 1976, VNA; *Lects*, 255; Henry Gelman to VN, April 2, 1955; Wetzsteon, "Nabokov as Teacher," 243.

42. *Lects*, 78–79.

43. Appel and Newman, 242.

44. *Lects*, 147; Appel, "Remembering Nabokov," 24; *Lects*, 210.

45. VN to Mischa Fayer, Middlebury College, July 12, 1955, VNA.

46. Appel, "Remembering Nabokov," 16–17.

47. Appel and Newman, 243.

48. *Lects*, 382; *LectsR*, 240.

49. *Lects*, 251.

50. *Lects*, 381.

51. 1950 diary, October 16 and 24, VNA.

52. VN to KW and E. B. White, October 25, 1950, E. B. White Collection, Cornell.

53. *Lolita*, 132.

54. MS, LCNA.

55. KW to VN, November 16, 1950, VNA.

56. *Lects*, 63–64, and unpublished lecture notes, VNA.

57. *SL*, 106.

58. 1950 diary, November 27–28, VNA.

59. Gerald Clarke interview with VN, September 1974, from TS in VNA; Daniel R. Hunter to BB, November 16, 1990.

60. Unpublished lecture notes, VNA.

61. Wetzsteon, "Nabokov as Teacher," 244.

62. *Lects*, 134, 385, 134–35.

63. 1951 Yearbook, VNA.

64. Cf. *SO*, 31.

65. 1951 diary, January 19–20, VNA.

66. 1951 Yearbook, January 31.

67. Unpublished notes, VNA.

68. VéN to KW, February 13, 1951, VNA.

69. 1951 Yearbook, February 21.

70. *NWL*, 259; cf. *NWL*, 252.

71. Harper and Bros. to Gollancz, March 3, 1951, VNA.

72. 1951 Yearbook. Story pub. *Hudson Review* 11 (Winter 1958–1959): 491–503; repr. *TD*, 219–38.

73. VN to KW, March 10, 1951, VNA.

74. *SL*, 116–17.

75. VN to Tatyana Karpovich, February 8, and Mikail Karpovich to VN, March 27, 1951, VNA.

76. *Metamorphosis*, trans. A. L. Lloyd, preface by Paul Goodman (New York: Vanguard, 1946), from VN copy, VNA.

77. Unpublished lecture notes, VNA; 1951 diary, April 18.

78. 1951 diary, April 28; BB interview with Avgusta Jaryc, April 1983; VN

to Sigismund Sluszka, April 10, 1951, VNA; Albert Parry, *NRS*, July 9, 1978, 2.

79. Buxbaum interview; 1948 diary, January 13, VNA.

80. BB interviews with Avgusta Jaryc and Milton Cowan, April 1983, and with Marc Szeftel, May 1983.

81. Unpublished lecture notes, VNA; 1951 Yearbook, February 18; VN to KW, September 25, 1955, VNA.

82. VN to Roman Grynberg, September 11, 1950, ColB.

83. 1951 diary, May 25; *New York Herald Tribune*, May 20, 1951; Appel, "Nabokov: A Portrait," 12; BB interview with Appel, April 1983.

84. *NWL*, 261–62.

CHAPTER 10. FINDING TIME FOR LOLITA

1. *Perepiska*, 67; VéN to KW, February 13, and VN to KW, June 8, 1951, VNA.

2. Diary, VNA; Gordon H. Fairbanks, Helen E. Shadick, and Zulefa Yedigar, *A Russian Area Reader for College Classes* (New York: Ronald Press, [1951]).

3. VN to Grynberg, June 9, 1951, ColB; *NWL*, 264.

4. *SL*, 120–21, and VN correspondence with Finley and Levin, June–November 1951, VNA.

5. *SL*, 121; *Libération*, August 31, 1986; diary, September 2–6, 1951, VNA.

6. "Nearctic Members," 513; *NWL*, 264; BB interview with DN, December 1981.

7. Page-a-Day Diary, VNA.

8. Ibid.

9. Robert Hughes interview with VN, September 1965, from TS, VNA; Alan Nordstrom interview with VN, "My Child *Lolita*," *Ivy*, February 1959, 28.

10. "Female of *Sublivens*," 35; *PF*, 36–37; VéN to Igor Trofimov, March 21, 1980, VNA.

11. "Female of *Sublivens*," 35, 36; *Perepiska*, 69; VN to Mark Aldanov, August 1951, ColB; *NWL*, 265; VN to P. Sheldon Remington, June 23, 1953, VNA.

12. *Lolita*, 310; *NWL*, 265.

13. *NWL*, 266; *SL*, 122; Petzoldt-Exum certificate, August 16, 1951, VNA; DN to BB, September 22, 1988. DN, *CC*, 306, misdates this to 1949.

14. *NWL*, 265–66; *SL*, 122; BB interview with VéN, January 1985.

15. *SL*, 121.

16. *NWL*, 265; VéN to Doussia Ergaz, September 2, 1951, VNA.

17. Mizener, "Professor Nabokov," 56.

18. VN to Vera Alexandrova, September 13, 1951, VNA.

19. *NWL*, 266; Cornell Board of Trustees to VN, April 28, 1951, VNA; Leonard Cottrell to VN, May 4, 1951, VNA.

20. VN to John Finley, October 6, 1951, VNA; unpublished note, VNA;

diary, October 4 and 7–9, 1951, VNA; *SO*, 55, 128; Mizener, "Professor Nabokov," 56.

21. BB interview with VéN, October 1982; *Time*, May 23, 1969, 89.

22. VN to Henry Allan Moe, October 8, to KW, November 2, and to Doussia Ergaz, October 30, 1951, VNA.

23. *NWL*, 270; Bishop, "Nabokov at Cornell," 237; *SL*, 124.

24. VN to KW, November 2, 1951; pub. *New Yorker*, February 2, 1952; repr. *ND*, 197–212.

25. *NWL*, 267; KW to VN, November 26, 1951, VNA.

26. VN to KW, November 29, 1951, VNA.

27. *New Yorker* to Mrs. T. L. Slaugh, February 28, and VN to KW, March 10, 1952, VNA.

28. Diary, VNA; VéN to Judith Matlack, October 29, 1951, VNA; *NRS* [ca. December 10, 1951]; *SL*, 127–28 and VN-Covici correspondence, October 1951–January 1952, VNA.

29. *Lolita* MS notes, LCNA; diary, 1951, VNA; Field, *Life in Art*, 328; Penelope Gilliatt interview with VN, *Vogue*, December 1966, 280; Hans-Peter Riklin interview with VN, January 5, 1970, from TS, VNA.

30. *NWL*, 269, 270; Henry Allan Moe to VN, April 9, and VN to Pascal Covici, January 20, 1952, VNA.

31. *NWL*, 272; VN to Morris Bishop, February 21, 1952, VNA.

32. Sarton, *Fur Person*, 8.

33. Field, *VN*, 268. Field writes that "Tom Jones eventually came to live in *Pale Fire*," although Kinbote's cat there is black, not tiger-striped, and spurned, not pampered, by Kinbote. Cf. Marina Naumann, "Novel Cat Connections," *Nabokovian* 22 (1989): 18–20.

34. VN to Morris Bishop, February 21, 1952, VNA; BB interview with Ivan Nabokoff, January 1985; Yuri Ivask to BB, August 21, 1983.

35. Harry Levin to VN, June 27, 1951, VNA; Field, *VN*, 239; *DQ*, 1, 4.

36. *DQ*, 72.

37. *NWL*, 272; Field, *Life*, 264; Harry Levin, *NYTBR*, November 16, 1980; BB interview with Levin, February 1987; Levin to BB, July 23, 1990; Gennadi Barabtarlo to BB, June 11, 1990.

38. *DQ*, 110, 112.

39. *LectsR*, 164–65; *Lects*, 86–87.

40. *Perepiska*, 68 (cf. *SL*, 122); diary, February 9, 1952, VNA; Notes for Work in Progress, VNA; BB interview with Elena Levin, March 1983; Field, *Life*, 7; DN, *CC*, 306; DN to BB, October 14 and 17, 1990.

41. BB interviews with Harry and Elena Levin, March 1983, and with Mary McCarthy, January 1985.

42. Richard Wilbur to BB, August 30, 1990.

43. *NWL*, 278, 311; BB interview with Harry Levin, March 1983.

44. Diary, 1952, VNA; Richard Ellmann to VN, January 2, 1975, VNA; VN to Morris Bishop, February 21, 1952, VNA; Field, *Life*, 262.

45. *NWL*, 272; *Nouvelle Gazette* (Brussels), February 24, 1952; *Paris-Normandie-Rouen*, March 14, 1952, and album of reviews, February–March 1952, VNA.

46. Archibald MacLeish to VN, November 27, 1951, VNA; VN to KW,

March 10, 1952, VNA; "Restoration" and "Pity the elderly grey translator" MSS, VNA; VN correspondence with Wellesley College, February–March 1952, and with the University of Toronto, March–April 1952, VNA; Field, *Life*, 247.

47. Henry Allan Moe to VN, April 9, 1952, VNA; diary, VNA; VéN to Jason Epstein, September 17, 1960, VNA; VN to Pascal Covici, April 11, 1952, VNA; *SL*, 132–34.

48. *NWL*, 276.

49. Diary, VNA; VéN to Isabel Stephens, July 5, 1952; DN, *CC*, 307.

50. *NWL*, 277, 278.

51. VéN to Hans Epstein, January 1953, VNA; VéN to Isabel Stephens, July 5, 1952; "Butterfly Collecting in Wyoming," 50; DN to BB, October 17, 1990.

52. "Migratory Species," 51–52.

53. VéN to Isabel Stephens, July 5, 1952.

54. "Butterfly Collecting in Wyoming," 50.

55. Diary, VNA; VéN to Doussia Ergaz, July 19, 1952, VNA; *SL*, 134.

56. "Butterfly Collecting in Wyoming," 49; VN to James Laughlin, August 16, 1952; *NWL*, 277; VN to Grynberg, August 10, 1972, ColB; VéN to Yvonne Davet, August 1952, VNA; VéN to John Fischer, August 13, 1952, VNA.

57. Familial Matters Folder, VNA; Bishop, "Nabokov at Cornell," 236; BB interviews with Alison Bishop, April 1983, and with Harry Levin, March 1983; DN to BB, October 17, 1990.

58. Diary, VNA.

59. VN to Covici, October 14 and November 3, 1952, VNA; *SL*, 391.

60. *NWL*, 268.

61. VN to George Hessen, October 1, 1952, VNA; Notes for Work in Progress, VNA; Trahan, "Laughter from the Dark," 179.

62. Diary, VNA; *NRS*, December 18, 1952; DN, *CC*, 308–9.

63. Appel, "Remembering Nabokov," 18.

64. Robert Hughes interview with VN, September 1965, from TS, VNA; Sylvia Berkman to VéN, February 26, 1953, VNA.

65. VN to KW, February 16, 1953, VNA; VN to Ambassador Hotel, December 10, 1955, VNA; Morris Bishop to VN and VéN, February 26, 1953, VNA.

66. *NWL*, 280; diary, VNA; *SL*, 136.

67. *NWL*, 281; diary, VNA.

68. Sarton, *Fur Person*, 9.

69. Diary, VNA; *NWL*, 280.

70. VN to Donald Eff, May 1, 1953, VNA; *NWL*, 281; VN to Roman Jakobson, May 5, 1955, VNA.

71. VN to Pascal Covici, May 6, 1953, VNA; *SM*, 12, 195–96; diary, VNA.

72. VéN to Alice James, May 17, 1953, VNA, and to Karpovich, June 17, 1953, ColB.

73. *SL*, 139; "Nearctic Members," 496.

74. Notes for Work in Progress, VNA; *NWL*, 282; VéN to Yvonne Davet, June 20, 1953, VNA; VéN to Rosemary Mizener, June 17, 1953, VNA; *SL*, 139.

75. VN to KW, July 26, 1953, to William Maxwell, August 16, 1953, VNA; *SL*, 208.

76. VN to KW, July 26, 1953; *SL*, 140.

77. *Life*, April 13, 1959; VéN to Alison Bishop [ca. July 21, 1953], VNA; *Los Angeles Mirror Evening News*, July 31, 1959.

78. VN to Morris Bishop, July 21, 1953, VNA; Notes for Work in Progress, VNA; *SL*, 139; diary, November 12, 1953; VéN to Karpovich, June 17, 1953, ColB.

79. Notes for Work in Progress, VNA.

80. Diary, VNA; Heine, "Nabokov as Teacher."

81. VN to EW, October 15, 1953, Yale; *SL*, 138-39; VN to KW, November 7, 1953, VNA.

82. VéN to Mrs. Saltus, November 20, 1953; *SL*, 139; VN to William Sale, October 26, 1953, VNA; VéN to Colette Duhamel, December 9, 1953, VNA.

CHAPTER 11. LOLITA

Epigraphs: *NWL*, 298; *Newsweek*, November 24, 1958.

1. Written 1950–1953; pub. Paris: Olympia Press, 1955. Edition cited, New York: Putnam's, 1958.

2. Trilling, "The Last Lover," 19.

3. *SM*, 290.

4. Christopher Ricks, "Profferings," *TLS*, October 10, 1968, 1154. Julian Barnes repeats Ricks's point in *Flaubert's Parrot* (London: Jonathan Cape, 1984).

5. Davies, "Mania for Green Fruit," *Victoria Daily Times*, January 17, 1959.

6. Trilling, "The Last Lover," 12.

7. *SO*, 94.

8. Stella Estes letter to VN, VNA; echoed by Trilling and others.

9. *LectsR*, 309.

10. See editorial, *New Republic*, October 27, 1958.

11. Cf. VéN note, Page-a-Day Diary, September 17, 1958, VNA.

12. *Gift* has a similar formulation, but not the exact one I recall but cannot locate.

13. Appel, *AnL*, lxvii.

14. Proffer, *Keys to Lolita*, and Appel, *AnL*, mark the Carmen and Quilty trails. Appel in particular traces manner and matter and most of the book's allusions with insight and wit.

15. Appel, *AnL*, 326.

CHAPTER 12. LOLITA *INTO PRINT*, PNIN *ONTO PAPER*

1. VN-Covici correspondence, November 1953–January 1954, VNA; *NWL*, 285.

2. *SL*, 142–43; VéN to KW, January 26, 1954, VNA; KW to VéN, February 1, 1954, Bryn Mawr.

3. Sukenick, *Down and In*, 76–81; BB interview with Samuel Anderson, February 1987.

4. VN to KW, February 3, 1954, VNA; *SL*, 150.

5. VéN to Jacqueline Chalaire, Doubleday, August 30, 1956, VNA; *SL*, 143; Covici to VN, March 25, 1954, VNA.

6. Appel, "Remembering Nabokov," 20–21.

7. "Vnov' ya posetil . . ." ("Again I have visited . . .").

8. Cf. Grayson, *Nabokov Translated*, 141.

9. Cf. *SM*, 12; *SL*, 149; *DB*, pub. New York: Chekhov Publishing House, 1954.

10. VN–Wallace Brockway correspondence, March 20–June 5, 1954, VNA.

11. *SL*, 149.

12. Appel, "Remembering Nabokov," 19 (bracketed material in original), 29.

13. Diary, VNA; Morris Bishop to VN, August 15, 1958, VNA; VN to George Hessen, April 26, 1954, and to Yuri Ivask, February 21, 1956, VNA; *University Daily Kansan*, April 20 and 22, 1954.

14. *Lectures on Ulysses*, page preceding p. 1; *SO*, 71; *Lects*, 306, 322.

15. Quennell, 12; BB interview with Appel, February 1987; VN's annotated *Ulysses*, VNA.

16. Notes for Work in Progress, VNA; Mizener, *Cornell Alumni News*, September 1983, 56; diary, September 18, 1954, VNA.

17. VéN to Gordon Lacy, August 23, 1954, VNA; *NWL*, 285; *SL*, 253; DN, CC, 315.

18. *NWL*, 285; *SL*, 150; VN to James Laughlin, July 21, 1954, VNA; DN, CC, 315.

19. *SL*, 146; VN to Wallace Brockway, July 25, 1954, VNA; *SL*, 148; BB interview with DN, December 1981; DN, CC, 311.

20. Wallace Brockway to VN, June 29, 1954, VNA; VN to KW, February 3, 1954, VNA; *SL*, 147; VéN to Doussia Ergaz, August 6, 1954; *SO*, 270.

21. VéN to Gordon Lacy, August 23, 1954, VNA; *NWL*, 286–87; diary, VNA.

22. Notes for Work in Progress, VNA; *NYTBR*, May 7, 1984. VN sent the book to Laughlin on July 21.

23. VéN to KW, September 30, 1954, VNA; Brower to VN, March 26, 1957, VNA. "Problems of Translation" pub. *Partisan Review*, Autumn 1955.

24. CornUA, Proceedings of the Board of Trustees.

25. *Perepiska*, 79; *NWL*, 290; Roger Straus to VN, November 11, 1954, VNA. Straus later misremembered that he *had* thought the book publishable (*NYTBR*, May 7, 1984).

26. BB interview with Harry and Elena Levin, February 1987. The Levins heard the story from both Wilson and Nabokov.

27. BB interview with Jason Epstein, March 1983; *N1*; *NWL*, 288.

28. *NWL*, 290, 293, 298.

29. *SL*, 154; Rahv to VN, November 18, 1954, VNA.

30. *NYTBR*, May 7, 1984.

31. Notes for Work in Progress, and exam script, January 1955, Literature 311, VNA.

32. Pub. April 23, 1955.

33. VN to Tatiana Terentiev, November 1 and 10, 1954, VNA.

34. VN to Doussia Ergaz, February 16, 1955, VNA; *SO*, 270; Doussia Ergaz to VN, April 19, 1961, VNA.

35. *SL*, 156; VN to Covici, May 1, 1955, VNA; *NWL*, 293; VN to Anna Kallinn, BBC, May 7, June 5, and July 15, 1955, VNA.

36. *NWL*, 290; Ergaz to VN, April 26 and 28, 1955, VNA.

37. Girodias, "Pornologist on Olympus," 56; Kenneth Allsop, "I Am a Pornographer," 595; Girodias, *Preuves*, January 1963.

38. Ergaz to VN, May 13 and 24, and VN to Ergaz, May 24, 1955, VNA.

39. *SO*, 271.

40. Cited in Ergaz to VN, May 13, 1955.

41. Ergaz to VN, April 28, and VN to Ergaz, May 24, 1955.

42. Bishop, "Nabokov à Cornell"; Morris Bishop to Alison Bishop, May 18, 1955, CornUA; Alison Bishop, in Gibian and Parker, 217.

43. VN to Ergaz, June 4, 1955, to Ivan Obolensky, April 1, 1958, and to Walter Minton, September 19, 1957, VNA; *SO*, 268.

44. VéN to Sylvia Berkman [ca. early August 1955], VNA; Helga Chudacoff interview with VN, September 1974, from TS in VNA; BB interview with Sylvia Berkman, April 1983.

45. VéN to Sylvia Berkman [ca. early August 1955], VNA.

46. VN to Epstein, March 7, 1955, VNA; *SL*, 160-61; Epstein to VN, June 28, 1955, VNA; BB interview with DN, December 1981; VéN to Isabel Stephens, October 6, 1955, VNA.

47. VéN to Covici, June 20, and to Sylvia Berkman [ca. early August 1955], VNA.

48. VN to Ergaz, July 12, 1955, VNA; *SL*, 175; VN to Girodias, July 12, 1955, VNA.

49. VéN to Ada Gregg, July 18, and to Isabel Stephens, October 6, 1955, VNA.

50. Notes for Work in Progress, VNA; VN to Girodias, July 23, 1955, VNA.

51. VN to William Maxwell, July 24, 1955, VéN to Jacqueline Chalaire, August 30, 1956, 1951 Year Book ("February 27"), and VN to Girodias, July 25, 1955, VNA; VéN to Elena Wilson, August 6, 1955, Yale; VN to Covici, August 20, 1955, VNA; Tompkins County Memorial Hospital bill, VNA.

52. BB interview with Stephen Jan Parker, February 1987; *SO*, 84-85.

53. EW, *Upstate*, 161; EW, *Letters on Literature and Politics*, 577.

54. VN to William Maxwell, August 23, 1955, VNA; "Pnin Gives a Party" pub. November 12, 1955.

55. *SL*, 177; VN to EW, August 31, 1955, VNA; VN to KW, September 25, 1955, VNA.

CHAPTER 13. PNIN

1. Written 1953-1955; pub. serially in *New Yorker* (chap. 1, November 28, 1953; chap. 3, April 23, 1955; chap. 4, October 15, 1955; chap. 6, November 12, 1955); in book form, New York: Doubleday, 1957. For a lovingly detailed

line-by-line commentary and a discussion of the novel's paradoxes and principles, see Barabtarlo, *Phantom of Fact*.

2. *MUSSR*, 321.

3. Charles Nicol provided the first and best outline of the novel's squirrel pattern before Barabtarlo in "Pnin's History," 93–105. My own interpretations of the pattern frequently differ from those Nicol suggests.

4. *SL*, 159.

5. First noted by Rowe, *Nabokov's Spectral Dimension*, 62.

CHAPTER 14. LOLITA *SPARKS*

Epigraph: *SL*, 197.

1. *SL*, 437.

2. *NWL*, 214.

3. BB interview with Alfred Appel, April 1983; VN to Andrew Field, February 3, 1967.

4. BB interview with Appel, April 1983.

5. Parry, "Pamyati Vladimira Nabokova."

6. Adams, "Nabokov's Show."

7. BB interview with Ephim Fogel, April 1983. The professor was David Lee Clark.

8. VN draft letter to Morris Bishop, February 21, 1952, VNA.

9. Adams, "Nabokov's Show"; BB interview with Elizabeth Lonsdale Webster, April 1983; DN to BB, October 17, 1990.

10. BB interviews with James McConkey and with M. H. Abrams, April 1983.

11. Fogel, in Gibian and Parker, 231; BB interview with Fogel, April 1983.

12. Kahn, in Gibian and Parker, 229; BB interview with Kahn, April 1983.

13. Demorest, "Administering Professor Nabokov," 56.

14. George, "Remembering Nabokov," 479–92; VéN to BB, March 31, 1989; Robert M. Adams to BB, August 31, 1989.

15. VN to Marie Schébéko, September 21, and to Doussia Ergaz, October 8, 1955, VNA.

16. *NWL*, 297; *SL*, 209; VN to KW, October 9, 1955, and VéN to Gus Lobrano, October 25, 1955, VNA.

17. *SL*, 182.

18. *NWL*, 296; KW to VN, November 21, 1955; *SL*, 180–81; E. B. White to BB, April 20, 1983.

19. Diary, 1956, VNA.

20. VéN to Tatiana Terentiev, February 4, 1956, ColB.

21. Diary; VéN to Elena Wilson, April 20, 1956, Yale.

22. BB interview with Harry and Elena Levin, March 1983; EW, *Letters on Literature and Politics*, 723.

23. DN, "Translating with Nabokov," 147; diary; BB interviews with VéN, February 1983, and with DN, April 1983.

24. VN to Roman Jakobson, March 30, 1955, to KW and to Mark Aldanov, April 30, 1956, VNA.

25. Notes for Work in Progress, VNA; *Sunday Express*, January 29, 1956; *Spectator*, February 10, 1956; *NYTBR*, February 26, 1956; *NWL*, 298.

26. Field, *VN*, 308; Doussia Ergaz to VéN, February 22 and March 12, 1956, VNA.

27. *NYTBR*, March 11, 1956; VéN to Girodias, March 15, and to Doussia Ergaz, April 21, 1956, VNA.

28. VN correspondence with BBC, October 1955–March 1956, VNA; diary; VéN to Elena Wilson, April 20, 1956, Yale.

29. *NWL*, 296; *SL*, 183.

30. Edith Dale to VéN, February 9, 1956, VéN to Yvonne Davet, June 12, VN to Mark Aldanov, September 7, 1956, VNA; *NWL*, 299–300.

31. *SL*, 186.

32. VN to Jason Epstein, July 7, to KW, August 7, and VéN to Amy Kelly, September 18, 1956, VNA.

33. VéN to Amy Kelly, September 18, 1956, VNA.

34. VN to Reuben Brower, August 30, and to Thomas Wilson, September 14, 1956, VNA.

35. VéN to Sylvia Berkman, September 7, 1956, VNA; diaries.

36. VéN to Sylvia Berkman, September 7, 1956.

37. *SL*, 190–91.

38. Field, *VN*, 289.

39. Doussia Ergaz to VN, July 24, 1956, VNA.

40. VéN to Doussia Ergaz, October 26, 1956, VNA; BB interview with Jason Epstein, March 1983; *SL*, 191n.

41. VN to Epstein, September 13, 1956, VNA; *NWL*, 304.

42. VN to Epstein, October 24 and November 12, 1956, VNA.

43. Girodias to VN, August 13 and September 12, 1956, VNA; Nemerov, *New York Times*, October 30, 1956.

44. John Hollander, *Partisan Review*, Fall 1956; Ergaz to VéN, October 31, 1956, VNA.

45. VéN to Ergaz, November 8, 1956; *SL*, 194.

46. *Arts* (Paris), January 16, 1957; *SL*, 201; *Saturday Review*, June 22, 1957.

47. Cornell Faculty Survey, 1956–1957, VNA; Eleanor Billmeyer interview with VN, February 28, 1957, from TS, VNA.

48. *NWL*, 306; VN to Roman Grynberg, January 19, 1957, VNA; diary.

49. Exam script and Notes for Work in Progress, VNA; Daniel R. Hunter to BB, November 16, 1990.

50. Elena Levin to VéN, February 20, 1957, VNA; Field, *Life*, 263; Harry Levin in Donoghue, "VN: The Great Enchanter," from TS, VNA.

51. BB interview with Lauriston and Ruth Sharp, April 1983; VN to Andrew Field, June 12, 1970, VNA.

52. Girodias to VN, February 8 and March 5, VNA; *SL*, 200.

53. *SL*, 208–9; pub. *New Yorker*, July 6, 1957; repr. *PP*, 177–79.

54. *SL*, 206; Epstein to VN, March 6, 1957, VNA.

55. VN to Epstein, August 24, 1956, VNA.

56. VéN to Gus Lobrano, October 25, 1955, and to Sylvia Berkman, October 1956, VNA; MS note, Shoebox 1, VNA.

57. *SO*, 31; *Pale Fire* MS, LCNA.

58. *SL*, 212-13.

59. VN to KW, April 30, 1957, VNA.

60. *Newsweek*, March 11, 1957, VNA.

61. VN to Doussia Ergaz, March 24, 1957, VNA.

62. Daryl Turgeon to VéN, February 10, 1966, VNA.

63. Fogel, in Gibian and Parker, 233.

64. Diary; Notes for Work in Progress, VNA; McConkey, "Nabokov and 'The Window,' " 30; BB interviews with McConkey and Appel, April 1983; Field, *Life*, 276.

65. Unpublished lecture notes, VNA; see also BB, "Nabokov at Cornell," 138-41.

66. Reuben Brower to VN, March 26, 1957, VNA; *SO*, MS, VNA; pub. as "Zametki perevodchika [Notes of a Translator]," and "Zametki perevodchika—II [Notes of a Translator—II]."

67. Girodias to VN, March 12, 1957, VNA.

68. VéN to Ergaz, March 17, and VN to Epstein, April 16, 1957, VNA.

69. VN to John Barrett, April 18, 1957, Bollingen Collection, LC; *NWL*, 311.

70. *SL*, 216; George Hessen to VN, June 20, 1956, VNA; BB interview with VéN, February 1983; Field, *VN*, 303.

71. Appel, "Remembering Nabokov," 23; Rosemary Mizener to BB, August 26, 1983; BB interview with M. H. Abrams, April 1983.

72. *NWL*, 72; EW, *Upstate*, 157; "Zametki perevodchika," 131.

73. *Upstate*, 160; "Zametki perevodchika—II," 39.

74. *SO*, 248; BB interview with VéN, December 1986.

75. *Upstate*, 161.

76. *SL*, 220-21; *NWL*, 317.

77. VN to Reuben Brower and to KW, July 18, 1957, VNA; BB interview with Ruth Sharp, April, 1983; LCNA; *NWL*, 320.

78. VN to Epstein, May 1, 1957, VNA; *Saturday Review*, June 22, 1957; *SL*, 217.

79. *SL*, 222; VN to Ergaz, September 10, 1957, VéN to Ergaz, July 30, 1957, Epstein to VN, June 24, 1957, VNA.

80. VN, *Cornell Daily Sun*, October 3, 1958.

81. LCNA; BB interview with Lauriston and Ruth Sharp, April 1983; Shoebox 1, VNA.

82. Diary; Girodias to VN, and VN to Girodias, September 14, 1957, VNA.

83. VéN to Girodias, September 11, 1957, VN to Walter Minton, September 7, 1957, VNA; *SL*, 220, 225.

84. *SL*, 228-29, 232-35; VN correspondence with Girodias, October–November, 1957, VNA.

85. Marc Szeftel, "*Lolita* at Cornell"; VéN to Epstein, December 22, 1957; Kahn, in Gibian and Parker, 229-30; BB interview with Kahn, April 1983;

Field, *VN*, 305; comments on Katz novel cited and reproduced in bookseller Randy F. Weinstein's catalogue, *Lives of Works that Matter*, 30.

86. Richard Schickel, *Reporter*, November 28, 1957; VN to Vaun Gillmor [ca. December 4, 1957], Bollingen Collection, LC.

CHAPTER 15. EUGENE ONEGIN

Epigraphs: *SO*, 252, 242.

1. *SO*, 106.

2. *NG*, 29.

3. Unpublished lectures, VNA.

4. In *EO*, 2:527, VN produces a four-line sample of a rhymed translation he dates 1950. His retrospective datings are often very approximate, and he seems in fact to have decided by 1948, before beginning at Cornell, to translate *EO* only in prose.

5. *SO*, 38; *NWL*, 205, 227; VN to Jakobson, January 16, 1950, VNA.

6. *SL*, 130.

7. *SO*, 13; *NWL*, 311; *SL*, 342.

8. See *SO*, 256.

9. "Zametki perevodchika"; "Zametki perevodchika—II"; "The Servile Path," Brower, *On Translation*.

10. Arndt, *Eugene Onegin*; VN, "On Translating Pushkin: Pounding the Clavichord."

11. Bayley, *Observer*, November 29, 1964; EW, *NYRB*, July 15, 1965; VN and EW, "The Strange Case of Nabokov and Wilson"; VN, "Nabokov's Reply."

12. Diaries, 1966–1967, VNA; *SL*, 482.

13. Revised ed., trans. Babette Deutsch with Avrahm Yarmolinsky (Harmondsworth: Penguin, 1964).

14. Harmondsworth: Penguin, 1979.

15. *The Triple Thinkers* (1952; Harmondsworth: Penguin, 1962), 51.

16. *SO*, 233.

17. *NYRB*, February 3, 1983.

18. James Boswell, *Life of Johnson*, ed. R. W. Chapman (Oxford: Oxford University Press, 1970), 742.

19. *Encounter*, May 1965.

20. BB interview with Epstein, March 1983.

21. *NWL*, 290.

22. 1:x (1964).

23. A point made in Alexander Gerschenkron's review article, "A Manufactured Moment?"

24. *SO*, 253.

25. Ibid.

26. Ibid., 254.

27. Ibid., 255–56.

28. 2:186.

29. *NWL*, 311.

30. 1:x.

31. VNA.

32. BB interview with Elena Levin, March 1983.

33. 1:8.

34. "Problems of Translation," 496; unpublished Russian lecture, VNA; Gerschenkron, "A Manufactured Moment?" 337.

35. Bayley, *Observer*, November 29, 1964; Brown, "Pluck and Polemics," 313.

36. See Clayton, *Alexander Pushkin's "Eugene Onegin,"* 68.

37. 2:392.

38. Brown, *Russian Literature of the Romantic Period*, 3:414 n. 32.

39. 2:339–40.

40. 1:10.

41. *SO*, 118, 10.

42. VNA.

43. 1:8.

44. 3:19–20.

45. 3:11–12.

46. 2:73.

47. 2:149.

48. 2:275, 280; 3:241.

49. 2:152, 150–51.

50. *SO*, 264–65.

51. 3:101.

52. 2:146; 3:173, 32–33.

53. 3:290.

54. 2:181.

55. 3:505, 506; 2:119.

56. 3:290; 2:322, 204.

57. 3:290.

58. 1:59.

59. Unpublished lecture notes, VNA; 3:349, 363; unpublished lecture notes.

60. 3:409.

61. 2:47–48; for critique of Chizhevski, see, e.g., 2:80.

62. 3:320; 2:164; 3:363.

63. 2:79; *SO*, 266; 3:191–92.

64. 3:42; 2:177; 3:353; *SL*, 348.

65. 2:110.

66. "Zametki perevodchika—II," 131–32.

67. 2:33, 162–63.

68. 3:65.

69. 3:471–72.

70. Victor Terras, "Puškin's 'Feast During the Plague' and Its Original: A Structural Confrontation," in Andrej Kodjak and Kiril Taranovsky, eds., *Al-*

exander Puškin: A Symposium on the 175th Anniversary of His Birth (New York: New York University Press, 1976), 208–9.

71. See Pushkin, *Sobranie sochineniy* (Moscow: 1962), 7:208. Pushkin bought *Specimens of the Table Talk of the Late Samuel Taylor Coleridge* (2 vols., London: John Murray, 1835) in the year it came out. See the Coleridge entry for June 24, 1827.

72. *New Statesman*, January 19, 1968.

73. Brown, *Russian Literature of the Romantic Period*, 3:188; Ricks, "Nabokov's Pushkin."

74. Nabokov firmly dismisses the idea that a foot in an iambic line can be anything but an iamb, whatever the actual accents of the words within the foot. The line is the unit of meter as the organism is of life, and a variant accent does not create a new foot (pyrrhic, trochaic, or spondaic) any more than a man with one leg constitutes the start of a new species. In iambic verse the *expectation* of an unstressed syllable followed by a stressed syllable persists throughout the line, and if word accents do not correspond to the expected stresses, the feet still remain iambic. Nabokov could have made this point much more concisely than he does. He then introduces new names for the three possible kinds of irregular iambic foot: a foot without accents he terms a "scud"; a foot with an initial accent on the metrically unstressed first syllable with no accent on the metrically stressed second syllable constitutes a "tilt" (or a "tilted scud"); and a foot with two accents becomes a "false spondee."

75. For "tilts" and "false spondees," see previous note.

76. On the pretext that in both variations, the expected metrical stress on the second syllable is unaccented. But the metrically *un*stressed first syllable is unaccented in scuds and accented in tilts—which makes all the difference.

77. 3:461.

78. 3:501.

CHAPTER 16. LOLITA *EXPLODES*

Epigraph: *SL*, 259.

1. "The Lolita Case," *Time*, November 17, 1958; Page-a-Day Diary, VNA.

2. *SL*, 236–37.

3. VéN to Minton, September 3, and VN to Minton, November 10, 1958, VNA; *SL*, 228.

4. Girodias press release, January 15, 1958, and VN to Michel Mohrt, January 1, 1958, VNA.

5. VéN to Isabel Stephens, March 18, 1958, and Vaun Gillmor to VN, January 28, 1958, VNA.

6. VN to Epstein, February 12, 1958; "What Hath 'Lolita' Wrought?" *Elmira Telegram*, December 14, 1958; VN and VéN to Isabel Stephens, March 18, and VN to Natalia de Peterson [ca. March 1958], VNA.

7. Notes for Work in Progress, VNA.

8. VN diary, March 15, 1958; Abrams, in Gibian and Parker, 221; Robert M. Adams to BB, August 31, 1989.

9. Rosemary Mizener to BB, August 26, 1983.

10. BB interview with Black, April 1983.

11. VN to Epstein, March 30, 1958, VNA; diary, April 8, 1958; Doussia Ergaz to VN, March 21 and April 4, 1958, VNA.

12. Demorest, "Administering Professor Nabokov," 8.

13. Notes for Work in Progress, VNA.

14. Cited in VéN to Rachel Adams, March 28, 1958, VNA; Alfred Appel to VN, October 17, 1970, VNA; Abrams, in Gibian and Parker, 220; Ross Wetzsteon to BB, March 1987; LectsR MS, VNA; Robert M. Adams, August 31, 1989.

15. VN to Wahlström and Witrand, January 9 and May 1, 1958, VNA; NWL, 325–26; VéN to Agnes Perkins, April 29, 1958, VNA.

16. Page-a-Day Diary, VNA.

17. NWL, 324; VéN to Agnes Perkins, April 29, 1958.

18. VN to Minton, May 10, 1958, VNA.

19. Page-a-Day Diary, VNA.

20. Phyllis Meras interview with VN, May 13, 1962, from TS in VNA; DN to BB, October 18, 1990.

21. Page-a-Day Diary, VNA.

22. VéN to Sylvia Berkman, August 25, and to Filippa Rolf, September 25, 1958, VNA.

23. VN to Doussia Ergaz, July 8, 1958, VNA; Brenner, "Nabokov," Page-a-Day Diary, VNA.

24. Page-a-Day Diary, VNA.

25. VéN to Minton, August 13, 1958, VNA.

26. SL, 257; Page-a-Day Diary, VNA.

27. Page-a-Day Diary, VNA; SL, 259; VéN to Amy Kelly, April 19, 1961, VNA.

28. VN to Minton, September 3, 1958, VNA; SL, 260; Page-a-Day Diary, VNA; Life International, April 13, 1959; VéN to Morris and Alison Bishop, April 15, 1959, VNA.

29. Page-a-Day Diary, VNA.

30. Ibid.; Ada, 361, 227.

31. Page-a-Day Diary, VNA.

32. Minton to VN, September 16, 1958, VNA.

33. "Vladimir Nabokov denies Lolita Obscene," Register (New Haven, Conn.), January 18, 1959; VN correspondence with LC, September 1958–February 1959, VNA, inc. SL, 270–71.

34. BB interviews with Elizabeth Lonsdale Webster and with Peter Kahn, April 1983; Parker, cited in Field, VN, 279, and cf. Parker, "In the Interest of Accuracy."

35. Cornell Sun, October 3, 1958.

36. SL, 262–64. Declaring that "Nabokov waited until he was on the verge of leaving Cornell before registering his complaint formally," Field insinuates (VN, 280) that VN dared to complain only when he no longer needed to rely

on his Cornell salary. He does not know that VN protested as early as June 1951 (to Milton Cowan, head of Cornell's Division of Languages; see above, p. 199), or that the timing of the September 1958 protest reflects not only his students' inability to answer his test, but also Richard Leed's provokingly inaccurate claims in the *Cornell Sun*. Field also cites a student's twenty-year-old recollection that the test included a fill-in passage "from *The Gift*, and thus was not in the least a simple test!" (*VN*, 279)—a much more colorful story than the modest truth that the test was fair and straightforward. Nabokov had taught elementary Russian at Wellesley, and knew what could be expected.

37. Stephen Jan Parker, lecture notes, October 1, 1958.

38. VN diary; Page-a-Day Diary, VNA; VN to Minton, September 8, 1958.

39. VN diary; Page-a-Day Diary, VNA.

40. Patricia Blake, in Max Hayward, *Writers in Russia: 1917–1978* (New York: Harcourt Brace Jovanovich, 1983), p. l; VN to Robert Bingham, November 8, 1958, VNA; Adamovich, *NZ* 134 (1979): 98. Pasternak's fiction had been unfavorably compared to VN's as far back as a comment by "Gulliver" (Nina Berberova), *Vozrozhdenie*, June 18, 1931.

41. VN to Epstein, August 26, 1958, VNA; *SL*, 264; *SO*, 206; VN to Roy Basler, April 9, 1959, and to Robert Bingham, November 8, 1958.

42. VN to KW, October 16, 1958, VNA; cf. also Szeftel, "*Lolita* at Cornell."

43. Guy de Mallac, *Boris Pasternak: His Life and Art* (Norman, Okla.: Oklahoma University Press, 1981), 231–35.

44. *SO*, 205; Page-a-Day Diary, VNA; Russian *Lolita*, 298.

45. *SL*, 288.

46. *New Yorker*, November 15, 1958. In his review Wilson strongly censured the translation, and in the process misconstrued a simple but crucial phrase that in the words of one critic could be "clearly understood by a first-year Russian student" (Blake, in Hayward, *Writers in Russia*, lv).

47. *New York Times*, November 10, 1958; *Time*, March 2, 1959; Minton to VN, September 24, 1958, VNA.

48. *SL*, 198; Page-a-Day Diary, VNA; *Observer*, November 30, 1958.

49. Page-a-Day Diary, VNA; *SL*, 588; *Newsweek*, November 24, 1958; VN to Minton, March 3, 1958, VNA; *SL*, 261.

50. *Cornell Sun*, November 20, 1958; VN to Sylvia Berkman, Mikhail Karpovich, Victor Lange, Harry Levin, Marc Slonim, Gleb Struve, and Aileen Ward, November 1958, VNA; Page-a-Day Diary, VNA.

51. Page-a-Day Diary, VNA; VN to Minton, December 3, 1958; *RLSK*, 39; Field, *VN*, 309.

52. *Daily Express*, December 17, 1958.

53. VéN to Morris and Alison Bishop, April 15, 1959, VNA; BB interview with Herbert Gold, April 14, 1983; Minton to VN, January 7, 1959, VNA.

54. Page-a-Day Diary, VNA; Gold, "Nabokov Remembered," 46–48, and "Vladimir Nabokov"; BB interview with Gold, April 1983.

55. *SL*, 276; *Veckojournalen*, February 27–March 6, 1959.

56. VN to *Hudson Review*, January 2, 1959, VNA; *SL*, 277.

57. VN to Minton, January 8 and 12, 1959, VNA.

58. Gross, "Portrait of a Publisher." Weidenfeld's recollections are somewhat muddled: he did plan a strategy for *Lolita*, but most of it had been put into operation before he met VN (in March 1959).

59. *Spectator*, January 9, 1959; *Times* (London), January 23, 1959.

60. Weidenfeld to VN, January 7, 1959, VNA; *SL*, 273.

61. Weidenfeld to VN, January 7, 1959; *Time*, March 2, 1959.

62. *NWL*, 327; VéN to Epstein, January 18, 1959; Page-a-Day Diary, VNA.

63. Page-a-Day Diary, VNA; VéN to Epstein, January 18, 1959, and VN to Minton, February 6, 1959, VNA.

64. VéN to Sylvia Berkman, February 2, 1959; unpublished notes, VNA.

65. Yearbook, 1951, VNA.

66. Gold, "Nabokov Remembered," 58.

67. Page-a-Day Diary, VNA.

68. *Ibid.*; *People*, March 22, 1959.

69. VéN to Gallimard, February 28 and March 4, 1959, VNA.

70. BB interview with Weidenfeld, March 1983; Page-a-Day Diary, VNA; Weidenfeld to VN, March 5, 1959, VNA.

71. Diary, March 4.

72. *NWL*, 327.

73. VéN to Morris and Alison Bishop, May 20, and to Lisbet Thompson, May 24, 1959, VNA; Page-a-Day Diary, VNA.

74. VN to Nicolas Nabokov, May 12, and to John Franclemont, May 31, 1959, VNA; Page-a-Day Diary, VNA; BB interview with VéN, January 1985.

75. VN to Minton, May 18, 1959, VNA.

76. VéN to Amy Kelly, June 11, 1959, VNA.

77. *Sports Illustrated*, September 14, 1959, E5–E8.

78. VN to Boyle, June 6, and to George Hessen, July 10, 1959, VNA.

79. VN to Minton, May 30, 1959, VNA.

80. Unpublished notes, VNA; Stephen Parker interview with VN, October 1971, from TS, VNA; B. Buison Ribling to Mina Turner, July 9, 1959, VNA.

81. VéN to EW, June 30, 1959, Yale; EW to VéN, July 1959, VNA; *SL*, 293.

82. VN to Minton, July 14, 1959, VNA; *LS*, vii; unpublished notes, VNA.

83. VéN to Sidney Posel, July 30, to James Harris, August 12, and to Kittredges, August 12, 1959, VNA.

84. VN to Minton, August 4, 1959, VNA; *LS*, vii; DN to BB, January 26, 1989.

85. VéN to Sidney Posel, August 4, 1959, and VéN to Robert Boyle, August 12, 1959, VNA; VN diary.

86. *NYTBR*, August 23, 1959.

87. William McGuire to John Barrett, September 14, 1959, Bollingen Collection, LC.

88. *NWL*, 327.

89. Page-a-Day Diary, VNA; VéN to Morris and Alison Bishop, September 22, 1959, VNA; Robert Hughes interview with VN, September 1965, from TS, VNA.

CHAPTER 17. CHASED BY FAME

Epigraph to Part 2: *SO*, 177–78.

1. Diary, 1959, VNA; VéN to Jason Epstein, October 15, 1959, VNA.

2. *SL*, 300.

3. Ibid., 300–301.

4. VéN to Walter Minton, October 15, 1959, VNA; *SM*, 14.

5. VéN to Filippa Rolf, October 15, 1959, VNA.

6. VéN to Ledig-Rowohlt, October 19, and to Jason Epstein, October 27, 1959, VNA.

7. BB interview with Ivan and Claire Nabokoff, January 1985.

8. Girodias, "Pornologist on Olympus," 147; *SO*, 211–12; BB interview with Ledig-Rowohlt, January 1982; VéN to BB, February 28, 1989.

9. Doussia Ergaz to VN, April 19, 1961, VNA; Girodias, "Pornologist on Olympus"; VN, "Olympic Game," 211–12; VéN to Minton, November 9, 1959, VNA.

10. Shakhovskoy, *V poiskakh Nabokova*, 49–50; BB interviews with VéN, June 1982, and with Irina Komarov and Zinaida Shakhovskoy, March 1983.

11. Shakhovskoy, "Le cas Nabokov," 668; *CE*, 214, 216.

12. Shakhovskoy, "Le cas Nabokov"; *Lects*, 373; *Lolita*, 177–78, 317.

13. "Pustynya," *NZ* 111 (June 1973); BB interview with Zinaida Shakhovskoy, March 1983. Despite Zinaida Shakhovskoy's manifest failure to understand Nabokov, and apparently because of her readiness to fill out her ignorance of the facts of his life with jaundiced speculation, Andrew Field declares her sorry compilation "one of the essential books written on Nabokov" (*VN*, 384).

14. *V poiskakh Nabokova*, 57; BB interview with Irina Komarov, March 1983; Komarov to VN, October 26, 1959, VNA; VN diary; BB interview with Evgenia Cannac, March 1983.

15. Diary; BB interview with Ledig Rowohlt, January 1982.

16. J. F. Bergery to VN [ca. October 21, 1959], VNA; *SL*, 303; BB interview with Alain Robbe-Grillet, March 1987; Field, *VN*, 350; *SO*, 174.

17. VN to Alan Pryce-Jones [ca. October 10, 1959], VéN to Minton, November 9, 1959, VN notes for Andrew Field, June 12, 1970, VéN to Sylvia Berkman, December 4, 1959, and Nigel Nicolson to VN, October 30, 1959, VNA.

18. George Weidenfeld to VN, September 28, 1959, and VéN to Minton, November 26, 1959, VNA; Weidenfeld, cited in Gross, "Portrait of a Publisher"; *NWL*, 329.

19. Nigel Nicolson to Andrew Field, October 23, 1970, cited in Field, *VN*, 310; BB interview with George Weidenfeld, March 1983; VéN to Lisbet Thompson, December 1, 1959, VNA.

20. Diary; VéN to Minton, November 9, to Lisbet Thompson, December 1, to Sylvia Berkman, December 4, and to Hélène Massalsky, December 4, 1959, VNA; and to William McGuire, November 16, 1959, Bollingen Collection, LC.

21. VéN to George Weidenfeld, November 23, 1959, to John Sutro, November 16, 1959, VNA, and to William McGuire, November 16, 1959.

22. VéN to Hélène Massalsky, December 4, to Joan de Peterson, November 25, and to Kirill Nabokov, November 26, 1959, VNA; *Ada*, 477.

23. Diary, 1962, VNA; *LS*, vii–viii; *SL*, 309; Familial Matters Folder, VNA.

24. VN to William McGuire, Bollingen Collection, LC, and to George Hessen, January 28, 1960, VNA; VéN to Lisbet Thompson, December 1, and to Sylvia Berkman, December 4, 1959, VNA.

25. *Ada*, 342.

26. *SL*, 365–66.

27. VNA.

28. Robert Hughes interview with VN, September 1965, from TS in VNA.

29. *Le nouveau candide*, November 23–30, 1961; BB interview with Peter Ustinov, December 1986; *SL*, 359.

30. *SL*, 303.

31. *SL*, 510; Kubrick to VN, December 8, VN cable and VéN letter to Kubrick, December 10, 1959, VNA.

32. Arnoldo Mondadori to VéN, November 27, 1959, VNA; DN to BB, February 28, 1989; VéN to Mariagloria Sears, December 24, 1959, VNA.

33. VéN to Arnoldo Mondadori, December 1 and 6, and to Irving Lazar, December 31, 1959, VNA.

34. VéN to Minton, January 1, 1960, Elena Sikorski to VN, October 24, Kirill Nabokov to VN, November 10, and VéN to Kirill Nabokov, November 26, 1959, VNA; DN to BB, February 28, 1989.

35. Notes for Work in Progress, VNA; Szeftel, "*Lolita* at Cornell"; *PP*, 147.

36. Diary; VéN to Joan de Peterson, January 29, 1960, VNA.

37. *SL*, 307–8.

38. Stanley Kubrick to VéN, January 7, 1960, VéN to Joan de Peterson, March 31, 1960, and to Lazar, December 1, 1959, VNA; Mondadori correspondence, January–February 1960, and Clairouin correspondence, 1960–1962, VNA; *Le phare* (Brussels), February 7, 1960.

39. *SL*, 309; VéN to Mariagloria Sears, February 7, 1960, VNA.

40. *SL*, 310–11.

41. VéN to Kirill Nabokov, March 27, 1960, VNA; *LS*, viii.

42. VN to Minton, February 1, VéN to Minton, March 8, and to Jason Epstein, March 15, 1960, VNA.

43. *LS*, ix.

44. VéN to Morris and Alison Bishop, March 14, 1960, VNA; *LS*, xiii; VN to EW, October 10, 1960, Yale; VN to Samuil Rosoff, October 10, 1960, and VéN to Joan de Peterson, September 30, 1960, VNA.

45. *LS*, ix; VéN to George Hessen, March 15, 1960, VNA; Familial Matters Folder, VNA; *NWL*, 330; VéN to Minton, April 5, 1960, VNA.

46. Iseman correspondence, June–August 1960, Kubrick to VN, January 17, 1966, Robert Badinter correspondence, 1960–1962, Mondadori and Gallimard correspondence, April–May 1960, VNA.

47. BB interview with Lazar, August 1989; Gordon Ackerman, "Nabokov

and the Innocent European," *Weekly Tribune*, January 28, 1966; Appel, *NDC*, 58; VéN to Morris and Alison Bishop, July 21, 1960.

48. *LS*, ix; VéN to Jason Epstein, July 9, 1960, and VN to John Franclemont, October 3, 1960, VNA.

49. *SL*, 316; *Time*, October 10, 1960, 22; *LS*, x–xi; VéN notes, July 12, Kubrick to VN, July 13, 1960, VNA; *SL*, 317–18, 322; VéN to Lazar, December 15, 1960, VNA.

50. *LS*, x and xiii; screenplay published New York: McGraw-Hill, 1974.

51. *LS* MS, VNA.

52. Ibid.

53. VN to Samuil Rosoff, October 10, VéN to Joseph Iseman, September 3, VN to Robert McGregor, September 4, VéN to Amy Kelly, July 24, 1960, and VN to Irving Lazar, February 7, 1961, VNA.

54. *SL*, 322; VN to Hessen, September 15, 1960, VNA.

55. *Los Angeles Times*, September 29, 1960; *Perepiska*, 104; *LS*, xi; diary; Janine Colombo interview with VN, *L'information d'Israel*, February 3, 1961.

56. DN, *CC*, 313; *SL*, 323–34.

57. *Newsweek*, January 3, 1972.

58. Diary; VN to Hellens, October 30, 1960, Hellens to VN, February 11, 1961, VNA.

59. VN to Samuil Rosoff, October 10, 1960; *Perepiska*, 104; *LS*, xi.

60. Diary; Notes for Work in Progress, VNA; VéN to Jacqueline Stephens, September 15, 1961, VNA.

61. Diary; VéN to Michel Mohrt, December 18, 1960.

62. BB interview with VéN, March 1982; *PF*, MS, LCNA; *SO*, 55.

63. VéN to Minton, December 2, 1960, and to Filippa Rolf, November 2, 1961, VNA; *Daily Express*, April 8, 1961.

64. VéN to Michael Scammell, January 30, and VN to EW, February 27, 1961, VNA.

65. VéN to Joan de Peterson, February 23, 1961, VNA; *Daily Express*, April 8, 1961; diary, January 8, 1961, VNA.

66. VN to Monique Grall, January 19, 1961, VNA.

67. VéN to Filippa Rolf, July 29, 1969, and February 17, 1965, VN to Joan Daly, June 7, 1969, VNA.

68. VéN to Michel Mohrt, January 1961, VNA; VN to William McGuire, January 30, 1961, Bollingen Collection, LC; *SL*, 324; VN to William Maxwell, February 1961, VNA.

69. VN to Minton, February 18, 1961, VNA; VN interview in untraced newspaper clipping [ca. June 1962].

70. VéN to Joan de Peterson, April 23, and to Lisbet Thompson, April 7, 1961, VNA; *LS*, xii; diary, April 8, 1961; *Nice-Matin*, April 13, 1961.

71. VéN to Amy Kelly, April 19, 1961, VNA; DN to BB, December 24, 1982; Pavarotti, *Pavarotti*, 57–61; VéN to Elena Levin, June 10, 1961, VNA.

72. VéN to Ledig Rowohlt, May 4, to Minton and to Filippa Rolf, May 12, 1961, VNA; *SL*, 331–32.

73. Diary.

74. VéN to Lisbet Thompson, July 12, 1961, VNA.

75. VéN to Elena Levin, June 10, to Joan de Peterson, July 22, to Stanley Kubrick, May 4, and to Lisbet Thompson, June 14, 1961, VNA; Musée zoologique, Lausanne.

76. Diary; VéN to Joan de Peterson, July 22, and to Filippa Rolf, August 6, 1961, VNA; BB interview with ES, January 1985.

77. VéN to Filippa Rolf, August 6, and to Michael Scammell, August 3, 1961, VNA.

78. Diary; VéN to Kubrick, August 15, and to Lisbet Thompson, August 21, 1961, VNA.

79. VN interview in unidentified newspaper clipping [ca. June 1962]; PF, MS, LCNA; cf. PF, 232.

80. Diary; VéN to Joan de Peterson, August 28, 1961, VNA.

81. VéN to Anna Feigin, September 18, to Lisbet Thompson, October 1, and to Michael Scammell, September 14, 1961, VNA.

82. VéN to Karin Hartnell, October 1, 1961, VNA.

83. VéN to Joan de Peterson, August 28, to Anna Feigin, September 18, and to Joseph Iseman, December 9, 1961, VNA; SL, 331; Journal de Montreux, January 23, 1964; Journal de Genève, March 13, 1965.

84. VéN to Kubrick, May 4, and to Lisbet Thompson, June 12, VN to Lazar, December 12, VéN to George Weidenfeld, October 19 and November 4, 1961, VNA.

85. VéN to Joseph Iseman, December 9, 1961, VNA; BB interview with Jaqueline Callier, December 1982.

86. VéN to Pantheon Books, November 10, 1961, VNA.

87. VN to Minton, December 6, 1961, VNA.

CHAPTER 18. PALE FIRE

1. Written 1960–1961; pub. New York: Putnam's, 1962.

2. SO, 283.

3. "The real real story" is Mary McCarthy's phrase, in her celebrated essay on Pale Fire ("A Bolt from the Blue"). She was the first to spring many of Pale Fire's surprises, but she sparked so brightly with the excitement of discovery that the novel generates that she soon short-circuited sense.

4. At the end of his 1962 diary, Nabokov drafted some phrases for possible interviews: "I wonder if any reader will notice the following details: 1) that the nasty commentator is not an ex-king and not even Dr. Kinbote, but Prof. Vseslav Botkin, a Russian and a madman. . . ."

5. For a standard treatment of paranoia, I have drawn on the Encyclopaedia Britannica, 1962 ed., which VN certainly mined on occasion (he cites it in Ada).

6. In his 1962 diary, VN also noted of Kinbote: "He commits suicide before completing his Index, leaving the last entry without p[age] ref[erences]."

7. Realism and the Aim of Scientific Discovery, vol. 1 of Postscript to the Logic of

Scientific Discovery, ed. W. W. Bartley III (London: Hutchinson, 1983), 168–69.

8. *SO*, 11.

9. I have stolen the point from Harry Levin, *Shakespeare Survey* 26 (1973): 89.

10. *Ada*, 361.

11. This link was noted by Julia Bader, in her *Crystal Land*, 46.

12. Noticing the shimmer of relationships between the two parts, Andrew Field (*Nabokov: His Life in Art*) made a good guess at Shade as the disguised author of the commentary, but did not ask *why* Shade would invent a persona for a commentary, and remained content with evidence so slight as often to compel disbelief. He even states that "the most cogent argument for the essential unity of poem with commentary are the rejected draft portions of the poem which Kinbote cites and which, if they are Shade's, would prove—in direct contradiction to the poem itself—that the old poet was indeed on the verge of writing a poem about Zembla" (300). Field seems not to notice that the variants are labeled "K's contribution" (i.e., Kinbote's fabrication) in the index and are risibly flat in their versification. Julia Bader makes a far better, though somewhat patchy, case in *Crystal Land*.

13. See for instance Stegner, *Escape into Aesthetics*; Grabes, *Fictitious Biographies*; and Tammi, *Problems of Nabokov's Poetics*.

14. *SM* MS, VNA.

15. *Gift*, 322.

16. *RLSK*, 204–5.

17. *Lolita*, 317.

18. Bodenstein, " 'The Excitement of Verbal Adventure,' " 149.

19. I am grateful to Professor Forrest Scott for making me think harder about Alice's Red King.

20. VN to Andrew Field, September 26, 1966, VNA.

21. See *VNRY*, 189–93.

CHAPTER 19. MASK AND MAN

1. *SO*, 55.

2. VéN to BB, March 11, 1989.

3. *SO*, 197.

4. Bernard Pivot interview with VN, May 1975, from TS in VNA; diary, February 7, 1967, VNA.

5. VN to Teddy Kollek, October 3, 1974, VNA.

6. *SO*, 109, 27–28, 149.

7. BB interviews with Margaret Newstead, February 1983, with Bart Winer, April 1983, with Carlo Barozzi, February 1983, and with Jaqueline Callier, December 1982.

8. *SO*, xi; George Feifer interview with VN, *Saturday Review*, November 27, 1976, 24.

9. *SO*, 28; Field, *VN*, 355.

10. *Ada*, 421; *SO*, 29.

11. Alan Levy interview with VN, April 1971, from TS in VNA; diary, April 22, 1965; Field, *Life*, 23.

12. Robert Hughes interview with VN, September 1965, from TS, VNA; *SO*, 43, 29.

13. Bollingen correspondence, October 1961, Bollingen Collection, LC; BB interview with Winer, April 1983; VN to William McGuire, January 7, 1962, Bollingen Collection, LC.

14. Diary.

15. VéN to Minton, January 4, 1962, VNA.

16. VéN to Minton, January 23, 1962, VNA.

17. *Publishers' Weekly*, January 15 and February 26, 1962; *New York Post*, January 31, 1962.

18. VéN note, February 20, 1962, VNA; Mason, *Before I Forget*, 430.

19. VéN to Doussia Ergaz, March 4, and VN to A. C. Spectorsky, April 24, 1962, VNA.

20. VN to George Hessen, March 27, 1962, VNA.

21. VéN to Minton, April 16, and to Irving Lazar, April 15, 1962, VNA.

22. VN diary; *Newsweek*, June 25, 1962; McCarthy, "A Bolt from the Blue"; VN to William McGuire, October 28, 1962.

23. Alvarez and Appel "identified" as VN by Alvarez, *Saturday Review*, June 13, 1970; Appel also by Gore Vidal (*Matters of Fact and Fiction*, New York: Random House, 1977); Brien, by George Gomari, *New Statesman*, December 22, 1967; Field, by Alan Brien, *New Statesman*, December 8, 1967; Mary McCarthy, by Scammell, *Encounter*, April 1963; Proffer, by a *TLS* anonym, October 10, 1968; Scammell, by Herbert Gold, *Saturday Evening Post*, February 11, 1967; Wilson, by Stephen Jones, *NYRB*, July 26, 1965, and by Wilson himself, in an unpublished letter to *New Statesman* [ca. December 1967], Yale; *Ada*, 542.

24. VéN to Morris and Alison Bishop, May 26, and to Joan de Peterson, July 24, 1962, VNA; *SO*, 3; *LS*, xii; diary.

25. *LS*, xii; VN cited by Kubrick, *Observer*, June 24, 1962.

26. *New York Times*, cited in *Observer*, July 1, 1962, and *Time*, July 13, 1962.

27. *Newsweek*, January 3, 1972; *Der Spiegel*, October 5, 1987, 238.

28. Diary, 1962.

29. VéN to Lisbet Thompson, July 16, 1962, VNA.

30. Helga Chudacoff interview with VN, June 1974, from TS in VNA; *SO*, 200.

31. VéN to Minton, July 8, 1962, VNA; *SL*, 339; diary; *Bookstand* [ca. November 1962], BBC.

32. Rosoff to VN, June 15, and VN to Rosoff, August 31, 1963, VNA; diary; VN notes for Andrew Field, June 12, 1970, VNA.

33. *Perepiska*, 105; VéN to Topazia Markevitch, August 24, 1962, VNA; BB interview with Ustinov, December 1986; VN to Gold, August 25, 1962, VNA.

34. VéN to Lisbet Thompson, November 8, 1963, and to Joseph Iseman, October 7, 1962, VNA.

35. Memorandum, May 27, 1964, and VN to McGuire, September 28, 1962, Bollingen Collection, LC.

36. VéN to Lisbet Thompson, November 11, 1962, VNA; DN to BB, March 11, 1989; VN diary; VéN to Suzanne Ustinov, October 14, 1962, VNA; BB interview with Peter Ustinov, December 1986.

37. Cited in Gross, "Portrait of a Publisher."

38. Weidenfeld to VéN, November 20, 1962, VNA.

39. Minton to VN, September 27, and VéN to Minton, November 4, 1962, VNA.

40. VéN to Jane Rowohlt, November 4, 1962, VNA; VéN to BB, March 11, 1989.

41. VN to McGuire, October 28, 1962, Bollingen Collection, LC.

42. VN to McGuire, December 1, 1962, Bollingen Collection, LC.

43. Ibid.

44. BB interview with Winer, April 1983.

45. VN to McGuire, December 1, 1962; BB interview with Winer, April 1983.

46. VéN to William Maxwell, November 14 and 21, 1962, VNA.

47. SL, 342; VN to William Maxwell, January 10, 1963, VNA.

48. VéN to Weidenfeld, January 12, and to Vittorio Sereni, March 22, VN to Grynberg, January 29, and to Minton, April 5, 1963, VNA.

49. Diary; Micha to VN, February 28, and VéN to Micha, March 21 and May 11, and Dieter Zimmer to VéN, August 20, 1963, VNA; SO, 20. Rowohlt changed his mind about the bibliography and had it published as a separate pamphlet at the end of 1963.

50. VéN to DN, December 5, 1962; diary; VéN to BB, March 11, 1989; Butterflies of Europe MS, VNA.

51. VN to Doussia Ergaz, May 6, and to McGuire, May 18, 1963, VNA.

52. NYTBR, May 26, 1963; Robert Gutwillig, New York Herald Tribune, May 26, 1963.

53. VéN to Isabel Stephens, May 22, and to Morris and Alison Bishop, June 23, 1963, VNA; Nabokov Collection, Lausanne; diary; Ada, 552.

54. Diary; Nabokov Collection, Lausanne; VN to McGuire, "September" [August] 10, 1963, Bollingen Collection, LC; VN to Winer, August 21, 1963, SL, 347–49.

55. VéN to Minton, July 30, 1963, VNA; diary; Associated Rediffusion correspondence, July–August 1963, VNA.

56. VN to Max Gissen, September 10, and to Weidenfeld, September 10 and 18, 1963, VNA; N1.

57. Diary; Butterflies of Europe MS, VNA.

58. VN to Micha, December 5, 1963, VNA.

59. Ghislaine Micha to VN [ca. December 8], and VN to René and Ghislaine Micha, December 11, 1963, VNA.

60. VN to Minton, December 15, 1963, and Rowohlt to VéN and DN, July 7, 1977, VNA; BB interview with Margaret Newstead, February 1983; Alan Levy interview with VN, April 1971, from TS in VNA.

61. Diary.

62. VéN to Arndt, July 8, 1959, VNA; VN to McGuire, October 14, 1963, Bollingen Collection, LC.

63. *NG*, 61, 153.

64. *SO*, 331, 334–35.

65. VN to Weidenfeld, December 31, 1963; *Butterflies of Europe* MS, VNA.

66. Diary.

67. Coindreau to VN, January 6, 1965, VN to Girard, October 19, 1963, VN notes for Coindreau and Girard, January 11, 1965, VNA.

68. Coindreau to VN, January 6, and VN to Coindreau, January 14, 1964, and VN notes, January 11, 1965, VNA.

69. VN notes to Coindreau and Girard, January 11, 1965, VNA.

70. Rowohlt to VéN, January 22, 1964, and July 7, 1977, VNA.

71. Diary; VN to William Maxwell, January 16, 1964, and Minton to VN, December 1963, VNA.

72. Louba Schirman to VéN, September 17, 1964, and VN to Nicholas Thompson, October 12, 1964, VNA.

73. VéN to Morris and Alison Bishop, February 1964, VNA; DN to BB, March 11, 1989; BB interview with Ustinov, December 1986.

74. De Liso to VN, February 28, 1964, VNA; VN letter to *Life*, pub. December 5, 1949, repr. *SL*, 93–94; *SO*, 168.

75. Minton to VN, July 6, 1964 (Weidenfeld had mooted the project in October 1963), VéN to Joan Daly, August 8, 1964, and to Lee Stevens, February 7, 1965, VNA.

76. Morris Bishop to Alison and Richard Jolly, April 6, 1964, Bishop Collection, CornUA.

77. William Maxwell to VN, April 1964, VNA.

78. *SM*, 178; Field, *Life*, 6–7; *SM* MS, VNA.

79. BB interview with Peter Lubin, May 1983.

80. A cassette of VN's reading is available from the Poetry Room, Harvard; for Levin's introduction, see his *Grounds for Comparison*; Field, *Life*, 7; BB interview with Sylvia Berkman, April 1983; William Maxwell to VN, April 1964, VNA.

81. ES to VN, April 28, 1964, VNA.

82. VéN to McGuire, May 11, 1964, VNA. Only a few, the earliest copies to be bound, received the ribbons.

83. VéN to Nathalie Nabokoff, June 19, and to Henri-Louis de la Grange, August 17, 1964, VNA; *Butterflies of Europe* MS, VNA; diary.

84. VéN to A. C. Spectorsky, June 19, 1964, VNA.

85. VN to Jason Epstein, August 2, 1964, VNA.

86. VN to Peter de Peterson, September 8, 1964, VéN to Weidenfeld, October 27, 1964, VNA.

87. *New Republic*, September 26, 1964.

88. *SO*, 50.

89. *SL*, 359–60.

CHAPTER 20. ADA STIRS

1. Robert Hughes interview with VN, September 1965, from TS, VNA.

2. VéN to Jane Howard, October 19, 1964, VNA.

3. VéN to Walter Minton, July 13, 1964, and unpublished notes, VNA.

4. Notes for Work in Progress, VNA.

5. VéN to Weidenfeld, October 27, and to Minton, November 17, 1964, VNA.

6. Diary, March 28, 1965, Girodias to Barney Rosset, December 10, 1964, and VN to Minton, December 21, 1964, VNA.

7. VéN to Hélène Massalsky, December 9, to Filippa Rolf, November 29, 1964, to William Maxwell, January 13, 1965, and to Lisbet Thompson, February 26, 1965, VNA.

8. VN to Weidenfeld, January 30, and to Nicholas Thompson, February 14, VéN to Securité publique, Lausanne, February 7, VN to Minton, February 16, 1965, VNA; *Despair*, 8 (cf. Grayson, *Nabokov Translated*); *PP*, 183; diary, March 28, 1965, VNA.

9. Russian *Lolita*, translated 1963–1965, pub. New York: Phaedra, 1967.

10. "Little Girl Migrates," *New Republic*, January 20, 1968.

11. *Lolita*, 318–19.

12. Russian *Lolita*, 296. The translation is my own; for complete English text, see trans. by Earl D. Sampson in Rivers and Nicol, 188–94.

13. For negative Russian appraisals, see Ellendea Proffer, "Nabokov's Russian Readers," 253–60; for positive: BB interview with Berberova, April 1983; Barabtarlo, "Onus Probandi"; 26; TS report of Shikhovtsev lecture, 1986, VNA.

14. Brown, "Little Girl Migrates," 20; Weidle, *Russkaya mysl'* 29 (December 1977): 10.

15. VN to Bertrand Thompson, March 21, 1965, VNA; Nakhimovsky and Paperno, *English-Russian Dictionary of Nabokov's Lolita*.

16. VéN to Filippa Rolf, March 15, 1965; diary.

17. VéN to William Maxwell, May 9, to Ledig Rowohlt, June 1, to Minton, June 8 and May 14, 1965, VNA; DN to Marinel sisters, June 5, 1965, Juliar Collection; *Augusta Chronicle*, January 2, 1972; DN, *CC*, 315; DN to BB, March 5, 1989.

18. *SL*, 374; EW's review appeared in *NYRB*, July 15, 1965.

19. Letters to Editor, *New Statesman*, January 22, 1965 (VN), April 9, 1965 (Deutsch), and April 23, 1965 (VN).

20. "Pluck and Polemics," 313.

21. Ibid.

22. In *An Edmund Wilson Celebration*, ed. John Wain (Oxford: Phaidon, 1978), 7.

23. *N1*.

24. *NWL*, 150, 214.

25. *NWL*, 58; EW to Roman Grynberg, May 20, 1962, ColB; *NWL*, 51–52, 63, 183.

26. *NWL*, 186, 276; EW, *Upstate*, 161–62; *SO*, 218.

27. Wilson, *New Yorker*, April 29, 1967; VN diary, May 20, 1967, VNA.

28. VN's letter of May 26, 1958 (incorrectly dated in *NWL* March 24, 1958) received no reply, and VN then wrote again on March 2, 1959, *NWL*, 327; VN to EW, October 10, 1960, Yale; Grynberg to VN, August 6, 1962, VNA.

29. VN to William McGuire, September 16, 1962, and September 30, 1963, Bollingen Collection, LC.

30. *SL*, 356, 358.

31. Notes for Work in Progress, VNA; Field, *VN*, 358; EW, *Letters on Literature and Politics*, 652.

32. *EO*, 2:429; *NYRB*, August 26, 1965.

33. Patricia Blake, introduction to Hayward, *Writers in Russia*, lvi–lviii; *NYRB*, August 26, 1965.

34. *Inquiry*, July 9–23, 1979, 23.

35. "Nabokov's Reply," *Encounter*, February 1966, 80–89; *SO*, 241, 247.

36. *SO*, 252, 256–57.

37. *Observer*, February 6, 1966; *Daily Telegraph*, February 14, 1966; VN to Weidenfeld, December 3, 1963, VNA.

38. Letters to Editor, *NYRB*, January 20, 1966 (VN), February 17, 1966 (EW), *New Statesman*, January 5, 1968 (EW), January 19, 1968 (VN); Grynberg to VN, December 4, VéN to Grynberg, December 25, 1965, VNA; draft letter to EW, *EO* MS, VNA; diary, VNA.

39. VéN to Weidenfeld, July 8, VN to George Hessen, July 16, 1965; *SO*, 136.

40. DN, *Enchanter*, 110–11; BB interview with Weidenfeld, March 1983; VéN to Weidenfeld, September 9 and 15, 1965, VNA.

41. MS, VNA.

42. VéN to Filippa Rolf, March 15, 1965, VNA.

43. Phaedra correspondence, September 13–23, 1965, VNA.

44. Hughes correspondence, August–September 1965, VNA.

45. *SO*, 51–61. The following excerpts are from the typed transcripts, VNA, and from the film itself.

46. Hughes to VN and VéN, October 19, 1965, VNA; *SL*, 381–82.

47. VN to Hughes, December 31, 1965, January 10 and February 9, 1966, VNA.

48. *SL*, 378.

49. *SL*, 380–81.

50. Diary, January 1 and March 10, 1966, VNA.

51. VéN to Oscar de Liso, December 5, 1965; *WI* galleys, VNA; *WI* foreword; Radio Liberty correspondence, December 1965–January 1967, VNA.

52. VéN to Louba Schirman, December 14, 1965. Girodias's article had appeared in *Evergreen Review*, September 1965, under the first title and in his anthology *The Olympia Reader* under the second.

53. *SO*, 310.

54. *Ada*, 211. Note the recurrence of the "tumbler" applied to Apostolski

(SM, 232) in the double entendre of *Ada*'s "tumbling the foliage, '*troussant la raimée,*' as Sore, the ribald night watchman, expressed it."

55. Diary, January 5–13, 1966.

56. *SO,* 272, 277. For the date of composition, diary January 29–February 15, 1966, VNA. Pub. *Evergreen Review,* February 1967, after *NYRB* and *Encounter* rejected it for fear of libel action.

57. "Speranza" MS, VNA; *SL,* 378; VéN to William Maxwell, February 3, 1966, VNA; Lowell, "Nine Poems"; Blake, in Hayward, *Writers in Russia,* lxiii–lxiv; VN letter to editor, *Encounter,* May 1966, 91; VN to Struve, November 14, 1966, VNA; *Ada,* 412.

58. Diary, February 5, 1966; unpublished notes, VNA.

59. *SO,* 122.

60. Putnam's correspondence, 1965–1967.

61. *Escape into Aesthetics.*

62. VN to Field, February 18, 1966, VNA.

63. VéN to Roman Grynberg, September 28, 1966.

64. Diary, April 8–11, 1966.

65. For VN on Hurd, see *Lolita,* 201; on Balthus, *SO,* 167; on Steinberg, VN to William Maxwell, March 17, 1966, VNA.

66. VéN to Filippa Rolf, April 11, and to Louba Schirman, April 11, 1966, VNA; *SO,* 169; VéN to Morris and Alison Bishop, November 29, 1966, VNA; BB interview with VéN, January 1980; VéN to BB, March 5, 1989.

67. VéN to Hélène Massalsky, May 19, and to Bishops, November 29, 1966, VNA; diary.

68. VéN to Bishops, November 29, to Hélène Massalsky, June 10, and to Sonia Slonim, June 17, 1966, VNA; diary; VéN to Barley Alison, July 10, and to Hélène Massalsky, July 28, 1966, VNA.

69. "Nabokov," *Vogue,* December 1966, 224–29, 279–81; *SL,* 395.

70. VN to Barley Alison, September 4, 1966, VNA; Halsman, *Halsman,* 80; Yvonne and Philippe Halsman to VN and VéN, November 11, 1968, VNA; Gold, "Nabokov Remembered," 52.

71. "The Artist in Pursuit of Butterflies," *Saturday Evening Post,* February 11, 1967, 83; Gibian and Parker, 49–50.

72. *Saturday Evening Post,* February 11, 1967, 82.

73. *Saturday Evening Post,* March 25, 1967, 6; repr. *SL,* 404–6.

74. Diary, October 13, 1966; VéN to Penelope Gilliatt, October 27, 1966, VNA; Field, *Life in Art;* VéN to Field, September 18, and to Sonia Slonim, June 17, VN to Field, September 26, 1966, VNA.

75. Proffer, *Keys to Lolita; Wisconsin Studies in Contemporary Literature.*

76. "Nabokov's Puppet Show," 1967; Appel, *AnL;* "*Ada* Described." His *Nabokov's Dark Cinema* contains much valuable information on and discussion of VN, but has moved beyond literary criticism into a very personal reflection on the relationship between high and low culture—VN on the one hand and film, comics, and advertising on the other—in America and in Appel's life.

77. Diary; Zimmer interview TS, VNA.

78. VéN to Lisbet Thompson, October 25, 1966; diary, October 25, 1966, VNA.

CHAPTER 21. FLYING HIGH

1. Putnam's correspondence, 1965–1967, VNA.

2. VéN to James Street, October 27, 1966, and to Minton, May 3, 1967, and Minton to VéN, May 23, 1967, VNA.

3. Diary; *Encounter*, February 1966, 80, repr. *SO*, 242–43; *EO* MS, VNA.

4. VéN to Ledig Rowohlt, November 21, 1966, VNA; diary.

5. Lee Stevens and James Street to VéN, December 17, VN to Minton, December 22, and Putnam's correspondence, 1966, VNA.

6. VN to Minton, December 26, 1966, and January 13, 1967, and VéN to Joan Daly, March 5, 1967, VNA.

7. *New Republic*, January 14 and 21, 1967; VéN to Appel, January 24, 1967, VNA.

8. *KQK*, ix.

9. Diary; VN to Minton, April 19, 1967, VNA. For other appraisals of VN's revisions, see Grayson, *Nabokov Translated*, and Carl Proffer, "A New Deck for Nabokov's Knaves," 293–309.

10. *Mary*, xii–xiii; "An Aggressively Private Person."

11. *KQK*, 169–70, *KDV*, 165–66. VN identified "Ronald" as Hingley to Carl and Ellendea Proffer (BB interview with Proffers, April 1983).

12. Weidenfeld to V and VéN, February 3, VéN to Field, January 28, and VN to Field, February 3 and 5, 1967, VNA.

13. VéN to Robert Shankland, March 20, 1967, VNA, and to Anna Feigin, July 10, 1967, private collection.

14. Diary; Kemeny to VN, February 28 and March 14, 1967, VNA.

15. VéN to Elena Levin, July 21, 1967, VNA; *SL*, 412.

16. ES to VN, May 5, VN to ES, May 5, 1967 (*Perepiska*, 108–10); VéN to Peter Kemeny, June 6, 1967, VNA.

17. Louba Schirman to VéN, April 17, Kemeny to VN and VéN [ca. April 29 and May 19, 1967], VN to Ed Booher, August 21, 1967, VNA.

18. VéN to Alison Bishop, July 16, 1967, VNA; *SO*, 333; diary.

19. Ed Booher to VN and VéN, July 26, 1967, VNA.

20. VéN to Hotel Savoy, Chamonix, June 25 [for July?], 1967, VNA.

21. VéN to Ed Booher, August 26, and to Gleb Struve, September 4, 1967, VNA.

22. Diary; VéN to Anna Feigin, October 4, 1967, VNA.

23. Phyllis Christiansen to BB, June 15 and August 7, 1983, BB interview with Phyllis Christiansen, April 1983; diary.

24. BB interview with Alfred Appel, April 1983; diary, September 13, 1967.

25. *SO*, 109–10; *Perepiska*, 113; diary, December 23, 1967; Pierre Dommergues interview with VN, *Les Langues modernes* 62, no. 1 (January–February 1968): 96; Martin Esslin interview with VN, *New York Times*, May 12, 1968, 4.

26. VéN to Vivian Crespi, March 11, 1967; BB interview with ES, July 1979; diary, November 4, 1967. For the scrabble-and-portents theme, see my *Nabokov's Ada: The Place of Consciousness*.

27. BB interview with Frank Taylor, April 1983.

28. Diary.

29. Iseman and McGraw-Hill correspondence, November–December 1967, VNA; DN to BB, October 25, 1990.

30. Diary, January 11, 1969; *Perepiska*, 112–14; VéN to Ledig Rowohlt and to Joseph Iseman, December 20, 1967, VNA.

31. VéN to Field, December 6, 1967, VNA; diary; Field, "World of Vladimir Nabokov."

32. VéN to Minton, October 29, and to Joan Daly, July 2, 1967, VNA; *Izobretenie Val'sa* MS, VNA.

33. *New York Times*, January 12, 1968; Martin Esslin interview with VN, *New York Times*, May 12, 1968, 4; Ed Booher to VN, January 26, 1968, VNA.

34. Diary; *Annotated Lolita* TS, and Appel to VN, May 31, 1975, VNA.

35. BB interview with Alfred Appel, April 1983.

36. Diary.

37. VéN to Anna Feigin, January 29, 1968, private collection; Sonia Slonim to VéN, March 8, VéN to Elizaveta Marinel, March 12, and to Alison Bishop, March 13, 1968, VNA; diary.

38. Diary; VéN to Filippa Rolf, May 5, 1968, and to Marie Schébéko, June 30, 1971.

39. VéN to William Maxwell, April 16, 1968, VNA; diary; VéN to Heather Grierson, May 2, 1968, VNA.

40. VéN to Field, April 17, Field to VN, April 28, VéN to Field, May 21, 1968, VNA.

41. Diary, April 19, 1968; Irving Lazar to David Wolper, April 23, 1968, VNA; *Publisher's Weekly*, June 3, 1968; Weeks to VN, May 17, VéN to Frank Taylor, May 29, Robie Macauley to VN, November 20 and December 28, 1968, VNA.

42. Lazar correspondence, June–August 1968, VNA; BB interview with Lazar, August 1989.

43. Diary; VéN to Marie Schébéko, May 3, 1968, VNA, and to Elizaveta Marinel, May 6, 1968, Juliar Collection; VéN to Irving Lazar, August 18, to Field, May 21 and August 17, and to *Russkaya Mysl'*, August 1, 1968, VNA; diary; VéN to Morris and Alison Bishop, August 4, and to Peter Kemeny, July 2, 1968, VNA.

44. VéN to Appel, July 8, 1968, VNA; diary, July 19, 1968; VéN to Elizaveta Marinel, July 11, 1968, Juliar Collection.

45. VéN to Kemeny, July 2, 1968, and to Minton, June 17, 1972, Dan Erickson to VN, July 26, 1968, and VéN to Erickson, July 27, 1968, VNA.

46. Diary; VéN to David Merrick and Alan Delyun, August 17, to Irving Lazar, August 18, 1968, and to Domenico Porzio, October 20, 1969, VNA.

47. VéN to David Merrick and Alan Delyun, August 17, 1968; diary, October 5, 1968.

48. Diary; Lazar to VéN, September 10, 1968, VNA; Frederic Raphael to BB, August 28, 1987.

49. VéN to Frank Taylor, October 10, and VN to Taylor, October 27, 1968, VNA; *SO*, 122.

50. Philippe and Yvonne Halsman to VN and VéN, November 11, 1968, VNA.

CHAPTER 22. ADA

1. Written 1965–1968; pub. *Ada or Ardor: A Family Chronicle* (New York: Mc-Graw-Hill, 1969). To the Penguin edition (Harmondsworth: 1970), Nabokov adds notes to the book under the pseudonym "Vivian Darkbloom."

2. *SO*, 179.

3. "Van Loves Ada, Ada Loves Van."

4. *KQK*, viii.

5. *SM*, 290.

6. *SO*, 121.

7. *Nabokov's Ada*. See esp. chaps. 7–10.

8. See ibid., 104–7.

9. See ibid., chaps. 9–10.

10. Chaps. 11–13.

11. See *Nabokov's Ada*, 169–78.

12. See ibid., chap. 12.

13. For the chief links between Lucette and Aqua, see ibid., 126–32.

14. *NG*, 142.

15. Unpublished lepidopterological notes [ca. 1943], VNA.

16. *PF*, 265.

CHAPTER 23. TIDYING UP

1. *SL*, 445.

2. Diary; BB interview with Jaqueline Callier, February 1983.

3. BB interview with Jaqueline Callier, February 1983.

4. Field correspondence with VN and VéN, August–October 1968, VNA; Dieter Zimmer interview with VN, October 1966, from TS in VNA; *SO*, 124; VéN to Dean of Ithaca, November 13, 1968, and May 5, 1969, VNA.

5. *SO*, 294; Notes for Work in Progress, VNA; Field, *Life*, 32.

6. BB interview with Carl Proffer, April 1983; diary, January 1, 1970, VNA.

7. Diary, November 28–29, 1968, VNA.

8. Diary; VéN to Frank Taylor, November 30, 1968, VNA; *SL*, 440.

9. BB interview with Taylor, April 1983; Anthony Velie to VN, January 3 and 16, 1969, VNA; *New York Post*, December 6, 1968; Grunwald to VN, February 7, 1969, VNA.

10. Diary; Field, *Life*, 8–9. In *N1*, VN corrected Field's erroneous address for the Montreux Palace.

11. Diary; *Time*, May 23, 1969, 48–49; VN to Frank Taylor, April 7, and VéN to Taylor, April 10, 1969, VNA.

12. "Ultimate masterpiece," *Houston Chronicle*, May 11, 1969; "culminating statement," *This World*, May 18, 1969; "greatest novel," *Denver Post*, May 11, 1969; Kazin, *Saturday Review*, May 10, 1969.

13. Bishop to VN, June 5, 1969, VNA.

14. Toynbee, *Observer*, October 5, 1969; McCarthy, *Listener*, November 25, 1971; see also *Time*, May 3, 1971.

15. Dickstein, *New Republic*, June 28, 1967; *SO*, 146; *NYRB*, July 10, 1969.

16. *SO*, 120.

17. Carl Proffer to VN and VéN, March 17 and May 5, 1969, Robert Shankland to VéN, March 24, 1971, VNA; Gleb Struve, *Russkaya mysl'*, April 17, 1969.

18. BB interview with Bart Winer, April 1983; VéN to Alfred Appel and VN to Field, October 1, 1969, VNA.

19. VéN to A. A. Goldenweiser, June 18, 1969, VNA; diary; VN to Rowohlt, June 2 and September 19, 1969, Rowohlt to VN, June 29, 1971, VNA.

20. VéN to Elizaveta Marinel, August 2, 1969, Juliar Collection; VéN to William McGuire [ca. late June], VNA; *SL*, 455.

21. *SO*, 150, 217.

22. BB interview with Proffers, April 1983.

23. Diary, August 12, 1969, and "Notes to *Ada*" MS, VNA. After VN's death it was republished in Rivers and Nicol.

24. BB interview with Karlinsky, May 1983; Karlinsky to BB, June 30, 1990.

25. *NYRB*, December 4, 1969; repr. *SO*, 283. Cf. Lowell's "Nine Poems."

26. Diary, October 7 and August 4–17, 1969.

27. Fayard correspondence, October 1969, Mondadori correspondence, September 1969–March 1970, VN to Frank Taylor, November 11, 1969, and VéN to Richard Adams, January 9, 1970, VNA.

28. *New York Times*, May 1, 1969; Taylor to VN, September 5, 1969, VNA; Gerald Clarke interview with VN, September 17, 1974, from TS in VNA.

29. *SL*, 528; Field, *VN*, 370; Scammell, *Solzhenitsyn*, 906.

30. Concise *EO* MS, and VN to Taylor, January 11, 1970, VNA.

31. Notes for Work in Progress, VNA.

32. *PP* MS, VNA.

33. Diary; VN to Frank Taylor, December 9 and 13, 1969; *PP* MS.

34. *PP* 14, 15.

35. VN to C.H.O'D. Alexander, September 14, 1967, to C. R. Flood, March 22, 1973, and to E. R. Beal, May 22, 1972, VN to Frank Taylor, January 11, 1970, VNA; Spassky, *Russkaya mysl'*, March 10, 1983, 16; chess notes, VNA.

36. Diary.

37. *SL*, 460; BB interview with Appel, April 1983; *Triquarterly* 17 (Winter 1970), repr. as Appel and Newman; VN to Appel, February 28, 1970, VNA; diary; *SO*, 294, 287, 288. Steiner's essay appeared in *Encounter*, August 1966.

38. Diary; *SO*, 169.

39. VéN to A. A. Goldenweiser, June 12, and to Harry and Elena Levin, June 21, 1970, VNA.

40. Diary; VéN to Irving Lazar, February 1, 1970, and to Joseph Iseman, February 6, 1970, VN to Lerner, January 4, 1971, VNA.

41. Diary.

42. Ibid.

43. *Los Angeles Times*, August 7, 1977.

44. Caption, *Saturday Review of the Arts*, January 1973, 40; VN to Alfred Appel, August 3, 1970, VNA.

45. Diary.

46. Rivers and Nicol, 16–17.

47. Quennell, 21.

48. Rivers and Nicol, 16.

49. *Novel*, Spring 1971, 209.

50. Rivers and Nicol, 11; BB interview with Appel, April 1983; Rivers and Nicol, 16; *SO*, 163–64.

51. *SO*, 168–69; diary; VéN to Peter Kemeny, June 16, 1972, VNA.

52. Pub. *Times Higher Educational Supplement*, October 23, 1970, 19; Collins correspondence, August–September 1970, VNA.

53. VéN to Anne Murphy, November 19, 1970, VNA.

54. Diary; VéN to Anne Murphy, November 19, and to Nicolas Nabokov, November 15, 1970, VNA; *SO*, 166, 217.

55. Diary; VN to Field, August 24, 1970, VNA.

56. VN interview with Paul Sufrin, September 1971, from TS in VNA; Field, *Life*, 32.

57. Field, *Life*, 12, 10; BB interview with VéN, November 1986.

58. James Salter interview with VN, *People*, March 17, 1975. Field, *Life*, 13, recorded VN as straight-faced in making his comment about the blood of Peter the Great. DN reported VéN's recollection of VN's playfulness, *TLS*, January 6, 1978; Field replied, *TLS*, January 27, 1978; VéN reiterated her account in interview with BB, November 1986.

59. VéN to George Hessen, October 31, 1970, VNA.

60. Field, *Life*, 9–15; N2; Field to VN, January 23, 1971, VNA.

61. VéN correspondence with A. A. Goldenweiser, 1968–1970; VN to Rosoff, August 31, 1963, VNA.

62. *SL*, 476, and Levavi correspondence, November–December 1970, diary, April 20, 1971, VNA; *SL*, 478.

63. VéN to John Cady, January 6, 1971, VNA.

64. Diary, February–March 1971, VNA.

65. *SO*, 178, 203; diary; *Vogue*, April 1972, 78; VN to Alden Whitman, April 3, 1971, and VéN to Andrew Field, May 9, 1971, VNA.

66. VN to Karlinsky, April 15, 1971, VNA; BB interview with Karlinsky, May 1983.

67. Parker to VN, April 25, 1971, VNA; BB interview with Parker, February 1987.

68. VéN to Alan Levy, April 26, 1971; diary; VéN to Anne Murphy, July 7, 1971, VNA.

69. Diary; Israel Shenker, *Words and Their Masters* (Garden City, N.Y.: Doubleday, 1974), 24.

70. Diary; Alan Levy interview with VN, *New York Times Magazine*, October 31, 1971.

71. Quennell, 129.

72. New York: New York University Press, 1971.

73. Pub. *NYRB*, October 7, 1971; repr. *SO*, 304–07.

74. *NWL*, 332.

75. EW, *Letters on Literature and Politics*, 733.

76. *NYTBR*, November 7, 1971. For some of EW's comments, see p. 312 (and *Upstate*, 156–62).

77. *SO*, 218.

78. Diary; correspondence with Fayard and Bureau Littéraire Clairouin, September–November 1971, VNA.

79. VéN to Irving Lazar, March 5, 1972, VNA; *SO*, 185; VéN to Alden Whitman, October 6, 1971, VNA.

80. Diary; *EO* MS, VNA.

81. VéN to George Weidenfeld, January 5, and to Anne Murphy, January 17, 1972, VNA; diary; VéN to Peter Kemeny, March 3, 1972; *TT* MS, VNA.

CHAPTER 24. TRANSPARENT THINGS

1. Written 1969–1972; pub. New York: McGraw-Hill, 1972.

2. A point noted by Michael Rosenblum in "Finding What the Sailor Has Hidden," 222.

CHAPTER 25. REINVENTING A LIFE

Epigraphs: SO, 156; *PF*, 256.

1. Notes for Work in Progress, VNA.

2. Diary; VN to William McGuire, May 10, 1972, VNA.

3. SSN to VN, May 15, June 6 and 7, 1972, and Field to SSN, July 15, 1971, VNA.

4. *Glory*, xiii; *Time*, January 24, 1972; Field, *Life in Art*, 123.

5. VéN to Field, January 21, 1972, and VN to *Time*, March 27, 1972, VNA.

6. Field to VN, April 21, 1972, VéN to Field, May 9, Field to VN and VéN, May 18, 1972, VNA; Vladimir Zenzinov to VN, June 15, July 5 and 16, 1935, LCNA; *Pamyati Amalii Osipovny Fondaminskoy*, Paris: privately printed, 1937.

7. Appel and Newman, 356.

8. Diary; SSN to VN, October 14, 1972, VNA.

9. VN to Field, July 24, 1972, VNA.

10. Diary; BB interview with Elena Sikorski, June 1979.

11. Field to VN, August 16, VN to Field, September 8, 1972, VNA.

12. Field to VN, August 25, 1968, VNA; *SL*, 517–18.

13. Diary, September 25, 1972.

14. Diary, October 2–4, 1972; VN to Dan Lacy, January 31, 1973, VNA.

15. Edmund White to VN, October 24, 1973, VNA; *Saturday Review of the Arts*, January 6, 1973, 4.

16. Diary, November 5–17, 1972; pub. *Saturday Review of the Arts*, January 6, 1973, repr. *SO*, 308–14.

17. Gerald Clarke interview with VN, *Esquire*, July 1975, 133; BB interview with White, March 1988.

18. BB interview with Alfred Appel, April 1983.

19. Diary, November 24, 1972; Robert Evett, *Washington Daily News*, November 19, 1972; Updike, *New Yorker*, November 18, 1972.

20. Diary; VN to Edmund White, December 4, 1972, VNA.

21. Diary, January 5, 11, and 18, 1973, VNA.

22. Diary; VN to Field, January 31, 1973.

23. Those curious to understand the depth of Nabokov's frustration over the next three years of wrangling first with Field and then with Field's editors may wish to know what was wrong with Field's work. Three examples must suffice.

Exhibit A. Throughout 1922, Germany's rapid inflation quickened its pace until it reached grotesque proportions late in 1923, when *Rul'*, the newspaper that V. D. Nabokov had founded and his son contributed to so often, jumped from four thousand marks at the beginning of August to five million marks at the end of September and two billion marks in December. Curiously, the cost of living in Germany had been very low in real terms in the early days of the inflation, and Russian émigrés had thronged to Berlin in such numbers that the city became the overwhelming center of émigré life, émigré writing, and émigré publishing. But the chaos of hyperinflation during late 1923 and the increase in the real cost of living at the end of the year, after the revaluation of the mark (the price of *Rul'* fell at a stroke to twenty pfennings), prompted Russians to leave the city in droves, so that by mid-1924 Paris had become and remained the center of émigré culture until Hitler's army rearranged Europe. But Nabokov stayed put in Berlin, determined not to dilute his Russian by moving to a city where he could speak the local language perfectly. He was the only major Russian writer to remain, and in this self-imposed isolation he developed over the next few years from promise to greatness.

Although the German inflation had such a major effect on Russian émigré culture and on Nabokov's own circumstances, although its date could be checked in any encyclopedia, Field assumed the inflation began in 1929, in sympathy with the Wall Street crash. He somehow managed to persist in this misconstruction despite all the evidence even a superficial researcher of the period could discover, and even despite *Rul'* itself, the prime source for Nabokov's life and milieu in these years. In his corrections to Field's manuscript, Nabokov supplied the true date in the one passage where the inflation was explicitly assigned a year—averse to chronology, Field generally eschewed dates—but despite this correction Field did not change any of the various *other* passages that were based on his strange misconception. Winding up for a peroration at the end of his chapter on Nabokov in Germany, for instance, he alludes to the sizable sum received in 1929 for the German translation of *King, Queen, Knave*, and pictures the Nabokovs "standing on this little islet of security while the swiftly rising never-ending German inflation eddied and ripped around them" (Field, *Life*, 183). Did it not matter that the inflation had actually occurred six years earlier, as he had just been informed?

Exhibit B. With the income from the German translations of *Mary* and *King, Queen, Knave* in mind, Field declares: "Nineteen twenty-eight and twenty-nine were good years. . . . His collection of short stories and poems, *The Return of Chorb*, was published in Russian, and, what was most important, Ilya Fondaminsky, one of the editors of the main émigré publication, *Contemporary Annals*, made a trip to Berlin from Paris, one of the main purposes of which was to recruit Sirin's work for the journal, which he did with a vigorous Russian slap on his knee. Prior to that only some poems by Nabokov had appeared in *Contemporary Annals*. A long and generally happy association with the journal began with the appearance of his novella *The Eye* in 1930, followed by his first major novel, *The Defense*" (Field, *Life*, 183). In fact, Fondaminsky's trip to Berlin took place in the summer of 1930, and involved not the completed manuscript of *The Defense* (as Field identifies it when he returns to this scene: *Life*, 214) but the incomplete manuscript of *Glory*. Nabokov recounts the incident lucidly and accurately in his foreword to *Glory*, where the whole point of the story is that by this stage in Nabokov's career, Fondaminsky and *Sovremennye zapiski* (*Contemporary Annals*) were prepared to accept his work for publication even before its completion.

In the few lines cited above, Field obscures a host of salient facts about Nabokov's artistic career. He makes nonsense of the first meeting between Nabokov and Fondaminsky, the man who, as Nabokov would later declare, "did more for Russian émigré literature than any other" (*SM*, 286–87). He distorts beyond recognition the real story of Nabokov's association with *Sovremennye zapiski*, the most important of émigré journals, the place of first publication of his last seven Russian novels, and the source of most of his literary income for his last ten years as an émigré writer. Prior to Fondaminsky's trip, Field declares, only some poems by Nabokov had appeared in *Sovremennye zapiski*. A few lyrics had indeed been published there in 1921 and 1922, but Nabokov's bibliographer should have known that in 1927 the journal had also published his story "Terror" and his long verse novella "A University Poem." As his bibliographer and biographer, Field should certainly have known that *before* Fondaminsky called on him in Berlin, Nabokov had published the whole of *The Defense* in *Sovremennye zapiski*, and had already had *The Eye* accepted there. The first installment of *The Defense* in November 1929 had produced an immediate and extraordinary reaction: novelist Nina Berberova had felt at once that by its publication alone the emigration was saved, immortalized, justified; Ivan Bunin declared that Nabokov had "snatched a gun and done away with the whole older generation, myself included"; Georgy Adamovich and Georgy Ivanov had launched their notorious attack on this upstart crow. (See *VNRY*, 343–44, 350.) But Field manages to knock down the signposts at this turning point of Nabokov's reputation by declaring that *The Eye* preceded *The Defense* in *Sovremennye zapiski* and implying that *The Defense* remained unpublished there until late 1930 or 1931.

There is nothing elusive about the correct sequence of Nabokov's novels in 1929–1930: *The Defense* was written in the spring and summer of 1929, and published in *Sovremennye zapiski* in 1929–1930; *The Eye* written in the winter of 1929–1930, and published in *Sovremennye zapiski* late in 1930; *Glory* written in the spring, summer, and fall of 1930, and published in *Sovremennye zapiski* in 1931. All these facts are recorded in Nabokov's own published autobiographical writings and confirmed by the letters he had made available to Field. Once again, for no reason whatsoever, Field jumps at the wrong inference—*if* Fondaminsky came to Berlin to buy Nabokov's work for *Sovremennye zapiski, then* none of his work could have appeared there already—and realigns the facts to fit his mistaken scenario. Had he checked in *Speak, Memory*, in the forewords to *The Defense, The Eye*, and *Glory*, had he even consulted his own *Nabokov: A Bibliography*, he could not have made these multiple errors. He does not even attend to the inconsistencies within his own fudged facts: *if* Fondaminsky had taken away the manuscript of *The Defense*, as he misstates, why according to his version did *The Eye* appear first?

In his third book on Nabokov, Field fails to record correctly the order in which the man's novels appeared, let alone to chart the growth of his reputation or the development of his art.

Exhibit C. While still living in Berlin in 1936, Nabokov undertook a reading tour to Paris early in the year. Field records that "a French as well as a Russian evening was held in February 1936" (*Life*, 205). Correct: at the French evening, Nabokov read "Mademoiselle O," his memoir of his French governess. But Field immediately begins to conflate that 1936 reading with another much more celebrated reading a year later, after Nabokov had left Berlin. In February 1937, Nabokov would be called on at the last minute for a different French reading and would be delighted to see in the sparse audience rounded up at the last moment the figure of James Joyce sitting in the audience amidst the Hungarian football team. Field transfers Joyce's presence back to the 1936 reading, although this contradicts his own later report (*Life*, 209–10) that Nabokov did *not* meet Joyce in February 1936. He has managed to reduce the well-known story of the strange first encounter of two of the greatest writers of the century to a muddled mirage. (See *VNRY*, 424, for 1936 reading, 431 and 434 for "Pouchkine" and 1937 reading.)

Field also has Nabokov during the 1936 reading deliver his *1937* lecture on Pushkin, "Pouchkine, ou le vrai et le vraisemblable." "It was the centenary of the poet's death," Field explains. Although trained as a Russian scholar, he does not note the mismatch between 1837, the most famous date in Russian literary history, and 1936.

For his account of the 1936 reading, Field silently drew on one of Nabokov's letters to his mother. The account ends with Field's one acknowledged quotation from the letter, Nabokov's comment to his mother that in the course of the reading "applause came like bomb explosions." In fact, Nabokov had written something far more vivid: "My reading . . . was interrupted by applause during which the organizer's old and nervous bulldog would fly out of the hall like a bomb" (VN to EIN, March 23, 1935 [for 1936], VNA).

Field had no other source for the 1936 reading than the letter Nabokov showed him. It gives no warrant whatsoever for Field's confusion of this reading with the 1937 Pushkin lecture, which would not be conceived, let alone written, until many months later, or for Joyce's presence, or for the clichéd comparison of applause and explosions.

When Field could manage to garble common historical knowledge (the German inflation), Nabokov's accurate published recollections (Fondaminsky's visit), or a straightforward account Nabokov had himself set down in a letter just after the event (the 1936 reading), and all for no reason other than his own negligence, it is no wonder that Nabokov would have to shudder again and again at the innumerable distortions in Field's versions of information supplied to him in conversation, and at second or third hand, decades after the event.

24. Field to VN, February 10, 1973, VNA; diary; N1.

25. Field to VN, January 23, 1971, VNA.

26. LectsR, 138.

27. Field to VéN, March 3, 1967, VNA.

28. VéN to Field, November 16, 1966, VNA; Simon Karlinsky to BB, August 22 and December 19, 1988.

29. Field, Life, 115; DB, 169; Field, Life, 121; N1. Field corrected his error about VN's age and level of entry into Tenishev in Life, 112, 114.

30. Field, Life, 71. See VNRY, 77 and 543 n. 41.

31. N1.

32. VéN to Field, May 21, 1968, and March 3, 1969, VNA.

33. Field to VN, July 9, 1973, VNA.

34. VéN to Field, March 10, 1973, VNA.

35. VéN to Joseph Iseman, September 11, 1972, and VN to Dan Lacy, January 31, 1973, VNA; diary.

36. VN to Benjamin Houston, April 2, 1973, VNA.

37. Diary, April 20, 1973.

38. Field to VN, May 7, and VN to Field, May 14, 1973, VNA.

39. VN to Joan Daly, May 28, 1973, VNA.

40. VN to Alfred Appel, June 15, 1973, VNA; diary; VéN to Richard Adams, July 7, 1973, VNA.

41. VN to Fred Hills, August 1, 1973, VNA.

42. Field to VN, July 9, 1973, VNA.

43. 1951 Year Book, March 25, VNA.

44. *SL*, 517.

45. *N1*; Field, *Life*, 124, 227.

46. Diary, September 4–5, 1973; BB interview with Karlinsky, May 1983; *LATH*, 209.

47. *SL*, 519.

48. Clarence Brown, *Trenton Times*, September 30, 1990.

49. New York: Crown.

50. Field to VN, July 9, 1973.

51. Dmitri Nabokov was the first to explode Field's claim in his *Observer* review, April 26, 1987; DN to BB, October 27, 1990.

52. Diary, September 17–22, 1973; VN to Weidenfeld, September 24, 1973, VNA.

53. Diary; VN to Fred Hills, November 3, 1973, VNA; *SL*, 521.

54. *LATH*, MS, VNA.

55. Diary.

56. *SL*, 528; Field, *VN*, 370; diary; VéN to Gerald Clarke, July 14, 1975, VNA.

57. VéN to William McGuire, March 8, and to Dan Lacy, March 12, 1974, VNA; diary.

CHAPTER 26. LOOK AT THE HARLEQUINS!

1. Written 1973–1974, pub. New York: McGraw-Hill, 1974.

2. *New Statesman*, April 25, 1975.

3. *SM*, 40.

4. *LATH*, 8, has "confined madman," a misprint for "confirmed." See Gerald Clarke interview with VN, *Esquire*, July 1975, 131.

5. Pierre Dommergues interview with VN, *Les Langues modernes*, January–February 1968, 99.

6. *SM*, 295.

7. BB interview with Alfred Appel, April 1983.

8. Field, *Life*, 34.

9. *Stikhi*, 106–7; see *VNRY*, 206–8.

10. VN to Ledig Rowohlt, May 2, 1975.

11. *SM*, 152, 215, 225, 230.

12. See *VNRY*, 250–54.

CHAPTER 27. UNANSWERED QUESTIONS

Epigraphs: Helga Chudacoff interview with VN, April 17, 1974, from TS, VNA; *RLSK*, 170.

1. VéN to Alfred and Nina Appel, March 18, 1974, VNA; diary, April 30, 1974; VN to Hills, May 10, 1974, VNA.

2. Diary, May 5–13, 1974; VéN to Marie Schébéko, April 25, 1974, VNA.

3. VN to William McGuire, May 15, 1974; unpublished chess notes, VNA; diary, May 15, 1974.

4. *NWL*, 2; VéN to Elena Wilson, May 3, 1974, VNA; diary.

5. Clairouin correspondence, May 1974; diary.

6. VN to Fred Hills, May 10, 1974; VNA; diary, May 31 and June.

7. VN to Fred Hills, June 18, 1974, and VéN to Peter Kemeny, October 9, 1974, VNA; diary, June 7–8 and 21, 1974.

8. BB interview with Hills, April 1983.

9. Appel, "Remembering Nabokov," 26–27.

10. BB interviews with Appel, April 1983.

11. *SL*, 532–34; VN to Henri Hell, October 21, 1974, VNA; BB interview with Appel, 1983.

12. Diary; VéN to Peter Kemeny, October 9, 1974; DN to BB, October 28, 1990.

13. Diary, August 21, 1974; BB interviews with VéN, December 1986, with Appel and with William McGuire, April 1983.

14. Diary and interview file, VNA.

15. VéN to Carl and Ellendea Proffer, November 11, 1974, Carl Proffer to VN and VéN, June 10, 1975, VNA.

16. Proffer, *Widows of Russia*, 48–49.

17. VéN, *Russkaya mysl'*, July 6, 1978.

18. *Observer*, May 26, 1974, repr. *SL*, 531.

19. *SL*, 540–41; Carl Proffer "Maramzin Trial," *NYRB*, March 6, 1975; Maramzin, "On Being Free," *NYRB*, January 22, 1976; BB interview with Carl Proffer, April 1983.

20. Diary; BB interviews with VéN, June and September 1982.

21. Diary, August 8, 1974.

22. *SL*, 527–28; Scammell, *Solzhenitsyn*, 907; VN diary, October 10, 1974.

23. Diary, October 27 and November 4, 1974; *SL*, 537, 539; diary, November 23 and 27, 1974.

24. VN and VéN to Isabel and Rockwell Stephens, December 18, 1974, VNA; VéN to Irving Lazar, February 3, to William and Paula McGuire, March 29, to Peter Kemeny, April 9, and to Gordon Lish, *Esquire*, February 11, 1975, VNA; BB interview with DN, December 1981.

25. *SL*, 548; diary.

26. VN correspondence with Kollek, September 1974–April 1976.

27. VéN to Marie Schébéko, April 2, 1975, VNA, and to Elizaveta Marinel-Allan, September 30 and December 14, 1974, Juliar Collection.

28. VéN to Joan Daly, February 3, 1975, VNA.

29. *SL*, 544–45, 555–58, and VN correspondence with Joseph Iseman and Joan Daly, December 1974–April 1976, VNA.

30. VN correspondence with Iseman and Daly, 1973–1976.

31. BB interview with Loo, March 1983.

32. VéN to Marie Schébéko, April 2, 1975; diary; Alexender Bakhrakh to BB, August 17, 1983, and BB interview with Ivan Nabokoff, January 1985; Pivot, in *Le Soir* (Brussels), September 14, 1983.

33. *L'Exprès*, June 9–15, 1975.

34. VéN to Beverly Loo, June 16, 1975, VNA; BB interview with VéN, February 1983, and with Louba Schirman, January 1985.

35. *SL*, 552; BB interview with Jaqueline Callier and with Martin and Margaret Newstead, February 1983.

36. BB interview with VéN, February 1983; Hôpital de Montreux to VN, October 13, 1975; VéN to Blue Cross–Blue Shield, February 10, 1976, VNA; VN to John Cady, November 3, 1975, VéN to Weidenfeld, June 16, 1976, VNA; *SL*, 554.

37. VN to Hills, December 4, 1975, VNA; diary, December 1, 1975; VéN to Dan Lacy, July 28, VN to Hills, January 23, and VéN to Andrey Sinyavsky, January 30, 1976, VNA; diary, January 26, 1976; *SL*, 554; diary, February 2, 1976; VN to Hills, February 16, 1976, VNA.

38. VéN to Carl and Ellendea Proffer, January 21 and March 12, 1976, Carl Proffer to VN and VéN, March 22, 1976.

39. VéN to Dan Lacy, January 16, 1976, and Elena Wilson to Karlinsky, February 3, 1976, VNA.

40. Diary, April 3 and 7, 1976; VéN to Gleb Struve, April 26, 1976, Hoover; VéN to Hills, April 20, 1976, VNA; *SL*, 560.

41. Charles Fecher, *Catholic Review*, June 1, 1973; O'Hara, *Canto*, Spring 1977.

42. Cf. reviews of Field: Denis Donoghue, *NYRB*, August 3, 1967 ("terms which I would wish to reserve for the greatest writers. But he does not produce the evidence"); Michael Wood, *New Society*, December 14, 1967 ("Its central suggestion is that Nabokov writes only about artists. . . . unbelievably unhelpful"); Julian Moynahan, *Partisan Review*, Summer 1968 ("asserts that the fiction is mainly concerned with the business of making art. . . . This is plainly wrong and drastically limits the value of Field's study as criticism").

43. *KQK*, viii.

44. *SO*, 34.

45. Gene Bell, *Nation*, May 31, 1975; Christopher Lehmann-Haupt, *New York Times*, May 30, 1977.

46. Diary, May 1 and 11, 1976; VéN to William McGuire, June 5, 1976, VNA; diary, May 15 and 30, 1976.

47. VéN to Elizaveta Marinel-Allan, May 27, 1976, Juliar Collection; VN to Fred Hills, June 15, VéN to Beverly Loo, June 8, VéN to Blue Cross–Blue Shield, November 9, 1976, VNA.

48. *SL*, 560; VN to Pyke Johnson, December 8, 1975, VNA; McGuire, *Bollingen*, 226.

49. *New York Times*, October 30, 1976, repr. *SL*, 562.

50. VN to Fred Hills, November 8, 1976; diary, September 21, 1976; William F. Buckley, *National Review*, July 22, 1977; VéN to Blue Cross–Blue Shield, November 9, 1976, VNA; DN to BB, October 28, 1990.

51. VéN to Carl Proffer and Ellendea Proffer, July 25, and to Dan Lacy, July

28, and VéN to Alfred Appel, August 9, 1976, and to Lena Levin, August 11, 1977, VNA.

52. BB interview with VéN, February 1983; medical certificate, October 11, 1976, VNA.

53. Diary; BB interview with Loo, March 1983.

54. Diary; Ardis correspondence, October–December 1976, and verse albums, VNA.

55. Diary, October 29, 1976, VéN to Marie Schébéko, October 30, VN to Fred Hills, November 8, and VéN to Bernard de Fallois, November 5, 1976, VNA.

56. Hugh A. Mulligan interview with VN, syndicated, *Hanover Star Bulletin*, January 9, 1977, and elsewhere.

57. *SL*, 562; VN to Teddy Kollek, December 10, 1976, VNA; Robert Robinson interview with VN, *Listener*, March 24, 1977; BB interview with William McGuire, April 1983; diary, January 31, 1977.

58. VéN to William McGuire and to Elena Wilson, February 28, 1977, and to Jonathan Gillet, February 25, 1977, VNA; DN, in Quennell, 128; Stephen Jan Parker to VéN, May 29, 1977.

59. DN, in Quennell, 134; VN to Teddy Kollek, March 26, 1977, VNA.

60. Ibid.; diary, March 19, 1976; VéN to Ledig Rowohlt, April 6, 1977, VNA.

61. Diary; VéN to Shura Barbetti, May 4, 1977, VNA; BB interview with Carl Proffer, April 1983; Carl Proffer to VN and VéN, June 1, 1977, VNA.

62. BB interviews with VéN, February 1983, and with ES, September 1982.

63. Medical certificate, September 8, 1977, VNA.

64. VéN to Joan Daly, June 17, and to J. D. O'Hara, June 15, 1977, VNA; BB interview with VéN, February 1983, and with DN, February 1987; VéN to Alfred Appel, June 20, 1977, VNA.

65. VéN to Beverly Loo, June 27, and to Stephen Jan Parker, June 22, 1977; BB interview with VéN, February 1983; DN, in Quennell, 136.

66. DN, in Quennell, 136.

67. Ibid.; medical certificate, September 8, 1977, VNA.

68. Medical certificate, September 8, 1977, VNA; BB interview with VéN, February 1983; VéN to Louise Fürrer, July 4, 1977, VNA; Quennell, 136.

69. Medical certificate, September 8, 1977, VNA.

70. *In Memoriam: Vladimir Nabokov, 1899–1977*; BB interview with Loo, March 1983.

71. Alfred Appel to VéN, July 1, 1982, VNA.

72. Vladimir Nabokov, *Drugie berega: Stikhi i Proza*, rec. 2, read by Vadim Muratov (Melodia, 1989).

73. DN to BB, October 28, 1990.

74. Diary, December 1, 1974.

75. "Vtoroe prilozhenie k *Daru*" MS, LCNA.

76. *IB*, 209.

BIBLIOGRAPHY

THE VAST bulk of my time in researching this biography was spent either with Nabokov's published works or with the unpublished materials in his archives in Montreux. However, it may be useful to specify what else has proved relevant.

The bibliography therefore lists all written materials consulted for Nabokov's life or the lives of his forebears in the preparation of both *Vladimir Nabokov: The Russian Years* and *Vladimir Nabokov: The American Years*, and any critical commentary on Nabokov's works cited in either volume. Section I below lists archival, library, and museum collections consulted; section II, periodicals searched through at length; section III, books and articles relevant to Nabokov's family, especially his father, Vladimir Dmitrievich Nabokov, and grandfather, Dmitri Nikolaevich Nabokov; section IV, works by Nabokov; and section V, books and articles either relevant to Nabokov's life or cited in relation to his work.

The standard bibliography of Nabokov's works is Michael Juliar's *Vladimir Nabokov: A Descriptive Bibliography* (New York: Garland, 1986), to which additions and annual supplements are made in the journal *The Nabokovian*. *The Nabokovian* also supplements Samuel Schuman's much less comprehensive bibliography of Nabokov criticism, *Vladimir Nabokov: A Reference Guide* (Boston: G. K. Hall, 1979). A new annotated bibliography of Nabokov criticism, by Stephen Jan Parker, is forthcoming from Garland Press.

I. ARCHIVAL, LIBRARY, AND MUSEUM COLLECTIONS

ACADEMY OF SCIENCES LIBRARY, LENINGRAD

Yunaya mysl' (Tenishev school magazine).

BRYN MAWR COLLEGE LIBRARY

Katharine A. White Collection. VN letters; TS of unpublished chapter of *Conclusive Evidence*.

CAMBRIDGE UNIVERSITY

Cambridge University Archives
Council, examination, lodging-house, matriculation, and tutorial records.

Trinity College Archives
Admissions records; Magpie and Stump Debating Society records.

CENTRAL STATE ARCHIVE OF LITERATURE AND ART, MOSCOW

Aykhenvald Collection. VN letter to Yuli Aykhenvald.
Dioneo Collection. VDN letters to Dioneo.
Makeev Collection. VN letters to Makeev.
L. F. Panteleev Collection. VDN letters.
Rech' Collection. Galleys and proofs of VN's *Stikhi* (1916).

CENTRAL STATE ARCHIVE OF THE OCTOBER REVOLUTION, LENINGRAD

Tenishev School Collection. Fund 2811. Class list.

CENTRAL STATE HISTORICAL ARCHIVE, LENINGRAD

Mikhail Chubinsky Collection. VDN letters.

CENTRAL STATE HISTORICAL ARCHIVE OF THE CITY OF LENINGRAD

Imperial School of Jurisprudence Collection. Fund 355. Materials relating to V. D. Nabokov's employment.
Office of the City Governor of St. Petersburg Collection. Fund 569.
Office of the Governor-General of St. Petersburg Province Collection. Fund 253.
Petrograd Ecclesiastical Consistory Collection. Fund 19. Records of VN's birth and christening.
St. Petersburg Land Tenure Commission Collection. Fund 297.
St. Petersburg City Council Collection. Fund 513.
St. Petersburg Nobility Collection. Fund 536.
Tenishev School Collection. Fund 176. Marks and comments on pupils, timetables, etc.

COLUMBIA UNIVERSITY LIBRARY

Bakhmeteff Archive
Mark Aldanov Collection. Klaus Mann, Nicolas Nabokov, VN, VéN, and Edmund Wilson letters.

Avgusta Damanskaya Collection. VDN letters.

Mstislav Dobuzhinsky Collection. Dobuzhinsky and VN letters.

Alexis Goldenweiser Collection. Goldenweiser, VN, and VéN letters.

Roman Grynberg Collection. Grynberg, VN, and Edmund Wilson letters.

Abram Kagan Collection. VN letters.

Mikhail Karpovich Collection. VN and VéN letters.

Manfred Kridl Collection. VN letter.

Herbert Machiz Collection. VéN letter.

Paul Milyukov Collection. VDN letters.

Dmitri Dmitrievich Nabokov Collection. Family documents.

Vladimir Nabokov Collection. Manuscript of "Pamyati Amalii Osipovny Fondaminskoy."

Sofia Panina Collection. Nikolay Astrov memoir of VDN; VDN letters to Ivan Petrunkevich.

Sergey Potresov Collection. VN letter.

Fyodor Rodichev Collection. EIN letters.

Russian National Committee Collection. KDN letters.

Evgeny Sablin Collection. VN letters.

Ariadna Tyrkova-Williams Collection. KDN and VDN letters.

Union of Russian Journalists and Writers in Paris Collection. VN receipts.

George Vernadsky Collection. VN letters to Mikhail Rostovtzeff and Vernadsky.

Avrahm Yarmolinsky Collection. VN letters.

Vladimir Zenzinov. VéN letters, VN letters, and lecture TS.

Other

Random House Collection. VN letters; reader's report on early version of *Bend Sinister*.

Lionel Trilling Collection. VN letters.

CORNELL UNIVERSITY

Comstock Hall
VN lepidoptera collection.

Olin Library
Morris Bishop Collection. VN limerick.

William Forbes Collection. VN letters.

Proceedings of Board of Trustees.

E. B. White Collection. VN letters.

Romance Studies Department
Archives.

HARVARD UNIVERSITY

Houghton Library
Vladimir Nabokov Collection. VN letter to William James; VN note on *Madame Bovary*; TS of "Lines Written in Oregon."

734   BIBLIOGRAPHY

Lamont Library
Poetry Room. VN tapes.

Museum of Comparative Zoology
VN lepidoptera collection.

Slavic Department
Letters and other materials relating to VN's course at Harvard, 1951–1952.

INSTITUTE OF RUSSIAN LITERATURE AND ART (PUSHKINSKIY DOM), LENINGRAD

K. K. Arsen'ev Collection. VDN letters.
E. P. Karpov Collection. VDN letter.
A. F. Koni Collection. VDN letters.
Russkaya mysl' Collection. VDN letter.
M. V. Vatson Collection. VDN letter.

LIBRARY OF CONGRESS

Manuscript Division
Bollingen Collection. Materials relating to VN's *Eugene Onegin*.
Vladimir Nabokov Collection. Substantial collection of VN MSS and letters.
    Restricted.
Vladimir Nabokov Correspondence File. VN's correspondence with library
    over deposit of his papers.
Vozdushnye puti Collection. VéN MS notes.
Zinaida Shakhovskoy Collection. VN letters.

Music Division
Sergey Koussevitzky Collection. VN letters.
Sergey Rachmaninoff Collection. VN letters and TS.

PRINCETON UNIVERSITY

Firestone Library
Allen Tate Collection. VN letters.

ROZHDESTVENO KRAEVEDCHESKIY MUZEY

Photographs of the Nabokov family and estates.

SALTYKOV-SHCHEDRIN STATE PUBLIC LIBRARY, LENINGRAD

Tenishev school handbooks.
Yunaya mysl' (Tenishev school magazine).

Manuscript Division
N. S. Tagantsev Collection. VDN letters.
P. L. Vaksel Collection. VDN letters.
Fund 1000. V. A. Ratkov-Rozhnov memoirs. On Dmitri Nikolaevich Nabokov.

Plekhanov House
P. B. Struve Collection. VDN letters.

STANFORD UNIVERSITY

Hoover Institution
Constitutional Democratic Party Collection. Records of émigré activity.
Crimean Regional Government Collection. Minutes and memoir.
Boris Nicolaevsky Collection. VDN letters; VN letters to Nina Berberova.
Russian Review Collection. Dmitri Mohrenschildt letter to VN.
Gleb Struve Collection. VéN letters and VN letters and MSS.
Mark Vishnyak Collection. VéN and VN letters.

UNIVERSITY OF ILLINOIS LIBRARY, URBANA

Philip Mosely Collection. VN letters.
Sophia Pregel-Brynner Collection. VéN letter.
Vadim Rudnev Collection. VN letters.

UNIVERSITÉ DE LAUSANNE

Musée cantonal zoologique. VN lepidoptera collection.

UNIVERSITY OF TEXAS, AUSTIN

Harry Ransom Humanities Research Center
Jason Epstein Collection. VéN and VN letters.
Harper's Collection. VN letters.
Edward Weeks Collection. VéN and VN letters.

VLADIMIR NABOKOV ARCHIVES

VN's early (1915–1928) and late (mid-1960s on) MSS; principal collection of
his correspondence, diaries, etc. (1919 on); VDN documents (1890–1922).
Private. In 1991 this material became part of the Berg Collection of the New
York Public Library. Restricted.

WELLESLEY COLLEGE ARCHIVES

Administrative reports, VN biographical file, oral history interviews with VN
associates.

YALE UNIVERSITY

Beinecke Rare Book and Manuscript Library
Nina Berberova Collection. VN letters to Khodasevich.
Vladimir Nabokov Collection. *Ada* TS.
Edmund Wilson Collection. Nabokov letters to Wilson.

II. PERIODICALS

Arkhiv russkoy revolyutsii. Berlin. Emigré journal.
Atlantic Monthly. Boston. Monthly.

Berliner Adressbuch. Berlin. Annual.
Beseda. Berlin. Emigré journal.
Blagonamerennyy. Brussels. Emigré journal.
Cambridge Review. Cambridge, England. Weekly.
Cambridge University Reporter. Cambridge, England. Irregular.
Chisla. Paris. Emigré journal.
Cornell Alumni News. Ithaca, N.Y. Monthly.
Cornell Daily Sun. Ithaca, N.Y. Daily.
The Cornellian. Ithaca, N.Y. Annual.
Cornell Reports. Ithaca, N.Y. Quarterly.
Dni. Berlin, then Paris. Emigré daily, then weekly.
Encounter. London. Monthly.
Esquire. Chicago. Monthly.
Ezhegodnik gazety rech'. St. Petersburg. Annual.
Golos emigranta. Berlin. Emigré journal.
Golos minuvshego na chuzhoy storone. Paris. Emigré journal.
Golos Rossii. Berlin. Emigré daily.
Grani. Berlin. Emigré journal.
Grani. Frankfurt. Postwar émigré quarterly.
The Granta. Cambridge, England. Weekly.
Gryadushchaya Rossiya. Paris. Emigré journal.
The Harvard Crimson. Cambridge, Mass. Daily.
Illyustrirovannaya Rossiya. Paris. Emigré weekly.
Illyustrirovannaya zhizn'. Paris. Emigré weekly.
Istorik i sovremennik. Berlin. Emigré journal.
Izvestia S.-Peterburgskoy gorodskoy dumy. St. Petersburg.
Knizhnyy ukazatel'. Prague. Emigré monthly.
Kontinent. Paris. Emigré quarterly, 1974– .
The Last Word. Wellesley, Mass. Monthly.
Legenda. Wellesley, Mass. Annual.
Lepidoperists' Society News. New Haven, Conn. Irregular.
Mech'. Warsaw. Emigré weekly.
Minuvshee. Paris. Journal.
Mosty. Munich. Postwar émigré journal.
Museum of Comparative Zoology. Annual Report. Cambridge, Mass. Annual.
Nabokovian. Lawrence, Kans. Semi-annually.
Na chuzhoy storone. Berlin, then Prague. Emigré journal.
Nakanune. Berlin. Pro-Soviet émigré daily, then weekly.
Nash mir. Berlin. Emigré weekly.
Nash vek. Berlin. Emigré weekly.
New Republic. New York. Weekly.
New Russia. London. Weekly.
New Yorker. New York. Weekly.
New York Review of Books. New York. Semi-monthly.

New York Sun. New York. Daily.
New York Times. New York. Daily.
Nov'. Tallinn. Emigré journal.
Novaya gazeta. Paris. Emigré weekly.
Novaya russkaya kniga. Berlin. Emigré monthly.
Novoe russkoe slovo. New York. Emigré daily.
Novoe slovo. Berlin. Pro-Nazi émigré weekly.
Novoe vremya. St. Petersburg. Daily.
Novyy grad. Paris. Emigré journal.
Novyy korabl'. Paris. Emigré journal.
Novyy zhurnal. New York. Postwar émigré journal.
Obshchee delo. Paris. Emigré daily.
Opyty. New York. Postwar émigré journal.
Partisan Review. New York. Monthly.
Perezvony. Riga. Emigré journal.
Playboy. Chicago. Monthly.
Poslednie novosti. Paris. Emigré daily.
Pravo. St. Petersburg. Weekly.
The Problemist. London. Bi-monthly.
Psyche. Boston. Lepidopterological quarterly.
Rech'. St. Petersburg. Daily.
Rossia. Paris. Emigré weekly.
Rossiya i slavyanstvo. Paris. Emigré weekly.
Rul'. Berlin. Emigré daily.
The Russian. London. Weekly.
Russkaya kniga. Berlin. Emigré monthly.
Russkaya mysl'. Moscow. Prerevolutionary monthly.
Russkaya mysl'. Sofia, then Prague, then Paris. Emigré monthly.
Russkaya mysl'. Paris. Postwar émigré weekly.
Russkaya zarubezhnaya kniga. Prague. Emigré journal.
Russkie vedomosti. Moscow. Prerevolutionary daily.
Russkie zapiski. Paris. Emigré journal.
Russkiy v Anglii. London. Emigré semi-monthly.
Russkoe ekho. Berlin. Emigré weekly.
Sankt-peterburgskie vedomosti. St. Petersburg. Daily.
Segodnya. Riga. Emigré daily.
Sem' dney v illyustratsiyakh. Paris. Emigré weekly.
Sovremennye zapiski. Paris. Emigré journal.
Spalding's Cambridge Directory. Cambridge, England. Annual.
Spolokhi. Berlin. Emigré monthly.
Stanford University Bulletin. Stanford. Quarterly.
Stolitsa i usad'ba. St. Petersburg. Semi-monthly.
Students' Hand Book. Wellesley, Mass. Annual.
Students' Handbook. Cambridge, England. Annual.
Teatr i zhizn'. Berlin. Emigré semi-monthly.
Time. New York. Weekly.

Vereteno. Berlin. Emigré journal.
Veretyonysh. Berlin. Emigré journal.
Versty. Paris. Emigré journal.
Ves' Peterburg. St. Petersburg. Annual.
Vestnik Evropy. St. Petersburg. Monthly.
Vestnik partii narodnoy svobody. St. Petersburg. Weekly.
Vestnik prava. St. Petersburg. Monthly.
Vladimir Nabokov Research Newsletter. See *Nabokovian*.
Volya Rossii. Prague. Emigré weekly, then journal.
Vozdushnye puti. New York. Postwar émigré journal.
Vozrozhdenie. Paris. Emigré daily.
Vozrozhdenie. Paris. Postwar émigré monthly.
Vremennik obshchestva druzey russkoy knigi. Paris. Emigré journal.
Vremya. Berlin. Emigré weekly.
We. Wellesley, Mass. Monthly.
Wellesley Alumnae Magazine. Wellesley, Mass. Quarterly.
Wellesley College Bulletin. Wellesley, Mass. Quarterly.
Wellesley College News. Wellesley, Mass. Weekly.
Yaltinskiy golos. Yalta. 1918. Daily.
Yunaya mysl'. St. Petersburg. Irregular.
Zhar-ptitsa. Berlin, then Paris. Emigré journal.
Zhurnal ugolovnogo prava i protsessa. St. Petersburg. Quarterly.
Zveno. Paris. Emigré weekly, then monthly.

III. THE NABOKOV FAMILY

Adresnaya kniga goroda S. Peterburga na 1895 g. St. Petersburg, 1895.
Al'manakh sovremennykh russkikh gosudarstvennykh deyateley. St. Petersburg: Goldberg, 1897.
Armstrong, Terence. Letter to Editor. "Nabokov." *TLS*, October 21, 1977, 1239.
Aronson, Grigory. *Rossiya nakanune revolyutsii*. New York, 1962.
Arseniev, K. K. *Za chetvert' veka, 1871–1894*. Petrograd, 1915.
Astrov, Nikolay. "V. D. Nabokov." Unpublished lecture, March 28, 1932. Panina Collection, ColB.
Baddeley, John F. *Russia in the "Eighties": Sport and Politics*. London: Longmans, Green, 1921.
Baedeker, Karl. *La Russie: Manuel du voyageur*. Leipzig: Karl Baedeker, 1897.
———. *Russland: Handbuch für Reisende*. Leipzig: Karl Baedeker, 1901.
Belchikov, N. F. *Dostoevsky v protsesse Petrashevtsev*. Moscow: Nauka, 1971.
Bensman, Stephen J. "The Constitutional Ideas of the Russian Liberation Movement: The Struggle for Human Rights during the Revolution of 1905." Ph.D. diss., University of Wisconsin, Madison, 1977.
Bogdanov, Nikolay. "Krymskoe kraevoe pravitel'stvo." Unpublished memoir. Hoover.

Brinkley, George. *The Volunteer Army and Allied Intervention in South Russia, 1917–1921.* Notre Dame: University of Notre Dame Press, 1966.

Browden, Robert Paul, and Alexander Kerensky, eds. *The Russian Provisional Government, 1917: Documents.* Stanford: Stanford University Press, 1961.

Davydov, Aleksandr. *Vospominaniya.* Paris, 1982.

Demidov, I. "Blagorodnoe sertse." *Poslednie novosti,* March 30, 1922, 2.

Deutsch [Deich], Leo. *Sixteen Years in Siberia: Some Experiences of a Russian Revolutionist.* Trans. Helen Chisholm. 1903; repr. Westport, Conn.: Hyperion, 1977.

Dolgorukov, K. Paul. "K kharakteristike V. D. Nabokova." *Russkaya mysl'* 6–7 (1922): 268–72.

Dostoevsky, Fyodor. *Pis'ma.* Ed. A. S. Dolinin. 4 vols. Moscow and Leningrad, 1928.

Dvoryanstvo i krepostnoy stroy v Rossii. Moscow: Nauka, 1975.

Feoktistov, Evgeny. *Vospominania E. M. Feoktistova: Za kulisami politiki i literatury, 1848–1896.* Ed. Y. Oksman. Leningrad: Priboy, 1929.

Ferrand, Jacques, and Sergey S. Nabokov. *Les Nabokov: Essai généalogique.* Paris, 1982.

"Fond imeni V. D. Nabokova." *Russkaya mysl'* 8–12 (1922): 271–72.

Frank, Joseph. *Dostoevsky: The Years of Ordeal, 1850–1859.* Princeton: Princeton University Press, 1983.

Fuks, Viktor. *Sud i politsiya.* 2 vols. Moscow: Universitetskaya tipografiya, 1889.

Ganfman, M. L. "V. D. Nabokov." *Rul',* March 30, 1922, 1.

Gertsen, A. I. *Sobranie sochineniy v 30 tomakh.* Moscow: Akademiya Nauk, 1959.

Gronsky, P. P. "Borets za pravo." *Poslednie novosti,* March 30, 1922, 2.

Gruzenberg, O. O. "Moya pamyatka o V. D. Nabokove." *Rul',* April 2, 1922, 1.

———. *Vchera: Vospominaniya.* Paris: Dom knigi, 1938.

Healy, Ann Erickson. *The Russian Aristocracy in Crisis, 1905–1907.* Hamden, Conn.: Archon, 1976.

Hessen, Iosif. "Let sorok nazad." *Zarya* 2 (1942).

———. "Pamyati druga." *Rul',* March 30, 1922, 1.

———. *Sudebnaya reforma.* St. Petersburg: Gershunin, 1905.

———. "V dvukh vekakh." *Arkhiv russkoy revolyutsii* 22 (1937).

Hessen, Vladimir. *V borbe za zhizn' (zapiski emigranta).* New York: Rausen, 1974.

Hickman, Jarmila. "D. N. Nabokov, Minister of Justice, 1878–1885, in the Context of the Reform of 1864." Unpublished Master's thesis, Manchester, 1982.

Ikonnikov, Nikolay. *Noblesse de Russie: Les Nabokov.* Paris: 1960.

K. "Sobranie pamyati V. D. Nabokova." *Nash vek,* April 3, 1932, 7.

Kerensky, Alexander. *The Kerensky Memoirs: Russia and History's Turning Point.* London: Cassell, 1966.

Kharlamov, V. "Na slavnom postu." *Poslednie novosti,* March 30, 1922, 2.

Kislinsky, N. A. *Nasha zheleznodorozhnaya politika*. 4 vols. St. Petersburg, 1902.

Koni, A. F. *Sobranie sochineniy*. 8 vols. Moscow: Yuridicheskaya literatura, 1966–1969.

Krishevsky, N. "V Krymu (1916-1918 g.)." *Arkhiv russkoy revolyutsii*, 13 (1924).

Kucherov, Samuel. *Courts, Lawyers, and Trials under the Last Three Tsars*. New York: Praeger, 1953.

Kulisher, Evgeny. "Pamyati V. D. Nabokova." *Poslednie novosti*, April 19, 1932, 4.

Kuropatkin, A. N. "Dnevnik A. N. Kuropatkina." *Krasnyy arkhiv* 2 (1922).

L., B. "Sobesedovanie o russkoy intelligentsii." *Rul'*, February 9, 1922, 2.

Leikin, V. *Petrashevtsy*. Moscow, 1924.

Maklakov, Vasily. *The First State Duma*. 1939; trans. Mary Belkin, Bloomington: Indiana University Press, 1964.

Makletsov, A. "V. D. Nabokov, kak uchyonyy kriminalist." *Rossiya i slavyanstvo*, April 23, 1932, 2.

————. "V. D. Nabokov—uchyonyy." *Rul'*, April 8, 1922, 1–2.

Meshchersky, Kn.V.P. *Moi vospominaniya*. 2 vols. St. Petersburg, 1897–1898.

Milyukov, Paul. "Pamyati starogo druga." *Poslednie novosti*, April 1, 1922, 2.

————. "Pamyati V. D. Nabokova." *Poslednie novosti*, March 28, 1925, 1.

————. *Political Memoirs, 1905–1917*. Ed. Arthur Mendel. Ann Arbor: University of Michigan Press, 1967.

————. "V. D. Nabokov (k godovshchine smerti)." *Poslednie novosti*, March 28, 1923, 2–3.

————. *Vospominaniya (1859–1917)*. 2 vols. New York: Chekhov Publishing House, 1955.

Milyutin, D. A. *Dnevnik D. A. Milyutina*. Ed. P. A. Zaionchkovsky. 4 vols. Moscow, 1947–1950.

Ministerstvo yustitsii za sto let, 1802–1902. St. Petersburg: Senatskaya tipografiya, 1902.

Mogilyansky, N. "V. D. Nabokov (iz vospominaniy)." *Poslednie novosti*, April 1, 1922, 2.

Nabokov, Dmitri Vladimirovich. Letter to Editor. "Nabokov." *TLS*, January 6, 1978.

————. Letter to Editor. "Nabokov." *TLS*, March 17, 1978.

Nabokov, Konstantin Dmitrievich. *Ispytaniya diplomata*. Stockholm, 1921.

———— [as "C. Nabokoff"]. *The Ordeal of a Diplomat*. London: Duckworth, 1921.

Nabokov, Sergey Sergeevich. "Iz perepiski K. D. Nabokova s S. Vitte i dr." In Shakhovskoy et al., *Russkiy al'manakh*, 414–19.

Nabokov, Vladimir Dmitrievich. "Deyatelnost' partii narodnoy svobody v gosudarstvennoy dume." *Vestnik partii narodnoy svobody*, October 1, 1906, 1603.

————. "Duel' i ugolovnyy zakon." *Pravo*, December 13–20, 1909, 2729–44, 2833–47.

————. *Elementarnyy uchebnik osobennoy chasti russkogo ugolovnogo prava*. St. Petersburg: Senatskaya tipografiya, 1903.

————. "Iz vospominaniy o teatre: Napravnik." *Teatr i zhizn'* 9 (April 1922).

————. "Iz vospominaniy o teatre (za 35 let)." *Teatr i zhizn'* 1–2 (September 1921).

————. *Iz voyuyushchey Anglii*. Petrograd: Union, 1916.

————. "Kishinyovskaya krovavaya banya." *Pravo*, April 27, 1903, 1283–85.

————. "Mery sotsial'noy zashchity protiv retsidivistov." *Zhurnal ugolovnogo prava i protsessa* 1 (1913): 1–29.

————. "Moskovskie khudozhniki." *Teatr i zhizn'* 5–6 (December 1921).

————. "Nishchenstvo i brodyazhestvo, kak nakazuemye prostupki." *Zhurnal Sankt-Peterburgskogo yuridicheskogo obshchestva* 3 (1895): 9–73.

————. "Peterburgskaya gimnaziya sorok let tomu nazad (stranichka vospominaniy)." *Novaya rossiya* 1 (April 1922).

———— [as translator]. *Pis'ma Imperatritsy Aleksandry Fyodorovny k Imperatoru Nikolayu II*. 2 vols. Berlin: Slovo, 1922.

————. "Pis'ma V. D. Nabokova iz Krestov k zhene: 1908 g." Ed. VN, *Vozdushnye puti* 4 (1965).

————. "Plotskie prestupleniya." *Vestnik prava* 32 (1902): 129–89.

————. "Po povodu 'Krymskykh ocherkov.' " *Golos Rossii*, September 30, 1920.

————. "Proekt ugolovnogo ulozheniya i smertnaya kazn'." *Pravo*, January 30, 1900, 257–63.

————. "Raboty po sostavleniyu sudebnykh ustavov: Obshchaya kharakteristika sudebnoy reformy." In N. V. Davydov and N. N. Polyansky, eds., *Sudebnaya reforma*, Moscow: Ob'edinenie, 1915.

————. *Sbornik statey po ugolovnomu pravu*. St. Petersburg: Obshchestvennaya pol'za, 1904.

————. *Sistematicheskiy katalog biblioteki Vladimira Dmitrievicha Nabokova*. St. Petersburg: Tovarishchestvo khudozhestvennoy pechati, 1904; supplement, 1911.

————. *Soderzhanie i metod nauki ugolovnogo prava: Zadachi akademicheskogo prepodavaniya*. St. Petersburg, 1896.

————. "Sovremennoe polozhenie i takticheskoe zadachi k.d.-skoy partii." *Pravo*, October 25, 1905, 3404.

————. "Teatral'nyy Peterburg." *Teatr i zhizn'* 7 (January 1922), 8 (March 1922).

————. *Tyuremnye dosugi*. St. Petersburg, 1908.

————. "Vremennoe pravitel'stvo." *Arkhiv russkoy revolyutsii*, 1 (1922); trans. and ed. Virgil D. Medlin and Steven L. Parsons in *V. D. Nabokov and the Russian Provisional Government*. New Haven: Yale University Press, 1976.

———— and A. I. Kaminka. *Vtoraya gosudarstvennaya duma*. St. Petersburg: Obshchestvennaya pol'za, 1907.

———— and I. I. Petrunkevich. *Rechi I. Petrunkevicha i V. Nabokova: Iz dumskikh otchetov*. St. Petersburg: Tipografiya Busselya, 1907.

———— et al. *Svoboda pechati pri obnovlennom stroe*. St. Petersburg, 1912.

Nemanov, L. "V. D. Nabokov." *Poslednie novosti*, March 30, 1922, 2.

Nemirovich-Danchenko, Vasily. "U soyuznikov. (Poezdka russkikh pisateley v 1916 godu v Angliyu, Frantsiyu, i Italiyu.)" *Istorik i sovremennik* 4 (1923): 98–133.

Nol'de, Baron B. E., "V. D. Nabokov v 1917 g." In Nol'de, *Dalekoe i blizkoe* (Paris, 1930); trans. in Medlin and Parsons, *V. D. Nabokov and the Russian Provisional Government*.

Novgorodtsev, P. "Pamyati Vladimira Dmitrievicha Nabokova." *Russkaya mysl'*, 4 (1922).

Obolensky, V. "Neschastnaya Rossiya." *Poslednie novosti*, March 30, 1922, 2.

Obshchiy morskoy spisok. Vol. 7. St. Petersburg, 1893.

Oldenburg, S. S. *The Last Tsar*. Ed. Patrick J. Rollins, trans. Leonid I. Mihalap and Patrick J. Rollins. 4 vols. Gulf Breeze, Fla.: Academic International Press, 1975–1978.

Pares, Bernard. *My Russian Memoirs*. 1931; repr. New York: AMS, 1969.

———. *Russia and Reform*. London, 1907.

Pasmanik, Daniil. *Revolyutsionnye gody v Krymu*. Paris: privately printed, 1926.

Pearson, Raymond. *The Russian Moderates and the Crisis of Tsarism, 1914–1917*. London: Macmillan, 1977.

Pearson, Thomas S. *Russian Officialdom in Crisis: Autocracy and Local Self-Government, 1861–1900*. Cambridge: Cambridge University Press, 1989.

Petrunkevich, I. I. "Iz zapisok obshchestvennogo deyatelya." *Arkhiv russkoy revolyutsii* 21 (1934).

Pihatcheff. *See* Pykhachev.

Pipes, Richard, ed. *Revolutionary Russia*. Cambridge: Harvard University Press, 1968.

———. *Struve: Liberal on the Left, 1870–1905*. Cambridge: Harvard University Press, 1970.

Pobedonostsev, Konstantin. *K. P. Pobedonostsev i ego korrespondenty: Pis'ma i zapiski*. Moscow: Gosudarstvennoe Izdatelstvo, 1923.

Polovtsov, A. A. *Dnevnik gosudarstvennogo sekretarya A. Polovtsova*. 2 vols. Moscow: Nauka, 1966.

"Protsess 169 deputatov pervoy gosudarstvennoy dumy: Rech' V. D. Nabokova." *Vestnik partii narodnoy svobody*, December 18, 1907, 2118.

Pykhachev, Véra [née Nabokov]. *Sem' let vo vlasti tyomnoy sily*. Belgrade: Novoe Vremya, 1929. Trans. by Janet Crawford under the title Véra Pihatcheff, *Memoirs*. Rowsley: The Bibliophilia Library, 1935.

Riha, Thomas. "*Riech'*: A Portrait of a Russian Newspaper." *Slavic Review* 22 (1963): 663–82.

———. *A Russian European: Paul Milyukov in Russian Politics*. Notre Dame: University of Notre Dame Press, 1969.

Rosenberg, William G. *Liberals in the Russian Revolution: The Constitutional Democratic Party, 1917–1921*. Princeton: Princeton University Press, 1974.

Russkiy biograficheskiy slovar'. St. Petersburg: Imperatorskoe russkoe istoricheskoe obshchestvo, 1914.

Samuel, Maurice. *Blood Accusation*. New York: Knopf, 1966.

Savelov, L. M. *Biografischeskiy ukazatel' po istorii, geraldike i rodoslovoyu rossiyskogo dvoryanstvo*. 2d ed. Ostrogozhsk: Azarovoy, 1897.

Shaposhnikov, N. V. *Heraldica*. St. Petersburg: Pozharov, 1900.

Shchegolev, P. E., ed. *Petrashevtsy v vospominaniyakh sovremennikov*. Moscow: Gosudarstvennoe izdatels'tvo, 1926.

"Sobranie pamyati V. D. Nabokova." *Nash vek*, April 3, 1932, 7.

Struve, Peter. "Geroicheskoe nachalo lichnogo podviga." *Obshchee delo*, April 7, 1922, 1.

———. "Pamyati Vladimira Dmitrievicha Nabokova." *Russkaya mysl'*, 1922, 4.

Sudebnye ustavy 20 noyabrya 1864 g.: Za pyat'desyat let. 2 vols. Petrograd: Senatskaya tipografiya, 1914.

Tatarinov, V. "V. D. Nabokov i russkaya emigratsiya." *Golos emigranta* 12 (April 1922): 8.

———. "Sobranie natsional'nogo soyuza v Berline." *Rul'*, July 12, 1921, 5.

Timberlake, Charles, ed. *Essays on Russian Liberalism*. Columbia: University of Missouri Press, 1972.

Troitsky, N. A. *Tsarism pod sudom progressivnoy obshchestvennosti, 1866–1895 gg*. Moscow: Mysl', 1979.

Trotsky, Leon. *The History of the Russian Revolution*. Trans. Max Eastman. 3 vols. London: Victor Gollancz, 1932.

Tseretelli, I. V. *Vospominanie o fevralskoy revolyutsii*. Paris: Mouton, 1963.

Tyrkova-Williams, Ariadna. *From Liberty to Brest-Litovsk*. London: Macmillan, 1919.

———. *Na putyakh k svobode*. New York: Chekhov Publishing House, 1952.

———. "V. D. Nabokov i pervaya duma." *Russkaya mysl'* 6–7 (1922): 272–83.

Valuev, P. A. *Dnevnik P. A. Valueva, ministra vnutrennykh del 1861–1876*. Moscow, 1901.

———. *Dnevnik, 1877–1884*. Petrograd, 1919.

Vinaver, Maxim. "Pamyati Vladimira Dmitrievicha Nabokova." *Poslednie novosti*, March 30, 1922, 2.

Vinogradoff, Igor. "The Circumstantial Evidence." *TLS*, October 7, 1977.

———. Letter to Editor. "Nabokov." *TLS*, February 17, 1978.

Vitte, Sergey. *Vospominaniya*. 3 vols. Moscow: Izdatel'stvo sotsial'no-ekonomicheskoy literatury, 1960.

Wonlar-Larsky, Nadine [née Nadezhda Nabokov]. *The Russia that I Loved*. London, n.d.

Yablonovsky, Aleksandr. "V. D. Nabokov." *Vozrozhdenie*, April 2, 1931, 3.

Zaionchkosky, P. A. *The Russian Autocracy in Crisis, 1878–1882*. 1964; trans. Gary M. Hamburg, Gulf Breeze, Fla.: Academic International Press, 1979.

———. *The Russian Autocracy under Alexander III*. 1970; trans. David A. Jones, Gulf Breeze, Fla.: Academic International Press, 1976.

Zhurnal zasedaniya gorodskoy dumy. St. Petersburg, 1905, 9.

"Zhurnal zasedaniya soveta ministrov Krymskogo kraevogo pravitel'stva." *Arkhiv russkoy revolyutsii* 2 (1921): 135–41.

IV. VLADIMIR NABOKOV: WORKS

Ada or Ardor: A Family Chronicle. New York: McGraw-Hill, 1969.

Anya v strane chudes. [Trans. of *Alice in Wonderland* by Lewis Carroll.] Berlin: Gamayun, 1923.

"Authors' Authors." *NYTBR*, December 5, 1976, 4.

Bend Sinister. 1947; repr. with VN introduction, New York: Time, 1964.

"Butterfly Collecting in Wyoming, 1952." *Lepidopterists' News* 7 (1953): 49–52. Repr. *SO*.

Camera Obscura. Trans. Winifred Roy. London: John Long, 1936.

Conclusive Evidence. New York: Harper & Bros., 1951.

The Defense. Trans. Michael Scammell with VN. New York: Putnam's, 1964.

Despair. Trans. VN. New York; Putnam's, 1966.

Details of a Sunset and Other Stories. Trans. DN with VN. New York: McGraw-Hill, 1976.

Drugie berega. New York: Chekhov Publishing House, 1954.

The Enchanter. Trans. DN. New York: Putnam's, 1986.

Eugene Onegin. Trans. with commentary by VN. 4 vols. New York: Bollingen, 1964. Rev. ed. Princeton: Princeton University Press, 1975.

The Eye. Trans. DN with VN. New York: Phaedra, 1965.

"The Female of *Lycaeides Argyrognomon Sublivens*." *Lepidopterists' News* 6 (1952): 35. Repr. *SO*.

"A Few Notes on Crimean Lepidoptera." *Entomologist* 53 (February 1920): 29–33.

The Gift. Trans. Michael Scammell and DN with VN. New York: Putnam's, 1963.

Glory. Trans. DN with VN. New York: McGraw-Hill, 1971.

Gorniy put'. Berlin: Grani, 1923.

Grozd'. Berlin: Gamayun, 1922.

Invitation to a Beheading. Trans. DN with VN. New York: Putnam's, 1959.

King, Queen, Knave. Trans. DN with VN. New York: McGraw-Hill, 1968.

Laughter in the Dark. Trans. and rev. VN. Indianapolis: Bobbs-Merrill, 1938.

Lectures on Don Quixote. Ed. Fredson Bowers. New York: Harcourt Brace Jovanovich/Bruccoli Clark, 1983.

Lectures on Literature. Ed. Fredson Bowers. New York: Harcourt Brace Jovanovich/Bruccoli Clark, 1980.

Lectures on Russian Literature. Ed. Fredson Bowers. New York: Harcourt Brace Jovanovich/Bruccoli Clark, 1981.

Lectures on Ulysses. Bloomfield Hills, Mich.: Bruccoli Clark, 1980.

Letter to Editor. *Cornell Daily Sun*, October 3, 1958.

Letter to Editor. "Nabokov's Onegin." *Encounter*, May 1966, 91–92.

Letter to Editor. "Nabokov v. Deutsch." *New Statesman*, January 22, 1965, 112.

Letter to Editor. "Pushkin v. Deutsch." *New Statesman*, April 23, 1965.

Letter to Editor. "Pushkin's English." *New Statesman*, January 19, 1968.

Letter to Editor. "Translation." *NYRB*, January 20, 1966.

Letter to Editor. *Observer*, May 26, 1974.

Letter to Editor. "Olympic Game." *Playboy*, July 1961. Repr. *SO*.

Letter to Editor. *Saturday Evening Post*, March 25, 1967, 6.

Lolita. 1955; New York: Putnam's, 1958.

Lolita [Russian]. New York: Phaedra, 1967.

Lolita: A Screenplay. New York: McGraw-Hill, 1974.

"*Lolita* and Mr. Girodias." *Evergreen Review*, February 1967, 37–41. Repr. *SO*.

Look at the Harlequins! New York: McGraw-Hill, 1974.

"*Lysandra Cormion*, A New European Butterfly." *Journal of the New York Entomological Society*, September 1941, 265–67.

The Man from the USSR and Other Plays. Trans. DN. New York: Harcourt Brace Jovanovich/Bruccoli Clark, 1984.

Mary. Trans. Michael Glenny with VN. New York: McGraw-Hill, 1970.

"Migratory Species Observed in Wyoming, 1952." *Lepidopterists' News* 7 (1953): 51–52.

Nabokov's Dozen. New York: Doubleday, 1958.

"Nabokov's Reply." *Encounter*, February 1966, 80–89. Repr. *SO*.

"The Nearctic Forms of *Lycaeides Hüb*[ner] (Lycaenidae, Lepidoptera)." *Psyche*, September–December 1943, 87–99.

"The Nearctic Members of the Genus *Lycaeides* Hübner." *Bulletin of the Museum of Comparative Zoology* 101 (1949): 479–541.

"A New Species of *Cyclargus* Nabokov (Lycaenidae, Lepidoptera)." *The Entomologist* 81 (December 1948): 273–80.

Nikolay Gogol. Norfolk, Conn.: New Directions, 1944.

Nikolka Persik. [Trans. of Romain Rolland, *Colas Breugnon*.] Berlin: Slovo, 1922.

Nine Stories. New York: New Directions, 1947.

"Notes on the Lepidoptera of the Pyrénées Orientales and the Ariège." *Entomologist* 64 (1931): 255.

"Notes on the Morphology of the Genus *Lycaeides*." *Psyche*, September–December 1944, 104–38.

"Notes on Neotropical *Plebejinae* (Lycaenidae, Lepidoptera)." *Psyche*, March–June 1945, 1–61.

"Notes to *Ada* by Vivian Darkbloom." In *Ada*, Harmondsworth: Penguin, 1970.

"O Khodaseviche." *SZ* 69 (1939): 262–64.

"On Adaptation." *NYRB*, December 4, 1969. Repr. in *SO*.

"On a Book Entitled *Lolita*." *Anchor Review* 2 (June 1957). Repr. in *Lolita*, New York: Putnam's, 1958.

"On Inspiration." *Saturday Review of the Arts*, January 6, 1973, 30, 32. Repr. *SO*.

"On Learning Russian." *Wellesley Magazine*, April 1945, 191–92.

"On Some Inaccuracies in Klots' *Field Guide*." *Lepidopterists' News* 6 (1952): 41. Repr. *SO*.

"On Translating Pushkin: Pounding the Clavichord." *NYRB*, April 30, 1964, 14–16. Repr. *SO*.

"Opredeleniya." TS, LCNA.

"Painted Wood." *Carrousel* 2 (1923): 9–10.

Pale Fire. New York: Putnam's, 1962.

"Pamyati A. M. Chornogo." *Poslednie novosti*, August 13, 1932, 3.

"Pamyati I. V. Gessena." *NRS*, March 31, 1943, 2.

"Pamyati Yu. I. Aykhenval'da." *Rul'*, December 23, 1928, 5.

Perepiska s sestroy. Ann Arbor: Ardis, 1985.

Pnin. Garden City, N.Y.: Doubleday, 1957.

Poems and Problems. New York: McGraw-Hill, 1971.

"Postscript to the Russian Edition of *Lolita*." Trans. Earl D. Sampson, in Rivers and Nicol, 188–94.

"Pouchkine, ou le vrai et le vraisemblable." *Nouvelle revue française*, March 1937, 362–78.

"Problems of Translation: 'Onegin' in English." *Partisan Review*, Autumn 1955, 496–512.

The Real Life of Sebastian Knight. Norfolk, Conn.: New Directions, 1941.

"Rebel's Blue, Bryony White." *Times Educational Supplement*, October 23, 1970, 19. Repr. *SO*.

"Reputations Revisited." *TLS*, January 21, 1977, 66.

A Russian Beauty and Other Stories. Trans. DN and Simon Karlinsky with VN. New York: McGraw-Hill, 1973.

Selected Letters, 1940–1977. Ed. DN and Matthew J. Bruccoli. New York: Harcourt Brace Jovanovich/Bruccoli Clark Layman, 1989.

"The Servile Path." In *On Translation*, ed. Reuben A. Brower. Cambridge: Harvard University Press, 1959, 97–110.

Soglyadatay. Paris: Russkie zapiski, 1938.

"Some New or Little-Known Nearctic *Neonympha*." *Psyche*, September–December 1942, 61–80.

The Song of Igor's Campaign [anon.]. Trans. VN. New York: Vintage, 1960.

Speak, Memory: An Autobiography Revisited. New York: Putnam's, 1966.

Stikhi. Petrograd: privately printed, 1916.

Stikhi. Ann Arbor: Ardis, 1979.

Stikhotvoreniya, 1929–1951. Paris: Rifma, 1952.

"The Strange Case of Nabokov and Wilson." *NYRB*, August 26, 1965, 25–26.

Strong Opinions. New York: McGraw-Hill, 1973.

Three Russian Poets. Norfolk, Conn.: New Directions, 1945. Enlarged ed., under the title *Pushkin, Lermontov, Tyutchev*, London: Lindsay Drummond, 1947.

Transparent Things. New York: McGraw-Hill, 1972.

Tyrants Destroyed and Other Stories. Trans. DN with VN. New York: McGraw-Hill, 1975.

[Untitled]. In *Pamyati Amalii Osipovny Fondaminskoy*. Paris: privately printed, 1937, 69–72.

Vesna v Fial'te i drugie rasskazy. New York: Chekhov Publishing House, 1956.

Vozvrashchenie Chorba: Rasskazy i stikhi. Berlin: Slovo, 1930.

The Waltz Invention. Trans. DN with VN. New York: Phaedra, 1966.

"What Faith Means to a Resisting People." *Wellesley Magazine*, April 1942, 212.

"Zametki perevodchika." *Opyty* 8 (1957): 36–49.

"Zametki perevodchika—ii." *NZ* 49 (1957): 130–44.

Nabokov, Vladimir Vladimirovich, and Andrey Balashov. *Dva puti*. Petrograd: privately printed, 1918.

Nabokov, Vladimir Vladimirovich, and Edmund Wilson. *Nabokov-Wilson Letters*. Ed. Simon Karlinsky. New York: Harper & Row, 1979.

INTERVIEWS WITH VN (SEE ALSO *SO*)

Ackerman, Gordon. *Weekly Tribune*, January 28, 1966.

All, Nikolay. *NRS*, June 23, 1940.

Appel, Alfred, Jr. *Novel*, Spring 1971, 209–22. Repr. in *SO*.

Belleval, Guy de. *Journal de Genève*, March 13, 1965.

Beretzky, Nurit. *Ma'ariv*, January 19, 1970. TS, VNA.

Boyle, Robert. *Sports Illustrated*, September 14, 1959, E5–E8.

Bronowski, Jacob, August 1963. TS, VNA.

Chudacoff, Helga. *Die Welt*, September 26, 1974. TS, VNA.

Clarke, Gerald. *Esquire*, July 1975.

Colombo, Janine. *L'Information d'Israel*, February 3, 1961.

Davis, Douglas. *National Observer*, June 29, 1964, 17.

Dommergues, Pierre. *Les Langues modernes* 62 (January–February 1968): 92–102.

Duffy, Martha. *Time*, May 23, 1969.

Esslin, Martin. *NYTBR*, May 12, 1968, 4–5, 50–51.

Feifer, George. *Saturday Review*, November 27, 1976, 20–26.

Gilliatt, Penelope. *Vogue*, December 1966.

Givan, Charles. *Los Angeles Times*, August 7, 1977.

Gold, Herbert. *Saturday Evening Post*, February 11, 1967, 81–85.

Guérin, Anne. *L'Exprès*, January 26, 1961.

Hoffman, Kurt. Bayerishcher Rundfunk, May 1972.

Holmes, David. BBC, November 5, 1959. TS, VNA.

Hughes, Robert. National Educational Television, January 1966. TS, VNA.

Jannoud, Claude. *Le Figaro littéraire*, January 13, 1973.

Jaton, Henri. Radio Suisse Romande, October 5, 1963. TS, VNA.

Kulakofsky, Beth. *Wellesley College News*, March 21, 1941, 8.

Laansoo, Mati, CBC, 1973. Published in *Vladimir Nabokov Research Newsletter* 10 (1983).

Levy, Alan. *New York Times Magazine*. October 31, 1971. TS, VNA.

Macrae, Rosalie. *Daily Express*, April 8, 1961.

Mercadie, Claude. *Nice-Matin*, April 13, 1961.

Morini, Simona. *Vogue*, April 15, 1972, 74–79.

Mulligan, Hugh. Conducted November 1976. TS, VNA.

Nordstrom, Alan. *Ivy* (New Haven), February 1959, 28.

O'Neil, Paul. *Life International*, April 13, 1959, 63–69.

Petchek, Willa. *Observer Magazine*, May 30, 1976.

Pivot, Bernard. French television, "Apostrophes," TF-1, May 30, 1975. TS, VNA.

Reese, Katharine. *We* (Wellesley College), December 1943, 32.

Safarik, Bernard. Swiss German television, 1974. MS, VNA.

Salter, James. *People*, March 17, 1975, 60–64.

Schroeder-Jahn. German television, 1966. TS, VNA.

Shenker, Israel. In Shenker, *Words and Their Masters*, Garden City, N.Y.: Doubleday, 1974.

Smith, Peter Duval. BBC, November 1962. Partially repr. in *SO*. TS, VNA.

Tabozzi, Roberto. *Panorama*. Conducted October 16, 1969. TS, VNA.

[Unsigned]. *Journal de Montreux*, January 23, 1964.

[Unsigned]. *Newsweek*, November 24, 1958, 114–15.

Whitman, Alden. Unpublished interview, October 6, 1971. VNA.

Zimmer, Dieter. *Die Zeit*, November 1, 1966. TS, VNA.

V. VLADIMIR NABOKOV: SECONDARY SOURCES

A., A. "Vladimir Nabokov (Sirin) igraet N. N. Evreynova." *Russkaya mysl'*, December 29, 1977.

Abrams, Meyer H. In Donoghue, "VN: The Great Enchanter."

——. In "Remembering Nabokov," in Gibian and Parker, 218–21.

Adamovich, Georgy. *Kommentarii*. Washington, D.C.: Victor Kamkin, 1967.

——. *Odinochestvo i svoboda*. New York: Chekhov Publishing House, 1955.

Adams, Robert M. "Nabokov's Show." *New York Review of Books*, December 18, 1980.

Aletrus [Irina Guadanini]. "Tunnel'." *Sovremennik* 3 (1961): 6–23.

Alloy, V. "Iz arkhiva V. V. Nabokova." *Minuvshee* 8 (1989): 274–81.

Allsop, Kenneth. "I Am a Pornographer." *Spectator*, October 21, 1960.

Amis, Martin. "Out of Style." *New Statesman*, April 25, 1975.

Appel, Alfred, Jr. "*Ada* Described." In Appel and Newman, 160–86.

——, ed. *The Annotated Lolita*. New York: McGraw-Hill, 1970.

——. "Backgrounds of *Lolita*." In Appel and Newman, 17–40.

——. "Conversations with Nabokov." *Novel*, Spring 1971, 209–22.

——. "Memories of Nabokov." *TLS*, October 7, 1977, 1138–42. Repr. as "Remembering Nabokov," in Quennell.

——. "Nabokov: A Portrait." *Atlantic*, September 1971. Repr. in Rivers and Nicol.

——. *Nabokov's Dark Cinema*. New York: Oxford University Press, 1974.

——. "Nabokov's Puppet Show." *New Republic*, January 14 and 21, 1967.

Appel, Alfred, Jr., and Charles Newman, eds. *Triquarterly* 17 (Nabokov Special Issue, 1970). Repr. as *Nabokov: Criticism, Reminiscences, Translations, and Tributes*. Evanston, Ill.: Northwestern University Press, 1970.

Arbatov, Z. "Nollendorfplatzkafe." *Grani* 41 (1959): 106–22.

Arndt, Walter, trans. *Eugene Onegin*. New York: Dutton, 1963.

Bader, Julia. *Crystal Land: Artifice in Nabokov's English Novels*. Berkeley: University of California Press, 1972.

Baedeker, Karl. *Russia with Teheran, Port Arthur, and Peking: Handbook for Travellers*. Leipzig: Karl Baedeker, 1914.

Bakhrakh, Aleksandr. "Ot Sirina k Nabokovu." *Russkaya mysl'*, December 29, 1977, 8–10. Repr. in Bakhrakh, *Po pamyati, po zapisyam: Literaturnye portrety*. Paris: La Presse Libre, 1980.

Barabtarlo, Gennadi. "*Onus Probandi*." *Russian Review* 47 (1988): 237–52.

———. *Phantom of Fact: A Guide to Nabokov's Pnin*. Ann Arbor: Ardis, 1989.

Bayley, John. *Observer*, November 29, 1964.

Berberova, Nina. *The Italics Are Mine*. Trans. Philippe Radley. New York: Harcourt Brace & World, 1969.

———. *Kursiv moy*. 1972; 2d ed. 2 vols. New York: Russica, 1983.

———. "Nabokov in the Thirties." In Appel and Newman, 220–33.

Bethea, David. *Khodasevich: His Life and Art*. Princeton: Princeton University Press, 1983.

Bishop, Alison. In "Remembering Nabokov," in Gibian and Parker, 216–17.

Bishop, Morris. "Nabokov à Cornell." *L'Arc* 24 (1964): 62–64.

———. "Nabokov at Cornell." In Appel and Newman, 234–39.

Blake, Patricia. Introduction to *Writers in Russia: 1917–1978*, by Max Hayward. New York: Harcourt Brace Jovanovich, 1983.

Bodenstein, Jurgen. " 'The Excitement of Verbal Adventure': A Study of Vladimir Nabokov's English Prose." Ph.D. diss., Heidelberg, 1977.

Boegeman, Margaret Byrd. "*Invitation to a Beheading* and the Many Shades of Kafka." In Rivers and Nicol, 105–24.

Boyd, Brian. ". . . and the eluding." *TLS*, April 24, 1987, 432–33.

———. "Emigré Responses to Nabokov, (i)–(iv)." *Nabokovian* 17–20 (Fall 1986–Spring 1988).

———. Letter to Editor. "Novel with Cocaine." *TLS*, March 6, 1987, 241.

———. Letter to Editor. "Vladimir Nabokov." *TLS*, June 17–23, 1988, 677.

———. "Nabokov at Cornell." In Gibian and Parker, 119–44.

———. "Nabokov Bibliography: Aspects of the Emigré Period." *Vladimir Nabokov Research Newsletter* 11 (Fall 1983): 21–24.

———. *Nabokov's Ada: The Place of Consciousness*. Ann Arbor: Ardis, 1985.

———. "Nabokov's Russian Poems: A Chronology." *Nabokovian* 21 (Fall 1988): 13–28.

———. "The Problem of Pattern: Nabokov's *Defense*." *Modern Fiction Studies* 33 (Winter 1987): 575–604.

———. *Vladimir Nabokov: The Russian Years*. Princeton: Princeton University Press, 1990.

Breasted, Barbara, and Noëlle Jordan. "Vladimir Nabokov at Wellesley." *Wellesley Magazine*, Summer 1971, 22–26.

Brenner, Conrad. "Nabokov: The Art of the Perverse." *New Republic*, June 23, 1958, 18–21.

Brown, Clarence. "Little Girl Migrates." *New Republic*, January 20, 1968, 19–20.

———. "Love-Hate Letters." *Saturday Review*, June 23, 1979.

———. "Pluck and Polemics." *Partisan Review*, February 1973, 311–14.

Brown, William Edward. *A History of Russian Literature of the Romantic Period*. Ann Arbor: Ardis, 1986.

Brown, William L., Jr. In "Remembering Nabokov," in Gibian and Parker, 224–26.

B[uckley], W[illiam] F. "VN-RIP." *National Review*, July 22, 1977, 820.

Bunin, Ivan, and Vera Bunin. *Ustami Buninykh*. Ed. M. Grin. 3 vols. Frankfurt: Possev, 1977–1982.

Burgess, Anthony. "Dorogoi Bunny, Dear Volodya. . . ." *Inquiry*, July 9, 1979, 23–24.

———. "Pushkin & Kinbote." *Encounter*, May 1965, 74.

Cannac, Evgenia. "Berlinskiy 'Kruzhok poetov' (1928–33)." In Shakhovskoy et al., *Russkiy al'manakh*, 363–66.

Clayton, J. Douglas. *Alexander Pushkin's "Eugene Onegin."* Toronto: University of Toronto Press, 1985.

Cowan, Milton. In "Remembering Nabokov," in Gibian and Parker, 222–23.

Croisé, Jacques. *See* Shakhovskoy, Zinaida.

Daiches, David. In Donoghue, "VN: The Great Enchanter."

———. "Nabokov à Cornell." *L'Arc* 24 (1964): 65–66.

Davies, Robertson. "Mania for Green Fruit." *Saturday Night*, October 11, 1958.

Davis, Linda H. *Onward and Upward: A Biography of Katharine S. White*. New York: Harper & Row, 1987.

Davydov, Sergey. *Teksty-matreshki Vladimira Nabokova*. Munich: Otto Sagner, 1982.

Dembo, L. S. See *Wisconsin Studies in Contemporary Literature*.

Demorest, Jean-Jacques. "Administering Professor Nabokov." *Arts and Sciences* (Cornell) 4, no. 2 (1983): 8.

Deutsch, Babette. Letter to Editor. *New Statesman*. April 9, 1965.

———, trans., with Avrahm Yarmolinsky. *Eugene Onegin*. Harmondsworth: Penguin, 1964.

Don-Aminado [Aminado Shpolyansky]. *Poezd na tret'em puti*. New York: Chekhov Publishing House, 1954.

Donoghue, Denis. "VN: The Great Enchanter." BBC broadcast, March 17, 1982, featuring M. H. Abrams, David Daiches, Alex de Jonge, Alfred Kazin, Harry Levin, William McGuire, Dmitri Nabokov, Sergey Sergeevich Nabokov, Véra Nabokov, and Bart Winer.

Duffy, Martha. "An Old Daydream." *Time*, January 24, 1972, 58–59.

Elledge, Scott. *E. B. White: A Biography*. New York: Norton, 1984.

Ellmann, Richard. *James Joyce*. 2d ed. New York: Oxford University Press, 1982.

Fedotov, G. P. "I. I. Fondaminskiy v emigratsii." *Novyy zhurnal* 18 (1948): 317–29.

Field, Andrew. "Foreword: The Nabokov Mafia." In *VN: The Life and Art of Vladimir Nabokov*. London: Futura, 1988.

———. Letter to Editor. "Nabokov." *TLS*, January 27, 1978.

———. Letter to Editor. "Real Life of an Author." *Observer*, May 3, 1987, 17.

——. *Nabokov: His Life in Art*. Boston: Little, Brown, 1967.

——. *Nabokov: His Life in Part*. New York: Viking, 1977.

——. "Russia's 'Other' Poets." *New Leader*, August 1963.

——. *VN: The Life and Art of Vladimir Nabokov*. New York: Crown, 1986.

——. "The World of Vladimir Nabokov." *Literary Guild Magazine*, Spring 1969.

Fitch, Noel Riley. *Sylvia Beach and the Lost Generation: A History of Literary Paris in the Twenties and Thirties*. New York: Norton, 1983.

Fleishman, Lazar. *Boris Pasternak*. Berkeley and Los Angeles: University of California Press, 1990.

Fleishman, Lazar, Robert Hughes, and Olga Raevsky-Hughes, eds. *Russkiy Berlin, 1921–1923*. Paris: YMCA, 1983.

Fogel, Ephim. In "Remembering Nabokov," in Gibian and Parker, 231–33.

Franclemont, John G. In "Remembering Nabokov," in Gibian and Parker, 227–28.

Frank, S. "Pamyati Yu. I. Aykhenval'da." *Rul'*, December 17, 1929.

Freund, Gisèle, and V. B. Carleton. *James Joyce in Paris: His Final Years*. London: Cassell, 1966.

Garric, Alain. "Nabokov l'enchanteur." *Libération*, August 30–31, 1986, 26–28.

——. "Roman avec Nabokov." *Libération*, December 26, 1985, 21–24.

George, Emery. "Remembering Nabokov: An Interview with Victor Lange." *Michigan Quarterly Review* 25 (1986): 479–92.

Gerschenkron, Alexander. "A Manufactured Moment?" *Modern Philology*, May 1966, 336–47.

Gessen. *See* Hessen, Iosef.

Gezari, Janet K. "Roman et problème chez Nabokov." *Poétique* 5 (1974): 96–113.

Gibian, George, and Stephen Jan Parker, eds. *The Achievements of Vladimir Nabokov*. Ithaca: Cornell Center for International Studies, 1984.

Gill, Brendan. *Here at the New Yorker*. New York: Random House, 1975.

Girodias, Maurice. Letter to Editor. *Life*, July 6, 1959.

——. "*Lolita*, Nabokov, and I." *Evergreen*, September 1965. Repr. as "A Sad, Ungraceful History of *Lolita*," in *The Olympia Reader*. New York: Grove, 1965.

——. "Pornologist on Olympus." *Playboy*, April 1961.

Gold, Herbert. "The Artist in Pursuit of Butterflies." *Saturday Evening Post*, February 11, 1967.

——. "Nabokov Remembered: A Slight Case of Poshlost." In Gibian and Parker, 45–59.

——. "Vladimir Nabokov, 1899–1977." *NYTBR*, July 31, 1977.

Grabes, Herbert. *Fictitious Biographies: Vladimir Nabokov's English Novels*. The Hague: Mouton, 1977.

Grayson, Jane. *Nabokov Translated: A Comparison of Nabokov's Russian and English Prose*. Oxford: Oxford University Press, 1977.

Green, Hannah. "Mister Nabokov." *New Yorker*, February 14, 1977, 32–35. Repr. in Quennell.

Gross, Miriam. "Portrait of a Publisher." *Observer*, October 19, 1980.

Grumbach, Doris. *The Company She Kept*. London: Bodley Head, 1967.

Guerra, René. "A Propos d'une pièce oubliée de Vladimir Nabokov: *L'Evénement*." *Slovo* (Paris) 6 (1984): 121–46.

Halsman, Yvonne. *Halsman: Portraits*. New York: McGraw-Hill, 1983.

Heine, T. C., Jr. "Nabokov as Teacher." *Cornell Alumni News*, April 1977, 10.

Hessen, Iosif. *Gody izgnaniya: Zhiznennyy otchyot*. Paris: YMCA, 1981.

Hingley, Ronald. "An Aggressively Private Person." *NYTBR*, January 15, 1967.

Hodges, Ronald W., et al., eds. *Check List of the Lepidoptera of America North of Mexico*. London: E. W. Classey and Wedge Entomological Research Foundation, 1983.

Holt, Terry. "Shades of Nabokov." *Cornell Reports* 17 (Summer 1983): 2–3.

Hughes, Robert P. "Notes on the Translation of *Invitation to a Beheading*." In Appel and Newman, 284–92.

In Memoriam: Vladimir Nabokov, 1899–1977. New York: McGraw-Hill, 1977.

Ioann, Archbishop ["Strannik"]. "Nachalo Nabokoviany." *Russkaya mysl'*, June 1, 1978, 10.

Ivask, Yuri. "Razgovory's Adamovichem," *NZ* 134 (1979): 92–101.

———. "V. V. Nabokov." *NZ* 128 (September 1977): 272–76.

J., C. "Publishers' Confessions—Rejections I Regret." *NYTBR*, May 7, 1984.

Jarrell, Randall. *Randall Jarrell's Letters*. Ed. Mary Jarrell. Boston: Houghton Mifflin, 1985.

Johnson, D. Barton. *Worlds in Regression: Some Novels of Vladimir Nabokov*. Ann Arbor: Ardis, 1985.

Johnston, Charles, trans. *Eugene Onegin*. Harmondsworth: Penguin, 1979.

Jonge, Alex de. In Donoghue, "VN: The Great Enchanter."

Kahn, Peter. In "Remembering Nabokov," in Gibian and Parker, 229–30.

Karlinsky, Simon. Introduction to *NWL*, 1–25.

———. *Marina Tsvetaeva: The Woman, Her World, and Her Poetry*. Cambridge: Cambridge University Press, 1985.

Karlinsky, Simon, and Alfred Appel, Jr., eds. *The Bitter Air of Exile: Russian Writers in the West, 1922–1972*. 1973; rev. ed. Berkeley: University of California Press, 1977.

Kazin, Alfred. In Donoghue, "VN: The Great Enchanter."

———. "Vladimir Nabokov: Wisdom in Exile." *New Republic*, July 23, 1977, 12–14.

Klots, Alexander B. *A Field Guide to the Butterflies of North America, East of the Great Plains*. Boston: Houghton Mifflin, 1951.

Kovalevsky, P. E. *Zarubezhnaya Rossia*. Paris: Librairie des Cinq Continents, 1971, and *Dopolnitel'nyy vypusk*, 1973.

Krishevsky, N. "V Krymu (1916–1918 g.)." *Arkhiv russkoy revolyutsii* 13 (1924): 71–124.

Lambert, J. W., and Michael Ratcliffe. *The Bodley Head, 1887–1987*. London: Bodley Head, 1987.

Landau, Grigory. "Pamyati Yu. I. Aykhenval'da." *Rul'*, December 23, 1928, 5.

———. "Rul'." *Vozrozhdenie*, December 1, 1931, 2–3.

Laqueur, Walter. *Russia and Germany: A Century of Conflict*. London: Weidenfeld & Nicolson, 1965.

Levin, Harry. In Donoghue, "VN: The Great Enchanter."

———. *Grounds for Comparison*. Cambridge: Harvard University Press, 1972.

———. "Shakespeare's Misanthrope." *Shakespeare Survey* 26 (1973): 89–94.

Lowell, Robert. "Nine Poems by Ossip Manderstamm." *NYRB*, December 23, 1965.

McCarthy, Mary. "A Bolt from the Blue." *New Republic*, June 4, 1962. Repr. in *The Writing on the Wall*, New York: Harcourt, Brace & World, 1970.

McConkey, James. "Nabokov and 'The Window of the Mint.' " In Gibian and Parker, 29–43.

McDunnough, J. "New North American Eupithecias 1 (Lepidoptera, Geometridae)." *Canadian Entomologist* 77 (September 1945): 168–76.

McGuire, William. *Bollingen: An Adventure in Collecting the Past*. Princeton: Princeton University Press, 1982.

———. In Donoghue, "VN: The Great Enchanter."

Makovsky, Sergey. *Na Parnase serebryannogo veka*. Munich: Tsentral'noe ob'edinenie politicheskikh emigrantov iz SSSR, 1962.

Maksimova, E. "Muza Nabokova." *Izvestia*, August 9, 1989, 6.

———. "Ya ne znala, chto ya russkaya." *Izvestia*, April 8, 1989, 6.

Malmstad, John. "The Historical Sense and Xodasevič's Deržavin." In V. F. Khodasevich, *Derzhavin*. Munich: Wilhelm Fink, 1975, v–xviii.

———. "Iz perepiski V. F. Khodasevicha (1925–1938)." *Minuvshee* 3 (1987): 262–91.

Mandelstam, Osip. *The Prose of Osip Mandelstam*. Trans. Clarence Brown. Princeton: Princeton University Press, 1965.

Markevitch, Igor. *Etre et avoir été*. Paris: Gallimard, 1980.

Marshall, Sidney Smith. "Yellow-Blue Väse: A Reminiscence about Vladimir Nabokov." *Wellesley Alumnae Magazine*, Fall 1977, 25–26.

Mason, James. *Before I Forget*. London: Hamish Hamilton, 1981.

Mizener, Arthur. "Professor Nabokov." *Cornell Alumni News*, September 1977, 56.

Morozov, Tatiana. "Pamyati Iriny Yurievny Guadanini." *Russkaya mysl'*, May 12, 1977.

Nabokov, Dmitri Vladimirovich. "Close Calls and Fulfilled Dreams: Selected Entries from a Private Journal." *Antaeus* 61 (Autumn 1988): 229–323.

———. "Did He Really Call His Mum Lolita?" *Observer*, April 26, 1987.

———. In Donoghue, "VN: The Great Enchanter."

———. "A Few Things that Must Be Said on Behalf of Vladimir Nabokov." In Rivers and Nicol, 35–42.

———. Introduction to *SL*, ix–xviii.

Nabokov, Dmitri Vladimirovich. "Nabokov." Letter to Editor. *TLS*, January 6, 1978.

———. "Nabokov and the Theater." In *MUSSR*, 3–26.

———. "On a Book Entitled *The Enchanter*." In *The Enchanter* by VN, 97–127.

———. "On Revisiting Father's Room." *Encounter*, October 1979. Repr. in Quennell, 126–36.

———. "A Rejoinder." *National Review*, January 30, 1987, 42–43.

———. "Translating with Nabokov." In Gibian and Parker, 145–77.

Nabokov, Nicolas. *Bagazh: Memoirs of a Russian Cosmopolitan*. New York: Atheneum, 1975.

Nabokov, Sergey S. In Donoghue, "VN: The Great Enchanter."

Nabokov, Véra. In Donoghue, "VN: The Great Enchanter."

———. Letter to Editor. *Russkaya mysl'*, July 6, 1978, 10.

———. Letter to Editor. *Russkaya mysl'*, December 13, 1985, 14.

———. Letter to Editor. *Insight*, December 22, 1986.

———. "Predislovie." In *Stikhi* by VN. Ann Arbor: Ardis, 1979, 3–4.

Nabokov, Véra and Dmitri. Letter to Editor. "Novel with Cocaine." *TLS*, December 20, 1985, 1455.

Nakhimovsky, Alexander, and Slava Paperno. *An English-Russian Dictionary of Nabokov's Lolita*. Ann Arbor: Ardis, 1982.

Nekrasov, Viktor. "Beseda v 'Grand-Otele.' " *NRS*, April 10, 1983, 5.

Nicol, Charles. "Pnin's History." *Novel*, Spring 1971, 197–208. Repr. *Critical Essays on Vladimir Nabokov*, ed. Phyllis Roth. Boston: G. K. Hall, 1984, 93–105.

Niven, David. *Go Slowly, Come Back Quickly*. Garden City, N.Y.: Doubleday, 1981.

Noel, Lucie Léon. "Playback." In Appel and Newman, 209–19.

Obolensky, Vladimir. "Krym v 1917–1920 g.g." *Na chuzhoy storone* 5 (1924): 5–40; 6 (1924): 53–72; 7 (1924): 81–110.

Ofrosimov, Yuri. "Pamyati poeta." *NZ* 84 (1966): 290–93.

Oliver, Edith. "Notes on a Marginal Friendship." In *An Edmund Wilson Celebration*, ed. John Wain. Oxford: Phaidon, 1978, 3–16.

Orndorff, William. "Lolita's Home?" Letter to Editor. *Cornell Alumni News*, February 1984.

Ossorguine-Bakounin, Tatiana. *L'emigration russe en Europe: Catalogue collectif des périodiques en langue russe, 1855–1940*. Paris: Institut d'etudes slaves, 1976.

"Pamyati Yu. I. Aykhenval'da." *Nash vek*, January 1, 1932, 5.

Paperno, Slava, and John V. Hagopian. "Official and Unofficial Responses to Nabokov in the Soviet Union." In Gibian and Parker, 99–117.

Parker, Stephen Jan. "In the Interest of Accuracy." *Cornell Alumni News*, March 1981, 13–14.

———. "Professor Nabokov: A Review Essay." *Vladimir Nabokov Research Newsletter* 8 (Spring 1982): 38–45.

Parry, Albert. "Chitateli pishut." *NRS*, September 10, 1978.

———. "Pamyati Vladimira Nabokova." *NRS*, July 9, 1978, 2.

Paul, Sherman. *Edmund Wilson: A Study of Literary Vocation in Our Time*. Urbana: University of Illinois Press, 1965.

Pavarotti, Luciano. *Pavarotti: My Own Story*. With William Wright. Garden City, N.Y.: Doubleday, 1981.

Peterson, Ronald E. "Time in *The Gift*." *Vladimir Nabokov Research Newsletter* 9 (Fall 1982): 36–40.

Pifer, Ellen. *Nabokov and the Novel*. Cambridge: Harvard University Press, 1980.

Poltoratzky, N. P., ed. *Russkaya literatura v emigratsii: Sbornik statey*. Pittsburgh: University of Pittsburgh Press, 1972.

Proffer, Carl R. *Keys to Lolita*. Bloomington: Indiana University Press, 1968.

———. "A New Deck for Nabokov's Knaves." In Appel and Newman, 293–309.

———. *The Widows of Russia and Other Writings*. Ann Arbor: Ardis, 1987.

Proffer, Ellendea. "Nabokov's Russian Readers." In Appel and Newman, 253–60.

Prokosch, Frederick. *Voices: A Memoir*. New York: Farrar Straus Giroux, 1983. (Invented "memoir" of VN.)

Quennell, Peter, ed. *Vladimir Nabokov: A Tribute*. London: Weidenfeld & Nicolson, 1979.

Quine, W. V. *The Time of My Life: An Autobiography*. Cambridge: MIT Press, 1985.

Raeff, Marc. "Russian Culture in Emigration." Unpublished TS.

Raevsky, Nikolay. "Vospominaniya o Vladimire Nabokove." *Prostor* 2 (February 1989): 112–17.

Rampton, David. *Vladimir Nabokov*. Cambridge: Cambridge University Press, 1984.

Reichard, Gladys, Roman Jakobson, and Elizabeth Werth. "Language and Synesthesia." *Word* 5 (August 1949).

"Remembering Nabokov." Reminiscences by Meyer H. Abrams, Alison Bishop, William L. Brown, Jr., J. Milton Cowan, Ephim Fogel, John G. Franclemont, and Peter Kahn. In Gibian and Parker, 215–33.

Ricks, Christopher. "Nabokov's Pushkin." *New Statesman*, December 25, 1964, 995.

Rivers, J. E., and Charles Nicol, eds. *Nabokov's Fifth Arc: Nabokov and Others on His Life's Work*. Austin: University of Texas Press, 1982.

Rosenblum, Michael. "Finding What the Sailor Has Hidden: Narrative as Patternmaking in *Transparent Things*." *Contemporary Literature* 19 (1978).

Rowe, William Woodin. *Nabokov's Spectral Dimension*. Ann Arbor: Ardis, 1981.

Sale, Roger. *Chicago Sun-Times*, October 25, 1981.

Sarton, May. *The Fur Person*. 1957: repr. New York: Norton, 1978.

Scammell, Michael. *Solzhenitsyn: A Biography*. New York: Norton, 1984.

Schapiro, Leonard. Preface to *Writers in Russia: 1917–1978*, by Max Hayward. Ed. Patricia Blake. New York: Harcourt Brace Jovanovich, 1983.

Sedykh, Andrey. "U V. V. Sirina." *NRS*, December 5, 1982.

Sexton, David. "Nabokov in Trinity." *Trinity Review*, 1980, 8–9.

Shakhovskoy, Zinaida. "Le Cas Nabokov, ou la blessure de l'exil" [as Jacques Croisé]. *La Revue des deux mondes*, August 15, 1959.

———. *La folle Clio*. Paris: Presses de la Cité, 1966.

———. *Une Manière de vivre*. Paris: Presses de la Cité, 1965.

———. *Otrazheniya*. Paris: YMCA, 1975.

———. "Pustynya." *NZ* 111 (June 1973): 27–33.

———. "V. I Pol' i 'Angel'skie stihi' Vl. Nabokova." In Shakhovskoy et al., *Russkiy al'manakh*, 230–35.

———. *V poiskakh Nabokova*. Paris: La presse libre, 1979.

———. [Untitled]. *Russkaya mysl'*, December 29, 1977, 8.

Shakhovskoy, Zinaida, René Guerra, and Eugene Ternovsky, eds. *Russkiy al'manakh*. Paris, 1981.

Shcherbina, V. R. *Literaturnoe nasledstvo*. Vol. 84: *Ivan Bunin*. Moscow: Nauka, 1973.

Shumikhin, S. V. "Pis'mo Very i Vladimira Nabokovykh Yu. I Aykhenval'du." *Nashe nasledie* 2 (1988): 113.

Smith, Gerald S. "Nabokov and Russian Verse Form." *Russian Literature Triquarterly* 24 (1991): 271–305.

Spoto, Donald. *The Dark Side of Genius: The Life of Alfred Hitchcock*. Boston: Little, Brown, 1983.

Stanford University Bulletin. Fiftieth Annual Register: 1940–1941. Stanford: Stanford University, [1940].

Stegner, Page. *Escape into Aesthetics: The Art of Vladimir Nabokov*. New York: Dial Press, 1966.

Strannik. *See* Ioann, Archbishop.

Struve, Gleb. "Dnevnik chitatelya: K istorii russkoy zarubezhnoy literatury: Ob odnom maloizvestnom zhurnale." *NRS*, June 5, 1979.

———. "Dnevnik chitatelya: Pamyati V. V. Nabokova." *NRS*, July 17, 1977, 5, 8.

———. "Iz moikh vospominaniy ob odnom russkom literaturnom kruzhke v Berline." *NRS*, October 4, 1981. Repr. in *Tri yubileya Andreya Sedykh*, ed. Leonid Rzhevsky. New York: Literaturnyy Fond, 1982, 189–94.

———. "K smerti V. V. Nabokova." *NRS*, August 7, 1977, 5.

———. *Russkaya literatura v izgnanii*. 1956; 2d ed., Paris: YMCA, 1984.

Struve, Nikita. "K razgadke odnoy literaturnoy tayny: *Roman s kokainom* M. Ageeva." *Vestnik russkogo khristianskogo dvizheniya* 144 (1985): 165–79.

———. *Ossip Mandelstam*. Paris: Institut d'etudes slaves, 1982.

———. "Spor vokrug V. Nabokova i *Roman s kokainom*." *Vestnik russkogo khristianskogo dvizheniya* 146 (1985): 156–75.

Sukenick, Ronald. *Down and In: Life in the Underground*. New York: Beech Tree Books, 1987.

Sweeney, Susan. [Untitled note.] *Nabokovian* 16 (Spring 1986): 14–15.

Szeftel, Marc. "*Lolita* at Cornell." *Cornell Alumni News*, November 1980, 27–28.

Tammi, Pekka. *Problems of Nabokov's Poetics: A Narratological Analysis*. Helsinki: Academia Scientiarum Fennica, 1985.

Timashev, Nikolay. "M. M. Karpovich." *NZ* 59 (1959): 192–95.

Tolstoy, Alexandra. *Out of the Past*. Trans. and ed. Katherine Strelsky and Catherine Wolkonsky. New York: Columbia University Press, 1981.

Trahan, Elizabeth Welt. "Laughter from the Dark: A Memory of Vladimir Nabokov." *Antioch Review* 43 (Spring 1985): 175–82.

Trevelyan, G. M. *Trinity College: An Historical Sketch*. Cambridge: Trinity College, 1943; repr. 1983.

Trilling, Lionel. "The Last Lover." *The Griffin*, August 1958.

Triquarterly, Special Nabokov Issue, 17 (Winter 1970). Repr. as Appel and Newman.

Tsvetaeva, Marina. "Poet o kritike." *Blagonamerennyy* 2 (1926).

Updike, John. "Grandmaster Nabokov." *New Republic*, September 26, 1964, 15–18.

———. Introduction to *Lects*.

———. "Van Loves Ada, Ada Loves Van." *New Yorker*, August 2, 1969.

Ustinov, Peter. *Dear Me*. London: Heinemann, 1977.

Venn, J. A. *Alumni Cantabrigiensis*. Cambridge: Cambridge University Press, 1947.

Vestermann, William. "Nabokov's Second Fiancée Identified." *American Notes and Queries*, September–October 1985.

Vishnyak, Mark. *Gody emigratsii, 1919–1969, Paris–New York*. Stanford: Hoover, 1970.

———. *"Sovremennye zapiski": Vospominaniya redaktora*. Bloomington: Indiana University, School of Slavonic and East European Studies, 1957.

"Vladimir Nabokov—A Profile." *The Last Word* (Wellesley), April 1943, 19–21.

"Vladimir Nabokov Visits Spelman." *Spelman Messenger*, November 1942, 5–9.

Vrangel, Baroness Ludmila. *Vospominaniya i starodavnie vremena*. Washington, D.C.: Victor Kamkin, 1964.

Weaver, Warren. *Alice in Many Tongues: The Translations of Alice in Wonderland*. Madison: University of Wisconsin Press, 1964.

Weeks, Edward. "The Peripatetic Reviewer," *Atlantic Monthly*, January 1967.

Weidle, Vladimir. "Pervaya *Lolita*." *Russkaya mysl'*, December 29, 1977, 9.

Weinstein, Randy F. *Lives of Works that Matter*. Southfield, Mass.: privately printed, 1989.

Wetzsteon, Ross. "Nabokov as Teacher." In Appel and Newman, 240–46.

———. "Vladimir Nabokov: A Student's Recollection." *Cornell Alumni News*, February 1968, 12–15.

Williams, Robert C. *Culture in Exile: Russian Emigrés in Germany*. Ithaca: Cornell University Press, 1972.

Wilson, Edmund. *The Fifties: From Notebooks and Diaries of the Period*. Ed. Leon Edel. New York: Farrar, Straus, and Giroux, 1983.

———. *The Forties: From Notebooks and Diaries of the Period*. Ed. Leon Edel. New York: Farrar, Straus, and Giroux, 1983.

Wilson, Edmund. *Letters on Literature and Politics, 1912–1972.* Ed. Elena Wilson. New York: Farrar, Straus, and Giroux, 1977.

———. Letter to Editor. *New Statesman*, January 5, 1968.

———. Letter to Editor. *NYRB*, February 17, 1966.

———. "The Strange Case of Pushkin and Nabokov." *NYRB*, July 15, 1965, 3–6.

———. *Upstate: Records and Recollections of Northern New York.* New York: Farrar, Straus, and Giroux, 1971.

———. *A Window on Russia.* London: Macmillan, 1973.

Winer, Bart. In Donoghue, "VN: The Great Enchanter."

Wisconsin Studies in Contemporary Literature, Special Nabokov Issue, Spring 1967. Repr. as *Nabokov: The Man and His Work*, ed. L. S. Dembo. Madison: University of Wisconsin Press, 1967.

Zaleski, Philip. "Nabokov's Blue Period." *Harvard Magazine*, July–August 1986, 34–38.

Zenzinov, Vladimir. "Pamyati I. I. Fondaminskogo-Bunakova." *NZ* 18 (1948): 299–316.

Zveers, A., ed. "Perepiska I. A. Bunina s M. A. Aldanovym." *NZ* 155 (184): 131–46.

INDEX

THROUGHOUT the index, "N" stands for Vladimir Vladimirovich Nabokov. His works are listed under his name. Subentries entitled "N's addresses in" denote the span of time that he occupied each residence, and they are arranged chronologically.

Brian Boyd

VLADIMIR NABOKOV
The Russian Years

'Masterly, inspiring first volume of a two-volume critical life of Nabokov that lays open the heart and art of a writer as have few biographies since Richard Ellmann's *James Joyce*... A benchmark of biographical excellence'
Kirkus

'Very readable – this biography is lucidly written and very objective, bearing in mind the author's obvious devotion to his subject. It would seem that, once the second volume is published, there will be little more to say about Nabokov'
Sunday Telegraph

'As a biography Boyd's book can hardly be surpassed. It is a definitive life of the man and a superby documented chronicle of his time'
New York Times

'Scholarly, sympathetic, full of insight'
Financial Times

VINTAGE